Less managing. More teaching. Greater learning.

INSTRUCTORS...

Would you like your **students** to show up for class **more prepared**?
(Let's face it, class is much more fun if everyone is engaged and prepared...)

Want an **easy way to assign** homework online and track student **progress**?
(Less time grading means more time teaching...)

Want an **instant view** of student or class performance?
(No more wondering if students understand...)

Need to **collect data and generate reports** required for administration or accreditation?
(Say goodbye to manually tracking student learning outcomes...)

Want to **record and post your lectures** for students to view online?
(The more students can see, hear, and experience class resources, the better they learn...)

With **McGraw-Hill's *Connect*,**

INSTRUCTORS GET:

- Simple **assignment management**, allowing you to spend more time teaching.
- **Auto-graded** assignments, quizzes, and tests.
- **Detailed visual reporting** where student and section results can be viewed and analyzed.
- Sophisticated **online testing** capability.
- A **filtering and reporting** function that allows you to easily assign and report on materials that are correlated to learning objectives and Bloom's taxonomy.
- An easy-to-use **lecture capture** tool.
- The option to **upload course documents** for student access.

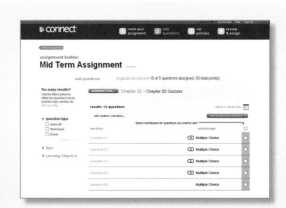

Strategic Human Resource Management
Canada

Gaining a Competitive Advantage |

Search   1st Edition

RAYMOND A. NOE
Ohio State University

BARRY GERHART
University of Wisconsin—Madison

JOHN R. HOLLENBECK
Michigan State University

PATRICK M. WRIGHT
Cornell University

LINDA E. ELIGH
University of Western Ontario

Chapter contributors:
James G. Knight LL.B, *Partner, Filion Wakely Thorup Angeletti LLP,* and
Natasha Savoline LL.B

McGraw-Hill
Ryerson
Connect. Learn. Succeed.

Strategic Human Resource Management:
Gaining a Competitive Advantage
Canadian Edition

Statistics Canada information is used with the permission of Statistics Canada. Users are forbidden to copy the data and redisseminate it, in an original or modified form, for commercial purposes, without permission from Statistics Canada. Information on the availability of the wide range of data from Statistics Canada can be obtained from Statistics Canada's Regional Offices, its World Wide Web site at www.statcan.gc.ca, and its toll-free access number 1-800-263-1136.

The Internet addresses listed in the text were accurate at the time of publication. The inclusion of a Web site does not indicate an endorsement by the authors or McGraw-Hill Ryerson, and McGraw-Hill Ryerson does not guarantee the accuracy of the information presented at these sites.

ISBN-13: 978-0-07-096336-8
ISBN-10: 0-07-096336-3

1 2 3 4 5 6 7 8 9 10 TCP 1 9 8 7 6 5 4 3 2

Printed and bound in Canada.

Care has been taken to trace ownership of copyright material contained in this text; however, the publisher will welcome any information that enables them to rectify any reference or credit for subsequent editions.

Executive Sponsoring Editor: Kim Brewster
Marketing Manager: Cathie Lefebvre
Developmental Editors: Tracey Haggert & Lori McLellan
Senior Editorial Associate: Christine Lomas
Supervising Editor: Jessica Barnoski
Photo/Permissions Research: Indu Arora
iLearning Sales Specialist: Catherine Renaud
Copy Editor: Karen Rolfe
Production Coordinator: Lena Keating
Cover Design: Katherine Strain
Interior Design: Katherine Strain
Page Layout: Bookman Typesetting Co. Inc.
Printer: Transcontinental Printing Group

Library and Archives Canada Cataloguing in Publication

Strategic human resource management : gaining a competitive advantage / Raymond A. Noe .... [et al.]. — 1st Canadian ed.

Includes bibliographical references and index.
ISBN 978-0-07-096336-8

1. Personnel management—Textbooks. I. Noe, Raymond A.

HF5549.S76 2012   658.3   C2011-906892-3

In tribute to the life and ways of my parents
— R. A. N.

*To my parents, Harold and Elizabeth, my wife, Patty,
and my children, Jennifer, Marie, Timothy, and Jeffrey*
— J. R. H.

*To my parents, Robert and Shirley, my wife, Heather,
and my children, Chris and Annie*
— B. G.

*To my parents, Patricia and Paul, my wife, Mary,
and my sons, Michael and Matthew*
— P. M. W.

*To my husband, Norman who supports and encourages me
in everything I do. And to my children Blake, Meredith, and
Ryan (and their growing families) who inspire me and
help me envision the workforce of the future.*
— L. E. E.

RAYMOND A. NOE is the Robert and Anne Hoyt Designated Professor of Management at The Ohio State University. He was previously a professor in the Department of Management at Michigan State University and the Industrial Relations Center of the Carlson School of Management, University of Minnesota. He received his BS in psychology from The Ohio State University and his MA and Ph.D. in psychology from Michigan State University. Professor Noe conducts research and teaches undergraduate as well as MBA and Ph.D. students in human resource management, managerial skills, quantitative methods, human resource information systems, training, employee development, and organizational behaviour. He has published articles in the *Academy of Management Journal, Academy of Management Review, Journal of Applied Psychology, Journal of Vocational Behavior,* and *Personnel Psychology*. Professor Noe is currently on the editorial boards of several journals including *Personnel Psychology, Journal of Applied Psychology,* and *Journal of Organizational Behavior*. Professor Noe has received awards for his teaching and research excellence, including the Herbert G. Heneman Distinguished Teaching Award in 1991 and the Ernest J. McCormick Award for Distinguished Early Career Contribution from the Society for Industrial and Organizational Psychology in 1993. He is also a fellow of the Society of Industrial and Organizational Psychology.

JOHN R. HOLLENBECK received his Ph.D. in Management from New York University in 1984, and is currently the Eli Broad Professor of Management at the Eli Broad Graduate School of Business Administration at Michigan State University. Dr. Hollenbeck has published over 75 articles and book chapters on the topics of work motivation and group behaviour with more than 45 of these appearing in the most highly cited refereed outlets. According to the Institute for Scientific Research, this body of work has been cited over 1,700 times by other researchers. He was the acting editor at *Organizational Behavior and Human Decision Processes* in 1995, the associate editor at *Decision Sciences* between 1998 and 2004, and the editor of *Personnel Psychology* from 1996 to 2002. He currently serves on the editorial board of the *Academy of Management Journal, Academy of Management Review, Journal of Applied Psychology, Personnel Psychology, and Organizational Behavior and Human Decision Processes*. Dr. Hollenbeck's teaching has been recognized with several awards, including the Michigan State University Teacher-Scholar Award in 1987 and the Michigan State University Distinguished Faculty Award in 2006. Dr. Hollenbeck is currently a Fellow of the Academy of Management, the American Psychological Association, and the Society of Industrial and Organizational Psychology.

BARRY GERHART is the Bruce R. Ellig Distinguished Chair in Pay and Organizational Effectiveness and Director of the Strategic Human Resources Program at the University of Wisconsin—Madison. He was previously the Frances Hampton Currey Chair in Organizational Studies at the Owen School of Management at Vanderbilt University and Associate Professor and Chairman of the Department of Human Resource Studies, School of Industrial and Labor Relations at Cornell University. He received his BS in psychology from Bowling Green State University in 1979 and his Ph.D. in industrial relations from the University of Wisconsin—Madison in 1985. His research is in the areas of compensation/rewards, staffing, and employee attitudes. Professor Gerhart has worked with a variety of organizations, including TRW, Corning, and Bausch & Lomb. His work has appeared in the *Academy of Management Journal, Industrial Relations, Industrial and Labor Relations Review, Journal of Applied Psychology, Personnel Psychology,* and *Handbook of Industrial and Organizational Psychology,* and he has served on the editorial boards of the *Academy of Management Journal, Industrial and Labor Relations Review,* and the *Journal of Applied Psychology*. He was a co-recipient of the 1991 Scholarly Achievement Award, Human Resources Division, Academy of Management.

PATRICK M. WRIGHT is Professor of Human Resource Studies and Director of the Center for Advanced Human Resource Studies in the School of Industrial and Labor Relations at Cornell University. He was formerly Associate Professor of Management and Coordinator of the Master of Science in Human Resource Management program in the College of Business Administration and Graduate School of Business at Texas A&M University. He holds a BA in psychology from Wheaton College and an MBA and a Ph.D. in organizational behaviour/human resource management from Michigan State University. He teaches, conducts research, and consults in the areas of personnel selection, employee motivation, and strategic human resource management. His research articles have appeared in journals such as the *Academy of Management Journal, Journal of Applied Psychology, Organizational Behavior and Human Decision Processes, Journal of Management,* and *Human Resource Management Review.* He has served on the editorial boards of *Journal of Applied Psychology* and *Journal of Management* and also serves as an ad hoc reviewer for *Organizational Behavior and Human Decision Processes, Academy of Management Journal,* and *Academy of Management Review.* In addition, he has consulted for a number of organizations, including Whirlpool Corporation, Amoco Oil Company, and the North Carolina state government.

LINDA E. ELIGH has been a Lecturer in the Dan Program in Management and Organizational Studies, Faculty of Social Science, at the University of Western Ontario for over ten years. She regularly teaches compensation and benefits management, training and development, organizational behaviour and strategic human resource management to undergraduates. Linda has also taught extensively in the Diploma in Human Resources Management Program at the University of Guelph where her students have been a lively mixture of undergraduates and mid-career professionals. Linda holds a BA with a major in sociology and a Certificate in Personnel and Industrial Relations from the University of Guelph, and an MA in Leadership and Training from Royal Roads University. Earlier professional and work experience includes six years in various law firms in Alberta, and 14 years as a human resources practitioner with a Canadian division of Johnson & Johnson. She also provided consulting, training, and facilitation services to a broad array of private- and public-sector clients in Ontario for over eight years. In 2004, Linda co-authored HR eSource™, an online, bilingual Human Resources training program sponsored jointly by HRSDC and the HRPA. The project, which was described as an innovative union of an expert system and e-learning, won a 2007 WOW! Award from the Canadian Society for Training and Development. In addition to formal work experience, for many years Linda has expanded her knowledge of organizational culture, management issues, and workplace behaviours while providing volunteer leadership to numerous boards and committees in areas as diverse as the arts, mental health and addiction services, family and children's services, and economic and workforce development. She currently serves on the Operations Committee and Board of Directors of the Thames Valley Children's Centre in London Ontario. Linda has also been a member of the Human Resources Professionals Association (HRPA) for over 20 years.

BRIEF CONTENTS

CONTENTS

The Canadian economy is still recovering from the 2008 recession, with unemployment still higher than anticipated despite job-stimulus programs. Although the prime rate remains low to stimulate spending, consumer confidence is only moderate and experts warn that personal debt levels in Canada have reached record highs. Others predict that the country's inflated real estate market is due for a major correction; also, periodic (and dramatic) stock market fluctuations create constant challenges for organizations with massive pension obligations, and an aging population trying to save for retirement. There is growing concern that the United States, Canada's largest trading partner, may be heading for the second wave of a double-dip recession, creating further barriers to Canadian economic recovery.

The U.S. economy—as well as the economies of most other countries across the globe—experienced severe job loss and a drop in consumer confidence fuelled by the subprime mortgage scandal and the collapse of the stock market. Many well-known companies in the financial and manufacturing sectors, such as AIG, Lehman Brothers, General Motors, and Chrysler—underwent massive restructuring, received bailout money (resulting in increased government ownership), and struggled against the threat of bankruptcy. The massive downturn in the economy forced many companies to downsize their workforces, delay plans for new operations and growth, and closely scrutinize human resource budgets to cut unnecessary programs and costs. This occurred even in companies such as G.E., Google and Microsoft, which are known for gaining a competitive advantage through their human resource practices and are included on many business magazines' lists of "The 100 Best Companies to Work For" (on both sides of the border.) However, the employment situation in the United States has now reached its lowest ebb in 70 years, with 14 million people now unemployed, and with only one job vacancy for every five people searching for work.

At the same time that companies on both sides of the border are taking steps to deal with the current economic conditions, they are also paying closer attention to how to engage in business practices that are economically sound but sustainable; that is, business practices that are ethical, protect the environment, and contribute to the communities from which the business draws financial, physical, and human resources needed to provide its product and services. Consumers are demanding accountability in business practices: making money for shareholders should not involve abandoning ethics, ruining the environment, or exploiting employees from developing countries!

Regardless of whether a company's strategic direction involves downsizing, restructuring, growth, or a merger or acquisition, how human resources are managed is crucial for providing "value" to customers, shareholders, employees, and the community in which they are located. Our definition of "value" includes not only profits but also employee growth and satisfaction, additional employment opportunities, stewardship of the environment, and contributions to community programs. If a company fails to effectively use its financial capital, physical capital, and human capital to create "value," it will not survive. The way a company treats its employees (including those who are forced to leave their jobs) will influence the company's public reputation and brand as a responsible business, especially in a poor economy. For example, organizations such as Canada Post, which is facing future pension obligations twice its current revenue along with constant erosion of such revenue to courier companies and e-business, is sticking with its recruiting, training and development, and employee recognition plans. Canada Post is also ensuring that all employees (including top-level managers) understand their responsibility to share the effort and sacrifices (such as two-tiered wage plans and diluted pension programs) required to sustain the businesses.

We believe that all aspects of human resource management—including how companies interact with the environment; acquire, prepare, develop, and compensate employees; and design and evaluate work—can help companies meet their competitive challenges and create value. Meeting challenges is necessary to create value and to gain a competitive advantage.

THE COMPETITIVE CHALLENGES

The challenges that organizations face today can be grouped into three categories:

- **The sustainability challenge.** Sustainability refers to the ability of a company to survive and exceed in a dynamic competitive environment without sacrificing or creating a threat to the resources of its employees, the community, or the environment. Sustainability depends on how well a company meets the needs of those who have an interest in seeing that the company succeeds. Challenges to sustainability include the ability to deal with economic and social changes; engage in responsible and ethical business practices; efficiently use natural resources and protect the environment; provide high-quality products and services; and develop methods and measures (also known as metrics) to determine if the company is meeting stakeholder needs. Companies in today's economy use mergers and acquisitions, growth, and downsizing to successfully compete. Companies rely on skilled workers to be productive, creative, and innovative and to provide high-quality customer service; their work is demanding and companies cannot guarantee job security. One issue is how to attract and retain a committed, productive workforce in turbulent economic conditions that offer opportunity for financial success, but which can also turn sour, making every employee expendable. Forward-looking businesses are capitalizing on the strengths of a diverse workforce. The examples of LivEnt, Norbourg, and NorTel in Canada and Enron and WorldCom in the United States provide a vivid example of how sustainability depends on ethical and responsible business practices, including the management of human resources. And the recent troubles experienced by Research in Motion remind us that shareholders are much less willing to "wait and see" than in the past, and are now quickly taking management to task and demanding explanations when share values dive. Another important issue is how to meet financial objectives through meeting both customer and employee needs. To meet the sustainability challenge, companies must engage in human resource management practices that address short-term needs but help ensure the long-term success of the firm. The development and choice of human resource management practices should support business goals and strategy.
- **The global challenge.** Companies must be prepared to compete with companies from around the world, either in Canada or abroad. Companies must both defend their domestic markets from foreign competitors and broaden their scope to encompass global markets. Recent threats to and successes of Canadian businesses (consider the auto and steel industries) have proven that globalization is a continuing challenge.
- **The technology challenge.** Using new technologies such as computer-aided manufacturing, virtual reality, expert systems, and the Internet can give companies an edge. New technologies can result in employees "working smarter" as well as providing higher-quality products and more efficient services to customers. Companies that have realized the greatest gains from new technology have human resource management practices that support the use of technology to create what is known as high-performance work systems. Work, training programs, and reward systems often need to be reconfigured to support employees' use of new technology. The three important aspects of high-performance work systems are (1) human resources and their capabilities, (2) new technology and its opportunities, and (3) efficient work structures and policies that allow employees and technology to interact. Companies are also using e-HRM (electronic HRM) applications to give employees more ownership of the employment relationship through the ability to enroll in and participate in training programs, change benefits, communicate with co-workers and customers online, and work "virtually" with peers in geographically different locations.

We believe that organizations must successfully deal with these challenges to create and maintain value, and the key to facing these challenges is a motivated, well-trained, and committed workforce.

THE CHANGING ROLE OF THE HUMAN RESOURCE MANAGEMENT FUNCTION

The human resource management (HRM) profession and practices have undergone substantial change and redefinition. Many articles written in both the academic and practitioner literature have been critical of the traditional HRM function. Unfortunately, in many organizations HRM services are not providing value but instead are mired down in managing trivial administrative tasks. Where this is true, HRM departments can be replaced with new technology or outsourced to a vendor who can provide higher-quality services at a lower cost. Although this recommendation is indeed somewhat extreme (and threatening to both HRM practitioners and those who teach human resource management!), it does demonstrate that companies need to ensure that their HRM functions are creating value for the firm.

Technology should be used where appropriate to automate routine activities, and managers should concentrate on HRM activities that can add substantial value to the company. Consider employee benefits: Technology is available to automate the process by which employees enroll in benefits programs and to keep detailed records of benefits usage. This use of technology frees up time for the manager to focus on activities that can create value for the firm (such as how to control costs resulting from absenteeism and reduce workers' compensation claims).

Although the importance of some HRM departments is being debated, everyone agrees on the need to successfully manage human resources for a company to maximize its competitiveness. Several themes emerge from our conversations with managers and our review of research on HRM practices. First, in today's organizations, managers themselves are becoming more responsible for HRM practices and most believe that people issues are critical to business success. Second, many managers believe that their HRM departments are not well respected because of a perceived lack of competence, business sense, and contact with operations. A study by Deloitte Consulting and *The Economist* Intelligence Unit found that only 23 percent of business executives believe that HR currently plays a significant role in strategy and operational results. Third, many managers believe that for HRM practices to be effective they need to be related to the strategic direction of the business. This text emphasizes how HRM practices can and should contribute to business goals and help to improve product and service quality and effectiveness.

Our intent is to provide students with the background to be successful HRM professionals, to manage human resources effectively, and to be knowledgeable consumers of HRM products. Managers must be able to identify effective HRM practices to purchase these services from a consultant, to work with the HRM department, or to design and implement them personally. The text emphasizes how a manager can more effectively manage human resources and highlights important issues in current HRM practice.

We think this book represents a valuable approach to teaching human resource management for several reasons:

- The text draws from the diverse research, teaching, work and consulting experiences of five authors who have worked as human resource practitioners, and taught human resource management to undergraduates, traditional day MBA students as a required and elective course, and more experienced managers and professional employees in weekend and evening MBA and diploma programs. The teamwork approach gives a depth and breadth to the coverage that is not found in other texts.
- Human resource management is viewed as critical to the success of a business. The text emphasizes how the HRM function, as well as the management of human resources, can help companies gain a competitive advantage.
- The book discusses current issues such as e-HRM, talent management, diversity, and employee engagement, all of which have a major impact on business and HRM practice.

- Strategic human resource management is introduced early in the book and integrated throughout the text.
- Examples of how new technologies are being used to improve the efficiency and effectiveness of HRM practices are provided throughout the text.
- We provide examples of how companies are evaluating HRM practices to determine their value.

ORGANIZATION

This text is built on the foundations of the most successful HRM text in the United States. Now in its seventh edition, Noe, Hollenbeck, Gerhart, and Wright's *Human Resource Management: Gaining a Competitive Advantage* continues to set the bar for textbooks on this subject. The Canadian edition, *Strategic Human Resource Management: Gaining a Competitive Advantage*, takes that solid foundation and places it squarely in a Canadian context. This edition has been fully reworked and rewritten to reflect the Canadian HR reality. It is shorter, to accommodate the Canadian semester, and it is written from a Canadian perspective, to address the needs of the Canadian student and instructor. Structured around four parts, *Strategic Human Resource Management: Gaining a Competitive Advantage* (Canadian edition) is organized as follows:

Part 1 begins with an introductory chapter that provides a detailed discussion of the global, new-economy, stakeholder, and work-system challenges that influence companies' abilities to successfully meet the needs of shareholders, customers, employees, and the community. We discuss how the management of human resources can help companies meet the competitive challenges.

The remainder of Part 1 focuses on a discussion of the environmental forces that companies face in attempting to capitalize on their human resources as a means to gain competitive advantage. The environmental forces include the strategic direction of the business, the legal environment, the type of work performed, and physical arrangement and planning of the work.

A key focus of the strategic human resource management chapter is highlighting the role that staffing, performance management, training and development, and compensation play in different types of business strategies. The chapter concludes by emphasizing how HRM practices should be aligned to help the company meet its business objectives and that the HRM function needs to have a customer focus to be effective and to be seen as a valuable business partner.

A key focus of the legal chapter is enhancing managers' understanding of human rights legislation and the many implications for managing human resources, such as employment and pay equity, sexual harassment, and accommodations for employees with disabilities. The various types of discrimination and ways they have been interpreted by the courts are discussed. The advantages of effectively managing and promoting diversity are also discussed.

The chapter on analysis and design of work and human resources planning emphasizes how work systems can improve company competitiveness by alleviating job stress and by improving employees' motivation and satisfaction with their jobs. Job analysis, job design, and the process required to develop a human resource plan is discussed, along with the strengths and weaknesses of staffing options such as outsourcing, use of contingent workers, and downsizing. The chapter concludes by illustrating how the HRM function itself can be transformed into a more strategic partner through integration of technology, outsourcing, and job redesign,

Part 2 deals with the acquisition, assessment, and development of human resources, including recruitment and selection, training and development, and managing employee engagement and performance. In the chapter on recruitment and selection, strategies for recruiting talented employees are emphasized together with the important role played by the recruiter and ways to minimize errors in employee selection and placement to improve the company's competitive position. Selection-method standards such as validity and reliability are discussed in easily understandable terms without compromising the technical complexity of these issues. The chapter also discusses selection methods such as interviews and various types of tests (including personality, honesty, and drug tests) and compares them on measures of validity, reliability, generalizability, utility, and legality.

The chapter on training and strategic development of people describes the components of effective training systems and the manager's role in determining employees' readiness for training, creating a positive learning environment, and ensuring that training is used on the job. The advantages and disadvantages of different training methods are described, such as e-learning and mobile training. The discussion of employee development introduces the student to how assessment, job experiences, formal courses, and mentoring relationships are used to develop employees.

The chapter on managing employee engagement and performance explores how companies can determine the value of employees and capitalize on their talents through retention and development strategies. The discussion of performance management examines the strengths and weaknesses of performance management approaches using comparison, attributes, results, or behaviours. The discussion of retention and separation emphasizes how managers can maximize employee productivity and satisfaction to avoid absenteeism and turnover. The use of employee surveys to monitor job and organizational characteristics that affect satisfaction and subsequently retention is also discussed. The chapter concludes with a discussion of fairness, as well as discipline procedures and alternative dispute resolution.

Part 3 covers rewarding and compensating human resources, including designing pay structures, recognizing individual contributions, and providing benefits. Here we explore how managers should decide the pay rate for different jobs, given the company's compensation strategy and the worth of jobs. The advantages and disadvantages of merit pay, gainsharing, and skill-based pay are discussed. The chapter on recognizing employee contributions with pay examines how pay influences individual employees and various strategies for recognizing employee contributions, as well as the advantages and disadvantages of pay for performance. The link between incentive plans and the balanced scorecard is discussed, as well as the importance of clear communication in compensation management. This chapter also addresses the controversy surrounding managerial and executive pay. The benefits chapter highlights the different types of benefits provided by Canadian employers— both mandatory government-sponsored benefits and voluntary employer-sponsored benefits. The chapter discusses reasons for the growth of such benefits and how benefit costs can be contained. Benefits plan design and effective communication is emphasized if the true nature and value of benefits is to be realized by employees.

Part 4 covers special topics in human resource management, including collective bargaining and labour relations, safe and productive workplaces, and the challenges involved in managing human resources globally. The collective bargaining and labour relations chapter focuses on traditional issues in labour–management relations, such as union structure and membership, the organizing process, and contract negotiations. It also addresses new union agendas and less adversarial approaches to labour–management relations. The chapter on safe workplaces describes Canadian legislation governing safety in occupational settings, as well as current attitudes and approaches relating to health and safety in the workplace. The roles and responsibilities of various stakeholders are described, along with the strategic importance of wellness programs and the scope and implications of workplace violence. Finally, the chapter on managing human resources globally examines social and political changes such as the introduction of the euro in the European Community, the emergence of new low-cost labour markets that have caused companies to do business on a global scale, and the need to manage expatriate employees effectively in order to remain competitive. Selecting, preparing, and rewarding employees effectively for foreign assignments is described, along with the need to provide cross cultural-training at various stages of the assignment. In addition, the need to effectively repatriate such employees is emphasized if the company hopes to obtain a full return of its investment in expatriate employees and the global businesses they manage.

ACKNOWLEDGMENTS

As the Canadian edition of *Strategic Human Resource Management: Gaining a Competitive Advantage* is launched, it is important to acknowledge those who made it a reality. The process started with the vision and entrepreneurial spirit of Kim Brewster, executive sponsoring editor Management/ Business of McGraw-Hill Ryerson, Higher Education Division, who developed the marketing information and business plan that inspired confidence that a new perspective for teaching human resource management was required in the Canadian textbook market. Tracey Haggert, our Canadian developmental editor, helped us in making major decisions regarding the book, and made writing this book an enjoyable and lively process. Lori McLellan, in-house developmental editor, was equally instrumental in managing the process around the supplements to the text and deserves our gratitude as well. We also worked with an all-star development and project management team, including Jessica Barnoski, supervising editor, Editorial, Design, Production and freelance copy editor Karen Rolfe. Their oversight, suggestions, and patience kept the Canadian author focused on providing a high-quality Canadian edition while meeting the publication deadline.

The authors wish to thank Jamie Knight LL.B and Natasha Savoline LL.B for their legal expertise in researching and revising the following chapters: The Legal Environment: Equality and Human Rights (c. 3), Collective Bargaining and Labour Relations (c. 11), and Safe, Secure, and Productive Workplaces (c. 12).

In addition to the feedback from over 120 instructors in the U.S. market over seven editions, we have also had many Canadian faculty members from colleges and universities around the country provide feedback on various aspects of the Canadian edition of this textbook. We would like to thank these instructors who gave of their time to review the text throughout the development process. Their helpful comments and suggestions have helped to make this a better text:

Gordon Barnard	Durham College
Vivien Corwin	Royal Roads University
Stephen Friedman	York University, Schulich
Stefan Groschi	University of Guelph
Lisa Guglielmi	Seneca College
Lisa Keeping	Wilfrid Laurier University
Joshua Knapp	University of Lethbridge
Joanne Leck	University of Ottawa
Don Maccormac	University of P.E.I.
Sara Mann	University of Guelph
Marc Mentzer	University of Saskatchewan
Preiti Phulphagar Momaya	Centennial College
Melanie Peacock	Mt. Royal University
Jacqueline Power	University Windsor
Maria Rotundo	University of Toronto, Rotman
Carol Ann Samhaber	Algonquin College
Piers Steel	University of Calgary
Amy Tucker	Thompson Rivers University
Krista Uggerslev	University of Manitoba
Thea Vakil	University of Victoria
Anil Verma	University of Toronto, Rotman
Chantal Westgate	McGill University

The Canadian edition of *Strategic Human Resource Management: Gaining a Competitive Advantage* was developed to teach students how to face and meet a variety of challenges within their organizations and how to gain a competitive advantage for their companies.

Throughout this text, the pedagogy focuses on HRM practices and strategies companies can employ to be competitive. These vignettes, boxes, cases, and applications are found in every chapter and provide excellent real-business examples to underscore key concepts throughout the text.

"COMPETING THROUGH …" FEATURES

The chapter's key pedagogical boxes are designed around the three biggest challenges faced by organizations today—**sustainability**, **globalization**, and **technology**.

The **"Competing Through Sustainability," "Competing Through Globalization,"** and **"Competing Through Technology"** boxes highlight organizations—Canadian and international—that are leading the way with HR policies and practices that address these challenges. Their practical relevance and timeliness to HR issues are essential for student learning in the classroom.

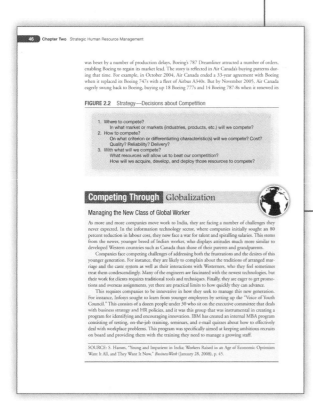

IN-CHAPTER FEATURES

Learning objectives at the beginning of each chapter inform students about the key concepts they should understand after reading through the chapter.

Throughout each chapter, a design element calls out where the learning for each learning objective begins in the text. This element will guide students in their comprehension of the chapter topics and provide a reminder of the learning objectives throughout the chapter.

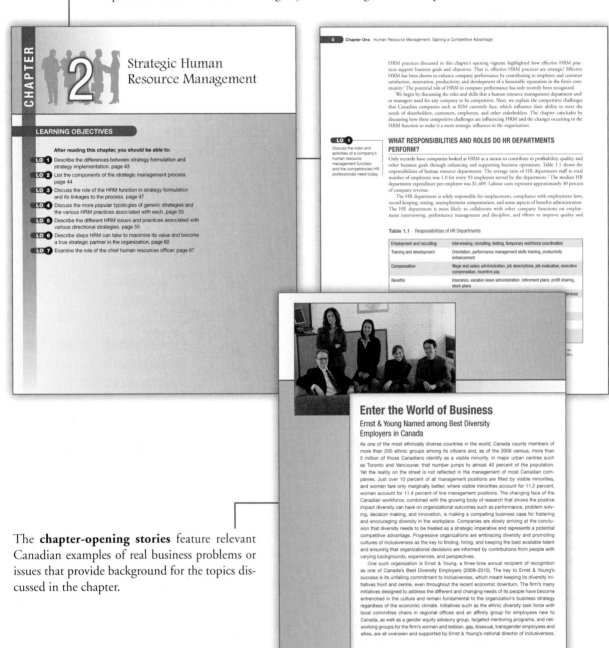

CHAPTER

2

Strategic Human Resource Management

LEARNING OBJECTIVES

After reading this chapter, you should be able to:

LO 1 Describe the differences between strategy formulation and strategy implementation. page 43

LO 2 List the components of the strategic management process. page 44

LO 3 Discuss the role of the HRM function in strategy formulation and its linkages to the process. page 47

LO 4 Discuss the more popular typologies of generic strategies and the various HRM practices associated with each. page 50

LO 5 Describe the different HRM issues and practices associated with various directional strategies. page 55

LO 6 Describe steps HRM can take to maximize its value and become a true strategic partner in the organization. page 62

LO 7 Examine the role of the chief human resources officer. page 67

---

6   Chapter One   Human Resource Management: Gaining a Competitive Advantage

HRM practices discussed in this chapter's opening vignette highlighted how effective HRM practices support business goals and objectives. That is, effective HRM practices are strategic! Effective HRM has been shown to enhance company performance by contributing to employee and customer satisfaction, innovation, productivity, and development of a favourable reputation in the firm's community.[1] The potential role of HRM in company performance has only recently been recognized.

We begin by discussing the roles and skills that a human resource management department and/or managers need for any company to be competitive. Next, we explain the competitive challenges that Canadian companies such as RIM currently face, which influence their ability to meet the needs of shareholders, customers, employees, and other stakeholders. The chapter concludes by discussing how these competitive challenges are influencing HRM and the changes occurring in the HRM function to make it a more strategic influence in the organization.

LO 1
Discuss the roles and activities of a company's human resource management function and the competencies HR professionals need today.

WHAT RESPONSIBILITIES AND ROLES DO HR DEPARTMENTS PERFORM?

Only recently have companies looked at HRM as a means to contribute to profitability, quality, and other business goals through enhancing and supporting business operations. Table 1.1 shows the responsibilities of human resource departments. The average ratio of HR department staff to total number of employees was 1.0 for every 93 employees served by the department.[2] The median HR department expenditure per employee was $1,409. Labour costs represent approximately 30 percent of company revenue.

The HR department is solely responsible for outplacement, compliance with employment laws, record keeping, testing, unemployment compensation, and some aspects of benefits administration. The HR department is most likely to collaborate with other company functions on employment interviewing, performance management and discipline, and efforts to improve quality and

Table 1.1   Responsibilities of HR Departments

Employment and recruiting	Interviewing, recruiting, testing, temporary workforce coordination
Training and development	Orientation, performance management skills training, productivity enhancement
Compensation	Wage and salary administration, job descriptions, job evaluation, executive compensation, incentive pay
Benefits	Insurance, vacation leave administration, retirement plans, profit sharing, stock plans

Enter the World of Business
Ernst & Young Named among Best Diversity Employers in Canada

As one of the most ethnically diverse countries in the world, Canada counts members of more than 200 ethnic groups among its citizens and, as of the 2006 census, more than 5 million of those Canadians identify as a visible minority. In major urban centres such as Toronto and Vancouver, that number jumps to almost 40 percent of the population. Yet the reality on the street is not reflected in the management of most Canadian companies. Just over 10 percent of all management positions are filled by visible minorities, and women fare only marginally better; where visible minorities account for 11.2 percent, women account for 11.4 percent of line management positions. The changing face of the Canadian workforce, combined with the growing body of research that shows the positive impact diversity can have on organizational outcomes such as performance, problem solving, decision making, and innovation, is making a compelling business case for fostering and encouraging diversity in the workplace. Companies are slowly arriving at the conclusion that diversity needs to be treated as a strategic imperative and represents a potential competitive advantage. Progressive organizations are embracing diversity and promoting cultures of inclusiveness as the key to finding, hiring, and keeping the best available talent and ensuring that organizational decisions are informed by contributions from people with varying backgrounds, experiences, and perspectives.

One such organization is Ernst & Young, a three-time annual recipient of recognition as one of Canada's Best Diversity Employers (2008–2010). The key to Ernst & Young's success is its unfailing commitment to inclusiveness, which meant keeping its diversity initiatives front and centre, even throughout the recent economic downturn. The firm's many initiatives designed to address the different and changing needs of its people have become entrenched in the culture and remain fundamental to the organization's business strategy regardless of the economic climate. Initiatives such as the ethnic diversity task force with local committee chairs in regional offices and an affinity group for employees new to Canada, as well as a gender equity advisory group, targeted mentoring programs, and networking groups for the firm's women and lesbian, gay, bisexual, transgender employees and allies, are all overseen and supported by Ernst & Young's national director of inclusiveness.

The **chapter-opening stories** feature relevant Canadian examples of real business problems or issues that provide background for the topics discussed in the chapter.

By highlighting and defining **key terms in the margin**, in context and as part of the chapter discussion, students are more easily able to master the language of HR.

Chapter Two Strategic Human Resource Management 49

Ltd. in their day-to-day tasks and longer-range planning activities. The overall company mission statement acts as a compass that aligns the company worldwide, despite geographic distance.

connect

Learn more about the overall corporate values that guide Merck Frosst Canada Ltd. and its mission and values mission statement online with Connect.

An organization's **goals** are what it hopes to achieve in the medium- to long-term future; they reflect how the mission will be operationalized. The overarching goal of most profit-making companies in North America is to maximize stockholder wealth. But companies have to set other long-term goals in order to maximize stockholder wealth.

Goals
What an organization hopes to achieve in the medium- to long-term future.

External analysis consists of examining the organization's operating environment to identify the strategic opportunities and threats. Examples of opportunities are customer markets that are not being served, technological advances that can aid the company, and labour pools that have not been tapped. Threats include potential labour shortages, new competitors entering the market, pending legislation that might adversely affect the company, and competitors' technological innovations.

External Analysis
Examining the organization's operating environment to identify strategic opportunities and threats.

Internal analysis attempts to identify the organization's strengths and weaknesses. It focuses on the quantity and quality of resources available to the organization—financial, capital, technological, and human resources. Organizations have to honestly and accurately assess each resource to decide whether it is a strength or a weakness.

Internal Analysis
The process of examining an organization's strengths and weaknesses.

External analysis and internal analysis combined constitute what has come to be called the SWOT (strengths, weaknesses, opportunities, threats) analysis. After going through the SWOT analysis, the strategic planning team has all the information it needs to generate a number of strategic alternatives. The strategic managers compare these alternatives' ability to attain the organization's strategic goals; then they make their **strategic choice.** The strategic choice is the organization's strategy; it describes the ways the organization will attempt to fulfill its mission and achieve its long-term goals.

Strategic Choice
The organization's strategy; the ways an organization will attempt to fulfill its mission and achieve its long-term goals.

Many of the opportunities and threats in the external environment are people related. With fewer and fewer highly qualified individuals entering the labour market, organizations compete for not only customers but also employees. It is HRM's role to keep close tabs on the external environment for human resource–related opportunities and threats, especially those directly related to the HRM function: potential labour shortages, competitor wage rates, government regulations affecting employment, and so on. For example, North American companies are finding that more and more high school graduates lack the basic skills needed to work, which is one source of the "human capital shortage."[18] However, not recognizing this environmental threat, many companies have encouraged the exit of older, more skilled workers while hiring less skilled younger workers who require basic skills training.[19]

An analysis of a company's internal strengths and weaknesses also requires input from the HRM function. Today companies are increasingly realizing that their human resources are one of their most important assets. A company's failure to consider the strengths and weaknesses of its workforce may result in its choosing strategies it is not capable of pursuing.[20] However, some research has demonstrated that few companies have achieved this level of linkage.[21] For example, one company chose a strategy of cost reduction through technological improvements. It built a plant designed around a computer-integrated manufacturing system with statistical process controls.

Although this choice may seem like a good one, the company soon learned otherwise. It discovered that its employees could not operate the new equipment because 25 percent of the workforce was functionally illiterate.[22] Other companies do internal analysis well, however, and make a point of investing in workforce capability so workers have the right skills when the company is ready to implement a particular strategy. For example, Standens Limited, mentioned in Chapter 1, forms alliances with educational institutions to keep its workforce learning, which has ensured the company did not make the same mistake.

"Evidence-Based HR" sections within the chapters highlight the growing trend to demonstrate how HR contributes to a company's competitive advantage. Evidence-Based HR shows how HR decisions are based on data and not just intuition. The company examples show how HR practices influence the company's bottom line or key stakeholders including shareholders, employees, customers, or the community.

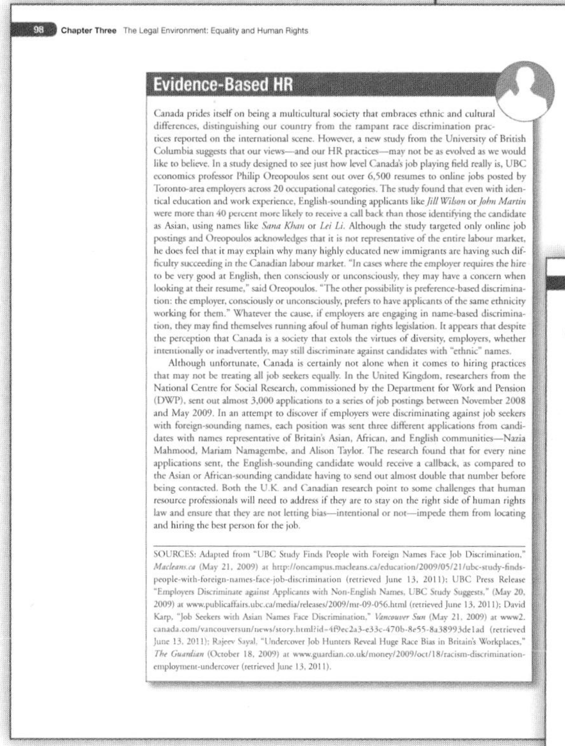
98 Chapter Three The Legal Environment: Equality and Human Rights

Evidence-Based HR

Canada prides itself on being a multicultural society that embraces ethnic and cultural differences, distinguishing our country from the rampant race discrimination practices reported on the international scene. However, a new study from the University of British Columbia suggests that our views—and our HR practices—may not be as evolved as we would like to believe. In a study designed to see just how level Canada's job playing field really is, UBC economics professor Philip Oreopoulos sent out over 6,500 resumes to online jobs posted by Toronto-area employers across 20 occupational categories. The study found that even with identical education and work experience, English-sounding applicants like *Jill Wilson* or *John Martin* were more than 40 percent more likely to receive a call back than those identifying the candidate as Asian, using names like *Sana Khan* or *Lei Li*. Although the study targeted only online job postings and Oreopoulos acknowledges that it is not representative of the entire labour market, he does feel that it may explain why many highly educated new immigrants are having such difficulty succeeding in the Canadian labour market. "In cases where the employer requires the hire to be very good at English, then consciously or unconsciously, they may have a concern when looking at their resume," said Oreopoulos. "The other possibility is preference-based discrimination: the employer, consciously or unconsciously, prefers to have applicants of the same ethnicity working for them." Whatever the cause, if employers are engaging in name-based discrimination, they may find themselves running afoul of human rights legislation. It appears that despite the perception that Canada is a society that extols the virtues of diversity, employers, whether intentionally or inadvertently, may still discriminate against candidates with "ethnic" names.

Although unfortunate, Canada is certainly not alone when it comes to hiring practices that may not be treating all job seekers equally. In the United Kingdom, researchers from the National Centre for Social Research, commissioned by the Department for Work and Pension (DWP), sent out almost 3,000 applications to a series of job postings between November 2008 and May 2009. In an attempt to discover if employers were discriminating against job seekers with foreign-sounding names, each position was sent three different applications from candidates with names representative of Britain's Asian, African, and English communities—Nazia Mahmood, Mariam Namagembe, and Alison Taylor. The research found that for every nine applications sent, the English-sounding candidate would receive a callback, as compared to the Asian or African-sounding candidate having to send out almost double that number before being contacted. Both the U.K. and Canadian research point to some challenges that human resource professionals will need to address if they are to stay on the right side of human rights law and ensure that they are not letting bias—intentional or not—impede them from locating and hiring the best person for the job.

SOURCES: Adapted from "UBC Study Finds People with Foreign Names Face Job Discrimination," *Macleans.ca* (May 21, 2009) at http://oncampus.macleans.ca/education/2009/05/21/ubc-study-finds-people-with-foreign-names-face-job-discrimination (retrieved June 13, 2011); UBC Press Release "Employers Discriminate against Applicants with Non-English Names, UBC Study Suggests," (May 20, 2009) at www.publicaffairs.ubc.ca/media/releases/2009/mr-09-056.html (retrieved June 13, 2011); David Karp, "Job Seekers with Asian Names Face Discrimination," *Vancouver Sun* (May 21, 2009) at www2.canada.com/vancouversun/news/story.html?id-4f9ec2a3-e33c-470b-8e55-8a38993de1ad (retrieved June 13, 2011); Rajeev Sayal, "Undercover Job Hunters Reveal Huge Race Bias in Britain's Workplaces," *The Guardian* (October 18, 2009) at www.guardian.co.uk/money/2009/oct/18/racism-discrimination-employment-undercover (retrieved June 13, 2011).

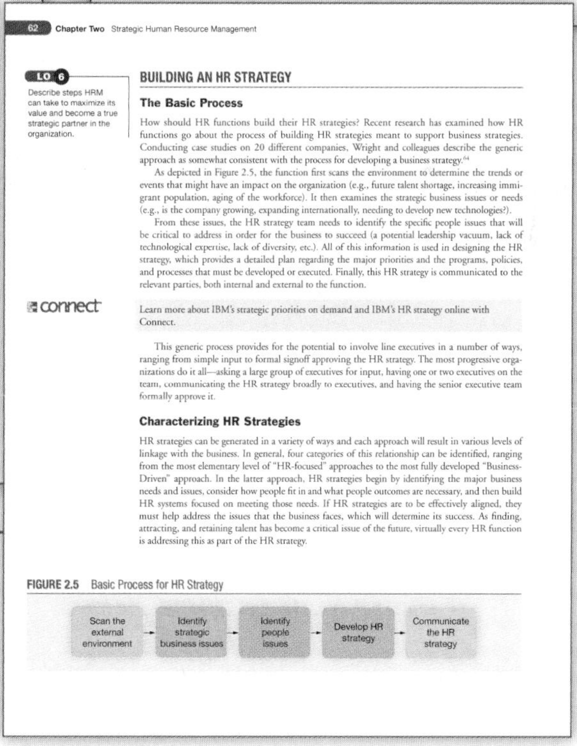
62 Chapter Two Strategic Human Resource Management

LO 6
Describe steps HRM can take to maximize its value and become a true strategic partner in the organization.

BUILDING AN HR STRATEGY

The Basic Process

How should HR functions build their HR strategies? Recent research has examined how HR functions go about the process of building HR strategies meant to support business strategies. Conducting case studies on 20 different companies, Wright and colleagues describe the generic approach as somewhat consistent with the process for developing a business strategy.[64]

As depicted in Figure 2.5, the function first scans the environment to determine the trends or events that might have an impact on the organization (e.g., future talent shortage, increasing immigrant population, aging of the workforce). It then examines the strategic business issues or needs (e.g., is the company growing, expanding internationally, needing to develop new technologies?).

From these issues, the HR strategy team needs to identify the specific people issues that will be critical to address in order for the business to succeed (a potential leadership vacuum, lack of technological expertise, lack of diversity, etc.). All of this information is used in designing the HR strategy, which provides a detailed plan regarding the major priorities and the programs, policies, and processes that must be developed or executed. Finally, this HR strategy is communicated to the relevant parties, both internal and external to the function.

connect

Learn more about IBM's strategic priorities on demand and IBM's HR strategy online with Connect.

This generic process provides for the potential to involve line executives in a number of ways, ranging from simple input to formal signoff approving the HR strategy. The most progressive organizations do it all—asking a large group of executives for input, having one or two executives on the team, communicating the HR strategy broadly to executives, and having the senior executive team formally approve it.

Characterizing HR Strategies

HR strategies can be generated in a variety of ways and each approach will result in various levels of linkage with the business. In general, four categories of this relationship can be identified, ranging from the most elementary level of "HR-focused" approaches to the most fully developed "Business-Driven" approach. In the latter approach, HR strategies begin by identifying the major business needs and issues, consider how people fit in and what people outcomes are necessary, and then build HR systems focused on meeting those needs. If HR strategies are to be effectively aligned, they must help address the issues that the business faces, which will determine its success. As finding, attracting, and retaining talent has become a critical issue of the future, virtually every HR function is addressing this as part of the HR strategy.

FIGURE 2.5 Basic Process for HR Strategy

Connect references throughout the chapters direct students online to find more information on specific topics and provide a direct link between text material and McGraw-Hill Ryerson's online teaching and learning platform.

END-OF-CHAPTER FEATURES

The **"A Look Back"** segment encourages students to recall the chapter's opening story and apply it to what they have just learned.

Discussion Questions are useful for more than just review purposes, as these questions challenge students to apply concepts in the chapter to their own lives and experiences.

The *leader of the HR function* is the role in which CHROs spent the most time, but it is not seen as one that has the greatest impact. This role deals with ensuring that the HR function is aligning its activities and priorities toward the needs of the business, and it usually entails meeting with direct reports to provide guidance and check on progress. However, CHROs increasingly rely on their direct reports to design and deliver HR services while they shift their attention to advising and counselling the top executive team.

Liaison to the board entails all of the activities in which CHROs engage with the board of directors, including discussions of executive compensation, CEO performance, CEO succession, and performance of other members of the executive leadership team. This role is increasing in importance, although it has a long way to go before equalling the strategic adviser, talent architect, and counsellor/confidante/coach roles.

The role of *workforce sensors* entails taking the pulse of the employee population to identify any morale or motivation issues. This is a role in which CHROs do not spent much time, and few viewed it as having the greatest impact on the business.

Finally, CHROs to some extent become the face of the organization to outside constituents such as labour unions, nongovernmental organizations, and the press. They spend the least amount of time in the *representative of the firm* role.

The new strategic role for HRM presents both opportunities and challenges. HRM has the chance to profoundly impact the way organizations compete through people. On the other hand, with this opportunity comes serious responsibility and accountability.[76] HRM functions of the future must consist of individuals who view themselves as businesspeople who happen to work in an HRM function, rather than HRM people who happen to work in a business.

A Look Back

Transforming GM

In the beginning, GM's plan for changing its business model included plans to lay off 47,000 employees worldwide, close five additional plants in North America, and eliminate four of the company's eight brands. In addition, the company conducted talks with the UAW and CAW to restructure $20 billion in obligations to retired hourly workers. Still, the bondholders of GM felt that the company was not going far enough. They wanted to see even greater cuts, as well as a reduction in commitments to the legacy workforce. Without that, they felt GM couldn't survive over the long term.

By March 2009, GM of Canada Ltd. and the CAW had agreed to cuts that would translate into hundreds of millions of dollars in savings in order to qualify for bailout monies and to "take bankruptcy off the table once and for all." Such concessions negotiated by the CAW added to the $400 million in savings (over three years) that GM workers had already given up in their 2008 contract. The new deal cut average hourly wages and benefits to around $69 per hour per GM worker. Another week of special holidays was sacrificed along with a special $1,700 annual bonus, and wages and cost-of-living allowance was frozen for the term of the agreement. The annual bonus money was redirected to pay health costs of the legacy workforce. Those still actively working agreed to pay $360 per year in health care premiums. Retirees and surviving spouses saw their pensions and cost-of-living increases frozen, and going forward they will pay $180 per year in health care premiums. In addition...

Key Terms

Adverse-effect discrimination, 85	Direct discrimination, 85	Pay equity, 112
Bona fide occupational qualification (BFOQ), 89	Discrimination, 84	Psychological harassment, 102
	Diversity management, 113	
	Employment equity, 106	Reasonable accommodation, 87
Canadian Charter of Rights and Freedoms (the Charter), 82	Employment systems review, 111	Sexual harassment, 100
	Harassment, 98	Systemic discrimination, 86
	Human rights, 82	Undue hardship, 88

Discussion Questions

1. You smell alcohol when greeting one of your employees on the way into work in the morning. What do you do? What are your obligations under human rights legislation? How do these legal obligations affect your HRM duties and your responsibilities to the organization and other employees?

2. You are tasked with hiring a new sales force for one of the company's new products. Your boss informs you that the CEO has given express instructions to hire people who have similar characteristics to the target market. The consumers are young, attractive, white professionals. What do you do? What are the potential legal implications of your possible courses of action?

3. Some companies have dress codes that require men to wear suits and women to wear dresses. Is this discriminatory? Why?

4. The concept of a bona fide occupational requirement can require that different standards be applied to different employees (e.g., In the *Meiorin* case the court found that different standards should apply to women versus men.) Do you agree with this approach? Why? What are some alternatives?

5. Sexual harassment can be found even where a victim voluntarily participates in the offending conduct, including having sexual intercourse with the harasser. Do you think this is fair? Why?

6. A major complaint of employers of the duty to accommodate under human rights legislation is that the costs of making reasonable accommodations will reduce their ability to compete with businesses (especially foreign ones) that do not face these requirements. Is this a legitimate concern? How should employers and society weigh the costs and benefits of the duty to accommodate?

7. Both employment equity and pay equity legislation target certain designated groups for preferential treatment. Do you think this is necessary? Do you think this is fair? Why?

8. Your organization is located in a major city centre with a culturally diverse population, but your company employs few visible minorities. You are the HR manager with overall responsibility for staffing. How can you tap into the diverse talent pool outside the company's doorstep to attract, recruit, and retain visible minorities and ensure that their talent is dispersed throughout all levels of your organization?

Self-Assessment Exercise

Take the following self-assessment quiz. For each statement, circle T if the statement is true or F if the statement is false. Then check your answers with the answer key below.

What do you know about sexual harassment?

1. A man cannot be the victim of sexual harassment.	T	F
2. The harasser must be the victim's manager or a manager in another work area.	T	F
3. Sexual harassment charges can be filed only by the person who directly experiences the harassment.	T	F
4. The best way to discourage sexual harassment is to have a policy that discourages employees from dating each other.	T	F
5. Sexual harassment is not a form of sex discrimination.	T	F
6. After receiving a sexual harassment complaint, the employer should let the situation cool off before investigating the complaint.	T	F
7. Sexual harassment is illegal only if it results in the victim being laid off or receiving lower pay.	T	F
8. An employer has no obligation to investigate a complaint of sexual harassment if it believes that the allegations are untrue.	T	F
9. Sexual harassment does not include incidents between employees outside the workplace.	T	F
10. Sexual harassment cannot occur between employees who have a history of having engaged in a consensual sexual relationship.	T	F
11. Conduct will not be found to comprise sexual harassment where the complainant has provoked the behaviour by wearing inappropriately revealing attire at work or by flirting or joking with the alleged perpetrators.	T	F
12. A person cannot be expected to know that his or her conduct is offensive if the complainant never raised any objection to it.	T	F

Answer Key: Did you notice that none of the statements above are true? If you circled "F" for all ten statements, congratulations! You know the difference between facts and fiction about sexual harassment. Try quizzing friends who haven't read this chapter and compare results.

Exercising Strategy: Home Depot's Bumpy Road to Equality

Home Depot is the largest home-products firm selling home repair products and equipment for the do-it-yourselfer. Founded 20 years ago, it now boasts 100,000 employees and more than 900 warehouse stores nationwide. The company's strategy for growth has focused mostly on one task: build more stores. In fact, an unwritten goal of Home Depot executives was to position a store within 30 minutes of every customer in the United States. In addition, Home Depot has tried hard to implement a strategy of providing superior service to its customers. The company has prided itself on hiring people who are knowledgeable about home repair and who can teach customers how to do home repairs on their own. This strategy, along with blanketing the country with stores, has led to the firm's substantial advantage over competitors.

But Home Depot ran into some legal problems. During the company's growth, a statistical anomaly has emerged. About 70 percent of the merchandise employees (those directly involved in selling lumber,...

Self-Assessment Exercises encourage students to apply and experience HR concepts and to evaluate their own skills.

Exercising Strategy cases feature a mix of "classic" HR strategic triumphs and newer Canadian organizations, and offer insight into the HR strategy of the companies profiled.

Exercising Strategy: Transforming the Business and HR at Xerox

In 1958, Xerox launched the Xerox 914, the first automatic, plain-paper office copier. This product went on to become the top-selling industrial product of all time. Xerox's successful xerography technology gave it a sustainable competitive advantage that endured for years. However, all good things must come to an end, and in Xerox's case, that end was the late 1990s. By 2000, Xerox experienced its biggest slide in history, and the consensus among analysts within the industry was that Pat Nazemetz was working with "an unsustainable business model," meaning unless things changed drastically, Xerox would soon cease to exist. In 2000 Xerox had $17.1 billion in debt, with only $154 million in cash on hand. By 2001, Xerox's stock, which had peaked at $63, fell to about $4—a loss of more than 90 percent of its market capitalization. And as if that was not enough, it also faced an accounting investigation by the Securities and Exchange Commission for how it accounted for its customer leases on copiers.

Enter new VP of HR Pat Nazemetz in 1999 and new CEO Anne Mulcahy in 2000 to try to right a sinking ship. Mulcahy put the company on a starvation diet. This entailed selling major operations in China and Hong Kong, reducing global headcount to 61,100 from 91,500 through selloffs, early retirements, and layoffs, and implementing drastic cost controls. While Mulcahy's strategy has brought Xerox back to life (2005 saw Xerox triple its net income to $360 million and $978 million by 2005) as an organization, the HR function had to drive the change in the business while simultaneously transforming the function.

While many HR functions look to outsource, Xerox transformed its HR function largely internally. According to Nazemetz, outsourcing providers say, "Let us in, let us take over your HR function and we can take 10 percent to 30 percent out of your cost base.' We began trimming down, finding synergies and opportunities to get more efficient. We found the savings ourselves."

The largest single savings came from consolidating and expanding the HR Service Center. The Center began with purely transactional work (e.g., record keeping), then added Web-based processes to handle routine work. The Center now conducts research and analysis of HR operations and handles employee-relations issues. This has enabled HR to reduce headcount without reducing levels of service.

Also, as with any organization that has shed 30 percent of its workforce, employee morale was an issue. Even before the fall, HR had been taking the pulse of employees through its "hearts and minds" surveys. This intranet-based survey tapped into a number of employee attitudes and sought to identify the problem areas for HR and line executives to focus on. Employees noted concerns with items such as "Company supports risk-taking," "Company considers impact on employees," "Senior-management behaviour is consistent with words," and "Trust level is high."

"People often ask me how Xerox has found success," says Mulcahy. "My answer is that you have to have a strategy and a plan, but [more importantly], what you really need is excellence of execution, and that starts and ends with a talented, motivated group of people aligned around a common set of goals. Our HR people came through with a series of alignment workshops and retention incentives just when we needed them [to] make Xerox the stronger, better company it is today."

The Xerox that exists today has grown considerably and restored its reputation for innovation. After its recent acquisition of Affiliated Computer Services (ACS), the company now employs 130,000 employees in 160 countries around the world. And the talented people Mulcahy refers to include employees such as Party Calkins, a chemist hired in 1993, who stayed the course and helped the company find its moorings once again. During the troublesome years, she says, Xerox became obsessed with the concept of remanufacturing to eliminate warehouses of old copiers and parts, and to design its products to be sustainable over time among multiple owners. Culkins, along with inspired Xerox engineers and designers, set a goal of 90 percent reusability of all used parts and pieces of Xerox copiers, developed the company's Signature Analysis technology, and began building

Questions

1. If Home Depot was correct in that it was not discriminating, but simply filling positions consistent with those who applied for them (and very few women were applying for merchandising positions), given your reading of this chapter, was the firm guilty of discrimination? If so, under what theory?

2. How does this case illustrate the application of new technology to solving issues that have never been tied to technology? Can you think of other ways technology might be used to address diversity/employment equity issues?

Managing People: Civility in the Workplace

In some Canadian jurisdictions, there are now health and safety laws dealing with workplace violence, workplace harassment, and even psychological harassment. All Canadian jurisdictions have human rights laws that prohibit discriminatory practices and harassment based on prohibited grounds such as race, cultural background, age, and disability. Another way to approach the same kind of objective that motivated these kinds of legislative initiatives is to focus on creating and fostering a civil workplace.

The issue of civility, or more likely incivility, in the workplace has made it onto the radar at an increasing number of organizations in Canada and beyond. Presumably, every organization would agree that treating colleagues with respect and courtesy is an unwritten—or even written—rule at any workplace; however, a recent study concluded that 10 percent of workers reported experiencing uncivil behaviours on a daily basis and 20 percent said they were targets of incivility weekly. Those employees experiencing this kind of behaviour in the workplace report higher stress levels, greater rates of absenteeism, and lower productivity. Over time, chronic exposure to incivility can lead to withdrawal behaviours, with some employees eventually leaving their jobs. Likewise, researchers argue that what begins as a little rude behaviour can escalate into retaliatory behaviours between colleagues ("You ignored my suggestion in that meeting and were sarcastic about it, so I am going to make sure you don't get invited to the informal team lunch") and even spiral into much more serious toxic behaviours including sabotage, overt manifestations of discrimination, or even assault. And legal challenges founded on disrespect, discrimination, and wrongful dismissal can generally be blamed on the kinds of poor working relationships that are the hallmark of an uncivil workplace.

Experts feel that the real challenge lies in convincing some organizations to make creating and sustaining a civil workplace a priority. Many continue to perceive incivility among coworkers as "personality conflicts" and something that will get worked out among colleagues. In light of the effect that incivility can have on productivity, employee well-being, and the overall functioning of the organization—as well as the potential legal implications of tacitly supporting an uncivil workplace—more and more companies are addressing the issue head on by acknowledging it and implementing policies or creating programs that foster a civil workplace.

In the health-care industry, an uncivil workplace transcends employee issues to have repercussions for both patient care and patient outcomes. Following the implementation of a successful initiative designed for the U.S. Veteran Affairs Administration, the CREW (Civility, Respect and Engagement at Work) program was reworked and revamped to suit the needs of Canada's health-care system. Headed by Dr. Michael Leiter, a professor of psychology and the director of Acadia's Centre for Organizational Research and Development in Halifax, the CREW project was implemented at nine health-care centres including three hospitals in Nova Scotia and two in Ontario.

The program was structured around being aware of and modifying behaviours that are within the control of any given workgroup—how coworkers and managers treat one another. The program

Managing People cases look at incidents and problems faced by real companies and encourage students to critically evaluate each situation and to apply the chapter content.

SUPPLEMENTS FOR STUDENTS AND INSTRUCTORS

Strategic Human Resource Management: Gaining a Competitive Advantage, Canadian edition, offers students and instructors a comprehensive ancillary and technology package, including a wealth of new material housed on *Connect*, created by Grace O'Farrell of the University of Winnipeg. Further supplementary materials such as the **Manager in the Hot Seat Resources**, and the **Management Asset Gallery** are also available for use with the text.

Connect

McGraw-Hill *Connect*™ is a web-based assignment and assessment platform that gives students the means to better connect with their coursework, with their instructors, and with the important concepts that they will need to know for success now and in the future.

With *Connect*, instructors can deliver assignments, quizzes, and tests online. Nearly all the questions from the text are presented in an auto-gradeable format and tied to the text's learning objectives. Instructors can edit existing questions and author entirely new problems. Track individual student performance—by question or assignment or in relation to the class overall—with detailed grade reports. Integrate grade reports easily with Learning Management Systems (LMS) such as WebCT and Blackboard. And much more.

By choosing *Connect*, instructors are providing their students with a powerful tool for improving academic performance and truly mastering course material. *Connect* allows students to practise important skills at their own pace and on their own schedule. Importantly, students' assessment results and instructors' feedback are all saved online—so students can continually review their progress and plot their course to success.

Connect also provides 24/7 online access to an eBook—an online edition of the text—to aid them in successfully completing their work, wherever and whenever they choose.

KEY FEATURES

Simple Assignment Management

With *Connect*, creating assignments is easier than ever, so you can spend more time teaching and less time managing.

- Create and deliver assignments easily with selectable end-of-chapter questions and test bank material to assign online.
- Streamline lesson planning, student progress reporting, and assignment grading to make classroom management more efficient than ever.
- Go paperless with the eBook and online submission and grading of student assignments.

Smart Grading

When it comes to studying, time is precious. *Connect* helps students learn more efficiently by providing feedback and practice material when they need it, where they need it.

- Automatically score assignments, giving students immediate feedback on their work and side-by-side comparisons with correct answers.
- Access and review each response; manually change grades or leave comments for students to review.
- Reinforce classroom concepts with practice tests and instant quizzes.

Instructor Library

The *Connect* Instructor Library is your course creation hub. It provides all the critical resources you'll need to build your course, just how you want to teach it.

- Assign eBook readings and draw from a rich collection of textbook-specific assignments.
- Access instructor resources, including ready-made PowerPoint presentations and media to use in your lectures.
- View assignments and resources created for past sections.
- Post your own resources for students to use.

eBook

Connect reinvents the textbook learning experience for the modern student. Every *Connect* subject area is seamlessly integrated with *Connect* eBooks, which are designed to keep students focused on the concepts key to their success.

- Provide students with a *Connect* eBook, allowing for anytime, anywhere access to the textbook.
- Merge media, animation, and assessments with the text's narrative to engage students and improve learning and retention.
- Pinpoint and connect key concepts in a snap using the powerful eBook search engine.
- Manage notes, highlights, and bookmarks in one place for simple, comprehensive review.

INSTRUCTOR RESOURCES

Connect is a one-stop shop for instructor resources, including:

- **Instructor's Manual:** Written by the Canadian text author Linda Eligh, the Instructor's Manual accurately represents the text's content and supports instructors' needs. Each chapter includes the learning objectives, glossary of key terms, a chapter synopsis, complete lecture outline, and solutions to the end-of-chapter discussion questions. Answers to questions and some teaching suggestions are also included for chapter features such as A Look Back, Managing People, and Exercising Strategy. Some teaching suggestions are also included with each chapter.

- **EZ Test Computerized Test Bank:** Written by Grace O'Farrell, University of Winnipeg, this flexible and easy-to-use electronic testing program allows instructors to create tests from book-specific items. The Test Bank contains a broad selection of multiple choice, true/false, and essay questions, and instructors may add their own questions as well. Each question identifies the relevant page reference and difficulty level. Multiple versions of the test can be created and printed.
- **Powerpoint™ Presentations:** Prepared by Roberta Wheeler, Fanshawe College, these robust presentations offer high quality visuals from the text and highlight key concepts from each chapter to bring key HR concepts to life.
- **Video Presentations:** This video package contains carefully selected segments from current Canadian and international sources. It is an excellent supplement to lectures and useful for generating in-class discussion. See the Video summary information and teaching notes, which have been prepared to accompany the video package (also available on DVD).

Connect for Students

By choosing *Connect*, instructors are providing their students with a powerful tool for improving academic performance and truly mastering course material. Noe *Connect* allows students to study and practise important skills at their own pace and on their own schedule with additional material, online quizzing, video streaming, a searchable glossary, newsfeeds, and study exercises.

Tegrity

Tegrity is a service that makes class time available all the time by automatically capturing every lecture in a searchable format for students to review when they study and complete assignments. With a simple one-click start-and-stop process, you capture all computer screens and corresponding audio. Students replay any part of any class with easy-to-use browser-based viewing on a PC or Mac. Educators know that the more students can see, hear, and experience class resources, the better they learn. With Tegrity, students quickly recall key moments by using Tegrity's unique search feature. This search helps students efficiently find what they need, when they need it across an entire semester of class recordings. Help turn all your students' study time into learning moments immediately supported by your lecture. To learn more about Tegrity, watch a two-minute Flash demo at http://tegritycampus.mhhe.com, and consult your local *i*Learning Sales Specialist.

Course Management

McGraw-Hill Ryerson offers a range of flexible integration solutions for Blackboard, WebCT, Desire2Learn, Moodle, and other leading learning management platforms. Please contact your local McGraw-Hill Ryerson *i*Learning Sales Specialist for details.

Create

McGraw-Hill's Create Online gives you access to the most abundant resource at your fingertips— literally. With a few mouse clicks, you can create customized learning tools simply and affordably. McGraw-Hill Ryerson has included many of our market-leading textbooks with Create Online for ebook and print customization as well as many licensed readings and cases. For more information, go to www.mcgrawhillcreate.com.

CourseSmart

CourseSmart brings together thousands of textbooks across hundreds of courses in an ebook format providing unique benefits to students and faculty. By purchasing an ebook, students can save up to 50 percent off the cost of a print textbook, reduce their impact on the environment, and gain access to powerful Web tools for learning, including full-text search, notes, and highlighting, and email tools for sharing notes between classmates. For faculty, CourseSmart provides instant access to review and compare textbooks and course materials in their discipline area without the time, cost, and environmental impact of mailing print copies. For further details, contact your *i*Learning Sales Specialist or go to www.coursesmart.com.

CHAPTER

Human Resource Management: Gaining a Competitive Advantage

LEARNING OBJECTIVES

After reading this chapter, you should be able to:

LO 1 Discuss the roles and activities of a company's human resource management function and the competencies HR professionals need today. page 6

LO 2 Discuss the implications of changes in the economy, the makeup of the labour force, environmental issues, and ethics for company sustainability. page 11

LO 3 Discuss how human resource management helps meet the needs of various stakeholders. page 19

LO 4 Discuss some of the challenges companies must overcome and the strategies required to compete in the global marketplace. page 23

LO 5 Identify the challenges of technology and discuss high-performance work systems. page 26

LO 6 Discuss the transformation of the HRM function. page 29

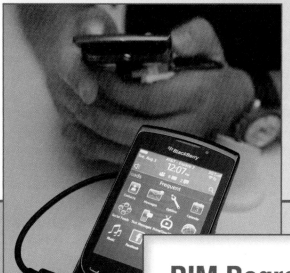

RIM Regroups for Organizational Change

After apparently cruising unscathed through the depths of a global recession and chalking up a 35 percent increase in revenue and a 29.8 percent increase in net income in 2009, Research in Motion (RIM), the legendary Canadian wireless communications company founded in 1984 by CEO Mike Lazaridis, found itself facing another major challenge in its corporate evolution 18 months later. RIM is the Waterloo, Ontario–based designer and manufacturer of the highly addictive BlackBerry® and the Blackberry® Playbook™, as well as radio modems, software development tools, and other hardware and software for businesses and large enterprises. Although still in a very strong financial position with no debt and earnings of US$3.4 billion, some analysts and long-term investors were suggesting RIM has seen its best days and calling for a leadership review. The reason? In a news release timed around its June shareholders' meeting, the company revised expectations downward, quoting Co-CEO Jim Balsillie as saying, "Fiscal 2012 has gotten off to a challenging start." Despite reassurances that innovation was still a priority at RIM, the company's lowered expectations became a subject of hot debate.

Detractors claimed co-CEOs Lazaridis and Balsillie were distracted and the company missed the boat in its launch of the Blackberry® Playbook™. Some pointed out that RIM's workforce had become bloated after the previous ten years of voracious growth, a valid argument since RIM's workforce had grown to 17,000 employees. Critics also said the company had lost irretrievable market share to Apple's iPhone® and to devices running Google's Android® mobile operating system. Defenders maintained that RIM had surmounted major business challenges in the past (e.g., questions about security that threatened emerging business in the Middle East and expensive patent battles). And even though share prices were now under $30, they said the company was still strong, especially since QNX Software Systems had been acquired.

To reassure investors, RIM also promised to streamline operations across the organization, including a headcount reduction. Reallocating resources would enable better focus on RIM's strategic objectives and speed up new product introductions. Although that is what shareholders needed to hear, it could not be good news for employees. A public announcement to reduce headcount had the potential to undermine the very foundation of RIM's past success—its relationship with thousands of talented employees. At the very least, it signalled change was in the wind for RIM, something Microsoft and Apple had faced in previous decades.

When controversy and the spectre of "rightsizing" swirls around any company, managers and human resources professionals usually begin to focus on filling essential positions only, and on retaining top performers. For RIM, such talent was key to generating the promised "accelerated product innovations." Much of the talent RIM had acquired in the previous ten years had signed on to realize the company's recruitment promise to "be part of a cutting-edge, global team and ... have the opportunity to work with leading innovators in [the] industry." RIM's job was now to keep as much top talent as possible while it rallied to restore shareholder confidence. No question, RIM's competitors would be willing to poach some of the bright workers who had been hired from over 350 universities around the world—employees such as one promising young student hired, whom Lazaridis later learned had the highest marks in engineering in China!

Also at risk was the culture at RIM, which was one of respect for the talented and determined knowledge workers in its employ. Over the years, RIM had created an employment value proposition asking that employees be willing to take risks, draw deep within themselves, and persevere in the face of adversity, striving always to reach a personal best. In response, employees had always been rewarded for loyalty and hard work. For example, to motivate new employees (including thousands of co-op and internship students over the years), the employment relationship begins with receiving a free BlackBerry® smartphone, which is theirs as long as they are employed by the company. In addition to competitive pay packages, employees are treated to numerous social activities and celebrations such as a huge annual Christmas party, occasional rock concerts featuring top performers, 100 percent tuition subsidization, profit sharing and year-end bonuses, and much more. Employees also get access to the Healthy® RIM program, where, again, employees are challenged to step up to the plate to maximize return on investment.

The well-earned commitment of 17,000 employees who made up the workforce at RIM certainly plays a role in explaining the phenomenal growth of RIM, and the determination of RIM's leaders to fly in the face of foreign governments and defend user security. But with the company's reputation on the line, it was especially important to be left with what Lazaridis once summarized as "enough critical mass, the right people, the right culture." As RIM's managers and HR professionals began the task of streamlining operations, more than a few observers no doubt recalled the sentiments of co-CEO and founder Mike Lazaridis, who once said, "There's nothing more valuable than incredibly talented, gifted, trained, and motivated people." Words of wisdom, certainly, but when a company finds itself caught in the crosshairs of intense market scrutiny, there are indeed tough choices to be made.

SOURCES: Canada's Top 100 Employers, 2011 RIM Company profile at http://www.eluta.ca/top-employer-rim (retrieved July 18, 2011); R. McQueen, *BlackBerry: The Inside Story of Research in Motion,* (Toronto: Key Porter Books, 2010); A. Sweeny, *BlackBerry Planet: The Story of Research in Motion and the Little Device That*

Took the World by Storm (Toronto: John Wiley & Sons Canada, 2009); RIM corporate website: http://www.rim.com/company/ Media and Careers/Why RIM?: "RIM's Executive Team"; RIM Annual Report 2010 at http://www.rim.com/investors/documents/pdf/annual/2010rim_ar.pdf; RIM Annual Report 2011 at http://www.rim.com/investors/documents; C. Sorensen and J. Kirby, "Can RIM Recover?" *Maclean's*, (July 6, 2011), at http://www2.macleans.ca/2011/07/06/can-rim-recover (retrieved July 18, 2011).

INTRODUCTION

RIM illustrates the key role that human resource management (HRM) plays in determining the survival, effectiveness, and competitiveness of North American businesses. **Competitiveness** refers to a company's ability to maintain and gain market share in its industry. RIM's human resource management practices are helping support the company's business strategy and provide services and products the customer values. The value of a product or service is determined by its quality and how closely the product fits customer needs.

Competitiveness is related to company effectiveness, which is determined by whether the company satisfies the needs of stakeholders (groups affected by business practices). Important stakeholders include stockholders, who want a return on their investment; customers, who want a high-quality product or service; employees, who desire interesting work and reasonable compensation for their services; and the community, which wants the company to contribute to activities and projects, and minimize pollution of the environment. Companies that do not meet stakeholders' needs are unlikely to have a competitive advantage over other firms in their industry.

Human resource management (HRM) refers to the policies, practices, and systems that influence employees' behaviour, attitudes, and performance. Many companies refer to HRM as involving "people practices." Figure 1.1 emphasizes that there are several important HRM practices. The strategy underlying these practices needs to be considered to maximize their influence on company performance. As the figure shows, HRM practices include analyzing and designing work, determining human resource needs (HR planning), attracting potential employees (recruiting), choosing employees (selection), teaching employees how to perform their jobs and preparing them for the future (training and development), rewarding employees (compensation), evaluating their performance (performance management), and creating a positive work environment (employee relations). The

Competitiveness
A company's ability to maintain and gain market share in its industry.

Human Resource Management (HRM)
Policies, practices, and systems that influence employees' behaviour, attitudes, and performance.

FIGURE 1.1 Human Resource Management Practices

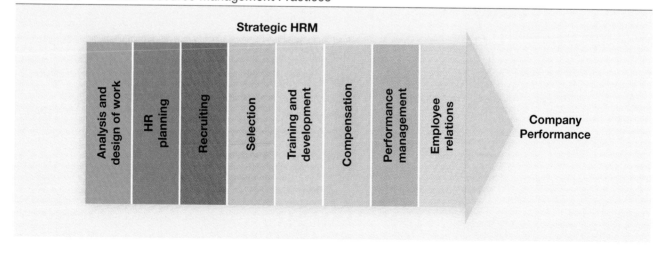

HRM practices discussed in this chapter's opening vignette highlighted how effective HRM practices support business goals and objectives. That is, effective HRM practices are strategic! Effective HRM has been shown to enhance company performance by contributing to employee and customer satisfaction, innovation, productivity, and development of a favourable reputation in the firm's community.[1] The potential role of HRM in company performance has only recently been recognized.

We begin by discussing the roles and skills that a human resource management department and/ or managers need for any company to be competitive. Next, we explain the competitive challenges that Canadian companies such as RIM currently face, which influence their ability to meet the needs of shareholders, customers, employees, and other stakeholders. The chapter concludes by discussing how these competitive challenges are influencing HRM and the changes occurring in the HRM function to make it a more strategic influence in the organization.

LO 1

Discuss the roles and activities of a company's human resource management function and the competencies HR professionals need today.

WHAT RESPONSIBILITIES AND ROLES DO HR DEPARTMENTS PERFORM?

Only recently have companies looked at HRM as a means to contribute to profitability, quality, and other business goals through enhancing and supporting business operations. Table 1.1 shows the responsibilities of human resource departments. The average ratio of HR department staff to total number of employees was 1.0 for every 93 employees served by the department.[2] The median HR department expenditure per employee was $1,409. Labour costs represent approximately 30 percent of company revenue.

The HR department is solely responsible for outplacement, compliance with employment laws, record keeping, testing, unemployment compensation, and some aspects of benefits administration. The HR department is most likely to collaborate with other company functions on employment interviewing, performance management and discipline, and efforts to improve quality and

Table 1.1   Responsibilities of HR Departments

Employment and recruiting	Interviewing, recruiting, testing, temporary workforce coordination
Training and development	Orientation, performance management skills training, productivity enhancement
Compensation	Wage and salary administration, job descriptions, job evaluation, executive compensation, incentive pay
Benefits	Insurance, vacation leave administration, retirement plans, profit sharing, stock plans
Employee services	Employee assistance programs, relocation services, outplacement services
Employee and community relations	Attitude surveys, labour relations, publications, compliance with employment law, discipline
Personnel records	Information systems, records
Health and safety	Safety inspection, drug testing, health, wellness
Strategic planning	International human resources, forecasting, planning, mergers and acquisitions

SOURCE: Based on SHRM-BNA Survey No. 66, "Policy and Practice Forum: Human Resource Activities, Budgets, and Staffs, 2000–2001," *Bulletin to Management*, Bureau of National Affairs Policy and Practice Series, June 28, 2001, Washington, DC: Bureau of National Affairs.

productivity. Large companies are more likely than small ones to employ HR specialists, with benefits specialists being the most prevalent. Other common specializations include recruitment, compensation, and training and development.[3]

Many different roles and responsibilities can be performed by the HR department depending on the size of the company, the characteristics of the workforce, the industry, and the value system of company management. The HR department may take full responsibility for human resource activities in some companies, whereas in others it may share the roles and responsibilities with managers of other departments such as finance, operations, or information technology. In some companies the HR department advises top-level management; in others the HR department may make decisions regarding staffing, training, and compensation after top managers have decided relevant business issues.

Learn more about the responsibilities and roles performed by HR departments online with Connect.

CONNECT

WHAT COMPETENCIES DO HR PROFESSIONALS NEED?

In Canada, the Canadian Council of Human Resources Associations has conducted exhaustive research over the years to identify competencies for Canadian HR professionals. The profession's seven functional areas of knowledge, skills, abilities and other attributes (KSAOs) were captured in the Human Resources Professionals in Canada Body of Knowledge along with the Required Professional Capabilities (RPCs®) that form the "core capabilities of the HR profession as well as HR policies and practice used in Canada."[4] These RPCs provide a basis of certifying human resources professionals in Canada and were most recently revised and approved by the CCHRA in October 2007.

In the global picture, HR professionals need to have the six competencies shown in Figure 1.2 These are the most recent competencies identified by the Human Resource Competency Study (HRCS) which has identified HR competencies for the past 20 years. The study is conducted by the Society for Human Resource Management (SHRM) in partnership with Dave Ulrich and associates and is "the longest running and most extensive global HR competency study in existence."[5] Ulrich is an HR thought leader whose many awards include being listed in The Thinkers 50 as one of the World's Top 50 Business Thinkers in 2009. He was also awarded the Nobels Colloquia Prize for Leadership on Business and Economic Thinking in 2010.[6] The SHRM is the world's largest human resource management association, providing extensive services to HR professionals around the world, and often partnering with the CCHRA, the HRPA, and other provincial human resources organizations in Canada to conduct research about human resources.

The competencies are shown as a three-tier pyramid with the Credible Activist competency the most important for high performance as an HR professional and effective HR leader. Demonstrating these competencies can help HR professionals show managers that they are capable of helping the HR function create value, contribute to the business strategy, and shape the company culture. Although great emphasis is placed on the strategic role of HR, effective execution of the operational executor competency—necessary administrative service including filling open jobs, paying employees, benefits enrolment, keeping employee records, and completing legally required paperwork (such as T4s and Employment Equity reports)—is still important. As we discuss later, technological advances have made available e-HRM and human resource information systems, which make administration of services more efficient and effective and free up time for HR to focus on strategic issues. Successful HR professionals must be able to share information, build relationships, and influence persons both inside and outside the company, including managers, employees, community members, schools, customers, vendors, and suppliers.

FIGURE 1.2   HRCS Competency Study—Six Competencies for the HR Profession

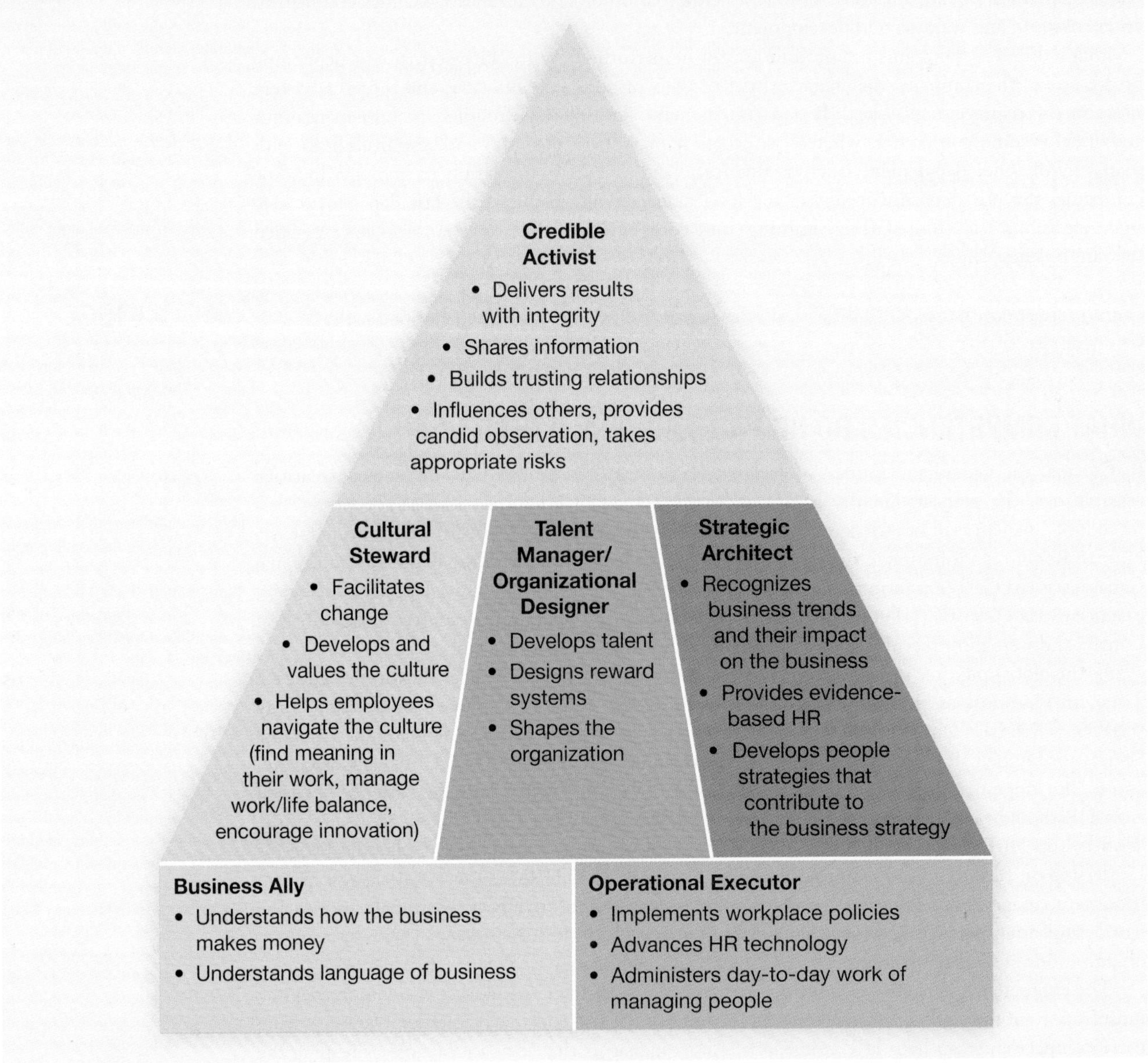

Credible Activist
- Delivers results with integrity
- Shares information
- Builds trusting relationships
- Influences others, provides candid observation, takes appropriate risks

Cultural Steward
- Facilitates change
- Develops and values the culture
- Helps employees navigate the culture (find meaning in their work, manage work/life balance, encourage innovation)

Talent Manager/ Organizational Designer
- Develops talent
- Designs reward systems
- Shapes the organization

Strategic Architect
- Recognizes business trends and their impact on the business
- Provides evidence-based HR
- Develops people strategies that contribute to the business strategy

Business Ally
- Understands how the business makes money
- Understands language of business

Operational Executor
- Implements workplace policies
- Advances HR technology
- Administers day-to-day work of managing people

SOURCE: Based on R. Grossman, "New Competencies for HR," *HR Magazine* (June 2007), pp. 58–62; HR Competency Assessment Tools at http://www2.shrm.org/competencies/index.asp.

Sometimes helping employees can involve crisis management activities such as those HR professionals had to perform during and following the 9/11 crisis in 2001 and pandemics such as SARS, the Avian flu, and H1N1. Other issues include natural disasters and the potential for terrorism. For example, after dealing with firebomb threats in one of its Ottawa branches, the Royal Bank of Canada (RBC) took proactive steps to avoid trouble during the G20 Summit held in Toronto in June 2010. Taking advice from G20 organizers, RBC prioritized the safety of its clients and employees and drew upon its business continuity plan to fend off any interruption in service that might have occurred. HR advised managers to reduce staff in the Toronto core, being creative to find ways for employees to work from home or assigning staff to alternate work sites out of the downtown core. Such actions proved wise as RBC's employees, clients, and service were unaffected by rioting and violence that took place in the heart of Toronto's financial district as G20 leaders met a few blocks away.[7]

EVOLUTION OF THE HRM FUNCTION

The amount of time that the HRM function devotes to administrative tasks is decreasing, and its roles as a strategic business partner, change agent, and employee advocate are increasing.[8] HR managers face two important challenges: shifting their focus from current operations to strategies for the future[9] and preparing non-HR managers to develop and implement human resource practices.

Traditionally, the HRM department (also known as "Personnel" or "Employee Relations") was primarily an administrative expert and employee advocate. Human resource management was primarily reactive; that is, human resource issues were a concern only if they directly affected the business. Although that still remains the case in many companies that have yet to recognize the competitive value of human resource management, other companies believe that HRM is important for business success and therefore have expanded the role of HRM as a change agent and strategic partner.

As part of its strategic role, one of the key contributions that HR can make is to engage in evidence-based HR. **Evidence-based HR** refers to demonstrating that human resources practices have a positive influence on the company's bottom line or key stakeholders (employees, customers, community, shareholders). This helps show that the money invested in HR programs is justified and that HR is contributing to the company's goals and objectives. Evidence-based HR requires collecting data on metrics such as productivity, turnover, accidents, employee attitudes, and medical costs,

Evidence-based HR
Demonstrating that human resource practices have a positive influence on the company's bottom line or key stakeholders (employees, customers, community, and shareholders).

Evidence-Based HR

Holt Renfrew, Canada's 170-year-old luxury goods retailer, realized after considerable reflection that its 14 percent vacancy rate might have something to do with the fact that it wasn't doing enough to appeal to its "young, hip, and fashionable" workforce, the majority of which were female. Looking to fix the problem, the company started by revamping its compensation structure. After making base salaries more competitive, the company added a new twist—variable commissions designed to appeal to individual preferences. The benefits program was tweaked next, adding services such as teeth whitening and Botox that appeal to the fashion-conscious young women the company wants to attract. The company also added more sales and management courses to its employee development program to support faster career growth. The result of such attention to issues of motivation, rewards, and career development? In just two years, the number of Holt's sales associates with annual sales of $1 million increased from only 9 to an impressive 43 percent, and its vacancy rate dropped to just 1 percent. With such improvements, the company is now well positioned to attract and retain the top associates it needs to serve its unique and highly affluent customers.

Sources: Based on P. Sullivan, "Human Capital: Creating a Culture of Engagement," *HR Professional,* 25(2) (February/March 2008), p. 49; http://www.holtrenfrew.com/holts/pages/careers/careers-at-holts. dot?language_id=1&url=66216#I-Thrive.

and showing their relationship with HR practices. This provides evidence that HR is as important to the business as finance, accounting, and marketing. HR decisions should be made on the basis of data and not just intuition. The "Evidence-Based HR" feature in this chapter illustrates how Holt Renfrew's human resource practices improved the company's ability to attract and retain the right employees, and substantially increased revenue. Throughout each chapter of the book, we provide examples of evidence-based HR.

Why have HRM roles changed? Managers see HRM as the most important lever for companies to gain a competitive advantage over both domestic and foreign competitors. Consider the evidence of a 2008 Ekos survey among senior executives from over 1,000 businesses across Canada where three-quarters of those surveyed reported that HR professionals on their staff helped to achieve the financial well-being of the company. They indicated they believe there is a strategic advantage to having a human resources professional on their staff and that human resources professionals are very important to both the day-to-day function and overall success of their organization.[10]

THE HRM PROFESSION

There are many different types of jobs in the HRM profession. A survey conducted by the Society of Human Resource Management (SHRM) to better understand what HR professionals do found that the primary activities of HR professionals are performing the HR generalist role (providing a wide range of HR services), with fewer involved in other activities such as the HR function at the executive level of the company, training and development, HR consulting, and administrative activities.[11]

HR salaries vary depending on education and experience as well as the type of industry. Some positions involve work in specialized areas of HRM such as recruiting, training, compensation, or labour relations. HR generalists with a bachelor's degree and at least four years experience make a base salary falling in a range of $53,900–$69,600.[12] Generalists usually perform the full range of HRM activities, including recruiting, training, compensation, and employee relations. Most HR professionals chose HR as a career because they found HR appealing as a career, they wanted to work with people, or they were asked by chance to perform HR tasks and responsibilities.[13]

connect   Learn more about median salaries for HRM positions online with Connect.

A university degree is held by the vast majority of HRM professionals, many of whom also have completed postgraduate work. Business typically is the field of study (human resources or industrial relations), although some HRM professionals have degrees in the social sciences (economics or psychology), the humanities, or law. Those who have completed graduate work have master's degrees in HR management, business management, or a similar field. This is important because to be successful in HR, it is important to speak the same language as the other business functions. HRM professionals have to have credibility as business leaders, which means being able to understand finance and build a business case for HR activities. A well-rounded educational background will likely serve a person well in an HRM position. As one HR professional noted:

> One of the biggest misconceptions is that it is all warm and fuzzy communications with the workers. Or that it is creative and involved in making a more congenial atmosphere for people at work. Actually it is both of those some of the time, but most of the time it is a big mountain of paperwork which calls on a myriad of skills besides the "people" type. It is law, accounting, philosophy, and logic as well as psychology, spirituality, tolerance, and humility.[14]

Many top-level managers and HR professionals believe that the best way to develop the future effective professionals needed in HR is to take employees with a business point of view and train them. For example, United Parcel Services (UPS) wants its leaders to move up in the company with lifelong careers in many different functions.[15] The senior vice president for human resources at UPS started out loading trucks and became a delivery truck driver and delivery supervisor before he moved to several HR positions. He then joined the legal department and served as general counsel before he took the top HR position at UPS. At companies such as General Electric and Citigroup, and Baxter Corporation (Canada), training programs are used to develop HR professionals' skills. Also, HR professionals often rotate through job assignments in non-HR functions to help them learn about the business and become more strategic business partners.[16]

Professional certification in HRM is less common than membership in professional associations, but individuals working in the field of HR in Canada increasingly seek to acquire the Certified Human Resources Professional (CHRP) Designation. As many of the 21,000 individuals[17] who have acquired the designation can confirm, acquiring the CHRP designation can both increase earnings and accelerate career progress. A recent study commissioned by the Human Resources Professionals Association (HRPA) found that employers pay 3 to 4 percent more (to employees in the same job) to those holding the designation than they do to non-CHRP holders. Another survey by the Canadian Council of Human Resources Association (CCHRA) of 1,500 employees working for Toronto banks found that "More than one half of HR Directors and HR vice-presidents hold a CHRP, while slightly more than one-third of HR generalists have the designation. Employers recognize the value of the designation."[18]

Learn more about the CHRP advantage and comparison of base salaries between holders and nonholders of the CHRP designation online with Connect.

connect

COMPETITIVE CHALLENGES INFLUENCING HUMAN RESOURCE MANAGEMENT

Three competitive challenges that companies now face will increase the importance of human resource management practices: the challenge of sustainability, the global challenge, and the technology challenge. These challenges are shown in Figure 1.3 on page 12.

The Sustainability Challenge

LO 2

Discuss the implications of changes in the economy, the makeup of the labour force, environmental issues, and ethics for company sustainability.

Sustainability
The ability of a company to survive and exceed in a dynamic competitive environment, based on an approach to organizational decision making that considers the company's ability to make a profit without sacrificing the resources of its employees, the community, or the environment.

Traditionally, sustainability has been viewed as one aspect of corporate social responsibility related to the impact of the business on the environment.[19] However, we take a broader view of sustainability, as first described in the Preface of this book. **Sustainability** refers to a company's ability to survive and succeed in a dynamic competitive environment, without sacrificing the resources of its employees, the community, or the environment.[20] Sustainable company success is based on how well the company meets the needs of its stakeholders. Stakeholders include employees, customers, the community, shareholders, and all of the other parties that have an interest in seeing that the company succeeds. Sustainability includes the ability to deal with economic and social changes, engage in responsible and ethical business practices, provide high-quality products and services, and, of course, practise environmental responsibility. It also requires establishing methods to determine and ensure that the company is meeting stakeholders' needs. For example, it may mean being more accountable and transparent around compensation of the CEO and senior corporate officers, by using plain language to describe such arrangements in the company's annual proxy circular. Or it could mean ensuring that employee and customer needs are given top priority when a merger (or acquisition) takes place, so that the merged entity actually delivers increased value to all stakeholders, *and sustains that value over time.* It could also mean doing everything possible to protect employees and their jobs in an economic downturn, taking pains to avoid the high cost of turnover and the inevitable loss of

FIGURE 1.3   Competitive Challenges Influencing Canadian Companies

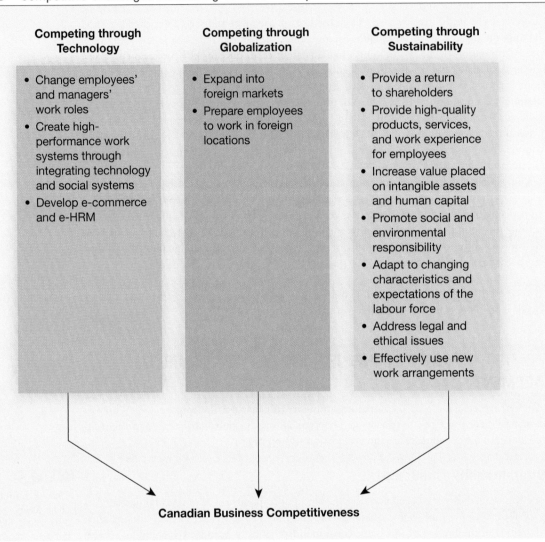

Competing through Technology

- Change employees' and managers' work roles
- Create high-performance work systems through integrating technology and social systems
- Develop e-commerce and e-HRM

Competing through Globalization

- Expand into foreign markets
- Prepare employees to work in foreign locations

Competing through Sustainability

- Provide a return to shareholders
- Provide high-quality products, services, and work experience for employees
- Increase value placed on intangible assets and human capital
- Promote social and environmental responsibility
- Adapt to changing characteristics and expectations of the labour force
- Address legal and ethical issues
- Effectively use new work arrangements

Canadian Business Competitiveness

commitment among employees who remain. We will summarize a few of these key issues here, and you may be sure these and other issues will come up again in future chapters.

Several changes in the economy have important implications for human resource management. These include the changing structure of the economy, the development of e-business, and more growth in professional and service occupations. Growth in these occupations means that skill demands for jobs have changed, with knowledge becoming more valuable. Remaining competitive in a global economy also requires demanding work hours and changes in traditional employment patterns. The creation of new jobs, aging employees leaving the workforce, slow population growth, and a lack of employees who have the skills needed to perform the jobs in greatest demand means that demand for employees will exceed supply. This has created a "war for talent" that has increased the attention companies pay to attracting and retaining human resources.

Economic Changes   When the global economy was plunged into a major recession in 2008, Canada seemed to experience considerably less shock than other countries, such as the United States where the economic downturn was the worst since the years following World War II. The economies of China and India also slowed, and Europe, Mexico, and Japan slipped into recession. The Canadian experience was much less painful, with less unemployment and fewer job losses (400,000) than expected, speeding the labour market toward almost full recovery by mid-2010. One notable exception has been manufacturing, where unemployment levels held fast at well below pre-recession levels.[21]

However, as the initial effects of the recession fade in Canada, other domestic concerns have emerged, such as high levels of personal debt and emerging fears that the Canadian housing market may be poised for a serious downturn in the future. Canada is part of a complex global economy and must react to the transformations occurring in the external environment, including the possibility of another "double-dip" recession if bailouts and stimulus spending are not enough to avoid further downturns. In addition, many worry that unprecedented high debt levels among governments around the world will lead to high inflation and tax burdens in the future.

The implications of these economic developments for human resource management are far reaching. The low level of Canadian job loss (compared to other countries) during the recession provides a clue about the real concerns of Canadian employers before and during the recession. In a Conference Board study conducted between September 2008 and January 2009, 167 employers indicated that after considering their organization's strategic objectives, their top HR challenges over the next three to five years included attracting, recruiting, and retaining employees; leadership capacity; and the aging workforce. And over the long term, employers ranked strategic workforce planning, succession management, management/leadership development, and knowledge transfer and management as their top five HR priorities. These survey results indicate that Canadian employers are not so much concerned with survival but, rather, sustainable growth.[22]

To cope with recession, the Conference Board indicates that employers resisted letting go of key talent, opting instead to tough it out.[23] Many companies, such as Standen's Limited of Calgary, whose story is described in the "Competing through Sustainability" box in this chapter, used creative means to avoid layoffs of highly skilled employees. Others implemented creative cost control such as unpaid leaves, suspending pension plan contributions, restructuring benefit plans, and cutting training budgets. Going forward, more companies will at least closely monitor the size of their workforce, more carefully consider plans for new operations and growth, and constantly monitor human resource budgets to eliminate waste and seize opportunities.

Employment and Occupational Growth Projections and Skill Requirements.   The competition for labour is affected by the growth and decline of industries, jobs, and occupations. Competition for labour is also influenced by the number and skills of persons available for full-time work. Projections indicate that although labour force growth in Canada will continue until 2011, it will sink to less than 1 percent in 2014 and continue to decline thereafter.[24] Aging boomers will retire at an increasing rate, reaching 2.6 percent annually by 2014. The current rate of national labour force participation (67.4 percent) is now seen as a peak, and imbalances between supply and demand within various sectors are expected to become serious by 2020.[25]

The future North American labour market will be both a knowledge economy and a service economy.[26] There will be many high-education professional and managerial jobs and low-education service jobs. Boundaries between knowledge and service work are blurring, creating "technoservice" occupations that combine service technology and software application. Software application engineers, technical support, engineering, and people in scientific consulting jobs work directly with customers, and customers influence the product design process.

For example, in 2006, more than 75 percent of Canadians were employed in the service sector, and this sector will continue to lead job growth until at least 2016. The most growth will occur in computer systems design and related services, professional business services, other professional services, and health.[27] Jobs in goods-producing industries such as forestry and manufacturing have been under downward pressure due to global competition or economic turmoil, although construction, mining, and oil and gas extraction (and the support services associated with these industries) are expected to grow above the general economy-wide average.[28]

connect

Learn more about Canada's fastest-growing occupations between 2005 and 2015 online with Connect.

Between 2010 and 2015, about two-thirds of job openings are expected to occur in management or in occupations usually requiring postsecondary education (university, college, or apprenticeship training). The number of people in the workforce with a university degree is projected to continue rising and will comprise nearly a quarter of the entire labour force by 2015. Management and occupations requiring college or apprenticeship training or high school will experience moderate growth, and the lowest-skill occupations, requiring only on-the-job training, will weaken to less than 1 percent of all job openings.[29]

A growing area of concern for the future is whether employers will be able to access the right people with the right skills at the right time, as aging workers leave full-time employment and other workers are needed to replace them, and as the nature of work continues to transform. For example, changing skills requirements have become a key concern in the manufacturing sector, an industry many of us might be tempted to describe as "producing goods and selling them to customers."[30] Not so, says the Canadian Manufacturers and Exporters (CME), which says it is now a "knowledge-based and service intensive business where success depends on delivering customer solutions, not simply on producing things."[31]

As far back as 2004, a Management Issues Survey conducted by the CME revealed that 42 percent of respondents believed limited availability of skilled and experienced personnel would be a strategic issue changing fundamental business practices over the next five years.[32] All survey respondents agreed that the core competencies required of the manufacturing workforce would change substantially, and by the year 2020 would include key skills such as:

- A mix of creative problem-solving capabilities, technical know-how, and business skills, as well as an ability to interact with colleagues and customers;
- A higher degree of technical and technological expertise as production systems become more automated and interconnected, and as workplaces incorporate advanced technologies such as nanotechnology, biotechnology, microelectronics, and robotics;
- Multilingual and multicultural skills, as business operations expand on a more global basis;
- Management skills in the fields of manufacturing processes, supply chains, product and knowledge development, financing, and global business.[33]

Increased Value Placed on Intangible Assets and Human Capital.   Today more and more companies are interested in using intangible assets and human capital as a way to gain an advantage over competitors. A company's value includes three types of assets that are critical for the company to provide goods and services: financial assets (cash and securities), physical assets (property, plant, equipment), and intangible assets. Table 1.2 on page 16 provides examples of intangible assets. **Intangible assets** include human capital, customer capital, social capital, and intellectual capital. Intangible assets are equally or even more valuable than financial and physical assets but they are difficult to duplicate or imitate.[34] By one estimate, up to 75 percent of the source of value in a company is in intangible assets.[35]

Intangible Assets
A type of company asset including human capital, customer capital, social capital, and intellectual capital.

Competing Through Sustainability

Managing without Layoffs

As one of North America's largest manufacturers of full-line leaf springs, suspension components, trailer axles, and agricultural tillage tools, an observer might be tempted to say that Standen's Limited of Calgary is not only a highly sustainable business, but also, in fact, a model of sustainability. Founded in 1924, the company now boasts around 500 employees located in plants and distribution centres in Canada, the United States, and China. Standen's models the future of Canadian manufacturing, leading the industry with numerous technological innovations. For example, the company was one of the first leaf-spring manufacturers to embrace computer-assisted design (CAD). Now much of the specialized manufacturing machinery and software development programs used by Standen's are designed and made in-house at its new state-of-the-art facility in Calgary's industrial district. The company also sponsors ongoing education for its employees and partners with SAIT Polytechnical to create apprenticeship and leadership development opportunities and to encourage imagination and lifelong learning.

Standen's leaves nothing to chance, having registered to ISO/TS 16490 Automotive and ISO 9001:2008 Quality international standards, as well as ISO14011 Environmental standards. In fact, it boasts that it has been using environmentally friendly practices for 85 years, recycling steel, paper, and other consumables; burning natural gas; and using computer-controlled heat-treating of steel to eliminate waste of energy and materials.

Standen's is passionate about retaining its highly skilled employees, believing that its people and "the value they add to our organization are the key to our success." No doubt the company's 85-year emphasis on job security for contributing employees prompted one employee testimonial found on the company's website, saying: "I have been able to rely on Standen's for stability and growth while raising four children in an uncertain world." Such statements are rare indeed these days.

That's why, during two very challenging years of the global recession, Standen's embraced a creative way to keep 100 percent of staff employed. In March 2009 the company joined a federal government Work Sharing program designed to help companies avoid temporary layoffs. Employees worked a shorter workweek but experienced less financial loss when employment insurance was used to subsidize the company's payroll during the downturn. This allowed Standen's to pay all 475 employees for four days, even though they worked a three-day week due to low production demand, with the company gradually resuming full payroll as business improved. As John Simpson, director of Personnel and HR said, "The whole objective here was how can we weather this recession and keep everybody employed." The HR department's creative solution allowed the company to survive the downturn with minimal inconvenience to all stakeholders involved. When business ramps up to its usual pace, Standen's highly skilled employees will be ready and eager to rise with the tide of competition once again—illustrating the key role HR can play in meeting the challenges of sustainability.

SOURCES: Standen's corporate website: www.standens.com (job security/training and development/ what our employees are saying); S. Dobson. "Employers in Holding Pattern," *Canadian HR Reporter*, 23(5), (March 2010) pp. 1, 10, retrieved August 19, 2010, from ABI/INFORM Global. (Document ID: 2004016481).

Table 1.2 Examples of Intangible Assets

HUMAN CAPITAL	SOCIAL CAPITAL
• Tacit knowledge	• Corporate culture
• Education	• Management philosophy
• Work-related know-how	• Management practices
• Work-related competence	• Informal networking systems
CUSTOMER CAPITAL	**INTELLECTUAL CAPITAL**
• Customer relationships	• Patents
• Brands	• Copyrights
• Customer loyalty	• Trade secrets
• Distribution channels	• Intellectual property

SOURCES: Based on L. Weatherly, *Human Capital: The Elusive Asset* (Alexandria, VA: 2003 SHRM Research Quarterly); E. Holton and S. Naquin, "New Metrics for Employee Development," *Performance Improvement Quarterly* 17 (2004), pp. 56–80; M. Huselid, B. Becker, and R. Beatty, *The Workforce Scorecard* (Boston: Harvard University Press, 2005).

Intangible assets have been shown to be responsible for a company's competitive advantage. Human resource management practices such as training, selection, performance management, and compensation have a direct influence on human and social capital through influencing customer service, work-related know-how and competence, and work relationships.

For example, consider companies in the airline industry. Canadian-owned WestJet Airlines is one of the most profitable airlines in North America and, despite continuous pressures on the highly competitive airline industry in general, WestJet has expanded every year to its current 69 destinations in Canada, the United States, Mexico, and the Caribbean.[36] One of the distinctions between WestJet and its competitors is how it treats its employees. The company has been named one of Canada's Most Admired Corporate Cultures in each year from 2005 to 2008 and was selected as one of the 50 Best Employers in Canada in Hewitt Associates 2010 Best Employer Study.[37] WestJet's strategic plan includes investing in and fostering the growth, development, and commitment of its people, and its encouragement of ownership among its employees means that 82 percent of eligible WestJetters own shares in the company. Ferio Pugliese, WestJet vice president People and Culture makes it clear that the company understands the vital link between intangible assets and profits, saying: "The culture at WestJet is built on transparency, inclusion, and caring. It's important for us that our owners—our WestJetters, believe the company they work for cares about them and strives to provide opportunities for genuine open communication on a regular basis. We believe engagement comes from taking personal accountability for what you do, day in and day out. When employees are involved and cared for, they take pride in their work and it shows up in areas like safety and guest experience. Our success and profitability to date supports this notion and for that we sincerely thank every member of our WestJet family."[38]

Intangible assets have been shown to be related to a company's bottom line. A study by the American Society for Training and Development of more than 500 publicly traded U.S.–based companies found that companies that invested the most in training and development had a shareholder return 86 percent higher than companies in the bottom half and 46 percent higher than the market average.[39]

In addition to building human capital, companies need to be able to adapt to change. *Change* refers to the adoption of a new idea or behaviour by a company. Technological advances, changes in the workforce or government regulations, globalization, and new competitors are among the many factors that require companies to change. Change is inevitable in companies as products, companies, and entire industries experience shorter life cycles.[40] For example, in July 2010, General Motors closed its only remaining plant in Windsor, Ontario, once considered to be the capital of Canada's automotive industry. This also put 500 employees out of work and shifted production of transmissions to another plant. It was the end of an era, since GM employed 7,000 workers at the peak of its 90-year history in that city.[41] In the same month, it announced production of the Opel Astra in Russia, adding a fourth model to its new production facility in St. Petersburg, established in November 2008.[42]

Changes in Employment Expectations. The need for companies to make rapid changes as a result of new technologies, competitors, and customer demands has played a major role in reshaping the employment relationship.[43] New or emergent business strategies that result from these changes cause companies to merge, acquire new companies, grow, and in some cases downsize and restructure. This has resulted in changes in the employment relationship. The **psychological contract** describes what an employee expects to contribute and what the company will provide to the employee for these contributions.[44] Unlike a sales contract, a psychological contract is not written. Traditionally, companies expected employees to contribute time, effort, skills, abilities, and loyalty. In return, companies would provide job security and opportunities for promotion. However, in the new economy a new type of psychological contract is emerging.[45] The competitive business environment demands frequent changes in the quality, innovation, creativeness, and timeliness of employee contributions and the skills needed to provide them. This has led to restructuring, mergers and acquisitions, and often layoffs and longer hours for many employees. Companies demand excellent customer service and high productivity levels. Employees are expected to take more responsibility for their own careers, from seeking training to balancing work and family. In exchange for top performance and working longer hours without job security, employees want companies to provide flexible work schedules; comfortable working conditions; more autonomy in accomplishing work, training, and development opportunities; and financial incentives based on how the company performs. Employees realize that companies cannot provide employment security, so they want employability—that is, they want their company to provide training and job experiences to help ensure that employees can find other employment opportunities.

> **Psychological Contract**
> Expectations of employee contributions and what the company will provide in return.

These changing expectations and an underlying cynicism felt by employees has been aggravated by the recession. A Towers Watson 2010 Global Workforce Study scanning 20,000 full-time employees in 22 global markets revealed that employees are staying put "with significant numbers of employees sacrificing the prospect of career growth for a secure job right now." However, the survey also found that "confidence in leaders and managers is disturbingly low—particularly in terms of the interpersonal aspects of their respective roles."[46] Further, 12 percent of top-performing employees had serious intentions to leave their current employer, while a further 17 percent felt uncertain about whether to stay or not. The report warns that top talent may be poised to flee once the recession is past, and that organizations shouldn't acquire a false sense of security since "competition for top performers has not flagged."[47] These studies indicate problems with employee engagement.

Concerns with Employee Engagement. **Employee engagement** refers to the degree to which employees are fully involved in their work and the strength of their commitment to their job and the company.[48] The Conference Board defines it as "a heightened emotional and intellectual connection that an employee has for his/her job, organization, manager, or co-workers that, in turn influences him/her to apply additional discretionary effort to his/her work."[49] Employees who are engaged in their work and committed to the company they work for give companies a competitive

> **Employee Engagement**
> The degree to which employees are fully involved in their work and the strength of their commitment to their job and the company.

advantage including higher productivity, better customer service, and lower turnover.[50] What is the state of employee engagement in North American and global companies? In a nutshell—not good! Between 2007 and 2009, a CLC global survey of 200,000 employees around the world revealed that the number of employees indicating they are highly disengaged has risen from 8 percent to 21 percent. The study also revealed that since the beginning of 2008, proactive discretionary effort by employees has decreased 60 percent.[51] Under such circumstances, the human resource challenge is how to build a committed, productive workforce in the face of low morale and the turbulent economic conditions that produce it. In other words, HR departments must somehow take advantage of the fact that people are staying put to build increased employee engagement and reduce cynicism before the economy gains steam and opportunities elsewhere begin to look inviting enough that top performers decide to jump ship.

Talent Management

A systematic planned strategic effort by a company to attract, retain, develop, and motivate highly skilled employees and managers.

Talent Management.   **Talent management** refers to a systematic planned strategic effort by companies to attract, retain, develop, and motivate highly skilled employees and managers.

Companies report that the most important talent management challenges they face are identifying employees with managerial talent and training and developing them for managerial positions.[52] Many companies do not have employees with the necessary competencies to manage in a global economy.[53] That is, such managers need to be self-aware and able to build international teams, create global management and marketing practices, and interact and manage employees from different cultural backgrounds. For example, one of the new paradigms identified by the Canadian Manufacturers and Exporters is global integration, meaning that manufacturers are expanding their focus beyond domestic/North American markets to include global markets. This means dealing with global customers, participating in global networks, and reaching out globally for the best in technology, skills, and cost structures. At the same time, future challenges include the lack of people with a combination of technical, business, language and cultural skills, and a tendency for smaller Canadian businesses to use consultants for global business issues rather than to build competency inhouse in these areas.[54] The role of Human Resources in resolving issues such as these, along with succession planning and leadership development will be discussed again in much greater detail in Chapter 6.

Use of Part-Time Employment and Alternative Work Arrangements.   The need to avoid layoffs, decrease costs and/or increase profits, and, in the recession, simply to survive, has led many workplaces to implement more part-time employment and nonstandard work arrangements. **Alternative work arrangements** include the hiring of independent contractors, on-call workers, temporary workers, and contract company workers. Temporary employment grew rapidly from the late 90s, and by 2007 almost 13 percent of working Canadians were employed on a temporary basis (term, contact, casual, or seasonal jobs), with term or contract employees making up the majority of all temporary workers.[55] In addition, the number of core-age employees hired on a part-time basis has more than doubled in the past 30 years, reaching just over 18 percent of the total workforce by 2007.[56] This hints at the growing reliance on alternative hiring practices and the key role of strategic human resources planning in ensuring sustainability as well as growth of the organization, topics discussed in chapters 4 and 5.

Alternative Work Arrangements

Independent contractors, on-call workers, temporary workers, and contract company workers who are not employed full-time by the company.

Demanding Work, but with More Flexibility.   The globalization of the world economy and the development of e-commerce have made the notion of a 40-hour workweek obsolete. As a result, companies need to be staffed 24 hours a day, 7 days a week. Employees in manufacturing environments and service call centres are being asked to move from 8- to 12-hour days or to work afternoon or midnight shifts. Similarly, professional employees face long hours and work demands that spill over into their personal lives. Smartphones and pagers bombard employees with information and work demands. These intrusions often result in erosion of family life, greater employee stress, less satisfied employees, loss of productivity, and higher turnover—all of which are costly for companies. Human Resources professionals are challenged to facilitate more flexible work schedules, protect employees' free time, and use employees' work time more productively. Implementing flexible hours, weekend work, job sharing, telecommuting, and a host of other approaches must become part of the strategic human resources planning process, and also factor into planning of compensation and benefits as well as recruitment and retention strategies.

Meeting the Needs of Stakeholders: Shareholders, Customers, Employees, and Community As we mentioned earlier, company effectiveness and competitiveness are determined by whether the company satisfies the needs of stakeholders. Stakeholders include shareholders (who want a return on their investment), customers (who want a high-quality product or service), and employees (who desire interesting work and reasonable compensation for their services). The community (which wants the company to contribute to activities and projects and minimize pollution of the environment) is also an important stakeholder.

LO 3

Discuss how human resource management helps meet the needs of various stakeholders.

Measuring Performance to Stakeholders: The Balanced Scorecard. One way to measuring performance for stakeholders is to implement the **balanced scorecard,** a means of performance measurement that gives managers an indication of the performance of a company based on the degree to which stakeholder needs are satisfied; it depicts the company from the perspective of internal and external customers, employees, and shareholders.[57] The balanced scorecard is important because it brings together most of the features that a company needs to focus on to be competitive. These include being customer focused, improving quality, emphasizing teamwork, reducing new product and service development times, and managing for the long term.

Balanced Scorecard
A means of performance measurement that gives managers a chance to look at their company from the perspectives of internal and external customers, employees, and shareholders.

The balanced scorecard differs from traditional measures of company performance by emphasizing that the critical indicators chosen are based on the company's business strategy and competitive demands. Companies need to customize their balanced scorecards based on different market situations, products, and competitive environments.

The balanced scorecard can be useful in managing human resources. Communicating the scorecard to employees gives them a framework that helps them see the goals and strategies of the company, how these goals and strategies are measured, and how they influence the critical indicators. The balanced scorecard should be used to (1) link human resource management activities to the company's business strategy and (2) evaluate the extent to which the HRM function is helping the company meet its strategic objectives. Later in this book you will find examples of organizations that utilize the Balanced Scorecard to measure and reward employee performance.

Learn more about the balanced scorecard online with Connect.   connect

Social Responsibility. Increasingly, companies are recognizing that social responsibility can help boost a company's image with customers, gain access to new markets, and help attract and retain talented employees. Companies thus try to meet shareholder and general public demands that they be more socially, ethically, and environmentally responsible. For example, the Royal Bank of Canada's RBC Blue Water Project® is a ten-year $50 million grant program supporting not-for-profit organizations that protect watersheds and provide or ensure access to clean drinking water. In addition, its Children's Mental Health Project grant program demonstrates commitment of resources to children who are among the most vulnerable in Canadian society.[58] Commitments such as these and other highly responsible corporate behaviour has led to RBC being named as one of the "Best 50 Corporate Citizens" in Canada in June 2010 and to rank among the 2010 Global 100 List of the Most Sustainable Corporations in the World.[59] In contrast, other companies such as BP are viewed less positively due to perceptions that they are responsible for extensive environmental damage.

HR professionals play an important role in developing sustainable business practices and programs such as providing employees with training on environmental stewardship, being energy efficient, and collaborating when times are tough.

Customer Service and Quality Emphasis To compete in today's economy, whether on a local or global level, companies need to provide a quality product or service. If companies do not adhere to quality standards, their ability to sell their product or service to vendors, suppliers, or customers will be restricted. Some countries even have quality standards that companies must meet in order to conduct business there. **Total quality management (TQM)** is a cooperative companywide effort to continuously improve the ways people, machines, and systems accomplish work.[60] The HRM function plays a pivotal role in the implementation of TQM, competition for quality awards, pursuit of international standards certification, and implementation of various business strategies to improve the quality of process outputs.

> **Total Quality Management (TQM)**
> A cooperative companywide effort to continuously improve the ways people, machines, and systems accomplish work.

One of the most important ways to improve customer satisfaction is to improve the quality of employees' work experiences, an HRM responsibility. Research shows that satisfied employees are more likely to provide high-quality customer service. Customers who receive high-quality service are more likely to be repeat customers. Organizations that understand this equation are Diversicare Canada Management Services of Mississauga and the Region of Peel. Both won the 2009 Order of Excellence award from the National Quality Institute, Canada's national authority on quality and best practices in the workplace.[61] This hallmark recognition is the result of state-of-the-art human resources practices that create a culture of quality through continuous integrated improvements in employee satisfaction and customer satisfaction, cost savings, decreases in turnover, and much more.

Changing Demographics and Diversity of the Workforce Company performance on the balanced scorecard and TQM are influenced by the characteristics of its workforce. The labour force of current employees is often referred to as the internal labour force. Employers identify and select new employees from the external labour market through recruiting and selection. The external labour market includes persons actively seeking employment. As a result, the skills and motivation of a company's internal labour force are influenced by the composition of the available labour market (the external labour market). The skills and motivation of a company's internal labour force determine the need for training and development practices and the effectiveness of the company's compensation and reward systems.

Two important changes in the demographics and diversity of the workforce are projected. First, the average age of the workforce will increase. Second, the workforce will become more diverse in terms of gender, range of abilities, and racial composition, as immigration and other factors continue to affect the size and diversity of the workforce.

Aging of the Workforce. The labour force will continue to age, due mainly to large numbers of baby boomers in the workforce who are approaching retirement age, and an increasing tendency for older workers to keep on working. The size of the 16–24 youth population will decrease to its lowest level by 2027 (just over 10 percent of the total population), the same year that the number of Canadians aged 55 or older will increase to one in three of all Canadians.[62] The number of 55-and-older workers increased 43 percent between 2001 and 2006, comprising over 15 percent of the workforce,[63] and the number of over-65 workers is expected to double by 2015 from its 2005 levels.[64] The reasons are many. Older individuals are leading healthier and longer lives than in the past, and they are more educated than past generations, which provides them with the opportunity (in favourable labour market conditions) to work longer. And of course, some will continue working because they haven't set aside enough for retirement.

Increased Diversity of the Workforce.

Increased diversity of the Canadian workforce means many things and is created by a number of dynamic factors, often occurring simultaneously. For example:

Employment of individuals with disabilities has been increasing in recent years, as employers and others strive to create more accessible and inclusive workplaces.

- The number of women who work outside the home has increased steadily over the years and women now comprise 47.3 percent of the workforce.[65]
- The employment rate for Aboriginal people has also been increasing for individuals from all Aboriginal groups (Inuit, Métis, and First Nations) since 2001. The unemployment rate of this group of Canadians is currently 19 percent, much higher than the national average.[66]
- Employment of people with disabilities has also increased in the past ten years, although people with disabilities are also still much more likely to be unemployed or out of the labour force than others in the general population (35.2 percent).[67]
- Immigrants now comprise about one-fifth of Canada's labour force[68] and by 2031 approximately one in four of all persons living in Canada will be foreign born. Of the foreign-born group, 55.4 percent will have come from Asia, 20 percent from Europe, and 13.9 percent from Africa. Within the foreign-born group, 71 percent will be visible minorities, bolstering overall growth of visible minorities in Canada to between 25 to 28 percent of Canada's total population by 2031.[69]

The implications of the changing labour market for managing human resources are far reaching. Because labour market growth will be primarily older workers, women, Aboriginal people, visible minorities, and individuals with disabilities, Canadian companies will have to ensure that employees and human resource management systems are free of bias to capitalize on the perspectives and values that such groups can contribute to improving product quality, customer service, product development, and market share. Managing cultural diversity involves many different activities, including creating a respect-based organizational culture that values diversity, ensuring that HRM systems are bias-free, facilitating higher career involvement of women, promoting knowledge and acceptance of cultural differences, ensuring involvement in education both within and outside the company, and dealing with employees' resistance to diversity.[70] In addition, how diversity issues are managed has implications for creativity, problem solving, retaining good employees, and developing markets for the firm's products and services. The bottom line is that to gain a competitive advantage, companies must harness the power of the diverse workforce. The implication of diversity for HRM practices will be highlighted throughout this book.

Learn more about how managing cultural diversity can provide competitive advantage online with Connect.   connect

Legal and Ethical Issues   Five main areas of the legal environment have influenced human resource management over the past 25 years.[71] These areas are employment equity legislation, employee health and safety, compensation and benefits, employee privacy, and job security. Attention is also likely to continue to be focused on human rights issues relating to age, gender, religion, visible minorities, and individuals with disabilities.

Although women are now almost half of the workforce and are advancing into top management ranks, "glass ceilings" still prevent them from getting the experiences necessary to move to top management positions.[72] Research indicates that while 37 percent of management occupations are now filled by women, only 6.4 percent of the heads of FP 500 companies are women.[73] Thus, we are likely to see more challenges to gender discrimination focusing on lack of access to training and development and promotional opportunities that are needed to be considered for top management posts.

An area of litigation that will continue to have a major influence on HRM practices involves job security. Since the mid-90s when companies began to close plants and lay off employees because of restructuring, technology changes, or financial crisis, cases dealing with wrongful dismissal of employees have increased. As the age of the workforce increases, the number of cases dealing with age discrimination in layoffs, promotions, and benefits will likely rise. Employers' work rules, recruitment practices, and performance evaluation systems will need to be revised to ensure that these systems do not falsely communicate employment agreements the company does not intend to honour (such as lifetime employment) or discriminate on the basis of age.

Many decisions related to managing human resources are characterized by uncertainty. Ethics can be considered the fundamental principles by which employees and companies interact.[74] These principles should be considered in making business decisions and interacting with clients and customers.

As a result of corporate scandals at LivEnt, Norbourg, Enron, and more recently AIG, Lehman Brothers, and Goldman Sachs, current interests in ethics focus on transparency, corporate governance, honesty in accounting systems, and even criminal behaviour. But ethics are complicated in a world dominated by global trade, and there are various levels of commitment to ethics that companies may wish to make. HRM involvement is essential if companies wish to move beyond a compliance-based stance on ethics toward a "value-based" approach where expectations and transmission of ethical behaviour become integral to the company culture. This notion was confirmed in the results of Hewitt's 2008 Best Employer in Canada survey, which focused on corporate governance. Survey results indicated that organizations with higher engagement are more effective in implementing people-related aspects of good corporate governance. They do so by making their values very clear to employees, as well as relating everything back to such values "to reinforce how upholding the organization's values help[s] them run a more successful enterprise."[75] HRM plays a pivotal role in creating and sustaining employee engagement and if "great sustainability in the face of business challenges"[76] is indeed one of the key benefits of employee engagement, as Hewitt concluded from its analysis of Best Employer studies around the world, then the HRM function is an essential component for achieving that goal.

Because of linkage between ethics and the HRM function, HR professionals must begin by examining what constitutes ethical behaviour within their own profession. Human resource managers must satisfy three basic standards for their practices to be considered ethical.[77] First, HRM practices must result in the greatest good for the largest number of people. Second, employment practices must respect basic human rights of privacy, due process, consent, and free speech. Third, managers must treat employees and customers equitably and fairly. Human resources professionals interested in accessing more specific information about professional conduct can access the HRPA Professional Rules of Conduct published in June 2009 on the association's website at www.hrpa.ca. The Rules incorporate the HRPA's Code of Ethics for Human Resources Professionals. The National Code of Ethics of the CCHRA can be found at http://www.chrp.ca on the "I am a CHRP" page and through links on individual HR Association websites. Throughout the book we highlight ethical dilemmas in human resource management practices.

The Global Challenge

LO 4

Discuss some of the challenges companies must overcome and the strategies required to compete in the global marketplace.

Companies are finding that to survive they must compete in international markets as well as fend off foreign corporations' attempts to gain ground in North America. To meet these challenges, Canadian businesses must develop global markets, use their practices to improve global competitiveness, and better prepare employees for global assignments.

Every business must be prepared to deal with the global economy. Global business expansion has been made easier by technology; the Internet allows data and information to be instantly accessible around the world. The Internet, e-mail, and video conferencing enable business deals to be completed between companies thousands of miles apart.

Globalization is not limited to any particular sector of the economy, product market, or company size.[78] Companies without international operations may buy or use goods that have been produced overseas, hire employees with diverse backgrounds, or compete with foreign-owned companies operating within Canada.

Businesses around the world are attempting to increase their competitiveness and value by increasing their global presence, often through strategic alliances, mergers, and acquisitions. The "Competing through Globalization" box shows how Canadian clothing manufacturer neon buddha™ successfully competes through offshoring, astute use of technology, and sustainable business and environmental practices that benefit many stakeholders.

Entering International Markets

Many companies are entering international markets by exporting their products overseas, building manufacturing facilities or service centres in other countries, entering into alliances with foreign companies, and engaging in e-commerce. Developing nations such as Taiwan, Indonesia, and China may account for more than 60 percent of the world economy by 2020.[79] According to the Conference Board of Canada, Canada lags significantly in this area, with its share of global foreign direct investment slipping from 11 percent in 1978 to only 3 percent by 2008.[80] Such poor performance is the result of low productivity and low capacity for innovation. There are notable exceptions, such as Research in Motion (RIM), which is moving into China, India, Eastern Europe, the Middle East, Southeast Asia, and Latin America.[81]

Global companies are struggling to both find and retain talented employees, especially in emerging markets but the demand for talented employees often exceeds supply. Also, companies often place successful North American managers in charge of overseas operations, but these managers lack the cultural understanding necessary to attract, motivate, and retain talented employees. To cope with these problems, companies are taking creative approaches to improve cultural understanding. For example, IBM draws more than two-thirds of its revenue from outside the United States and is seeking to build team leadership in order to compete in emerging markets around the world. IBM's Corporate Service Program donates the time and service of about 600 employees for projects in countries such as Turkey, Romania, Ghana, Vietnam, the Phillipines, and Tanzania.[82] The goal of the program is to develop a leadership team that learns about the needs and culture of these countries, while at the same time providing valuable community service. For example, eight IBM employees from five countries travelled to Timisoara, Romania. Each employee was assigned to help a different company or nonprofit organization.

Some companies are also offering cross-cultural training to better prepare managers and their families for overseas assignments, and ensuring that training and development opportunities are available for global employees. These and more HRM issues associated with global issues will be discussed in Chapter 13.

Competing Through Globalization

Offshoring with a Conscience

How does a Canadian company with headquarters in St. Catharines, Ontario, that makes women's clothing designed for travel, home, work, and yoga compete successfully with giants in the fashion industry around the world? Simple—it puts together a business model that is hard if not impossible, to replicate, and then gives away 1 percent (gross) of everything it sells. Sound unlikely?

Consider Pure & Co., maker of neon buddha™ lifestyle clothing, which offshores the production and management of Canadian-designed garments to a team of 300 women in Chiang Mai, Thailand, as well as partnering with a further 4,500 Thai women knitters who work from their homes to produce works of art under the company's other label Pure Handknit.® The company also has an office in the Philippines that handles customer service as well as IT (information technology) functions 24 hours a day to support its offices and customers in Canada, the United States, the United Kingdom, Australia, and Thailand. Guided by a stated belief in karma, the company operates with a progressive management style that encourages staff to take initiative, and then supports that energy with respect, training, and the freedom to make mistakes. The employment deal includes company-paid health care and maternity leave; free English classes for employees and their families and friends (the company has a full-time English teacher from San Francisco), and support for formal education. But since karma is a two-way street, employees are cautioned they must be willing to take responsibility for their department and "contribute for the greater good of the company, its community, and the environment."

In addition to providing for its employees, Pure & Co. acts as a role model in other areas. The company markets its fashion lines around the world through teamwork, partnerships, and sustainable business practices. Such practices include giving back to Thai communities where the company operates through nongovernmental grass-roots organizations such as the Mirror Foundation and the Mae Tao Clinic, which provides free health care for refugees and migrant workers. Pure & Co.'s highly creative President Sébastien Sirois rationalizes giving away 1 percent of gross sales because it is "measurable and simple." Besides, he adds, it's the right thing to do when the company has "the chance to give hope and opportunity for others."

For Pure & Co., competing globally also includes caring about the environment. Materials are routinely recycled and excess fabric is donated to selected nongovernmental organizations and women's groups that can create income-generating projects. The company also plants trees and strives to lessen carbon emissions by shipping more products by sea. By the end of 2010 the company's new completely green dye house will be ready for use, an event wholeheartedly embraced by the local farming community of San Kampheng, just outside Chiang Mai. For a number of reasons, it marks the first time a neighbourhood has actually welcomed a dye house into its farming community. Power will be provided by a 2 MW (2,000,000 watts per hour) biomass power plant that will turn local agricultural waste (straw, corncobs, rice husk, etc.) into electricity and bring income to local farmers. The complex will not only be 100 percent self-sufficient with respect to power, but also produce extra power to be sold to the national grid, replacing electricity currently produced by coal.

As for success, neon buddha™ and Pure Handknit® garments seem to appeal strongly to customers all around the world. Retailers offering its timeless and chic designs range from

Neiman Marcus in the United States to small independently owned shops in the Gulf Islands in British Columbia, where one of the authors of this textbook bought a neon buddha™ pullover. The purchase ensured that two Canadian organizations made a profit, women and men in a developing country would continue to have work, and the world would be a better place.

SOURCES: Based on information from http://www.neonbuddha.net/ourcauses; http://pureandco.com/careers/ /www.maetaoclinic.org/about us; www.mirrorartgroup.org/cms and Dye House Facility Fact Sheet, July 26, 2010.

Offshoring

Offshoring refers to the exporting of jobs from developed countries, such as Canada and the United States to countries where labour and other costs are lower. India, China, Russia, Mexico, Brazil, and the Philippines are some of the destination countries for offshored jobs. Why are jobs offshored?[83] The main reason is labour costs. Workers in some other countries earn a fraction of the wages of North American workers performing the same job. For example, Indian computer programmers receive about $10 an hour compared to $60 per hour earned by North American programmers. Other reasons include the availability of a highly skilled and motivated workforce. Both India and China have high numbers of engineering and science graduates. While Canada has recently boosted the number of graduates in science, math, computer science, and engineering disciplines to just over 22 percent of all graduates, less than 7 percent graduate from engineering and engineering trades, which is very low compared to Finland (16 percent) or Sweden (14 percent).[84] The competition from emerging countries looms large, considering China graduated 325,000 engineers in 2004, five times as many as in the United States and that India graduates 2 million English-speaking students with strong technical and quantitative skills each year.[85] Finally, cheap global telecommunications costs allow companies with engineers 6,000 miles away to complete design work and interact with other engineers as if they were located in the office down the hall.

> **Offshoring**
> Exporting jobs from developed countries to countries where labour and other costs are lower.

Initially, offshoring involved low-skilled manufacturing jobs with repeatable tasks and specific guidelines for how the work was to be completed. North American offshoring now includes high-skilled manufacturing jobs and is also prevalent in the service and information technology sectors. For example, in contrast to computer and printer manufacturer Hewlett-Packard, which hired its first foreign workers 20 years after its founding in 1939, search engine Google employed people outside the United States just three years after its 1998 start.[86]

For the past 40 years or so, Canada has engaged far more in materials offshoring than service offshoring. However, since 2003 service offshoring has become an increasingly important practice among Canadian business services (excluding software and computer use), financial services, and insurance. In addition, although service offshoring is still low in comparison (15 percent) to materials offshoring), it has been growing at a rate of 12 percent per year while materials offshoring has been increasing at just under 9 percent per year.[87] Canadian industry offshoring is primarily to the United States (68 percent), with the balance going to the United Kingdom, Japan, and other OECD countries.[88]

Although companies may be attracted to offshoring because of lower labour costs, a number of other issues must be considered that have implications for the HRM function. First, can employees in the offshored locations provide a level of customer service that is the same as or higher than customers receive from Canadian operations? Second, would offshoring demoralize Canadian employees such that the gains from offshoring would be negated by lower motivation, lower satisfaction, and higher turnover? Third, are local managers adequately trained to motivate and retain offshore employees? Fourth, what is the potential effect, if any, of political unrest in the countries in which operations are offshored? Will employees be safe there? Fifth, what effect would offshoring have on the public image of the company? Would customers or potential customers avoid purchasing products or services because they believe offshoring costs Canadian employees their jobs, or exploits foreign child workers? Would offshoring have an adverse effect on recruiting new employees?

While there has been considerable debate across North America about whether offshoring results in loss of jobs or creates new jobs, a 2008 study by Baldwin and Gu concluded that material and services offshoring has no effect on employment in Canada.[89] Baldwin and Gu also concluded globalization and technological change related to information and communications technologies, discussed next, as well as integration of world economies, are key drivers behind offshoring. Smaller entrepreneurial companies are finding that offshoring helps them expand their business.

LO 5

Identify the challenges of technology and discuss high-performance work systems.

The Technology Challenge

Technology has reshaped the way we play (e.g., games on the Internet), communicate (e.g., smart phones), plan our lives (e.g., electronic calendars that include Internet access), and where we work (e.g., small, powerful personal computers allow us to work at home, while we travel, and even while we lie on the beach). The Internet has created a new business model—e-commerce—in which business transactions and relationships can be conducted electronically. The Internet is a global collection of computer networks that allows users to exchange data and information. For example, customers can now read the *Vancouver Sun* and many local newspapers online; send online greeting cards; purchase clothes, flowers, and airline tickets on the Web; and even arrange to have a shopping service pick up groceries and deliver them. Companies can connect with job candidates across the world on Internet and company-specific job boards, and employees can connect with friends, family, and coworkers using social networking software such as Facebook and Twitter.

How and Where People Work Advances in sophisticated technology along with reduced costs for the technology are changing many aspects of human resource management. Technological advances in electronics and communications software have made possible mobile technology such as smartphones and iPods as well as improving the Internet. For example, the staff of neon buddha™ are distributed all across the globe, but coworkers keep things moving around the clock using highly integrated computer technology, cellphones, and Skype to hold meetings and exchange information. They even have a virtual watercooler on a secure site so that staff can socialize across the miles.[90] The Internet and the Web allow employees to send and receive information as well as to locate and gather resources, including software, reports, photos, and videos. The Internet gives employees instant access to experts with whom they can communicate and to newsgroups, which are bulletin boards dedicated to specific areas of interest, where employees can read, post, and respond to messages and articles. Internet sites also have home pages—mailboxes that identify the person or company and contain text, images, sounds, and video.

Robotics, radio frequency identification, and nanotechnology and computer-assisted design such as that used by Standen's in Calgary are transforming manufacturing.[91] Technology has also made equipment easier to operate, helping companies cope with skill shortages and allowing older workers to postpone retirement. For example, consider working a grader construction vehicle (which is used to smooth and level dirt on roadways and other construction projects). Older vehicle models required operating as many as 15 levers in addition to a steering wheel and several foot pedals, leaving operators with sore backs and shoulders at the end of the day. Caterpillar's latest version of the grader includes redesigned controls that use only two joysticks and eliminate the physical demands of pushing pedals and turning a steering wheel. Besides reducing the physical demands, the redesign of the grader without a steering wheel resulted in operators having better visibility of the steel blade, and switches for lights, windshield wipers, and the parking brake could be grouped together in one place in the cab.

Technology is pushing the boundaries of artificial intelligence, speech synthesis, wireless communications, and networked virtual reality.[92] Realistic graphics, dialogue, and sensory cues can now be stored on tiny, inexpensive computer chips. These advances have the potential for freeing workers from going to a specific location to work and from traditional work schedules. For example, a recent survey found that 37 percent of employers offer telecommuting on a part-time basis and 23 percent on a full-time basis.[93] Telecommuting has the potential to increase employee productivity, encourage family-friendly work arrangements, and help reduce traffic and air pollution. But at the same time, technologies may result in employees being on call 24 hours a day, 7 days a week. Many companies are taking steps to provide more flexible work schedules to protect employees' free time and to more productively use employees' work time.

High-Performance Work Systems New technology causes changes in skill requirements and work roles, and often results in redesigning work structures (e.g., using work teams).[94] **High-performance work systems** maximize the fit between the company's social system (employees) and its technical system.[95] For example, computer-integrated manufacturing uses robots and computers to automate the manufacturing process. The computer allows the production of different products simply by reprogramming the computer. As a result, labourer, material handler, operator/assembler, and maintenance jobs may be merged into one position. Computer-integrated manufacturing requires employees to monitor equipment and troubleshoot problems with sophisticated equipment, share information with other employees, and understand the relationships between all components of the manufacturing process.[96] Consider the changes Canon Inc., known for office imaging, computer peripherals, and cameras, has made to speed up the development and production process.[97] Canon is using a procedure called concurrent engineering, where production engineers work together with designers. This allows them to more easily exchange ideas to improve a product or make it easier to manufacture. Canon also now has production employees work in "cells," where they perform multiple tasks and can more easily improve the production process. Previously, employees worked in an assembly line controlled by a conveyor belt. The new cell system requires lower parts inventory and less space, cutting factory operating and real estate costs. Also, employees are more satisfied working in cells because they feel more responsibility for their work.

Working in Teams and Partnerships. Through technology, the information needed to improve customer service and product quality becomes more accessible to employees. This means that employees are expected to take more responsibility for satisfying the customer

High-Performance Work Systems
Work systems that maximize the fit between the company's social system (employees) and technical system.

Technology speeds up completion of projects and even makes it possible for virtual teams to work around the clock if members are located around the globe.

and determining how they perform their jobs. One of the most popular methods for increasing employee responsibility and control is work teams, and partnerships including virtual work teams.

Work teams involve employees with various skills who interact to assemble a product or provide a service. Work teams may assume many of the activities usually reserved for managers, including selecting new team members, scheduling work, and coordinating activities with customers and other units in the company.

Besides changing the way that products are built or services are provided within companies, technology has allowed companies to form partnerships with one or more other companies, resulting in teamwork that reaches beyond boundaries within companies and even countries as employees form virtual teams. **Virtual teams** refer to teams that are separated by time, geographic distance, culture, and/or organizational boundaries and that rely almost exclusively on technology (e-mail, Internet, videoconferencing) to interact and complete their projects. Virtual teams can be formed within one company, such as Pure & Co., mentioned in "Competing through Globalization," whose sales representatives and management communicate virtually with one another, customers and suppliers located in Canada, the United States, Australia, the United Kingdom, Thailand, and Philippines.[98] A company may also use virtual teams in partnerships with suppliers or competitors to pull together the necessary talent to complete a project or speed the delivery of a product to the marketplace. For example, the Pure & Co. transportation network allows 4,500 knitters in Thailand to work in their villages while the company delivers specs and yarn to them, then picks up the finished product for centralized quality control and distribution.[99]

Software developers are positioning employees around the world with clusters of three or four facilities, six to eight hours apart, to keep projects moving 24 hours a day.[100] The intent is to increase productivity and reduce project completion time by allowing employees to focus continuously on projects through using highly talented engineers who can work in their own time zone and location without having to move to a different country or work inconvenient hours. Also, globally distributed projects can draw on employees from many different cultures, backgrounds, and perspectives, helping to produce services and products that can better meet the needs of global customers. The challenges are how to organize work so that teams in different locations and different work shifts can share tasks with minimum interaction.

Changes in Skill Requirements.
High-performance work systems have implications for employee selection and training of employees at all levels as skill requirements change over time. For example, employees need job-specific knowledge and basic skills to work with the equipment created with the new technology. Because technology is often used as a means to achieve product diversification and customization, employees must have the ability to listen and communicate with customers. Interpersonal skills, such as negotiation and conflict management, and problem-solving skills are more important than physical strength, coordination, and fine motor skills—previous job requirements for many manufacturing and service jobs. Although technological advances have made it possible for employees to improve products and services, managers must be taught how to empower employees to make changes. In addition, use of new technology and work designs such as work teams and virtual teams need to be supported by cross-training, which refers to training employees in a wide range of skills so they can fill any of the roles needed to be performed on the team.

Changes in Company Structure and Reporting Relationships.
The traditional design of North American companies emphasizes efficiency, decision making by managers, and dissemination of information from the top of the company to lower levels. However, this structure is not effective in the current work environment, in which personal computers give employees immediate access to information needed to complete customer orders or modify product lines. In the adaptive organizational structure, employees are in a constant state of learning and performance improvement. Employees are free to move wherever they are needed in the company. The adaptive organization is characterized

Virtual Teams
Teams that are separated by time, geographic distance, culture, and/or organizational boundaries and rely almost exclusively on technology for interaction between team members.

by a core set of values or a vital vision that drives all organizational efforts.[101] Previously established boundaries between managers and employees, employees and customers, employees and vendors, and the various functions within the company are abandoned. Employees, managers, vendors, customers, and suppliers work together to improve service and product quality and to create new products and services. Line employees are trained in multiple jobs, communicate directly with suppliers and customers, and interact frequently with engineers, quality experts, and employees from other functions.

Increased Use and Availability of e-HRM and Human Resource Information Systems (HRIS) **Electronic human resource management (e-HRM)** refers to the processing and transmission of digitized information used in HRM, including text, sound, and visual images from one computer or electronic device to another. New technologies and advances in software, including avatars, collaborative social networks, and mobile technologies such as iPods, are influencing training, development, work design, recruiting, and other aspects of HR.

> **Electronic Human Resource Management (e-HRM)**
> The processing and transmission of digitized information used in HRM.

For example, Capital One, a U.S. financial service company, uses an audio learning program that allows employees to learn through their iPods at their own convenience.[102] The company has also developed a mobile audio learning channel, which supplements competency-based and leadership and management programs and other existing company training courses. It is also used to ensure that employees receive information when they need it.

Companies continue to use human resource information systems to store large quantities of employee data including personal information, training records, skills, compensation rates, absence records, and benefits usages and costs. A **human resource information system (HRIS)** is a system used to acquire, store, manipulate, analyze, retrieve, and distribute information related to a company's human resources.[103] An HRIS can support strategic decision making, help the company avoid lawsuits, provide data for evaluating policies and programs, and support day-to-day HR decisions. The "Competing through Technology" box shows how IBM has used technology to create a Workforce Management Initiative (WMI), a single integrated and highly cost effective approach to hiring, managing, developing, and deploying IBM's global workforce.

> **Human Resource Information System (HRIS)**
> A system used to acquire, store, manipulate, analyze, retrieve, and distribute information related to a company's human resources.

Learn more about the implications of e-HRM for HRM practices online with Connect.

 connect

Competitiveness in High-Performance Work Systems. Human resource management practices that support high-performance work systems include employee selection, performance management, training, work design, and compensation. These practices are designed to give employees skills, incentives, knowledge, and autonomy. Research studies suggest that high-performance work practices are usually associated with increases in productivity and long-term financial performance.[104] Research also suggests that it is more effective to improve HRM practices as a whole, rather than focus on one or two isolated practices (such as the pay system or selection system).[105] There may be a best HRM system, but whatever the company does, the practices must be aligned with each other and be consistent with the system if they are to positively affect company performance.[106] We will discuss this alignment in more detail in chapters 2 and 4.

HRM AT THE CROSSROADS

> **LO 6**
> Discuss the transformation of the HRM function.

Throughout this chapter we have emphasized how human resource management practices can help companies gain a competitive advantage. We have also discussed the best of current research and practice to show how they may contribute to a company's competitive advantage, and how the role of the HRM function has been evolving over time. Most HR executives have recognized the need to make the function's major role into one that is much more strategic.

Competing Through Technology

HR Drives Success at IBM

In the technology world, change is constant, fast, and difficult to manage, so running the human resource function in a company such as IBM presents a tremendous set of challenges. However, for the past 11 years, J. Randall MacDonald has taken on this challenge, driving change in the business and change in HR.

Since joining IBM, the company has moved from predominantly manufacturing computers to a software and services company. Such a strategic shift requires an entirely new set of organizational capabilities and, consequently, different kinds of people with different skills. In addition, the company has consistently increased its global footprint with decreasing employment in North America and vast increases in areas such as central Europe, China, and India. This "global transformation" cannot work by having seemingly unconnected operations in 170 countries, each practically working in a vacuum. Rather, the company needs to be nimble, ready to meet and exceed client expectations around the world quickly and effectively. In his role as chief human resource officer, MacDonald has overseen a function that has added value through this transformation.

For example, the company provides an intranet port called Learning @IBM Explorer that offers individual career guidance and learning plans, underwriting the company's extensive approach to individual and career development.

However, one particularly innovative HR project that has added immense value to IBM's business strategy occurred when MacDonald co-led a technology project aimed at creating a single, integrated approach to hiring, managing, developing, and deploying IBM's global workforce. The result, called the "Workforce Management Initiative (WMI)," proved to be a leading-edge innovation no one else had done within HR. Key components of the system include the Global Opportunity Marketplace, which speeds up processing of thousands of job applications and the job offers made every day. Expertise Assessments provides a consistent taxonomy to describe skills; the ability to measure talent supply and demand; and a built-in, integrated approach to sharing talent data across each of the applications within the WMI application suite. Professional Marketplace provides a more efficient, effective way to find and deploy skilled IBMers needed to help solve clients' problems or respond to their requests. Over the past three years, WMI has saved the company more than $276 million.

MacDonald is clear about why the company invested $100 million in the WMI project, saying, "This is the first time HR ever directly contributed to the strategy at IBM. What's the proof point? HR converting the strategy into execution."

SOURCE: Tom Starner, "A Passion at the Helm," October 16, 2008, http://www.hreonline.com/HRE/story .jsp?storyId=136568343&query=IBM.

For those still in doubt, Table 1.3 provides several questions that managers can use to determine if HRM is playing a strategic role in the business. If these questions have not been considered, it is highly unlikely that (1) the company is prepared to deal with competitive challenges or (2) human resources are being used to help a company gain a competitive advantage. The bottom line for evaluating the relationship between human resource management and the business strategy is to consider this question: "What is HR doing to ensure that the right people with the right skills are doing the right things in the jobs that are important for the execution of the business strategy?"[107]

Table 1.3 Questions Used to Determine If Human Resources Are Playing a Strategic Role in the Business

1. What is HR doing to provide value-added services to internal clients?
2. What can the HR department add to the bottom line?
3. How are you measuring the effectiveness of HR?
4. How can we reinvest in employees?
5. What HR strategy will we use to get the business from point A to point B?
6. What makes an employee want to stay at our company?
7. How are we going to invest in HR so that we have a better HR department than our competitors?
8. From an HR perspective, what should we be doing to improve our marketplace position?
9. What's the best change we can make to prepare for the future?

SOURCES: Data from A. Halcrow, "Survey Shows HR in Transition," *Workforce*, June 1988, p. 74; P. Wright, *Human Resource Strategy: Adapting to the Age of Globalization* (Alexandria, VA: Society for Human Resource Management Foundation, 2008).

The HRM function now appears to be at a crossroads. Virtually every HRM function in top companies is going through a transformation process to create a function that can play this new strategic role while successfully fulfilling its other roles. In fact, according to a recent study, 64 percent of HR executives said that their HRM function is in a process of transformation.[108] This transformation process is occurring globally. As the role of HRM in administration has decreased, other roles such as practice development and strategic business partnering have increased. One of the most comprehensive studies ever conducted regarding HRM concluded that "human resources is being transformed from a specialized, standalone function to a broad corporate competency in which human resources and line managers build partnerships to gain competitive advantage and achieve overall business goals."[109]

To understand the transformation going on in HRM, one must understand HRM activities in terms of their strategic value. One way of classifying these activities is depicted in Figure 1.4. Transactional activities (the day-to-day transactions such as benefits administration, record keeping, and employee services) are low in their strategic value. Traditional activities such as performance management, training, recruiting, selection, compensation, and employee relations are the nuts and bolts of HRM. These activities have moderate strategic value because they often form the practices and systems to ensure strategy execution. Transformational activities create long-term capability and adaptability for the firm. These activities include knowledge management, management development, cultural change, and strategic redirection and renewal. Obviously, these activities comprise the greatest strategic value for the firm and it is these areas where HRM must spend more time if it is to maximize its contribution to the strategic management of the organization.

MEETING COMPETITIVE CHALLENGES THROUGH HRM PRACTICES

In this introductory chapter we have discussed the global, technological, and sustainability challenges North American companies are facing, and emphasized that management of human resources plays a critical role in determining companies' success in meeting these challenges. For example, to meet the sustainability challenge, companies need to weather difficult economic changes and figure out how to retain key staff until the economy improves. To meet all three challenges, companies need to capitalize on the diversity of values, abilities, and perspectives that employees bring to the workplace.

FIGURE 1.4 Categories of HRM Activities and Percentages of Time Spent on Them

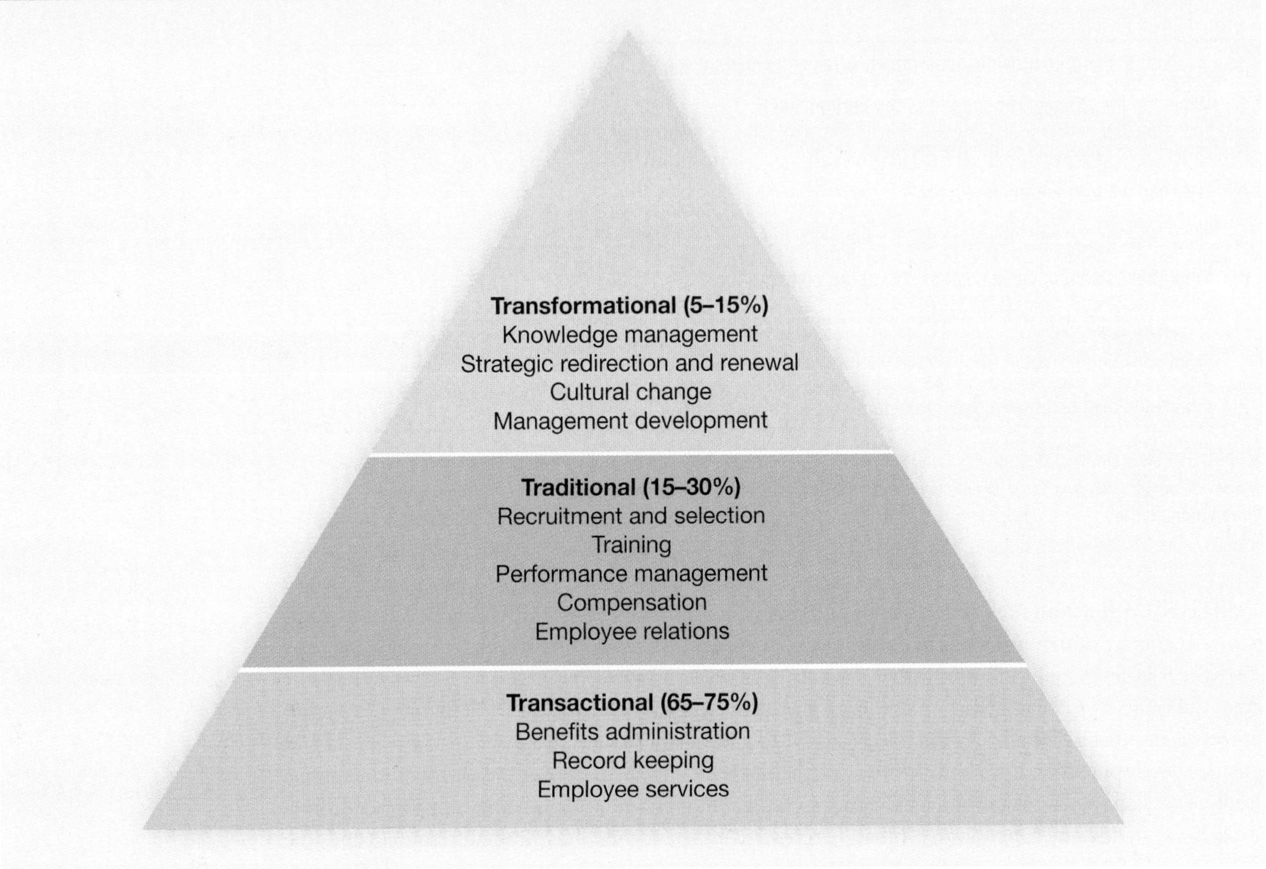

Transformational (5–15%)
Knowledge management
Strategic redirection and renewal
Cultural change
Management development

Traditional (15–30%)
Recruitment and selection
Training
Performance management
Compensation
Employee relations

Transactional (65–75%)
Benefits administration
Record keeping
Employee services

SOURCE: P. Wright, G. McMahan, S. Snell, and B. Gerhart, *Strategic Human Resource Management: Building Human Capital and Organizational Capability.* Technical report. Cornell University, 1998.

In Chapter 2 we will discuss the strategic management process that takes place at the organization level and the role of HRM in this process. We will also address what the HRM function must do to move away from its traditional transactional approach shown in Figure 1.4 to become truly strategic in its orientation. We will explain how HR executives such as those found in more progressive companies have begun to view the HRM function as a strategic business unit, defining that business in terms of their customer base, their customers' needs, and the technologies and structural changes required to satisfy customers' needs. The sustainability, global, and technological challenges facing companies today are daunting indeed. However, the chapters ahead are designed to equip you with the information and motivation you need to see the big picture and the invaluable role that the HRM function can play in building human capital. It's a realization Research in Motion made back in 2001 when it ramped up the role of HR in the organization and created a new position that would also be part of its executive team—its first vice president of HR. Don Morrison, chief operating officer of RIM supported the move, saying the company needed leadership and expertise in this area to bring it to another level, adding "In all well-run companies this is done."[110]

If companies such as RIM are an indication of what HRM can do to help companies grow and change, clearly there has never been a more exciting time to be in HR. Welcome aboard!

A Look Back

In its 25 years of existence, Research in Motion (RIM) has experienced innumerable challenges while becoming an "overnight success" with its famous BlackBerry® smart phone. Market share of the smartphone has surpassed other tech giants like Apple and Nokia in the past but new challenges have arisen. RIM's market share is challenged daily by emerging smart-phone technology (especially in the number of downloadable "apps" available), and the soaring tablet market is a major focus. In addition, the company has recently done battle with less democratic international governments willing to ban the product unless provided with access in order to intercept and monitor user messaging.

1. What HR practices do you believe are the most critical in helping RIM to fend off competitors and continue its impressive growth?

2. Could RIM be as successful without its current HR practices? Explain?

3. Do you think the culture and HR practices RIM uses to support its employees would be as successful in other industries such as health care or education? Explain why or why not.

Summary

This chapter introduced the roles and activities of a company's human resource management function and emphasized that effective management of human resources can contribute to a company's business strategy and competitive advantage. To successfully manage human resources, individuals need personal credibility as business leaders, business knowledge, understanding of the business strategy, technology knowledge, and the ability to deliver HR services. Human resource management practices should be evidence based, that is, based on data showing the relationship between the practice and business outcomes related to key company stakeholders (employees, customers, community, and shareholders). In addition to contributing to a company's business strategy, human resource practices are important for helping companies deal with sustainability, globalization, and technology challenges. The sustainability challenges are related to the economy, the changing characteristics and expectations of the labour force, the value placed on intangible assets and human capital, and meeting stakeholder needs (return to shareholders, social responsibility, high-quality products and services, and ethical practices). Global challenges include entering international markets, and offshoring. Technology challenges include using new technologies to support flexible and virtual work arrangements and high-performance work systems.

In this chapter we have explored the various changing roles of the HRM function. HRM today must play roles as an administrative expert, employee advocate, change agent, and strategic partner. The function must also deliver transactional, traditional, and transformational services and activities to the firm, and it must be both efficient and effective. The chapter concludes by explaining that the HRM function is at a crossroads where HRM professionals must hold up the mirror and ask if the HRM function plays a strategic role in the business, and to realize the key role HRM has to play in meeting business challenges of sustainability, technology, and globalization.

Key Terms

Alternative work arrangements, 18	Electronic HRM (e-HRM), 29	High-performance work systems, 27
Balanced scorecard, 19	Employee engagement, 17	Human resource information system (HRIS), 29
Competitiveness, 5	Evidence-based HR, 9	

Human resource management (HRM), 5

Intangible assets, 14

Offshoring, 25

Psychological contract, 17

Sustainability, 11

Talent management, 18

Total quality management (TQM), 20

Virtual teams, 28

Discussion Questions

1. Traditionally, human resource management practices were developed and administered by the company's human resource department. Line managers are now playing a major role in developing and implementing HRM practices. Why do you think non-HR managers are becoming more involved in developing and implementing HRM practices?

2. Staffing, training, compensation, and performance management are important HRM functions. How can each of these functions help companies succeed in meeting the global challenge, the challenge of using new technology, and the sustainability challenge?

3. What are intangible assets? How are they influenced by human resource management practices?

4. What is "evidence-based HR"? Why might an HR department resist becoming evidence based?

5. Do you agree with the statement "Employee engagement is something companies should be concerned about only if they are making money"? Explain.

6. What is sustainability? How can HR practices help a company become more socially and environmentally conscious? How can HR practices facilitate ethical business decisions?

7. Explain the implications of each of the following labour force trends for HRM: (1) aging workforce, (2) diverse workforce, (3) skill imbalances.

8. What role do HRM practices play in a business decision to expand internationally?

9. What might a quality goal and high-performance work systems have in common in terms of HRM practices?

10. What factors should a company consider before offshoring? What are the advantages and disadvantages of offshoring?

11. What are virtual teams and how do they contribute to sustainability? Provide an example of a virtual team mentioned in this chapter.

12. Is HRM becoming more strategic? Explain your answer.

Self-Assessment Exercise: Do You Recognize Unethical Actions?

Ethics are complicated in a global marketplace and companies vary in terms of their commitment to ethics. This makes it essential for HRM to become involved if companies wish to move beyond mere compliance and toward a more sustainable, "value-based approach" where expectations and transmission of ethical behaviour become integral to the company culture. Consider your own knowledge of ethics and how well prepared you might be if presented with an ethical dilemma. How ethical are you?

Instructions: Read each of the following descriptions of individuals' actions. For each, circle whether you believe the behaviour described is ethical or unethical.

1. A company president found that a competitor had made an important scientific discovery that would sharply reduce the profits of his own company. The president hired a key employee of the competitor in an attempt to learn the details of the discovery.	Ethical Unethical

2. To increase profits, a general manager used a production process that exceeded legal limits for environmental pollution.	Ethical Unethical
3. Because of pressure from her brokerage firm, a stockbroker recommended a type of bond that she did not consider to be a good investment.	Ethical Unethical
4. A small business received one-quarter of its revenues in the form of cash. On the company's income tax forms, the owner reported only one-half of the cash receipts.	Ethical Unethical
5. A corporate executive promoted a loyal friend and competent manager to the position of divisional vice president instead of a better qualified manager with whom she had no close ties.	Ethical Unethical
6. An employer received applications for a supervisor's position from two equally qualified applicants. The employer hired the male applicant because he thought some employees might resent being supervised by a female.	Ethical Unethical
7. An engineer discovered what he perceived to be a product design flaw that constituted a safety hazard. His company declined to correct the flaw. The engineer decided to keep quiet, rather than taking his complaint outside the company.	Ethical Unethical
8. A comptroller selected a legal method of financial reporting that concealed some embarrassing financial facts. Otherwise, those facts would have been public knowledge.	Ethical Unethical
9. A company paid a $350,000 "consulting" fee to an official of a foreign country. In return, the official promised to help the company obtain a contract that should produce a $10 million profit for the company.	Ethical Unethical
10. A member of a corporation's board of directors learned that his company intended to announce a stock split and increase its dividend. On the basis of this favourable information, the director bought additional shares of the company's stock. Following the announcement of the information, he sold the stock at a gain.	Ethical Unethical

Now score your results. How many actions did you judge to be unethical?

All of these actions are unethical. The more of the actions you judged to be unethical, the better your understanding of ethical business behaviour.

SOURCE: Based on S. Morris et al., "A Test of Environmental, Situational, and Personal Influences on the Ethical Intentions of CEOs," *Business and Society* 34 (1995), pp. 119–47.

Exercising Strategy: Focused Retention Strategies

The recent recession has served to remind employers that retention of key talent is critical not only to survival, but also to keeping growth neurons firing while the economy is idling. In any case, with over a million boomers poised to retire, or phasing out of the workforce in the next three to four years, employers know that things will continue to heat up in what may soon become a job seekers' job market. At the same time it's crucial to avoid unnecessary recruitment costs until better conditions for growth return, which means retaining good employees by ensuring they are as engaged as possible. But engagement can mean different things to different people and retention strategies can vary in terms of what actually makes employees want to stay put. Each company must look carefully at what works for it and gather as much information as possible to form the best strategies possible.

One company that has been rated above average in employee engagement is Ceridian Canada Ltd., a business process outsourcing company and one of Canada's Top 100 Employers. To maintain and increase engagement, the company utilizes a number of strategic human resource practices such as providing individual online performance reviews (from managers trained in the process) every six months. Such reviews also provide employees with the ability to give confidential feedback on their manager's performance. The process encourages ongoing dialogue between managers and employees. Employees who are top performers are recognized with unique awards and gift certificates and the company also has a peer recognition program in which employees can nominate one another for awards and prizes and the chance to win a paid vacation to a resort as part of the annual "President's Club Award."

An in-house employee satisfaction survey also provides insight into what is important to employees, along with a second, externally conducted confidential employee satisfaction and engagement survey. Both surveys are done every 12 months, providing ample opportunity for the company to gather the information needed to quickly make any adjustments needed. What makes these approaches especially important is that Ceridian's workforce consists mostly of experts in the area of payroll and benefits who spend their workdays providing advice and services to other human resource professionals.

Questions:

1. Why might the opportunity to provide feedback with respect to their manager's performance help with retention of Ceridian employees? Is it fair to managers?

2. Do you think it is a good idea to present top performers with awards and gift certificates? Is there a downside to this practice?

3. What is the value of having a peer recognition program such as the one Ceridian sponsors for its employees?

SOURCES: Based on P. Sullivan, "Human Capital: Creating a Culture of Engagement," *HR Professional*, 25(2), (February/March 2008), p. 49; http://www.holtrenfrew.com/holts/pages/careers/careers-at-holts.dot?language_id=1&url=66216#I-Thrive; Canada's Top 100 Employers 2011 (National) at http://www.eluta.ca/top-employer-ceridian-canada.

Managing People: Helping Health-Care Workers Avoid Role Overload

A recent study in Canada's Health Sector by Linda Duxbury and Chris Higgins involving over 1,400 employees in four Ottawa hospitals revealed that only 25 percent of participants felt they were strongly supported by their employers when coping with something called role overload—the combination of "too many responsibilities and not enough time to attend to them." This means that 75 percent of study participants felt they could be getting more (42 percent) or a lot more (33 percent) support to deal with job-related stress. According to the study, role overload is a combination of inadequate staff and equipment, poor communication, high expectations, and unpredictable, complex work with high task interdependence. Add in an urgent culture that seems to tolerate only a "can do" attitude (despite constant downsizing and restructuring), public scrutiny, and life-or-death consequences, and you have stressed-out workers. If there isn't support at home, then the result can be difficulty coping on both fronts—work and home—or total overload. The study also revealed that 80 percent of managers surveyed feel overloaded and stressed, a situation they said is aggravated by a lack of role clarity. Duxbury describes this as the need to be everything to everyone, and she says it is the result of having too large a span of control and in some cases from being responsible for staff around the clock.

The study's results are even more concerning when considered in the context of an aging population. Baby boomers now working in hospitals will soon begin to retire or phase out of full-time work, at the same time as demands on the health care system increase due to growing numbers of aging patients needing complex levels of care. One such situation occurred recently in the Timmins and District Hospital when hospital beds suddenly began filling with patients who belonged in nursing homes. Instead of the 85 percent occupancy the hospital had planned for, in a matter of months the hospital found itself with 110 percent occupancy. Much like the Ottawa study, nurses rapidly began to burn out in a difficult and unpredicted situation. So the obvious question seems to be: If the majority of people who currently care for the physically and mentally ill are now experiencing role overload, and the majority of their managers also report feeling overwhelmed and unable to provide the support they know their employees need, how bad will things get in Canada's future health-care system?

Duxbury and Higgins are emphatic that the solution is not just a matter of adding more staff. In fact, they believe that is the worst thing that can happen. For things to improve, they say change must be focused on two key areas: "the immediate manager and the organizational culture." Higgins believes this is important because "the employees with the most supportive managers have fewer problems than those with non-supportive managers, in any industry." Greg Earles, vice president of HR and organizational effectiveness at Queensway Carleton Hospital, one of the hospitals studied, notes that to do this, the right change management process would have to be in place because employees must understand and be equipped to deal with the change, and they might need to "lead and be champions of change."

Emma Pavlov, senior vice president of Toronto's University Health Network (UHN), a three-site hospital with 14,000 employees, would no doubt agree, but might add that for a change management process to be effective, managers must first acquire change management skills, so they can model the way, and feel less overwhelmed in the bargain. UHN is so committed to supporting managers it has already partnered with Toronto's Rotman School of Management to create a mandatory annual Leadership Development program for all directors and managers. Change management is a core component of the program. Pavlov and her team have also worked hard to change adversarial union/management relations over the past 12 years by creating a clear strategy to change the relationship and then implementing mandatory training for all new managers on collaborative labour relations. Mike Resetar, chief human resources officer at Timmins and District Hospital, and his team have also built a collaborative labour relations process. Other initiatives include Weight Watchers, yoga and a walking club, flexible scheduling, mentoring, and financial support for nurses to upgrade their skills. At Bluewater Health in Sarnia, Director of HR Colleen Cook describes alleviating the stresses of shift work for older nurses by involving them in projects that remove the need to be on rotation for awhile.

Duxbury and Higgins have sounded the warning: workers in health care are feeling the pressure of role overload, and their insights offer much to think about for both policy makers and HRM in health-care settings. The solutions implemented by Toronto's University Health Network, Bluewater Health, and Timmins and District Hospital offer hope for HR strategies focussed on the future. But as the Ottawa study portends, there is still much to be done if we are avoid losing valuable health-care workers to stress and role overload

Questions

1. Based on your experience in the health-care system, do you find the results of Duxbury and Higgins's study to be surprising? Why or why not?
2. Does the approach taken to change management put in place by Toronto University Health Network seem effective? What else might need to be done?
3. How might more collaborative labour relations at UHN and Timmins and District Hospital help to reduce or avoid role overload among employees and managers in these health-care settings? Could such an approach help with total overload among those employees who lack support at home? If so, what difference would it make?

SOURCES: Based on S. Dobson, "Health Workers Overloaded: Study," *Canadian HR Reporter* (March 8, 2010), pp. 3, 8; D. McCutcheon "Health Care HR," *HR Professional*, 26 (June/July 2009) p. 45; L. Duxbury, C. Higgins & S. Lyons, *The Etiology and Reduction of Role Overload in Canada's Health-Care Sector* (Ottawa: Carleton University, 2010).

Practise and learn online with Connect.

CHAPTER 2

Strategic Human Resource Management

Enter the World of Business

GM's Attempt to Survive

The auto industry in North American has recently faced a financial crisis, to the point that General Motors, the once-great, world-leading automobile manufacturer, had to declare bankruptcy in the United States and received $30 billion in government aid under the Troubled Asset Relief Program (TARP). While GM Canada did not declare bankruptcy, it received $3 billion in temporary loans from the Canada Development Investment Corporation and from the Government of Ontario, funds that were proportional to the bailout offered by the U.S. government. When the dust had settled, the U.S. Treasury Department had temporarily acquired 61 percent ownership of General Motors Company, and the Canadian government had acquired another 12 percent, inspiring a new nickname—"Government Motors." The bailouts were meant to be a stopgap only—something to get GM through the next few years while management tried to restructure the company in a way it will make it viable for the long term. What kind of restructuring was required? In essence, GM needed to create a new business model that will enable the company to sell enough cars at a high enough price to cover its costs—and it is the costs that have been killing GM.

Critics of GM talk about the fact that GM has had higher labour costs than its foreign competitors. This is true, but misleading. GM's average hourly wage for its existing workforce has been reasonably competitive. However, the two aspects that made GM uncompetitive were its benefit costs (in particular, health care) and, most importantly, the cost of its legacy workforce.

A legacy workforce describes the former workers (i.e., those no longer working for the company) to whom the firm still owes financial obligations. Over the years, both the Canadian Auto Workers (CAW) and the United Auto Workers (UAW) unions negotiated collective agreements with GM that provided substantial retirement benefits for former GM workers. In particular, retired GM workers were covered under defined-benefit plans that guaranteed a certain percentage of their final (preretirement) salary as a pension payment as long as they live, as well as having the company pay health-care premiums. In addition, the contract specified that workers were entitled to retire at full pension after 30 years of service. That meant that someone who started at age 18 could retire at age 48 and, according to actuarial tables, potentially get 30 more years of pension and health insurance for the 30 years he or she worked.

This might have seemed sustainable when the projections were that GM would continue growing its sales and margins. However, since the 1970s, foreign competitors have been eating away at the market share of North American automakers. Between 1996 and 2004, the Big Three automakers (GM, Ford, and Chrysler) lost 13 percent of the market, job losses were mounting, and technology and globalization were taking their toll. GM's U.S. sales figures have been in constant, increasing decline since 1999. At last the CAW began to see the future in different, more realistic terms and, in 2004, Buzz Hargrove entered negotiations with a different mindset. He chose to negotiate the first deal among the Big Three with Ford because the CAW enjoyed the best relationship with that company. However, talks resulted in the lowest wage hikes in the history of the CAW along with a net job loss of 1,100 workers. In its deal with Ford, the CAW "signalled a dramatic shift in focus from getting the most money in wages, pensions, and benefits, to getting a deal that tried to save jobs—or at the very least to mitigate the loss." The deal signalled the end of an era.

Following the bailouts, GM struggled to come up with a new business model. In addition to the legacy workforce, it was saddled with a significant number of plants with thousands of employees who had become completely unnecessary, given the volume of cars GM can produce and sell. Unfortunately, those excess resources were located in Canada as well, where the first plant to open was GM Annex in Windsor, 90 years ago, followed over the years by 12 other plants in other Ontario cities and Quebec. Clearly, massive change was about to happen as GM began to face up to government demands that the company examine its assumptions surrounding overall auto sales, market share as it corresponds to its current product mix, and all long-term product plans, in return for loans that give the company time to do so.

So the crisis that faced GM could be summarized as one of falling revenues and stable, or even increasing, fixed costs (considering the existing workforce as well as the legacy workforce). GM's remaining 12,000 employees in Canada, along with their American counterparts, found themselves counting on a miracle. Eventually, like a phoenix rising from the smouldering ashes of the old GM, hope emerged. On July 10, 2009, an entirely new entity was incorporated called the General Motors Company. By November 2010, it made a successful $23 billion public offering on major stock exchanges, raising funds that allowed the company to make substantial repayments on government loans.

In the new company's *Annual Report* for 2010, Daniel F. Akerson, chairman and CEO, describes the new business model as one with "a lower cost structure, a stronger balance sheet and a dramatically lower risk profile." He goes on to point out that in its first full year of operation, the new business model helped the General Motors Company achieve net income attributable to common stockholders of $4.7 billion, sales of $135.6 billion, and earnings per share of $2.89, after reducing debt by more than $11 billion, and making a $4 billion cash contribution to improve pension funding levels. Akerson indicated that future growth will be based on three key areas: developing great new products for customers worldwide, engaging more effectively with customers, and focusing on financial discipline.

SOURCES: P. Ingrassia "GM's Plan: Subsidize Our 48-Year Old Retirees," *The Wall Street Journal* (February 19, 2009) at http://online.wsj.com/article/SB123500874299418721.html; S. Terlep and N. King, "Bondholders Say GM's Plan Fails to Tackle Issues," *The Wall Street Journal* (February 19, 2009) at http://online.wsj.com/article/SB123500467245718075.html?mod=testMod.; Norman DeBono, "Paradigm Shift," *London Free Press*

(September 17, 2005); "GM Closes Windsor Plant, Ending an Era," CBC News Business (July 28, 2010), at http://www.cbc.ca/news/business/story/2010/07/28/wdr-gm-plant-closing.html (retrieved June 10, 2011); "The Governments of Canada and Ontario Reject Automakers' Restructuring Plans" (March 30, 2009), Ottawa, Industry Canada News Release; General Motors Company 2010 *Annual Report,* "This Is the New GM."

INTRODUCTION

As the General Motors example illustrates, business organizations exist in an environment of competition. They can use a number of resources to compete with other companies. These resources are physical (such as plant, equipment, technology, and geographic location), organizational (the structure, planning, controlling, and coordinating systems, and group relations), and human (the experience, skill, and intelligence of employees). It is these resources under the control of the company that provide competitive advantage.[1]

The goal of strategic management in an organization is to deploy and allocate resources in a way that gives it a competitive advantage. As you can see, two of the three classes of resources (organizational and human) are directly tied to the human resource management function. As Chapter 1 pointed out, the role of human resource management is to ensure that a company's human resources provide a competitive advantage. Chapter 1 also pointed out some of the major competitive challenges that companies face today. These challenges require companies to take a proactive, strategic approach in the marketplace.

To be maximally effective, the HRM function must be integrally involved in the company's strategic management process.[2] This means that human resource managers should (1) have input into the strategic plan, both in terms of people-related issues and in terms of the ability of the human resource pool to implement particular strategic alternatives; (2) have specific knowledge of the organization's strategic goals; (3) know what types of employee skills, behaviours, and attitudes are needed to support the strategic plan; and (4) develop programs to ensure that employees have those skills, behaviours, and attitudes.

We begin this chapter by discussing the concepts of business models and strategy and by depicting the strategic management process. Then we discuss the levels of integration between the HRM function and the strategic management process in strategy formulation. Next, we review some of the more common strategic models and, within the context of these models, discuss the various types of employee skills, behaviours, and attitudes, and the ways HRM practices aid in implementing the strategic plan. Then we explain various steps the HRM function must take to create and sustain a truly strategic HRM function. Finally, we examine the role of the leader of the HRM function, the chief human resources officer.

WHAT IS A BUSINESS MODEL?

A business model is a story of how the firm will create value for customers and, more importantly, how it will do so profitably. We often hear or read of companies that have "transformed their business model" in one way or another, but what that means is not always clear. To understand this, we need to grasp a few basic accounting concepts.

First, fixed costs are generally considered the costs that are incurred regardless of the number of units produced. For instance, if you are producing widgets in a factory, you have the rent you pay for the factory, depreciation of the machines, the utilities, the property taxes, and so on. In addition, you generally have a set number of employees who work a set number of hours with a specified level of benefits, and while you might be able to vary these over time, on a regular basis you pay the same total labour costs whether your factory runs at 70 percent capacity or 95 percent capacity.

Second, you have a number of variable costs, which are those costs that vary directly with the units produced. For instance, all of the materials that go into the widget might cost a total of $10, which means that you have to charge at least $10 per widget, or you cannot even cover the variable costs of production.

Third is the concept of "contribution margins," or margins. Margins are the difference between what you charge for your product and the variable costs of that product. They are called contribution margins because they are what contributes to your ability to cover your fixed costs. So, for instance, if you charged $15 for each widget, your contribution margin would be $5 ($15 price − $10 variable cost).

Fourth, the gross margin is the total amount of margin you made and is calculated as the number of units sold times the contribution margin. If you sold 1,000,000 units, your gross margin would then be $5,000,000. Did you make a profit? That depends. Profit refers to what is left after you have paid your variable costs and your fixed costs. If your gross margin was $5,000,000, and your fixed costs were $6,000,000, then you lost $1,000,000.

Competing Through Technology

Retailers Leverage Technology to Lower Labour Costs

As the economic turmoil continues to force companies to better manage their labour costs, retailers are finding that information technology can enable them to schedule their workforce in ways that maximize customer service while minimizing labour costs. Retailers around the world from every industry segment—including Air Canada, Walmart, GameStop, IKEA, and Payless—use "scheduling optimization software" solutions to drive store productivity, control labour costs, and minimize compliance risk. These systems integrate data such as the number of customers at different hours of the day, the time needed to sell certain products, and/or the time needed to unload a truck to help predict how many workers a store needs at any given hour. This enables the stores to cut costs by having fewer unnecessary paid employees during slow times. Nikki Baird of Forrester Research Inc. says, "There's been a new push for labour optimization. You want to have the flexibility to more closely match ... shifts to when the demand is there." For instance, in a test of 39 stores, Walmart found that 70 percent of customers said the checkout experience had improved. Walmart spokeswoman Sarah Clark states, "The advantages are simple. We will benefit by improving the shopping experience by having the right number of associates to meet our customers' needs when they shop our stores."

And far from being a solution that exploits workers, the advanced schedule optimization in fact creates the best-fit employee schedules based on employee skills, availabilities, and work/life preferences. It also helps retailers to effectively comply with federal and provincial employment standards, and with corporate policies covering employee scheduling, shifts, meals, breaks, union requirements, and the use of minor-age employees.

Research by Kronos found that 71 percent of the respondents found that such workforce management technology helps them control their labour costs, but more interestingly, 88 percent said that their store associates have reacted positively to the scheduling technology.

SOURCES: "Kronos® for Retail Schedules 1.5 Million Associates," *Computer Technology Journal* (January 29, 2009), p. 275; "Air Canada Improves Scheduling Efficiency and Crewmember Satisfaction with Altitude PBS™" at http://www.kronos.com/Case-Study/Air-Canada.aspx (retrieved October 11, 2010).

One can easily see how, given the large component that labour costs are to most companies, reference to business models almost inevitably leads to discussions of labour costs. These can be the high cost associated with current unionized employees in developed countries within North America or Europe or, in some cases, the high costs associated with a legacy workforce. For instance, the Big Three automakers have huge numbers of retired or laid-off workers for whom they still have the liability of paying pensions and health care benefits. This is a significant component of their fixed-cost base, which makes it difficult for them to compete with other automakers that either have fewer retirees to cover or have no comparable costs because their home governments provide pensions and health care. The "Competing through Technology" box describes how a number of retailers are using technology to effectively match employee schedules to customer traffic in order to effectively serve their customers in an efficient manner, and keep labour costs as low as possible.

Learn more about GM's redesigned business model online with Connect.

MC Graw Hill **connect**™

WHAT IS STRATEGIC MANAGEMENT?

LO 1
Describe the differences between strategy formulation and strategy implementation.

Many authors have noted that in today's competitive market, organizations must engage in strategic planning to survive and prosper. *Strategy* comes from the Greek word *strategos,* which has its roots in military language. It refers to a general's grand design behind a war or battle. In fact, one dictionary defines strategy as the "skillful employment and coordination of tactics" and as "artful planning and management."[3]

Strategic management is a process, an approach to addressing the competitive challenges an organization faces. It can be thought of as managing the "pattern or plan that integrates an organization's major goals, policies, and action sequences into a cohesive whole."[4] These strategies can be either the generic approach to competing or the specific adjustments and actions taken to deal with a particular situation.

First, business organizations engage in generic strategies that often fit into some strategic type. One example is "cost, differentiation, or focus."[5] Another is "defender, analyzer, prospector, or reactor."[6] Different organizations within the same industry often have different generic strategies. These generic strategy types describe the consistent way the company attempts to position itself relative to competitors.

However, a generic strategy is only a small part of strategic management. The second aspect of strategic management is the process of developing strategies for achieving the company's goals in light of its current environment. Thus, business organizations engage in generic strategies, but they also make choices about things such as how to scare off competitors, keep competitors weaker, react to and influence pending legislation, deal with various stakeholders and special interest groups, lower production costs, raise revenues, decide what technology to implement, and determine how many and what types of people to employ. Each of these decisions may present competitive challenges that have to be considered.

Strategic management is more than a collection of different strategic models. It is a process for analyzing a company's competitive situation, developing the company's strategic goals, and devising a plan of action and allocation of resources (human, organizational, and physical) that will increase the likelihood of achieving those goals. This kind of strategic approach should be emphasized in human resource management. HR managers should be trained to identify the competitive issues the company faces with regard to human resources and to think strategically about how to respond.

Strategic human resource management (SHRM) can be thought of as "the pattern of planned human resource deployments and activities intended to enable an organization to achieve its goals."[7] For example, many firms have developed integrated manufacturing systems such as advanced

Strategic Human Resource Management (SHRM)
A pattern of planned human resource deployments and activities intended to enable an organization to achieve its goals.

manufacturing technology, just-in-time inventory control, and total quality management in an effort to increase their competitive position. However, these systems must be run by people. SHRM in these cases entails assessing the employee skills required to run these systems and engaging in HRM practices, such as selection and training, that develop these skills in employees.[8] To take a strategic approach to HRM, we must first understand the role of HRM in the strategic management process.

Components of the Strategic Management Process

LO 2

List the components of the strategic management process.

Strategy Formulation
The process of deciding on a strategic direction by defining a company's mission and goals, its external opportunities and threats, and its internal strengths and weaknesses.

Strategy Implementation
The process of devising structures and allocating resources to enact the chosen strategy.

The strategic management process has two distinct yet interdependent phases: strategy formulation and strategy implementation. During **strategy formulation** the strategic planning groups decide on a strategic direction by defining the company's mission and goals, its external opportunities and threats, and its internal strengths and weaknesses. They then generate various strategic alternatives and compare those alternatives' ability to achieve the company's mission and goals. During **strategy implementation,** the organization follows through on the chosen strategy. This consists of structuring the organization, allocating resources, ensuring that the firm has skilled employees in place, and developing reward systems that align employee behaviour with the organization's strategic goals. Both of these strategic management phases must be performed effectively. It is important to note that this process does not happen sequentially. As we will discuss later with regard to emergent strategies, this process entails a constant cycling of information and decision making. Figure 2.1 presents the strategic management process.

In recent years organizations have recognized that the success of the strategic management process depends largely on the extent to which the HRM function is involved.[9]

Linkage between HRM and the Strategic Management Process

The strategic choice really consists of answering questions about competition—that is, how the firm will compete to achieve its missions and goals. These decisions consist of addressing the issues of where to compete, how to compete, and with what to compete, which are described in Figure 2.2.

Although these decisions are all important, strategic decision makers often pay less attention to the "with what will we compete" issue, resulting in poor strategic decisions. For example, in the 1980s PepsiCo acquired the fast-food chains of Kentucky Fried Chicken, Taco Bell, and Pizza Hut ("where to compete" decisions) in an effort to increase its customer base. However, it failed to adequately recognize the differences between its existing workforce (mostly professionals) and that of the fast-food industry (lower-skilled people and high-schoolers) as well as its ability to manage such a workforce. This was one reason that PepsiCo spun off the fast-food chains in 1998. In essence, it had made a decision about where to compete without fully understanding what resources would be needed to compete in that market.

Boeing illustrates how failing to address the "with what" issue resulted in problems in its "how to compete" decisions. When the aerospace firm's consumer products division entered a price war with Airbus Industrie, it was forced to move away from its traditional customer service strategy toward emphasizing cost reduction.[10] The strategy was a success on the sales end as Boeing received large numbers of orders for aircraft from firms such as WestJet, Delta, Continental, Southwest, and Singapore Airlines. However, it had recently gone through a large workforce reduction (thus, it didn't have enough people to fill the orders) and did not have the production technology to enable the necessary increase in productivity. The result of this failure to address "with what will we compete" resulted in the firm's inability to meet delivery deadlines and the ensuing penalties it had to pay to its customers. After all the dust settled, for the first time in the history of the industry, its chief rival Airbus sold more planes than Boeing in 2003. Luckily, Boeing was able to overcome this stumble, in large part because of a number of faux pas on the part of Airbus. When Airbus's behemoth A380

FIGURE 2.1 A Model of the Strategic Management Process

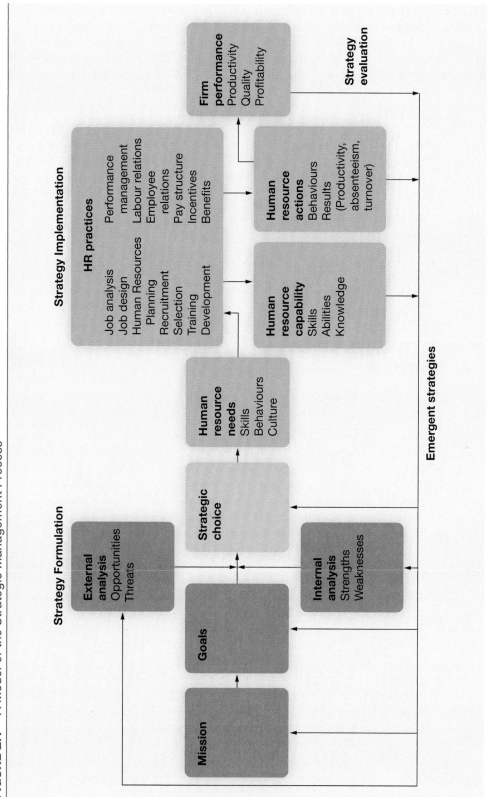

was beset by a number of production delays, Boeing's 787 Dreamliner attracted a number of orders, enabling Boeing to regain its market lead. The story is reflected in Air Canada's buying patterns during that time. For example, in October 2004, Air Canada ended a 33-year agreement with Boeing when it replaced its Boeing 747s with a fleet of Airbus A340s. But by November 2005, Air Canada eagerly swung back to Boeing, buying up 18 Boeing 777s and 14 Boeing 787-8s when it renewed its

FIGURE 2.2 Strategy—Decisions about Competition

1. Where to compete?
   In what market or markets (industries, products, etc.) will we compete?
2. How to compete?
   On what criterion or differentiating characteristic(s) will we compete? Cost? Quality? Reliability? Delivery?
3. With what will we compete?
   What resources will allow us to beat our competition?
   How will we acquire, develop, and deploy those resources to compete?

Competing Through Globalization

Managing the New Class of Global Worker

As more and more companies move work to India, they are facing a number of challenges they never expected. In the information technology sector, where companies initially sought an 80 percent reduction in labour cost, they now face a war for talent and spiralling salaries. This stems from the newer, younger breed of Indian worker, who displays attitudes much more similar to developed Western countries such as Canada than those of their parents and grandparents.

Companies face competing challenges of addressing both the frustrations and the desires of this younger generation. For instance, they are likely to complain about the traditions of arranged marriage and the caste system as well as their interactions with Westerners, who they feel sometimes treat them condescendingly. Many of the engineers are fascinated with the newest technologies, but their work for clients requires traditional tools and techniques. Finally, they are eager to get promotions and overseas assignments, yet there are practical limits to how quickly they can advance.

This requires companies to be innovative in how they seek to manage this new generation. For instance, Infosys sought to learn from younger employees by setting up the "Voice of Youth Council." This consists of a dozen people under 30 who sit on the executive committee that deals with business strategy and HR policies, and it was this group that was instrumental in creating a program for identifying and encouraging innovation. IBM has created an internal MBA program consisting of testing, on-the-job training, seminars, and e-mail quizzes about how to effectively deal with workplace problems. This program was specifically aimed at keeping ambitious recruits on board and providing them with the training they need to manage a growing staff.

SOURCE: S. Hamm, "Young and Impatient in India; Workers Raised in an Age of Economic Optimism Want It All, and They Want It Now," *BusinessWeek* (January 28, 2008), p. 45.

wide-body fleet. By April 2007, Air Canada had exercised half of its options to buy 50 Boeing 787 Dreamliners, making Air Canada the largest customer of the Dreamliner in North America, and third in the world behind Qantas and All Nippon Airways.[11] The "Competing through Globalization" box describes the challenges firms face in competing for talent in a global labour market.

Role of HRM in Strategy Formulation

As the preceding examples illustrate, often the "with what will we compete" questions present ideal avenues for HRM to influence the strategic management process. This might be through either limiting strategic options or forcing thoughtfulness among the executive team regarding how and at what cost the firm might gain or develop the human resources (people) necessary for such a strategy to be successful. For example, HRM executives at PepsiCo could have noted that the firm had no expertise in managing the workforce of fast-food restaurants. The limiting role would have been for these executives to argue against the acquisition because of this lack of resources. On the other hand, they might have influenced the decision by educating top executives as to the costs (of hiring, training, and so on) associated with gaining people who had the right skills to manage such a workforce.

A firm's strategic management decision-making process usually takes place at its top levels, with a strategic planning group consisting of the chief executive officer, the chief financial officer, the president, and various vice presidents. However, each component of the process involves people-related business issues. Therefore, the HRM function needs to be involved in each of those components. One recent study of 115 strategic business units within *Fortune* 500 corporations found that between 49 and 69 percent of the companies had some link between HRM and the strategic planning process.[12] However, the level of linkage varied, and it is important to understand these different levels.

Four levels of integration seem to exist between the HRM function and the strategic management function: administrative linkage, one-way linkage, two-way linkage, and integrative linkage.[13] These levels of linkage will be discussed in relation to the different components of strategic management. The linkages are illustrated in Figure 2.3.

LO 3

Discuss the role of the HRM function in strategy formulation and its linkages to the process.

FIGURE 2.3 Linkages of Strategic Planning and HRM

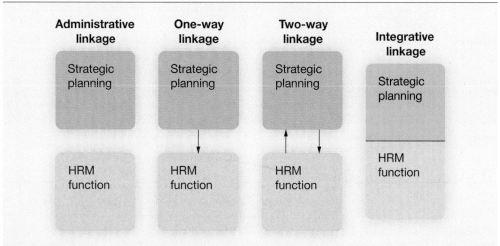

SOURCE: Adapted from K. Golden and V. Ramanujam, "Between a Dream and a Nightmare: On the Integration of the Human Resource Function and the Strategic Business Planning Process," *Human Resource Management* 24 (1985), pp. 429–51.

Administrative Linkage In administrative linkage (the lowest level of integration), the HRM function's attention is focused on day-to-day activities. The HRM executive has no time or opportunity to take a strategic outlook toward HRM issues. The company's strategic business planning function exists without any input from the HRM department. Thus, in this level of integration, the HRM department is completely divorced from any component of the strategic management process in both strategy formulation and strategy implementation. The department simply engages in administrative work unrelated to the company's core business needs.

One-Way Linkage In one-way linkage, the firm's strategic business planning function develops the strategic plan and then informs the HRM function of the plan. Many believe this level of integration constitutes strategic HRM—that is, the role of the HRM function is to design systems and/or programs that implement the strategic plan. Although one-way linkage does recognize the importance of human resources in implementing the strategic plan, it precludes the company from considering human resource issues *while* formulating the strategic plan. This level of integration often leads to strategic plans that the company cannot successfully implement.

Two-Way Linkage Two-way linkage allows for consideration of human resource issues during the strategy formulation process. This integration occurs in three sequential steps. First, the strategic planning team informs the HRM function of the various strategies the company is considering. Then HRM executives analyze the human resource implications of the various strategies, presenting the results of this analysis to the strategic planning team. Finally, after the strategic decision has been made, the strategic plan is passed on to the HRM executive, who develops programs to implement it. The strategic planning function and the HRM function are interdependent in two-way linkage.

Integrative Linkage Integrative linkage is dynamic and multifaceted, based on continuing rather than sequential interaction. In most cases, the HRM executive is an integral member of the senior management team. Rather than an iterative process of information exchange, companies with integrative linkage have their HRM functions built right into the strategy formulation and implementation processes. It is this role that we will discuss throughout the rest of this chapter.

Thus, in strategic HRM, the HRM function is involved in both strategy formulation and strategy implementation. The HRM executive gives strategic planners information about the company's human resource capabilities, and these capabilities are usually a direct function of the HRM practices.[14] This information about human resource capabilities helps top managers choose the best strategy because they can consider how well each strategic alternative would be implemented. Once the strategic choice has been determined, the role of HRM changes to the development and alignment of HRM practices that will give the employees the necessary skills to implement the strategy.[15] In addition, HRM practices must be designed to elicit actions from employees in the company.[16] In the next two sections of this chapter we show how HRM can provide a competitive advantage in the strategic management process.

STRATEGY FORMULATION

Five major components of the strategic management process depicted in Figure 2.1 are relevant to strategy formulation.[17] The first component is the organization's mission. The mission is a statement of the organization's reason for being; it usually specifies the customers served, the needs satisfied and/or the values received by the customers, and the technology used. The mission statement is often accompanied by a statement of a company's vision and/or values, such as the mission and values of Merck & Co. that guide over 1,400 employees of Montreal-based Merck Frosst Canada

Ltd. in their day–to-day tasks and longer-range planning activities. The overall company mission statement acts as a compass that aligns the company worldwide, despite geographic distance.

Learn more about the overall corporate values that guide Merck Frosst Canada Ltd. and its mission and values mission statement online with Connect.

An organization's **goals** are what it hopes to achieve in the medium- to long-term future; they reflect how the mission will be operationalized. The overarching goal of most profit-making companies in North America is to maximize stockholder wealth. But companies have to set other long-term goals in order to maximize stockholder wealth.

External analysis consists of examining the organization's operating environment to identify the strategic opportunities and threats. Examples of opportunities are customer markets that are not being served, technological advances that can aid the company, and labour pools that have not been tapped. Threats include potential labour shortages, new competitors entering the market, pending legislation that might adversely affect the company, and competitors' technological innovations.

Internal analysis attempts to identify the organization's strengths and weaknesses. It focuses on the quantity and quality of resources available to the organization—financial, capital, technological, and human resources. Organizations have to honestly and accurately assess each resource to decide whether it is a strength or a weakness.

External analysis and internal analysis combined constitute what has come to be called the SWOT (strengths, weaknesses, opportunities, threats) analysis. After going through the SWOT analysis, the strategic planning team has all the information it needs to generate a number of strategic alternatives. The strategic managers compare these alternatives' ability to attain the organization's strategic goals; then they make their **strategic choice.** The strategic choice is the organization's strategy; it describes the ways the organization will attempt to fulfill its mission and achieve its long-term goals.

Many of the opportunities and threats in the external environment are people related. With fewer and fewer highly qualified individuals entering the labour market, organizations compete for not only customers but also employees. It is HRM's role to keep close tabs on the external environment for human resource–related opportunities and threats, especially those directly related to the HRM function: potential labour shortages, competitor wage rates, government regulations affecting employment, and so on. For example, North American companies are finding that more and more high school graduates lack the basic skills needed to work, which is one source of the "human capital shortage."[18] However, not recognizing this environmental threat, many companies have encouraged the exit of older, more skilled workers while hiring less skilled younger workers who require basic skills training.[19]

An analysis of a company's internal strengths and weaknesses also requires input from the HRM function. Today companies are increasingly realizing that their human resources are one of their most important assets. A company's failure to consider the strengths and weaknesses of its workforce may result in its choosing strategies it is not capable of pursuing.[20] However, some research has demonstrated that few companies have achieved this level of linkage.[21] For example, one company chose a strategy of cost reduction through technological improvements. It built a plant designed around a computer-integrated manufacturing system with statistical process controls.

Although this choice may seem like a good one, the company soon learned otherwise. It discovered that its employees could not operate the new equipment because 25 percent of the workforce was functionally illiterate.[22] Other companies do internal analysis well, however, and make a point of investing in workforce capability so workers have the right skills when the company is ready to implement a particular strategy. For example, Standens Limited, mentioned in Chapter 1, forms alliances with educational institutions to keep its workforce learning, which has ensured the company did not make the same mistake.

Goals
What an organization hopes to achieve in the medium- to long-term future.

External Analysis
Examining the organization's operating environment to identify strategic opportunities and threats.

Internal Analysis
The process of examining an organization's strengths and weaknesses.

Strategic Choice
The organization's strategy; the ways an organization will attempt to fulfill its mission and achieve its long-term goals.

Thus, with an integrative linkage, strategic planners consider all the people–related business issues before making a strategic choice. These issues are identified with regard to the mission, goals, opportunities, threats, strengths, and weaknesses, leading the strategic planning team to make a more intelligent strategic choice. Although this process does not guarantee success, companies that address these issues are more likely to make choices that will ultimately succeed.

Recent research has supported the need to have HRM executives integrally involved in strategy formulation. One study of U.S. petrochemical refineries found that the level of HRM involvement was positively related to the refinery manager's evaluation of the effectiveness of the HRM function.[23] A second study of manufacturing firms found that HRM involvement was highest when top managers viewed employees as a strategic asset and associated with reduced turnover.[24] However, both studies found that HRM involvement was unrelated to operating unit financial performance.

Research has indicated that few companies have fully integrated HRM into the strategy formulation process.[25] As we've mentioned, companies are beginning to recognize that in an intensely competitive environment, managing human resources strategically can provide a competitive advantage. Thus, companies at the administrative linkage level will either become more integrated or face extinction. In addition, companies will move toward becoming integratively linked in an effort to manage human resources strategically.

It is of utmost importance that all people–related business issues be considered during strategy formulation. These issues are identified by the HRM function. Mechanisms or structures for integrating the HRM function into strategy formulation may help the strategic planning team make the most effective strategic choice. Once that strategic choice is determined, HRM must take an active role in implementing it. This role will be discussed in the next section.

STRATEGY IMPLEMENTATION

LO 4

Discuss the more popular typologies of generic strategies and the various HRM practices associated with each.

After an organization has chosen its strategy, it has to execute that strategy—make it come to life in its day-to-day workings. The strategy a company pursues dictates certain HR needs. For a company to have a good strategy foundation, certain tasks must be accomplished in pursuit of the company's goals, individuals must possess certain skills to perform those tasks, and these individuals must be motivated to perform their skills effectively.

The basic premise behind strategy implementation is that "an organization has a variety of structural forms and organizational processes to choose from when implementing a given strategy," and these choices make an economic difference.[26] Five important variables determine success in strategy implementation: organizational structure; task design; the selection, training, and development of people; reward systems; and types of information and information systems.

As we see in Figure 2.4, HRM has primary responsibility for three of these five implementation variables: task, people, and reward systems. In addition, HRM can directly affect the two remaining variables: organizational structure, and types of information and information systems. First, for the strategy to be successfully implemented, the tasks must be designed and grouped into jobs in a way that is efficient and effective.[27] Second, the HRM function must ensure that the organization is staffed with people who have the necessary knowledge, skill, and ability to perform their part in implementing the strategy. This goal is achieved primarily through human resources planning, recruitment, selection and placement, training, development, and career development. In addition, the HRM function must develop performance management and reward systems that lead employees to work for and support the strategic plan. In other words, the role of the HRM function becomes one of (1) ensuring that the company has the proper number of employees with the levels and types of skills required by the strategic plan[28] and (2) developing "control" systems that ensure that those employees are acting in ways that promote the achievement of the goals specified in the strategic plan.[29]

FIGURE 2.4 Variables to Be Considered in Strategy Implementation

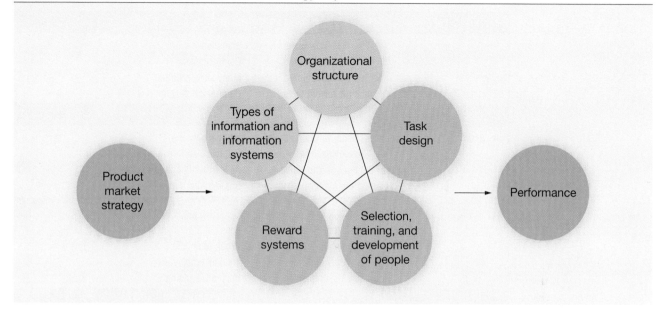

In essence, this is what has been referred to as the "vertical alignment" of HR with strategy. Vertical alignment means that the HR practices and processes are aimed at addressing the strategic needs of the business. But the link between strategy and HR practices is primarily through people. For instance, as IBM moved from being a manufacturer of personal computers to being a fully integrated service provider, the types of people it needed changed significantly. Instead of employing thousands of workers in manufacturing or assembly plants, IBM increasingly needed software engineers to help write new "middleware" programs, and an army of consultants who could help corporate customers to implement these systems. In addition, as IBM increasingly differentiated itself as being the "integrated solutions" provider (meaning it could sell the hardware, software, consulting, and service for a company's entire information technology needs), employees needed a new mindset that emphasized cooperating across different business divisions rather than running independently. Thus, the change in strategy required different kinds of skills, different kinds of employees, and different kinds of behaviours.

How does the HRM function implement strategy? As Figure 2.1 shows, it is through administering HRM practices: job analysis and design, recruitment and selection processes, training and development programs, performance management systems, reward systems (pay structure, incentives and benefits), and employee and labour relations programs. The details of each of these HRM practices, as well as human resources planning (discussed in Chapter 4) are the focus of the rest of this book. At this point we will present some research about HRM practices and their role in strategy implementation. We will then discuss the various strategies companies pursue and the types of HRM systems congruent with those strategies, focusing first on how the different types of strategic models are implemented and then on the HRM practices associated with various directional strategies.

HRM Practices

The HRM function can be thought of as having six menus of HRM practices, from which companies can choose those most appropriate for implementing their strategy. Each of these menus refers to a particular functional area of HRM mentioned above.[30] These menus are presented in Table 2.1.

Table 2.1 Menu of HRM Practice Options

JOB ANALYSIS AND DESIGN		
Few tasks	↔	Many tasks
Simple tasks	↔	Complex tasks
Few skills required	↔	Many skills required
Specific job descriptions	↔	General job descriptions
RECRUITMENT AND SELECTION		
External sources	↔	Internal sources
Limited socialization	↔	Extensive socialization
Assessment of specific skills	↔	Assessment of general skills
Narrow career paths	↔	Broad career paths
TRAINING AND DEVELOPMENT		
Focus on current job skills	↔	Focus on future job skills
Individual orientation	↔	Group orientation
Train few employees	↔	Train all employees
Spontaneous, unplanned	↔	Planned, systematic
PERFORMANCE MANAGEMENT		
Behavioural criteria	↔	Results criteria
Developmental orientation	↔	Administrative orientation
Short-term criteria	↔	Long-term criteria
Individual orientation	↔	Group orientation
PAY STRUCTURE, INCENTIVES, AND BENEFITS		
Pay weighted toward salary and benefits	↔	Pay weighted toward incentives
Short-term incentives	↔	Long-term incentives
Emphasis on internal equity	↔	Emphasis on external equity
Individual incentives	↔	Group incentives
LABOUR RELATIONS AND EMPLOYEE RELATIONS		
Collective bargaining	↔	Individual bargaining
Top-down decision making	↔	Participation in decision making
Formal due process	↔	No due process
View employees as expense	↔	View employees as assets

SOURCES: Adapted from R. S. Schuler and S. F. Jackson, "Linking Competitive Strategies with Human Resource Management Practices," *Academy of Management Executive* 1 (1987), pp. 207–19; and C. Fisher, L. Schoenfeldt, and B. Shaw, *Human Resource Management*, 2nd ed. (Boston: Houghton Mifflin, 1992).

As you can see, there are a wide range of HRM choices available to managers. As one example, the pay system has an important role in implementing strategies. First, a high level of pay and/or benefits relative to that of competitors can ensure that the company attracts and retains high-quality employees, although this might have a negative impact on the company's overall labour costs.[31] Second, by tying pay to performance, the company can elicit specific activities and levels of performance from employees.

In a study of how compensation practices are tied to strategies, researchers examined 33 high-tech and 72 traditional companies. They classified them by whether they were in a growth stage (greater than 20 percent inflation-adjusted increases in annual sales) or a maturity stage. They found that high-tech companies in the growth stage used compensation systems that were highly geared toward incentive pay, with a lower percentage of total pay devoted to salary and benefits. On the other hand, compensation systems among mature companies (both high-tech and traditional) devoted a lower percentage of total pay to incentives and a high percentage to benefits.[32]

When it comes to employee relations, companies can choose to treat employees as an asset that requires investment of resources or as an expense to be minimized.[33] They have to make choices about how much employees can and should participate in decision making, what rights employees have, and what the company's responsibility is to them. The approach a company takes in making these decisions can result in it either successfully achieving its short- and long-term goals or ceasing to exist.

Recent research has begun to examine how companies develop sets of HRM practices that maximize performance and productivity. For example, one study of automobile assembly plants around the world found that plants that exhibited both high productivity and high quality used "HRM best practices," such as heavy emphasis on recruitment and hiring, compensation tied to performance, low levels of status differentiation, high levels of training for both new and experienced employees, and employee participation through structures such as work teams and problem-solving groups.[34] Another study found that HRM systems composed of selection testing, training, contingent pay, performance appraisal, attitude surveys, employee participation, and information sharing resulted in higher levels of productivity and corporate financial performance, as well as lower employee turnover.[35] Finally, a recent study found that companies identified as some of the "best places to work" had higher financial performances than a set of matched companies that did not make the list.[36] Similar results have also been observed in a number of other studies.[37]

In addition to the relationship between HR practices and performance in general, in today's fast-changing environment, businesses have to change quickly, requiring changes in employees' skills and behaviours. In one study the researchers found that the flexibility of HR practices, employee skills, and employee behaviours were all positively related to firm financial performance, but only the skill flexibility was related to cost efficiency.[38] While these relationships are promising, the causal direction has not yet been proven. For instance, while effective HR practices should help firms perform better, it is also true that highly profitable firms can invest more in HR practices.[39] The research seems to indicate that while the relationship between practices and performance is consistently positive, we should not go too far out on a limb arguing that increasing the use of HRM practices will automatically result in increased profitability.[40]

Strategic Types

As we previously discussed, companies can be classified by the generic strategies they pursue. It is important to note that these generic "strategies" are not what we mean by a strategic plan. They are merely similarities in the ways companies seek to compete in their industries. Various typologies (classifications of strategic types) have been offered, but we focus on the two generic strategies proposed by Porter: cost and differentiation.[41]

According to Michael Porter of Harvard, competitive advantage stems from a company's being able to create value in its production process. Value can be created in one of two ways. First, value can be created by reducing costs. Second, value can be created by differentiating a product or service in such a way that it allows the company to charge a premium price relative to its competitors. This leads to two basic strategies. According to Porter, the "overall cost leadership" strategy focuses on becoming the lowest-cost producer in an industry. This strategy is achieved by constructing efficient large-scale facilities, reducing costs through capitalizing on the experience curve, and controlling overhead costs and costs in areas such as research and development, service, sales force, and advertising. This strategy provides above-average returns within an industry, and it tends to bar other firms' entry into the industry because the firm can lower its prices below competitors' costs.

The "differentiation" strategy, according to Porter, attempts to create the impression that the company's product or service is different from that of others in the industry. The perceived differentiation can come from creating a brand image, from technology, from offering unique features, or from unique customer service. If a company succeeds in differentiating its product, it will achieve above-average returns, and the differentiation may protect it from price sensitivity. For instance, Dell Computer Company built its reputation on providing the lowest-cost computers through leveraging its supply chain and direct selling model. However, recently the company has seen its share eroding as the consumer market grows and HP has offered more differentiated, stylish-looking computers sold through retail outlets where customers can touch and feel them. In addition, Apple has differentiated itself through its own operating system that integrates well with peripheral devices such as the iPod and iPhone. In both cases, these companies can charge a premium (albeit higher for Apple) over Dell's pricing.[42]

HRM Needs in Strategic Types

Role Behaviours
Behaviours that are required of an individual in his or her role as a jobholder in a social work environment.

While all of the strategic types require competent people in a generic sense, each of the strategies also requires different types of employees with different types of behaviours and attitudes. As we noted earlier, different strategies require employees with specific skills and also require these employees to exhibit different "role behaviours."[43] **Role behaviours** are the behaviours required of an individual in his or her role as a jobholder in a social work environment. These role behaviours vary on a number of dimensions. Additionally, different role behaviours are required by the different strategies, as illustrated in Table 2.2 below:

Thus, companies engaged in cost strategies, because of the focus on efficient production, tend to specifically define the skills they require and invest in training employees in these skill areas. They also rely on behavioural performance management systems with a large performance-based compensation component. These companies promote internally and develop internally consistent pay systems with high pay differentials between superiors and subordinates. They seek efficiency through worker participation, soliciting employees' ideas on how to achieve more efficient production.

Table 2.2 Employee Role Behaviours Required to Support Company Strategies (New)

COST STRATEGY	DIFFERENTIATION STRATEGY
High concern for quantity	Moderate concern for quantity
Short-term focus	Long-term focus
Comfortable with stability	Tolerance for ambiguity
Risk averse	Risk taker
Comfortable with performing relatively repetitive work independently or autonomously	Highly creative; developing new ideas, cooperating with others, taking a balanced approach to process and results.

SOURCE: Based on R. Schuler and S. Jackson, "Linking Competitive Strategies with Human Resource Management Practices," *Academy of Management Executive* 1 (1987), pp. 207–19.

Differentiation companies will seek to generate more creativity through broadly defined jobs with general job descriptions. They may recruit more from outside, engage in limited socialization of newcomers, and provide broader career paths. Training and development activities focus on cooperation. The compensation system is geared toward external equity, as it is heavily driven by recruiting needs. These companies develop results-based performance management systems and divisional–corporate performance evaluations to encourage risk taking on the part of managers.[44]

Directional Strategies

As discussed earlier in this chapter, strategic typologies are useful for classifying the ways different organizations seek to compete within an industry. However, it is also necessary to understand how increasing size (growth) or decreasing it (downsizing) affects the HRM function. For example, the top management team might decide that they need to invest more in product development or to diversify as a means for growth. With these types of strategies, it is more useful for the HRM function to aid in evaluating the feasibility of the various alternatives and to develop programs that support the strategic choice.

Companies have used four possible categories of directional strategies to meet objectives.[45] Strategies emphasizing market share or operating costs are considered "concentration" strategies. With this type of strategy, a company attempts to focus on what it does best within its established markets and can be thought of as "sticking to its knitting." Strategies focusing on market development, product development, innovation, or joint ventures make up the "internal growth" strategy. Companies with an internal growth strategy channel their resources toward building on existing strengths. Those attempting to integrate vertically or horizontally or to diversify are exhibiting an **"external growth" strategy,** usually through mergers or acquisitions. This strategy attempts to expand a company's resources or to strengthen its market position through acquiring or creating new businesses. Finally, a "divestment," or **downsizing,** strategy is one made up of retrenchment, divestitures, or liquidation. These strategies are observed among companies facing serious economic difficulties and seeking to pare down their operations. The human resource implications of each of these strategies are quite different.

External Growth Strategy
An emphasis on acquiring vendors and suppliers or buying businesses that allow a company to expand into new markets.

Downsizing
The planned elimination of large numbers of personnel, designed to enhance organizational effectiveness.

Concentration Strategies   **Concentration strategies** require that the company maintain the current skills that exist in the organization. This requires that training programs provide a means of keeping those skills sharp among people in the organization and that compensation programs focus on retaining people who have those skills. Appraisals in this strategy tend to be more behavioural because the environment is more certain, and the behaviours necessary for effective performance tend to be established through extensive experience.

Concentration Strategy
A strategy focusing on increasing market share, reducing costs, or creating and maintaining a market niche for products and services.

Internal Growth Strategies   **Internal growth strategies** present unique staffing problems. Growth requires that a company constantly hire, transfer, and promote individuals, and expansion into different markets may change the necessary skills that prospective employees must have. In addition, appraisals often consist of a combination of behaviours and results. The behavioural appraisal emphasis stems from the knowledge of effective behaviours in a particular product market, and the results appraisals focus on achieving growth goals. Compensation packages are heavily weighted toward incentives for achieving growth goals. Training needs differ depending on the way the company attempts to grow internally. For example, if the organization seeks to expand its markets, training will focus on knowledge of each market, particularly when the company is expanding into international markets. On the other hand, when the company is seeking innovation or product development, training will be of a more technical nature, as well as focusing on interpersonal skills

Internal Growth Strategy
A focus on new market and product development, innovation, and joint ventures.

such as team building. Joint ventures require extensive training in conflict resolution techniques because of the problems associated with combining people from two distinct organizational cultures.

Mergers and Acquisitions Increasingly we see both consolidation within industries and mergers across industries. One example of the former occurred in June 2009 with a merger between Watson Wyatt (7,700 employees in 34 countries) and Towers Perrin (6,300 employees in 26 countries). This move combined two global professional service firms whose business is to advise clients on how to improve performance through effective people, risk, and financial management. The new combined firm of Towers Watson is expected to "benefit from the scale of the combined companies," and to reap around $80 million in "pretax annual synergies" as a result of the merger.[46]

Citicorp's merger with Traveller's Group in 1998 to form Citigroup is an example of two firms from different industries (pure financial services and insurance) combining to change the dynamics within both. In Canada, such "cross-pillar bank/insurance mergers" have been denied for public policy reasons since the late 90s and, given the struggles of Citicorp following its merger, and the still-strong health of Canada's banking industry, it seems to have been a good move on the part of the Canadian government. Whatever the type, one thing is certain—mergers and acquisitions are on the increase, and HRM needs to be involved.[47] In addition, like the Towers Watson deal, these mergers frequently consist of global megamergers, in spite of some warnings that these might not be effective.

"People issues" may be one of the major reasons that mergers do not always live up to expectations. Some companies now heavily weigh firm cultures before embarking on a merger or acquisition. In addition to the desirability of HRM playing a role in evaluating a merger opportunity, HRM certainly has a role in the actual implementation of a merger or acquisition. The "Competing through Sustainability" box illustrates how Montreal-based Yellow Pages Group involves HRM at each stage of a merger or acquisition to avoid problems usually associated with such corporate deals.

Training in conflict resolution is also necessary when companies engage in an external growth strategy. All the options for external growth consist of acquiring or developing new businesses, and these businesses often have distinct cultures. Thus many HRM programs face problems in integrating and standardizing practices across the company's businesses. The relative value of standardizing practices across businesses must be weighed against the unique environmental requirements of each business and the extent of desired integration of the two firms. Surprises abound when companies get to the implementation stage. For example, when it comes to pay practices, a company may desire a consistent internal wage structure to maintain employee perceptions of equity in the larger organization. On the other hand, it may be faced with adapting North American pay practices to fit into the culture and expectations of employees in another country where the acquisition takes place. For example, LaFarge North America gathered unexpected insights when the company tried to implement its global compensation system in a plant it acquired in India. There the company discovered that the company's incentive system itself was not motivational or valued by the employees. Rather, what truly motivated the employees was receiving their incentive cheques personally, in a private meeting, and having the cheque handed to them by the highly revered plant owner, a distant member of a royal family.[48]

Of course, one of the most sensitive issues around mergers and acquisitions is the expectation on the part of employees that their jobs may soon be deemed redundant and downsizing begins.

Downsizing Of increasing importance to organizations in today's competitive environment is HRM's role in downsizing or "rightsizing." The number of organizations undergoing downsizing has increased significantly in North America. While there are a number of reasons companies may choose to downsize, mergers and acquisitions are often precursors of a workforce purge. One recent example is Suncor, which acquired Petro-Canada in August 2009 to become the second-largest

Competing Through Sustainability

Mergers and Acquisitions: Amateurs Need Not Apply

Companies that are truly experienced in mergers and acquisitions have learned over time that ensuring sustainability of such deals means involving HRM at the "get-go." Sustainability means retention of key talent, achieving cultural alignment and integration of companies involved, maintaining engagement of employees, and ensuring revenue growth, among other results. HR's role is to anticipate and meet the needs of employees on both sides of the deal and, in so doing, create a solid foundation to meet the needs of other stakeholders involved, such as customers, managers, and shareholders. That means getting HR involved as soon as the soft breeze of a merger begins to waft its way across the strategic horizon. Yellow Pages Group, based in Montreal, is just such an organization.

At Yellow Pages, HRM is included right from the first step, at the intention-to-purchase stage. Once a deal is clearly emerging, HRM begins due diligence, which includes "identifying potential risks and liabilities and any potential integration issues in terms of alignment of things like working conditions, benefits, and pensions." Then, at a more mature stage, but before the deal is closed, HRM steps in again to do what Vice President of HR Josee Dykun refers to as "a thorough cultural assessment, looking at the visions, the values, the ones that are unspoken as well as those that are more concrete, the work processes." At this second stage, the task for Dykun and her team is to put together an integration plan while being sensitive to the needs and feelings of individuals in the target company. That's because most people who are going to be impacted will now be well into a predictable case of premerger jitters. Finally, once the deal is official, Dykun's team launches a swift, assertive, and thorough communication plan designed to address the WHIFM ("What's in it for me?") all stakeholders have firmly on their minds. Everyone needs to know what the new corporate vision is and where they will fit in personally.

Bob Bundy of Mercer Human Resources Consulting says that if a merger or acquisition is to meet everyone's expectations, cultural integration and change must get top billing and anticipating behaviour patterns among individuals involved in the deal is one of the first things to be considered. Bundy ought to know since he leads Mercer's M&A consulting services businesses. However, he cautions that it is just one aspect of a systematic approach to facilitating successful mergers, saying, "To accelerate the impact of culture necessary for successful integration requires adherence to a process that must include clarifying the context of the deal, identifying the right behaviours, pulling the right levers to drive those behaviours and managing the change required." Mercer uses a series of eight distinct steps that include measuring and reinforcing change outcomes as the final touch, but experience has taught them that it isn't always a linear process. Circumstances, experience and judgment have shown them that steps can and will be done out of sequence to make the deal work. Especially in large-scale M&As, Bundy notes, each party coming to the table brings a lot of cultural baggage. As Dykun's approach indicates, who better to deal with cultural baggage than HRM?

SOURCES: Based on Uyen Vu, "HR's Role in Mergers, Acquisitions," *Canadian HR Reporter* (December 4, 2006), p. 17; and B. Bundy, "Integrating Cultures in M&Ss," *Canadian HR Reporter* (December 4, 2006), p. 19. Reprinted by permission of *Canadian HR Reporter*. © Copyright Thomson Reuters Canada Ltd., (November 1, 2010), Toronto, Ontario, 1-800-387-5164. Web: www.hrreporter.com.

company in Canada. Initially, Suncor's CEO Rick George indicated the company would be cutting $300 million in operating costs. However, by early 2010, George announced that the company would actually slash $400 million, in part by terminating 2,000 employees by the end of the year.[49]

Downsizing can be good for a company, but it also presents numerous dilemmas. For example, during the massive "war for talent" that went on during the late 1990s, especially within the dot.com industry, firms sought to become "employers of choice," to establish "employment brands," and to develop "employee value propositions" as ways to ensure that they would be able to attract and retain talented employees. However, when a company downsizes it means that one important question facing firms is, How can we develop a reputation as an employer of choice, and engage employees to the goals of the firm, while laying off a significant portion of our workforce? How firms answer this question will determine how they can compete by meeting the stakeholder needs of their employees.

In addition, despite the increasing frequency of downsizing, research reveals that it is far from universally successful for achieving the goals of increased productivity and increased profitability. For example, a survey conducted by the American Management Association revealed that only about one-third of the companies that went through downsizings actually achieved their goal of increased productivity. Another survey by the AMA found that over two-thirds of the companies that downsize repeat the effort a year later.[50] Finally, research by the consulting firm Mitchell & Company found that companies that downsized during the 1980s lagged the industry average stock price in 1991.[51] Thus it is important to understand the best ways of managing downsizings, particularly from the standpoint of HRM if the outcome is to benefit the company's overall strategy.

While downsizing is painful and controversial, it also provides opportunities and for that reason downsizing can demonstrate to top-management decision makers the value of the company's human resources to its ultimate success. The role of HRM is to effectively manage the process in a way that makes this value undeniable. We discuss specific reasons for downsizing, its implications as a labour force management strategy, and HRM's role in the process in Chapter 4.

Strategy Evaluation and Control

A final component to the strategic management process is that of strategy evaluation and control. Thus far we have focused on the planning and implementation of strategy. However, it is extremely important for the firm to constantly monitor the effectiveness of both the strategy and the implementation process. This monitoring makes it possible for the company to identify problem areas and either revise existing structures and strategies or devise new ones. In this process we see emergent strategies appear as well as the critical nature of human resources in competitive advantage.

THE ROLE OF HUMAN RESOURCES IN PROVIDING STRATEGIC COMPETITIVE ADVANTAGE

Thus far we have presented the strategic management process as including a step-by-step procedure by which HRM issues are raised prior to deciding on a strategy and then HRM practices are developed to implement that strategy. However, we must note that human resources can provide a strategic competitive advantage in two additional ways: through emergent strategies and through enhancing competitiveness.

Emergent Strategies

Having discussed the process of strategic management, we also must distinguish between intended strategies and emergent strategies. Most people think of strategies as being proactive, rational decisions aimed toward some predetermined goal. The view of strategy we have presented thus far in the chapter focuses on intended strategies. Intended strategies are the result of the rational decision-making process used by top managers as they develop a strategic plan. This is consistent with the definition of strategy as "the pattern or plan that integrates an organization's major goals, policies, and action sequences into a cohesive whole."[52] The idea of emergent strategies is evidenced by the feedback loop in Figure 2.1.

Most strategies that companies espouse are intended strategies. For example, when Howard Schultz founded Starbucks, he had the idea of creating a third place (between work and home) where people could enjoy traditional Italian-style coffee. He knew that the smell of the coffee and the deeper, darker, stronger taste would attract a new set of customers to enjoy coffee the way he thought it should be enjoyed. This worked, but as Starbucks grew, customers began asking if they could have non-fat milk in their lattes, or if they could get flavour shots in their coffees. Schultz swore that such things would essentially pollute the coffee and refused to offer them. Finally, after repeated requests from his store managers who kept hearing customers demanding such things, Schultz finally relented.[53]

Emergent strategies, on the other hand, consist of the strategies that evolve from the grassroots of the organization and can be thought of as what organizations actually do, as opposed to what they intend to do. Strategy can also be thought of as "a pattern in a stream of decisions or actions."[54] For example, when Honda Motor Company first entered the North American market with its 250-cc and 350-cc motorcycles in 1959, it believed that no market existed for its smaller 50-cc bike. However, the sales on the larger motorcycles were sluggish, and Japanese executives running errands in one major city on Honda 50s attracted a lot of attention, including that of a buyer with a major retailer. Honda found a previously undiscovered market as well as a new distribution outlet (general retailers) that it had not planned on. This emergent strategy gave Honda a 50 percent market share by 1964.[55] The distinction between intended and emergent strategies has important implications for human resource management.[56] The new focus on strategic HRM has tended to focus primarily on intended strategies. Thus HRM's role has been seen as identifying for top management the people-related business issues relevant to strategy formulation and then developing HRM systems that aid in the implementation of the strategic plan.

However, most emergent strategies are identified by those lower in the organizational hierarchy. It is often the rank-and-file employees who provide ideas for new markets, new products, and new strategies. HRM plays an important role in facilitating communication throughout the organization, and it is this communication that allows for effective emergent strategies to make their way up to top management. For example, Starbucks' Frappucino was a drink invented by a store employee; Starbucks leaders (including Schultz) thought it was a terrible idea. They fought it in a number of meetings, but the employee kept getting more and more information supporting her case for how much customers seemed to like it. The leaders finally gave the go-ahead to begin producing it, and it has become a $1-billion-a-year product, and one that has contributed to the Starbucks brand.[57]

Enhancing Firm Competitiveness

A related way in which human resources can be a source of competitive advantage is through developing a human capital pool that gives the company the unique ability to adapt to an ever-changing environment. Recently managers have become interested in the idea of a "learning organization," in which people continually expand their capacity to achieve the results they desire.[58] This requires the company to be in a constant state of learning through monitoring the environment, assimilating information, making decisions, and flexibly restructuring to compete in that environment. Companies that develop such learning capability have a competitive advantage. Although certain organizational information-processing systems can be an aid, ultimately the people (human capital) who make up the company provide the raw materials in a learning organization.[59]

Thus, the role of human resources in competitive advantage should continue to increase because of the fast-paced change characterizing today's business environment. Since the early 90s the Big Three auto manufacturers have improved the quality of their cars to compete with the Japanese,[60] and they have also developed more flexible and adaptable manufacturing systems so that they can respond to customer needs more quickly. This flexibility of the manufacturing process allows the emergent strategy to come directly from the marketplace by determining and responding to the exact mix of customer desires. It requires, however, that the company have people in place who have the skills to similarly adapt quickly.[61] As Howard Schultz, the founder and chairman of Starbucks, says, "If people relate to the company they work for, if they form an emotional tie to it and buy into its dreams, they will pour their heart into making it better. When employees have self-esteem and self-respect they can contribute so much more; to their company, to their family, to the world."[62] This statement exemplifies the increasing importance of human resources in developing and maintaining competitive advantage.[63]

STRATEGIC MANAGEMENT OF THE HRM FUNCTION

So far we have discussed the strategic management process that takes place at the organization level and the role of HRM in this process. We have also described the various levels of linkage that HRM may occupy with respect to the strategic planning process the company uses. Recall that in strategic HRM the HRM function is part of an integrative linkage where, in most cases, the HRM executive becomes an integral part of the senior management team, and the HR department is involved in both strategy formulation and implementation. However, for the HRM function to become truly strategic in its orientation, it must earn the integrative linkage role by being strategic in conducting its own business of HR. That is, it must view itself as a separate business entity and engage in strategic management in an effort to effectively serve the organization's various internal customers. Only when the HRM function is perceived by the CEO and others in the organization to be a strategically run business unit within the organization will it earn its "place at the table." Note how the results of several 2009 Towers Watson surveys on HR involvement in mergers and acquisitions described in the "Evidence-Based HR" feature support this notion.

To achieve this separation, one recent trend within the field of HRM, consistent with the total quality management philosophy, is for the HR executive to take a customer-oriented approach to implementing the function. In other words, the strategic planning process discussed earlier in this chapter, which takes place at the level of the business, can also be performed within the HRM function. HR executives in more progressive companies have begun to view the HRM function as a strategic business unit and have tried to define that business in terms of their customer base, their customers' needs, and the technologies required to satisfy customers' needs.

A customer orientation is one of the most important changes in the HRM function's attempts to become strategic. It entails first identifying customers, which can include line managers who require HRM services; the strategic planning team that requires the identification, analysis, and recommendations regarding people-oriented business problems; and employees, because the rewards they receive from the employment relationship are determined and/or administered by the HRM department.

In addition, the products of the HRM department must be identified. For example, line managers want to have high-quality employees committed to the organization and employees want compensation and benefit programs that are consistent, adequate, and equitable, and they want fair promotion decisions.

Finally, the technologies through which HRM meets customer needs vary depending on the need being satisfied. Essentially, a customer service orientation provides a means for the HRM function to specifically identify who its customers are, what customers' needs are being met, and how well those needs are being met.

Evidence-Based HR

In 2009 Towers Perrin conducted several online surveys on the people-related risks in mergers and acquisitions. The surveys included more than 100 Canadian finance executives and 118 Canadian HR executives in companies that had completed at least one merger and or acquisition in the previous three years. Participants were asked a number of questions about the level of involvement of HR in various stages of deals considered to be either very successful or less successful. The responses from both finance and HR executives reporting on successful deals were then compared with responses from executives reporting on less successful deals. Survey analysts point out that companies undertake such deals for a wide variety of reasons, from product, service, or channel expansion to talent or capability acquisition. However, the ultimate objectives of all such deals are improved financial and shareholder return on investment (ROI). At the end of the day, the success of a merger or acquisition is measured against stakeholder expectations for deal outcomes, and by the extent to which it helped the company achieve the growth objectives that prompted the deal in the first place. Among all respondents in the survey, 52 percent felt their deals were successful, while 38 percent indicated deals were fairly successful, and 10 percent were not very, or not at all successful.

The results of the study clearly indicate ways that HR can effectively support successful completion of mergers and acquisitions, as well as areas where HR can improve. For example, HR supported 65 percent of successful deals by effectively and openly communicating with employees throughout the transition, and in 56 percent of such deals by initiating and implementing ways to retain key employees. And in over 40 percent of successful deals, HR was credited with assigning the best resources to the integration team, influencing the effectiveness of senior leaders involved, and deploying human capital effectively at all stages of the deal. These results contrast sharply with companies completing less successful deals in every area where effective HR support was reported, indicating that getting HR involved early and often in a merger or acquisition can influence the outcomes substantially. For example, HR was reported as being helpful in influencing the effectiveness of senior leadership in only 15 percent of less successful deals, and of deploying human capital at all stages in only 19 percent of deals that could have gone a lot better.

Towers Perrin also examined whether hindsight offered insight with respect to HR involvement in M&As, asking the question "What would improve the results of your next deal?" Of those respondents who had completed very successful deals 56 percent indicated they would improve knowledge of HR about mergers and acquisitions, a sentiment endorsed by 47 percent of those who hadn't fared as well in their deals. When asked if they could improve the results of the next deal by improving the business acumen of HR, over 40 percent of both successful and unsuccessful dealmakers agreed they would improve business acumen of HR before they went through it again.

The study concluded that companies completing successful deals seemed to have an HR function that was fully tuned into the key objectives and strategy of the deal and that was skilled in guiding leadership and managing the people issues involved (leadership, communication, talent management). It also appeared that the HR functions in such companies had developed effective processes for managing people that were in sync with the goals and expectations of company leaders. In other words, the HR function in such companies was definitely seen as an asset to the process.

SOURCES: M. Tougas, J. Kissack, L. Lynch, L. Samaroo, and E. D'Amours, "Mastering the People Risks in M&A: The Heart of a Deal," Towers Watson 2010; and "Positioning for M&A Success: Putting People into the Equation," *M&A Pulse Report*, Towers Watson, December 2009 (originally published by Towers Perrin), pp. 2–8.

Describe steps HRM
can take to maximize its
value and become a true
strategic partner in the
organization.

BUILDING AN HR STRATEGY

The Basic Process

How should HR functions build their HR strategies? Recent research has examined how HR functions go about the process of building HR strategies meant to support business strategies. Conducting case studies on 20 different companies, Wright and colleagues describe the generic approach as somewhat consistent with the process for developing a business strategy.[64]

As depicted in Figure 2.5, the function first scans the environment to determine the trends or events that might have an impact on the organization (e.g., future talent shortage, increasing immigrant population, aging of the workforce). It then examines the strategic business issues or needs (e.g., is the company growing, expanding internationally, needing to develop new technologies?).

From these issues, the HR strategy team needs to identify the specific people issues that will be critical to address in order for the business to succeed (a potential leadership vacuum, lack of technological expertise, lack of diversity, etc.). All of this information is used in designing the HR strategy, which provides a detailed plan regarding the major priorities and the programs, policies, and processes that must be developed or executed. Finally, this HR strategy is communicated to the relevant parties, both internal and external to the function.

Learn more about IBM's strategic priorities on demand and IBM's HR strategy online with Connect.

This generic process provides for the potential to involve line executives in a number of ways, ranging from simple input to formal signoff approving the HR strategy. The most progressive organizations do it all—asking a large group of executives for input, having one or two executives on the team, communicating the HR strategy broadly to executives, and having the senior executive team formally approve it.

Characterizing HR Strategies

HR strategies can be generated in a variety of ways and each approach will result in various levels of linkage with the business. In general, four categories of this relationship can be identified, ranging from the most elementary level of "HR-focused" approaches to the most fully developed "Business-Driven" approach. In the latter approach, HR strategies begin by identifying the major business needs and issues, consider how people fit in and what people outcomes are necessary, and then build HR systems focused on meeting those needs. If HR strategies are to be effectively aligned, they must help address the issues that the business faces, which will determine its success. As finding, attracting, and retaining talent has become a critical issue of the future, virtually every HR function is addressing this as part of the HR strategy.

FIGURE 2.5   Basic Process for HR Strategy

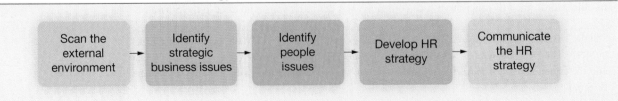

Learn more about approaches to developing an HR strategy online with Connect.

Evaluating HRM Effectiveness

The strategic decision-making process for the HRM function requires that decision makers have a good sense of the effectiveness of the current HRM function. This information provides the foundation for decisions regarding which processes, systems, and skills of HR employees need improvement. Often HRM functions that have been heavily involved in transactional activities for a long time tend to lack systems, processes, and skills for delivering state-of-the-art traditional activities and are unable to contribute in the transformational arena. Thus diagnosis of the effectiveness of the HRM function provides critical information for its strategic management.

In addition, having good measures of the function's effectiveness provides other valuable benefits.[65] Evaluation is a sign to other managers that the HRM function really cares about the organization as a whole and is trying to support operations, production, marketing, and other functions of the company. Information regarding cost savings and benefits is useful to prove to internal customers that HRM practices contribute to the bottom line. Such information is also useful for gaining additional business for the HRM function, all of which helps with marketing the function. Evaluation also helps determine whether the HRM function is meeting its objectives and effectively using its budget and thus provides accountability.

Two approaches are commonly used to evaluate the effectiveness of HRM practices: the audit approach and the analytic approach. The **audit approach** focuses on reviewing the various outcomes of the HRM functional areas. Both key indicators and customer satisfaction measures are typically collected. The development of electronic employee databases and information systems has made it much easier to collect, store, and analyze the functional key indicators than in the past, when information was kept in file folders or unlinked software programs.

If the HRM function desires to be more customer oriented as part of the strategic management process, then a logical source of effectiveness data can be the customers. One important internal customer is the employees of the firm. Many organizations use their regular employee attitude survey as a way to assess the employees as users/customers of the HRM programs and practices.[66] In addition, many firms now use surveys of top-line executives as a better means of assessing the effectiveness of the HRM function. The top-level line executives can see how the systems and practices are impacting both employees and the overall effectiveness of the firm from a strategic standpoint. This can also be useful for determining how well HR employees' perceptions of their function's effectiveness align with the views of their line colleagues.

Audit Approach
Type of assessment of HRM effectiveness that involves review of customer satisfaction or key indicators (such as turnover rate or average days to fill a position) related to an HRM functional area (such as recruiting or training).

Learn more about examples of key indicators and customer satisfaction measures for HRM functions online with Connect.

Another approach is the **analytic approach**, which focuses on either (1) determining whether the introduction of a program or practice (such as a training program or a new compensation system) has the intended effect or (2) estimating the financial costs and benefits resulting from an HRM practice. For example, we will explore how companies can determine a training program's impact on learning, behaviour, and results in Chapter 6. The second strategy involves determining the dollar value of the training program, taking into account all the costs associated with the program. Using this strategy, we are not concerned with how much change occurred but rather with the dollar value (costs versus benefits) of the program.

The analytic approach is more demanding than the audit approach because it requires the detailed use of statistics and finance.

Analytic Approach
Type of assessment of HRM effectiveness that involves determining the impact of, or the financial cost and benefits of, a program or practice.

IMPROVING HRM EFFECTIVENESS

Once a strategic direction has been established and HRM's effectiveness evaluated, leaders of the HRM function can explore how to improve its effectiveness in contributing to the firm's competitiveness. Often the improvement focuses on the traditional and transactional aspects of the pyramid depicted in Figure 1.4 First, within each activity, HRM needs to improve both the efficiency and effectiveness in performing each of the activities. Second, often there is a push to eliminate as much of the transactional work as possible (and some of the traditional work) to free up time and resources to focus more on the higher-value-added transformational work. Redesign of the structure (reporting relationships) and processes (through outsourcing and information technology) enables the function to achieve these goals simultaneously. Figure 2.6 depicts this process. We will discuss each of these approaches briefly.

Restructuring to Improve HRM Effectiveness

Traditional HRM functions were structured around the basic HRM sub functions such as staffing, training, compensation, appraisal, and labour relations. Each of these areas had a director who reported to the VP of HRM, who often reported to a VP of finance and administration. However, for the HRM function to truly contribute strategically to firm effectiveness, the senior HR person must be part of the top management team (reporting directly to the chief executive officer), and there must be a different structural arrangement within the function itself.

A recently developed generic structure for the HRM function is depicted in Figure 2.7, which divides the HRM function effectively into three divisions: the centres for expertise, the field

FIGURE 2.6 Improving HRM Effectiveness

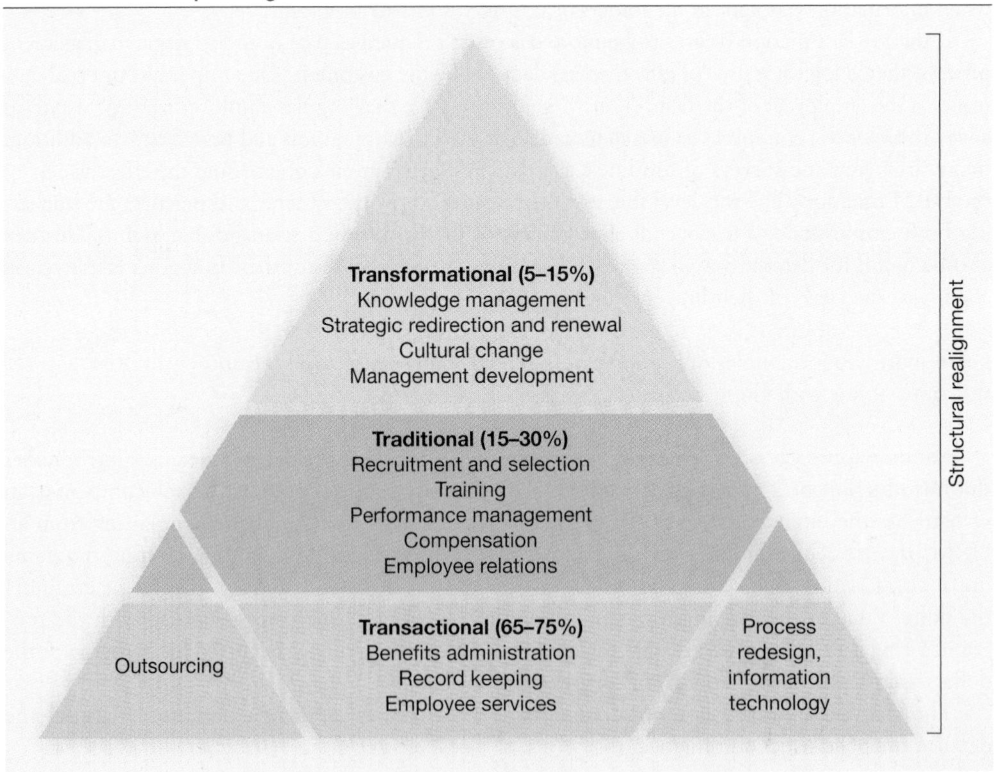

FIGURE 2.7 Old and New Structures for the HRM Organization

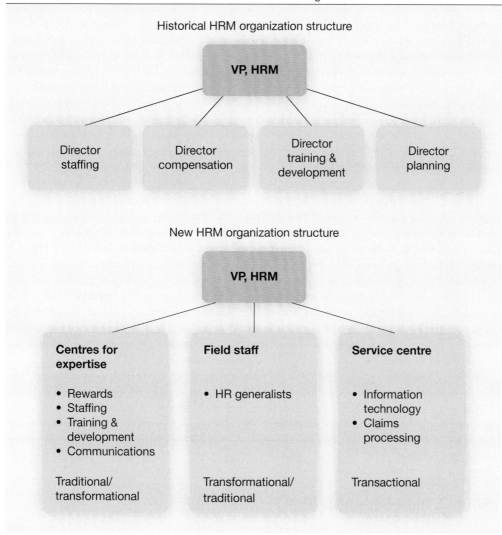

SOURCE: P. Wright, G. McMahan, S. Snell, and B. Gerhart, *Strategic Human Resource Management: Building Human Capital and Organizational Capability.* Technical report. Cornell University, 1998.

generalists, and the service centre.[67] Such structural arrangements improve service delivery through specialization. Centre for expertise employees can develop current functional skills without being distracted by transactional activities, and generalists can focus on learning the business environment without having to maintain expertise in functional specializations. Finally, service centre employees can focus on efficient delivery of basic services across business units.

Outsourcing to Improve HRM Effectiveness

Restructuring the internal HRM function and redesigning the processes represent internal approaches to improving HRM effectiveness. However, increasingly HR executives are seeking to improve the effectiveness of the systems, processes, and services the function delivers through

Outsourcing
The practice of having another company (a vendor, third-party provider, or consultant) provide services.

outsourcing. **Outsourcing** refers to the practice of having another company (a vendor, third-party provider, or consultant) provide services. One study suggests that 80 percent of companies now outsource at least one HR activity.[68] The HR responsibilities most likely to be outsourced completely include employee assistance and counselling, flexible spending account administration, and background and criminal background checks. Outsource providers such as ADP, Accenture HR Services, Convergys, and Hewitt provide payroll services as well as recruiting, training, record managements, and expatriation. The primary reasons for outsourcing are to save money and spend more time on strategic business issues, such as identifying new business opportunities; assessing possible merger, acquisition, or divestiture strategies; or working on recruiting and developing talent.[69] As a result, HR functions related to these areas such as employee development, performance management, communications plans and strategies, policy development and implementation, and organizational development are outsourced least frequently.

When outsourcing occurs, the outsourcing partner chosen is expected to provide the service more cheaply or effectively than it can be performed internally. Usually this is because outsourced providers are specialists who are able to develop extensive expertise that can be leveraged across a number of companies. For example, when the Canadian Imperial Bank of Commerce contracted with Electronic Data Systems (EDS) Corporation to take over payroll, benefits administration, and other HR processing for the Toronto-based bank, the bank had 30 incompatible HR systems and had not invested in e-HRM (use of the Web for HR operations).[70] EDS revised the bank's payroll, benefits, executive compensation, and human resources information technology systems, and it created my.HR, a Web portal used by managers and employees. Use of EDS has not required any additional costs over the bank's yearly HR budget. When the bank outsourced payroll, it cut 200 jobs from its centralized HR staff, leaving the remaining HR staff to focus on strategic issues such as recruiting, training, and union contract negotiations. The centralized staff members moved over to EDS.

We must also point out that although the outsourcing of HR is expected to grow, many contracts have ended because of lack of understanding of the outsourcing provider's capabilities, failure to reach goals such as anticipated cost reductions, and poor delivery of services.[71] A key aspect of any outsourcing decision is an understanding of the company's vision for HR and an assessment of the costs of performing HR functions within the company compared with the potential savings through outsourcing.

PROCESS REDESIGN AND NEW TECHNOLOGIES

In addition to structural arrangements, process redesign enables the HRM function to more efficiently and effectively deliver HRM services. Process redesign often uses information technology, but information technology applications are not a requirement. Process design is a critical tool for improving any process in a company and will be discussed in depth in Chapter 4 as a technique to be incorporated with analysis and design and human resources planning. However, in making the transition to a more strategic HRM function, it is also important to integrate the process into continuous improvement of the HRM function.

Reengineering
Review and redesign of work processes to make them more efficient and improve the quality of the end product or service.

Reengineering is a complete review of critical work processes and redesign to make them more efficient and able to deliver higher quality. Reengineering is especially critical to ensuring that the benefits of new technology can be realized. Applying new technology to an inefficient process will not improve efficiency or effectiveness. Instead, it will increase product or service costs related to the introduction of the new technology.

Reengineering can be used to review the HRM department functions and processes, or it can be used to review specific HRM practices such as work design or the performance management system. The four steps of the reengineering process are shown in Figure 2.8.

FIGURE 2.8 The Reengineering Process

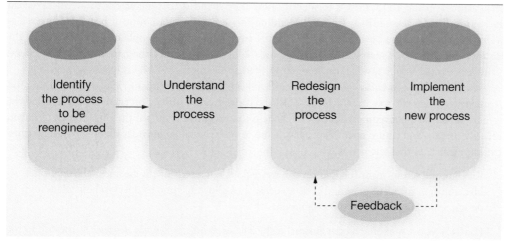

Like all other business processes, the HRM function has the capacity to increase effectiveness over time through integration of new technology, especially in the area of administration. Several new and emerging technologies can help improve the effectiveness of the HRM function. **New technologies** are current applications of knowledge, procedures, and equipment that have not been used previously. New technology usually involves automation—that is, replacing human labour with equipment, information processing, or some combination of the two, and it may even include use of new applications, such as the growth of Web 2.0 applications on the Internet.

For example, the role of HRM in administration is decreasing as technology is used for many administrative purposes, such as managing employee records and allowing employees to get information about and enrol in training, benefits, and other programs. Advances in technology such as the Internet have decreased the HRM role in maintaining records and providing self-service to employees.[72] **Self-service** refers to giving employees online access to information about HR issues such as training, benefits, compensation, and contracts; enrolling online in programs and services; and completing online attitude surveys.

In HRM, technology has already been used for three broad functions: transaction processing, reporting, and tracking; decision support systems; and expert systems.[73] We will discuss these and many other emerging technologies being applied to HRM in Chapter 4. In addition, you will find mention of specific improvements that can be made to various functions of HR through prudent integration of technology in each chapter where the issue is relevant. For now, it is enough to realize that HR is no different than any other department in the organization in that continuous improvement is essential if the department is to maximize its contribution to the organization. This can be done only through awareness, determination, effective measurement, process redesign, and integration of new technology where appropriate.

THE ROLE OF THE CHIEF HUMAN RESOURCE OFFICER

Having discussed the increasing importance of HR and the new strategic role of HR professionals, we now examine the role of the leader of the HR function. These chief human resource officers (CHROs) bear the responsibility for leading the HR function as well as ensuring that HR systems and processes deliver value to the company. Only recently have researchers attempted to examine what these HR leaders do and how they affect the business.

New Technologies
Current applications of knowledge, procedures, and equipment that have not been previously used. Usually involves replacing human labour with equipment, information processing, or some combination of the two.

Self-Service
Giving employees online access to HR information, online enrollment in programs and services, and completing online attitude surveys.

LO 7

Examine the role of the chief human resources officer.

A recent survey identified seven roles that CHROs have to play to one degree or another, and then asked Fortune 150 CHROs to identify how they spend their time across those roles. As can be seen in Figure 2.9, CHROs reported spending the second-most amount of time (21 percent) as a *strategic adviser* to the executive team. This role entails sharing the people expertise as part of the decision-making process, as well as shaping how the human capital of the firm fits into its strategy. This also was the role that was most frequently cited as having the greatest impact on the firm.

The role of *talent architect* also sees a significant portion of time spent (17 percent) and was also frequently cited as the role in which the CHRO has the greatest impact on the business. Playing the role of talent architect requires that CHROs help the executive team see the importance of talent, identify present and future talent gaps, and come to own the talent agenda. One CHRO described the importance of this role this way:

> Keeping the senior team focused on the strategic talent needs of the business allows proper identification of talent gaps and future needs, thus allowing time to develop best talent and design appropriate experiential assignments.[74]

CHROs report spending as much time in the role of *counsellor/confidante/coach* as they do in the talent architect role (17 percent), and a number of CHROs listed this role as one of the roles with the greatest impact. This role seemingly is a broad one, and it can entail anything from behavioural or performance counselling to being the personal sounding board for the CEO. Perhaps as pressure mounts on CEOs from investors and analysts, the CHRO is the most trusted adviser for personal advice or simply to listen to the CEO's problems. One poignant comment regarding this role was:

> If I do my job right, I am the copper wire that connects all the outlets of the firm together effectively. This includes OD work (which some might put in the strategic adviser category), performance counselling and relationship building, business consulting and the strategic elements of talent acquisition and planning.[75]

FIGURE 2.9 Percentage of Time CHROs Spend in Each Role

The *leader of the HR function* is the role in which CHROs spent the most time, but it is not seen as one that has the greatest impact. This role deals with ensuring that the HR function is aligning its activities and priorities toward the needs of the business, and it usually entails meeting with direct reports to provide guidance and check on progress. However, CHROs increasingly rely on their direct reports to design and deliver HR services while they shift their attention to advising and counselling the top executive team.

Liaison to the board entails all of the activities in which CHROs engage with the board of directors, including discussions of executive compensation, CEO performance, CEO succession, and performance of other members of the executive leadership team. This role is increasing in importance, although it has a long way to go before equalling the strategic adviser, talent architect, and counsellor/confidante/coach roles.

The role of *workforce sensors* entails taking the pulse of the employee population to identify any morale or motivation issues. This is a role in which CHROs do not spent much time, and few viewed it as having the greatest impact on the business.

Finally, CHROs to some extent become the face of the organization to outside constituents such as labour unions, nongovernmental organizations, and the press. They spend the least amount of time in the *representative of the firm* role.

The new strategic role for HRM presents both opportunities and challenges. HRM has the chance to profoundly impact the way organizations compete through people. On the other hand, with this opportunity comes serious responsibility and accountability.[76] HRM functions of the future must consist of individuals who view themselves as businesspeople who happen to work in an HRM function, rather than HRM people who happen to work in a business.

A Look Back

Transforming GM

In the beginning, GM's plan for changing its business model included plans to lay off 47,000 employees worldwide, close five additional plants in North America, and eliminate four of the company's eight brands. In addition, the company conducted talks with the UAW and CAW to restructure $20 billion in obligations to retired hourly workers. Still, the bondholders of GM felt that the company was not going far enough. They wanted to see even greater cuts, as well as a reduction in commitments to the legacy workforce. Without that, they felt GM couldn't survive over the long term.

By March 2009, GM of Canada Ltd. and the CAW had agreed to cuts that would translate into hundreds of millions of dollars in savings in order to qualify for bailout monies and to "take bankruptcy off the table once and for all." Such concessions negotiated by the CAW added to the $400 million in savings (over three years) that GM workers had already given up in their 2008 contract. The new deal cut average hourly wages and benefits to around $69 per hour per GM worker. Another week of special holidays was sacrificed along with a special $1,700 annual bonus, and wages and cost-of-living allowance was frozen for the term of the agreement. The annual bonus money was redirected to pay health costs of the legacy workforce. Those still actively working agreed to pay $360 per year in health care premiums. Retirees and surviving spouses saw their pensions and cost-of-living increases frozen, and going forward they will pay $180 per year in health care premiums. In addition, both GM workers and retirees are now required to pay a greater portion of actual health and dental services utilized under their plans.

Questions

1. Our opening vignette indicated that the new General Motors Company has achieved a lot using its new business model. Visit the company's website and download a copy of the 2010 Annual Report (http://investor.gm.com/stockholder-information). Do you think the new business model, as described by the CEO Daniel Akerson in the 2010 Annual Report is enough to make the company truly sustainable over time? Explain your answer.

2. How might GM change the way it manages its workforce as part of its transformation?

3. Notice that little of the discussion dealt with GM's products. What would a few extremely successful products do for GM's business model? What would a line of mediocre or poor products do to this transformation process?

SOURCE: S. Terlep and N. King, "Bondholders Say GM's Plan Fails to Tackle Issues," *The Wall Street Journal* (February 19, 2009) at http://online.wsj.com/article/SB123500467245718075. html?mod=testMod; T. Van Alphen, "Auto Union to Freeze Pay at GM," *Toronto Star* (March 9, 2009) at www.thestar.com/News/Canada/article/598763 (retrieved June 7, 2011); "Landmark Auto Deal" Canadian Press video at http://www.thestar.com/videozone/598802--landmark-auto-deal October 20, 2010, (retrieved June 7, 2011).

Summary

A strategic approach to human resource management seeks to proactively provide a competitive advantage through the company's most important asset: its human resources. While human resources are the most important asset, they are also usually the single largest controllable cost within the firm's business model. The HRM function needs to be integrally involved in the formulation of strategy to identify the people-related business issues the company faces. Once the strategy has been determined, HRM has a profound impact on the implementation of the plan by developing and aligning HRM practices that ensure that the company has motivated employees with the necessary skills. Finally, the emerging strategic role of the HRM function requires that HR professionals in the future develop business, professional–technical, change management, and integration competencies.

If HR wants to maximize its value to the organization, it must "have all its ducks in a row," which means building an HR strategy that involves input from line executives. HR must measure its effectiveness using recognized methods of evaluation such as the audit approach or the analytic approach. There must be continuous improvement of the HRM process, using a variety of methods such as restructuring, process redesign, outsourcing and maximal use of new technologies. Finally, a critical component of integrated linkage between strategic organizations and their HRM function is the role of the chief human resource officer. When the CHRO has a "seat at the table," organizations and HR have true potential for achieving organizational goals.

Key Terms

Analytic approach, 63
Audit approach, 63
Concentration strategy, 55
Downsizing, 55
External analysis, 49
External growth strategy, 55
Goals, 49

Internal analysis, 49
Internal growth strategy, 55
New technologies, 67
Outsourcing, 66
Reengineering, 66
Role behaviours, 54

Self-service, 67
Strategic choice, 49
Strategic human resource
    management (SHRM), 43
Strategy formulation, 44
Strategy implementation, 44

Discussion Questions

1. Pick one of your university or college's major sports teams (such as football, basketball, hockey, or soccer). How would you characterize that team's generic strategy? How does the composition of the team members (in terms of size, speed, ability, and so on) relate to that strategy? What are the strengths and weaknesses of the team? How do they dictate the team's generic strategy and its approach to a particular game?

2. Do you think that it is easier to tie human resources to the strategic management process in large or in small organizations? Why?

3. How can strategic management within the HRM department ensure that HRM plays an effective role in the company's strategic management process?

4. What types of specific skills (such as knowledge of financial accounting methods) do you think HR professionals will need to have the business, professional-technical, change management, and integrative competencies necessary in the future? Where can you develop each of these skills?

5. What are some of the key environmental variables that you see changing in the business world today? What impact will those changes have on the HRM function in organizations?

6. How can the processes for strategic management discussed in this chapter be transplanted to manage the HRM function?

7. Why do you think that few companies take the time to determine the effectiveness of HRM practices? Should a company be concerned about evaluating HRM practices? Why? What might people working in the HRM function gain by evaluating the function?

8. Some argue that outsourcing an activity is bad because the activity is no longer a means of distinguishing the firm from competitors. (All competitors can buy the same service from the same provider, so it cannot be a source of competitive advantage.) Is this true? If so, why would a firm outsource any activity?

9. Examine the seven roles of the CHRO, which they have to play to one degree or another. Can you see yourself in this position one day? What do the various roles played by the CHRO tell us about HRM's role in strategy formulation and implementation?

10. Based on discussions of mergers and acquisitions contained in this chapter, what do you think is the most important contribution the HR function can offer to effectively support such deals? What can those in charge of the HR function do to gain involvement in various stages of planning and execution of such deals? Assuming they are invited to contribute, what expectations might various stakeholders have of HR before, during, and after the merger or acquisition takes place?

Self-Assessment Exercise

Think of a company you have worked for, or find an annual report for a company you are interested in working for. (Many companies post their annual reports online at their website.) Then answer the following questions.

Questions

1. How has the company been affected by the trends discussed in this chapter?

2. Does the company use the strategic HR practices recommended in this chapter?

3. What else should the company do to deal with the challenges posed by the trends discussed in this chapter?

Exercising Strategy: Transforming the Business and HR at Xerox

In 1958, Xerox launched the Xerox 914, the first automatic, plain-paper office copier. This product went on to become the top-selling industrial product of all time. Xerox's successful xerography technology gave it a sustainable competitive advantage that endured for years. However, all good things must come to an end, and in Xerox's case, that end was the late 1990s. By 2000, Xerox experienced its biggest slide in history, and the consensus among analysts within the industry was that Xerox was working with "an unsustainable business model," meaning unless things changed drastically, Xerox would soon cease to exist. In 2000 Xerox had $17.1 billion in debt, with only $154 million in cash on hand. By 2001, Xerox's stock, which had peaked at $63, fell to about $4—a loss of more than 90 percent of its market capitalization. And as if that was not enough, it also faced an accounting investigation by the Securities and Exchange Commission for how it accounted for its customer leases on copiers.

Enter new VP of HR Pat Nazemetz in 1999 and new CEO Anne Mulcahy in 2000 to try to right a sinking ship. Mulcahy put the company on a starvation diet. This entailed selling major operations in China and Hong Kong, reducing global headcount to 61,100 from 91,500 through selloffs, early retirements, and layoffs, and implementing drastic cost controls. While Mulcahy's strategy has brought Xerox back to life (2003 saw Xerox triple its net income to $360 million and $978 million by 2005) as an organization, the HR function had to drive the change in the business while simultaneously transforming the function.

While many HR functions look to outsource, Xerox transformed its HR function largely internally. According to Nazemetz, outsourcing providers say, "'Let us in, let us take over your HR function and we can take 10 percent to 30 percent out of your cost base.' We began trimming down, finding synergies and opportunities to get more efficient. We found the savings ourselves."

The largest single savings came from consolidating and expanding the HR Service Center. The Center began with purely transactional work (e.g., record keeping), then added Web-based processes to handle routine work. The Center now conducts research and analysis of HR operations and handles employee-relations issues. This has enabled HR to reduce headcount without reducing levels of service.

Also, as with any organization that has shed 30 percent of its workforce, employee morale was an issue. Even before the fall, HR had been taking the pulse of employees through its "hearts and minds" surveys. This intranet-based survey tapped into a number of employee attitudes and sought to identify the problem areas for HR and line executives to focus on. Employees noted concerns with items such as "Company supports risk-taking," "Company considers impact on employees," "Senior-management behaviour is consistent with words," and "Trust level is high."

"People often ask me how Xerox has found success," says Mulcahy. "My answer is that you have to have a strategy and a plan, but [more importantly], what you really need is excellence of execution, and that starts and ends with a talented, motivated group of people aligned around a common set of goals. Our HR people came through with a series of alignment workshops and retention incentives just when we needed them [to] make Xerox the stronger, better company it is today."

The Xerox that exists today has grown considerably and restored its reputation for innovation. After its recent acquisition of Affiliated Computer Services (ACS), the company now employs 130,000 employees in 160 countries around the world. And the talented people Mulcahy refers to include employees such as Patty Calkins, a chemist hired in 1993, who stayed the course and helped the company find its moorings once again. During the troublesome years, she says, Xerox became obsessed with the concept of remanufacturing to eliminate warehouses of old copiers and parts, and to design its products to be sustainable over time among multiple owners. Culkins, along with inspired Xerox engineers and designers, set a goal of 90 percent reusability of all used parts and pieces of Xerox copiers, developed the company's Signature Analysis technology, and began building parts and copiers with more than one life in mind. Savings have added up to hundreds of millions of dollars over time, and the focus on remanufacturing and reuse now dominates the design process of almost all Xerox products. By 2009, Mulcahy and CEO Ursula Burns noted in the company's 2009 *Report on Global Citizenship*, "We were an early leader in the sustainability movement because we thought it was the right thing to do for the environment. But we discovered something else along the way. Every one of our innovations ended up either saving us money or creating new markets and new revenue. We found, in other words, that we don't have to choose between the environment and profit. We can do both. "And in the past three years alone, Xerox has brought over 100 products to the market, in 2007 it won the National Medal of Technology, and in 2009 it was named the world's most admired company in the computer industry by *Fortune* magazine, citing its reputation for use of corporate assets, quality of management, and social responsibility.

Questions

1. What were some of the challenges presented by the massive downsizing that occurred at Xerox?

2. Based on results of the past ten years, do you think Xerox was able to regain both the "hearts and minds" of employees following the dark period of downsizing?

3. Visit the career page in the main Xerox company website, at www.xeroxcareers.com. Then examine this chapter's discussion of various linkages possible between strategic planning and HRM. Based on what you see on the Career page for Xerox, and what you have learned above, what type of linkage do you think Xerox's HRM function has with planning and implementation of strategy at Xerox? Explain your reasons for thinking this way.

SOURCES: Based in part on A. Werbach, *Strategy for Sustainability: A Business Manifesto,* Harvard Business School Publishing, 2009, pp. 170–17; US Xerox website; and http://www.xeroxcareers.com/about-us/default.aspx.

Managing People: Emerging Market Financiers— Passing Gear on the On Ramp

Indications are surfacing that North American financial institutions may be at the dawn of a whole new era of competition—one in which "the rules" may change drastically in terms of who does business with whom. Some are calling it "Globalization 2.0," and what's different about stage 2 is that international lending and investment patterns threaten to move beyond the traditional east–west or north–south reciprocal economic relationships that North Americans have always assumed would be their right. In fact, capital flow is starting to go in new directions that reflect the increasing strength of "emerging markets" such as China, India, and Russia. As entrepreneurs gain strength in emerging markets by exploiting opportunities in their own backyard, they are also going after vast opportunities in other emerging markets such as Africa. In so doing, they are also beginning to see advantages that go along with securing financing from strengthening banks in China, Russia, and Nigeria. This approach is called "emerging-market cross-pollination," or as one cynical prophet succinctly described it: "Mumbai, Dubai, Shanghai, or good-bye." Note that New York, London, and Toronto don't appear in that list of financial centres. It appears that if Canadian banks aren't alert, they could soon be bypassed altogether. Aggressive and geographically closer emerging market lenders could soon become preferred partners among locally based industry leaders. As companies in emerging markets grow, they could be become much less patient with east–west cultural differences that prolong or stall financing. With opportunities in the developing world materializing every day, why not seek financing closer to home among increasingly robust and aggressive financial institutions that are happy to accommodate? Companies in India seeking to exploit opportunities in South Africa or Russia could bypass North American and U.K. lenders altogether in favour of lenders who have an intuitive and much better understanding of their needs.

At least one Canadian bank seems to have taken an important step in the right direction to forestall such possibilities. In February 2007, the Royal Bank of Canada announced the appointment of Zabeen Hirji as chief human resources officer, giving her responsibility for enterprise-wide human resources functions and strategies. As the bank's new CHRO, Hirji became one of the organization's ten executive officers charged with "setting overall strategic direction of RBC," so the bank has placed her firmly among those who will grapple with such complex competitive issues.

Although Hirji's appointment was the logical next step in a steadily progressive 30-year career with RBC that included assignments in retail banking, credit cards, operations, and strategy before landing in HR, her personal background also adds considerable strategic value to RBC and the challenges it now faces offshore. What makes Hirji so perfect for her new role in HR is that she is an East Indian Muslim who speaks Katchi, a traditional Indian language her grandmother taught her. Born in Tanzania, Hirji's early memories include listening to her father, a soft-drink manufacturer, talk business every night at the dinner table. After he died at the age of 43, Hirji's mother decided to immigrate to Canada in 1974, taking 14-year-old Hirji and her siblings with her. Hirji says her approach to "think big and take action to get there" is something she learned from her mother and grandmother, both independent and spirited women who taught her to take control of her life, saying "the ball was in my court." That may be why she decided to build on her analytical and math inclinations by pursuing an MBA at Simon Fraser University. Later she accepted a job at RBC and soon realized that banking seemed to suit her and that she liked working at RBC.

After becoming the senior vice president human resources in 2001, Hirji acquired a reputation as a trailblazer, introducing flextime, working from home, and promotion from within at the bank. Hirji wanted to use her role to influence RBC people strategies, to begin "breaking down the barriers, for giving people, regardless of their gender or ethnicity, the chance to fulfill their potential." She and her team made significant progress. RBC can now say that "one third of the executives are women, half of all senior management are female, and nine percent of senior managers are visible minorities." Hirji encourages others to be their best by leveraging what is unique about them, saying "… look at who you are and make the most of it. Think not of limits, but of creating maximum value from yourself, and everything you do."

Diversity and Hirji's role in creating an inclusive environment are part of the bank's growth platform where human capital and customers (domestic and international) are inextricably linked. At RBC diversity is seen as a business, social, and demographic imperative. The social and business reasons include treating people with respect and "enabling people to unlock their potential so they achieve their aspirations," which helps attract and retain top talent (like Zabeen Hirji). Appreciation of diversity is also essential for how individuals and teams are led and for how creativity and innovation can be increased among naturally analytical minds. Diversity is seen as a management tool that leverages both similarities and differences among RBC's nearly 70,000 employees and helps it outperform the competition. However, in explaining why diversity is also a "Demographic Imperative" RBC reveals insights for how it plans to fend off threats from the previously mentioned "emerging-market cross-pollination," saying:

- Today's workforce and marketplace is a dynamic mix of different cultures, ages, races, lifestyles, genders, and more.
- Statistics emerging from recent U.S. and Canadian census and labour force reports prove that our consumer base and talent pools are shifting.
- These visible demographic differences, as well as emerging market realities, continuously create new customer and employee needs.

In short, management at RBC believes that leveraging diversity is the right and smart thing to do, and that "from a business vantage point, to best serve the market, one must 'employ the market.'"

Certainly Zabeen Hirji seems to be the right person, in the right place, at the right time to lead RBC's human capital management into what promises to be a volatile future. By placing her in charge of its workforce and including her in the executive team, RBC has positioned itself about as well as it can to ensure RBC remains a player no matter how much or where the game changes.

SOURCES: Based on C. Freeland, "Globalization 2.0: Emerging-Market Cross Pollination," *The Globe and Mail*, Report on Business (October 1, 2010); Zabeen Hirji: Dwelling in Two Rooms, Women'sPost.ca (October 2, 2008), at http://www.womenspost.ca/articles/profiles/zabeen-hirji-dwelling-two-rooms (retrieved June 7, 2010); "Why Diversity Matters," at http://www.rbc.com/diversity/why-does-diversity-matter.html (retrieved June 7, 2010); D. Kelly, "'Fulfilling Potential' Vital to Royal Bank's Senior Vice-President of Human Resources," *The Globe and Mail* (November 25, 2008) at http:www.triec.ca/news/story/69 (retrieved June 7, 2010).

Questions

1. Why do Zabeen Hirji's unique personal qualities and background give RBC a competitive advantage in the future? What difference does it make that she became a member of the executive team?

2. How does RBC's focus on diversity influence the way it manages people? Its human resource practices?

3. What does the statement "to best serve the market, one must employ the market" mean now for RBC? In the future?

 **Practise and learn online with Connect.**

The Legal Environment: Equality and Human Rights

LEARNING OBJECTIVES

After reading this chapter, you should be able to:

LO 1 Describe how various levels of government shape the legal environment for HRM in Canada. page 79

LO 2 Explain the importance of the Canadian Charter of Rights and Freedoms and human rights legislation, and their implications for HRM. page 82

LO 3 Discuss what constitutes discrimination and requirements for reasonable accommodation. page 84

LO 4 Explain various concepts of discrimination and HRM's role in prevention and elimination of such behaviours. page 85

LO 5 Explain employment equity legislation and describe the four designated groups. page 106

LO 6 Describe what is required to implement and promote employment equity programs. page 110

LO 7 Explain pay equity and its implications for HRM. page 112

LO 8 Develop approaches for managing and promoting diversity effectively. page 113

Enter the World of Business

Ernst & Young Named among Best Diversity Employers in Canada

As one of the most ethnically diverse countries in the world, Canada counts members of more than 200 ethnic groups among its citizens and, as of the 2006 census, more than 5 million of those Canadians identify as a visible minority. In major urban centres such as Toronto and Vancouver, that number jumps to almost 40 percent of the population. Yet the reality on the street is not reflected in the management of most Canadian companies. Just over 10 percent of all management positions are filled by visible minorities, and women fare only marginally better; where visible minorities account for 11.2 percent, women account for 11.4 percent of line management positions. The changing face of the Canadian workforce, combined with the growing body of research that shows the positive impact diversity can have on organizational outcomes such as performance, problem solving, decision making, and innovation, is making a compelling business case for fostering and encouraging diversity in the workplace. Companies are slowly arriving at the conclusion that diversity needs to be treated as a strategic imperative and represents a potential competitive advantage. Progressive organizations are embracing diversity and promoting cultures of inclusiveness as the key to finding, hiring, and keeping the best available talent and ensuring that organizational decisions are informed by contributions from people with varying backgrounds, experiences, and perspectives.

One such organization is Ernst & Young, a three-time annual recipient of recognition as one of Canada's Best Diversity Employers (2008–2010). The key to Ernst & Young's success is its unfailing commitment to inclusiveness, which meant keeping its diversity initiatives front and centre, even throughout the recent economic downturn. The firm's many initiatives designed to address the different and changing needs of its people have become entrenched in the culture and remain fundamental to the organization's business strategy regardless of the economic climate. Initiatives such as the ethnic diversity task force with local committee chairs in regional offices and an affinity group for employees new to Canada, as well as a gender equity advisory group, targeted mentoring programs, and networking groups for the firm's women and lesbian, gay, bisexual, transgender employees and allies, are all overseen and supported by Ernst & Young's national director of inclusiveness.

These initiatives continued to flourish even as the economy tanked. According to Fiona Macfarlane, Ernst & Young's people leader in Canada, "One of the lessons learned from the changing economy over the past year or two is that diversity is actually a tool for strengthening your business. A collaboration of different perspectives and points of view enables business leaders to challenge the old ways of thinking and drive the innovation that is going to propel us into the new economy."

As the economy slowly recovers, Ernst & Young feels that those businesses that continued to promote inclusiveness and diversity through the downturn are now at a great advantage as economic conditions improve. Its "people-first" culture of inclusion, and its strong support for its diverse team, means Ernst & Young is poised for continued success. "There is growth potential right now, but businesses can only capitalize on this upturn if they equip themselves with strong people," says Macfarlane. "Companies hoping to attract and keep the best talent need to listen to and learn from their employees. This can best be achieved in a culture of inclusiveness."

Beyond the obvious benefits to the bottom line, cultivating diversity lends itself to a more positive workplace for employees. For Ernst & Young, meeting the divergent needs of its people has been a valuable tool for attracting—and retaining—excellent employees and for making sure that Ernst & Young was able to both weather the economic storm and find itself in a position to take advantage of growth opportunities now that the skies appear to be clearing.

SOURCES: Adapted from "Lessons in Diversity Prime Businesses to Thrive in the Upturn: Ernst & Young," Ernst & Young News Releases (March 23, 2010) at www.ey.com/CA/en/Newsroom/News-releases/2010-Best-Diversity-Employers; Fiona McFarlane, Diane Sinhuber, and Tanya Khan (2010) *Diversity Briefing: Questions for Directors to Ask* (Toronto: The Canadian Institute of Chartered Accountants) at www.ey.com/Publication/vwLUAssets/DirectorBriefingDiversity/$FILE/DirectorBriefingDiversity.pdf; "Flexibility, Inclusiveness, Learning—All Business Essentials: Ernst & Young" Ernst & Young News Releases (April 13, 2010) at www.ey.com/CA/en/Newsroom/News-releases/2010-Best-Workplaces.

INTRODUCTION

In Chapter 1, we discussed the environment of the HRM function, and we noted that several environmental factors affect an organization's HRM function. One is the legal environment, particularly the laws affecting the management of people. As indicated by troubles with workplace discrimination and harassment in many workplaces, legal issues can cause serious problems for a company's success and survival. In this chapter, we first present an overview of the Canadian legal system, noting the different legislative bodies, regulatory agencies, and judicial bodies that determine the legality of certain HRM practices. We then discuss the major laws, adjudicative bodies, and policy determinations that govern these practices.

One point to make clear at the outset is that managers often want a list of "dos and don'ts" that will keep them out of legal trouble. They rely on rules such as, "Don't ever ask a female applicant if she is married" without understanding the "why" behind these rules. Clearly, certain practices are illegal or inadvisable, and this chapter will provide some valuable tips for avoiding discrimination and harassment lawsuits. However, such lists are not compatible with a strategic approach to HRM and are certainly not the route to developing a competitive advantage; they are simply mechanical reactions to the situations. Our goal is to provide an understanding of how the legislative, regulatory, and judicial systems work to define equal employment opportunity and human rights law. Beyond the strict letter of the law, our goal is to stimulate discussion about acting in accordance with the "spirit" of the law, which should be consistent with notions of ethical business practices. Armed with this understanding, a manager is better prepared to manage people within the limits imposed by the legal system and the broader expectations of the evolving society within which businesses operate. Effective management of human resources creates competitive advantage. Rather than viewing the legal system as a constraint, firms that embrace the concept of diversity in spirit and not merely as technical compliance with the strict letter of the law should find that they are able to leverage the differences among people to the benefit of the employees and the business that employs them.

THE LEGAL SYSTEM IN CANADA

LO 1

Describe how various levels of government shape the legal environment HRM in Canada.

The foundation for the Canadian legal system is set forth in the *Constitution Act*, 1867, which is the supreme law of the country and affects HRM in three ways. First, it delineates a citizen's constitutional rights, on which the government cannot impinge.[1] In this respect, most individuals are aware of the Canadian Charter of Rights and Freedoms, which is part of the *Constitution Act*, 1982, and guarantees persons in Canada the right to equality and basic freedoms in their interactions with government.

Second, the Constitution established three major and ongoing governing bodies: the legislative, executive, and judicial branches. The Constitution explicitly defines the roles and responsibilities of each of these branches. Each branch has its own areas of authority, but these areas have often overlapped, and the borders between the branches are often blurred.

Third, the Constitution divides law-making power and functions in Canada between the federal government and the provinces and territories. The federal Parliament is assigned power over matters of general or national importance[2] and the provinces are assigned matters of more local concern involving "property and civil rights."[3] This encompasses employment and labour laws such as those relating to trade unions, minimum wages, hours of work, workers' compensation, paid vacations, industrial standards, and a range of other laws that govern the workplace, including human rights. Employees of the federal government and its agencies as well as other federally regulated employers are governed by federal labour and employment legislation. However, this comprises only a small percentage of working Canadians. The great majority of employees in Canada are governed by provincial or territorial labour and employment legislation.

Further distinguishing Canada from several other western legal regimes is the presence of two distinct legal systems: (1) the Civil Code in Quebec and (2) the common law in the remainder of the country. Quebec's Civil Code is based upon a comprehensive written code of rules and principles, while the common law is based on precedent-setting judge-made law. Another unique feature of the Canadian law system is the operation of a separate criminal law system governed by the federal Criminal Code of Canada and the civil law system governing all other aspects of the law.

Legislative Branch

The legislative branch of the federal government consists of the Parliament of Canada, which includes the House of Commons, which is elected; the Senate, which is appointed; and the Queen or her representative, the governor general. In the provinces, the same process applies but the Queen's provincial representative is called the lieutenant governor. At the provincial/territorial level, the legislative branch consists of the provincial legislatures. The federal, provincial, and territorial legislatures develop laws that govern many HRM activities. Most laws in Canada are first scrutinized and discussed by the Cabinet, then presented for debate and approval by members of the House of Commons and the Senate. Before a bill becomes a law, the Queen or her representative, the

Governor General, must approve or "assent to" it. By constitutional convention, such assent always follows the advice of the government. It should be noted that municipalities, based on authority delegated by provincial legislatures, also make laws, typically called bylaws. These bylaws are not generally significant to HRM activities, but sometimes have local impact.

Enacted legislation, regulations, and bylaws are paramount over common law. In this respect, legislation overrides court judgments; however, courts interpret the application of legislation. In the end, all laws must conform to the Constitution. A court or judge may find that a statute is unconstitutional and declare that statute to be null and void or otherwise direct a framework for changes. It is then the responsibility of the legislative branch to amend the offending legislation or enact new legislation if it deems it to be appropriate.

connect

Learn more about how statutory laws emerged online with Connect.

Executive Branch

The Constitution vests executive power in Canada in the Queen and calls for its exercise by the Governor General and Privy Council. In our democratic society, this is merely a constitutional convention. The real executive power rests with the Cabinet. The Cabinet, at the federal level, consists of the prime minister and ministers who are answerable to Parliament for government activities. Ministers are also responsible for government departments, such as the Department of Finance and the Department of Justice. At the provincial/territorial level, the executive branch consists of the Premier and Cabinet in each such jurisdiction. The executive branch is responsible for administering and enforcing the laws and policies passed by Parliament and the legislatures. Most importantly, the executive branch determines regulations under legislation and makes appointments to the administrative agencies and tribunals that are responsible for enforcing legislation, such as human rights commissions and tribunals.

When particularly sensitive cases or those involving a significant constitutional issue come before the Court, the Attorney General, representing the executive branch, argues for certain preferred outcomes.

Judicial Branch

The judiciary in Canada is separate from all other branches of government. All government action is subject to judicial scrutiny. The judiciary comprises federally and provincially appointed judges who interpret and apply the law and the Constitution, and provide impartial adjudication of disputes. In labour and employment law, much of the adjudication is handled outside the court system by administrative tribunals that are granted particular responsibility for the adjudication of disputes arising under specific legislation. These tribunals include human rights tribunals, labour relations boards, employment standards tribunals, pay equity tribunals, and workers' compensation boards. In unionized workplaces, most disputes are adjudicated by privately appointed arbitrators. These administrative tribunals and arbitrators have significant authority to make final and binding decisions, subject to judicial review by the courts on very limited grounds.

The judicial branch consists of the court system, which has four levels, illustrated in Figure 3.1. The first level comprises the civil and criminal provincial courts, which are typically divided within each province into various divisions defined by the subject matter of the cases they were created to hear or by their specific jurisdiction, such as a Small Claims Division, a Family Division, and a Criminal Division. The second level consists of courts of first instance such as the Federal Court, the Tax Court of Canada and provincial and territorial Superior Courts of general jurisdiction. The third level comprises appellate courts including the Federal Court of Appeal and provincial appellate courts.

FIGURE 3.1   Outline of Canada's Court System

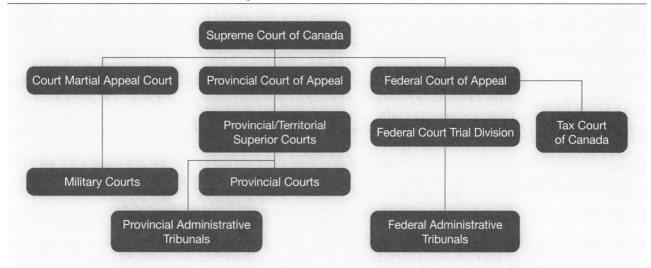

SOURCE: Canada's System of Justice, Figure: Outline of Canada's Court System, page 16, http://www.justice.gc.ca/eng/dept-min/pub/just/07.html. Department of Justice Canada, 2005. Reproduced with the permission of the Minister of Public Works and Government Services Canada, 2011.

The top level consists of the Supreme Court of Canada, which is our country's highest court. It is a national general court of appeal for Canada, and is the final level of appeal. Decisions of the Supreme Court of Canada are binding and their applicability can be overturned only through legislation.

Learn more about appointment of judges in Canada online with Connect.

Having described the legal system that affects the management of HRM, we now explore some laws that regulate HRM activities, particularly equality and human rights laws. We first discuss the major laws that mandate equality and human rights in Canada. Then we examine the agencies involved in enforcing these laws. This leads us into a discussion of some relevant court cases. Finally, we explore some issues in respect of these areas of the law facing today's managers.

PROTECTING HUMAN RIGHTS

Through their elected governments, Canadians have decided that protecting the rights of individuals in a modern and civilized society necessarily includes protection of the rights of people to live the lives they want to live. People should be able to live without facing inequitable treatment for reasons unrelated to personal merit, provided that those protections do not unduly interfere with the rights of others. As such, whatever an individual's racial and cultural background, sex or sexual preferences, age, or physical or mental disabilities, Canadian society is vigilant of the rights of all people to participate in society to the full extent of their true abilities, subject only to the legitimate rights and aspirations of other participants in society. This recognition and protection of individual rights and freedoms appears in human rights legislation at both federal and provincial/territorial levels of government, and forms a crucial part of the legislative fabric that underlies the legal foundation of Canadian society. Human rights in the employment context are protected by the Canadian Charter of Rights and Freedoms as well as human rights legislation in force in each jurisdiction across Canada.

LO 2

Explain the importance of the Canadian Charter of Rights and Freedoms and human rights legislation and their implications for HRM.

The Canadian Charter of Rights and Freedoms
A constitutional entrenchment of fundamental rights and freedoms of all Canadians.

The Canadian Charter of Rights and Freedoms

Entrenched in the Constitution in 1982, the **Canadian Charter of Rights and Freedoms** (Charter) forms part of the Constitution of Canada. The *Charter* protects fundamental freedoms of all Canadians such as freedom of religion, expression and association; democratic rights including the right to vote; mobility rights such as the right to live and work in any province; legal rights including the right to life, liberty, and security of the person; equality rights including the right to equal protection and benefit of the law without discrimination and, in particular, without discrimination based on race, national or ethnic origin, colour, religion, sex, age, or mental or physical disability; language rights; and Aboriginal rights. It is the equality rights in section 15 of the *Charter* that underpin human rights legislation throughout Canada. In light of the similarity of the equality rights in the *Charter* and the rights found in human rights legislation, the case law and principles involving section 15 of the *Charter* can be relied upon in interpreting human rights legislation.[4] Further, the Supreme Court of Canada has stated that the rights protected by human rights legislation must encompass the rights protected by section 15 of the *Charter*.[5]

As a part of the Constitution, the *Charter* takes precedence over other laws. Legislation that is found to conflict with the *Charter* can be ruled invalid by the courts unless it falls within one of two exceptions. First, legislation that offends the *Charter* can withstand scrutiny provided it can be demonstrably justified as a reasonable limit in a free and democratic society.[6] Second, Parliament or a provincial legislature may specifically exempt a statute, or a provision thereof, from the application of the *Charter* for a limited period of time under the *Charter*'s "notwithstanding" clause.[7] This latter exemption has rarely been invoked.

One important point regarding the *Charter* is that it applies only to government action and actors, not directly to private individuals, businesses, or other organizations. Accordingly, only federal and provincial/territorial governments, as well as municipal governments are legally bound by the *Charter*'s constitutional rights and freedoms. However, courts have interpreted government in a fairly broad manner such that the *Charter* has been applied not only to purely governmental actors and institutions such as federal and provincial governments, but also to entities in which governments play a substantial role such that it may be said the entity is inherently governmental, or where the entity acts in furtherance of a specific government program or policy. This could include, for example, public schools and universities, public hospitals and other care facilities, and Crown corporations.

 **connect**

Learn more about the Canadian Bill of Rights, the first human rights protection for Canadians at the federal level, online with Connect.

HUMAN RIGHTS LEGISLATION

Human Rights
Personal and private rights protected by government through legislation aimed to ensure that individuals are treated equally and can participate freely in society in a manner free from discrimination and harassment based on prescribed grounds such as race; colour; religion or creed; sex; sexual orientation; age; disability; marital status; family status; national, ethnic, or place of origin; or criminal record.

Human rights legislation refers to the government's attempt to ensure that all individuals are treated equally and can participate freely in society in a manner free from discrimination and harassment. To achieve this objective, the legislation prohibits discrimination or harassment in respect of several areas including employment.[8] Each of the ten provinces, the three territories, and the federal government has enacted its own human rights legislation. While prohibited grounds of discrimination and harassment vary slightly by jurisdiction, as do the precise terms used as set out in Table 3.1, all statutes prohibit discrimination and harassment on the basis of race; colour; religion or creed; sex; sexual orientation; age; disability; marital status; and national, ethnic, or place of origin. Sexual harassment is also forbidden.[9] Some jurisdictions also prohibit discrimination or harassment based on other grounds such as family status, language, social condition or origin, source of income, association, political belief, and a criminal record or pardoned conviction. In summary, while every

Table 3.1   Prohibited Grounds of Discrimination

GROUND	FEDERAL	ALBERTA	BRITISH COLUMBIA	MANITOBA	NEW BRUNSWICK	NEWFOUNDLAND & LABRADOR	NOVA SCOTIA	ONTARIO	PRINCE EDWARD ISLAND	QUEBEC	SASKATCHEWAN	NORTHWEST TERRITORIES	NUNAVUT	YUKON TERRITORY
Age	•	•	•	•	•	•	•	•	•	•	•	•	•	•
Disability	•	•	•	•	•	•	•	•	•	•	•	•	•	•
Race	•	•	•	•	•	•	•	•	•	•	•	•	•	•
Colour	•	•	•	•	•	•	•	•	•	•	•	•	•	•
Religion	•	•	•	•	•	•	•		•	•	•	•	•	•
Creed				•		•	•	•	•	•	•	•	•	•
Sex/Gender	•	•	•	•	•	•	•	•	•	•	•	•	•	•
Sexual Orientation	•	•	•	•	•	•	•	•	•	•	•	•	•	•
Gender Identity			•	•								•		
Family Status	•	•	•	•		•	•	•		•	•	•	•	•
Marital Status	•	•	•	•	•	•	•	•	•	•	•	•	•	•
Family Affiliation												•		
Language												•		
Place of Origin		•	•	•				•			•	•	•	
National/ Ethnic Origin	•			•	•	•	•	•	•	•		•	•	•
Ancestry		•	•	•	•			•			•	•	•	•
Nationality/Citzenship				•				•			•	•	•	
Civil Status						•				•				
Social Origin						•								
Social Condition				•							•	•		
Political Beliefs			•	•	•	•	•		•	•		•		•
Criminal Conviction	•		•					•	•	•		•	•	•
Source of Income/Receipt of Social Assistance		•		•			•		•			•		•
Actual or Presumed Association with a Protected Group				•			•							•

*Sexual harassment is prohibited in all jurisdictions.

employer and employee in Canada is governed by human rights legislation, the extent of the protections afforded depends on the particular legislation that applies. Because such a varied patchwork of laws applicable in the realm of human rights exists, seeking expert or legal advice is always a prudent course of action.

Human rights legislation is not as sweeping as the Charter, although Quebec's Charter of Human Rights and Freedoms guarantees many similar rights and freedoms. However, unlike the Charter, human rights legislation does not simply apply to actions of the government; rather, it extends protection for individuals against human rights violations to include private persons and corporations. Given the fundamental rights it was enacted to protect, human rights legislation is viewed as quasi-constitutional legislation—that is, fundamental law taking precedence over all other statutes in force in each jurisdiction, except the Charter. Similarly, human rights legislation has primacy over any collective agreement or contract in place between workplace parties. Human rights protections affect almost every aspect of the employment relationship, and thus HRM, making it critical that employers and their representatives, as well as employees and unions, understand and comply with their respective rights and obligations pursuant to the applicable legislation. Given the fundamental status afforded human rights in Canada, an infringement on those rights is not taken lightly and can result in substantial penalties and damages upwards of tens of thousands of dollars.

DISCRIMINATION

LO 3

Discuss what constitutes discrimination and requirements for reasonable accommodation.

Discrimination

A restriction, preference, or distinction based on a prohibited ground, which results in unequal treatment and denies an individual his or her right to the equal protection and benefit of guaranteed human rights and freedoms.

How would you know if you were the victim of discrimination? Assume that you have applied for a job and were not hired. How do you know if the organization decided not to hire you because you are unqualified, or less qualified than the individual ultimately hired, or simply because the person in charge of the hiring decision "didn't like your type"? Discrimination is a multifaceted issue. It is often difficult to determine the extent to which unfair discrimination affects an employer's decisions.

Discrimination is a fluid and flexible concept, the precise definition of which is defined in the human rights statutes of only three provinces: Manitoba, Nova Scotia, and Quebec. A general definition of discrimination can be ascertained by reference to these statutes, as well as the policies of human rights bodies across Canada and the case law that has interpreted the legislation. Generally, discrimination is a restriction, preference, or distinction based on a prohibited ground, which results in unequal treatment and denies an individual his or her right to the equal protection and benefit of guaranteed human rights and freedoms. It is illegal for employers to treat employees differently based on any prohibited ground in respect of terms and conditions of employment such as pay, promotion, hiring, training, and dismissal.

Discriminatory conduct can be direct or indirect. Neither intention nor motivation to discriminate is required. Rather, discrimination occurs provided even part of the reason for the differential treatment is based on a prohibited ground. An employer who dismisses an employee because of a legitimate reorganization of the workplace while also taking into consideration that it would be better to retain younger workers who have more energy and are not so near to retirement has engaged in discrimination based on age. Moreover, discrimination can occur where an individual is being discriminated against because of a perception, although incorrect, that he or she is a member of a group sharing the characteristic of a prohibited ground of discrimination, even though the person being discriminated against is not actually a member of that group.[10] An employee fired after testing positive in a drug screening test because of a perception that he was a drug addict (considered a disability under human rights legislation) would be a victim of discrimination based on a perceived rather than actual disability.

Three types of discrimination have emerged from human rights legislation and its application and interpretation by decision makers including courts, tribunals and labour arbitrators: (1) direct discrimination; (2) adverse-effect or constructive discrimination; and (3) systemic discrimination. In practice, there is no distinction by decision makers between the different kinds of discrimination in respect of the legal tests and burdens at play in assessing a claim of discrimination.[11] Nonetheless, an understanding of the different forms that discrimination can take is a valuable tool for HRM in recognizing and addressing discrimination in the workplace.

Learn more about a decision made by the Nova Scotia Human Rights Commission Board of Inquiry addressing discrimination online with Connect.

Direct Discrimination

Direct discrimination exists in employment when a party implements a rule, practice, preference, or restriction that on its face treats a person differently or unequally based on a prohibited ground such as race, sex, or the like. For example, if a company fails to hire women with school-age children (claiming the women will be frequently absent), but hires men with school-age children, the applicants are being treated differently based on sex. Another example would be an employer who checks the references and investigates the conviction records of visible-minority applicants but does not do so for white applicants. In these examples, notice that (1) people are being treated differently and (2) the differential treatment is deliberate.

Employers are also prohibited from engaging in direct discrimination through the use of a third party, most commonly an employment agency. For example, directing an employment agency to screen applicants for employment based on a prohibited ground of discrimination such as age or sex constitutes direct discrimination and is prohibited.

Individuals may also be subject to direct discrimination because of their association with others who are members of a group identified by a personal characteristic protected under human rights legislation. A man denied a promotion because his wife is black or a woman refused a job opportunity because of a perception that her husband who has a disability will require that she take too much time away from work are victims of discrimination by association.

The "Competing through Globalization" box on page 86 illustrates how some companies in France are changing their approach to recruitment to overcome obstacles around diversity management and to prevent discrimination in hiring.

Adverse-Effect Discrimination

A rule, practice, preference, or restriction that is neutral on its face may inadvertently or indirectly operate in a manner that discriminates against an employee or group of employees sharing a common personal attribute that is protected as a prohibited ground of discrimination. This is called "**adverse-effect discrimination**" or "constructive discrimination." A policy that all employees be available for work on Friday evenings and Saturdays is not discriminatory on its face, but adversely discriminates against members of certain religions that observe Sabbath given that their religion prevents them from working on those days. A requirement that employees wear a uniform with a hat adversely discriminates against members of the Sikh religion for whom wearing a turban is a mandatory part of their faith. Accordingly, a policy adopted in good faith for legitimate business reasons that is equally applicable to all employees to whom it is intended to apply may be discriminatory if it affects an employee or group of employees differently than others to whom it applies.

Adverse-effect discrimination demonstrates that equal treatment does not necessarily mean treating all individuals the same. For example, if, for some practical reason, you hired individuals based on their height, you may not have intended to discriminate against anyone, and yet using height would have a disproportionate impact on certain protected groups. Women tend to be shorter than men, so fewer women will be hired. Certain ethnic groups, such as those of Asian ancestry, also tend

Direct Discrimination
A rule, practice, preference, or restriction that on its face treats a person differently or unequally based on a prohibited ground of discrimination.

LO 4

Explain various concepts of discrimination and HRM's role in prevention and elimination of such behaviours.

Adverse-Effect Discrimination
A rule, practice, preference, or restriction that is neutral on its face, but which inadvertently or indirectly operates in a manner that discriminates against an employee or group of employees on a prohibited ground of discrimination.

Competing Through Globalization

Seeking Diversity in France

The year 2006 saw a string of violent protests and riots in and around Paris as poor ethnic (mostly North African) residents sought to express their dissatisfaction with their current state. Now a number of companies and the government are working together to try to effectively manage the diverse workforce and potentially reduce the economic disparities that exist in this "egalitarian" society.

The basic problem stems from what appears to be widespread discrimination in employment among French companies. According to research conducted by Jean-Francois Amadieu, a professor of sociology at the University of Paris, job candidates with North African–sounding names have one-third the chance of getting an interview compared to those with French-sounding names. He concludes that a significant number of French firms could be rightfully sued for discrimination.

As an example, Manuella Arulnayagam graduated from engineering school in 2003 and spent a year sending out her résumé. The daughter of Sri Lankan immigrants, she did not receive a single interview. In fact, at one job fair, a recruiter took one glance at her résumé and dropped it in the garbage can. She states, "Throughout my whole life and studies I never wanted to believe that my name or my address could be a problem."

One of the potential obstacles to better managing diversity in France actually stems from the legal system. In the interest of ensuring equality, French law precludes collecting information on race, ethnicity, religion, and other characteristics. However, this makes it difficult for French employers to proactively recruit or target particular minority groups.

One solution has been to go straight to the so-called *banlieues,* or poor immigrant neighbourhoods, to attempt to recruit minority workers. Firms such as the cosmetic maker L'Oreal send managers to high schools in poor areas to coach students in writing résumés and proper behaviour in job interviews.

In addition, more progressive HR departments in companies such as insurer AXA or carmaker Peugeot automatically strip personal data that might imply racial or ethnic status from résumés before forwarding them to recruiters. If those making the decisions to offer interviews do not know the ethnicity of the applicant, they cannot discriminate on that basis.

SOURCE: M. Valla, "France Seeks Path to Workplace Diversity," *The Wall Street Journal* (January 3, 2007), p. A2.

---

to be shorter than those of European ancestry. Thus, your "neutral" employment practice will have an adverse impact on certain protected groups.

This is not to imply that simply because a selection practice has an adverse impact, it is necessarily illegal. Some characteristics (such as height) are not equally distributed across race and gender groups; however, the important question is whether the characteristic is a legitimate requirement for the job.

Systemic Discrimination

Systemic Discrimination
Unintentional discrimination that arises from a pattern of behaviour that is rooted in established stereotypes, attitudes, and value systems that perpetuates the relative disadvantage of a protected group.

Systemic discrimination closely resembles adverse-effect or constructive discrimination in that it is neither deliberate nor blatant. Unlike adverse-effect discrimination, systemic discrimination is not based on a particular employer rule, practice, preference, or restriction. Rather, discrimination arises from a pattern of behaviour that is rooted in established stereotypes, attitudes, and value systems that perpetuates the relative disadvantage of a protected group. Systemic discrimination is so deeply entrenched in the culture and norms of the workplace that it is often difficult to detect. Pay inequities between jobs traditionally performed by women and those traditionally performed by men despite equivalent skill and educational requirements is an example of systemic discrimination.

REASONABLE ACCOMMODATION

Human rights legislation imposes on employers the positive obligation of **reasonable accommodation**, commonly referred to in the human rights arena as the duty to accommodate. The duty requires that employers make adjustments to their policies, practices, and expectations to ensure that an employee is not subject to discriminatory treatment based on a prohibited ground of discrimination. An employee with a sleep disorder may no longer be able to work the night shift while an employee returning to work after suffering an illness or injury may not be able to perform his or her former job or work full-time hours. An employer may also need to alter dress codes or break policies to accommodate employees' religious beliefs in terms of personal appearance and prayer practices. Tables 3.2 and 3.3 provide examples of reasonable accommodation and what it does not include.

Reasonable Accommodation Adjustments that employers are legally obligated to make to their policies, practices, and expectations to ensure that an employee is not subject to discriminatory treatment based on a prohibited ground of discrimination. Commonly referred to as the duty to accommodate.

Table 3.2 Examples of Reasonable Accommodation

- Altering shift schedules
- Providing leaves of absence
- Granting days off for religious observance
- Modifying the physical and ergonomic aspects of the workplace
- Modifying work tasks
- In some cases, bundling or assembling a series of tasks together from other jobs to create a modified position
- Supplying assistive devices
- Placing an employee in a modified job
- Providing retraining
- Transferring the employee to an alternative job (whether inside or outside the bargaining unit)
- Modifying the employee's attendance or performance standards
- Making exceptions to standard policies and practices (e.g., dress codes, break schedules)

Table 3.3 Reasonable Accommodation Does Not Include

- Creating an unproductive modified position
- Retaining an employee who will not be able to return to work in the foreseeable future based on sufficient and valid medical information
- Creating a permanent new position
- Providing perfect accommodation in the eyes of the employee
- Providing accommodation that imposes undue hardship on the employer

Undue Hardship

Employers have a duty to accommodate employees to the point of **undue hardship**. Employers also bear the onus of proving in a claim of discrimination that undue hardship was met. Undue hardship is an onerous and stringent standard that requires an exhaustive search for all accommodative alternatives, but does not entitle an employee to perfect or preferred accommodation. Rather, an employee's right to accommodation has limits and must be balanced against an employer's right to efficiently and safely operate its business. Factors relevant to a determination of whether the duty to accommodate to the point of undue hardship has been satisfied vary by jurisdiction and by the forum in which the claim of discrimination is being heard. For example, the federal statute limits the applicable factors to health, safety, and cost similar to the Ontario legislation, which considers only cost, health and safety, and outside sources of funding. However, where an allegation of discrimination is being adjudicated by a court or labour arbitrator, the court or arbitrator may consider a broader range of factors in determining whether accommodation will cause undue hardship, including public safety; employee safety; size and resources of the organization; financial costs; disruption of operations; substantial interference with the rights of other employees or individuals (e.g., under a collective agreement); availability of government funding; and morale problems of other employees brought about by the accommodation, although this factor will be disregarded if it is based on discriminatory attitudes.[12] Financial cost, safety, and the size of the employer's operations are typically allotted more weight by decision makers than other factors. Provisions of a collective agreement and the legitimate operational requirements of a workplace are given some weight. However, there is little persuasive value associated with the defence of employee morale. The issue of the interchangeability of the workforce and operations has generally been included within a consideration of the size of the employer. The larger the employer's operation, the greater the expectation that it will be able to meet its duty to accommodate the employee given its greater resources and accommodation options. As a consequence, what will constitute undue hardship varies from case to case.

When the Supreme Court of Canada issued its decision in *British Columbia (Public Service Employee Relations Commission) v. BCGSEU*[13]("*Meiorin*"), almost ten years ago, it heralded a new "unified approach" to the analysis of discrimination. Gone was the distinction between direct and adverse-effect discrimination. Employers were required to accommodate employees to the point of undue hardship in all cases. However, the decision in *Meiorin* suggested that employers might be required to establish that it was "impossible" to accommodate a disabled employee in order to make out the undue hardship defence. This premise was put to the test in a recent decision of the Supreme Court in which the Court clarified its earlier statements and confirmed that an employer need not show that accommodation is "impossible."[14] Rather, the Court reaffirmed that an employer can expect employees to perform their part of the employment bargain, provided that the employer makes the necessary effort to accommodate those who require it. When it becomes evident that an employee cannot "fulfill the basic obligations associated with the employment relationship for the foreseeable future," it is not discriminatory for an employer to end the relationship.

The search for accommodation is a multiparty inquiry involving the employer, the employee, and, where applicable, the union. While the primary burden rests on the employer, all parties are expected to cooperate in and facilitate the search for reasonable accommodation. Moreover, accommodation must be assessed on a case-by-case basis.

Failure to accommodate to the point of undue hardship constitutes a violation of human rights laws in all jurisdictions. The concept of accommodation to the point of undue hardship necessarily implies that employers will have to endure some hardship before the duty to accommodate will be met. The duty to accommodate is a continuous obligation that must be monitored, reviewed, and revised according to the employee's and the employer's changing circumstances. Most importantly, when an employer is required to accommodate an employee, it is essential that a diligent, proactive, and sincere effort is made to accommodate the employee in a manner that respects the employee's dignity and self-worth.

Bona Fide Occupational Qualification

In addition to the defence of undue hardship, an employer can justify discriminatory treatment if it can demonstrate that it is a **bona fide occupational qualification (BFOQ)**. To be a valid BFOQ, the standard must be a necessary rather than simply a preferred characteristic of the job. If one were hiring an individual to hand out towels in a women's locker room, being a woman would be a BFOQ, as would a requirement that employees who will be selling liquor be of a certain age. A rule that drivers and pilots have acceptable vision would also likely qualify as a BFOQ.

Bona Fide Occupational Qualification
A qualification that is necessary to the performance of a particular job.

The Supreme Court of Canada set out a three-part test for establishing that a discriminatory rule, standard, or requirement is a BFOQ:

1. The standard was adopted for a purpose rationally connected to job performance;
2. The standard was adopted in an honest and good-faith belief that it was necessary to the fulfillment of that legitimate work-related purpose; and
3. The standard is reasonably necessary to accomplish that legitimate purpose. This includes a requirement to demonstrate that the individual cannot be accommodated without undue hardship.[15]

Once a complainant alleging discrimination has made out a *prima facie* case that discrimination occurred, the onus shifts to the employer to satisfy the BFOQ test on a balance of probabilities. Although neither the duty to accommodate nor the defence of a BFOQ are explicitly set out in every human rights statute, the case law has made clear that these principles and standards apply to each and every case of discrimination. To understand how the legal principles regarding discrimination are applied in the law, let's look at how an actual case alleging discrimination would proceed.

The Complainant's Burden   As in most legal cases, the complainant (sometimes called the applicant) has the burden of proving that the respondent has committed an illegal act. This is the idea of a "prima facie" case. In a case of discrimination, the complainant meets the prima facie burden by demonstrating that he or she was subject to discrimination by virtue of an employer policy, practice, preference, or restriction, or that the standard in question disproportionately affects a protected group relative to the majority group. The complainant must show a nexus between the discrimination and a prohibited ground. In addition, the complainant must present evidence to show that other employment practices could sufficiently meet the employer's goal without adverse impact.

The Respondent's Defence   Once the complainant has made the prima facie case of discrimination, the burden shifts to the respondent to demonstrate that the discriminatory act was based on a BFOQ based on the three-part test set out by the Supreme Court of Canada. In respect of meeting the undue hardship standard required of the third step of the test, the respondent must base its case on the factors applicable in the particular jurisdiction and forum in which the case is being heard.

Learn more about the difficulties of using a BFOQ as a defence by viewing *Wiens v. Inco Metals Co.* online with Connect.

⊞ connect

The Complainant's Reply   If the respondent can demonstrate that the rule or standard is a BFOQ, the burden shifts back to the complainant to prove that the reason offered by the respondent to justify its discriminatory conduct was not in fact the genuine reason for its decision, but merely a "pretext" or excuse for its actual discriminatory decision. The complainant also has the opportunity to reply to the respondent's arguments to clarify any conflicting evidence, and to respond to any new evidence put forward by the respondent that the complainant did not address when it presented its case.

To demonstrate how the principles of discrimination play out in practice, let's have a look at two precedent-setting real cases of discrimination decided by Canada's highest court—the Supreme Court of Canada.

British Columbia (Public Service Employee Relations Commission) v. B.C.G.S.E.U. ("Meiorin").

As noted above, this landmark Supreme Court of Canada case established a new unified approach to cases of discrimination, eliminating the distinction between direct and adverse-effect (and systemic) discrimination.[16] The decision mandates that reasonable accommodation be considered in every case of discrimination. Meiorin was a female forest firefighter with the province of British Columbia who was dismissed after three years of good service when she failed after four attempts to pass part of a newly implemented uniform aerobic standards test. Meiorin failed to run 2.5 kilometres in 11 minutes by 49.4 seconds. Meiorin argued that the test discriminated against women. In particular, Meiorin asserted that men had an unfair advantage in such tests because women, on average, have less aerobic capacity. About 70 percent of men passed the exam on the first try, compared to only about 35 percent of the women. Meiorin also maintained that the fitness exam was not a good measure of her abilities in the field because they were not related to the actual requirements of the job. The government argued that the fitness test was a BFOQ.

Meiorin was successful in demonstrating a *prima facie* case by showing that the aerobic standard had a disproportionately negative effect on women as a group. Meiorin adduced evidence to show that, owing to physiological differences, most women have a lower aerobic capacity than most men and that, unlike most men, most women cannot sufficiently improve their aerobic capacity with training to meet the aerobic standard. Shifting the burden to the government, the Supreme Court of Canada held that the government presented no credible evidence to show that the prescribed aerobic capacity was necessary for either men or women to perform the work of a forest firefighter safely and efficiently. In particular, the evidence did not permit a decision as to whether men and women required the same minimum level of aerobic capacity to perform a forest firefighter's tasks safely and efficiently. Moreover, the government failed to establish that it would experience undue hardship if a different standard were used. The Court ordered Meiorin be reinstated and paid five years in back pay.

This case illustrates how similarly situated individuals (in this case, men and women) can be treated differently by the application of a uniform standard with the differences in treatment based on sex, and emphasizes that individual assessment is necessary. The same analysis applies to other prohibited grounds of discrimination. Let's look at a case of religious discrimination.

Central Alberta Dairy Pool v. Alberta Human Rights Commission.

Although decided before the unified approach was adopted by the Supreme Court of Canada in *Meiorin*, the *Central Alberta Dairy Pool* decision applied a similar approach under the provisions of the Alberta human rights statute then in force and remains a leading case addressing religious discrimination today. The complainant, Jim Christie, was employed for almost three years in the production operations of the respondent's milk processing plant in Wetaskiwin, Alberta. He became a prospective member of the World Wide Church of God in February 1983, which observed Sabbath and other holy days during the year. Members of the faith were expected to not work on these days, although the Church did not impose sanctions for those who were required or chose to work. Christie was granted his request to work the early shift on Fridays in order that his work schedule not conflict with the onset of his Sabbath. He was also granted one of two requested days off surrounding the Easter holiday. The second day, Easter Monday, was denied for reasons of plant operating needs. The employer argued that Mondays were particularly busy days at the plant given that surplus milk that arrived on the weekend had to be canned promptly on Monday to prevent spoilage and, thus, lost profits. Mondays were also busy shipping days.

The Court was satisfied that Christie raised a *prima facie* case. Christie showed the existence of a bona fide religion and his genuine commitment to it, he gave adequate notice of his religious requirements to the employer, and he made an effort to accommodate the employer to the extent possible without being required to compromise his beliefs.

The employer failed to show that the standard was a BFOQ in the Court's view, because it could not prove that it accommodated Christie to the point of undue hardship. The Court refused to conclude that Christie's request to be absent Easter Monday could not be accommodated in light of the existence of the employer's established contingency plan for dealing with sporadic Monday absences. If the employer could cope with an employee being sick or away on vacation on Mondays, the Court held that it could certainly accommodate a similarly isolated absence of an employee like Christie due to a valid religious obligation.

The decision illustrates that there need be no intention to discriminate to ground a finding of discrimination. The decision also makes clear that an employer may be required to make exceptions to legitimate and reasonable uniformly applied policies in order to meet its onerous legal obligations pursuant to the duty to accommodate under human rights legislation.

To facilitate a greater understanding of discrimination in employment, let's take a closer look at some of the more common prescribed prohibited grounds of discrimination.

Religion or Creed

As demonstrated in *Central Alberta Dairy Pool*, individuals with strong religious beliefs often find that some observations and practices of their religion come into direct conflict with their work duties. Some religions forbid individuals from working on the Sabbath day or other holy days when the employer schedules them for work. Others might have beliefs that preclude them from shaving or cutting their hair, which might conflict with a company's dress code, as does a religious requirement to wear certain attire (a turban, for example). Spiritual and aboriginal faiths can be protected under this ground, as well as atheism. However, faiths that promote hatred or violence or that contravene the Criminal Code are not likely to garner the protection of human rights laws. Like other forms of discrimination, religious discrimination can arise not only from the conduct of the employer and its representatives, but also from the actions of coworkers.[17]

Examples of reasonably accommodating a person's religious obligations might include redesigning work schedules (most often accommodating those who cannot work on holy days), providing alternative testing dates for applicants, not requiring union membership and/or allowing payment of "charitable contributions" in lieu of union dues, or altering certain dress or grooming requirements. Note that although an employer is required to make reasonable accommodation, it need not be that which is preferred or suggested by the employee.

In one case, an employee working for Shopper's Drug Mart was fired when his religious beliefs clashed with his assigned work tasks.[18] Raymond Jones, a Jehovah's Witness, refused to assist in decorating the store for Christmas given that the holiday was offensive to his religion. After refusing to set out poinsettas at the front of the store, Jones was told to complete the task or face immediate dismissal. Jones left and filed a human rights complaint. The British Columbia Human Rights Tribunal found that Jones's faith prohibited him from decorating the store for Christmas. He was therefore discriminated against when he was fired for refusing to put out the poinsettas. The employer failed to meet the standard of undue hardship given that the supervisor who had asked Jones to put the poinsettas out admitted that he completed the task in only a few minutes. The employer was ordered to pay Jones more than $30,500 in damages.

Competing Through Sustainability

The Advantages of Going Green

In 2010, eight Canadian companies made the Global 100 list of most sustainable privately held companies, placing Canada fourth among 22 countries "The Global 100 are charting out a new prosperity agenda reconciling the mega-trend of sustainability with the mega-institution of the corporation. The kicker: sustainability can be a market-beating strategy, as the Global 100's substantial out-performance demonstrates," says Toby Heaps, editor-in-chief of *Corporate Knights*, the Toronto-based magazine that publishes the Global 100 rankings. While sustainability comes with a cost, companies are learning how to turn waste streams into revenue streams through new technologies, renewable energy, and bio-fuels.

"Increased focus on sustainable operations from larger corporations has been driven by public demand," says Vanessa Magness, an accounting professor at Toronto's Ryerson University, whose research focuses on environmental accounting and establishing links between pollution, profit, and disclosure. Magness adds that "companies are realizing that reducing their environmental footprint improves the marketability of their products."

TransAlta Corp.'s headquarters in downtown Calgary is powered by a southern Alberta wind farm. It's an unexpected power source for a 95-year-old electricity company, but Urs Schön, a utilities analyst with the SAM Group in Zurich, Switzerland, says that TransAlta isn't your typical North American power generator when we're talking about sustainability activities.

Schön places TransAlta among the top 16 electrical utilities worldwide for sustainability and the $2.8 billion, 51-plant firm has consistently placed on the Dow Jones Sustainability Index.

TransAlta's performance is due, in large part, to being a forerunner in environmental initiatives based on the credo that sustainability is an exercise in balancing the needs of the environment and the needs of the economy. TransAlta recognizes that climate change has forced us to reevaluate how we generate energy to power our cities, heat our homes, and fuel our cars. TransAlta calls this the "Triple E" equation—a view that society's economic growth is directly tied to energy consumption and environmental impact.

In 2009, with the acquisition of Canadian Hydro Developers, TransAlta became the largest publicly traded provider of renewable energy in Canada. In addition to quarterly reports on its greenhouse gas emissions, TransAlta also publishes its sulphur dioxide and particulate matter emissions, water intake and discharge, and employee injuries. "Many North American utility companies don't report these items, or if they do, the data is only released once a year," says Schön. "TransAlta's reporting shows high-level management has reflected on those issues and is taking them into account in their decisions on an ongoing basis." TransAlta's environmental conscience has proven helpful to not only stakeholders but also the bottom line. Early and proactive measures to reduce the company's impact on air pollution by decreasing its reliance on coal and increasing its use of natural gas to fuel its plants, as well as investing in projects that offset emissions and other new technologies, have enabled TransAlta to reduce its net greenhouse gas emissions significantly.

In doing so, the company has built up a portfolio of credits to sell into the market. Installing a sulphur dioxide scrubber at its Centralia, Wa. plant in 2000 has not only reduced SO2 emissions by more than 60 percent, but also allowed the company to trade its excess allowances into the U.S. market for "several millions of dollars per year," says Don Wharton, TransAlta's director of sustainable development.

Additionally, the company has found profitable ways to recycle its waste, selling several thousand tons of fly ash (a coal mining by-product that otherwise would be disposed of back into the mine) to regional cement and concrete manufacturers in Alberta and the Western United States, saving several million dollars in production costs.

Beyond benefits to the environment, TransAlta investors are seeing gains too. Even more impressive to Schön is TransAlta's willingness to move away from coal-heavy electricity generation altogether.

"In terms of total capital expenditure, [the company] has higher investments in renewable sources than other companies in the field," says the analyst. This means TransAlta's investments in green initiatives such as wind power could be powering more than just the company's headquarters—it could very well be powering its reputation as a global leader.

PricewaterhouseCoopers is doing its share to help Canadian companies implement sustainability principles in their organizations through its Green Business/PricewaterhouseCoopers Executive Roundtable on Sustainability as well as educating companies on sustainable business solutions. The roundtable serves as a forum for the exchange of ideas about environmental initiatives—what works and what doesn't and the underlying strategies that make these programs a success—while also reinforcing the benefits, financial and otherwise, of sustainability. Rewarding employees for environmental practices such as purchasing hybrid vehicles or biking to work, a focus on educating and engaging employees in environmental responsibility initiatives, and promoting an understanding of how a commitment to sustainability reduces the company's risk, enhances its public image, and assists the organization in capitalizing on opportunities to enhance the bottom line are just some of the topics of discussion that participants can expect. As Blair Feltmate, Director of Sustainable Development at OPG says, "Wherever you have operations in the world, the expectation is that you've worked to minimize your environmental footprint, you've demonstrated that you care about your employees and you care about the communities in which you operate. And if you can't demonstrate that meaningfully, the probability of you being granted a licence to operate ongoing is very much limited."

SOURCES: TransAlta "2009 Report on Sustainability" at www.transalta.com/sites/default/files/TransAlta-summary-report-on-sustainability-2009.pdf); Robert Colman, "Embedding Sustainable Practices," *Green Business*, (September 2008); adapted from June Morrow, "Clean and Green: TransAlta's Decision to Adopt Eco-friendly Policies Is Paying Off," *Canadian Business Online* (February 22, 2006) at www.canadian business.com/managing/strategy/article.jsp?content=20060222_120924_5288; Matt Powell, "Canada Takes Fourth in Global Sustainability Rankings," *Canadian Manufacturing* (February 11, 2011).

Disability

Disability is defined differently in each human rights statute, but always includes both a physical and mental disability. Regardless of the precise definition of disability in the applicable legislation, decision makers have interpreted disability quite broadly to include most illnesses or injuries that affect a person's ability to perform significant life functions, such as employment. Temporary illnesses such as the flu or a common cold will not fall within the definition of a disability. Rather, a disability under human rights laws is generally one that is ongoing and significant, although episodic conditions such as epilepsy and seasonal allergies are also included. Afflictions such as drug and alcohol addiction are also protected under the ground of disability. However, recreational use of these substances is not. In recent years, a heightened recognition of the protection afforded mental disabilities has taken place in the human rights arena given the increased awareness and understanding of these illnesses in society in general. For example, in 2008, ADGA Group Consultants Inc. was ordered to pay more than $80,000 to IT Specialist Paul Lane when it was found to have discriminated against him on the basis of mental disability, after it fired him four days after he informed his manager that he had bipolar disorder.[19]

Experience tells us that most accommodations are relatively inexpensive. What are some examples of reasonable accommodation with regard to disabilities? One example is providing readily accessible facilities such as ramps and/or elevators for disabled individuals to enter the workplace. Job restructuring might include eliminating marginal tasks, shifting these tasks to other employees, redesigning job procedures, or altering work schedules. An employer might reassign a disabled employee to a job with essential job functions he or she could perform, or might accommodate applicants for employment who must take tests through providing alternative testing formats, providing readers, or providing additional time for taking the test. In addition, readers, interpreters, or technology that offers reading assistance might be given to a disabled employee. An employer could also allow or encourage employees to provide their own accommodation such as bringing a guide dog to work. Leaves of absences are another form of accommodation and can include time off to attend rehabilitation treatment for drug and alcohol addiction.

The "Competing Through Technology" box describes how Scotiabank has evolved in its approach to accommodation over the years and how technology increasingly makes jobs more accessible for those with disabilities.

connect

Learn more about human rights in a sample case based on disability online with Connect.

Competing Through Technology

Tapping into the Diverse Human Talent Pool

Pina D'Intino remembers the day as if it was yesterday, even though ten years have passed. One minute she could see everything around her, the next she was plunged into permanent darkness. D'Intino was scheduled to have surgery for acute congenital glaucoma, a rare form of glaucoma occurring at birth that can usually be corrected with surgery. Things did not turn out the way she expected them to. She lost her sight soon after the surgery, and, for just a moment, her way in life. "I was right back to square one and coming back to work with a disability is relearning everything. Even relearning to walk all over again," says D'Intino, who worked for Scotiabank.

Although her employer was already making strides toward creating a work environment accessible to people with a disability, "It wasn't just a learning experience for myself; it was a learning experience for my managers and my peers," says the 46-year-old mother of three, referring to the decade-long process of change. "They were very difficult discussions at the time," she says, describing her return to work. "The bank didn't have anyone at my level at the time with full blindness, and was trying to assess how much of my current work I could still do and how much had to be modified or whether it was time to start something completely new." Patience and perseverance helped D'Intino build a new career path.

In the next decade, she would serve as something of a lightning rod to help make the bank a leader in the rapidly developing field of workplace accessibility. She remembers the day she made the pitch to the bank's IT executive team on the need for implementing accessibility guidelines. "We actually brought them into a room, shut off the lights, took off their glasses, then made them look at our own website and some commonly used websites," she says. "Then we showed them how a little accommodation can go a long way...like changing the font or colour background on the monitor meant they could read the screen without sitting six inches away from it." Now, D'Intino practises what she preaches as senior manager of Scotiabank's specialized IT program designed to make computers the friend of every employee, no matter their disability. The program, Enabling Solutions and Support Management, was set up a few years ago and works to a strict set of international guidelines on accessibility.

The arguments for moving to greater accessibility for people with disabilities are strong. There are 1.85 million people in Ontario with a disability, according to the Ontario Ministry of Community and Social Services. The disabilities run the full gamut from physical handicaps to hearing loss and sight impairment to mental health disability and learning or intellectual dysfunctions, such as dyslexia, for example. Given an accommodating workplace, people with disabilities can be often be superior in their performance; one study concluded 90 percent of people with disabilities did as well or better at their jobs than their nondisabled coworkers. They represent not only a potential pool of valuable employees but also add up to a significant proportion of Scotiabank's 12.5 million customers in 50 countries. Here in Canada, nationwide figures indicate that people with disabilities have an estimated spending power of about $25 billion annually.

The kind of breakthrough software available to D'Intino and any other employee with disabilities at Scotiabank includes a screen reader called JAWS that gives an audio confirmation of what the employee has just written on his or her computer screen; computer voice-recognition called Dragon Naturally Speaking; electronic pointers that will perform the task of a mouse for physically handicapped employees; specialized phones to assist people with hearing loss; and Braille keyboards and label printers for those with impaired vision.

D'Intino says that her most valuable tool in the workplace is Gilligan. He's her four-year-old standard poodle service dog. He brings her safely to and from work and helps her navigate the office complex. "He also become a stress reliever for a lot of people," she says with a laugh. "What's really cool now is that people are a lot more aware around our service dogs and how they should act around them."

D'Intino says it's part of the dramatic change in public attitude to people with a disability.

"We're seeing more and more creative solutions to integrating people and a lot more flexibility in the workplace," she says. "It is certainly much better than when I started my journey 10 years ago."

"Do we still have ways to go? We will always have a way to go," D'Intino says.

SOURCE: Adapted from Paul Dalby, "A 'Lightning Rod' for Bank's Diversity" thestar.com, February 19, 2009, (www.thestar.com/Business/article/589480). Reprinted by permission of the author, Paul Dalby, a Warkworth-based writer.

Age and Accommodation

There is a misconception that older employees are less productive, of less worth, and less receptive and adaptable to change and training. However, the experience, ideas, and productivity of older employees are often invaluable. Age discrimination may occur at the hiring stage if an employee is declined employment because of a perception that the employee's age limits career potential or if the employee is viewed as overqualified due to lengthy experience. Using objective criteria in hiring practices can help reduce this problem. Given the rapidly aging workforce, the retention of valuable older employees during the transition to retirement has become a pressing issue. Flexible

As the Canadian population ages and baby boomers either don't want to or can't afford to retire, mandatory retirement policies are likely to find themselves being challenged under the *Charter* as a violation of the right to equality under section 15.

work arrangements such as reduced workweeks or workdays, flextime, compressed workweeks, working from home, leaves of absence, contract employment, job sharing, and part-time schedules can prove to be to the mutual benefit of the employer and the employee. Such arrangements may also be necessary to allow older employees to care for elderly family members such as parents, spouses, or same-sex partners. Modifying an older employee's job or transferring the employee to a less-demanding job can also be appropriate provided that it is not carried out in a discriminatory manner or for reasons that infringe human rights laws.

Older workers can also face discrimination surrounding retirement. Several mandatory retirement policies have been challenged as discriminatory. To mount a challenge to a mandatory retirement policy, the prescribed age of mandatory retirement must fall within the definition of age protected in the applicable human rights statute. For example, in jurisdictions where the definition of age in the statute includes an upper limit of age 65, policies imposing mandatory retirement at age 65 cannot be challenged under the legislation. Where such a challenge can be mounted, only policies that can be justified by the employer as a BFOQ will survive scrutiny. This requires demonstrating a correlation between older age and the essential duties of the job and showing that individual assessments would constitute undue hardship. While such policies have been upheld in the case of police[20] and firefighters[21] based on the correlation between age and physical fitness, it will be difficult to justify similar policies in the corporate world. Mandatory retirement policies have also been challenged under the *Charter* as violation of the right to equality under section 15.[22] While the policies are invariably found to infringe the right to equality guaranteed by the *Charter*, their success in withstanding scrutiny depends on a case-by-case assessment of whether they can be justified under section 1 of the *Charter* as a reasonable limit in a free and democratic society in the circumstances.

Family Status

Family status has different meanings in different jurisdictions. In most jurisdictions it is defined as the parent and child relationship. However, in others, family status is defined by blood, marriage, and adoption. Moreover, the interpretation and application of family status as a prohibited ground of discrimination varies considerably across the country. Discrimination based on family status may arise in a number of ways in respect of an individual's employment such as differential treatment based on one's status as a single parent, the granting of family benefits under an insurance plan or collective agreement, antinepotism policies (although they are explicitly permitted in Ontario and can be upheld in other jurisdictions based on a BFOQ), rigid employer policies that do not provide reasonable flexibility for accommodation of legitimate and pressing family responsibilities, and an employee's association with his or her spouse (e.g., where the spouse has a conflict or legal issue with the employer, takes a job with a competitor, becomes ill and needs care, or has engaged in criminal behaviour).

National/Ethnic Origin, or Place of Origin

The prohibition against discrimination based on national/ethnic origin, or place of origin protects individuals from discrimination based on where they were born, raised, or reside, along with related characteristics. These protected grounds frequently intersect with the prohibited grounds of colour, race, citizenship, and religion or creed. Immigrants with foreign job experience or academic credentials are frequently subject to discrimination based on national/ethnic origin, or place of origin when applying for jobs in Canada. With the influx of immigrants in Canada, the issue of foreign-trained employees' access to professions and trades is becoming more common. Although some of the barriers limiting access to professions and trades are created by the government, others are presented by employers who prefer to hire Canadian-trained applicants. To justify its preference, the employer may have to demonstrate that local training or education is a reasonable or BFOQ, such that it will be impossible to accommodate the foreign-trained applicant without undue hardship.

Race and Colour

The concept of race includes not only skin colour and physical features, but also characteristics such as accent or manner of speech, name, beliefs and practices, diet, clothing and grooming, place of origin, and citizenship. Individuals who are perceived to be members of a certain race are also protected, regardless of whether or not the individual identifies with that race. In addition to discrimination by way of racial harassment, discrimination based on race and colour may arise if an employment decision or the manner in which an employee is treated by the employer or its representatives is any way motivated by considerations of the employee's race or colour. For example, an East Indian employee with superior qualifications who is bypassed for a promotion in favour of a white candidate, or an employer policy or practice of refusing employment to individuals of certain races or to candidates who are not proficient in English, is likely to constitute discrimination based on race or colour where the conduct cannot be justified as a BFOQ. In addition, a workplace in which visible minorities are concentrated in low-level positions, but are significantly underrepresented in management, may indicate the existence of systemic discrimination based on race or colour. Recently, the Quebec Human Rights Tribunal ordered Bombardier Inc. to pay $319,000 to a Pakistan-born pilot who was discriminated against on grounds of ethnic and national origin when he was denied training by the company because the United States considered him to be a security threat.[23] The award included a $50,000 payment for punitive damages—the largest awarded in the Tribunal's history.

The "Evidence-Based HR" box on page 98 summarizes research evidence about tendencies towards racial discrimination in Canada and the United Kingdom.

Evidence-Based HR

Canada prides itself on being a multicultural society that embraces ethnic and cultural differences, distinguishing our country from the rampant race discrimination practices reported on the international scene. However, a new study from the University of British Columbia suggests that our views—and our HR practices—may not be as evolved as we would like to believe. In a study designed to see just how level Canada's job playing field really is, UBC economics professor Philip Oreopoulos sent out over 6,500 resumes to online jobs posted by Toronto-area employers across 20 occupational categories. The study found that even with identical education and work experience, English-sounding applicants like *Jill Wilson* or *John Martin* were more than 40 percent more likely to receive a call back than those identifying the candidate as Asian, using names like *Sana Khan* or *Lei Li*. Although the study targeted only online job postings and Oreopoulos acknowledges that it is not representative of the entire labour market, he does feel that it may explain why many highly educated new immigrants are having such difficulty succeeding in the Canadian labour market. "In cases where the employer requires the hire to be very good at English, then consciously or unconsciously, they may have a concern when looking at their resume," said Oreopoulos. "The other possibility is preference-based discrimination: the employer, consciously or unconsciously, prefers to have applicants of the same ethnicity working for them." Whatever the cause, if employers are engaging in name-based discrimination, they may find themselves running afoul of human rights legislation. It appears that despite the perception that Canada is a society that extols the virtues of diversity, employers, whether intentionally or inadvertently, may still discriminate against candidates with "ethnic" names.

Although unfortunate, Canada is certainly not alone when it comes to hiring practices that may not be treating all job seekers equally. In the United Kingdom, researchers from the National Centre for Social Research, commissioned by the Department for Work and Pension (DWP), sent out almost 3,000 applications to a series of job postings between November 2008 and May 2009. In an attempt to discover if employers were discriminating against job seekers with foreign-sounding names, each position was sent three different applications from candidates with names representative of Britain's Asian, African, and English communities—Nazia Mahmood, Mariam Namagembe, and Alison Taylor. The research found that for every nine applications sent, the English-sounding candidate would receive a callback, as compared to the Asian or African-sounding candidate having to send out almost double that number before being contacted. Both the U.K. and Canadian research point to some challenges that human resource professionals will need to address if they are to stay on the right side of human rights law and ensure that they are not letting bias—intentional or not—impede them from locating and hiring the best person for the job.

SOURCES: Adapted from "UBC Study Finds People with Foreign Names Face Job Discrimination," *Macleans.ca* (May 21, 2009) at http://oncampus.macleans.ca/education/2009/05/21/ubc-study-finds-people-with-foreign-names-face-job-discrimination (retrieved June 13, 2011); UBC Press Release "Employers Discriminate against Applicants with Non-English Names, UBC Study Suggests," (May 20, 2009) at www.publicaffairs.ubc.ca/media/releases/2009/mr-09-056.html (retrieved June 13, 2011); David Karp, "Job Seekers with Asian Names Face Discrimination," *Vancouver Sun* (May 21, 2009) at www2.canada.com/vancouversun/news/story.html?id=4f9ec2a3-e33c-470b-8e55-8a38993de1ad (retrieved June 13, 2011); Rajeev Sayal, "Undercover Job Hunters Reveal Huge Race Bias in Britain's Workplaces," *The Guardian* (October 18, 2009) at www.guardian.co.uk/money/2009/oct/18/racism-discrimination-employment-undercover (retrieved June 13, 2011).

Sex

Discrimination based on sex in today's workplaces is less commonly based on a blatant refusal to hire women for certain positions and more frequently related to workplace standards that inadvertently discriminate against women, as was the case in *Meiorin*. Pay inequities between men and women performing the same or equally valuable work are also a common form of sex discrimination. However, sex discrimination can be more overt such as a refusal to hire or promote a woman who is pregnant because she will be taking maternity leave, or a refusal to reinstate a woman once her maternity leave ends. Similarly, pregnant women may be denied certain positions based on an ill-conceived perception that certain jobs are not appropriate or safe for pregnant women or the fetus. While this concern may be well intentioned and legitimate in certain cases, it will be justified only where objective, medical, and perhaps scientific evidence can support such a conclusion. Conversely, discrimination can also occur where a pregnant woman is *refused* reassignment from a job that is known to pose risks to her or her unborn baby. Gender discrimination also falls within the protection afforded individuals based on sex. Gender discrimination might occur in cases of the treatment of transgendered individuals such as transsexuals or cross-dressers. A nightclub in British Columbia was found to have discriminated against a pre-operative male to female transsexual on grounds of sex and disability by denying her access to the women's washroom.[24] The decision suggested that protection against sex discrimination applies broadly to include those who are victims of discrimination because they fall outside the traditional male or female gender categories. The decision also demonstrates that discrimination is not limited to the biological definition of gender, but encompasses the broader social context.

Learn more about discrimination based on sex online with Connect.

Sexual Orientation

Sexual orientation includes heterosexual, gay, lesbian, and bisexual orientation. The laws protecting individuals based on their sexual orientation have progressed rapidly, propelled by changing societal standards and challenges to discriminatory stereotypes. However, gays and lesbians in particular continue to be victimized by society's lingering discriminatory stereotypes and attitudes. Discrimination based on sexual orientation is most prevalent in the workplace in the form of harassment, as well as the denial of career advancements and in some cases dismissal, merely because of the individual's real, or perceived, sexual orientation. In one case, an offer of permanent employment was withdrawn when the woman openly displayed that she was a lesbian.[25] In another, a man was fired when he disclosed that he was gay.[26] Moreover, discrimination based on sexual orientation is aggravated when combined with discrimination based on another prohibited ground, or stereotypes such as the unfounded view that AIDS is a disease predominantly afflicting gay men.

The principles related to discrimination based on sexual orientation have developed primarily through case law involving the denial of benefits to same-sex couples. The statutes conferring benefits to couples indirectly discriminated against same-sex couples by defining "spouse" in a manner that did not apply to same-sex partners. Many of these restrictive definitions have been struck down by the courts and replaced with statutory provisions that expand the traditional heterosexual model of marriage and cohabitation to encompass gay and lesbian relationships. As a consequence, it is discriminatory today to deny spousal benefits such as employment and pension benefits to the same-sex partners of an employee.[27]

Special Interest Organizations

Some statues make special provisions for special interest organizations such as religious, philanthropic, educational, fraternal, or social institutions or organizations that are primarily engaged in serving the interests of persons identified by a prohibited ground of discrimination. For example, a Catholic school can hire only teachers of the Catholic faith. Similarly, it is generally reasonable for a denominational organization such as a church, mosque, temple, or synagogue to hire only members of its faith to serve as leaders in the organization. However, this exemption is unlikely to apply in the case of employees for whom religious denomination cannot be justified as a BFOQ, such as a janitor.

HARASSMENT

Harassment
A type of discrimination that involves any verbal or physical conduct that offends an employee, which is unwelcome or that a reasonable person should have known to be unwelcome, and that is related to a prohibited ground of discrimination.

Harassment is a type of discrimination that involves any verbal or physical conduct that offends an employee, which is unwelcome or that a reasonable person should have known to be unwelcome, and that is related to a prohibited ground of discrimination. Accordingly, while intention may be an aggravating factor, it is not required. Harassment is generally behaviour that fails to respect an individual's dignity and self-worth and that humiliates, demeans, or embarrasses someone. Table 3.4 provides examples of such behaviours. Many statutes require that harassment be a "course" of conduct such that it is most often found to have occurred based on a pattern of harassing behaviour. However, harassment can include one isolated serious incident.

However, harassment does not include appropriate and reasonable management and supervision of employees carried out in good faith and for legitimate work-related purposes, such as that related to discipline, performance management, the distribution and assignment of work, and the lawful operation of employment policies and practices, or a collective agreement.

Like other forms of discrimination, employers are responsible for ensuring that their workplaces remain free of harassment. This includes protecting employees from harassment not only by its own employees, but also by third parties such as contractors or service technicians.[28] Employers that learn of harassment in the workplace must take immediate and diligent action to rid the workplace of the offending behaviour. This will invariably include a thorough investigation, followed by appropriate remedial measures. Corrective action can take many forms such as disciplining or, where appropriate, dismissing those responsible for the harassment, changing reporting structures where an employee has been subject to harassment by a superior, transferring an employee to separate the harasser from the victim, educating management and other employees about harassment including through human rights training and by drawing attention to the employer's harassment policy, and making amendments to any existing policy where required. Employees who have been subject to harassment may also require time off to cope with the emotional impact of the offending behaviour.

Table 3.4   Examples of Harassment

• Unwelcome remarks, jokes, name calling, gestures, or innuendos related to a prohibited ground of discrimination (e.g., age, race, sexual orientation, disability, religion, etc.)
• Unwanted physical contact such as touching or pushing
• Refusal to interact with an individual based on a prohibited ground of discrimination
• Threats, intimidation, coercion, or verbal abuse
• Taunting
• Humiliating or demeaning treatment
• Abuse of power such as the vindictive and unfair distribution of work assignments or conduct that sabotages an employee's ability to perform at work

Table 3.5 Costs of Harassment

• Direct negative impact on employees and on a company's profitability
• Employees who are being harassed can suffer from headaches, ulcers, tension, depression, insomnia, and other illnesses that either keep them away from work or reduce their well-being and productivity
• An employee who is being harassed may resign, which penalizes that individual financially, and means that a new employee must be trained
• If harassment is an ongoing problem, it may affect morale and lead to a decrease in productivity and high staff turnover
• Damages awarded by a tribunal, court, or labour arbitrator to compensate the victim of the harassment

SOURCE: Canadian Human Rights Commission, "Anti-Harassment Policies for the Workplace: An Employer's Guide," (March 2006) at www.chrc-ccdp.ca/pdf/ahpoliciesworkplace_en.pdf (accessed June 13, 2011).

In addition to the damages that may be awarded against an employer by a tribunal, court, or labour arbitrator to compensate an employee who was a victim of harassment, harassment produces many more detrimental and disruptive costs for the organization, some examples of which are set out in Table 3.5.

Sexual Harassment

Sexual harassment is any unwanted verbal comment or physical contact of a sexual nature, or that is based on a person's sex or gender that the harasser knew was unwelcome or reasonably ought to have known was unwelcome. Examples are provided in Table 3.6. Sexual harassment can generally take place in one of two ways. First, "quid pro quo" sexual harassment can occur when some kind of benefit (or punishment) is made contingent on the employee's submitting (or not submitting) to sexual

Sexual Harassment
Any unwanted verbal comment or physical contact of a sexual nature, or that is based on a person's sex or gender that the harasser knew was unwelcome or reasonably ought to have known was unwelcome.

Table 3.6 Examples of Sexual Harassment

• Images of naked or scantily clad women (or men) in the workplace
• Sexually explicit images in the workplace
• Sexually explicit jokes or jokes with sexual overtones
• Sexually explicit comments
• Sexual posturing
• Questions about a person's sex life
• Unwanted persistent pursuit of a date
• Derogatory comments based on sex or gender
• Unwanted personal attention from coworkers or employer representatives
• Leering
• Unwanted physical contact such as touching, patting, or pinching
• Unwanted sexual comments, jokes, or advances, including from a person of the same sex
• Promises of work-related benefits in return for sexual acts or a sexual relationship
• Sexual and physical assault

advances. For example, a male manager tells his female secretary that if she has sex with him, he will help her get promoted, or he threatens to fire her if she fails to do so. Submission to such conduct is made either explicitly or implicitly a term or condition of an individual's employment, submission to or rejection of such conduct by an individual is used as the basis for employment decisions affecting such individual, or such conduct has the purpose or effect of unreasonably interfering with an individual's work performance or creating an intimidating, hostile, or offensive working environment. A one-time occurrence of quid pro quo harassment can be sufficient to violate human rights laws.[29]

The *Barnes v. Thomas Stratton Warehousing Co. Inc.* case illustrates *quid pro quo* sexual harassment.[30] Barnes was a new employee who was advised by her supervisor during the first week of her employment that she could "thank [her] ass" for the job. The supervisor also told Barnes that a full-time job was dependent on her agreeing to have sex with him, and that she would have to wear short skirts to sell the company's product. The Newfoundland Board of Inquiry found the supervisor and the corporate employer liable for sexual harassment.

A more subtle, and possibly more pervasive, form of sexual harassment is that which creates a "poisoned" or "hostile" working environment. This occurs when someone's behaviour in the workplace creates an environment that makes it difficult for someone of a particular sex to work. Many complainants in sexual harassment lawsuits have alleged that men ran their fingers through the complainants' hair, made suggestive remarks, and physically assaulted them by touching them inappropriately. Other examples include having pictures of naked women posted in the workplace, using offensive sexually explicit language, or using sex or gender-related jokes or innuendoes in conversations. Generally, this type of sexual harassment requires a course or pattern of harassing conduct rather than merely a one-time occurrence.[31] However, a serious one-time incident can be sufficient to constitute sexual harassment. In one such case, an employer presented himself naked to his employee and tried to persuade her to have sex with him.[32]

These types of behaviours are actionable under human rights legislation because they treat individuals differently based on their sex or gender. However, the list is not in any way exhaustive. Like other forms of discrimination, the types of behaviour that can ground a finding of sexual harassment are interpreted broadly by decision makers.[33] In addition, although most harassment cases involve male-on-female harassment, harassment can also entail female-on-male harassment and same-sex harassment. For example, husband and wife owners of a security firm were found to have sexually harassed one of their female employees.[34]

In addition, Menzies Chrysler Incorporated of Whitby, Ontario, and two of its male used car salesmen were recently ordered to pay $50,000 to a male complainant when Graham was found to have subjected the complainant to a sexually hostile and poisoned work environment, and his supervisor, Lyons, knew of the behaviour and did nothing to stop it. The evidence revealed that Graham had a pattern of parading naked in front of the complainant while thrusting and gyrating his hips towards him in a sexual manner and making related sexual suggestions to the complainant, and generally subjected the complainant to lewd, inappropriate comments of a sexual nature. Pornography was also rampant in the workplace. The respondents argued that the conduct was "just fun" and "horseplay," and could not be sexual harassment because the sexualized locker-room atmosphere was created in an all-male environment. In the respondents' view, it was simply "good-natured fun between 'the boys.'"[35]

In order to constitute sexual harassment, the evidentiary burden on the complainant is to demonstrate that the impugned behaviour was (1) a course of vexatious conduct or comment, (2) by an employer or employer's agent, (3) unwelcome or ought to be known to be unwelcome and (4) related to sex or gender.[36] From this, there are four critical issues to be proven in each of these cases. First, the behaviour must be sexual in nature. This can include discrimination based on sex or gender.

Second, to constitute discrimination, the conduct must be severe enough on a one-time basis, or consist of a sufficient pattern or course of conduct to create a poisoned, hostile work environment.

A third critical issue is that the harassment must have been unwelcome. Decision makers use an objective standard that consists of assessing whether a reasonable person in the position of the harasser would have known his or her behaviour to be unwelcome. Notably, the fact that the behaviour was consensual or appeared to be condoned by the complainant does not preclude a finding of sexual harassment. Decision makers begin with a view that sexual advances do not belong in the workplace and thus are unwelcome. A complainant's history of joining in similar behaviour, including engaging in sexually explicit conversations or even sexual intercourse with the harasser is not determinative of whether the conduct was unwelcome. This is particularly the case in relationships involving a power imbalance or where the conduct is of such a degrading nature that the complainant is not held to the requirement to expressly object to the unwelcome conduct.[37] Passivity or voluntariness in engaging in or failing to expressly reject sexual conduct is not to be confused with consent.

Learn more about a case involving issues of sexual harassment, passivity, and consent online with Connect.

The fourth issue that decision makers must determine is whether and to what extent the organization is liable for the actions of its employees. Employers are generally held liable for harassment by their employees regardless of whether they knew of the offending behaviour. Where an employer knew of the behaviour and failed to take appropriate steps to remedy the problem, the penalties imposed on the employer will be much more severe.

To ensure a workplace free from sexual harassment, organizations can follow some important steps. First, the organization can develop and communicate a policy that makes it very clear that sexual harassment will not be tolerated in the workplace. Second, all employees, new and old, can be trained to identify inappropriate workplace behaviour. Third, the organization can develop a mechanism for reporting sexual harassment that encourages people to speak out. Fourth, management can prepare to take prompt disciplinary action against those who commit sexual harassment as well as appropriate action to protect the victims of sexual harassment.[38]

Learn more about sexual harassment in the workplace online with Connect.

Psychological Harassment

Jurisdictions including Quebec[39] and Saskatchewan[40] explicitly prohibit psychological harassment with a purpose of eliminating violence and bullying in the workplace. The Quebec statute defines psychological harassment as "any vexatious behaviour in the form of repeated and hostile or unwanted conduct, verbal comments, actions or gestures, that affects an employee's dignity or psychological or physical integrity and that results in a harmful work environment for the employee."[41] Psychological harassment can creep into the management of employees if supervisors and managers are not trained properly to steer clear of aggressive or harsh management styles. To reduce the likelihood of a finding of psychological harassment by an employer, employees must be treated in a respectful manner by superiors. Performance management and criticisms must be legitimate, communicated in a way that does not demean or humiliate the employee, and provide the employee with a sufficient understanding of the issues and the necessary assistance to improve.

Psychological Harassment
Vexatious behaviour in the form of repeated and hostile or unwanted conduct, comments, actions, or gestures, that affects an employee's dignity or psychological or physical integrity and that adversely affects an employee's work environment.

Discrimination and Harassment Policy

Establishing an effective discrimination and harassment policy is the first step to maintaining a discrimination and harassment-free workplace. Figure 3.2 sets out a helpful checklist in respect of the essential components of policy.

FIGURE 3.2 Checklist for a Discrimination and Harassment Policy

☐ Policy statement—management supports a discrimination and harassment-free workplace

☐ A summary of the law

☐ Employees' responsibilities and rights

☐ Supervisors', managers', and employers' responsibilities

☐ An undertaking that allegations of discrimination and harassment will be dealt with seriously, speedily, and confidentially

☐ Descriptions of discriminatory and harassing behaviour

☐ Procedures—guidelines and manners of proceeding under the policy

☐ Remedies, corrective action, and safeguards

☐ Protection against victimization or retaliation for employees who complain of discrimination or harassment, or who testify in an investigation

☐ Selection of objective, neutral, and trusted discrimination and harassment counsellors, mediators, and investigators

☐ Communication and circulation of the policy to all employees and managers, current and new

☐ Education of all staff about discrimination and harassment and the policy

☐ Monitoring—a commitment to periodic revision and review of the policy

SOURCE: Adapted from Canadian Human Rights Commission, "Anti-Harassment Policies for the Workplace: An Employer's Guide, Part 4: Checklist for an Anti-Harassment Policy: Medium and Large Organizations" at www.chrc-ccdp.ca/publications/anti_harassment_part3-eng.aspx#part4 (accessed June 13, 2011). Reproduced with the permission of the Minister of Public Works and Government Services, 2011.

REPRISAL FOR PARTICIPATION AND OPPOSITION

Suppose you overhear a supervisor in your workplace telling someone that he refuses to hire women because he knows they are just not cut out for the job. Or you are present when your colleagues utter racial slurs at a fellow worker or make sexualized remarks to a female employee about her personal appearance. Believing this to be illegal discrimination, you face a dilemma. Should you come forward and report this statement? Or if someone else files a lawsuit for discrimination, should you testify on behalf of the complainant? What happens if your employer threatens to fire you if you do anything?

Human rights laws protect you. All human rights statutes provide that employers cannot retaliate against employees for exercising any of their lawful rights under human rights legislation. This may include complaining that you have been the subject of discrimination or harassment—typically the first step for an employee who believes he or she has been the victim of discriminatory or harassing behaviour—filing or threatening to file a human rights complaint, opposing an employer's or fellow worker's perceived illegal employment practice or participating in a proceeding, whether on your own or another's behalf, related to an alleged violation of human rights laws. Participation might include, for example, testifying in an investigation, hearing, court, tribunal, or arbitration proceeding regarding an illegal employment act. Clearly, the purpose of these provisions is to protect employees from employers' threats and other forms of intimidation aimed at discouraging employees from bringing to light acts they believe to be illegal. This is known in law as a "reprisal." A reprisal might take the form of being singled out for unfair treatment at work, being unjustifiably passed over for an employment opportunity or being fired, making the workplace so intolerable that the employee feels forced to quit, or perhaps being made the subject of false rumours or accusations at work or even in public.

These cases can be extremely costly for companies because they allege acts of intentional discrimination, and therefore, in addition to damages for the acts of discrimination or harassment, complainants are entitled to further damages specific to the reprisal.

This does not mean that employees have an unlimited right to talk about how racist or sexist their employers are. The courts tend to frown on employees whose activities result in a poor public image for the company unless those employees had attempted to use the organization's internal channels—approaching one's manager, raising the issue with the HRM department, and so on—before going public.

ENFORCEMENT OF HUMAN RIGHTS

Human rights laws are enforced by the applicable statutory and adjudicative bodies in each jurisdiction. Some jurisdictions have both a human rights commission and tribunal or board of inquiry. Human rights commissions or tribunals can take on any number of functions such as administering the human rights statute, investigating and resolving human rights complaints, sponsoring or conducting human rights research, developing human rights guidelines, and promoting education and awareness about human rights laws and issues. In some jurisdictions, these roles are shared between two bodies—usually a human rights commission and a human rights tribunal or board of inquiry. In such a case, the tribunal or board of inquiry takes on the role of the decision maker carrying out the adjudication and resolution of human rights disputes; any remaining duties are typically within the purview of the commission. This division in duties has been in place in Ontario since amendments to the Human Rights Code in December 2006, which assigned the Human Rights Tribunal with responsibility for all aspects of the complaint and resolution process, while the remaining duties fall within the power of the Human Rights Commission. Moreover, Ontario is unique in that it has a Human Rights Legal Support Centre for the purpose of providing human rights legal support services throughout the province. Parties that are dissatisfied with a decision made by a human rights administrative body can appeal that decision. The precise appeal procedures and forums to which the appeal can be made differ by jurisdiction.

Human Rights Remedies

Human rights bodies across the country have broad powers to remedy human rights violations. While the precise remedies vary, they often include monetary damages for lost wages and other employment benefits, as well as lost employment opportunities, and general damages for hurt feelings and mental anguish. Only four jurisdictions permit punitive or exemplary damages.[42] Other jurisdictions have explicitly rejected this view of damages in favour of a view that human rights remedies are intended to compensate the victim rather than punish the wrongdoer.[43] Nonmonetary remedies might include an order that the offender cease his or her behaviour now and in the future, develop human rights plans and policies, educate and train employees about human rights, apologize to the victim, amend offending provisions of a collective agreement, reinstate the victim or provide the victim with an employment opportunity that was improperly denied. An employer's history of compliance or noncompliance with human rights laws may also affect the types and extent of any remedies ordered.

HUMAN RIGHTS PROTECTIONS IN OTHER LEGISLATION

Human rights protections can also be found in other employment-related provincial legislation beyond human rights statutes. Labour relations statutes prohibit discrimination in respect of union membership and lawful union activity. Unions' duty of fair representation precludes unfair, arbitrary, or discriminatory treatment in respect of its representation of union members. Moreover, the Ontario statute prohibits any discrimination that offends the Human Rights Code or the Charter.[44] Ontario also has the Ontarians with Disabilities Act, 2001 (ODA), which applies to the Government of Ontario including its ministries, agencies, and services. ODA is an attempt by the government to support the rights of persons of all ages with disabilities by improving opportunities for persons with disabilities and providing for their involvement in the identification, removal, and prevention of barriers to their full participation in society. Initiatives involve barrier-free buildings, structures, and premises; accessibility of goods and services; providing information in an accessible format; and the development of annual accessibility plans. However, ODA will eventually be superseded by the Accessibility for Ontarians with Disabilities Act, 2005 (OADA), which will extend protections throughout the public and private sector in Ontario. (The ODA remains in full force until the 20-year period allowed for full implementation of all standards set by the OADA is complete.) The statute provides for the establishment of accessibility standards by regulation and applies to persons or organizations that employ other persons; deal with the public by providing goods, services, facilities, or accommodation; own or occupy premises that are open to the public; or engage in a business, activity, or undertaking prescribed by regulation. Compliance with all regulations is required by 2025. In addition, some workplace health and safety legislation such as occupational health and safety and workers' compensation statutes prohibit discriminatory treatment of workers. Equality in the workplace is also promoted through employment equity and pay equity legislation, discussed in further detail below.

<table>
<tr><td>

LO 5

Explain employment equity legislation and describe the four designated groups.

</td></tr>
</table>

EMPLOYMENT EQUITY

Propelled by the Royal Commission on Equality in Employment report by Judge Rosalie Abella in 1984, employment equity legislation in Canada aims to provide equality in employment to four historically disadvantaged groups: (1) women; (2) Aboriginal people; (3) people with disabilities; and iv) visible minorities. The Abella report indicated that these groups were subject to disadvantages such as high unemployment rates, lower-than-average salaries, and concentration in low-status jobs with little potential for career advancement. The report later became the foundation of the Employment Equity Act, 1986, which applied to only federally regulated private employers, but was later amended as the Employment Equity Act, 1995 (EEA), broadening its application to the federal public service and adding an audit compliance system. Beyond the right to be free from discrimination in employment guaranteed by the Charter and human rights legislation, **employment equity** legislation proactively targets the four designated groups to require or encourage preferential treatment in employment practices. Rather than requiring equal treatment, it requires an accommodation of differences in striving for true equality.

Employment Equity
Initiatives that proactively target women, Aboriginal people, people with disabilities, and visible minorities to require or encourage preferential treatment in employment practices in an effort to achieve equality in employment.

Quebec also has employment equity legislation aimed at granting equal access in employment to (1) women, (2) handicapped persons, (3) Aboriginal people, (4) visible minorities, and (5) people whose mother tongue is neither French nor English and who belong to a designated group other than Aboriginal peoples or visible minorities.[45]

The Four Designated Groups

The four designated groups were identified in the Abella report because of historical disadvantage in achieving fair and equitable employment practices. Traditionally, the advancement of these individuals to higher-paying, managerial, executive, and professional positions has been obstructed by an invisible "glass ceiling,"—that is, organizational or attitudinal bias that prevents their progression to these higher-level positions. Employment equity legislation aims to break through this ceiling and provide these individuals with equal opportunities in employment.

Figure 3.3 illustrates the representation of the designated groups in the Canadian workforce as a whole versus federally regulated employers in past years. The table indicates that the representation of the designated groups in the workforce of federally regulated employers has increased, suggesting that employment equity initiatives have had some degree of success.

Let's take a closer look at the disadvantages faced by the four designated groups.

WOMEN

Historically, women have been segregated into lower-level and lower-paying jobs. In 2009, 67 percent of employed women worked in teaching, nursing and related health occupations, clerical or other administrative positions, or sales and service occupations.[46] In contrast, 31.0 percent of employed men worked in these fields. The *2009 Catalyst Census: Financial Post 500 Women Board Directors* (2010) examined women's representation on corporate boards at the most profitable companies in Canada. The Census, illustrated in Figure 3.4, indicates that women are underrepresented in all leadership positions in these companies. Despite women comprising 47.4 percent of the Canadian labour force, only 14.0 percent of board of director seats in these companies were held by women in 2010, and 41.9 percent of companies did not have a single woman on the board (not shown).

These figures are symbolic of the representation of women in particular types of employment in the labour force overall. Statistics demonstrate that although women have made gains in professional occupations, they are less likely to hold permanent full-time work or be employed in managerial positions and they earn less money than their male counterparts.[47] For example, in 2008, the average earnings for full-year, full-time female workers was $44,700. For male workers, the average was $62,600.[48] Women earned an average of 71.3 percent of men's earnings.[49] In 2008, 45 percent of men versus only 27.1 percent of women working in permanent full-time employment in the federally regulated private sector earned more than $60,000.[50] Moreover, 78.7 percent of the women employed in this sector versus 90 percent of the men held full-time employment. These facts highlight that women continue to face obstacles in achieving equality in employment today.

FIGURE 3.3 Representation of Designated Groups 1992–2008

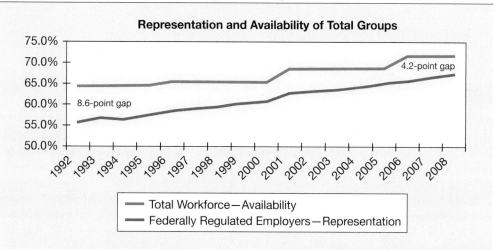

SOURCE: Canadian Human Rights Commission, *Impact of the Employment Equity Act and of the CHRC Employment Equity Program over the Years*, March 2010 at www.chrc-ccdp.ca/pdf/eer_reme-eng.pdf (accessed June 13, 2011). Reproduced with the permission of the Minister of Public Works and Government Services, 2011.

FIGURE 3.4 The Catalyst Pyramid: Canadian Women in Business

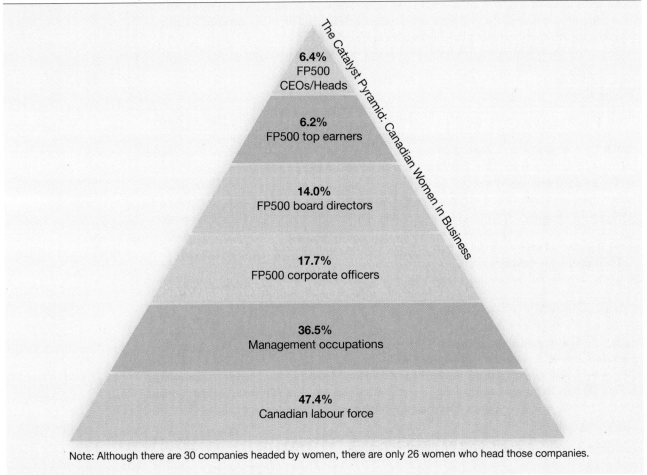

The Catalyst Pyramid: Canadian Women in Business

6.4%
FP500
CEOs/Heads

6.2%
FP500 top earners

14.0%
FP500 board directors

17.7%
FP500 corporate officers

36.5%
Management occupations

47.4%
Canadian labour force

Note: Although there are 30 companies headed by women, there are only 26 women who head those companies.

SOURCES: Catalyst Research (2011); Catalyst, "2010 Census of Women Corporate Officers and Top Earners of the FP500," (2011); Catalyst, "2009 Catalyst Census: Financial Post 500 Women Board Directors," (2010); Statistics Canada, "282-0010," CANSIM (2011).

ABORIGINAL PEOPLE

Aboriginal people continue to be underrepresented in employment, tend to be promoted less often, and earn less than their non-Aboriginal counterparts.[51] The 2006 Census by Statistics Canada indicated that the unemployment rate of Aboriginal people was 14.8 percent compared to only 6.3 percent for the non-Aboriginal population. The Census also revealed that the average income of full-time permanent Aboriginal employees lagged behind that of their non-Aboriginal colleagues, with Aboriginal employees earning 80.8 percent of full-time, permanent non-Aboriginal workers' salaries. Moreover, Aboriginal people have a propensity to be concentrated in clerical and semiskilled manual work. Aboriginal women face even greater obstacles than Aboriginal men given that they face the combined effect of inequities affecting both women and Aboriginal people.[52] Given that statistics indicate that the Aboriginal population is growing up to six times more rapidly than the general population,[53] the gaps that Aboriginal people face in respect of employment equity will only continue to widen if the inequalities that they face are not properly addressed.

PEOPLE WITH DISABILITIES

Approximately 4.4 million Canadians reported living with a disability in 2006, comprising 14.3 percent of the population.[54] This number is growing and, with an increased awareness of disabilities in society in general as well as an aging population, this number can be expected to rise. People with disabilities have a high degree of nonparticipation in the labour market, and are only about half as likely to be employed as nondisabled people. Specifically, studies indicate that about 45 percent of work-aged disabled individuals are participating in the labour market versus 80 percent of the non-disabled population. Employees with a disability tend to earn approximately 17.6 percent less than their nondisabled counterparts. However, this gap varies depending on the severity of the disability. In addition to inequities in pay, workers with a disability are also somewhat more likely to face inequality on the job in respect of opportunities for promotion and training.[55]

VISIBLE MINORITIES

Despite the fact that visible minorities tend to be more highly educated, they have a higher unemployment rate than non-visible minorities—8.6 percent compared to 6.6 percent.[56] Foreign-born visible minorities experience an even greater discrepancy in respect of education and employment as illustrated in the Evidence-Based HR box earlier in this chapter. Canadian employers are resistant to viewing the skills of visible minorities as transferable to the Canadian marketplace. Moreover, visible minorities are far less likely to be employed in jobs of a comparable skill level, and equally educated visible minorities receive lower salaries than their nonvisible minority counterparts. Overall, visible minorities continue to face barriers in being hired and advancing in employment. The 2006 Census indicated that 16.2 percent of the population is a visible minority and, if current growth trends continue, it is predicted that one in every five Canadians will be a visible minority by the year 2017,[57] growing to one-third of the population by 2031.[58] Given this rapid growth, the inequities hindering visible minorities in the workplace will remain at the forefront of discussions on employment equity. Recognizing the worth of Canada's diverse talent pool will be critical to the future success of Canadian organizations.

The Employment Equity Act (EEA)

The EEA is federal legislation that applies to only federally regulated industries and employers, and federal contractor organizations that are provincially regulated suppliers of goods and services with at least 100 employees in Canada that bid on or receive federal contracts initially valued at $200,000 or more. Accordingly, provincially regulated organizations are beyond its reach.

The EEA has been criticized by some as promoting inequality rather than equality by giving preferential treatment to some groups. However, proponents of the EEA suggest that the preferential treatment it mandates is necessary to right historic disadvantages and achieve genuine equality in society. In Canada, the *Charter* and human rights legislation explicitly exempt employment equity initiatives from being characterized as discriminatory action.

The EEA requires all federally regulated companies to report annually on the workforce distribution of the four designated groups, which is reviewed by the Canadian Human Rights Commission.[59] The commission is responsible for ensuring compliance with the act. Distinguishing employment equity from affirmative action in the United States, employment equity initiatives in Canada are not tied to satisfying controversial quotas. Rather, under employment equity legislation, employers are required to identify and eliminate employment barriers in respect of the four designated groups, which result from the employer's employment systems, policies, and practices.[60] By requiring that employers implement positive policies and practices and make reasonable accommodations, the goal of the EEA is to have the employer's workforce reflect the representation of the designated groups in the overall Canadian workforce. However, employers are not required to implement initiatives that would impose undue hardship, create new positions in their workforce, or hire or promote unqualified persons.[61]

In striving to achieve employment equity, the EEA imposes on employers several statutory duties including (1) collection of workforce information; (2) analysis of the workforce to determine the degree of underrepresentation of designated group members; (3) review of employment systems, policies, and practices; (4) preparation of an employment equity plan; (5) implementation and monitoring of the plan; (6) periodic review and revision of the plan; (7) provision of information about employment equity to the workforce; (8) consultation with employee representatives; and (9) establishment and maintenance of employment equity records.

LO 6

Describe what is required to implement and promote employment equity programs.

Employment Equity Programs

Employment equity programs are mandated only in respect of those organizations governed by the EEA and the Quebec employment equity statute. The program is intended to set out measurable and detailed steps for implementing and achieving employment equity in the workplace.

There are seven steps to establishing and implementing an effective employment equity program,[62] which are reviewed below.

STEP ONE: OBTAIN THE COMMITMENT OF SENIOR MANAGEMENT

A key to the success of any organizational initiative including employment equity is the buy-in of senior management. It is critical to maintain and communicate the support of senior executives to employees, which is best done through the establishment and distribution of an employment equity policy or a comprehensive letter to all employees signed by the chief executive officer. This helps to foster support for diversity, promote an understanding about employment equity, and encourage employees to provide their input to the employment equity initiative. It is critical that responsibility for overseeing and administering the program be assigned to a senior executive, who in turn should delegate administrative functions of the program to a designated group of employees.

connect

Learn more about a statement of commitment to employment equity online with Connect.

STEP TWO: ESTABLISH A MECHANISM FOR CONSULTATION AND COLLABORATION

Consultation and collaboration with employee representatives or the union is required by the EEA.[63] Employment equity committees are an effective way to facilitate employment equity discussion, as are other joint labour–management committees and forums. To be effective and valid, consultation and collaboration must be ongoing, taking place throughout the planning, implementation, and revision and review of the program.

STEP THREE: CONDUCT A WORKFORCE SURVEY

The workforce survey involves asking employees to complete a voluntary questionnaire regarding whether or not they are members of one of the designated groups. The collection of information is by self-identification only. That is, only employees who identify themselves to the employer, or agree to be identified as a member of one of the designated groups, may be deemed as such for the purposes of employment equity. Moreover, any such information collected is strictly confidential and limited in use by the employer for the purposes of implementing employment equity in its organization.

STEP FOUR: UNDERTAKE A WORKFORCE ANALYSIS

Once the workforce survey is complete, the information must be analyzed to determine how the representation of designated groups in each occupational group in the employer's workforce compares to the representation of these groups in the particular segments in the external labour force from which the employer is expected to draw employees, or the Canadian workforce as a whole. This allows the employer to determine if designated groups are underrepresented in particular occupations within its organization or its workforce overall. External data such as information from Statistics Canada is used to assist employers with this analysis. A proper analysis of the data can also help the employer in identifying if it is having difficulty recruiting members of designated groups into certain jobs, whether they are concentrated in certain jobs in the organization or if there is a higher turnover rate of these individuals in respect of particular positions.

STEP FIVE: COMPLETE AN EMPLOYMENT SYSTEMS REVIEW

An **employment systems review** is an in-depth assessment of all of the employer's systems, policies, and practices, both formal and informal, written and unwritten, as well as collective agreements, and of the manner in which these are implemented, in order to identify barriers to the full participation of designated group members in employment with the employer. The review must also include attitudes and behavioural barriers that may be limiting the employment opportunities of designated group members. Barriers can be intentional or unintentional and have the effect of excluding or imposing a disadvantage on members of designated groups in the workplace. At a minimum, employment systems reviews will typically include a look at recruitment, selection, and hiring; promotion and transfers; training and development; performance evaluation systems; discipline; termination, resignation, and retirement of employment; salaries and benefits; and accommodation of designated groups. The review often involves interviews with employees, union representatives and management, and sometimes focus groups.

Employment Systems Review
An in-depth assessment of all of the employer's systems, policies, and practices, both formal and informal, written and unwritten, as well as collective agreements, and of the manner in which these are implemented, in order to identify barriers to the full participation of designated group members in employment with the employer.

STEP SIX: DEVELOP AND IMPLEMENT AN EMPLOYMENT EQUITY PLAN

The plan contains the solutions to the problems identified through the employment systems review. With the workforce analysis and employment systems review in hand, employers are armed with the information they need to develop positive and realistic goals and timetables for the achievement of employment equity within their organizations. While goals can be expressed as numbers or percentages, they are not quotas and there is no automatic penalty when employers fall short of achieving their targets. Rather, goals are a measure used to assist in planning and evaluating employment equity initiatives. Plans must contain five essential components as set out in Table 3.7.

Employers are required by the EEA to make all reasonable efforts to implement the plan. What constitutes reasonable efforts will vary based on the particular circumstances. However, where ongoing commitment, support, and progress in respect of achieving the plan and complying with the provisions of the EEA can be demonstrated, the standard of reasonable effort is likely to be satisfied.

Table 3.7 Key Elements of An Employment Equity Plan

An employment equity plan must contain:
1. Positive policies, practices, and reasonable accommodations to be instituted in the short term for the hiring, training, promotion, and retention of designated group members.
2. Short-term measures to be taken by the employer to eliminate employment barriers identified during the review of its employment systems, policies, and practices.
3. A timetable for the implementation of the positive policies and practices and measures to eliminate employment barriers.
4. Short-term numerical goals for the hiring and promotion of designated group members in each occupational category where underrepresentation exists.
5. Longer-term goals for increasing designated group member representation, including a strategy for achieving those goals. These goals may be numerical, qualitative, or both.

SOURCES: Human Resources and Skills Development Canada, "*Guidelines for the Employment Equity Act and Regulations, Guideline 7: Employment Equity Plan,*" at www.hrsdc.gc.ca/eng/lp/lo/lswe/we/legislation/guidelines/gdln7.shtml (accessed June 13, 2011); Employment Equity Act, s.10. Reproduced with the permission of the Minister of Public Works and Government Services, 2011.

STEP SEVEN: MONITOR, REVIEW, AND REVISE THE PLAN

Monitoring and reviewing the plan in conjunction with all workplace parties is essential to assessing the plan's effectiveness in making progress in achieving employment equity. In the absence of careful monitoring, even the best laid plans will fail. With an effective monitoring system, the plan can be revised as necessary to address ineffective strategies or changing circumstances.

connect

Learn more about one company's approach to employment equity online with Connect.

LO 7

Explain pay equity and its implications for HRM.

PAY EQUITY

Women have historically been paid lower wages than men. While the wage gap has narrowed over the years, women still earn approximately 71 cents for every dollar earned by men—a figure that has stayed relatively constant since 1999 to the chagrin of pay equity advocates.[64] However, the earnings gap varies depending on the type of occupation. For example, in 2008, women working in medicine and health-related occupations earned approximately 57 percent as much as men in those occupations and women in business and finance occupations earned only 59 percent of the earnings of their male counterparts. In nonprofessional occupations such as sales and service, women earned about 57 percent of men. While earnings for men and women with a university degree were higher, women still earned approximately 30 percent less than their male counterparts.

Pay Equity
Equal pay for work of equal value.

Pay equity legislation recognizes that work traditionally performed by women has been undervalued as compared with male-dominated jobs, and aims to eliminate systemic gender disparities in pay. All jurisdictions have some form of equal-pay legislation addressing wage inequalities between men and women. While statutes in all jurisdictions promote equal pay for equal work, some jurisdictions have statutes that focus on the work performed and require equal pay for similar or substantially similar work[65] (e.g. male orderlies with nurses' aides). This differs from pay equity legislation in force in other jurisdictions, which invokes a broader analysis of comparing the value of different male- and female-dominated jobs and requiring equal pay for work of equal value[66] (e.g. female-dominated clerical work compared with the male-dominated work of mechanics).

Pay equity legislation is generally enforced through a complaint-based system, meaning that someone has to file a complaint in order to trigger the statutes' enforcement mechanisms. Pay equity programs use a gender-neutral evaluation system to determine which jobs in the employer's organization hold the same value to the employer. The particular criteria by which value is measured vary by jurisdiction, but include some variation of the concepts of skill, effort, and responsibility. Using this system, employers are required to identify pay equity gaps, take steps to close those gaps, and maintain pay equity over time.

Neglecting to correct pay equity gaps can be costly. In 2006, Bell Canada reached an agreement with the Communications, Energy, and Paperworkers Union for more than $100 million in a longstanding pay equity dispute affecting approximately 4,700 workers.[67] In 2005, the Canadian Human Rights Tribunal awarded approximately $150 million in pay equity adjustments dating back 22 years to about 6,000 current and former clerical employees of Canada Post. The Federal Court overturned the Tribunal's decision in February 2010.[68] However, the final word on the matter has not yet been heard as the Supreme Court of Canada has agreed to hear the union's appeal.

MANAGING DIVERSITY

Diversity management is a strategic initiative designed to capitalize on an organization's diverse talent pool. A diverse workforce offers tremendous advantages to an organization not only in terms of varied perspectives and approaches, but also in skill sets and relationships as well as the ability to relate to cultural groups and business communities. Diversity programs are not only beneficial to the internal organization; a successful diversity management plan can affect how the public, partners and customers view the organization, boosting its public image and its profits.

Diversity Management
A strategic initiative designed to capitalize on an organization's diverse talent pool.

Employees of Hewlett-Packard (HP) Canada know that if they discriminate against their colleagues there will be serious and swift consequences. The company's dedication to diversity is one way that it attracts new hires. HP Canada's work through the Safe Space program—a course designed to foster an inclusive environment for gay, lesbian, bisexual, and transgender workers—earned it the title of one of Canada's Best Diversity Employers for 2008.[69] This program is just one of the ways HP Canada creates a safe and inclusive work environment for its employees.

How do companies like HP Canada develop and maintain an effective diversity management program? Below we outline six keys to a successful diversity management plan.

Commitment from the Top

One of the keys to HP Canada's diversity program is a visible commitment from the top—a vital component of any successful corporate initiative. Management has to "walk the talk" and must be accountable to its employees to ensure that it maintains an atmosphere that respects and promotes diversity. Because of this commitment at HP Canada, every report of any conduct that offends the diversity culture at the company is addressed promptly and taken seriously. Such an immediate and resolute approach to defeating conduct in opposition of diversity initiatives is essential.

LO 8

Develop approaches for managing and promoting diversity effectively.

Communication

Open communication is another aspect that is critical to an effective diversity management system. Creating avenues and opportunities for employees to freely voice concerns without fear of reprisal is essential. The system cannot function if employees are hesitant to voice their views and come forward with complaints. To encourage frank and open discussion, those in leadership positions should initiate dialogue and not merely wait for issues to be brought to their attention. Without this dialogue, meaningful change cannot be made. An effective way to facilitate open dialogue about diversity issues is mentoring programs, particularly reverse mentoring programs where junior-level employees are matched with senior members of the organization for the precise purpose of creating a culture of awareness and understanding about diversity issues. Advisory committees are also a valuable vehicle for communication. Boeing Canada Technology has an employment equity and diversity team that meets biweekly to discuss diversity initiatives.[70]

Develop and Implement Diversity Initiatives

Diversity initiatives are virtually endless in type and scope because they are particular to the individual organization. This can make the task of embarking on diversity management daunting. One of the best and most strategic ways to begin the process of developing a diversity program is benchmarking. Learning from those who have had success about what works and what doesn't is critical to making an organization's road to success a little less bumpy than those who have ventured along the path to diversity before. Focusing on the best in diversity management will provide an organization with a competitive advantage.

Every year, Canada's Top 100 Employers project[71] names 100 Canadian employers as best in diversity. Studying and learning from the diversity management initiatives of these and similar employers, and adapting their practices to other organizations, is a far more effective process than attempting to start from scratch. As examples from the best in diversity management demonstrate, diversity initiatives should be built into all aspects of the organization from day-to-day interactions to policies and formal processes including, for example, flexible work practices to address family commitments, selection, hiring, retention, and accommodation.

Ensure a System of Support

In addition to addressing concerns and complaints about diversity from a sensitive and supportive stance, support groups are an important tool in assisting individual employees in coping with ignorance, bigotry, and harassment, as well as feeling more comfortable in bringing diversity issues to light. The gender equity advisory group, targeted mentoring programs, and networking groups for women and lesbian, gay, bisexual, and transgender (LGBT) employees established by Ernst & Young, referenced at the beginning of the chapter, are examples. Intuit Canada established a, LGBT network to provide support and professional development opportunities, as well as a women's network to provide peer mentoring and skills development. Moreover, Proctor & Gamble hosts employee networks for Asian, French, LGBT, black, and Latino groups.[72] Such groups make employees feel more valued in the organization and, at the same time, assist in meeting diversity objectives and improve morale, productivity, loyalty, and service.

Evaluate and Revise Objectives

Setting objectives that can be evaluated and revised is imperative. Absent these markers, an organization cannot properly assess whether its diversity program is achieving its intended results. Just as a company tracks revenue in the business, it should track head count, staff levels, and the diversity mix so that it can determine what is working well and what is not. Speaking to members of diversity task forces or advisory groups where they have been established is also critical, as is seeking feedback from employees regarding their perception of diversity within the organization. Requiring managers to report regularly on progress in meeting diversity objectives makes diversity a priority. Moreover, measurable objectives allow not only for evaluation, but also for rewarding a commitment to achieving diversity success—another method of enforcing the organization's commitment to diversity and increasing its visibility throughout the organization. KPMG has a diversity advisory board that meets quarterly to help direct the company's diversity, inclusion, and equity strategy.

The Royal Bank of Canada (RBC) has a diversity leadership council that meets quarterly, and Telus Corporation has a diversity steering committee and working council to develop and implement diversity-related human resources programs.[73]

Diversity Training and Education

Common to virtually every successful diversity program is a commitment to comprehensive and ongoing diversity training and education. Training that emphasizes management's steadfast commitment to diversity and enables all members of the organization to understand, support, and achieve diversity initiatives provides the organization with the means to achieve a successful diversity management program. Sensitization to diversity, misconceptions about diversity, and communicating how diversity can affect the bottom line are just some of the common aspects of diversity training. Conflict management training, focused on working effectively with the opposite gender and different cultures, is also an effective way to improve the efficiency and productivity of cross-gender and cross-cultural work teams and environments. Research tells us that homogeneous groups make better decisions than diverse groups unless diverse groups are trained in how to capitalize on their diversity.[74] Canadian Pacific Railway hosts a variety of information sessions on topics such as aboriginal spirituality, Islam, Judaism, Buddhism, and learning disabilities. Ernst & Young holds regular leadership training conferences for visible minority and female employees, and HSBC Bank Canada provides training to senior employees on how to develop talented employees from diverse groups.[75]

CURRENT ISSUES REGARDING DIVERSITY AND EQUAL EMPLOYMENT OPPORTUNITY

Because of ongoing changes in Canada's demographics, the composition of most organizations is also becoming increasingly diverse. Statistics Canada predicts that one in four Canadians will be age 65 or older by the year 2031.[76] By the same year, it is estimated that one-third of Canada's population will represent a visible minority.[77] Recently, there has also been more focus on mental health. For example, in British Columbia, while disability remains the most cited ground of human rights complaints, in 2008, mental disabilities formed the basis for approximately 14 percent of disability complaints in British Columbia—a 20 percent increase from 2004–2005.[78] As the characteristics of Canada's population continue to change in conjunction with an increased emphasis on diversity and human rights, greater focus will be placed on important human rights and equality issues such as mandatory retirement and the value of older employees, recognition of foreign qualifications, and the reasonable accommodation of employees with mental disabilities.

A Look Back

Ernst & Young's Lessons in Diversity

At the opening of this chapter, we referred to Ernst & Young's commitment to making diversity a priority across its organization. Ernst & Young's dedication to diversity not only earned it the distinction of being one of Canada's Best Diversity Employers three years running, but also has contributed significantly to the company being recognized as a top employer on various other fronts. The company was also the recipient of several other recent awards including Canada's Top 100 Employers 2010, Best Workplaces in Canada 2009, Alberta's Best Workplaces 2010, Canada's Top Campus Employers 2009, and Progressive Employer of Canada 2009. One of the keys to Ernst

& Young's success includes reverse mentoring programs where junior employees act as mentors to senior leaders at the firm to help foster understanding and awareness of issues such as generational differences, sexual orientation, religion, culture, and gender. A rampant culture of inclusiveness including yearly inclusiveness training and an ethnic diversity taskforce have also helped Ernst & Young create a culture that respects and cultivates diversity.

The initiatives taken by Ernst & Young are an example of the various diversity initiatives that have been implemented by many Canadian employers including Canada's 35 Best Diversity Employers of 2009, such as Hewlett-Packard, RBC, Telus Corporation, and KPMG. Like Ernst & Young, all of these employers have come to recognize that making diversity a priority is not only morally and ethically sound, but also a strategic HRM initiative that reaps significant rewards for the organization.

Questions

1. Despite diversity initiatives such as those at Ernst & Young, women remain significantly underrepresented in the boardrooms of the majority of Canadian businesses and earn less on average than their male counterparts. How would you address these issues in your organization?

2. Experience tells us that complementary skills add value to an organization. Diverse groups have been shown to outperform those made up exclusively of members who share similar abilities. How would you ensure that your organization capitalizes on the diverse talent pool?

3. What issues and/or ethical dilemmas might arise in creating and implementing programs such as those put into practice at Ernst & Young?

4. How can an organization address resistance by employees, discriminatory or otherwise, to diversity programs?

SOURCES: "Flexibility, Inclusiveness, Learning—All Business Essentials: Ernst & Young," Ernst & Young News Release (April 13, 2010) at www.ey.com/CA/en/Newsroom/News-releases/2010-Best-Workplaces (retrieved June 13, 2011); Rachel Caballero and Richard Yerema, "Chosen as One of Canada's Best Diversity Employers for 2010," (March 23, 2010) at www.eluta.ca/diversity-at-ernst-young (retrieved June 13, 2011); "Canada's Best Diversity Employers," canadianimmigrant.ca, at www.canadianimmigrant.ca/careers/workplaceissues/article/3252 (retrieved June 13, 2011).

Summary

Viewing employees as a source of competitive advantage results in dealing with them in ways that are ethical and legal including providing a workplace in which discrimination and harassment are strictly prohibited. An organization's legal environment—especially the laws regarding equality and human rights—has a particularly strong effect on its HRM function. HRM is concerned with the management of people, and government is concerned with protecting individuals. One of HRM's major challenges, therefore, is to perform its function within the legal constraints imposed by the government. Given the ramifications of violating equality and human rights laws (and the moral requirement to treat people fairly regardless of their sex or race), HR and line managers need a good understanding of the legal requirements and prohibitions in order to manage their businesses in ways that are sound, both financially and ethically. Organizations that do so effectively will definitely have a competitive advantage.

Key Terms

Adverse-effect
    discrimination, 85
Bona fide occupational
    qualification
    (BFOQ), 89
Canadian Charter of
    Rights and Freedoms
    (the Charter), 82

Direct discrimination, 85
Discrimination, 84
Diversity management, 113
Employment equity, 106
Employment systems
    review, 111
Harassment, 100
Human rights, 82

Pay equity, 112
Psychological
    harassment, 103
Reasonable
    accommodation, 87
Sexual harassment, 101
Systemic discrimination, 86
Undue hardship, 88

Discussion Questions

1. You smell alcohol when greeting one of your employees on the way into work in the morning. What do you do? What are your obligations under human rights legislation? How do these legal obligations affect your HRM duties and your responsibilities to the organization and other employees?

2. You are tasked with hiring a new sales force for one of the company's new products. Your boss informs you that the CEO has given express instructions to hire people who have similar characteristics to the target market. The consumers are young, attractive, white professionals. What do you do? What are the potential legal implications of your possible courses of action?

3. Some companies have dress codes that require men to wear suits and women to wear dresses. Is this discriminatory? Why?

4. The concept of a bona fide occupational requirement can require that different standards be applied to different employees (e.g., In the *Meiorin* case the court found that different standards should apply to women versus men.) Do you agree with this approach? Why? What are some alternatives?

5. Sexual harassment can be found even where a victim voluntarily participates in the offending conduct, including having sexual intercourse with the harasser. Do you think this is fair? Why?

6. A major complaint of employers about the duty to accommodate under human rights legislation is that the costs of making reasonable accommodations will reduce their ability to compete with businesses (especially foreign ones) that do not face these requirements. Is this a legitimate concern? How should employers and society weigh the costs and benefits of the duty to accommodate?

7. Both employment equity and pay equity legislation target certain designated groups for preferential treatment. Do you think this is necessary? Do you think this is fair? Why?

8. Your organization is located in a major city centre with a culturally diverse population, but your company employs few visible minorities. You are the HR manager with overall responsibility for staffing. How can you tap into the diverse talent pool outside the company's doorstep to attract, recruit, and retain visible minorities and ensure that their talent is dispersed throughout all levels of your organization?

Self-Assessment Exercise

Take the following self-assessment quiz. For each statement, circle T if the statement is true or F if the statement is false. Then check your answers with the answer key below.

What do you know about sexual harassment?

1. A man cannot be the victim of sexual harassment. T F

2. The harasser must be the victim's manager or a manager in another work area. T F

3. Sexual harassment charges can be filed only by the person who directly experiences the harassment. T F

4. The best way to discourage sexual harassment is to have a policy that discourages employees from dating each other. T F

5. Sexual harassment is not a form of sex discrimination. T F

6. After receiving a sexual harassment complaint, the employer should let the situation cool off before investigating the complaint. T F

7. Sexual harassment is illegal only if it results in the victim being laid off or receiving lower pay. T F

8. An employer has no obligation to investigate a complaint of sexual harassment if it believes that the allegations are untrue. T F

9. Sexual harassment does not include incidents between employees outside the workplace. T F

10. Sexual harassment cannot occur between employees who have a history of having engaged in a consensual sexual relationship. T F

11. Conduct will not be found to comprise sexual harassment where the complainant has provoked the behaviour by wearing inappropriately revealing attire at work or by flirting or joking with the alleged perpetrators. T F

12. A person cannot be expected to know that his or her conduct is offensive if the complainant never raised any objection to it. T F

Answer Key: Did you notice that none of the statements above are true? If you circled "F" for all ten statements, congratulations! You know the difference between facts and fiction about sexual harassment. Try quizzing friends who haven't read this chapter and compare results.

Exercising Strategy: Home Depot's Bumpy Road to Equality

Home Depot is the largest home-products firm selling home repair products and equipment for the do-it-yourselfer. Founded 20 years ago, it now boasts 100,000 employees and more than 900 warehouse stores nationwide. The company's strategy for growth has focused mostly on one task: build more stores. In fact, an unwritten goal of Home Depot executives was to position a store within 30 minutes of every customer in the United States. In addition, Home Depot has tried hard to implement a strategy of providing superior service to its customers. The company has prided itself on hiring people who are knowledgeable about home repair and who can teach customers how to do home repairs on their own. This strategy, along with blanketing the country with stores, has led to the firm's substantial advantage over competitors.

But Home Depot ran into some legal problems. During the company's growth, a statistical anomaly has emerged. About 70 percent of the merchandise employees (those directly involved in selling lumber, electrical supplies, hardware, and so forth) were men, whereas about 70 percent of operations employ-ees (cashiers, accountants, back-office staff, and so forth) were women. Because of this difference in the late '90s, several years ago a lawsuit was filed on behalf of 17,000 current and former employees as well as up to 200,000 rejected applicants. Home Depot explained the disparity by noting that most female job applicants had experience as cashiers, so they were placed in cashier positions; most male applicants express an interest in or aptitude for home repair work such as carpentry or plumbing. However, law-yers argued that Home Depot was reinforcing gender stereotyping by hiring in this manner.

More recently, five former Home Depot employees sued the company, charging that it had dis-criminated against visible-minority workers at two stores in southeast Florida. The five alleged that they were paid less than white workers, passed over for promotion, and given critical performance reviews based on race. "The company takes exception to the charges and believes they are without merit," said Home Depot spokesman Jerry Shields. However, the company faced other racial dis-crimination suits as well, including one filed by the Michigan Department of Civil Rights.

To avoid such lawsuits in the future, Home Depot could have resorted to hiring and promoting by quota, ensuring an equal distribution of employees across all job categories—something that the company wanted to avoid because such action would undermine its competitive advantage. However, the company has taken steps to broaden and strengthen its own nondiscrimination policy by adding sexual orientation to the written policy. In addition, company president and CEO Bob Nardelli (until 2007) announced in the fall of 2001 that Home Depot would take special steps to protect benefits for its more than 500 employees serving in the Army reserves who had been activated. "We will make up any difference between their Home Depot pay and their military pay if it's lower," said Nardelli. "When they come home [from duty], their jobs and their orange aprons are waiting for them."

In settling the gender discrimination suit, the company agreed to pay $65 million to women who had been steered to cashiers' jobs and had been denied promotions. In addition, the company promised that every applicant would get a "fair shot." Home Depot's solution included leveraging technology to make better hiring decisions that ensure the company is able to maximize diversity.

Home Depot instituted its Job Preference Program, an automated hiring and promotion system, across all its stores at a cost of $10 million. It set up kiosks where potential applicants can log on to a computer, complete an application, and undergo a set of prescreening tests. This process weeds out unqualified applicants. Then the system prints out test scores along with structured interview questions and examples of good and bad answers for the managers interviewing those who make it through the prescreening. In addition, the Home Depot system is used for promotions. Employees are asked to constantly update their skills and career aspirations so they can be considered for pro-motions at nearby stores.

The system has been an unarguable success. Managers love it because they are able to get high-quality applicants without having to sift through mounds of résumés. In addition, the system seems to have accomplished its main purpose. The number of female managers has increased 30 percent and the number of minority managers by 28 percent since the introduction of the system. In fact, David Borgen, the co-counsel for the complainants in the original lawsuit, states, "No one can say it can't be done anymore, because Home Depot is doing it bigger and better than anyone I know."

SOURCES: "Home Depot Says Thanks to America's Military; Extends Associates/Reservists' Benefits, Announces Military Discount," company press release (October 9, 2001); S. Jaffe, "New Tricks in Home Depot's Toolbox?" *BusinessWeek* Online (June 5, 2001) at www.businessweek.com; "HRC Lauds Home Depot for Adding Sexual Orientation to Its Non-discrimination Policy," Human Rights Campaign (May 14, 2001) at www.hrc.org; "Former Home Depot Employees File Racial Discrimination Lawsuit," *Diversity at Work* (June 2000) at www.diversityatwork.com; "Michigan Officials File Discrimination Suit against Home Depot," *Diversity at Work* (February 2000) at www.diversityatwork.com; M. Boot, "For Complainants' Lawyers, There's No Place Like Home Depot," *The Wall Street Journal,* interactive edition (February 12, 1997).

Questions

1. If Home Depot was correct in that it was not discriminating, but simply filling positions consistent with those who applied for them (and very few women were applying for merchandising positions), given your reading of this chapter, was the firm guilty of discrimination? If so, under what theory?

2. How does this case illustrate the application of new technology to solving issues that have never been tied to technology? Can you think of other ways technology might be used to address diversity/employment equity issues?

Managing People: Civility in the Workplace

In some Canadian jurisdictions, there are now health and safety laws dealing with workplace violence, workplace harassment, and even psychological harassment. All Canadian jurisdictions have human rights laws that prohibit discriminatory practices and harassment based on prohibited grounds such as race, cultural background, age, and disability. Another way to approach the same kind of objective that motivated these kinds of legislative initiatives is to focus on creating and fostering a civil workplace.

The issue of civility, or more likely incivility, in the workplace has made it onto the radar at an increasing number of organizations in Canada and beyond. Presumably, every organization would agree that treating colleagues with respect and courtesy is an unwritten—or even written— rule at any workplace; however, a recent study concluded that 10 percent of workers reported experiencing uncivil behaviours on a daily basis and 20 percent said they were targets of incivility weekly. Those employees experiencing this kind of behaviour in the workplace report higher stress levels, greater rates of absenteeism, and lower productivity. Over time, chronic exposure to incivility can lead to withdrawal behaviours, with some employees eventually leaving their jobs. Likewise, researchers argue that what begins as a little rude behaviour can escalate into retaliatory behaviours between colleagues ("You ignored my suggestion in that meeting and were sarcastic about it, so I am going to make sure you don't get invited to the informal team lunch") and even spiral into much more serious toxic behaviours including sabotage, overt manifestations of discrimination, or even assault. And legal challenges founded on disrespect, discrimination, and wrongful dismissal can generally be blamed on the kinds of poor working relationships that are the hallmark of an uncivil workplace.

Experts feel that the real challenge lies in convincing some organizations to make creating and sustaining a civil workplace a priority. Many continue to perceive incivility among coworkers as "personality conflicts" and something that will get worked out among colleagues. In light of the effect that incivility can have on productivity, employee well-being, and the overall functioning of the organization—as well as the potential legal implications of tacitly supporting an uncivil workplace—more and more companies are addressing the issue head on by acknowledging it and implementing policies or creating programs that foster a civil workplace.

In the health-care industry, an uncivil workplace transcends employee issues to have repercussions for both patient care and patient outcomes. Following the implementation of a successful initiative designed for the U.S. Veteran Affairs Administration, the CREW (Civility, Respect and Engagement at Work) program was reworked and revamped to suit the needs of Canada's health-care system. Headed by Dr. Michael Leiter, a professor of psychology and the director of Acadia's Centre for Organizational Research and Development in Halifax, the CREW project was implemented at nine health-care centres including three hospitals in Nova Scotia and two in Ontario.

The program was structured around being aware of and modifying behaviours that are within the control of any given workgroup—how coworkers and managers treat one another. The program began with questionnaires in which the employees rated the level of civility and support received by their coworkers and supervisors. Over the course of the program, the information was then acted on through a series of weekly half-hour meetings facilitated by members of the staff themselves and in which concerns surrounding treatment, support, and civility, and its impact on employees and on work, were discussed. As Dr. Leitner explains, "Each meeting set a target: 'Here is the way we want to react around each other; keep that in mind and work on it for the week and report back on your experiences at the next meeting,'"

In follow-up surveys, a sense of increased civility prevailed within the CREW teams and incidences of incivility among coworkers and between employees and managers decreased significantly, dropping by as much as 30 percent in some teams. Similarly, perceived stress levels (down by 15 percent), intention to quit, and absenteeism (down by 15 percent during the CREW program) all decreased in the group within the CREW program; whereas, in the control group, these metrics stayed relatively unchanged.

Because we spend so much time at work, the type of working relationship we enjoy with our coworkers and managers colours our overall work experience and can impact the level of health and safety we feel at work. It may seem obvious, but as the CREW project demonstrated, when individuals are exposed to civil behaviours in the workplace and are given an opportunity to work on sustaining them, they feel better overall and are healthier and happier at work. These kinds of improved relationships mean a better workplace and could have positive outcomes for organizational commitment and engagement levels at work. And, it doesn't take much to accomplish. Experts agree that both organizations and individual employees have a relatively straightforward role to play in creating and sustaining a civil workplace. Organizations need to ensure that civility becomes an organizational priority, and one that is discussed regularly and publicly in meetings from the boardroom to the shop floor. To support this, companies need to create and socialize an acceptable code of conduct with clear enforcement standards and repercussions for any uncivil behaviour. Standards need to be enforced consistently and resources need to be made available for everything from protecting whistle-blowers to introducing workplace civility initiatives. For employees, it's really a matter of following the "golden rule" and treating others as you would like to be treated by being respectful, professional, courteous, and supportive.

To an uncomfortable extent, our society celebrates individual self-expression without taking sufficient account of how an individual interacts with other individuals in a group setting. Some of our role models, including actors, musicians, and even politicians, are able to get away with and even be celebrated for conduct that is demeaning and disrespectful to other individuals or recognizable groups of people. Sometimes their conduct has no target whatsoever, but is simply boorish and worthy of nothing but pity, and yet they are cheered for their individuality. In the workplace, both as a matter of law and good sense, it is civil, sensible, and respectful conduct that ought to win our applause and approval—that is the kind of behaviour that is good for business and most likely to create a workplace environment that operates within legal expectations, particularly in terms of human rights and modern health and safety laws.

SOURCES: Arla Day, Michael P. Leiter, Heather K. Spence Laschinger, and Debra Gilin Oore, "Developing Healthy Workplaces: What's Civility Got to Do with It?" *Good Company* (February 11, 2010) at www.phwa.org/resources/goodcompany/newsletter/article/158 (accessed June 13, 2011); Michael Leitner, *CREW Improves What Really Matters* at www.qwqhc.ca/uploads/CREW Improves What Really Matters-633828213885625000.pdf (accessed March 2, 2011); Immen Wallace "Defusing the Uncivil workplace" *CTV News* at www.ctv.ca/generic/generated/static/business/article1886834.html (accessed June 13, 2011); Lisa Spiegel *CREW: Civility, Respect and Engagement at Work* at www.qwqhc.ca/knowledge-exchange-practices-details.aspx?id=75 (accessed June 13, 2011).

Questions

1. In a multicultural workplace, what forms of incivility could give rise to human rights issues?

2. Staying with the multicultural workplace, discuss how an employer could work with employees in a proactive and mutually beneficial way to try to build bridges of understanding so that comments and actions are not taken out of context or misinterpreted in the journey from one cultural group to another.

3. Consider how rude remarks or jokes that feature "put-downs" of people from other cultures or with different sexual orientation might constitute not simply a lack of civility, but also a violation of human rights legislation in terms of being discriminatory or even the basis for a harassment complaint.

4. What measures should an employer take to create a civil and respectful workplace?

5. What kind of training and follow-up might be suitable so that a workplace is not only civil and respectful, but also complies with legislative requirements in terms of how the employer and management team members treat employees, and also how employees treat each other?

Analysis and Design of Work and Human Resource Planning

Enter the World of Business

Job Design: Back to the Future at Toyota

In 2007, Toyota Motor Corporation surpassed General Motors as the world's largest car-maker. This was the accomplishment of a long-term goal that could be obtained only through a strong focus on rapid growth and expansion. However, in the process of focusing on this goal, many insiders at Toyota believed that the organization was straying from some of its core values, especially as this related to the organization's structure and design of jobs. In fact, in 2009, Toyota reported its first annual operating loss since 1938, and due to the economic recession, the company had so much extra capacity that it had to lay off workers for the first time since 1950. As industry observer Tokai Gakuin, noted, "Toyota was so focused on becoming the world's largest automaker that it failed to cut production quickly enough in 2008, as the economic crisis struck the United States, its largest market."

The steps that the company took to restore profitability provide a lesson in how to compete via organizational design and job design. First, with respect to manufacturing jobs, the fast-paced expansion of Toyota's plants both in Japan and North America was, in some cases, purchased at the price of reduced quality standards. The number of recalls for manufacturing defects tripled in the last three years, and quality ratings by analysts such as J.D. Powers and Associates slipped noticeably. Toyota had to issue a series of recalls for vehicles all around the world between November 2009 and August of 2010 because of faulty accelerator pedals, problems with "all-weather" floor mats, brakes, steering-column components, defective front-drive shafts (in Tacoma pickup trucks), issues with stability control programs, and more. In response, the company streamlined jobs, tightened job descriptions and enhanced training programs in a way that slowed production but increased quality. For example, quality control inspectors were required to put on a glove and massage the door of every Camry in a soft circular motion in search of tiny dents for roughly 15 minutes prior to sending the car further down the production line.

With respect to sales jobs, because of Toyota's ambitious quotas, sales personnel often used high-pressure techniques to get customers to purchase cars more quickly, and then, after the sale was made, often handed over the cars without properly inspecting them. Thus, even when customers loved their cars, they often hated their car-buying experience. Toyota quickly responded to this problem by sending out five-person evaluation teams to sales units that were ranked low in customer satisfaction and reanalyzed all the jobs in those units—all the way from the top manager to the car washer. In each case, the team tried to redesign the way jobs were done to create a personal link between each customer and each person who was responsible for the car, all of which resulted in slower sales but happier customers.

Finally, with respect to managerial jobs, Toyota's middle-level managers made the case that in contrast to the organization's traditional, slow, consensus-based, decision-making process with a long-term focus, too many recent decisions were made single-handedly by the president, Katsuaki Watanabe. For example, middle-level managers noted how Watanabe quickly flip-flopped on where to build factories, first increasing production overseas when the Japanese yen was strong (and hence making production in Japan more expensive), and then quickly reverting production back within North America when the yen lost value. Because currency exchange rates fluctuate a great deal over short time periods, the short-term gain in profitability often resulted in long-term inefficiencies associated with starting up and closing factories. Watanabe was eventually replaced as president by Akio Toyoda, the grandson of the organization's founder, Kiichiro Toyoda, who promised to restore the organization's traditional approach to organizational structure and job design.

In early 2011, however, Toyota's found itself facing another major crisis when a devastating earthquake and tsunami hit Japan on March 11. The natural disaster made a direct hit on an area that encompassed Toyota's production base, causing an immediate shutdown of four subsidiary plants that produce parts and vehicles. Fortunately, there were no injuries but the company's dealers, suppliers, and many other partners were also affected by the damage. The company immediately formed an emergency task force to assess the extent of damage and its impact to its employees and all aspects of the business. By March 14 the company suspended all vehicle production in Japan. Although manufacturing of replacement parts started up again by March 22, suspension of vehicle production continued into late April. However, when new vehicle production did resume, it was on a limited basis at 50 percent volume because of parts availability. The impact slowly spread overseas, and on April 19 production was interrupted in Canada, where scheduling now included a reduced, three-day workweek with production levels held at 50 percent in the days the plant was up and running. In addition, all North American plants would suspend production for one week in late May. By April 22, the company announced that "after an in-depth analysis of its suppliers affected by the earthquake and tsunami ... global production will begin to ramp up as soon as July in Japan and August in North America, with all models back to normal production by November or December 2011." With the worst of the crisis now seemingly behind them, Toyota's leaders are still faced with ongoing availability problems of approximately 150 electronic, rubber, and plastic-related parts affecting new-vehicle production. And although the company has announced that it plans to continue securing parts from its original suppliers, it has also indicated that it will consider substituting parts from other suppliers. In such an event, concerns with quality will no doubt once again come under intense scrutiny as Toyota struggles to restore stability to its sales and production facilities worldwide.

SOURCES: D. Welch, "Staying Paranoid at Toyota," *BusinessWeek,* July 2, 2007, pp. 80–82; I. Rowley, "Even Toyota Isn't Perfect," *BusinessWeek,* January 11, 2007, pp. 33–36; N. Shirouzu, "Toyota to Change Leader Amid Sales Slump," *The Wall Street Journal,* December 28, 2008, pp. A1–A2; N. Shirouzu and J. Murphy, "A

Scion Drives Toyota Back to the Basics," *The Wall Street Journal,* February, 24, 2009, pp. B1–B3; Toyota USA Newsroom, http://pressroom.toyota.com/Safety-Recall; www.toyota.ca, Company Info/News and Event: News and updates from March 13–April 22, 2011.

INTRODUCTION

In Chapter 2, we discussed the processes of strategy formulation and strategy implementation. Strategy formulation is the process by which a company decides how it will compete in the market-place; this is often the energizing and guiding force for everything it does. Strategy implementation is the way the strategic plan gets carried out in activities of organizational members. We noted five important components in the strategy implementation process, three of which are directly related to the human resource management function (task design, selection training, and development of people and reward systems) and two that are directly *influenced* by HRM (organizational structure and types of information and decision processes), Thus, in this chapter we will discuss two HRM practices utilized to make strategy associated with task design and organizational structure become reality: job analysis and design and human resources planning.

The chapter begins with a three-part discussion about the analysis and design of work, and reveals considerations that go into making informed decisions about how to create and link jobs. Next, the important role of human resources planning is discussed. Factors that influence the supply and demand for labour are explained, as well as what HRM can do to create and execute human resource plans and policies that support their firm's competitive advantage in a dynamic environment.

It should be clear from the outset of this discussion that there is no "one best way" to design jobs and structure organizations. The organization needs to create a fit between its environment, competitive strategy, and philosophy on the one hand, and its jobs and organizational design on the other. For example, in our opening story, we saw how Toyota became number 1 in sales volume by following one approach, but then changed this approach when it decided to put more emphasis on quality and customer satisfaction. Failing to design effective organizations and jobs has important implications for competitiveness. Many years ago, some believed that the difference between North American auto producers and their foreign competitors could be traced to North American workers; however, when companies like Toyota and Honda came into North America and demonstrated clearly that they could run profitable car companies with North American workers, the focus shifted to processes and organization. It is now clear that the success of many of these non–North American firms was attributable to how they structured the work and designed their organizations. For example, Toyota's plants in Cambridge and Woodstock, Ontario, differ in many ways from the General Motors plant in Oshawa, but the nature of the workforce is not one of them.[1]

The fields of job analysis and job design have extensive overlap, yet in the past they have been treated differently.[2] Job analysis has focused on analyzing existing jobs to gather information for other human resource management practices such as selection, training, performance appraisal, and compensation. Job design, on the other hand, has focused on redesigning existing jobs to make them more efficient or more motivating to jobholders.[3] Thus job design has had a more proactive orientation toward changing the job, whereas job analysis has had a passive, information-gathering orientation. We will show in this chapter how these two approaches are interrelated, but first we must look at "big-picture" issues related to work-flow analysis and organizational structure.

WORK-FLOW ANALYSIS AND ORGANIZATION STRUCTURE

In the past, HR professionals and line managers have tended to analyze or design a particular job in isolation from the larger organizational context. *Work-flow design* is the process of analyzing the tasks necessary for the production of a product or service, prior to allocating and assigning these tasks to

LO 1

Analyze an organization's structure and work-flow process, identifying the output, activities, and inputs in the production of a product or service.

a particular job category or person. Only after we thoroughly understand work-flow design can we make informed decisions regarding how to initially bundle various tasks into discrete jobs that can be executed by a single person.

Organization structure refers to the relatively stable and formal network of vertical and horizontal interconnections among jobs that constitute the organization. Only after we understand how one job relates to those above (supervisors), below (subordinates), and at the same level in different functional areas (marketing versus production) can we make informed decisions about how to redesign or improve jobs to benefit the entire organization.

Finally, work-flow design and organization structure have to be understood in the context of how an organization has decided to compete. Both work-flow design and organization structure can be leveraged to gain competitive advantage for the firm, but how one does this depends on the firm's strategy and its competitive environment.

Analyzing Work Flow: Work Outputs, Processes, and Inputs

Nearly all organizations have a common need to clearly identify the outputs of work, to specify the quality and quantity standards for those outputs, and to analyze the processes and inputs necessary for producing outputs that meet the quality standards.[4] This concept of a work-flow process is depicted in Figure 4.1 and provides an approach for analyzing the work process of a department as a means of examining jobs in the context of an organization.

Work Outputs   Every work unit—whether a department, team, or individual—seeks to produce some output that others can use. An output is the product of a work unit and can be an identifiable

FIGURE 4.1   Developing a Work-Unit Activity Analysis

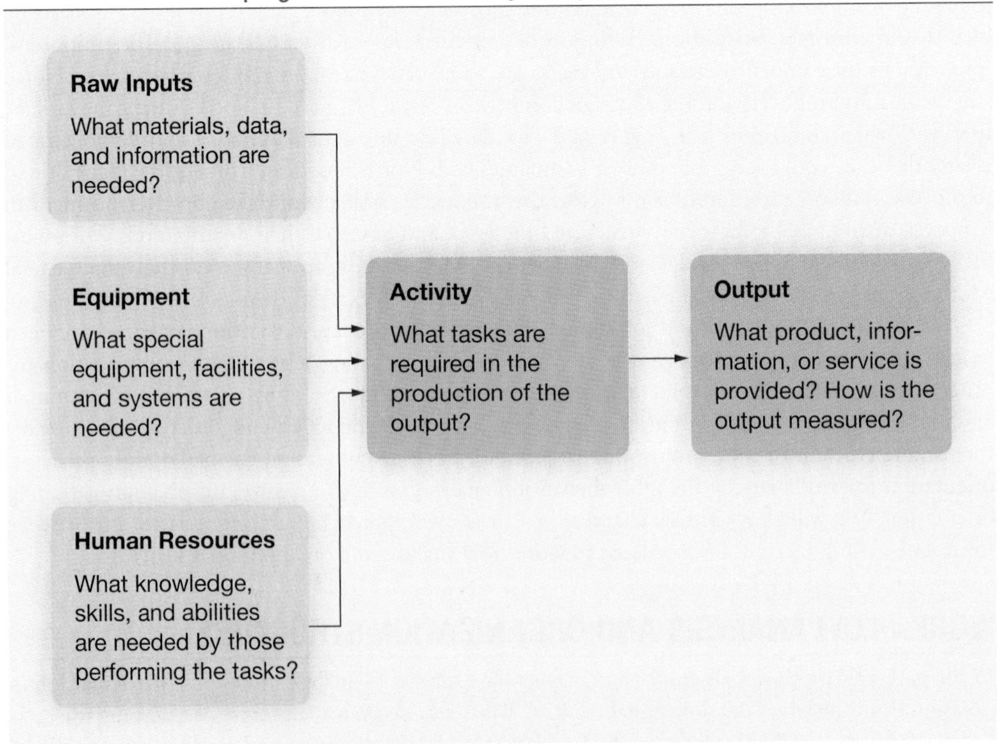

thing (a completed purchase order, an employment test, or a hot, juicy hamburger) or a service (lawn cutting, selling a home, cutting hair). We often picture an organization only in terms of the product that it produces, and then we focus on that product as the output. For example, at Toyota it is an automobile. However, merely identifying an output or set of outputs is not sufficient. Once these outputs have been identified, it is necessary to specify standards for the quantity or quality of these outputs.

Learn more about analyzing work outputs using ProMES online with Connect. **connect**

Work Processes   Once the outputs of the work unit have been identified, it is possible to examine the work processes used to generate the output. The work processes are the activities that members of a work unit engage in to produce a given output. Every process consists of operating procedures that specify how things should be done at each stage of the development of the product. These procedures include all the tasks that must be performed in the production of the output. The tasks are usually broken down into those performed by each person in the work unit. Of course, in many situations where the work that needs to be done is highly complex, no single individual is likely to have all the required skills. In these situations, the work may be assigned to a team, and team-based job design is becoming increasingly popular in contemporary organizations.[5] In addition to providing a wider set of skills, team members can back each other up, share work when any member becomes overloaded, and catch each other's errors. However, for teams to be effective, it is essential that the level of task interdependence (how much they have to cooperate) matches the level of outcome interdependence (how much they share the reward for task accomplishment).[6] Teams also have to be given the autonomy to make their own decisions in order to maximize the flexible use of their skill and time and thus promote problem solving.[7] In addition, even in teams it is critical to establish individual accountability of behaviour.[8]

Again, to design work systems that are maximally efficient, a manager needs to understand the processes required in the development of the products for that work unit. Often, as workloads increase within a work group, the group will grow by adding positions to meet these new requirements. However, when the workload lightens, members may take on tasks that do not relate to the work unit's product in an effort to appear busy. Without a clear understanding of the tasks necessary to the production of an output, it is difficult to determine whether the work unit has become overstaffed. Understanding the tasks required allows the manager to specify which tasks are to be carried out by which individuals and eliminate tasks that are not necessary for the desired end. This ensures that the work group maintains a high level of productivity.

Work Inputs   The final stage in work-flow analysis is to identify the inputs used in the development of the work unit's product. As shown in Figure 4.1, these inputs can be broken down into the raw inputs, equipment, and human resources needed to perform the tasks. *Raw inputs* consist of the materials that will be converted into the work unit's product. *Equipment* refers to the technology and machinery necessary to transform the raw materials into the product. The final inputs in the work-flow process are the *human resources*; that is, the skills and abilities necessary to perform the tasks. Obviously, the human resources consist of the workers available to the company, but increasingly organizations are recruiting the inputs of customers as a critical input in designing processes and products.

To compete successfully, organizations often have to scour the world for the best raw materials, the best equipment, and the people with the best skills, and then try to integrate all of this seamlessly in the work processes that merge all these factors. IBM has been in the forefront of incorporating new technologies to get leaner, and it has also searched far and wide for people with the best sets of skills as well. Some low-skill call centre jobs that IBM needs are done by workers from China, Brazil, or

Eastern Europe, depending on where the call originates and the language spoken by the customer. The key to this strategy is not just going where one can get cheap labour, but, instead, going where one can get the exact kind of labour needed at the best price. As noted by Robert Moffat, IBM's senior vice president, "Some people think the world is centered in India and that's it. Globalization is more than that. Our customers need the right skills, in the right place at the right time."[9] This approach is evident in those IBM operations that require high-skill employees who have to work in close proximity to customers. For example, IBM Canada's K–12 Education maintains staff across Canada to provide Technical Support Services. These services include toll-free numbers for customer telephone support, websites for patching, and on-site technical support to help with training and problem solving.[10]

Indeed, research consistently shows that creating a good fit between the skills and values of workers and the tasks and missions they are assigned is a powerful determinant of organizational success that cannot be taken lightly.[11] As the "Competing through Globalization" box shows, new technologies such as "innovation portals" can help promote the speed with which global teams can be created, coordinated, and monitored to enhance organizational effectiveness.

connect

Learn more about analyzing work inputs online with Connect.

Competing Through Globalization

Innovation Portals: Creating Openings for Global Teams

Due to the increased complexity of work, as well as the increased demand to compete based upon speed, most organizations have changed the job design process from one focused on individual, stand-alone jobs to jobs that were designed for teams. Increasingly, however, the globalization of product and labour markets has created additional pressure for quick collaboration within global teams. One response to this demand has been the creation of "innovation portals," that is, technology that helps individual employees with a problem or innovative idea to tap into the global network of talent within the organization or even outside its own boundaries.

For example, at IBM, innovation portals take the form of specially designated "chat rooms," where any employee with a new idea or project can recruit team members, line up resources, and tap into market research or engineering skills available anywhere within this large and sprawling multinational firm. An entrepreneurial IBM employee can often create a virtual global team with cross-functional skills to tackle some problem in as little as two hours. For example, in one case, when a client needed to launch a new service that would allow video streaming for cell phones, an IBM project leader was able to organize a 20-person team that included staff from 10 different countries in just two weeks. The entire project was completed within two months. On average, IBM's own internal research suggests that the use of such portals has decreased the length of time it takes to get projects up and running from six months to 30 days. In the last three years alone, IBM has employed more than 90,000 workers in such global teams, and these groups have been responsible for leading 70 new businesses and creating 10 new products.

Because of its size and global scope, IBM tends to use its portals to create teams where all the members are IBM employees. This is often not an option for smaller firms that are not international in their scope. Hence, many smaller firms use innovation portals to link specialists within their own companies to independent contractors or specialists in other companies. There are many different models for such global collaboration, but the key dimensions by which most differ involve how the problem is structured and how dominant any one member of the team is in terms of command and control. For example, the "Orchestra Model" of global teams is one where there is a well-structured problem and one dominant member of the team who controls the process. A Boeing 787 project used a portal owned by Boeing to recruit partners from the company's own list of suppliers but also included independent contractors to help develop components for Boeing's new airplane. Boeing was clearly in control of this well-scripted and planned project, but it was able to reach far outside its own local talent base to create global teams for accomplishing complex tasks.

Alternatively, some portals follow a "Jam Session Model" of global teaming, where the problem is unstructured and there are no dominant members. For example, the Tropical Disease Initiative was an innovation portal project where many different academics and scientists concerned about fighting global diseases came together to take on diseases that were not widespread enough to create a strong profit potential for commercial pharmaceutical teams. This democratically led community of scientists tended to focus not on well-structured problems (e.g., curing malaria), but instead on emergent opportunities, where some new finding in the scientific literature was studied for its potential to provide assistance in treating any of a large number of diseases off a fixed list of "unprofitable diseases."

Regardless of what model is employed, innovation portals create opportunities to create global teams that can accomplish tasks that are well beyond the scope of any one of its members.

SOURCES: P. Engardio, "Managing a Global Workforce," *BusinessWeek* (August 20, 2007), pp. 48–51; J. Marquez, "Connecting a Virtual Workforce," *Workforce Management* (September 22, 2008), pp. 18–28; S. Nambison and M. Sawhney, *The Global Brain* (Philadelphia, PA: Wharton School Publishing, 2008).

Organization Structure

Whereas work-flow design provides a longitudinal overview of the dynamic relationships by which inputs are converted into outputs, organization structure provides a cross-sectional overview of the static relationships between individuals and units that create the outputs. Organization structure is typically displayed via organizational charts that convey both vertical reporting relationships and horizontal functional responsibilities.

Dimensions of Structure Two of the most critical dimensions of organization structure are centralization and departmentalization. **Centralization** refers to the degree to which decision-making authority resides at the top of the organizational chart as opposed to being distributed throughout lower levels (in which case authority is *decentralized*). **Departmentalization** refers to the degree to which work units are grouped based on functional similarity or similarity of work flow.

Learn more about organizing a business school online with Connect.

Centralization
Degree to which decision-making authority resides at the top of the organizational chart.

Departmentalization
Degree to which work units are grouped based on functional similarity or similarity of work flow.

Structural Configurations Although there are an infinite number of ways to combine centralization and departmentalization, two common configurations of organization structure tend to emerge in organizations. The first type, referred to as a *functional structure,* is shown in Figure 4.2 on page 132. A functional structure, as the name implies, employs a functional departmentalization scheme with relatively high levels of centralization. High levels of centralization tend to go naturally with functional departmentalization because individual units in the structures are so specialized that

FIGURE 4.2 The Functional Structure

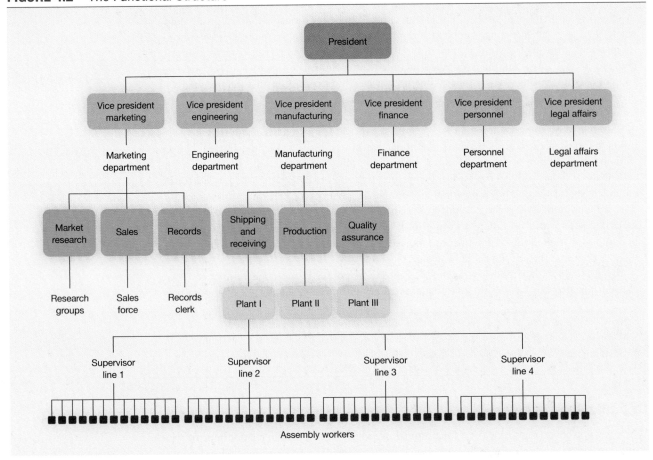

SOURCE: Adapted from J. A. Wagner and J. R. Hollenbeck, *Organizational Behavior: Securing Competitive Advantage*, 3rd ed. (New York: Prentice Hall, 1998).

members of the unit may have a weak conceptualization of the overall organization mission. Thus, they tend to identify with their department and cannot always be relied on to make decisions that are in the best interests of the organization as a whole.

Alternatively, a second common configuration is a *divisional structure,* an example of which is shown as Figure 4.3. Divisional structures combine a divisional departmentalization scheme with relatively low levels of centralization. Units in these structures act almost like separate, self-sufficient, semiautonomous organizations. The organization shown in Figure 4.3 is divisionally organized around different products, but organizations can also be divisionally organized around geographic regions or around different clients.

connect

Learn more about structural configurations online with Connect.

Because of their work-flow focus, their semiautonomous nature, and their proximity to a homogeneous consumer base, divisional structures tend to be more flexible and innovative. They can detect and exploit opportunities in their respective consumer base faster than the more centralized

FIGURE 4.3   Divisional Structure: Product Structure

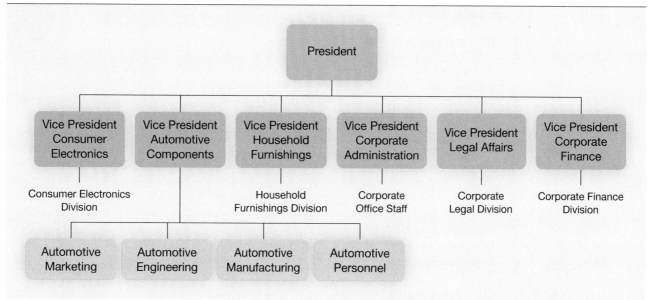

SOURCE: Adapted from J. A. Wagner and J. R. Hollenbeck, *Organizational Behavior: Securing Competitive Advantage,* 3rd ed. (New York: Prentice Hall, 1998).

functionally structured organizations. The perceived autonomy that goes along with this kind of structure also means that most employees prefer it and feel they are more fairly treated than when they are subject to centralized decision-making structures.[12] See the "Competing through Sustainability" box on page 134, which explains how Microsoft converted from a functional structure to a divisional structure.

On the downside, divisional structures are not very efficient because of the redundancy associated with each group carrying its own functional specialists. Also, divisional structures can "self-cannibalize" if the gains achieved in one unit come at the expense of another unit. For example, Kinko's stores are structured divisionally with highly decentralized control. Each manager can set his or her own price and has autonomy to make his or her own decisions. But the drawback to this is lack of coordination in the sense that "every Kinko's store considers every other Kinko's store a competitor; they vie against each other for work, they bid against each other, competing on price."[13]

Functional structures are most appropriate in stable, predictable environments, where demand for resources can be well anticipated and coordination requirements between jobs can be refined and standardized over consistent repetitions of activity. This type of structure also helps support organizations that compete on cost, because efficiency is central to making this strategy work. Divisional structures are most appropriate in unstable, unpredictable environments, where it is difficult to anticipate demands for resources, and coordination requirements between jobs are not consistent over time. This type of structure also helps support organizations that compete on differentiation or innovation, because flexible responsiveness is central to making this strategy work. To increase their flexibility, many contemporary organizations are changing their direction away from functional structures to more divisional structures, but this is often more difficult than it seems.[14] In many cases, norms and habits that are often created by the original structure persist even after the boxes on the organizational chart have been rearranged, and the cultural influences can be as important as structural influences when it comes to determining outcomes of such transitions.[15]

Competing Through Sustainability

Microsoft Gets Its "Mojo" Back

Throughout the 1990s, revenue growth at Microsoft averaged more than 30 percent per year, making it one of the most successful business organizations in the world. However, with success comes new challenges, and both external and internal pressures created problems that eventually cut into Microsoft's dominance. Internally, as the organization increased in size and scope, the decision-making process at Microsoft was slowing to a crawl, and Microsoft experienced turnover among key personnel, many of whom became millionaires as the company grew, but whose intrinsic motivation was low because they did not feel that they had enough autonomy in their jobs. As one manager noted, "In the past, the system was optimized for people to get stuff done. Now, everybody is always preparing for a meeting." Left unattended, such issues threaten the economic side of any company's sustainability, or what Adam Werbach, an expert in sustainability describes as "thriving in perpetuity." The loss of key talent undermines the firm's ability to compete when good people and their ideas are snapped up by competitors, and in high-tech businesses rapid decision making is essential for developing new products and getting them to market first.

To turn this situation around, CEO Steve Ballmer took unprecedented steps in strategically restructuring the organization to respond to these new competitive pressures. The question guiding this reorganization was how best to divvy up the 55,000 Microsoft employees and define their jobs so that innovation and productivity could be maximized, while turnover and bureaucratic impediments could be minimized. Turning first to the organization's structure, it was clear that Microsoft was too centralized given its current size.

Ballmer wanted to decentralize the organization and create a large number of semiautonomous business divisions (e.g., a Personal Computer Division, a Server Division, a Gaming Division) that had responsibility for their own profit and loss figures. Some leaders at Microsoft initially resisted this move, however, because they felt that all Microsoft products had to work seamlessly together, and independent divisions would not provide for effective coordination and collaboration across units. Ballmer realized, "We'd have to come up with a structure unlike anything out there, to simultaneously give divisions enough autonomy to manage themselves, yet make it easier for them to cooperate and integrate the technology."

The solution was a structure that relied on seven autonomous divisions that were supported by a new concept in work-flow design that formalized how product development would both proceed within divisions and then be transferred across divisions. The seven divisions divided the work up into separate units for operating systems (Windows Client), desktop applications (Information Worker), business services (Business Solutions), servers systems (Server and Tools), mobile devices (Mobile and Embedded Devices), Internet services (MSN), and X-Box and other gaming applications (Home Entertainment). Within each unit, a new product development process called the Software Engineering Strategy laid out a universally applied procedure that dictated how a project moved from the "incubator phase" to the "definer phase" to the "owner phase," stipulating where the "participants," "reviewers," and "coaches" should provide input into the process.

One of the immediate results of the new structure was that it clearly revealed how much money was being lost in certain divisions such as MSN and the Home Entertainment Divisions relative to the tried-and-true Windows Client Division. Although disheartening in some cases, this at least provided a benchmark from which to measure improvement as the divisions moved forward. More critically, however, these structural changes at the organization level spilled down to individual jobs, both clarifying who was supposed to do what and motivating individuals to sink or swim in their new, more autonomous roles.

The 2005 reorganization wasn't a magic bullet that provided instant relief, but it helped reduce the turnover rates among the key players by increasing their intrinsic motivation. As one of Microsoft's new division leaders noted, all the new divisional managers "sense a chance to do one last great thing in their working lives." And such motivation would be needed when the company's much-flawed Vista operating system was finally launched in 2007, after a painful six-year development process. Born within the old Microsoft structure and culture, teams worked simultaneously on Vista features, in isolation from one another and oblivious to each other's schedules. Small wonder the end product proved to be incompatible with printers, device drivers, and more. More than just an embarrassing flop, it opened the door to humiliation as Apple responded with aggressive "I'm a Mac" ads, insinuating Microsoft was an old geezer whose day was done. Even worse, the corporate market opted to skip the Vista upgrade altogether. By 2008 Ballmer tweaked the structure a bit more and the company downsized 5,000 workers—a first for Microsoft.

Then, in October 2009 (after Microsoft's first decrease in fiscal revenue ever from 2008's $60 billion to 2009's $58.4 billion), Windows 7 was launched. Vista's successor was the result of a much faster three-year development cycle and a much more open approach to product development that included beta testing among 8 million users prior to liftoff. Windows 7 was highly compatible, had "cool" features and needed less computing horsepower than Vista. Market analysts predicted that about 25 percent of corporate customers would be upgrading within two years.

But Windows 7 wasn't Microsoft's only resurgence in 2009. That summer the company launched a record-setting number of new products such as Zune (Microsoft's MP3 player), and Bing (a new search engine), and entered the retail market to compete with Apple stores. The company also launched a number of overhauls of existing products such as Windows Server and cut a landmark search engine deal with Yahoo. By late 2010 sales rebounded to $62.8 billion and the company was focused on the right thing: consumers. As Darren Houston, vice president of the consumer and online division says, "The new way forward is about listening to consumers, creating things that people really want." Sounds like a plan that might compensate for Apple's lead in smartphones and the tablet market. In the high-tech world, the race is always on, but at the end of Q3 2010, Microsoft sales are strong again.

SOURCES: J. Greene, "Microsoft's Midlife Crisis," *BusinessWeek,* April 19, 2004, pp. 88–98; J. Kerstetter, "Gates and Ballmer on Making the Transition," *BusinessWeek,* April 19, 2004, pp. 96–97; G. B. Schlender, "Ballmer Unbound: How Do You Impose Order on a Giant Runaway Mensa Meeting?" *Fortune,* January 26, 2004, pp. 117–24.; C. Campbell, "How Microsoft Got Hip," *Maclean's,* October 26, 2009, p. 44; Microsoft Company Record, Hoover's Online, accessed November 1, 2010; R. Guth, "Ballmer Ponders Changes at Microsoft; Chief's Conundrum: Central Planning, or Unit Autonomy," *Wall Street Journal,* June 27, 2008, p. B6; J. O'Brien and K. Thai, "Microsoft Reboots," *Fortune,* 160(8), 98–108. R. Waters, "Microsoft Sales Strength Eases Wall St. Concerns," *Financial Times,* London (UK); October 29, 2010, p. 22; A. Werbach, *Strategy for Sustainability*, Harvard Business Press, Boston, 2009, p. 9.

Structure and the Nature of Jobs Finally, moving from big-picture issues to lower-level specifics, the type of organization structure also has implications for the design of jobs. Jobs in functional structures need to be narrow and highly specialized. Workers in these structures (even middle managers) tend to have little decision-making authority or responsibility for managing coordination between themselves and others. The choice of structure also has implications for people who assume the jobs created in functional versus divisional structures. For example, managers of divisional structures often need to be more experienced or high in cognitive ability relative to managers of functional structures.[16] Finally, flatter structures also have implications for organizational culture in terms of ethics and accountability.

In our next section, we cover specific approaches for analyzing and designing jobs. Although all of these approaches are viable, each focuses on a single, isolated job. These approaches do not necessarily consider how that single job fits into the overall work flow or structure of the organization. Thus, to use these techniques effectively, we have to understand the organization as a whole. Without this big-picture appreciation, we might redesign a job in a way that might be good for that one job but out of line with the work flow, structure, or strategy of the organization. In an effectively structured organization, people not only know how their job fits into the bigger picture, but also how everyone else fits as well. Thus, when one of Microsoft's managers says, "I'm not confused about who to go to in order to get something done—there's greater clarity now," this is a sign that the new structure may be meeting the internal needs of the organization's members.[17]

connect Learn more about the structure and nature of jobs online with Connect.

LO 2

Understand the importance of job analysis in strategic human resource management.

Job Analysis
The process of getting detailed information about jobs.

JOB ANALYSIS: THE BUILDING BLOCK OF HRM

Job analysis refers to the process of getting detailed information about jobs. The process has deep historical roots—going all the way back to Socrates. In his description of a "just" state, Socrates argued that society needed to recognize three things: (1) that individuals differ in their abilities; (2) unique aptitude requirements exist for different occupations; and (3) in order to achieve high-quality performance, society must attempt to place people in occupations that best suit their aptitudes. In other words, for society (or an organization) to succeed, it must have detailed information about the requirements of jobs (through job analysis) and it must ensure that a match exists between the job requirements and individuals' aptitudes (through selection).[18]

Job analysis is such an important activity to HR managers that it has been called the building block of everything that HRM does.[19] This statement refers to the fact that almost every human resource management program or activity requires some type of information that is gleaned from job analysis: selection, performance appraisal, labour relations, health and safety, training and development, job evaluation, career planning, compliance with human rights legislation, work redesign, and human resource planning. For example, in human resource planning (a topic covered in the last half of this chapter), planners analyze an organization's human resource needs in a dynamic environment and develop activities that enable a firm to adapt to change. This planning process requires accurate information about the levels of skill required in various jobs to ensure that enough individuals are available in the organization to meet the human resource needs of the strategic plan.[20]

While job analysis is clearly important to the HR department's various activities, it is also of pivotal importance to line managers who rely on the various "products" of HRM to do their jobs well. First, managers must have detailed information about all the jobs in their work group to understand the work-flow process. Second, managers need to understand the job requirements to make intelligent hiring decisions since managers will often interview prospective applicants and recommend who should receive a job offer. Third, a manager is responsible for ensuring that each individual is performing satisfactorily (or better). This requires the manager to evaluate how well each person is performing and to provide feedback to those whose performance needs improvement. Again, this requires that the manager clearly understand the tasks required in every job. Finally, it is also the manager's responsibility to ensure that the work is being done safely, knowing where potential hazards might manifest themselves and creating a climate where people feel free to interrupt the production process if dangerous conditions exist.[21]

Learn more about the importance of job analysis to HRM activities online with Connect.

Nature and Sources of Job Analysis Information

While many sources of information are useful in conducting job analysis, two types of information are especially useful: job descriptions and job specifications. A **job description** is a list of the tasks, duties, and responsibilities (TDRs) that a job entails. TDRs are observable actions. For example, a clerical job requires the jobholder to type on a computer keyboard. If you were to observe someone in that position for a day, you would certainly see some word processing or data input occurring. Detailed information about the work performed in the job (that is, the TDRs) makes it possible for a manager and others to determine how well an individual is meeting each job requirement.

Job Description
A list of the tasks, duties, and responsibilities that a job entails.

Learn more about sample job descriptions online with Connect.

A **job specification** is a list of the knowledge, skills, abilities, and other characteristics (KSAOs) that an individual must have to perform the job. *Knowledge* refers to factual or procedural information that is necessary for successfully performing a task. A *skill* is an individual's level of proficiency at performing a particular task. *Ability* refers to a more general enduring capability that an individual possesses. Finally, *other characteristics* might be personality traits such as one's achievement motivation or persistence. Thus KSAOs are characteristics about people that are not directly observable; they are observable only when individuals are carrying out the TDRs of the job. If someone applied for the clerical job discussed, you could not simply look at the individual to determine whether he or she possessed keyboarding skills. However, if you were to observe that individual creating a new document, you could assess the keyboarding skill level. When a manager is attempting to fill a position, it is important to have accurate information about the characteristics a successful jobholder must have, which requires focusing on the KSAOs of each applicant.

Job Specification
A list of the knowledge, skills, abilities, and other characteristics (KSAOs) that an individual must have to perform a job.

In performing job analysis, one question that often arises is: Who should make up the group of incumbents that are responsible for providing the job analysis information? Whatever job analysis method you choose, the process of job analysis entails obtaining information from people familiar with the job. We refer to these people as *subject-matter experts* because they are experts in their knowledge of the job.

In general, it will be useful to go to the job incumbent to get the most accurate information about what is actually done on the job. This is especially the case when it is difficult to monitor the person who does the job. However, particularly when the job analysis will be used for compensation purposes, incumbents might have an incentive to exaggerate their duties. Thus, you will also want to ask others familiar with the job, such as supervisors, to look over the information generated by the job incumbent. This serves as a check to determine whether what is being done is congruent with what is supposed to be done in the job. One conclusion that can be drawn from this research is that incumbents may provide the most accurate estimates of the actual time spent performing job tasks. However, supervisors may be a more accurate source of information about the importance of job duties. Incumbents also seem more accurate in terms of assessing safety-related risk factors associated with various aspects of work, and in general the further one moves up the organizational hierarchy, the less accurate the risk assessments.[22] Although job incumbents and supervisors are the most obvious and frequently used sources of job analysis information, other sources, such as customers, can be helpful, particularly for service jobs. Finally, when it comes to analyzing skill levels, external job analysts who have more experience rating a wide range of jobs may be the best source.[23] Depending on the job, additional information could be derived from company documentation such as accident reports, customer complaint summaries or anything else that is helpful. Such information would provide additional, valuable information to various methods of conducting job analysis, or even provide multisource validation.[24]

LO 3

Choose the right job analysis technique for a variety of human resource activities.

Job Analysis Methods

There are various methods for analyzing jobs and no "one best way." In this section, we discuss four ways to analyze jobs: the job analysis interview, observation and self-reports, the National Occupational Classification (NOC), and the position analysis questionnaire. Although most managers would not have time to use each of these techniques in the exact manner suggested, the four provide some anchors for thinking about both quantitative and qualitative approaches, as well as whether a task or person-based approach should be used in conducting job analysis.

Job Analysis Interview   The job analysis interview is a highly accessible, qualitative approach that even small companies without a formal HRM function can implement using simple guidelines for the process. Job analysis interviews are usually conducted using a job analysis questionnaire to provide consistency in the type of data collection across all jobs being analyzed. The process may be done by a professional job analyst or an in-house job analysis committee under the guidance of HRM. A job analysis committee could include a supervisor and/or manager, several employees, and a union representative if appropriate. Interviews may be done one-on-one, or with groups, or even a combination.

connect

Learn more about job analysis interview questionnaires online with Connect.

Observation and Self-Reports   Information gleaned from job analysis interviews is often combined with two other sources of information—observation and self-reports (such as diary entries or work logs) of job incumbents. For example, a job analyst or supervisor may interview and then observe a group of Technical Service Representatives (TSRs) working in a call centre to better understand and even measure work activities, the working environment itself (noisy, interruptions, stressful), work stoppages caused by equipment failures, etc. The TSRs could also be asked to keep a diary of every activity they undertake and to estimate the time spent on each activity, recording the same interruptions or downtimes on phones due to equipment failure. In some jobs, employees regularly keep logs that track their daily activities; these logs can also provide information. In the case of TSRs, call activity is often contained in computerized call logs that record frequency and length of calls, hang-ups etc.

The National Occupational Classification   Creating job descriptions and job specifications (the primary outputs of job analysis) from data collected through interviews, observation, and other sources can be a daunting task. However, Human Resources and Skills Development Canada has created a very helpful resource to assist in finding the right words and phrases to accurately describe tasks and responsibilities. The National Occupational Classification (NOC) is a database that organizes the work Canadians do into over 30,000 job titles and into 520 occupational descriptions. Each occupational description is assigned a four digit code based on the NOC classification matrix.

The NOC code is useful to employers because it is integrated with occupational statistics concerning labour market information applicable to human resources planning, career counselling, recruitment, and compensation or pay equity issues. Once the code is determined, users can easily locate occupational profiles written in standardized language to begin writing job descriptions and specifications. Such profiles contain general descriptions of the occupation, the kinds of workplaces where the occupation is found, sample job titles, main duties of the occupational group, employment requirements, and other additional information. Human Resources and Skills Development Canada (HRSDC) has made the process of writing job descriptions easier by providing a downloadable "Job Descriptions: An Employers Handbook" (2007) PDF document free on the NOC website.[25]

In addition, since each occupational profile is also linked to labour market information, employers, employees, unions, and job seekers can check national wage information, projected labour supply and demand, changes in levels of employment over time and a range of other information. For example, accessing the Canadian Occupational Projection System (COPS) through the "Working in Canada" tool provided by the Government of Canada will help employers anticipate specific skill shortages. This supports the processes of job design and human resources planning, making it easier to be more proactive and less vulnerable when faced with labour supply fluctuations.[26]

Learn more about how NOC codes are assigned online with Connect.

McGraw Hill **connect**™

Position Analysis Questionnaire (PAQ)   We finish this section with the PAQ, a quantitative technique that is also one of the broadest and most well-researched instruments for analyzing jobs. Moreover, its emphasis on inputs, processes, relationships, and outputs is consistent with the work-flow analysis approach that we used in leading off this chapter (Figure 4.1 on p. 128).

The PAQ is a standardized job analysis questionnaire containing 194 items.[27] These items represent work behaviours, work conditions, and job characteristics that can be generalized across a wide variety of jobs. They are organized into six sections:

1. *Information input* —Where and how a worker gets information needed to perform the job.
2. *Mental processes*—The reasoning, decision making, planning, and information processing activities that are involved in performing the job.
3. *Work output*—The physical activities, tools, and devices used by the worker to perform the job.
4. *Relationships with other persons*—The relationships with other people required in performing the job.
5. *Job context*—The physical and social contexts where the work is performed.
6. *Other characteristics*—The activities, conditions, and characteristics other than those previously described that are relevant to the job.

The job analyst is asked to determine whether each item applies to the job being analyzed. The analyst then rates the item on six scales: extent of use, amount of time, importance to the job, possibility of occurrence, applicability, and special code (special rating scales used with a particular item). These ratings are submitted to the PAQ headquarters, where a computer program generates a report regarding the job's scores on the job dimensions.

Research has indicated that the PAQ measures 32 dimensions and 13 overall dimensions of jobs (such as clerical, technical, or supervisory activities), and that

While observing this group of window assemblers would be a useful way to gather job data, conducting individual and/or group interviews with both workers and supervisors would be essential to gather accurate data. Because of the physical nature of the work shown here, accurate job specifications would also be especially important for other HRM activities such as effective hiring and prevention of work-related injuries.

a given job's scores on these dimensions can be very useful. The significant database has linked scores on certain dimensions to scores on subtests of the General Aptitude Test Battery (GATB). Thus, knowing the dimension scores provides some guidance regarding the types of abilities that are necessary to perform the job. Obviously, this technique provides information about the work performed in a format that allows for comparisons across jobs, whether those jobs are similar or dissimilar. Another advantage of the PAQ is that it covers the work context as well as inputs, outputs, and processes.

However, the PAQ has some disadvantages. One problem is that to fill out the test, an employee needs the reading level of a college or university graduate; this disqualifies some job incumbents from the PAQ. In fact, it is recommended that only job analysts trained in how to use the PAQ should complete the questionnaire, rather than job incumbents or supervisors. Indeed, the ratings of job incumbents tend to be lower in reliability relative to ratings from supervisors or trained job analysts.[28] A second problem associated with the PAQ is that its general, standardized format leads to rather abstract characterizations of jobs. Thus it does not lend itself well to describing the specific, concrete task activities that comprise the actual job, and it is not ideal for developing job descriptions or redesigning jobs. HRM or managers in a small company doing job analysis for the first time would probably look for a simpler and more accessible tool to gather job information, such as the job analysis interview described earlier.

connect

Learn more about the Position Analysis Questionnaire (PAQ) online with Connect.

LO 4

Identify the tasks performed and the skills required in a given job.

Dynamic Elements of Job Analysis

Although we tend to view jobs as static and stable, in fact, jobs tend to change and evolve over time. Those who occupy or manage the jobs often make minor, cumulative adjustments to the job that try to match either changing conditions in the environment or personal preferences for how to conduct the work.[29] Indeed, although there are numerous sources for error in the job analysis process,[30] most inaccuracy is likely to result from job descriptions simply being outdated. For this reason, in addition to statically defining the job, the job analysis process must also detect changes in the nature of jobs.

For example, in today's world of rapidly changing technology, products, and markets, some people have begun to question whether the concept of "the job" is simply a social artifact that has outlived its usefulness. Indeed, many researchers and practitioners are pointing to a trend referred to as "dejobbing" in organizations. This trend consists of viewing organizations as a field of work needing to be done rather than a set of discrete jobs held by specific individuals. Also, jobs tend to change with changes in the economy in the sense that economic downturns tend to be associated with organizational downsizing efforts. Research suggests that successful downsizing efforts almost always entail some changes in the nature, and not just the number, of jobs.[31] In fact, in the most recent recession of 2008, the new job requirements for the reduced set of jobs left over after downsizing efforts tend to be broader in scope and come with less close supervision relative to the jobs prior to the economic downturn.[32] Failure to take into consideration the nature of the new jobs created after downsizing events is critical because, without support from HR, survivors of downsizing events tend to be less committed to the organization and have higher rates of subsequent turnover when the economy returns to normal.[33]

LO 5

Understand the different approaches to job design and various trade-offs that may be required.

JOB DESIGN

So far we have approached the issue of managing work in a passive way, focusing only on understanding what gets done, how it gets done, and the skills required to get it done. Although this is necessary, it is a very static view of jobs, in that jobs must already exist and that they are already

Evidence-Based HR

Faster Teams Ensure the Purse Stays "Sold"

Louis Vuitton is a maker of top-of-the-line bags and purses sold in high-end retail stores such as Toronto's Holt Renfrew, and in high-traffic tourist locations such as Louis Vuitton Banff or at the Hotel Vancouver. In its original work system, the company designed work processes centred on individuals. Each Vuitton worker did highly specialized tasks such as cutting leather and canvas, stitching seams, attaching the handle, and so on. Then, when each person was finished, he or she would sequentially send the bag to the next person in line. A typical line would be staffed by 20 to 30 people. In 2006, the company switched to a team-based design where teams of six to nine people work together simultaneously to assemble the bags. Workers are cross-trained in multiple tasks and can flexibly change roles and shift production from one bag to another if any one bag becomes a "hit" and another becomes a "dud." The length of time it took to produce the same bags dropped from eight days to one day, and Vuitton customers, who had often had to be placed on waiting lists for the most popular products, were able to get their hands on the product much more quickly. This speed to market is critical given the emotional nature of this purchase—after all, if one is ready to spend $700 on a tote bag, it is best not to have to delay that decision.

SOURCE: Based on C. Passariello, "Louis Vuitton Tries Modern Methods on Factory Line," *The Wall Street Journal*, October 9, 2006, pp. A1, A15; www.louisvuitton.com.

assumed by the stakeholders involved to be structured in the one best way. However, a manager may often be faced with a situation in which the work unit does not yet exist, requiring jobs within the work unit to be designed from scratch. Sometimes workloads within an existing work unit are increased, or work group size is decreased while the same workload is required. Finally, sometimes the work is not being performed in the most efficient manner. In these cases, a manager may decide to change the way that work is done in order for the work unit to perform more effectively and efficiently. This requires redesigning the existing jobs, such as the decision at Louis Vuitton to switch to a team-based job design, described in the "Evidence-Based HR" box.

Job design is the process of defining how work will be performed and the tasks that will be required in a given job. **Job redesign** refers to changing the tasks or the way work is performed in an existing job. To effectively design jobs, one must thoroughly understand the job as it exists (through job analysis) and its place in the larger work unit's work-flow process (work-flow analysis). Having a detailed knowledge of the tasks performed in the work unit and in the job, a manager then has many alternative ways to design a job. This can be done most effectively through understanding the trade-offs between certain design approaches.

Research has identified four basic approaches that have been used among the various disciplines (such as psychology, management, engineering, and ergonomics) that have dealt with job design issues.[34] Although these four approaches comprehensively capture the historical approaches to this topic, one still needs to go beyond such broad category levels to get a full appreciation of the exact nature of jobs and how they can be changed.[35] All jobs can be characterized in terms of how they fare according to each approach; thus a manager needs to understand the trade-offs of emphasizing one approach over another. In the next section we discuss each of these approaches and examine the implications of each for the design of jobs. Table 4.1 displays how jobs are characterized along each

Job Design
The process of defining the way work will be performed and the tasks that will be required in a given job.

Job Redesign
The process of changing the tasks or the way work is performed in an existing job.

Table 4.1 Major Elements of Various Approaches to Job Design

The mechanistic approach	The ergonomic/ biological approach
Specialization	Physical demands
Skill variety	Ergonomics
Work methods autonomy	Work conditions
The motivational approach	The perceptual–motor approach
Decision-making autonomy	Job complexity
Task significance	Information processing
Interdependence	Equipment use

SOURCE: From Michael A. Campion and Paul W. Thayer, "Job Design: Approaches, Outcomes, and Trade-Offs," *Organizational Dynamics,* Winter 1987, Volume 15, No. 3. Copyright © 1987, with permission from Elsevier.

of these dimensions. The Work Design Questionnaire (WDQ), a specific instrument that reliably measures these and other job design characteristics, is available for companies wishing to comprehensively assess their jobs on these dimensions.[36]

Mechanistic Approach

The mechanistic approach has roots in classical industrial engineering. *Scientific management* was one of the earliest and best-known statements of the mechanistic approach.[37] It advocated taking a scientific approach (such as conducting time-and-motion studies) to identify the most efficient movements for workers to make. Once the "one best way" to perform the work was identified, workers were selected based on their ability to do the job, trained in the standard "one best way" to perform the job, and offered monetary incentives to motivate them to work at their highest capacity.

The scientific management approach evolved into the mechanistic approach, which results in simple, meaningless jobs that reduce an organization's need for and dependence on high-skilled individuals. If a worker leaves, a new employee can be trained to perform the job quickly and inexpensively. Many jobs structured this way are performed in developing countries where low-skilled and inexpensive labour is abundant.

Motivational Approach

The motivational approach to job design has roots in organizational psychology and management literature and, in many ways, emerged as a reaction to mechanistic approaches to job design. It focuses on the job characteristics that affect psychological meaning and motivational potential, and it views attitudinal variables (such as satisfaction, intrinsic motivation, job involvement, and behavioural variables such as attendance and performance) as the most important outcomes of job design. The prescriptions of the motivational approach focus on increasing the meaningfulness of jobs through interventions such as job enlargement, job enrichment, and the construction of jobs around sociotechnical systems.[38]

A model of how motivational job design affects employee reactions is the "Job Characteristics Model," developed by Richard Hackman and Greg Oldham[39], which is illustrated in Figure 4.4. According to this model, jobs can be described in terms of five characteristics. *Skill variety* is the extent to which the job requires a variety of skills to carry out the tasks. *Task identity* is the degree to which a job requires completing a "whole" piece of work from beginning to end. *Autonomy* is the degree to which the job allows an individual to make decisions about the way the work will be carried out. *Feedback* is the extent to which a person receives clear information about performance effectiveness from the work itself. *Task significance* is the extent to which the job has an important impact on the lives of other people. Although all five characteristics are important, the belief that the task is significant because performing it well leads to outcomes one values may be the most critical motivational aspect of work.[40] This can often be enhanced by making it clear to the worker how his or her job affects other people, whether they are customers, coworkers, or society in general.[41]

These five job characteristics determine the motivating potential of a job by affecting the three critical psychological states of experienced meaningfulness, responsibility, and knowledge of results. According to the job characteristics model, when the core job characteristics (and thus the critical psychological states) are high, individuals will have a high level of internal work motivation. This is expected to result in higher quantity and quality of work as well as higher levels of job satisfaction.[42] Of the three critical psychological states, research suggest that "experienced meaningfulness may be the most important when it comes to managing work-related stress."[43]

Job design interventions emphasizing the motivational approach tend to focus on increasing the meaningfulness of jobs. Much of the work on job enlargement (broadening the types of tasks

FIGURE 4.4 The Job Characteristics Model

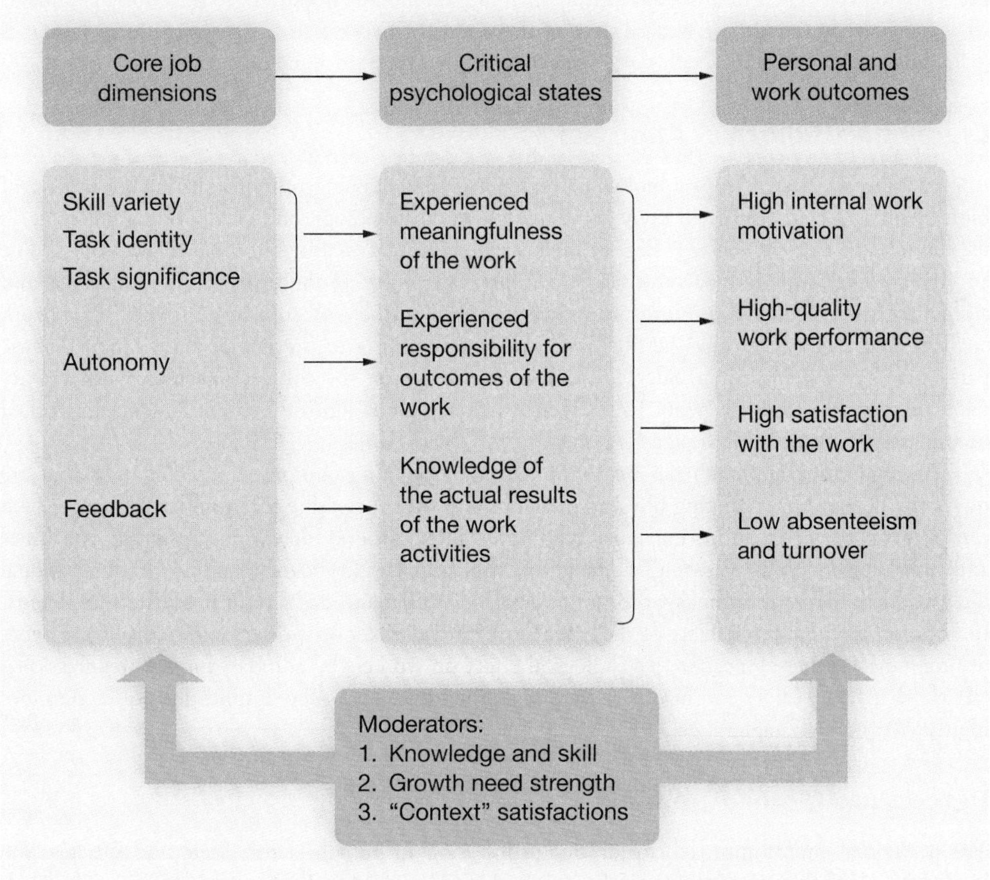

SOURCE: J. RICHARD HACKMAN & GREG R. OLDHAM, WORK REDESIGN, 1st, © 1980. Printed and electronically reproduced by permission of Pearson Education, Inc., Upper Saddle River, New Jersey.

performed), job enrichment (adding complexity and meaningfulness to a person's work), and self-managing work teams (empowering workers by adding more decision-making authority to jobs), has its roots in motivational work design. In self-managing work teams, leadership is not the sole prerogative of one person, but rather is distributed throughout the team, and research shows that this can enhance group performance—especially in service jobs where there is a great deal of direct interpersonal interaction between team members and clients.[44] Not all workers respond positively to enriched jobs like these because they require some degree of flexibility and responsiveness to other people, but with the right workers, interventions such as these have been found to have dramatic effects on employee motivation.[45]

In some cases, even work that may not be that interesting can be made significant by clarifying the link between what workers do and the outcomes of their work, perhaps far down the chain. For example, in medicine, a stent is an expandable wire form or perforated tube that is inserted into an artery to help promote blood flow after a heart operation. The actual work that goes into stent production is an assembly-line process where each worker does a very small and, some might argue, boring task. To help increase the meaningfulness of this work, however, the company sponsors a party each year where line workers get to meet people whose lives were saved by the stents that were produced on that line. This is often a moving emotional experience for both parties and helps the employees see the impact of their work in a context where this would not naturally happen.[46] Thus, although at some point it might be necessary to pay workers in order to motivate them, it is even more important to show job incumbents why their jobs are important. Indeed, one of the secrets behind effective transformational leaders is their ability to help workers see the larger meaning in what they are doing on a day-to-day basis.[47]

Ergonomic/Biological Approach

Approaching job design from a biological perspective and drawing primarily from the sciences of biomechanics (i.e., the study of body movements), work physiology, and occupational medicine, is usually referred to as *ergonomics*. **Ergonomics** is the science of creating a proper fit between people and their work, taking into account safety, comfort, ease of use, productivity and performance, and aesthetics.[48] The goal is to minimize physical strain on workers by structuring the physical work environment around the way the human body works, seeking to prevent physical fatigue, aches, pains, and health complaints. Such research focuses more on the context in which work activity takes place rather than the work itself. Hence issues such as lighting, space, and hours worked become salient issues in job design.[49]

Ergonomics
The science of creating a proper fit between people and their work, taking into account safety, comfort, ease of use, productivity and performance, and aesthetics.

The ergonomic approach has been applied in redesigning equipment used in jobs that are physically demanding, reducing physical demands and thus increasing the numbers of people who can perform them. In addition, many ergonomic interventions focus on redesigning machines and technology, such as adjusting the height of the computer keyboard to minimize occupational illnesses (such as carpal tunnel syndrome) or designing chairs and desks to fit posture requirements. In addition to the direct effects of these kinds of interventions on worker well-being, these types of programs also have a positive psychological effect on workers by emphasizing an organizational climate that values safety and health.[50] We discuss the health and safety implications of ergonomics in greater detail in Chapter 12.

Perceptual–Motor Approach

The perceptual–motor approach to job design has roots in human-factors literature. Whereas the biological approach focuses on physical capabilities and limitations, the perceptual–motor approach focuses on human mental capabilities and limitations. The goal is to design jobs in a way that ensures they do not exceed people's mental capabilities and limitations. This approach generally tries to improve reliability, safety, and user reactions by designing jobs to reduce their information-processing requirements. In designing jobs, one looks at the least capable worker and then constructs job requirements that an individual of that ability level could meet. Similar to the mechanistic approach, this approach generally decreases the job's cognitive demands.

Recent changes in technological capacities hold the promise of helping to reduce job demands and errors, but in some cases, these developments have actually made the problem worse. The term "absence presence" has been coined to refer to the reduced attentive state that one might experience when simultaneously interacting with multiple media. For example, someone might be talking on a cell phone while driving a car, or surfing the net while attending a business meeting, or checking e-mail while preparing a presentation. In all these cases, the new technology serves as a source of distraction from the primary task, reducing performance and increasing the opportunities for errors.[51] Indeed, research shows that on complex tasks, even very short interruptions can break one's train of thought and derail performance. Thus, e-mail servers that have a feature that signals the arrival of each incoming message might best be turned off if the job incumbent cannot resist the temptation to interrupt ongoing activity.[52]

In addition to external disruptions, information processing errors are also increased in any context that requires a "handoff" of information from one person to another, and thus managers and work teams involved will need to create processes to ensure errors are decreased.

Learn more about job design online with Connect.

HUMAN RESOURCE PLANNING

Of course, employers and human resource managers do not exist in a vacuum. In many cases, global movements, political pressures, cultural preferences, and product market developments all simultaneously influence the supply and demand for labour. This dynamic nature of managing human resources makes the field challenging and difficult, but such complexity also provides a great opportunity to carve out unique and sustainable sources of competitive advantage if managers want to find a better way of doing business relative to their competitors. Such firms grow and prosper, while those that fail to forecast the future and plan accordingly risk going out of business.

Accordingly, we now turn our attention to factors that influence the supply and demand for labour, and, in particular, what human resources managers can do in terms of planning and executing human resource policies that give their firms competitive advantage in a dynamic environment.

Two of the major ways that societal trends and events affect employers are through (1) consumer markets, which affect the demand for goods and services, and (2) labour markets, which affect the supply of people to produce goods and services. In some cases, the market might be characterized by a labour surplus. In other cases, the market may be characterized by a shortage of labour. Reconciling the difference between the supply and demand for labour presents a challenge for organizations, and how they address this will affect their overall competitiveness.

There are three keys to effectively utilizing labour markets to one's competitive advantage. First, companies must have a clear idea of their current configuration of human resources. In particular, they need to know the strengths and weaknesses of their present stock of employees. Second, organizations must know where they are going in the future and be aware of how their present configuration of human resources relates to the configuration that will be needed. Third, where there are discrepancies between the present configuration and the configuration required for the future, organizations need programs that will address these discrepancies. Under conditions of a labour surplus, this may mean creating an effective downsizing intervention. Under conditions of a labour shortage, this may mean waging an effective recruitment campaign.

The remainder of this chapter looks at tools and technologies that can help an organization develop and implement effective strategies for leveraging labour market "threats" into opportunities to gain competitive advantage. We will lay out the actual steps that go into developing and implementing a human resource plan, taking into account recent trends and practices (such as downsizing, employing temporary workers, outsourcing, and flexible work arrangements) that can have a major impact on the firm's bottom line and overall reputation.

THE HUMAN RESOURCE PLANNING PROCESS

LO 6

Discuss how to align a company's strategic direction with its human resource planning and determine the labour demand and supply for workers in various job categories.

An overview of human resource planning is depicted in Figure 4.5. The process consists of forecasting, goal setting and strategic planning, and program implementation and evaluation. We discuss each of these stages in the next sections of this chapter.

Forecasting

Forecasting
The attempts to determine the supply of and demand for various types of human resources to predict areas within the organization where there will be future labour shortages or surpluses.

The first step in the planning process is **forecasting**, as shown in the top portion of Figure 4.5. In personnel forecasting, the HR manager attempts to ascertain the supply of and demand for various types of human resources. The primary goal is to predict areas within the organization where there will be future labour shortages or surpluses.

Forecasting, on both the supply and demand sides, can use either statistical methods or judgmental methods. Statistical methods are excellent for capturing historic trends in a company's demand for labour, and under the right conditions they give predictions that are much more precise than those that could be achieved through subjective judgments of a human forecaster. On the other hand, many important events that occur in the labour market have no historical precedent; hence, statistical methods that work from historical trends are of little use in such cases. For example, because the depth and scope of the recession in 2008 was larger than anyone had experienced since the Great Depression in the 1930s, making predictions about how big General Motors needed

FIGURE 4.5 Overview of the Human Resource Planning Process

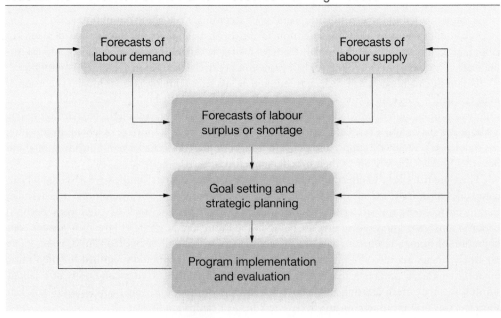

to be and what kinds of products it should be selling led to contentious debate. With no historical precedent, one must rely on the pooled subjective judgments of experts, and their "best guesses" might be the only source from which to make inferences about the future. Typically, because of the complementary strengths and weaknesses of the two methods, companies that engage in human resource planning use a balanced approach that includes both statistical and judgmental components.

Determining Labour Demand   Typically, demand forecasts are developed around specific job categories or skill areas relevant to the organization's current and future state. Once the job categories or skills are identified, the planner needs to seek information that will help predict whether the need for people with those skills or in that job category will increase or decrease in the future. Organizations differ in the sophistication with which such forecasts are derived.

At the most sophisticated level, an organization might have statistical models that predict labour demand for the next year given relatively objective statistics on leading indicators from the previous year. A **leading indicator** is an objective measure that accurately predicts future labour demand. For example, a manufacturer of automobile parts that sells its product primarily to the Big Three automakers would use several objective statistics on the Big Three automakers for one time period to predict how much demand there would be for the company's product at a later time period. Inventory levels, sales levels, employment levels, and price levels at the Big Three in one year might predict the demand for labour in the production assembler job category in the next year.

> **Leading Indicator**
> An objective measure that accurately predicts future labour demand.

Using historical records, one might use multiple regression techniques to assess the best predictive model for estimating demand for production assemblers from information on sales levels, inventory levels, employment levels, and price levels at the Big Three. Since this is not a statistics book, we simply note here that this technique will convert information of four or more leading indicators into a single predicted value for demand for production assemblers that is optimal—at least according to the historical data. For example, the demand for nurses in a community can historically be predicted very well by knowing the average age of the community members. Thus, if the average age of Canadian citizens is going up, which it is, then one can expect an increase in the need for nurses. Statistical planning models are useful when there is a long, stable history that can be used to reliably detect relationships among variables. However, these models almost always have to be complemented by subjective judgments of people who have expertise in the area. There are simply too many "once-in-a-lifetime" changes that have to be considered and that cannot be accurately captured in statistical models. For example, terrorism and instability in the Middle East, combined with an unprecedented demand for oil in emerging economies such as China and India, have resulted in increasingly high and unpredictable energy prices. This in turn has led to a resurgence of interest in nuclear power, even among developing nations. Past concerns about the safety of nuclear power plants may resurface, however, and increasing reliance on solar power and wind farms make it difficult to predict strictly from historical trends whether the demand for workers trained in nuclear power technology will increase.[53]

Learn more about long-term and day-to-day forecasting using statistical methods based on historical trends online with Connect.

Determining Labour Supply   Once a company has projected labour demand, it needs to get an indicator of the firm's labour supply. Determining the internal labour supply calls for a detailed analysis of how many people are currently in various job categories (or who have specific skills) within the company. This analysis is then modified to reflect changes in the near future caused by retirements, promotions, transfers, voluntary turnover, and terminations.

Transitional Matrix

Matrix showing the proportion (or number) of employees in different job categories at different times.

As in the case of labour demand, projections for labour supply can be derived either from historical statistical models or through judgmental techniques. One type of statistical procedure that can be employed for this purpose involves transitional matrices. **Transitional matrices** show the proportion (or number) of employees in different job categories at different times. Typically these matrices show how people move in one year from one state (outside the organization) or job category to another state or job category.[54]

Table 4.2 shows a hypothetical transitional matrix for a parts manufacturer, focusing on seven job categories. Although these matrices look imposing at first, you will see that they are easy to read and use in determining the internal labour supply. A matrix like the one in this table can be read in two ways. First, we can *read the rows* to answer the question "Where did people in this job category in 2008 go by 2011?" The rows also reveal career progression patterns within the firm, such as when employees progress from production assembler to production manager and to assistant plant manager. Next, the matrix can also be read *from top to bottom (in the columns)* to answer the question "Where did the people in this job category in 2011 come from (Where were they in 2008)?" Reading matrix columns helps to understand how promotable existing employees seem to be and to what extent the company must rely on external hiring to fill positions.

Matrices such as these are extremely useful for charting historical trends in the company's supply of labour. More importantly, if conditions remain somewhat constant, they can also be used to plan for the future. For example, if we believe that we are going to have a surplus of labour in the production assembler job category in the next three years, we note that by simply initiating a freeze on external hires, the ranks of this position will be depleted by 20 percent on their own. Similarly, if we believe that we will have a labour shortage in the area of sales representatives, the matrix informs us that we may want to (1) decrease the amount of voluntary turnover in this position, since 35 percent of those in this category leave every three years (2) speed the training of those in the sales apprentice job category so that they can be promoted more quickly than in the past, and/or (3) expand external recruitment of individuals for this job category, since the usual 20 percent of job incumbents drawn from this source may not be sufficient to meet future needs. As with labour demand, historical precedents for labour supply may not always be reliable indicators of future trends. Thus, statistical forecasts of labour supply also need to be complemented with judgmental methods.

Table 4.2 A Hypothetical Transitional Matrix for an Auto Parts Manufacturer

2008	2011							
	(1) SALES MGR.	(2) SALES REP.	(3) SALES APPREN.	(4) ASST. PLANT MGR.	(5) PROD. MGR.	(6) PROD. ASSEMBLER	(7) CLERICAL	(8) NOT IN ORGANI-ZATION
1. Sales manager	.95							.05
2. Sales representative	.05	.60						.35
3. Sales apprentice		.20	.50					.30
4. Assistant plant manager				.90	.05			.05
5. Production manager				.10	.75			.15
6. Production assembler					.10	.80		.10
7. Clerical							.70	.30
8. Not in organization	.00	.20	.50	.00	.10	.20	.30	

Learn more about Table 4.2 online with Connect.

MGraw Hill connect

Determining Labour Surplus or Shortage Once forecasts for labour demand and supply are known, the planner can compare the figures to ascertain whether there will be a labour shortage or labour surplus for the respective job categories. When this is determined, the organization can determine what it is going to do about these potential problems. For example, it is relatively easy to predict from historical data that in the future, Canada is likely to experience a shortage of nurses, police officers, and firefighters as thousands of boomers begin to phase into retirement. In contrast, overcapacity problems related to automobile production would suggest that there will be a labour surplus of autoworkers in the future. Similarly, the most recent data on overcapacity problems in the semiconductor industry point to the fact that there is likely to be a surplus of workers in that industry as well.[55]

LO 7

Discuss various ways of eliminating a labour surplus and avoiding a labour shortage.

Goal Setting and Strategic Planning

The second step in human resource planning is goal setting and strategic planning, as shown in the middle of Figure 4.5 on page 146. The purpose of setting specific quantitative goals is to focus attention on the problem and provide a benchmark for determining the relative success of any programs aimed at redressing a pending labour shortage or surplus. The goals should come directly from the analysis of labour supply and demand and should include a specific figure for what should happen with the job category or skill area and a specific timetable for when results should be achieved.

The auto parts manufacturer hypothesized in Table 4.2, for instance, might set a goal to reduce the number of individuals in the production assembler job category by 50 percent over the next three years. Similarly, the firm might set a goal to increase the number of individuals in the sales representative job category by 25 percent over the next three years.

Once these goals are established, the firm needs to choose from the many different strategies available for redressing labour shortages and surpluses. Table 4.3 shows some of the options available to a human resource planner when seeking to reduce the workforce or to avoid a labour shortage.

Table 4.3 Options for Reducing Expected Labour Surplus and Labour Shortage

OPTIONS FOR REDUCING AN EXPECTED LABOUR SURPLUS			OPTIONS FOR AVOIDING AN EXPECTED LABOUR SHORTAGE		
OPTION	SPEED	HUMAN SUFFERING	OPTION	SPEED	REVOCABILITY (EASE OF CHANGE)
1. Downsizing	Fast	High	1. Overtime	Fast	High
2. Pay reductions	Fast	High	2. Temporary employees	Fast	High
3. Demotions	Fast	High	3. Outsourcing	Fast	High
4. Transfers	Fast	Moderate	4. Retrained transfers	Slow	High
5. Work sharing	Fast	Moderate	5. Turnover reductions	Slow	Moderate
6. Hiring freeze	Slow	Low	6. New external hires	Slow	Low
7. Natural attrition	Slow	Low	7. Technological innovation	Slow	Low
8. Early retirement	Slow	Low	8. Flexible work arrangements	Fast	High
9. Retraining	Slow	Low			

This stage is critical because the many options available to the planner differ widely in their expense, speed, effectiveness, amount of human suffering, and revocability (how easily the option chosen can be changed or undone). For example, if the organization can anticipate a labour surplus far enough in advance, it may be able to freeze hiring and then just let natural attrition adjust the size of the labour force. If successful, an organization may be able to avoid layoffs altogether, so that no one has to lose a job.

One of the difficulties that General Motors experienced was that when faced with a surplus of labour, the company was contractually obligated to send workers to the JOBS bank program, where they got paid for not working. In contrast, Toyota sent all of its surplus workers to training programs where they upgraded their skills. Toyota workers took classes in a host of areas including safety procedures, productivity improvement workshops, materials handling, as well as decision making and ethics.[56]

Unfortunately for many workers, in the past decade the typical organizational response to a surplus of labour has been downsizing, which is fast but high in human suffering. The widespread use of downsizing is a contributing factor to escalating levels of personal debt and personal bankruptcies in North America. Beyond this economic impact, the psychological impact spills over and affects families, increasing the rates of divorce, child abuse, and drug and alcohol addiction.[57] The typical organizational response to a labour shortage has been either hiring temporary employees or outsourcing, responses that are fast and easy to change. Given the pervasiveness of these choices, we discuss them next.

Downsizing   Recall that in Chapter 2, we defined downsizing as the planned elimination of large numbers of personnel to enhance organizational effectiveness. Although one tends to think of downsizing as something that a company turns to in times of recession like that seen in 2008 and 2009, in fact, many organizations engaged in downsizing in the 2002–2007 time period. During that period, in more than 80 percent of the cases where downsizing took place, the organizations initiating the cutbacks were making a profit at the time.

Surveys indicate four major reasons that organizations engaged in downsizing. First, many organizations are looking to reduce costs, and because labour costs represent a big part of a company's total costs, this is an attractive place to start. For example, the CBC reduced its workforce by 800 jobs in the spring of 2010.[58] Second, in some organizations, introducing technological changes, or closing outdated or nonprofitable facilities has reduced the need for labour. In addition, technology has been employed to move work that one might think was not particularly mobile, and which reduced the need for labour. For example, Pepsico has converted many of its full-service Pizza Hut restaurant locations into small pizza take-out depots that receive orders from customers phoning a single centralized telephone number. A third reason for downsizing was that, for economic reasons, some firms have changed the domestic location of where they conduct business. Some of this shift was from one region of Canada or the United States to another where labour is less expensive (such as moving a call centre from California to New Brunswick or Newfoundland.) And, fourth, downsizing also occurs when jobs have been moved out of Canada altogether, when offshoring has occurred.

Although downsizing has an immediate effect on costs, much of the evidence suggests that it has negative effects on long-term organizational effectiveness and thus sustainability, especially for some types of firms. For example, in firms that are high in research and development intensity, downsizing has been linked to lower long-term organizational profits,[59] and in the service industries requiring high levels of customer contact, the impact is exacerbated.[60] The negative effect of downsizing on firm performance was especially high among firms that engaged in high-involvement work practices, such as employing teams and pay-for-performance incentives. Thus, the more a firm attempts to compete through its human resources, the more devastating the impact of layoffs is on productivity.[61]

There are at least three reasons most downsizing efforts fail to live up to expectations in terms of enhancing firm performance, and can sometimes even threaten the very sustainability of the organization. First, although the initial cost savings are a short-term plus, the long-term effects of an improperly managed downsizing effort can be negative. Downsizing not only leads to a loss of talent, but also in many cases disrupts the social networks needed to promote creativity and flexibility.[62] Second, many downsizing campaigns let go of people who turn out to be irreplaceable assets. In fact, one survey indicated that in 80 percent of the cases, firms wind up replacing some of the very people who were let go. Indeed, the practice of hiring back formerly laid-off workers has become so routine that many organizations are increasingly using software formerly used for tracking job applicants to track their laid-off employees.[63] A third reason downsizing efforts often fail is that employees who survive the purges often become narrow-minded, self-absorbed, and risk-averse. Motivation levels drop off because any hope of future promotions—or even a future—with the company dies out. Many employees also start looking for alternative employment opportunities.[64]

The negative publicity associated with a downsizing campaign can also hurt the company's image in the labour market, making it more difficult to recruit employees later. In an age of blogs and text messaging, the once-private practice of laying off employees is becoming increasingly transparent and organizational mistakes are likely to become highly public.[65] Unfortunately, many employers execute layoffs in ways that make matters worse. For example, in September 2006, Radio Shack human resource managers decided to inform 400 people by e-mail that they were laid off.[66] This made a dehumanizing event even more dehumanizing, and the negative publicity that attended this decision was damaging to the company's image at a time when it was already undergoing a considerable amount of turmoil.

To avoid some of these problems, it is best to avoid indiscriminate across-the-board cuts, and instead perform surgical strategic cuts that not only reduce costs, but also improve the firm's competitive position.

Early Retirement Programs and Buyouts   Another popular means of reducing a labour surplus is to offer an early retirement program. As discussed in Chapter 1, the average age of the Canadian workforce is increasing. However, even though many baby boomers are approaching traditional retirement age, this group seems to have no intention of retiring any time soon.[67]

Although an older workforce has some clear advantages for employers in terms of experience and stability, it also poses problems. First, older workers are sometimes more costly than younger workers because of their higher seniority, higher medical costs, and higher pension contributions. When the value of the older workers' experience clearly offsets these costs, such employees are viewed as an asset to the business, and employers will see benefit in employing them. However, if the additional experience offered by older workers does not offset such costs, employers will see little benefit in employing them since it becomes difficult to pass these costs to consumers. Second, because older workers typically occupy the best-paid jobs, they sometimes prevent the hiring or block the advancement of younger workers, leaving the organization in a perilous position whenever the older workers decide to retire.

In the face of such demographic pressures, many employers try to induce voluntary attrition among their older workers through early retirement incentive programs. These programs come in an infinite variety. Depending on how lucrative they are, they meet with varied success. Although some research suggests that these programs do induce attrition among lower-performing older workers, to a large extent, the success of such programs is contingent upon accurate forecasting. Although mistakes in either direction can be costly, an underenrolled program creates an additional set of problems if employees start to think that they should wait it out and hope for an even better package further down the line. This makes the process of calculating one's future labour supply much more complex. As one HR manager notes, "It's a very dicey issue. You have to encourage people to leave and tell them this is the best offer you are going to get."[68] For this and other reasons, many early retirement programs are simply converted into buyouts for specific workers that have nothing to do with age.

■ connect™

Learn more about why boomers aren't retiring anytime soon online with Connect.

Employing Temporary Workers   Whereas downsizing has been a popular method for reducing a labour surplus, hiring temporary workers and outsourcing has been the most widespread means of eliminating a labour shortage. Temporary employment affords firms the flexibility needed to operate efficiently in the face of swings in the demand for goods and services. In addition to flexibility, hiring temporary workers offers several other advantages:

- The use of temporary workers frees the firm from many administrative tasks and financial burdens associated with being the "employer of record."
- Small companies that cannot afford their own testing programs often get employees who have been tested by a temporary agency.
- Many temporary agencies train employees before sending them to employers, which reduces training costs and eases the transition for both the temporary worker and the company.
- Because the temporary worker has little experience in the host firm, he or she brings an objective perspective to the organization's problems and procedures that is sometimes valuable. Temporary employees can sometimes help employers benchmark and improve employer practices by describing how a problem was dealt with effectively by a previous (temporary) employer.

Certain disadvantages to employing temporary workers need to be overcome to effectively use this source of labour. For example:

- In the service sector, low levels of commitment to the organization and its customers on the part of temporary employees often spills over and reduces the level of customer loyalty.[69]
- There is often tension between a firm's temporary employees and its full-time employees. For example, many universities employ temporary, part-time faculty to provide teaching support to full-time faculty who need time to conduct research. This leads to problems of union representation and two-tiered pay systems. In addition, full-time faculty perceive part-time workers as a threat because their availability reduces the need to hire new Ph.D. graduates into full-time positions.

Of course, in attempting to convince full-time employees that they are valued and not about to be replaced by temporary workers, the organization must take care not to create the perception that temporary workers are second-class organizational citizens. HR staff can also prevent feelings of a two-tiered society by ensuring that the temporary agency provides benefits to the temporaries that are at least minimally comparable to those enjoyed by the full-time workers with whom they interact. This not only reduces the benefit gap between the full-time and part-time workers but also helps attract the best part-time workers in the first place.

■ connect™

Learn more about employing temporary workers and managing related problems online with Connect.

Outsourcing and Offshoring   Whereas a temporary employee can be brought in to manage a single job, in other cases a firm may be interested in getting a much broader set of services performed by an outside organization or the process of outsourcing, first discussed in Chapter 2. Outsourcing is a logical choice when a firm simply does not have certain expertise and is not willing to invest time and effort into developing it. For example (ironically), companies increasingly outsource many of their human resource management tasks to outside vendors who specialize in efficiently performing many of the more routine administrative tasks associated with this function. Cost savings in this area are easily obtained because rather than purchase and maintain their own specialized hardware and software, as well as specialized staff to support such systems, companies can time-share the facilities and expertise of a firm that focuses on this technology.

In this way, a moderate-size company that might otherwise need to have a 15- to 30-person HR staff can get by with just 5 to 7 people devoted to HR because it shares services with outside firms such as Ceridian or Accenture,[70] thus benefiting from economies of scale. In addition to managing the size of the HR unit, the hope is also that this frees up HR managers to focus on more strategic issues.

In other cases, outsourcing is aimed at simply reducing costs by hiring less expensive labour to do the work, and, more often than not, this means moving the work outside the country. Offshoring is a special case of outsourcing where the jobs that move leave one country and go to another. This kind of job migration has always taken place; however, rapid technological changes have made the current trends in this area historically unprecedented.

Although initially many jobs that were outsourced were low scope and simple jobs, increasingly, higher-skilled work is being done overseas, such as legal research, accounting work (preparation of tax returns) and numerous other knowledge-based activities. Indeed, the stereotype that call centre staffing is the only type of work being offshored is increasingly invalid, as countries such as China, India, and those in Eastern Europe try to climb the skill ladder of available work. For example, call centre work has decreased to less than half its original volume in India, and the growth is now in higher-paying contracts dealing with business process improvement, processing mortgages, handling insurance claims, overseeing payrolls, and reading X-rays and other medical tests.[71] Many of the simple call centre jobs that moved to India are either moving deeper into the rural Indian villages [72] or, ironically, moving back to North America, a process called "homeshoring."

When making the decision to offshore a product or service, organizations consider several critical factors. Many who failed to look before they leaped onto the offshoring bandwagon have been disappointed by their results. Quality control problems, security violations, and poor customer service experiences have in many cases wiped out all the cost savings attributed to lower wages, and more. There are several steps a company should take to ensure the success of this strategy. First, when choosing an offshore vendor, usually the bigger and older the better. Small overseas upstarts often promise more than they can deliver and take risks that one is unlikely to see in larger, more established contractors.[73] Second, do not offshore any work that is proprietary or requires tight security. One software developer that hired an Indian firm to debug its programs later found that the firm copied the software and sold it under its own brand name.[74] In general, the work that is outsourced needs to be "modular" in the sense that the work is self-contained and does not require the outsourcing firm to provide any information that is best kept secret for competitive reasons.[75] Third, it is generally a good idea to start small and then monitor the work very closely, especially in the beginning. Typically, if problems are to develop, they manifest themselves quickly to those who are paying close attention.[76]

Rather than treating offshored work as just a cost-containment strategy, firms are increasingly looking for "transformational offshoring," which promotes growth and opens up avenues of new revenue. That is, the increased sophistication of outsourcing firms means that they are better able to partner with companies on an equal basis in developing innovative and unique ways to do business. This development has prompted one CEO to note that "I think we will end up with companies that deliver products faster, at lower cost, and are better able to compete against anyone in the world."[77]

connect

Learn more about trends in offshoring online with Connect.

Altering Pay and Hours   Companies facing a shortage of labour may be reluctant to hire new full-time or part-time employees. Under some conditions, these firms may have the option of trying to garner more hours from the existing labour force. Despite having to pay workers time-and-a-half for overtime production, employers see this as preferable to hiring and training new employees—especially if they are afraid that current demand for products or services may not extend to the future. Also, for a short time at least, many workers enjoy the added compensation. However, over extended periods, employees experience stress and frustration from being overworked in this manner. At some point, most employers in North America will have to respond to a labour shortage with an increase in wages, which then has to be passed on to consumers in terms of an increase in price.

In the face of a labour surplus, organizations can sometimes avoid layoffs if they can get their employees to take pay cuts. (Recall the Work Sharing solution put in place by Standen's Limited described in Chapter 1.) Alternatively, a company can avoid layoffs and hold the pay rate constant by reducing the number of hours of all the workers. Similar types of "furloughs" also occur from time to time among professional workers.

connect

Learn more about altering pay and hours online with Connect.

Flexible Work Arrangements   Another strategy associated with job design and human resources planning is the implementation of flexible work arrangements (FWAs). Because FWAs also help employees cope with the stress of work and family, the topic is often discussed under the umbrella of work–life balance. Regardless of how it is classified, employers that choose to implement various types of FWAs can achieve a range of objectives. Reasons for implementing FWAs range from work–life balance initiatives to the need to increase productivity or the desire to maximize physical resources. FWAs include a variety of options that all have one thing in common—they provide flexibility to employers and/or employees with respect to scheduling and location of work being done. Most types of FWAs can exist for whatever duration the employer finds useful on an individual or group basis, and are easily reversible by the employer when their purpose has been served.

FWAs help employers increase retention of valuable employees by giving them more control over when and where they complete the work assigned to them. Popular options include telecommuting, flexible work schedules, and compressed workweeks, to name a few.

Telecommuting is the practice of using technology to complete work traditionally done in the workplace in another location, such as the employee's home. For example, a journalist may work from home (or her cottage during the summer months) using a telephone, computer, software, fax, and other equipment provided by her employer. Benefits for the employee include greater autonomy over when and how work actually gets done, fewer indirect expenses such as clothing, gas, and meals that accompany commuting to work each day, and the ability to spend more time at home and in her community. The employer can save costs normally spent on dedicated office space and increased productivity from an employee who has more control over time and interruptions. Of course, the success of such arrangements depends on the level of trust that exists between the employer and employee, and whether or not the employee continues to meet employer expectations with respect to quantity and quality of work done.

Flexible work schedules and compressed workweeks are other types of flexible work arrangement options. A **flexible work schedule** is a work arrangement whereby an employer permits an employee to select alternative start and end times to the firm's normally scheduled workday, with the proviso that the required total hours will be worked each day, and the employee is present during

Telecommuting
The practice of using technology to complete work traditionally done in the workplace in another location, such as the employee's home.

Flexible Work Schedules
A work arrangement whereby an employer permits an employee to select alternative start and end times to the firm's normally scheduled workday, with the proviso that the required total hours will be worked each day and the employee will be present during core business hours (usually 10 a.m. to 3 p.m.) established by the employer.

core business hours (usually 10 a.m. to 3 p.m.) established by the employer. However, flexible work schedules are not just limited to hours worked in a day. They can be designed to accommodate whatever both parties want and can agree to. For example, some employers are open to flexing the total months worked over an entire year (a flexyear arrangement), increasing the ability to retain employees who may be going back to school or older employees phasing into retirement.

Another flexible work schedule arrangement is job sharing, in which two people doing the same job agree to share one job between them, each working a reduced workweek. In the event of an economic downturn and labour surplus, such an arrangement would help an employer to retain two trained employees (for the cost of one) until the economy picks up. It would also enable the employees involved to spend more time on family or volunteer interests, but still hold their place in the employer's workforce. Thus, if the employer and employees can work out an agreement that works for everyone, it is just a matter of formalizing the arrangements.

Compressed workweeks are arrangements whereby employees work the same number of hours normally expected in a traditional five-day workweek, except that the workload is compressed into fewer days of the week, with longer hours worked each day. In other words, the workload remains constant but is completed in fewer days, with employees working longer hours each day. For example, the traditional five-day, eight hour per day workweek that many of us are familiar with could instead be worked as a four-day workweek with employees working 10 hours per day. Such an arrangement may help employers to increase capacity of existing buildings and equipment to be put into use for the additional four hours per day, and even to increase production to a sixth day if two crews work a "four tens" shift. This may allow an organization time to build production levels before investing in additional human capital, equipment, and facilities. And even though it can be tiring to work four ten-hour days in a row, employees may be quite happy to do so, knowing that every weekend is a long weekend.

It would also appear that there is evidence to support the use of FWAs to prevent turnover and to increase job satisfaction among employees. In their 2009 study of the costs and benefits (ROI) of work–life balance practices, Canadian researchers Donna Lero, Julia Richardson, and Karen Korabik indicated that among the 6,322 Canadian employers participating in the Workplace and Employee Survey (WES) for the years 1999–2003, "flexible work hours were available to 54% of female employees and 58% of male employees with roughly two thirds of all employees using this option when it was available."[78] In addition, telecommuting work was available to 11 percent of employees and used by just under 6 percent. Results also indicated that among men "use of one or more [FWA] practices and use of a compressed workweek was associated with more promotions and use of one or more practices and a flexible work schedule was associated with lower rates of quitting. Among women, higher job satisfaction and a lower quit rate was predicted by use of one or more practices and use of a FWA. Compressed-week employees also had lower quit rates."[79]

Program Implementation and Evaluation

The programs developed in the strategic-choice stage of the process are put into practice in the program-implementation stage, shown at the bottom of Figure 4.5 on page 146. A critical aspect of program implementation is to make sure that one individual is held accountable for achieving the stated goals and has the necessary authority and resources to accomplish this goal. It is also important to have regular progress reports on the implementation to be sure that all programs are in place by specified times and that the early returns from these programs are in line with projections.

The final step in the planning process is to evaluate the results. Of course, the most obvious evaluation involves checking whether the company has successfully avoided any potential labour shortages or surpluses. Although this bottom-line evaluation is critical, it is also important to go beyond it to see which specific parts of the planning process contributed to success or failure.

Compressed Workweeks
Work schedule arrangements whereby employees work the same number of hours normally expected in a traditional five-day workweek, except that the workload is compressed into fewer days of the week, with longer hours worked each day.

The Special Case of Employment Equity Planning

Workforce Utilization Review
A comparison of the proportion of workers in protected subgroups with the proportion that each subgroup represents in the relevant labour market.

We have argued that human resource planning is an important function that should be applied to an organization's entire labour force. It is also important to plan for various subgroups within the labour force. For example, employment equity plans forecast and monitor the proportion of various designated group members, such as women and people with disabilities, who are in various job categories and career tracks. The proportion of workers in these subgroups can then be compared with the proportion that each subgroup represents in the relevant labour market. This type of comparison is called a **workforce utilization review**. This process can be used to determine whether there is any subgroup whose proportion in the relevant labour market is substantially different from the proportion in the job category.

Competing Through Technology

Technology and Fatigue Risk Management

When it comes to human resources planning, historical data is useful not only for making long-term predictions of labour demand in broad categories such as nursing, policing, or retailing but also is a critical issue in the airline industry, where cost control is a matter of survival and where mental fitness of crew members is regulated to protect the public. While technology is essential for increasing productivity, it can also provide a reliable mechanism for organizations such as Air Canada that provide flight services in a highly regulated industry where failure to comply can mean deadly mistakes and loss of life. When trying to match crew members to flights, airlines need to meet both contractual obligations and regulatory requirements, such as originating with institutions Transport Canada. Implementation of policies, guidelines, and training on fatigue risk management are seen as the responsibility of both senior management and employees. In addition, ineffective crewmember scheduling also plays havoc with the personal life of employees, decreasing job satisfaction and increasing organizational turnover.

Assigning 3,100 pilots to hundreds of flights, required flight simulator training, and recurrent line training every month used to be a difficult manual process until Air Canada helped Kronos® launch Altitude PBS™ (Preferential Bidding System). The company's comprehensive rostering system virtually "revolutionized crewmember scheduling," according to James Tarapasky, Air Canada's manager of crew scheduling automation and process. The new software ensured compliance with regulatory limits governing time off and maximum "stick" time for pilots, while eliminating monthly overlap flying conflicts whenever they occur. Customized bid options in the system allow crew members to bid for certain days off, be specific about flight pairings, and select whom they want to fly with. It all adds up to a much more satisfying work schedule for crew members while honouring a seniority-based system specified in the Air Canada contract. A new web-based bidding option will also enable pilots to put bids in from anywhere in the world. Such features prompted Tarapasky to say that Altitude PBS™ "presents a flight package that is workable, flyable and productive. We are 100 percent federally and contractually compliant, which is a must." Such attention to detail, along with crewmember satisfaction, is no doubt one of the many reasons independent air safety consultants have named Air Canada the world's safest airline.

SOURCES: "Air Canada Improves Scheduling Efficiency and Crewmember Satisfaction with Altitude PBS," www.kronos.com/generic-htcontent.aspx?id=521&terms=Air+Canada (accessed November 2, 2010); Fatigue Risk Management System for the Canadian Aviation Industry, Policies and Procedures Development Guidelines; Transport Canada, TP 14576E (April 2007), www.tc.gc.ca/media/documents/ca-standards/14576e.pdf (accessed June 14, 2011).

If such an analysis indicates that some group—for example, Aboriginal Canadians—makes up 35 percent of the relevant labour market for a job category but that this same group constitutes only 5 percent of the actual incumbents in that job category in that organization, then this is evidence of underutilization. Underutilization could come about because of problems in selection or from problems in internal movement, and this could be seen via the transitional matrices discussed earlier in this chapter.

This kind of review is critical for many different reasons. First, many firms adopt a voluntary approach to employment equity to make sure underutilization does not occur and to promote diversity. Second, companies might also engage in utilization reviews because they are legally required to do so by virtue of size or contracts with the federal government. Third, a requirement to implement an employment equity plan can be mandated by the courts as part of the settlement of discrimination complaints, as occurred with CN in 1987.[80] Employment equity plans are not without controversy, and to avoid problems they should be accompanied by effective communication plans spelling out the benefits such programs bring to the organizational competitiveness and the larger society.

Learn more about employment equity planning online with Connect.

connect

IMPROVING JOB DESIGN AND HR PLANNING USING HRM INFORMATION SYSTEMS AND E-HRM

LO 8

Discuss the types of new technologies that can be considered in redesigning jobs organization-wide, and planning of the HRM function.

We know downsizing, restructuring, and reengineering often result in productivity improvements. However, new technology plays a big role by allowing companies to find leaner, more flexible ways of operating.[81] A study of companies in a variety of industries found that investments in computers provided a better return than investments in other kinds of capital.[82] Technology requires companies to have appropriately skilled and motivated people and streamlined work processes. In some cases, technology is replacing human capital.[83] An example of this is robotics used in manufacturing, or the introduction of automated attendant systems that have reduced or eliminated the need for receptionists in many organizations. The "Competing Through Technology" box illustrates how Air Canada uses technology to improve human resource planning and to reduce administration errors associated with complex crew scheduling.

The HRM function is no different from other departments in the organization when it comes to productivity improvements. In Chapter 2, we mentioned briefly the new and emerging technologies that are available to improve the effectiveness of the HRM function in the organization through automation and information processing. Such technologies can be very helpful in assembling data needed by others in the organization for job analysis and design and human resource planning. Furthermore, technological innovations such as interactive voice technology or constantly emerging specialized HR software are essential tools that should be considered when the HRM department engages in job analysis and design and human resources planning for its own internal purposes.

In HRM, technology has been used in the past for three broad functions: transaction processing, reporting, and tracking; decision support systems; and expert systems.[84] In addition, the newest technologies being applied to HRM now include interactive voice technology, client–server architecture, relational databases, imaging, and development of specialized software. These technologies improve effectiveness through increasing access to information, improving communications, and improving the speed with which HRM transactions and information can be gathered. They can also reduce costs and facilitate

Technology has helped employers find leaner, more flexible ways of working. Human resource professionals have many new options such as interactive voice technology to streamline HR functions.

the administration of HRM functions such as job design and human resources planning, recruiting, training, and performance management and other HR activities. Such technology enables

- Employees to gain complete control over their training and benefits enrolments and employees, and managers to access information and knowledge as needed when making decisions
- The creation of a paperless employment or "personnel office" as information resides in a virtual environment
- Streamlining the HRM department's work (e.g., delivering paystubs online)
- Allowing employees and managers to select the type of media they want to use to send and receive information (such as newsletters, paystubs, payment of benefits claims)
- Flexibility—in many cases, work can be completed at any time and place
- Closer monitoring of employees' work[85]

As discussed in Chapter 2, outsourcing of HRM activities provided one mechanism for reducing the burden of transactional activities. However, today the focus is on using information technology to handle these tasks in-house. Information systems once run only by the HRM function are now evolving into employee self-serve systems. Employees can access an HRIS system and make their benefit enrolment, changes, or claims online. This in turn permits HRM staff to focus on more strategic actions such as designing more motivational compensation systems.

FIGURE 4.6 Change in Delivery

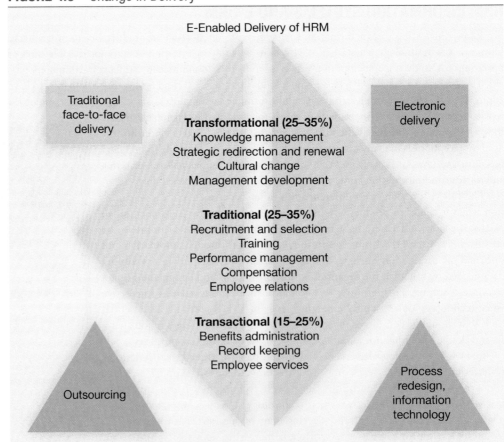

E-Enabled Delivery of HRM

Traditional face-to-face delivery

Electronic delivery

Transformational (25–35%)
Knowledge management
Strategic redirection and renewal
Cultural change
Management development

Traditional (25–35%)
Recruitment and selection
Training
Performance management
Compensation
Employee relations

Transactional (15–25%)
Benefits administration
Record keeping
Employee services

Outsourcing

Process redesign, information technology

In addition, the speed requirements of e-business force HRM functions to explore how to leverage technology for the delivery of both traditional and transformational HRM activities. This does not imply that over time all HRM will be executed over the Web; however, a number of HRM activities currently delivered via paper or face-to face communications can be moved to the Web with no loss (and even gains) in effectiveness and efficiency. The e-enabled delivery model of HRM illustrated in Figure 4.6 serves to illustrate how jobs and responsibilities can shift (when compared with Figure 2.6 on page 64) when technology is added into the mix. Clearly HRM has as much to gain as any department in the organization, and, in fact, should lead the way in demonstrating the advantages of factoring new technology into analysis and design of jobs and/or human resources planning.

Learn more about new technologies available for use in HRM online with Connect.

A Look Back

This chapter opened with a vignette that illustrated the trade-offs associated with alternative methods for organizational design and job design. We showed how one type of design was associated with larger production quantity at Toyota, but that an alternative type of design was better suited for maximizing production quality. The more recent problems faced by Toyota in resolving complex issues around supply of new motor vehicle parts (raw inputs) and availability of human resources emphasizes the importance of having a highly functional organizational structure that supports fast and effective decision making, especially when the company is quickly thrust into a crisis situation. Throughout the chapter we also illustrated how other companies made decisions to change organizational structure or job design (such as Microsoft and IBM) that have affected a whole host of different outcomes, especially issues such as human resources planning. We also examined various options employers have available to them to resolve both a surplus and shortage of labour that occur over time, each having consequences that must be addressed after implementation. The role of technology was also discussed in terms of improving job design and HR planning and in assisting HRM in acquiring, storing, and retrieving key information when needed.

Questions

1. In the opening vignette for this chapter, you learned about the recalls and quality problems Toyota was working hard to correct prior to the earthquake that occurred in Japan on March 11, 2011. Considering what you have learned in this chapter, what do you consider to be the most important job and organizational design decisions Toyota made in its attempt to gain control over quality issues?

2. What challenges in the way of human resources planning probably emerged from Toyota's struggles with organizational structure and job design? What types of human resource planning issues emerged when the company was faced with a major natural disaster?

3. Toyota's business has both a production aspect related to building cars, and a customer service aspect associated with selling cars, and these issues exist on a global basis. Using the work-unit activity analysis flowchart illustrated in Figure 4.1 on page 128, describe some of the problems created by the earthquake that Toyota had to resolve (and may continue to struggle with for some time).

4. Examine Table 4.3 on page 149 and decide which options Toyota utilized in managing labour supply and production issues following the earthquake. How revocable, or easy to change, were such options? Do you believe any other options might have been more effective under the circumstances? Explain your answer.

Summary

The analysis and design of work is one of the most important components to developing and maintaining a competitive advantage. Strategy implementation is virtually impossible without thorough attention devoted to work-flow analysis, job analysis, and job design. Managers need to understand the entire work-flow process in their work unit to ensure that the process maximizes efficiency and effectiveness. To understand this process, managers also must have clear, detailed information about the jobs that exist in the work unit, and the way to gain this information is through job analysis. Equipped with an understanding of the work-flow process and the existing job, managers can redesign jobs to ensure that the work unit is able to achieve its goals while individuals within the unit benefit from the various work outcome dimensions such as motivation, satisfaction, safety, health, and achievement. Job analysis is also the foundation of all human resource activities, such as ensuring compliance with legislation, effectively recruiting and selecting job applicants, engaging in effective labour relations, deciding on training objectives, managing performance, and compensating employees (to name a few).

Human resource planning uses labour supply and demand forecasts to anticipate labour shortages and surpluses. It also entails programs that can be utilized to reduce a labour surplus (such as downsizing and early retirement programs) and eliminate a labour shortage (such as bringing in temporary workers or expanding overtime). When done well, human resource planning can enhance the success of the organization while minimizing the human suffering resulting from poorly anticipated labour surpluses or shortages. There are a number of options available to managers to adjust for shortages and surpluses in labour supply, which vary in the consequences for both employees and the organization itself. One popular solution is the implementation of flexible work arrangements, which can provide win-win solutions for everyone involved, and can be fairly easy to undo when circumstances change. Various types of technology play a significant role in designing jobs that take cost out of the operation and result in greater productivity throughout the organization. The HRM function has many options available to increase its own value in the organization and to increase job satisfaction for HRM professionals.

Key Terms

Centralization, 131
Compressed workweeks, 155
Departmentalization, 131
Ergonomics, 144
Flexible work schedules, 154
Forecasting, 146

Job analysis, 136
Job description, 137
Job design, 141
Job redesign, 141
Job specification, 137
Leading indicator, 147

Telecommuting, 154
Transitional matrix, 148
Workforce utilization
review, 156

Discussion Questions

1. Assume you are the manager of a fast-food restaurant. What are the outputs of your work unit? What are the activities required to produce those outputs? What are the inputs?

2. Based on Question 1, consider the cashier's job. What are the outputs, activities, and inputs for that job?

3. Consider the "job" of college or university student (or choose another job that you know quite a bit about). Perform a job analysis on this job. What are the tasks required in the job? What are the knowledge, skills, and abilities necessary to perform those tasks? What environmental trends have influenced the job over the past ten years, and how did such trends change the skill requirements? Finally, consider whether flexible work arrangements discussed in the chapter could be included in this job's design.

4. Discuss how the following trends are changing the skill requirements for managerial jobs in Canada: (a) increasing use of computers (b) increasing international competition (c) increasing work–family conflicts.

5. Why is it important for a manager to be able to conduct a job analysis? What are the negative outcomes that would result from not understanding the jobs of those reporting to the manager?

6. What are the trade-offs between the different approaches to job design? Which approach do you think should be weighted most heavily when designing jobs?

7. For the cashier job in Question 2, which approach to job design was most influential in designing that job? In the context of the total work-flow process of the restaurant, how would you redesign the job to more heavily emphasize each of the other approaches?

8. Discuss the effects that an impending labour shortage might have on the following three subfunctions of human resource management: selection and placement, training and career development, and compensation and benefits. Which subfunction might be most heavily impacted? In what ways might these groups develop joint cooperative programs to avert a labour shortage?

9. Discuss the costs and benefits associated with statistical versus judgmental forecasts for labour demand and labour supply. Under what conditions might either of these techniques be infeasible? Under what conditions might both be feasible, but one more desirable than the other?

10. As more of the information systems once run only by the HRM function evolve into employee self-serve systems, what do you think is lost and/or gained from an employee's point of view? From an HRM point of view?

Self-Assessment Exercise

The chapter described how the National Occupational Classification (NOC) provided by Human Resources and Skills Development Canada can help employers conduct job analysis and the writing of job descriptions and job specifications. In addition, the NOC enables employers to easily access labour market projections that estimate the future supply and demand of labour for each of the occupational profiles. The system was also designed to help job seekers. To see if you think this NOC 2006 system meets the goal of promoting the effective education, training, counselling, and employment needs of the Canadian workforce, visit the NOC website at www.noc.com.

Look up the NOC listing for your current job, a past job, or your dream job (or as close to it as you can get among the occupational descriptions provided). List the skills identified for that job. For each skill, evaluate how well your own experiences and abilities enable you to match the job requirements. Then check the "Working in Canada" report for the same occupational description. What are the outlook and prospects for the job longer term? What kind of national wage information exists? What volume of job openings are predicted versus the projected number of job seekers over the next eight to ten years? What else can you find?

Exercising Strategy: From Big Blue to Efficient Blue

While downsizing and the change management processes that go along with it have become both mainstream and expected in today's business practices, it wasn't always that way. Such practices were learned painfully during the '90s as technology revolutionized the environment and accelerated the forces of globalization. Companies scrambled to come up with the money to invest in technology, reduce the size of their workforce, and generally "stay in the game." Companies such as Kodak became uncompetitive in a few short years because they failed to embrace new technologies, or waited too long to react. IBM did make the transition, however, and became a model for others caught in the same dilemmas. The story of how IBM and its HRM function changed in that time is presented below as a classic tale of HRM leadership during a period of corporate revolution we can all still learn from.

IBM was long known as "Big Blue" because of its size, in terms of both the number of employees and the amount of revenue and costs associated with its operations. However, as the old saying goes, "the bigger they are, the harder they fall." In the early 90s IBM racked up over $8 billion in losses when it was blindsided by the switch in consumer preferences from mainframe computers to smaller, networked personal computers.

The incoming CEO, Lou Gerstner, needed to engineer one of the greatest turnarounds in modern business; he started with a new vision of what the company would become, as well as a strategy for getting where the company needed to be. The strategy had both an external aspect, focused on changing from an old-fashioned manufacturing company to a modern service provider, and an internal aspect of restructuring operations to reduce costs and promote efficiencies.

Nowhere was this internal strategy change felt more strongly than in the HR division. The HRM function at IBM was large, decentralized, and regionally based, with branch offices all over the world employing over 3,500 people. By the year 2000 there was only one single, centralized unit employing fewer than 1,000 people.

The key to the successful downsizing effort was IBM's emphasis on matching size changes with changes in structure and the substitution of technology for labour. Instead of interacting face-to face with the local human resources office, all communication would be technologically mediated and directed to the central HRM facility via telephone, e-mail, or fax. Moreover, user-friendly software was developed to help employees answer their questions without any other human involvement.

The sprawling, geographically dispersed units were replaced with an efficient three-tier system. The first tier was composed of broadly trained human resource generalists who received telephone calls from any of IBM's 700,000 HRM "customers" (employees) and tried to respond to any queries that could not be handled via the automated system. The second tier, a smaller number of highly trained specialists (in areas such as retirement planning, occupational safety requirements, or selection standards), took any calls that exceeded the knowledge level of the generalists. Finally, the third tier consisted of even a smaller number of top executives charged with keeping the HRM practices in line with the overall corporate strategy being developed by Gerstner.

Amazingly, despite the radical downsizing of this unit, employee satisfaction with service actually increased to over 90 percent, and Gerstner singled out the reengineering of this department as a success story that should serve as a benchmark to the rest of the company's divisions. Moreover, the restructuring and redesign of these IBM jobs have formed a blueprint for many other HRM departments in other organizations.

Questions

1. In terms of our discussion of organizational structure, in what ways did the structure at IBM change under Lou Gerstner, and what impact did this have on individual jobs?
2. Compare and contrast the direction of structural change at IBM with the direction of change we saw in the structural realignment at Microsoft (also discussed in the chapter).
3. Since both IBM and Microsoft achieved their goals by changing their structures and job design in opposite directions, what does this say about the relationship between organization structure and job design? About organizational performance and job satisfaction on the other?

SOURCES: S. N. Mehta, "What Lucent Can Learn from IBM," *Fortune* (June 25, 2001), p. 40; G. Flynn, "Out of the Red, Into the Blue," *Workforce* (March 2000), pp. 50–52; P. Gilster, "Making Online Self-Service Work," *Workforce* (January 2001), pp. 54–61; J. Hutchins, "The U.S. Postal Service Delivers an Innovative HR Strategy," *Workforce* (October 2000), pp. 116–118.

Managing People: ROWE-ing up the (Ottawa) River

Netflix, the online video rental service that entered the Canadian market in October 2010, is widely recognized as an employer that tends to give a wide degree of autonomy to managers. CEO Reed

Hastings tends to pay managers very well and gives them unlimited vacation time. They are also free to structure their own compensation package (cash versus stock) as well as the way they do their own work. In return, Hastings expects extremely high performance and accountability. Indeed, as marketing manager Heather McIlhany notes, "Netflix has a tough but fulfilling culture that will only work with fully formed adults who are not looking for a place to hide or pass the buck." This combination of freedom and responsibility among its workers has helped Netflix fight off many competitors, including Walmart, which briefly ventured into the online video rental business. Many thought that Walmart would put an end to Netflix, but after several years of failing to make inroads into this market, Walmart pulled out in 2007 and referred all of its former customers to Netflix. Indeed, the Netflix launch in Canada had many speculating that the day of the franchised video rental store is gone forever. With Rogers on-demand options and now Netflix, why would anyone stop at the video store after picking up the pizza and settling in for the usual TGIF home movie festival?

With IBM and Best Buy already joining Netflix in redefining job expectations and workflow, some observers already says it's "the end of clock punching." Certainly Peter Hadwen, a workplace consultant in Ottawa for the past 20 years, feels that the time has come for more organizations to see the wisdom of a "results-only work environment" (ROWE). Make your goals, get results for the boss—and you've done your job. No need to attend pesky meetings. No need to show up at 8:30 a.m., or answer those phones for co-workers. Quite the opposite, since ROWE is based on employees setting their own schedules and flexing work around that consideration *first*. If another week skiing doesn't interfere with getting that project in on time—book another week at Whistler!

While those of us bound to an 8 to 5 desk might hoot in disbelief (and envy!), early research indicates that ROWE workplaces have reported "more job satisfaction and job organization."

Observers say that ROWE is more efficient for managers, who spend much less time overseeing the behaviours and schedules of employees. Indeed, ROWE employees work roughly the same number of hours as in the days before ROWE, despite being released from clocks, schedules, and other annoying expectations. Stephen Harville, another workplace consultant, says Canadian employers are beginning to explore the merits of ROWE, but are cautious. For Harville, however, the answer is simple. He thinks ROWE may be the key to remaining competitive in a volatile world, saying, "If you're going to work more effectively, you better be ready to make adjustments, especially when it comes to the relationship between work and production and job satisfaction and success."

SOURCES: M. Conlin, "Netflix: Flex to the Max," *BusinessWeek* (September 24, 2007), pp. 72–74; and L. Bourgon, "The End of Clock-Punching?" *Canadian Business* (September 27, 2010).

Questions

1. What changes, if any, might need to occur if you were writing job descriptions for a ROWE workplace? Would job descriptions be of any value at all?

2. Are there any legal concerns HRM might have to deal with (around job descriptions and work objectives) if an organization becomes a ROWE workplace? What other challenges might HRM need to identify and overcome?

3. How might various HRM activities such as performance management be affected if a ROWE approach were adapted at your workplace? What about human resources planning?

4. Which approach to job design does the concept of ROWE seem to fit best–mechanistic, motivational, ergonomic/biological, or perceptual motor?

5. If an organization using the ROWE approach was forced to downsize its workforce, would the ROWE approach still work? Why or why not?

 **Practise and learn online with Connect.**

5 Recruitment and Selection

LEARNING OBJECTIVES

After reading this chapter, you should be able to:

LO 1 Describe the various recruitment policies that organizations adopt to make job vacancies more attractive. page 168

LO 2 List the various sources from which job applicants can be drawn, their relative advantages and disadvantages, and the methods for evaluating them. page 171

LO 3 Explain the recruiter's role in the recruitment process, challenges the recruiter faces, and the opportunities available. page 177

LO 4 Establish the basic standards of selection methods, including reliability, validity, and generalizability. page 180

LO 5 Discuss how the particular characteristics of a job, organization, or applicant affect the utility of any test. page 183

LO 6 List the common methods used in selecting human resources and the degree to which each method meets selection method standards. page 184

LO 7 Describe the various legal requirements in recruitment processes and selection decisions. page 197

Enter the World of Business

Meyers Norris Penny: Values-Driven Recruitment

It's an enviable Canadian success story that young accounting graduates and business clients are drawn to in large numbers. Small wonder. Three highly competent and entrepreneurial accountants dream big, work hard, and put together a unique and different business model for an accounting and business advisory firm that eventually causes both the company and their clients to grow exponentially. Then one day, the company (by now known as Meyers Norris Penny) discovers it has become the largest public accountancy and business advisory firm headquartered in Western Canada, and the seventh largest in all of Canada. Even better, in 2010, it is recognized as one of the Hewitt 50 Best Employers in Canada.

So with a company history like that you'd think it would be an obvious target for young undergraduates seeking employment—sort of a "build-it-and-they'll-come" kind of story. Actually, MNP didn't reach its current size doing things that way. MNP is all about finding out first what's good for the client and, it seems, what's good for future employees as well. That was evident in the firm's 2008 fall campus recruitment campaign, which featured posters and pamphlets spread liberally across university and college campuses asking only one simple, irresistible question: "What do you want?" Typical answers include: "I want to make partner by the time I'm 30," and "I want to do more than just cash and receivables in my first year." The result of so clearly understanding the target market was a record number of high-calibre applications, a highly satisfying outcome for Bob Twerdun and his HRM team. Like other HRM departments in Canadian accounting firms, they know just how tight the labour market has been over the past five years.

Once students arrived at information sessions, articling students and partners representing MNP facilitated sessions by listening first, then providing students with information and personal testimonials on what the company could do to make their dreams come true. Twerdun, for example, told students who asked "the partner question" that he would be retiring in about eight years, and added that "if you join the company right now, you could make partner before I'm gone." That's an answer students can understand and base decisions on. It's also a far cry from the usual broadcast approach used at information sessions and job fairs, where participating companies compete with stats and information and students are quickly overwhelmed. MNP's sessions were more like a tennis game, with students serving the first ball, and then having more control over subsequent volleys across the net. It served as an important signal that if they joined the company, they will have some say in their future and get clear information on how to meet and exceed expectations. The 2008 fall cross-campus recruitment campaign netted MNP 180 high-quality hires—proof the campaign sent out an accurate message about MNP. Further evidence the company's approach was effective and unique was received in the form of an Employer of Choice Marketing award (for overall advertising campaign), sponsored by CanWest-owned *Working*, a recruitment advertising network based in Toronto.

MNP's on-campus approach was consistent with the company's 60-year history of integrity, growth, and partnership. Ron Meyers, Don Penny, and Daryl Ritchie are revered as "the intrepid leaders" of MNP's journey, "each bringing the right strengths to the firm at the right time and each allowing his successor to start from an advantaged position." Their combined efforts served to increase volume and locations, expand firm services, tighten niches, and retool governance and structure—whatever was needed at various critical junctures in the firm's growth. The company's growth was fuelled with mergers and organic growth that brought the company to its current state—rather like the hiring process in which new employees are acquired or merge their future with the firm and then both the employee and the firm continue to grow. With such an approach to recruitment then, it's not surprising that over time, organic growth has outstripped merger growth, and the company has doubled the volume of the merged organizations.

The promise of growth discussed at recruitment sessions is supported by substance at MNP. New hires can count on access to leadership development, performance management, professional development, and wellness initiatives. For example, the firm's MNP University offers 150 courses along with generous funding so that people can come together for training from all across the organization. In addition, "performance management includes two reviews per year that establish a clear connection between achievement and annual goals and bonuses," combined with a transparent career transition process that helps employees chart the coveted path from manager to partner. Even more important, such programs are backed up by "enthusiastic and committed managers and partners who are delivering those programs." No wonder the company found itself on Hewitt's 50 Best Employers list the first time it threw its name into the hat in 2010. But perhaps the greatest insight into why job seekers might choose MNP over other companies is in Twerdun's reaction to making the "50 Best" list. Twerdun saw the Hewitt recognition as confirmation that "we were able to embed our values or help people new to the organization understand [and internalize] our values." In a post-Enron world, students would view the top priority placed on values as accounting-speak for job security and a rewarding career. And if values-oriented recruits choose MNP over others, then the value proposition propels a virtuous circle. The process of attracting the right people with the right skills (and matching values) at the right time is both complete and self-perpetuating. As one of Canada's 50 Best Employers, Meyers Norris Penny—which officially changed its name to MNP on June 6, 2011—can rest assured that its message is clear, and that it can choose from the best— even in the tightest of labour markets for bright young accounting grads.

SOURCES: S. Klie, "Firm Asks Students "What Do You Want?," *Canadian HR Reporter* (May 5, 2008), pp. 9–10; S. Dobson, "Engagement Drives Top Employers," *Canadian HR Reporter* (January 26, 2009), p. 8;

Telephone interview with Bob Twerdun and Kathryn Edwards (August 24, 2010); Meyers Norris Penny Values Statement at www.mnp.ca/about/vision-and-values (retrieved October 29, 2010).

INTRODUCTION

Our opening vignette reveals some of the complex challenges involved in attracting job seekers to vacancies within an organization during the recruitment process. When companies are faced with filling new or existing positions they must be both strategic and efficient in getting the message out about the job vacancy and what the company can offer, or they risk losing bright candidates to competitors. For example, when searching for experienced accountants, competitors can be almost any company in any industry. When going on campus, competitors can be other accounting firms or any firm that wants to hire young accounting graduates. Once a pool of candidates has been located, however, a new challenge arises: how to separate the best from all candidates and get an offer out to the right person before a competitor lures them away. Moreover, who has time for recruitment anyway, when the needs of business demand one`s time and attention? Unless there is a systematic process in place for both attracting an adequate pool of qualified job seekers and then determining which of the applicants is the right one to hire, and getting him or her to accept an offer of employment, precious time and money can be wasted.

This chapter will provide an overview of key techniques and issues to consider in both the recruitment and selection process. In the first half of this chapter we familiarize you with the process by which individuals find and choose jobs and, like Myers Norris Penny in our opening vignette, the role of recruitment in HRM in reaching these individuals and shaping their choices. The second part of the chapter focuses on ways to minimize errors in employee selection and placement and, in doing so, improve your company's competitive position.

THE HUMAN RESOURCE RECRUITMENT PROCESS

As our discussion of human resources planning in Chapter 4 indicated, it is difficult to always anticipate exactly how many (if any) new employees will have to be hired in a given year in a given job category. The role of human resource recruitment is to build a supply of potential new hires that the organization can draw on if the need arises. Thus, **human resource recruitment** is defined as any practice or activity carried on by the organization with the primary purpose of identifying and attracting potential employees. It thus creates a buffer between planning and actual selection of new employees.

Human Resource Recruitment Any practice or activity carried on by the organization with the primary purpose of identifying and attracting potential employees.

Recruitment activities are designed to affect (1) the number of people who apply for vacancies, (2) the type of people who apply for them, and/or (3) the likelihood that those applying for vacancies will accept positions if offered. The goal of an organizational recruitment program is to ensure that the organization has a number of reasonably qualified applicants (who would find the job acceptable) to choose from when a vacancy occurs.

The goal of recruiting is not simply to generate large numbers of applicants. If the process generates a sea of unqualified applicants, the organization will incur great expense in personnel selection (as discussed more fully later in the chapter), but few vacancies will actually be filled. This problem of generating too many applicants is often promulgated by the use of wide-reaching technologies such as the Internet to reach people. The goal of personnel recruitment is not to finely discriminate among reasonably qualified applicants either. Recruiting new personnel and selecting new personnel are both complex processes. Each task is hard enough to accomplish successfully, even when one is well focused. Organizations explicitly trying to do both at the same time will probably not do either well. For example, research suggests that recruiters provide less information about the company when conducting dual-purpose interviews (interviews focused on both recruiting and selecting applicants).[1] Also, applicants apparently remember less information about the recruiting organization after dual-purpose interviews.[2] Finally, applicants respond less positively to highly structured interviews, and yet this is precisely the type of interview that has the highest validity in terms of making effective screening decisions.[3]

Because of strategic differences among companies (see Chapter 2), the importance assigned to recruitment may differ. In general, however, as shown in Figure 5.1, all companies have to make decisions in three areas of recruiting: (1) personnel policies, which affect the kinds of jobs the company has to offer; (2) recruitment sources used to solicit applicants, which affect the kinds of people who apply; and (3) the characteristics and behaviours of the recruiter. These, in turn, influence both the nature of the vacancies and the nature of the people applying for jobs in a way that shapes job choice decisions.[4]

LO 1

Describe the various recruitment policies that organizations adopt to make job vacancies more attractive.

Human Resource Policies

Human resource policies (sometimes referred to as *personnel policies*) is a generic term used to refer to organizational decisions that affect the nature of the vacancies for which people are recruited. Research on recruitment makes one thing clear: the characteristics of the vacancy are more important than recruiters or recruiting sources when it comes to predicting job choice decisions.

Internal versus External Recruiting: Job Security   One desirable feature of a vacancy is that it provides ample opportunity for advancement and promotion. One organizational policy that affects this is the degree to which the company "promotes from within"; that is, recruits for upper-level vacancies internally rather than externally.

We discuss internal versus external recruiting both here and in the section "Recruitment Sources" later in this chapter because this policy affects the nature of both the job and the individuals who apply. For now, we focus on the effects that "promote from within" policies have on job characteristics, noting that such policies make it clear to applicants that there are opportunities for advancement within the company. These opportunities spring not only from the first vacancy but also from the vacancy created when a person in the company fills that vacancy. Similarly, during downtimes,

FIGURE 5.1   Overview of the Individual Job Choice—Organizational Recruitment Process

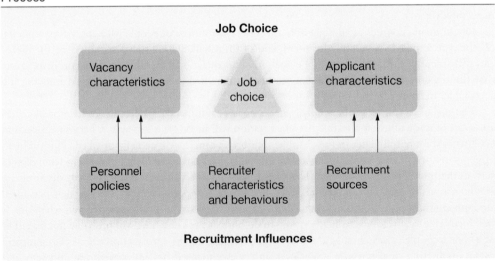

organizations with strong internal recruiting orientations typically have developed information systems that support reassigning potentially dislocated workers to different jobs in the company.

Extrinsic and Intrinsic Rewards   Because pay is an important job characteristic for almost all applicants, companies that take a "lead-the-market" approach to pay—that is, a policy of paying higher-than current-market wages—have a distinct advantage in recruiting. Pay can also make up for a job's less desirable features—for example, paying higher wages to employees who have to work midnight shifts. These kinds of specific shift differentials and other forms of more generic compensating differentials will be discussed in more detail in later chapters that focus on compensation strategies. We merely note here that "lead" policies make any given vacancy more attractive to applicants.

Increasingly, organizations that compete for applicants based on pay do so using pay forms other than wages and salary. In the 1990s many employers attempted to recruit employees with promises of stock option plans but this has become a much less attractive option since the 2001 recession and the turbulence of the stock market.

One rather noticeable recruitment campaign using pay forms to attract recruits took place between 2002 and 2003 in Canada. In an effort to attract high-quality recruits to the Regular Force, the Department of National Defence in Canada launched an aggressive ad campaign across Canada offering $20,000 enrolment bonuses to individuals qualified in 15 professional trades (such as millwrights, electricians, and even X-ray technicians.) Later, to attract Engineering and Science students, the Army upped the ante in at least one university newspaper, offering students a $40,000 recruitment bonus, and saying "Students can receive a salary, paid tuition, books, and guaranteed employment upon graduation." But by far the most enticing offer was reserved for future medical officers. In 2002, the Canadian Army offered a $225,000 enrolment bonus to physicians licensed to practice in Canada, if they felt eager to take on a challenge and sign up for a "chance to serve overseas and to help others during United Nations operations." For those eager applicants who took the DND up on their tempting offer, the phrase "Show Me the Money!" would soon be followed by "You're in the Army now."[5]

Employer Branding   Organizations often advertise specific vacancies (discussed next in the section "Recruitment Sources"). Sometimes, however, organizations advertise just to promote themselves as a good place to work in general.[6] Employer branding, or image advertising, is particularly important for companies in highly competitive labour markets. Recall that Meyers Norris Penny, the company described in the opening vignette, ramped up its profile in the labour market by competing successfully in Hewitt's Best Employers in Canada study. It also developed an award winning on-campus recruitment campaign, creating a highly cohesive message about what MNP has to offer to top talent comparing employers in a very tight labour market.

However, employer branding is also important for companies that perceive themselves as having a tired, bad, or controversial image. For example, Commissionaires is a Canadian, private, not-for-profit firm offering 37 different types of security and security-related services that finds meaningful work for retired veterans. However, after realizing it was having trouble recruiting its target market, market research in 2005 revealed that the company was inaccurately perceived to be a department of the federal government. As a result, the retired veterans who should have been attracted to the firm that could find them meaningful work had an uncomplimentary idea of the company and the type of business it does. Executive Director Doug Briscoe discovered potential applicants thought the company offered only "... the most menial of security guarding tasks. They weren't aware that we're in all these other lines of business."[7] After hiring Brand Matters, an external branding company in Toronto, the company acquired a new image through use of more energetic colours and a new motto ("Trusted Everyday Everywhere"), and it established more effective and appealing ways to communicate the real nature of work available through Commissionaires. The end result gave the company an image that both the company and the employees "would really rally behind."[8] Indeed, research evidence suggests that the impact of company image on applicant reactions ranks second only to the nature of the work itself.[9]

Even though it does not provide any information about any specific job, image advertising is often effective because job applicants develop ideas about the general reputation of the firm (i.e., its brand image) and then this spills over to influence their expectations about the nature of specific jobs or careers at the organization.[10]

According to Patrick Sullivan, CEO of Workopolis in Toronto, organizations need to take three important steps to build an employment brand: "(1) Define the target audience; (2) Develop a set of reasons why the organization is more attractive to that audience than other organizations, and: (3) incorporate those reasons into all recruitment efforts and the organization's career website."[11] After taking these steps, one way of implementing a very strong brand is to compete in events such as Mediacorp's Canada's Top 100 Employers annual competitions and employer conferences. When a company applies to participate in this competition, it must analyze and describe its value proposition to job seekers in areas such as recognition, career development, working conditions, benefits, work–life balance and other demanding criteria set by an advisory board of prestigious scholars and practitioners in the field of HRM. The company's employment offerings are then compared to other applicants; the top 100 are chosen each year and featured on the Mediacorp website.[12]

The process of doing an internal analysis and subjecting a summary of HRM practices to scrutiny can be time consuming, but there are a number of paybacks that make it very worthwhile. For example, when Meyers Norris Penny (MNP) participated in the Hewitt's 50 Best Employers in Canada study, the process prompted the company to carefully examine what makes employees successful at MNP. Bob Twerdun, vice president of Human Capital, recalls that the analytical process required to make a submission to the Hewitt study resulted in the company taking "the next, more positive step of establishing measures of success for employee's current and future roles."[13] Another outcome Twerdun and his HRM team valued was the feedback from team members, which provided internal validation.[14]

Research suggests that the language associated with a organization's brand image is often similar to personality trait descriptions might be used to describe another person (such as *innovative, competent,* or *sincere*).[15] These perceptions influence the degree to which individuals feels attracted to the organization, especially if there appears to be a good fit between the traits of the applicant and the traits that describe the organization.[16] Applicants seem particularly sensitive to issues of diversity and inclusion in these types of advertisements; hence, organizations that advertise their image need to ensure that the actors in their advertisements reflect the broad nature of the labour market constituencies to whom they are trying to appeal in terms of race, gender, and culture.[17] Indeed, since the inception of the Canada's Top 100 Employer's research and project website by Richard Yerema and Mediacorp Canada Inc., the competition has been expanded to include categories such as Canada's Best Diversity Employers, Canada's Greenest Employers, Top Employers for Canadians Over 40, and other areas of differentiation that help employers match up with more than one target audience.

Although sometimes it is said that there is no such thing as bad publicity, this is not always true when it comes to recruiting. Although, in general, familiarity is better than lack of familiarity, applicants seem to be especially sensitive to bad publicity; thus, advertising campaigns are often used to try to send a positive message about the organization.[18] Although a firm can try to create an image using television advertisements or Web pages, research suggests that face-to-face contact (such as that provided by job fairs) is a much stronger avenue to enhance an organization's image.[19] For example, following Canadian-born *Avatar* director James Cameron's highly publicized trip to the Alberta oil sands to inspect the environmental effects of this method of oil extraction, and highly negative news coverage of ducks drowning in Syncrude's tailings ponds, the Canadian Association of Petroleum Producers (CAPP) began a series of television and print advertisements to influence public perception. CAPP's ads featured highly skilled and knowledgeable young engineers and other professionals proudly describing the solutions that the petroleum industry is implementing in the oil sands to prevent or contain damage to the environment. Thus the Canadian public and potential target applicants for jobs at in oil sands development were provided with alternative and more positive perspectives to help them make decisions about the company and its activities.

Recruitment Sources

LO 2

List the various sources from which job applicants can be drawn, their relative advantages and disadvantages, and the methods for evaluating them.

The sources from which a company recruits potential employees are a critical aspect of its overall recruitment strategy. The total labour market is expansive; any single organization needs to draw from only a fraction of it. The number and nature of job seekers who apply for an organization's vacancies will be affected by how (and to whom) the organization communicates its vacancies. The type of person who is likely to respond to a job advertised on the Internet may be different from the type of person who responds to an ad in the classified section of a local newspaper. In this section we examine the different sources from which recruits can be drawn, highlighting the advantages and disadvantages of each.

Internal versus External Sources   We discussed internal versus external sources of recruits earlier in this chapter and focused on the positive effects that internal recruiting can have on recruits' perceptions of job characteristics. We will now discuss this issue further, but with a focus on how using internal sources affects the kinds of people who are recruited.

In general, relying on internal sources offers a company several advantages. First, it generates a sample of applicants who are well known to the firm. Second, these applicants are relatively knowledgeable about the company's vacancies, which minimizes the possibility of inflated expectations about the job. Third, it is generally cheaper and faster to fill vacancies internally.

With all these advantages, you might ask why any organization would ever employ external recruiting methods. There are several good reasons. First, for entry-level positions and perhaps even for some specialized upper-level positions, there may not be any internal recruits from whom to draw. Second, bringing in outsiders may expose the organization to new ideas or new ways of doing business. Using only internal recruitment can result in a workforce whose members all think alike and who therefore may be poorly suited to innovation.[20]

Finally, recruiting from outside sources is a good way to strengthen one's own company and weaken one's competitors at the same time. This strategy seems to be particularly effective during bad economic times, where "countercyclical hiring" policies create once-in-a-lifetime opportunities for acquiring talent.[21] For example, during the most recent recession, many firms that were top performers—and hence able to weather the storm better than their lower-performing competitors—viewed this as an excellent opportunity to poach the highest-performing individuals within struggling companies.[22] Thus, for many organizations, times of crisis and turbulence are the best time to shine by leveraging their current talent and success to bring in more talent and achieve even greater success over the long term.[23]

Direct Applicants and Referrals   **Direct applicants** are people who apply for a vacancy without prompting from the organization. **Referrals** are people who are prompted to apply by someone within the organization. These two sources of recruits share some characteristics that make them excellent sources from which to draw.

First, many direct applicants are to some extent already "sold" on the organization. Most of them have done some homework and concluded that there is enough fit between themselves and the vacancy to warrant their submitting an application. This process is called self-selection. A form

Direct Applicants
People who apply for a job vacancy without prompting from the organization.

Referrals
People who are prompted to apply for a job by someone within the organization.

of aided self-selection occurs with referrals. Many job seekers look to friends, relatives, and acquaintances to help find employment, and evoking these social networks can greatly aid the job search process for both the job seeker and the organization.[24] Current employees (who are knowledgeable of both the vacancy and the person they are referring) do their homework and conclude that there is a fit between the person and the vacancy; they then sell the person on the job. Indeed, research shows that new hires that used at least one informal source reported having greater prehire knowledge of the organization than those who relied exclusively on formal recruitment sources. These kinds of word-of-mouth endorsements from credible sources seem to have a particularly strong effect early in the recruitment process when people are still unfocused in their search process.[25] Ironically, as more and more recruiting is accomplished via impersonal sources such as the Internet, the ability to draw on personal sources of information on recruits is becoming even more valuable. A 2008 survey conducted by HRinfodesk, a Canadian payroll and employment law website, reflects this duality. Among the 259 companies surveyed, Internet job boards (32.8 percent) just barely surpassed employee referrals (31.7 percent) as the survey participants' most successful recruitment source. It seems that while the Internet is becoming more popular, many job organizations still rely heavily on employee endorsements to make a good hire.[26]

When one figures into these results the low costs of such sources, they clearly stand out as one of the best sources of new hires, and some employers even offer financial incentives to current employees for referring applicants who are accepted and perform acceptably on the job (e.g., stay 180 days).[27] Other companies play off their good reputations in the labour market to generate direct applications. In the war for talent, some employers that try to entice one new employee from a competitor will often try to leverage that one person to try to entice even more people away. The term "liftout" has been coined for this practice of trying to recruit a whole team of people. Liftouts are seen as valuable because the company acquires a completely functional team.[28] Indeed, the team chemistry and coordination that often takes years to build is already in place after a liftout, and this kind of speed provides competitive advantage. Of course, having a whole team lifted out of your organization is devastating, because customers are frequently next to leave, following the talent; hence firms have to work hard to ensure that they can retain their critical teams.

Advertisements in Newspapers and Periodicals   Advertisements to recruit personnel are ubiquitous, even though they typically generate less desirable recruits than direct applications or referrals—and do so at greater expense. However, because few employers can fill all their vacancies with direct applications and referrals, some form of advertising is usually needed. Moreover, an employer can take many steps to increase the effectiveness of this recruitment method.

The two most important questions to ask in designing a job advertisement are, What do we need to say? and To whom do we need to say it? With respect to the first question, many organizations fail to adequately communicate the specifics of the vacancy. Ideally, individuals reading an ad should get enough information to evaluate the job and its requirements, allowing them to make a well-informed judgment regarding their qualifications. This could mean running long advertisements, which costs more. However, these additional costs should be evaluated against the costs of processing a huge number of applicants who are not reasonably qualified or who would not find the job acceptable once they learn more about it.

Perhaps the biggest problem with most advertisements is that they are often written to be excessively demanding in terms of the actual skill requirements that are needed for the work, unnecessarily decreasing the number of legitimate applicants. Some have estimated that roughly half of the labour shortage in certain engineering fields can be traced to this problem. For example, as one recruiter of software engineers noted with respect to his company's search policy, "I say smart people can learn sister applications, but there is a reluctance among hiring managers to see that. If they use an SAP database system, they won't even look at someone with experience with PeopleSoft."[29]

In terms of whom to reach with this message, the organization placing the advertisement has to decide which medium it will use. The classified section of local newspapers is a commonly used medium. It is a relatively inexpensive means of reaching many people within a specified geographic area who are currently looking for work (or at least interested enough to be reading the classifieds). On the downside, this medium does not allow an organization to target skill levels very well. Typically, classified ads are read by many people who are either over- or underqualified for the position. Moreover, people who are not looking for work rarely read the classifieds, and thus this is not the right medium for enticing people away from their current employers. Targeted journals and periodicals may be better than general newspapers at reaching a specific part of the overall labour market, although the lead time required may be a drawback. In addition, employers are also using television—particularly cable television—as a reasonably priced way of reaching people.

Electronic Recruiting There are many ways to employ the Internet for recruiting purposes, and increasingly organizations are refining their use of this medium. In fact, a survey of HR executives indicated that electronic job boards were the most effective source of recruits for 36 percent of the respondents, well ahead of local newspapers (21 percent), job fairs (4 percent), and walk-ins and referrals (1 percent).[30]

Obviously, one of the easiest ways to get into "e-cruiting" is to simply use the organization's own Web page to solicit applications. In this way, organizations can fine-tune their recruitment message and focus on specific types of applicants. For example, the interactive nature of this medium allows individuals to fill out surveys that describe what they are looking for and what they have to offer. These surveys can be "graded" immediately and recruits can be given direct feedback about how well they are matched for the organization. Research shows that this type of immediate feedback is helpful both to recruits and to the organization, by quickly and cheaply eliminating misfits for either side.[31] Indeed, customizing e-cruiting websites to increase the possibility for attracting job seekers whose values match the employer's values, and whose skills match requirements of current job vacancies is probably their best feature.[32]

Of course, smaller and less well-known organizations may not attract any attention to their own websites; thus, for them, this is not a good option. A second way for organizations to use the Web is to interact with the large, well-known job sites such as Workopolis.com, Monster.ca, or CareerBuilder.ca. These sites attract a vast array of applicants, who submit standardized resumes that can be electronically searched using key terms. Applicants can also search for companies in a similar fashion; the hope, of course, is that there may be a match between the employer and the applicant. The biggest downside to these large sites, however, is their sheer size and lack of differentiation. Because of this limitation of the large sites, smaller, more tailored websites called "niche boards" focus on certain industries, occupations, or geographic areas. For example, the Society of Certified Management Accountants (CMA) has a website for each province that includes a members-only job page that helps job seekers with a CMA designation and up-to-date membership link to employers placing ads on the organization's job board.[33]

The increased familiarity of Web devotees with Web logs (blogs) has created other opportunities for recruiters to reach out and have public or semipublic conversations with recruits. Microsoft's senior recruiter for marketing, Heather Hamilton, manages a blog that describes what it is like to work at a marketing career at Microsoft. Interested candidates can read what she posts, and then ask questions or provide their own information. This allows many other "passive" applicants to see the answers to previous questions or what other people who are applying to the organization are like. In one week alone, this blog was viewed by over 25,000 people and, as Hamilton notes, "the big thing for me is reach. ... as a recruiter, I could be on the phone all day every day and not be able to reach that many people."[34]

The growing use of iPods has also opened up a new and rich avenue to get information from employer to applicant via podcasts. Podcast can be used to reach out to a large number of people;

Competing Through Technology

Social Recruiting: Potential for Big ROI

Social media presents many marketing channels that offer employers high potential for external employment branding and spreading the word about job openings. In a world where speed of response really matters, recruiters can build a pool of applicants in a much shorter time than when using only traditional methods of advertising and recruitment. The four social networks most utilized by recruiters include Facebook.com (600 million active users), Twitter.com (175 million users), LinkedIn.com (80 million users), and YouTube, which currently attracts over 110 million unique visits per day in the United States. Each social network was designed for various uses and functions, but companies usually leverage their impact by using several such networks simultaneously, and linking them to corporate websites. Using more than one encourages corporate messages to go viral to reach the widest audience possible. For example, a company may post an interesting video on YouTube about the company, provide information that points to it on the company's Facebook career page, and reinforce that by sending out "tweets" (messages using 140 characters or less) on Twitter. In addition, the content created will often be designed to motivate subscribers of all three sites to forward the message to a relevant number of friends, who in turn, it is hoped, will do the same thing.

In addition to having the most subscribers overall, Facebook has been especially successful in Canada, where it enjoys greater market penetration than in any other country in the world. Almost 50 percent of Canadians spend at least an hour a day on the site (visiting multiple times per day), so it represents a rich market for reaching Canadian job applicants quickly. And because Canadian Facebook users also maintain an average 190 "friends" each (compared to the average of 130 elsewhere in the world), and interact more often with brands than in other countries, the site represents an important channel for reinforcing recruitment strategies launched in other ways. For large companies that create a well-tended and interactive presence in Facebook, the potential to improve recruiting can be great. Companies use a variety of techniques to make their Facebook pages interactive in some way, which increases traffic to everything the company wishes to point to, including corporate websites where expanded information on careers and jobs may be posted. For example, Starbucks' Facebook site garners 16.3 million hits per month, and Tim Horton's boasts 1.2 million Facebook fans, giving both companies broad exposure to a marketplace of not only coffee lovers (and their friends), but also a huge audience of potential employees. Facebook helps create word-of-mouth marketing. Users who discover something they find useful (such as a coupon for free coffee, a funny video, or a job posting) can forward the information to friends in an instant. Marketing experts say that such shared messages are 68 percent more likely to be remembered because they've been shared by a friend, making them a powerful tool in attracting potential applicants.

Creators of Twitter.com never intended the site to be a social network site, but the company's 200 million original subscribers quickly decided how the "tweet" function could best be used. Although the average subscriber spends around 12.5 minutes per month on the site, the general feeling in the high-tech community is that the full potential of Twitter has yet to be fully realized. Twitter allows computer-generated tweets to reach job applicants quickly and drives them to more information.

The YouTube website is an online video community that offers companies the chance to post a longer audio visual message about the company. YouTube provides an opportunity to feature benefits of the culture and work environment and to reach users who may not even think to go to the company's official website. However, anyone can post a video on YouTube, so the potential for harm to company image is also a very real possibility. For example, a sensational video captured on a smartphone at 3 p.m. and posted on YouTube can be on the national news within hours if picked up by more traditional media. Therefore, experts advise that whether companies use this site for recruitment or not, they need to scan this site regularly to ensure they know what is being said about them by others who are posting videos on YouTube.

LinkedIn.com started as a professional social network where individuals could post career profiles with current contact information so they could be readily accessed and shared by others. The database of profiles provides a ready source of resumes to anyone hunting for talent. For small companies and start-ups, it's a free source of talent who have made it clear they want to be contacted. For example, Mobilicity, a young Canadian wireless communications service provider, hired its director of Human Resources after accessing her LinkedIn profile and approaching her. Even at the interview stage, the company never asked for her full resume. Since then she has hired over three-quarters of the company's rapidly expanding national workforce using social media channels discussed here. The experience of Mobilicity illustrates that even small companies can leverage social media to their advantage.

Professional recruiters especially like social media because they feel more in control. They can search LinkedIn for profiles during the short period before responses to postings in other social media channels pour in. Along the way, they get a huge amount of help from complete strangers who are motivated to help others based on the inherent expectations of social networking to "pay it forward."

However, success in such channels comes with experience, and often with following advice from experts with a profound understanding of the advantages and pitfalls of social media. Those more experienced in such formats advise HR managers to start slowly, adding "social recruiting" carefully to their traditional recruitment methods and blending such methods with other recruitment efforts and overall company marketing where possible. After they have some experience using various forms of social media themselves and understand its impact, they will see possibilities more clearly. Next, they should develop a deliberate and well-thought-out strategy that allows them to control the message. That includes identifying the needs of their target market (e.g., 18- to 24-year-olds or 34- to 54-year-olds?), crafting the right response and message to answer such needs, and then choosing the best social media channels to reach that audience. It's not just knowledge-based industries that can exploit social media. Compass Group Canada and McDonald's have both found they can reach service workers more effectively by placing a strong emphasis on social media. For example, McDonalds maintains a substantial presence on Facebook and, after identifying that young people who are a major part of its target audience value a sense of individuality and belonging, it ensured that employment brand information contained in all relevant media emphasized choice in uniforms, flexibility in schedules, and the potential for scholarships. Such targeted messaging to young people in the social media channels most natural for them created a much stronger response from the specific audience they wanted to attract. Compass has made considerable progress using social media to recruit, reducing time-to-hire by half, from an average 45 days to around 28, a significant achievement.

Social recruiting has become so prevalent that companies who have not yet ventured into social networking may soon need to consider adding it to their recruitment approaches. It is also becoming clear that marketing to consumers is not much different than marketing employment branding since the combination reaches both active and passive job seekers. With projections that by 2031 only two Canadians will remain in the workforce for every four active workers today, understanding how to use social media will undoubtedly become increasingly essential as the much-rumoured war for talent reaches full engagement.

SOURCES: K. Peters, "Public Image Ltd.," *HR Professional*, Vol. 25, No. 1, (December 2007/January 2008), pp. 24–30; L. Young, "Sphere of Influence, Using Social Media to Win the War for Talent," *HR Professional*, Vol. 28, No. 2, (February 2011), pp. 28–34; S. Moretti, QMI Agency, "Facebook Using Canada as Testing Ground," *London Free Press* (November 4, 2010); J. Hempel, "Trouble at Twitter," *Fortune* (May 2, 2011), pp. 66–76.

however, the rich nature of the media—which employs color, sound, and video—is much more powerful than a simple text-only e-mail. "Podcasts really make the job description come alive," notes Dan Finnigan, a general manager at HotJobs.com (recently acquired by Monster.com), and the ability to describe the organization's culture is so much more emotionally charged with this media relative to mere words on a page.[35]

Social and professional networking sites such as Facebook and LinkedIn represent new important avenues for employers to reach out to targeted groups of both passive and active job seekers in their own environments, and the impact of these sites on the role of recruitment is growing daily.[36] While Facebook does not allow employers to create pages as members, it does allow them to purchase pages in order to create what is called a "sponsored group." Ernst & Young's sponsored group page has been joined by more than 5,000 Facebook users, who can access information about Ernst & Young and chat with recruiters from the company in a blog-like manner.[37] Unlike more formal media, the conversations held here are very informal and serve as an easy first step for potential recruits to take in their relationship with the company. The "Competing through Technology" box on page 174 provides more information on how companies can use social media to ramp up their Internet presence and add to more traditional methods such as those described here.

As with any new and developing technology, all of these approaches present some unique challenges. From an employer's perspective, the interactive, dynamic, and unpredictable nature of blogs and social networking sites means that people who have negative things to say about the organization can join the conversations, and this can be difficult to control. The biggest liability from the applicant's perspective is the need to protect his or her identity, because this medium has also been a haven for identity thieves, who post false openings in the hope of getting applicants to provide personal information.[38] In general, an applicant interacting with these types of sites should never provide a social insurance number, set up bank accounts, or submit to security checks until he or she has visited the employer in person.

Public and Private Employment Agencies Human Resources and Skills Development Canada (HRSDC) helps unemployed Canadians find work through its online Job Bank, located on the Service Canada website. The Job Bank is a free public service allowing employers and job seekers to connect online. Canadians seeking work can now create an online account to access useful aids such as Resume Builder, so they can present a strong summary of their skills and other attributes. They can also access Job Alert to access thousands of job advertisements, and use Career Navigator to obtain guidance regarding suitable career options. Employers can match their job requirements with the skills of applicants using another service called Job Match. Both job seekers and employers can also access labour market information including trends in employment and compensation linked to the National Occupational Classification (NOC) discussed in Chapter 4.[39]

Public employment agencies such as the HRSDC's Job Bank serve primarily the blue-collar labour market; private employment agencies perform much the same service for the white-collar labour market. Unlike public agencies, however, private employment agencies charge the organization for the referrals.

One type of private employment agency is the executive search firm (ESF). These agencies are often referred to as *headhunters* because, unlike the other sources we have examined, they operate almost exclusively with people who are currently employed. Dealing with executive search firms is sometimes a sensitive process because executives may not want to advertise their availability for fear of their current employer's reaction. Thus, ESFs serve as an important confidentiality buffer between the employer and the recruit. Along with newspapers and classified advertisements, ESFs may have suffered the most damage in recent years due to the combination of reduced employment levels (due to the recent recession) on the one hand and increased use of low-cost electronic search vehicles on the other. Many have questioned whether ESFs have a viable business model, given the recent changes in the economy and in technology.[40]

Colleges and Universities

Most colleges and universities have placement services that seek to help their graduates obtain employment. Indeed, on-campus interviewing, following information sessions such as those provided by Meyers Norris Penny, the company in our chapter-opening vignette, is the most important source of recruits for entry-level professional and managerial vacancies.[41] Organizations tend to focus especially on colleges and universities that have strong reputations in areas for which they have critical needs (e.g., chemical engineering, public accounting, or the like).[42]

Many employers have found that to effectively compete for the best students, they need to do more than just sign up prospective graduates for interview slots. One of the best ways to establish a stronger presence on a campus is with a college or university internship program. For example, IBM and Research in Motion (RIM) sponsor internship opportunities through a variety of universities and often hire these interns for full-time positions when they graduate. These kinds of programs allow an organization to get early access to potential applicants and to assess their capacities directly. Another way of increasing one's presence on campus is to participate in university job fairs. In general, a job fair is a place where many employers gather for a short time to meet large numbers of potential job applicants. Although job fairs can be held anywhere (such as at a hotel or convention centre), campuses are ideal locations because of the many well educated, yet unemployed, individuals who live and study there. Job fairs are an inexpensive means of generating an on-campus presence and provide one-on-one dialogue with potential recruits—dialogue that could not be achieved through less-interactive media such as newspaper ads. Finally, as more organizations attempt to compete on a global level, the ability to recruit individuals who will be successful both at home and abroad is a growing concern. Many organizations believe that a university or college campus is one of the best places to search for this type of transportable talent, since such campuses are temporary homes to large numbers of international students who have already proven they can adapt and succeed in a foreign environment.

Evaluating the Quality of a Source

Because there are few rules about the quality of a given source for a given vacancy, it is generally a good idea for employers to monitor the quality of all their recruitment sources. One means of accomplishing this is to develop and compare yield ratios for each source.[43] Yield ratios express the percentage of applicants who successfully move from one stage of the recruitment and selection process to the next. Comparing yield ratios for different sources helps determine which is best or most efficient for the type of vacancy being investigated. Data on cost per hire are also useful in establishing the efficiency of a given source.[44]

Table 5.1 shows hypothetical yield ratios and cost-per-hire data for five recruitment sources. For the job vacancies generated by this company, the best two sources of recruits are local universities and employee referral programs. Newspaper ads generate the largest number of recruits, but relatively few of these are qualified for the position. Recruiting at nationally renowned universities generates highly qualified applicants, but relatively few of them ultimately accept positions. Finally, executive search firms generate a small list of highly qualified, interested applicants, but this is an expensive source compared with other alternatives.

Recruiters

The last part of the model presented in Figure 5.1 on page 168 that we will discuss is the recruiter, noting that the recruiter often gets involved late in the process. In many cases, by the time a recruiter meets some applicants, they have already made up their minds about what they desire in a job, what the current job has to offer, and their likelihood of receiving a job offer.[45]

LO 3

Explain the recruiter's role in the recruitment process, challenges the recruiter faces, and the opportunities available.

Table 5.1 Hypothetical Yield Ratios for Five Recruitment Sources

	RECRUITING SOURCE				
	LOCAL UNIVERSITY	RENOWNED UNIVERSITY	EMPLOYEE REFERRALS	NEWSPAPER AD	EXECUTIVE SEARCH FIRMS
Resumes generated	200	400	50	500	20
Interview offers accepted	175	100	45	400	20
Yield ratio	87%	25%	90%	80%	100%
Applicants judged acceptable	100	95	40	50	19
Yield ratio	57%	95%	89%	12%	95%
Accept employment offers	90	10	35	25	15
Yield ratio	90%	11%	88%	50%	79%
Cumulative yield ratio	90/200 45%	10/400 3%	35/50 70%	25/500 5%	15/20 75%
Cost	$30,000	$50,000	$15,000	$20,000	$90,000
Cost per hire	$333	$5,000	$428	$800	$6,000

Moreover, many applicants approach the recruiter with some degree of skepticism. Knowing that it is the recruiter's job to sell them on a vacancy, some applicants may discount what the recruiter says relative to what they have heard from other sources (such as friends, magazine articles, and professors). For these and other reasons, recruiters' characteristics and behaviours seem to have less impact on applicants' job choices than we might expect.

Recruiter's Functional Area. Most organizations must choose whether their recruiters are specialists in human resources or experts at particular jobs (e.g., supervisors or job incumbents). Some studies indicate that applicants find a job less attractive and the recruiter less credible when he is an HRM specialist.[46] This does not completely discount an HRM specialist's role in recruiting, but it does indicate that such specialists need to take extra steps to ensure that applicants perceive them as knowledgeable and credible.

Recruiter's Traits. Two traits stand out when applicants' reactions to recruiters are examined. The first, which could be called "warmth," reflects the degree to which the recruiter seems to care about the applicant and is enthusiastic about his or her her potential to contribute to the company. The second characteristic could be called "informativeness." In general, applicants respond more positively to recruiters who are perceived as warm and informative. These characteristics seem more important than demographic characteristics such as age, sex, or race, which have complex and inconsistent effects on applicant responses.[47]

Recruiter's Realism. Perhaps the most well-researched aspect of recruiting deals with the level of realism that the recruiter incorporates into the message. Because the recruiter's job is to attract candidates, there is some pressure to exaggerate the positive features of the vacancy while downplaying the negative features because applicants are highly sensitive to negative information. On the other hand, if the recruiter goes too far in a positive direction, the candidate can be misled and lured into taking the job under false pretenses.[48] This can lead to a serious case of unmet expectations and a high turnover rate.[49] In fact, unrealistic descriptions of a job may even lead new job incumbents to believe that the employer is deceitful.[50]

Many studies have looked at the capacity of "realistic job previews" to circumvent this problem and help minimize early job turnover. On the whole, the research indicates that realistic job previews do lower expectations and can help reduce future turnover in the workforce.[51] Certainly, the idea that one can go overboard in selling a vacancy to a recruit has merit. However, the belief that informing people about the negative characteristics of the job will totally "inoculate" them to such characteristics seems unwarranted, based on the research conducted to date.[52] Thus we return to the conclusion that an organization's decisions about personnel policies that directly affect the job's attributes (pay, security, advancement opportunities, and so on) will probably be more important than recruiter traits and behaviours in affecting job choice. Indeed, research indicates that structured interventions that help applicants simply make good decisions about which jobs are best for them may work out best for both employers and applicants. That is, helping applicants better understand their own needs and qualifications and then linking this to the current openings may be best in the long run for all concerned, even if it does not result in an immediate hire.[53]

Enhancing Recruiter Impact. Although research suggests that recruiters do not have much influence on job choice, this does not mean recruiters cannot have an impact. For example, in contexts where applicants already have high awareness of the organization because its products are well known, the impact of the recruiter is weaker than in contexts where the applicant has low product awareness.[54] Organizations can take several steps to increase the impact that recruiters have on those they recruit. First, recruiters can provide timely feedback. Applicants react very negatively to delays in feedback, often making unwarranted attributions for the delays (such as, the organization is uninterested in the application). Second, recruiting can be done in teams rather than by individuals. As we have seen, applicants tend to view line personnel (job incumbents and supervisors) as more credible than personnel specialists, so these kinds of recruiters should be part of any team. On the other hand, personnel specialists have knowledge that is not shared by line personnel (who may perceive recruiting as a small part of their "real" jobs), so they should be included as well.

THE SELECTION PROCESS

The recruitment process is complete once an adequate pool of qualified candidates have applied for the organization's vacant position(s). Next, managers and others who need to be involved will then begin the process of selecting the best candidate. **Selection** is the process by which an organization attempts to identify applicants with the necessary knowledge, skills, abilities, and other characteristics that will help it achieve its goals.

Any organization that intends to compete through people must take the utmost care with how it chooses organizational members. These decisions have a critical impact on the organization's ability to compete, and on each applicant's life. These decisions are too important to be left to the whim of untrained individuals, or to an outsourcing firm. Such a decision is not only unfair to applicants who may be wrongly denied jobs, but also a questionable business practice because it hurts the firm's ability to compete. Jack Welch, the legendary former CEO at General Electric said it best:

> What could possibly be more important than who gets hired? Business is a game, and as with all games, the team that puts the best people on the field and gets them playing together wins. It's that simple.[55]

Selection
The process by which an organization attempts to identify applicants with the necessary knowledge, skills, abilities, and other characteristics that will help it achieve its goals.

Thus, the purpose of this section is to show how to minimize errors in employee selection and placement and, in so doing, improve a company's competitive position. We begin by focusing on five standards that should be met by any selection method. The chapter then concludes by evaluating several common selection methods according to those standards.

SELECTION METHOD STANDARDS

LO 4

Establish the basic standards of selection methods, including reliability, validity, and generalizability.

Several generic standards should be met in any selection process. We focus on five: (1) reliability, (2) validity, (3) generalizability, (4) utility, and (5) legality. The first four build on each other in the sense that the preceding standard is often necessary but not sufficient to support the one that follows. This is less the case with legal standards; however, a thorough understanding of the first four standards helps us understand the rationale underlying legality, the fifth standard. We discussed legal issues at length in Chapter 3 and will discuss compliance with the law during both recruitment and selection (legality) as our last topic in this chapter.

Reliability

Much of the work in personnel selection involves measuring characteristics of people to determine who will be accepted for job openings. For example, we might be interested in applicants' physical characteristics (such as strength or endurance), their cognitive abilities (such as mathematical ability or verbal reasoning capacity), or aspects of their personality (such as their initiative or integrity). Whatever the specific focus, in the end we need to quantify people on these dimensions (assign numbers to them) so we can order them from high to low on the characteristic. Once people are ordered in this way, we can decide whom to hire and whom to reject.

Reliability
The consistency of a performance measure; the degree to which a performance measure is free from random error.

One key standard for any measuring device is its reliability. We define **reliability** as the degree to which a measure is free from random error. If a measure of some supposedly stable characteristic such as intelligence is reliable, then the score a person receives based on that measure will be consistent over time and in different contexts.

Estimating the Reliability of Measurement   Most measurement in personnel selection addresses complex characteristics such as intelligence, integrity, and leadership ability. However, to appreciate some of the complexities in measuring people, we will consider something concrete in discussing these concepts: the measurement of height. Let's say the first person we measure turns out to be 6 feet 1 and ¼ inches tall. It would not be surprising to find out that someone else measuring the same person a second time, perhaps an hour later, found this applicant's height to be 6 feet and ¾ inches. The same applicant, measured a third time, maybe the next day, might be measured at 6 feet 1 and ½ inches tall.

As this example makes clear, even though the person's height is a stable characteristic, we get slightly different results each time he is assessed. This means that each time the person is assessed, we must be making slight errors. If a measurement device were perfectly reliable, there would be no errors of measurement. If we used a measure of height that was not as reliable as a ruler—for example, guessing someone's height after seeing her walk across the room—we might see an even greater amount of unreliability in the measure. Thus *reliability* refers to the measuring instrument (a ruler versus a visual guess) rather than to the characteristic itself.

connect

Learn more about estimating the reliability of measurement as well as the standards for reliability online with Connect.

Validity

We define **validity** as the extent to which a performance measure is related to performance on the job. A measure must be reliable if it is to have any validity. On the other hand, we can reliably measure many characteristics (such as height) that may have no relationship to whether someone can perform a job. For this reason, reliability is a necessary but insufficient condition for validity.

Criterion-Related Validation   One way of establishing the validity of a selection method is to show that there is an empirical association between scores on the selection measure and scores for job performance. If there is a substantial correlation between test scores and job-performance scores, **criterion-related validity** has been established.[56]

Learn more about criterion-related validity online with Connect.

Criterion-related validity studies come in two varieties. **Predictive validation** seeks to establish an empirical relationship between test scores taken *prior* to being hired and eventual performance on the job. Because of the time and effort required to conduct a predictive validation study, many employers are tempted to use a different design. **Concurrent validation** assesses the validity of a test by administering it to people already on the job and then correlating test scores with existing measures of each person's performance. The logic behind this strategy is that if the best performers currently on the job perform better on the test than those who are currently struggling on the job, the test has validity. (Figure 5.2 on page 182 compares the two types of validation study.)

Despite the extra effort and time needed for predictive validation, it is superior to concurrent validation for a number of reasons, First, job applicants (because they are seeking work) are typically more motivated to perform well on the tests than are current employees (who already have jobs). Second, current employees have learned many things on the job that job applicants have not yet learned. Therefore, the correlation between test scores and job performance for current employees may not be the same as the correlation between test scores and job performance for less-knowledgeable job applicants. Third, current employees tend to be homogeneous—that is, similar to each other on many characteristics. Thus, on many of the characteristics needed for success on the job, most current employees will show restriction in range. This restricted range makes it hard to detect a relationship between test scores and job performance scores because few of the current employees will be very low on the characteristic you are trying to validate. For example, if emotional stability is required for a nursing career, it is quite likely that most nurses who have amassed five or six years' experience will score high on this characteristic. Yet to validate a test, you need both high test scorers (who should subsequently perform well on the job) and low test scorers (who should perform poorly on the job). Thus, although concurrent studies can sometimes help anticipate the results of predictive studies, they do not serve as substitutes.

Learn more about determining how much validity is enough through tests of statistical significance online with Connect.

Content Validation   When sample sizes are small, an alternative test validation strategy, content validation, can be used. **Content validation** is performed by demonstrating that the items, questions, or problems posed by the test are a representative sample of the kinds of situations or problems that occur on the job. A test that is content valid exposes the job applicant to situations that are likely to occur on the job, and then tests whether the applicant currently has sufficient knowledge, skill, or ability to handle such situations.

FIGURE 5.2 Graphic Depiction of Concurrent and Predictive Validation Designs

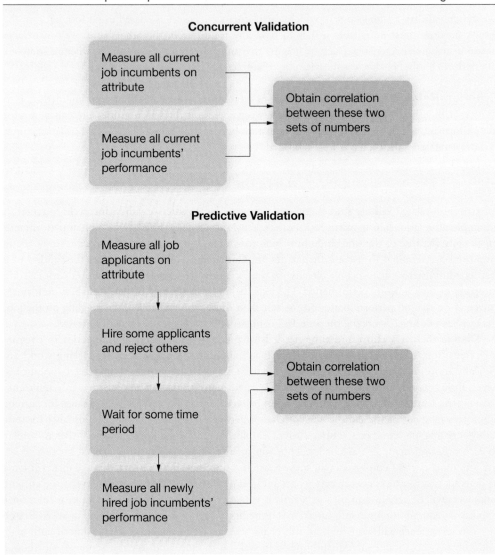

For example, a general contracting firm that constructed tract housing needed to hire a construction superintendent.[57] This job involved organizing, supervising, and inspecting the work of many subcontractors involved in the construction process. The tests developed for this position attempted to mirror the job. One test was a scrambled subcontractor test, where the applicant had to take a random list of subcontractors (roofing, plumbing, electrical, fencing, concrete, and so on) and put them in the correct order that each should appear on the site. A second test measured construction error recognition. In this test, the applicant went into a shed that was specially constructed to have 25 common and expensive errors (such as faulty wiring and upside-down windows) and recorded whatever problems she could detect.

Many of the new simulations that organizations are using are essentially computer-based role-playing games, where applicants play the role of the job incumbent, confronting the exact types of people and problems real-live job incumbents would face. The simulations are just like traditional role-playing games (e.g., Dungeons and Dragons), and the applicant's reactions and behaviours are scored to see how well they match with what one would expect from the ideal employee.[58] Because the content of these tests so closely parallels the content of the job, one can safely make inferences from one to the other. Although criterion-related validity is established by empirical means, content validity is achieved primarily through a process of expert judgment; that is, by drawing upon the knowledge of individuals who have the most accurate and intimate knowledge and experience of the job in question.

The ability to use content validation in small sample settings makes it generally more applicable than criterion-related validation. However, content validation has two limitations. First, one assumption behind content validation is that the person who is to be hired must have the knowledge, skills, or abilities at the time she is hired. Second, because subjective judgment plays such a large role in content validation, it is critical to minimize the amount of inference involved on the part of judges. Thus the judges' ratings need to be made with respect to relatively concrete and observable behaviours (for example, "applicant detects common construction errors" or "arranges optimal subcontractor schedules").

Generalizability

Generalizability is defined as the degree to which the validity of a selection method established in one context extends to other contexts. Thus, the SAT, used primarily in the United States, may be a valid predictor of someone's academic performance (e.g., in an undergraduate program), but, does this same test predict performance in graduate programs? If the test does not predict success in this other situation, then it does not "generalize" to this other context. Thus, rather than rely on the SAT for all types of programs, separate tests such as the GMAT, LSAT, MCAT, and GRE may be needed for particular types of graduate schools.

There are three primary "contexts" over which we might like to generalize: different situations (jobs or organizations), different samples of people, and different time periods. Just as reliability is necessary but not sufficient for validity, validity is necessary but not sufficient for generalizability.

Learn more about further research on generalizability online with Connect.

Generalizability
The degree to which the validity of a selection method established in one context extends to other contexts.

Utility

Utility is the degree to which the information provided by selection methods enhances the bottom-line effectiveness of the organization. Strategic approaches to human resource management place a great deal of importance on determining the financial worth of human capital and great strides have been made in assessing this value.[59] In general, the more reliable, valid, and generalizable the selection method is, the more utility it will have. On the other hand, many characteristics of particular selection contexts enhance or detract from the usefulness of given selection methods, even when reliability, validity, and generalizability are held constant.

Many factors relate to the utility of a test. For example, the value of the product or service produced by the job incumbent plays a role: the more valuable the product or service, the more value there is in selecting the top performers. The cost of the test, of course, also plays a role. More expensive tests will on average have less utility unless they produce more valid predictions.

Learn more about how characteristics of particular selection contexts impact utility online with Connect.

LO 5

Discuss how the particular characteristics of a job, organization, or applicant affect the utility of any test.

Utility
The degree to which the information provided by selection methods enhances the effectiveness of selecting personnel in real organizations.

LO 6

List the common methods used in selecting human resources and the degree to which each method meets selection method standards.

TYPES OF SELECTION METHODS

Now that we have described four of the five common or generic standards by which selection measures can be judged, we examine the common selection methods used in various organizations and discuss their advantages and disadvantages in terms of these standards.

Interviews

A selection interview has been defined as "a dialogue initiated by one or more persons to gather information and evaluate the qualifications of an applicant for employment." The selection interview is the most widespread selection method employed in organizations, and there have been literally hundreds of studies examining its effectiveness.[60]

Unfortunately, the long history of research on the employment interview suggests that, without proper care, it can be unreliable, low in validity, and biased against a number of different groups.[61] Moreover, interviews are relatively costly because they require at least one person to interview another person, and these persons have to be brought to the same geographic location. Finally, in terms of legality, the subjectivity embodied in the process, as well as the opportunity for unconscious bias effects, often makes applicants upset, particularly if they fail to get a job after being asked apparently irrelevant questions. Employers can also get into trouble in interview contexts when they do not pose the exact same questions to all applicants, since bias might be revealed in the nature of questions asked.[62] In the end, subjective selection methods such as the interview must be validated by traditional criterion-related or content validation procedures if they show any degree of adverse impact.

Fortunately, more recent research has pointed to a number of concrete steps that one can employ to increase the utility of the personnel selection interview.[63] First, HR staff should keep the interview structured, standardized, and focused on accomplishing a small number of goals. That is, they should plan to come out of each interview with quantitative ratings on a small number of dimensions that are observable (such as interpersonal style or ability to express oneself) and avoid ratings of abilities that may be better measured by tests (such as intelligence). In addition to coming out of the interview with quantitative ratings, interviewers should also have a structured note-taking system that will aid recall when it comes to justifying the ratings.[64]

Second, interviewers can utilize different types of questions to increase their knowledge and judgment about how the applicant may behave on the job if hired. Two types of interview questions commonly used are behavioural description interview questions and situational interview questions. **Behavioural description interviews (BDI)** are structured interviews using open-ended, experienced-based questions that focus on what the applicant has done in the past in an attempt to predict future behaviour. Such questions are phrased so that interview candidates are forced to describe something they have actually done before to resolve a problem or situation that forms the content of the question being asked in the interview. Hence the candidate's answer is specific about what she *did do,* not what she *might do* if faced with the same or similar situation again. Such questions are used because "the best predictor of future performance is past performance in similar circumstances."[65] Thus, when a candidate describes how he or she has handled a situation in the past, interviewers are presented with information that they can accept as evidence of future behaviour. If any ambiguity exists, interviewers can probe further for more information (since the event actually happened) and can even include it in reference checking if desired. Paul C. Green, an expert in competency development and competency-based systems notes that using behaviour description interview questions is much more strategic than using less specific, nonbehavioural questions. He says that "the behavioural language provides the basis for linking organizational identity to the interviewing system," and that effective behaviour interviews require more input from senior

Behavioural Description Interviews (BDI)
Structured interviews posing open-ended, experience-based questions that focus on what the applicant has done in the *past*.

management and thus are more likely to integrate the core values of the organization to the hiring process. In effect, behavioural language serves as an integrator between organizational strategies and human resource systems and tools (such as job descriptions, job interviews, performance appraisals, and training and development objectives). There is also considerable evidence that behavioural-based interviews are both reliable and valid.[66]

Interviewers can also ask questions dealing with specific situations that are likely to arise in the future on the job, and use these to determine what the person is likely to do in that situation. These types of **situational interview** items or dilemmas (future job-based issues, questions, or problems likely to arise on the job) have been shown to have quite high predictive validity.[67]

Table 5.2 provides examples of both behaviour description interview questions (experience based) and situational interview questions (future-based). Research suggests that both types of questions can show validity but that behavioural (experience-based) questions often outperform situational (future-oriented) questions. Experience-based items also appear to reduce some forms of impression management, such as ingratiation, better than future-oriented items.[68] Regardless of the past or future frame, an additional benefit of such questions is their standardization, and the concrete behavioural nature of the information that is collected mean that they can be effectively employed, even by those who have little training in psychological assessment.[69]

Behavioural interviews can be particularly effective when assessing sensitive issues dealing with the honesty and integrity of candidates. Clearly, simply asking people directly whether they have integrity will not produce much in the way of useful information. However, questions that pose ethical dilemmas and ask respondents to discuss how they dealt with such situations in the past

Situational Interview
An interview procedure where applicants are confronted with specific future-based issues, questions, or problems that are likely to arise on the job.

Table 5.2 Examples of Behavioural (Experience-Based) and Situational (Future-Based) Interview Questions

BEHAVIOUR DESCRIPTION INTERVIEWS (BDI) (EXPERIENCE-BASED)	
Motivating employees:	"Think about an instance when you had to motivate an employee to perform a task that he or she disliked but that you needed to have done. How did you handle that situation?"
Resolving conflict:	"What was the biggest difference of opinion you ever had with a co-worker? How did you resolve that situation?"
Overcoming resistance to change:	"What was the hardest change you ever had to bring about in a past job, and what did you do to get the people around you to change their thoughts or behaviours?"
SITUATIONAL INTERVIEWS (FUTURE-BASED)	
Motivating employees:	"Suppose you are working with an employee who you know greatly dislikes performing a particular task. You need to get this task completed, however, and this person is the only one available to do it. What would you do to motivate that person?"
Resolving conflict:	"Imagine that you and a co-worker disagree about the best way to handle an absenteeism problem with another member of your team. How would you resolve that situation?"
Overcoming resistance to change:	"Suppose you had an idea for change in work procedures that would enhance quality, but some members of your work group were hesitant to make the change. What would you do in that situation?"

When more than one person is able to interview a candidate for a position, there is significant advantage in removing any errors or biases that a single individual might make in choosing the correct person for the job. In today's technological world, it is becoming easier for multiple people to give their input in an interview by watching a video or listening via conference call if they cannot be there in person.

are often revealing in terms of how different people deal with common dilemmas. For example, by stating, "We have all observed someone stretching the rules at work, so give me two examples of situations in which you faced this dilemma and how you dealt with it," the interviewer forces the applicant to reveal how he or she deals with ethical dilemmas as an observer. Since the person is an observer and not the perpetrator in this case, he or she will be less defensive in terms of revealing how he or she deals with ethical issues. When assessing sensitive characteristics like this, research suggests that it is often best to wait until later in the interview to pose such questions, after some degree of rapport has been established and the candidate is less self-conscious.[70]

It is also important to use multiple interviewers who are trained to avoid many of the subjective errors that can result when one human being is asked to rate another. Many employers are now videotaping interviews and then distributing the tapes (rather than moving the applicants) around. This is seen by some as a cost-effective means of allowing numerous raters to evaluate the candidate under standard conditions.[71]

Limiting the subjectivity of the process is central to much of this training, and research suggests that it is best to ask interviewers to be "witnesses" of facts that can later be integrated via objective formulas, as opposed to being "judges" allowed to idiosyncratically weigh how various facts should be combined to form the final recommendation.[72] In addition to being a witness, the interviewer sometimes has to be the "crown prosecutor," because in some cases the interviewees may be motivated to try to present an overly positive, if not outright false, picture of their qualifications. People seem to be particularly prone to present false information when the competition for jobs is high, and data on resume fraud indicates a spike in detected fraud during the recent recession of 2007. Part of this spike was attributable to the behaviour of applicants, but part of it was also due to the ease with which employers can access basic information on applicants from sources such as Google.[73] The data from a 2006 survey of executive recruiters bears this out and reveals that it is common practice for employers to search the Web for information on applicants. In fact, 35 percent of those respondents stated that they eliminated candidates based upon what they learned from Web searches—up from 25 percent the year before.[74] Some of this is attributable directly to content placed on blogs or social networking sites, where the person may have disclosed information that a previous employer may have wanted to keep confidential (e.g., product launches, production problems, personnel matters, and so on). In other cases, the content of the person's digital identity may be at odds with the image or corporate culture that is being promoted by the organization.

connect

Learn more about managing your digital identity online with Connect.

Interviewers need to be critical and look for inconsistencies or gaps in stories or experiences from those who are providing information. Increasingly, interviewers are seeking training that helps them detect nonverbal signs that someone is trying to be deceptive, such as hand tremors, darting eyes, mumbled speech, and failing to maintain eye contact, which may be a cause for concern and increased scrutiny.[75]

Reference Checking, Biographical Data, and Application Blanks

Just as few employers would think of hiring someone without an interview, nearly all employers also use some method for getting background information on applicants before an interview. This information often can be solicited from the people who know the candidate through reference checks.

The evidence on the reliability and validity of reference checks suggests that these are, at best, weak predictors of future success on the job. The main reason for this low validity is that the evaluations supplied in most reference letters are so positive that it is hard to differentiate applicants. This problem with reference letters has two causes. First, the applicant usually gets to choose who writes the letter and can thus choose only those writers who think the highest of her abilities. Second, because letter writers can never be sure who will read the letters, they may fear that supplying damaging information about someone could come back to haunt them.

Thus, it is clearly not in the past employer's interest to reveal too much information beyond job title and years of service. In general, the validity of reference checks increases when the employer goes beyond the list provided by the applicant, and employers who rely heavily on this source tend to seek a large number of references and contact those people directly by phone for a more interactive and, possibly, open and anonymous exchange of information.[76] Many organizations outsource this activity to agencies that specialize in background checking, including verifying educational qualifications, past job performance and employment history, credit rating, obtaining a driver's abstract, etc. Doing so may provide more extensive information and in a timelier manner than employers can manage themselves. This allows employment offers to be extended more quickly, based on the best information possible about the candidate being offered the job.

The evidence on the utility of biographical information collected directly from job applicants is much more positive, especially for certain outcomes such as predicting turnover.[77] The low cost of obtaining such information significantly enhances its utility, especially when the information is used in conjunction with a well-designed, follow-up interview that complements, rather than duplicates, the biographical information bank.

Again, as with the interview, the biggest concern with the use of biographical data is that applicants who supply the information may be motivated to misrepresent themselves. Background checks can help on this score, but many firms that provide background checks are unreliable themselves. Because of this, as you can see in the "Competing through Globalization" box on page 188, in some countries, this is not even a viable option.

It is important to remember, however, that background checks offer no guarantee, because of the increased sophistication of those in the dishonesty business. For example, there are now websites that will not only provide fake degrees, but also staffed telephone numbers that will provide further bogus information to callers. Some universities and prison systems have even been hacked into by companies that try to insert or delete their clients' names from databases.[78]

Although it is not a panacea, to some extent forcing applicants to elaborate on their responses to biodata questions can sometimes be helpful.[79] A good elaboration forces applicants to support their answers with evidence that includes names of other people involved, dates, locations, and objective evidence that would support a thorough cross-checking. Thus, rather than just asking someone if they have ever led a sales team, an elaborated item would require the applicant to name all members of the team, where and when the team was together, and what sales they accomplished, citing specific products, figures, and customers. The evidence suggests that forced elaboration reduces the traditional measures of faking behaviour.[80]

Competing Through Globalization

Background Checks in Europe? Mind Your Own Business

Applicant background checks that are thoroughly done are increasingly important when screening for jobs in North America. While some HRM professionals conduct references themselves, many have begun outsourcing the task to professional reference-checking firms, and one doesn't have to look far to understand why. For example, when a counterfeit ring was broken up by York Regional Police in Markham, Ontario, they discovered forged immigration documents and fake university degrees and transcripts so convincing that even university officials accepting applications were fooled. That means that unless an employer's referencing process included verifying the degree or transcript directly from the educational institutions involved, the deception would go undetected.

And that's just one thing that Canadian employers worry about. Add to this the possibility of unwittingly hiring an individual with a violent background, applicants with serious credit problems, or people who don't have the legal right to work in Canada. Unless employers know how to avoid such pitfalls, they may hire convincing liars with dubious backgrounds. For example, an internal study of referencing data gathered by Infocheck in Canada several years ago found that 40 percent of applicants had various problems revealed in their driver's record, 27 percent had poor credit issues, and almost 20 percent had been fired by previous employers. No wonder the reference-checking industry has grown substantially in North America, especially as recent reports of home-grown terrorists make employers even more skittish.

One sees much less of this kind of problem outside North America, despite much longer exposure and experience with terrorism. In Europe, criminal background checks are limited, credit screening is rare, and call centre interviews with former co-workers and bosses is unheard of. There are several reasons for these differences between Europe and North America: First, in terms of values and culture, in Europe, the applicant's right to privacy trumps the organization's right to know. While privacy legislation has recently created more constraints around all HRM practices in Canada, background checks are legal and employers are still advised to do them, as long as the employee signs a consent form in advance. But things are different in Europe, where individual privacy is more closely guarded and protected. Thus, a North American firm that seeks an employee's consent to do a background check is likely to be denied in Europe, and performing the check without consent would be illegal in many countries.

Second, relative to North America, there are far fewer incidences of workplace violence reported in Europe, and the rates of theft and fraud are also much lower. While the lower incidence reporting of such events may be influenced by culturally specific interpretations of what constitutes workplace violence, it still influences European attitudes and barriers around background checks. Similarly, there is a general notion that Europeans tend to carry less debt, perhaps because background checks for credit problems rarely turn up applicants whose financial situation is so dire that one might be afraid of trusting them around money. While some have suggested this notion is also worth revisiting in light of real and looming debt crises in various European countries, it is an issue that has yet to be revealed. However, in North America, debt levels are known to have reached an all-time high. Many North Americans, if screened on their credit card balances, would risk being rejected as viable hires given most standards adopted by companies that do background checks.

Third, although the greater deference to individual privacy would seem to put the employer at a disadvantage, on the other side of the equation, the legal concept of negligent hiring is also largely unheard of in Europe. (Negligent hiring occurs when an employer hires an unqualified or unsuitable person for a job, and thus exposes others to serious risk or harm.) This reduces the need for employers to show copious amounts of due diligence in order to protect themselves legally. As in any country, individual employees in Europe may run afoul of the law or commit egregious acts; however, this is an issue between the offender and the law, and a person's employer is rarely held legally responsible for his or her actions.

Finally, if the legal motivation to perform due diligence and avoid negligent hiring suits is taken out of the picture, the decision to do a background check lies solely on its perceived value in screening out future problems. That's because experience shows information collected by firms doing background checks can be inaccurate and there is objective evidence that the effectiveness of these checks in preventing future problems is weak. (For example, most fraud is committed by long-term employees who know the firm well, not repeat offenders who move from place to place. Thus, only 7 percent of convicted fraud perpetrators had any criminal record whatsoever prior to the offence they were convicted of, and hence they would not be caught in any screen.) Despite such evidence, however, the use of background checks is likely to remain entrenched as a uniquely North American tradition. Due diligence rules!

SOURCES: F. Hanson, "Worker Screening Limited Overseas," *Workforce Management* (February 16, 2009), p. 37; F. Hanson and G. Hernandez, "Caution Amid the Credit Crunch," *Workforce Management* (February 16, 2009), pp. 35–36; C. Terhune, "The Trouble with Background Checks," *BusinessWeek* (June 9, 2009), p. 58; V. Tsang, "No More Excuses," *Canadian HR Reporter* (May 23, 2005) p. R5; S. Hall and A. Miedema, "But I Thought You Checked?" *Canadian HR Reporter* (May 21, 2007), p. 18; S. Klie, "Weeding out the Fakes," *Canadian HR Reporter* (May 7, 2007), p. 1.

Physical Ability Tests

Although automation and other advances in technology have eliminated or modified many physically demanding occupational tasks, many jobs still require certain physical abilities or psychomotor abilities. In these cases, tests of physical abilities may be relevant to not only predicting performance but also predicting occupational injuries and disabilities.[81] There are seven classes of tests in this area: those that evaluate (1) muscular tension, (2) muscular power, (3) muscular endurance, (4) cardiovascular endurance, (5) flexibility, (6) balance, and (7) coordination.[82]

The criterion-related validities for these kinds of tests for certain jobs are quite strong.[83] Unfortunately, these tests, particularly the strength tests, are likely to have an adverse impact on some applicants with disabilities and many female applicants. For example, roughly two-thirds of all males score higher than the highest-scoring female on muscular tension tests.[84]

As a result, there are three interrelated questions to ask in deciding whether to use these kinds of tests if the employer wishes to prevent discrimination in hiring. First, is the physical ability being assessed a reasonable and necessary requirement for performing the job (a *bona fide occupational requirement* (BFOR) of the position), and is it mentioned prominently enough in the job description? The Canadian Human Rights Act does not require employers to hire individuals who cannot perform essential job functions, as long as the employer can demonstrate that the job description is accurate evidence of the essential functions (BFOR) of the job. For example, the Canadian Human Rights Commission Guide to Screening and Selection in Employment states that "a job may require a certain level of colour vision in order to be performed safely and efficiently, thereby precluding from consideration a person who does not meet this standard."[85] Second, is it possible to accommodate an individual who is unable to perform the essential job function without undue hardship to the firm? Finally, is there a probability that failure to adequately perform the job would result in some risk to the safety or health of the applicant, co-workers, or clients?

Competing Through Sustainability

Police Recruiting: Give Peace a Chance

Maintaining an adequate level of policing in Canada is about to become much more difficult, and not because crime is on the increase. Rather, it is the fact that thousands of police officers are nearing retirement age and they will have to be replaced if Canadians are to continue to enjoy their relatively peaceful standard of living. But replacing so many police officers won't be easy for a number of reasons.

One reason such large-scale recruitment is difficult is because attracting high-quality candidates to what is perceived as a tough job has always been a problem. One recent policing study revealed that only 3 percent of candidates in the youth sector see policing as a career that would interest them. To find qualified candidates, police organizations are using innovative ideas to attract diverse types of recruits to their cities. For example, the Hamilton Police Service tries to attract laid-off steel workers. Former employees of Stelco and Dofasco, caught in the downturn of the steel industry, are increasingly willing to consider a second career in policing, where there is no shortage of work. Applicants in their 30s and early 40s are still young enough to anticipate a full career as a police officer. Efforts among the First Nations community in areas such as Sudbury include having a full-time aboriginal liaison officer show young people a targeted recruitment video. Other officers spend three months mentoring immigrants who express an interest in policing to help them make up their minds. The Vancouver Police Department is experimenting with technologically generated recruitment, holding information sessions in the virtual world of Second Life, as avatars tell avatars what it means to choose a career in policing. The jury is still out on how effective such a method is. As Constable Howard Chow of the VPD says, applicants ultimately "still have to come in and face the same questions and go through the same procedures as the 21-year-old guy who's wanted to be a police officer his whole life."

Once recruited, going through the Constable Selection Process is complicated. Applicants must pass a 12-step process of assessment before perhaps receiving an offer to join the force. This includes psychological and aptitude assessments, and evaluation of analytical thinking, communications, behavioural and physical readiness, and vision and hearing. To encourage and assist interested applicants who may worry about successfully passing the physical assessment part of the selection process, the Hamilton Police Service has a solution. The service has developed a Physical Readiness for Employment in Policing (PREP) program designed to encourage potential recruits who fear they don't have "the right stuff" physically to get hired. The PREP program also contains a personal touch to ensure enthusiastic recruits don't drift away because of lack of contact. Instead, the Hamilton PD matches PREP participants with an officer-mentor who helps recruits prepare for both the physical testing and the interview process.

Many police departments across Canada have already begun offering existing officers "stay pay," in hopes they will delay retirement. Retention bonuses are a good strategy, but money alone isn't enough to keep older workers on the job, and police departments will no doubt need to reshape their organizations so that older workers can contribute for as long as possible. Peter Cappelli and Bill Novelli, authors of *Managing the Older Worker: How to Prepare for the New Organizational Order,* argue that what makes older workers stay on the job or, like former Stelco and Dofasco workers, enter new fields like policing, is a desire to be valued, remain mentally sharp, and to be productive. However, like many people who have worked for many years, they will also want to work less. That may or may not fly in the world of policing where criminals work 24/7 to stir up trouble. Regardless, police department recruiters in cities all across Canada will need to be very creative and persuasive if they are to retain older officers who find themselves reporting to 30-year-olds with much less experience. But as Cappelli and Novelli say, in the face of a labour shortage in policing, "If you ignore [boomers], you're ignoring a third of the workforce." Sounds like police recruitment officers will need to find a way to convince existing officers that walking the beat or chasing criminals is where they want to be for the next few years. Either that or the rest of us may indeed have to "bite the bullet" and live with less protection in the next decade.

SOURCES: D. Harder, "Recruiting in Age of Social Networking," *Canadian HR Reporter*, (April 21, 2008), p. 13; D. Mccutcheon, "Industry Insider: Police Personnel," *HR Professional* (April/May 2009), p. 37; J. Budak, "Not on Company Time, Gramps," *Canadian Business* (October 11, 2010), p. 79.

Cognitive Ability Tests

Cognitive ability tests differentiate individuals based on their mental rather than physical capacities. Cognitive ability has many different facets, although we will focus only on three dominant ones. **Verbal comprehension** refers to a person's capacity to understand and use written and spoken language. **Quantitative ability** concerns the speed and accuracy with which one can solve arithmetic problems of all kinds. **Reasoning ability**, a broader concept, refers to a person's capacity to invent solutions to many diverse problems.

Some jobs require only one or two of these facets of cognitive ability. Under these conditions, maintaining the separation among the facets is appropriate. For example, the verbal requirements associated with many jobs in the North American economy have increased over the years, but this has occurred at a time when we have witnessed decreases in scores on standardized tests measuring these skills.[86] For example, a survey of more than 400 large firms suggested that as many as 30 percent of the applicants for entry-level positions have such poor reading and writing scores that it would be impossible to put them on the job without remedial training.[87] If this is the only cognitive ability that is related to the job, then this would be the only one that should be used to make decisions. However, many jobs that are high in complexity require most, if not all, of the facets, and hence one general test is often as good as many tests of separate facets.[88] Highly reliable commercial tests measuring these kinds of abilities are widely available, and they are generally valid predictors of job performance in many different kinds of contexts, including widely different countries.[89] The validity of these kinds of tests is related to the complexity of the job, however, in that one sees higher criterion-related validation for complex jobs than for simple jobs. The predictive validity for these tests is also higher in jobs that are dynamic and changing over time and thus require adaptability on the part of the job incumbent.[90]

For example, the jobs of top-level executives could be fairly characterized as complex and dynamic, and analytic problem solving has consistently been shown to be a major predictor of success in this occupation.[91] Despite this, many of the top executive MBA programs in North America have dropped the use of the GMAT in recent years.[92] The schools traditionally explain eliminating this screen in terms of placing more emphasis on diversity and experience relative to sheer brain power. However, due to the lucrative nature of these programs in terms of generating revenue for the schools, some have suggested that this is primarily a ploy to reduce barriers to entry, admit more students, and generate more revenue. This strategy may backfire, however, if the students who are eventually brought into these programs become a burden to their classmates or a liability to future employers. Indeed, there is some evidence that the ability to screen on general cognitive ability is

Cognitive Ability Tests
Tests that include three dimensions: verbal comprehension, quantitative ability and reasoning ability.

Verbal Comprehension
A person's capacity to understand and use written and spoken language.

Quantitative Ability
The speed and accuracy with which one can solve arithmetic problems of all kinds.

Reasoning Ability
A person's capacity to invent solutions to many diverse problems.

the single greatest virtue associated with the most selective schools, and that controlling for this, the MBA degree itself is not a valid predictor for long-term executive success.[93]

Personality Inventories

While ability tests attempt to categorize individuals relative to what they can do, personality measures tend to categorize individuals by what they are like. Research suggests that there are five major dimensions of personality, known as "the Big Five": (1) extroversion, (2) adjustment, (3) agreeableness, (4) conscientiousness, and (5) inquisitiveness. Table 5.3 lists each of these with a corresponding list of adjectives that fit each dimension.

Although it is possible to find reliable, commercially available measures of each of these traits, the evidence for their validity and generalizability is mixed at best.[94] For example, conscientiousness, which captures the concepts of self-regulation and self-motivation, is one of the few factors that displays any validity across a number of different job categories, and many real-world managers rate this as one of the most important characteristics they look for in employees. (People high in conscientiousness show more stamina at work, which is helpful in many occupations.) Despite this, the use of personality traits in selection contexts has risen over the years.[95] Part of this is attributable to the wider use of team-based structures that put more emphasis on collaboration at work. In contexts where task interdependence between individuals is stressed, personality conflicts become more salient and disruptive relative to situations where individuals are working alone.[96]

Me
Graw connect   Learn more about personality inventories online with Connect.
Hill

The concept of "emotional intelligence" is another form of assessment related to personality inventories, and has been used to describe people who are especially effective in fluid and socially intensive contexts. Emotional intelligence is traditionally conceived of having five aspects: (1) self-awareness (knowledge of one's strengths and weaknesses), (2) self-regulation (the ability to keep disruptive emotions in check), (3) self-motivation (how to motivate oneself and persevere in the face of obstacles), (4) empathy (the ability to sense and read emotions in others), and (5) social skills (the ability to manage the emotions of other people). Daniel Goleman, one of the primary proponents of this construct, noted that "in the new workplace, with its emphasis on flexibility, teams and a strong customer orientation, this crucial set of emotional competencies is becoming increasingly essential for excellence in every job in every part of the world."[97] Although there is not a great deal of direct empirical research on emotional intelligence, there is a great deal of overlap between many of its dimensions and aspects of the Big Five, and there is a large body of evidence regarding these.

The use of personality measures as screening devices has also increased because of the increased use of multinational structures and the increase in the number of jobs that require that people work in foreign locales. The number of people who are asked to work outside their own country has

Table 5.3 The Five Major Dimensions of Personality Inventories

1.	Extroversion	Sociable, gregarious, assertive, talkative, expressive
2.	Adjustment	Emotionally stable, nondepressed, secure, content
3.	Agreeableness	Courteous, trusting, good-natured, tolerant, cooperative, forgiving
4.	Conscientiousness	Dependable, organized, persevering, thorough, achievement-oriented
5.	Inquisitiveness	Curious, imaginative, artistically sensitive, broad-minded, playful

increased steadily over time and, more often than not, the decision of whom to send where is based primarily on technical skills. However, in one large study of expatriates working in Hong Kong, Japan, and Korea, high levels of emotional stability and openness to experience were two of the strongest predictors of adjustment and performance, and these tended to trump technical expertise when it came to predicting who would succeed and fail. In this study, the cost of an adjustment failure (i.e., someone who has to come home prior to finishing his or her assignment) was estimated at over $150,000 per person, and hence the stakes are high in this context.[98]

Finally, the validity for almost all of the Big Five factors in terms of predicting job performance also seems to be higher when the scores are not obtained from the applicant but are instead taken from other people.[99] The lower validity associated with self-reports of personality can be traced to three factors. First, people sometimes lack insight into what their own personalities are actually like (or how they are perceived by others), so their scores are inaccurate or unreliable. Second, people's personalities sometimes vary across different contexts. Thus, someone may be very conscientious when it comes to social activities such as planning a family wedding or a fraternity party, but less conscientious when it comes to doing a paid job. Someone else may work hard at the office, and

Evidence-Based HR

It is essential to collect empirical evidence and validate personality tests in specific contexts rather than assuming that they will work because a commercial developer of such tests says so. For example, one context where measures of personality have been validated with empirical evidence is in the context of franchise operations. A franchise operation is usually part of a national chain (e.g., Tim Hortons, Canadian Tire) but is run locally in an entrepreneurial fashion by a single individual. Successful national franchise chains often select potential franchisees carefully from among numerous applicants to ensure the long-term success of new and existing franchises and to protect the viability and reputation of the franchise brand and image. Not everyone who expresses interest in buying a franchise is successful in passing various levels of screening that may be in place. While sufficient financing would certainly be one criteria for selection, there are often many other factors that come into play, depending on the selectivity of the franchisor.

Evidence within this industry indicates that the amount of revenue each franchise generates varies widely, despite the similarity of product, advertising, and size across the corporation. To learn why this was the case, one franchise operator distributed a set of personality items to all current franchisees and identified each item that distinguished those generating revenue in the top 80th percentile from those whose revenue generation placed them in the bottom 20th percentile. The distinguishing items were then used to select future franchisees who tended to resemble the current high performers and not the current low performers, resulting in an increase in annual royalties per franchise from $6,500 a month to $52,000. (Note that this is a concurrent design, and an example of a criterion-related validity study, discussed earlier) Thus, such an approach enabled the franchisor to identify those applicants more likely to become high performers when running a company franchise, ensuring greater success for the overall operation, and a greater likelihood of success for new franchisees.

SOURCE: J. Bennett, "Do You Have What It Takes?" *The Wall Street Journal,* (September 19, 2006), p. R11.

then not lift a finger to do household chores. Third, unlike intelligence tests, people are much better at "faking" their responses to personality items.[100] Research suggests that when people fill out these inventories when applying for a job, their scores on conscientiousness and emotional stability are much higher relative to when they are just filling out the same questionnaires anonymously for research purposes.[101]

Several steps can be used to try to reduce faking. For example, if employers simply warn applicants that they are going to cross-check the applicants' self-ratings with other people, this seems to reduce faking.[102] Also, the degree to which people can fake various personality traits is enhanced with questionnaires, and one sees much less faking of traits when interviewers are assessing the characteristics.[103]

All of this reinforces the idea that it is better to obtain this information from people other than the job applicant, and that it is better to use this information to reject low scorers but not necessarily hire all higher scorers on the basis of self-reports alone.[104]

Work-Sample Tests

Work-sample tests attempt to simulate the job in a prehiring context to observe how the applicant performs in the simulated job. The degree of fidelity in work samples (accuracy and similarity to the physical and mental challenges of the actual work the test is meant to represent) can vary greatly. In some cases, applicants respond to a set of standardized hypothetical case studies and role-play how they would react to certain situations.[105] Often these standardized role-plays employ interactive video technology to create "virtual job auditions."[106] In other cases, the job applicants are brought to the employers' location and actually perform the job for a short time period as part of a "job tryout."[107] Finally, although not generally considered a test, the practice whereby employers hire someone on a temporary basis and then, after a rather long trial (six months to a year), hire that person permanently is in essence an extended work-sample test.[108]

In some cases, employers will sponsor competitions where contestants (who at this point are not even considered job applicants) vie for attention by going head-to-head in solving certain job-related problems. These sorts of competitions have been common in some industries such as architecture and fashion design, but their use is spreading to many other business contexts. These competitions tend to be cost effective in generating a lot of interest, and some have attracted as many as 1,000 contestants who bring their talents to bear on specific problems faced by the employing organization.[109] Competitions are particularly well suited for assessing and "discovering" young people who may not have extended track records or portfolios to evaluate.

As part of its own fight in the war for talent, Google sponsors an event called "Google Code Jam," which attracts more than 10,000 contestants a year from all over the world. This one-day competition requires contestants to work to solve some very difficult programming problems under relatively high levels of time pressure. For example, finalists have to develop software that would perform unique and difficult searches employing a minimum number of "clicks" or develop a complex interactive war game from scratch in under two hours. The winner of the contest receives $7,000 and a guaranteed job at Google's prestigious Research and Development Center, but, in fact, Google usually winds up hiring more than half of the 50 finalists each year (although that is not guaranteed). The finalists in this contest represent the best of the best in terms of the world's top programmers, and as Robert Hughes, director of the Code Jam, notes, "Wherever the best talent is, Google wants them."[110]

With all these advantages of work-sample tests come two drawbacks. First, by their very nature, the tests are job specific, so generalizability is low. Second, partly because a new test has to be developed for each job and partly because of their nonstandardized formats, these tests are relatively expensive to develop. It is much more cost effective to purchase a commercially available cognitive ability test that can be used for a number of different job categories within the company than to develop a test for each job. For this reason, some have rated the utility of cognitive ability tests higher than work-sample tests, despite the latter's higher criterion-related validity.

In the area of managerial selection, work-sample tests are typically the cornerstone in assessment centres. Generically, the term **assessment centre** is used to describe a wide variety of specific selection programs that employ multiple selection methods to rate either applicants or job incumbents on their managerial potential. Someone attending an assessment centre would typically experience work-sample tests such as an in-basket test which contains samples of typical day-to-day problems the applicant would be expected to handle if hired, and several tests of more general abilities and personality. Because assessment centres employ multiple selection methods, their criterion-related validity tends to be quite high. Assessment centres seem to tap a number of different characteristics, but "problem-solving ability" stands out as probably the most important skill determined via this method.[111] The idiosyncratic and unique nature of the different exercises, however, has led some to suggest that the exercises themselves should be scored for winners and losers without making any reference to higher-order characteristics such as skills, abilities, or traits.[112] Research indicates that one of the best combinations of selection methods includes work-sample tests with a highly structured interview and a measure of general cognitive ability. The validity coefficient expected from such a combined battery often exceeds .60.[113]

> **Assessment Centre**
> A process in which multiple raters evaluate employees' performance on a number of exercises.

Honesty Tests and Drug Tests

Many problems that confront society also exist within organizations, which has led to two new kinds of tests: honesty tests and drug-use tests. Theft in organizations has always been a problem, especially in the retail industry where theft is very difficult to control. Many companies formerly employed polygraph tests, or lie detectors, but in many places these are now illegal. For example, the Employment Standards Act of Ontario forbids the use of lie detector tests, which it defines as "an analysis, examination, interrogation or test taken or performed by means of or in conjunction with a device, instrument or machine, whether mechanical, electrical, electromagnetic, electronic or otherwise, and that is taken or performed for the purpose of assessing or purporting to assess the credibility of a person."[114] However, the banning of such tests did not eliminate the problem of theft by employees. As a result, the paper-and-pencil honesty-testing industry was born.

Paper-and-pencil honesty tests come in a number of different forms, and more recently such tests have been computerized for ease of administration and scoring. Some directly emphasize questions dealing with past theft admissions or associations with people who stole from employers. Other items are less direct and tap more basic traits such as social conformity, conscientiousness, or emotional stability.[115] Some sample items are shown in Table 5.4. A large-scale independent review of validity studies suggests they can predict both theft and other disruptive behaviours. Another

Table 5.4 Sample Items from a Typical Integrity Test

1.	It's OK to take something from a company that is making too much profit.
2.	Stealing is just a way of getting your fair share.
3.	When a store overcharges its customers, it's OK to change price tags on merchandise.
4.	If you could get into a movie without paying and not get caught, would you do it?
5.	Is it OK to go around the law if you don't actually break it?

SOURCE: From *Inc.: The Magazine for Growing Companies.* Copyright © 1992 by Mansueto Ventures LLC. Reproduced with permission of Mansueto Ventures LLC via Copyright Clearance Centre.

positive feature of these tests is that one does not see large differences attributable to race or sex, so they are not likely to have an adverse impact on these demographic groups.[116]

As is the case with measures of personality, some people are concerned that job applicants confronting an honesty test can fake their way to a passing score. The evidence does support this. However, it is not clear that this affects the validity of the predictions made using such tests. That is, it seems that despite this built-in bias, scores on the test still predict future theft. Thus, the test is still seen to be valid for detecting which applicants are prone to theft since the effect of the faking bias is not large enough to detract from the test's validity.[117]

Regardless of whether such tests are valid or useful in predicting future theft, integrity tests are controversial and should be selected and administered with care. In addition, some are not for use with current employees. When using paper-and-pencil honesty tests, employers need to ensure that they select a test designed to detect and predict the behaviours they are concerned about for the job in question (e.g., theft, lying, disciplinary problems). Canadian researcher Victor Catano advises employers to consider the practical side of managing such tests, since many proprietary tests can be administered on site but must be returned to the publisher for scoring and interpretation. He also recommends they be used as an *additional* tool along with other types of tests, and as a last step in the selection process when trying to decide between two equally qualified candidates.[118] In fact, one study found that the validity of integrity tests increased significantly when used to supplement cognitive ability tests.[119] In addition, while apparently legal in Canada, employers should be aware that in the late 90s a former employee of Sobeys filed a human rights complaint against the company based on her failure to pass a paper-and-pencil honesty test when she reapplied to work with the company at a later date.[120]

As with theft, there is a growing perception of the problems caused by drug use among employees. The major controversies surrounding drug tests involve not only concerns about reliability and validity but also whether they represent an unreasonable search and seizure, a violation of human rights, and/or an invasion of privacy. Urinalysis and blood tests are invasive procedures, and accusing someone of drug use is a serious matter.

So why would companies still try to use drug testing in Canada? There are four reasons, which include (1) screening of job applicants for ingestion of illegal drugs, as a condition of employment; (2) to see if impairment was the cause of an accident or near miss, or as a condition of return to work if prior history exists and the employee is in a safety-sensitive position; (3) testing employees whose on-the-job performance is suffering, if drug abuse is suspected to be the reason for poor job behaviours; and (4) random drug testing, in which employees are randomly tested after being selected by a computer.[121]

Arguments in favour of pre-employment drug testing include the need to protect the safety of workers and the general public, such as those employed in the transportation industry or in the oil fields. However, one Alberta oil patch case involving pre-employment drug screening as a precondition of employment (conducted by Kellogg, Brown & Root (KBR) a global supplier of engineering, procurement, and construction services in the hiring of John Chiasson) wound up in the courts for over five years, demonstrating that the practice of drug testing can prove to be litigious, even when employers test for job-related reasons and have employee and public safety in mind.

Justifying drug testing of *any* kind in Canada is difficult to do. Employers considering the use of drug tests would be well advised to make sure that their drug-testing programs conform to some general rules. First, these tests should be administered systematically to all applicants for the same job. Second, testing seems more defensible for jobs that involve safety hazards associated with failure to perform.[122] Test results should be reported back to the applicant, who should be allowed an avenue of appeal (and perhaps retesting). Tests should be conducted in an environment that is as unintrusive as possible, and results from those tests should be held in strict confidence. Finally, when testing current employees, the program should be part of a wider organizational program that provides rehabilitation counselling.[123] However, as the Chiasson case illustrates, even when companies such as KBR try to "follow the rules," the process of drug testing can prove to be an expensive minefield that some may choose to avoid, especially since drug testing doesn't target common factors that impact job performance such as sleep deprivation, family problems, and mental illness.

You will find an extensive discussion of the legality of drug testing for pre-employment purposes in Chapter 12, as well as random testing, for-cause testing, or postincident testing. As the discussion in that chapter indicates, pre-employment drug testing is generally impermissible, and is found to be valid only when there is sufficient concern about safety *and* when three stringent conditions required by the Supreme Court of Canada are satisfied.

Learn more about problems with drug testing online with Connect.

ConnecT

COMPLIANCE WITH THE LAW DURING RECRUITMENT AND SELECTION

LO 7

Describe the various legal requirements in recruitment processes and selection decisions.

The final standard that any recruitment and selection method should adhere to is legality, meaning *compliance* with a variety of federal and provincial laws. Many issues related to recruiting and selecting employees effectively under Canadian laws were discussed generically in Chapter 3. These included requirements of employers to provide equal employment opportunities under the Canadian Human Rights Act, and to meet accessibility requirements contained in the recently passed Employment Accessibility Standard developed under the Accessibility for Ontarians with Disabilities Act, 2005 (and similar provisions in other provinces) Our discussion in Chapter 3 was broad and dealt with legal aspects in all areas of human resource management. In this chapter we focus more narrowly on issues that relate directly to recruitment and selection methods.

Legal Considerations. There are at least four issues employers must pay attention to if they want to be sure they are complying with human rights legislation and other laws that apply to activities involved in recruiting job applicants, conducting the selection process, and making job offers to successful candidates. These include (1) preventing discrimination against applicants, (2) respecting the privacy of applicants, (3) increasing accessibility to the position for all potential applicants and accommodating individuals with disabilities, and (4) communicating hiring agreements clearly. Such considerations apply from the moment a job vacancy becomes known and the firm decides how to advertise the job opening, right through to the moment when a job offer is extended to the individual chosen for hire. Compliance with the law is important but it also makes good business sense, since many people applying for a job are also potential customers or clients. To prevent problems, companies are well advised to be as inclusive as possible, and to extend respect to applicants in every way, including the following.

1. **Recruiting: Advertise job vacancies widely, using a variety of methods, in order to attract a diverse number and type of applicants.** Many firms rely on word-of-mouth advertising because they believe it is inexpensive and fast. Rather than advertise jobs formally in a public venue, they rely exclusively on chance "walk-ins" and referrals from friends or existing employees. In this way, the company severely limits access to knowledge of job opening and directly or indirectly discriminates as "acceptable" applicants are encouraged to apply for the job on face value alone. Hundreds of others who may be much more qualified will never even see a description of the job vacancy. There are many cost-effective ways to eliminate such discriminatory practices, and to increase access to a job vacancy exponentially, such as regularly posting both a written and audio version of the job in a specially designated

"Careers" area of the company website, or on online job boards. This would make it easy for many more job seekers to access the ad, including those who are vision impaired, or who have limited mobility. Aboriginal people, visible minorities, and women (with Internet access) would also have greater access to knowledge of the job opening as well. The company can also list the job with a hiring agency that advertises widely and regularly receives voluntary applications from thousands of qualified people.

To specifically increase accessibility during recruitment, employers should provide clear information about essential job duties in job ads, and they should also be prepared to demonstrate how external recruitment efforts enable applicants with disabilities to find information about job vacancies. Job postings should contain language to the effect that "individual accommodation will be provided to applicants who are selected for assessement."[124] Finally, applicants granted an interview should also be told that assessment and selection materials and processes can be made available in an accessible format if they so wish, and then provided if requested.

2. **Selection: Train interviewers in advance to use valid and reliable interview questions.** By using consistent, job-related questions with all applicants, the company will go a long way toward avoiding discrimination and also increase the likelihood of hiring the best-qualified candidate. Managers and others involved in interviewing should be trained in advance to conduct effective interviews and also to recognize unfair questions that violate human rights legislation. An excellent resource for all involved in interviewing is the *Guide to Screening and Selection in Employment*, a publication available free online through the Canadian Human Rights Commission. The guide illustrates clearly which questions interviewers should avoid asking because they are discriminatory, and offers effective alternative questions that still provide information that helps differentiate among candidates. For example, rather than asking candidates if they have child care arrangements in place in order to determine their availability for work, ask all applicants if they can meet attendance requirements for the job (which should be clear in the job advertisement or stated clearly by the interviewer during the interview).

3. **Selection: Use only reliable and valid selection applicant testing methods.** Earlier we described various selection tests and the importance of validating those over time so that they are both accurate and reliable in differentiating candidates. The employer must ensure that all selection testing methods actually measure accurately and reliably whether the candidate can perform the essential duties of the position, and when a job offer is finally extended to the candidate, it must inform the applicant of the company's accommodation procedures.[125]

4. **Selection: Respect applicants' human rights and right to privacy.** Employers are also subject to the provisions of Personal Information Protection Electronic Documents Act 2005 (PIPEDA), which requires employers to respect issues of consent and privacy. Therefore they must weigh carefully the information needed about an applicant. For example, is a credit check really required to determine an applicant's employability?

The recruitment and selection process inherently requires that employers collect confidential personal and professional information about applicants. Thus the company has an ethical and legal responsibility (under PIPEDA) to do several things. First, employers should obtain signed consent in advance to obtain references from former employers and others about the applicant, and it should clarify how such information will be used once obtained. Once the information is obtained, employers are obliged to protect applicant privacy by limiting access to the informatoin to only those directly involved in the interview and hiring process. All resumes, recruitment files, interview notes, testing results, referencing information, candidate comparison charts, and other records should be stored in a way that ensures they will remain confidential. When such records (both paper and digital) are finally disposed of, the company has an obligation to do so in a way that ensures that private information of applicants never falls into the hands of others for whom it was not intended. To avoid problems, companies should be able to demonstrate (through accurate records) how and when private information has been disposed of.

5. **Selection: Manage risk—Clarify the terms of an offer of employment in a confirmation letter to the new employee.** Once a verbal offer has been extended, confirm what everyone agreed to in writing. Then have the new employee sign the offer letter and keep the letter on file. For other, more complex, employment offers, have a specialist in employment law draft the letter or contract and supervise the terms of offer. Include any special conditions in the letter or contract and make it a matter of record rather than simply a verbal promise that may prove subject to selective recall at a later date. Some employers use this confirmation letter to reinforce the need for confidentiality, moral conduct, and other key expectations of employees.

Clearly, it can take time to understand all the various laws that govern HRM practices involved in attracting, selecting, and hiring individuals to fill job vacancies, but it is essential to put proactive, systematic processes in place to avoid trouble. Respecting and protecting the rights of people who express interest in working for the company is the right thing to do, and when policies and procedures are in place, they quickly become standard operating procedures. Continuous training of people newly involved in the process of hiring is also essential, however, to manage risks associated with hiring and to ensure that practices are followed. Finally, specialists in employment law abound, and HRM should find a firm they trust and can work well with, and consult the specialists as necessary. As John Martelli, senior legal counsel and corporate privacy officer at Bruce Power says, "Employees have become much more litigious over the last 15 years. They know their rights, in part because of the Internet."[126]

A Look Back

In the chapter-opening vignette, we saw how employer branding that is well aligned with the operating mission and vision of an accounting firm ensured that the company was able to attract a sufficient number of suitable applicants even in a tight labour market for young accounting graduates. However, MNP was (and continues to be) careful to promise only what it can deliver when speaking to graduates in on-campus recruitment information sessions. The results were impressive—the company was able to attract a large number of recruits to ensure the firm's continued strong growth, and its campaign was so well implemented that the company won an award for its efforts.

Questions

1. Based on the information provided, why do you think young accounting grads were attracted to MNP? What role did the recruiters play while on-campus?

2. What types of interview questions would you recommend that HRM and managers ask when interviewing on-campus job seekers? What questions do you think students should ask during an interview?

3. Which selection testing methods might be most appropriate to ensure the best applicants are chosen from the many new graduates who were recruited on-campus by MNP? Have you heard of other selection tests used on new graduates that are not mentioned in Chapter 5? Explain your answer.

4. What steps could the HRM team at MNP take to ensure they are getting the most accurate and truthful information from applicants before making job offers?

Summary

Human resource recruiting is a continuous activity that creates an applicant pool for the organization that serves as kind of a buffer zone in the event of a labour shortage. Organizational recruitment programs affect applications through personnel policies (such as promote-from-within policies or due process provisions) that affect the attributes of the vacancies themselves (contract, part time, full time, etc.). They can also impact the nature of people who apply for positions by using different recruitment sources (such as recruiting from universities versus advertising in newspapers). Finally, organizations can use recruiters to influence individuals' perceptions of jobs (by eliminating misconceptions or clarifying uncertainties) or perceptions of themselves (changing the value the applicant places on rewards for various work outcomes).

In this chapter we examined the five critical standards with which all personnel selection methods should conform: reliability, validity, generalizability, utility, and legality. We also looked at nine different selection methods currently used in organizations and evaluated each with respect to these five standards. Table 5.5 summarizes these selection methods and can be used as a guide in deciding which test to use for a specific purpose. Although we discussed each type of test individually, it is important to note in closing that there is no need to use only one type of test for any one job. Indeed, managerial assessment centres use many different forms of tests over a two- or three day period to learn as much as possible about candidates for important executive positions. As a result, highly accurate predictions are often made, and the validity associated with the judicious use of multiple tests is higher than for tests used in isolation.

Table 5.5   A Summary of Selection Methods

METHOD	RELIABILITY	VALIDITY	GENERALIZABILITY	UTILITY	LEGALITY
Interviews	Low when unstructured and when assessing nonobservable traits	Low if unstructured and nonbehavioural	Low	Low, especially because of expense	Low because of subjectivity and potential interviewer bias; also, lack of validity makes job-relatedness low
Reference checks	Low, especially when obtained from letters	Low because of lack of range in evaluations	Low	Low, although not expensive to obtain	Those writing letters may be concerned with charges of libel
Biographical information	High test–retest, especially for verifiable information	High criterion-related validity; low in content validity	Usually job specific, but have been successfully developed for many job types	High; inexpensive way to collect vast amounts of potentially relevant data	May have adverse impact; thus often develop separate scoring keys based on sex or race
Physical ability tests	High	Moderate criterion-related validity; high content validity for some jobs	Low; pertain only to physically demanding jobs	Moderate for some physical jobs; may prevent expensive injuries and disability	Often have adverse impact on women and people with disabilities; need to establish job-relatedness

(continued on next page)

Table 5.5 A Summary of Selection Methods (continued)

METHOD	RELIABILITY	VALIDITY	GENERALIZABILITY	UTILITY	LEGALITY
Cognitive ability tests	High	Moderate criterion-related validity; content validation inappropriate	High; predictive for most jobs, although best for complex jobs	High; low cost and wide application across diverse jobs in companies	Research indicates adverse impact on minority groups in United States although decreasing over time
Personality inventories	High	Low to moderate criterion-related validity for most traits; content validation inappropriate	Low; few traits predictive for many jobs, except conscientiousness	Low, although inexpensive for jobs where specific traits are relevant	Low because of cultural and sex differences on most traits, and low job-relatedness in general
Work-sample tests	High	High criterion and content validity	Usually job specific, but have been successfully developed for many job types	High, despite the relatively high cost to develop	High because of low adverse impact and high job-relatedness
Honesty tests	High	Moderately valid with respect to a number of criteria	Moderate; predictive about potential for dysfunctional job-related behaviour among job applicants	High, although many tests must be submitted to publisher for correct interpretation	No apparent legislative barriers; however, one human rights complaint filed in Nova Scotia in late 90s
Drug tests	Low; drug tests are often unreliable and many are considered inaccurate regarding current impairment or usage level; conditions under which test is administered can also affect reliability	Low due to lack of reliability	Low due to lack of reliability and validity	Expensive, but perceived to yield high payoffs for health and safety-related risks to organization; must first establish direct relationship to job to justify testing	To meet legal scrutiny, testing policy must have a clear and legitimate purpose; highly invasive and violates human rights unless a direct relationship to job performance exists; also risks being discriminatory

Key Terms

Discussion Questions

1. Recruiting people for jobs that entail international assignments is increasingly important for many companies. Where might one go to look for individuals interested in these types of assignments? How might recruiting practices aimed at these people differ from those one might apply when targeting an "average" recruit?

2. Discuss the relative merits of internal versus external recruitment. What types of business strategies might best be supported by recruiting externally, and what types might call for internal recruitment? What factors might lead a firm to decide to switch from internal to external recruitment or vice versa?

3. We examined many different types of selection methods in this chapter. Assume that you were just rejected for a job based on one of these methods. Obviously, you might be disappointed and angry regardless of what method was used to make this decision, but can you think of two or three methods that might leave you most distressed? In general, why might the acceptability of the test to applicants be an important standard to add to the five we discussed in this chapter?

4. Videotaping applicants in interviews is becoming an increasingly popular means of getting multiple assessments of that individual from different perspectives. Can you think of some reasons that videotaping interviews might also be useful in evaluating the interviewer? What would you look for in an interviewer if you were evaluating one on videotape?

5. Distinguish between concurrent and predictive validation designs, discussing why the latter is preferred over the former. Examine each of the selection methods discussed in this chapter and determine whether the choice of validation design employed impacts the validity of each method. Which is most affected?

6. Some have speculated that in addition to increasing the validity of decisions, employing rigorous selection methods has symbolic value for organizations. What message is sent to applicants about the organization through its hiring practices, and how might this message be reinforced by recruitment programs that occur before selection and training programs that occur after selection?

Self-Assessment Exercise

Most employers have to evaluate hundreds of resumes each week. If you want your resume to have a good chance of being read by prospective employers, you must invest time and energy not only in its content, but also in its format. Your resume could even be viewed as your first "interview" since it is your first opportunity to gain the attention of employers who will receive it. Review your resume and answer yes or no to each of the following questions.

1. Does it avoid typos and grammatical errors?
2. Does it avoid using personal pronouns (such as "I" and " me")?
3. Does it clearly identify what you have done and accomplished?
4. Does it highlight your accomplishments rather than your duties?
5. Does it exceed two pages in length?
6. Does it have correct contact information?
7. Does it have at least 1-inch (2 cm) margins?

8. Does it use a maximum of two typefaces or fonts?

9. Does it use bullet points to emphasize your skills and accomplishments?

10. Does it avoid use of underlining?

11. Does it include information about your volunteer and leadership experiences?

12. Is the presentation consistent? (e.g., If you use bold italics for the name of your most recent workplace, do you do that for previous workplaces as well?)

The more "yes" answers you gave, the more likely your resume will attract an employer's attention and get you a job interview!

Learn more about your most prominent traits in another Self-Assessment Exercise online with Connect.

Exercising Strategy: Mining for Gold: A Network Approach to Assessing Employee Value

Traditional approaches to validating employment tests and methods have relied on subjective appraisals from supervisors as the primary criterion. A test was valid if it predicted what future supervisors are likely to say about that person after having worked with him or her for a short time. As you might imagine, and as we will see in much more detail in Chapter 7, the perceptions of these supervisors are often biased, unreliable, and based on incomplete information. Therefore, one might question what the ability to predict what supervisors are likely to say about a briefly known subordinate actually implies, and why the need for finding an alternative, more reliable, valid, and less biased criterion has been an ongoing concern in the area of human resources.

Increasingly, the combination of social networking software—and the technology to analyze data that can be collected by this software—is ushering in a new age of methods to determine employee value. *Data mining,* that is, the process of electronically going through massive amounts of data generated by networked computers, has proven valuable in many areas of business. In the area of operations, it has been used to streamline supply chains. In marketing, it has been used to more effectively target audiences. Now, in the area of human resource management, it is being used to identify who are the most important and valuable employees within the firm, or who is likely to be successful. It also reveals how employees might act even before they get the notion to act—such as calling in sick, or deciding to resign. Such an approach is called predictive analytics, and the process relies on "temporal reasoning" that occurs as the technology sorts through mounds of digital data to determine what is going to happen in the future. Predictive analytics reveals connections among bytes of information gleaned from web page visits, e-mails, employee data, blogs, Twitter pages and social networking sites such as Facebook that contain assorted types of information about the employee and perhaps even friends of that employee. However, experts caution that the science of data mining isn't always perfect (as election results will tell us). For example, Tom Davenport, one expert in the field of analytics, points out that, "The person who resigns may not be the person you predicted would resign at all."

That's not a concern at Microsoft, though—at least not yet. The company has software that allows them to code who talks to whom, how often, and about what content. This allows HRM to see who tends to originate ideas (spark plugs), who seems to build on them and pass them on (super-connectors), and who seems to hold them up (bottlenecks). Deciding who should get credit for a great idea has always been a contentious and controversial process in organizations that rely on subjective appraisals; however, with this new "process tracing technology," once the market identifies an idea as a winner, the organization can go back and objectively determine its source and trajectory.

In addition to tracing specific ideas, this software also, over the longer haul, can be used to help identify who is at the centre and who is at the periphery of the organization's social network. For example, at IBM, someone who is routinely copied on ideas from a large number of people, from a large number of different departments, and from many different sources (supervisors, peers, subordinates, and clients) is identified as someone who must be playing a major leadership role in the organization. Once identified, these people are fast-tracked for future leadership roles and shielded from downsizing efforts such as those that marked the 2008 recession. Although, as is the case with any objective indicator, one might be able to game this system in different ways, in general, this shows the desire that some companies have to go beyond the single subjective impression of a supervisor when it comes to determining the value of every employee or new hire.

SOURCES: S. Baker, "How Much Is That Worker Worth," *BusinessWeek* (March 23, 2009), pp. 46–48; S. Baker, "Putting a Price on Social Networks," *BusinessWeek* (April 8, 2009), pp. 45–47; S. Baker, "Reading the Body Language of Leadership," *BusinessWeek* (March 30, 2009), p. 48.; J. Kirby, "Corporate Mind Games," *Macleans*, (September 23, 2010) at www2.macleans.ca/2010/09/23/corporate-mind-games/ (retrieved June 23, 2011).

Questions

1. Would you be concerned if you accepted a job at an organization and found out later that you had been "data mined" in the selection process? Why or why not?

2. Is it ethical for companies to trace every digital move an employee makes, or to sort through every byte of information that can be found about an individual? Explain your answer.

3. If data mining were to be restricted, what legislation might allow this to happen? What could a company do to overcome such restrictions?

4. What could you do to ensure that only positive data could be mined about your background? What can you do if negative information is already available in digital format that could be mined?

Managing People: Bridging the Generation Gap

Dutch employment agency Randstad, which entered the Montreal market in 1997, teams newbies with older staff to great effect. For a pair of colleagues born four decades apart, Penelope Burns and Rinath Benjamin spend a lot of time together. Burns, 68, and Benjamin, 29, are sales agents for Randstad. They sit inches apart, facing each other. They hear every call the other makes. They read every e-mail the other sends or receives. Sometimes they finish each other's sentences.

This may seem a little strange, but the unconventional pairing is all part of Randstad's effort to ensure that its 20-something employees—the flighty, praise-seeking Generation Y that we have read so much about—fit in and, more to the point, stick around. The company, which has been expanding in North America, is hoping to win the hearts, minds, and loyalty of its young employees by teaming them up with older, more experienced hands. Every new sales agent is assigned a partner to work with until their business has grown to a certain size, which usually takes a few years. Then they both start over again with someone who has just joined the company. "This makes the corporate world more personal, approachable," says Randstad CEO Stef Witteveen. "It's easier for the Gen Yers to identify with their jobs. They don't drown in their cubicles."

Randstad has been pairing up people almost since it opened for business four decades ago. The founder's motto was "Nobody should be alone." The original aim was to boost productivity by having sales agents share one job and trade off responsibilities. The system has been refined over the years and now each week one person is out making sales calls, and the other is in the office interviewing potential workers and handling the paperwork. Then they switch.

Randstad brought its partnership program to North America in the late 1990s, and now boasts numerous branches in six Canadian provinces. But it wasn't until two years ago, once Randstad had integrated the personnel from the various firms it had acquired, that it began recruiting new employees. In 2006, for example, it hired about 600 people, 420 of whom are in their 20s. Knowing that these Gen-Yers need lots of attention in the workplace, Randstad executives figured that if they shared a job with someone whose own success depended on theirs, they were certain to get all the nurturing they required. Such an approach acknowledges what experts are saying, that for Gen Y the psychological contract is embedded in relationships within the organization, not the organization itself.

No Touchdowns Allowed

Of course, Randstad doesn't simply put people together and hope it all works out. First it figures out who will play well with other people. To assess that, the human resources department conducts extensive interviews and requires candidates to shadow a sales agent for half a day. "We have certain questions that we look for them to answer with *we* instead of *I*," says HRM Chief Genia Spencer. "Somebody who needs to be recognized as the star, who needs personal achievement and doesn't like to share that, won't work in a unit. Partners cannot compete with each other." One question Randstad asks is: What's your most memorable moment while being on a team? "If they answer: 'When I scored the winning touchdown,' that's a deal killer," says Spencer. "Everything about our organization is based on the team and group."

Before joining Randstad in January 2006, Benjamin had worked for six years as a sales agent at Verizon. When she first heard about Randstad's partnering program she was a little apprehensive. "It was completely different. I was used to being responsible for everything," she says. "Here you are forced to be open, to tell everything." But Burns knew they could work together. "I tested her during the interview to see if she had a sense of humour, if I could tease her a little bit and she would know it was to relieve the tension." Burns has been an agent at Randstad since 1998 and has been in the business for some two decades. She is feisty and competitive. Benjamin is quick, direct, confident. She's big on e-mail, texting, and her BlackBerry.

One of the most compelling features of Randstad's partnering program is that neither person is "the boss." And both are expected to teach the other.

Burns:	People think I run the works. I don't. She trains me as much as I train her.
Benjamin:	We have a great rapport. She's like my grandmother.
Burns:	You can get cynical when you've been in the business as long as I have. She doesn't let me get that way.
Benjamin:	During our training, we learn that we are each other's boss. The biggest shock was to have someone asking what I'm doing all the time. Now I'm over that.

Soon after Benjamin started, she suggested they begin to use the electronic payroll system Randstad offers to save time and reduce their paperwork. Burns hesitated: She had been filling out time sheets for the talent (as the temporary employees are called) and wasn't sure how they would take to the new task. But Benjamin persuaded her it would ultimately be simpler for everyone. "You don't have to drag me into the future, just give me a little push," says Burns. Now, when someone hasn't logged on in time, Burns calls and says: "Rinath says you have to get your time sheet in."

Burns, who has had a couple of other partners, says the younger agents are often impatient. "They want to tell clients about problems before we have a solution. Sometimes new people don't realize that's not a good idea." She says Benjamin wants to act quickly, but hasn't made that mistake. "She tells me to take a breath," says Benjamin.

Gaining Perspective

Randstad encourages people to solve problems with their partners and breaks up teams only when the situation is fairly dire—when, say, one person is sabotaging the other or when productivity suffers because of constant bickering. In those cases, which the company says are rare, the uncooperative partner usually ends up leaving the company.

Even so, Randstad's ability to keep its employees has improved. The company used to have a retention rate of 50 percent, which is the industry standard. In the past year, its rate has increased to 60 percent. "We have determined a clear connection between being in a unit and feeling more successful and productive," says Spencer.

CEO Witteveen, who is 44, acknowledges that some managers resist having to accommodate the idiosyncrasies of Gen Y. "It's natural to think: 'Why should I do all these kinds of things for them? No one did that for me.' You have to get over that. You have to think beyond your own feelings of fairness. It's about improving the relationship with the employee." He says he, too, had to learn to appreciate the concerns of the younger generation even though he gets practice at home. "I have two Gen-Y kids, and they come with all the features," he says.

Questions

1. Personnel selection decisions typically are based on the fit for one person for one job. In what way does Randstad's use of partnership teams alter the typical way one might think about selection decisions?

2. What are some personal characteristics that might be viewed positively when staffing a single job, but that might actually be viewed negatively when staffing partnership teams?

3. Randstad deliberately creates variance in age when forming partnership teams. In what ways might younger workers and older workers be in a position to uniquely support each other when working in sales teams?

4. Other than age, what other types of traits or abilities might one want to see when creating variance in partnership teams?

SOURCES: Susan Berfield, "Bridging the Generation Gap," *BusinessWeek* (September 1, 2007), pp. 60–61; www.randstad.com/about-us (retrieved October 26, 2010); www.randstad.ca/about/randstad_canada_group.aspx (retrieved October 26, 2010); www.randstad.ca/branches/branch_locator.aspx (retrieved October 26, 2010).

connect **Practise and learn online with Connect.**

6 Training and Strategic Development of People

Enter the World of Business

Retention Tactics at Accenture Reap Huge ROI

Accenture Consulting has offices in 150 cities around the globe in countries such as Argentina, Botswana, South Korea, Poland, Canada, and the United States, and it encourages employees to spend time with clients—not in their own offices. If employees want to spend time in one of the consulting firm's offices, they have to make a reservation for a desk! Accenture has a virtual management workforce of 204,000 employees in 120 countries who, at any one time, are working at different times and places around the world. Accenture's consultants analyze client's business needs and design and implement solutions. The consultants work in teams depending on the size of the client and the project. While the work and travel can be exciting, it also can take a heavy toll on the consultants; many eventually choose to take a stable job, often with one of the clients with whom they have worked. Although a consultant deciding to work for a client can help Accenture keep and maybe even add new business, Accenture loses money when talented employees leave.

To prevent such turnover, Accenture has taken a number of steps, including making a heavy investment in employee learning. The company is so committed to this approach to retention that in 2007 it published a book entitled *Return on Learning: Training for High Performance at Accenture* explaining how it achieved a 353 percent "return on learning" (i.e., a return on the company's investment of money, time, and interest in the learning of its employees.) In 2008, Accenture invested over $900 million in training and professional development (12 million hours of learning, or an average of 78 hours per year of customized learning per employee). From the moment employees join Accenture they continuously improve their marketable skills and begin to develop specialist knowledge through a series of training activities designed to fit the unique needs of each employee at his or her particular career level. In addition, training delivered through a wide variety of methods is integrated with job experience and constant feedback, ensuring constant professional growth.

Accenture also reduces turnover by helping consultants manage their careers to recognize and take advantage of opportunities within the company. For example, after orientation every new hire is assigned a career counsellor, a more senior Accenture employee in the same line of business who is available to meet face-to-face or electronically to discuss current work and potential career opportunities. Accenture's performance and compensation system encourages senior employees to make time in their schedules for career counselling. Every employee at Accenture is evaluated on people development skills as part of the annual performance review, which is tied to a percentage of pay increase. To encourage career development, Accenture's human resources department is focusing on communicating the different available career paths to employees more effectively. Also, the company's career counsellors attend mandatory one-day training on the different career paths at Accenture. Accenture has replaced the old "get promoted or leave" approach with a philosophy that emphasizes how its multiple workforces each contribute to the business in a different, but complementary, way. The company's business strategy depends on these different workforces blending together as an integrated whole, to help it and its clients achieve higher levels of performance. As a result, Accenture now has many different opportunities that vary in both the type of work (consulting, technology, and outsourcing) and the type of client being served (for-profit and not-for-profit businesses).

Accenture's Careers Marketplace website was developed to provide employees with information about changing careers within the company, and it provides links to unfilled positions. For example, one of the videos on the website explains how an employee has moved within the company from consulting to business operations work to human resources. The employee discusses how each move helped her develop her skills and experience. Accenture also recognizes the important role of nonwork life in a successful career. For example, Accenture has a leave program (Future Leave) through which employees can arrange for part of their paycheques to be set aside for up to three months of future time off. The company also asks employees to evaluate how well the company is doing in providing them with a high-quality life as well as to rank issues such as diversity, reputation, work, rewards, and career development in order of personal importance. This helps Accenture determine the work/life balance of employees. The surveys are also used by career counsellors in their discussions with employees.

Altogether, Accenture's training and development tactics are designed to give employees as many reasons as possible to resist tempting offers from other employers when they emerge.

SOURCES: Based on J. Marquez, "Accentuating the Positive," *Workforce Management* (September 22, 2008), pp. 18–25; Accenture's website at www.accenture.com; S. Needleman, "New Career, Same Employer," *The Wall Street Journal* (April 21, 2008), p. B9.; D. Vanthournout, Kurl Olson, John Ceisel, Andrew White, Tad Waddington, Thomas Barfield, Samir Desai, and Craig Mindrum, *Return on Learning: Training for High Performance at Accenture,* B2Books, Agate Publishing (2006); "Great Place to Work" at http://careers3.accenture.com/ Careers/Canada/People-At-Accenture/Great-Place-To-Work/default.htm (retrieved November 22, 2010); "About Accenture," at http://careers3.accenture.com/Careers/Global/About-Accenture/default.htm (retrieved November 29, 2010).

INTRODUCTION

As the Accenture Consulting example illustrates, training, employee development, and career management are key contributors to a company's competitive advantage by helping employees understand their strengths, weaknesses, and interests and by showing them how new jobs, expanded job responsibilities, and career paths are available to them to meet their personal growth needs. Clearly, learning is an essential part of Accenture's business strategy. Training helps employees at Accenture develop specific skills that enable them to succeed in their current job, but the company also recognizes that learning involves not only formal training courses but also job experiences and interactions between employees. This helps retain valuable employees who might otherwise leave to join clients or competitors. In addition, there is both a direct and an indirect link between training and development and business strategy and goals. For example, training can help employees develop skills needed to perform their jobs, which directly affects the business, and employee development is key to ensuring that employees have the competencies necessary to serve customers and create new products and customer solutions. However, employee development is also important to ensure that companies have the managerial talent needed to successfully execute a growth strategy. Regardless of the business strategy, training and development are important for retaining talented employees.

To provide context, we begin this chapter by discussing the relationship between training, development, and careers. Next, we look at systematic approaches to training. Finally, we examine various approaches to employees' development and discuss some special issues in employee development.

THE RELATIONSHIP AMONG TRAINING, DEVELOPMENT, AND CAREERS

LO 1

Discuss the relationship between training and development and how the two can contribute to companies' business strategy.

Training and Development

In general, **training** refers to a planned effort by a company to facilitate employees' learning of job-related competencies. These competencies include knowledge, skills, or behaviours that are critical for successful job performance. The goal of training is for employees to master the knowledge, skill, and behaviours emphasized in training programs and to apply them to their day-to-day activities. If training is to offer a competitive advantage, it should be used in a broader way, as a mechanism for creating and sharing knowledge (as with Accenture). It should create intellectual capital, which includes basic skills (skills needed to perform one's job), advanced skills (such as how to use technology to share information with other employees), and an understanding of the customer or manufacturing system, and self-motivated creativity.[1]

Development refers to formal education, job experiences, relationships, and assessment of personality and abilities that help employees prepare for the future. The Accenture Consulting example illustrates that although development can occur through participation in planned programs, it often results from performing different types of work or serving new clients. Because it is future oriented, it involves learning that is not necessarily related to the employee's current job.[2]

Table 6.1 shows the differences between training and development. Traditionally, training focuses on helping employees' performance in their current jobs. Development prepares them for other positions in the company and increases their ability to move into jobs that may not yet exist.[3] Development also helps employees prepare for changes in their current jobs that may result from

Training
A planned effort to facilitate the learning of job-related knowledge, skills, and behaviour by employees.

Development
The acquisition of knowledge, skills, and behaviours that improve an employee's ability to meet changes in job requirements and in client and customer demands.

Table 6.1 Comparison between Training and Development

	TRAINING	DEVELOPMENT
Focus	Current	Future
Use of work experiences	Low	High
Goal	Preparation for current job	Preparation for changes in current job
Participation	Required	Voluntary

new technology, work designs, new customers, or new product markets. Development is especially critical for talent management, particularly for senior managers and employees with leadership potential (recall our discussion of attracting and retaining talent in Chapter 1). Companies report that the most important talent management challenges they face include developing existing talent and attracting and retaining existing leadership talent.[4]

It is important to note, however, that as training continues to become more strategic (that is, related to business goals), the distinction between training and development will blur. At the same time, both training and development will be required and will focus on current and future personal and company needs.

Now that you have some context, we begin our discussion of training by emphasizing the conditions through which training practices can help companies gain competitive advantage and how managers can contribute to a high-leverage training effort and create a learning organization. We then describe a systematic and effective approach to training design, including a review of training methods to choose from and the importance of training evaluation. Finally, we conclude our discussion of training by focusing on two special training issues, managing diversity and socializing employees.

HIGH-LEVERAGE TRAINING STRATEGY: A SYSTEMATIC APPROACH

It has been estimated that 85 percent of jobs in North America and Europe require extensive use of knowledge, meaning that employees are now required to share knowledge and to use it creatively to modify products and services, or to understand the service or product development system. Therefore, many companies have adopted the broader perspective on training described earlier, known as high-leverage training. **High-leverage training** is linked to strategic business goals and objectives, uses an instructional design process to ensure that training is effective, and compares or benchmarks the company's training programs against training programs in other companies.[5]

High-leverage training practices also help to create working conditions that encourage continuous learning. **Continuous learning** requires employees to understand the entire work system including the relationships among their jobs, their work units, and the company (Continuous learning is similar to the idea of service or product development system understanding mentioned earlier).[6] Employees are expected to acquire new skills and knowledge, apply them on the job, and share this information with other employees.

The emphasis on high-leverage training has been accompanied by a movement to link training to performance improvement or business strategy.[7] That is, training is used to improve employee performance, which leads to improved business results. Training is seen as one of several possible solutions to improve performance; other solutions can include such actions as changing the job or increasing employee motivation through pay and incentives, topics covered chapters 4, 8, and 9

High-Leverage Training
Training practice that links training to strategic business goals, has top management support, relies on an instructional design model, and is benchmarked to programs in other organizations.

Continuous Learning
A learning system that requires employees to understand the entire work process and expects them to acquire new skills, apply them on the job, and share what they have learned with other employees.

Learn more about high-leverage training and continuous learning online with Connect.

Figure 6.1 shows the strategic training and development process with examples of strategic initiatives, training activities, and metrics. The strategic training and development process involves identifying strategic training and development initiatives that will help achieve the business strategy. Employees participate in specific training and development activities that support these initiatives. The final step of the process involves collecting measures or metrics. The metrics are used to determine if training helped contribute to goals related to the business strategy. This may be particularly important when companies begin using web-based training or developing websites for knowledge

FIGURE 6.1 The Strategic Training and Development Process

sharing. These newer learning strategies rely on learners being able to be self-directed in the learning process, and to learning without direct help from instructors. Hence, the outcomes are initially less predictable. Evaluation of such strategies will help determine when such strategies are appropriate and helpful, and when they are not.

DESIGNING EFFECTIVE TRAINING ACTIVITIES

A key characteristic of training activities that contribute to competitiveness is that they are created using one of several well-known systems of instructional design,[8] or what is referred to as a training design process. **Training design process** refers to a systematic approach for developing training programs. Instructional System Design (ISD) and the ADDIE model (analysis, design, development, implementation, evaluation) are two specific types of training design processes with which you may be familiar. Table 6.2 presents the six steps of the training design process (and the purpose of each), which emphasizes that effective training practices involve more than just choosing the most popular or "colourful" training method.

Learn more about the training design process online with Connect.

Needs Assessment

The first step in the instructional design process, **needs assessment**, refers to the process used to determine if training is necessary. Figure 6.2 shows the reasons or pressure points (causes) and outcomes resulting from needs assessment. As we see, many different "pressure points" suggest that training is necessary. These pressure points include performance problems, new technology, customer requests (internal or external) for training, new legislation, new jobs, new products, or lack of basic skills (among employees) as well as support for the company's business strategy (e.g., growth, global business expansion). Note that these pressure points do not guarantee that training is the correct solution.

Table 6.2 The Training Design Process

STEPS IN TRAINING PROCESS	PURPOSE OF THE STEP
1. Needs assessment • Organizational analysis • Person analysis • Task analysis	Step 1 is essential to determine if training is needed, or if another solution could be more effective.
2. Ensuring employees' readiness for training • Attitudes and motivation to learn • Supportive work environment	Step 2 is required to ensure that employees have the motivation to learn and a supportive work environment to master training content.
3. Creating a learning environment • Identification of learning objectives and training outcomes • Meaningful content • Practice and feedback • Observation and interaction with others • Administering and coordinating program • Training committed to memory	Step 3 addresses whether the training session (or the learning environment) has the factors necessary for learning to occur.
4. Ensuring transfer of training • Self-management strategies • Peer and manager support (There are things managers, employees, and trainers should be doing before, during, and after training to ensure transfer occurs.)	Step 4 ensures that trainees apply the content of training to their jobs. This requires support from managers and peers for the use of training content on the job as well as getting the employee to understand how to take personal responsibility for skill improvement. (Thus, the conditions that facilitate transfer of learning in a training program should be planned *before* training takes place.)
5. Selecting training methods • Presentation methods • Hands-on methods • Group methods	Step 5 involves choosing the right training methods (from a wide variety of methods), to create the most appropriate learning environment for achieving the training objectives.
6. Evaluating training programs • Identification of training outcomes and evaluation design • Return on investment	Step 6 is necessary to determine whether training achieved the desired learning outcomes and/or financial objectives.

Organizational Analysis
A process for determining the business appropriateness of training.

Person Analysis
A process for determining whether employees need training, who needs training, and whether employees are ready for training.

Task Analysis
The process of identifying the tasks, knowledge, skills, and behaviours that need to be emphasized in training.

Needs assessment typically involves organizational analysis, person analysis, and task analysis.[9] Organizational analysis considers the context in which training will occur. That is, **organizational analysis** involves determining the business appropriateness of training, given the company's business strategy, its resources available for training, and support by managers and peers for training activities.

Person analysis helps identify who needs training. **Person analysis** involves (1) determining whether performance deficiencies result from a lack of knowledge, skill, or ability (a training issue) or from a motivational or work-design problem; (2) identifying who needs training; and (3) determining employees' readiness for training. **Task analysis** includes identifying the important tasks and knowledge, skill, and behaviours that need to be emphasized in training for employees to complete their tasks.

FIGURE 6.2   The Needs Assessment Process

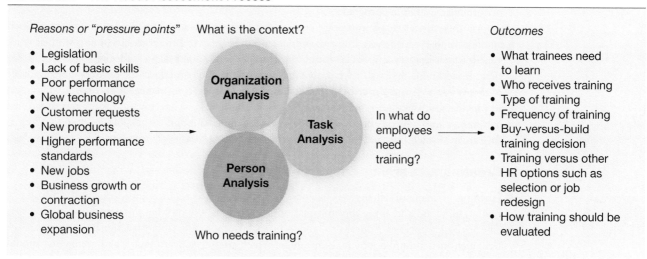

Reasons or "pressure points"

- Legislation
- Lack of basic skills
- Poor performance
- New technology
- Customer requests
- New products
- Higher performance standards
- New jobs
- Business growth or contraction
- Global business expansion

What is the context?

Organization Analysis

Task Analysis

Person Analysis

In what do employees need training?

Who needs training?

Outcomes

- What trainees need to learn
- Who receives training
- Type of training
- Frequency of training
- Buy-versus-build training decision
- Training versus other HR options such as selection or job redesign
- How training should be evaluated

Person analysis and task analysis are often conducted at the same time because it is often difficult to determine whether performance deficiencies are a training problem without understanding the tasks and the work environment. As shown in Figure 6.2, needs assessment shows who needs training and what trainees need to learn, including the tasks in which they need to be trained plus knowledge, skill, behaviour, or other job requirements. Needs assessment helps determine whether the company will purchase training from a vendor or consultant or develop training using internal resources.

Learn more about needs assessment online with Connect.

Ensuring Employees' Readiness for Training

The second step in the training design process is to evaluate whether employees are ready to learn. *Readiness for training* refers to whether (1) employees have the personal characteristics (ability, attitudes, beliefs, and motivation) necessary to learn program content and apply it on the job and (2) the work environment will facilitate learning and not interfere with performance.

Although managers are not often trainers, they play an important role in influencing employees' readiness for training. **Motivation to learn** is the desire of the trainee to learn the content of the training program.[10] Various research studies have shown that motivation is related to knowledge gain, behaviour change, or skill acquisition in training programs.[11] Of course, employees' motivation to learn in training activities is also influenced by the degree to which they have essential skills such as strong cognitive abilities, and the reading and writing skills needed to understand the content of a training program. Employers may wish to conduct a literacy audit as part of ensuring training readiness.

Managers need to ensure that employees' motivation to learn is as high as possible. One way they can do this is by ensuring employees' self-efficacy. **Self-efficacy** is the employees' belief that they can successfully learn the content of the training program. For example, training employees to use equipment for computer-based manufacturing represents a potential threat, especially if employees are intimidated by new technologies and do not have confidence in their ability to master

Motivation to Learn
The desire of the trainee to learn the content of a training program.

Self-Efficacy
The employees' belief that they can successfully learn the content of a training program.

the skills needed to use the technology. Research has demonstrated that self-efficacy is related to performance in training programs.[12]

Another critical factor impacting employee training motivation is the work environment itself and how employees perceive it. For example, employees may feel there are constraints in their work situation that hold them back such as lack of proper tools, equipment, budgetary support, and/or time. In addition, they will have individual perceptions about the level of social support available to them before, during, or after training takes place. This refers to managers' and peers' willingness to provide feedback and reinforcement.[13] It is in the manager's interest to ensure any situational constraints are removed and that trainees receive as much support as possible from co-workers so they are motivated to acquire new work behaviours in the training environment.

Creating a Learning Environment

Learning permanently changes behaviour. For employees to acquire knowledge and skills in the training program and apply this information in their jobs, the training program must include specific learning principles. Educational and industrial psychologists and instructional design specialists have identified a number of conditions under which employees learn best,[14] and events that should occur, including (1) trainees need to know why they should learn (learning objectives and training outcomes); (2) training programs need meaningful content (3) training should provide opportunities for practice and feedback (4) trainees need to observe experience and interact with others; (5) training should include good program coordination and administration, and (6) trainees need to commit training content to memory.

connect

Learn more about motivation, self-efficacy, and creating a learning environment online with Connect.

Ensuring Transfer of Training

Transfer of Training
The use of knowledge, skills, and behaviours learned in training on the job.

Transfer of training, the fourth step in the training design process, refers to on-the-job use of knowledge, skills, and behaviours learned in training. As Figure 6.3 shows, transfer of training is influenced by the climate for transfer, manager support, peer support, opportunity to use learned capabilities, technological support, and self-management skills. As we discussed earlier, learning is influenced by the learning environment (such as meaningfulness of the content and opportunities for practice and feedback) and employees' readiness for training (for example, their motivation to learn and whether or not the learning environment facilitates learning). If no learning occurs in the training program, transfer is unlikely.

Climate for Transfer
Trainees' perceptions of characteristics of the work environment (social support and situational constraints) that can either facilitate or inhibit use of trained skills or behaviour.

One way to think about the work environment's influence on transfer of training is to consider the overall climate for transfer. **Climate for transfer** refers to trainees' perceptions about a wide variety of characteristics of the work environment that facilitate or inhibit use of trained skills or behaviour. These characteristics include manager and peer support, opportunity to use skills, and the consequences for using learned capabilities.[15] Research has shown that transfer of training climate is significantly related to positive changes in behaviours following training.

Opportunity to Perform
Trainees are provided with or actively seek experience using newly learned knowledge, skills, or behaviour.

Opportunity to use learned capabilities (**opportunity to perform**) refers to the extent to which the trainee is provided with or actively seeks experience with newly learned knowledge, skill, and behaviours from the training program,[16] and it is influenced by both the work environment and trainee motivation. One way trainees can use learned capabilities is through assigned work experiences (problems or tasks) that require their use. The trainees' manager usually plays a key role in determining work assignments. Opportunity to perform is also influenced by the degree to which

FIGURE 6.3   Work Environment Characteristics Influencing Transfer of Training

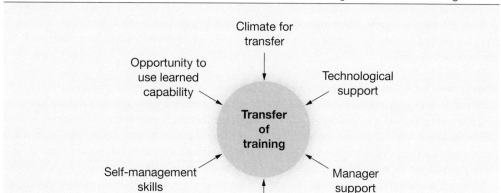

trainees take personal responsibility to actively seek out assignments that allow them to use newly acquired capabilities. Trainees given many opportunities to use training content on the job are more likely to maintain learned capabilities than trainees given few opportunities.[17]

Technology can also be utilized to assist with transfer of training. One example is **electronic performance support systems (EPSS)**, which are computer applications that can provide skills training, information access, and expert advice.[18] EPSS may be used to enhance transfer of training by giving trainees an electronic information source that they can refer to as needed as they attempt to apply learned capabilities on the job.

Finally, training programs should prepare employees to self-manage their use of new skills and behaviours on the job.[19] Specifically, within the training program, trainees should set goals for using skills or behaviours on the job, identify conditions under which they might fail to use them, identify the positive and negative consequences of using them, and monitor their use of them. Also, trainees need to understand that it is natural to encounter difficulty in trying to use skills on the job; relapses into old behaviour and skill patterns do not indicate that trainees should give up. Finally, because peers and supervisors on the job may be unable to reward trainees using new behaviours or to provide feedback automatically, trainees need to create their own reward system and ask peers and managers for feedback.

Electronic Performance Support Systems (EPSS)
Computer applications that can provide skills training, information access, and expert advice.

Learn more about transfer of training online with Connect.

Selecting Training Methods

The fifth step in the instructional design method is selecting design methods. A number of different methods can help employees acquire new knowledge, skills, and behaviours. Although the use of new technology-based methods of training has been growing in recent years, along with the tendency for self-directed study, instructor-led classroom training still remains the most frequently used method.

Regardless of whether the training method is traditional or technology based, for training to be effective it must be based on the training design model shown in Table 6.2.

Presentation Methods
Training methods in which trainees are passive recipients of information.

Presentation Methods **Presentation methods** refer to methods in which trainees are passive recipients of information. Presentation methods include traditional classroom instruction, including distance learning; audiovisual techniques; and mobile technology such as iPods and PDAs. These are ideal for presenting new facts, information, different philosophies, and alternative problem-solving solutions or processes.

Instructor-Led Classroom Instruction. Classroom instruction typically involves having the trainer lecture a group. In many cases the lecture is supplemented with question-and-answer periods, discussion, or case studies. Traditional classroom instruction is one of the least expensive, least time-consuming ways to present information on a specific topic to many trainees. The more active participation, job-related examples, and exercises that the instructor can build into traditional classroom instruction, the more likely trainees will learn and use the information presented on the job.

Another way to offer instructor-led training is through distance learning, often used by geographically dispersed companies. Distance learning features two-way communications between people and enables companies to provide information about new products, policies, or procedures as well as skills training and expert lectures to field locations.[20] It currently involves various types of technology, including teleconferencing, webcasting,[21] and individualized, personal computer–based training.[22]

Learn more about instructor-led presentation methods online with Connect.

Audiovisual Techniques. *Audiovisual instruction* includes overheads, slides, and video. It has been used for improving communications skills, interviewing skills, and customer-service skills and for illustrating how procedures (such as welding) should be followed. However, video is rarely used alone; it is usually used in conjunction with lectures to show trainees real-life experiences and examples. Video is also a major component of behaviour modelling and interactive video instruction.

Mobile Technologies: iPods and PDAs. Mobile technologies such as iPods and PDAs allow training and learning to occur naturally throughout the workday or at home, allow employees to be connected to communities of learning, and give employees the ability to learn at their own pace by reviewing material or skipping over content they know.[23] The typical users for mobile learning include employees who are part of a workforce that spends most of its time travelling; visiting customers, clients, or various company locations (such as sales, security officers, executives, or inspectors); or who have limited time available to spend in traditional training activities or e-learning.

Some of the challenges of using mobile technology for learning include ensuring that employees know when and how to take advantage of the technology; encouraging communication, collaboration, and interaction with other employees in communities of practice; and ensuring that employees can connect to a variety of networks no matter their location or the mobile device they are using.[24]

Mobile technology is useful not only for entertainment, but also for employees who travel and need to be in touch with the office. iPods and PDAs also give employees the ability to listen to and participate in training programs at their leisure.

Hands-on Methods **Hands-on methods** are training methods that require the trainee to be actively involved in learning. Hands-on methods include on-the-job training, simulations, business games and case studies, behaviour modelling, interactive video, and e-learning (Web-based training.) These methods are ideal for developing specific skills, understanding how skills and behaviours can be transferred to the job, experiencing all aspects of completing a task, and dealing with interpersonal issues that arise on the job.

On-the-Job Training (OJT)

On-the-job training (OJT) refers to new or inexperienced employees learning through observing peers or managers performing the job and trying to imitate their behaviour. OJT can be useful for training newly hired employees, upgrading experienced employees' skills when new technology is introduced, cross-training employees within a department or work unit, and orienting transferred or promoted employees to their new jobs.

OJT takes various forms, including self-directed learning programs and apprenticeships (both are discussed later in this section.) OJT is an attractive training method because, compared to other methods, it needs less investment in time or money for materials, trainer's salary, or instructional design. Managers or peers who are job knowledge experts are used as instructors. As a result, it may be tempting to let them conduct the training as they believe it should be done. However, such training may be unstructured and ineffective.

OJT must be structured to be effective. Table 6.3 shows the steps of structured OJT. Because OJT involves learning by observing others, successful OJT is based on the principles emphasized by social learning theory. These include the use of a credible trainer, a manager or peer who models the behaviour or skill, communication of specific key behaviours, practice, feedback, and reinforcement. Some companies may utilize computerized simulations or other forms of virtual reality to accomplish objectives that are part of OJT training, allowing employees to observe and practise tasks, receive feedback, and correct mistakes in a safe virtual environment. Since many jobs today are knowledge based and utilize computers as an integral way of accomplishing work, it can be an effective form or part of OJT. We discuss this and the role of virtual reality later in this section.

Hands-On Methods
Training methods that actively involve the trainee in learning.

On-the-Job Training (OJT)
New or inexperienced employees learning through observing peers or managers performing the job and trying to imitate their behaviour.

Table 6.3 Steps in On-the-Job Training

PREPARING FOR INSTRUCTION	
1. Break down the job into important steps. 2. Prepare the necessary equipment, materials, and supplies.	3. Decide how much time you will devote to OJT and when you expect the employees to be competent in skill areas.

ACTUAL INSTRUCTION	
1. Tell the trainees the objective of the task and ask them to watch you as you demonstrate it. 2. Show the trainees how to do it without saying anything. 3. Explain the key points or behaviours. (Write out the key points for the trainees, if possible.) 4. Show the trainees how to do it again. 5. Have the trainees do one or more parts of the task and praise them for correct reproduction (optional).	6. Have the trainees do the entire task and praise them for correct reproduction. 7. If mistakes are made, have the trainees practise until accurate reproduction is achieved. 8. Praise the trainees for their success in learning the task.

SOURCES: Based on W. J. Rothwell and H. C. Kazanas, "Planned OJT Is Productive OJT," *Training and Development Journal* (October 1990), pp. 53–55; P. J. Decker and B. R. Nathan, *Behaviour Modelling Training* (New York: Praeger Scientific, 1985).

Self-Directed Learning
A program in which employees take responsibility for all aspects of learning.

Self-directed learning involves having employees take responsibility for all aspects of learning—when it is conducted and who will be involved. Self-directed learning for salespeople could involve reading newspapers or trade publications, talking to experts, or surfing the Internet to find new ideas related to the sales industry.[25] Also, self-directed learning could involve the company providing salespeople with information such as databases and training courses and seminars, but they are in charge of taking the initiative to learn. Because the effectiveness of self-directed learning is based on the employee's motivation to learn, companies may want to provide seminars on the self-directed learning process, self-management, and how to adapt to the environment, customers, and technology to better facilitate the process.

Apprenticeship
A work-study training method with both on-the-job and classroom training.

Apprenticeship is a provincially regulated work-study training method made up of two parts, on-the-job training and classroom training. To qualify, applicants complete an in-school portion, usually around 10 percent of the program, in a certified learning institution. Institutionalized training complements the on-the-job training experience (the remaining 90 percent), which is provided under the instruction of a certified journeyperson in the trade. It takes between two and five years to become a certified journeyperson in Canada, depending on the trade.[26] Apprenticeships can be sponsored by individual companies or by groups of companies cooperating with a union. The majority of apprenticeship programs are in the skilled trades, such as plumbing, carpentry, electrical work, and bricklaying.

The OJT portion involves assisting a certified tradesperson (a journeyman) at the work site, and follows the guidelines for effective on-the-job training, using[27] modelling, practice, feedback, and evaluation. First, the employer verifies that the trainee has the required knowledge of the operation or process. Next, the trainer (a certified journeyperson in the trade) demonstrates each step of the process, emphasizing safety issues and key steps. The trainer provides the apprentice with the opportunity to perform the process until all are satisfied that the apprentice can perform it properly and safely.

Simulation
A training method that represents a real-life situation, allowing trainees to see the outcomes of their decisions in an artificial environment.

Simulations. A **simulation** is a training method that represents a real-life situation, with trainees' decisions resulting in outcomes that mirror what would happen if the trainee were on the job. In effective simulations, the job situation is represented with both physical and psychological accuracy. Simulations, which allow trainees to see the impact of their decisions in an artificial, risk-free environment, are used to teach production and process skills as well as management and interpersonal skills.

At United Parcel Service (UPS), technology has made the drivers' job more complex.[28] They have to handle the truck safely, be proficient on the DIAD (handheld computer), and understand how to stay safe during a package delivery. As a result, UPS developed the Integrad Training Center. Integrad includes a package car simulator (replicating the famous UPS brown delivery trucks) designed to teach new hires how to load and unload packages from shelves, the floor, and the rear door—meeting company time standards for such activities while minimizing stress and strain that cause injuries. The average driver has to step off and on the truck at least 120 times on his or her route, which can strain ankles if done incorrectly. Trainees deliver packages with trainer and trainees serving as customers in a simulated town with stores, streets, and even a loading dock.

Virtual Reality
Computer-based technology that provides trainees with a three-dimensional learning experience. Trainees operate in a simulated environment that responds to their behaviours and reactions.

A recent development in simulations is the use of virtual reality technology. **Virtual reality** is a computer-based technology that provides trainees with a three-dimensional learning experience. Using specialized equipment or viewing the virtual model on the computer screen, trainees move through the simulated environment and interact with its components.[29] Technology is used to stimulate multiple senses of the trainee.[30] Devices relay information from the environment to the senses. For example, audio interfaces, gloves that provide a sense of touch, treadmills, or motion platforms are used to create a realistic, artificial environment. Devices also communicate information about the trainee's movements to a computer. These devices allow the trainee to experience the perception of actually being in a particular environment.

Stapoil, a Norwegian oil company, has an oil platform in Second Life, an online virtual community mentioned in Chapter 5, that allows trainees to walk around it. Stapoil uses the oil platform for safety training. It catches fire, and employees have to find lifeboats to safely exit the platform.[31] British Petroleum (BP) used Second Life to train new gas station employees in the safety features of gasoline storage tanks and piping systems.[32] BP builds three-dimensional replicas of the tank and pipe systems normally found at a gas station. In the virtual world, trainees are able to see the underground storage tanks and piping systems and observe how safety devices control gasoline flow, which they could never do in real life.

Business Games and Case Studies. Situations that trainees study and discuss (case studies) and business games in which trainees must gather information, analyze it, and make decisions are used primarily for management skill development.

Games stimulate learning because participants are actively involved and the games mimic the competitive nature of business. The types of decisions that participants make in games include all aspects of management practice, including labour relations (such as agreement in contract negotiations), marketing (the price to charge for a new product), and finance (financing the purchase of new technology).

Most documentation on learning from games is anecdotal.[33] Games may give team members a quick start at developing a framework for information and help develop cohesive groups. For some groups (such as senior executives), games may be more meaningful training activities (because the game is realistic) than presentation techniques such as classroom instruction.

Behaviour Modelling. Research suggests that behaviour modelling is one of the most effective techniques for teaching interpersonal skills.[34] Each training session, which typically lasts four hours, focuses on one interpersonal skill, such as coaching or communicating ideas. Each session presents the rationale behind key behaviours, a videotape of a model performing key behaviours, practice opportunities using role-playing, evaluation of a model's performance in the videotape, and a planning session devoted to understanding how the key behaviours can be used on the job. In the practice sessions, trainees get feedback regarding how closely their behaviour matches the key behaviours demonstrated by the model. The role-playing and modelled performance are based on actual incidents in the employment setting in which the trainee needs to demonstrate success.

Interactive Video. Interactive video combines the advantages of video and computer-based instruction. Instruction is provided one-on-one to trainees via a personal computer. Trainees use the keyboard or touch the monitor to interact with the program. Interactive video is used to teach technical procedures and interpersonal skills. The training program may be stored on a DVD or the company intranet.

E-Learning. **E-learning** or online learning refers to instruction and delivery of training by computers through the Internet or company intranets.[35] E-learning includes Web-based training, distance learning, virtual classrooms, and use of CD-ROMs and DVDs. E-learning can include task support, simulation training, distance learning, and learning portals. There are three important characteristics of e-learning. First, e-learning involves electronic networks that enable information and instruction to be delivered, shared, and updated instantly. Second, e-learning is delivered to the trainee via computers with Internet technology. Third, it focuses on learning solutions that go beyond traditional training to include electronic links to information and tools that improve performance.

E-Learning
Instruction and delivery of training by computers through the Internet or company intranet.

■ connect

Learn more about hands-on presentation methods online with Connect.

Blended Learning. Because of the limitations of online learning related to technology (e.g., insufficient bandwidth, lack of high-speed Web connections), trainee preference for face-to-face contact with instructors and other learners, and employees' inability to find unscheduled time during their workday to devote to learning from their desktops, many companies are moving to a hybrid, or blended, learning approach. *Blended learning* combines online learning, face-to-face instruction, and other methods for distributing learning content and instruction. The "Competing Through Technology" box shows how blended learning is benefitting the TD Bank Group by providing both tangible and indirect benefits.

Learning Management System (LMS)
Technology platform that automates the administration, development, and delivery of a company's training program.

Learning Management System. A **learning management system** (LMS) refers to a technology platform that can be used to automate the administration, development, and delivery of all of a company's training programs. An LMS can provide employees, managers, and trainers with the ability to manage, deliver, and track learning activities.[36] LMSs are becoming more popular for several reasons. An LMS can help companies reduce travel and other costs related to training, reduce time for program completion, increase employees' accessibility to training across the business, and provide administrative capabilities to track program completion and course enrolments. An LMS allows companies to track all of the learning activity in the business. For example, FedEx Kinkos has an LMS.[37] The company has document and shipping centres around the world and employs more than 20,000 people. Its LMS includes a software package that allows creation of individualized training for each employee, schedules classrooms, tracks employee progress, manages all aspects of the training curriculum, and delivers e-learning courses. Employees have access via personal computer to their personal learning plans based on their job, what their manager requires, and their own personal interests.

Group- or Team-Building Methods
Training techniques that help trainees share ideas and experiences, build group identity, understand the dynamics of interpersonal relationships, and get to know their own strengths and weaknesses and those of their co-workers.

Group- or Team-Building Methods Group- or team-building methods are training methods designed to improve team or group skills and effectiveness. Training is directed at improving the trainees' skills as well as team effectiveness. In group-building methods, trainees share ideas and experiences, build group identity, understand the dynamics of interpersonal relationships, and get to know their own strengths and weaknesses and those of their co-workers. Group techniques focus on helping teams increase their skills for effective teamwork. A number of training techniques are available to improve work group or team performance, to establish a new team, or to improve interactions among different teams. They include trust falls (in which each trainee stands on a table and falls backward into the arms of fellow group members), paintball games, NASCAR pit crews, cooking, obstacle courses and even drumming. All involve examination of feelings, perceptions, and beliefs about the functioning of the team; discussion; and development of plans to apply what was learned in training to the team's performance in the work setting. Group-building methods often involve experiential learning. Experiential learning training programs involve gaining conceptual knowledge and theory; taking part in a behavioural simulation; analyzing the activity; and connecting the theory and activity with on-the-job or real-life situations.[38] Group-building methods fall into three categories: adventure learning, team training, and action learning.

Adventure Learning
Learning focused on the development of teamwork and leadership skills by using structured outdoor activities.

Adventure Learning. **Adventure learning** develops teamwork and leadership skills using structured outdoor activities.[39] Adventure learning appears to be best suited for developing skills related to group effectiveness, such as self-awareness, problem solving, conflict management, and risk taking. Adventure learning may involve strenuous, challenging physical activities such as dogsledding

Competing Through Technology

Preventing Bank Heists through Blended Learning

Many companies, recognizing the strengths and weaknesses of face-to-face instruction and technology-based training methods, are using both in a blended-learning approach to training. As the following example illustrates, technology-based training can be used to provide consistent delivery of training content involving transfer of information (knowledge and skills) to geographically dispersed employees who can work at their own pace, practise, and in some cases collaborate with the trainer and trainee online. Then trainees can be brought to a central location for face-to-face training (classroom, action learning, games, and role-plays), which can emphasize the application of knowledge and skills using cases and problems that require the application of training content.

Recently TD Bank decided to use blended learning to speed up design and delivery of essential training in robbery prevention when it was faced with an escalating number of bank heists at the peak of the recession. Talk about being under siege! Nancy Nazer, vice president of Leadership Development and Learning Strategies at TD Bank in Toronto knew that quick but thorough action was needed, and implemented a needs analysis to start. Although such training had always existed, and in fact the bank's Hazard Prevention Program stated that " Special training to prepare for branch robberies is given to branch employees on a regular basis to ensure they are prepared at all times," clearer objectives were identified for the new bank robbery training program. These included (1) reduce the number of robberies (2) enhance risk-management practices (3) improve robbery prevention overall, and (4) reduce financial losses. In focus groups, needs analysts also learned that the program should deal with post-event issues as well— important finding they hadn't anticipated.

To ensure they had the best content and methods, course designers partnered with the RCMP and an armed robbery association. The course designer also wanted to make the learning process as realistic as possible since the ultimate training evaluation could be a life-or-death situation when a customer service representative found him- or herself face-to-face with a seasoned criminal. At such times, everyone hopes they can respond in a safe and effective way to keep the situation under control.

By November 2008 the pilot program was ready and included e-learning, instructor-led discussions, scripted role-play scenarios, debriefs, informal discussions and ongoing coaching. Nazer felt that the blended approach provided "more comprehensive learning because it wasn't just a one-time event, it was more fulsome to go beyond just the awareness."

By January 2009, TD Bank launched the training to its 33,000 employees. Employees were instructed to complete a 30 minute e-learning portion (including video footage) that dealt with what to do before, during and after a robbery, and the master test required an 80 percent pass rate before taking in-branch training, the next step of the program. Hour–long, in-class sessions located in branches included time spent reviewing the self-directed computer-based lessons. Learners could then clarify issues with instructors, ask questions, and take part in role-plays with co-workers. Debriefing ensured understanding, and a second in-class session took place again six months later. With the initial training done, annual refreshers were the next step and are required of all employees. So far the results are encouraging, with participants averaging 80 percent and above.

Of course, the proof of effectiveness in such a program is in how well employees can handle an actual robbery in progress. By late 2010 Nazer was feeling very positive, saying "... in the last few weeks we have had a number of 'attempted' robberies (two already today!) The reason these are only 'attempts' is that people are using their learnings from the robbery awareness training."

While the new training program produced tangible benefits such as "a 41 percent reduction in cash losses" in 2009 over 2008, and 11 percent fewer robberies, indirect benefits emerged as well. Nazer believes that using the blended approach has raised expectations for future modules. It has reinforced her commitment to accessing the latest and best data possible for content, and to providing the best and latest technology possible so that learning is easier and faster for TD Bank employees.

SOURCES: Based on S. Dobson, "Learning to Avoid the Bad Guys," *Canadian HR Reporter* (November 29, 2010), p. 24; TD Financial Group Corporate Responsibility Report, Workplace Health and Safety, at www.td.com/corporateresponsibility/crr2008/pdf/emp_health_safety.pdf (retrieved January 7, 2011).

or mountain climbing. It can also use structured individual and group outdoor activities such as climbing walls, going through rope courses, making trust falls, climbing ladders, and travelling from one tower to another using a high-wire device.

The physically demanding nature of adventure learning and the requirement that trainees often have to touch each other in the exercises may increase the company's risk for negligence claims due to personal injury, intentional infliction of emotional distress, and invasion of privacy, and therefore companies should plan such programs with care and be aware of their legal responsibilities before proceeding.

Team Training. Team training coordinates the performance of individuals who work together to achieve a common goal. Such training is an important issue when information must be shared and individuals affect the overall performance of the group. For example, in the military as well as the private sector (think of nuclear power plants or commercial airlines), much work is performed by crews, groups, or teams. Success depends on coordination of individual activities to make decisions, team performance, and readiness to deal with potentially dangerous situations (such as an overheating nuclear reactor).

ⓜ connect

Learn more about experiential learning, adventure learning, and team training methods online with Connect.

Action Learning
Teams work on an actual business problem, commit to an action plan, and are accountable for carrying out the plan.

Action Learning. In **action learning**, teams or work groups get an actual business problem, work on solving it and commit to an action plan, and are accountable for carrying out the plan.[40] Typically, action learning involves between 6 and 30 employees; it may also include customers and vendors. There are several variations on the composition of the group. In one variation the group includes a single customer for the problem being addressed. Sometimes the groups include cross-functional team members (members from different company departments) who all have a stake in the problem. Or the group may involve employees from multiple functions who all focus on their own functional problems, each contributing to helping solve the problems identified.

Six Sigma Training
An action training program that provides employees with defect-reducing tools to cut costs and certifies employees as green belts, champions, or black belts.

Six Sigma and black belt training programs involve principles of action learning. **Six Sigma training** provides employees with measurement and statistical tools to help reduce defects and cut costs.[41] Six Sigma is a quality standard with a goal of only 3.4 defects per million processes. There are several levels of Six Sigma training, resulting in employees becoming certified as green belts, champions, or black belts.[42] To become black belts, trainees must participate in workshops and complete written assignments coached by expert instructors. The training involves four 4-day sessions over about 16 weeks. Between training sessions, candidates apply what they learn to assigned projects and then use them in the next training session. Trainees are also required to complete not only oral and written exams but also two or more projects that have a significant impact on the company's bottom line. After completing black belt training, employees are able to develop, coach, and lead Six Sigma teams; mentor and advise management on determining Six Sigma projects; and provide Six Sigma tools and statistical methods to team members. After black belts lead several project teams, they can take additional training and be certified as master black belts. Master black belts can teach other black belts and help senior managers integrate Six Sigma into the company's business goals.

McKesson Canada, an award-winning provider of logistics services, software applications, and automation solutions in the Canadian health-care marketplace, has wholeheartedly adopted the Six Sigma training program. The company has trained 15 to 20 black belts across the company and returned them to their original business units as their team's Six Sigma representatives.[43] When the two-year commitment as Six Sigma representative ends, the black belts are reassigned to the business at higher positions, helping to spread the approach throughout the organization and ensuring that key leaders are committed to the Six Sigma philosophy. In most divisions of the company, Six Sigma training is mandated for senior vice presidents, who attend training that introduces Six Sigma and details how to identify a potential Six Sigma project. Across the company, every manager and director is expected to attend basic training. The Six Sigma effort has produced savings ever since inception of the program in 1999. [44]

Evaluating Training Programs

The sixth, and last, step in the instructional design process is evaluating training programs. Examining the outcomes of a program helps in evaluating its effectiveness. These outcomes should be related to the program objectives, which help trainees understand the purpose of the program. **Training outcomes** can be categorized as cognitive outcomes, skill-based outcomes, affective outcomes, results, and return on investment.[45] Which training outcomes measure is best? The answer depends on the training objectives. For example, if the instructional objectives identified business-related outcomes such as increased customer service or product quality, then results outcomes should be included in the evaluation.

> **Training Outcomes**
> A way to evaluate the effectiveness of a training program based on cognitive, skill-based, affective, and results outcomes.

Ernst & Young's training function uses knowledge testing for all of the company's e-learning courses, which account for 50 percent of training.[46] New courses and programs use behaviour transfer and business results. Regardless of the program, the company's leaders are interested in whether the trainees feel that it was a good use of their time and the company's money and whether they would recommend it to other employees. The training function automatically tracks these outcomes because managers expect that training activities have a positive impact on business results (such as client satisfaction) and employee engagement (reduced turnover).

Learn more about evaluating training methods online with Connect.

OTHER SPECIAL TRAINING ISSUES AND EMPLOYEE ONBOARDING

To meet the competitive challenges of sustainability, globalization, and technology discussed in Chapter 1, companies must successfully deal with several special training issues. Such special training include managing workforce diversity, socializing and orienting new employees, and preparing employees to work in different cultures abroad. In the next section of this chapter we will discuss managing workforce diversity and socializing and orienting new employees. However, we will

> **LO 3**
>
> Explain the importance of organizational socialization, the onboarding process, and other special training solutions.

reserve our discussion of preparing employees to work in different cultures to Chapter 13, Managing Human Resources Globally.

Managing Workforce Diversity

Diversity can be considered to be any dimension that differentiates a person from another.[47] Therefore, managing diversity requires implementing various activities to help employees embrace (understand and accept) differences and variety in others, including age, ethnicity, education, sexual orientation, work style, race, gender, abilities, and more.

Managing Diversity
The process of creating an inclusive environment that allows all employees to contribute to organizational goals and experience personal growth.

Managing diversity involves creating an inclusive environment that allows all employees to contribute to organizational goals and experience personal growth. This environment includes access to jobs as well as fair and positive treatment of all employees. The company must develop employees who are comfortable working with people from a wide variety of backgrounds. Managing diversity may require changing the company culture. It includes the company's standards and norms about how employees are treated, competitiveness, results orientation, innovation, and risk taking. The value placed on diversity is grounded in the company culture.

Compliance with human rights legislation and the requirement for many companies to complete annual employment equity plans, discussed in Chapter 3, is a predictable first step to successfully managing a diverse workforce, but companies need to ensure that

- Employees understand how their values and stereotypes influence their behaviour toward members of the four designated groups and with respect to other differences (e.g., differences in age).
- Employees gain an appreciation of cultural differences among themselves.
- Behaviours that isolate or intimidate designated group members improve.

Diversity Training
Training designed to improve employee attitudes about diversity and/or develop skills needed to work with a diverse workforce.

This can be accomplished through diversity training programs. **Diversity training** is training designed to improve employee attitudes about diversity and/or develop skills needed to work with a diverse workforce. The goals of diversity training are (1) to eliminate values, stereotypes, and managerial practices that inhibit employees' personal development and therefore (2) to allow employees to contribute to organizational goals regardless of their race, sexual orientation, gender, family status, religious orientation, or cultural background.[48] Diversity training programs differ according to whether attitude or behaviour change is emphasized.[49]

Attitude Awareness and Change Program
Program focusing on increasing employees' awareness of differences in cultural and ethnic backgrounds, physical characteristics, and personal characteristics that influence behaviour toward others.

Attitude awareness and change programs focus on increasing employees' awareness of differences in cultural and ethnic backgrounds, physical characteristics (such as disabilities), and personal characteristics that influence behaviour toward others. The assumption underlying these programs is that, by increasing their awareness of stereotypes and beliefs, employees will be able to avoid negative stereotypes when interacting with employees of different backgrounds. The programs help employees consider the similarities and differences between cultural groups, examine their attitudes toward employment equity, or analyze their beliefs about why employees from designated groups are successful or unsuccessful in their jobs. Many of these programs use DVDs and experiential exercises to increase employees' awareness of the negative emotional and performance effects of stereotypes, values, and behaviours on designated group members.

Behaviour-Based Program
A program focusing on changing the organizational policies and individual behaviours that inhibit employees' personal growth and productivity.

Behaviour-based programs focus on changing the organizational policies and individual behaviours that inhibit employees' personal growth and productivity. These programs can take three approaches.

One approach is to identify incidents that discourage employees from working to their potential. Groups of employees are asked to identify specific promotion opportunities, sponsorship, training opportunities, or performance management practices that they believe were handled unfairly. Their views regarding how well the work environment and management practices value employee differences and provide equal opportunity may also be collected. Another approach is to teach managers and employees basic rules of behaviour in the workplace.[50] For example, managers and employees should learn that it is inappropriate to use statements and engage in behaviours that directly or indirectly convey disrespect for others. A third approach is **cultural immersion:** sending employees directly into communities where they can interact with persons of different abilities or races, or from different cultures and nationalities.

Learn more about diversity training and how to create a successful diversity training program online with Connect.

Cultural Immersion
A behaviour-based diversity program that sends employees into communities where they interact with persons from different cultures, races, and nationalities.

Socialization, Orientation, and Onboarding Programs

Organizational socialization is the process by which new employees are transformed into effective members of the company. Effective socialization involves being prepared to perform the job effectively, learning about the organization, and establishing work relationships.

Socialization and orientation programs play an important role in socializing employees. Orientation involves familiarizing new employees with company rules, policies, and procedures. Typically, a program includes information about the company, department in which the employees will be working, and the community the employees will live in (if a transfer is involved). Onboarding refers to the orientation process for newly hired managers.

Although the content of orientation programs is important, the process of orientation cannot be ignored. Too often, orientation programs consist of completing payroll forms and reviewing human

Organizational Socialization
A process by which new employees are transformed into effective members of the company.

Evidence-Based HR

Arrow Targets Cost-Effective Orientation Programs

Arrow Electronics—an electronics component and computer products company (known as Arrow North American Components in Canada) with 11,000 employees in more than 200 locations in 53 countries—used to have a five-day orientation that introduced the industry and Arrow's culture, values, and history to new employees. However, the program was not cost-effective because it was limited to the company's North American employees, which meant all new employees had to travel to one location to attend the program. Arrow now delivers the same content through an interactive computer game. New employees can view modules on industry basics, corporate history, and culture. Each module is followed by a quiz-show-based game to assess what employees learned, and they receive immediate feedback. The program is self-paced, can be accessed around the world, and can be completed in several different languages. Total costs for game development were approximately 10 percent of what had been spent on the classroom orientation. Thus the development of an alternative and engaging method of delivery of the company's orientation program has contributed to Arrow's bottom line (and ongoing competitiveness), and to ensuring that all employees receive the same information around the world. At the same time it has provided new employees with a much more convenient and flexible way to learn about the company they are joining, without having to travel or be away from home for five or more days.

SOURCE: J. Arnold, "Gaming Technology Used to Orient New Hires," *SHRM 2009 HR Trendbook* (Alexandria, VA: Society for Human Resource Management), pp. 36–38. Reprinted with the permission of *HR Magazine* published by the Society for Human Resource Management, Alexandria, VA.

resources policies with managers or human resource representatives. Although these are important activities, the new employee has little opportunity to ask questions, interact with peers and managers, or become familiar with the company's culture, products, and service. Effective orientation programs actively involve the new employee. An important characteristic of effective orientation is that peers, managers, and senior co-workers are actively involved in helping new employees adjust to the work group.[51]

Orientation programs must also be cost effective. See the Evidence-Based HR box and note how Arrow Electronics reduced the cost of orientation. IBM uses Second Life for new hires to learn about corporate culture and business processes by having their avatars attend meetings, watch presentations, and interact with other avatars in a virtual IBM community.

connect

Learn more about socialization and orientation online with Connect.

LO 4

Explain how employee development contributes to strategies related to employee retention, developing intellectual capital, and business growth.

EMPLOYEE DEVELOPMENT

As we explained earlier, training is invaluable to help employees become better at their current jobs. However, companies must do everything they can to retain top-performing employees and position the organization to adapt quickly to changes in the environment. One of the most important ways to accomplish both is to invest in continuing employee development. Accordingly, we now turn our attention to the topic of career development, a process that goes a long way to ensure retention of a company's most talented employees as well as sustainability of the organization itself.

Development and Careers

Traditionally, careers have been described in various ways.[52] Careers have been described as a sequence of positions held within an occupation (for example, a university faculty member can hold assistant, associate, and full professor positions). Careers have also been described in the context of mobility within an organization. For example, an engineer may begin her career as a staff engineer. As her expertise, experience, and performance increase, she may move through advisory engineering, senior engineering, and senior technical positions. Finally, careers have been described as a characteristic of the employee. Each employee's career consists of different jobs, positions, and experiences.

Protean Career
A career that is based on self-direction with the goal of psychological success in one's work.

Today's careers are known as protean careers.[53] A **protean career** is based on self-direction with the goal of psychological success in one's work. Employees take the most responsibility for managing their careers. For example, an engineer may decide to take a sabbatical from her position to work in management at United Way for a year. The purpose of this assignment could be to develop her managerial skills as well as help her personally evaluate if she likes managerial work more than engineering.

Changes in the psychological contract between employees and their companies have influenced the development of the protean career.[54] A psychological contract is the expectations that employers and employees have about each other. Today's psychological contract rarely provides employees with job security even if they perform well. Instead, companies offer employees opportunities to attend training programs and participate in work experiences that can increase their employability with their current and future employers. For example, the term *blue-collar work* has always meant manufacturing work, but technology has transformed the meaning dramatically.[55] Traditional assembly-line jobs that required little skill and less education have been sent overseas. Today's blue-collar workers are more involved in customized manufacturing.

Because companies need to be more responsive to customers' service and product demands, employees need to develop new skills rather than rely on a static knowledge base. The types of knowledge an employee needs have changed.[56] In the traditional career, "knowing how" (having the appropriate skills and knowledge to provide a service or produce a product) was critical. Although knowing how remains important, employees also need to "know why" and "know whom." "Knowing why" refers to understanding the company's business and culture so the employee can develop and apply knowledge and skills that can contribute to the business. "Knowing whom" refers to relationships the employee may develop to contribute to company success. These relationships may include networking with vendors, suppliers, community members, customers, or industry experts. Learning to "know whom" and "know why" requires more than formal courses and training programs. Learning and development in the protean career are increasingly likely to involve relationships and job experiences rather than formal courses.

The emphasis on continuous learning, learning beyond "knowing how," and changes in the psychological contract are altering the direction and frequency of movement within careers (the career pattern).[57] These new career patterns mean that developing employees (as well as employees taking control of their own careers) will require more opportunities to (a) determine their interests and skill strengths and weaknesses, and (b) based on this information, seek appropriate development experiences that will likely involve job experiences and relationships *as well as* formal courses.

The most appropriate view of today's careers are that they are "boundaryless and often change."[58] A career is now likely to include movement across several employers and different occupations. One study found that 60 percent of employees of all ages rate time and flexibility as very important reasons for staying with a company.[59] But Gen-Xers (those in their mid-20s to late 40s) were more likely to leave a job than baby boomers (those in their late-40s to mid 60s). Some 51 percent of employees under age 40 reported they were looking for a new job within the next year, compared to only 25 percent of those 40 or older.

As this discussion shows, to retain and motivate employees companies need to provide a system to identify and meet employees' development needs. This is especially important to retain good performers and employees who have potential for managerial positions. This system is often known as a **career management** or *development planning system*. We discuss these systems in detail later in the chapter.

> **Career Management System**
> A system to retain and motivate employees by identifying and meeting their development needs (also called *development planning systems*).

Learn more about protean careers and boundaryless careers online with Connect.

APPROACHES TO EMPLOYEE DEVELOPMENT

> **LO 5**
> Discuss current trends in using formal education for development.

Four approaches are used to develop employees: formal education, assessment, job experiences, and interpersonal relationships.[60] Many companies use a combination of these approaches. Figure 6.4 shows the frequency of use of some employee development practices. Larger companies are more likely to use leadership training and development planning more frequently than smaller companies.

Keep in mind that although much development activity is targeted at managers, all levels of employees may be involved in development. For example, most employees typically receive performance appraisal feedback (a development activity related to assessment) at least once per year. Here and in Chapter 7 we will discuss how, as part of the appraisal process employees are asked to complete individual development plans outlining (1) how they plan to change their weaknesses and (2) their future plans (including positions or locations desired and education or experience needed). Next we explore each type of development approach.

Formal Education

Formal education programs include off-site and on-site programs designed specifically for the company's employees, short courses offered by consultants or universities, executive MBA programs,

> **Formal Education Programs**
> Employee development programs, including short courses offered by consultants or universities, executive MBA programs, and university programs.

FIGURE 6.4 Frequency of Use of Some Employee Development Practices

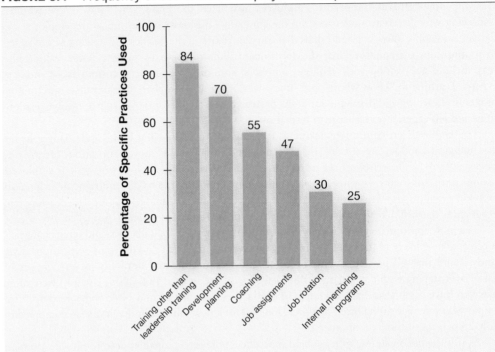

SOURCE: Based on E. Esen and J. Collison, *Employee Development* (Alexandria, VA: SHRM Research, 2005).

and university programs in which participants live at the university while taking classes. These programs may involve lectures by business experts, business games and simulations, adventure learning, and meetings with customers.

Many companies, such as the Bank of Montreal (BMO) rely primarily on in-house development programs offered by training and development centres or corporate universities, rather than sending employees to programs offered by public universities.[61] These companies rely on in-house programs because they can be tied directly to business needs, can be easily evaluated using company metrics, and can get senior-level management involved.

BMO has invested more than $400 million in training and development, including building the Institute for Learning, at two campuses (Toronto and Chicago), with high-tech classrooms, rooms to accommodate out-of-town employees, a presentation hall, restaurants, and a gym.[62] Each year 8,000 employees receive training at the Institute for Learning. A wide range of individual courses and focussed programs are offered that are linked to the bank's business strategies. They include management leadership training, risk management training, project management programs, and a four-year MBA program in financial services offered through a partnership with the Dalhousie School of Management and the Institute for Canadian Bankers. BMO believes the programs provide immediate benefit to the company because they often require participants to provide solutions to issues the company is facing. Evaluation and feedback are used to determine the success of specific programs. BMO uses many different types of evaluation including skill tests and performance evaluations conducted by managers after the participant returns to the job to determine transfer of training. BMO also looks at the relationship between the bank's education spending and its performance. Employee surveys are used to determine the quality and relevance of programs.

Leadership, entrepreneurship, and e-business are the most important topics in executive education programs. Programs directed at developing executives' understanding of global business issues and management of change are other important parts of executive development.[63]

Learn more about formal education programs as an employee development approach online with Connect.

‖ connect

Assessment

Assessment involves collecting information and providing feedback to employees about their behaviour, communication style, or skills.[64] The employees, their peers, managers, and customers may provide information. Assessments are used for several reasons. First, assessment is most frequently used to identify employees with managerial potential and to measure current managers' strengths and weaknesses. Assessment is also used to identify managers with the potential to move into higher-level executive positions, and it can be used with work teams to identify the strengths and weaknesses of individual team members and the decision processes or communication styles that inhibit the team's productivity. Assessments can help employees understand their tendencies, needs, the type of work environment they prefer, and the type of work they might prefer to do.[65] This information, along with the performance evaluations they receive from the company, can help employees decide what type of development goals might be most appropriate for them (e.g., leadership position, increased scope of their current position).

Companies vary in the methods and the sources of information they use in developmental assessment. Many companies use employee performance evaluations. Companies with sophisticated development systems use psychological tests to measure employees' skills, interests, personality types, and communication styles. Self, peer, and managers' ratings of employees' interpersonal styles and behaviours may also be collected. Popular assessment tools include personality tests, the Myers-Briggs Type Indicator®, assessment centres, Benchmarks®, performance appraisals, and 360-degree feedback.

Personality Tests Tests are used to determine if employees have the personality characteristics necessary to be successful in specific managerial jobs or jobs involving international assignments. Personality tests typically measure five major dimensions: extroversion, adjustment, agreeableness, conscientiousness, and inquisitiveness (see Table 5.3 on page 192).

Myers-Briggs Type Indicator® Personality Inventory **Myers-Briggs Type Indicator® Personality Inventory (MBTI)®** is the most popular psychological assessment tool for employee development. As many as 2 million people take the MBTI assessment tool in North America each year. The personality assessment consists of more than 100 questions about how the person feels or prefers to behave in different situations (such as "Are you usually a good 'mixer' or rather quiet and reserved?"). The MBTI assessment tool is based on the work of Carl Jung, a psychiatrist who believed that differences in individuals' behaviour resulted from preferences in decision making, interpersonal communication, and information gathering. These concepts were further developed by the mother–daughter team of Katharine C. Briggs and Isabel Briggs Myers, who are credited with developing the MBTI Inventory. The MBTI is a self-scored forced-choice inventory through which one rates oneself along four different dimensions.[66]

The MBTI assessment tool is a valuable tool for understanding communication styles and the ways people prefer to interact with others. Because it does not measure how well employees perform their preferred functions, it should not be used to appraise performance or evaluate employees'

LO 6

Relate how assessment of personality type, work behaviours, and job performance can be used for employee development.

Assessment
Collecting information and providing feedback to employees about their behaviour, communication style, or skills.

Myers-Briggs Type Indicator® Personality Inventory (MBTI)®
A personality assessment tool used for team building and leadership development that identifies employees' preferences for energy, information gathering, decision making, and lifestyle.

promotion potential. Furthermore, MBTI assessment tool types should not be viewed as unchangeable personality patterns.

connect

Learn more about Myers Briggs Type Indicator® Personality Inventory (MBTI) online with Connect.

Assessment Centre
A process in which multiple raters evaluate employees' performance on a number of exercises.

Assessment Centre   At an **assessment centre** multiple raters or evaluators (assessors) evaluate employees' performance on a number of exercises.[67] An assessment centre is usually an off-site location such as a conference centre. From 6 to 12 employees usually participate at once. Assessment centres are primarily used to identify whether employees have the personality characteristics, administrative skills, and interpersonal skills needed for managerial jobs. Assessment centres are also increasingly being used to determine if employees have the necessary skills to work in teams.

Assessment centre exercises are designed to measure employees' administrative and interpersonal skills. Skills typically measured include leadership, interpersonal, problem-solving, administrative and personal skills. Assessment methods include exercises such as in-basket and scheduling exercises (which test an applicant's ability to prioritize issues that typically arrive on their desk each day), leaderless group discussions, and personality tests and role-plays; managers usually serve as assessors.

Research suggests that assessment centre ratings are related to performance, salary level, and career advancement.[68] Assessment centres may also be useful for development because employees who participate in the process receive feedback regarding their attitudes, skill strengths, and weaknesses.[69] Such feedback provides valuable insight that may fuel both personal and professional growth, depending on what the employee chooses to do with the information. For example, Steelcase, the office furniture manufacturer with 750 employees in Canada,[70] uses assessment centres for first-level managers. The assessment centre activities include in-basket exercises, interview simulation, and a timed scheduling exercise requiring participants to fill positions created by absences. Managers are also required to confront an employee on a performance issue, getting the employee to commit to improve. Because the exercises relate closely to what managers are required to do at work, feedback given to managers based on their performance in the assessment centre can target specific skills or competencies that they need to be successful managers.

Benchmarks©
An instrument designed to measure the factors that are important to managerial success.

Benchmarks©   **Benchmarks©** is an instrument designed to measure the factors that are important to being a successful manager. The items measured by Benchmarks are based on research that examines the lessons executives learn at critical events in their careers.[71] The Benchmarks instrument includes items that measure managers' skills in dealing with subordinates, acquiring resources, and creating a productive work climate. The instrument shows the 16 skills and perspectives believed to be important for becoming a successful manager, such as "Doing whatever it takes," or "Being a Quick Study." These skills and perspectives have been shown to be related to performance evaluations, bosses' ratings of promotability, and actual promotions received.[72] To get a complete picture of managers' skills, the managers' supervisors, peers, and the managers themselves all complete the instrument. A summary report presenting the self-ratings and ratings by others is provided to the manager, along with information about how the ratings compare with those of other managers. A development guide with examples of experiences that enhance each skill and how successful managers use the skills is also available.

Performance Appraisal
The process through which an organization gets information on how well an employee is doing his or her job.

Performance Appraisals   As we will discuss further in Chapter 7, **performance appraisal** is the process of measuring employees' performance. Performance appraisal information can also be useful for employee development under certain conditions.[73] When used for developmental purposes, the appraisal system must tell employees specifically about their performance problems and how they can improve their performance. This includes providing a clear understanding of the differences between current performance and expected performance, identifying causes of the performance discrepancy, and developing action plans to improve performance. Managers must be trained in frequent performance feedback and also need to monitor employees' progress in carrying out action plans.

The appraisal starts with a planning meeting between employee and manager. The strategic initiatives of the department are discussed, along with the employee's role. The employee and manager agree on around four personal objectives that will help the department reach its goals as well as key performance outcomes related to the employee's job description. Competencies the employee needs to reach the personal objectives are identified. The manager and employee jointly develop a plan for improving or learning the competencies. During the year, the manager and employee monitor the progress toward reaching the performance and personal objectives and achievement of the learning plan. Pay decisions made at the end of each year are based on the achievement of both performance and learning objectives.

In Chapter 7 we will discuss the trend towards upward feedback and 360-degree feedback systems in the performance appraisal process, excellent mechanisms for stimulating employee development. However, for now we will simply say that regardless of the assessment method used, the information must be shared with the employee for development to occur. Along with assessment information, the employee needs suggestions for correcting skill weaknesses and using skills already learned. These suggestions might be to participate in training courses or develop skills through new job experiences. Based on the assessment information and available development opportunities, employees should develop action plans to guide their self-improvement efforts.

Job Experiences

Most employee development occurs through **job experiences**[74]: relationships, problems, demands, tasks, or other features that employees face in their jobs. A major assumption of using job experiences for employee development is that development is most likely to occur when there is a mismatch between the employee's skills and past experiences and the skills required for the job. To succeed in their jobs, employees must stretch their skills—that is, they are forced to learn new skills, apply their skills and knowledge in a new way, and master new experiences.[75] New job assignments help take advantage of employees' existing skills, experiences, and contacts, while helping them develop new ones.[76]

Most of what we know about development through job experiences comes from a series of studies conducted by the Center for Creative Leadership.[77] Executives were asked to identify key career events that made a difference in their managerial styles and the lessons they learned from these experiences. The key events included those involving the job assignment (such as fixing a failing operation), those involving interpersonal relationships (getting along with supervisors), and the specific type of transition required (situations in which the executive did not have the necessary background).

Figure 6.5 shows the various ways that job experiences can be used for employee development. For companies with global operations (multinationals), it is not uncommon for employee development to involve international assignments that require frequent travel or relocation.

Learn more about job demands and what employees can learn from them online with Connect.

Enlarging the Current Job **Job enlargement** refers to adding challenges or new responsibilities to employees' current jobs. This could include special project assignments, switching roles within a work team, or researching new ways to serve clients and customers. For example, an engineering

---

LO 7

Explain how job experiences can be used for skill development.

Job Experiences
The relationships, problems, demands, tasks, and other features that employees face in their jobs.

Job Enlargement
Adding challenges or new responsibilities to an employee's current job.

FIGURE 6.5 How Job Experiences Are Used for Employee Development

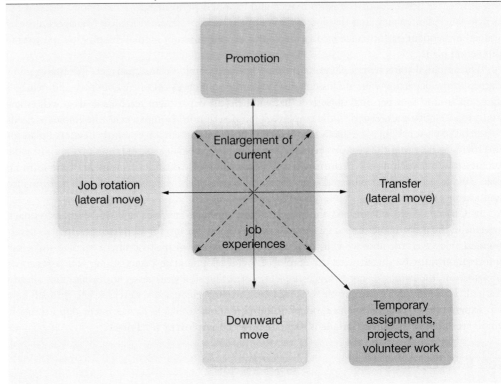

employee may join a task force developing new career paths for technical employees. Through this project work, the engineer may lead certain aspects of the challenge undertaken by the task force (such as reviewing the company's career development process). As a result, the engineer not only learns about the company's career development system, but also uses leadership and organizational skills to help the task force reach its goals. Some companies are enlarging jobs by giving two managers the same responsibilities and job title and allowing them to divide the work (two-in-a-box).[78] This helps managers learn from a more experienced employee; helps companies fill jobs that require multiple skills; and, for positions requiring extensive travel, ensures that one employee is always on site to deal with work-related issues. For example, at Cisco Systems, the head of the Cisco routing group, who was trained as an engineer but now works in business development, shared a job with an engineer. Each employee was exposed to the other's skills, which has helped both perform their jobs better.

Job Rotation

The process of systematically moving a single individual from one job to another over the course of time. The job assignments may be in various functional areas of the company or movement may be between jobs in a single functional area or department.

Job Rotation **Job rotation** gives employees a series of job assignments in various functional areas of the company or movement among jobs in a single functional area or department.

Job rotation helps employees gain an overall appreciation of the company's goals, increases their understanding of different company functions, develops a network of contacts, and improves problem-solving and decision-making skills.[79] It has also been shown to be related to skill acquisition, salary growth, and promotion rates.[80] But there are a number of potential problems with job rotation for both the employee and the work: (1) the rotation may create a short-term perspective on problems and solutions by rotating employees and their peers; or (2) employees' satisfaction and motivation may be adversely affected because they find it difficult to develop functional specialties and don't spend enough time in one position to receive a challenging assignment.

Transfers, Promotions, and Downward Moves Upward, lateral, and downward mobility is available for development purposes in most companies.[81] In a **transfer**, an employee is assigned a job in a different area of the company. Transfers do not necessarily increase job responsibilities or compensation. They are likely lateral moves (a move to a job with similar responsibilities). **Promotions** are advancements into positions with greater challenges, more responsibility, and more authority than in the previous job. Promotions usually include pay increases.

Transfers may involve relocation within Canada or to another country. Relocation can be stressful not only because the employee's work role changes, but if the employee is in a two-career family, the spouse must find new employment. Also, relocations disrupt employees' daily lives, interpersonal relationships, and work habits.[82] The employee and perhaps spouse have to find new housing, shopping, health care, and leisure facilities, and they may be many miles from the emotional support of friends and family. They also have to learn a new set of work norms and procedures; they must develop interpersonal relationships with their new managers and peers; and they are expected to be as productive in their new jobs as they were in their old jobs even though they may know little about the products, services, processes, or employees for whom they are responsible.

A **downward move** occurs when an employee is given less responsibility and authority.[83] This may involve a move to another position at the same level (lateral demotion), a temporary cross-functional move, or a demotion because of poor performance. Temporary cross-functional moves to lower-level positions, which give employees experience working in different functional areas, are most frequently used for employee development. For example, engineers who want to move into management often take lower-level positions (such as shift supervisor) to develop their management skills.

Because of the psychological and tangible rewards of promotions (such as increased feelings of self-worth, salary, and status in the company), employees are more willing to accept promotions than lateral or downward moves. Promotions are more readily available when a company is profitable and growing. When a company is restructuring or experiencing stable or declining profits—especially if numerous employees are interested in promotions and the company tends to rely on the external labour market to staff higher-level positions—promotion opportunities may be limited.[84]

Temporary Assignments, Projects, Volunteer Work, and Sabbaticals Temporary assignments take a variety of forms such as special company projects, volunteer work or even a **sabbatical**, which is a leave of absence from the company to renew or develop skills. One company that supports sabbaticals is Maple Reinders, a values-driven engineering, construction, and design firm located in Mississauga. The company's values statement emphasizes the importance of "being honest, ethical, safe, generous, responsible, candid and open,"[85] according to Company President Mike Reinders. To demonstrate its commitment to social responsibility the company contributes to Habitat for Humanity, and it also helps finance mission-oriented sabbaticals for employees who wish to put their own effort behind special projects. For example, Barbara Kerkhof, a proposals manager who has been with the company for 16 years, was sent by the company to Churuzapa, Peru in 2007 to help build a community centre at the edge of the Amazon rainforest. The final result, which included masonry walls, columns, trusses and a roof, was up and operating in just six days. Kerkhof and her colleagues also visited local families, taking food, clothes, and toys and of course, friendship. Kerkhof found her sabbatical very worthwhile, saying, "It was this combination of physical construction and cultural connection that made it such a meaningful trip."[86] Employees on sabbatical, such as Kerkhof, often receive full pay and benefits. The practice lets employees get away from the day-to-day stresses of their jobs and acquire new skills and perspectives. Sabbaticals also allow employees more time for personal pursuits such as writing a book or spending more time with young children. Sabbaticals are common in a variety of industries ranging from consulting firms to the fast-food industry.[87]

Transfer
The movement of an employee to a different job assignment in a different area of the company.

Promotions
Advancement into positions with greater challenge, more responsibility, and more authority than the employee's previous job.

Downward Move
A job change involving a reduction in an employee's level of responsibility and authority.

Sabbatical
A leave of absence from the company to renew or develop skills.

Competing Through Globalization

Going around the World Develops Leadership Skills

PricewaterhouseCoopers (PwC) designed the Ulysses program in response to the interconnected global challenges. The program's key objectives are to develop responsible leaders who are able to assume senior international leadership roles; who understand the role of business in influencing the economic, political, social, and environmental well-being of world communities and markets; and who can deliver responsible and sustainable business solutions. Ulysses participants are selected from around the world on the basis of their leadership skills and potential within the local firm. Typically they are in their first 10 years of partnership; they come from different regions and countries; and their expertise varies across accounting and finance, strategy, tax advisory, and management consultancy. The Ulysses program involves sending participants to developing areas of the world for eight weeks to use their business skills to benefit locals and learn how to overcome barriers, connect with clients from different cultures, and identify answers to very difficult problems. Partners are forced to take on projects outside their areas of expertise. The partners work on projects in multicultural teams in developing countries in collaboration with local social or governmental organizations, social entrepreneurs, and international institutions.

The cost to PwC is $15,000 per participant for travel and expenses plus three months of salary, which continues uninterrupted, even while the employee is focussed on developmental projects not directly related to his or her usual job. Each partner also spends two weeks in training to prepare for the trip and debriefing when they return. For example, one partner was sent to a village in Namibia, Africa, along with partners from Mexico and the Netherlands to help village leaders deal with the community's AIDS crisis. The partner helped the village leaders understand what was needed to get support from the community for AIDS prevention programs. Other projects have involved working with an ecotourism collective in Belize, small organic farmers in Zambia, and an organization in Ghana to alleviate the suffering of people with mental illnesses, and promoting rural development through microfinancing and entrpreneurship in Paraguay. PwC has evidence showing that the program is a success and is working on developing more measures such as impact on productivity rates.

Progress in meeting leadership goals set by program participants before they attend the program is evaluated. All 24 participants are still working at PwC, half have been promoted, and most have new job responsibilities. The ability of participants to win contracts with global clients appears to have improved. Participants believe that the experience has helped them better relate to their colleagues and clients. The partner who worked on the AIDS project has seen how slowly decisions are made in other places, which has helped him become more patient with his peers at work. Also, he now favours face-to-face conversations over e-mail because it is more valuable for building trust—a lesson learned in Namibia, where there was no electricity, e-mail, or PowerPoint.

SOURCES: Based on J. Hempel, "It Takes a Village—and a Consultant," *BusinessWeek* (September 6, 2004), pp. 76–77; J. Marquez, "Companies Send Employees on Volunteer Projects Abroad to Cultivate Leadership Skills," *Workforce Management* (November 2005), pp. 50–51. Also see "The Ulysses Project" and related links at www.pwc.com, the website for PricewaterhouseCoopers (retrieved April 6, 2009).

Volunteer assignments can also be used for development. Volunteer assignments may give employees opportunities to manage change, teach, have a high level of responsibility, and be exposed to other job demands. For PricewaterhouseCoopers, volunteer assignments and involvement with community projects helps the company live its corporate values[88] (see the "Competing Through Globalization" box). To encourage employees to volunteer with an organization or project of their choice, the company supports them with a $300 donation as long as they give over 50 hours of their time a year, or the equivalent of 3 hours per week. Besides providing valuable services to community organizations, PWC believes volunteer assignments help employees improve team relationships and develop leadership and strategic thinking skills.

Interpersonal Relationships

Employees can also develop skills and increase their knowledge about the company and its customers by interacting with a more experienced organization member. Mentoring and coaching are two types of interpersonal relationships used to develop employees.

Mentoring   A **mentor** is an experienced, productive senior employee who helps develop a less experienced employee (the protégé). Most mentoring relationships develop informally as a result of interests or values shared by the mentor and protégé. Research suggests that employees with certain personality characteristics (such as emotional stability, the ability to adapt their behaviour based on the situation, and high needs for power and achievement) are most likely to seek a mentor and be an attractive protégé for a mentor.[89] Mentoring relationships can also develop as part of a planned company effort to bring together successful senior employees with less experienced employees.

Developing Successful Mentoring Programs.   Although many mentoring relationships develop informally, one major advantage of formalized mentoring programs is that they ensure access to mentors for all employees, regardless of gender, race or abilities. An additional advantage is that participants in the mentoring relationship know what is expected of them.[90] One limitation of formal mentoring programs is that mentors may not be able to provide counselling and coaching in a relationship that has been artificially created.[91] To overcome this limitation, it is important that mentors and protégés spend time discussing work styles, their personalities, and their backgrounds, which helps build the trust needed for both parties to be comfortable with their relationship.[92] Mentors should be chosen based on interpersonal and technical skills. They also need to be trained.[93]

Both mentors and protégés can benefit from a mentoring relationship. Research suggests that mentors provide career and psychosocial support to their protégés. **Career support** includes coaching, protection, sponsorship, providing challenging assignments, exposure, and visibility. **Psychosocial support** includes serving as a friend and a role model, providing positive regard and acceptance, and creating an outlet for the protégé to talk about anxieties and fears. Additional benefits for the protégé include higher rates of promotion, higher salary, and greater organizational influence.[94]

Mentor programs socialize new employees, increase the likelihood of skill transfer from training to the work setting, and provide opportunities for women and minorities to gain the exposure and skills needed to move into managerial positions.

Some companies have initiated group mentoring programs. In **group mentoring programs**, a successful senior employee is paired with a group of four to six protégés. One potential advantage of the mentoring group is that protégés can learn from each other as well as from a more experienced senior employee. Also, group mentoring acknowledges the reality that it is difficult for one mentor to provide an employee with all the guidance and support necessary. Group mentoring provides a

Competing Through Sustainability

Powerful Lessons from Mentoring

One of the key components of sustainability is the cultural aspect, which includes building a positive employee relations climate that protects and values diversity in all its forms. This includes being open to diverse perspectives from all levels of the organization and from all external stakeholders. If the company is to be managed well, it must prepare for and fend off external shocks to its long-term survival and competitiveness. This requires gathering as much information as possible and soliciting the support and cooperation of important stakeholders, such as employees. Hence, it is important to include women (and other members of designated groups) in senior management roles, and to listen to employees on issues that are important to them. If women and other newcomers are to be welcomed in leadership roles and their credibility accepted, it is important to prepare them so that biased expectations and barriers do not get in their way.

For a variety of reasons, the progress of women and other designated groups into senior management positions has been slow. In Canada women hold only 17.7 percent of senior corporate officer positions among Financial Post 500 Leadership companies, in part because they comprise only 36.5 percent of management, professional and related positions. It is rare for a woman in Canada to hold the title vice president of Human Resources. It is even rarer for that same woman to be named to Canada's Most Powerful Women's Top 100 list created by the Women's Executive Network (WXN) (Corporate Executive category) for three consecutive years, and then be placed in the WXN Hall of Fame (2009). But these are the lofty heights that Stacey Allerton Firth has ascended to since 2003 and where she fits quite comfortably. She has done so while overseeing 7,400 employees at Ford Motor Company in Canada, and working with the CAW there to transform the labour relations climate into one of transparency and collaboration. As vice president HR, Allerton Firth provided the leadership needed on the corporate side to reach an agreement that supported Ford's vision for a sustainable and competitive business environment in Canada, while at the same time protecting employees' interests. In her role as lead negotiator in the 2005 and 2008 negotiations with the CAW, she believed that if negotiators on both sides were to be able to wade through the negotiations productively and reach consensus over difficult issues, they could do so effectively only in a context of trust and respect. With extensive experience with Ford on both sides of the border, Allerton Firth has gained insight on leveraging the more team-oriented and collaborative decision-making approach of Ford in Canada. In addition, she has indicated that she truly believes the union helps balance management perspective, saying "I think that the union is helpful in many respects, despite the fact that we do not agree on all issues. They can be a voice and resource for employees that, in their absence, might not otherwise be as clearly heard. We absolutely view the union as an organization that we respect and whose views and ideas are important to us in terms of achieving our goals." Hardly an approach one would deem power driven, so how did Allerton Firth make the list?

According to Pamela Jeffery, founder of WXN, the word *power* is meant to indicate "how a woman drives an organization's results, improves her community and mentors and coaches the next generation of women leaders." That helps to understand why Allerton Firth repeatedly made the list, but there are other puzzles to resolve. For example, how did she navigate the pitfalls of the male-dominated automotive sector to emerge such a high-profile winner? Well, it wasn't easy, but Allerton Firth attributes much of her success in rising to the top and building her leadership style to the formal and informal mentors who have supported her since starting her career with Ford in 1990. They were there when the view wasn't clear, helping her focus.

Allerton Firth notes that she got some reality checks from those who had her interests firmly in mind, saying, "I had some pretty candid feedback from some mentors about some of the strategies I was picking and what the impact of those strategies would be, and some additional considerations that I really took to heart, "She adds, "I'm not sure I would have seen those blind spots on my own." One of the primary lessons she learned from a male mentor in the industry was the importance of networking—a lesson she took to heart. Like most women in business, there are always distractions from work, home or family that seem more important than getting out to a meeting or a breakfast to meet and greet. But Allerton Firth's mentor convinced her that building a solid network was worth the time and effort, and he was right. Firth came to understand that women spend too much time waiting for what they want. She says, "You have to go get the responsibility and the authority and the power. You can't wait for somebody to come and offer it to you." Such clearheadedness is no doubt the reason Allerton Firth was destined to win in the Corporate Executive Category of the WXN Top 100 list. She contributed significantly to the management and strategic direction of Ford Canada; demonstrated vision and leadership there and throughout her career; contributed to the financial performance of her organization in the most recent fiscal year; and finally, demonstrated commitment to her community. There is no question Allerton Firth did all of that and more.

Such support and insight from Allerton Firth's mentors are part of the reason she ensures there is a formal mentoring program at Ford; she understands its link to sustainability. It's also why she works hard to be as approachable as possible among Ford's employees. By engaging with employees in more casual environments such as the company gym or cafeteria, she hopes they will recognize her and feel comfortable approaching her if they need her. Doing so also helps to keep her "in the know" about small things, which can lead to big things that may impact the next set of negotiations. Engaging frequently with employees also provides her with a diversity of perspective that is important to the long-term goals of the company.

SOURCES: S. Klie, "HR Execs Land on Most Powerful Women List," *Canadian HR Reporter* (January 11, 2011), p. 1; A. Werbach, *Strategy for Sustainability*, Harvard Business Press, 2009, p. 11; Canada's Most Powerful Top Women—100 at www.top100women.ca/?w=top100.selection; Catalyst, Canadian Women in Business Pyramid and associated research (March 2011) at www.catalyst.org/publication/198/canadian-women-in-business (retrieved May 14, 2011); M. Luft, Channel Editor, Honeycomb Connect, Corporate H.R. Officers (C.H.R.O.M.E.), Profile: Stacey Allerton-Firth, Ford Motor Company of Canada (April 7, 2006) at www.honeycombconnect.com/Human_Resources/document_4668.ashx?page=Human_Resources_home&datasource=91 (accessed May 14, 2011).

development network for employees: a small group an employee can use for mentoring support and who also have an interest in each others' learning and development. The mentor helps protégés understand the organization, guides them in analyzing their experiences, and helps them clarify career directions. Each protegé may complete specific assignments, or the group may work together on a problem or issue.[95] The "Competing through Sustainability" box shows how mentoring can lead to exponential growth for individuals and help women take on senior roles in organizations.

Learn more about mentoring online with Connect.

Coaching   A **coach** is a peer or manager who works with an employee to motivate, help develop skills, and provide reinforcement and feedback. A coach can play three roles[96]: developing high potential managers, acting as a sounding board for managers, or specifically trying to change behaviours

Coach
A peer or manager who works with an employee to motivate, help develop skills, and provide reinforcement and feedback.

that are making managers ineffective.[97] Part of coaching may be one-on-one with an employee (such as giving feedback). Coaches help employees learn for themselves; this involves helping them find experts who can assist with the employees' concerns and teaching them how to obtain feedback from others Third, coaching may involve providing resources such as mentors, courses, or job experiences the employee may not be able to gain access to without the coach's help. Becton Dickinson, Canada, a medical technology company that sells medical supplies, devices, laboratory equipment, and diagnostic products to health care institutions, uses peer coaching as part of its leadership development programs.[98] The topics discussed include job challenges as a development method, ambiguity as a change agent, and how to influence others. Evaluation of the peer coaching has found that coaches gain confidence in their abilities and participants learn about the topics discussed.

connect

Learn more about coaching online with Connect.

LO 9

Discuss the steps and responsibilities in the development planning process.

CAREER MANAGEMENT AND DEVELOPMENT PLANNING SYSTEMS

Effective career management and development planning systems include important design features, such as positioning the system as a response to a business need; ensuring that employees and managers participate in development of the system; and ensuring that a large diverse talent pool is created as a result of the process. In addition, the career management process should follow a systematic approach, implementing steps such as self-assessment, reality check, goal setting and action planning, and for which both the company and the employee bear responsibility to create mutually successful outcomes.

Steps in the Career Management Process

While companies' career management systems vary in the level of sophistication and the emphasis they place on different components of the process, most systems include at least the steps shown in Figure 6.6, Steps and Responsibilities in the Career Management Process.

Self-Assessment   *Self-assessment* refers to the use of information by employees to determine their career interests, values, aptitudes, and behavioural tendencies. It often involves psychological tests such as the Myers-Briggs Type Indicator (described earlier in the chapter), the Strong-Campbell Interest Inventory, and the Self-Directed Search. The Strong-Campbell Interest Inventory helps employees identify their occupational and job interests; the Self-Directed Search identifies employees' preferences for working in different types of environments (such as sales, counselling, landscaping, and so on). Tests may also help employees identify the relative values they place on work and leisure activities. Through the assessment, a development need can be identified. This need can result from gaps between current skills and/or interests and the type of work or position the employee wants.

Reality Check   Reality check refers to the information employees receive about how the company evaluates their skills and knowledge and where they fit into the company's plans (e.g., potential promotion opportunities, lateral moves). Usually this information is provided by the employee's manager as part of performance appraisal. It is not uncommon in well-developed career management systems for the manager to hold separate performance appraisals and career development discussions.

Goal Setting   *Goal setting* refers to the process of employees developing short- and long-term career objectives. These goals usually relate to desired positions (such as *become sales manager within three years*), level of skill application (*use budgeting skills to improve the unit's cash flow problems*), work setting (*move to corporate marketing within two years*), or skill acquisition (*learn how to use the company's human resource information system*). These goals are usually discussed with the manager and written

FIGURE 6.6 Steps and Responsibilities in the Career Management Process

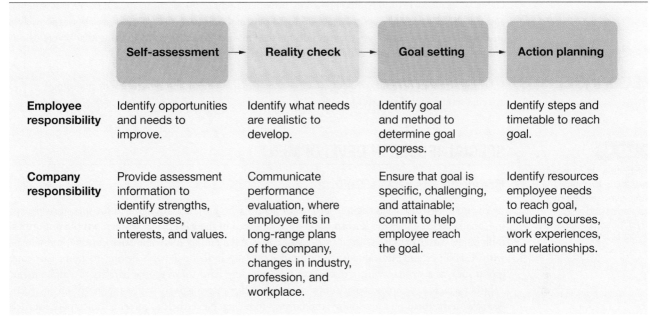

	Self-assessment	Reality check	Goal setting	Action planning
Employee responsibility	Identify opportunities and needs to improve.	Identify what needs are realistic to develop.	Identify goal and method to determine goal progress.	Identify steps and timetable to reach goal.
Company responsibility	Provide assessment information to identify strengths, weaknesses, interests, and values.	Communicate performance evaluation, where employee fits in long-range plans of the company, changes in industry, profession, and workplace.	Ensure that goal is specific, challenging, and attainable; commit to help employee reach the goal.	Identify resources employee needs to reach goal, including courses, work experiences, and relationships.

into a development plan. A development plan for a product manager usually includes descriptions of strengths and weaknesses, career goals, and development activities for reaching the career goal.

Action Planning   During this phase, employees determine how they will achieve their short-and long-term career goals. Action plans may involve any one or a combination of development approaches discussed in the chapter (such as enrolling in courses and seminars, getting additional assessment, obtaining new job experiences, or finding a mentor or coach).[99] The development approach used depends on the needs and developmental goal. General Mills and the Toronto-Dominion Bank are good examples of various approaches to career management and development planning systems.

General Mills' development plan follows a process in which each employee completes a development plan that asks employees to consider four areas:

- *Professional goals and motivation:* What professional goals do I have? What excites me to grow professionally?
- *Talents or strengths:* What are my talents and strengths?
- *Development opportunities:* What development needs are important to improve?
- *Development objectives and action steps:* What will be my objective for this plan? What steps can I take to meet the objectives?

Managers and employees are encouraged to discuss the development plan at least once a year. Speakers, online tools, and workshops to help employees complete the development plan and prepare for a development discussion with their managers increase the visibility and emphasize the importance of the development planning process.

The Toronto-Dominion Bank partnered with Barbara Moses, a career expert and author of numerous books on career issues, to create its Career Advisor website on the company's intranet. The site includes powerful self-assessment tools, career advice, and coaching from several of Moses' best-selling books, and is designed to help employees reflect on their goals and create an action plan that is realistic and feasible to move up to the next rung on their own personal career ladder. The site contains numerous learning categories such as Know Yourself, Overcome Career Distress, Find Great Work, Coach Others etc. The tools provided include 90 learning modules, 39 assessments, and the ability for employees to create up to 18 personal reports as they learn more about themselves and decide what career moves they should make. The site proved to be so inviting that several thousand people accessed it in the first few weeks alone.[100]

■ connect™

Learn more about design factors of effective career management and development planning systems online with Connect.

LO 10

Discuss what companies are doing for special employee development issues and to help dysfunctional managers.

SPECIAL ISSUES IN DEVELOPMENT

Breaking the Glass Ceiling

In Chapter 3 we discussed the four groups of people who have been designated for special treatment in Canada because they are known to be disadvantaged in the workplace: women, visible minorities, individuals with disabilities, and Aboriginal people. As unemployment statistics indicate, individuals with disabilities and Aboriginal people (and especially individuals who belong to more than one group such as a woman with a disability) are struggling hard to overcome barriers to employment. Efforts to increase employment among such job seekers have gained increasing attention in recent years, with the focus on accessibility and fairness in hiring. Nevertheless, career advancement for such individuals is a much lower priority so far, unless companies are very focussed on managing diversity.

However, it has long been known that two of the designated groups, women and visible minorities, are frequently disadvantaged when they try to advance to higher-level positions once they acquire time and experience on the job. For example, as noted earlier, although women represented 47.4 percent of the Canadian workforce, they filled just under 37 percent of management occupations, and only 6.4 percent of FP500 companies were headed by women.[101] Thus, a major development issue facing companies today is how to get women and visible minorities, already present in significant numbers in the Canadian workforce, into upper-level management positions—or how to break the **glass ceiling**. With growing awareness of diversity, the issue has become even more important. Knowledge acquired from helping women and minorities advance in organizations also provides the information necessary to increase fairness for individuals with disabilities and Aboriginal employees. It will no doubt also assist Lesbian, Gay, Bisexual, and Transgendered/Transsexual (LGBT) peoples, who were added in 2007 as a "fifth group" in the assessment criteria for the Canada's Best Diversity Employers competition. The 2011 list of winners for this competition, which recognizes Canadian employers with exceptional workplace diversity and inclusiveness programs, now includes over 40 employers. Individual profiles of companies on the website illustrate how companies such as KPMG, Mount Sinai Hospital, and Shell Canada are breaking the glass ceiling and barriers to employment.[102]

The glass ceiling is a barrier to advancement to the higher levels of the organization. With respect to women and minorities, findings so far indicate this barrier may be due to stereotypes or company systems that adversely affect the development of members of these two groups.[103] Where women are concerned, the glass ceiling actually is created at very early stages in their careers and is likely caused by lack of access to training programs, appropriate developmental job experiences, and developmental relationships (such as mentoring).[104] Research has found no gender differences in access to job experiences involving transitions or creating change.[105] However, male managers receive significantly more assignments involving high levels of responsibility (high stakes, managing business diversity, handling external pressure) than female managers of similar ability and managerial level. Also, female managers report experiencing more challenge due to lack of personal support (a type of job demand considered to be an obstacle that has been found to relate to harmful stress) than male managers. Career encouragement from peers and senior managers does help women advance to the higher management

Glass Ceiling
A barrier to advancement to higher-level jobs in the company that adversely affects women and minorities. The barrier may be due to lack of access to training programs, development experiences, or relationships (e.g., mentoring).

levels.[106] Managers making developmental assignments need to carefully consider whether gender biases or stereotypes are influencing the types of assignments given to women versus men.

Women and visible minorities often have trouble finding mentors because of their lack of access to the "old boy network," managers' preference to interact with other managers of similar status rather than with line employees, and intentional exclusion by managers who have negative stereotypes about women's and minorities' abilities, motivation, and job preferences.[107] Potential mentors may view minorities and women (or members of other designated groups) as a threat to their job security because they believe employment equity plans give those groups preferential treatment. However, as we have noted earlier, a well-designed mentoring program can go a long way toward overcoming such problems and facilitating upward movement for employees who have been traditionally disadvantaged in the workplace.

Learn more about breaking the glass ceiling online with Connect.

Succession Planning

Many companies are losing sizable numbers of upper-level managers due to retirement and company restructurings. They are also finding that their middle managers are not ready to move into upper management positions due to skill weaknesses or lack of experience. This shows the importance of succession planning. **Succession planning** refers to the process of identifying and tracking high-potential employees and helps organizations in several different ways[108]: it requires senior management to systematically review leadership talent in the company; it ensures that top-level managerial talent is available; and it provides a set of development experiences that managers must complete to be considered for top management positions, which avoids premature promotion of managers. Succession planning systems also help attract and retain managerial employees by providing them with development opportunities. Table 6.4 shows the process used to develop a succession plan.

Succession Planning
The identification and tracking of high-potential employees capable of filling higher-level managerial positions.

Helping Managers with Dysfunctional Behaviours

A number of studies have identified managerial behaviour that can cause an otherwise competent manager to be a "toxic" or ineffective manager. Such behaviour includes insensitivity to others, inability to be a team player, arrogance, poor conflict management skills, inability to meet business

Table 6.4   The Process of Developing a Succession Plan

1.   Identify the positions included in the plan.
2.   Identify the employees included in the plan.
3.   Develop standards to evaluate positions (e.g., competencies, desired experiences, desired knowledge, developmental value).
4.   Determine how employee potential will be measured (e.g., current performance and potential performance).
5.   Develop the succession planning review.
6.   Link the succession planning system with other human resource systems, including staffing systems, training and development, performance management, and compensation.
7.   Determine what feedback will be provided to employees.
8.   Evaluate the succession plan.

SOURCES: Based on B. Dowell, "Succession Planning," in *Implementing Organizational Interventions,* ed. J. Hedge and E. Pulaskos (San Francisco: Jossey-Bass, 2002), pp. 78–109; R. Barnett and S. Davis, "Creating Greater Success in Succession Planning," *Advances in Developing Human Resources* 10 (2008), pp. 721–739.

objectives, and inability to change or adapt during a transition.[109] For example, a skilled manager who is interpersonally abrasive, aggressive, and an autocratic leader may find it difficult to motivate subordinates, may alienate internal and external customers, and have trouble getting ideas accepted by superiors. These managers are in jeopardy of losing their jobs and have little chance of future advancement because of their dysfunctional behaviour. Typically, a combination of assessment, training, and counselling is used to help managers change the dysfunctional behaviour.

A Look Back

The chapter opener described Accenture Consulting's training programs and career management and employee development efforts, which are aimed at retention of key talent within the organization. Training also includes ensuring employees know they should be out in the field with clients, not hidden away in an office at Accenture, an approach that the company recognizes can take a heavy toll on employees. To prevent turnover, Accenture has invested heavily in various forms of training, and the company helps consultants understand what they can do to proactively manage their own careers. The company has also created a career website that helps employees understand the career options available to them, and the need to incorporate nonwork life as part of the planning process. Finally, the company evaluates the various strategies in place to assist employees in both personal and professional development and to understand how it impacts retention at Accenture.

Based on what you have learned in this chapter, answer the questions below. You may find it useful to visit the career page of Accenture Consulting Canada to read profiles of people working at Accenture, including their roles and responsibilities, and what a day in their life with Accenture is like. The company's main career page can be found at: http://careers.accenture.com/ca-en/Pages/index.aspx.

Questions

1. What role does the extensive investment in training made by Accenture play in its overall strategic objectives?

2. How might job experiences acquired from working with clients at their workplaces to resolve unique and specific client problems, help consultants at Accenture develop both professionally and personally over time?

3. Based on what you have learned in this chapter and from the contents of Accenture's career page, what could or should be included in the development plan that a consultant at Accenture might complete with his or her career counsellor? Explain your suggestions.

4. Would the development activities for the highest performing consultants vary from the activities used for satisfactorily performing consultants? Why? Explain the differences.

Summary

Technological innovations, new product markets, and a diverse workforce have increased the need for companies to re-examine how their training practices contribute to learning. In this chapter we discussed a systematic approach to training, including needs assessment, design of the learning environment, consideration of employee readiness for training, and transfer-of-training issues. We reviewed numerous training methods and stressed that the key to successful training was to choose a method that would best accomplish the objectives of training. We also emphasized how training can contribute to effectiveness through establishing a link with the company's strategic direction.

Orientation and onboarding programs help transform new employees into effective members of the company. Managing diversity is a training issue that is relevant given company needs to capitalize on a diverse workforce and a global labour market.

This chapter also emphasized the various development methods that companies use: formal education, assessment, job experiences, and interpersonal relationships. Most companies use one or more of these approaches to develop employees. Formal education involves enrolling employees in courses or seminars offered by the company or educational institutions. Assessment involves measuring the employee's performance, behaviour, skills, or personality characteristics. Job experiences include job enlargement, rotating to a new job, promotions, or transfers. A more experienced, senior employee (a mentor) can help employees better understand the company and gain exposure and visibility to key persons in the organization. Part of a manager's job responsibility may be to coach employees. Regardless of the development approaches used, employees should have a development plan to identify (1) the type of development needed (2) development goals (3) the best approach for development, and (4) whether development goals have been reached. For development plans to be effective, both the employee and the company have responsibilities that need to be completed. Other issues to consider include creating more opportunities for women and other members of designated groups or "breaking the glass ceiling," as well as linking the company's training and development efforts to a succession plan. Managers who exhibit dysfunctional behaviours represent another challenge and their habits should be identified early. When training and development interventions are implemented, such managers receive a second chance to get performance back in line with expectations, thus preventing unnecessary turnover within the management group of an organization.

Key Terms

Action learning, 224
Adventure learning, 222
Apprenticeship, 220
Assessment centre, 232
Assessment, 231
Attitude awareness and
    change program, 226
Behaviour-based
    program, 226
Benchmarks©, 232
Career management
    system, 229
Career support, 237
Climate for transfer, 216
Coach, 239
Continuous learning, 212
Cultural immersion, 227
Development, 211
Diversity training, 226
Downward move, 235
E-learning, 221
Electronic performance
    support system
    (EPSS), 217

Formal education
    programs, 229
Glass ceiling, 242
Group mentoring
    programs, 237
Group- or team-building
    methods, 222
Hands-on methods, 219
High-leverage training, 212
Job enlargement, 233
Job experiences, 233
Job rotation, 234
Learning management
    system (LMS), 222
Managing diversity, 226
Mentor, 237
Motivation to learn, 215
Myers-Briggs Type Indicator
    personality inventory
    (MBTI), 231
Needs assessment, 213
On-the-job training
    (OJT), 219

Opportunity to perform, 216
Organizational analysis, 214
Organizational
    socialization 227
Performance appraisal, 232
Person analysis, 214
Presentation methods, 218
Promotions, 235
Protean career, 228
Psychosocial support, 237
Sabbatical, 235
Self-directed learning, 220
Self-efficacy, 215
Simulation, 220
Six Sigma training, 224
Succession planning, 243
Task analysis, 214
Training design process, 213
Training outcomes, 225
Training, 211
Transfer of training, 216
Transfer, 235
Virtual reality, 220

Discussion Questions

1. "Melinda," bellowed Roger, "I've got a problem and you've got to solve it. I can't get people in this plant to work together as a team. As if I don't have enough trouble with the competition and delinquent accounts, now I have to put up with running a zoo. It's your responsibility to see that the staff gets along with each other. I want a human relations training proposal on my desk by Monday." If you were Melinda, how would you determine the need for human relations training? How would you determine whether you actually had a training problem? Why else might the plant feel like a "zoo"?

2. Ziptronex, a retail electronics store, recently invested a large amount of money to train sales staff to improve customer service. The skills emphasized in the program include how to greet customers and determine their needs, and demonstrate product convenience. The company wants to know whether the program is effective. What stage of the strategic training and development process would help the company acquire this information? What kinds of information would it acquire?

3. To improve product quality, a company is introducing a computer-assisted manufacturing process into one of its assembly plants. The new technology is likely to substantially modify jobs. Employees will also be required to learn statistical process control techniques. The new technology and push for quality will require employees to attend numerous training sessions. More than 50 percent of the employees who will be affected by the new technology completed their formal education more than 10 years ago. Only about 5 percent of the company's employees have used the tuition reimbursement benefit. How should management maximize employees' readiness for training?

4. Assume you are general manager of a small fish-cleaning company in Newfoundland. Most training is unstructured and occurs on the job. Currently, senior fish cleaners are responsible for teaching new employees how to perform the job. Your company has been profitable in spite of challenges to the fishing industry, but recently wholesale fish dealers that buy your product have been complaining about the poor quality of your fresh fish. For example, some fillets have not had all the scales removed and abdomen parts remain attached to the fillets. You have decided to change the on-the-job training received by the fish cleaners. How will you modify the training to improve the quality of the product delivered to the wholesalers?

5. What learning condition do you think is most important for *your* learning to occur? Which is least critical? Why?

6. What types of assessment tools are popular with employers in the employee development process? Which one would you like to try? Why do you think it might be useful to you?

7. Many employees are unwilling to relocate because they like their current community, and spouses and children prefer not to move. Yet employees need to develop new skills, strengthen skills, and be exposed to new aspects of the business to prepare for management positions. How could an employee's current job be changed to develop management skills?

8. Why do companies develop formal mentoring programs? What are the potential benefits for the mentor? For the protégé? Does all mentoring have to be company sponsored? Explain your answers.

9. What is the organization's role in each stage of the career management process? What is the employee's responsibility at each stage?

10. What are some examples of glass ceiling issues that still remain in organizations? What would you recommend to eliminate such problems, and to help even the playing field for women in the workplace?

Self-Assessment Exercise:

In the chapter we discussed the need for learners to be motivated so that training will be effective, along with a variety of factors that impact motivation and influence transfer of training to on-the-job behaviours. What is your motivation to learn and how well is the learning transferring to your actual performance as student? Find out by answering the following questions. Read each statement and indicate how much you agree with it, using the following scale:

5 = Strongly Agree	4 = Somewhat Agree	3 = Neutral	2 = Somewhat Disagree	1 = Strongly Disagree

1. I believe it is important to put forth my best effort when completing projects or assignments in my classes.	5	4	3	2	1
2. When I start each semester, I set goals for myself about what I hope to achieve in each course.	5	4	3	2	1
3. When I'm involved in courses and can't understand something, I get so frustrated that I stop trying to learn.	5	4	3	2	1
4. I frequently explore the online learning material provided by textbook publishers to expand my learning beyond what may be offered in class.	5	4	3	2	1
5. The student development centre of my university or college provides workshops for skills related to writing various types of exams, taking notes in class, writing essays and reports, and doing research through the online library catalogue.	5	4	3	2	1
6. I take full advantage of resources provided through the student development centre listed above to increase my skills and abilities as a student.	5	4	3	2	1
7. I often make an appointment with my instructors during the semester to discuss questions I have so we can get to know each other a little better and I can receive feedback.	5	4	3	2	1
8. I often make an appointment to review my exams after writing them to see what I can do to improve.	5	4	3	2	1
9. I take an active part in exercises and discussions during class (or online) and sometimes ask questions in class.	5	4	3	2	1
10. I often initiate or join small study groups among my classmates before exams.	5	4	3	2	1

If you circled 4 or 5 in response to questions 1 and 2, 4, and 6–10, you are probably quite motivated to learn and have fairly high self-efficacy, meaning you believe that you can successfully learn the content from a training program.

However, if you circled a 4 or 5 in response to Question 3, and/or circled 2 or a 1 for Questions 5 or 6, there may well be barriers in your learning environment that prevent you from feeling motivated or prevent transfer of learning to exam and assignment results.

If you circled a 4 or 5 in response to questions 4–8 and 10, you are quite aware of supportive tools, equipment, and individuals in your student "work environment" and you take advantage of the various supports provided. Conversely, circling a 3, 2, or 1 for these questions indicate you have not considered the supports for learning around you, or decided to take advantage of them.

If you circled a 4 or 5 in response to questions 1, 4, 7–9, you are a person who is proactive about gaining practice and seeking feedback in your learning environment. Circling a 3, 2 or 1 for these questions may indicate you could do much more to enhance your learning environment.

If you circled a 4 or 5 in response to questions 1, 9 and 10, you actively seek opportunities to perform in order to help transfer your course learning to outcomes valuable to you.

If you circled a 4 or 5 in response to questions 1–2, and 4–10 (and/or circled a 1 or 2 in response to question 3) you are good at self-management. This includes taking the time to set goals and to seek feedback from peers, and your "manager" (instructor) even when it is not offered, and you do not give up easily.

This short exercise was designed to help you think of your student activities as a "job" in which there are various supports available that enhance your motivation to learn, as well as constraints that make learning a challenge. In addition, you have opportunities to self-manage your behaviours to overcome obstacles in your learning environment and to enhance transfer of learning in your courses. For example, you can seek support from peers and instructors even if it is not offered, you can seek opportunities to perform (use your learning) in as many ways as possible, and you can seek out whatever technological supports may exist to help you in your "job" as a student.

Exercising Strategy: Safeway Ensures Inclusive Opportunities to "Bring Home the Bacon"

Consider Safeway's efforts to break the glass ceiling for women, visible minorities and people with disabilities. Safeway has 1,775 grocery stores in North America. Women make up 57 percent of the 12,000 full-time employees in Canada Safeway, and visible minorities another 22 percent. In addition, the company now employs 600 Canadians with disabilities. But Safeway knows that hiring from designated groups is just the start, and has been working diligently for some time to ensure such individuals receive the preparation and support they need to break the glass ceiling and be selected to join the company's management team.

For example, to meet the challenges of competitors such as specialty grocers and big-box, low-price competitors such as Walmart, and recognizing that 70 percent of its customers were women, Safeway took steps to help develop women for advancement into management. Championing Change for Women: An Integrated Strategy, includes programs that focus on leadership development, mentoring, and work/life balance. Safeway typically promotes from within and has focused on the retail level as a source for potential managers through the company's Retail Leadership Development (RLD) program. Ninety percent of Safeway's 1,800 store managers moved up through the company's management ranks through the program, and all but 1 of the company's 10 division presidents began their careers working in one of the stores.

To help women and visible minorities achieve top-level management positions, the RLD was used to increase the number of members of such designated groups who participate and complete the program. Those who complete the program are assigned to a store or an assistant manager position that can lead to corporate-level leadership positions. To help support women's efforts to gain leadership positions, Safeway ensures that women who work part-time and use flexible schedules have similar opportunities for coaching, advancement, and development as employees who have traditional work schedules. The company also realized that frequent relocations did not work for some employees, especially women. As a result, rejecting a relocation to a different location is no longer considered a career-ending decision.

Safeway also provides a women's leadership network for women interested in advancing into management. The network sponsors events such as presentations at company locations that highlight the success of Safeway women and provide learning opportunities. Executives who attend these presentations meet with women who have been identified as candidates for management positions and are targeted for development opportunities in stores. These discussions focus on the women's career interests, and the executives suggest job opportunities and encourage the women to apply for positions that can help them advance to the next management level. Safeway's mentoring program emphasizes that a manager's first protégé should be a woman because of the lack of female mentors. Safeway's work/life balance program, which includes flextime, allows all women, regardless of their family status, to have a healthy balance between work and life. Safeway also realizes that its managers are responsible for helping women reach management positions. As a result, all managers attend a Managing Diversity Workshop and are evaluated on their success in meeting diversity goals. Managers who reach their targets can increase their pay bonus by 10 percent.

Safeway's women's initiative has been successful. Since 2000, the number of female store managers has increased by 42 percent. The number of women who have qualified for and completed the RLD program increased 31 percent over the past five years. A research report commission by Safeway showed that the program increased the company's sales and earnings. By enhancing its reputation as an employer of choice for women and visible minorities, Safeway received the Catalyst Award, which is presented annually to outstanding companies that promote the career advancement of women and minorities.

Efforts to develop the potential of employees with disabilities are still at an early stage, but appear to be integrated with other glass ceiling efforts described above. For example, Safeway Canada managers volunteer on the boards of organizations that build awareness and opportunities, such as the Manitoba Business Leadership Network and "EmployAbilities" in Edmonton. The company also maintains a diversity website on its intranet to ensure all employees have the information they need to be more inclusive of everyone, All told, Safeway's efforts have earned it recognition as one Canada's Best Diversity Employers 2010, among a small group of only 46 Canadian employers so far.

Questions

1. Why is it important for employees at Safeway in Canada to break the glass ceiling?

2. At what stage of an employee's relationship with Safeway do traditional barriers faced by women, visible minorities, and individuals with disabilities need to be broken down or removed? What are those barriers?

3. Although we have no information on the extent of employment of Aboriginal people (the fourth designated group) at Safeway, what role do managers have in creating a more inclusive workplace, and ensuring that members of all four designated groups have a fair chance for advancement at Safeway?

SOURCES: A. Pomeroy, "Cultivating Female Leaders," *HR Magazine* (February 2007), pp. 44–50; Top 100 Employers in Canada 2010, Employer Review Canada Safeway Limited, www.eluta.ca/diversity-at-canada-safeway (retrieved November 29, 2010).

Managing People: Multifaceted Messaging about Diversity at Sodexo

Canadian companies everywhere are working hard to help their employees embrace diversity to increase organizational effectiveness, prevent conflict, and ensure fairness in the workplace. However, it takes a multifaceted approach to get it right. Sodexo efforts in this area so far have resulted in being named one of the Top 50 Companies for Diversity by Diversity Inc., and earned it gold-level status for Progressive Aboriginal Relations with the Canadian Council for Aboriginal Business (CCAB).

As the leading food and facilities management company in North America, with more than 750 locations in Canada, Sodexo is the company of choice, for thousands of universities, health care facilities and senior communities, corporations and remote sites. With such a diverse array of clients, Sodexo views diversity as important for the company to meet business growth targets. For that reason, diversity and inclusion are core elements of the business strategy.

The objectives of the company's efforts to manage diversity are related to the business, employees, shareholders, and community. For example, the objectives include understanding and living the business case for diversity and inclusion; increasing awareness of how diversity relates to business challenges; creating and fostering a diverse work environment by developing management practices that drive hiring, promotion, and retention of talent; engaging in relationship management and customer service to attract and retain diverse clients and customers; and partnering with businesses run by women and visible minorities to deliver food and facility management services.

Sodexo separates employment equity and compliance training from diversity education. Every three years, employees are required to take employment equity refresher courses. Top management is also involved in and committed to managing diversity. The senior executives program includes ongoing classroom training that is reinforced with community involvement, sponsoring employee groups, and mentoring diverse employees. Executives are engaged in learning the business case for diversity and are personally held accountable for the company's diversity agenda. Every manager takes an eight-hour introductory class (Spirit of Diversity). Other learning opportunities are available, including three- to four-hour learning labs that include topics such as cross-cultural communications, sexual orientation in the workplace, generations in the workplace, and gender in the workplace. The company's learning and development team develops customized learning solutions for different functions and work teams. For example, a course related to selling to a diverse client base was developed and offered to the sales force, and a cross-cultural communications program was provided for recruiters.

In addition to diversity training activities, Sodexo has six employee network groups that provide a forum for employees' professional development and sharing input and ideas to support the company's diversity efforts. Sodexo's Champions of Diversity program rewards and recognizes employees who advance diversity and inclusion.

To emphasize the importance of diversity for the company at Sodexo, each manager has a diversity scorecard that evaluates his or her success in recruitment, retention, promotion, and development of all employees. The scorecard includes both quantitative goals as well as evaluation of behaviours such as participating in training, mentoring, and doing community outreach. A proportion of managers' pay bonuses is determined by success in these areas.

Sodexo has found that its diversity training and efforts to manage diversity are having a positive impact on business results. Its mentoring program has led to increased productivity, engagement, and retention of women and visible minorities. In fact, there was an estimated return on investment of $19 for every dollar spent on the program. As a result, Sodexo also has been awarded several new business contracts and retained clients because of its involvement in managing diversity.

SOURCES: R. Anand and M. Winters, "A Retrospective View of Corporate Diversity Training from 1964 to the Present," *Academy of Management Learning & Education,* 7 (2008), pp. 356–372; Dolezalek, "The Path to Inclusion." Also, see www.sodexousa.com. and Sodexo Culture at www.sodexo.ca/caen/aboutus/culture/culture.asp (retrieved November 29, 2010).

Questions

1. How does Sodexo's approach to managing diversity impact its bottom line? How might it influence business growth?
2. What role does training play in helping employees accept diversity?
3. How is diversity tied to employee development? How is it tied to other HR functions?

Practise and learn online with Connect.

7 Managing Employee Engagement and Performance

Enter the World of Business

Engagement Follows Love

Six years ago things looked pretty grim as Razor Suleman, founder of I Love Rewards, took stock of the company's situation. Morale was so low at this company that builds web-based rewards and recognition programs that even Suleman decided he would look for a job. With only 12 employees and turnover at 40 percent, Suleman realized that I Love Rewards "was probably the worst company on the planet to work for" and that if a worst-company competition existed, I Love Rewards would top the list. It doesn't get much more ironic than that.

Fortunately for Suleman, one of his employees challenged him to create a vision for the company. Suleman responded by drafting a five-page plan to "recruit, retain, and inspire great people" and to become a global leader in employee recognition, which proved to be a turning point that transformed the tiny company's future. At the heart of this transformation was Suleman's sudden realization that even though the company was marketing employee-recognition software and recognition consulting services, he had neglected to create a recognition program for his own team. What was he thinking? Suleman's epiphany became the springboard for a host of innovative changes designed to create total engagement among I Love Rewards' present and future employees. Those changes also created a role model for current and future customers. Suleman realized that if employees were expected to convince customers to break the gold-watch-for-long-service paradigm and really ignite the concept of performance-based rewards, then clearly the company had to walk the talk. Thus Suleman's focus became winning the heads and hearts of his own employees, and making I Love Rewards a great place to work and an inspiration to clients.

Company revenues have doubled annually in the last few years, and sales now exceed $25 million; the current workforce (80-plus employees) and customer base (over 100) have grown exponentially; and the company is now expanding into the United States. The list of awards the company has won started growing in 2007. For example, the company made the 2009 WorldBlu List of Most Democratic Workplaces™, and recently placed first in AON Hewitt's annual Best Small and Medium Employers list (in the Greater Toronto Area), because researchers found the company's employees to be so highly motivated and enthusiastic about the company and their jobs. According to the Top 100 Reasons to Work with Us on the company website, the employees really like their coworkers, citing the highly focused, great team they work with as #1. But they also value being asked for input into the company's Master Plan (#9), quarterly open forums with the senior leadership team (#14), the annual two-day company retreat (#82), and "awesome challenges" to look forward to every day (#96). The list is very, very long. Seems like Suleman started something with that five-page plan he drafted. Today the people management practices at I Love Rewards are completely aligned with the business of I Love Rewards. And no one is happier than the employees, except maybe the customers, who know they can trust a company whose CEO has learned what employee engagement really is and how to make it happen.

SOURCES: Based on www.iloverewards.com/company/top-100-reasons-to-work-with-us; P. Brent, "Turnaround Began When Company Hit Rock Bottom," *Toronto Star* (November 20, 2010) p. M4; R. Suleman, "Building a Successful Recognition Program," *Canadian HR Reporter* (October 4, 2010), pp. 27–28.

INTRODUCTION

Every executive recognizes the need for satisfied, loyal customers. If the firm is publicly held, it is also safe to assume that every executive appreciates the need to have satisfied, loyal investors. Customers and investors provide the financial resources that allow the organization to survive. However, unlike Razor Suleman, not every executive understands the need to generate satisfaction and loyalty among employees, because retention rates among employees are related to retention rates among customers.[1] In fact, research has established a direct link between employee retention rates and sales growth[2] and companies such as I Love Rewards that win multiple awards and are cited as one of the "100 Best Companies to Work For" routinely outperform their competition on many other financial indicators of performance.[3] Research indicates that sustained (at least 10 years) competitive advantage in capital markets is directly attributable to successfully managing the workforce.[4] Job satisfaction and retention are also related to organizational performance.[5] This is especially the case in service industries, where disgruntled workers often create large numbers of dissatisfied customers.[6] Lack of experience and cohesiveness within work units destroys efficiency, and the costs associated with constantly replacing workers erodes a firm's competitive position.[7] Indeed, study after study has shown a direct causal connection between poor worker attitudes on the one hand, and poor customer service on the other.[8]

Thus, this chapter begins by examining what managers can do to increase engagement among employees, influencing them to stay with the organization. Here the focus is on avoiding **voluntary turnover**; that is, turnover initiated by employees (often those whom the company would prefer to keep). We discuss what causes employees to be become dissatisfied and "mysteriously" begin to withdraw from their employers. Next, the key role of performance management is examined with respect to identifying top performers and ensuring continued growth and retention of such key talent so the investment isn't lost to competitors. The importance of feedback is also discussed, along with various interventions designed to improve the performance of mediocre and poorly performing employees.

However, since another hallmark of successful firms is their ability and willingness to dismiss employees who are engaging in counterproductive behaviour, we then turn our attention to **involuntary turnover**; that is, turnover initiated by the organization (often among people who would prefer to stay). Indeed, it is somewhat ironic that one of the keys to retaining productive employees is ensuring that these people are not being made miserable by supervisors or co-workers who are engaging in unproductive, disruptive, or dangerous behaviour. In such situations, managers have a responsibility to end things as effectively as possible, allowing all stakeholders to go their separate ways. Thus our chapter concludes with a frank discussion about discipline and termination of

Voluntary Turnover
Turnover initiated by employees (often whom the company would prefer to keep).

Involuntary Turnover
Turnover initiated by the organization (often among people who would prefer to stay).

poorly performing employees, emphasizing various legal difficulties employers need to be aware of when concluding the employment relationship.

DRIVING ENGAGEMENT: PREVENTING VOLUNTARY TURNOVER

Describe what influences employee satisfaction, possible causes of job withdrawal, and how to measure employee engagement.

In this section we focus on a topic employers should be obsessed with—preventing employees who are highly valued by the organization from leaving (and perhaps even joining the competition). A 2010 Conference Board survey of 349 Canadian companies measured average turnover in the private sector at 9.1 percent and 5.7 percent in the public sector, averaging 8.2 percent overall (down from 9.7 percent in the pre-recession period of 2008.)[9] At the organizational level, turnover results in lowered work unit performance, which, in turn, harms the firm's financial performance.[10] This causal chain is especially strong when the organization is losing its top performers. Research suggests that some of the organization's top performers are up to 300 percent more productive than average employees, and retaining these workers is especially difficult.[11] Moreover, in organizations that rely on teams or long-term customer contacts, the loss of workers who are central to employee teams or customer networks can be especially disruptive.[12]

To understand why good employees leave we begin by examining the job withdrawal process that characterizes voluntary employee turnover, and we illustrate the central role that job satisfaction plays in this process. Replacing workers is an expensive undertaking, and recent estimates place this cost at roughly $50,000 for professional or managerial workers and $25,000 for clerical or manufacturing employees.[13] Replacement costs are just a tip of the iceberg, however, when it comes to the costs of job dissatisfaction and turnover. One recent study showed that firms in the top quartile in terms of employee job satisfaction had profit rates that were 4 percent higher than firms in the bottom quartile. There is also a demonstrable relationship between employee satisfaction and customer satisfaction at the individual level,[14] and turnover rates and customer satisfaction at the organizational level.[15] Indeed, the whole employee satisfaction–firm performance relationship can become part of a virtuous cycle, where firms with more highly satisfied employees perform better and increase their profits, which in turn they use to shore up employee pay and benefits—further adding to their competitive advantage.[16] We will discuss what aspects of job satisfaction seem most critical to retention and how employee feedback surveys can be used to strategically manage engagement and prevention of voluntary turnover.

Learn more about additional survey results online with Connect.

connect

Process of Job Withdrawal

Recall that in Chapter 1 we defined employee engagement as the degree to which employees are fully involved in their work and the strength of their job and company commitment. Employers who care about retaining good employees will naturally want to be aware of signs to watch for when engagement begins to wane. What causes engagement to fizzle out? What does lack of engagement look like? Generally it begins when employees become dissatisfied with something and begin to withdraw from the job in one way or another.

Job withdrawal is a set of behaviours that dissatisfied individuals enact to avoid the work situation. The right side of Figure 7.1 on page 256 shows a model grouping the overall set of behaviours into three categories: behaviour change, physical job withdrawal, and psychological job withdrawal. We present the various forms of withdrawal in a progression, as if individuals try the next category only if the preceding form of withdrawal is either unsuccessful or impossible to implement. This theory of **progression of withdrawal** has a long history and many adherents.[17]

Progression of Withdrawal
Theory that dissatisfied individuals enact a set of behaviours in succession to avoid their work situation.

FIGURE 7.1 An Overall Model of the Job Dissatisfaction–Job Withdrawal Process

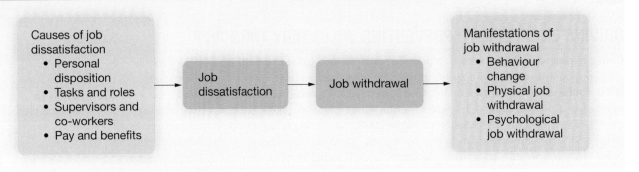

One might expect that an employee's first response to dissatisfaction would be to try to change the conditions that generate the dissatisfaction which can lead to, or cause change in, their behaviour. For example, there may be a supervisor–subordinate confrontation, or even conflict, as dissatisfied workers try to bring about changes in policy or upper-level personnel. Indeed, as shown in the "Competing through Globalization" box, there are many different ways people might "voice" their concerns, and people from different cultures approach this in different ways. Where employees are unionized, it can lead to an increased number of grievances being filed,[18] a topic we discuss in Chapter 11. Although at first this type of conflict can feel threatening to the manager, on closer inspection, this is really an opportunity for the manager to learn about and perhaps solve an important problem.

However, if job conditions cannot be changed, a dissatisfied worker may attempt to solve the problem through physical withdrawal—leaving the job. This could take the form of an internal transfer if the dissatisfaction is job specific (the result of an unfair supervisor or unpleasant working conditions). On the other hand, if the source of the dissatisfaction relates to organization-wide policies (lack of job security or below-market pay levels), then turnover is likely. However, someone who is dissatisfied with the job or organization might not be able to jump to another job right away but will instead disengage temporarily (through absenteeism or tardiness).

When dissatisfied employees are unable to change their situation or remove themselves physically from their jobs, they may psychologically disengage themselves from their jobs until a better opportunity comes along.[19] Although they are physically on the job, their minds may be somewhere else. If the primary dissatisfaction has to do with the job itself, the employee may display a very low level of job involvement. However, if the dissatisfaction is with the employer as a whole, the employee will display a low level of organizational commitment. For example, individuals who feel they have been unjustly treated by their employer often respond by reducing their level of commitment and often look for an opportunity to quit their jobs.[20]

Researchers debate various aspects of the withdrawal process, including the concept of progression, and the impact of critical incidents on pushing an employee from just being dissatisfied to making a decision to leave the company. Regardless of what specific theory one endorses, there is a general consensus that withdrawal behaviours are clearly related to one another, and they are all at least partially caused by job dissatisfaction.[21]

connect

Learn more about research findings on progression of withdrawal online with Connect.

Competing Through Globalization

French Workers Stage "Bossnappings" to Voice Concerns

North American companies doing business in France may need to make rather shocking adjustments to what can be expected when employees voice concerns about senior-level personnel or their decisions. Indeed, the behaviour changes associated with this particular source of job dissatisfaction can be extreme when compared to North America, and could be regarded as the zenith of job withdrawal—especially by the person or persons who become the focus of dissatisfied employees.

When heavy construction manufacturer Caterpillar announced that it would shed 733 jobs in plants in Grenoble, France, in April 2009, the workers at the site kidnapped their bosses and held them hostage. Although this may seem like an unreasonable act to many outside that country, in fact, the Caterpillar incident was the fourth kidnapping of bosses that had occurred in France in 2009. Earlier that year, managers at Sony were also held hostage by their workers at their plant and 3M manager Roc Rousselet of the Pithivier plant was locked in his office for two days while irate workers bargained for better severance packages and improved working conditions for those who would stay. The CEO of the firm that controls Gucci and Yves St. Laurent was surrounded and sequestered by workers while in his car, and anger about a plant closing in Reims motivated angry workers to storm a management meeting and treat their bosses to an egging.

Kidnapping one's bosses is technically a crime in France. Yet, despite this, kidnapping of bosses is tolerated by both police and organizational executives as a negotiating strategy for establishing the "social plan" that is also legally mandated by law in the case of company layoffs. The social plan is a document negotiated between union and management listing the amount of severance pay workers are to receive, as well as the support they will be provided in terms of finding new jobs or training. When the union does not like the terms being offered, some resort to kidnapping to draw media attention to their cause. Although Caterpillar France attributed the layoffs in the Grenoble site to a 55 percent loss in orders caused by the recession, and indicated it planned to eliminate 20,000 positions worldwide, members of the CGT union saw it differently. One union representative explained, "At a time when the company is making a profit and distributing dividends to shareholders we want to find a favourable outcome for all the workers and know as quickly as possible where we are going." This is often an effective strategy, and Caterpillar increased the amount of severance granted to workers from 37 million euros to 47 million euros to resolve the situation. Regardless, French President Nicolas Sarkozy displayed little patience for such "aggravating matters that are contrary to the law" and called for a stop to "bossnappings."

Although kidnapping one's boss may sound barbaric, in fact, there are strong cultural norms for how such a kidnapping works, and both sides of the negotiation play by a certain set of unspoken rules. The workers never engage in any outright violence against the bosses and treat them with as much respect and dignity as the basic nature of a kidnapping would allow. Kidnappings rarely last more than two or three days, and cots are often brought in so that people do not have to sleep on the floor. The kidnapped executives are allowed to contact their families as much as they like and, in cases of health-related issues (such as hostages with heart problems), receive any treatment that might be necessary. In return, the company never calls in the police and never presses for criminal charges against the workers.

Canadian executives would never think of being kidnapped by their workers. However, French history is littered with revolutions, and the idea of protest is ingrained in the minds of French workers and management alike. Indeed, as one former kidnapped CEO, Maurice Levy, noted, "Protest is inscribed in the genes of French culture. In the past, peasants protested against their lords. Today, the difference is that the lords are chief executives."

SOURCES: "French Caterpillar Workers Detain Bosses in France," Associated Press, *The Globe and Mail* (March 31, 2009) p. B13; L. Abboud and M. Colchester, "French Bosses Beseiged as Worker Anger Rises," *The Wall Street Journal* (April 1, 2009), p. A1; D. Gauthier-Villars and L. Abboud, "In France, the Bosses Can Become Hostages," *The Wall Street Journal* (April 3, 2009), pp. A1–A2; J. Leeder, "Economic Uncertainty Boils over in Workplace," *The Globe and Mail* (March 26, 2009), p. B1; "Head of 3M's French Unit Set Free After Being Held Hostage," *The Globe and Mail* (March 27, 2009), p. B8; Sarkozy Tells French: No More "Bossnappings," Agence France Presse, *The Globe and Mail* (April 8, 2009), p. B8.

Job Satisfaction and Job Withdrawal

As we see in Figure 7.1 on page 256 the key driving force behind loss of engagement and all the different forms of job withdrawal is job dissatisfaction. This is the opposite of **job satisfaction,** which we define as a pleasurable feeling that results from the perception that one's job fulfills or allows for the fulfillment of one's important job values.[22] This definition reflects three important aspects of job satisfaction. First, job satisfaction is a function of *values,* defined as "what a person consciously or unconsciously desires to obtain." Second, this definition emphasizes that different employees have different views of which values are important, and this is critical in determining the nature and degree of their job satisfaction. One person may value high pay above all else; another may value the opportunity to travel; another may value staying within a specific geographic region. The third important aspect of job satisfaction is perception. An individual's perceptions may not be a completely accurate reflection of reality, and different people may view the same situation differently, depending on their own frame of reference.

Job Satisfaction
A pleasurable feeling that results from the perception that one's job fulfills or allows for the fulfillment of one's important job values.

■ connect™

Learn more about how people are influenced by their frame of reference online with Connect.

Sources of Job Dissatisfaction

Many things can cause dissatisfaction among employees. Managers and HR professionals need to be aware of these so they can raise job satisfaction, increase engagement, and reduce employee withdrawal. This is an issue that is particularly salient in the current economy where pressures to raise productivity have pushed many workers to the limit. In a 2010 Conference Board Survey of 167 employers that conduct engagement surveys, key areas identified by employees as needing the most improvement were recognition (25 percent), career opportunities (23 percent), effectiveness of management (20 percent), development opportunities (20 percent), and compensation and benefits (18 percent).[23] Survey results such as this will vary, depending on the time and place they are conducted, and the types of companies included in the survey. However, sources of job dissatisfaction most under the control of all employers at any point in time include basic issues such as providing safe working conditions, pay and benefits, supervisors and co-workers, and the tasks and roles the employee is assigned.

In Chapter 12, we discuss extensively the employee's right to *safe working conditions*, and the employer's role in enforcing health and safety legislation and in implementation of health and safety awareness programs. We wish to reinforce here that the perception and reaction of the organization's own employees to the safety of their working conditions has implications for satisfaction, retention, and competitive advantage that go well beyond merely meeting the legal requirements. That is, if applicants or job incumbents conclude that their health or lives are at risk because of the job, attracting and retaining workers will be impossible. Employers may also provide employee assistance programs to promote overall health and wellness to reduce health care–related expenditures. These programs more than pay for themselves over time, and firms that emphasize health and wellness send workers a clear signal that they care about them, strengthening the employer–employee relationship. The strategic link between employee engagement and retention and wellness programs is reinforced in the "Exercising Strategy" feature on page 296.

Pay and benefits is another critical area where employers can directly influence job satisfaction. For most employees, pay is not only a primary source of income, but also an indicator of status. The standing of an employee's pay relative to others within the organization, or the standing of their pay relative to others doing similar work for other employers, can become more important than the level of pay itself.[24] Thus, for some people, pay is a reflection of self-worth, so pay satisfaction takes on critical significance when it comes to retention.[25] Satisfaction with benefits is another important dimension of overall pay satisfaction. However, since employees can easily underrate the value of their benefits package, it is critical to make benefits not only highly salient to employees, but also to link them to the organization's strategic direction.

Supervisors and co-workers are the two primary groups of people in an organization who affect job satisfaction. A person may be satisfied with her supervisor and co-workers because she shares the same values, attitudes, and philosophies as they do, or because they provide the social support she needs to achieve her own goals. It is worth noting that job satisfaction can be derived simply from congruence among supervisors and subordinates at one level,[26] and considerable research indicates that social support is a strong predictor of job satisfaction and lower employee turnover.[27] In contrast, abusive supervision is a major cause of turnover, and some organizations find that they can reduce turnover in some units by 25 percent to 33 percent in a single year simply by removing a specific supervisor who lacks interpersonal skills.[28] Thus, because supervisors and other more experienced workers exert such a powerful influence on the organization's culture, some organizations are going to great lengths to develop the mentoring and coaching skills of these individuals.[29] Note that SaskEnergy, featured in "Managing People" on page 298, introduced a coaching program to make its work environment more welcoming and to ensure employee commitment. Likewise, because incivility and lack of interpersonal skills among co-workers or team members can also create job dissatisfaction, many organizations foster team building both on and off the job (such as softball or hockey teams). The idea is that group cohesiveness and support for individual group members will be increased through exposure and joint efforts. Although management certainly cannot ensure that each stressed employee develops friends, employers can make it easier for employees to interact—a necessary condition for developing friendship and rapport. In fact, results of surveys indicate that endorsing the item "Most of my closest friendships are with people at work" is one of the most powerful tools for predicting low turnover.[30]

Employers also have direct control over the *tasks and roles* of employees, and as a predictor of job dissatisfaction, nothing surpasses the nature of the task itself.[31] Many aspects of a task have been linked to dissatisfaction, but we will focus here on the complexity of the task, the amount of flexibility in where and when the work is done, and, finally, the value the employee puts on the task.[32]

With a few exceptions, there is a strong positive relationship between task complexity and job satisfaction. That is, the boredom generated by simple, repetitive jobs that do not mentally challenge the worker leads to frustration and dissatisfaction.[33] One of the major interventions aimed at reducing job dissatisfaction is **job enrichment**, which increases job complexity. As the term suggests, this intervention is directed at jobs that are "impoverished" or boring because of their repetitive nature

Job Enrichment
The process of enriching jobs that are boring, repetitive, or low in scope through interventions such as ensuring workers have opportunities for input into important organizational decisions involving their work.

or low scope. Many job enrichment programs are based on the job characteristics theory discussed earlier in Chapter 4. For example, many job enrichment programs provide increased opportunities for workers to have input into important organizational decisions that involve their work, and this has been routinely found to reduce role conflict and ambiguity. In some cases, job enrichment programs may have to be complemented with training programs to ensure people have the skills to expand their jobs. In general, skills training gives job incumbents the ability to better predict, understand, and control events occurring on the job, which in turn increases their ability to make their own decisions.[34]

Another task-based intervention that increases job complexity and engagement is job rotation, which was discussed in Chapter 6. Although employees may not feel capable of putting up with the dissatisfying aspects of a particular job indefinitely, they often feel they can do so temporarily. Job rotation can do more than simply spread out the dissatisfying aspects of a particular job; it can increase work complexity for employees and provide valuable cross-training in jobs so that employees eventually understand many different jobs. This makes for a more flexible workforce and increases workers' appreciation of the other tasks that have to be accomplished for the organization to complete its mission.[35]

Because of the degree to which nonwork roles often spill over and affect work roles, and vice versa, a second critical aspect of work that affects satisfaction and retention is the degree to which scheduling is flexible. To help employees manage their multiple roles, companies have turned to a number of family-friendly policies to both recruit new talent and hold onto the talent they already have. These policies may include provisions for child care and elder care, extended maternal and paternal leaves, and flexible work arrangements such as those discussed in Chapter 4.[36] Note how some employers are helping employees achieve work/life balance by easing the burden of child and elder care in the "Competing Through Sustainability" box.

Finally, by far, the most important aspect of work in terms of generating satisfaction is the degree to which it is meaningfully related to core values of the worker. The term **prosocial motivation** is often used explicitly to capture the degree to which people are motivated to help other people. When people believe that their work has an important impact on other people, they are much more willing to work longer hours.[37] This prosocial motivation could be directed toward helping co-workers and has been found to relate to helping behaviour.[38] This form of motivation can also be triggered by recognizing that one's work has a positive impact on those who benefit from one's service, such as customer or clients.[39] In contrast, when their social needs are thwarted, employees often react negatively and in self-defeating ways that drive people further from them.[40] Thus, if employers wish to ensure greater job satisfaction, they can design jobs that are more meaningful to employees, and provide team training, which underscores the importance of helping behaviours in the workplace.

Prosocial Motivation
The degree to which people are energized to do their jobs because it helps other people.

connect Learn more about sources of job dissatisfaction online with Connect.

Employee Engagement Surveys

Many employers wish to measure the level of engagement and job satisfaction among employees and do so by conducting regular employee engagement surveys. For example, in the 2010 Conference Board Survey among 167 employers mentioned earlier in this chapter, 74 percent of organizations "regularly use employee surveys to measure employee engagement, employee satisfaction and work culture," with a median response rate to such surveys by employees of 76 percent. The majority of that group conduct such surveys annually or every second year.[41] Although such employers face a number of design decisions, such as what measures to use and what facets of satisfaction to measure, a systematic, ongoing program of *employee survey research* should be a prominent part of any human

Competing Through Sustainability

Parents, Kids, and Caring Companies

For new mothers returning to work there is nothing more stressful than searching for manageable child care arrangements or the thought of turning that tiny cherub over to a complete stranger. Then there is the other end of the spectrum—trying to care for elderly parents who have reached a point where they can't safely be left alone. But how to do that when you work full time, carry a lot of responsibility, and may be in a job that requires frequent travel? The problem can seem insurmountable unless you're lucky enough to work for a very understanding and resourceful employer that helps ease the burden by providing work/life balance programs and access to emergency caregivers when a crisis crops up.

That's the kind of employer that Ernst & Young, RBC Financial Group, Cassels Brock, and Deloitte & Touche have each proven to be. Each maintains a membership with Kids and Company, an innovative care provider founded in 2002. The company operates on a business-to-business model that provides full-service daycare centres accessible only by employees of corporate clients. Corporate clients pay $5,000–$10,000 per year for membership fees and about half also subsidize a portion of parents' fees of $1,000 per month. By 2008 the client list included numerous law firms, most of the Big Six banks, all of the Big Four accounting firms, and multinationals such as Coca-Cola and Procter & Gamble. Corporate memberships provide employees with access to guaranteed high-quality child care at any of the Kids & Company Locations. Employers can also purchase up to two weeks worth of emergency backup child care days for $350/year for children under 13 years of age. There's also a Nanny care program if families want a well qualified in-home caregiver, and a meals-to-go service available through a partnering firm. That would certainly ease the tension for a harried parent picking up a toddler at 5 p.m.

One of the key attractions of Kids and Company's services is that it provides emergency backup care for stress-filled days when unanticipated issues interrupt normal child or eldercare arrangements. KPMG's National Director of Total Rewards, Geri Markvoort, believes that the service signals to employees that the company cares for them and enhances KPMG's long-standing status as an employer of choice. Norma Tombari of RBC Financial Group notes Kids and Company's services have been "well received by RBC employees who have used the service."

For parents, such as Robert Betteridge, of Calgary law firm Burnet, Duckworth & Palmer, the service meant he and his physician wife could get on with their professional lives and continue to enjoy their role as parents. And for Betteridge there was an extra perk to the arrangement others would envy. Because his downtown office was in close proximity to his son's daycare, he occasionally encountered the daycare group when he was making his way to a destination. Bettridge describes the situation with a chuckle, saying "It's funny walking out for a coffee and every once in awhile I run into my son on the rope chain." Such moments can have dual outcomes; strengthening the bond between father and son while reinforcing that same father's commitment to a caring employer. For an employer who has made the difficult and often expensive decision to support employees through partners like Kids and Company, such moments also make it all worthwhile.

SOURCES: V. Galt, "Top-Ranked Bosses Know How to 'Walk the Talk,'" *The Globe and Mail* (October 28, 2006), p. B13; Kids and Company website: Our People at https://www.kidsandcompany.ca/index.php/about/people/ (retrieved July 8, 2011); D. Carlson, "Perks for Prospects," *Financial Post*, May 16, 2007; R. Spence, " No. 1 Profile, A Need for Speed," Profit Magazine Canada's Fastest Growing Companies, *Profit Magazine* (June 2008) p. 56.

resource strategy for a number of reasons. First, it allows the company to monitor trends over time and thus prevent problems in the area of voluntary turnover before they happen. For example, the level of satisfaction with promotion opportunities in the company might have eroded over time, whereas the satisfaction with co-workers has improved. If there was a strong relationship between satisfaction with promotion opportunities and voluntary turnover among high performers, this would constitute a threat that the organization might need to address via some of the techniques discussed in Chapter 6.

A second reason for undertaking an ongoing program of employee engagement surveys is that they provide a means of empirically assessing the impact of changes in policy (such as introduction of a new performance appraisal system) or personnel (e.g., introduction of a new CEO) on worker attitudes. Such a comparison would be invaluable when a merger has taken place, for example, and would provide the information necessary to know what employers should keep on doing and what needs to be changed.

Third, when these surveys incorporate standardized scales, they often allow the company to compare itself with others in the same industry along these dimensions. Again, if the survey reveals major differences between the organization and the industry as a whole (on overall pay levels, for example), the company can react and change its policies before there is a mass exodus of people moving to the competition.

Although findings such as these are leading more companies to do such surveys, conducting an organizational opinion survey is not something that should be taken lightly. Especially in the beginning, surveys such as this often raise expectations. If people fail to see any timely actions taken on matters identified as problems in the survey, satisfaction is likely to be even lower than it would be in the absence of a survey.

Finally, although the focus in this section has been on surveys of current employees, any strategic retention policy also has to consider surveying people who are about to become ex-employees. Exit interviews with departing workers can be a valuable tool for uncovering systematic concerns that are driving retention problems. If properly conducted, an exit interview can reveal the reasons people are leaving, and perhaps even set the stage for their later return.[42] If a recruiter has information about what caused a specific person to leave (such as an abusive supervisor or a lack of family-friendly policies), when the situation changes, the person may be willing to come back.[43] Indeed, in the war for talent, the best way to manage retention is to engage in a battle for every valued employee, even in situations when it looks like the battle may have been lost.

connect™ Learn more about design of employee engagement surveys online with Connect.

MANAGING PERFORMANCE

Companies that seek competitive advantage through employees must be able to manage the behaviour and results of all employees. Traditionally, the formal performance appraisal system was viewed as the primary means for managing employee performance. Performance appraisal was an administrative duty performed by managers and was primarily the responsibility of the human resource function. Managers now view performance appraisal as an annual ritual—they quickly complete the form and use it to catalogue all the information they have collected on an employee over the previous year, which may include negative information. Because they may dislike confrontation and feel that they don't know how to give effective evaluations, some managers spend as little time as possible giving employees feedback. Not surprisingly, most managers and employees dislike performance appraisals. Some of the reasons include the lack of consistency of use of performance appraisals across the company; inability to differentiate among different performance levels; and the inability of the appraisal system to provide useful data for development, to help employees build their skills and competencies, or to build engagement among employees and a high-performance culture.[44]

Some have argued that all performance appraisal systems are flawed to the point that they are manipulative, abusive, autocratic, and counterproductive. Table 7.1 shows some of the criticism of performance appraisals and how the problems can be fixed. It is important to realize that the deficiencies shown in Table 7.1 are not the result of evaluating employee performance. Rather, they result from how the appraisal system is developed and used. If done correctly, performance appraisals can provide valuable benefits to both employees and the company.

An important part of appraising performance is to establish employee goals, which should be tied to the company's strategic goals. The performance appraisal process tells top performers that they are valued by the company. It requires managers to at least annually communicate to employees their performance strengths and deficiencies. A good appraisal process ensures that all employees doing similar jobs are evaluated according to the same standards. The use of technology, such as the Internet, can reduce the administrative burden of performance appraisal and improve the accuracy of performance reviews. Also, a properly conducted appraisal can help the company identify the strongest and weakest employees. It can help legally justify many HRM decisions such as promotions, salary increases, discipline, and layoffs. *Fortune* magazine annually ranks the most globally admired companies. The Hay Group, which produces the Global Most Admired report for *Fortune,* says the companies on the list have chief executive officers who understand that performance measurement is about learning how to motivate people and linking performance to rewards. Many of the executives report that performance measurement encourages collaboration and cooperation. They believe performance measures help companies focus on operational excellence, customer loyalty, and development of people.

We believe that performance appraisal is only one part of the broader process of performance management. We define **performance management** as the process through which managers ensure that employees' activities and outputs are congruent with the organization's goals. Performance management is central to gaining competitive advantage.

Performance Management
The means through which managers ensure that employees' activities and outputs are congruent with the organization's goals.

Table 7.1 Problems and Possible Solutions in Performance Management

PROBLEM	SOLUTION
Discourages teamwork	Make collaboration a criterion on which employees will be evaluated.
Evaluators are inconsistent or use different criteria and standards	Provide training for managers; have the HR department look for patterns on appraisals that suggest bias or over- or underevaluation.
Only valuable for very good or very poor employees	Evaluate specific behaviours or results to show specifically what employees need to improve.
Encourages employees to achieve short-term goals	Include both long-term and short-term goals in the appraisal process.
Manager has complete power over the employee	Managers should be appraised for how they appraise their employees.
Too subjective	Evaluate specific behaviour or results.
Produces emotional anguish	Focus on behaviour; do not criticize employees; conduct appraisal on time.

SOURCES: Based on G. Latham, J. Almost, S. Mann, and C. Moore, "New Developments in Performance Management," *Organizational Dynamics* 34 (2005), pp. 77–87; J. A. Siegel, "86 Your Appraisal Process?" *HR Magazine* (October 2000), pp. 199–202.

However, if a company's performance management process is to avoid the problems described above and to accomplish the goal of linking employee activities and outputs to organizational strategy for competitive advantage, we believe an *effective* performance management system will have three parts: defining performance, measuring performance, and feeding back performance information. Why three distinct activities? First, a performance management system specifies which aspects of performance are relevant to the organization, primarily through job analysis (discussed in Chapter 4). Second, it measures those aspects of performance through **performance appraisal**, the process through which an organization gets information on how well an employee is doing his or her job. Third, it provides feedback to employees through **performance feedback** sessions so they can adjust their performance to the organization's goals. Performance feedback is also fulfilled through tying rewards to performance via the compensation system (such as through merit increases or bonuses), a topic to be covered in Chapters 8 and 9.

Performance Appraisal
The process through which an organization gets information on how well an employee is doing his or her job.

Performance Feedback
The process of providing employees information regarding their performance effectiveness.

Thus we will now examine a variety of approaches to performance management. First we present a model of performance that helps us examine the purposes of performance management systems. Then we discuss specific performance measures criteria, and approaches to measuring performance and the strengths and weaknesses of each. We also look at various sources of performance information. The errors resulting from subjective assessments of performance (rater errors) are presented, as well as the means for reducing those errors. Then we discuss some various aspects of performance feedback. Finally, we address the development and implementation of a legally defensible performance management system.

■ connect™ Learn more about the practice of performance management online with Connect.

AN ORGANIZATIONAL MODEL OF PERFORMANCE MANAGEMENT

LO 2

Identify the major determinants of individual performance and the general purposes of performance management.

For many years, researchers in the field of HRM and industrial–organizational psychology focused on performance appraisal as a measurement technique.[45] The goal of these performance appraisal systems was to measure individual employee performance reliably and validly. This perspective, however, tended to ignore some important influences on the performance management process. Thus, we begin this section by presenting the major purposes of performance management from an organizational rather than a measurement perspective. To do this, we need to understand the process of performance management. Figure 7.2 presents our process model of performance management in organizations.

As the figure shows, individuals' attributes—their skills, abilities, and so on—are the raw materials of performance. For example, in a sales job, an organization wants someone who has good interpersonal skills and knowledge of the products. These raw materials are transformed into objective results through the employee's behaviour. Employees can exhibit desired behaviours only if they have the necessary knowledge, skills, abilities, and other characteristics. Thus, employees with good product knowledge and interpersonal skills can talk about the advantages of various brands and can be friendly and helpful (not that they necessarily display those behaviours, only that they *can* display them). On the other hand, employees with little product knowledge or indifferent interpersonal skills cannot effectively display those behaviours. The objective results are the measurable, tangible outputs of the work, and they are a consequence of the employee's or the workgroup's behaviour. In our example, a salesperson who displays the correct behaviours will likely make a number of sales.

Another important component in our organizational model of the performance management system is the organization's strategy. The link between performance management and the organization's strategies and goals is often neglected. Chapter 2 pointed out that most companies pursue some type of strategy to attain their revenue, profit, and market share goals. Divisions, departments, workgroups, and individuals within the company must align their activities with these strategies and goals. If they are not

FIGURE 7.2   Model of Performance Management in Organizations

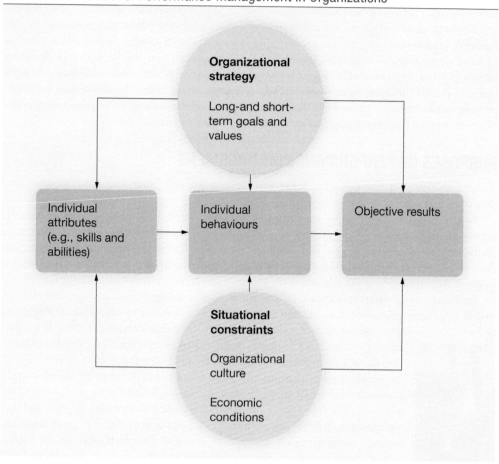

aligned, then the likelihood of achieving the goals becomes small. How is this link made in organizations? Primarily by specifying what needs to be accomplished and what behaviours must be exhibited for the company's strategy to be implemented. This link is being recognized as necessary more and more often, through the increasing popularity of **performance planning and evaluation (PPE) systems.** PPE systems seek to tie the formal performance appraisal process to the company's strategies by specifying at the beginning of the evaluation period the types and level of performance that must be accomplished to achieve the strategy. Then at the end of the evaluation period, individuals and groups are evaluated based on how closely their actual performance met the performance plan. In an ideal world, performance management systems would ensure that all activities support the organization's strategic goals.

Finally, our model notes that situational constraints are always at work within the performance management system. As discussed previously, an employee may have the necessary skills and yet not exhibit the necessary behaviours. Sometimes the organizational culture discourages the employee from doing effective things. Workgroup norms often dictate what the group's members do and the results they produce. On the other hand, some people are simply not motivated to exhibit the right behaviours. This often occurs if the employees do not believe their behaviours will be rewarded with pay raises, promotions, and so forth. Finally, people may be performing effective behaviours, and yet the right results do not follow. For example, an outstanding salesperson may not have a large volume of sales because the economy is bad and people are not buying.

Performance Planning and Evaluation (PPE) System
Any system that seeks to tie the formal performance appraisal process to the company's strategies by specifying at the beginning of the evaluation period the types and level of performance that must be accomplished in order to achieve the strategy.

Thus, as you can see in Figure 7.2 on page 265, employees must have certain attributes to perform a set of behaviours and achieve certain results. To gain competitive advantage, the attributes and results must be tied to the company's strategy. Regardless of the job or company, effective performance management systems measure performance criteria (such as sales) as precisely as possible. Effective performance management systems also serve a strategic function by linking performance criteria to internal and external customer requirements. Effective performance management systems include a process for changing the system based on situational constraints. Besides serving a strategic purpose, performance management systems also have administrative and developmental purposes. We next examine the various purposes of performance management systems.

PURPOSES OF PERFORMANCE MANAGEMENT

There are three purposes of performance management systems: strategic, administrative, and developmental.

First and foremost, a performance management system should link employee activities with the organization's goals. One of the primary ways strategies are implemented is through defining the results, behaviours, and, to some extent, employee characteristics that are necessary for carrying out those strategies, and then developing measurement and feedback systems that will maximize the extent to which employees exhibit the characteristics, engage in the behaviours, and produce the results.

Performance management is critical for companies to execute their talent management strategy, that is, to identify employees' strengths and weaknesses, link employees to appropriate training and development activity, and reward good performance with pay and other incentives. As we mentioned in Chapter 1, talent management is critical for competitiveness. Performance management systems can even help develop global business.

Performance management is critical for executing a talent management system and involves one-on-one contact with managers to ensure that proper training and development are taking place.

Secondly, organizations use performance management information (performance appraisals, in particular) in many administrative decisions: salary administration (pay raises), promotions, retention/termination, layoffs, and recognition of individual performance.[46] Despite the importance of these decisions, however, many managers, who are the source of the information, see the performance appraisal process only as a necessary evil they must go through to fulfill their job requirements. They feel uncomfortable evaluating others and feeding those evaluations back to the employees. Thus, they tend to rate everyone high or at least rate them the same, making the performance appraisal information relatively useless.

While we have emphasized that performance management is key to talent management in organizations, a third purpose of performance management is to develop employees who are *ineffective* at their jobs. When employees are not performing as well as they should, performance management seeks to improve their performance. The feedback given during a performance evaluation process often pinpoints the employee's weaknesses. Ideally, however, the performance management system identifies not only any deficient aspects of the employee's performance but also the causes of these deficiencies—for example, a skill deficiency, a motivational problem, or an obstacle holding the employee back.

Managers are often uncomfortable confronting employees with their performance weaknesses. Such confrontations, although necessary to the effectiveness of the work group, often strain everyday working relationships. Giving high ratings to all employees enables a manager to minimize such conflicts, but then the developmental purpose of the performance management system is not fully achieved.[47]

Learn more about purposes of performance management systems online with Connect.

connect

PERFORMANCE MEASURES CRITERIA

LO 3

Identify the five criteria for gauging effective performance management systems.

In Chapter 4 we discussed how, through job analysis, one can analyze a job to determine exactly what constitutes effective performance. Once the company has determined, through job analysis and design, what kind of performance it expects from its employees, it needs to develop ways to measure that performance. This section presents the criteria underlying job performance measures. Later sections discuss approaches to performance measurement, sources of information, and errors.

Although researchers, practitioners, and others differ about criteria to use to evaluate performance management systems, we believe that five stand out: strategic congruence, validity, reliability, acceptability, and specificity.

Strategic congruence is the extent to which a performance management system elicits job performance that is congruent with the organization's strategy, goals, and culture. If a company emphasizes customer service, then its performance management system should assess how well its employees are serving the company's customers. Strategic congruence emphasizes the need for the performance management system to guide employees in contributing to the organization's success. This requires systems flexible enough to adapt to changes in the company's strategic position. Most companies' appraisal systems remain constant over a long time and through a variety of strategic emphases. However, when a company's strategy changes, its employees' behaviour needs to change too.[48] The fact that appraisal systems often do not change may account for why many managers see performance appraisal systems as having little impact on a firm's effectiveness.

Strategic Congruence
The extent to which the performance management system elicits job performance that is consistent with the organization's strategy, goals, and culture."

Learn more about strategic congruence online with Connect.

connect

Validity is the extent to which a performance measure assesses all the relevant—and only the relevant—aspects of performance. This is often referred to as "content validity." As you can see in Figure 7.3, the circle on the right side of the figure represents "true" job performance—all the aspects of performance relevant to success in the job. On the other hand, companies must use some measure of performance, such as a supervisory rating of performance on a set of dimensions or

Validity
The extent to which a performance measure assesses all the relevant—and only the relevant—aspects of job performance.

FIGURE 7.3   Contamination and Deficiency of a Job Performance Measure

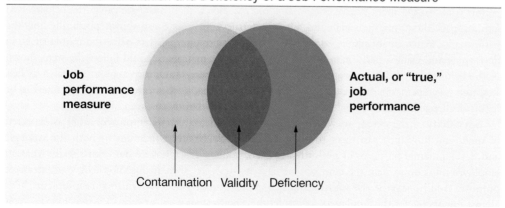

Job performance measure

Actual, or "true," job performance

Contamination   Validity   Deficiency

measures of the objective results on the job (represented by the circle on the left side of the figure). Validity is concerned with maximizing the overlap between actual job performance and the measure of job performance (the green portion in the figure).

For a performance measure to be valid, it must not be deficient or contaminated. A performance measure is deficient if it does not measure all aspects of performance (the blue portion in the figure). An example is a system at a large university that assesses faculty members based more on research than teaching, thereby relatively ignoring a relevant aspect of performance.

A contaminated measure evaluates irrelevant aspects of performance or aspects that are not job related (the gold portion in the figure). The performance measure should seek to minimize contamination, but its complete elimination is seldom possible. An example of a contaminated measure is the use of actual sales figures for evaluating salespersons across very different regional territories. Often sales are highly dependent upon the territory (number of potential customers, number of competitors, economic conditions) rather than the actual performance of the salesperson. A salesperson who works harder and better than others might not have the highest sales totals because the territory simply does not have as much sales potential as others. Thus, these figures alone would be a measure that is strongly affected by things beyond the control of the individual employee.

Reliability

The consistency of a performance measure; the degree to which a performance measure is free from random error.

Reliability refers to the consistency of a performance measure. One important type of reliability is *interrater reliability:* the consistency among the individuals who evaluate the employee's performance. A performance measure has interrater reliability if two individuals give the same (or close to the same) evaluations of a person's job performance. Evidence seems to indicate that most subjective supervisory measures of job performance exhibit low reliability.[49] With some measures, the extent to which all the items rated are internally consistent is important (*internal consistency reliability*).

In addition, the measure should be reliable over time (*test–retest reliability*). A measure that results in drastically different ratings depending on when the measures are taken lacks test–retest reliability. For example, if salespeople are evaluated based on their actual sales volume during a given month, it would be important to consider their consistency of monthly sales across time. What if an evaluator in a department store examined sales only during May? Employees in the lawn and garden department would have high sales volumes, but those in the men's clothing department would have somewhat low sales volumes. Clothing sales in May are traditionally lower than other months. One needs to measure performance consistently across time.

Acceptability

The extent to which a performance measure is deemed to be satisfactory or adequate by those who use it.

Acceptability refers to whether the people who use a performance measure accept it. Many elaborate performance measures are extremely valid and reliable, but they consume so much of managers' time that the managers refuse to use them. Alternatively, those being evaluated by a measure may not accept it. Acceptability is affected by the extent to which employees believe the performance management system is fair. As Table 7.2 shows, there are three categories of perceived fairness: procedural, interpersonal, and outcome fairness. The table also shows specifically how the performance management system's development, use, and outcomes affect perceptions of fairness. In developing and using a performance management system, managers should follow the steps shown in the column labelled "Implications" in Table 7.2 to ensure that the system is perceived as fair. Research suggests that performance management systems that are perceived as unfair are likely to be legally challenged, be used incorrectly, and decrease employee motivation to improve.[50]

Specificity

The extent to which a performance measure gives detailed guidance to employees about what is expected of them and how they can meet these expectations.

Specificity is the extent to which a performance measure tells employees what is expected of them and how they can meet these expectations. Specificity is relevant to both the strategic and developmental purposes of performance management. If a measure does not specify what an employee must do to help the company achieve its strategic goals, it does not achieve its strategic purpose. Additionally, if the measure fails to point out employees' performance problems, it is almost impossible for the employees to correct their performance.

Table 7.2 Categories of Perceived Fairness and Implications for Performance Management Systems

FAIRNESS CATEGORY	IMPORTANCE FOR PERFORMANCE MANAGEMENT SYSTEM	IMPLICATIONS
Procedural fairness	Development	• Give managers and employees opportunity to participate in development of system. • Ensure consistent standards when evaluating different employees. • Minimize rating errors and biases.
Interpersonal fairness	Use	• Give timely and complete feedback. • Allow employees to challenge the evaluation. • Provide feedback in an atmosphere of respect and courtesy.
Outcome fairness	Outcomes	• Communicate expectations regarding performance evaluations and standards. • Communicate expectations regarding rewards.

SOURCE: Adapted from S. W. Gilliland and J. C. Langdon, "Creating Performance Management Systems That Promote Perceptions of Fairness," in *Performance Appraisal: State of the Art in Practice,* ed. J. W. Smither. Copyright © 1998 by Jossey-Bass, Inc. This material is used by permission of John Wiley & Sons, Inc.

APPROACHES TO MEASURING PERFORMANCE

The model of performance management presented in Figure 7.2 on page 265 shows that we can manage performance by focusing on employee attributes, behaviours, or results. In addition, we can measure performance in a relative way, making overall comparisons among individuals' performance. In this section we explore the comparative, attribute, behavioural, and results approaches to measuring and managing performance, discussing the techniques that are associated with each approach and evaluating these approaches against the criteria of strategic congruence, validity, reliability, acceptability, and specificity.

The Comparative Approach

The comparative approach to performance measurement requires the rater to compare an individual's performance to that of others. This approach usually uses an overall assessment of an individual's performance or worth and seeks to develop some ranking of the individuals within a work group. At least three techniques fall under the comparative approach: ranking, forced distribution, and paired comparison.

Ranking *Simple ranking* requires managers to rank employees within their departments from highest performer to poorest performer (or best to worst). *Alternation ranking,* on the other hand, consists of a manager looking at a master list of employees, deciding who is the best employee, and placing that person as number one on a new (blank) list that will eventually rank all employees from highest performer to poorest performer (or best to worst). That employee's name is then crossed off the master list of employees. From the remaining names on the master list, the manager then decides

LO 4

Discuss the traditional approaches to performance management and how to select the most effective approach for a given situation.

who the worst employee is and places that person's name at the *bottom* of the new list that will eventually rank all employees as noted above. The manager then crosses that name off the master list. The manager then examines the remaining names on the master list of employees and decides who the next best employee is and places that name beneath the first name on the new list, thus ranking the two best performers among all employees against each other. The next worst performer is then selected, and that person's name is placed just above the worst performer in ranking. The process continues, with the manager alternating back and forth among remaining names on the master list until all employees under consideration have been ranked from highest performer to lowest performer (or best to worst) on the new list.

Forced Distribution   The *forced distribution* method also uses a ranking format, but employees are ranked in groups. This technique requires the manager to put certain percentages of employees into predetermined categories. Forced distribution was popularized by former General Electric CEO Jack Welch, who insisted that GE annually identify and remove the bottom 10 percent of the workforce. Such performance ranking takes several forms. Most commonly, employees are grouped into three, four, or five categories, usually of unequal size, indicating the best workers, the worst workers, and one or more categories in between. For example, at General Electric managers were to place employees into top (20 percent), middle (70 percent), and bottom (10 percent) categories. The bottom 10 percent usually receive no bonuses. The forced distribution method forces managers to categorize employees based on distribution rules determined by the company (such as those designated by GE), not on their performance. Forced distribution systems force managers to distinguish between employees, which avoids an entitlement mentality for pay, rewards, and development activities. However, even if a manager's employees are all above-average performers, the manager is forced to rate some employees as "Not Acceptable."

Advocates of these systems say that they are the best way to identify high-potential employees who should be given training, promotions, and financial rewards and to identify the poorest performers who should be helped to perform better through appropriate feedback and development, or asked to leave. Top-level managers at many companies have observed that despite corporate performance and return to shareholders being flat or decreasing, compensation costs have continued to spiral upward and performance ratings continue to be high. They question how there can be such a disconnect between corporate performance and employees' evaluations and compensation. Forced distribution systems provide a mechanism to help align company performance and employee performance and compensation. Employees in the bottom 10 percent cause performance standards to be lowered, influence good employees to leave, and keep good employees from joining the company.

A forced distribution system helps managers tailor development activities to employees based on their performance. For example, as shown in Table 7.3, poor performers are given specific feedback about what they need to improve in their job and a timetable is set for their improvement. If they do not improve their performance, they are dismissed. Top performers are encouraged to participate in development activities such as job experiences, mentoring, and completion of leadership programs which will help prepare them for top management positions. The use of a forced distribution system is seen as a way for companies to increase performance, motivate employees, and open the door for new talent to join the company to replace poor performers.[51] Advocates say these systems force managers to make hard decisions about employee performance based on job-related criteria, rather than to be lenient in evaluating employees. Critics, on the other hand, say the systems in practice are arbitrary, risk being illegal if not implemented carefully, and cause poor morale.[52] For example, one workgroup might have 20 percent poor performers while another might have only high performers, but the process mandates that 10 percent of employees be eliminated from both groups. Also, in many forced distribution systems an unintended consequence is the bottom category tends to

Table 7.3   Performance and Development Based on Forced Distribution and Ranking

RANKING OR DISTRIBUTION CATEGORY	PERFORMANCE AND DEVELOPMENT PLAN
A Above average: exceptional; A1 performer	• Accelerate development through challenging job assignments • Provide mentor from leadership team • Recognize and reward contributions • Praise employees for strengths • Consider leadership potential • Nominate for leadership development programs
B Average: meets expectations; steady performer	• Offer feedback on how to become a high performer • Encourage development of strengths and improvement of weaknesses • Recognize and reward employee contributions • Consider enlarging job
C Below expectations: poor performance	• Give feedback and agree upon what specific skills, behaviour, and/or results need to be improved, with timetable for accomplishment • Move to job that better matches skills • Ask to leave the company

SOURCES: Based on B. Axelrod, H. Handfield-Jones, and E. Michaels, "A New Game Plan for C Players," *HBR,* (January 2002), pp. 80–88; A. Walker, "Is Performance Management as Simple as ABC?" *T + D,* (February 2007), pp. 54–57; T. De Long and V. Vijayaraghavan, "Let's Hear It for B Players," *HBR,* (June 2003), pp. 96–102.

consist of members of designated groups such as visible minorities, women, and people over 40 years of age, causing human rights complaints. Finally, it is difficult to rank employees into distinctive categories when criteria are subjective or when it is difficult to differentiate employees on the criteria (such as teamwork or communications skills).

Paired Comparison   The *paired comparison* method requires managers to compare every employee with every other employee in the work group, giving an employee a score of 1 every time he or she is considered the higher performer. Once all the pairs have been compared, the manager computes the number of times each employee received the favourable decision (i.e., counts up the points), and this becomes the employee's performance score.

The paired comparison method tends to be time consuming for managers and will become more so as organizations become flatter with an increased span of control. For example, a manager with 10 employees must make 45 ($10 \times 9/2$) comparisons. However, if the group increases to 15 employees, 105 comparisons must be made.

The Attribute Approach

The attribute approach to performance management focuses on the extent to which individuals have certain attributes (characteristics or traits) believed desirable for the company's success. The techniques that use this approach define a set of traits—such as initiative, leadership, and competitiveness—and evaluate individuals on them.

Graphic Rating Scales   The most common form that the attribute approach to performance management takes is the *graphic rating scale.* Table 7.4 on page 272 shows a graphic rating scale used in a manufacturing company. As you can see, a list of traits is evaluated by a five-point (or some other number of points) rating scale. The manager considers one employee at a time, circling the number that signifies how much of that trait the individual has. Graphic rating scales can provide a number of different points (a discrete scale) or a continuum along which the rater simply places a check mark (a continuous scale).

Note that in the example shown in Table 7.4, raters are forced to decide for themselves what constitutes "excellent" or "poor" performance for an employee, since there is nothing to guide them in differentiating among each of the ratings, other than their personal values and observation of the employee. The subjective nature of such appraisals means they may be challenged, especially if termination of the employee is an eventual outcome. This means managers must ensure they have sufficient data or evidence on record to demonstrate how the appraisal is significantly related to actual work behaviour.

To get around such problems, variations on the method have been developed, such as the mixed-standard scale. To create a mixed-standard scale, relevant performance dimensions are defined and then statements are developed representing good, average, and poor performance along each dimension. These statements are then mixed with the statements from other dimensions on the actual rating instrument. Using this type of appraisal format, the rater should be able to compare any employee's performance to the standardized statements, resulting in less subjective and more accurate appraisals. Note that mixed-standard scales were originally developed as trait-oriented scales. However, this same technique has been applied to instruments using behavioural rather than trait-oriented statements (which we discuss next) as a means of reducing rating errors in performance appraisal.[53]

The Behavioural Approach

The behavioural approach to performance management attempts to define the behaviours an employee must exhibit to be effective in the job. The techniques used for this approach define those

Table 7.4 Example of a Graphic Rating Scale

The following areas of performance are significant to most positions. Indicate your assessment of performance on each dimension by circling the appropriate rating.

PERFORMANCE DIMENSION	RATING				
	DISTINGUISHED	EXCELLENT	COMMENDABLE	ADEQUATE	POOR
Knowledge	5	4	3	2	1
Communication	5	4	3	2	1
Judgment	5	4	3	2	1
Managerial skill	5	4	3	2	1
Quality performance	5	4	3	2	1
Teamwork	5	4	3	2	1
Interpersonal skills	5	4	3	2	1
Initiative	5	4	3	2	1
Creativity	5	4	3	2	1
Problem solving	5	4	3	2	1

behaviours and then require managers to assess the extent to which employees exhibit them. We discuss three techniques that rely on the behavioural approach.

Critical Incidents   The *critical incidents* technique requires managers to keep a record of specific examples of effective and ineffective performance on the part of each employee. Here's an example of an incident described in the performance evaluation of an appliance repair person:

> A customer called in about a refrigerator that was not cooling and was making a clicking noise every few minutes. The technician pre-diagnosed the cause of the problem and checked his truck for the necessary parts. When he found he did not have them, he checked the parts out from inventory so that the customer's refrigerator would be repaired on his first visit and the customer would be satisfied promptly.

These incidents give specific feedback to employees about what they do well and what they do poorly, and they can be tied to the company's strategy by focusing on incidents that illustrate best how to support that strategy. However, many managers resist having to keep a daily or weekly log of their employees' behaviour. It is also often difficult to compare employees because each incident is specific to that individual.

Behaviourally Anchored Rating Scales   A *behaviourally anchored rating scale (BARS)* builds on the critical incidents technique. It is designed to specifically define performance dimensions by developing behavioural anchors associated with different levels of performance.[54] These are statements describing examples of job-related behaviours that serve as a foundation (anchor) for making comparisons with actual employee behaviour in a performance appraisal.

To develop a BARS, we first gather a large number of critical incidents that represent effective and ineffective performance on the job. These incidents are classified into performance dimensions, and those that experts agree clearly represent a particular level of performance are used as behavioural examples (or anchors) to guide the rater. The manager's task is to rate an employee's performance along each dimension. This rating becomes the employee's score for that dimension. An example of a BARS is presented in Figure 7.4 on page 274.

Behavioural anchors have advantages and disadvantages: they can increase interrater reliability by providing a precise and complete definition of the performance dimension. However, they can bias information recall—that is, behaviour that closely approximates the anchor is more easily recalled than other behaviour.[55] Research has also demonstrated that managers and their subordinates do not make much of a distinction between BARS and trait scales.[56]

Assessment Centres   You will recall that in Chapter 6 we pointed out that assessment centres are usually used for selection and promotion decisions. However, they have also been used as a technique for measuring managerial performance.[57] At an assessment centre, individuals usually perform a number of simulated tasks, such as leaderless group discussions, in-basket management, and role-playing. Assessors observe the individuals' behaviour and evaluate their skill or potential as managers.

The advantage of assessment centres is that they provide a somewhat objective measure of an individual's performance at managerial tasks. In addition, they allow specific performance feedback, and individualized developmental plans can be designed.

The Results Approach

The results approach focuses on managing the objective, measurable results of a job or work group. This approach assumes that subjectivity can be eliminated from the measurement process and

FIGURE 7.4 Task-BARS Rating Dimension: Patrol Officer

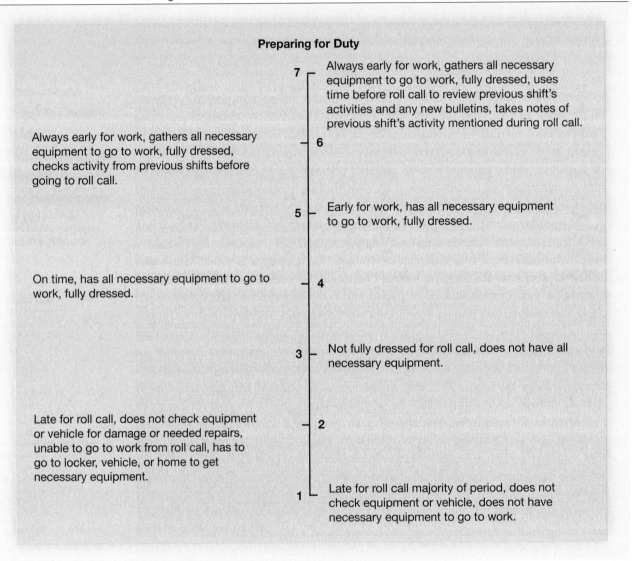

SOURCE: Adapted from R. Harvey, "Job Analysis," in *Handbook of Industrial & Organizational Psychology,* 2nd ed., ed. M. Dunnette and L. Hough (Palo Alto, CA: Consulting Psychologists Press, 1991), p. 138.

that results are the closest indicator of one's contribution to organizational effectiveness.[58] We now examine one type of performance management system that use results: management by objectives.

Management by Objectives *Management by objectives (MBO)* is popular in both private and public organizations.[59] The original concept was developed in a large accounting firm and was called a "manager's letter." The process consisted of having all the subordinate managers write a letter to their superiors, detailing what their performance goals were for the coming year and how they planned to achieve them.[60]

In an MBO system, the top management team first defines the company's strategic goals for the coming year. These goals are passed on to the next layer of management, and these managers define the goals they must achieve for the company to reach its goals. This goal-setting process cascades down the organization so that all managers set goals that help the company achieve its goals.[61] These goals are used as the standards by which an individual's performance is evaluated.[62]

MBO systems have three common components.[63] They require specific, difficult, objective goals. (An example of MBO-based goals used in a financial service firm is presented in Table 7.5). The goals are not usually set unilaterally by management but with the managers' and subordinates' participation. The manager gives objective feedback throughout the rating period to monitor progress toward the goals.

Research on MBO has revealed two important findings regarding its effectiveness.[64] Of 70 studies examined, 68 showed productivity gains, while only 2 showed productivity losses, suggesting that MBO usually increases productivity. Also, productivity gains tend to be highest when there is substantial commitment to the MBO program from top management: an average increase of 56 percent when commitment was high, 33 percent when commitment was moderate, and 6 percent when commitment was low.

Clearly, MBO can have a very positive effect on an organization's performance. Considering the process through which goals are set (involvement of staff in setting objectives), it is also likely that MBO systems effectively link individual employee performance with the firm's strategic goals.

In summary, organizations can take four approaches to measuring performance: comparative, attribute, behavioural and results. Table 7.6 on page 276 summarizes the various approaches to measuring performance based on the criteria we set forth earlier (strategic congruence, validity, reliability, acceptability and specificity) and illustrates each approach's strengths and weaknesses.

Learn more about approaches to measuring performance and evaluation of approaches to performance measurement online with Connect.

CHOOSING A SOURCE FOR PERFORMANCE INFORMATION

Whatever approach to performance management is used, it is necessary to decide whom to use as the source of the performance measures. Each source has specific strengths and weaknesses. We discuss five primary sources: managers, peers, subordinates, self, and customers.

Managers

Managers are the most frequently used source of performance information. It is usually safe to assume that supervisors have extensive knowledge of the job requirements and that they have had adequate opportunity to observe their employees—in other words, that they have the ability to rate

LO 5

Discuss the advantages and disadvantages of the different sources of performance information.

Table 7.5 An Example of a Management by Objectives (MBO) Measure of Job Performance

KEY RESULT AREA	OBJECTIVE	% COMPLETE	ACTUAL PERFORMANCE
Loan portfolio management	Increase portfolio value by 10% over the next 12 months	90	Increased portfolio value by 9% over the past 12 months
Sales	Generate fee income of $30,000 over the next 12 months	150	Generated fee income of $45,000 over the past 12 months

Table 7.6 Evaluation of Approaches to Performance Measurement

| | CRITERIA | | | | |
APPROACH	STRATEGIC CONGRUENCE	VALIDITY	RELIABILITY	ACCEPTABILITY	SPECIFICITY
Comparative	Poor, unless manager takes time to make link	Can be high if ratings are done carefully	Depends on rater, but usually no measure of agreement used	Moderate; easy to develop and use but resistant to normative standard	Very low
Attribute	Usually low; requires manager to make link	Usually low; can be fine if developed carefully	Usually low; can be improved by specific definitions of attributes	High; easy to develop and use	Very low
Behavioural	Can be quite high	Usually high; minimizes contamination and deficiency	Usually high	Moderate; difficult to develop, but accepted well for use	Very high
Results	Very high	Usually high; can be both contaminated and deficient	High; main problem can be test–retest; high, though timing of measure is important	High; usually developed with input from those to be evaluated	High regarding results, but low regarding behaviours necessary to achieve them

SOURCES: Snell, "Control Theory in Strategic Human Resource Management: The Mediating Effect of Administrative Information," *Academy of Management Journal* 35 (1992), pp. 292–327.; P. Wright, J. George, S. Farnsworth, and G. McMahan, "Productivity and Extra-Role Behavior: The Effects of Goals and Incentives on Spontaneous Helping," *Journal of Applied Psychology* 78, no. 3 (1993), pp. 374–381; Latham and Wexley, *Increasing Productivity through Performance Appraisal.*

their employees. In addition, because supervisors have something to gain from the employees' high performance and something to lose from low performance, they are motivated to make accurate ratings[65] even if they don't always achieve that result, for one reason or another. Finally, feedback from supervisors is strongly related to performance and to employee perceptions of the accuracy of the appraisal if managers attempt to observe employee behaviour or discuss performance issues in the feedback session.[66] However, problems with using supervisors as the source of performance information can occur where the supervisor does not have an adequate opportunity to observe the employee performing his job duties. Also, some supervisors may be so biased against a particular employee that to use the supervisor as the sole source of information would result in less-than-accurate measures for that individual. Favouritism is a fact of organizational life, but it is one that must be minimized as much as possible in performance management.[67] Thus, one way to reduce any chance of favouritism is to not rely on only a supervisor's evaluation of an employee's performance.

Peers

Another source of performance information is the employee's co-workers. Peers are an excellent source of information in a job such as law enforcement, where the supervisor does not always observe the employee. Peers have expert knowledge of job requirements, and they often have the most opportunity to observe the employee in day-to-day activities. Peers also bring a different perspective to the evaluation process, which can be valuable in gaining an overall picture of the individual's performance. In fact, peers have been found to provide extremely valid assessments of performance in several different settings.[68] However, friendships among peers may increase potential to bias ratings.[69] In addition, when evaluations are made for administrative decisions, peers often feel uncomfortable being both rater and ratee. When these ratings are used only for developmental purposes, however, peers react favourably.[70]

Subordinates

Subordinates are an especially valuable source of performance information when managers are evaluated. Subordinates often have the best opportunity to evaluate how well a manager treats employees. **Upward feedback** refers to appraisals that involve collecting subordinates' evaluations of managers' behaviour or skills. One study found that managers viewed receiving upward feedback more positively when receiving feedback from subordinates who were identified, but subordinates preferred to provide anonymous feedback. When subordinates were identified, they inflated their ratings of the manager.[71] However, when subordinates are identified, and thus given such power over their managers, it places the manager in a difficult situation,[72] which can lead to managers' emphasizing employee satisfaction over productivity. However, this happens only when administrative decisions are made from these evaluations. As with peer evaluations, it is a good idea to use subordinate evaluations only for developmental purposes and, to reduce fear of retribution, it is important to use anonymous evaluations and at least three subordinates for each manager.

Upward Feedback
Managerial performance appraisal that involves subordinates' evaluations of the manager's behaviour or skills.

Self

Although self-ratings are not often used as the sole source of performance information, they can still be valuable.[73] Obviously, individuals are aware of their own behaviour, and they usually have access to information regarding their results on the job. Self-evaluation gives employees the opportunity to explain to their manager what they have done well and to request training for areas they believe they need to improve. Managers find that self-evaluation by employees helps managers make more appropriate performance ratings based on the discussion and feedback they receive from employees.[74] However, self-ratings tend to be inflated. Indeed, research has found that self-ratings for personal traits as well as overall performance ratings tend to be lenient compared to ratings from other sources.[75] Thus, the best use of self-ratings is as a prelude to the performance feedback session to get employees thinking about their performance and to focus discussion on areas of disagreement.

Customers

As discussed in Chapter 1, service industries are expected to account for a major portion of job growth.[76] As a result, many companies are involving customers in their evaluation systems. Because of the unique nature of services—the product is often produced and consumed on the spot—supervisors, peers, and subordinates often do not have the opportunity to observe employee behaviour. Instead, the customer is often the only person present to observe the employee's performance and thus is the best source of performance information.

Using customer evaluations of employee performance is most appropriate when an employee's job requires direct service to the customer or linking the customer to other services within the company, or when the company is interested in gathering information to determine what products and services the customer wants.[77] However, customer surveys can be expensive; therefore, many companies conduct such evaluations only once a year and for a short time.

In conclusion, the best source of performance information often depends on the particular job. Managers should choose the source or sources that provide the best opportunity to observe employee behaviour and results. Often, eliciting performance information from a variety of sources results in a performance management process that is accurate and effective. In fact, one recent popular trend in organizations, especially in the area of management development, is the use of 360-degree appraisals.[78]

The 360-Degree Feedback Process

360-Degree Feedback Systems
A performance appraisal system for managers that includes evaluations from a wide range of persons who interact with the manager. The process includes self-evaluations as well as evaluations from the manager's boss, subordinates, peers, and customers.

In **360-degree feedback systems**, employees' behaviours or skills are evaluated not only by subordinates but also by peers, customers, bosses, and themselves. The raters complete a questionnaire asking them to rate the employee on a number of different dimensions. The major advantage of the technique is that it provides a means for minimizing bias in an otherwise subjective evaluation technique. It has been used primarily for strategic and developmental purposes.[79]

For example, the 360-degree process provides an opportunity for upward feedback to managers and hence is useful as a management development tool. This technique consists of having multiple raters (boss, peers, subordinates, customers) provide input into a manager's evaluation. The benefits of 360-degree feedback include collecting multiple perspectives of managers' performance, allowing employees to compare their own personal evaluations with the views of others, and formalizing communications about behaviours and skills ratings between employees and their internal and external customers. Several studies have shown that performance improves and behaviour changes as a result of participating in upward feedback and 360-degree feedback systems.[80] The most change occurs in individuals who receive lower ratings from others than they gave themselves (overraters).

In effective 360-degree feedback systems, reliable or consistent ratings are provided, raters' confidentiality is maintained, the behaviours or skills assessed are job related (valid), the system is easy to use, and managers receive and act on the feedback.[81] Technology allows 360-degree questionnaires to be delivered to the raters via their personal computers. This increases the number of completed questionnaires returned, makes it easier to process the information, and speeds feedback reports to managers.

Regardless of the assessment method used, the information must be shared with the employee for development to occur. Along with assessment information, the employee needs suggestions for correcting skill weaknesses and using skills already learned. These suggestions might be to participate in training courses or develop skills through new job experiences. Based on the assessment information and available development opportunities, employees should work with their managers to develop action plans to guide their self-improvement efforts.

connect Learn more about the 360-degree approach to performance appraisal online with Connect.

The "Competing Through Technology" box shows how several companies are using technology to speed up the administrative aspects of performance appraisals and to increase access to, and use of, performance information for employees and managers.

LO 6

Distinguish types of rating errors, and explain how to minimize each in a performance evaluation.

RATER ERRORS IN PERFORMANCE MEASUREMENT

Research consistently reveals that humans have tremendous limitations in processing information. Because we are so limited, we often use "heuristics," or simplifying mechanisms, to make judgments.[82] These heuristics, which appear often in subjective measures of performance, can lead to rater errors. Table 7.7 provides a summary of rater errors that can occur during performance appraisals. However, in addition to such rater errors, performance evaluations may also be purposefully distorted to achieve personal or company goals (appraisal politics), an error we discuss separately.

Table 7.7 Summary of Rater Errors in Performance Management

TYPE OF RATER ERROR	IMPLICATIONS OF THE RATER ERROR
Similar-to-me Error	Judging those who are similar to the rater more highly than those who are not. May lead to discriminatory decisions when similarity is based on demographic characteristics such as race or sex.[83]
Contrast Error	Comparing individuals with one another instead of against an objective standard. For example, a rater compares a completely competent performer with several peers who are outstanding and gives the competent employee lower-than-deserved ratings because of the outstanding colleagues.
Distributional Errors	The result of a rater's tendency to use only one part of the rating scale, making it difficult to distinguish among employees rated by the same person, and/or to compare the performance of individuals rated by different raters. Three types include *leniency error,* which occurs when a rater assigns high (lenient) ratings to all employees; *strictness error*, when a manager gives low ratings and holds all employees to unreasonably high standards; and *central tendency*, which occurs when a manager rates all employees in the middle of the scale.
Halo and Horns Errors	Failing to distinguish among different aspects of an employee's performance. *Halo effect* occurs when one *positive performance* aspect causes the rater to rate all other aspects of performance positively. For example, professors are rated as outstanding researchers because they are known to be outstanding teachers. Halo error leads to employees believing that no aspects of their performance need improvement. The *horns effect* occurs when one *negative aspect* results in the rater assigning low ratings to all the other aspects. Horns error makes employees frustrated and defensive.

Competing Through Technology

Going Paperless Increases the Effectiveness of Performance Management

Many companies are moving to Web-based and online paperless performance management systems. These systems have several advantages including helping companies ensure that performance goals at all levels of the organizations are aligned, providing managers with greater access to employee performance information and tools for understanding and using the data, and improving the efficiency of appraisal systems.

The Sandy Hill Community Health Centre (SHCHC) in Ottawa was an early adapter of "paperless performance reviews," choosing to rethink the organization's approach to performance management, which, like many organizations, was based on handwritten performance appraisals. Performance appraisal at Sandy Hill was a rigorous 360-degree process where as many as six people might be assessing one employee. Employees liked the 360-degree appraisals, but they were becoming far too labour intensive. Moreover, if Sandy Hill was to continue satisfying requirements of the Building Healthy Organizations (BHO) accreditation process for appraisals to be completed every two years, something had to change. After a brief pilot program using a competency-based paper format, managers realized they valued the 360-degree process and set about finding a way to preserve that aspect of employee evaluations. Matthew Garrison, HR Director of SHCHC, researched roughly 25 web-based tools and finally settled on UK-based Quask software (now Perfectforms). Its simplicity and the low price ($1,200 all in, in 2004) appealed to Garrison and others involved in selecting and designing the new system. What cinched the decision to go with Quask was that the health centre's managers could choose appraisal form content as well as the rating scale. This gave the organization flexibility unmatched by any other system considered at the time. Finally, information from the system could be exported into spreadsheets and used for planning and other purposes. After some tinkering, the system was finalized, approved, and launched within two months. Over the next three months, appraisal completion rates spiked as managers hustled to bring things up to date. To complement the faster administrative process, managers continue to conduct face-to-face meetings with employees to review past performance and plan future objectives.

When the Regional Municipality of York took the plunge to use an online performance management system, managers sought a system that was easy to use and intuitive for all stakeholders. The Halogen software system was implemented within a month using a series of low-risk phases. Effort was expended by those involved in designing the system to retain the integrity and appearance of past forms used by managers to ease transition of the process online. Following a one-year trial phase, a further 300 employees were added. Feedback surveys revealed 90 percent satisfaction with users of the system, and 70 percent said that it saved time. Within a year the recommendation to roll it out across the entire organization was almost unanimous. SNC-Lavalin O&M also chose Halogen to reinforce its pay-for-performance approach, increase retention, and improve its succession-planning activities.

Web-based performance management systems tend to increase completion rates of performance appraisals, which means employees and managers can move forward with a clear understanding of goals and expectations, and managers can feel confident in implementing development plans for their reports. However, as online systems have evolved and improved, they have come to include far more than just a faster and more efficient process for completing a performance appraisal. Effective web-based software should have the capability of being integrated with compensation, succession planning, and goal management throughout the organization. That is, there should be reporting capabilities that allow easy tracking of completion rates, linkages between individual and organizational goals, and timely data to inform the company's succession-planning process.

The market has matured tremendously since Sandy Hill Community Health Centre was shopping for a web-based performance appraisal system. Now there are a dizzying array of such systems, with integrated talent management capabilities that significantly leverage the value of performance appraisals. It is also easier now to find what Matthew Garrison was looking for—a flexible web-based performance management system that allows stakeholders to design something everyone likes without having to involve IT or the system vendor. Any online performance management system requires employees and managers to change how they use performance appraisal information—that is, to recognize and use performance information beyond once- or twice-a-year performance appraisals. Finally, to increase usage of any new system, it is important to train employees and managers and communicate how the system can be used.

SOURCES: "Paperless Performance Reviews," *HR Professional* (February 2005); D. Robb, "Appraising Appraisal Software," *HR Management,*(October 2008), pp. 65–70; P. Loucks, "Plugging into Performance Management," *Canadian HR Reporter* (February 26, 2007), p. 21; Halogen Software Website, Case Studies at www.halogensoftware.com/customers/case-studies.

Appraisal Politics

Appraisal politics refer to evaluators purposefully distorting a rating to achieve personal or company goals. Research suggests that several factors of the appraisal system and the company culture promote such activity. Appraisal politics are most likely to occur when raters are accountable to the employee being rated, there are competing rating goals, and a direct link exists between performance appraisal and highly desirable rewards. Appraisal politics also are likely to occur if top executives tolerate distortion or are complacent toward it, and if distortion strategies are part of "company folklore" and are passed down from senior employees to new employees.

Reducing Rater Errors and Politics, and Increasing Reliability and Validity of Ratings

Organizations can take two training approaches to reduce rater errors.[84] *Rater error training* attempts to make managers aware of rating errors and helps them develop strategies for minimizing those errors.[85] These programs consist of having the managers view videotaped vignettes designed to elicit rating errors such as contrast error (comparing individuals with one another instead of against an objective standard). Managers then make their ratings and discuss how the error influenced the rating. Finally, they get tips on how to avoid committing those errors. This approach has been shown to be effective for reducing errors, but there is evidence that reducing rating errors can also reduce accuracy of performance ratings.[86]

Rater accuracy training, also called *frame-of-reference training,* attempts to emphasize the multidimensional nature of performance and thoroughly familiarize raters with the actual content of various performance dimensions. This involves providing examples of performance for each dimension and then discussing the actual or "correct" level of performance that the example represents.[87] Accuracy training seems to increase accuracy, provided that the raters also are held accountable for ratings, job-related rating scales are used, and raters keep records of the behaviour they observe.[88]

Learn more about reducing rater errors in performance appraisals online with Connect.

PERFORMANCE FEEDBACK

Once the expected performance has been defined and employees' performance has been measured, it is necessary to feed that performance information back to the employees so they can correct any deficiencies. The performance feedback process is complex and provokes anxiety for both the manager and the employee. Few of us feel comfortable sitting in judgment of others. The thought of confronting others with what we perceive to be their deficiencies causes most of us to shake in our shoes. If giving negative feedback is painful, receiving it can be excruciating—thus the importance of the performance feedback process.

The Manager's Role in an Effective Performance Feedback Process

If employees are not made aware of how their performance is not meeting expectations, their performance will almost certainly not improve; in fact, it may get worse. Effective managers provide specific performance feedback to employees in a way that elicits positive behavioural responses. To provide effective performance feedback, managers should consider the recommendations contained in Table 7.8 on page 282.[89]

To these recommendations, we add the following research insights. When employees participate in the feedback session, they are consistently satisfied with the process. (Recall our discussion of fairness earlier in this chapter.) Participation includes allowing employees to voice their opinions of

---

Appraisal Politics
A situation in which evaluators purposefully distort ratings to achieve personal or company goals.

LO 7
Conduct an effective performance feedback session.

Table 7.8 Recommendations for Providing Effective Performance Feedback

Feedback Should Be Given Frequently, Not Once a Year.

Take responsibility to correct performance deficiencies immediately on becoming aware of them. If performance is subpar in January, waiting until December to appraise the performance could mean an 11-month productivity loss.

Provide the employee with such frequent performance feedback that he or she already knows almost exactly what his or her formal evaluation will be.

Create the Right Context for the Discussion.

Choose a neutral location for the constructive feedback session, so the employee does not associate the manager's office with unpleasant conversations.

Position the meeting as an opportunity to discuss the employee's role, your role as manager, and the relationship between the two of you, and point out that the meeting is meant to be an open dialogue.

Ask the Employee to Rate His or Her Performance Before the Session.

Have the employee complete a self-assessment before the feedback session. After reflecting on his or her performance over the past rating period (including both strengths and weaknesses) the employee is better equipped to participate fully in the feedback session.

Once the formal evaluation is underway, utilize the self-assessment by focusing discussion on areas where disagreement exists, which will help to create a more efficient session.

Encourage the Subordinate to Participate in the Session.

Rather than taking a "tell-and-sell" approach (where managers tell the employees how they have rated them and then justify these ratings), choose one of the following options, which allow more participation in the session by the subordinate:

- Adopt a "tell-and-listen" approach in which managers tell employees how they have rated them and then let the employees explain their side of the story. (Somewhat participative.)
- Adopt a "problem-solving" approach, by working with the employee to solve performance problems in an atmosphere of respect and encouragement. (Most participative.)

Recognize Effective Performance through Praise.

To give accurate performance feedback, recognize effective performance as well as poor performance.

Praising effective performance provides reinforcement for that behaviour and adds credibility to the feedback by making it clear that the manager is not only identifying performance problems.

Resist the urge to focus only on performance problems. This should never be the case.

Focus on Solving Problems.

Work with the employee to determine the actual cause of poor performance, and then agree on how to solve it.

Remember that each cause (lack of equipment, poor sales pitch, difficult co-worker) requires a different solution. Without a problem-solving approach, the correct solution might never be identified.

Focus Feedback on Behaviour or Results, Not on the Person.

To avoid defensiveness, focus the discussion on the employee's job behaviours or results, not perceived personal traits of the employee. (For example, rather than saying, "You're screwing up! You're just not motivated," focus on the actual issue or results the employee did not handle well, saying, "You did not meet the deadline that you agreed to because you spent too much time on another project.")

Minimize Criticism.

Resist the temptation to reel off a litany of offences when an individual's performance is below standard and some criticism must take place.

Once the employee agrees that a change is in order, encourage ownership of the problem and move into problem-solving mode.

Agree to Specific Goals and Set a Date to Review Progress

Help the employee establish a goal you can both agree to, and that provides strong motivation for the individual about future performance.

Set a specific follow-up date to review the employee's progress toward meeting the goal, and to provide added incentive to take the goal seriously, and work to achieve it.

the evaluation, as well as discuss performance goals. One study found that, other than satisfaction with one's supervisor, participation was the single most important predictor of satisfaction with the feedback session.[90] Finally, the importance of goal setting in the feedback session cannot be overemphasized. It is one of the most effective motivators of performance.[91] Research has demonstrated that it results in increased satisfaction, motivation to improve, and performance improvement.[92]

WHAT MANAGERS CAN DO TO DIAGNOSE PERFORMANCE PROBLEMS AND MANAGE EMPLOYEES' PERFORMANCE

LO 8

Identify the cause of a performance problem or lack of engagement.

In addition to understanding how to give employees effective performance feedback, managers need to be able to diagnose the causes of performance problems so they can initiate appropriate actions to improve and maintain employee performance. Giving performance feedback to marginal employees is often only the first step to improving their performance. Additional action or support from the manager or the organization is frequently necessary to head things in the right direction. However, to solve any problem effectively, the first step is to identify the actual problem is to be solved. Once the actual problem is identified, there is a much greater chance of solving the problem effectively. Therefore, if managers want to choose appropriate actions to help an underperforming employee, they must first make an accurate diagnosis of what is causing the employee to underperform. The process begins in each case with examining a variety of possible causes of poor performance.

Diagnosing the Causes of Poor Performance

Excluding external issues over which an employee has no control (such as a downturn in the economy), there are many different reasons for an employee's poor performance. For example, poor performance can be due to lack of employee ability, misunderstanding of performance expectations, lack of feedback, or the need for training, as with an employee who does not have the knowledge and skills needed to meet the performance standards. It is important to consider whether the poor performance is detrimental to the business. That is, is poor performance critical to completing the job and does it affect business results? If it is detrimental, then the next step is to conduct a performance analysis to determine the cause of poor performance. The different factors that should be considered in analyzing poor performance are shown in Figure 7.5 on page 284. For example, if an employee understands the expected level of performance, has been given sufficient feedback, understands the consequences, but lacks the knowledge and skills needed to meet the performance standard, this suggests that the manager may want to consider training the employee to improve performance, moving the employee to a different job that better fits that person's skills, or discharging the employee and making sure that selection methods to find a new employee measure the level of knowledge and skills needed to perform the job.

After conducting the performance analysis, managers should meet with the employee to discuss the results, agree to the next steps that the manager and employee will take to improve performance (e.g., training, providing resources, giving more feedback), discuss the consequences of failing to improve performance, and set a timeline for improvement. This type of discussion is most beneficial if it occurs more frequently than the quarterly or yearly performance review, so performance issues can be quickly dealt with before they have adverse consequences for the company (and the employee). Next, we discuss the actions that should be considered for different types of employees.

Actions for Managing Employees' Performance

Marginal employees are those employees who are performing at a bare minimum level because of a lack of ability and/or motivation to perform well.[93] Table 7.9 on page 285 shows actions for the

Marginal Employee
An employee performing at a barely acceptable level because of lack of ability and/or motivation to perform well, not poor work conditions.

FIGURE 7.5   Factors to Consider in Analyzing Poor Performance

Input

Does the employee recognize what he or she is supposed to do?

Are the job flow and procedures logical?

Do employees have the resources (tools, equipment, technology, time) needed for successful performance?

Are other job demands interfering with good performance in this area?

Employee Characteristics

Does the employee have the necessary skills and knowledge needed?

Does the employee know why the desired performance level is important?

Is the employee mentally, physically, and emotionally able to perform at the expected level?

Feedback

Has the employee been given information about his or her performance?

Is performance feedback relevant, timely, accurate, specific, and understandable?

Performance Standard/Goals

Do performance standards exist?

Does the employee know the desired level of expected performance?

Does the employee believe he or she can reach the performance standard?

Consequences

Are consequences (rewards, incentives) aligned with good performance?

Are the consequences of performance valuable to the employee?

Are performance consequences given in a timely manner?

Do work group or team norms encourage employees not to meet performance standards?

SOURCES: Based on G. Rummler, "In Search of the Holy Performance Grail," *Training and Development* (April 1996), pp. 26–31; C. Reinhart, "How to Leap over Barriers to Performance," *Training and Development* (January 2000), pp. 20–24; F. Wilmouth, C. Prigmore, and M. Bray, "HPT Models: An Overview of the Major Models in the Field," *Performance Improvement* 41 (2002), pp. 14–21.

manager to take with four different types of employees. As the table shows, in considering ways to improve performance, managers need to take into account whether employees lack ability, motivation, or both. To determine an employee's level of ability, a manager should consider if he or she has the knowledge, skills, and abilities needed to perform effectively. Lack of ability may be an issue if an employee is new or the job has recently changed. To determine employees' level of motivation,

Table 7.9 Ways to Manage Employees' Performance

		ABILITY	
		HIGH	**LOW**
MOTIVATION	**High**	**Solid performers** • Reward good performance • Identify development opportunities • Provide honest, direct feedback	**Misdirected effort** • Coach • Frequent performance feedback • Set goals • Train or arrange temporary assignment for skill development • Restructured job assignment
		Underutilizers • Give honest, direct feedback • Provide counselling • Use team building and conflict resolution	**Deadwood** • Withhold pay increases • Demotion • Outplacement • Fire
	Low	• Link rewards to performance outcomes • Offer training for needed knowledge or skills • Manage stress levels	• Specific, direct feedback on performance problems

SOURCE: Based on M. London, *Job Feedback* (Mahwah, NJ: Lawrence Erlbaum Associates, 1997), pp. 96–97. Used by permission.

managers need to consider if employees are doing a job they want to do and if they feel they are being appropriately paid or rewarded. A sudden negative change in an employee's performance may indicate personal problems.

Employees with high ability and motivation are likely good performers (*solid performers*). Table 7.9 emphasizes that managers should not ignore employees with high ability and high motivation; they should provide development opportunities to keep these employees satisfied and effective. Poor performance resulting from lack of ability but not motivation (*misdirected effort*) may be improved by skill development activities such as training or temporary assignments. Managers with employees who have the ability but lack motivation (*underutilizers*) need to consider actions that focus on interpersonal problems or incentives. These actions include making sure that incentives or rewards that the employee values are linked to performance and making counselling available to help employees deal with personal problems or career or job dissatisfaction. Chronic poor performance by employees with low ability and motivation (*deadwood*) indicates that outplacement or firing may be the best solution.

DEVELOPING AND IMPLEMENTING A SYSTEM THAT FOLLOWS LEGAL GUIDELINES

We now discuss the legal issues and constraints affecting performance management. Because performance measures play a central role in administrative decisions such as promotions, pay raises, discipline, and termination, employees who sue an organization, or lodge a human rights complaint over these decisions, may ultimately attack the measurement systems on which the decisions were made.

While it might be tempting to think our neighbours to the south are more inclined to engage in lawsuits, Canadian employees are currently perceived as becoming more litigious, and many HR professionals believe they will become even more so in the future. For example, a 2010 survey of 533 *Canadian HR Reporter* readers and members of the Human Resources Professionals Association asked respondents if they felt employees are becoming more litigious than five years ago. Almost half (47.5 percent) of respondents indicated they feel employees are becoming more litigious, and 22.2 percent feel they are much more litigious. However, when asked to look forward to 2015, almost 30 percent said they believe employees will become much more litigious, with 49 percent indicating employees will become more willing to duke it out using lawyers.[94] Figure 7.6 illustrates the issues respondents identified as problems most likely to lead to litigation. The most common human rights complaints related to employment are based on mental or physical disabilities, with family status, religious beliefs and race cited next.

In discrimination suits, the plaintiff often alleges that the performance measurement system unjustly discriminated against the plaintiff because of personal characteristics. Many performance measures are subjective, and we have seen that individual biases can affect them, especially when those doing the measuring harbour biases based on age, gender, race, or a range of other possible stereotypes.

Employers should also be aware that although the survey puts human rights complaints as the third biggest concern below wrongful dismissals, legal professionals involved in human rights and employment law are seeing major changes in the numbers and frequency of human rights complaints and an increase in the amount of awards or settlements.[95] There are a number of reasons for this, including changes in the way human rights complaints are heard. Since B.C. and Ontario no longer have human rights commissions, complainants in those provinces can now file complaints directly through human rights tribunals that are designed to assist disputing parties with formal mediation, or where mediation fails, to serve as an independent quasi-judicial court system. As such, human rights tribunals provide complainants with a venue for getting evidence heard and obtaining a ruling on the validity of the complaint. Tribunals can also impose consequences on employers where a human rights violation has occurred. For complainants, such provincial tribunals provide a more efficient and accessible process for airing human rights cases than filing a complaint through

FIGURE 7.6 Problematic Litigation Issues

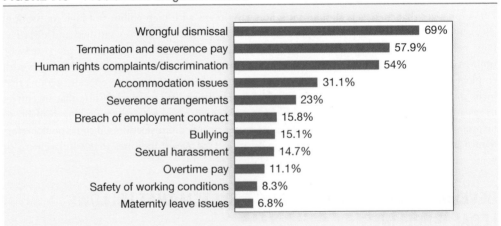

SOURCE: C. Balthazard, "Legal Fever Catching," Pulse Survey, *Canadian HR Reporter* (November 1, 2010), p. 11. Reprinted with permission of *Canadian HR Reporter*. © Copyright Thomson Reuters Canada Ltd., (November 1, 2010), Toronto, Ontario, 1-800-387-5164. Web: www.hrreporter.com.

a human rights commission. Thus it has become easier and more feasible to hold an employer accountable where human rights violations have occurred.[96] Another significant development is that human rights tribunals have been allowed to award legal fees to complainants who win their cases. Although this development was successfully appealed at the Supreme Court Level in April 2010, the law currently remains unclear in B.C. and employers are clearly more vulnerable to decisions with significantly higher awards to successful complainants.[97] One such case described in the "Evidence-based HR" box illustrates how closely integrated human rights issues and perceptions of discrimination are with wrongful dismissal suits, and the high cost paid by employers who underestimate how carefully to approach terminations involving employees with disabilities.

Learn more about developing and implementing a legally defensible performance management system online with Connect.

≣ connect

Electronic Monitoring for Performance Management

An increasing trend in companies involves using sophisticated electronic tracking systems to ensure that employees are working when and how they should be. Electronic tracking systems include security cameras, hand and fingerprint recognition systems, global positioning systems (GPS), network forensic software that monitors and plays back employee activity on computer screens, and systems that can track employees using handheld computers and other mobile devices. The systems are used on both blue-collar and white-collar employees,[98] and there are a host of reasons that employers want to monitor employees in the workplace. These reasons include concerns about

LO 9

List the major elements that contribute to perceptions of fairness and explain how to apply these in organizational contexts involving discipline and dismissal.

Evidence-Based HR

Employers who wish to terminate employees with disabilities should proceed with care, and even more so when the employment contract appears to be thwarted or obstructed by medical conditions such as depression or stress. In all disability-related terminations, legal experts advise employers to consider key factors including (1) the nature and period of employment of the employee, and the terms of the employment contract; (2) the importance of the employee's position; (3) the nature of the employee's illness or disability; (4) and the employer's duty to accommodate. The financial impact for an employer of not doing so can be regrettable indeed.

Consider *Senyk v. WFG Agency Network*. In this situation, WFG Agency Network terminated a female employee (Senyk) after she had been on long-term disability for two years. Her dismissal notice arrived by e-mail from her supervisor without any final discussion of her situation. Senyk responded by filing a discrimination complaint with the B.C. human rights tribunal and was awarded $35,000 in damages for injury to dignity, as well as all of her legal fees and expenses. Mike Weiler, an associate counsel at Vancouver law firm Boughton, explains that the award was much higher than similar awards in the past. He also warns, "These decisions coming down are quite substantive, they're quite broad-based, and I get the impression that the remedies are going to continue to increase."

SOURCES: S. Dobson, "Human Rights Costs Growing Concern," *Canadian HR Reporter* (July 12, 2010) p.1, 16; and N. Chsherbinin, "Disability-related Dismissals Can Be Frustrating," *Canadian Employment Law Today*, (September 22, 2010), p. 1.

security of company information, the need to investigate employee misconduct, prevention of fraud and criminal use of computers, and the desire to monitor productivity.[99]

Despite the potential increased productivity and efficiency benefits that can result from these systems, they still present privacy concerns, and they are subject to scrutiny in five areas of law: privacy, labour relations, human rights, evidence admissibility, and criminal law.[100] Moreover, critics argue that these systems threaten to reduce the workplace to an electronic sweatshop in which employees are treated as robots that are monitored to maximize productivity for every second they are at work. Also, electronic monitoring systems such as GPS threaten employees' rights and dignity to work without being monitored.

To avoid an expensive brush with the law or at least unnecessarily negatively impacting employee morale, employers should consider a number of questions *before* implementing electronic monitoring in any form, and deal with concerns proactively. Questions to be asked include (1) Is there a less intrusive alternative that will achieve the same ends? (2) What employment laws might apply to electronic monitoring being considered? (3) Will the technology being considered actually deliver on desired goals? (4) What policies should be created, and what communication with employees should occur before implementation? (5) How might electronic monitoring affect employee morale and the company's image?[101]

MANAGING INVOLUNTARY TURNOVER

Despite a company's best efforts in the area of personnel selection, training, and design of compensation systems, some employees will occasionally fail to meet performance requirements or will violate company policies while on the job. When this happens, organizations need to invoke a discipline program that could ultimately lead to the individual's discharge. For a number of reasons, discharging employees can be a very difficult task that needs to be handled with the utmost care and attention to detail.

As hinted at above, legal aspects to this decision can have important repercussions for the organization. In Canada, employers can terminate an employee for any reason they choose as long as the termination doesn't breach any contracts in force, including employment contracts, collective agreements, or statutes such as human rights law.[102]

Unless there is a formal employment contract in place that outlines the terms for separation, or if the employer cannot prove "cause" for termination, the employer is bound to provide reasonable notice of termination to the employee or provide compensation in lieu of notice. The amount of notice is defined in employment standards acts across Canada and the paid period of notice is designed to allow the employee enough time to find a replacement job with similar pay and working conditions. The longer the employee has been working in the job from which he or she is terminated, the longer the period of notice required.

However, if an employer terminates an employee for "just cause," no severance pay is required, so the courts are extremely vigilant about what constitutes "just cause," and the onus is clearly on the employer to prove "just cause exists beyond the balance of probabilities."[103] Failure to provide adequate explanation for "just cause" could expose the employer to a wrongful dismissal suit as the employee attempts to mitigate damages to reputation, lost wages or salary, and perceived mental damage. Therefore, employers are well advised to not only understand generally what constitutes "just cause" but also to seek legal advice prior to terminating an employee even if the situation appears to be an open-and-shut case.

All of the following reasons provide "cause" for dismissal, but all are wide open for interpretation by the courts, and employers have a habit of engaging in wishful thinking, or misinterpret their situation to fit each of the categories listed here. **Just cause** is a legal term that means an employer has a

Just Cause
A legal term meaning an employer has a justifiable (and legally defensible) reason for terminating an employee without providing reasonable notice or payment in lieu of notice.

justifiable (and legally defensible) reason for terminating an employee without providing reasonable notice or payment in lieu of notice. General reasons for just cause include:[104]

Serious misconduct—There is clear and established evidence the employee is guilty of dishonesty, theft or assault, harassment or sexual harassment.

Incompetence (or habitual neglect of duty)—In spite of clearly communicated reasonable job requirements, and where performance problems have been communicated to the employee and assistance offered, with time allowed for improvement, the employee cannot or refuses to meet job expectations.

Conflict of interest (incompatible conduct at work)—While at work the employee engages in activities that conflict with, compromise, or compete with the employer's business or interests.

Wilful disobedience—An employee wilfully challenges or disobeys a manager's clearly provided instructions. (Does not apply to all situations. For example, as discussed in Chapter 12, workers have the right to refuse unsafe work under Canadian Occupational Health and Safety legislation as long as the right is not being abused)

If the employee sues for **wrongful dismissal**, an allegation against a former employer by a terminated employee that wrongful termination of the employment contract has occurred due to failure (on the part of the employer) to provide just cause for termination of employment, and the employer cannot prove just cause beyond the balance of probabilities, the employee will be entitled to damages, which can be substantial, depending on a wide variety of factors.

Because it takes time to build a case for dismissal for cause, employers will react in different ways. For example, some endure long stretches of poor performance in order to create the extensive paper trail to support termination of employment. While HR professionals often point the finger of blame at supervisors who have not done a diligent job documenting past performance problems, supervisors often turn around and accuse HR of never being satisfied with the amount of evidence provided by supervisors. Moreover, keeping poor performers in their roles does not directly affect HR professionals every day, like it does supervisors, who have to watch helplessly as the morale of the rest of the workforce erodes. Indeed, there is nothing more corrosive to team-based structures than wide variability in effort and performance between different members, and hence it is somewhat ironic that the key to prompting and sustaining a collaborative and productive culture is the firm's right to terminate poor or troublesome employees.

Another reaction is to initiate punitive actions short of termination, in an effort to get the employee to quit on his or her own. This reaction is often a result of frustrated supervisors, who, unable to fire someone because of cautions from HR, resort to punishing the employee in other ways. This might include giving the person a low-level work assignment, a downsized office, or some other form of undesirable treatment. The problem with this approach, however, is that it might be construed as "constructive dismissal" and the employer could be sued for this.

Constructive dismissal is now defined as "a unilateral and fundamental change to a material term or condition of employment."[105] The definition and perspective of the courts makes this an ambiguous area of the law. Generally, however, a unilateral change is one that is imposed on the employee without any warning or negotiation, and where the employee has not consented to or worked for a substantial period of time (one to three months) under the changed conditions. The term *fundamental* means the employee has been forced to bear a significant change to the employment arrangement without consenting to it. Finally, the term *material* includes salary, bonus, commission, title, and responsibilities, but can also include benefits plans, office and administrative support, and reporting arrangements. Hence employers may be found guilty of constructive dismissal if they attempt to (1) demote an employee; (2) reduce compensation (by more than

Wrongful Dismissal
An allegation against a former employer by a terminated employee that wrongful termination of the employment contract has occurred due to failure (on the part of the employer) to provide just cause for termination of employment.

Constructive Dismissal
A unilateral and fundamental change to a material term or condition of employment.

10 percent); (3) force the employee to take a job in a different location that forces the employee to move; or (4) impose significant and negative changes in daily work.[106] Imposing or failing to halt serious and ongoing poor treatment of an employee has also been interpreted as constructive dismissal and links to harassment or failure to stop harassment by forcing the employee to work in a toxic environment. Essentially the courts view such failure to protect an employee as a breach of contract.[107] Finally, we will point out that we have only brushed the surface of reasons an employer should tread cautiously when terminating an employee. Judgment can be negatively influenced by ego needs combined with heightening of emotions in many situations. It makes sense to assume nothing and seek legal counsel prior to severing an employment arrangement.

A third reaction is to pay off the employee with thousands of dollars in excess severance pay in return for waiving his or her right to sue for wrongful dismissal. That is, even if the employer feels the case is unwarranted, in order to avoid litigation itself, the employer may offer the terminated employee an amount that is significant enough to persuade that individual to waive his or her right to sue. The problem with this strategy is that it sets the expectation that all poor performers are entitled to compensation on their way out the door, and this eventually increases the amount of potential future litigation by rewarding frivolous charges. As we have seen in this chapter, this strategy may grossly overestimate the plaintiff's probability of winning such a case. A more effective and sustainable strategy for employers is to develop a reputation that they will defend the firm's right to terminate low performers, rather than invite bullying by an overly aggressive lawyer or employee.

Given the critical financial and personal risks associated with employee dismissal, it is easy to see why the development of a standardized, systematic approach to discipline and termination is critical to all organizations. These decisions should not be left solely to the discretion of individual managers or supervisors. In the next section we explore aspects of an effective discipline and discharge policy.

connect

Learn more about wrongful dismissal online with Connect.

Fairness and Principles of Justice

Earlier in this chapter, when discussing acceptability of performance measures criteria, we touched on the notion of justice, particularly as this relates to the notions of outcome justice, procedural justice, and interactional justice. There we noted that employees are more likely to respond positively to negative feedback regarding their performance if they perceive the appraisal process as being fair on these three dimensions. Obviously, because fairness is important with respect to ongoing feedback, this is even more critical in the context of a final termination decision. Therefore, we will revisit the three types of fairness perceptions here, with an emphasis on how these need to be operationalized in effective discipline and discharge policies that support the type of "psychological contracts" that tend to govern employer–employee relationships.[108]

Outcome Fairness
The judgment that people make with respect to the outcomes received relative to the outcomes received by other people with whom they identify.

As we noted earlier, **outcome fairness** refers to the judgment that people make with respect to the *outcomes received* relative to the outcomes received by other people with whom they identify (referent others). Clearly, a situation where one person is losing his or her job while others are not is conducive to perceptions of outcome unfairness on the part of the discharged employee. The degree to which this potentially unfair act translates into the type of anger and resentment that might spawn retaliation in the form of violence or litigation, however, depends on perceptions of procedural and interactional justice.[109]

Procedural Justice
A concept of justice focusing on the methods used to determine the outcomes received.

Whereas outcome justice focuses on the ends, procedural and interactional justice focus on means. If methods and procedures used to arrive at and implement decisions that impact the employee negatively are seen as fair, the reaction is likely to be much more positive than if this is not the case. **Procedural justice** focuses specifically on the *methods used to determine the outcomes received*. Table 7.10 details six key principles that determine whether people perceive procedures as

Table 7.10   Six Determinants of Procedural Justice

1. **Consistency.** The procedures are applied consistently across time and other persons.
2. **Bias suppression.** The procedures are applied by a person who has no vested interest in the outcome and no prior prejudices regarding the individual.
3. **Information accuracy.** The procedure is based on information that is perceived to be true.
4. **Correctability.** The procedure has built-in safeguards that allow one to appeal mistakes or bad decisions.
5. **Representativeness.** The procedure is informed by the concerns of all groups or stakeholders (co-workers, customers, owners) affected by the decision, including the individual being dismissed.
6 **Ethicality.** The procedure is consistent with prevailing moral standards as they pertain to issues such as invasion of privacy or deception.

being fair. Even given all the negative ramifications of being dismissed from one's job, the person being dismissed may accept the decision with minimum anger if the procedures used to arrive at the decision are consistent, unbiased, accurate, correctable, representative, and ethical. When the procedures for the decisions are perceived in this fashion, the individual does not feel unfairly singled out, and this helps maintain his or her faith in the system as a whole, even if he or she is unhappy with the specific decision that was triggered by the system.[110]

Whereas procedural justice deals with how a decision was made, **interactional justice** refers to the *interpersonal nature of how the outcomes were implemented.* For example, in many documented cases, after giving employees the news of their termination, employers immediately have security guards whisk them out of the building with their various personal items haphazardly thrown together in cardboard boxes. This strips the employees of their dignity, as well as their job, and employees who witness this happen to a co-worker show a drastically lower level of organizational commitment from that day forward.[111] When the decision is explained well and implemented in a fashion that is socially sensitive, considerate, and empathetic, this helps defuse some of the resentment that might come about from a decision to discharge employees. As one human resource director noted, the key is to ensure that the affected individual "walks out with their dignity and self-respect intact."[112] Going through these steps is especially important if the individual who is being managed is already high in hostility, and hence a threat to respond in violent fashion.[113] Indeed, beyond the context of employee termination, the use of systems that promote procedural and interactive justice across the organization results in more satisfied employees,[114] a more productive workforce,[115] and a more collaborative and innovative organizational culture.[116]

Interactional Justice
A concept of justice referring to the interpersonal nature of how the outcomes were implemented.

Learn more about principles of fairness online with Connect.

Progressive Discipline and Alternative Dispute Resolution

Except in the most extreme cases, employees should generally not be terminated for a first offence. Rather, termination should come about at the end of a systematic discipline program. Effective discipline programs have two central components: documentation (which includes specific publication of work rules and job descriptions that should be in place prior to administering discipline) and progressive punitive measures. Thus, as shown in Table 7.11 on page 292, punitive measures should be taken in steps of increasing magnitude, and only after having been clearly documented. This may start with an unofficial warning for the first offence, followed by a written reprimand for additional offences. At some point, later offences may lead to a temporary suspension. Before a company suspends an employee, it may even want to issue a last-chance notification, indicating that the next

Table 7.11   An Example of a Progressive Discipline Program

OFFENCE FREQUENCY	ORGANIZATIONAL RESPONSE	DOCUMENTATION
First offence	Unofficial verbal warning	Witness present
Second offence	Official written warning	Document filed
Third offence	Second official warning, with threat of temporary suspension	Document filed
Fourth offence	Temporary suspension and "last chance notification"	Document filed
Fifth offence	Termination (with right to go to arbitration)	Document filed

**Alternative Dispute
Resolution (ADR)**
A method of resolving disputes
that does not rely on the legal
system. Often proceeds through
the four stages of open door
policy, peer review, mediation,
and arbitration.

offence will result in termination. Such procedures may seem exasperatingly slow, and they may fail to meet the manager's emotional need for quick and satisfying retribution. In the end, however, when problem employees are discharged, the chance that they can prove they were discharged for poor cause has been minimized.

At various points in the discipline process, the individual or the organization might want to bring in outside parties to help resolve discrepancies or conflicts. As a last resort, the individual might invoke the legal system to resolve these types of conflicts, but in order to avoid this, some companies are turning to **alternative dispute resolution (ADR)** techniques that show promise in resolving disputes in a timely, constructive, cost-effective manner. Alternative dispute resolution can take on many different forms, but in general, ADR proceeds through the four stages shown in Table 7.12. Each stage reflects a somewhat broader involvement of different people, and the hope is that the conflict will be resolved at earlier steps. However, the last step may include binding arbitration, where an agreed-upon neutral party resolves the conflict unilaterally if necessary.

Whereas ADR is effective in dealing with problems related to performance and interpersonal differences in the workplace, many of the problems that lead an organization to want to terminate an individual's employment relate to drug or alcohol abuse. In these cases, the organization's discipline and dismissal program should also incorporate an employee assistance program.

Table 7.12   Stages in Alternative Dispute Resolution

Stage 1: Open-door policy

The two people in conflict (e.g., supervisor and subordinate) attempt to arrive at a settlement together. If none can be reached, they proceed to

Stage 2: Peer review

A panel composed of representatives from the organization that are at the same level of those people in the dispute hears the case and attempts to help the parties arrive at a settlement. If none can be reached, they proceed to

Stage 3: Mediation

A neutral third party from outside the organization hears the case and, via a nonbinding process, tries to help the disputants arrive at a settlement. If none can be reached, the parties proceed to

Stage 4: Arbitration

A professional arbitrator from outside the organization hears the case and resolves it unilaterally by rendering a specific decision or award. Most arbitrators are experienced employment lawyers or retired judges.

Employee Assistance and Wellness Programs

An **employee assistance program (EAP)** is a referral service that supervisors, managers, or employees can use to seek professional treatment for various problems. You will recall from Chapter 3 that alcohol and substance abuse are both viewed as a disability under human rights legislation, and thus discipline related to such problems usually involves facilitating rehabilitation efforts through the company's employee assistance program. EAPs have been evolving since the 1950s, and many are now fully integrated into companies' overall health benefits plans, serving as gatekeepers for benefits utilization, disability and absence monitoring, and wellness programs.[117] EAPs vary widely, but most share some basic elements. First, the programs are usually identified in company documentation such as employee handbooks. Supervisors (and union representatives, where relevant) are trained to use the referral service for employees whom they suspect of having physical or mental health–related problems (such as depression) or substance abuse issues. Employees are also trained to use the system to make self-referrals when necessary. Finally, costs and benefits of the programs (as measured in positive employee outcomes such as return-to-work rates) are evaluated, typically annually. Wellness programs are discussed in depth in Chapter 12, and we provide evidence of the link between such programs and increased productivity, employee engagement, and retention in the Exercising Strategy feature at the end of this chapter.

> **Employee Assistance Programs (EAPs)**
> Employer programs that attempt to ameliorate problems encountered by workers who are drug dependent, alcoholic, or psychologically troubled.

Outplacement Counselling

The terminal nature of an employee discharge not only leaves the person angry, but also leads to confusion as to how to react and regarding what happens next. If the employee feels there is nothing to lose and nowhere else to turn, the potential for violence or litigation is higher than most organizations are willing to tolerate. Therefore, many organizations provide **outplacement counselling,** which tries to help dismissed employees manage the transition from one job to another. There is a great deal of variability in the services offered via outplacement programs, typically including career counselling, job search support, résumé critiques, job interviewing training, and provision of networking opportunities. Although it may seem counterintuitive to help someone find new jobs after just concluding they did not perform well in their last job, most outplacement services frame this as just a bad fit between a person and the job, and work to find jobs where the fit is better.[118] Outplacement counselling is aimed at helping people realize that losing a job is not the end of the world and that other opportunities exist. Indeed, for many people, losing a job can be a critical learning experience that plants the seed for future success.

> **Outplacement Counselling**
> Counselling to help displaced employees manage the transition from one job to another.

A Look Back

The chapter opener on I Love Rewards discussed the vision statement created by CEO and founder Razor Suleman that seemed to be the catalyst for turning things around at I Love Rewards. Since that event, the company has grown significantly and continues to build its success story through expansion south of the Canadian border.

Questions

1. Review the reasons that employees disengage from their jobs and lose commitment to their employers. How might the changes put in place at I Love Rewards help attract and retain employees to I Love Rewards? Is there anything else you think the company could do to increase engagement among its employees?

2. Visit the company's website at www.iloverewards.com and in the "Company" section review the Top One Hundred Reasons To Work with Us at I Love Rewards. Which of the first 25 or so reasons listed seem most important to you and what you might value in a workplace? Explain why.

3. Assuming that performance appraisals would be done effectively at I Love Rewards, do you think they would play a meaningful role in maintaining engagement among employees? Would they prevent voluntary turnover? Explain why or why not.

Summary

Organizations can gain competitive advantage by strategically managing the retention process so that voluntary turnover among high performers is kept to a minimum. Voluntary turnover reflects a separation initiated by the individual, often when the organization would prefer that the person stay a member. Voluntary turnover can be minimized by taking action to increase employee engagement, and measuring and monitoring employee levels of satisfaction with critical facets of job and organization, and then addressing any problems identified by engagement surveys.

Measuring and managing performance is a challenging enterprise and another key to gaining competitive advantage. Performance management systems serve strategic, administrative, and developmental purposes—their importance cannot be overestimated. A performance measurement system should be evaluated against the criteria of strategic congruence, validity, reliability, acceptability, and specificity. Measured against these criteria, the comparative, attribute, behavioural, and results approaches have different strengths and weaknesses. Thus, deciding which approach and which source of performance information are best depends on the job in question. Effective managers need to be aware of the issues involved in determining the best method or combination of methods for their particular situations. In addition, once performance has been measured, a major component of a manager's job is to feed that performance information back to employees in a way that results in improved performance rather than defensiveness and decreased motivation. Managers should take action based on the causes for poor performance: ability, motivation, or both. In addition, managers must ensure that their performance management system can meet legal scrutiny, especially if it is used to discipline or terminate poor performers.

Finally, this chapter examined issues related to employee separation. Involuntary turnover reflects a separation initiated by the organization, often when the individual would prefer to stay a member of the organization. Retaliatory reactions to organizational discipline and dismissal decisions can be minimized by implementing these decisions in a manner that promotes feelings of procedural and interactive justice. Both discipline and termination efforts can be assisted by employee assistance programs and help with outplacement counselling when all efforts for turning a poor employee's performance around have been exhausted.

Key Terms

360-degree feedback systems 278
Acceptability, 268
Alternative dispute resolution (ADR), 292
Appraisal politics, 281
Constructive dismissal, 289
Employee assistance programs (EAPs), 293
Interactional justice, 291
Involuntary turnover, 254
Job enrichment, 259
Job satisfaction, 258
Just cause, 288
Marginal employee, 283

Discussion Questions

1. Organizational turnover is generally considered a negative outcome, and many organizations spend a great deal of time and money trying to reduce it. What situations would indicate that an increase in turnover might be just what an organization needs? Given the difficulty of terminating employees, what organizational policies might promote the retention of high-performing workers but promote voluntary turnover among low performers?

2. Two popular interventions for enhancing worker satisfaction are job enrichment and job rotation. What are the critical differences between these interventions, and under what conditions might one be preferable to the others?

3. If off-the-job stress and dissatisfaction begin to create on-the-job problems, what are the rights and responsibilities of the human resource manager in helping the employee to overcome these problems? Are intrusions into such areas an invasion of privacy, a benevolent and altruistic employer practice, or simply a prudent financial step taken to protect the firm's investment?

4. Employee engagement surveys are designed to measure employee engagement at a given point in time, within departments or specific areas of the company, and to help employers detect signs of job dissatisfaction as early as possible. What could an employer do if such a survey reveals dissatisfaction with pay and benefits? With supervisors or coworkers?

5. What sources of performance information might be effective in evaluating faculty members' performance?

6. The performance of students is usually evaluated with an overall results measure of grade point average. How is this measure contaminated? How is it deficient? What other measures could be used to more adequately evaluate student performance?

7. Think of the last time you had a conflict with another person, either at work or at school. Using the guidelines for performance feedback, how would you provide effective performance feedback to that person?

8. Why might a manager intentionally distort appraisal results? What would you recommend to minimize this problem?

9. Electronic monitoring is one method of monitoring employee performance. Do you agree that such methods may present privacy concerns? Explain your answer.

10. The discipline and termination procedures described in this chapter are systematic but rather slow. In your opinion, are there some offences that should lead to immediate dismissal? What offenses are they and how would you justify this to a court if you were an employer sued for wrongful dismissal?

Self-Assessment Exercise

How do you like getting feedback? To test your attitudes toward feedback, take the following quiz. Read each statement, and write A next to each statement you agree with. If you disagree with the statement, write D.

_____ 1.   I like being told how well I am doing on a project.

_____ 2.   Even though I may think I have done a good job, I feel a lot more confident when someone else tells me so.

_____ 3.   Even when I think I could have done something better, I feel good when other people think well of me for what I have done.

_____ 4.   It is important for me to know what people think of my work.

_____ 5.   I think my instructor would think worse of me if I asked him or her for feedback.

_____ 6.   I would be nervous about asking my instructor how she or he evaluates my behaviour in class.

_____ 7.   It is not a good idea to ask my fellow students for feedback; they might think I am incompetent.

_____ 8.   It is embarrassing to ask other students for their impression of how I am doing in class.

_____ 9.   It would bother me to ask the instructor for feedback.

_____ 10.   It is not a good idea to ask the instructor for feedback because he or she might think I am incompetent.

_____ 11.   It is embarrassing to ask the instructor for feedback.

_____ 12.   It is better to try to figure out how I am doing on my own, rather than to ask other students for feedback.

For statements 1–4, add the total number of As:

For statements 5–12, add the total number of As:

For statements 1–4, the greater the number of As, the greater your preference for and trust in feedback from others. For statements 5–12, the greater the number of As, the greater the risk you believe there is in asking for feedback.

How might this information be useful in understanding how you react to feedback in school or on the job?

SOURCES: Based on D. B. Fedor, R. B. Rensvold, and S. M. Adams, "An Investigation of Factors Expected to Affect Feedback Seeking: A Longitudinal Field Study," *Personnel Psychology* 45 (1992), pp. 779–805; and S. J. Asford, "Feedback Seeking in Individual Adaptation: A Resource Perspective," *Academy of Management Journal* 29 (1986), pp. 465–487.

Exercising Strategy: Weighing in for Healthy Employees

Awareness of the need for workplace wellness programs has gained considerable ground in recent years as managers have become more aware of links to productivity, employee engagement, retention, and both short- and long-term disability to the organization. For example, a study of 403 Canadian employers in 2004 revealed that 20 percent offered comprehensive healthy workplace programs and another 5 percent had implemented health screening among employees, double the results found in 2000.

However, a study done in 2007 of 153 accountants, general managers, and HR managers in the auto parts industry by the Richard Ivey School of Business resulted in findings that surprised even the researchers about who supports such programs and why. It seems that senior HR managers (51 percent) supported workplace health programs because such interventions help the bottom line. However, in what seemed like a role reversal, corporate accounting managers indicated such programs should be implemented "out of a sense of moral social responsibility." Strangely, cost-reduction strategies did not even enter the picture for these senior accounting managers. The general managers in the study supported such programs for both reasons—moral responsibility and bottom-line implications. More recent studies indicate there are plenty of reasons to support both camps.

For example, research compiled by the Canadian Healthy Workplace Council around the same time as the Ivey study provides many reasons that creating a healthier workplace is a good strategy. Of interest to the bottom-line advocates: in 2006 Canadian employees averaged 9.7 lost workdays for personal reasons, or the equivalent of 102 million workdays, with the cost of each long-term absence from work estimated at $8,800. However, comprehensive, well-promoted and successful workplace health programs "result in average reductions in sick leave, health plan costs, workers' compensation and disability costs of just over 25%." Another source reports that every $1.00 investment in wellness returns payback of $4.50.

Evidence for the moral social responsibility side comes from studies of rising rates of obesity (24 percent of adults over 18 in 2004) and the $4.3 billion impact on the health system when both direct and indirect costs are included. In mid-2010 the Canadian Mental Health Association reported that mental illness affects one in five Canadians, with a cost to employers of 35 million workdays ($51 billion per year). Supporting both arguments, a study done by the Centre for Addiction and Mental Health indicate that mental illness is the reason for more lost days than any other chronic illness and that, in Ontario, the average cost to organizations for a single instance of short-term disability originating with a mental health issue is almost $18,000.

Although the Ivey study reported significant interest and support by managers for wellness programs, there are many other managers who balk at the idea. For such doubters, more information on the costs and benefits of such initiatives should be considered. One source places the cost of wellness programs at between $150 and $200/employee/year (based on the range of $75,000 to $100,000 per year for employers with 500 employees). A growing and diverse array of employers have weighed the ROI against such costs, and decided supporting employee health and well-being is the strategic and right thing to do. Laura Thanasse, senior vice-president, Total Rewards at Scotiabank (60,000 employees) links it to strategy, saying, "Our overall HR strategy is having engaged employees. Having engaged employees means that we need healthy employees." Robert Meggy, president and CEO of the Great Little Box Company in Vancouver (220 employees) links the company's numerous wellness initiatives (free gym, basketball court, 10-kilometre Sun Run, weight control programs) to retention, saying, "If you take more of an interest in people, people stay longer." Finally, Bayer Canada (1,000 employees), has been pleased with the results of launching its Life at Work program, a response to a 2005 employee survey that made work/life balance an issue. After seeing reductions in both long- and short-term disability costs, the company became interested in doing an employee health survey to anticipate how additional programs might be utilized to address health risks such as high blood cholesterol levels.

Regardless of the reasons for implementing a wellness program, it seems as if the chances of living longer will increase substantially for employees whose employers care enough to examine the issues and either improve the bottom line, or fulfil a larger sense of moral responsibility, through health and wellness.

Questions

1. What might account for the "role reversal" results in the Ivey study, where HR managers supported implementation of wellness programs based on bottom-line impact and senior accounting managers supported such initiatives for reasons of moral social responsibility?

2. Based on the content of this chapter, what types of strategies and interventions might help to reduce the need for and cost of mental health-related leaves?

SOURCES: S. Klie, HR Focuses on Bottom Line of Wellness, *Canadian HR Reporter* (July 26, 2007), p. 3; D. Brown, "Finding out Causes of Poor Health, First Step to Cutting Benefit Costs, *Canadian HR Reporter* (October 25, 2004), pp. 5, 7; HR Leaders Talk, "Obesity in the Workplace," *Canadian HR Reporter* (January 26, 2009) p. 13; "A Coordinated Action Agenda for Healthy Workplaces," The Graham Lowe Group Inc. and Canadian Healthy Workplace Council (October 2007) www.grahamlowe.ca/documents/208 (retrieved January 28, 2011); S. Dobson, HR by the Numbers, "Mental Health Leave Most Costly," *Canadian HR Reporter* (October 4, 2010), p. 4.

Managing People: Coaching Drives Cosy Climate at SaskEnergy

SaskEnergy, the provincial Crown corporation that distributes natural gas in Saskatchewan, has a well-earned reputation for innovation in the rather conservative and conventional utility sector. And clearly HR plays a big role in the amount of energy employees of SaskEnergy take to their tasks every day. Margot Almas, director of Employee and Organizational effectiveness, explains how SaskEnergy views the engagement equation, saying, "Our people provide our service, our service drives our growth, and our growth ensures our future. Therefore our future depends on an engaged and committed workforce." However, when an engagement survey produced lower than expected scores on two important issues—managing performance and employee recognition—it was clear there was a need for action or the utility would not be able to achieve ambitious strategic objectives. Almas and the senior management team swung into action.

Working with a consultant, four key areas were prioritized for improvement: (1) recognizing both individual and team contributions; (2) ensuring SaskEnergy is perceived as a positive and welcoming work environment; (3) ensuring SaskEnergy is perceived as an organization that encourages and supports lifelong learning; and (4) ensuring success in a tight labour market through total commitment of the hearts and minds of employees.

Introducing a long-term coaching program seemed to offer an overarching solution to achieve all four goals. Launching the program included integrated assessments, workshops, long-term peer-to-peer coaching triangles, and follow-up evaluations, such as coaching assessments. Top management support and active involvement ensured that more than 200 managers at SaskEnergy jumped on board, a key driver of the ultimate success of the program. Smaller but reinforcing initiatives included Generation Energy, a group that employees under 30 were encouraged to join. Participants gained opportunities for volunteer work, mentorship, and networking, which help this younger generation see the reasons for commitment to corporate goals. Providing opportunities for more control over work schedules also helps with attraction and retention. For example, 10 employees at SaskEnergy have entered job-sharing arrangements, working one week on, followed by one week off.

SaskEnergy's intense focus on increasing engagement produced significant and rewarding ROI, when in 2008 the organization conducted another engagement survey and achieved the highest level of participation ever in a survey. But two scores in particular stood out: 73 percent of employees indicated SaskEnergy is "a good place to work," and 86 percent said they were proud to work there. Bingo! And if Almas's engagement = future equation is any indicator, future also equals growth at SaskEnergy.

Questions:

1. Why do you think SaskEnergy and the consultants hired to develop solutions to low employee survey results decided to launch a long-term coaching program? Would you welcome such a program if it was implemented in the organization where you work? Why?

2. Go to the Canada's Top 100 Employers website and examine the profile of SaskEnergy in the section containing Saskatchewan's Top Employers for 2011 at www.canadastop100.com/sk/. What other types of flexible work arrangements does the utility offer besides job-sharing arrangements?

3. Based on the organization's profile on the Saskatchewan section of Canada's Top 100 Employers website noted above, if you lived in Regina, would you consider working for SaskEnergy? Why or why not?

SOURCES: Based on L. Finkelstein, "Coaching SaskEnergy to Higher Performance," *Canadian HR Reporter*, December 1, 2008), p. 23; and K. Lunau, "When the Going Gets Tough," Macleans.ca, (October 14, 2009) at www2.macleans.ca/2009/10/14/when-the-going-gets-tough/ (retrieved July 11, 2011).

 **Practise and learn online with Connect.**

Pay Structure Decisions

The Home Depot China Announcement
家得宝中国发布仪式

Enter the World of Business

The Home Depot Makes Inroads into China

The business model at the Home Depot is built around homes, and the hope that people will be buying homes, selling homes, and improving homes. Thus, despite problems with the real estate market in some parts of North America, and a world recession that had The Home Depot reporting a 66 percent drop in first-quarter profits, and a 7 percent drop in sales (May 2008), management could feel satisfied with its decision to expand into China. It could also be especially satisfied that it had appointed Cape Breton–born Annette Verschuren, President of The Home Depot Canada, as President of The Home Depot China. But why Verschuren and why China?

Verschuren seemed like a clear choice to head up the company's venture into China for this retailer of do-it-yourself home products and services. After all, Verschuren had built an impressive track record while growing the company's presence in Canada from a few stores in 1996 to its current 166 stores and 30,000 employees. After building the Canadian operation from the ground up, she was a logical choice to repeat that feat in China—where opportunities for home products and especially contract services are limitless.

In 2007, the company bought 12 Home Way stores in Northern China and began designing a prototype for the hundreds of stores it plans to build throughout China. The timing seemed right to penetrate a market just beginning to emerge, one supported by a new middle class for whom home ownership is becoming possible at last. As China continues building thousands of apartment "shells," those purchasing such spaces will need help finishing the interior surface before each can be called a home. This will create a vast market for contract services that The Home Depot China will be well positioned to provide, along with complementary home and building products Canadians have long taken for granted.

However, doing business in China requires more than just building stores. Experts such as Irv Beiman, Ph.D., of eGate Consulting Shanghai Ltd. caution that large western multinationals should anticipate major human resource challenges such as problems with retention, teamwork, and even developing functional capability. He says this is due in part to "high turnover and the fact that compensation incentives are based on functional job performance rather than strategic performance measured against an employee's key performance objectives."

Verschuren seems to have done her homework. The first thing she did was to hire a manager with experience in building supercentres in Asia and to establish a local leadership team. However, looking back on the company's approach during the first six months, Verschuren acknowledges the lack of human resources policy development, saying, "The HR piece is one of the most important parts of our roll-out in China." She says the company started by taking care of its people first, doing things such as cleaning up facilities and building employee lunchrooms and proper bathrooms. Then the focus turned to communicating the company's values, creating job descriptions, and launching a performance management system. Another important step was making adjustments to salaries, which helped the company deal with historical notions that pay increases are based on favouritism and the notion that everyone gets the same amount. Verschuren also acknowledges the hard work required to establish HR systems, saying, "There is so much we are doing in terms of introducing policy and procedures. There was definitely a lack of that, so we're bringing in what makes sense in China." The goal for Verschuren is to capture what she sees as "the stunning energy and passion of the Chinese," something she sees as achievable by creating trust in leadership, through transparency and shared values. This will provide the foundation for employee teamwork and retention, both essential components for successful expansion over the long haul.

So this Cape Breton native seems to have found the right strategy as she works to establish The Home Depot in a market that some might call the "Wild East," but whose annual economic growth is projected at 9.9 percent for 2010 and 8.3 percent for 2011 (compared to 3.5 percent and 2.9 percent respectively for Canada.) And perhaps because she is a woman, Verschuren's capable presence will also help to change the notoriously chauvinist business environment in China. In a country where women have faced great difficulties, there seems little doubt that Verschuren will demonstrate that women are capable of strong leadership in the face of great odds.

SOURCES: Based on M. Birchall-Spencer, "Interview: Annette Verschuren, President of The Home Depot Canada and the Home Depot China, Discusses Her Leadership Strategy and the Retailer's Expansion into China," *HR Professional* (August/September 2008), vol. 25, no. 5, pp. 41–46; E. Kelly, "The New Frontier," *HR Professional* (August/September 2008), vol. 25, no. 5, p. 26; "Creating a Sustainable Rewards and Talent Management Model," 2010 Global Talent Management and Rewards Study, Towers Watson, 2010.

<table>
<tr><td>LO 1</td></tr>
</table>

Describe the main decision areas and concepts in strategic compensation management.

INTRODUCTION

From the employer's point of view, pay is a powerful tool for furthering the organization's strategic goals. First, pay has a significant impact on employee attitudes and behaviours. It influences the kind of employees who are attracted to (and remain with) the organization, and it can be a powerful tool for aligning current employees' interests with those of the broader organization. Second, employee compensation is typically a significant organizational cost and thus requires close scrutiny. As Table 8.1 shows, total compensation (cash and benefits) averages 22 percent of revenues and varies both within and across industries. In the chapter opener, The Home Depot's goal is to build a stable and low-cost workforce to support massive expansion opportunities in China. Building a compensation strategy there includes changing long-standing employee attitudes about the origin of pay increases, the need to improve individual performance, the need to work together with others

Table 8.1 Total Compensation as a Percentage of Revenues

INDUSTRY	PERCENTILE		
	25TH	50TH	75TH
Hospitals/health care	43%	46%	49%
Manufacturing	22	27	34
Insurance/health care	6	8	11
All industries	13	22	32

SOURCES: Data from Saratoga Institute, *Human Capital Benchmarking Report 2000;* and Saratoga/Pricewaterhouse Coopers, *Key Trends in Human Capital: A Global Perspective, 2006.*

in a team, and the linkage between individual and team performance and pay. At the same time, like all other North American employers, The Home Depot is under pressure to reduce labour costs domestically, without jeopardizing its relationship with its workforce. For example, it also wants to have an efficient workforce in place and ready to go when the real estate market and the urge for home improvements picks up again.

From the employees' point of view, policies having to do with wages, salaries, and other earnings affect their overall income and thus their standard of living. Both the level of pay and its seeming fairness compared with others' pay are important. Pay is also often considered a sign of status and success. Employees attach great importance to pay decisions when they evaluate their relationship with the organization. Therefore, pay decisions must be carefully managed and communicated.

Pay decisions can be broken into two areas: pay structure and individual pay. In this chapter we focus on **pay structure,** which in turn entails a consideration of pay level and job structure. **Pay level** is defined here as the average pay (including wages, salaries, and bonuses) of jobs in an organization. (Benefits could also be included, but these are discussed separately in Chapter 10.) **Job structure** refers to the relative pay of jobs within an organization. Consider the same two jobs in two different organizations. In Organization 1, jobs A and B are paid an annual average compensation of $40,000 and $60,000, respectively. In Organization 2, the pay rates are $45,000 and $55,000, respectively. Organizations 1 and 2 have the same pay level (an average of $50,000), but the job structures (relative rates of pay) differ.

Both pay level and job structure are characteristics of organizations and reflect decisions about jobs rather than about individual employees. This chapter's focus is on why and how organizations attach pay policies to jobs. In the next chapter we look within jobs to discuss the different approaches that can determine the pay of individual employees as well as the advantages and disadvantages of these different approaches.

Why is the focus on jobs in developing a pay structure? As the number of employees in an organization increases, so too does the number of human resource management decisions. In determining compensation, for example, each employee must be assigned a rate of pay that is acceptable in terms of external, internal, and individual equity (defined later) and in terms of the employer's cost. Although each employee is unique and thus requires some degree of individualized treatment, standardizing the treatment of similar employees (those with similar jobs) can help greatly to make compensation administration and decision making more manageable and more equitable. Thus pay policies are often attached to particular jobs rather than tailored entirely to individual employees.

Pay Structure
The relative pay of different jobs (job structure) and how much they are paid (pay level).

Pay Level
The average pay, including wages, salaries, and bonuses, of jobs in an organization.

Job Structure
The relative pay of jobs within an organization.

EQUITY THEORY AND FAIRNESS

In discussing the consequences of pay decisions, it is useful to keep in mind that employees often evaluate their pay relative to that of other employees. Equity theory suggests that people evaluate the fairness of their situations by comparing them with those of other people.[1] According to the theory, a person (P) compares her own ratio of perceived outcomes (O) (pay, benefits, working conditions) to perceived inputs (I) (effort, ability, experience) to the ratio of a comparison other (o).

$$OP/IP <, >, \text{ or } = O_o/I_o?$$

If P's ratio (O_p/I_p) is smaller than the comparison other's ratio (O_o/I_o), under-reward inequity results. If P's ratio is larger, over-reward inequity results, although evidence suggests that this type of inequity is less likely to occur and less likely to be sustained because P may rationalize the situation by re-evaluating her outcomes less favourably or inputs (self-worth) more favourably.[2]

The consequences of P's comparisons depend on whether equity is perceived. If equity is perceived, no change is expected in P's attitudes or behaviour. In contrast, perceived inequity may cause P to restore equity. Some ways of restoring equity are counterproductive, including (1) reducing one's own inputs (not working as hard) (2) increasing one's outcomes (such as by theft) (3) leaving the situation that generates perceived inequity (leaving the organization or refusing to work or cooperate with employees who are perceived as over-rewarded).

Equity theory's main implication for managing employee compensation is that to an important extent, employees evaluate their pay by comparing it with what others get paid, and their work attitudes and behaviours are influenced by such comparisons.

Another implication is that employee perceptions determine their evaluation. The fact that management believes its employees are paid well compared with those of other companies does not necessarily translate into employees' beliefs. Employees may have different information or make different comparisons than management.

Two types of employee social comparisons of pay are especially relevant in making pay level and job structure decisions (see Table 8.2). First, *external equity* pay comparisons focus on what employees in other organizations are paid for doing the same general job. Such comparisons are likely to influence the decisions of applicants to accept job offers as well as the attitudes and decisions of employees about whether to stay with an organization or take a job elsewhere (see chapters 5 and 7). The organization's choice of pay level influences its employees' external pay comparisons and their

Table 8.2   Pay Structure Concepts and Consequences

PAY STRUCTURE DECISION AREA	ADMINISTRATIVE TOOL	FOCUS OF EMPLOYEE PAY COMPARISONS	CONSEQUENCES OF EQUITY PERCEPTIONS
Pay level	Market pay surveys	External equity	External employee movement (attraction and retention of quality employees); labour costs; employee attitudes
Job structure	Job evaluation	Internal equity	Internal employee movement (promotion, transfer, job rotation); cooperation among employees; employee attitudes

consequences. A market pay survey is the primary administrative tool organizations use in choosing a pay level.

Second, *internal equity* pay comparisons focus on what employees within the same organization, but in different jobs, are paid. Employees make comparisons with lower-level jobs, jobs at the same level (but perhaps in different skill areas or product divisions), and jobs at higher levels. These comparisons may influence general attitudes of employees; their willingness to transfer to other jobs within the organization; their willingness to accept promotions; their inclination to cooperate across jobs, functional areas, or product groups; and their commitment to the organization. The organization's choice of job structure influences its employees' internal comparisons and their consequences. Job evaluation is the administrative tool organizations use to design job structures.

In addition, employees make internal-equity pay comparisons with others performing the same job. Such comparisons are most relevant to the next chapter, which focuses on using pay to recognize individual contributions and differences.

We now turn to ways to choose and develop pay levels and pay structures, the consequences of such choices, and the ways two administrative tools—market pay surveys and job evaluation—help in making pay decisions.

DEVELOPING PAY LEVELS

Describe the major administrative tools used to manage employee compensation.

Market Pressures

Any organization faces two important competitive market challenges in deciding what to pay its employees: product market competition and labour market competition.

Product Market Competition   First, organizations must compete effectively in the product market. In other words, they must be able to sell their goods and services at a quantity and price that will bring a sufficient return on their investment. Organizations compete on multiple dimensions (quality, service, and so on), and price is one of the most important dimensions. An important influence on price is the cost of production.

An organization that has higher labour costs than its product market competitors will have to charge higher average prices for products of similar quality. Thus, for example, if labour costs are 30 percent of revenues at Company A and Company B, but Company A has labour costs that are 20 percent higher than those of Company B, we would expect Company A to have product prices that are higher by $(0.30 \times 0.20) = 6$ percent. At some point, the higher price charged by Company A will contribute to a loss of its business to competing companies with lower prices (such as Company B). In the automobile industry, labour-related expenses per vehicle (including retiree and active worker benefits such as health care) recently averaged $606 higher for the Big Three (General Motors, Ford, and Chrysler) than for Japanese producers Toyota, Nissan, and Honda. This labour cost advantage is a major factor in the pretax profit advantage per vehicle of $2,271 that these Japanese producers held over the Big Three.[3] Recently, however, North American producers have negotiated drastic changes (on both sides of the border) with their workers to improve competitiveness. For example, after bargaining successfully with the UAW in March 2009 for reductions in hourly labour costs (from $60 to $55 per hour immediately and down to $50 by 2011), Ford went to the CAW in November 2009 and threatened to pull out of Canada. Canadian production comprises about 13 percent of all Ford production in North America.[4] Hence by October, the CAW was forced to reopen a concessionary contract made just 18 months earlier and concede to a second cost-cutting agreement with "cuts to benefits, a reduction in vacation, break times and co-pays on health care, all of which were pattern items from the agreements with Chrysler and General Motors."[5] Japanese and European producers in North America are thought to be currently in the $48 to $49 range.

Therefore, *product market competition* places an *upper bound* on labour costs and compensation. This upper bound is more constrictive when labour costs are a larger share of total costs and when demand for the product is affected by changes in price (i.e., when demand is *elastic*). Although costs are only one part of the competitive equation (productivity is just as important), higher costs may result in a loss of business. In the absence of clear evidence on productivity differences, costs need to be closely monitored.

What components make up labour costs? A major component is the average cost per employee. This is made up of both direct payments (such as wages, salaries, and bonuses) and indirect payments (such as the Canada/Quebec Pension Plans (CPP/QPP), Worker's Compensation insurance, and Employment Insurance). A second component of labour cost is the staffing level (number of employees). Not surprisingly, financially troubled organizations often seek to cut costs by focusing on one or both components. Staff reductions, hiring freezes, wage and salary freezes, and sharing benefits costs with employees are several ways of enhancing the organization's competitive position in the product market.

Labour Market Competition   A second important competitive market challenge is *labour market competition*. Essentially, labour market competition is the amount an organization must pay to compete against other companies that hire similar employees. These labour market competitors typically include not only companies that have similar products but also those in different product markets that hire similar types of employees. If an organization is not competitive in the labour market, it will fail to attract and retain employees of sufficient numbers and quality. For example, even if a computer manufacturer offers newly graduated electrical engineers the same pay as other computer manufacturers, if automobile manufacturers and other labour market competitors offer salaries $5,000 higher, the computer company may not be able to hire enough qualified electrical engineers. Labour market competition places a *lower bound* on pay levels.

Employees as a Resource

Because organizations have to compete in the labour market, they should consider their employees not only as a cost but also as a resource in which the organization has invested and from which it expects valuable returns. Although controlling costs directly affects an organization's ability to compete in the product market, the organization's competitive position can be compromised if costs are kept low at the expense of employee productivity and quality. Having higher labour costs than your competitors is not necessarily bad if you also have the best and most effective workforce, one that produces more products of better quality.

Pay policies and programs are one of the most important human resource tools for encouraging desired employee behaviours and discouraging undesired behaviours. Therefore, they must be evaluated not only in terms of costs but also in terms of the returns they generate—how they attract, retain, and motivate a high-quality workforce. For example, if the average revenue per employee in Company A is 20 percent higher than in Company B, it may not be important that the average pay in Company A is 10 percent higher than in Company B.

Pay Levels: Deciding What to Pay

Although organizations face important external labour and product market pressures in setting their pay levels, a range of discretion remains.[6] How large the range is depends on the particular competitive environment the organization faces. Where the range is broad, an important strategic decision is whether to pay above, at, or below the market average. The advantage of paying above the market average is the ability to attract and retain the top talent available, which can translate into a highly effective and productive workforce. The disadvantage, however, is the added cost.[7]

Under what circumstances do the benefits of higher pay outweigh the higher costs? According to **efficiency wage theory,** one circumstance is when organizations have technologies or structures that depend on highly skilled employees. For example, organizations that emphasize decentralized decision making may need higher-calibre employees. Another circumstance where higher pay may be warranted is when an organization has difficulties observing and monitoring its employees' performance. It may therefore wish to provide an above-market pay rate to ensure the incentive to put forth maximum effort. The theory is that employees who are paid more than they would be paid elsewhere will be reluctant to shirk because they wish to retain their good jobs.[8]

Efficiency Wage Theory
A theory stating that wages influence worker productivity.

Market Pay Surveys

To compete for talent, organizations use **benchmarking,** a procedure in which an organization compares its own practices against those of the competition. In compensation management, benchmarking against product market and labour market competitors is typically accomplished through the use of one or more pay surveys, which provide information on going rates of pay among competing organizations.

Benchmarking
Comparing an organization's practices against those of the competition.

The use of pay surveys requires answers to several important questions:[9]

1. Which employers should be included in the survey? Ideally, they would be the key labour market and product market competitors.
2. Which jobs are included in the survey? Because only a sample of jobs is ordinarily used, care must be taken that the jobs are representative in terms of level, functional area, and product market. Also, the job content must be sufficiently similar.
3. If multiple surveys are used, how are all the rates of pay weighted and combined? Organizations often have to weight and combine pay rates because different surveys are often tailored toward particular employee groups (labour markets) or product markets. The organization must decide how much relative weight to give to its labour market and product market competitors in setting pay.

Several factors affect decisions on how to combine surveys.[10] Product market comparisons that focus on labour costs are likely to deserve greater weight when (1) labour costs represent a large share of total costs (2) product demand is elastic (it changes in response to product price changes) (3) the supply of labour is inelastic, and (4) employee skills are specific to the product market (and will remain so). In contrast, labour market comparisons may be more important when (1) attracting and retaining qualified employees is difficult and (2) the costs (administration, disruption, and so on) of recruiting replacements are high.

As this discussion suggests, knowing what other organizations are paying is only one part of the story. It is also necessary to know what those organizations are getting in return for their investment in employees. To find that, some organizations examine ratios such as revenues/employees and revenues/labour cost. However, comparing these ratios across organizations requires caution. For example, different industries rely on different labour and capital resources. So comparing the ratio of revenues to labour costs of a petroleum company (capital intensive, high ratio) to a hospital (labour intensive, low ratio) would be like comparing apples and oranges. But within industries, such comparisons can be useful. Besides revenues, other return-on-investment data might include product quality, customer satisfaction, and potential workforce quality (such as average education and skill levels).

Rate Ranges   As the preceding discussion suggests, obtaining a single "going rate" of market pay is a complex task that involves a number of subjective decisions; it is both an art and a science. Once a market rate has been chosen, how is it incorporated into the pay structure? Typically—especially

Rate Ranges
Different employees in the same job may have different pay rates.

for white-collar jobs—it is used for setting the midpoint of pay ranges for either jobs or pay grades (discussed next). Market survey data are also often collected on minimum and maximum rates of pay as well. The use of **rate ranges** permits a company to recognize differences in employee performance, seniority, training, and so forth in setting individual pay (discussed in the next chapter). For some blue-collar jobs, however, particularly those covered by collective bargaining contracts, there may be a single rate of pay for all employees within the job.

Benchmark Jobs and Nonbenchmark Jobs   In using pay surveys, it is necessary to make a distinction between two general types of jobs: benchmark jobs (key jobs) and nonbenchmark jobs (nonkey jobs). **Benchmark jobs** have relatively stable content and—perhaps most importantly—are common to many organizations. Therefore, it is possible to obtain market pay survey data on them. Note, however, that to avoid too much of an administrative burden, organizations may not gather market pay data on all such jobs. In contrast to benchmark jobs, **nonbenchmark jobs** are, to an important extent, unique to organizations; thus, by definition, they cannot be directly valued or compared through the use of market surveys. Therefore, they are treated differently in the pay-setting process.

Benchmark Jobs
Key jobs used in pay surveys, that have relatively stable content and are common to many organizations.

Nonbenchmark Jobs
Jobs that are unique to organizations and that cannot be directly valued or compared through the use of market surveys.

Developing a Job Structure

Although external comparisons of the sort we have been discussing are important, employees also evaluate their pay using internal comparisons. So, for example, a vice president of marketing may expect to be paid roughly the same amount as a vice president of information systems because they are at the same organizational level, with similar levels of responsibility and similar impacts on the organization's performance. Recall that job structure can be defined as the relative worth of various jobs in the organization, based on these types of internal comparisons. We now discuss how such decisions are made.

Job Evaluation
An administrative procedure used to measure internal job worth.

Job Evaluation   One typical way of measuring internal job worth is to use an administrative procedure called **job evaluation.** Compensation managers have developed five main types of job evaluation over time, and compensation consulting firms have developed customized versions of these approaches for use with their own clients. We shall focus our attention here on the three types of job evaluation most commonly used by organizations: (1) ranking (2) classification/grade description, and (3) the point method.

Both ranking and classification are qualitative approaches that require comparison of whole jobs to each other and rely to a considerable extent on the judgment of individuals involved in the job evaluation process. However the point method provides a quantitative approach in which each job is assigned a unique point value based on a detailed analysis of that job's **compensable factors,** or the characteristics of jobs that an organization values and chooses to pay for. After breaking the job down into compensable factors, evaluators assign each a point value according to a predetermined points table in a job evaluation manual. The final step is to add together all points assigned to compensable factors, which determines the point value of the overall job.[11]

Compensable Factors
The characteristics of jobs that an organization values and chooses to pay for.

All three approaches will result in a hierarchical job structure, and the place a job assumes in the hierarchy depends on its internal relative worth to the organization. The choice of job evaluation method should be carefully thought out in advance and matched to the organization's long-term needs and overall strategy. It is important to remember that job evaluation is not a one-time process. Each time a new job is created, it must be evaluated to determine its internal worth relative to existing jobs in the organization before assuming its place on the structure. In addition, individual or groups of existing jobs may need to be re-evaluated from time to time as changes occur in the jobs themselves or as the organization grows and responds to its environment. For example, a job or group of jobs may change substantially with the addition of new technology, or the organization may make an acquisition and need to integrate a number of new jobs into its existing structure. Finally, if the organization is subject to provincial or federal pay equity legislation, it is wise to pick a job evaluation approach that includes as little room for subjectivity (and gender bias) as possible. That is because job evaluation is the basis for establishing the organization's pay structure and, hence, a job's position in the hierarchy will also determine the amount of pay incumbents will receive.

As you will see, of the three most commonly used methods of job evaluation, only the point method truly stands up to the scrutiny of pay equity legislation. Therefore, we begin with a brief description of the ranking and classification methods, followed by a more detailed explanation of the point method.

Ranking Method   Ranking is the simplest and cheapest of all job evaluation approaches, at least initially. For that reason, it will often be chosen by a small firm or startup with few jobs to evaluate, as a quick and easy way to begin comparing the internal relative worth of the organization's jobs. Sometimes called "whole job ranking,"[12] it consists of asking a committee of job evaluators to examine job descriptions of all the jobs in the organization and rank the jobs from highest to lowest value to the organization, until a job structure is created. Two variations of this approach include *alternation ranking* and *paired comparison*. Using the *alternation ranking* method, evaluators begin by examining all jobs in the organization; on the basis of what they know about the job, they decide which seems to be the most valuable job in the organization (e.g., sales manager), as well as which job is the least valuable to the organization (e.g., shipping clerk). Then the next most valuable job in the organization is determined (sales representative) and placed in order beneath the most valuable job, and the next least valuable job is placed in order above the least valuable job (warehouse coordinator). The ranking process continues until all jobs have been examined and placed. Ultimately, evaluators create a hierarchical job structure in which all jobs are ranked as accurately as possible according to what evaluators think is their internal relative worth to the organization.

Paired comparison is another whole-job ranking method that works better when there are many more jobs to be considered, and is more rigorous.[13] The main difference in this approach is that each individual job is methodically compared to each other job in the organization one by one on a matrix, to determine which is more valuable. Jobs are then ranked from highest to lowest depending on the outcomes of the many specific comparisons. New jobs can later be added to the structure, based on the same process.

The accuracy of the ranking process depends on the number of people involved and the criteria established (if any) for deciding which job is more valuable than another. Raters first must agree on criteria for ranking, which may or may not be possible. Further, as the process continues, it will become increasingly more difficult to discern the difference among jobs that are ranked closer to the middle. While decisions about the most and least valuable jobs may seem obvious to many, the differences among jobs in the middle of the structure can be much more subtle and it may be hard to reach consensus about which job is ranked higher. Due to the subjectivity involved and since there is no clear reason why one job ranks higher than another, it will not meet the specific requirements of comparing jobs on the basis of skills, effort, responsibility, and working conditions required to do the job. In addition, ranking provides little basis for justification for pay differences when employees ask tough questions. Not being able to explain pay differences in an adequate way may lead to employee doubts about the validity and fairness of the process that determined the rank of their job. Under such circumstances, employers might also determine the paycheque resulting from the job structure to be unacceptable as well. Hence, managers of organizations that decide to use ranking as a first approach to job evaluation may well find themselves repeating the entire process at a later date, using a more defensible and acceptable method for creating a job structure.

Classification (Grade Description) Method   Many large public-sector organizations such as the federal government, universities, colleges, and government agencies use the classification (or grade description) method of job evaluation. The classification (grade description) method uses generic organization-wide descriptions to classify jobs into groups with other similar jobs that fit the same generalized description. The process begins by creating general classes of jobs, such as administrative, managerial, professional, and technical, that exist in all such organizations, and writing a number of grade descriptions for each class. All general class descriptions should be clearly written so that managers and others can easily classify which major class the job fits into. For example, the general description should be clear enough to help a manager understand how to correctly classify a payroll administrator (administrative) or a mechanic (technical), or a general manager (managerial).

Once a clear description of each class is established, a series of grade descriptions for each class is written to further differentiate the level of skill, experience, complexity, and responsibility required for jobs placed in each grade. For example, in a large university, it might be determined that all the jobs in the organization classified as administrative can be categorized using four different grades or levels within that classification (grades I, II, III and IV). However, in the technical class, seven different grades may be required to adequately classify jobs, since technical jobs might include greater discernment among levels of complexity. In any class, it might be important to add a grade or two for jobs in which there is responsibility for the work of others (supervising others, project leadership, etc.). Once class and grade descriptions are written for all types of jobs in the organization, salary maximums and minimums are then set for each classification and grade and adjusted annually, or according to collective bargaining agreements. The number of classifications and grades within each class, and their descriptions, are unique to each organization and can vary considerably.

The advantage of such systems is that, once in place, they provide organizations with a universal and easy approach for coping with hundreds (even thousands) of jobs in a more efficient and cost-effective manner. The system is much more defensible than ranking since both job rank and compensation are based on universally agreed-upon and transparent classification and grade descriptions that have been reviewed and agreed to by key stakeholders. For example, in public-sector organizations it is common to see the job classification and grade included as part of a job posting, allowing applicants to determine whether the pay might be the same or higher than the current job they hold when they consider applying for the position. Managers have written descriptions to fall back on as the basis of discussion with employees when questions arise, and have guidelines for promotion and raises when an employee is progressing in his or her role or performing better than others.

However, if class or grade descriptions are too broad, there is room for error and conflict when initially classifying a job, and such classifications can be difficult and time consuming to change in large bureaucratic organizations. By the same token, if class and grade descriptions are too detailed, the system becomes very cumbersome, allowing little flexibility for managers or the organization to cope with external pressures on hiring such as globalization or shortages of labour. Finally, the system does not allow comparison of jobs from different job families (a scientist's job vs. a clerical job) which makes it very difficult to meet pay equity challenges. Since many public-sector organizations are also highly unionized, this is a key consideration, given that many challenges are likely to occur no matter how well the class and grade descriptions are written. If an organization wishes to establish a job evaluation system that is more bulletproof in meeting the requirements of pay equity, it may be better served by the point method, which we discuss next.[14]

The Point Method   As mentioned earlier, the point method is based on breaking an individual job down into the key characteristics of jobs that an organization values, or its compensable factors. Compensable factors are derived from the organization's job analysis and resulting job descriptions as well as the weight assigned to each compensable factor. The weighted value of each factor is determined in advance and integrated into a point matrix system, along with short descriptions of each compensable factor (and each ascending degree of skill or competency level represented in the matrix for each compensable factor). All information is then encompassed in a job evaluation manual for use by managers and other stakeholders when it is time to evaluate a job or group of jobs in the organization.

Most point-method systems begin with four key characteristics that are universal to all jobs: skill, effort, responsibility, and working conditions. These four universal factors are then broken down into subfactors that managers and others believe are key to various groups of jobs and which generally also reflect the culture and values of the organization. For example, skill is often broken down into two subfactors that are required characteristics in all jobs—Education and Experience. However, an organization may wish to add Complexity as a third subfactor, as shown in Table 8.3. Likewise, Effort is often broken down into mental and physical effort, which helps to differentiate further among jobs in an organization. It is best to use benchmark jobs in the organization when deciding on compensable factors, since these are common jobs that are unlikely to change much over time, and will help create a system that accommodates most jobs. Once the number and type of subfactors is agreed to, each subfactor must then be broken down into degrees or levels that may come into play for that subfactor. For example, the subfactor of Experience shown in Table 8.3 is divided into seven degrees (or levels of experience that are required for various jobs across an organization). The organization must then write definitions for each degree chosen (seven definitions) so that jobs can be compared accurately to the matrix. For more subjective types of subfactor/degree descriptions such as Responsibility, the job evaluation manual will usually contain a series of short, but more detailed descriptions to help job evaluators differentiate the value of one job over another.

The next step is to create a point table (or scoring system) that affixes a point band reflecting an increasing value for each degree of the compensable factor. (That will ensure that if a PhD is required for a job compared to the point matrix that it garners considerably higher points than a job that requires only two years of postsecondary education.) However, in order to generate a point band for scoring each compensable factor, job evaluators often first apply a weighting scheme to account for the differing importance of the compensable factors to the organization.

Weights can be generated in two ways. First, *a priori* weights can be assigned, which means factors are weighted using expert judgments about the importance of each compensable factor. Second,

Table 8.3 Sample Points Table for Nine Compensable Factors

COMPENSABLE FACTOR	WEIGHT	DEGREES (LEVELS)						
		1	2	3	4	5	6	7
Education	15	15	30	45	60	75	90	115
Experience	10	10	20	30	40	50	60	70
Complexity	10	10	20	30	40	50	60	
Mental Effort	5	5	10	15	20	25	30	35
Physical Effort	5	5	10	15	20	25	30	
Supervision	15	15	30	45	60	75		
Financial	15	15	30	45	60	75		
Decision Making	15	15	30	45	60	75	90	
Working Conditions	10	10	10	15	20	25	30	35

weights can be derived empirically based on how important each factor seems in determining pay in the labour market. (Statistical methods such as multiple regression can be used for this purpose.) Table 8.3 provides a sample point table where the initial weighting of the compensable factor is the basis of an increasing point band for each of the nine compensable factors chosen for this system. Note that the point band in each case has been created by simply using the initial weight assigned for each factor as the basic number of points for Degree 1, and then simply multiplying that basic number across the band by the Degree itself. For example, Education is weighted at 15 percent when determining job value, and therefore Education is valued at 15 points for Degree 1 on the point band. Thereafter, the point value of each ascending Degree level (of Education required) is increased by using the Degree level as the multiplication factor of the basic weight/point value of 15. (Education Degree 2 is worth 30 points, and so on). This is a simple way to reflect the increasing value or weight of each ascending degree of a compensable factor.[15]

Once the job evaluation manual has been created, containing definitions for compensable factors and their various degrees, and a matching point table with point bands has been created, salary grades can be created using point ranges as the basis of differentiating levels. For example, Salary Grade 3 is made up of jobs valued at or between 365 and 395 points. When the job evaluation manual has been finalized with all stakeholders' input and approval, training should take place so that users (participants in job evaluation committees) feel comfortable with the new system and are ready to evaluate jobs accurately. Benchmark jobs will usually be evaluated first, providing an established understanding of the value of standard jobs in the organization, before evaluating nonbenchmark jobs, which may have unique qualities that require additional considerations.[16]

Table 8.4 shows an example of a three-factor job evaluation system applied to three jobs. Note that the jobs differ in the levels of experience, education, and complexity required. Summing the scores on the three compensable factors provides an internally oriented assessment of relative job worth in the organization. In a sense, the computer programmer job is worth 41 percent (155/110 − 1) more than the computer operator job, and the systems analyst job is worth 91 percent (210/110 − 1) more than the computer operator job. Whatever pay level is chosen (based on benchmarking and competitive strategy), we would expect the pay differentials to be somewhat similar to these percentages. The internal job evaluation and external survey-based measures of worth can, however, diverge, depending on a number of factors such as how recently jobs have been compared to the external market, labour market shortages, the company's pay level decisions, and so on.

Developing a Pay Structure

In the example in Table 8.5, there are 15 jobs, 10 of which are benchmark (key) jobs. For these jobs, both pay survey and job evaluation data are available. For the five nonbenchmark jobs, by definition, no survey data are available, only job evaluation information. Note that, for simplicity's sake, we work with data from only two pay surveys and we use a weighted average that gives twice

Table 8.4   Example of a Three-Factor Job Evaluation System

| | COMPENSABLE FACTORS | | | |
JOB TITLE	EXPERIENCE	EDUCATION	COMPLEXITY	TOTAL
Computer operator	40	30	40	110
Computer programmer	40	50	65	155
Systems analyst	65	60	85	210

Table 8.5 Job Evaluation and Pay Survey Data

JOB	KEY JOB?	JOB TITLE	JOB EVALUATION	SURVEY 1 (S1)	SURVEY 2 (S2)	SURVEY COMPOSITE (2/3*S1 + 1/3*S2)
A	y	Computer operator	110	$2,012	$1,731	$1,919
B	y	Engineering tech I	115	2,206	1,908	2,106
C	y	Computer programmer	155	2,916	2,589	2,807
D	n	Engineering tech II	165	—	—	—
E	n	Compensation analyst	170	—	—	—
F	y	Accountant	190	3,613	3,099	3,442
G	y	Systems analyst	210	4,275	3,854	4,134
H	n	Computer programmer—senior	225	—	—	—
I	y	Director of personnel	245	4,982	4,506	4,823
J	y	Accountant—senior	255	5,205	4,270	4,893
K	y	Systems analyst—senior	270	5,868	5,652	5,796
L	y	Industrial engineer	275	5,496	4,794	5,262
M	n	Chief accountant	315	—	—	—
N	y	Senior engineer	320	7,026	6,572	6,875
O	n	Senior scientist	330	—	—	—

SOURCE: Adapted from S. Rynes, B. Gerhart, G.T. Milkovich, and J. Boudreau, *Current Compensation Professional Institute* (Scottsdale, AZ: American Compensation Association, 1988). Reprinted with permission.

as much weight to survey 1 (an example of a choice or strategy compensation analysts might make when reviewing the value or origin of various surveys for their purposes.) Also, our example works with a single structure. Many organizations have multiple structures that correspond to different job families (such as clerical, technical, and professional) or product divisions.

How are the data in Table 8.5 combined to develop a pay structure? First, it is important to note that both internal and external comparisons must be considered in making compensation decisions. However, because the pay structures suggested by internal and external comparisons do not necessarily converge, employers must carefully balance them. Studies suggest that employers may differ significantly in the degree to which they place priority on internal- or external-comparison data in developing pay structures.[17]

At least three pay-setting approaches, which differ according to their relative emphasis on external or internal comparisons, can be identified: market survey data, adjusted pay policy line, and pay grade.[18]

Market Survey Data   The approach with the greatest emphasis on external comparisons (market survey data) is achieved by directly basing pay on market surveys that cover as many key jobs as possible. For example, the rate of pay for job A in Table 8.6 on page 314 would be $1,919; for job B, $2,106; and for job C, $2,807. For nonbenchmark jobs (jobs D, E, H, M, and O), however, pay

Table 8.6   Pay Midpoints under Different Approaches

JOB	KEY JOB?	JOB TITLE	JOB EVALUATION	(1) SURVEY POLICY	(2) PAY MIDPOINTS POLICY	(3) GRADES
A	y	Computer operator	110	$1,919	$1,835	$2,175
B	y	Engineering tech I	115	2,106	1,948	2,175
C	y	Computer programmer	155	2,807	2,856	3,310
D	n	Engineering tech II	165	3,083	3,083	3,310
E	n	Compensation analyst	170	3,196	3,196	3,310
F	y	Accountant	190	3,442	3,650	3,310
G	y	Systems analyst	210	4,134	4,104	4,444
H	n	Computer programmer—senior	225	4,444	4,444	4,444
I	y	Director of personnel	245	4,823	4,898	4,444
J	y	Accountant—senior	255	4,893	5,125	5,579
K	y	Systems analyst—senior	270	5,796	5,465	5,579
L	y	Industrial engineer	275	5,262	5,579	5,579
M	n	Chief accountant	315	6,486	6,486	6,713
N	y	Senior engineer	320	6,875	6,600	6,713
O	n	Senior scientist	330	6,826	6,826	6,713

SOURCE: Adapted from S. Rynes, B. Gerhart, G. T. Milkovich, and J. Boudreau, *Current Compensation Professional Institute* (Scottsdale, AZ: American Compensation Association, 1988). Reprinted with permission.

Pay Policy Line
A mathematical expression that describes the relationship between a job's pay and its job evaluation points.

survey information is not available, and we must proceed differently. Basically, we develop a market **pay policy line** based on the key jobs (for which there are both job evaluation and market pay survey data available). As Figure 8.1 shows, the data can be plotted with a line of best fit estimated. This line can be generated using a statistical procedure (regression analysis). Doing so yields the equation –$661 + $22.69 × job evaluation points. In other words, the predicted monthly salary (based on fitting a line to the key job data) is obtained by inserting the number of job evaluation points into this equation. Thus, for example, job D, a nonbenchmark job, would have a predicted monthly salary of –$661 + $22.69 × 165 = $3,083.

As Figure 8.1 also indicates, it is not necessary to fit a straight line to the job evaluation and pay survey data. In some cases, a pay structure that provides increasing monetary rewards to higher-level jobs may be more consistent with the organization's goals or with the external market. For example, nonlinearity may be more appropriate if higher-level jobs are especially valuable to the organization and the talent to perform such jobs is rare. The curvilinear function in Figure 8.1 is described by the equation

Natural logarithm of pay = $6.98 + (0.006 × job evaluation points)

Adjusted Pay Policy Line   A second pay-setting approach that combines information from external and internal comparisons is to use the market pay policy line to derive pay rates for both benchmark and nonbenchmark jobs that reflect the firm's intended pay level policy (above, at, or

FIGURE 8.1   Pay Policy Lines, Linear and Natural Logarithmic Functions

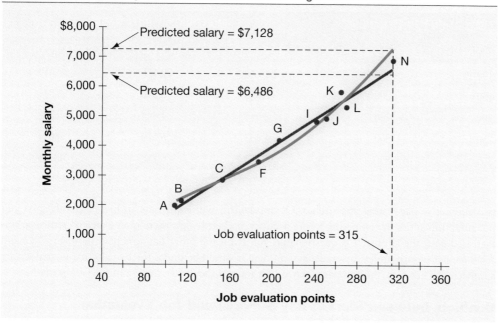

below market rates). To do this, the compensation manager uses the market pay policy line as a starting point, and then draws a new line above or below the market pay policy line by whatever percentage it takes to ensure the adjusted pay policy line puts the company's pay level intentions into practice. For example, if the company claims that its policy is to pay 15 percent above the market rate, the compensation manager would shift the entire market pay policy line upward by 15 percent. This creates a new, firm-specific pay policy line that provides a more accurate foundation for setting pay rates 15 percent above market rates, as intended. This approach differs from the first approach in that actual market rates are no longer used for benchmark jobs. This introduces a greater degree of internal consistency into the structure because the pay of all the jobs is directly linked to the number of job evaluation points and also incorporates the firm's pay level policy.

Pay Grades   A third approach is to group jobs, into a smaller number of pay classes or **pay grades.** Table 8.7 on page 316 (see also Table 8.6, last column), for example, demonstrates one possibility: a five-grade structure. Each job within a grade would have the same rate range (i.e., would be assigned the same midpoint, minimum, and maximum). The advantage of this approach is that the administrative burden of setting separate rates of pay for hundreds (even thousands) of different jobs is reduced. It also permits greater flexibility in moving employees from job to job without raising concerns about, for example, going from a job having 230 job evaluation points to a job with 215 job evaluation points. What might look like a demotion in a completely job-based system is often a nonissue in a grade-based system. Note that the **range spread** (the distance between the minimum and maximum) is larger at higher levels, in recognition of the fact that performance differences are likely to have more impact on the organization at higher job levels (see Figure 8.2 on page 316).

The disadvantage of using grades is that some jobs will be underpaid and others overpaid. For example, in Table 8.6 on page 314, job C and job F both fall within the same grade. The midpoint for job C under a grade system is $3,310 per month, or $503 or $454 *more* than under the

Pay Grades
Jobs of similar worth or content grouped together for pay administration purposes.

Range Spread
The distance between the minimum and maximum amounts in a pay grade.

Table 8.7   Sample Pay Grade Structure

PAY GRADE	JOB EVALUATION POINTS RANGE		MONTHLY PAY RATE RANGE		
	MINIMUM	MAXIMUM	MINIMUM	MIDPOINT	MAXIMUM
1	100	150	$1,740	$2,175	$2,610
2	150	200	2,648	3,310	3,971
3	200	250	3,555	4,444	5,333
4	250	300	4,463	5,579	6,694
5	300	350	5,370	6,713	8,056

two alternative pay-setting approaches. Obviously, this will contribute to higher labour costs and potential difficulties in competing in the product market. Unless there is an expected return to this increased cost, the approach is questionable. Job F, on the other hand, is paid between $132 and $340 *less* per month under the grades system than it would be under the two alternative pay-setting approaches. Therefore, the company may find it more difficult to compete in the labour market.

LO 3

Explain the importance of competitive labour market and product market forces in compensation decisions.

Conflicts between Market Pay Surveys and Job Evaluation

An examination of Table 8.6 on page 314 suggests that the relative worth of jobs is quite similar overall, whether based on job evaluation or pay survey data. However, some inconsistencies typically arise, and these are usually indicated by jobs whose average survey pay is significantly below or above the pay policy line. The closest case in Table 8.6 is job L, for which the average pay falls significantly

FIGURE 8.2   Sample Pay Grade Structure

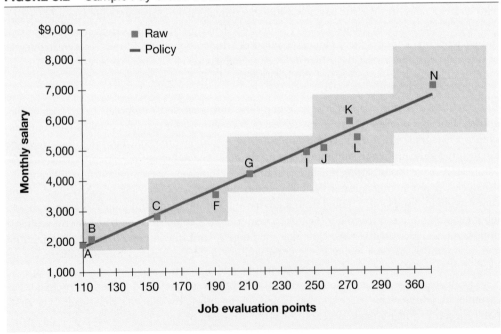

below the pay policy line. One possible explanation is that a relatively plentiful supply of people in the labour market are capable of performing this job, so the pay needed to attract and retain them is lower than would be expected given the job evaluation points. Another kind of inconsistency occurs when market surveys show that a job is paid higher than the policy line (such as job K). Again, this may reflect relative supply and demand, in this case driving pay higher.

How are conflicts between external and internal equity resolved, and what are the consequences? The example of the vice presidents of marketing and information technology may help illustrate the type of choice faced. The marketing VP job may receive the same number of job evaluation points, but market survey data may indicate that it typically pays less than the information technology VP job, perhaps because of tighter supply for the latter. Therefore, does the organization pay salaries based on the market survey (external comparison) or on the job evaluation points (internal comparison)?

Emphasizing the internal comparison would suggest paying the two VPs the same. In doing so, however, either the VP of marketing would be "overpaid" or the VP of information technology would be "underpaid." The former drives up labour costs (product market problems); the latter may make it difficult to attract and retain a quality VP of information technology (labour market problems).

Another consideration has to do with the strategy of the organization. For example, in many large multinational organizations the marketing function is critical to success. Thus, even though the market for marketing VPs is lower than that for information technology VPs, an organization may choose to be a pay leader for the marketing position (pay at the 90th percentile, for example) but only meet the market for the information technology position (perhaps pay at the 50th percentile). In other words, designing a pay structure requires careful consideration of which positions are most central to dealing with critical environmental challenges and opportunities in reaching the organization's goals.[19]

What about emphasizing external comparisons? Two potential problems arise. First, the marketing VP may be dissatisfied because she expects a job of similar rank and responsibility to that of the information technology VP to be paid similarly. Second, it becomes difficult to rotate people through different VP positions (for training and development) because going to the marketing VP position might appear as a demotion to the VP of information technology.

There is no one correct solution to such dilemmas. Each organization must decide which objectives are most essential and choose the appropriate strategy. However, there seems to be a growing sentiment that external comparisons deserve greater weight because organizations are finding it increasingly difficult to ignore market competitive pressures.

Monitoring Compensation Costs

Pay structure influences compensation costs in a number of ways. Most obviously, the pay level at which the structure is pegged influences these costs. However, this is only part of the story. The pay structure represents the organization's intended policy, but actual practice may not coincide with it. Take, for example, the pay grade structure presented in Table 8.7. The midpoint for grade 1 is $2,175, and the midpoint for grade 2 is $3,310. Now, consider the data on a group of individual employees in Table 8.8 on page 318. One frequently used index of the correspondence between actual and intended pay is the **compa-ratio,** computed as follows:

Compa-Ratio
An index of the correspondence between actual and intended pay.

Grade compa-ratio = Actual average pay for grade/Pay midpoint for grade

The compa-ratio directly assesses the degree to which actual pay is consistent with the pay policy. A compa-ratio *less than* 1.00 suggests that actual pay is *lagging* behind the policy, whereas a compa-ratio *greater than* 1.00 indicates that pay (and costs) *exceeds* that of the policy. Although there

Table 8.8 Compa-Ratios for Two Grades

EMPLOYEE	JOB	PAY	MIDPOINT	EMPLOYEE COMPA-RATIOS
	Grade 1			
1	Engineering tech I	$2,306	$2,175	1.06
2	Computer programmer	2,066	2,175	.95
3	Engineering tech I	2,523	2,175	1.16
4	Engineering tech I	2,414	2,175	1.11
	Average			**1.07**
	Grade 2			
5	Computer programmer	3,906	3,310	1.18
6	Accountant	3,773	3,310	1.14
7	Accountant	3,674	3,310	1.11
	Average			**1.15**

may be good reasons for compa-ratios to differ from 1.00, managers should also consider whether the pay structure is allowing costs to get out of control.

Learn more about monitoring compensation costs online with Connect.

Globalization, Geographic Region, and Pay Structures

Market pay structures can differ substantially across countries both in terms of their level and in terms of the relative worth of jobs. Compared with the labour markets in Germany and Canada, markets in Mexico and Korea provide much lower levels of pay overall and much lower payoffs to skill, education, and advancement. These differences create a dilemma for global companies. For example, should a German engineer posted to Korea be paid according to the standard in Germany or Korea? If the Germany standard is used, a sense of inequity is likely to exist among peers in Korea. If the Korea market standard is used, it may be all but impossible to find a German engineer willing to accept an assignment in Korea. Typically, expatriate pay and benefits (such as housing allowance and tax equalization) continue to be linked more closely to the home country. However, this link appears to be slowly weakening and now depends more on the nature and length of the assignment.[20]

Most companies doing business internationally have either formal or informal policies that provide for pay differentials based on geographic location.[21] These differentials are intended to prevent inequitable treatment of employees who work in more expensive parts of Canada, and around the world. Calculating differences among exotic locations is a complex matter and requires considerable research, or the help of relocation consultants who work with such information constantly. The "Evidence-Based HR" box describes various insights gathered from a study of multinational organizations regarding trends in global consistency with respect to compensation policies and job evaluation, or job levelling.

Table 8.9 provides sample information from the Xpatulator.com website, which provides free international cost-of-living overviews and rank information on 13 cost-of-living baskets and 300 locations globally. The information shown provides some idea of how various cities around the

Table 8.9 Global Comparison of Most Expensive Places to Live and Hardship Index (January 2011)

RANKING AS MOST EXPENSIVE PLACE IN WORLD TO LIVE.	CITY	COST OF LIVING INDEX (WHERE AVAILABLE)	HARDSHIP INDEX*
1	Tokyo, Japan	158.4	20% (some hardship)
2	Caracas, Venezuela		40% (extreme hardship)
3	Hong Kong, China	129.4	20% (some hardship)
5	Moscow, Russia		30% (high degree of hardship)
12	Seoul, Republic of Korea		30% (high degree of hardship)
16	London, England		10% (minimal hardship)
19	Shanghai, China		30% (high degree of hardship)
33	New York City, USA	100	10% (minimal hardship)
37	Toronto, Canada		10% (minimal hardship)
54	Vancouver, Canada		10% (minimal hardship)
61	Brisbane, Australia		10% (minimal hardship)
89	Dubai, UAE	89.7	20% (some hardship)
96	Boston, USA		10% (minimal hardship)
109	Mumbai, India		30% (high degree of hardship)
110	Ottawa, Canada		10% (minimal hardship)
126	Beijing, China		30% (high degree of hardship)
175	Tbilisi, Repub. of Georgia		30% (high degree of hardship)
180	Mexico City, Mexico		30% (high degree of hardship)
284	Tianjin, China	61.4	30% (high degree of hardship)

*Measurement of hardship people are likely to experience in global terms at this location.

SOURCE: www.xpatulator.com (retrieved February 23, 2011).

world compare against each other as "the most expensive place in the world to live," as well as the comparative amount of hardship an expatriate can expect to encounter if required to live there.

A wide variety of issues contribute to what influences the cost of living in each location. For example, Xpatulator.com reports that even though the cost of education is reasonable in Tokyo, the high cost of groceries, health care, and household accommodation make it the most expensive city in the world to live in. Likewise, although the cost of furniture and appliances, education, recreation and culture are relatively inexpensive in Hong Kong, health care and household accommodation (again) make it the third most expensive city in the world. However, Hong Kong is apparently an easier place to live than Moscow, which offers a high degree of hardship when compared internationally.[22] The "hardship index" offers yet another consideration that might enter into compensation negotiations. All comparative information helps employers decide if a premium should be added to persuade expatriates to take an assignment, and how much the premium should be. Certainly, where extreme differences in the cost of daily living exist, some expenses may be handled separately from compensation differentials.

We have hinted here about a few of the complications related to compensation issues when handling expatriate assignments and relocations. Ensuring such employees have key information and even receive their paycheques and other payments on time is another important aspect of expatriate assignments. See the "Competing Through Technology" box to learn more about the technical handling of such issues.

Geographic location is an important factor for Human Resources to consider when establishing a pay structure. For example, Vancouver ranks 54th among 300 cities in terms of how expensive it is to live there, reinforcing that employers need to factor in living costs when deciding upon salaries in order to hire a strong workforce.

Evidence-Based HR

Global organizations as diverse as Research in Motion, The Home Depot, Microsoft, and other large multinational firms struggle with how much to emphasize global consistency in compensation and talent management programs versus incorporating local variations. Companies might tend toward global consistency among reward and talent management practices due to concerns around alignment and governance, efficiency and cost management, quality, talent mobility and complexity. For those companies still deciding which way to go, the results of a recent Towers Watson Global Talent Management and Rewards Study may provide some interesting perspectives, and lend deeper appreciation for the role of job evaluation in global human resources.

The 2010 survey drew from a research base of 1,176 HR professionals holding responsibility for compensation and benefits or talent management among the domestic (42 percent), international (23 percent), and global (35 percent) companies involved. Findings revealed multinationals tend to develop global consistency among programs for senior management such as performance and succession management, long- and short-term incentives, and leadership development. However, for "other" employees, such companies were more likely to emphasize global consistency in organization-wide job evaluation (also called job levelling in the survey), competency models, and base pay. In addition, establishing global consistency in these practices appears to form the foundation for global consistency in other areas such as performance management and short-term incentives implemented below the top management level. Thus, one apparent conclusion is that decisions around the degree and type of global consistency to emphasize in reward and talent practices appear to be linked to job level. Additionally, there appears to be "a strong connection between globally consistent job levelling and consistency in career pathing, the way work gets done, how work is evaluated and how employees are rewarded." Finally, even though many respondents ranked their talent management systems as not very effective, the researchers concluded that when a globally consistent job-levelling system exists, it "provides a framework and starting point for greater alignment and integration of talent management programs in general, leading to improved effectiveness."

SOURCE: "Creating a Sustainable Rewards and Talent Management Model," 2010 Global Talent Management and Rewards Study, pp. 18–19. Towers Watson, 2010.

Competing Through Technology

Using SaaS to remove the Sass from Expatriate Management

It's one thing to create a pay structure and assign individual pay rates, but it's another thing altogether to administer such issues effectively, especially when employees work in remote locations such as part of an oil drilling crew in Libya, or are assigned to a country with primitive infrastructure. When the complexities of managing global compensation, payroll, and the costs of expatriate assignments are considered, it's a wonder any human resources managers or compensation specialists are willing to take on the task. To start with, there are unique compliance issues that arise with each assignment, depending on the country or the region to which an employee is assigned. Add to that renewal deadlines, visa and work permits, tax issues, income security issues, equity plans, and assignment packages that vary considerably in terms of compensation and benefits provided. Toss in the need to integrate reporting, payroll and expense management with existing home-country administrative processes, and it becomes clear why headaches can be anticipated. Finally, the cost of overseas relocation equates to 7–10 percent of overall employee costs. So how *does* one measure the effectiveness of expatriate programs after all is said and done? Better not to ask, perhaps.

Adopting human capital management systems (HCMS) delivered through cloud computing seems to be a growing solution to expatriate program management. Cloud computing is an IT processing service provided by an external network host that links computing devices (desktops, laptops, and mobile devices) of a subscriber organization together via the Internet. In this way it provides subscribers and their employees with consistent levels of computing power, multiple common software applications, and files of information, without the aggravation of managing the network or software installations in-house. Moving a company's HCMS into a cloud environment is done by consolidating all employee data into one system using software-as-a-service (SaaS) platforms. A SaaS system uses noncustomizable software delivered through the cloud network host. However, despite the inability to customize the software, users say that managing global payroll and HR systems is simpler and more efficient. Even better, the "cloud" sheds a ray of transparency and light on expense management for all stakeholders involved because everyone shares the same applications and files needed to manage expenses, regardless of their location in the world or the computing device they use to input or access the information (e.g., smartphone, desktop computer, tablet, etc.). Of course, access to information is based on security levels that are built into the system, even though the applications are hosted externally.

SaaS is a kind of a turnkey technology solution, since the company does not have to develop or install the solution in-house, something that can take considerable time and resources, such as internal IT experts. It is often the next technological step for companies that want to move away from human resource information systems (HRIS), used exclusively by HR and payroll staff, and toward human resource management systems (HRMS) which allow all employees and managers in the organization to access security-controlled information in a self-service fashion. For an expatriate in Singapore, it means being able to check one's paycheque online anytime anywhere in the world, or to file a monthly expense report. For managers, information from any internal system can then be included in expense reporting mechanisms when it comes time to track the expatriate assignment at head office. Financial data and other information can also be incorporated into the overall SaaS chosen, like any self-managed enterprise-wide system (ERP), and once employee or other data is loaded into the system, maintenance and updates are completely managed by the vendor off-site.

SaaS systems fill a gap that existed when managing expatriate groups since there was little to choose from other than localized payroll systems and expensive broad enterprise wide platforms. One example cited by researchers at the Forum for Expatriate Management (FEM) is that of changing tax laws, which can create compliance risks when there are multiple systems to manage. However, with a SaaS, if a certain country's tax laws change, the code base used for payments gets entered once by the system administrator and is then available in real time whenever users access it around the world. The system also reduces the huge challenges of trying to keep track of where employees are in the world, where they will be paid, and what the tax withholding and reporting requirements are in their current location. FEM describes SaaS as a kind of miracle to clear away expatriate chaos, saying, "Having a standardized platform from which the latest data in local languages and currencies can be extracted enables businesses to become more efficient, generate useful reports, control costs and better understand statistical norms such as where expatriates are and how much the company is spending."

A global survey of HR service delivery and technology done in 2010 by Towers Watson of 456 organizations (half of which were global or multinational firms) revealed that 52 percent of respondents are currently using SaaS, or are planning to. Current adopters enthuse about "quick implementation, better functionality, ease of managing on an ongoing basis, lower ongoing costs and never needing an upgrade." However, remaining survey participants list various concerns some might refer to as "cloud illusions," as their reason for resistance. These include data security concerns, having no ability to customize the system, and the need to rely on a single vendor. For such organizations SaaS may not be the answer, or perhaps it is simply a matter of finding the right vendor to overcome concerns. For managers around the world, however, SaaS sheds a new and promising light on the difficult task of managing and evaluating expatriate assignments.

SOURCE: Based on I. Turnbull, "The Evolution of HR Technology: 'Sexy' Is Out, Functionality Is In, *Canadian HR Reporter* (November 2, 2010), p. 14; S. Dobson, "Technology Eases Relocation Process, *Canadian HR Reporter* (May 17, 2010), 19.; and "Shaping the HR Service Delivery and Technology of Tomorrow... Today," *HR Service Delivery and Technology Survey Research Report*, p. 10, Towers Watson, 2010. NA-2010-16686.

THE IMPORTANCE OF PROCESS: PARTICIPATION AND COMMUNICATION

LO 4

Discuss the significance of process issues such as communication in compensation management.

Designing effective compensation programs and solving problems related to compensation are complex matters that typically require collecting, sorting, and reporting a great deal of information before deciding what to do. For this reason, compensation management has been criticized for following the simplistic belief that "if the right technology can be developed, the right answers will be found."[23] In reality, however, any given pay decision is rarely obvious to the diverse groups that make up organizations, regardless of the decision's technical merit or basis in theory. Of course, it is important when changing pay practices to decide which program or combination of programs makes most sense, but how such decisions are made and how they are communicated also matter.[24]

Participation

Employee participation in compensation decision making can take many forms. For example, employees may serve on task forces charged with recommending and designing a pay program. They may also be asked to help communicate and explain its rationale. This is particularly true in the case of job evaluation as well as many of the programs discussed in the next chapter. To date, employee participation in pay-level decisions remains fairly rare.

It is important to distinguish between participation by those affected by policies and those who must actually implement the policies. Managers are in the latter group (and often in the former group at the same time). As in other areas of human resource management, line managers are typically responsible for making policies work. Their intimate involvement in any change to existing pay practices is, of course, necessary.

Communication

A dramatic example of the importance of communication was found in a study of how an organization communicated pay cuts to its employees and the effects on theft rates and perceived equity.[25] Two organization units received 15 percent across-the-board pay cuts. A third unit received no pay cut and served as a control group. The reasons for the pay cuts were communicated in different ways to the two pay-cut groups. In the "adequate explanation" pay-cut group, management provided a significant amount of information to explain its reasons for the pay cut and also expressed significant remorse. In contrast, the "inadequate explanation" group received much less information and no indication of remorse. The control group received no pay cut (and thus no explanation).

The control group and the two pay-cut groups began with the same theft rates and equity perceptions. After the pay cut, the theft rate was 54 percent higher in the "adequate explanation" group than in the control group. But in the "inadequate explanation" condition, the theft rate was 141 percent higher than in the control group. In this case communication had a large, independent effect on employees' attitudes and behaviours.

Communication is likely to have other important effects. We know, for example, as emphasized by equity theory, that not only actual pay but also the comparison standard influences employee attitudes.[26] Under two-tier wage plans, employees doing the same jobs are paid two different rates, depending on when they were hired. Moreover, the lower-paid employees do not necessarily move into the higher-paying tier. Common sense might suggest that the lower-paid employees would be less satisfied, but this is not necessarily true. In fact, a study by Peter Cappelli and Peter Sherer found that the lower-paid employees were more satisfied on average.[27] Apparently, those in the lower tier used different (lower) comparison standards than those in the higher tier. The lower-tier employees compared their jobs with unemployment or lower-paying jobs they had managed to avoid. As a result, they were more satisfied, despite being paid less money for the same work. This finding does not mean that two-tier wage plans are likely to be embraced by an organization's workforce. It does, however, support equity theory through its focus on the way employees compare their pay with other jobs and the need for managers to take this into consideration. Employees increasingly have access to salary survey information, which is likely to result in more comparisons and thus a greater need for effective communication.

Managers play the most crucial communication role because of their day-to-day interactions with their employees. Therefore, they must be prepared to explain why the pay structure is designed as it is and to judge whether employee concerns about the structure need to be addressed with changes to the structure. One common issue is deciding when a job needs to be reclassified because of substantial changes in its content. If an employee takes on more responsibility, she will often ask the manager for assistance in making the case for increased pay for the job.

Learn more about communication regarding compensation online with Connect.

LO 5

Describe new developments in the design of pay structures.

CURRENT CHALLENGES

Problems with Job-Based Pay Structures

The approach taken in this chapter, that of defining pay structures in terms of jobs and their associated responsibilities, remains the most widely used in practice. However, job-based pay structures have a number of potential limitations.[28] First, they may encourage bureaucracy. The job description sets out specific tasks and activities for which the incumbent is responsible and, by implication, those for which the incumbent is not responsible. Although this facilitates performance evaluation and control by the manager, it can also encourage a lack of flexibility and a lack of initiative on the part of employees: "Why should I do that? It's not in my job description." Second, the structure's hierarchical nature reinforces a top-down decision-making and information flow as well as status differentials, which do not lend themselves to taking advantage of the skills and knowledge of those closest to production. Third, the bureaucracy required to generate and update job descriptions and job evaluations can become a barrier to change because wholesale changes to job descriptions can involve a tremendous amount of time and cost. Fourth, the job-based pay structure may not reward desired behaviours, particularly in a rapidly changing environment where the knowledge, skills, and abilities needed yesterday may not be very helpful today and tomorrow. Fifth, the emphasis on job levels and status differentials encourages promotion-seeking behaviour but may discourage lateral employee movement because employees are reluctant to accept jobs that are not promotions or that appear to be steps down.

Responses to Problems with Job-Based Pay Structures

Delayering and Banding   In response to the problems caused by job-based pay structures, some organizations are **delayering,** or reducing the number of job levels to achieve more flexibility in job assignments and in assigning merit increases. These broader groupings of jobs are also known as *broad bands*. Table 8.10 shows how banding might work for a small sample of jobs. IBM's change to broad bands in the late 90s was accompanied by a change away from a point-factor job evaluation system to a more streamlined approach to evaluating jobs, as Figure 8.3 shows.

Delayering
Reducing the number of job levels within an organization.

Table 8.10 Example of Pay Bands

TRADITIONAL STRUCTURE		BANDED STRUCTURE	
GRADE	TITLE	BAND	TITLE
14	Senior accountant	6	Senior accountant
12	Accountant III		
10	Accountant II	5	Accountant
8	Accountant I		

SOURCE: P. LeBlanc, *Perspectives in Total Compensation 2,* no. 3 (March 1992), pp. 1–6. Used with permission of the National Practice Director, Sibson & Company, Inc.

FIGURE 8.3 IBM's Simplified Job Evaluation Approach

Below is an abbreviated schematic illustration of the new—and simple—IBM job evaluation approach:

POSITION REFERENCE GUIDE

Band	Skills required	Leadership/Contribution	Scope/Impact
1			
2			
3			
4			
5			
6			
7			
8			
9			
10			

Factors: Leadership/Contribution

Band 06: Understand the mission of the professional group and vision in own area of competence.
Band 07: Understand the departmental mission and vision.
Band 08: Understand departmental/functional mission and vision.
Band 09: Has vision of functional or unit mission.
Band 10: Has vision of overall strategies.

Both the bands and the approach are global. In the U.S., bands 1–5 are nonexempt; bands 6–10 are exempt. Each cell in the table contains descriptive language about key job characteristics. Position descriptions are compared to the chart and assigned to bands on a "best fit" basis. There are no points or scoring mechanisms. Managers assign employees to bands by selecting a position description that most closely resembles the work being done by an employee using an online position description library.

That's it!

SOURCE: A. S. Richter, "Paying the People in Black at Big Blue," *Compensation and Benefits Review,* May–June 1998, pp. 51–59. Copyright © 1998 by Sage Publications, Inc. Reprinted with permission of Sage Publications, Inc.

At the same time, IBM greatly reduced the bureaucratic nature of the system, going from 5,000 job titles and 24 salary grades to a simpler 1,200 jobs and 10 bands. Within their broad bands, managers were given more discretion to reward high performers and to choose pay levels that were competitive in the market for talent.

One possible disadvantage of delayering and banding is a reduced opportunity for promotion. Therefore, organizations need to consider what they will offer employees instead. In addition, to the extent that there are separate ranges within bands, the new structure may not represent as dramatic a change as it might appear. These distinctions can easily become just as entrenched as they were under the old system. Broad bands, with their greater spread between pay minimums and maximums, can also lead to weaker budgetary control and rising labour costs. Alternatively, the greater spread can permit managers to better recognize high performers with high pay. It can also permit the organization to reward employees for learning.

Paying the Person: Pay for Skill, Knowledge, and Competency   A second, related response to job-based pay structure problems has been to move away from linking pay to jobs and toward building structures based on individual characteristics such as skill or knowledge.[29] Competency-based pay is similar but usually refers to a plan that covers **exempt employees** (such as managers), or employees not covered by the Employment Standards Act in their jurisdiction. The basic idea is that if you want employees to learn more skills and become more flexible in the jobs they perform, you should pay them to do it. (See Chapter 6 for a discussion of the implications of skill-based pay systems on training.) However, according to Gerald Ledford Ph.D., a recognized authority on human capital issues (including compensation), it is "a fundamental departure" from job-based pay because employees are now "paid for the skills they are capable of using, not for the job they are performing at a particular point in time."[30].

Skill-based pay systems, or pay based on the skills employees acquire and are capable of using, seem to fit well with the increased breadth and depth of skill that changing technology continues to bring.[31] For example, in a production environment, workers might be expected not only to operate machines but also to take responsibility for maintenance and troubleshooting, quality control, even modifying computer programs.[32] Toyota concluded years ago that "none of the specialists [e.g., quality inspectors, many managers, and foremen] beyond the assembly worker was actually adding any value to the car. What's more ... assembly workers could probably do most of the functions of specialists much better because of their direct acquaintance with conditions on the line."[33]

In other words, an important potential advantage of skill-based pay is its contribution to increased worker flexibility, which in turn facilitates the decentralization of decision making to those who are most knowledgeable. It also provides the opportunity for leaner staffing levels because employee turnover or absenteeism can now be covered by current employees who are multiskilled.[34] In addition, multiskilled employees are important in cases where different products require different manufacturing processes or where supply shortages or other problems call for adaptive or flexible responses—characteristics typical, for example, of many newer so-called advanced manufacturing environments (such as flexible manufacturing and just-in-time systems).[35] More generally, it has been suggested that skill-based plans also contribute to a climate of learning and adaptability and give employees a broader view of how the organization functions. Both changes should contribute to better use of employees' know-how and ideas. Consistent with the advantages just noted, a field study found that a change to a skill-based plan led to better quality and lower labour costs in a manufacturing plant.[36]

Of course, skill-based and competency-based approaches also have potential disadvantages.[37] First, although the plan will likely enhance skill acquisition, the organization may find it a challenge to use the new skills effectively. Without careful planning, it may find itself with large new labour costs but little payoff. In other words, if skills change, work design must change as quickly to take full advantage. Second, if pay growth is based entirely on skills, problems may arise if employees "top out" by acquiring

Exempt Employees
Employees who are not covered by the Employment Standards Act. Exempt employees are not eligible for overtime pay.

Skill-Based Pay
Pay based on the skills employees acquire and are capable of using.

all the skills too quickly, leaving no room for further pay growth. (Of course, this problem can also afflict job-based systems.) Third, and somewhat ironically, skills-based plans may generate a large bureaucracy—usually a criticism of job-based systems. Training programs need to be developed. Skills must be described, measured, and assigned monetary values. Certification tests must be developed to determine whether an employee has acquired a certain skill. Finally, as if the challenges in obtaining market rates under a job-based system were not enough, there is almost no body of knowledge regarding how to price combinations of skills (versus jobs) in the marketplace. Obtaining comparison data from other organizations will be difficult until skill-based plans become more widely used.

Can the Canadian Labour Force Compete?

LO 6

Explain where Canada stands from an international perspective on pay issues.

We often hear that Canadian labour costs are simply too high to allow Canadian companies to compete effectively with companies in other countries. The average hourly labour costs (cash and benefits) for manufacturing production workers in Canada and in other advanced industrialized and newly industrialized countries are given in Table 8.11 in U.S. dollars:[38]

Based solely on a cost approach, it would perhaps make sense to try to shift many types of production from a country such as Germany to other countries, particularly the newly industrialized countries. Would this be a good idea? Not necessarily. There are several factors to consider.

Instability of Country Differences in Labour Costs   First, note that relative labour costs are very unstable over time. For example, in 1985, Canadian labour costs were (10.95/9.57) or 14 percent greater than those of (West) Germany. But by 1990, the situation was reversed significantly, with (West) German labour costs exceeding those of Canada by (21.53/15.95), or 35 percent, and remaining higher. Did German employers suddenly become more generous while Canadian

Table 8.11   Average Hourly Labour Costs (Cash and Benefits), Manufacturing Production Workers in Canada and Other Industrialized Countries

	1985	1990	1995	2000	2005	2007
Industrialized						
Canada	$10.95	$15.95	$16.10	$16.04	$23.82	$28.91
United States	13.01	14.77	17.19	19.76	23.65	24.59
Czech Republic				2.83	6.11	8.20
Germany[a]	9.57	21.53	30.26	23.38	33.00	37.66
France	7.52	15.49	20.01	15.70	24.63	28.57
Japan	6.43	12.64	23.82	22.27	21.76	19.75
Newly industrialized						
Mexico	1.60	1.80	1.51	2.08	2.63	2.92
Hong Kong[b]	1.73	3.20	4.82	5.63	5.65	5.78
South Korea	1.25	3.82	7.29	8.19	13.56	16.02
China					0.62[c]	0.81

[a] West Germany for 1985 and 1990 data.
[b] Special Administrative Region of China.
[c] 2006

employers clamped down on pay growth? Not exactly. Because all our figures are expressed in U.S. dollars, currency exchange rates influence such comparisons, and these exchange rates often fluctuate significantly from year to year. For example, in 1985, when German labour costs were around 86 percent of those in Canada, the Canadian dollar was worth 2.14 German marks. But in 1990 the Canadian dollar was worth 1.38 German marks. With the difference in the Canadian dollar to the German mark, labour costs in Canada were lower when measured "apples to apples" in U.S. currency. In any event, relative to countries such as Germany, Canadian labour costs are now a bargain; this explains, in part, decisions by Brose, a German family-owned international automotive supplier, to set up its first Canadian production facilities in London, Ontario, in 2005, where labour costs were lower than Germany's by a substantial amount (30 percent). The euro, Germany's current currency, has fluctuated from €1 = CDN$1.43 at the end of 2000, to €1 = CDN$1.30 by the end of 2005 and back up to €1= CDN$1.37 by early 2011, reinforcing the higher labour cost in Germany relative to Canada (when expressed in Canadian dollars).[39]

Skill Levels Second, the quality and productivity of national labour forces can vary dramatically. This is an especially important consideration in comparisons between labour costs in industrialized countries like Canada and developing countries such as Mexico. For example, in 2010 the high school graduation rate for individuals 25–64 in Canada was 87 percent versus 34 percent in Mexico.[40] Thus, lower labour costs may reflect the lower average skill level of the workforce; certain types of skilled labour may be less available in low-labour cost countries. On the other hand, any given company needs only enough skilled employees for its own operations. Some companies have found that low labour costs do not necessarily preclude high quality.

Productivity Third, and most directly relevant, are data on comparative productivity and unit labour costs, essentially meaning labour cost per hour divided by productivity per hour worked. One indicator of productivity is gross domestic product (or total output of the economy) per person, adjusted for differences in purchasing power. On this measure, Canada fares well. These figures (in U.S. dollars) for 2009 are represented in Figure 8.4. The combination of lower labour costs and higher productivity translates into lower unit labour costs in Canada than in Japan and western Europe.[41]

Nonlabour Considerations Fourth, any consideration of where to locate production cannot be based on labour considerations alone. For example, although the average hourly labour cost in Country A may be $15 versus $10 in Country B, if labour costs are 30 percent of total operating costs and nonlabour operating costs are roughly the same, then the total operating costs might be $65 (50 + 15) in Country A and $60 (50 + 10) in Country B. Although labour costs in Country B are 33 percent less, total operating costs are only 7.7 percent less. This may not be enough to compensate for differences in skills and productivity, customer wait time, transportation costs, taxes, and so on. Further, the direct labour component of many products, particularly high-tech products (such as electronic components), may often be 5 percent or less. Thus the effect on product price-competitiveness may be insignificant.[42]

In fact, an increasing number of organizations have decided that it is more important to focus on nonlabour factors in deciding where to locate production. Product development speed may be greater when manufacturing is physically close to the design group. Quick response to customers (such as making a custom replacement product) is difficult when production facilities are on the other side of the world. Inventory levels can be dramatically reduced through the use of manufacturing methods like just-in-time production, but suppliers need to be in close physical proximity.

In addition to these considerations, the "Competing Through Globalization" box notes some concerns that should be examined in advance by firms that are considering offshoring jobs (including professional or knowledge worker jobs) primarily to reduce labour costs.

FIGURE 8.4 Gross Domestic Product per Person, 2009 OECD International comparison (USD)

Bar chart showing GDP per person (USD) by country:

- Average OECD: ~$31,000
- Mexico: ~$12,000
- Italy: ~$29,000
- France: ~$32,000
- Japan: ~$32,000
- Germany: ~$34,000
- United Kingdom: ~$34,500
- Canada: ~$37,500
- United States: ~$44,500

SOURCE: OECD in Figures, 2009 Edition as shown in Statistics Canada, "Canada at a Glance 2010, p. 13. Catalogue no. 12-581-XIE (PDF) ISSN: 1701-5766, Minister of Industry, 2010 at www45.statcan.gc.ca/2009/cgco_2009_009-eng.htm (retrieved February 5, 2011).

Competing Through Globalization

The 80/20 Rule Applies When Starting Operations Offshore

In the past few years, some glaring truths have emerged that drive decision making within companies such as The Home Depot (featured in our opening vignette), Brose, and others we have mentioned in earlier chapters to choose carefully where they plan to expand next. For example, one Towers Perrin study describes how most areas of Europe are struggling against the tide of economic downturns. One survey indicated 70 to 80 percent of companies have implemented a hiring freeze, roughly two-thirds are freezing salaries, and over half are cutting costs through layoffs. At least one-third are also considering workforce reductions over the next three years. On the other hand, China and India continue with strong economic growth, with much, much lower effort expended on cost cutting and cost management practices listed above. For example, only 6 percent of Indian or Chinese companies plan to reduce their workforce in the next three years. As well, there is Brazil, which is also experiencing strong economic growth, although Brazilians are engaging in a considerable amount of cost management for their own reasons. Another study conducted by PriceWaterhouseCoopers reports that (using GDP as a measure) between 2002 and 2009, the BRIC (Brazil, Russia, India, China) emerging economies grew by 83 percent, compared to Asia (62 percent); CEE Europe (47 percent); the United States (12 percent); and Canada, Western Europe and the United Kingdom (all at around 9 percent). Such figures are attention grabbing if you're looking for ideas to drive profit. So if a company decides to follow the numbers, and start up operations in Brazil, China, or India, what kinds of compensation and severance issues might it find in such low-wage economies now?

Rapidly escalating salaries would be one guess. A quick snapshot from a survey of merit increases done by Towers Perrin in 2010 reveals that for employees who met expectations, base pay increases in Canada averaged around 2.8 percent, but were considerably higher in Brazil (4.1 percent), and China and India (8.8 percent). As well, Canadians exceeding or far exceeding their employer expectations could expect a raise of 4.0 or 5.6 percent respectively (or roughly another 1.5 percent for each additional level of rating). In Brazil, top performers could expect a raise of 7.6 or 10.9 percent, averaging another 3.5 percent for each hike in performance status. However in both India and China, top performers in both categories could expect to receive increases of 12.6 and 17.7 percent respectively, adding over 4 or 5 percent for each higher level of performance rating. Thus salaries are clearly a dynamic area in faster-growth economies and, given increasing tendencies for Chinese workers to demand their rights and even strike for higher wages and working conditions, further escalation in labour costs seems inevitable.

And as wages soar upward in low-wage economies what kinds of severance arrangements figure into the equation when it comes time to terminate poor performers in those same areas? "Wildly varying" is a good answer. Experts suggest that offshoring employers start by making sure they are clear on at least the key areas such as who can be dismissed, understanding the legal and correct process for termination, requirements for a signed release, as well as "other considerations" such as local labour laws that may be very different than those in Canada. As we have discussed, in Canada termination is highly regulated under the Canada Labour Code and provincial Employment Standards Acts, and required notice periods and severance payments vary with length of employment and whether there is just cause for dismissal. In the larger hot economies, some laws exist, such as China's Labour Contract Law passed in January 2008, which attempted to increase the country's dismal record of human rights and dearth of employment laws. Now Chinese workers employed in the private sector must provide notice to their employers that they want to quit. Employers, on the other hand must provide 30 days' notice of termination to nonprobationary employees, and any termination indemnities are paid out on the basis of one month per year of service. Employers also cannot fire employees because of illness and there is a process for arbitration. India varies from this and Canadian law substantially, with employers having the power to terminate employment "at will," as in the United States (where employment-at-will policies state that either party in the employment relationship can terminate the employment relationship at any time regardless of cause). Despite this, however, a mandatory notice period is still required and it is illegal to terminate an employee on discriminatory grounds. In Brazil, employers must provide 30 days' notice and are responsible for accrued vacation, vacation bonus, Christmas bonus, and 50 percent of the balance accumulated during the individual's employment with the firm in an employee's severance fund (known as the Unemployment Guarantee Fund [FGTS]). Such "snapshots" of termination and severance pay requirements are just that, of course, but they help to illustrate the complexities of moving operations into countries where western employers have little or no previous experience. Needless to say, the rising cost of labour and a host of other issues, employment law, taxation, and cost-of-living issues leave much to be explored before venturing forth to gather riches.

SOURCES: Based on "Creating a Sustainable Rewards and Talent Management Model, 2010 Global Talent Management and Rewards Study, p. 3, Towers Watson, 2010; G. Ayraam, A. Ishak, and T. Appleyard, "Terminating Employees around the World," *Canadian HR Reporter* (April 6, 2009), p. 12; G. Waggott, "How to Say 'You're Fired' in 7 Languages, *Canadian HR Reporter* (April 5, 2010), p. 15; and Managing People in a Changing World, Key Trends in Human Capital—A Global Perspective—2010," p. 8, PriceWaterhouseCoopers, 2010.; International Labour Organizaiton: Brazil Country Summary: Profiles of National Legislation, at www.ilo.org/public/english/dialogue/ifpdial/info/termination/countries/brazil.htm (retrieved July 17, 2011).

LO 7

Explain the reasons for the controversy over executive pay.

Executive Pay

The issue of executive pay has received widespread attention in the press although there are very few top executives and their compensation accounts for only a small share of an organization's total labour costs. However, top executives have a disproportionate ability to influence organization performance, so decisions about their compensation are critical. For example, in its proxy circular released in February 2011, the TD Bank Group announced that Group President and Chief Executive Officer Ed Clark received an 8 percent increase in 2010, taking his total pay to $11.4 million. By the same token, the bank made a record profit of $4.64 billion and purchased the auto industry financier Chrysler Financial. This was a major expansion of the bank's strategy to push further into the United States, where it has a substantial presence in the retail banking and lending business. A few days later, the bank announced an increase in its quarterly dividend, the first in three years.[43]

Executive pay can also be symbolic because top executives are highly visible. What happens with their pay can influence the tone or culture of the organization. For example, Clark's increase correlates well with the bank's excellent performance in 2010, and the reward for top performance is clear. However, if the top executive's pay seems unrelated to the organization's performance, staying high even when business is poor, employees may not understand why some of their own pay should be at risk and depend on how the organization is performing.

How much do executives make? Table 8.12 on page 332 provides some data. Long-term compensation, typically in the form of stock plans, is the major component of CEO pay, which means that CEO pay varies with the performance of the stock market (see the "Change in S&P 500" column). Table 8.13 on page 332 lists a few of the top-paid Canadian CEOs.

TD Bank Group CEO Ed Clark made $11.4 million in 2010, a raise of 8 percent over 2009. The bank also reported profits of $4.64 billion and also substantially expanded its retail banking and lending business outside Canada.

Table 8.12 CEO Compensation

	CEO PAY							
YEAR	SALARY PLUS BONUS	STOCK GAINS	OTHER	TOTAL PAY	CHANGE IN CEO PAY	CHANGE IN S&P 500	WORKER PAY*	CEO PAY/ WORKER PAY**
2010	$2 million	$2 million	$2 million	$ 8 million	−27%	11	$33,429	239
2009	2 million	5 million	3 million	11 million	−15%	23	32,089	342
2008	3 million	6 million	3 million	13 million	−18%	−38	31,617	405
2007	4 million	8 million	4 million	16 million	34	5	30,682	508
2006	4 million	6 million	2 million	12 million	3	16	29,529	393
2005	3 million	6 million	2 million	11 million	51	5	28,305	399
2004	3 million	3 million	2 million	8 million	6	11	27,513	273
2003	3 million	3 million	1 million	7 million	−37	29	26,939	264
2002	3 million	7 million	1 million	11 million	−9	−22	26,351	429
2001	3 million	8 million	2 million	12 million	5	−12	25,677	483
2000	3 million	6 million	4 million	13 million	56	−9	25,013	524
1999	2 million	3 million	1 million	8 million	31	21	24,084	349
1995	2 million	1 million	1 million	3 million	25	38	20,804	144
1990	2 million	1 million	0.2 million	2 million	4	−3	18,187	132

SOURCES: CEO pay data from *Forbes* magazine website; Worker pay data from U.S. Bureau of Labour Statistics, *Employment and Earnings* (December 2010), Vol. 57, No. 12.

Through the year 1999, *Forbes* data pertained to the 800 largest U.S. companies. Beginning with year 2000, data pertain to the 500 largest U.S. companies.

*Worker pay data pertain to production workers in mining and logging and manufacturing, construction workers in construction, and nonsupervisory workers in the service-providing industries.

**Ratio of CEO pay to hourly employee pay.

Table 8.13 Highest-Paid Canadian CEOs, 2010 Compensation Ranking

CEO AND ORGANIZATION	TOTAL COMPENSATION
Edward Sampson, Niko Resources Ltd.	$16.5 million
Donald Walker, Magna International Inc.	16.2 million
Siegfried Wolf, Magna International Inc.	16.0 million
Richard Waugh, Bank of Nova Scotia	13.8 million
Steve Laut, Canadian National Resources Ltd.	13.1 million
Gordon Nixon, Royal Bank of Canada	11.9 million
William Doyle, Potash Corp. of Saskatchewan	11.6 million
Edmund Clark, Toronto-Dominion Bank	11.4 million
Glenn Chamandy, Gildan Activewear Inc.	11.2 million
Ronald Pantin, Pacific Rubiales Energy Corp.	11.1 million

SOURCE: J. McFarland, "Executive Compensation 2009: The Complete List," *Globe and Mail Update*, June 22, 2009; 2011, *The Globe and Mail*, Inc.

As Table 8.14 shows, Canadian top executives are well paid on a comparative basis internationally, but average roughly half that of U.S. executives, and slightly below France and Germany. (These figures are lower than those from business magazines such as *Forbes* because the latter reports refer only to larger companies.) The fact that the differential between top executive pay and that of an average manufacturing worker is so much higher in the United States than in some other countries has been described as creating a "trust gap"—that is, in employees' minds, a "frame of mind that mistrusts senior management's intentions, doubts its competence, and resents its self-congratulatory pay." For example, if comparing the Total Remuneration Multiple of the United States (39) to the other developed countries in Table 8.14, in Canada the differential is much lower (24) and on a par with France (23) and Germany (20). The differential issue becomes especially salient when many of the same companies with high executive pay simultaneously engage in layoffs or other forms of employment reduction. Employees ask, "If the company needs to cut costs, why not cut executive pay rather than our jobs?"[44] The issue is one of perceived fairness. One study reported that business units with higher pay differentials between executives and rank-and-file employees had lower customer satisfaction, which was speculated to result from employees' perceptions of inequity coming through in reduced levels of customer relations.[45]

Learn more about executive pay online with Connect.

LEGAL CONSTRAINTS ON COMPENSATION

So far we have discussed how employer policy implications influence the design of compensation to ensure that it supports and aligns with corporate strategy. However, as with all other areas of human resources management discussed in this textbook, employers must be aware of and comply with a variety of laws and regulations that govern compensation of employees. We turn our attention now

LO 8

Describe the regulatory framework for employee compensation.

Table 8.14   Total Remuneration of CEOs in Selected Countries (U.S. dollars)

COUNTRY	CEO TOTAL REMUNERATION	CEO/MANUFACTURING EMPLOYEE TOTAL REMUNERATION MULTIPLE
United States	$2,160,000	39
Canada	1,100,000	24
Mexico	1,000,000	60
Brazil	849,000	60
Argentina	431,000	45
France	1,200,000	23
Germany	1,180,000	20
China	211,000	36
India	291,000	51
Japan	543,000	11
Korea	584,000	23

Notes: Data based on a company with $500 million in sales; total remuneration includes salary, bonus, company contributions, perquisites, and long-term incentives. Table 8.14 values are based on much smaller companies than those in Table 8.12, thus explaining the table differences.

SOURCE: Towers Perrin, "2005–2006 Worldwide Total Remuneration," Stamford, CT, 2006.

Competing Through Sustainability

Learning the Hard Way about Employment Standards

When $30,000-a-year teller Dara Fresco decided she was going to go after her employer CIBC for $50,000 in unpaid overtime she felt she was owed after ten years of working for the bank, she found a lawyer willing to help her. Ultimately joined by a number of coworkers who shared her sentiments, she launched a class-action suit against the bank for $600 million. The plaintiffs claimed (1) the bank's overtime polices were unlawful and violated the Canada Labour Code; (2) completion of daily work frequently required employees to work overtime; and (3) CIBC's overtime policy dictated in order for overtime to be paid, prior approval was needed from one's manager. When Fresco's lawyer Douglas Elliott announced the lawsuit at a news conference, he described it as "groundbreaking" and "the largest unpaid overtime class action suit in Canadian history." Indeed, ground was broken, as at least four more overtime class-action suits followed in the wake of *Fresco v. Canadian Imperial Bank of Commerce*. KPMG, faced with similar allegations, settled for $10 million, but CIBC continues to fight back, as does the similarly accused Bank of Nova Scotia ($300 million) and CN Rail ($250 million).

As legions of lawyers for all parties pore over company records on overtime policies, work schedules, and records of overtime payments, the defendants struggle to disprove such allegations, while judges make wildly opposite decisions regarding certification. According to a legal view article authored by Lisa Bolton, a lawyer with a management-oriented employment and labour law firm in Toronto, that's because certification of a class action rests on the ability to "satisfy the court [that] common issues exist among proposed class members that can be determined on a class basis rather than an individual basis." Plaintiffs are also obliged to prove that a class action is the most efficient way to resolve the situation for everyone. The Ontario Supreme Court dismissed the case against CIBC based on the fact Fresco et al failed to satisfy commonality requirements. The judge said unpaid overtime was "not caused by an illegal policy," but rather because the bank failed (independent of the policy) "to pay for overtime hours that were either required or permitted to be worked." In other words, the bank failed to properly apply its overtime policy in individual circumstances. However, Scotiabank's policy on overtime was viewed to create a systemic barrier that applied to all Scotiabank employees in the class action, regardless of their individual circumstances, and so certification was granted. The main difference between the two was that CIBC's overtime policy allowed for approval of overtime hours *after they had been worked* even where there were extenuating circumstances. Regardless, Fresco (as lead plaintiff) planned to appeal the noncertification decision, and as of January 2011 no settlement had occurred. In the meantime, the suits against CN Rail and Scotiabank rage on.

In an attempt to understand how broad the problem of unpaid overtime might be (and hence how many CEOs might be looking over their shoulders), the Conference Board surveyed 267 Canadian organizations (in May 2008 and March 2009) of which 130 responded about their overtime practices. While 77 percent of respondents have written formal overtime compensation policies, 20 percent have only informal polices and 3 percent have no policies at all. That means that almost a quarter of respondents may be vulnerable to lawsuits. The survey also found that 70 percent of participants used job title as the basis for overtime eligibility, leaving the onus on the employer to prove that someone with "manager" in his or her title is actually performing as a manager, and thus exempt from overtime. Although around 75 percent of respondents use systems to track employee hours and 66 percent track amounts of overtime paid, only 38 percent indicated that overtime policies and procedures were tightly controlled, or that "overtime is an important issue and is squarely on managements' radar."

Employers who don't manage overtime responsibly could be in for a shock. Lawyers Meighan Ferris-Miles and Alison Adam of Shields, O'Donnell MacKillop in Toronto offer the following advice to stay out of trouble: (1) Be sure there is a mechanism in place for employees to get overtime approved *after the fact*—pre-authorization isn't always practical when overtime must be worked. Further, to avoid the spectre of establishing "common issue" among plaintiffs, make sure (2) policies on overtime allow for individual application and assessment; (3) be sure overtime policies are applied consistently; (4) analyze eligibility requirements and know the law on eligibility; (5) maintain accurate timesheets and have employees sign off on hours worked; and (6) create a system for authorizing and monitoring overtime and use discipline to reign in unauthorized overtime.

The class-action lawsuits currently plaguing several top employers in Canada remind us of the role that employment standards play in defining the timbre of the employment relationship. The problems encountered by KPMG, CIBC, CN, and Scotiabank remind us all of our duty to know and understand employment legislation, create sound policies and procedures that conform with the law, and train managers in their roles so that the law is upheld. If nothing else, class actions remind us that there is a big price to be paid for carelessness or neglect when it comes to overtime.

SOURCES: T. Cohen, "Teller Launches CIBC Suit," *The Toronto Star*, (June 6, 2007) at www.thestar.com/business/article/222030; S. Klie, "Overtime a Growing Concern; Conference Board Report," *Canadian HR Reporter* (September 7, 2009), Vol. 22, Iss. 15, p. 3; L. Bolton, "Making Sense of Overtime Class Actions," *Canadian HR Reporter* (June 14, 2010), Vol. 23, Iss. 12, p. 5; M. Ferris-Miles and A. Adam, "Preventing Overtime Class Actions," *HR Professional* (January 2011), Vol. 28, No. 1, p. 19; K. Thorpe, "Working 9 to 9: Overtime Practices in Canadian Organizations, Conference Board of Canada Briefing, August 2009, pp. 1–14.

---

to the network of provincial, federal, and territorial laws that affect employees and which employers must integrate into the design and implementation of all pay practices (including benefits, which will be discussed in Chapter 10.)

Employment and Labour Standards

In Canada, the Canada Labour Code defines the labour rights and responsibilities in all federally regulated businesses such as banks, marine shipping, transportation and communications systems, radio and television broadcasting, Crown corporations, fisheries, and many First Nation activities. The code covers 10 percent of Canadian workers. Employment standards for the remaining 90 percent of Canadian workers are defined by Employment Standards Acts enacted in each province or territory to ensure fairness in the workplace. The Canada Labour Code and each employment standards act come under the responsibility of either the Labour Program of Human Resources and Skills Development Canada (in partnership with Transport Canada and the National Energy Board) or the specific provincial Ministry of Labour, respectively. Both also provide information and guidance to employers through employment standards programs, and establish minimum standards employers must adhere to regarding **minimum wage**, hours of work, overtime, record keeping, vacation entitlement, public holidays, termination of employment and severance pay, pregnancy, parental and personal leave, and more. There are variations (and overlaps) among these laws and hence employers must ensure they are familiar and up to date with labour laws that apply to all aspects of the business

Minimum Wage
The lowest hourly wage an employer is legally allowed to pay an employee in the relevant province or territory of Canada for which such wages are determined.

in every location across Canada, and with the revisions that occur from time to time. For example, between 2008 to 2010, the minimum wage in most provinces and territories increased several times (e.g., three times in Ontario), but each province or territory enacted each such increase according to the unique conditions and designated needs of each province or territory.[46]

Finally, employers must take care in deciding whether a person working on their premises is classified as an employee or independent contractor.

Human Rights Legislation and Pay Equity

You will recall our explanation in Chapter 3 of various layers of human rights legislation that impose responsibility on employers to provide human resources systems and practices that are fair to all employees, and which integrate the principles of both employment equity and pay equity. Employers must also prevent both direct and indirect discrimination of any kind (based on sexual orientation, gender, religion etc.), and be especially vigilant with respect to the four designated groups who have been traditionally and persistently disadvantaged in the workplace—women, visible minorities, Aboriginal people, and individual with disabilities. This means human resources professionals and managers must ensure equitable treatment to all employees with respect to employment outcomes, such as all forms of compensation and benefits, as well as consideration for promotional and developmental opportunities that are indirectly related to compensation and benefits. Recall that the foundation for nondiscriminatory employment practices of all kinds (human resources planning, performance appraisals, training etc.) resides in eliminating systemic discrimination through a bias-free job analysis process (and/or job demands analysis) that in turn yields bias-free job descriptions. Remember that overstated job specifications set up unnecessary barriers that prevent individuals from accessing jobs, promotions, training and development, and the compensation that accompanies such opportunities. However, achieving equity requires constant vigilance, and issues such as closing the gender wage gap can be stubbornly elusive despite the best efforts of employers, the government, and advocacy and research conducted by special interest groups such as the National Association of Women and the Law (NAWL/ANFD). A Pay Equity Fact Sheet on NAWL's website points out that "more than 25 years after the adoption of the Canadian Human Rights Act, women working full-time still earn 71% of men's salaries, regardless of our age, occupation or education. For women of colour, Aboriginal women and women with a disability, the wage gap is even greater."[47]

Nevertheless, since the Pay Equity Act applies to all public-sector employers that are not federally regulated, and all private-sector employers with 10 or more employees that are not federally regulated, employers should make every effort to implement pay equity in their organizations. Thus employers must ensure that "jobs be evaluated and work mostly or traditionally done by women be compared to work mostly or traditionally done by men. If jobs are of **comparable worth,** then female jobs (such as nurse, teacher, childcare worker) must be paid at least the same as male jobs (such as truck driver, shipper, firefighter)."[48] Finally, jobs must evaluated based on the level of skill, effort, responsibility, and working conditions required to do the work.[49]

As with any regulatory influence, employers have concerns that employment and pay equity regulation obstructs market forces, which, according to economic theory, provide the most efficient means of pricing and allocating people to jobs. In theory, moving away from a reliance on market forces would result in some jobs being paid too much and others too little, leading to an oversupply of workers for the former and an undersupply for the latter. In addition, some empirical evidence suggests that a comparable worth policy would not have much impact on the relative earnings of women in the private sector.[50] One limitation of such a policy is that it targets single employers, ignoring that men and women tend to work for different employers.[51] To the extent that segregation

Comparable Worth
A public policy that advocates remedies for any undervaluation of women's jobs (also called pay equity).

by employer contributes to pay differences between men and women, comparable worth would not be effective. In other words, to the extent that sex-based pay differences are the result of men and women working in different organizations with different pay levels, such policies will have little impact.

Some work has focused on pinpointing where women's pay falls behind that of men. One finding is that the gender pay gap is wider where bonus and incentive payments (not just base salary) are examined. Other evidence indicates that women lose ground at the time they are hired and actually do better once they are employed for some time.[52] One interpretation is that when actual job performance (rather than the limited general qualification information available on applicants) is used in decisions, women may be less likely to encounter unequal treatment. If so, more attention needs to be devoted to ensuring fair treatment of applicants and new employees.[53] Some believe the notion of a "glass ceiling," discussed in Chapter 6, which allows women and members of other designated groups to come only within sight of the top echelons of management, but not advance to them. You will recall that mentoring programs have been suggested as one means of improving access. Indeed, one study found that mentoring had a significant positive effect on the pay of both men and women, with women receiving a greater payoff in percentage terms than men.[54]

Other Legal Requirements

There are also a number of other laws and regulations employers must comply with regarding compensation that we will mention here in brief since they are covered more extensively in other chapters as indicated.

For example, as our many examples of bargaining in the auto sector illustrate throughout this text, unions have a tremendous influence on compensation levels due to collective bargaining and settlements that occur among unionized organizations. However, their influence also is felt by non-unionized organizations, which feel pressured to raise wages and benefits to compete with unionized external competitors. Industrial relations law is defined by the Canada Labour Code and also through various provincial and territorial labour relations codes, acts, and labour relations boards.

Employers have an obligation to match current employees' contributions to the Canada/Quebec Pension Plan,[55] which provides the foundation for a modest government pension for all working Canadians, and to design, administer, and fund private-sector employee pension plans under Canadian pension plan legislation.

The Employment Insurance Act also requires employers to match employee contributions that combine to support Canada's employment insurance benefits programs. Such programs support individuals with temporary income after they have lost their jobs through no fault of their own, during skills-upgrading programs; while on pregnancy, maternal, or parental leave; or while on compassionate leave.[56]

Finally, workers' compensation legislation in each province and territory provides a no-fault, employer-funded program to protect employees from "the financial hardships associated with work-related injuries and occupational diseases."[57]

Although all such legislation is covered in other areas of this textbook in greater detail, such as Chapter 3, Chapter 10, and Chapter 12, we mention them here since all contribute additional pressure to payroll costs and thus influence budget-driven decisions related to human resources planning, hiring, design of compensation and provision of employer-provided benefits. Of course, no discussion of strategic compensation would be complete without a thorough review of approaches to incent and recognize top performers or the issues and options that should be considered when designing an effective employee benefits program. We address these topics in the next two chapters.

A Look Back

We began this chapter by showing how The Home Depot hopes to take advantage of low labour costs in China, while at the same time capturing massive new market opportunities for home building products and services among the emerging middle class in that country. Annette Verschuren, president of the company in China, knows that it will be necessary to replicate the same quality and commitment of its North American workforce if the company is to expand successfully in China, and she began by taking steps to create links between compensation and performance among employees. We also saw other strategies to control labour costs in these difficult times. For example, some financial services firms are shifting work to places such as India. We have seen in this chapter that pay structure decisions influence the success of strategy execution by influencing not only labour costs, but also employee perceptions of equity, and the way that different structures provide flexibility and incentives for employees to learn and be productive.

Questions

1. What types of changes have the companies discussed in this chapter made to their pay structures and administrative processes to support execution of their business strategies?

2. Would other companies seeking to better align their pay structures with their business strategies benefit from imitating the changes made at these companies? Provide an example of a company you are familiar with, or might have worked for, as well as the changes you think could or should be made.

Summary

In this chapter we have discussed the nature of the pay structure and its component parts, the pay level, and the job structure. Equity theory suggests that social comparisons are an important influence on how employees evaluate their pay. Employees make external comparisons between their pay and the pay they believe is received by employees in other organizations. Such comparisons may have consequences for employee attitudes and retention. Employees also make internal comparisons between what they receive and what they perceive others within the organization are paid. These types of comparisons may have consequences for internal movement, cooperation, and attitudes (such as organization commitment). Such comparisons play an important role in the controversy over executive pay, as illustrated by the focus of critics on the ratio of executive pay to that of lower-paid workers.

Pay benchmarking surveys and job evaluation are two administrative tools widely used in managing the pay level and job structure components of the pay structure, which influence employee social comparisons. Pay surveys also permit organizations to benchmark their labour costs against other organizations. Globalization is increasing the need for organizations to be competitive in both their labour costs and productivity.

The nature of pay structures is undergoing a fundamental change in many organizations. One change is the move to fewer pay levels to reduce labour costs and bureaucracy. Second, some employers are shifting from paying employees for narrow jobs to giving them broader responsibilities and paying them to learn the necessary skills.

Finally, a theme that runs through this chapter and the next is the importance of process in managing employee compensation. How a new program is designed, decided on, implemented, and communicated is perhaps just as important as its core characteristics.

Key Terms

Benchmark jobs, 308
Benchmarking, 307
Comparable worth, 336
Compa-ratio, 317
Compensable factors, 308
Delayering, 324
Efficiency wage theory, 307

Exempt employees, 326
Job evaluation, 308
Job structure, 303
Minimum wage, 335
Nonbenchmark jobs, 308
Pay grades, 315

Pay level, 303
Pay policy line, 314
Pay structure, 303
Range spread, 315
Rate ranges, 308
Skill-based pay, 326

Discussion Questions

1. You have been asked to evaluate whether your organization's current pay structure makes sense in view of what competing organizations are paying. How would you determine what organizations to compare your organization with? Why might your organization's pay structure differ from those in competing organizations? What are the potential consequences of having a pay structure that is out of line relative to those of your competitors?

2. Top management has decided that the organization is too bureaucratic and has too many layers of jobs to compete effectively. Which innovative alternatives to the traditional "job-based" approach to employee compensation can you suggest? List the advantages and disadvantages of these new approaches.

3. If major changes of the type mentioned in question 2 are to be made, what types of so-called process issues need to be considered? Of what relevance is equity theory in helping to understand how employees might react to changes in the pay structure?

4. Are executive pay levels unreasonable in Canada? Why or why not?

5. Your company plans to build a new manufacturing plant but is undecided where to locate it. What factors would you consider in choosing in which country (or province) to build the plant?

6. You have been asked to evaluate whether a company's pay structure is fair to women, or if a gender wage gap exists. How would you go about answering this question?

Self-Assessment Exercise

Consider your current job or a job you had in the past. For each of the following pay characteristics, indicate your level of satisfaction by using the following scale: 1 = very dissatisfied; 2 = somewhat dissatisfied; 3 = neither satisfied nor dissatisfied; 4 = somewhat satisfied; 5 = very satisfied.

_____ 1. My take-home pay

_____ 2. My current pay

_____ 3. My overall level of pay

_____ 4. Size of my current salary

_____ 5. My benefit package

_____ 6. Amount the company pays toward my benefits

_____ 7. The value of my benefits

_____ 8. The number of benefits I receive

_____ 9. My most recent raise

_____ 10. Influence my manager has over my pay

_____ 11. The raises I have typically received in the past

_____ 12. The company's pay structure

_____ 13. Information the company gives about pay issues of concern to me

_____ 14. Pay of other jobs in the company

_____ 15. Consistency of the company's pay policies

_____ 16. How my raises are determined

_____ 17. Differences in pay among jobs in the company

_____ 18. The way the company administers pay

Scoring:

These 18 items measure four dimensions of pay satisfaction. Find your total score for each set of item numbers to measure your satisfaction with each dimension.

Pay Level Total of items 1, 2, 3, 4, 9, 11:   _____

Benefits Total of items 5, 6, 7, 8:   _____

Pay Structure and Administration Total of items 12, 13, 14, 15, 17, 18:   _____

Pay Raises Total of items 10, 11, 16:   _____

Considering the principles discussed in this chapter, how could your company improve (or how could it have improved) your satisfaction on each dimension?

SOURCE: Based on H. G. Heneman III and D. P. Schwab, "Pay Satisfaction: Its Multidimensional Nature and Measurement," *International Journal of Psychology* 20 (1985), pp. 129–141.

Exercising Strategy: Shifting HR Information at Selkirk College

When Selkirk College in Castlegar, B.C., realized the vendor it had selected as a third-party payroll provider had decided to discontinue its product line, it made a critical decision—to bring the organization's payroll back in-house. The decision would mean developing and keeping all records and deposit files at the college, but it would also eliminate the costs associated with an external payroll. It would also give the college greater control over the data. The college looked for a system that could combine payroll with its other human resources data into one seamless system. That meant selecting an appropriate human resource management information system (HRIS) that could handle 580 staff who were spread out across eight campuses in B.C. Special considerations included the Selkirk's complex contracts with three bargaining units, complicated by the fact that some employees over-lapped several bargaining units.

To find the right system, Selkirk's selection team, including Liana Zwick, HR coordinator for the college, approached Vancouver Island University located in Nanaimo, B.C., which had already been using the "industrial strength" StarGarden HR/Payroll program designed for very complex pay and benefit issues that challenge local government, education, health, and unionized industries. The product had also been adopted by the City of St. John in Newfoundland, and other public-sector organizations in North America and Australia over the company's 20-year history. The University was only too happy to demonstrate how its system worked and provide feedback. Since the University's setup was similar to Selkirk's, the team was able to make an informed decision, knowing the company would have an efficient, combined HR and payroll system that was also user friendly.

The implementation team took full advantage of vendor-provided webinars, teleconferencing meetings, and site visits as they reached critical points around loading information into the system, starting up, parallel runs, and going live. Detail is crucial to success of such a project and the payroll staff worked hard to set up accurate tables, accruals, and tax code information in the new system while still running payrolls in the old system. After start up, lots of troubleshooting, and analysis, the system was launched in January 2010. Staff on both the payroll and HR side are pleased with the results of all their work. Benefits of the new system include easier-to-access information, greater confidence in data output, expanded and customizable reporting options, new automated features, a new employee self-service portal, and a soon-to-be implemented managers' portal. Both the self-service features and the ability to tweak the system when needed with a remote test-site have the endorsement of both the HR and payroll teams.

Like most HRIS installations, it was a lot of work for all involved. Zwick suggests that perhaps the process should have begun with estimating more accurately in advance the resources available versus the amount of work that such a project demands. In retrospect, having backup resources lined up in advance might have allowed for greater focus on the tasks required, faster learning about the system, and better troubleshooting. It's also a good idea to spend considerable time-testing complex issues, and thinking outside the box when it comes to troubleshooting scenarios, so the end product runs as smoothly as possible.

SOURCES: Based on S. Dobson, "Selkirk College Migrates to In-house HRIS system to Handle Complex Payroll," *Canadian HR Reporter* (June 14, 2010), pp. 23–24; and "StarGarden HR/Payroll Suite" located at www.stargarden.com.

Questions

1. What activities did the selection and implementation team from Selkirk College undertake to ensure the success of its transition to the new HRIS solution? Why did these activities help to make the transition easier?

2. What are the advantages and disadvantages of outsourcing the payroll function?

3. Given what you know about the decision to bring the payroll process back in-house at Selkirk College, do you think it was the right decision for the organization? Explain your answer.

4. What other options might have been chosen that you have learned about in this chapter?

Managing People: Corporate Pacific Xpress Inc.—Where Respect Drives Compensation

Coastal Pacific Xpress Inc. (CPx) is a trucking company with a difference. It starts with the company's mission statement: "Companies don't succeed—people do!" That's why owner Jim Mickey and partners Glen Parsons and Scott McIntosh were able to grow the company 500 percent in just five years leading up to 2005. It's also the reason that the Surrey-based company is now British Columbia's largest temperature-controlled carrier, with a state-of-the-art fleet of more than 250 trucks and 700 trailers, with customers that include Costco, Maple Leaf Foods, Safeway, Future Shop, and Best Buy. The company's egalitarian work environment comes from Mickey's belief that "if an employer treats employees with respect and dignity, they will work harder, which in turn will grow profits." Given that the company's revenue in 2010 was $120 million, it seems to be true.

It's a unique perspective in the much-beleaguered Canadian trucking industry that has struggled to adjust after deregulation in the mid-80s. As competition heated up, owners scrambled to take cost out of the business in order to lower their prices. New lower costs came mainly at a price to drivers, whose salaries plummeted from what was once regarded as "a solid living" to just $8 or $9 per hour. By 1987, critical driver shortages developed, as drivers found themselves no longer able to make a decent living. Morale sank as the average turnover in the industry rose to a whopping 135 percent and the ever-rising cost of diesel fuel added to the general misery.

But CPx has developed a better way to treat employees and still make a fair profit. It backs up its culture of respect with a strategic approach to recruitment and selection, training, and an innovative approach to compensation that aligns with everything else. In addition to paying competitive rates, the company adds additional amounts to base pay that are linked to small but important events that would otherwise lower driver compensation. These events include border crossings ($30), loading and unloading of trucks ($60), and the need to wait overnight ($250) while a customer scrambles to finish harvesting a crop. Add in an "industry-leading" benefits package mostly paid for by CPx, plus various other lifestyle features such as gym memberships. Drivers also receive diesel fuel subsidies that are charged to the customer, and amount to thousands of dollars on long hauls. Even more important, CPx is transparent and upfront with drivers on the topic, providing information and education on subsidies. (This is in contrast to some others in the industry who keep drivers in the dark in order to retain all or portions of subsidy payments.) And then there are the annual bonuses employees receive in years the company makes a profit. In 2005, that amounted to $400,000 divided among 400 loyal employees.

Underlying the company's strategic approach of respect in all facets of its relationship with employees is an additional relational component, rarely granted by other employers: CPx employees are empowered to fire an abusive customer if necessary. Mickey feels this is critical to maintaining a sense of community at CPx, saying, "You have to be fair and honest and take care of each other." And, given the amount of abuse many in the industry are known to have to take on a daily basis, perhaps this is the biggest reward of all.

SOURCES: Based on S. Klie, "'Employees First' at CPx," *Canadian HR Reporter* (September 26, 2005), pp. 1 & 3; Coastal Pacific Xpress company website: www.cpx.ca/pages/about-us/overview.php.

Questions

1. How would you describe the philosophy behind the compensation approach at Coastal Pacific Xpress? Where does it originate?

2. Do you think that the response of Coastal Pacific Xpress will continue to be sustainable in today's economy? Explain why or why not.

9 Recognizing Employee Contributions with Pay

Enter the World of Business

Canada Post Delivers a New Message

Like many large public-sector organizations, Canada Post, the largest federal crown Corporation in Canada, has looked to the future and been forced to realize the significant impact that baby boomers leaving the workforce will have on the organization. It has realized that 22,000 employees are expected to retire within the next ten years, and that current pension obligations are greater than two times revenue and still growing. At the same time, competition eats away at the business on a daily basis; the Internet diverts business away through downloading of goods that used to arrive by mail order; banks and utilities move steadily toward online payments; and courier companies aggressively work to take customers away. That's why, when Moya Greene assumed her role as Canada Post's new CEO in 2005, her direction regarding organizational core strategy was emphatic and crystal clear. Canada Post would need to (1) engage every one of its 70,000 employees (2) invest in its antiquated infrastructure, and (3) grow the business.

For Brad Smith, general manager, Compensation and Pay for Canada Post, this meant aligning all aspects of the organization's total reward system with corporate objectives so that the reward system would be a direct driver of employee engagement, enabling the other core strategic objectives to be achieved. The president made it clear that every person should know at all times what the goals of Canada Post were, how the company was doing, exactly what he or she as an individual could do on a daily basis to help achieve those goals, and finally what would be in it for them (the WHIFM). Since salaries and benefits comprise over 65 percent of the cost of operations (seven times more than transportation costs of the business), it was essential that there be a clear line of sight between employee expectations, the effort expended, and the compensation each employee received in return for that effort.

And so, by 2007, management began talks with the four main unions representing 97 percent of employees. Management's main point was that if Canada Post was to compete effectively in the future, it must make every front-line employee critically aware of how much each of them mattered, on a day-to-day basis, in sustaining the business. Management proposed adopting a balanced scorecard approach to measure financial, service performance, customer, and employee contributions to the business. These measurements would form the basis of a new Annual Performance Incentive Program designed to ensure that employees would be more involved in the business and share in its success. Taking a lesson from the failing auto industry, union negotiators saw the wisdom in creating a stake in the outcomes of Canada Post's business activities for the 53,000 full time core employees holding the fort against formidable competitors such as UPS and FedEx. With the balanced scorecard approach employees would have a new reason to step up performance. The stage was set—some new, key components had been added to the total reward program at Canada Post.

According to Smith, communication has become a key tool in building credibility of the program among employees. One of the first steps was to build a website to keep employees engaged all year long with monthly updates on corporate performance, and messages about how employees can improve their bonus. In mailings to employees' homes and one-on-one conversations with team leaders, employees are provided with Canada Post's objectives and details about how they will gain personal financial benefit from the company's bonus program. A special website calculator allows employees to input their salaries along with regularly updated corporate results to compute exactly how changes in performance will affect their personal bonus. The calculator helps simplify the incentive program and keeps the momentum going. When bonus payments are awarded, team leaders meet with employees individually, present the bonus cheque, and thank employees personally for their contributions. And to support that process, senior managers travel constantly to Canada Post facilities, talking to employee groups and individuals, and continuously reinforcing the message that every employee matters.

The next step was to communicate amounts and types of compensation being received more clearly, so that employees could understand the total value of all their rewards. Annual compensation statements were revised to show employees all the types and amounts of compensation they receive. The three-page statement begins with a summary of Canada Post's employee value proposition, titled "Competitive Total Compensation Package," an array of benefits available to all employees, including career opportunities, support for learning and development, and extensive health and safety training. The second page is a personalized statement of the employee's total compensation listing details of his or her pay and incentives, benefits, and individual participation in the retirement program. Finally, the third page provides a bar chart illustrating the total cost of all compensation compared to Canada Post's profits along with a succinct message pointing out that the corporation must be profitable in order to be sustainable.

Finally, to reinforce the corporate vision, an annual event known as "Employee Appreciation Week" was introduced. Along with other activities, team leaders deliver personalized thank-you cards to all employees, even the 20,000 or so temporary seasonal workers who help with the year-end crush. Both team leaders and employees commented on the benefit of such communications and that they have been changing relationships within the organization.

So, you might ask, has all this effort and engagement helped Canada Post meet Greene's three key objectives? The answer is both yes and no. Certainly, the organization has made tremendous progress toward becoming a performance-based culture, which emerged during Greene's five-year tenure. It also generated regular profits, cut costs by more than $500 million, and implemented a $2 billion upgrade to its infrastructure. culminating in the opening of its new, state-of-the-art mail processing plant in Winnipeg in June 2010. Certainly for Greene, a native of Newfoundland, things worked out very well—she was hired away to head England's Royal Mail. Greene was replaced in January 2011 by Deepak Chopra, former president and CEO of Pitney Bowes Canada and Latin America, with 15 years of global experience as a postal industry executive. Chopra's opening message to all employees reinforced the transformation that had occurred when he stated, "I see a culture of great pride, a culture of innovation and, more importantly, a culture of courage that is willing to transform the business."

And so it seemed that Canada Post could face the future with a new leader and a more effective approach to compensation that made it a key driver of employee engagement and the very sustainability of the organization. However, by March 2011, just a few months after Greene's departure, management and representatives from the Canadian Union of Postal Workers (CUPW) reached a standstill in negotiations toward a new collective agreement. Lower start rates and pension benefits proposed for future new hires became a key sticking point, and the union launched a series of 24-hour rotating strikes across Canada. After 11 days of disrupted postal service, Chopra announced a lockout. The dispute finally ended with back-to-work legislation and arbitration was introduced to settle remaining issues.

SOURCES: Webcast presentation October 26, 2010: "Getting Full Value from Total Rewards," Brad Smith, General Manager, Compensation and Pay, Canada Post, for the Conference Board of Canada at www.conferenceboard.ca; Canada Post Website: New Deal for New Employees and About us: News Release: "Canada Post Reports Profit in 2009 But Looks to a Challenging Year Ahead," (April 27, 2010); P. Waldie, "Moya Greene Sees Challenge in Royal Mail Posting," *The Globe and Mail* (June 17, 2010) at www.theglobe andmail.com/report-on-business/managing/moya-greene-sees-challenge-in-royal-mail-posting/article1608232/ (retrieved July 18, 2011); Deepak Chopra: Biography and Deepak Chopra: Message to Employees January 18, 2011, at www.infopost.ca/en/files/2011/01/EmployeeMessage_E.pdf (retrieved March 4, 2011); "Negotiations Between Canada Post and CUPW Break Off," Canada News Release June 22, 2011, at www.infopost.ca/en/files/2011/06/talks_break_off_june_22-e.pdf (retrieved July 16, 2011); Vanessa Lu, "Canada Post Workers Strike in Winnipeg," *Toronto Star* (June 3, 2011) at www.thestar.com/business/article/1001409--canada-post-workers-strike-in-winnipeg (retrieved July 16, 2011); "Getting Back to Work", Canada Post News Release (June 26, 2011) at www.infopost.ca/en/files/2011/06/talks_break_off_june_22-e.pdf (retrieved July 16, 2011); Erin Anderson and Josh O'Kane "Postal Service Expected to Start Tuesday," *The Globe and Mail* (June 27, 2011), p. A6.

INTRODUCTION

The opening story illustrates how even a heavily unionized government organization can use incentive compensation to motivate performance, while at the same time controlling fixed compensation costs and helping employees to understand their critical role in sustainability. It illustrates that public-sector organizations do not necessarily have to accept the inevitable—a buildup of massive pension deficits that will threaten future pensions and weigh heavily on taxpayers Canada-wide. Clearly it is possible to use compensation as a key tool in rallying the troops to fend off certain disaster. It certainly begs the question—which other private- and public-sector organizations should be moving in a similar direction and be much more strategic with compensation?

But the rotating strikes and lockout, which disrupted postal service for all Canadians throughout June 2011, also serve to remind us that such changes are seldom effected quickly and can certainly meet with resistance. This is especially true in public-sector organizations with a long history of job security and a large workforce comprising thousands of long-term employees. In such organizations, employees are only just beginning to understand how sustainability, technology, and globalization are impacting their jobs and those of future coworkers. Canada Post management chose to stand firm with its message about what it will take to remain competitive (and to protect jobs) in the future. It seems that compensation, in all its forms, is one of the mechanisms the organization will rely on to make the message clear.

Pay for Performance
Variable forms of pay designed to recognize and reward employees' performance that are based on measures of individual or group contributions to the organization's success; sometimes called *incentive pay, variable pay,* or *performance-based pay.*

The preceding chapter discussed setting pay for jobs. In this chapter we focus on **pay for performance** (sometimes called *incentive pay, variable pay, or performance-based pay*), or variable forms of pay designed to recognize and reward employees' performance that are based on individual or group contributions to the organization's success. That is, employees' pay does not depend solely on the jobs they hold. Instead, differences in performance (individual, group, or organization), seniority, skills, and so forth are used as a basis for differentiating pay among employees.[1] And as our opening story illustrates, union leaders are beginning to see the merit of performance pay since the sustainability of unions is also at stake.

Several key questions arise in evaluating different pay programs for recognizing contributions. First, what are the costs of the program? Second, what is the expected return (in terms of influences on attitudes and behaviours) from such investments? Third, does the program fit with the organization's human resource strategy and its overall business strategy? Fourth, what might go wrong with the plan in terms of unintended consequences? For example, will the plan encourage managers and employees to pay more attention to some objectives (e.g., short-term sales) than to some others (e.g., customer service and long-term customer satisfaction)?

Organizations have a relatively large degree of discretion in deciding how to pay, especially compared with the pay level decisions discussed in the previous chapter. The same organizational pay level (or "compensation pie") can be distributed (shared) among employees in many ways. Whether each employee's share is based on individual performance, profits, seniority, or other factors, the size of the pie (and thus the cost to the organization) can remain the same.

Regardless of cost differences, different pay programs can have very different consequences for productivity and return on investment. Indeed, a study of *how much* 150 organizations paid found not only that the largest differences between organizations had to do with *how* they paid, but that these differences also resulted in different levels of profitability.[2]

LO 1

Discuss how pay influences individual employees, and describe three theories that explain the effect of compensation on individuals.

HOW DOES PAY INFLUENCE INDIVIDUAL EMPLOYEES?

Pay plans are typically used to energize, direct, or control employee behaviour. Equity theory, described in the previous chapter, is relevant here as well. Most employees compare their own pay with that of others, especially those in the same job. Perceptions of inequity may cause employees to take actions to restore equity. Unfortunately, some of these actions (such as quitting or lack of cooperation) may not help the organization.

Three additional theories also help explain compensation's effects: reinforcement, expectancy, and agency theories.

Reinforcement Theory

E. L. Thorndike's law of effect states that a response followed by a reward is more likely to recur in the future. The implication for compensation management is that high employee performance followed by a monetary reward will make future high performance more likely. By the same token, high performance not followed by a reward will make it less likely in the future. The theory emphasizes the importance of an employee's actual experience of a reward, in terms of motivating future actions. Employers who promise rewards in return for high performance must be sure that employees actually receive the rewards promised when they perform well, and that employees who do not perform well do not receive rewards. Otherwise, the message employers are attempting to reinforce may be misconstrued or lost altogether.

Expectancy Theory

Although **expectancy theory** also focuses on the link between rewards and behaviours, it emphasizes expected (rather than experienced) rewards (hence the name *expectancy theory*). In other words, it focuses on the effects of incentives when they are offered by the organization. Behaviours (job performance) can be described as a function of ability and motivation. In turn, motivation is hypothesized to be a function of expectancy (the perceived link between effort and performance), instrumentality (perceived link between behaviours and pay), and valence perceptions (perceived value of rewards being offered versus behaviours expected by the organization). Compensation systems differ according to their impact on these motivational components. Generally speaking, the main factor is instrumentality: the link between behaviours and pay, or the beliefs employees hold that rewards will be received from the organization in return for behaviours requested. Valence of pay outcomes should remain the same under different pay systems. Expectancy perceptions (the perceived link between effort and performance) often have more to do with job design and training than pay systems. A possible exception would be skill-based pay, which directly influences employee training and thus expectancy perceptions.

Although expectancy theory implies that linking an increased amount of rewards to performance will increase motivation and performance, some authors have questioned this assumption, arguing that monetary rewards may increase extrinsic motivation but decrease intrinsic motivation. Extrinsic motivation depends on rewards (such as pay and benefits) controlled by an external source, whereas intrinsic motivation depends on rewards that flow naturally from work itself (such as performing interesting work).[3] In other words, paying a child to read books may diminish the child's natural interest in reading, and in the future the child may be less likely to read books unless there are monetary incentives. Although monetary incentives may reduce intrinsic motivation in some settings (such as education), the evidence suggests that such effects are small and probably not very relevant to most settings.[4] Therefore, while it is important to keep in mind that money is not the only effective way to motivate behaviour and that monetary rewards will not always be the answer to motivation problems, it does not appear that monetary rewards run much risk of compromising intrinsic motivation in most work settings.

Agency Theory

Agency theory focuses on the divergent interests and goals of all of the organization's stakeholders and the ways that employee compensation can be used to align these interests and goals. We cover agency theory in some depth because it provides especially relevant implications for compensation design.

An important characteristic of the modern corporation is the separation of ownership from management (or control). Unlike the early stages of capitalism, where owner and manager were often the same, today, with some exceptions (mostly smaller companies), most shareholders are far removed from the day-to-day operation of companies. Although this separation has important advantages (such as mobility of financial capital and diversification of investment risk), it also creates agency costs—the interests of the **principals** (owners) and their **agents** (managers) may no longer converge. What is best for the agent, or manager, may not be best for the owner.

Expectancy Theory
The theory that says motivation is a function of valence, instrumentality, and expectancy.

Agency Theory
A theory focussing on the divergent interests and goals of the organization's stakeholders and the ways that employee compensation can be used to align these interests and goals.

Principal
In agency theory, a person (e.g., an owner) who seeks to direct another person's behaviour.

Agent
In agency theory, a person (e.g., a manager) who is expected to act on behalf of a principal (e.g., an owner).

Agency costs can arise from two factors. First, principals and agents may have different goals (goal incongruence). Second, principals may have less than perfect information on the degree to which the agent is pursuing and achieving the principal's goals (information asymmetry).

Three examples of agency costs can occur in managerial compensation.[5] First, although shareholders seek to maximize their wealth, management may spend money on things such as perquisites (corporate jets, for example) or "empire building" (making acquisitions that do not add value to the company but may enhance the manager's prestige or pay). Second, managers and shareholders may differ in their attitudes toward risk. Shareholders can diversify their investments (and thus their risks) more easily than managers (whose only major source of income may be their jobs), so managers are typically more averse to risk. They may be less likely to pursue projects or acquisitions with high potential payoff. Another possibility is a preference on the part of managers for relatively little risk in their pay (high emphasis on base salary, low emphasis on uncertain bonuses or incentives). Indeed, research shows that managerial compensation in manager-controlled firms is more often designed in this manner.[6] Third, decision-making horizons may differ. For example, if managers change companies more than owners change ownership, managers may be more likely to maximize short-run performance (and pay), perhaps at the expense of long-term success. In a country such as China, these issues (and how they affect executive pay levels) have only recently begun to receive significant attention. (See the "Competing Through Globalization" box.)

Agency theory is also of value in the analysis and design of nonmanagers' compensation. In this case, interests may diverge between managers (now in the role of principals) and their employees (who take on the role of agents).

In designing either managerial or nonmanagerial compensation, the key question is, How can such agency costs be minimized? Agency theory says that the principal must choose a contracting scheme that helps align the interests of the agent with the principal's own interests (that is, it reduces agency costs). These contracts can be classified as either behaviour oriented (such as merit pay) or outcome oriented (share options, profit sharing, commissions, and so on).[7]

At first blush, outcome-oriented contracts seem to be the obvious solution. If profits are high, compensation goes up. If profits drop, compensation goes down. The interests of "the company" and employees are aligned. An important drawback, however, is that such contracts increase the agent's risk. And because agents are averse to risk, they may require higher pay (a compensating wage differential) to make up for it.[8]

Behaviour-based contracts, on the other hand, do not transfer risk to the agent and thus do not require a compensating wage differential. However, the principal must be able to overcome the information asymmetry issue noted previously and monitor with little cost what the agent has done. Otherwise, the principal must either invest in monitoring (e.g., add more supervisors) and information or structure the contract so that pay is linked at least partly to outcomes.[9]

Which type of contract should an organization use? It depends partly on the following factors:[10]

- *Risk aversion.* Risk aversion among agents makes outcome-oriented contracts less likely.
- *Outcome uncertainty.* Profit is an example of an outcome. Agents are less willing to have their pay linked to profits to the extent that there is a risk of low profits. They would therefore prefer a behaviour-oriented contract.
- *Job programmability.* As jobs become less programmable (less routine), outcome-oriented contracts become more likely because monitoring becomes more difficult.[11]
- *Measurable job outcomes.* When outcomes are more measurable, outcome-oriented contracts are more likely.
- *Ability to pay.* Outcome-oriented contracts contribute to higher compensation costs because of the risk premium.
- *Tradition.* A tradition or custom of using (or not using) outcome-oriented contracts will make such contracts more (or less) likely.

In summary, the reinforcement, expectancy, and agency theories all focus on the fact that behaviour–reward contingencies can shape behaviours. However, agency theory is of particular value in compensation management because of its emphasis on the risk–reward tradeoff, an issue that needs close attention when companies consider variable pay (performance-based) plans, which can carry significant risk.

Competing Through Globalization

Executive Pay Hits International Radar

In 2008, journalist Li Yuan conducted a two-hour interview with a senior Chinese banker on topics ranging from the (then) current global crisis to the growth of consumerism in China. The banker was fairly forthcoming, at least for a Chinese executive, until he was asked about his multi-million yuan ($1 is about seven yuan) compensation of the previous year. At that point, the banker clammed up. His silence amplified the growing awareness that while executive pay was a red hot topic in North America, provoking high drama between CEOs and outraged shareholders, it didn't hold a candle to China. There, Yuan said, disclosure of executive compensation among publicly traded Chinese companies commenced only a few years earlier, and had provoked an immediate and explosive reaction among the Chinese. It seems they were demanding to know what such pay had been based on and why executives could earn more than the state chairman. The remainder of Yuan's interview follows, along with his personal insights:

> The senior banker said he would be more than happy if his name weren't associated with the topic. On the one hand, he explained, top executives at public companies do make a lot more than executives at state-owned enterprises and government officials, not to mention the majority of ordinary Chinese. On the other hand, he said, people like him make far less than their counterparts on Wall Street and in Hong Kong. To attract and retain talented people who are increasingly moving around globally, public Chinese companies need to offer comparable salaries and bonuses. So the pay of executives like him are more or less a compromise between China's reality and market competition. "But how can I say this to those who make very little?" he asked. "They won't understand, and I don't expect them to understand."

> I see his point. I can't imagine China going back to the egalitarian society that we escaped 30 years ago, in which everybody received a salary based on their educational background and seniority, instead of their capabilities and achievements. Few people will work hard unless they know they will be rewarded, whether that reward is a bonus for a banker, power for a politician, or a harvest for a farmer. That's simply human nature, and China's economic growth in the past three decades is the best evidence of it.

> But I also understand why the unemployed, the middle class and lowly-paid government officials get angry at what they see as astronomical pay. The average annual income of urban workers in China last year was 24,932 yuan ($3,561), according to the National Bureau of State Statistics. Farmers and migrant workers make far less than that. Meanwhile, Shenzhen Development Bank Chairman and Chief Executive Frank Newman made roughly 23 million yuan ($3.3 million) in 2007, about 922 times the average urban pay, and Ping An Insurance Co. Chairman Ma Mingzhe made more than 66 million yuan ($9.3 million), or 2,647 times a regular worker's pay. (He donated 20 million yuan to a charity.)

The executive-compensation figures have triggered a public backlash. In an online vote on Sina.com, one of China's top portals, 93 percent of voters disapproved of the executive pay practices at Ping An and Shenzhen Development Bank.

Mr. Ma of Ping An has also been made a villain in Internet chat rooms and on online forums since his pay information became public late last month. "Is the 66 Million Yuan Pay an April Fool's Joke?" demands a post on the popular online forum Tianya.cn. ...

More importantly, some state-controlled public companies rely on monopolies and preferential government policies for their profits, so there's an understandable debate about whether these firms' government-appointed executives should get paid handsomely—and if their compensation should be linked to those "guaranteed" profits.

[These companies] need to answer the questions raised on online forums again and again: Do these officials deserve more than 10 times their government pay once they are appointed as CEOs of public companies? Do they have the managerial talent to be retained with shareholders' money? Is their loyalty to the government, or to their shareholders? If some of the bank's income comes from its monopoly position and preferential government policies, should the CEO be rewarded for that?

Yuan concludes by saying what we all know—that there are no easy answers to these questions. And while the western world and other industrial countries have been raging against this disparity (fruitlessly it seems) since the early 80s, China is just starting down this road. Moreover, Yuan observes, they are forced to make sense of it within a "backdrop of a complex asset structure and political system."

In another article published 18 months later, another journalist, Salil Tripathi, reports from yet another front in the war against executive compensation, saying, "Raging about executive pay is all the rage in India at the moment." Unlike China, there is nothing new here. This dialogue has been going on since 1991, when the government lifted restrictions on executive pay, making it easier for companies to pay senior managers more. Tripathi says that the result of less government interference (which had served only to drive executive pay underground) was to "set executives free to consume conspicuously." Of late, some have become publicly excessive in their spending and Tripathi reports that such excesses are "sparking angst about inequality."

There seems to be a global theme developing here. But while Yuan observes that the Chinese are becoming doggedly determined to get some answers and that "this in itself is encouraging," Mr. Tripathi is more cynical. He argues that the Indian government should keep its nose out of things and let the market set CEO pay. He says forcing CEOs to earn and spend less will simply shift things under the radar once again and the economy will pay the price, and proposed reforms will do nothing to help India's poor. Perhaps the Chinese should be taking notes from this example. Meanwhile, North Americans can wait patiently to see if there is anything new that emerges from these distant but familiar dialogues. Regardless of the cultural and other differences, when it comes to the topic of executive pay, we all seem to have a lot in common.

SOURCES: Based on Li Yuan, "Executive Pay Hits China's Radar," *The Wall Street Journal Online,* April 10, 2008. Copyright © 2008 by Dow Jones & Co., Inc. Reproduced with permission of Dow Jones & Co., Inc. via Copyright Clearance Center; and S. Tripathi, "Indian CEOs Get What they Deserve," *The Wall Street Journal Online* (October 29, 2009).

HOW DOES PAY INFLUENCE LABOUR FORCE COMPOSITION?

Traditionally, using pay to recognize employee contributions has been thought of as a way to influence the behaviours and attitudes of current employees, whereas pay level and benefits, which are discussed in Chapter 10, have been seen as a way to influence so-called membership behaviours. Membership behaviours are decisions employees make about whether to join an organization (become members) or remain with an organization (maintain membership). However, there is increasing recognition that individual pay programs may also affect the nature and composition of an organization's workforce.[12] For example, it is possible that an organization that links pay to performance may attract more high performers than an organization that does not link the two. There may be a similar effect with respect to job retention.[13]

Continuing the analysis, different pay systems appear to attract people with different personality traits and values.[14] Organizations that link pay to individual performance may be more likely to attract individualistic employees, whereas organizations relying more heavily on team rewards are more likely to attract team-oriented employees. The implication is that the design of compensation programs needs to be carefully coordinated with the organization and human resource strategy. Increasingly, both in Canada and abroad, employers are seeking to establish stronger links between pay and performance.

LO 2

Describe the fundamental pay programs for recognizing employees' contributions to the organization's success.

PAY-FOR-PERFORMANCE PROGRAMS

In compensating employees, an organization does not have to choose one program over another. Instead, a combination of programs is often the best solution. For example, one program may foster teamwork and cooperation but not enough individual initiative. Another may do the opposite. Used in conjunction, a balance may be attained. Such balancing of objectives, combined with careful alignment with the organization and human resource strategy, may help increase the probability that a pay-for-performance program has its intended effects and reduce the probability of unintended consequences and problems.[15]

Table 9.1 on page 354 provides an overview of the programs for recognizing employee contributions. Each program shares a focus on paying for performance. The programs differ according to three design features: (1) payment method (2) frequency of payout, and (3) ways of measuring performance. The table also speculates potential consequences of such programs for (1) performance motivation of employees (2) attraction of employees (3) organization culture, and (4) costs. Finally, there are two contingencies that may influence whether each pay program fits the situation: (1) management style and (2) type of work. We now discuss the different programs and some of their potential consequences in more depth.

LO 3

List the advantages and disadvantages of pay-for-performance programs.

Merit Pay

In **merit-pay** programs, annual pay increases are usually linked to performance appraisal ratings (see Chapter 8). Some type of merit-pay program exists in almost all organizations (although evidence on merit-pay effectiveness is surprisingly scarce).[16] As the chapter opening demonstrated, some employers have moved toward a form of merit pay that relies on bonuses rather than increases to base pay. One reason for the widespread use of merit pay is its ability to define and reward a broad range of performance dimensions. Indeed, given the pervasiveness of merit-pay programs, we devote a good deal of attention to them here.

Merit Pay
Annual increases to base pay that are usually linked to performance appraisal ratings.

Table 9.1   Programs for Recognizing Employee Contributions

	MERIT PAY	INCENTIVE PAY	PROFIT SHARING	OWNERSHIP	GAIN SHARING	SKILL-BASED
Design features						
Payment method	Changes in base pay	Bonus	Bonus	Equity changes	Bonus	Change in base pay
Frequency of payout	Annually	Weekly	Semiannually or annually	When share sold	Monthly or quarterly	When skill or competency acquired
Performance measures	Supervisor's appraisal of individual performance	Individual output, productivity, sales	Company profit	Company share returns	Production or controllable costs of stand-alone work unit	Skill or competency acquisition of individuals
Consequences						
Performance motivation	Relationship between pay and performance varies	Clear performance–reward connection	Stronger in smaller firms	Stronger in smaller firms	Stronger in smaller units	Encourages learning
Attraction	Over time pays better performers more	Pays higher performers more	Helps with all employees if plan pays out	Can help lock in employees	Helps with all employees if plan pays out	Attracts learning-oriented employees
Culture	Individual competition	Individual competition	Knowledge of business and cooperation	Sense of ownership and cooperation	Supports cooperation, problem solving	Learning and flexible organization
Costs	Requires well-developed performance appraisal system	Setting and maintaining acceptable standards	Relates costs to ability to pay	Relates costs to ability to pay	Setting and maintaining acceptable standards	Training and certification
Contingencies						
Management style	Some participation desirable	Control	Fits participation	Fits participation	Fits participation	Fits participation
Type of work	Individual unless group appraisals done	Stable, individual, easily measurable	All types	All types	All types	Significant skill depth or breadth

SOURCE: Adapted and modified from E. E. Lawler III, "Pay for Performance: A Strategic Analysis," in *Compensation and Benefits,* ed. L. R. Gomez-Mejia (Washington, DC: Bureau of National Affairs, 1989).

Merit Increase Grid
A grid that combines an employee's performance rating with the employee's position in a pay range to determine the size and frequency of his or her pay increases.

Basic Features   Many merit pay programs work off a **merit increase grid.** As Table 9.2 indicates, the size and frequency of pay increases are determined by two factors. The first factor is the individual's performance rating (because better performers should receive higher pay). The second factor is position in range (that is, an individual's compa-ratio). So, for example, an employee with a performance rating of EX and a compa-ratio of 120 would receive a pay increase of 9 to 11 percent. By comparison, an employee with a performance rating of EX and a compa-ratio of 85 would

Table 9.2 Example of Merit Increase Grid from Merck & Co., Inc.

PERFORMANCE RATING	SUGGESTED MERIT INCREASE PERCENTAGE			
	COMPA-RATIO 80.00–95.00	COMPA-RATIO 95.01–110.00	COMPA-RATIO 110.01–120.00	COMPA-RATIO 120.01–125.00
EX (Exceptional within Merck)	13–15%	12–14%	9–11%	To maximum of range
WD (Merck Standard with Distinction)	9–11	8–10	7–9	—
HS (High Merck Standard)	7–9	6–8	—	—
RI (Merck Standard Room for Improvement)	5–7	—	—	—
NA (Not Adequate for Merck)	—	—	—	—

SOURCE: From "Compensation and Performance Evaluation at Arrow Electronics" (Boston: Harvard Business School), Case 9-800-290. Copyright © 2000 by the President and Fellows of Harvard College. Reprinted with permission.

receive an increase of 13 to 15 percent. Note that the general magnitude of increases in such a table is influenced by inflation rates. Thus the percentage increases in such a grid would have been considerably lower in recent years. For example, in the Conference Board of Canada's 2011 Compensation Planning Outlook survey, of the 253 nonunionized companies granting salary increases, the average increase overall was 3.3 percent. However, "top performers" received an average 4.4 percent, while "satisfactory performers" received an average 2.8 percent, and "poor performers" received on average a mere 0.9 percent.[17]

One reason for factoring in the compa-ratio is to control compensation costs and maintain the integrity of the pay structure. If a person with a compa-ratio of 120 received a merit increase of 13 to 15 percent, she would soon exceed the pay range maximum. Not factoring in the compa-ratio would also result in uncontrolled growth of compensation costs for employees who continue to perform the same job year after year. Instead, some organizations think in terms of assessing where the employee's pay is now and where it should be, given a particular performance level. Consider Table 9.3. An employee who consistently performs at the EX level should be paid at 115 to 125 percent of the market (that is, a compa-ratio of 115 to 125). To the extent that the employee is far from that pay level, larger and more frequent pay increases are necessary to move the employee to the correct position. On the other hand, if the employee is already at that pay level, smaller pay increases will be needed. The main objective in the latter case would be to provide pay increases that are sufficient to maintain the employee at the targeted compa-ratio.

Table 9.3 Performance Ratings and Compa-ratio Targets

PERFORMANCE RATING	COMPA-RATIO TARGET
EX (Exceptional within Merck)	115–125
WD (Merck Standard with Distinction)	100–120
HS (High Merck Standard)	90–110
RI (Merck Standard Room for Improvement)	80–95
NA (Not Adequate for Merck)	None

SOURCE: From "Compensation and Performance Evaluation at Arrow Electronics" (Boston: Harvard Business School), Case 9-800-290. Copyright © 2000 by the President and Fellows of Harvard College. Reprinted with permission.

In controlling compensation costs, another factor that requires close attention is the distribution of performance ratings (see Chapter 8). In many organizations, 60 to 70 percent of employees fall into the top two (out of four to five) performance rating categories.[18] This means tremendous growth in compensation costs because most employees will eventually be above the midpoint of the pay range, resulting in compa-ratios well over 100. To avoid this, some organizations provide guidelines regarding the percentage of employees who should fall into each performance category, usually limiting the percentage that can be placed in the top two categories. These guidelines are enforced differently, ranging from true guidelines to strict forced-distribution requirements.

In general, merit-pay programs have the following characteristics. First, they identify individual differences in performance, which are assumed to reflect differences in ability or motivation. By implication, system constraints on performance are not seen as significant. Second, the majority of information on individual performance is collected from the immediate supervisor. Peer and subordinate ratings are rare and, where they exist, they tend to receive less weight than supervisory ratings.[19] Third, there is a policy of linking pay increases to performance appraisal results.[20] Fourth, the feedback under such systems tends to occur infrequently, often once per year at the formal performance review session. Fifth, the flow of feedback tends to be largely unidirectional, from supervisor to subordinate.

Learn more about merit pay online with Connect.

Criticisms of Traditional Merit-Pay Programs Criticisms of this process have been raised. For example, W. Edwards Deming, a leader of the total quality management movement, argued that it is unfair to rate individual performance because "apparent differences between people arise almost entirely from the system that they work in, not from the people themselves."[21] Examples of system factors include coworkers, the job, materials, equipment, customers, management, supervision, and environmental conditions. These are believed to be largely outside the worker's control, instead falling under management's responsibility. Deming argued that the performance rating is essentially "the result of a lottery."[22]

Deming also argued that the individual focus of merit pay discourages teamwork: "Everyone propels himself forward, or tries to, for his own good, on his own life preserver. The organization is the loser."[23] As an example, if people in the purchasing department are evaluated based on the number of contracts negotiated, they may have little interest in materials quality, even though manufacturing is having quality problems.

Deming's solution was to eliminate the link between individual performance and pay. This approach reflects a desire to move away from recognizing individual contributions. What are the consequences of such a move? It is possible that fewer employees with individual-achievement orientations would be attracted to and remain with the organization. One study of job retention found that the relationship between pay growth and individual performance over time was weaker at higher performance levels. As a consequence, the organization lost a disproportionate share of its top performers[24] In other words, too little emphasis on individual performance may leave the organization with average and poor performers.[25]

Thus, although Deming's concerns about too much emphasis on individual performance are well taken, one must be careful not to replace one set of problems with another. Instead, there needs to be an appropriate balance between individual and group objectives. At the very least, ranking and forced-distribution performance rating systems need to be considered with caution, lest they contribute to behaviour that is too individualistic and competitive.

Another criticism of merit-pay programs is the way they measure performance. If the performance measure is not perceived as being fair and accurate, the entire merit-pay program can break down. One potential impediment to accuracy is the almost exclusive reliance on the supervisor for providing performance ratings, even though peers, subordinates, and customers (internal and external) often have information on a person's performance that is as good as or better than that of the supervisor. A 360-degree performance feedback approach (discussed in Chapter 7) gathers feedback from each of these sources. To date, however, organizations have mainly used such data for development purposes and have been reluctant to use these multisource data for making pay decisions.[26]

In general, process issues appear to be important in administering merit pay. In any situation where rewards are distributed, employees appear to assess fairness along two dimensions: distributive (based on how much they receive) and procedural (what process was used to decide how much).[27] Some of the most important aspects of procedural fairness, or justice, appear in Table 9.4. These items suggest that employees desire clear and consistent performance standards, as well as opportunities to provide input, discuss their performance, and appeal any decision they believe to be incorrect.

Perhaps the most basic criticism is that merit pay does not really exist. High performers are not paid significantly more than mediocre or even poor performers in most cases,[28] something that certainly is demonstrated in the Conference Board survey results described in our earlier discussion of merit increase grids. For example, with a merit increase budget of 4 to 5 percent, suppose high performers receive 6 percent raises, versus 3.5 to 4 percent raises for average performers. On a salary of $40,000 per year, the difference in take-home pay would not be more than about $300 per year,

Table 9.4 Aspects of Procedural Justice in Pay Raise Decisions

INDICATE THE EXTENT TO WHICH YOUR SUPERVISOR DID EACH OF THE FOLLOWING:
1. Was honest and ethical in dealing with you.
2. Gave you an opportunity to express your side.
3. Used consistent standards in evaluating your performance.
4. Considered your views regarding your performance.
5. Gave you feedback that helped you learn how well you were doing.
6. Was completely candid and frank with you.
7. Showed a real interest in trying to be fair.
8. Became thoroughly familiar with your performance.
9. Took into account factors beyond your control.
10. Got input from you before a recommendation.
11. Made clear what was expected of you.
INDICATE HOW MUCH OF AN OPPORTUNITY EXISTED, AFTER THE LAST RAISE DECISION, FOR YOU TO DO EACH OF THE FOLLOWING THINGS:
12. Make an appeal about the size of a raise.
13. Express your feelings to your supervisor about the salary decision.
14. Discuss, with your supervisor, how your performance was evaluated.
15. Develop, with your supervisor, an action plan for future performance.

SOURCE: From R. Folger, and M.A. Konorsky, "Effects of Procedural and Distributive Justice on Reactions to Pay Raise Decisions," *Academy of Management Journal* 32 (1989), p. 115. Copyright © 1989 by Academy of Management (NY). Reproduced with permission of Academy of Management (NY) via Copyright Clearance Center.

or about $6 per week. Critics of merit pay point out that this difference is probably not significant enough to influence employee behaviours or attitudes. Indeed, as Figure 9.1 indicates, many employees do not believe there is any payoff to higher levels of performance.

Of course, small differences in pay can accumulate into large differences over time. The present value of the salary advantage would be $29,489 (based on a discount rate of 5 percent). For example, over a 30-year career, an initial annual salary difference of $740 with equal merit increases thereafter of 7 percent would accumulate into a career salary advantage of $75,738.[29] Whether employees think in these terms is open to question. But even if they do not, nothing prevents an organization from explaining to employees that what may appear to be small differences in pay can add up to large differences over time. It should also be kept in mind that merit ratings are often closely linked to promotions, which in turn are closely linked to salary. Thus, even in merit-pay settings where performance differences are not recognized in the short run, high performers are likely to have significantly higher career earnings.

Finally, the accumulation effect just described can also be seen as a drawback if it contributes to an entitlement mentality. Here the concern is that a big merit increase given early in an employee's career remains part of base salary "forever." It does not have to be re-earned each year, and the cost to the organization grows over time, perhaps more than either the employee's performance or the organization's profitability would always warrant. Merit bonuses (payouts that do not become part of base salary), in lieu of traditional merit increases, are thus used by some organizations instead.

Individual Incentives

Like merit pay, individual incentives reward individual performance, but with two important differences. First, payments are not rolled into base pay. They must be continuously earned and re-earned. Second, performance is usually measured as physical output (such as number of water faucets

FIGURE 9.1 Percentage of Employees Who Agree That Better Performance Leads to Better Increases

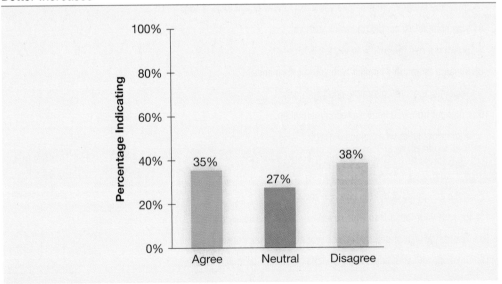

SOURCE: Hay Group, *Managing Performance: Survey of Employees in 335 Companies,* Philadelphia: Hay Group, 2002. Reprinted with permission.

produced) rather than by subjective ratings. Individual incentives have the potential to significantly increase performance. Locke and his colleagues found that monetary incentives increased production output by a median of 30 percent—more than any other motivational device studied.[30]

Nevertheless, individual incentives are relatively rare for a variety of reasons.[31] Most jobs (such as those of managers and professionals) have no physical output measure. Instead, they involve what might be described as "knowledge work." Second, many potential administrative problems (such as setting and maintaining acceptable standards) often prove intractable. Third, individual incentives may do such a good job of motivating employees that they do whatever they get paid for and nothing else. (See the Dilbert cartoon in Figure 9.2.) Fourth, as the name implies, individual incentives typically do not fit well with a team approach. Fifth, they may be inconsistent with the goals of acquiring multiple skills and proactive problem solving. Learning new skills often requires employees to slow or stop production. If the employees are paid based on production volume, they may not want to slow down or stop. Sixth, some incentive plans reward output volume at the expense of quality or customer service.

Therefore, although individual incentives carry potential advantages, they are not likely to contribute to a flexible, proactive, problem-solving workforce. In addition, such programs may not be particularly helpful in the pursuit of total quality management objectives.

Profit Sharing and Ownership

Profit Sharing   At the other end of the individual–group continuum are profit-sharing and share ownership plans. The four major types of profit-sharing plans in Canada include cash, deferred profit-sharing plans (DPSPs), employee profit-sharing plans (EPSPs), and combination plans. Examples of companies in Canada that have profit-sharing plans are The Home Depot, Digital Xtremes, Ceridian, and Vancouver City Savings Credit Union (VanCity).[32]

In **profit sharing,** payments are based on a measure of organization performance (profits), and the payments do not become part of the base salary. Profit sharing has two potential advantages. First, it may encourage employees to think more like owners, taking a broad view of what needs to be done to make the organization more effective. Thus, the sort of narrow self-interest encouraged by individual incentive plans (and perhaps also by merit pay) is presumably less of an issue. Instead, increased cooperation and citizenship are expected. Second, because payments do not become part of base pay, labour costs are automatically reduced during difficult economic times, and wealth is shared during good times. Consequently, organizations may not need to rely on layoffs as much to reduce costs during tough times.[33]

Profit Sharing
A compensation plan in which payments are based on a measure of organization performance (profits) and do not become part of the employees' base salary.

FIGURE 9.2   How Incentives Sometimes "Work"

SOURCE: DILBERT © Scott Adams/Dist. by United Feature Syndicate, Inc.

Does profit sharing contribute to better organization performance? The evidence is not clear. Although there is consistent support for a correlation between profit-sharing payments and profits, questions have been raised about the direction of causality,[34] which could be why Toyota doesn't have a profit-sharing plan even though they have been common in the auto industry. For example, although the most recent collective agreement negotiated by the CAW in 2009 with GM contains no provisions for a profit-sharing plan,[35] the plans continue to be part of the UAW agreements at Ford, Chrysler, and GM. However, payouts to workers in the three companies have differed significantly, with workers at GM receiving profit-sharing payments 1/15th the size received by the same type of worker at Chrysler. Is it because Chrysler workers perform 15 times better than their counterparts at GM that year? Probably not. Rather, auto workers are likely to view top management decisions regarding products, engineering, pricing, and marketing as directly influential and thus more important to the ultimate profitability of the organization than the assembly-line activities that make up their own jobs. As a result, with the exception of top (and perhaps some middle) managers, most employees are unlikely to see a strong connection between what they do and what they earn under profit sharing. This means that performance motivation is likely to change very little under profit sharing because employees perceive no value to themselves from profit sharing. Consistent with expectancy theory, motivation depends on a strong link between behaviours and valued consequences such as pay (instrumentality perceptions).

Another factor that reduces the motivational impact of profit-sharing plans is that most plans are of the deferred type. This may be why only 12 percent of the 323 companies offering short-term incentive plans in the Conference Board survey mentioned earlier offer profit-sharing plans, although it is not clear what type of plan they offer.[36]

Not only may profit sharing fail to increase performance motivation, but also employees may react very negatively when they learn that such plans do not pay out during business downturns.[37] First, they may not feel they are to blame because they have been performing their jobs well. Other factors are beyond their control, so why should they be penalized? Second, what seems like a small amount of risked pay for a manager earning $80,000 per year can be very painful to someone earning $15,000 or $20,000.

One solution some organizations choose is to design plans that have upside but not downside risk. In such cases, when a profit-sharing plan is introduced, base pay is not reduced. Thus, when profits are high, employees share in the gain, but when profits are low, they are not penalized. Such plans largely eliminate what is purported to be a major advantage of profit sharing: reducing labour costs during business downturns. During business upturns, labour costs will increase. Given that the performance benefits of such plans are not assured, an organization runs the risk under such plans of increasing its labour costs with little return on its investment.

In summary, although profit sharing may be useful as one component of a compensation system (to enhance identification with broad organizational goals), it may need to be complemented with other pay programs that more closely link pay to outcomes that individuals or teams can control (or "own"), particularly in larger companies. In addition, profit sharing runs the risk of contributing to employee dissatisfaction or higher labour costs, depending on how it is designed.

connect   Learn more about profit sharing online with Connect.

Ownership   Although comparative information is hard to find for Canada, recent data shows that 20 million Americans own shares in the company where they work.[38] Employee ownership is similar to profit sharing in some key respects, such as encouraging employees to focus on the success of the organization as a whole. In fact, with ownership, this focus may be even stronger. Like profit sharing, ownership may be less motivational the larger the organization. And because employees may not realize any financial gain until they actually sell their share (typically upon leaving the organization), the link between pay and performance may be even less obvious than under profit sharing. Thus, from a reinforcement theory standpoint (with its emphasis on actually experiencing rewards), the effect on performance motivation may be limited.

One way of achieving employee ownership is through **share options,** which give employees the opportunity to buy shares at a fixed price. Say the employees receive options to purchase shares at $10 per share in 2009, and the share price reaches $30 per share in 2014. They have the option of purchasing shares ("exercising" their share options) at $10 per share in 2014, thus making a tidy return on investment if the shares are then sold. If the share price goes down to $8 per share in the year 2014, however, there will be no financial gain. Therefore, employees are encouraged to act in ways that will benefit the organization.

For many years, share options had typically been reserved for executives in larger, established companies. More recently, there was a trend toward pushing eligibility farther down in the organization.[39] The trend definitely caught on in Canada as the Conference Board reported in 2000 that 56 percent of 142 companies in its survey had extended the plan to the management group below the executive group, and 19 percent extended it to nonmanagement employees.[40] Among start-up companies like those in the technology sector, these broad-based share option programs have long been popular and companies such as Microsoft attribute much of their growth and success to these option plans. Some studies suggest that organization performance is higher when a large percentage of top and midlevel managers are eligible for long-term incentives such as share options, which is consistent with agency theory's focus on the problem of encouraging managers to think like owners.[41] However, it is not clear whether these findings would hold up for lower-level employees, particularly in larger companies, who may see much less opportunity to influence overall organization performance.

In the 2011 Conference Board Survey mentioned earlier, 41 percent of the 170 private firms in the study offered traditional share options (down from 73 percent in 1998 when share options were soaring in popularity), and in most of these organizations eligibility rests primarily among senior executives.[42] However, the Golden Age of share options may be coming to an end. Investors have long questioned the historically favourable tax treatment of employee share options. In Canada, the Accounting Standards Board (AcSB) sets standards and because share options are an alternative form of compensation, they are also seen as an operating expense. Accordingly, they must be charged to the income statement for the period(s) for which the employee provides the associated service,[43] ensuring that shareholders receive accurate financial statements that take all liabilities into account.

Microsoft decided to eliminate share options in favour of share grants (gifts of shares to employees that they do not have to pay for). This is partly in response to the new accounting standards and partly in recognition of the fact that Microsoft's share price is not likely to grow as rapidly as it once did, making options less effective in recruiting, retaining, and motivating its employees. It appears that many companies are cutting back on share options overall, especially for nonexecutive employees. Those companies that continue to use broad-based share options have encountered difficulties in keeping employees motivated because of the steep decline in share prices that many have experienced.

Employee share ownership plans (ESOPs), under which employers give employees shares in the company, or sell them to employees at a discounted price, are the most common form of employee ownership.[44] In Japan, 91 percent of companies listed on Japanese stock markets have an ESOP, and these companies appear to have higher average productivity than non-ESOP companies.[45]

In Canada, there is an acknowledged lack of research to verify the extent of such plans, but such plans are definitely in use. For example, see the success that Apex Distribution has obtained using ESOPs in the "Evidence-Based HR" box. However, unlike share options, ESOPs are viewed under Canadian accounting standards as capital transactions (funds spent to improve or increase the life of company assets),[46] and are therefore charged to equity accounts.[47] Since equity accounts represent the value of company assets after all creditors claims have been satisfied, this ensures shareholders

Share Options
An employee ownership plan that gives employees the opportunity to buy the company's shares at a previously fixed price.

Employee Share Ownership Plan (ESOP)
An employee ownership plan that gives employers certain tax and financial advantages when shares are granted to employees.

and others are provided with an honest statement of the company's net assets. In their 2002 book, *Employee Ownership,* Canadian researchers Carol A. Beatty, Ph.D., and Harvey Schachter cite a well-known study done by the Toronto Stock Exchange in the mid-80s, which established that 63 percent of 821 firms in the study listed on the Toronto Stock Exchange had at least one type of employee equity program in place. Of these, 24 percent had share purchase plans and 54 percent had share option plans. The TSE found there were considerable benefits to launching an ESOP such as the fact that such companies' "five-year profit growth was 123 per cent higher, their net profit margin was 95 per cent higher and productivity measured by revenue per employee was 24 per cent higher than non ESOP companies, among other benefits."[48] Furthermore, according to Perry Phillips, president of the ESOP Association of Canada, the TSE study results compare closely to over 30 years of combined research done in the United States.[49] A Conference Board of Canada study done around the same time as the TSE research found 61 percent of publicly traded companies had share purchase plans.[50] A quick perusal of Canada's Top 100 Employers list reveals a number of companies that offer share purchase plans, such as uranium producer Cameco Corporation. Cameco provides the plan to nurture an ownership culture and makes it available to all employees. Telus Corporation (featured in "Managing People" at the end of this chapter), and Nexen Inc. also provide such plans.[51]

Some studies suggest that the positive effects of ownership are larger in cases where employees have greater participation,[52] perhaps because the "employee–owner comes to psychologically experience his/her ownership in the organization."[53]

Learn more about ESOPs online with Connect.

Gainsharing, Group Incentives, and Team Awards

Gainsharing

A form of compensation based on group or plant performance (rather than organizationwide profits) that does not become part of the employee's base salary.

Gainsharing   **Gainsharing** programs offer a means of sharing productivity gains with employees. Although there is no central registry of plans in Canada, one study cited by Milkovich, Newman, and Cole, reports they have been used by about 10 percent of Canadian employers.[54] A 2010 Conference Board survey revealed that only 7 percent of the 323 firms providing short-term incentive plans used gainsharing plans.[55] Although sometimes confused with profit-sharing plans, gainsharing differs in two key respects. First, instead of using an organization-level performance measure (profits), the programs measure group or plant performance, which is likely to be seen as more controllable by employees. Second, payouts are distributed more frequently and not deferred. In a sense, gainsharing programs represent an effort to pull out the best features of organization-oriented plans, such as profit sharing and individual-oriented plans, such as merit pay and individual incentives. Like profit sharing, gainsharing encourages pursuit of broader goals than individual-oriented plans do. But, unlike profit sharing, gainsharing can motivate employees much as individual plans do because of the more controllable nature of the performance measure and the frequency of payouts. Indeed, studies indicate that gainsharing improves performance.[56] However, not all companies find gainsharing plans to be the best fit with the philosophy, goals, and values of management, or the right conditions may not be in place for gainsharing to succeed. To understand why, we provide a brief history of how gainsharing came into existence in the first place.

The first known type of gainsharing plan was the Scanlon plan, developed in the 1930s by Joseph N. Scanlon, president of a local union at Empire Steel and Tin Plant in Mansfield, Ohio. The Scanlon Plan provides a monetary bonus to employees (and the organization) if the ratio of labour costs to the sales value of production is kept below a certain standard. Table 9.5 on page 364 shows a modified Scanlon plan (i.e., costs in addition to labour are included). Because actual costs ($850,000) were less than allowable costs ($907,500) in the first and second periods, there is a gain of $57,500. The organization receives 45 percent of the savings, and the employees receive the other

Evidence-Based HR

In the 13 years Apex Distribution Inc. has been in existence, it has grown exponentially from its three original locations to become the third-largest oil and gas service supplier in Western Canada. Now with more than 300 employees in 34 locations, the company placed 94th on the 2007 Profit 100 annual list of Canada's Fastest Growing Companies, which compared companies by percentage revenue growth from 2002–07. Apex also made the Financial Post list of 50 Best Managed Companies in Canada (2005 and 2008), which compared Canadian-owned and -managed companies with revenues over $10 million. How has this company moved into such elite company in such a short space of time? Company owner Don White attributes much of his company's growth to recruiting the best of the best and placing intense focus on customer service, along with implementing an ESOP early in the game. Since 2007, the company has expanded one of its largest product areas, the valve service business, across Alberta through acquisitions. It also expanded its product range and started pushing into Saskatchewan to service similar needs in the potash, diamond, gold, and refinery businesses. More recently, it has made significant progress venturing into the United States and is eyeing Australia for further international growth. Between 2005 and 2009, the company averaged year-over-year revenue growth of 60–70 percent that White says "has translated into bottom line or disciplined, profitable growth."

White is convinced that the Employee Share Ownership Plan he and two cofounders put in place right from the start back in 1999 is a key reason the company has been able to reach such heights. White admits that building the ESOP was a lot of work and it took time to understand how it was meant to work. In fact, disagreement about plan design created enough problems that White's two partners eventually left and sold their shares. However, White, the company, and its ESOP are still going strong with more than 130 employees owning shares, and some accumulating retirement nest eggs of $200,000 or more.

Was it worth it? If retention and growth are worth considering—absolutely! Up to the time it made the Profit 100 list, Apex had experienced zero turnover in the top management sales positions, in spite of the fact that the plan allows employees to sell their shares at any time. (This differs from artificial methods of retention designed into ESOP plans sponsored by some other companies that include a vesting period before shares actually transfer into the employee's name. Faced with time restrictions, employees stay put—but only until the shares are in their name.) And with revenue growth of 50 percent in 2005 and 100 percent in 2006, reaching $200 million in sales, it seems clear that White's determination to keep the ESOP broad based has made Apex an undisputed business leader in Western Canada and beyond.

SOURCES: Profit 100 Canada's Fastest-Growing Companies, CanadianBusiness.com: Profit 100 companies at http://list.canadianbusiness.com/rankings/profit100/2008/intro/Default.aspx?sp2=1&d1=d&sc1=9 (retrieved March 6, 2011); Financial Post 50 Best Management Companies, Apex Distribution Inc. profile by M. Bitti (February 3, 2009) at www.financialpost.com/reports/best-managed-companies/story.html?id=1248541; and https://www.canadas50best.com/en/Pages/Home.aspxon (retrieved March 6, 2011); and E. Beaton, "The Lure of ESOPs," *Profit Magazine* (June 1, 2007) at www.profitguide.com/article/4321--the-lure-of-esops--page1.

Table 9.5 Example of Gainsharing (Modified Scanlon Plan) Report

ITEMS	AVERAGE OF 1ST AND 2ND PERIODS	AVERAGE OF 2ND AND 3RD PERIODS
1. Sales in dollars	$1,000,000	$1,000,000
2. Inventory change and work in process	100,000	100,000
3. Sales value of production	1,100,000	1,100,000
4. Allowable costs (82.5% × 3 above)	907,500	907,500
5. Actual costs	850,000	917,500
6. Gain (4 − 5 above)	57,500	−10,000
7. Employee share (55% of 6 above)	31,625	−5,500
8. Monthly reserve (20% of 7 above) *If no bonus, 100% of 7 above	6,325	−5,500
9. Bonus to be distributed (7 − 8)	25,300	0
10. Company share (45% of 6 above)	25,875	−4,500
11. Participating payroll	132,000	132,000
12. Bonus percentage (9/11)	19.2%	0.0%
13. Monthly reserve (8 above)	6,325	−5,500
14. Reserve at the end of last period	0	6,325
15. Year-end reserve to date	6,325	825

SOURCE: From *Gainsharing and Goalsharing* by Kenneth Mericle. Copyright © 2004 by Praeger Publishers. Reproduced with permission by ABC-CLI0, LLC.

55 percent, although part of the employees' share is set aside in the event that actual costs exceed the standard in upcoming months (as line 5 in Table 9.5 shows did occur in the average of the second and third periods).

Following the success of the Scanlon plan, two additional designs emerged over time known as the Rucker Plan (1940s) and Improshare™(1970s), which was designed by industrial engineer and management consultant Michael Fein.[57] These two plans expanded the original concept, using different productivity standards and more complex formulas. Gainsharing plans and pay-for-performance plans in general often encompass more than just a monetary component. There is often a strong emphasis on taking advantage of employee know-how to improve the production process through teams and suggestion systems. A number of recommendations have been made about the organization conditions that should be in place for gainsharing to succeed. Commonly mentioned factors include (1) management commitment (2) a need to change or a strong commitment to continuous improvement (3) management's acceptance and encouragement of employee input (4) high levels of cooperation and interaction (5) employment security (6) information sharing on productivity and costs (7) goal setting (8) commitment of all involved parties to the process of change and improvement, and (9) agreement on a performance standard and calculation that is understandable, seen as fair, and closely related to managerial objectives.[58]

connect

Learn more about gainsharing online with Connect.

Team-based awards and incentives can be an effective way to recognize smaller groups of individuals who work together to achieve important organizational goals.

Group Incentives and Team Awards   Whereas gainsharing plans are often plant-wide, group incentives and team awards typically pertain to a smaller work group.[59] Group incentives (like individual incentives) tend to measure performance in terms of physical output, whereas team award plans may use a broader range of performance measures (such as cost savings, successful completion of product design, or meeting deadlines). As with individual incentive plans, these plans have a number of potential drawbacks. Competition between individuals may be reduced, but it may be replaced by competition between groups or teams. Also, as with any incentive plan, a standard-setting process must be developed that is seen as fair by employees, and these standards must not exclude important dimensions such as quality.

Balanced Scorecard

As the preceding discussion indicates, every pay program has advantages and disadvantages. Therefore, rather than choosing one program, some companies find it useful to design a mix of pay programs to create one that has just the right chemistry for the situation at hand. Relying exclusively on merit pay or individual incentives may result in high levels of work motivation but unacceptable levels of individualistic and competitive behaviour and too little concern for broader plant or organization goals. Relying too heavily on profit-sharing and gainsharing plans may increase cooperation and concern for the welfare of the entire plant or organization, but it may reduce individual work motivation to unacceptable levels. However, a particular mix of merit pay, gainsharing, and profit sharing could contribute to acceptable performance on all these performance dimensions.

LO 4

Describe how organizations combine incentive plans in a balanced scorecard.

Table 9.6   Illustration of Balanced Scorecard Incentive Concept

PERFORMANCE MEASURE	INCENTIVE SCHEDULE				
	TARGET INCENTIVE	PERFORMANCE	% TARGET	ACTUAL PERFORMANCE	INCENTIVE EARNED
Financial • Return on capital employed	$100	20% + 16–20% 12–16% Below 12%	150% 100% 50% 0%	18%	$100
Customer • Product returns	$ 40	1 in: 1,000 + 900–999 800–899 Below 800	150% 100% 50% 0%	1 in 876	$ 20
Internal • Cycle time reduction (%)	$ 30	9% + 6–9% 3–6% 0–3%	150% 100% 50% 0%	11%	$ 45
Learning and growth • Voluntary employee turnover	$ 30	Below 5% 5–8% 8–12%	150% 100% 50%	7%	$ 30
Total	$200				$195

SOURCE: F. C. McKenzie and M. P. Shilling, "Avoiding Performance Traps: Ensuring Effective Incentive Design and Implementation," *Compensation and Benefits Review*, July–August 1998, pp. 57–65. Copyright © 1998 by Sage Publications, Inc. Reprinted with permission of Sage Publications, Inc.

One approach that seeks to balance multiple objectives is the balanced scorecard (discussed in Chapter 1 and in the opening vignette of this chapter about Canada Post), which Kaplan and Norton describe as a way for companies to "track financial results while simultaneously monitoring progress in building the capabilities and acquiring the intangible assets they would need for future growth."[60]

Table 9.6 shows how a mix of measures might be used by a manufacturing firm to motivate improvements in a balanced set of key business drivers.

LO 5

Discuss issues related to performance-based pay for executives.

MANAGERIAL AND EXECUTIVE PAY

Because of their significant ability to influence organization performance, top managers and executives are a strategically important group whose compensation warrants special attention. In Chapter 8 we discussed how much this group is paid. Here we focus on the issue of how their pay is determined.

Business magazines such as *The Globe and Mail's Report on Business, Canadian Business, Forbes,* and *BusinessWeek* often publish a list of top executives who did the most for their pay and those who did the least. The latter group has been the impetus for much of the attention to executive pay. The problem seems to be that in some companies, top executive pay is high every year, regardless of profitability or stock market performance. One study, for example, found that CEO pay changes by $3.25 for every $1,000 change in shareholder wealth. Although this relationship was interpreted to mean that "the compensation of top executives is virtually independent of corporate performance, later work suggests this is not the case in most companies."[61]

How can executive pay be linked to organization performance? From an agency theory perspective, the goal of owners (shareholders) is to encourage the agents (managers and executives) to act in the best interests of the owners. This may mean less emphasis on noncontingent pay, such as base salary, and more emphasis on outcome-oriented "contracts" that make some portion of executive pay contingent on the organization's profitability or share performance.[62] Among midlevel and top managers, it is common to use both short-term bonus and long-term incentive plans to encourage the pursuit of both short- and long-term organization performance objectives. Indeed, the bulk of executive compensation comes from restricted shares, share options, and other forms of long-term compensation. Putting pay "at risk" in this manner can be a strong incentive. However, agency theory suggests that while too little pay at risk may weaken the incentive effect, too much pay at risk can also be a problem if executives take too large risks with firm assets.[63] The U.S. banking and mortgage industry problems that plunged the world into a global recession in late 2008 provide a salient example.

To what extent do organizations use such pay-for-performance plans, and what are their consequences? Research suggests that organizations vary substantially in the extent to which they use both long-term and short-term incentive programs. Further, greater use of such plans among top and midlevel managers was associated with higher subsequent levels of profitability. As Table 9.7 indicates, greater reliance on short-term bonuses and long-term incentives (relative to base pay) resulted in substantial improvements in return on assets.[64]

Earlier, we saw how the balanced scorecard approach could be applied to paying manufacturing employees. It is also useful in designing and measuring executive pay; CIBC provided clear evidence of this in its explanation of a new compensation framework for its senior executive team in the Executive Compensation section of the Management Proxy Circular

Executive pay is an area of compensation that has come under intense public and shareholder scrutiny in recent years as investors and others demand greater accountability and transparency.

Table 9.7 The Relationship between Managerial Pay and Organization Return on Assets

MANAGERIAL PAY MIX (RELATIVE TO BASE PAY)		CHANGE IN RETURN ON ASSETS	
BONUS/BASE RATIO	LONG-TERM INCENTIVE ELIGIBILITY	%	$a
10%	28%	5.2%	$250 million
20	28	5.6	269 million
10	48	5.9	283 million
20	48	7.1	341 million

[a]Based on the assets of the average *Fortune* 500 company in 1990.

SOURCE: B. Gerhart and G. T. Milkovich, "Organizational Differences in Managerial Compensation and Financial Performance," *Academy of Management Journal* 33 (1990), pp. 663–691.

for its Annual Shareholders' Meeting of February 2010. Table 9.8 illustrates the choice of performance measures the board utilized in Step 1 (Assessment of Business Performance) of the four-step process utilized for determining the annual cash bonus of its top executives. Note that while Table 9.8 shows sample measures used for CIBC Retail Markets, similar additional measures are also used for the CIBC and Wholesale Banking divisions. Such measures indicate that CIBC strives to meet its "strategic imperative of consistent and sustainable performance over the long term"[65] by balancing shareholder, customer, and employee objectives, and using past and leading indicators, as well as measures related to the organization's risk appetite goals.[66] The circular explains that the new compensation framework for senior executives is "based on our belief that executive pay should be tied to the creation of long-term value and that incentives should reward performance without encouraging undue risk-taking."[67] See the "Competing Through Sustainability" box, which describes recognition received by the CIBC for its efforts to improve reporting of executive compensation to shareholders.

Finally, there is significant pressure from regulators and shareholders to link pay and performance more effectively. As of December 31, 2008, the Canadian Securities Administrators (CSA) now requires disclosure of many types of compensation and benefits of top-paid executives. Changes include a new focus on providing total compensation numbers. Companies must not only disclose how their share price performed against a recognized share index over the previous five years, but also show how the compensation plan performed against the share index. Furthermore, amounts to be provided in the event of termination must actually be quantified, rather than stated only as a percentage, which is much less specific.[68]

Large institutional fund investors such as the various teachers' retirement fund boards, OMERS, OPSEU Pension Trust, and other members of the Canadian Coalition for Good Governance (CCGG) have created Guidelines for Building High Performance Boards, shown in Table 9.9. Originally drawn

Table 9.8   CIBC Business Performance Scorecard and Sample Measures for CIBC Retail Markets

PERFORMANCE CATEGORIES	MEASURES
Financial Performance (Reported and Adjusted) • Against Plan and Previous Year • Three Year Trend • Performance Relative to Peers	• Revenue • Net Income Before Tax • Net Income After Tax • Key Business Indicators (e.g., Loan Losses, Expenses, ROE)
Execution of Risk Appetite Strategy	Risk Metrics (e.g., Total consumer delinquencies (30+ days, 90+ days), Operational losses, Economic Profit, RAROC) [Risk-adjusted return on capital]
Customer Satisfaction • Against Plan and Previous Year • Three Year Trend • Performance Relative to Peers	• Customer Service Index • Market Share • Growth in Funds/Assets Managed
Employee Engagement • Against Plan and Previous Year • Three Year Trend • Performance Relative to Peers	• Employee Commitment Index from CIBC and SBU employee surveys • Employee Turnover

*Similar additional measures are also gathered for the CIBC and Wholesale Banking Divisions.

SOURCE: CIBC Management Proxy Circular, CIBC Notice of Annual Meeting of Shareholders (February 25, 2010), p. 38 at www.cibc.com/ca/pdf/about/proxy-circular-10.pdf (retrieved July 15, 2011).

Table 9.9 Canadian Coalition for Good Governance: Guidelines for Building High-Performance Boards

PRINCIPLE	GUIDELINES
A high performance board is accountable and independent.	Facilitate shareholder democracy.
	Ensure at least two thirds of directors are independent of management.
	Separate the roles of Chair and Chief Executive Officer.
A high performance board has experienced, knowledgeable and effective directors and committees, and the highest level of integrity.	Ensure that directors are competent and knowledgeable.
	Ensure that the goal of every director is to make integrity the hallmark of the company.
	Establish mandates for board committees and ensure committee independence.
	Establish reasonable compensation and share ownership guidelines for directors.
	Evaluate board, committee, and individual director performance.
A high performance board has clear roles and responsibilities.	Oversee strategic planning, risk management, and the hiring and evaluation of management.
	Assess the Chief Executive Officer and plan for succession.
	Develop and oversee executive compensation plans.
A high performance board engages with shareholders.	Report governance policies and initiatives to shareholders.
	Engage with shareholders within and outside the annual meeting.

SOURCE: 2010 Building High Performance Boards, Canadian Coalition for Good Governance, March 2010, www.ccgg.ca/site/ccgg/assets/pdf/CCGG_Building_High_Performance_Boards_Final_March_2010.pdf (retrieved March 2, 2011). Reprinted with permission.

up in 2005, and revised in 2010, the guidelines are designed to "promote good governance practices in Canadian public companies and the improvement of the regulatory environment to best align the interests of boards and management with those of their shareholders, and to promote the efficiency and effectiveness of the Canadian capital markets."[69] The guidelines are designed to ensure director independence from management. In the event that a firm's future is at risk, the board may well need to demonstrate its independence from management by taking dramatic action, which may include removing the chief executive. In the same spirit, the CCGG created the Executive Compensation Principles, shown in Table 9.10, to guide boards and other key stakeholders when designing an executive compensation program to create linkages between pay and performance.[70]

Table 9.10 Canadian Coalition for Good Governance: Executive Compensation Principles

Principle 1 "Pay for performance" should be a large component of executive compensation.
Principle 2 "Performance" should be based on measurable risk adjusted criteria, matched to the time horizon needed to ensure the criteria have been met.
Principle 3 Compensation should be simplified to focus on key measures of corporate performance.
Principle 4 Executives should build equity in their company to align their interests with shareholders.
Principle 5 Companies should limit pensions, benefits, and severance and change of control entitlements.
Principle 6 Effective succession planning reduces paying for retention.

SOURCE: Canadian Coalition for Good Governance, 2009 Executive Compensation Principles (March 2009) at www.ccgg.ca/site/ccgg/assets/pdf/2009_Executive_Compensation_Principles.pdf (retrieved March 2, 2011). Reprinted with permission.

Competing Through Sustainability

CIBC Raises the Bar in Corporate Governance

The Canadian Imperial Bank of Commerce (CIBC) has won numerous awards for everything from training excellence and to being a best employer for new Canadians to making the 2011 Financial Post Ten Best Managed Companies list. However, four awards in particular reveal an impressive trend around the bank's approach to corporate governance and responsibility to investors that other companies would do well to emulate.

First, CIBC is one of only 25 financial institutions around the world (and 11 in Canada), to be included in the Dow Jones Sustainability Index (DJSI), an honour the bank has earned for eight consecutive years. (The DJSI assesses and recognizes companies on the basis of stock performance as well as long-term economic, environmental, and social criteria.) Add to that being named one of Canada's 50 Most Socially Responsible Corporations when measured against environmental, social, and governance indicators in the annual Jantzi-*Maclean's* Corporate Social Responsibility Report. Third, the bank made the Corporate Knights Best 50 Corporate Citizens list for five years in a row. Finally, in 2010, it received a Governance Gavel Award from the Canadian Coalition for Good Governance (CCGG) for Best Disclosure of Approach to Executive Compensation. This last award may be the most meaningful, given the events of the past few years, and the general cynicism that has surrounded both levels of executive compensation and the ways in which organizations have reported them to their shareholders.

What was significant about CIBC's approach? For one thing, the bank's compensation philosophy was written in plain language. That's a refreshing change from the usual finance-speak found in most annual proxy circulars, which is then expanded upon and "explained" in plentiful footnotes in a font best described as Squint Hard 6, a smoke–and-mirrors practice that the CCGG says deemphasizes various elements of compensation. In addition, CIBC's 33-page section dedicated to explaining executive compensation also includes charts and clear explanations of base pay and complex layered incentives and perquisites. The Executive Compensation section opens with a three-page letter from the bank's chairman and the chair of the Compensation Committee that explains the bank's goals and compensation philosophy and practices for the current and preceding three years. Key statements, such as, "We have changed our compensation structure to be more consistent with our strategy and risk appetite" appear in boxes and bolded red print within the text of the letter, so they catch the reader's attention. The long-term perspective that helps shareholders make sense of current executive compensation is clearly set forth in numerous tables, charts, and summaries, one of which describes and compares the CIBC approach to both regulatory guidance and best practices. There is a section on the bank's fiscal performance for the year to help shareholders measure the return on their investment. And finally, should the information overwhelm shareholders, headlines serve as a quick reference tool on key issues covered. Therefore, if CIBC shareholders and interested others want comprehensive information on all forms of total direct and indirect compensation, they'll find it here. For example, they can follow the steps for how annual cash bonus targets for executives were calculated using four stages, beginning with an assessment of business performance and ending with a reasonability test (total direct compensation). In fact, reading through this section is almost a lesson in executive compensation, and it's easy to find on the Governance page of the bank's website. Clearly CIBC has raised the benchmark on clear communication about executive compensation.

SOURCES: D. Milstead, "And the Winner for Best Disclosure Is …," *The Globe and Mail* (November 3, 2010); CCGG Governance Gavel Awards, Canadian Coalition for Good Governance (July 2010) at www.ccgg.ca; CIBC Notice of Annual Meeting of Shareholders, Management Proxy Circular, pp. 28–61 at www.cibc.com/ca/pdf/about/proxy-circular-10.pdf (retrieved March 4, 2011); and About CIBC: Governance at www.cibc.com/ca/investor-relations/annual-reports.html.

PROCESS AND CONTEXT ISSUES

In Chapter 8 we discussed the importance of process issues such as communication and employee participation. Significant differences in how such issues are handled can be found both across and within organizations, suggesting that organizations have considerable discretion in this aspect of compensation management.[71] As such, it represents another strategic opportunity to distinguish one's organization from the competition.

LO 6

Explain the importance of process issues such as communication in compensation management.

Employee Participation in Decision Making

Consider employee participation in decision making and its potential consequences. Involvement in the design and implementation of pay policies has been linked to higher pay satisfaction and job satisfaction, presumably because employees have a better understanding of and greater commitment to the policy when they are involved.[72]

What about the effects on productivity? Agency theory provides some insight. The delegation of decision making by a principal to an agent creates agency costs because employees may not act in the best interests of top management. In addition, the more agents there are, the higher the monitoring costs.[73] Together, these suggest that delegation of decision making can be very costly.

On the other hand, agency theory suggests that monitoring would be less costly and more effective if performed by employees because they have knowledge about the workplace and behaviour of fellow employees that managers do not have. As such, the right compensation system might encourage self-monitoring and peer monitoring.[74]

Researchers have suggested that two general factors are critical to encouraging such monitoring: monetary incentives (outcome-oriented contracts in agency theory) and an environment that fosters trust and cooperation. This environment, in turn, is a function of employment security, group cohesiveness, and individual rights for employees—in other words, respect for and commitment to employees.[75]

Communication

Another important process issue is communication. Earlier, we spoke of its importance in the administration of merit pay, both from the perspective of procedural fairness and as a means of obtaining the maximum impact from a merit-pay program.[76] More generally, a change in any part of the compensation system is likely to give rise to employee concerns. Rumours and assumptions based on poor or incomplete information are always an issue in administering compensation, partly because of its importance to employee economic security and well-being. Therefore, in making any changes, it is crucial to determine how best to communicate reasons for the changes to employees. Some organizations now rely heavily on video or podcast messages from the chief executive officer to communicate the rationale for major changes. Brochures that include scenarios for typical employees are also used, as are focus group sessions where small groups of employees are interviewed to obtain feedback about concerns that can be addressed in later communication programs.

An issue at the heart of communication is also administration of any performance-based pay plan. No matter how well designed the plan is, people must know how much to expect and when. In earlier chapters we have discussed the importance of a good HRMS or HRIS system to administer payroll data, but sometimes more is needed. For example, sales compensation plans have a large percentage of performance-based pay and such plans are an important part of how business is acquired in all organizations. Hence, great care must go into designing such programs (often multilayered, complex, and linked to individual products) and also to ensuring accurate payouts. See the "Competing Through Technology" box, which describes one company that has designed software for use by sales management to take much of the pain out of designing and communicating performance-based pay in sales.

Competing Through Technology

Sales Compensation Software to the Rescue

If you asked a sales manager what he wanted most out of a sales performance management system, he'd probably tell you he wanted software that would help him design effective incentive systems quickly, and that would also calculate the total cost of the plan to the organization. It would include capabilities for sales analytics, audit, and compliance, and it would also allow sales reps to access a clear visual summary of closed and pending deals by product and customer, at any time. Ideally it would be a self-serve system that allowed sales reps to track exactly how much cash was coming their way. It would also have to be an accurate, flexible, and fast system that would inspire confidence. Spreadsheets would be history and there would be much more time for golf.

Such a system does exist, with Vericent's SPM (Sales Performance Management) software whose function is to reduce costs and increase the effectiveness of the sales management processes among its clients. The product originated with Don Shimmerman, who wanted to develop a software company that provided solutions to business problems. As an accountant who spent considerable time selling enhanced planning and budgeting systems to chief financial officers, he learned a lot about sales and software. He experienced difficulties in tracking his own commissions and getting paid correctly, so he tried to develop a solution. The resulting product, Varicent's SPM, added a new twist to the process of sales compensation planning and implementation called process automation, which goes far beyond the usual sales incentive calculations. Process automation helps sales managers figure out if a new compensation plan makes sense through enhanced analytics built into the software.

Varicent is said to work well for small to medium-sized companies. However, it is a particularly good fit among large, multinational customers such as Waste Management Inc., Robert Half International, Mitel, and Rogers, because these companies have a tremendous amount of incompatible data to deal with.

One company that acquired SPM was Getty, the well-known stock-photo agency. Before using SPM, Getty's compensation analysts had to work through 36 different Excel sheets to calculate commissions, and producing a report took days. After adopting Varicent's software, such problems went away according to Brian Parker, director of sales operations for Getty Images. Parker indicated that another reason Getty adopted the software was to build more strategic business plans that allowed for agile sales commissions better able to drive motivation. In addition, the new system allows him to analyze reports more quickly (with the click of a mouse) and to figure out what outcomes the company is getting from various sales incentives.

For these reasons, Varicent has continued to grow rapidly and earned considerable recognition, including the ISV/Software Solution of the Year in 2008 and #1 on *Profit*'s 100 Canada's Fastest Growing Companies list for 2009.

SOURCES: www.varicent.com/products-enterprise-overview.asp; M. Smith, "Sales Compensation Easier to Manage with Varicent 7" (June 18, 2010), Ventenna Research at http://marksmith.ventanaresearch.com/2010/06/18/sales-compensation-easier-to-manage-with-varicent-7 (retrieved July 15, 2011); and R. Spence, "No. 1 Profile: The Sales Doctors," *Profit Magazine* (June 2010) at www.canadianbusiness.com/entrepreneur/managing/article.jsp?content=20100528_160334_13500.

Pay and Process: Intertwined Effects

The preceding discussion treats process issues such as participation as factors that may facilitate the success of pay programs. At least one commentator, however, has described an even more important role for process factors in determining employee performance:

> Worker participation apparently helps make alternative compensation plans ... work better—and also has beneficial effects of its own. ... It appears that changing the way workers are treated may boost productivity more than changing the way they are paid.[77]

This suggestion raises a broader question: How important are pay decisions, per se, relative to other human resource practices? Although it may not be terribly useful to attempt to disentangle closely intertwined programs, it is important to reinforce the notion that human resource programs, even those as powerful as compensation systems, do not work alone.

Consider gainsharing programs. As described earlier, pay is often only one component of such programs. How important are the nonpay components?[78] There is ample evidence that gainsharing programs that rely almost exclusively on the monetary component can have substantial effects on productivity.[79] On the other hand, a study of an automotive parts plant found that adding a participation component (monthly meetings with management to discuss the gainsharing plan and ways to increase productivity) to a gainsharing pay incentive plan raised productivity. In a related study, employees were asked about the factors that motivated them to engage in active participation (such as suggestion systems). Employees reported that the desire to earn a monetary bonus was much less important than a number of nonpay factors, particularly the desire for influence and control in how their work was done.[80] A third study reported that productivity and profitability were both enhanced by the addition of employee participation in decisions, beyond the improvement derived from monetary incentives such as gainsharing.[81]

ORGANIZATION STRATEGY AND COMPENSATION STRATEGY: A QUESTION OF FIT

LO 7

List the major factors to consider in matching the pay strategy to the organization's strategy.

Although much of our focus has been on the general, or average, effects of different pay programs, it is also useful to think in terms of matching pay strategies to organization strategies. To take an example from medicine, using the same medical treatment regardless of the symptoms and diagnosis would be foolish. In choosing a pay strategy, management must consider how effectively it will further the organization's overall business strategy. Consider again the findings reported in Table 9.7 on page 367. The average effect of moving from a pay strategy with below-average variability in pay to one with above-average variability is an increase in return on assets of almost two percentage points (from 5.2 percent to 7.1 percent). But in some organizations, the increase could be smaller.

In Chapter 2 we discussed directional strategies, two of which were growth (internal or external) and concentration ("sticking to the knitting"). How should compensation strategies differ according to whether an organization follows a growth strategy or a concentration strategy? Table 9.11 on page 374 provides some suggested matches. Basically, a growth strategy's emphasis on innovation, risk taking, and new markets is linked to a pay strategy that shares risk with employees but also gives them the opportunity for high future earnings by having them share in whatever success the organization has.[82] This means relatively low levels of fixed compensation in the short run but the use of bonuses and share options, for example, that can pay off handsomely in the long run. Share options have been described as the pay program "that built Silicon Valley," having been used by companies such as Apple, Microsoft, and others.[83] When such companies become successful, everyone from top

Table 9.11 Matching Pay Strategy and Organization Strategy

	ORGANIZATION STRATEGY	
PAY STRATEGY DIMENSIONS	**CONCENTRATION**	**GROWTH**
Risk sharing (variable pay)	Low	High
Time orientation	Short-term	Long-term
Pay level (short run)	Above market	Below market
Pay level (long-run potential)	Below market	Above market
Benefits level	Above market	Below market
Centralization of pay decisions	Centralized	Decentralized
Pay unit of analysis	Job	Skills

SOURCE: Adapted from L. R. Gomez-Mejia and D. B. Balkin, *Compensation, Organizational Strategy, and Firm Performance* (Cincinnati: South-Western, 1992), Appendix 4b.

managers to secretaries can become millionaires if they own shares. Growth organizations are also thought to benefit from a less bureaucratic orientation, in the sense of having more decentralization and flexibility in pay decisions and in recognizing individual skills, rather than being constrained by job or grade classification systems. On the other hand, concentration-oriented organizations are thought to require a very different set of pay practices by virtue of their lower rate of growth, more stable workforce, and greater need for consistency and standardization in pay decisions. As noted earlier, Microsoft has eliminated share options in favour of share grants to its employees, in part because it is not the growth company it once was.

A Look Back

In this chapter, we discussed the potential advantages and disadvantages of different types of incentive or pay-for-performance plans. We also saw that these pay plans can have both intended and unintended consequences. Designing a pay-for-performance strategy typically seeks to balance the pros and cons of different plans and reduce the chance of unintended consequences. To an important degree, pay strategy will depend on the particular goals and strategy of the organization and its units. For example, Microsoft determined that its pay strategy needed to be revised (less emphasis on share options, more on share grants) to support a change in its business strategy and to recognize the slower-paced growth of its share price. At the beginning of this chapter, we saw that Canada Post is working to link pay to engagement, achievement of business metrics, and business growth. The organization's incentive plan is an important component of the organization's sustainability.

Questions

1. Does money motivate? Use the theories and examples discussed in this chapter to address this question.

2. Think of a company where you have worked and a job that you have held. Design an incentive plan for that company, or at least for the department in which you may have worked. What would be the potential advantages and disadvantages of your plan? If your money was invested in the company, would you adopt the plan?

Summary

Our focus in this chapter has been on the design and administration of pay-for-performance programs that recognize employee contributions to the organization's success. These programs vary as to whether they link pay to individual, group, or organization performance. Often, it is not so much a choice of one program or the other as it is a choice between different combinations of programs that seek to balance individual, group, and organization objectives.

Wages, bonuses, and other types of pay have an important influence on an employee's standard of living. This carries at least two important implications. First, pay can be a powerful motivator. An effective pay strategy can substantially promote an organization's success; conversely, a poorly conceived pay strategy can have detrimental effects. Second, the importance of pay means that employees care a great deal about the fairness of the pay process. A recurring theme is that pay programs must be explained and administered in such a way that employees understand their underlying rationale and believe it is fair. Effective communication is key to employee acceptance and buy-in of such programs, especially when new programs are introduced or when something is changing about design or administration of the program.

The fact that organizations differ in their business and human resource strategies suggests that the most effective compensation strategy will differ between organizations. Although benchmarking programs against the competition is informative, what succeeds in some organizations may not be a good idea for others. The balanced scorecard suggests the need for organizations to decide what their key objectives are and to use pay to support them.

Key Terms

Agency theory, 349
Agent, 349
Employee share ownership
  plan (ESOP), 361
Expectancy theory, 349
Gainsharing, 362
Merit increase grid, 354
Merit pay, 353
Pay for performance, 348
Principal, 349
Profit sharing, 359
Share options, 361

Discussion Questions

1. To compete more effectively, your organization is considering a profit-sharing plan to increase employee effort and encourage employees to think like owners. What are the potential advantages and disadvantages of such a plan? Would the profit-sharing plan have the same impact on all types of employees? Is the size of your organization an important consideration? Why or why not? What alternative pay programs should be considered?

2. Gainsharing plans have often been used in manufacturing settings but can also be applied in service organizations. How could performance standards be developed for gainsharing plans in hospitals, banks, insurance companies, and so forth?

3. Your organization has two business units. One unit is a long-established manufacturer of a product that competes on price and has not been subject to many technological innovations. The other business unit is just being started. It has no products yet, but it is working on developing a new technology for testing the effects of drugs on people via simulation instead of through lengthy clinical trials. Would you recommend that the two business units have the same pay programs for recognizing individual contributions? Why or why not?

4. Beginning with the opening vignette and continuing throughout the chapter, we have seen considerable evidence of how companies use various forms of pay for performance,

sometimes changing one that is already in place. Do you believe that changing a performance pay plan is risky? Why would a company change an existing plan or add a new one? Provide several examples.

Self-Assessment Exercise

Pay is only one type of incentive that can motivate you to perform well and contribute to your satisfaction at work. This survey will help you understand what motivates you at work. Consider each aspect of work and rate its importance to you, using the following scale: 5 = very important, 4 = somewhat important, 3 = neutral, 2 = somewhat unimportant, 1 = very unimportant.

Salary or wages	1	2	3	4	5
Cash bonuses	1	2	3	4	5
Boss's management style	1	2	3	4	5
Location of workplace	1	2	3	4	5
Commute	1	2	3	4	5
Job security	1	2	3	4	5
Opportunity for advancement	1	2	3	4	5
Work environment	1	2	3	4	5
Level of independence in job	1	2	3	4	5
Level of teamwork required for job	1	2	3	4	5
Other (enter your own):					
_____	1	2	3	4	5
_____	1	2	3	4	5
_____	1	2	3	4	5

Which aspects of work received a score of 5? A score of 4? These are the ones you believe motivate you to perform well and make you happy in your job. Which aspects of work received a score of 1 or 2? These are least likely to motivate you. Is pay the only way to motivate you?

_____

SOURCE: Based on the "Job Assessor" found at www.salarymonster.com (retrieved August 2002).

Exercising Strategy: Better Boards and More Competent Compensation Committees

Increasing regulatory and shareholder pressure on boards of directors regarding disclosure of executive compensation and actual linkage with corporate performance has generated questions about the roles and competence of directors, particularly when those directors also serve on compensation committees within boards. Directors are often highly motivated to do the right thing, but they also (rightfully) worry about the potential for damage to their personal reputations given the increasing weight of responsibility they carry. Those who serve on compensation committees have even greater reason for concern. To understand this better, we can start with examining the traditional mandate of compensation committees on boards.

While not all boards are the same and will vary according to the age and stage of development of the organization, according to Chris Howe of Hewitt Associates, most compensation committees will be responsible for meeting four to eight times per year to plan and carry out activities that include (1) setting performance goals for the CEO; (2) assessing CEO performance against such goals; (3) overseeing how the CEO performs the same activities with respect to other officers of the company; (4) reviewing and approving goals for all incentive programs, grants, and compensation programs for officers of the company; (5) overseeing succession planning if a process exists; and (6) ensuring disclosure obligations are met with respect to executive compensation. What directors bring to the table in terms of competence varies, depending on their role with the board and their own background. Howe points out that although committee members are often experienced executives, their knowledge of compensation is often based on their own personal experience, and they are not compensation or regulatory experts. For that reason, compensation committees are increasingly practising risk management by seeking the advice of executive compensation consultants. Such advisors provide advice on governance issues, regulatory reporting requirements, and appropriate levels of executive compensation. However, this may no longer be enough to protect the compensation committee, the board, and ultimately the organization. Howe suggests that perhaps it is time to add compensation experts to the composition of compensation committees, and to have them working on such issues well beyond the four to eight meetings a year held by the committee. It's not a bad idea and one that even unions have discovered is often necessary to engage in effective collective bargaining.

Another solution that is more broad based but that has considerable merit given all the issues (including directors' concern for personal or corporate liability) is to formally educate all directors on a board about their roles and responsibilities and good governance process. This would mean going way beyond the usual "board orientation," which is not usually extensive enough, to consider more of a team-based learning approach such as that offered by the Directors College, the first university-accredited corporate director development program in Canada. The Directors College was founded in 2003 as a joint effort between the Conference Board of Canada and McMaster's DeGroote School of Business. The Chartered Director (C.Dir.) program is both a residential and off-site experience, and the five-module program covers all the rules and regulations that directors need to know, and goes well beyond that. The behavioural side (such as political manipulation, factions among directors) that so often govern board dynamics negatively is thoroughly dealt with through in-class exercises and through a comprehensive board simulation exercise in the fifth module. There is also a final exam to ensure accountability and full engagement in the learning experience. The curriculum emphasizes the need to integrate corporate governance and corporate social responsibility. Directors learn how to extend their roles beyond just mediating between management and shareholders to effectively take other stakeholders into account as well.

The program, which has received extensive screening to qualify as a university program, is delivered by a faculty of professionals, corporate directors, and academic instructors who use a wide range of interactive learning techniques, including case studies, to ensure that transfer of training occurs and manifests as good governance practice in the boardroom.

While the composition of many boards has often been closely examined, both before and after members are selected, perhaps Howe's suggestion to add compensation experts to the mix, and the promise offered by the Directors' College, offer practical new perspectives for the current controversy surrounding not only executive compensation, but also the need for higher corporate performance overall. Certainly, being able to state in an annual report that members of a board have taken the time and personal effort to learn how to do the job properly would be welcomed by most shareholders. With the growth of knowledge-based organizations, shareholders have come to expect that corporate profits and growth are closely linked to the level of human capital the organization is able to attract. Perhaps steps should be taken to ensure that the people at the very top of the organization have the right skills to do the job they have been entrusted to do.

Questions

1. Go to the website of the Directors College at http://thedirectorscollege.com and examine the information you find there. Should companies ask new and existing members of their board of directors to obtain director certification? Why or why not?

2. If directors were better educated about their roles and responsibilities, or if compensation committees were required to have a compensation expert as part of their composition, do you think executive compensation would continue at the high levels it has reached in past years? Would boards place greater emphasis on succession planning? Explain your answers.

SOURCES: C. Howe, "Compensation Committees Face Increasing Challenges, Demands," *Canadian HR Reporter* (May 3, 2010) p. 21; The Directors' College website, "About Us," at http://thedirectorscollege.com/about/ (retrieved March 6, 2011).

Managing People: Telus Tweaks Short-Term Incentive Plan

With 26,000 unionized and nonunionized employees, annual revenues of just under $10 billion, and voluntary turnover of 13.3 percent, Telus Corporation has a lot at stake in the design of its total compensation package. That stake includes an award-winning, performance-based corporate culture that the company wants to remain intact. After all, the company's roots go back to 1906 when it was known as AGT, Alberta Government Telephones. After merging with BCTel in 1999, it not only became the second-largest telecommunications company in Canada, but also one of Canada's Top 100 Employers, a top diversity employer, and one of BC's top employers. The company's head office in Vancouver is exceptional as a workplace environment with a glass atrium that allows natural light to stream in, concierge services, an onsite fitness facility with trainers and massage therapy, a subsidized cafeteria with healthy meals—the list goes on and on.

Financial benefits at Telus are above average. The company maintains externally competitive salaries and employee salaries are reviewed annually. There are signing and referral bonuses, a share purchase plan, a defined-contribution pension plan, and various income security and other benefits. The company also provides a short-term incentive pay plan for which all unionized and nonunionized employees (including temporary employees) are eligible, which takes the form of a year-end bonus. However, even though the majority of employees were able to achieve plan targets for their personal goals in both 2008 and 2009, the company failed to hit its corporate performance in both years. Telus realized the plan was misaligned if employees were being rewarded even when the corporation was underperforming, and that meant changes were in order. A new plan was designed and implemented for the 2010 fiscal year.

The new plan is now more closely matched to the financial performance of Telus, and it is simpler and more transparent. It is also affordable, with funding now based on EBIT (a percentage of earnings before interest and taxes). In this spirit, the new incentive plan was launched using a budget of 6.5 percent of EBIT to be measured at the end of 2010, before calculating individual payouts. The intent was that employees would be more motivated to increase profitability at Telus in order to increase their own payouts. While incentive plan payouts are based on corporate performance for all employees in the plan at Telus, nonunionized employees can also receive a portion based on individual performance. All goals for the plan at both the corporate and personal levels are based on a balanced scorecard of both financial and nonfinancial measures, and the corporation has to achieve a minimum of 50 percent on each balanced scorecard measure before any particular metric can generate a payout. However, if the overall company misses target, employees will still achieve the part of the incentive plan based on personal achievement. Thus, when eligible employees excel they still get some level of payout regardless of corporate outcomes, but they stand to receive much more when the corporation hits target.

Telus's philosophy of one team, one plan guided the design of the new incentive plan and clearly the setting of goals at both the organizational and individual levels, with payouts for all when Telus meets target, reinforces that message. While tweaking an existing incentive plan is risky, it seems like there is a new plan in place that promises greater return on investment for all stakeholders.

Questions

1. What role does the short-term incentive plan at Telus play in its overall corporate performance? With employees?

2. Telus is a publicly traded corporation. Do you think shareholders would welcome the company's new short-term incentive plan? Why or why not?

3. It appears that unionized employees at Telus do not participate in the component of the plan based on individual objectives, but can still receive payouts based on overall performance. Why do you think unionized employees don't participate in this part of the plan? Is the plan still effective in your opinion? Explain your answer.

SOURCES: "Telus: Aligning Payouts with Corporate Performance," in *Making Short-Term Incentives Work for Your Organization*, The Conference Board of Canada (October 2010), p. 15; "Playing it Safe in the Face of an Unsteady Economic Recovery, Compensation Planning Outlook 2011," The Conference Board of Canada, pp. 7 & 8; Telus Corporation Profile, Top 100 Employers in Canada, at www.eluta.ca/top-employer-telus (retrieved March 8, 2011); "About Us," Telus Corporation website, www.telus.com.

 **Practise and learn online with Connect.**

Employee Benefits

After reading this chapter, you should be able to:

LO 1 Discuss the growth in benefits costs and the underlying reasons for that growth. page 383

LO 2 Describe the major provisions of government-sponsored, mandatory benefits programs. page 385

LO 3 Explain the various types of voluntary employer-sponsored benefits. page 390

LO 4 Explain different types of pension plans and current pension trends. page 391

LO 5 Discuss how employee benefits in Canada compare with other countries. page 398

LO 6 Discuss how to manage benefits effectively to control cost, influence productivity, and attract and retain good employees. page 400

LO 7 Explain the importance of effectively communicating the nature and value of benefits to employees. page 410

Enter the World of Business

Microsoft Moves into the Fast Lane with Flexible Benefits

When the HR team at Microsoft Canada began to redesign its benefits plan in 2008, they realized it was rather strange that the Canadian operations of a company that revolution-ized the way people process information through software 25 years ago was about follow a path hundreds of others had already tread. That is, they were about to move away from a traditional benefits plan in place since 1985 (when the company started up in Canada), and into the world of flexible benefits. The addition of a total rewards manager to the HR team was the catalyst for change.

As planning got underway, three goals informed the project. First, there was a desire to change to flexible benefits to better accommodate the needs of 1,400 very diverse employ-ees. Feedback from focus groups indicated they wanted to have more choice rather than a one-size-fits-all package, so that became a top priority. Second, it seemed to be time to update the content of the plan. Third, while the company didn't feel a need to cut back its benefits budget, there was a real desire to get more bang for the buck. With that in mind, AON Consulting (specialists in human capital management and insurance brokers) was selected to help with the redesign and guide the HR team in a change management activity that was part of their new more strategic role in the organization.

The company announced its intent to go to flexible benefits just as the recession began to emerge in 2008. Because of the timing, the news was greeted with some skepticism—largely from longer-term employees. Newer employees, however, welcomed the change since some had seen such plans in other companies and they knew it was a good move for Microsoft to make.

The HR management group worked closely with AON to ensure they had feedback on the design and issues that needed to be integrated into the entire process. Once the new design and project plan were completed, they had to be approved by senior management. Then, the plan went to focus groups, to gather employee reaction and feedback on specific issues.

When the final version of the plan was rolled out to all employees, HR staff involved used a hands-on, one-to-one approach that allowed employees to ask as many questions as they were needed. The process for enrollment included a clear step-by-step method that helped to overcome any remaining skepticism. The new plan design included giving employees a specific number of credits and then having them choose among three levels of coverage in health and dental care. It also included a change of insurance carriers and a new process of online filing and checking of claim statements, as well as outsourcing the overall benefit administration to AON. While there was a lot of new information for employees to absorb, it was all good news.

To help employees accept the change and complete the registration process, the HR-AON change team launched an extensive communications campaign, which started with the establishment of a dedicated website and toll-free hotline. Employee information sessions were held and informative e-mail newsletters were sent out explaining the new plan and providing help with decision making. Managers were also educated about the plan and helped by communicating with employees, which added depth to the process.

Overall, Carolyn Buccongello, director of HR at Microsoft, says implementation went very smoothly and employees were quick to embrace the concept of choice in benefits selection and other changes. She says they were also very excited about new offerings in the plan. And the outcome? "Six months later, we're thrilled with it," says Buccongello. Not only that, after moving to electronic filing and outsourcing claims administration, her team has freed up important time to plan the next big change project.

SOURCES: S. Dobson, "Microsoft Updates Benefits," *Canadian HR Reporter* (September 7, 2009) p. 19; 2010 Best Workplaces in Canada, Great Place to Work@ Institute Canada at www.greatplacetowork.ca/best/list-ca.htm (retrieved March 13, 2011); and "We Have You Covered," Microsoft Careers Canada website.

INTRODUCTION

Employee Benefits
Part of an organization's total compensation package and include both mandatory government-sponsored benefits and voluntary benefits such as life and disability insurance, extended health coverage, additional vacation pay, and a range of other options.

Flexible Benefits Plan
A benefits plan design that provides employees the chance to choose (within limits) among benefits offered by the employer, to help ensure the plan will more effectively meet the needs of all employees, and to help the employer contain costs.

Employee benefits are part of an organization's total compensation package and include both mandatory government-sponsored benefits and voluntary benefits such as life and disability insurance, extended health coverage, additional vacation pay, and a range of other options. If we think of benefits as a part of total employee compensation, many of the concepts discussed in the two previous chapters on employee compensation apply here as well. This means, for example, that both cost and behavioural objectives are important. The cost of benefits adds an average 44 percent to every dollar of payroll, thus accounting for about 30 percent of the total employee compensation package.[1] Controlling labour costs is not possible without controlling benefits costs. On the behavioural side, benefits seem to influence whether potential employees come to work for a company, whether they stay, when they retire—perhaps even how they perform (although the empirical evidence, especially on the latter point, is surprisingly limited).[2] Different employees look for different types of benefits. Employers need to regularly re-examine their benefits to see whether they fit the needs of today rather than yesterday. Our opening vignette on Microsoft Canada's decision to move to a flexible benefits plan and to update the content of the actual plan itself captures the importance of benefits to an organization's ability to recruit and retain top-level talent as the labour market tightens. A **flexible benefits plan** provides employees the chance to choose (within limits) among benefits offered by the employer, to help ensure the plan will more effectively meet the needs of all employees, and to help the employer contain costs. And of course the company's formal benefits plan provided through insurance carriers is complemented by dozens of other ways in which the company saves employees money while boosting their health and wellness. Such "other ways" include internally provided options such as an onsite gym and subsidized cafeteria, tuition reimbursement, and much more.

Although it makes sense to think of benefits as part of total compensation, benefits have unique aspects. First, there is the question of legal compliance. Although direct compensation is subject to government regulation, the scope and impact of regulation on benefits is far greater. Some benefits, such as Canada Pension and Employment Insurance, are mandated by law. Others, although not mandated, are subject to significant regulation or must meet certain criteria to achieve the most favourable tax treatment; these include pensions and savings plans. The heavy involvement of government in benefits decisions reflects the central role benefits play in maintaining economic security.

A second unique aspect of benefits is that organizations so typically offer them that they have come to be institutionalized. Providing medical and retirement benefits of some sort remains almost obligatory for many (e.g., large) employers. A large employer that did not offer such benefits to its full-time employees would be highly unusual, and the employer might well have trouble attracting and retaining a quality workforce.

A third unique aspect of benefits, compared with other forms of compensation, is their complexity. It is relatively easy to understand the value of a dollar as part of a salary, but not as part of a benefits package. The advantages and disadvantages of different types of medical coverage, pension provisions, disability insurance, and investment options for retirement funds are often difficult to grasp, and their value (beyond a general sense that they are good to have) is rarely as clear as the value of one's salary. Most fundamentally, employees may not even be aware of the benefits available to them; and if they are aware, they may not understand how to use them. When employers spend large sums of money on benefits but employees do not understand the benefits or attach much value to them, the return on employers' benefits investment will be fairly dismal.[3] Thus, one reason for giving more responsibility to employees for retirement planning and other benefits is to increase their understanding of the value of such benefits. However, there is a risk to this approach because employees may not really understand the choices they are making.

REASONS FOR BENEFITS GROWTH

LO 1

Discuss the growth in benefits costs and the underlying reasons for that growth.

In thinking about benefits as part of total compensation, a basic question arises: why do employers choose to channel a significant portion of the compensation dollar away from cash (wages and salaries) into benefits? Economic theory tells us that people prefer a dollar in cash over a dollar's worth of any specific commodity because the cash can be used to purchase the commodity or something else.[4] Thus, cash is less restrictive. Several factors, however, have contributed to less emphasis on cash and more on benefits in compensation. To understand these factors, it is useful to examine the growth in benefits over time and the underlying reasons for that growth.

Figure 10.1 on page 384 gives an indication of the overall growth in benefits. Note that in 1929, on the eve of the Great Depression, benefits added an average of only 3 percent to every dollar of payroll. By 1955 this figure had grown to 17 percent, and it has continued to grow, now accounting for almost 44 cents on top of every payroll dollar.

Many factors contributed to this tremendous growth.[5] First, significant growth occurred following World War II when wage and price controls instituted during the war, combined with labour market shortages, forced employers to think of new ways to attract and retain employees. Because benefits were not covered by wage controls, employers channelled more resources in this direction. Once institutionalized, such benefits tended to remain even after wage and price controls were lifted.

Second, the tax treatment of benefits programs is often more favourable for employees than the tax treatment of wages and salaries, meaning that a dollar spent on benefits has the potential to generate more value for the employees than the same dollar spent on wages and salaries. The **marginal tax rate** is the percentage of additional earnings that goes to taxes. Consider the hypothetical employee in Table 10.1 on page 384 and the effect on take-home pay of a $1,000 increase in salary. The total

Marginal Tax Rate
The percentage of an additional dollar of earnings that goes to taxes.

FIGURE 10.1 Growth of Employee Benefits, Percentage of Wages and Salaries and of Total Compensation, 1929–2011

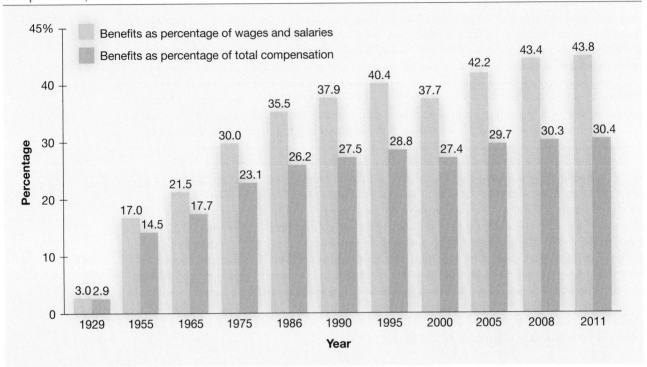

SOURCES: Data through 1990, U.S. Chamber of Commerce Research Center, *Employee Benefits 1990, Employee Benefits 1997, Employee Benefits 2000* (Washington, DC: U.S. Chamber of Commerce, 1991, 1997, and 2000). Data from 1995 onward, "Employer Cost for Employee Compensation," www.bls.gov.

effective marginal tax rate is higher for higher-paid employees and also varies according to province. (Nova Scotia is among the highest, with Nunavut at a mere 7 percent). A $1,000 annual raise for the employee earning $50,000 per year would increase net pay $631.00 ($1,000 × [1 − 0.3695]). In contrast, an extra $1,000 put into benefits would lead to an increase of $1,000 in "take-home benefits."

Employers, too, realize tax advantages from certain types of benefits. Although both cash compensation and most benefits are deductible as operating expenses, employers pay Canada Pension Plan contributions on 4.95 percent of the entire salary, Employer Health Taxes based on total payroll (salaries), as well as other taxes such as workers' compensation and unemployment compensation. However, no such taxes are paid on most employee benefits; the bottom line is that the employer may be able to provide more value to employees by spending the extra $1,000 on benefits instead of salary.

Table 10.1 Example of Marginal Tax Rates (2011) for an Employee Salary of $50,000 in Nova Scotia

	MARGINAL TAX RATE
Federal ($41,544–$83,088)	22.0%
Province (Nova Scotia) ($29,590–$59,180)	14.95%
Total tax rate	36.95%

The tax advantage of benefits also takes another form. Deferring compensation until retirement allows the employee to receive cash, but at a time (retirement) when the employee's tax rate is sometimes lower because of a lower income level. More important, perhaps, is that investment returns on the deferred money typically accumulate tax free, resulting in much faster growth of the investment.

A third factor that has influenced benefits growth is the cost advantage that groups typically realize over individuals. Organizations that represent large groups of employees can purchase insurance (or self-insure) at a lower rate because of economies of scale, which spread fixed costs over more employees to reduce the cost per person. Insurance risks can be more easily pooled in large groups, and large groups can also achieve greater bargaining power in dealing with insurance carriers or medical providers.

A fourth factor influencing the growth of benefits was the growth of organized labour in Canada from the 1930s through the 1950s. This was especially true following World War II when many soldiers who had left their jobs returned to work in industry. However, many became angry at the treatment they received from employers who failed to respect their contribution. Growing discontent caused many to join unions to secure better treatment, which greatly enhanced the unions' ability to organize workers and negotiate contracts with employers. Benefits were often a key negotiation objective. (Indeed, they still are. Benefits issues continue to be a common reason for work stoppages.) Unions were able to successfully pursue their members' interests in benefits, particularly when tax advantages provided an incentive for employers to shift money from cash to benefits. For unions, a new benefit such as medical coverage was a tangible success that could have more impact on prospective union members than a wage increase of equivalent value, which might have amounted to only a cent or two per hour. Also, many nonunion employers responded to the threat of unionization by implementing the same benefits for their own employees, thus contributing to benefits growth.

Finally, employers may also provide unique benefits as a means of differentiating themselves in the eyes of current or prospective employees. In this way, employers communicate key aspects of their culture that set them apart from the rest of the pack. Table 10.2 on page 386 shows some examples.

BENEFITS PROGRAMS

LO 2

Explain the major provisions of government-sponsored, mandatory benefits programs.

Most benefits fall into one of the following categories: mandatory government-sponsored benefits, voluntary employer-sponsored benefits, retirement, pay for time not worked, and family-friendly policies.[6]

Mandatory Government-Sponsored Benefits

Canada/Quebec Pension Plan (CPP/QPP) The **Canada/Quebec Pension Plan (CPP/QPP)** is a mandatory, government-sponsored pension plan funded by employers and employees, established in 1966 to provide a basic level of income security for working Canadians when they retire or become disabled. The Province of Quebec administers its own plan, the Quebec Pension Plan (QPP), but the two plans work together to ensure protection for all contributors. The CPP/QPP is designed to replace about 25 percent of a person's earnings from employment up to a maximum amount, which in 2011 (for retirees age 65) is $960 per month. To qualify for the CPP retirement pension individuals must have paid into the plan at least once during their working years. Self-employed persons can also contribute to the plan but they must pay both the employee and employer contributions into the plan, or 9.9 percent of eligible earnings. Following some changes made to the plan at the end of 2010, individuals now have more flexibility and can choose to begin receiving the pension between ages 60 and 70. However, if they choose to take benefits prior to age 65, and continue to work, they will need to meet certain earnings requirements. Benefit levels vary

Canada/Quebec Pension Plan (CPP/QPP)
A mandatory government-sponsored pension plan funded by employers and employees that provides a basic level of income security for working Canadians when they retire or become disabled; administered separately in Quebec.

Table 10.2   Differentiating via Benefits

Maternity Leave ("top up" to 75% for 52 weeks)	Deeley Harley-Davidson Canada
Pet plan insurance subsidy	Ceridian Canada Ltd.
Generous referral bonuses for successful referral of new candidate	The College of Physicians and Surgeons of Ontario
Exceptional training and development programs and a state-of-the-art training facility	Enbridge Inc.
A free stay at any company-run hotel	Four Seasons
Paid time off for volunteer work and matching employer contributions (up to $1,000) to employee's charity of choice	KPMG
Exceptional performers receive VIP trips to company-sponsored events and box seats at Bell Centre in Montreal	L'Oreal Canada Ltd.
Generous discounts off the lease or purchase of new vehicles (to $1,000) and for their family members (to $800)	Toyota Canada
Head office includes a 24/7 lounge complete with video games, foosball, billiards, and a DJ station for the company's monthly socials	Sophos Inc.
Provides a Stampede breakfast celebration including live entertainment, prizes, and breakfast served by top honchos	Shell Canada Inc.
Life Cycle account of $10,000 to help employees cross major thresholds such as buying first house or paying tuition	Xerox
Pays tuition subsidies and bonus of up to one month's salary to employees completing their professional project management designation	Siemens Canada Limited

SOURCE: Adapted frorm Brian Ballou and Norman H. Goodwin, "Quality of Work Life," *Strategic Finance,* October 2007, pp. 40–48.; and Top 100 Employers in Canada, 2011.

according to the length of an individual's contributory period and levels of earnings over the years, up to the maximum payable from the plan. However, with recent changes to the plan, as of January 2011, monthly CPP retirement pensions will increase by a larger percentage if taken after age 65.[7]

The CPP also provides disability benefits for contributors or their children. Payments to contributors stop when the individual dies, but survivor benefits include either a lump-sum death benefit of $2,500 or a survivor's pension and a children's benefit.

The plan is funded by contributions from both employers and employees. In 2011, each paid contributions of 4.95 percent (for a total of 9.9 percent) on the first $48,300 of the employee's earning, a figure known as the Yearly Maximum Pensionable Earnings (YMPE).

The CPP/QPP has been closely monitored since (then) Finance Minister Paul Martin made changes to the plan in the late 90s to ensure sustainability of the plan. Contribution rates were increased substantially to ensure adequate funding and a CPP Investment Board (CPPIB) was created to ensure the funds were effectively invested for high return in a well-diversified portfolio, and able to withstand market volatility. Sherry Cooper, a well-known Canadian economist, describes the CPP as a "model to the world."[8]

What are the behavioural consequences of CPP/QPP benefits? Because they are legally mandated, employers do not have discretion in designing this aspect of their benefits programs. However, CPP/QPP does affect employees' retirement decisions. The recent changes in eligibility age and benefits levels before and after age 65 will help older Canadians who wish to remain in the workforce longer. This may influence a larger pool of older workers to remain in the labour force for employers to tap into.

Employment Insurance (EI) Established under the Employment Insurance Act and subsequent amendments, the **Employment Insurance (EI)** program is a federal plan administered through federal–provincial and territorial agreements. Its main objectives are (1) to offset lost income during involuntary unemployment due to job loss, illness, or compassionate leave to care for gravely ill family members; (2) to provide maternity and parental benefits off the job due to pregnancy, childbirth, and adoption; (3) to help unemployed workers find new jobs; (4) to provide an incentive for employers to stabilize employment; and (5) to preserve investments in worker skills by providing income during short-term layoffs (which allows workers to return to their employer rather than start over with another employer).

The employment insurance program is financed through federal and provincial funding supported by payroll deductions of employee and employer contributions. In 2011 employees were required to contribute 1.78 percent of insurable earnings up to a maximum of $787, and employers were required to pay 1.4 times the employee contribution, or 2.49 percent of insurable earnings.

Unemployed workers are eligible for benefits if they (1) have a prior attachment to the workforce (have been without work for at least seven consecutive days or have worked a required number of hours in the previous 52 weeks); (2) are available and willing to work each day; (3) are actively seeking work (including registering with the local unemployment office); and (4) were not discharged for cause (such as wilful misconduct), did not quit voluntarily, and are not out of work because of a labour dispute. In December 2010 the federal government announced a significant enhancement to the plan. Under the Fairness for the Self-Employed Act, self-employed Canadians are now able to register for the EI plan and eligible for the special benefits of maternity, parental, sickness, and compassionate care.[9]

Benefits are administered by Service Canada on behalf of Human Resources and Skills Development Canada (HRSDC), which manages Employment Insurance. In the past few years, both claimants and employers have been able to access and submit required information and reports through a convenient Service Canada website. See the "Competing Through Technology" box to learn more about its features.

EI benefits are usually 55 percent of average eligible insurable weekly earnings in the past 14 to 26 weeks, to a maximum yearly amount, which was $44,200 in January 2011. Thus in 2011, the maximum weekly benefit for eligible claimants was $468. Following a two-week waiting period, benefits will be received for periods ranging between 14 to 45 weeks, depending on eligibility and on the regional rate of unemployment in the individual's area, and are taxable. Individuals receive compassionate care leave for up to 6 weeks, or if the individual is off work due to illness for up to 15 weeks.

Maternity benefits are paid for 15 weeks to the birth mother after a two-week waiting period, and can be combined with parental leave of up to another 35 weeks, for a total of 50 weeks overall. Parental leave may be taken by one parent to care for a newborn or adopted child, or shared as desired between both parents.[10] In January 2006, the Quebec Parental Insurance Plan (QPIP) replaced the federal EI program in Quebec and in that province birth mothers are provided with 18 weeks of maternity leave at 70 percent of average earnings to a maximum of $62,000 ($835 per week in 2009), with no waiting period. This can be combined with another 32 weeks of parental leave for either parent (37 weeks for adoptive parents), although the benefit rate drops to 55 percent after 7 weeks into the parental leave.[11]

Because unemployment insurance is, in effect, legally required, management's discretion is limited here, too. Management's main task is to do its part to sustain the system by avoiding unnecessary workforce reductions (e.g., by relying on the sorts of actions described in Chapter 4). The gradual enhancements over past years to the maternity and parental leave plan under EI were meant to help young families get a good start, but have also impacted employers in a number of ways. For example, these enhancements have led to women being absent from the workplace for longer periods of time

Employment Insurance (EI)
A mandatory, government-sponsored plan funded by employee and employer contributions that offsets lost income to eligible employees for reasons of job loss, illness, or compassionate leave, and that provides maternity and parental benefits and a variety of other employment initiatives.

Competing Through Technology

Pot of Gold: Service Canada Website

For regular users of the site, it seems hard to believe that the Service Canada website was created only in 2005. That's because users can become dependent on the site very quickly for both business and personal reasons, and forget that much of what is found there in just a few seconds could be very difficult to track down just a short while ago. Since this single-entry portal into a wide range of government programs (such as CPP/QPP and EI) was created, it has made accessing a growing number of services and programs much easier and more convenient for employees and organizations alike. For example, the site was designed to speed up service, and contains digital tools and forms that used to require considerable energy to acquire—if one knew where to go or whom to ask. It also allows employees, employers, the unemployed, and the retired to gain essential information, find and complete key documentation, and transact payments of many kinds using highly secure technology—much like online banking.

Search mechanisms enable navigation and quick access when searching for up-to-date phone numbers of government contacts. The site also provides information on the whereabouts of local Service Canada Centres for individuals who prefer a real person to answer questions or provide advice.

When it comes to employment alone, a quick glance down the sidebar of the Home Page reveals that key transitional moments in one's entire life cycle of employment can be facilitated by using the services provided among the thousands of links. Visitors to the site can choose from a Life Events shortlist of the most common milestones, such as Finding a Job, Raising a Family, Having a Baby, Retirement Planning, and Starting a Business. Just looking down the shortlist can provoke a rush of memories for those well along in their career—that first summer job, that first baby, opening an education account, deciding to start a business, and thinking about the years ahead (finally writing that novel). The list expands to a total of 17 Life Events, however, so anyone easily distracted could spend quite a while investigating them.

Services can also be selected by subject, such as Education and Training, Immigration, Personal Documents, and (again) Employment. A quick trip to these links reveals one can be connected to the means to apply for or renew a passport, or for employers, to complete and file a Record of Employment. Anyone who has tried either of these activities prior to 2005 and the launch of the website will appreciate the amount of convenience provided here—especially in completing such processes online.

On the Employment Insurance section of the site, individuals preparing for maternity, adoption, or parental leave, or to apply for income assistance after a job loss, will appreciate the ease of the online process.

When it comes time to start planning for retirement, the CPP section of the website provides essential information and lots of room for dreaming. Through this part of the site users can access their personal CPP Statement of Contributions. It also offers a Canadian Retirement Income Calculator toolkit that allows users to compute future income. Once all estimated sources of future income are loaded into the calculator tool, individuals can see if future income will be close to the 70 percent recommended by retirement planners, or whether it would be best to keep on working. Changes and updates to the CPP/QPP and other programs appear as soon as such programs are finalized, providing the most up-to-date information possible.

Accessibility is another important feature of the site. Users can listen to everything on the site by clicking on the Sidebar panel selections labelled "Page Tools" and "Read to Me," which enables auditory learners or those who are vision impaired to get the most out of the information offered. And of course the entire website is available in either English or French, including the ability to "Outils" and "Lisez-Moi."

The site is customized to the needs of a wide variety of users, including Aboriginal peoples, employers, families and children, newcomers to Canada, people with disabilities, seniors, service delivery partners, veterans, and students. Choosing the category you fit within is another easy way to access what is important quickly.

While it may seem odd to discuss a government website, this one offers so much it's hard not to get excited about it. For human resource managers and small business owners it provides a whole new way of working with employees ("Have you checked the Service Canada website for an explanation of how to renew your passport before you leave for Brazil?"). The vast amount of information directed at employers also assists in managing the needs of both employees and the business itself ("What grants are available for apprenticeship?") It also makes one's personal life a whole lot easier. Even if you aren't going to Brazil yourself, you can at least dream.

SOURCE: Service Canada Website, at www.servicecanada.gc.ca (in English or French). Reproduced with permission of the Minister of Public Works and Government Services, 2011.

as they choose to take full advantage of the plan. In addition, men have been opting to share the parental leave portion of the plan as they too choose to participate more fully in the early months of a new child's life. This has created challenges for employers with respect to productivity since such leave must often be covered using temporary workers. Employers have also had to face the issue of retention of valued workers who may opt not to return to work at the end of a leave.

Workers' Compensation
A mandatory government-sponsored insurance plan funded by employers that provides wage-loss benefits, health care, survivor benefits, and rehabilitative services to eligible employees with work-related injuries or diseases.

Workers' Compensation Workers' compensation laws cover job-related injuries and death.[12] Prior to enactment of these laws, workers suffering work-related injuries or diseases could receive compensation only by suing for damages. Moreover, the common-law defences available to employers meant that such lawsuits were not usually successful. In contrast, these laws operate under a principle of no-fault liability, meaning that an employee does not need to establish gross negligence by the employer. In return, employers receive immunity from lawsuits. (One exception is the employer who intentionally contributes to a dangerous workplace.) Employees are not covered when injuries are self-inflicted or stem from intoxication or obvious disregard for safety rules.[13]

Workers' compensation benefits fall into four major categories: (1) wage-loss benefits; (2) health care, (3) survivor benefits, and (4) rehabilitative services. Disability income, or wage-loss benefits, is typically 80–90 percent of net predisability earnings, although each province has its own maximum. In contrast to unemployment insurance benefits,

A key goal of workers' compensation is to assist workers injured on the job with lost income while they recover, and to guide employers in the return-to-work process, so that employees can make a safe and effective return to their pre-injury life.

disability benefits are tax free. The system is financed by employers who pay premiums generally calculated per $100 of insurable earnings related to average losses in each category. Premiums vary considerably since the cost to the employer is based on three factors. The first factor is the nature of the occupations and the risk attached to each. For example, employers operating logging businesses will pay much higher premiums than those in retail since there is a much greater risk of injury in the former, even when the highest safety standards are enforced. The second factor is the province where work is located since each province has its own Workplace Safety Insurance Board, and wage loss benefits vary by province. The third factor is the employer's experience rating.

The experience rating system again provides an incentive for employers to make their workplaces safer. Dramatic injuries (such as losing a finger or hand) are less prevalent than minor ones, such as sprains and strains. Back strain is the most expensive benign health condition in developed countries.[14] Many actions can be taken to reduce workplace injuries, such as work redesign and training; and to speed the return to health, and thus to work (e.g., exercise).[15] Some changes can be fairly simple (such as permitting workers to sit instead of having them bend over). It is also important to hold managers accountable (in their performance evaluations) for making workplaces safer and getting employees back to work promptly following an injury. See the discussion in Chapter 12 on safety awareness programs for some of the ways employers and employees are striving to make the workplace safer.

Voluntary Employer-Sponsored Benefits

LO 3

Explain the various types of voluntary employer-sponsored benefits

Private Group Insurance   As we noted earlier, group insurance rates are typically lower than individual rates because of economies of scale, the ability to pool risks, and the greater bargaining power of a group. This cost advantage, together with tax considerations and a concern for employee security, helps explain the prevalence of employer-sponsored insurance plans. We discuss two major types: medical insurance and disability insurance. Note that these programs are not legally required; rather, they are offered at the discretion of employers.

Extended Medical Insurance   Not surprisingly, public opinion surveys indicate that medical benefits are by far the most important benefit to the average person.[16] In one Canadian government survey that included almost 14 million employees, 50 percent were covered by three types of insurance: medical, dental and life/disability.[17]

Basic types of medical expenses typically covered under extended medical insurance include hospital expenses not covered by provincial hospital/medical plans such as semi-private and private room coverage. Other benefits that employers may offer include dental care, vision care, and prescription drug programs. Perhaps the most important issue in benefits management is the challenge of providing quality medical benefits while controlling costs, a subject we return to in a later section.

Short-Term Disability Plan
Benefits plans that provide income security to employees for short periods of absence from work due to nonwork-related illness or injury.

Long-Term Disability Plan
A form of income for longer periods of absence from work due to nonwork-related chronic illness or disability.

Disability Insurance   Two basic types of disability coverage exist—short-term disability and long-term disability.[18] **Short-term disability** plans provide income security to employees for short-term absence from work due to nonwork-related illness or injury. **Long-term disability** is a form of income protection for longer-term absences from work due to nonwork-related chronic illness or disability, and where applicable provides benefits until the maximum time specified in the long-term disability plan (e.g., a specific age such as 65 years old.). A 2009 Conference Board study of 255 medium-sized and large organizations across Canada indicated that 87 percent had short-term disability (STD) programs in place and about 99 percent had long-term disability plans in place.[19]

Of the companies with short-term disability plans, 62 percent of programs covered all employees, and 25 percent covered only some employees. The vast majority (86 percent) of programs were paid for by the employer, 3 percent were cost shared with employees, and 11 percent were paid for by employees themselves.[20] Short-term plans typically provide benefits for six months or less, at which point long-term plans take over so that income protection continues for as long as the employee's illness or disability continues and coverage is specified in the plan design. Maximum length of coverage for the short-term disability plans in the study ranged considerably from 10 to 104 weeks, although the average was 22 weeks. The salary replacement rates ranged between 60 to 100 percent, with the average at 84 percent.[21] The types of plans offered by companies vary. For example, plans may be self-insured (as were 55 percent of the short-term disability plans in the study), fully insured, or partially insured (hybrid plans). They may also be self-administered or be administrative services only (ASO) (where a company pays the benefits but outsources all claim processing and administration to an insurance company.) Of the long-term disability plans in the study, about two-thirds applied to all employees and the remaining one-third covered some employees. Funding of long-term disability plans has important tax implications since benefits are taxable if the employer pays the premium. This is important since most plans, like those in the study, cover only about 67 percent of an employee's predisability earnings. Thus, having to pay income tax on reduced earnings can create greater hardship. That could be why 45 percent of the plans in the study were paid for by employees alone, 41 percent were paid for by the employer or company, and the remaining 15 percent were cost shared.[22]

Regardless of how they are funded, access to such plans is vital to employees from an income security point of view. Disability benefits, especially long-term ones, must be coordinated with other programs, such as Employment Insurance, Canada Pension, and Workers Compensation.

Retirement

Earlier we discussed the Canada Pension Plan, a mandatory government program that provides retirement income. Although CPP can be a large component of the elderly's overall retirement income, private pension plans have grown in importance since the early 90s, reaching 32 percent of the average annual retirement income of Canadians 65 and older by 2006.[23] In one study that followed family income for individuals aged 54 to 56 (in 1983) until 2006 when they were between 77 to 79 years old, income sources changed over time. In their mid-50s more than 75 percent derived family income from earnings. By their mid-70s, around one-third of all income came from private pensions; about one-third was derived from public pensions (CPP); investments, capital gains and dividends accounted for almost 20 percent; and approximately 10 percent came from employment earnings.[24]

Employers have no legal obligation to offer private retirement plans, but many do. As we note later, if a private retirement plan is provided, it must be a **registered pension plan** according to the Income Tax Act and will be subject to pension standards legislation across Canada, in all ten provinces as well as the federal Pension Benefits Standards Act, 1985. (Pensions plans established for people employed in Yukon, the Northwest Territories, and Nunavut are regulated under the Office of the Superintendent of Financial Institutions Act.)[25] The main types of registered pension plans offered include defined benefit, money-purchase or defined contribution, and hybrid mixed plans, which are a combination of both defined-benefit and defined-contribution plans. In the past 30 years employers have been gradually shifting away from defined-benefit plans in Canada. For example, in 2006 only 30 percent of Canadian workers were covered by a defined-benefit plan, versus 41 percent in 1991. Changes have been more dramatic in the United Kingdom and in the United States.[26]

Defined-Benefit Pension Plan

A **defined-benefit pension plan** is an employer-sponsored and registered pension plan that guarantees (defines) a specified retirement benefit level to employees typically based on a combination of years of service and age as well as the employee's earnings level (usually the five highest earnings years). Often the amount guaranteed is 70 percent of whatever

LO 4

Explain different types of pension plans and current pension trends.

Registered Pension Plans
Retirement plans sponsored by employers that are registered according to the Income Tax Act and subject to federal and provincial pension standards legislation.

Defined-Benefit Pension Plan
An employer-sponsored and registered pension plan that guarantees (defines) a specified retirement benefit level to employees typically based on a combination of years of service and age as well as the employee's earnings level (usually the five highest earnings years).

years of previous earnings are utilized in the calculation. However, it can also be simply a guaranteed flat rate. For instance, an organization might guarantee a monthly pension payment of $1,500 to an employee retiring at age 65 with 30 years of service and an average salary over the final five years of $40,000. Table 10.3 illustrates shifts in private pension plan coverage in Canada in the 15 years prior to the last census, indicating that defined-benefits plans are gradually losing favour in the private sector, and being replaced by defined-contribution plans.

A 2010 Conference Board Survey of 379 public- and private-sector organizations reported that among private-sector organizations participating in the survey, 45 percent provided defined-benefit plans (versus 81 percent of public-sector organizations in the survey). In examining all organizations (both private and public sector) in the survey, 54 percent offered defined-benefits plans, with the average employer contribution being 8.8 percent of salary of plan members.[27]

Defined-benefit plans insulate employees from investment risk, which is borne by the company. Obviously, if the company has to pay out a guaranteed level of benefits upon retirement, it is in the company's best interest to fund the plan well and invest plan funds to the best advantage. However, in the event of severe financial difficulties that force the company to terminate or reduce employee pension benefits, plan members may be at serious risk. For example, if a company goes bankrupt, employees are considered to be the last creditors on the list, and in too many cases employees have found that the company defaulted on payments into the pension plan, leaving members with much, much less than they counted on in retirement.

Nortel is an example, with employees having no recourse but to take the company to court in a desperate attempt to recover what they once thought would be generous pensions. Although Nortel was granted creditor protection in January 2009, with plans to restructure, in June the company decided to discontinue operations and sell off assets. The Nortel Retirees and Former Employees Protection Canada (NRPC), which represents some 12,000 pensioners, 5,500 deferred pensioners, 450 employees on long-term disability, and the 1,500 severed and current employees (at the time) took action when shocked employees realized the plan was only 69 percent funded and they would be looking at a 31 percent decrease in benefits. Until the market downturn exposed such vulnerability, employees often didn`t understand the situation until they sought advice once the company applied for creditor protection or actually went bankrupt. As one representative of the NRPC pointed out, "This can happen to anyone, any reasonably sized company."[28]

Such tragedies have occurred in numerous smaller companies as well; according to one CBC documentary, loss of pension through bankruptcy has impacted over 11,000 people in the Hamilton area alone.[29] Unions, the Canadian Labour Congress, employee groups such as the NRPC, and NDP MP Pat Martin (Winnipeg Centre) have fought hard to gain more protection for employees. Martin introduced Bill C-281 as a private member's bill, calling for employees to be placed first on the list of creditors when assets were disbursed. As a result of such efforts, the Wage Earner Protection Program Act (WEPPA) and the Bankruptcy Insolvency Act (BIA) were passed in July 2008, granting employees priority over all other creditors for claims of outstanding wages (including salary commissions, compensation, unpaid employer pension contributions, unremitted employee

Table 10.3   Shifts in Canadian Pension Plan Coverage by Sector

	1991	2006	CHANGE
Private Sector			
DB Plan Members	86%	73%	13%
DC Plan members	14%	27%	13%

SOURCE: P. Gougeon, "Shifting Pensions," *Perspectives*, May 2009, p. 16 and 17, Statistics Canada Catalogue no. 75-001-X M.

pension deductions, and severance and termination pay) up to a maximum of $3,250. Amounts will be paid by Service Canada or the company estate after receivership. However, the bill does nothing to reimburse an employee's pension that has been accumulating for as much as 30 years.[30]

In March 2011, House of Commons Bill C-501 (Senate Bill S-214), An Act to Amend the Bankruptcy and Insolvency Act and other Acts (pension protection), had passed Second Reading and were making slow progress toward Third Reading. However, with the dissolution of Parliament in March 2011 for a general election, both bills were killed and will have to be reintroduced to the new session of Parliament. Both bills are designed to protect defined-benefit plan members by giving top priority to unfunded pension plan liabilities (among all creditors) when a company goes into bankruptcy proceedings.[31] There is still much controversy around such an approach since it can be argued that companies will be unable to get additional financing when they encounter problems, thus accelerating the decline of the business and the loss of jobs. However, for employees who are facing a bleak future after working, saving, and contributing to a pension plan their entire career, it seems like a very good idea.

Learn more about pension protection online with Connect.

Defined-Contribution Pension Plan   Unlike defined-benefit pension plans, **defined-contribution pension plans** do not promise a specific benefit level for employees upon retirement. Rather, an individual account is set up for each employee to which the employer provides a guaranteed size of contribution. The employee often contributes as well, and the funds are invested. However, since there is no further obligation for the employer, funds are often managed more conservatively. When it is time to retire, the total funds invested are withdrawn and used to purchase a retirement fund for the employee. The advantage of such plans for employers is that investment risk is shifted to employees and presents fewer administrative challenges because there is no need to calculate payments based on age and service. In the 2010 Conference Board survey of public- and private-sector organizations mentioned earlier, 52 percent of all organizations surveyed offered a defined-contribution plan, with the employer contribution of such plans averaging 7.4 percent of member salary.

As you will see from Table 10.4 on page 394, defined-contribution plans have been especially preferred among smaller Canadian companies, no doubt because of their desire to avoid long-term obligations. This preference could also be due to the fact that small companies tend to be younger, and might have been founded within the past 30 years when defined-contribution plans began to increase in favour. Some companies have both defined-benefit and defined-contribution plans. However, as the 2006 figures indicate, medium to large plans have clearly been shifting to defined-contribution plans in the past 20 years, while very large plans have shifted less than 1 percent.

There is a wide variety of defined-contribution plans, a few of which are briefly described here. One of the simplest is a *money purchase plan*, under which an employer specifies a level of annual contribution (such as 10 percent of salary). At retirement age, the employee is entitled to the contributions plus the investment returns. The term "money purchase" stems from the fact that employees often use the money to purchase an annuity rather than taking it as a lump sum. Profit-sharing plans and employee share ownership plans are also often used as retirement vehicles. Both permit contributions (cash and stock, respectively) to vary from year to year, thus allowing employers to avoid fixed obligations that may be burdensome in difficult financial times. However, such a lack of fixed obligations is not favourable to employees if shares have deflated in value at the point of retirement.

Defined-contribution plans continue to grow in importance, while, as we saw earlier, defined-benefit plans are viewed as riskier because of the huge responsibility to adequately fund such plans into the future. Defined-contribution plans put the responsibility for wise investing squarely on the shoulders of the employee. That is, the risk for funding an adequate retirement shifts to the employee, since there is no guarantee how much money will actually be in the plan by the time an individual retires.

Defined-Contribution Pension Plan
An employer-sponsored and registered pension plan in which an individual account is set up for each employee, to which the employer provides a guaranteed size of contribution; it may also include employee contributions.

Table 10.4   Shifting Canadian Pension Plan Coverage by Plan Size

	1991	2006
Small Plans		
DB Plans	45.6%	27.5%
DC Plans	54.4%	72.5%
Medium Plans		
DB Plans	79.3%	56.4%
DC Plans	20.7%	43.6%
Large Plans		
DB Plans	92%	76.9%
DC Plans	8%	23.1%
Very Large Plans		
DB Plans	98%	97.1%
DC Plans	2%	2.9%

SOURCE: P. Gougeon, "Shifting Pensions," *Perspectives*, May 2009, p. 19.

Several factors affect the amount of income that will be available to an employee upon retirement. First, the earlier the age at which investments are made, the longer returns can accumulate. As Figure 10.2 shows, an annual investment of $3,000 made between ages 21 and 29 will be worth much more at age 65 than a similar investment made between ages 31 and 39. Second, different investments have different historical rates of return. Between 1946 and 1990, the average annual return was 11.4 percent for stocks, 5.1 percent for bonds, and 5.3 percent for cash (bank savings accounts).[32] As Figure 10.2 shows, if historical rates of return were to continue, an investment in a mix of 60 percent stock, 30 percent bonds, and 10 percent cash between the ages of 21 and 29 would be worth almost four times as much at age 65 as would the same amount invested in a bank savings account. A third consideration is the need to counteract investment risk by diversification because stock and bond prices can be volatile in the short run. Although stocks have the greatest historical rate of return, that is no guarantee of future performance, particularly over shorter time periods. (This fact has become painfully obvious to many during the recent dramatic drop in stock market values around the world.) Thus some investment advisors recommend a mix of stock, bonds, and cash, as shown in the two columns on the left in Figure 10.2, to reduce investment risk. Younger investors may wish to have more stock, while those closer to retirement age typically have less stock in their portfolios. It's also important not to invest too heavily in any single stock.

Pension Design and Education   Although private pensions are not mandatory, those that are set up must meet certain requirements contained in both federal and provincial legislation, and the plan must also meet its own strategic objectives. Hence, various policy decisions must be made during the design process that ultimately create the company's unique pension offering. These include issues of eligibility, funding, the benefit formula, vesting, and portability.[33]

Eligibility.   One of the policy issues around plan design concerns who can join the plan and when. For example, how many years must an employee work for the organization before he or she becomes eligible to join the plan? Will part-time or contract employees be allowed to join the plan? If so, will they have the same eligibility period?

FIGURE 10.2   The Relationship of Retirement Savings to Age When Savings Begins and Type of Investment Portfolio

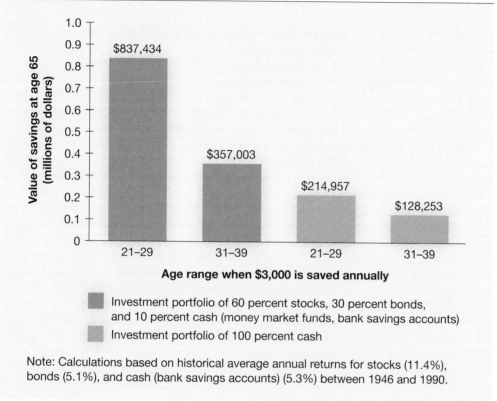

Investment portfolio of 60 percent stocks, 30 percent bonds, and 10 percent cash (money market funds, bank savings accounts)

Investment portfolio of 100 percent cash

Note: Calculations based on historical average annual returns for stocks (11.4%), bonds (5.1%), and cash (bank savings accounts) (5.3%) between 1946 and 1990.

Funding.   Plan design must include provisions for how the plan will be financed. Will it include both employee and employer contributions (contributory), or only employer contributions (non-contributory)? What rate of contribution is appropriate for the plan? Will the employer match the employee's contribution with a fixed amount or a percentage of salary or employee contribution?

Benefit Formula.   If an employer is providing a defined-benefit plan, the plan must specify how the amount of pension benefits will be calculated. In many plans the pension is based on an employee's final earnings. For example, the formula may use the highest salary in the last five years of membership in the plan, or an average of earnings in the last five years in the plan.

Vesting.   When employees become participants in a pension plan and work a specified minimum period of time, they earn a right to a pension upon retirement. These are referred to as **vesting rights**.[34] Vested employees have the right to their pension at retirement age, regardless of whether they remain with the employer until that time. Employee contributions to their own plans are always completely vested. However, the vesting of employer-funded pension benefits is governed by provincial pension legislation and most provinces require employer contributions to be vested by the time the employee has two years of service.

These requirements were put in place to prevent companies from terminating employees before they reach retirement age or before they reach their length-of-service requirements in order to avoid paying pension benefits. It should also be noted that transferring employees or laying them off as a means of avoiding pension obligations is not legal either, even if such actions are motivated partly by

Vesting Rights
Rights to a pension to be paid upon retirement earned by members of a pension plan once a specified minimum period of time has been worked with the employer sponsoring the plan (up to two years in Canada).

business necessity.[35] On the other hand, employers are free to vest earlier if they choose. However, if an employer experiences high quit rates during the first 18 months of employment, it may choose to vest at the two-year limit to minimize pension costs.

Portability.   Pension legislation now requires employers to make it easier to transfer the lump-sum value of an employee's pension amount (or the money in his or her defined-contribution account) to the pension plan of a new employer or into a locked-in RRSP (LIRA) with a recognized financial institution. The amount transferred out of the employee's plan depends on whether employer contributions are vested or not. When the employee is vested in the plan, all contributions and earnings on the employee's pension amount are transferred out of the plan. If the employee is not vested, only the employee's contributions and earnings on that amount will be portable.

Employers have increasing responsibility not only to design pension plans well, but also to educate employees about investing of their pension funds. To supplement existing legal requirements, in 2004 the Joint Forum of Financial Market Regulators issued new guidelines regarding the responsibility of employers for managing company pension and savings plans. These guidelines indicate that if an employer provides a defined-contribution plan, group RRSP, or deferred profit-sharing plan where members decide how their funds should be invested, the firm should be offering educational tools and information to employees. Employees need to know the meaning of important terms associated with both the pension and investment industries, the risk associated with various types of investments and general knowledge about market dynamics. They also need to understand management fees associated with various funds, how to compare the expected return on investment among various choices available, and how to plan for retirement.[36]

The traditional defined-benefit pension plan discourages employee turnover or delays it until the employer can recoup the training investment in employees.[37] Even if an employee's pension benefit is vested, it is usually smaller if the employee changes employers, mainly because the size of the benefit depends on earnings in the final years with an employer. It has also been suggested that pensions are designed to encourage long-service employees, whose earnings growth may eventually exceed their productivity growth, to retire. This is consistent with the fact that retirement benefits reach their maximum at retirement age.[38]

The fact that in recent years many employers have sought to reduce their workforces through early retirement programs is also consistent with the notion that pensions are used to retain certain employees while encouraging others to leave. One early retirement program approach is to adjust years-of-service credit upward for employees willing to retire, resulting in a higher retirement benefit for them (and less monetary incentive to work). These workforce reductions may also be one indication of a broader trend toward employees becoming less likely to spend their entire careers with a single employer.[39] On one hand, if more mobility across employers becomes necessary or desirable, the current pension system's incentives against (or penalties for) mobility may require modification. On the other hand, perhaps increased employee mobility will reinforce the continued trend toward defined-contribution plans, which have greater portability across employers.[40]

Of course, even if very small employers want to offer a pension plan, they cannot do so because of the time and resources required to design and administer a plan. This means that hundreds of thousands of Canadians who work for small companies, or who are self-employed, are denied the option of joining a company-sponsored pension plan. Instead they must resort to the next best option and try to build up enough savings for retirement through investments or RRSPs. In response to concerns of such individuals and following a nation-wide debate that included numerous stakeholders, the federal government developed a solution to the problem by creating a framework whereby any employer, and those who are self-employed, can participate in a defined-contribution pension plan. You'll find details about the new plan, announced in late December 2010, in the "Competing Through Sustainability" box.

Competing Through Sustainability

Hope for the Future: Registered Pooled Pension Plans

For some time there has been great debate about how to increase pension security for thousands of Canadians who do not have access to a private pension plan. In professional and government circles the phrase for this concern is "retirement income adequacy." Following extensive research on the topic by a group of finance ministers from British Columbia, Alberta, Manitoba, Ontario, and Nova Scotia (guided by a research director) provincial and territorial ministers meeting in December 2010, were able to come up with a framework for defined-contribution Pooled Registered Pension Plans (PRPPs) in Canada.

Still only broadly sketched out in terms of design and implementation, PRPPs offer strong hope to owners and employees of small business, and the self-employed, that they will soon have access to a low-cost retirement savings vehicle that can help them save for future retirement. Canadians previously excluded from Registered Pension Plans would no longer have to rely only on self-funded options such as RRSPs, personal investments, CPP, and Old Age Security and ongoing employment beyond age 65, the traditional age of retirement.

Once harmonized and implemented across all levels of government, the new plan will provide a straightforward, easy-to-access, low-cost pension plan that any employer can offer to employees. The lower investment management costs derived from creation of a large pooled fund will make it manageable for small employers. The plan design will ensure ease of portability if contributions need to be transferred between plans. This would assist those who are self-employed if they choose to take a job with an employer that has an existing pension plan or that participates in a PRPP. And, finally, the investment of pooled pension funds will be highly regulated and guided by administrators, trust companies, and insurance companies, with a fiduciary responsibility to ensure the most effective return on investment for plan members. While administrators will invest pension funds, plan members will have the opportunity to decide what their personal investment mix should be to meet personal objectives for retirement, and they will have personal accounts for record-keeping purposes. And, much like private pension plans already in existence among corporations, administrators of the PRPPs will provide educational tools and information to ensure the best investment choices are made.

While the new PRPP is indeed an exciting new option on the retirement horizon for all Canadians, there are those who still think this isn't enough to fill the gap of retirement savings that already exists in Canada. However, perhaps the decision to support financial literacy among Canadians is just as important as creating a new publicly administered pension plan. For example, in 2009, only 38 percent of Canadians contributed to an RRSP. If this is due to a poor understanding of the importance of setting aside retirement savings as early as possible during working years and of the tax benefits from making such investments, then perhaps the increased availability of financial education associated with PRPPs will finally reach those who have ignored such opportunities in the past. Regardless of which route currently unprotected Canadians choose to take (PRPPs or RRSPs) more education and another major option for retirement can only help.

SOURCES: "Framework for Pooled Registered Pension Plans," Department of Finance Canada, Publications and Reports, at www.fin.gc.ca/activty/pubs/pension/prpp-irpac-eng.asp; "Ensuring a Strong Retirement System, Support for Provinces and Territories While Moving Towards Budget Balance," Department of Finance Canada News Release at www.fin.gc.ca/n10/10-128-eng.asp; and S. Moretti, "Retirement Funding Gap a Concern," *London Free Press*, January 13, 2011.

McGraw connect

Learn more about vesting of pensions online with Connect.

LO 5

Discuss how employee benefits in Canada compare with those in other countries.

Pay for Time Not Worked

At first glance, paid vacation, holidays, sick leave, and so forth may not seem to make economic sense. The employer pays the employee for time not spent working, receiving no tangible production value in return. Therefore, some employers may see little direct advantage. Perhaps for this reason, a minimum number of vacation days (20) is mandated by law in the European Community. As many as 30 days of vacation is not uncommon for relatively new employees in Europe. By contrast, the legal minimum in Canada is mandated in provincial Employment Standards Acts. For example, in Ontario, the minimum provided is 10 days, but 15 days is typical for many large companies. Canadian workers must typically be with an employer for 20 to 25 years before they receive as much paid vacation as their western European counterparts.

Sick Leave Programs
Employer-sponsored benefit plans that often provide full salary replacement to employees for a limited period of time and which may be based on length of service.

Sick leave programs are employer-sponsored benefits plans that often provide full salary replacement for a limited period of time, usually not exceeding 26 weeks. The amount of sick leave is often based on length of service, accumulating with service (one day per month, for example). Sick leave policies need to be carefully structured to avoid providing employees with the wrong incentives. For example, if sick leave days disappear at the end of the year (rather than accumulate), a "use it or lose it" mentality may develop among employees, contributing to greater absenteeism. Organizations have developed a number of measures to counteract this.[41] Some allow sick days to accumulate, then pay employees for the number of sick days when they retire or resign. Employers may also attempt to communicate to their employees that accumulated sick leave is better saved to use as a bridge to long-term disability, because the replacement rate (the ratio of sick leave or disability payments to normal salary) for the former is typically higher. Sick leave payments may equal 100 percent of usual salary, whereas the replacement ratio for long-term disability might be 60 percent, so the more sick leave accumulated, the longer an employee can avoid dropping to 60 percent of usual pay when unable to work.

Although vacation and other paid leave programs help attract and retain employees, there is a cost to providing time off with pay, especially in a global economy. The fact that vacation and other paid leave practices differ across countries contributes to the differences in labour costs described in Chapter 8. Consider that, on average, in manufacturing, German workers work 297 fewer hours per year than their Canadian counterparts, and 562 fewer hours than workers in the Czech Republic! (See Figure 10.3.) In other words, German workers are at work approximately 7 fewer weeks per year than their Canadian counterparts and 14 fewer weeks than workers in the Czech Republic next door. It is not surprising then that German manufacturers such as Brose (mentioned in Chapter 8) have looked outside Germany in many cases for alternative production sites.

Family-Friendly Policies: Maternity Leave Top-Up

To ease employees' work/life conflict, organizations may use *family-friendly policies* such as family leave policies and child care. Although the programs discussed here would seem to be targeted to a particular group of employees, these programs often have "spillover effects" on other employees, who see them as symbolizing a general corporate concern for human resources, thus promoting loyalty even among employee groups that do not use the programs, and possibly resulting in improved organizational performance.[42]

Although Canadian employees can take maternity and parental leave for up to 50 weeks, the 55 percent of earnings (70 percent in Quebec) benefits received from EI are a significant decrease from net income. For this reason, some employers offer a "top-up" to employees, otherwise known

FIGURE 10.3 Average Annual Working Time in 2008 Relative to Canada

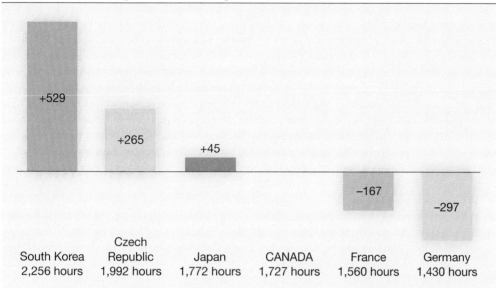

SOURCE: How Do OECD Labour Markets Perform? Table: Average Annual Working Time, Hours per Worker (last updated July 6, 2010). OECD Employment Outlook, Organization for Economic Cooperation and Development.

as Supplemental Unemployment Benefit (SUB), a government initiative linked directly with EI or QPIP benefits. Through a SUB plan, employers can supplement EI benefits during a period of unemployment that is caused by temporary stoppage of work, training, illness, injury or quarantine.[43]

A recent Employment Insurance Coverage Survey (EICS) indicated that in 2008, 20 percent of Canadian mothers with infants under 13 months receiving EI/QPIP benefits received a top-up from their employers. Of course, since the benefit is completely optional (or negotiated into a collective bargaining agreement), employers vary in their decisions about how much to top up EI benefits and for how long. The EI survey found that, on average, a top-up was offered for 19 weeks and employers provided $300 per week over and above EI being received by new mothers. (Note that men can also receive a top-up, but this was not measured in the survey discussed here.) In addition, women on maternity, adoption, or parental leave in Quebec are 2.7 times more likely to receive a top-up from their employers, where the first SUB plan of this type originated in 1979. Women working in unionized environments and for an organization with more than 500 employees are much more likely to receive a top-up. Finally, mothers working in the public sector are 5.7 times more likely to receive a top-up than those in the private sector, and the average length of a top-up is 22 weeks versus 12 weeks for women in the private sector.[44]

Employers offering top-ups to employees often do so for retention purposes, fearing the employees might decide not to continue working, or use the time off to seek a new job with another employer. Therefore, top-ups are usually offered on the condition that the employee will return to his or her job by a specific date, and that he or she will remain with the job for a specific period of time, or repay the top-up benefit. Top-ups seem to work from a retention standpoint since 96 percent of women on maternity leave who received a top-up returned to their original employer, versus 77 percent of those who had no top-up.[45]

Learn more about maternity leave and family-friendly policies online with Connect.

Child Care   Many Canadian companies, concerned about managing employment absence effectively or simply retaining valued employees following childbirth or adoption, look for ways to provide some form of child care support and they often combine it with other efforts to reintegrate new mothers (or fathers) back into the active workforce. The costs of child care vary across Canada, but usually are well over $50 per day.[46] Support comes from employers in several forms that vary in their degree of organizational involvement.[47] The lowest level of involvement offered is when an organization supplies and helps employees collect information about the cost and quality of available child care. At the next level, organizations provide vouchers or discounts for employees to use at existing child care facilities, or they may purchase membership in an organization that guarantees a certain number of daycare spaces for emergency backup day care. The TD Bank Financial Group offers employees pre-arranged emergency backup daycare in cities where the service is available,[48] and you will recall our discussion of services offered by Kid & Co in Chapter 7. At the highest level, firms provide child care at or near their worksites.

An organization's decision to staff its own child care facility should not be taken lightly. It is typically a costly venture with important liability concerns. Moreover, the results, in terms of reducing absenteeism and enhancing productivity, are often mixed.[49] One reason for this is that many organizations are "jumping on the day care bandwagon" without giving much thought to the best form of assistance for their specific employees.

LO 6

Discuss how to manage benefits effectively to control cost, influence productivity, and attract and retain good employees.

MANAGING BENEFITS: EMPLOYER OBJECTIVES AND STRATEGIES

Although the regulatory environment places some important constraints on benefits decisions, employers retain significant discretion and need to evaluate the payoff of such decisions.[50] As discussed earlier, however, this evaluation needs to recognize that employees have come to expect certain things from employers. Employers who do not meet these expectations run the risk of violating what has been called an "implicit contract" between the employer and its workers. If employees believe their employers feel little commitment to their welfare, they can hardly be expected to commit themselves to the company's success.

Clearly, there is much room for progress in the evaluation of benefits decisions.[51] Despite some of the obvious reasons for benefits—group discounts, regulation, and minimizing compensation-related taxes—organizations must spell out what they want their benefits package to achieve and then evaluate their results against their objectives. Research suggests that most organizations do not have written benefits objectives.[52] Obviously, without clear objectives to measure progress, evaluation is difficult (and less likely to occur). Table 10.5 provides an example of one organization's written benefits objectives.

Surveys and Benchmarking

As with cash compensation, an important element of benefits management is knowing what the competition is doing. Survey information on benefits packages is available from a wide variety of Human Resources Associations, the Conference Board of Canada, private consulting firms such as Towers Watson and KPMG, business associations (Board of Trade), labour associations, and government sources such as Statistics Canada (Labour Cost Surveys and Non-wage Benefits surveys) and Human Resources and Skills Development Canada. Increasingly, international comparison data is also available and provides insight into emerging markets that employers may be considering for expansion. To compete effectively in the product market, as discussed in Chapter 8, cost information is also necessary. Statistics Canada and the Bureau of Labor Statistics in the United States provide articles, survey information, and information on benefits costs for specific categories as well as breakdowns by industry, occupation, union status, and organization size. Figure 10.4 shows the breakdown of employee benefits cost (by category) for total benefits as a percentage of total compensation that appeared in Figure 10.1 on page 384 for 2011.

Table 10.5   One Company's Written Benefits Objectives

- To establish and maintain an employee benefit program that is based primarily on the employees' needs for leisure time and on protection against the risks of old age, loss of health, and loss of life.

- To establish and maintain an employee benefit program that complements the efforts of employees on their own behalf.

- To evaluate the employee benefit plan annually for its effect on employee morale and productivity, giving consideration to turnover, unfilled positions, attendance, employees' complaints, and employees' opinions.

- To compare the employee benefit plan annually with that of other leading companies in the same field and to maintain a benefit plan with an overall level of benefits based on cost per employee that falls within the second quintile of these companies.

- To maintain a level of benefits for non union employees that represents the same level of expenditures per employee as for union employees.

- To determine annually the costs of new, changed, and existing programs as percentages of salaries and wages and to maintain these percentages as much as possible.

- To self-fund benefits to the extent that a long-run cost savings can be expected for the firm and catastrophic losses can be avoided.

- To coordinate all benefits with social insurance programs to which the company makes payments.

- To provide benefits on a non contributory basis except for dependant coverage, for which employees should pay a portion of the cost.

- To maintain continual communications with all employees concerning benefit programs.

SOURCE: *Employee Benefits,* 3rd ed., Burton T. Beam Jr. and John J. McFadden. © 1992 by Dearborn Financial Publishing, Inc. Published by Dearborn Financial Publishing, Inc., Chicago. All rights reserved.

FIGURE 10.4   Employee Benefits Cost by Category, 2011

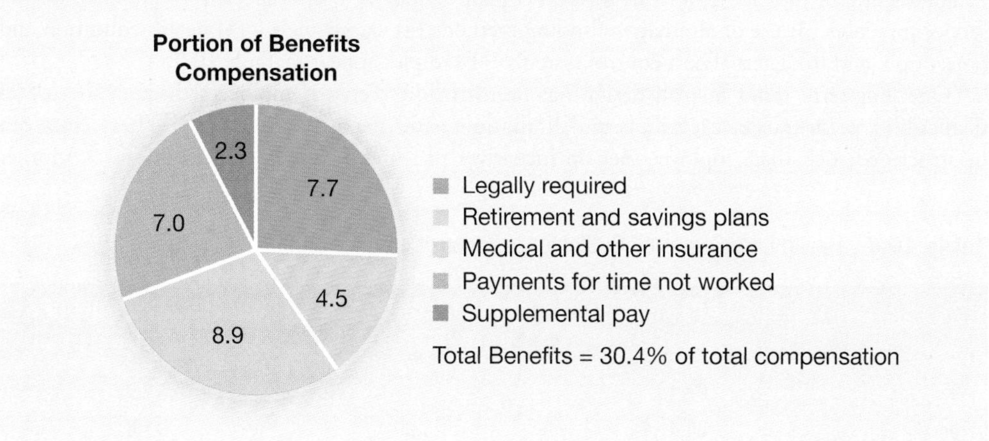

Portion of Benefits Compensation

- Legally required
- Retirement and savings plans
- Medical and other insurance
- Payments for time not worked
- Supplemental pay

Total Benefits = 30.4% of total compensation

SOURCE: "Employer Cost for Employee Compensation—March 2011" (News Release June 8, 2011) www.bls.gov.

Cost Control

In thinking about cost control strategies, it is useful to consider several factors. First, the larger the cost of a benefit category, the greater the opportunity for savings. Second, the growth trajectory of the benefit category is also important: even if costs are currently acceptable, the rate of growth may result in significant costs in the future. Third, cost containment efforts can work only to the extent that the employer has significant discretion in choosing how much to spend in a benefit category. For example, an employer could choose not to offer vision care in an extended medical plan to reduce benefits costs. On the other hand, much of the cost of legally required benefits (such as CPP/QPP) is relatively fixed to the number of employees on payroll, which constrains cost reduction efforts. Even with legally required benefits, however, employers can take actions to limit costs because of "experience ratings," which impose higher taxes on employers with high rates of unemployment or workers' compensation claims.

One benefit—medical and other insurance—stands out as a target for cost control for two reasons. Its costs are substantial; they have, except for the 1994 to 1999 period, grown at a significant pace, and this growth is expected to continue. Second, employers have many options for attacking costs and improving quality, which we discuss next.

Health Care: Controlling Costs and Improving Quality   As Table 10.6 indicates, Canada ranks in the lower middle among countries in terms of spending on health care (as a point of comparison, the United States is the top spender in the world.)

Canadian workers, like those in most western European countries that have nationalized health systems, receive public, hospital, and medical care benefits that provide for a range of needs including surgery, physician and nursing care, and prescription drugs administered in hospital. Employers often cover some of the balance of employee medical needs through extended health care including payment for many dental services and all or a portion of prescription drugs, vision care, registered massage therapy, psychological counselling, orthopedic shoes, and other services. Consequently, health insurance, like pensions, discourages employee turnover because not all employers provide health insurance benefits.[53]

Not surprisingly, the fact that many Canadians receive extended health care coverage through their employers has meant that many efforts at controlling costs and increasing quality and coverage have been undertaken by employers. These efforts, broadly referred to as managed care or cost containment, fall into six major categories: (1) plan design (2) use of specialty vendors and other service providers (3) use of alternative funding methods (4) claims review (5) health education and prevention, and (6) external cost control systems.[54] Examples appear in Table 10.7.

One long-term trend in plan design has been to shift costs to employees through the use of deductibles, coinsurance, exclusions and limitations, and maximum benefits.[55] These costs can be structured such that employees act on incentives to shift to less expensive options.[56] Another

Table 10.6   Health Care Costs and Outcomes in Various Countries (2009)

	LIFE EXPECTANCY AT BIRTH, FEMALE	INFANT MORTALITY RATE (PER 1,000)	HEALTH EXPENDITURES AS A PERCENTAGE OF GDP
Japan	86.4	2.4	8.5
France	84.4	3.9	11.8
Canada	**83.0**	**5.1**	**11.4**
Korea	83.8	3.5	6.9
Germany	82.8	3.5	11.6
United States	80.6	6.5	17.4
United Kingdom	82.5	4.6	9.8
Mexico	77.6	14.7	6.4

SOURCES: Organization for Economic Cooperation and Development, *OECD Health.* Data 2009, www.OECD.org and World Bank, *World Development Report 2009,* www.worldbank.org.

Table 10.7 Ways Employers Control Health Care Costs

PLAN DESIGN
Cost shifting to employees
Deductibles
Coinsurance
Exclusions and limitations
Maximum benefits
Cost reduction
Coordination of benefits
SPECIALTY VENDORS AND OTHERS
Disability management
Absence management
Lifestyle behaviour change
ALTERNATIVE FUNDING METHODS
Self-funding
CLAIMS REVIEW
HEALTH EDUCATION AND PREVENTIVE CARE
Health and wellness programs
Employee assistance programs (EAPs)
ENCOURAGEMENT OF EXTERNAL CONTROL SYSTEMS
Workers Compensation (Return to Work Programs)
Canadian Mental Health Association (Events and Initiatives)
Employer coalitions (e.g., regulating costs pharmacies can charge)

SOURCE: Adapted from B. T. Beam Jr. and J. J. McFadden, *Employee Benefits,* 3rd ed. (Chicago: Dearborn Financial Publishing, 1992) and from 2009/2010 Staying @Work Report, National Business Group on Health, Towers Watson 2010.

trend has been to focus on reducing, rather than shifting, costs through actions such as substituting generic drugs wherever possible for brand-name products, placing limits on biotech drugs, requiring prior authorization, and a range of other strategies. A very recent trend is the implementation of tiered formularies, meaning that instead of covering all drugs in a plan at one co-insurance rate, two or more groups ("baskets") of prescription drugs would be created and reimbursed at two or more different co-insurance levels.[57] There is also an increasing tendency to implement wellness initiatives to control rising costs of health plans. For example, a 2010 survey conducted by the International Foundation of Employee Benefits Plans (IFEBP) indicated that 78 percent of organizations offered wellness initiatives, which was up 17 percent over 2009. In addition, 20 percent of the organizations in the survey that were not offering wellness programs indicated they would probably offer them in the future.[58]

Employee Wellness Programs. Employee wellness programs (EWPs) are designed and sponsored by employers to focus on changing behaviours both during and outside work that could eventually lead to future health problems. EWPs are preventive in nature; they attempt to manage health care costs by decreasing employees' needs for services. Typically, these programs aim at specific health risks such as high blood pressure, high cholesterol levels, smoking, and obesity. They also

Employee Wellness Programs (EWPs)
Programs designed and sponsored by employers that focus on changing behaviours both during and outside work that could eventually lead to future health problems.

Many companies on Canada's Top 100 Employers' list provide fitness facilities to encourage stress management and healthy lifestyles.

try to promote positive health influences such as physical exercise and good nutrition.[59]

EWPs are either passive or active. Passive programs use little or no outreach to individuals, nor do they provide ongoing support to motivate employees to use the resources. Active wellness centres assume that behaviour change requires not only awareness and opportunity but also support and reinforcement.

One example of a passive wellness program is a health education program. These programs have two central goals: raising awareness levels of health-related issues and informing people on health-related topics. In these kinds of programs, a health educator usually conducts classes or lunchtime lectures (or co-ordinates outside speakers). Programs may also have various promotions (such as an annual mile run or a "smoke-out") or a newsletter that reports on current health issues.

Another kind of passive employee wellness program is a fitness facility: the company sets up a centre for physical fitness equipped with aerobic and muscle-building exercise machines and staffed with certified athletic trainers. The facility is publicized within the organization, and employees are free to use it on their own time. Digital Extremes, the leading game development studio, offers a fitness club subsidy and an incentive bonus of up to $450 to help employees act on good intentions and get fit. The Great Little Box Company in Vancouver offers a fully equipped, subsidized on-site fitness facility that includes personal trainers, an outdoor sand volleyball court, and a dock for employees who commute to work from Mitchell Island.[60] Health education classes related to smoking cessation and weight loss may be offered in addition to the facilities.

Although fitness facility programs are usually more expensive than health education programs, both are classified as passive because they rely on individual employees to identify their problems and take corrective action all by themselves. In contrast, active wellness centres assume that behaviour change also requires encouragement and assistance. One kind of active wellness centre is the outreach and follow-up model. It contains all the features of a passive model, but also has counsellors who handle one-on-one outreach and provide tailored, individualized programs for employees. Thus although the programs are voluntary, employees who make the choice to participate are given the assistance and feedback needed to continue improving their health, despite inevitable slumps in enthusiasm that may occur. Typically, tailored programs obtain baseline measures on various indicators (weight, blood pressure, lung capacity, and so on) and measure individuals' progress relative to these indicators over time. The programs set goals, provide guidance and encouragement to help participants maintain commitment, and provide small, symbolic rewards to individuals who meet their goals.

This encouragement needs to be particularly targeted to employees in high-risk categories (such as those who smoke, are overweight, or have high blood pressure) for two reasons. (First, a small percentage of employees create a disproportionate amount of health care costs; therefore, targeted interventions are more efficient. Targeted interventions can include smoking and weight-loss programs and even lunch-and-learn high-blood-pressure clinics. Second, research shows that those in high-risk categories are the most likely to perceive barriers (such as family problems or work overload)[61] to participating in company-sponsored fitness programs. Thus untargeted interventions are likely to miss the people that most need to be included. Therefore, even though employees must choose to participate, the existence of such programs in the workplace should increase both the opportunity and desire to participate over time. See the approach taken by Lighthouse Publishing Ltd. in Nova Scotia, featured in the "Evidence-Based HR" box.

Research on these different types of wellness centres leads to several conclusions.[62] First, the costs of health education programs are significantly less than those associated with either fitness facility programs or the follow-up model. Second, as indicated in Figure 10.5 on page 406, all three models are effective in reducing the risk factors associated with cardiovascular disease (obesity, high blood

Evidence-Based HR

Why would a small company with fewer than 50 employees who work in two different locations decide to launch a health and wellness program? And what chance would it even have for success? Lighthouse Publishing Ltd. decided to find out the answer to these questions when it had the opportunity to partner with its Regional Health Authority in assessing and evaluating the health of its employees, at no expense to the company. (By doing health assessments free of charge the partnership would also provide the Regional Health Authority access to a group of people in a workplace, one of several key settings identified for targeted interventions by the province in its Chronic Disease Prevention Strategy.) The assessment included a survey asking employees what types of health programs and activities they felt might meet their needs. With the results of the survey in hand, a committee of six people from different areas of the company began to plan solutions to employee concerns. Lighthouse Publishing assessed what it could realistically manage to meet those needs and decided to invest $2,000 in the health of its employees. A wide variety of small changes and programs were undertaken. Lighthouse focussed on four particular areas of interest—organizational health, obesity, fitness, and smoking. The biggest challenges were establishing credibility for the new plan and budget. After all, $2,000 doesn't go far when it comes to health and wellness programs. Changes included stocking a company fridge with healthy choices, holding BBQs each week, providing financial incentive for weight loss ("Pounds for Dollars"), promoting exercise through a "Walk at Work" program, and providing on-site addictions counselling along with free patches for smokers trying to quit. There were also private fitness classes and newsletters to keep enthusiasm high among the 75 percent of employees who ultimately decided to "get with the program." Those who wanted to put more "light" into Lighthouse lost 261 pounds in the weight-loss and fitness programs, and four of eight smokers in the company managed to quit. Morale definitely increased after the program began, the company's profile in the community has been raised, and the company has saved $6,000 on its extended health insurance premium so far. Not bad for a little publishing company in Bridgewater, Nova Scotia. And the return on the investment of $2,000? Priceless.

SOURCES: S. Klie, "Wellness Sees Positive Returns: Studies," *Canadian HR Reporter* (April 19, 2010), 8; and N. Stewart, "Beyond Benefits, Creating a Culture of Health and Wellness in Canadian Organizations," Conference Board of Canada Report (February 2010), pp. 15–16. "Nova Scotia Chronic Disease Prevention Strategy, October 31, 2003, Figure 3, p. 9 "Nova Scotia's Framework for Chronic Disease Prevention." at www.gov.ns.ca/hpp/publications/CDP_Strategy_Report_Final_October30.pdf (retrieved July 27, 2011).

FIGURE 10.5   The Cost and Effectiveness of Three Different Types of Employee Wellness Designs

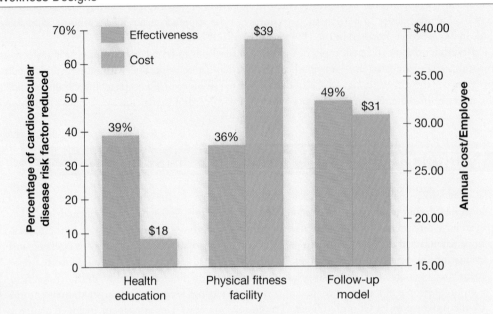

SOURCE: J. C. Erfurt, A. Foote, and M. A. Heirich, "The Cost Effectiveness of Worksite Wellness Programs for Hypertension Control, Weight Loss, Smoking Cessation and Exercise," *Personnel Psychology* 45 (1992), pp. 5–27. Used with permission.

pressure, smoking, and lack of exercise). However, the follow-up model is significantly better than the other two in reducing the risk factors. In the IFEBP survey mentioned earlier, 1 in 10 employers offering wellness initiatives attempted to measure the ROI on the investment, and 88 percent found a positive ROI.[63]

Whether the added cost of follow-up programs compared with health education programs is warranted is a judgment that only employers, employees, and unions can make. However, employers such as Sony and Quaker Oats believe that incentives are worth the extra cost, and their employees can receive up to several hundred dollars for reducing their risk factors. There appears to be no such ambiguity associated with the fitness facility model, however. This type of wellness centre costs as much or more than the follow-up model but is only as effective as the health education model. Providing a fitness facility that does not include systematic outreach and routine long-term follow-up to assist people with risk factors is not cost-effective in reducing health risks. "Attendants may sit in the fitness centre like the 'Maytag repairman' waiting for people to come."[64]

As an overall measure of wellness programs generally, one 2009 Towers Watson North American study of 352 human resources and/or health benefits managers (with 1,000 or more employees) provides some interesting findings on the impact of organizational commitment to wellness programs. The study includes 70 Canadian respondents who provided information on what they do in their organization to gain the "Health and Productivity Advantage." The study indicates that Canadian companies appear to be using more advanced approaches to absence, disability, and stress management, and Canadians place mental health issues on the same level as physical illnesses. They are also more likely to emphasize human resource practices and policies and hold both employees and

Competing Through Globalization

The Deadly Impact of Workplace Stress

When a company downsizes by more than 50,000 jobs in a ten-year period you can expect some negative things to happen, especially when 22,000 of those jobs disappeared between 2006 and 2008. But with 40 employees committing suicide due to work-related problems and another dozen attempting suicide, it seems clear that "downsizing" isn't quite the right term for what has been happening at France Telecom. What the company's union calls "pathogenic restructuring" has brought the former CEO, the deputy CEO, and the director of Human Resources under intense scrutiny by an investigating judge. Complaints by the union against management spurred a workplace investigation, and initial reports indicate that France Telecom implemented several particularly stressful forms of psychological pressure on employees, despite warnings from company doctors. One big stressor involved being forced to take a transfer, and in a 2008 workplace survey two-thirds of employees reported being "stressed out." An employee stabbed himself in a meeting, and another sent a goodbye e-mail to her father saying she couldn't take the restructuring.

Depending on the outcomes of the investigation, further investigation and an indictment may yet follow. How did France Telecom reach this point? As a huge government monopoly transitioning to private ownership, it is saddled with a workforce of 100,000 employees who basically have lifetime job guarantees, and labour force costs are already high in France. Thus, when jobs need to be restructured, a place must be found for displaced employees. In addition, tough-job security rules in France create additional pressure on organizations, such as making it difficult to terminate employees who aren't performing, or when business drops off, leading to an increase in short-term contract hiring.

Similar problems occurred at Peugeot, EDF, and Renault. At Renault, around 2007, three engineers killed themselves within a five-month period. Each had voiced concerns about excessive workloads, high-pressure management, exhaustion, and being humiliated during performance reviews. Now stress is rumoured to be on the rise at SNCF, a rail operator in France, where union representatives say that work conditions are declining and management isn't listening. After insisting the engineers' deaths were not caused directly by their work environment, Renault devised a $10 million plan to manage workplace stress, including adding to the workforce, and training 2,100 managers and their subordinates to avoid negative stress. The company also hired psychologists to work with senior management to recognize the signs of stress, and to help manage individuals caught up with it. Relaxation spots were created to help employees get away from the grind. By the spring of 2010, the management of France Telecom, operating under a new board, met with its unions and managed to reach agreement on several accords related to workforce mobility, stress, and work/life balance. More talks were planned, and closure of several small facilities was postponed. France Telecom also hired the same consulting firm that Renault did to deal with its suicide problem.

Canadians can scoff at such stories, saying they couldn't happen here. However, our workplaces are far from immune to the impact of stress. For example, in an employee survey at Toronto's University Health Network (UHN), 63 percent of employees responded that when it came to health, stress was their greatest concern. Similar results from Durham Region's Lakeridge Health Network, and the knowledge that mental health issues account for 30 to 40 percent of disability claims in Canada, remind us there is no room for complacency. Although stress-related disability claims are a long way from suicide, they do represent major loss of another kind—the absence of a coworker who used to look forward to showing up on the job and making a contribution.

SOURCES: M. Morra, "Return on Wellness," *HR Professional* (August/September 2009) pp. 21–24F. Glafour and T. Culpan, "The Man Who Makes Your iPhone," Bloomberg BusinessWeek (September 9, 2010) at www.businessweek.com/print/magazine/cdonte/10_38/b4195058423479 (retrieved March 20, 2011); M. Saltmarsh and D. Jolly (Paris); "France Telecom Suicides Prompt an Investigation," *The New York Times*; (April 10, 2010), Section B, Column 0, Business/Financial Desk, p. 3.; Schumpeter, "Hating What You Do," *The Economist* (October 10, 2009), p. 70.

managers accountable for creating, improving, and achieving a healthy workplace. The study looked at various levels of effectiveness achieved by improving health and productivity among participating companies and found that high-effectiveness companies had total returns to shareholders (TRS) over the previous five years of 14.8 percent, almost 5 percent more than low-effectiveness companies. In addition, high-effectiveness companies performed 55.5 percent better than peer competitors, and 34.2 percent better than the least-effective companies in the study. When unplanned lost workdays were examined, companies with the most effective health and productivity programs experienced 3.0 days, compared with 4.8 days among those with the lowest level of commitment to wellness. The high-effectiveness companies also reported 11 percent higher revenue per employee, and were more likely to have lower health care costs, less presenteeism (showing up to work despite being sick enough to stay home and underperforming on the job as a result), less absence due to disability, and lower turnover rates than their competitors.[65]

No matter what the cost or the return on investment however, wellness programs help employees to continue to thrive in economic downturns and during stressful organizational transitions. Any wellness program is better than no wellness program, a point made clear by the experience of French corporations discussed in the "Competing Through Globalization" box. Note how sharply these stories contrast with that of Lighthouse, described in the "Evidence-Based HR" box.

Health Care Costs and Quality: Ongoing Challenges. A global survey of medical trends done worldwide by Towers Watson in the fall of 2010 of 170 health insurers providing medical insurance solutions to employers provided information on the percentage increase in medical costs expected for 2011; the average increase in medical costs globally was projected to be 10.5 percent. This followed increases of 10.2 percent in 2009 and another 9.8 percent in 2010. In Canada, the increases have been quite a bit higher than the average, with increases of 12.5 percent in 2009 and again in 2010. However, in 2011, the costs will escalate higher with an increase of 13.3 percent.[66] Thus, control of health care costs is an ongoing challenge around the world. Drivers of cost increases found in the survey are many and range from higher costs due to new medical technologies to overuse of care available and poor employee health habits. Although specific reasons for Canada's expected increase in 2011 are not provided in the summary of the study, clearly Canada bears its fair share of such challenges.

Two important phenomena are often encountered in cost-control efforts. First, piecemeal programs may not work well because steps to control one aspect (such as medical cost shifting) may lead employees to "migrate" to other programs that provide medical treatment at no cost to them (such as workers' compensation). Second, there is often a so-called Pareto group, which refers to a small percentage (perhaps 20 percent) of employees being responsible for generating the majority (often 60 to 80 percent) of health care costs. Obviously, cost control efforts will be more successful to the extent that the costs generated by the Pareto group can be identified and managed effectively.[67]

Staffing Responses to Control Benefits Cost Growth   Employers may change staffing practices to control benefits costs. First, because benefits costs are fixed (in that they do not usually go up with hours worked), the benefits cost per hour can be reduced by having employees work more hours. However, there are drawbacks to having employees work more hours, such as the need to pay overtime. The provincial Employment Standards Acts, discussed in earlier chapters, require that nonexempt employees be paid time-and-a-half for hours in excess of 40 per week.

A second possible effect of ESA requirements (although this is more speculative) is that organizations will try to have their employees classified as exempt whenever possible (although such attempts may run afoul of ESAs). The growth in the number of salaried workers (many of whom are exempt) may also reflect an effort by organizations to limit the benefits cost per hour without having to pay overtime. A third potential effect is the growth in part-time employment and the use of temporary workers, which may be a response to rising benefits costs. Part-time workers are less likely to receive benefits than full-time workers although labour market shortages in recent years have reduced this difference.[68] Benefits for temporary workers are also usually quite limited.

Fourth, employers may be more likely to classify workers as independent contractors rather than employees, which eliminates the employer's obligation to provide legally required employee benefits. However, Canada Revenue Agency scrutinizes such decisions carefully, as Microsoft and other companies have discovered. Microsoft was compelled to reclassify a group of workers as employees (rather than as independent contractors) and to grant them retroactive benefits. Canada Revenue Agency looks at several factors, including the permanency of the relationship between employer and worker, how much control the employer exercises in directing the worker, and whether the worker offers services to only that employer. Permanency, control, and dealing with a single employer are viewed by Canada Revenue Agency as suggestive of an employment relationship.

Nature of the Workforce

Although general considerations such as cost control and "protection against the risks of old age and loss of health and life" (see Table 10.5 on page 401) are important, employers must also consider the specific demographic composition and preferences of their current workforces in designing their benefits packages.

At a broad level, basic demographic factors such as age and sex can have important consequences for the types of benefits employees want. For example, an older workforce is more likely to be concerned about (and use) medical coverage, life insurance, and pensions. A workforce with a high percentage of women of childbearing age may care more about parental leave top-ups. Young, unmarried men and women often have less interest in benefits generally, preferring higher wages and salaries.

Although some general conclusions about employee preferences can be drawn based on demographics, more finely tuned assessments of employee benefit preferences need to be done. One approach is to use marketing research methods to assess employees' preferences the same way consumers' demands for products and services are assessed.[69] Methods include personal interviews, focus groups, such as those Microsoft did in our opening vignette, and questionnaires. Relevant questions might include

- What benefits are most important to you?
- If you could choose one new benefit, what would it be?
- If you were given X dollars for benefits, how would you spend it?

As with surveys generally, care must be taken not to raise employee expectations regarding future changes. If the employer is not prepared to act on the employees' input, surveying may do more harm than good.

As discussed earlier, the benefits package may influence the future composition of the workforce. For example, a benefits package that has strong medical benefits and pensions may be particularly attractive to older people or those with families. An attractive pension plan may be a way to attract workers who wish to make a long-term commitment to an organization; where turnover costs are high, this type of strategy may have some appeal. On the other hand, a company that has very lucrative health care benefits may attract and retain people with high health care costs. Sick leave provisions may also affect the composition of the workforce. Organizations need to think about the signals their benefits packages send and the implications of these signals for workforce composition.

connect

Learn more about the nature of the workforce online with Connect.

LO 7

Explain the importance of effectively communicating the nature and value of benefits to employees.

Communicating with Employees

Effective communication of benefits information to employees is critical if employers are to realize sufficient returns on their benefits investments. Research makes it clear that current employees and job applicants often have a very poor idea of the benefits provisions available and the cost or market value of those benefits. One study asked employees to estimate both the amount contributed by the employer to their medical insurance and what it would cost the employees to provide their own health insurance. Table 10.8 shows that employees significantly underestimated both the cost and market value of their medical benefits. In the case of family coverage, employees estimated that the employer contributed $24, only 38 percent of the employer's actual contribution. This employer was receiving a very poor (perceived) return on its benefits investment: $0.38 for every $1.00 spent.[70] Although this

Table 10.8   Employee Perceptions versus Actual Cost and Market Value of Employer Contributions to Employee Medical Insurance

| | EMPLOYER CONTRIBUTION | | | MARKET VALUE[a] | | |
COVERAGE	ACTUAL	EMPLOYEE PERCEPTION	RATIO	ACTUAL	EMPLOYEE PERCEPTION	RATIO
Individual	$34	$23	68%	$ 61	$37	61%
Family	64	24	38	138	43	31

Note: Dollar values in table represent means across three different insurance carriers for individual coverage and three different carriers for family coverage.

[a]Defined as the amount a nonemployee would have to pay to obtain the same level of coverage.

SOURCE: Adapted from M. Wilson, G. B. Northcraft, and M. A. Neale, "The Perceived Value of Fringe Benefits," *Personnel Psychology* 38 (1985), pp. 309–320. Used with permission.

study was done in the mid-80s similar results were found in other studies reviewed in the early 90s and as late as 2007; one wonders whether today's employees are any more aware of this fact.

Organizations can help remedy the problem of employees' lack of knowledge about benefits and of course, there are many alternative ways to communicate benefits information (see Table 10.9). Nevertheless, most organizations spend little to communicate information about benefits, and much of this is spent on general written communications. Considering private-sector organizations spend a considerable amount per year on benefits, together with the complex nature of many benefits and the poor understanding of most employees, the typical communication effort may be inadequate.[71] On a more positive note, organizations are increasingly using Web-based tools to personalize and tailor communications to individual employees. In addition, effective use of traditional approaches (e.g., booklets) can have a large effect on employee awareness.[72]

Rather than a single standard benefits package for all employees, flexible benefit plans (cafeteria-style plans) permit employees to choose the types and amounts of benefits they want for themselves. The plans vary according to things such as whether minimum levels of certain benefits (such as health care coverage) are prescribed and whether employees can receive money for having chosen a "light" benefits package (or have to pay extra for more benefits). One example is vacation, where some plans permit employees to give up vacation days for more salary or, alternatively, purchase extra vacation days through a salary reduction.

What are the potential advantages of such plans?[73] First, employees gain a greater awareness and appreciation of what the employer provides them, particularly with plans that give employees a lump sum to allocate to benefits. Second, by permitting employee choice, there should be a better match between the benefits package and the employees' preferences. This, in turn, should improve employee attitudes and retention.[74] Third, employers may achieve overall cost reductions in their benefits programs. Cafeteria plans can be thought of as similar to defined-contribution plans, whereas traditional plans are more like defined-benefit plans. The employer can control the size

Table 10.9   Benefits Communication Media Examples for Different Audiences and Purposes

MEDIA	AUDIENCE	PURPOSE
Enrollment package	All employees (English and Other)	Announce changes or new hire enrollment only by deadline
Meetings	Local employees	Provide information on benefits and changes
Teleconference messaging	Remote employees	Provide information on benefits and changes
Intranet	All employees (personalized)	Provide information on benefits, training, and employment policies
E-mail alerts	Supervisors	Provide employees with information
Summary plan descriptions	All employees	Make available compliance information
Paycheque attachments	All employees	Provide information on benefits
Webcasts	Regional managers	Share context for changes and their roles and responsibilities

SOURCE: A. Parsons and K. Groh, "The New Road Effective Communications," *Compensation Benefits Review* 38 (2006), p. 57.

of the contribution under the former, but not under the latter, because the cost and utilization of benefits is beyond the employer's control. Costs can also be controlled by designing the choices so that employees have an incentive to choose more efficient options.

One drawback of cafeteria-style plans is their administrative cost, especially in the initial design and start-up stages. However, software packages and standardized flex-plans developed by consultants offer some help. Another possible drawback to these plans is adverse selection. Employees are most likely to choose benefits that they expect to need the most, or that are lacking under a spouse's plan. Someone in need of dental work would choose as much dental coverage as possible. As a result, employer costs can increase significantly as each employee chooses benefits based on their personal value. Another result of adverse selection is the difficulty in estimating benefits costs under such a plan, especially in small companies. Adverse selection can be controlled, however, by limiting coverage amounts, pricing benefits that are subject to adverse selection higher, or using a limited set of packaged options, which prevents employees from choosing too many benefits options that would be susceptible to adverse selection.

Flexible Spending Account
An account set up by an employer for each employee that permits pretax contributions to the account to be drawn on to pay for uncovered health care expenses (such as deductibles and copayments).

Flexible Spending Accounts   A **flexible spending account** is an account set up by an employer for each employee that permits pretax contributions to the account to be drawn on to pay for uncovered health care expenses (such as deductibles and copayments). Federal tax regulations require that funds in the health care and dependant care accounts be earmarked in advance and spent during the plan year. Remaining funds revert to the employer. Therefore, the accounts work best for employees who have predictable expenses. The major advantage of such plans is the increase in take-home pay that results from pretax payment of health and dependant-care expenses. Consider again the hypothetical employee with annual earnings of $50,000 and an effective total marginal tax rate of 37 percent from Table 10.1 on page 384. Table 10.10 illustrates the take-home pay from an additional $10,000 in salary with and without a flexible dependant-care account.

Therefore, the use of a flexible spending account saves the employee $1,850 ($3,150 − $1,300) per year.

MANAGING FUTURE BENEFITS COSTS

Overall pressure to manage all workforce costs and to control long-term disabilities to avoid the problems Nortel and GM faced have forced employers to make some tough choices. Increasing retiree health care costs have also led some companies to require white-collar employees and retirees to pay insurance premiums for the first time in history and to increase copayments and deductibles.

Table 10.10   Impact on Take-Home Pay of an Additional $10,000 in Salary With/Without Flexible Spending Care Account

	NO FLEXIBLE SPENDING CARE ACCOUNT	FLEXIBLE SPENDING CARE ACCOUNT
Salary portion	$10,000	$10,000
Pretax dependant-care contribution	0	−5,000
Taxable salary	10,000	5,000
Tax (37 percent)	−3,700	−1,850
After-tax cost of dependant care	−5,000	0
Take-home pay	$ 1,300	$ 3,150

Survey data indicate that some companies are ending retiree health care benefits altogether. For example, a Towers Watson study revealed that between 2005 and 2010 some employers opted to eliminate retiree health and benefits programs altogether. Other companies gradually reduced benefits or increased retiree contributions. For example, in 2010 a Towers Watson study noted a 6 percent increase over 2005 in companies reporting no retiree basic life coverage for employees. In addition, 39 percent of responding organizations provide no health care benefits for retirees—a 9 percent increase over 2005. One trend noted in the report was the implementation of a Health Spending Account (HSA), which provided greater ease in forecasting benefits costs (since employees are limited to a predefined amount held in their account), and helped to create more certainty about costs despite changes arising from trends in health and dental care and utilization.[75]

Obviously, major changes will hit the elderly hard, especially those with relatively fixed incomes. Not surprisingly, legal challenges have arisen, and pensioners have begun forming postretirement groups that monitor the profitability of their employer organizations, and changes such organization attempt to make in reduction of postemployment benefits. The Nortel group is just one example of employees who have begun to realize they cannot make assumptions about health care or pension benefits. The need to balance the interests of shareholders, current employees, and retirees in this area will be one of the most difficult challenges facing managers in the future.

A Look Back

We have seen that many organizations have become less paternalistic in their employee benefits strategies. In our opening vignette, Microsoft responded to employee feedback and changed its traditional benefits plan to a flexible benefits plan. However, when employees have more choice, they also now have more responsibility, and sometimes more risk, regarding their benefits choices. Recall that some of the longer-term Microsoft employees were skeptical when initially told about the change and became convinced only when they realized there were also more benefits offerings to choose from.

One change has been in the area of retirement income plans, where employers have moved toward greater reliance on defined-contribution plans. Such plans require employees to understand investing; otherwise, their retirement years may not be happy. The risk to employees is greater with defined-contribution plans, especially when the market becomes volatile, as it was in the early 80s and in the first ten years of this century. Companies use defined-contribution plans because they wish to avoid the major liabilities that can occur with defined-benefit pension plans, and which threaten the sustainability of the business. Defined-benefits plans also encourage an entitlement mentality that does not fit with other performance-based forms of compensation which link employee motivation to the overall performance of the company.

Although Microsoft was not motivated to reduce benefits in any way, many other companies have reduced or even eliminated health-care benefits to meet strategic objectives and remain competitive. In the area of health care, employers must be vigilant about rising costs. They may decide to increase the proportion of costs that employees pay, leading them to make better choices about health care. Again, the responsibility for anticipating this possibility increasingly falls to employees.

Questions

1. Why do employers offer benefits? How much responsibility should employers have for the health and well-being of their employees? Take the perspective of both a shareholder and an employee in answering this question.

2. If you were advising a new company on how to design its health care plan, what would you recommend?

Summary

Effective management of employee benefits is an important means by which organizations successfully compete. Benefits costs are substantial and continue to grow rapidly in some areas, and therefore control of such costs is necessary to compete in the product market. For example, employers are required by law to contribute to government-sponsored benefits such as the Canada/Quebec Pension Plan (CPP/QPP), Employment Insurance (EI), and Workers' Compensation.

At the same time, employers must offer a benefits package that permits them to compete in the labour market so that they can attract and retain good employees. Employers continue to be a major source of economic security for employees, often providing health and disability insurance, retirement benefits, and many other benefits. In doing so, employers are faced with an ongoing dilemma. On the one hand, they need to offer well-designed, attractive benefits; but on the other, they must ensure that such benefits do not create unfunded liabilities if the company experiences a downturn. For example, many employers have traditionally offered defined-benefits pension plans, which guarantees a defined level of retirement benefit to employees. However, recently more employers have begun shifting away from defined-benefits pension plans because they present significant risk if the company is unable to make pension contributions, or if the funds invested in the plan do not provide an adequate return. Recent volatility of world markets has prompted many employers to offer defined-contribution pension plans instead. Since such plans do not guarantee specific levels of retirement benefits, the risk of unfunded pension plan liabilities is eliminated for the employer. However, such plans shift risk to employees, and increasingly, retirement benefits will increasingly depend on the financial investment decisions employees make on their own behalf. Thus, employers have a responsibility to educate employees about pensions and to communicate such plans clearly.

Changes to benefits can have a tremendous impact on employees and retirees. Therefore, employers also carry a significant social responsibility in helping employees to make responsible benefits decisions. Health care benefit design has been changing in recent years; many employers now offer flexible benefits plans or flexible health spending accounts. Such plans aid in attracting and retaining quality employees, help to contain costs, and allow employees to tailor benefits to their own needs and stage of life. Effective communication of such plans can help make employees more aware of the actual value of their benefits as well as the costs associated with benefits to employers. Employee wellness programs focus on changing employee behaviours that could eventually lead to health problems and thus contribute to managing employer objectives associated with employee benefits.

Key Terms

Canada/Quebec Pension Plan (CPP/QPP), 385

Defined-benefit pension plan, 391

Defined-contribution pension plan, 393

Employee benefits, 382

Employee Wellness Programs (EWPs), 403

Employment Insurance (EI), 387

Flexible benefits plan, 382

Flexible spending accounts, 412

Long-term disability plan, 390

Marginal tax rate, 383

Registered pension plans, 391

Short-term disability plan, 390

Sick leave programs, 398

Vesting rights, 395

Workers' Compensation, 389

Discussion Questions

1. The opening vignette on Microsoft illustrates how moving to a flexible benefits plan can shift the relationship between employers and employees, as employees begin to take more responsibility for their own choices in benefits. What are the likely outcomes of this change? Where

does the social responsibility of employers end, and where does the need to operate more efficiently begin?

2. Your company, like many others, is experiencing double-digit percentage increases in health care costs. What suggestions can you offer that may reduce the rate of cost increases?

3. Why is communication of employee benefits so important? What sorts of programs can a company use to communicate more effectively? What are the potential positive consequences of more effective benefits communication?

4. What are the potential advantages of flexible benefits and flexible spending accounts? What are the potential drawbacks?

5. Although benefits account for a large share of employee compensation, many feel there is little evidence on whether an employer receives an adequate return on the benefits investment. One suggestion has been to link benefits to individual, group, or organization performance. Explain why you would or would not recommend this strategy to an organization.

Self-Assessment Exercise

One way companies determine which types of benefits to provide is to use a survey asking employees which types of benefits are important to them. Read the following list of employee benefits. For each benefit, mark an X in the column that indicates whether it is important to you or not.

Benefit	Important to Have	Not Important to Have	% Employers Offering
Dependant-care flexible spending account			70%
Flexible work schedule (described in Chapter 4)			64
Ability to bring child to work in case of emergency			30
Elder-care referral services			21
Adoption assistance			21
On-site child care centre			6
Gym subsidy			28
Vaccinations on-site (e.g., flu shots)			61
On-site fitness centre			26
Casual dress days (every day)			53
Organization-sponsored sports teams			39
Food services/subsidized cafeteria			29
Travel-planning services			27
Dry-cleaning services			15
Massage therapy services at work			12
Self-defence training			6
Concierge services			4

Compare your importance ratings for each benefit to the corresponding number in the right-hand column that indicates the percentage of employers that offer the benefit. Are you likely to find jobs that provide the benefits you want? Explain.

SOURCE: Based on Figure 2, "Percent of Employers Offering Work/Life Benefits (by Year)," in *Workplace Visions* 4 (2002), p. 3, published by the Society for Human Resource Management.

Exercising Strategy: Finding a Way for Legal Moms to Stay

There is a disturbing trend in the last ten years among women who go into the field of law; many don't stay there long. In fact, they are two to three times more likely to leave the profession than male lawyers. A 2009 study revealed that of the women who left private practice, 27 percent got out of law altogether; of women who left nonprivate practice, the figure was 25 percent. Work/life balance was the most cited reason for leaving. Although women now comprise 52 percent of Canadian law school graduates and 38 percent of all lawyers, it's becoming clear that the barriers to practising law over the long term are significant for women. Reasons for switching jobs or leaving the profession include the ever-familiar "glass ceiling," a male-dominated culture, and an unmet need for mentoring. However, the lack of accommodation for women in law who are also in the early stages of motherhood has created such significant problems that even the most determined among them may decide to leave the legal profession altogether.

While the personal cost of leaving a firm is significant for women, it is also hard on the bottom line of the firm itself. One 2005 study done by Catalyst reported the cost of losing an associate at $315,000, after taking into account the time and expense of recruitment, onboarding, development, and termination. Experts in the field note that it takes at least two years before new hires begin to earn their keep and if they leave shortly thereafter, it's a no-win situation.

Women trying to practise in small firms or as sole practitioners are especially vulnerable when it comes to maternity leave. For one thing, taking time off to have a baby makes it difficult to retain clients because there will be few or no colleagues to take over the workload. Even worse, having a baby can quickly become a financial nightmare. Although EI rules have now changed to include those who are self-employed for maternity and parental benefits, in the past they did not; women were forced to pay for their own leaves. Even with EI, the maximum benefit hardly comes close to the normal salary of a successful lawyer. Apple Newton-Smith (a criminal lawyer) and Susan Fraser (a civil litigator and administrative lawyer) are examples. By the time both returned to work after the birth of their second child, they were sinking into debt. Both went deep into their lines of credit, struggling without income for the months they took off, bearing costs associated with the practice itself, and dealing with stubborn accounts receivables. This was particularly true of Newton-Smith, who was often forced to wait months for legal aid to pay up on client files.

To resolve these problems, the Law Society of Upper Canada formed a Retention of Women in Private Practice Working Group, which ultimately came up with a number of solutions. First they proposed a two-pronged approach to support parental leave for women practising in very small firms, and who have no other benefits. The Judica Project was approved in 2008, providing parental benefits of $3,000 per month for three months to lawyers in firms of five or fewer, and it was funded by member contributions in an amount set by an actuary. In the first year, the fund was utilized by 75 women and 27 men. The program would flow for three years and then be evaluated. The second part of the plan involved creating practice locums, like those already in place for doctors. A registry was established of lawyers willing to step into the breach while new mothers attended to a smaller but equally demanding "client." In larger communities, lawyers often had no problem finding someone to take over files for the duration of a leave, but in small communities it could be a real problem, so the registry was a good idea.

No doubt the new EI rules, which now include self-employed persons, will reduce some of the financial burden for parental leave over time, as individuals pay into the plan long enough to qualify. However, there is still a gap of around $1,000 the Law Society will need to consider in its decision of whether or not to continue the fund. In addition, the general issue of work/life balance continues to persist. Despite the effort to get into law school and the added cost of getting yet another degree, women are leaving law, and it's not just about the money.

Questions

1. Why has the legal profession in Canada not realized until the last few years how maternity leaves affect women actively working in a law practice?

2. Are there any other types of professions in which women might experience the same problems? If so, what are they? Would the solutions devised by the Law Society work in other professions?

SOURCES: V. Berenyi, "Scales Tipped Against Women in Law," *Calgary Herald* (February 1, 2009); T. Crawford, "Women Lawyers Leaving in Droves," www.thestar.com (February 25, 2011); N. Fraser, "Leaving the Law over Lack of Maternity Leave," www.lexlo.ca (May 16, 2008).

Managing People: Big Help for a Big Problem

Substance abuse is a manager's worst nightmare, especially if there is no plan within the organization for how to deal with it. Many small companies find themselves in this position, and even managers in larger organizations will struggle if there is no employee assistance program to guide them. There is a substantial impact on the organization when substance abuse goes unaddressed, including higher usage of health benefits and greater levels of sick time, absenteeism, and tardiness. Other areas impacted include productivity, individual decision making, workplace morale, and safety. Substance abuse can also reflect negatively on the company's image and community relations.

Substance abuse and addictions such as gambling create a complex situation that emerges over time, but may ultimately present as a critical incident, such as a serious accident or violence in the workplace. Perhaps an employee begins exhibiting erratic behaviour or becomes unreliable, or work performance starts trending downward. This behaviour may be explained away as the result of too much stress or fatigue, or problems at home. What would tip off a manager that an addiction is the real reason for the behaviour he or she is seeing? Even if a manager suspects that substance abuse or addiction is part of the picture, how would he or she differentiate between an employee with a problem and a problem employee?

From the first moment a supervisor suspects that an employee has a problem with gambling or substance abuse, challenges arise that can seem overwhelming for managers. These include (1) accurately recognizing signs of problematic substance abuse; (2) understanding what actions to take to deal with it effectively and (3) ensuring that any actions taken are in compliance with privacy legislation, collective agreements, and any other legal constraints or policies that exist; (4) coping effectively if the situation manifests as a crisis; and (5) knowing what policies and resources exist to deal with the problem.

These issues are painful conundrums that have serious implications if organizations are unprepared. However, thanks to the Atlantic Canada Council on Addiction, employers can now download a free toolkit that will help them understand the issue and design an effective response before it lands on their doorstep. Funded by Health Canada, *Problematic Substance Use That Impacts the Workplace* is a comprehensive, step-by-step guide to help organizations understand problematic substance abuse and prepare for it ahead of time. The toolkit begins with Step 1 by explaining how to do a needs assessment based on four key questions such as "Are we prepared if we have a problem?" to find out what employee needs may exist as well as the organization's capacity to meet those needs. Step 2 guides employers in developing drug and alcohol policies, including suggested policy components, checklists, and a sample communication plan. Step 3 provides extensive information for educating employees. This is deemed a critical step in addressing problematic substance abuse, and includes prevention strategies aligned with comprehensive workplace health programs, and general information on the issue and its impact on work performance and personal life. This step explains how to help employees understand how to report a coworker, the types of supports available to employees and their families, and numerous other issues. Step 4 concerns supervisor training since supervisors are a key element in addressing the issue in the workplace. The training focuses on the role of the supervisor in handling problematic substance abuse, how to respond to a crisis, and developing and writing incident reports. Supervisors also need have a thorough knowledge of the company's policy on substance abuse, explain it to employees, and refer individuals for help. This step addresses avoiding excuses, appeals for sympathy, diversions, and emotional blackmail, as well as the right way to reintegrate employees who are returning to work. Step 5 addresses creating a support system and integrating health promotion, substance abuse prevention strategies, early identification, intervention, treatment, and reintegration. Finally, Step 6 guides employers in the process of evaluating the effectiveness of their approach to the problem once it has been implemented; measuring successes, addressing ongoing challenges, recognizing necessary modifications, and justifying continuing support for the program.

The toolkit includes checklists, including behavioural indicators to help recognize emerging problems, which are categorized under physical, psychosocial impact, and workplace performance and professional image, as well as indicators that identify progression and visible signs in the early, middle, and later phases of substance use. Samples are also provided of a communication poster, an incident report, and an evaluation survey to help employers begin. There is much here to help employers get past myths and assumptions and begin to take concrete action to preserve the health and productivity of employees at all levels of the organization. A quick review of even a few sections presents a convincing picture of why no organization should delay addressing problematic substance abuse and addiction in the workplace. And given the fact that substance abuse (alone) in Canada costs employers $24.3 billion a year, it may be worth the time to check it out.

Questions

Visit the Problematic Substance Abuse Step-by-Step Guide and Toolkit, which you will find at www.healthpei.ca/index.php3?number=publications&dept=&id=1823. Download the PDF version of the document and then answer the following questions.

1. What is problematic substance use and addiction, and what are two of the four myths associated with it?

2. List four physical behaviour indicators of problematic substance abuse, and three indicators linked to workplace performance and professional image. Would these be enough to be certain an employee had a serious problem with addiction? Explain your answer.

3. Why should employers address problematic substance abuse?

SOURCE: *Problematic Substance Abuse That Impacts the Workplace*, Atlantic Canada Council on Addiction, at www.healthpei.ca/photos/original/hpei_addic_kit.pdf,; M. Morra, "Return on Wellness," *HR Professional* (August/September 2009), pp. 21–24.

CHAPTER

11

Collective Bargaining and Labour Relations

Enter the World of Business

Framework of Fairness Agreement Takes Union–Management Relationship to the Next Level

In late 2007, in an unprecedented move in the unionized auto sector in North America, Frank Stronach, head of Magna International Inc., Canada's largest automotive systems and parts manufacturer, granted voluntary recognition to the Canadian Auto Workers (CAW), subject only to acceptance by a majority of Magna's 18,000 or so workers. In return, the workers gave up the right to strike. The company positioned the historic Framework of Fairness Agreement (FFA) with the CAW as a set of principles that established the needs of workers and business to be competitive, and that represented a new labour model which sought to preserve the key components of Magna's Fair Enterprise system, while ensuring proper checks and balances.

Stronach, chairman of Magna's board of directors, explained Magna's reasons for the paradigm-changing move, saying, "The traditional, confrontational model of labour relations is unproductive and wastes energy that would be better focused on creating the conditions which would be fair to employees and would ensure that Magna remains competitive in the global automotive industry." Stronach emphasized Magna's commitment to the agreement, saying, "Magna recognizes that the CAW has the ability to be an important ally in addressing the many competitive challenges our industry is facing, ensuring the needs of employees and society are balanced against the needs of our other stakeholders, namely customers, investors, and other business partners. We are pleased that the CAW is willing to embark with us on this groundbreaking agreement."

Bob White, founding president of the CAW, and past president of the Canadian Labour Congress, explained the CAW's reasoning behind the controversial agreement, saying, "Unions can't stay static (employers certainly don't). Unions must always take on new issues, and find new ways of making progress."

The FFA was set up to be introduced to employees in Magna's Canadian manufacturing divisions over the following two to three years. Magna divisional employees would have the opportunity to vote on approval of a new contract under the terms of the FFA, and to join the CAW. If the majority of workers in a facility voted in favour, the plant would then be covered by a Magna–CAW national collective agreement.

Key terms and conditions of the FFA included preservation of Magna's Fair Enterprises culture and operating principles, including sharing of the company's financial success through equity ownership; comprehensive no-strike, no lock-out provisions with unresolved collective bargaining issues being settled through final offer selection arbitration; progressive concern resolution; competitive wage and benefit principles; a concept tying annual wage adjustments to a manufacturing inflationary index, plant-specific performance measures, and competitive considerations; secret ballot voting on workplace issues; and depoliticization of the workplace and labour–management relations.

To meet the challenges of a global trading system that enables vehicles and parts to be imported to North America from developing countries where workers are exploited and paid nominal wages, the CAW and Magna also agreed to join forces in lobbying governments to rectify unfair global trading practices that threaten jobs and jeopardize the industry's future. Magna's gains included solid partnership with an influential union that had pragmatic bargaining expertise and a keen eye for economic and labour market analysis, as well as a successful track record in soliciting support from provincial and federal governments. Although workers were giving up the right to strike, they were also free to accept or reject the deal by a free vote. Like traditional collective agreements, terms under the FFA would be negotiated every three years, and ratified by secret ballot vote.

While critics were skeptical of workers relinquishing their most powerful economic weapon, Tim Armstrong, former deputy minister of labour and deputy minister of Industry, Trade and Technology in Ontario, said that where workers decided to choose an alternative method for resolving their differences and preserving job security, that preference should be respected. Workers were securing big gains in return, including provisions for significant employee involvement in the workplace, unprecedented access to information concerning Magna's operations, and the right to work with management on initiatives to increase job satisfaction and employment security. Members would get annual wage increases and high-quality benefits, be served by full-time local representatives, and benefit from the resources and programs of the CAW.

Don Walker, Magna co-CEO, said that Magna had been encouraged by the fact that CAW leadership had demonstrated understanding of the difficulties confronting manufacturers in an increasingly competitive, global environment. He pointed out the potential for substantial benefits to be realized by both parties in the agreement, saying, "This agreement will likely give the CAW increased membership and representation within Magna's Canadian divisions, while at the same time allowing us to maintain our competitiveness, through our entrepreneurial and flexible operating philosophy as we continue to work hard to support our customers and win new business."

Buzz Hargrove, then president of the CAW, was emphatically positive about the emerging "earthquake" in labour relations, saying, "Magna and the CAW will develop a new way of working together." He also reinforced advantages of the agreement, saying, "It will strengthen the CAW's ability to support auto parts workers at an incredibly challenging time, but in a way that also strengthens Canada's auto industry. Magna and the CAW have established an effective working relationship through our existing unionized facilities, and through our participation in joint industry initiatives such as the Canadian Automotive Partnership Council. The Framework of Fairness takes our relationship to the next level."

The FFA, if and when fully implemented, would cover up to 18,000 Magna production employees in about 45 manufacturing facilities in Ontario. Mindful of the concerns voiced by existing CAW members and other stakeholders who might ultimately be impacted by the union's major change in direction, Bob White reinforced the need to be open-minded, saying, "I think it is important to keep finding new strategies and innovations to make a positive difference in workers' lives, as long as workers have the ultimate say in determining whether they accept the union and the collective agreement, as they do in the CAW–Magna agreement."

Shortly after the historic agreement was signed, Buzz Hargrove retired, along with at least one other key CAW negotiator involved in the Magna deal, and the ground has shaken under the entire North American auto industry in other ways. Currently, few of Magna's facilities have actually joined the CAW beyond the handful of CAW units within Magna prior to the FFA. Perhaps this is because Magna's website prominently features an Employee Charter (in several languages), that outlines the principles and philosophy behind Magna's Fair Enterprise Culture, "in which employees and management share in the responsibility to ensure the success of the company." The charter features a hotline employees can call if they feel the charter's principles are not being met, and describes an employee advisory board that monitors and advises Magna's management to "ensure that Magna operates within the spirit of the Magna Employee's Charter and the principles of Magna's Corporate Constitution." With such a charter perhaps employees see no reason to involve the CAW. Regardless, the 2007 agreement forged between Magna and the CAW opened up new horizons for the future of labour relations in Canada, and perhaps around the world.

SOURCES: "New Agreement between Magna and CAW Union Aims to Change Confrontational Model of Labour Relations and Eliminate Strikes," *Canadian Driver* (October 16, 2007); "Unions Have to Innovate to Better Serve Workers," *TheStar.com*, October 30, 2007; "Time for Change," *canada.com* (November 1, 2007); Magna International Inc. Employee's Charter at www.magna.com/magna/en/responsibility/charter/pdf/Employee_Charter.pdf (retrieved June 29, 2011).

INTRODUCTION

The events at Magna in 2007 illustrate both the important role of labour relations in running a business and the influence of competitive challenges on the nature of labour relations. Global competition has forced a rethinking of core strategies. To be more competitive, employers must not only reduce cost but also improve quality. To do so, Magna needed to convince the CAW and its workers to cooperate in developing a new model of labour relations. It was decided by Magna and the CAW that successful employment relationships depended on embarking on this novel approach to labour relations and achieving a competitive level of efficiency. This common goal of mutual success was seized on to bind management and labour together in a search for improved competitiveness.

THE LABOUR RELATIONS FRAMEWORK

Describe what is meant by collective bargaining and labour relations.

It has been suggested that a successful industrial relations system consists of four elements: (1) an environmental context (technology, market pressures, and the legal framework, especially as it affects bargaining power); (2) participants, including employees and their unions, management, and the government; (3) a "web of rules" (rules of the game) that describe the process by which labour and management interact and resolve disagreements (such as the steps followed in settling contract grievances); and (4) ideology.[1] For the industrial relations system to operate properly, the three primary participants must, to some degree, have a common ideology (such as acceptance of some form of the capitalist system) and must accept the roles of the other participants. Acceptance does not translate into convergence of interests, however. To the contrary, some degree of worker–management conflict is inevitable because, although the interests of the two parties overlap, they also diverge in key respects (such as how to divide the economic profits).[2]

According to this view, an effective industrial relations system does not eliminate conflict. Rather, it provides institutions (and a "web of rules") that resolve conflict in a way that minimizes its costs to management, employees, and society. The collective bargaining system is one such institution, as are related mechanisms such as mediation, arbitration, and participation in decision making.

Labour–management relations exist on a continuum ranging from open conflict to cooperation/collaboration.[3] In an "open conflict" relationship, the parties have an extreme distrust and dislike for one another. In a "containment–aggression" relationship, distrust remains, but to a lesser extent and the parties' dislike for one another becomes antagonism. A relationship of "accommodation" is more courteous. However, it is still hindered by a lack of trust and acceptance of the other party. To progress through the continuum, the parties must seek and test new ways of working together to

FIGURE 11.1 A Labour Relations Framework

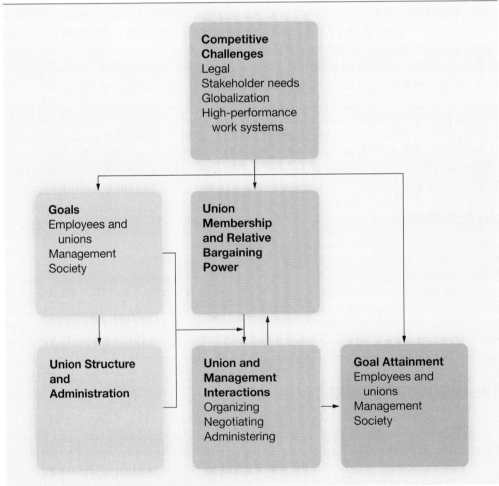

solve issues and problems of common concern. By undertaking this process, the parties can achieve a "cooperative" model. The final stage, "cooperation/collaboration," is characterized by a positive relationship where the parties trust and accept the legitimacy of each other's role and responsibilities and consciously strive for mutually satisfying solutions to problems within the context of a collective bargaining relationship.

A relationship that involves teamwork, a joint approach to solving labour relations issues, a mutual respect and recognition of each other's legitimate roles and differences, a system for handling and resolving conflict, and a joint effort in the management of workplace change will make great strides in achieving an effective labour relations model that will reap benefits for all workplace parties.

The labour relations framework depicted in Figure 11.1 highlights many aspects of the labour relations framework, including the important role of the environment (the competitive challenges); union, management, and societal goals; and a separation of union–management interactions into categories (union organizing, contract negotiation, contract administration) that can have important influences on one another but may also be analyzed somewhat independently. The model also highlights the important role that relative bargaining power plays in influencing goals, union–management interactions, and the degree to which each party achieves its goals. Relative bargaining power, in turn, is significantly influenced by the competitive environment (legal, social, quality, high-performance work systems, and globalization competitive challenges) and the size and depth of union membership.[4]

We now describe the components of this model in greater depth. The remainder of the chapter is organized into the following sections: the goals and strategies of society, management, and unions; union structure (including union administration and membership); the legal framework, perhaps the key aspect of the competitive environment for labour relations; union and management interactions (organizing, contract negotiation, contract administration); and labour relations outcomes. Environmental factors (other than legal ones) and bargaining power are discussed in the context of these sections. In addition, public-sector labour relations are discussed.

Evidence-Based HR

Labour: Everyone's Interests: Avoiding Labour Disputes

We have seen it happen many times. Sometimes the negotiating parties reach a deal or perhaps the employer tables its "last, best, and final offer," and the union reluctantly agrees to take it back to the membership for a ratification vote. The ratification meeting occurs. Loud voices and hot tempers prevail. The deal is turned down, whether or not the union has recommended it. Suddenly the employees are looking at shutting the company down with a strike as well as generating a major impact on other companies, the economy, and their own individual lives and families. When a strike starts, there is often no clear end in sight.

Often, there is no quick fix or easy solution to avoid unwanted or unintended impasses. Joel Cutcher-Gershenfeld, dean of the School of Labour and Employment Relations at the University of Illinois at Urban-Champaign, could offer some valuable wisdom to these collective bargaining parties so often at odds with each other's best interests. He has co-chaired Harvard University's Project on Negotiation in the Workplace and is a specialist in strategic negotiating in industrial relations. A component of this is interest-based negotiations (IBN), which is a bargaining strategy that continues to generate interest in North American workplaces. IBN's goal is to maximize interests on both sides of the collective bargaining table.

It is common for each side in traditional bargaining to open with positions that significantly overstate their needs and expectations. Step by step, each side inches toward a deal with incremental concessions. Bargaining can perpetuate ongoing disputes, as each side tries to read into settled (and yet often vague) language its own self-serving and mutually contradictory interpretations. The final result is frequently quite different from each side's starting point, which may undercut a negotiation team's mandate from its constituents and therefore take away future flexibility in achieving compromises.

Professor Cutcher-Gershenfeld endorses the IBN concept, which opens up the process and generates a wider range of solutions more likely to reflect and satisfy the interests of both sides. It begins before bargaining starts, as each side consults all stakeholders to determine where they can afford to be flexible and where they must remain firm. Teams from each side then bargain over how to bargain by setting ground rules and bargaining parameters. Often, it is useful to agree on joint fact gathering, as well as to share minutes and other information during the negotiation process. Technology can offer assistance in literally projecting the interests under discussion by PowerPoint or some other tool.

The Government of Saskatchewan is an example of an organization that supports IBN. The process is intended to promote an environment of open and clear communication that should help employers, employees, and trade unions maintain good working relationships or improve difficult relationships over the long term. In some situations, perhaps with government support, IBN can use a facilitator to guide the parties through an interest-based model to achieve a collective bargaining agreement. Overall, IBN is a process that continually returns focus to what the needs of all participants are, rather than supporting individual positions. IBN is a collaborative approach to problem solving, and an opportunity for people to sit down together and solve problems or reach resolution jointly, in a collaborative manner.

A few concepts that might help negotiators understand IBN include

- Positional negotiating versus interest based negotiating;
- Giving your picture and getting their picture;
- Blockers to moving from positional negotiating to interest-based negotiating; and
- A joint problem-solving model.

Teams should begin IBN negotiations with open-ended questions for each other, rather than a list of demands. Questions might focus on working together for a safe and productive workplace or on how to maximize production for the employer while sharing the resulting gains with workers. In this way, parties can focus the discussion on achieving the legitimate interests of each side and finding common ground in key issues, rather than retreating into inflexible positions. For example, instead of the employer focusing on the right to subcontract, IBN negotiating teams could jointly focus on how the existing employees can be the workforce of choice for the employer, both in terms of cost and quality.

Those with a more cynical mindset may conclude that some workplaces have too many historical issues to overcome in moving from a traditional adversarial, us-versus-them relationship to a more progressive, roundtable IBN process that focuses on "we" solutions. Those with an open mind may be more prepared to conclude that combative positions could give way to mutual gains; and positive thinking says that anything is negotiable, even the process itself.

SOURCE: Rachel Pulfer, "Labour: Everyone's Interests: Prevent Disputes with Smart Labour Talks," *Canadian Business Online* (April 23, 2007); and Government of Saskatchewan at www.aeei.gov.sk.ca/interest-based-negotiations.

GOALS AND STRATEGIES

Society

LO 2

Identify the labour relations goals of management, labour unions, and society.

In one sense, labour unions, with their emphasis on group action, do not fit well with the individualistic orientation of Canadian capitalism. However, industrial relations scholars such as Beatrice and Sidney Webb and John R. Commons argued in the late 1800s and early 1900s that individual workers' bargaining power was far smaller than that of employers, who were likely to have more financial resources and the ability to easily replace workers.[5] Effective institutions for worker representation (such as labour unions) were therefore seen as a way to make bargaining power more equal.

The major benefit of labour unions to society is the institutionalization of industrial conflict, which is therefore resolved in the least costly way. Thus, although disagreements between management and labour continue, it is better to resolve disputes through discussion (collective bargaining) than by battling in the streets. As an influential group of industrial relations scholars put it when describing the future of advanced industrial relations around the world, "Class warfare will be forgotten. The battles will be in the corridors instead of the streets, and memos will flow instead of blood."[6] In this sense, collective bargaining not only has the potential to reduce economic losses caused by strikes but also may also contribute to societal stability. For this reason, labour unions have often been viewed as an essential component of a democratic society. These were some of the beliefs that contributed to the introduction of the earliest labour relations legislation in Canada, namely the Trade Union Act of 1872, which gave workers the right to form unions and bargain with employers to set wages and working conditions. Various forms of legislation followed, much of it influenced by the passage of the National Labor Relations Act (the Wagner Act), in the United States in 1935. Then in 1948, the federal government enacted the Industrial Relations and Disputes Investigation Act, which became the dominant model for regulating labour and management activities and interactions in each of the provincial and territorial jurisdictions across Canada.

Although an industrial relations system based on collective bargaining has drawbacks, so too do the alternatives. Unilateral control by management sacrifices workers' rights. Extensive involvement of government and the courts can result in conflict resolution that is expensive, slow, and imposed by someone (a judge) with much less firsthand knowledge of the circumstances than either labour or management.

Learn more about the history of labour legislation in Canada online with Connect.

connect

Employers (Management)

Most employers want to discourage the unionization of their employees. Management discourages unions because it fears higher wage and benefit costs, the disruptions caused by strikes, and an adversarial relationship with its employees or, more generally, greater constraints placed on its decision-making flexibility and discretion. Historically, management has used two basic strategies to avoid unionization.[7] It may seek to provide employment terms and conditions that employees will perceive as sufficiently attractive and equitable so that they see little gain from union representation or it may aggressively oppose union representation, even where there is significant employee support for a union, such as demonstrated by Walmart in provinces such as Quebec and Saskatchewan.[8]

If management voluntarily recognizes a union, or if the union becomes certified by a labour relations board, the focus for management shifts from dealing with employees as individuals to employees as a group. Still, certain basic management objectives remain: controlling labour costs and increasing productivity (by keeping wages and benefits in check) and maintaining management prerogatives in important areas such as staffing levels and work rules. Management does not have the option of trying to decertify a union (that is, encouraging employees to vote out the union in a decertification election), even if it believes that the majority of employees no longer wish to be represented by the union. Rather, a decertification application must be initiated solely by employees without any employer influence, encouragement, or assistance.

Labour Unions

Labour unions seek, through collective action, to give workers a formal and independent voice in setting the terms and conditions of their work. Table 11.1 shows typical provisions negotiated by unions in collective bargaining contracts. Labour unions attempt to represent their members' interests in setting negotiation priorities.

Table 11.1 Typical Provisions in Collective Bargaining Contracts

Establishment and administration of the agreement	Wage determination and administration	Plant operations
Bargaining unit and plant supplements	General provisions	Work and shop rules
Contract duration and reopening and renegotiation provisions	Rate structure and wage differentials	Rest periods and other in-plant time allowances
Union security and dues check-off	Allowances	Health and safety
Special bargaining committees	Incentive systems and production bonus plans	Plant committees
Grievance procedures	Production standards and time studies	Hours of work and premium pay practices
Arbitration	Job classification and job evaluation	Shift operations
Mediation	Individual wage adjustments	Hazardous work
Strikes and lockouts	General wage adjustments during the contract period	Discipline and discharge
Contract enforcement		
	Job or income security	**Paid and unpaid leave**
Functions, rights, and responsibilities	Hiring and transfer arrangements	Vacations and holidays
Management rights clauses	Employment and income guarantees	Sick leave
Plant removal	Reporting and call-in pay	Statutory leaves
Subcontracting	Supplemental unemployment benefit plans	Bereavement and personal leave
Union activities on company time and premises	Regulation of overtime, shift work, etc.	Jury duty
Union–management cooperation	Reduction of hours to forestall layoffs	
Regulation of technological change	Layoff procedures; seniority; recall	**Employee benefit plans**
Advance notice and consultation	Worksharing in lieu of layoff	Health and insurance plans
	Attrition arrangements	Pension plans
	Promotion practices	Profit-sharing, stock purchase, and thrift plans
	Training and retraining	Bonus plans
	Relocation allowances	
	Severance pay and layoff benefit plans	**Special groups**
	Special funds and study committees	Apprentices and learners
		Workers with disabilities and older workers
		Women
		Union representatives
		Nondiscrimination clauses

SOURCE: Adapted from Harry Katz, Thomas Kochan, and Alexander Colvin, *An Introduction to Collective Bargaining and Industrial Relations* 4E, 2008. Copyright © 2008 The McGraw-Hill Companies.

A major goal of labour unions is bargaining effectiveness, because with it comes the power and influence to make the employees' voices heard and to effect changes in the workplace. The right to strike (both the threat and reality of strike action) is an important component of using bargaining power to create leverage. In turn, the success of a strike (actual or threatened) depends on the relative magnitude of the costs imposed on management versus those imposed on the union. A critical factor is the size of union membership. More members translates into a greater ability to halt or disrupt production and also generates greater financial resources for continuing a strike in the face of lost wages.

UNION STRUCTURE, ADMINISTRATION, AND MEMBERSHIP

A necessary step in discussing labour–management interactions is a basic knowledge of how labour and management are organized and how they function. Management has been described throughout this book. We now focus on labour unions.

National and International Unions

Most union members belong to a national or international union. In turn, most national unions are composed of multiple local units, and most are affiliated with provincial federations of labour, local labour councils, and/or the Canadian Labour Congress (CLC). Some unions associated with the CLC are also members of the American Federation of Labor and Congress of Industrial Organizations (AFL-CIO). National unions comprise 67 percent of Canada's union membership, while 27.6 percent of Canadian union members belong to international unions.[9] The remainder belong to independent local associations or directly chartered unions.

Trade unions generally have a localized structure. There is a central or national office run by the national executives of the union, which is responsible for the macro-level management of the union; for example, determining policy, distributing expertise and funding, assisting in organizing efforts, administering the union's finances, and managing relationships between the various branches of the union. The central or national office also typically maintains affiliations with umbrella labour organizations that, among other things, promote and advocate on behalf of the labour community in respect of social, political, and economic issues (e.g., federations of labour, the CLC). However, the union's day-to-day operations are run by the various branches or locals of the union and the local executive, as discussed below.

The structure of international unions is much the same as domestic unions with the exception of the international location of the parent union. The international union is typically based in the United States and has a Canadian national office. The union often has elected international officers, as well as Canadian union executives who determine and apply the international policies of the union. While the international union will have some common policies that apply equally to its American and Canadian locals, the Canadian offices and executives usually have autonomy to determine union policy in respect of the Canadian locals. Moreover, some international unions have district councils designed to address issues of regional interest and concern.

The largest labour unions in Canada (most of which are national unions) are listed in Table 11.2 on page 430. An important characteristic of a union is whether it is a craft or industrial union. The electrical workers' and carpenters' unions are examples of craft unions, meaning that the members all have a particular skill or occupation. Craft unions often are responsible for training their members (through apprenticeships) and for supplying craft workers to employers. Requests for carpenters, for example, would come to the union hiring hall, which would decide which carpenters to send out. Thus craft workers may work for many employers over time, their constant link being to the union. A craft union's bargaining power depends greatly on the control it can exercise over the supply of its workers.

Table 11.2 Largest Labour Unions in Canada—2010

NAME	NUMBER OF MEMBERS
Canadian Union of Public Employees	601,976
National Union of Public and General Employees	340,000
United Steel, Paper and Forestry, Rubber, Manufacturing, Energy, Allied Industrial and Service Workers International Union	280,000
United Food and Commercial Workers Canada	245,327
National Automobile, Aerospace, Transportation and General Workers Union of Canada (CAW Canada)	195,000
Public Service Alliance of Canada	188,462
Communications, Energy and Paperworkers Union of Canada	128,564
Fédération de la santé et des services sociaux	122,193
Teamsters Canada	113,851
Service Employees International Union	92,781
Alberta Union of Provincial Employees	79,004
Elementary Teachers' Federation of Ontario	73,325
FTQ Construction	69,914
Laborers' International Union of North America	68,650
Ontario Secondary School Teachers' Federation	63,113
Centrale des syndicats démocratiques (Syndicats à charte directe)	61,642
Fédération des syndicats de l'enseignement	60,000
Fédération interprofessionnelle de la santé du Québec	58,173
International Brotherhood of Electrical Workers	57,130
Fédération des employées et employés de services publics inc.	55,700
Canadian Union of Postal Workers	54,144
Ontario Nurses' Association	54,000
Alberta Teachers' Association	52,626
Professional Institute of the Public Service of Canada	50,306
United Brotherhood of Carpenters and Joiners of America	50,000
United Association of Journeymen and Apprentices of the Plumbing and Pipe Fitting Industry of the United States and Canada	49,905
British Columbia Teachers' Federation	47,021
UNITE HERE Canada	46,000
Christian Labour Association of Canada	45,000
International Union of Operating Engineers	41,993
Syndicat de la fonction publique du Québec	38,890
Ontario English Catholic Teachers' Association	38,500
International Association of Machinists and Aerospace Workers	36,597
Fédération du commerce inc.	36,274
Canadian Office and Professional Employees Union	34,000

SOURCE: Strategic Policy, Analysis, and Workplace Information Directorate, Labour Program, Human Resources and Skills Development Canada 2010 at www.hrsdc.gc.ca/eng/labour/labour_relations/info_analysis/union_membership/2010/unionmembership2010.shtml (retrieved August 7, 2011). Reproduced with the permission of the Minister of Public Works and Government Services, 2011.

By contrast, members of bargaining units represented by industrial unions tend to associate more closely with a single employer (and perhaps even a single location of a single employer) over the long term. Unlike craft unions, industrial unions are made up of members who are linked by their work in a particular industry (such as steelworkers and autoworkers). Typically they represent many different occupations. Membership in the union is a result of working for a particular employer in the industry. Changing employers is less common for industrial workers than it is among craft workers, and employees who change employers remain members of the same union only if they happen to move to other employers covered by that union. Whereas a craft union may restrict the number of members, to maintain higher wages, industrial unions try to organize as many employees in as wide a range of skills as possible.

Today, many unions—both craft and industrial—consist of white-collar or professional employees such as nurses, teachers, and office workers. Usually these white-collar employees are organized in separate bargaining units from their blue-collar counterparts. This could mean having both a blue-collar and a white-collar bargaining unit with a single employer or one group may remain nonunion. It also could mean that you have both a craft unit and an industrial unit with a single employer.

Local Unions

Even when a national union plays the most critical role in negotiating terms of a collective bargaining contract, negotiation occurs at the local level as well as over work rules and other issues that are locally determined. In addition, administration of the contract is largely carried out at the local union level including conducting membership drives and processing grievances. Consequently, the bulk of day-to-day interaction between labour and management takes place at the local union level.

The local of an industrial-based union may correspond to a single large facility or to a number of small facilities. In a craft-oriented union, the local may cover a city or a region. The local union typically elects officers (such as president, vice president, treasurer). Responsibility for contract negotiation may rest with the officers, or a bargaining committee may be formed for this purpose. Typically the national union provides assistance, ranging from background data about other settlements and technical advice to sending a representative to lead the negotiations.

Individual members' participation in local union meetings includes the election of union officials and strike votes. However, most union contact is with the shop steward, who is responsible for ensuring that the terms of the collective bargaining contract are enforced. The shop steward represents employees in grievances arising under the collective agreement. Another union position, the business representative, performs some of the same functions, especially if the union deals with multiple employers.

Union Security

The survival and security of a union depends on its ability to ensure a regular flow of new members and member dues to support the services it provides. Therefore, unions typically place high priority on negotiating two contract provisions with an employer that are critical to a union's security or viability: check-off provisions and union membership or contribution. First, under a **check-off provision**, the employer, on behalf of the union, is obligated to automatically deduct union dues from employees' paycheques.[10]

A second union security provision focuses on the flow of new members (and their dues). The strongest union security arrangement is a **closed shop**, under which a person must be a union member (and thus pay dues) before being hired. A **union shop** requires all existing and future employees to join and maintain membership in the union. An **agency shop**, based on the **Rand formula**, is similar to a union shop but does not require union membership, only that dues be paid by all members of

Check-off Provision
A union contract provision that requires an employer to deduct union dues from employees' paycheques.

Closed Shop
A union security provision requiring a person to be a union member before being hired.

Union Shop
A union security provision that requires all existing and future employees to join and maintain membership in the union.

Agency Shop or Rand Formula
A union security provision that requires an employee to pay union membership dues but not to join the union.

Maintenance of Membership
Union rules requiring members to remain members for a certain period of time (such as the length of the union contract).

Voluntary Check-Off
A union security provision wherein members of the union have union dues deducted by the employer only at their request, and there is no requirement to join the union.

the bargaining unit. **Maintenance of membership** rules do not require union membership but do require that employees who choose to join must remain members for a certain period of time (such as the length of the contract). **Voluntary check-off** does not require that employees join the union, and members of the union will have union dues deducted by the employer only at their request.

Union Membership and Bargaining Power

At the strategic level, management and unions meet head-on over the issue of union organizing. Increasingly, employers are actively resisting unionization in an attempt to control costs and maintain their flexibility. Unions, on the other hand, must organize new members and hold on to their current members to have the kind of bargaining power and financial resources needed to achieve their goals in future organizing and to negotiate and administer contracts with management.

Since the 1980s, when union membership was 38 percent of employment, membership has consistently declined as a percentage of employment. It now stands at 29.6 percent of all employment and 16 percent of private-sector employment.[11] Although union density rates in Canada have been steadily declining, they still remain more than twice that of the United States, which had a union density rate of only 12.3 percent in 2009.[12]

Several factors explain Canada's higher rate of union membership as compared to the United States. First, Canada has a much larger public-sector workforce—a group that is notoriously much easier to organize. Public-sector workers in Canada are among the most highly unionized workers with 71.2 percent of the public-sector workforce being unionized.[13] Differences in labour laws may also account for higher rates of unionization in Canada.[14] Overall, it has been suggested that certification procedures in Canada make it easier for unions to win representation votes. Moreover, Canada allows for a provision in collective agreements providing for mandatory union membership versus right-to-work laws in many areas of the United States that prohibit such a clause and provide workers a choice as to whether to join the union.

Table 11.3 provides a view of Canada's unionization rate as compared to several other countries as it stood in 2008.

LO 3

Explain the legal environment's impact on labour relations in Canada.

Legal Framework

Although competitive challenges have a major impact on labour relations, the legal framework of collective bargaining is an especially critical determinant of union membership and relative bargaining power. The efficient operation of this framework significantly impacts the degree to which employers, employees, and society are successful in achieving their goals. The legal framework also constrains union structure and administration and the manner in which unions and employers interact. Perhaps the most dramatic example of the influence of labour laws is the 1944 passage of Order-in-Council P.C. 1003 in Canada under the War Measures Act, which actively supported collective bargaining rather than impeding it. This order ushered in a new era of public policy in support of labour unions; it enshrined collective bargaining as the preferred mechanism for settling labour–management disputes. In conjunction with more favourable economic conditions after the war, union membership more than doubled between 1940 and 1946, from 362,000 to almost 832,000, reaching more than 1,000,000 in 1949.[15]

With increased membership came greater union bargaining power and, consequently, more success in achieving union goals. Within a few years, all jurisdictions in Canada had labour legislation espousing the right to join a trade union, creating rights and obligations of unions and employers in respect of labour relations including collective bargaining, and establishing regulatory bodies for the administration and enforcement of the statutes.

Table 11.3 International Unionization Rates (2008)

COUNTRY	RATE OF UNIONIZATION	COUNTRY	RATE OF UNIONIZATION
Denmark	67.6	Germany	19.1
Finland	67.5	Netherlands	18.9
Norway	53.3	Australia	18.6
Belgium	51.9	Switzerland	18.3
Luxembourg	37.4	Japan	1 .2
Italy	33.4	Hungary	16.8
Ireland	32.3	Slovak Republic	16.8
Austria	28.9	Poland	15.6
Canada	**27.1**	Spain	14.3
United Kingdom	27.1	Chile	13.6
Greece	24	United States	11.9
New Zealand	20.8	Korea	10.3
Portugal	20.4	France	7.7
Czech Republic	20.2	Turkey	5.8

Note: Numbers correspond to the ratio of wage and salary earners that are trade union members, divided by the total number of wage and salary earners.

SOURCE: Organisation for Economic Co-operation and Development, OECD.StatExtracts at http://stats.oecd.org/Index.aspx?DataSetCode=UN_DEN.

Although labour relations statutes have broad coverage, there are some notable exclusions. The types of employees that are excluded vary by jurisdiction and while they may not be covered by labour relations legislation of general application in one jurisdiction, they could be expressly included in another. Employees who perform sufficient managerial functions or who are employed in a confidential capacity in matters relating to labour relations are excluded.[16] Other employees excluded in some jurisdictions include, for example, domestic workers employed in a private home; persons employed in agriculture, hunting, or trapping;[17] persons employed in horticulture by an employer whose primary business is agriculture or horticulture; police;[18] firefighters; teachers, vice principals, and principals; provincial judges; Crown employees; and labour mediators or conciliators.[19] While some of these employees are excluded from labour relations statutes of general application, they are nonetheless covered by labour legislation specific to their particular occupation or profession. In the federal sector, professional employees are outside the scope of the statute.[20] Many provincial labour relations statutes similarly exclude professional employees including, for example, architects, dentists, engineers, land surveyors, and legal or medical professionals working in their professional capacity.[21]

Learn more about the underlying principles of Canadian Labour Legislation online with Connect.

Unfair Labour Practices—Employers

Labour relations legislation prohibits certain activities by both employers and labour unions. All jurisdictions have provisions within their labour relations statutes to prohibit an employer from adverse treatment toward an employee for engaging in union activities, or for asserting any other right the employee may have pursuant to the statute.[22] Generally, it is unlawful for employers or any person acting on their behalf to interfere with the formation or administration of a union or to contribute to a union.[23] Employers or any person acting on their behalf must also not discriminate against or refuse to employ or continue to employ an employee because the person was or is a member of a trade union or is a participant in lawful union activities.[24] This can include improper conduct that leads an employee to involuntarily resign akin to constructive dismissal. Furthermore, an employer must refrain from altering employment conditions so as to prevent an employee or potential employee from becoming a member of a trade union.[25] Employers similarly cannot threaten or penalize an employee because of the employee's choice to join or refrain from joining a union. In addition, closures, relocations, or contracting out effected to avoid the union are violations of the statutes, as is authorization, support, or encouragement of an unlawful lockout or similarly based threats.[26] Employer no-solicitation rules that prohibit union organizing during nonworking hours are generally unlawful, as are arbitrary restrictions upon access by union organizers to employer premises if those premises are generally accessible to the public. An exception exists in the rare circumstance where it can be proven that the organizing constitutes a genuine interference with the employer's ability to properly operate its business. Some examples of employer unfair labour practices are listed in Table 11.4.

Unfair Labour Practices—Labour Unions

Like employers, unions are forbidden from using intimidation or coercion to seek to compel a person to become, or refrain from becoming, a union member or from exercising any other lawful right pursuant to the labour relations statute.[27] The objective of the intimidating or coercive action does not necessarily have to be achieved for the labour board to find a violation of the statute. Moreover, just as employers are prohibited from interfering in unions, unions cannot interfere with the formation or administration of an employers' organization.[28] Certain specific duties and prohibitions exist in respect of unions[29] such as the duty to bargain in good faith; the prohibition against engaging in, threatening, or encouraging an unlawful strike; and the duty of fair representation and referral. In some jurisdictions, unions are also expressly prohibited from discriminating against a person in respect of membership in the union and in the imposition of any discipline. Unions may also be restricted in respect of the circumstances under which they can expel or suspend an employee's membership in the union, including where an employee is exercising his or her lawful rights pursuant to the statute. A union is prohibited from bargaining with the employer if it is not the bargaining agent of the employees it is purporting to represent, or if it knows or ought to know that another union is the bargaining agent of the bargaining unit. A union generally cannot require an employer to terminate the employment of an employee on the basis that the employee has been suspended or expelled from the union. In addition, in all jurisdictions but Saskatchewan, unions are prohibited from engaging in union organizing activities involving employees at the workplace during working hours, though in most jurisdictions unions may undertake such solicitation with the employer's consent. Special provisions apply in respect of employees who reside on employer property.

Duty of Fair Representation

While unions are obligated by the common law to treat their members fairly, the duty was codified in statute in most jurisdictions several decades ago, resulting in enforcement through the labour

Table 11.4 Examples of Employer Unfair Labour Practices

- Threatening employees with loss of their jobs or benefits if they join or vote for a union.
- Threatening to close down a plant if organized by a union.
- Questioning employees about their union membership or activities.
- Refusing to bargain with the union or engaging in tactics to sabotage or unreasonably delay negotiations.
- Spying or pretending to spy on union meetings.
- Granting wage increases or other benefits that are timed to discourage employees from forming or joining a union or during a statutory freeze.
- Altering terms and conditions of employment during a union organizing drive.
- Taking an active part in organizing a union or committee to represent employees.
- Providing preferential treatment or aid to one of several unions trying to organize employees.
- Firing employees for urging other employees to join a union or refusing to hire applicants because they are union members.
- Refusing to reinstate workers because the workers participated in a lawful strike.
- Closing a plant and opening the same operation at another plant with new employees because employees at the first plant joined a union.[30]
- Demoting or firing employees for filing an unfair labour practice or for testifying at a labour board hearing.
- Refusing to meet with union representatives because the employees are on strike.
- Refusing to supply union representatives with cost and other data concerning a group insurance plan covering employees.
- Announcing a wage increase without consulting the union.
- Failing to bargain about the effects of a decision to close one of employer's plants.

SOURCES: Jamie Knight, Brett Christen, Sharon Chilcott, and Paula Pettit, *Canada Labour Code: Quick Reference*, 2011 ed., (Toronto: Thomson Carswell); Jamie Knight, Ron LeClair, Gord Woods, and Roslyn McGilvery, *Ontario Labour Relations Act: Quick Reference*, 2011 ed., (Toronto: Thomson Carswell); Jeffrey Sack, C. Michael Mitchell, and Sandy Price, *1997, Ontario Labour Relations Board Law and Practice*, 3rd ed., (Markham, ON: LexisNexis Canada).

boards rather than the courts. Where such a statutory duty exists, the courts will not entertain a **duty of fair representation** action. Rather, the matter is within the exclusive jurisdiction of the labour relations board. Despite the statutory duty in most jurisdictions, a common law duty remains and the courts have given expression to what the duty entails. Briefly summarized, the common law duty consists of the following principles:

1. The union must fairly represent all members in the bargaining unit.
2. Where it is within the union's discretion to determine whether to refer a matter to arbitration, the member does not have a definite right to arbitration.
3. The union must exercise its discretion in good faith, honestly and objectively, while balancing the significance and outcome of the grievance from the perspective of the member with the legitimate interests of the union as a whole (e.g., the cost of proceeding to arbitration, the impact on other bargaining unit members, and the likelihood of success).
4. Arbitrary, capricious, discriminatory, or wrongful conduct on the part of the union is prohibited.
5. The union must represent the member in a fair and genuine manner with integrity and competence and absent any ill-will toward the member.

Duty of Fair Representation
A common law and statutory duty that the union fairly represent all employees in the bargaining unit, whether or not union members. Unions are prohibited from acting in an arbitrary, discriminatory, or unfair manner.

With the exception of New Brunswick and Prince Edward Island, unions in all Canadian jurisdictions have a statutory duty of fair representation that builds on the common law foundation.[31] Given the significant power unions acquire as bargaining representatives, the duty imposes a statutory obligation on unions to fairly represent all employees in the bargaining unit, including those who are not members of the union. Employees in the bargaining unit who believe they have been treated unfairly by the union can file a duty of fair representation application with the labour board.

Related to the duty of fair representation, where a union has the power to select, refer, assign, designate, or schedule persons to or at a workplace (typically, a union hiring hall in the construction, entertainment, or services industries), referrals must be fair and in accordance with any test applied in respect of the duty of fair representation. If an employee believes that the union has violated its duty of fair referral, the employee can file an application with the labour board.

connect Learn more about the duty of fair representation online with Connect.

Duty to Bargain in Good Faith

Duty to Bargain in Good Faith
A duty on employers and unions to make every reasonable effort to collectively bargain with the objective of reaching a collective agreement.

Employers and unions are required to bargain in good faith with each other with the objective of reaching an agreement as to the terms and conditions of a collective agreement. Most jurisdictions impose a statutory duty to bargain in good faith and a requirement that the parties make every reasonable effort to achieve their objective.[32] Some statutes also expressly provide that the parties must meet within a certain period of time following the date that notice to bargain was given. Employer recognition of the union as the employees' bargaining agent is obviously a necessary component of the duty, as is an agreement to meet. The duty is triggered by either party giving notice of its desire to bargain within the timelines prescribed by the statute, and survives a strike or lockout. Furthermore, some jurisdictions require that a provision for regular consultation during the term of the collective agreement be included in the agreement at the request of either party.

Enforcement

Enforcement of the labour relations statutes rests with the labour relations board in each jurisdiction, which is an independent, representational, and quasi-judicial tribunal with expertise in labour relations matters. The boards are typically composed of a tripartite panel including a neutral chairperson or a vice-chairperson, and appointees who are labour and employer representatives. However, there are many situations in which a chairperson or vice-chairperson may hear a case sitting alone.[33]

The major functions of a labour relations board include

1. Certification of trade unions, including all issues related to the organizing drive, membership cards, bargaining unit description, pre-vote campaign and conduct of the representation vote;
2. Termination of bargaining rights;
3. Resolving unfair labour practice complaints;
4. Determining employer status under the statute (e.g., in a sale of a business where there is a dispute over who is the employer);
5. Resolving duty of fair representation and fair referral complaints;
6. Resolving duty to bargain in good faith complaints including, where applicable, in respect of first contract arbitration;
7. Issuing remedies and declarations in respect of unlawful strikes, lockouts, and unlawful picketing;
8. Jurisdictional disputes between unions regarding the assignment of work; and
9. In some jurisdictions and in some situations, the referral of grievances to arbitration (i.e., British Columbia, Manitoba, and Ontario's construction industry).

Competing Through Technology

Labour Relations in the Face of Technological Changes

Technological change, while frequently necessary to compete in a global marketplace and sustain operational efficiency, can wreak havoc on workers. Aside from technology's obvious ability to result in human redundancy, new machines or processes are often frustrating to employees who suddenly find themselves ill equipped to meet work demands. New technology may also lead to increased workloads and pressures. The manner in which work is assigned and workers are supervised is no longer the same. Previously content workers may become disenchanted with their jobs, which they now find less meaningful and fulfilling. As worker morale and pride in their work plummets, employees feel disheartened by the lack of personal control over their new technology-dominated jobs. These new methods of work and overwhelming workloads also may trigger issues related to fairness in pay.

As these issues suggest, in the realm of labour relations and collective bargaining, technological change often becomes a contentious dispute between employers and unions. Seeking to protect the interests of their members, with job security high on their list of priorities, unions frequently challenge management's right to introduce new technologies and the manner in which management's implementation of these changes impacts workers.

In a unionized environment, a collective agreement governs the terms and conditions of work. As comprehensive as parties attempt to make their agreement, no agreement can cover all eventualities that may arise during the agreement's term. There always will be unanticipated conflicts of interest that do not fall within the scope of the clauses of the agreement and the dispute settlement procedures contained therein. These conflicts might include demands that were not conceded when the agreement was signed or issues that were not discussed or even contemplated at the bargaining table, some of which become apparent only after the agreement is signed. In either case, the result may be serious damage to the collective bargaining relationship.

Technological change is one such often unforeseen and unpredictable issue that may have a particularly negative effect on an organization's labour relations landscape. From a labour relations perspective, the exciting benefits of new technologies on an organization's profitability, productivity, and efficiency are counteracted by its all too frequent tendency to shrink the workforce and impose changes unwelcome and unsolicited by those workers most affected.

Because of its significant impact on the collective bargaining relationship, and the risk of disruption to labour relations, technological change can give rise to a statutory duty to bargain during the term of the collective agreement in some Canadian jurisdictions. The theory is that allowing parties to address contentious issues mid-contract alleviates some of the tension that would occur if parties were left to bargain these issues only once the collective agreement expired. In some cases, employers can be required to provide notice of the change. And while work stoppages mid-contract are permissible in certain jurisdictions in respect of technological change, parties must also comply with any provisions regarding notice to bargain in respect of the change.

Beyond statutory mandates to address the introduction of new technologies in the workplace, and in jurisdictions where no statutory provisions to address the issue exist, many workplace parties have taken the step of negotiating technological change clauses into their collective agreements. These clauses typically impose a duty upon management to disclose to the union impending plans to introduce technological change; they also frequently obligate management to consult, meet, and negotiate with the union in respect of the implementation and impact of the technological change. The hope is that workplace parties are able to negotiate a compromise that ideally maximizes the benefit of the purpose of the technological change while minimizing its detrimental impact on workers.

Whether such a clause is appropriate for a particular organization is subject to a contextual cost–benefit analysis. Certainly, such clauses will impose limits on management's ultimate freedom to introduce and implement new technology in any manner it sees fit. On the other hand, technological change provisions may lead to reduced labour conflict and disruption, while affording workers some say in how technological changes will impact their working lives.

SOURCE: H.D. Woods, "Technological Change and the Right to Strike," *Industrial Relations*, 27, no. 4 (1972), pp. 718–735.

A labour relations board does not initiate action. Rather, it responds to requests for action. Labour boards are generally considered masters of their own procedure and a board is empowered to manage board proceedings in the manner that it sees fit within the confines of administrative law principles such as the duty of fairness and the principles of natural justice. In carrying out their role, labour boards also undertake mediation and alternative dispute resolution in attempts to resolve disputes and in an effort to avoid a full-blown hearing.

McGraw Hill connect™

Learn more about remedial powers of labour boards online with Connect.

LO 4

Describe the major labour–management interactions: organizing, contract negotiations, and contract administration.

UNION AND MANAGEMENT INTERACTIONS: ORGANIZING

To this point we have discussed macro trends in union membership. Here we shift our focus to the more micro questions of why individual employees join unions and how the organizing process works at the workplace level.

Why Do Employees Join Unions?

Virtually every model of the decision to join a union focuses on two questions.[34] First, is there a gap between the pay, benefits, and other conditions of employment that employees actually receive versus what they believe they should receive? Second, if such a gap exists and is sufficiently large to motivate employees to try to remedy the situation, is union membership seen as the most effective or instrumental means of change? The outcome of many election campaigns hinges on how the majority of employees answer these two questions. Despite the obvious importance of compensation issues, some union organizing campaigns turn on other factors, such as poor communication by management or a fear of change, even when the change has brought, or likely will bring, improvements.

The Process and Legal Framework of Organizing

Certification

The process by which the labour board designates the union as the exclusive bargaining agent of employees in the bargaining unit.

Labour boards are responsible for ensuring that the organizing process follows certain steps and for **certification** of the union as the legally recognized bargaining agent for a unit of employees. At the most general level, the labour board holds a union representation vote if a prescribed minimum percentage of employees in the bargaining unit sign membership cards (the level of support required varies by jurisdiction and ranges from 35 percent to majority support).[35] In some jurisdictions, demonstrating a higher level of support than the minimum may permit the board to certify the union without a representation vote (i.e., automatic certification).[36]

Once a union has been certified as the exclusive representative of a group of employees, and where no collective agreement is in force, another union is barred from applying for certification to displace the certified union for a prescribed period of time ranging from six months to one year depending on the jurisdiction. If a collective agreement is in force, any displacement application may typically not occur until the last two or three months of the collective agreement's term, varying once again by jurisdiction and by the length of the term of the collective agreement. Similar time bars are in effect for applications to terminate the union's bargaining rights (i.e., decertification applications). The time bars serve to allow a newly certified union time to get a foothold and establish a relationship with union members and the employer.

While an application for certification to the labour board is the most common manner of acquiring bargaining rights, in many jurisdictions voluntary recognition is an alternative method by which a union can become the exclusive bargaining agent of employees in the bargaining unit.[37] **Voluntary recognition** occurs where the employer agrees in writing to recognize the union as the exclusive bargaining agent for a group of its employees. Once a union is voluntarily recognized, it becomes the exclusive bargaining agent for all employees in the bargaining unit, regardless of whether the employees are union members. However, the union might not be afforded certain rights and protections pursuant to the statute until a first collective agreement is finalized.

Labour boards are also responsible for determining the appropriate bargaining unit and the employees who are eligible to participate in organizing activities. A unit may cover employees in one facility or multiple facilities within a single employer, or the unit may cover multiple employers. Eligibility to vote varies by jurisdiction, but is within the exclusive discretion of the labour relations board. Eligibility may be determined by the employee's status as of the date of the application for certification, as of the date of the vote, or both. Employees absent from work, for example, on leaves of absence, workers' compensation, statutory leaves, and vacation may also be entitled to vote. Moreover, employees on layoff may be entitled to vote in some circumstances. Replacement workers employed during a legal strike or lockout or employees hired to replace a person who was unlawfully discharged likely will not be entitled to vote.

Labour boards customarily attempt to group together employees who have a community of interest in their wages, hours, and working conditions. In many cases, this grouping will be sharply contested, with management and the union jockeying to include or exclude certain employee subgroups in the hope of influencing the outcome of the vote.

Organizing Campaigns: Management and Union Strategies and Tactics Tables 11.5 and 11.6 on page 440 list common issues that arise during organizing campaigns. Unions attempt to persuade employees that their wages, benefits, treatment by employers, and opportunity to influence workplace decisions are not sufficient and that the union will be effective in obtaining improvements. Management emphasizes that it has provided a good package of wages, benefits, and so on. It also argues that, whereas a union is unlikely to provide improvements in such areas, it will likely lead to certain costs for employees, such as union dues and the income loss resulting from strikes.

Employers use a variety of methods to oppose unions in organizing campaigns, some of which may go beyond what the law permits, especially in the eyes of union organizers. Some employers use consultants and many use lawyers in an effort to defeat the union's campaign and keep its actions within the confines of permissible legal behaviour. It is not uncommon for unfair labour practices to be filed against an employer during an organizing campaign, regardless of whether the union's accusations are legitimate. Where legitimate, an employer unfair labour practice during a campaign can have a successful and legal "chilling effect" on the campaign, discouraging and dissuading employees from joining and voting for the union. Where the employer's actions are thought to have improperly influenced the outcome of the campaign through intimidation or coercion such that the true wishes of employees cannot be ascertained through a vote, some labour boards have the power to order

Voluntary Recognition
Voluntary recognition occurs where the employer agrees in writing to recognize the union as the exclusive bargaining agent of employees in the bargaining unit.

Table 11.5 Common Union Issues in Campaigns

UNION ISSUES
Union will prevent unfairness and will set up a grievance procedure and seniority system.
Union will improve unsatisfactory wages.
Union strength will give employees voice in wages, working conditions.
Union, not outsider, bargains for what employees want.
Union has obtained gains elsewhere.
Union will improve unsatisfactory sick leave and insurance.
Dues and initiation fees are reasonable.
Union will improve unsatisfactory vacations and holidays.
Union will improve unsatisfactory pensions.
Employer promises and good treatment may not be continued without union.
Employees choose union leaders.
Employer will seek to persuade or frighten employees to vote against union.
No strike without vote.
Union will improve unsatisfactory working conditions.
Employees have legal right to engage in union activity.

SOURCE: Adapted from John Fossum, *Labor Relations: Development, Structure and Process,* 1992. Copyright © 1992 The McGraw-Hill Companies.

Table 11.6 Common Management Issues in Campaigns

MANAGEMENT ISSUES
Improvements not dependent on unionization.
Wages good, equal to, or better than under union contract.
Financial costs of union dues outweigh gains.
Union is outsider.
Get facts before deciding; employer will provide facts and accept employee decision.
If union wins, strike may follow.
Loss of benefits may follow union win.
Strikers will lose wages; lose more than gain.
Unions not concerned with employee welfare.
Strike may lead to loss of jobs.
Employer has treated employees fairly and/or well.
Employees should be certain to vote.

SOURCE: Adapted from John Fossum, *Labor Relations: Development, Structure and Process,* 1992. Copyright © 1992 The McGraw-Hill Companies.

a second representation vote, automatically certify the union, or order other remedial measures.[38] Where allegations of an employer's unfair labour practice are not legitimate, they may nonetheless add fuel to the fire of the union's campaign by tainting employees' view of the employer and making the option of a union more attractive. At the other extreme, a labour board will not certify a union where it is of the view that the union is dominated or influenced by an employer to such an extent that the union cannot effectively represent the employees in the bargaining unit.[39]

In the context of an organizing drive, an employer has a right to free speech and can express its views on the union. However, an employer's views must be expressed without using coercion, intimidation, threats, promises, or undue influence. As a result, an employer must be cautious in determining what it says and how it is said, including how the content or manner of communications may be perceived by employees. The rationale for these limitations on free speech is rooted in an employer's dominant economic position over employees and the substantial influence its actions and communications inevitably have on a union's organizing drive. In light of the legal parameters, an employer must ensure that all information communicated is truthful. The employer can inform employees of their rights, and inform them of responsibilities that are associated with a union such as union dues, initiation fees, loss of income if a strike occurs, and picket-line duties. An employer can also correct untrue or misleading statements contained in union organizing material. However, for the most part, labour boards discourage any kind of significant employer activity during union organizing campaigns, especially if the employer through its actions appears to directly or indirectly raise a threat to job security.

Why would employers break the law? Some employers may believe that the consequences (such as back pay and reinstatement of workers) of doing so are minimal. Whether this is true in practice varies by the specific practice and precedent of each labour board. Others may simply be willing to take the risk in order to remain union free. In fact, some studies suggest that discrimination against employees involved in union organizing decreases union organizing success significantly and that the cost of back pay to union activists reinstated in their jobs is far smaller than the costs that would be incurred if the union managed to organize and gain better wages, benefits, and so forth.[40]

Still, labour boards attempt to maintain a noncoercive atmosphere under which employees feel they can exercise free choice. A labour relations board will set aside a vote result if it believes that either the union or the employer has created an atmosphere where the true wishes of employees cannot be ascertained. Examples of conduct that may lead to an election result being set aside include

- Threats to job security if the union is successful for the purpose of influencing the outcome of the vote or organizing activities;
- Granting or promising higher wages or benefits if the union is unsuccessful in its certification application;
- Anti-union statements beyond the limits of lawful employer free speech;
- The use of threats, intimidation, or coercion to influence votes or organizing activities.

Supervisors have the most direct contact with employees. Thus, as Table 11.7 on page 442 indicates, it is critical that they be proactive in establishing good relationships with employees if the company wishes to avoid union organizing attempts. It is also important for supervisors to know what not to do should a drive take place.

UNION AND MANAGEMENT INTERACTIONS: CONTRACT NEGOTIATION

The majority of contract negotiations take place between unions and employers that have been through the process before. In most cases, management has come to accept the union as an organization that it must work with. But when the union has just been certified and is negotiating its first contract, the situation can be very different. Sometimes parties are unable to negotiate a first

Table 11.7 What Supervisors Should and Should Not Do in an Organizing Drive

WHAT TO DO
Report any direct or indirect signs of union activity to a core management group.
Deal with employees by carefully stating the company's response to pro-union arguments. These responses should be coordinated by the company to maintain consistency and to avoid threats or promises.
Take away union issues by following effective management practice all the time: • Deliver recognition and appreciation. • Solve employee problems. • Protect employees from harassment or humiliation. • Provide business-related information. • Be consistent in treatment of different employees. • Accommodate special circumstances where appropriate. • Ensure due process in performance management. • Treat all employees with dignity and respect.
WHAT TO AVOID
Threatening employees with harsher terms and conditions of employment or employment loss if they engage in union activity.
Asking employees about pro-union or anti-union sentiments that they or others may have or reviewing union authorization cards or pro-union petitions.
Promising employees that they will receive favourable terms or conditions of employment if they forgo union activity.
Spying on employees known to be, or suspected of being, engaged in pro-union activities.

SOURCE: From J. A. Segal, *HR Magazine*, 1998 Copyright © 1998 by the Society for Human Resource Management. Reprinted with the permission of *HR Magazine*, published by the Society for Human Resource Management, Alexandria, VA, via the Copyright Clearance Center.

contract during this tentative time in their relationship. Many Canadian labour relations statutes provide for first-agreement arbitration, also referred to as first-contract arbitration.[41] This process uses an arbitration board to settle the terms and conditions of the parties' first collective agreement where the parties have been unable to do so on their own. However, labour boards have a strong preference to defer to parties to strike their own bargain. As a consequence, this remedy will be allowed only once the parties' ability to bargain a first collective agreement is genuinely futile, often where the employer refuses to recognize the union. The process of first-agreement arbitration is typically invoked only following attempts at board-assisted mediation or conciliation where no settlement is reached.

Collective agreements differ in their bargaining structures—that is, the range of employees and employers that are covered. In particular, collective agreements differ, first, according to whether narrow (craft) or broad (industrial) employee interests are covered. Second, they differ according to whether they cover multiple employers, a single employer with multiple locations (a single employer may have multiple locations, some union and some nonunion) or a single employer with only one location. Different structures have different implications for bargaining power and the number of interests that must be incorporated in reaching an agreement.

The determination of an appropriate bargaining unit varies on a case-by-case basis, the objective of which is to create a unit that can facilitate a viable and harmonious labour relations relationship.

Boards are granted wide discretion in this regard and are not constrained by any rigid defined criteria. However, generally a board will consider some or all of the following: (1) the community of interest among employees; (2) bargaining history; (3) the nature of the employer's business; (4) patterns in the industry or sector; (5) the wishes of the parties involved; (6) geographical distribution of the operation; (7) avoiding fragmentation; and (8) the appropriateness of the unit for overall labour relations purposes. Often several different bargaining units can be appropriate and the board is not constrained to choosing *the* most appropriate unit, merely *an* appropriate unit in the circumstances.

Community of interest is a set of shared interests among a group of employees that includes evidence of similarity in skills, interests, duties, and working conditions including methods of compensation; the physical and administrative structure of the employer; functional integration; and geography (i.e., are employees working in one or several locations?). Where community of interest is sufficiently distinct among a group of employees as compared to others in the bargaining unit such that the union would not be able to effectively represent all employees in one unit or where it would create the potential for serious labour relations instability, multiple bargaining units may result. For example, in some jurisdictions "blue-collar" and "white-collar" employees are typically separated into different bargaining units, as are outside sales personnel. Likewise, part-time, casual, and full-time employees also may be separated; office, clerical, and technical employees often have been grouped together, sometimes with salespeople.

Learn more about certifying craft unions as separate bargaining units online with Connect.

The Negotiation Process

Richard Walton and Robert McKersie suggested that labour–management negotiations could be broken into four subprocesses: distributive bargaining, integrative bargaining, attitudinal structuring, and intra-organizational bargaining.[42] **Distributive bargaining** focuses on dividing a fixed economic "pie" between the two sides. A wage increase, for example, means that the union gets a larger share of the pie, management a smaller share. It is a win–lose situation. **Integrative bargaining** has a win–win focus; it seeks solutions beneficial to both sides. So, if management needs to reduce labour costs, it could reach an agreement with the union to avoid layoffs in return for the union agreeing to changes in work rules that might enhance productivity.

Attitudinal structuring refers to the relationship and trust between labour and management negotiators. Where the relationship is poor, it may be difficult for the two sides to engage in integrative bargaining because each side hesitates to trust the other side to carry out its part of the deal. For example, the union may be reluctant to agree to productivity-enhancing work-rule changes to enhance job security if, in the past, it has made similar concessions but believes that management did not stick to its assurance of greater job security. Thus the long-term relationship between the two parties can have a very important impact on negotiations and their outcomes.

Intra-organizational bargaining reminds us that labour–management negotiations involve more than just two parties. Within management, and to an even greater extent within the union, different factions may have conflicting objectives. High-seniority workers, who are least likely to be laid off, may be more willing to accept a contract that is likely to lead to layoffs (especially if it also offers a significant pay increase for those whose jobs are not at risk). Less senior workers likely would feel very differently about this kind of trade-off. Thus union negotiators and leaders must simultaneously satisfy both the management side and their own internal constituencies. If they do not, they risk the union membership rejecting the contract, or they risk being voted out of office in the next election. Management, too, may not be of one mind about how to approach negotiations. Some will focus more on long-term employee relations, others will focus on cost control, and still others will focus on what effect the contract will have on stockholders.

Distributive Bargaining
The part of the labour–management negotiation process that focuses on dividing a fixed economic "pie."

Integrative Bargaining
The part of the labour–management negotiation process that seeks solutions beneficial to both sides.

Attitudinal Structuring
The aspect of the labour–management negotiation process that refers to the relationship and level of trust between the negotiators.

Intra-organizational Bargaining
The part of the labour–management negotiation process that focuses on the conflicting objectives of factions within labour and management.

Management's Preparation for Negotiations

Clearly, the outcome of contract negotiations will have important consequences for labour costs and labour productivity and, therefore, for the company's ability to compete in the product market. We can divide management preparation into the following seven areas, most of which have counterparts on the union side.[43]

1. *Establishing interdepartmental contract objectives:* The employer's industrial relations representatives need to meet with the accounting, finance, production, marketing, and other departments and set contract goals that will permit each department to meet its responsibilities toward achievement of the organization's overall objectives. As an example, finance may suggest a cost figure above which a contract settlement would seriously damage the company's financial health. The bargaining team needs to be constructed to take these various interests into account.

2. *Reviewing the old contract:* This step focuses on identifying provisions of the contract that might cause difficulties by hindering the company's productivity or flexibility or by leading to significant disagreements between management and the union. Such a review should include side agreements and practices that may be inconsistent with the express language of the agreement, as well as arbitration awards and settlements that have interpreted the agreement.

3. *Preparing and analyzing data:* Information on labour costs and the productivity of competitors, as well as data the union may emphasize, needs to be prepared and analyzed. The union data might include cost-of-living changes and agreements reached by other unions that could serve as a target. Data on employee demographics and seniority are relevant for establishing the costs of benefits such as pensions, health insurance, and paid vacations. Finally, management needs to know how much it would be hurt by a strike. How long will its inventory allow it to keep meeting customer orders? To what extent are other companies positioned to step in and offer replacement products? How difficult would it be to find replacement workers (where permissible) if the company decided to continue operations during a strike?

4. *Anticipating union demands:* Recalling grievances over the previous contract, having ongoing discussions with union leaders, and becoming aware of settlements at other companies are ways of anticipating likely union demands and developing potential counterproposals. To some extent, the entire negotiation process is about trying to identify union demands so that the company can determine whether or not meeting each such demand (or a reasonable collection of such demands) is preferable to a failed negotiation.

5. *Establishing the cost of possible contract provisions:* Wages have not only a direct influence on labour costs but often an indirect effect on benefit costs (such as pensions and paid vacation). Wage or benefit increases that seem manageable in the first year of a contract can accumulate to less manageable levels over time; this is especially so if benefits or premiums are tied to wages as a percentage calculation and there is no practical way to negotiate a lower level except through concession bargaining.

6. *Preparing for a strike:* If management intends to operate during a strike, it may need to line up replacement workers (in jurisdictions where such workers are permitted), increase its security, and determine how to deal with incidents on the picket line and elsewhere. If management does not intend to operate during a strike (or if the company will not be operating at normal levels), it needs to alert suppliers and customers and consider possible ways to avoid the loss of their business. This could even entail purchasing a competitor's product in order to have something to sell to customers.

7. *Determining strategy and logistics:* Decisions must be made about the amount of authority the negotiating team will have. What concessions can it make on its own, and which ones require it to check with top management? On which issues can it compromise, and on which can it not? What is the "drop-dead" point (or set of points in respect of various issues) where it is better to walk away than to settle? Decisions regarding meeting places and times also must be made.

Negotiation Stages and Tactics

Negotiations go through various stages and involve several bargaining meetings.[44] In some cases, many more people are present in the bargaining room in the early stages than in later stages. On the union side, this may give all the various internal interest groups a chance to participate and voice their goals. This, in turn, helps send a message to management about what the union feels it must do to satisfy its members, and it may also help the union achieve greater solidarity. Union negotiators often present an extensive list of proposals at an early stage, partly to satisfy their constituents and partly to arm themselves with issues on which they can show flexibility later in the process. Management may or may not present proposals of its own; sometimes it prefers simply to react to the union's proposals.

During the middle stages of bargaining, each side must make a series of decisions, even though the outcome remains uncertain. How important is each issue to the other side? How likely is it that disagreement on particular issues will result in a work stoppage? When and to what extent should one side signal its willingness to compromise on its position?

In the final stages, pressure for an agreement increases as the deadline for a strike or lockout approaches. Public negotiations may be only part of the process. Negotiators from each side may have private one-on-one or small-group meetings where public relations pressures are reduced. In addition, a neutral third party may become involved (typically through a government-supervised conciliation and/or mediation process). This third party is someone who can act as a go-between or facilitator, as well as a wise resource. In some cases, the only way for the parties to convince each other of their resolve (or to convince their own constituents of the other party's resolve) is to allow an impasse to occur.

Various books suggest how to avoid impasses by using mutual gains or integrative bargaining tactics. For example, *Getting to Yes*,[45] by Roger Fisher and William Ury, describes four basic principles:

1. People: Separate the people from the problem.
2. Interests: Focus on interests, not positions.
3. Options: Generate a variety of possibilities before deciding what to do.
4. Criteria: Insist that the results be based on some objective standard.

Once the union and management bargaining teams have agreed to the terms and conditions for a collective agreement, the agreement must be ratified by the bargaining unit. This takes place by way of a **ratification** vote. If a majority of bargaining unit members vote to accept the agreement struck between the bargaining teams, its terms are incorporated into a collective agreement, which will govern the terms and conditions of employment for the length of its term (at least a year and often three years or more). Although both unions and employers prefer to present a recommended settlement for ratification, sometimes unions will present the employer's final offer, either without a recommendation or even with a recommendation to reject the offer. In some situations, the employer also reserves a right to ratify a settlement proposed by the management bargaining team.

Ratification
A vote of bargaining unit members to accept a tentative collective agreement settlement reached between the union and management bargaining teams (or otherwise proposed for settlement).

Bargaining Power, Impasses, and Impasse Resolution

The conflicting goals are resolved through the negotiation process just described. An important determinant of the outcome of this process is the relative bargaining power of each party, which can be defined as the "ability of one party to achieve its goals when faced with opposition from some other party to the bargaining process."[46] In collective bargaining, an important element of power is the relative ability of each party to withstand a strike (or an employer lockout). Although strikes are rare (and lockouts rarer), the threat of a strike often looms large in labour–management negotiations. The relative ability to take a strike, whether or not one occurs, is an important determinant of bargaining power and, therefore, of bargaining outcomes.

Management's Willingness to Take a Strike

Management's willingness to take a strike comes down to two questions:

1. *Can the company remain profitable over the long run if it agrees to the union's demands?* The answer is more likely to be yes to the extent that higher labour costs can be passed on to consumers without losing business. This, in turn, is most likely when (1) the price increase is small because labour costs are a small fraction of total costs or (2) there is little price competition in the industry. Low price competition can result from regulated prices, from competition based on quality (rather than price), or from the union's organizing all or most of the employers in the industry, which eliminates labour costs as a price factor, so long as the union maintains a level playing field.

   Unions share part of management's concern with long-term competitiveness because a decline in competitiveness can translate into a decline in employment levels. On the other hand, the majority of union members may prefer to have higher wages, despite employment

Management has several factors to consider before taking a strike. Most negotiations do not result in a strike since it is often not in the best interest of either party.

declines, particularly if a minority of the members (those with low seniority) suffer more employment loss and the majority keep their employment with higher wages.

2. *Can the company continue to operate in the short run despite a strike?* Although "hanging tough" on its bargaining goals may pay off for management in the long run, the short-run concern is the loss of revenues and profits from production being disrupted and the potential longer-term loss of customers. The cost to strikers is a loss of wages and possibly a permanent loss of jobs depending on the extent of the economic impact of the strike on the employer's operations.

Bargaining outcomes also depend on the nature of the bargaining process and relationship, which includes the types of tactics used and the history of labour relations. The vast majority of labour–management negotiations do not result in a strike or lockout because a work stoppage is typically not in the best interests of either party. Furthermore, both the union and management usually realize that if they wish to interact effectively in the future, the experience of a work stoppage can be difficult to overcome. When strikes or lockouts do occur, the conduct of each party during the work stoppage can also have a lasting effect on labour–management relations. Violence by either side or threats of job loss by hiring replacements can make future relations difficult and acrimonious.

Learn more about conditions under which management is most able to take a strike online with Connect.

Impasse Resolution Procedures: Alternatives to Strikes

Given the substantial costs of work stoppages to both parties, procedures that resolve conflicts without strikes or lockouts have arisen in both the private and public sectors. Because many public-sector employees do not have the right to strike, alternatives are particularly important in that arena.

Three often-used impasse resolution procedures are conciliation, mediation, and arbitration. All rely on the intervention of a neutral third party. In most jurisdictions there is a process by which either party can proceed to **conciliation** by applying to the minister of labour for a conciliator to be appointed or one may be appointed on the direction of the minister.[47] A conciliator has no power to compel a settlement, but rather employs the power of persuasion and the threat of a work stoppage. Some unions (rarely, employers) will request for a conciliation officer appointment before consensual bargaining even begins, although they usually ask that the conciliation process not proceed until further notice. In some cases, the minister will issue a report informing the parties that a conciliation board will not be appointed. This is commonly referred to as a "no board" report. Most jurisdictions require conciliation or a "no-board report" as a mandatory prerequisite to a legal strike or lockout.

Mediation is the least formal of the dispute resolution procedures. Where contemplated by the labour relations statute, a mediator can be appointed to assist the parties in resolving collective bargaining disputes,[48] in some cases where either party makes a request, but usually on consent.[49] Typically, the minister of labour can appoint a mediator before a conciliation board has been assigned or a "no-board" report is issued. If the mediator is appointed after the appointment of a conciliation officer, which is the usual situation, the appointment of the conciliation officer is terminated. In some jurisdictions, with agreement of the parties, the conciliation officer will simply "change hats" and become the mediator. Whether the same person or a new appointee, the mediator does not really have any additional powers. In practice, mediators will try to be more persuasive than conciliation officers. They are assisted in this regard by the fact of an impending or existing work stoppage. Most mediators hold a meeting in the days preceding a work stoppage and, if unsuccessful, will remain in touch to try to reconvene during the work stoppage, whenever there appears to be an opening for settlement. A mediator has no formal authority but, rather, acts as a facilitator and go-between in negotiations.

Conciliation
A procedure for resolving collective bargaining impasses by which a conciliator with no binding authority acts as a facilitator and go-between in the negotiations; sometimes a necessary step before a legal strike or lockout can occur.

Mediation
A procedure for resolving collective bargaining impasses by which a mediator with no formal authority acts as a facilitator and go-between in the negotiations.

Arbitration
A procedure for resolving collective bargaining impasses by which an arbitrator chooses a binding solution to the dispute.

The most formal type of outside intervention is **arbitration**, under which a hearing is held and a binding solution is chosen by an arbitrator (or arbitration board). In some instances the arbitrator can fashion a solution (conventional arbitration). In other rare cases, the arbitrator must choose either the management's or union's final offer (final offer selection) on either the contract as a whole or on an issue-by-issue basis. In practice, this occurs only if the parties have expressly agreed to this method of arbitration. Traditionally, arbitrating the enforcement or interpretation of contract terms (rights arbitration) has been widely accepted, whereas arbitrating the actual writing or setting of contract terms (interest arbitration, our focus here) has been reserved for special circumstances. These include some public-sector negotiations involving "essential services," where strikes may be especially costly or pose risks to public order, health, safety, or welfare (e.g., police, firefighters, and hospital or nursing home personnel) and a very few private-sector situations, where strikes have been especially debilitating to both sides.[50] In an interest arbitration, the parties submit all outstanding issues that have been bargained to impasse to an interest arbitration panel that makes a final and binding decision regarding these issues. The three-person panel consists of a neutral third-party arbitrator typically selected by the parties as well as nominees on each side selected by the union and employer. Interest arbitration is intended to be an extension of the collective bargaining process such that it is meant to replicate, to the best extent possible, the agreement that would have been reached by the parties had they been able to negotiate the agreement on their own. One reason for avoiding greater use of interest arbitration is a strong belief that the parties closest to the situation (unions and management, rather than an arbitrator) are in the best position to effectively resolve their conflicts.

UNION AND MANAGEMENT INTERACTIONS: CONTRACT ADMINISTRATION

Grievance Procedure

Although the negotiation process (and the occasional work stoppage) receive the most publicity, the negotiation process typically occurs only every two or three years. By contrast, administration of the collective agreement goes on day after day, year after year. The two processes—negotiation and administration—are tightly connected. Vague or incomplete contract language developed in the negotiation process can make administration of the contract difficult. Such difficulties can, in turn, create conflict that can spill over into grievances, rights arbitration and the next negotiation process.[51] Furthermore, events during the negotiation process—strikes, the use of replacement workers, or violence by either side—can lead to ongoing management and labour difficulties in working successfully under a contract.

A key influence on successful contract administration is the grievance procedure for resolving labour–management disputes. Labour relations statutes across the country provide for the final and binding settlement by arbitration, without stoppage of work, of all differences between the parties arising from the interpretation, application, administration, or alleged violation of the agreement, including whether a matter is within the jurisdiction of the arbitrator (i.e., whether it is arbitrable) and including matters of employer-imposed discipline and discharge. Strikes during the life of a collective agreement are generally illegal. However, certain jurisdictions provide for rare exemptions in respect of disputes related to technological change[52] and reopener clauses in the collective agreement.[53] Strikes during the term of a contract can be especially disruptive because they are more unpredictable than strikes during the negotiation phase, which occur only at regular intervals and subject to clear procedures.

Beyond its ability to reduce strikes, the effectiveness of a grievance procedure can be judged using three criteria.[54] First, how well are day-to-day contract questions resolved? Time delays and

Competing Through Globalization

Labour Takes a Stand in China

Chinese workers are fighting for their rights—including higher wages and possibly collective bargaining rights—and rallying against subsistence wages, abysmal working conditions, and repressive work practices. These workers brought an unprecedented wave of strikes across the nation in 2010—halting production at car plants such as Honda and Toyota, and electronics component makers.

Strikes at Honda plants in May and June likely played a role in sparking the massive unrest, where striking workers made significant wage gains after walking off the job. Labourers at Honda Lock in Zhongshan, Guangdong province, called for a pay raise and improved collective bargaining rights when up to 500 workers demonstrated outside the gates of the plant. They demanded to elect their own labour representatives rather than the "enterprise union" imposed on all factories in China by company owners and the communist Chinese government. Workers want greater negotiating rights and a rise in base salary from 1,500 yuan (about $228 Canadian) to 2,000 yuan ($304 Canadian) a month.

In the weeks prior, South Korean carmaker Hyundai promised a 25 percent pay raise to end a strike by 1,000 employees at a supplier in Beijing. Employees of Foshan Fengfu Autoparts agreed to a pay raise of 366 yuan, an increase of about 23 percent on the previous monthly salary. Foxconn, an electronics supplier that manufactures for big North American companies such as Apple, Dell, and Hewlett-Packard, was hit by a spate of suicides among its workers and promised to increase salaries at its Shenzhen plant by nearly 70 percent if workers met certain conditions.

As reported by CTV News in June 2011, the staff at the four-star Gloria Plaza Hotel in Beijing decided they, too, had had enough. The hotel, which had done a thriving trade during the 2008 Olympic Games, unexpectedly announced it was shutting its doors for extensive renovations at the end of May, putting 400 people—almost all of them poor migrants from the countryside—out of work. Management at the hotel stated it would pay only the minimum severance package required by law. But the staff, who typically earned between 1,000 yuan ($155) and 1,800 yuan ($279) a month, decided they wanted more.

After years of donning smiles for guests who stayed in luxury suites while staff slept 20 to a room in a building over the parking garage, Gloria Plaza workers marched to the office of the company that owns the hotel and, when that didn't work, they did it again, and again. Eventually, their protests brought the concession they were demanding: a severance payment of up to several thousand yuan each, depending on length of service.

"The workers had not been treated fairly. We worked for a long time for such small payment. We needed to take action," said a 22-year-old electrician from Hebei province who would give only his family name, Chang. Despite the hotel's closure, Mr. Chang continued to live in the squalid Gloria Plaza dorm, which reeked of urine and uncollected garbage, while he searched for another job.

The Gloria Plaza labour action went almost unnoticed according to CTV, amid the series of strikes that forced the likes of auto giants Honda, Toyota, and Nissan to stop production at factories in China until they met worker demands. But the protests by Gloria Plaza workers were motivated by the same discontent that led those working assembly lines in the south of the country to walk off the job: a sense among China's tens of millions of low-wage workers that the time had come for them to share in China's economic success.

With more frequent strikes, China's workers have been getting their way, forcing double-digit wage hikes at Honda and Toyota. In response to the unrest, the Beijing government encouraged local governments to increase minimum wages; several had raised the minimum wage by as much as 20 percent since strikes at Honda in May. In the Yangtze River Delta, 2,000 workers walked off the job at a Taiwanese computer-parts plant in Shanghai's Pudong district. In Kunshan City, in Jiangsu, outside Shanghai, workers striking at a Taiwanese-owned rubber factory clashed with police. Workers also walked off the job at a Japanese industrial sewing machine plant in Xian and at a Taiwanese sporting goods factory in Jiujiang, in Jiangxi province. Although many more strikes and work stoppages occurred across the country, the unrest was largely unreported in the strictly controlled state-run media.

The Chinese government seems content to let the strikes happen, for now, but they have the potential to upend the low-wage economic model that has made China the "workshop of the world," according to CTV, and underpinned the country's astonishing economic growth over the past two decades. The worker unrest could also drive up prices for the ubiquitous made-in-China goods on store shelves in Canada and elsewhere, as manufacturers pass rising labour costs on to the consumer.

However, Beijing apparently sees greater risks in allowing worker grievances to fester. An editorial in the state-run *People's Daily* said the "made-in-China" model is "facing a turning point." Siding with the workers, the paper argued that it is time to rectify the country's widening gap between rich and poor, which some Chinese academics have argued is approaching the point where it poses a threat to social stability. "Rural migrant workers are the mainstay of China's industrial work force," Premier Wen Jiabao said in comments that were interpreted as a sign of the government's desire to see wages rise. "Our society's wealth and the skyscrapers are all distillations of your hard work and sweat. Your labour is glorious and should be respected by society at large."

If you examine the workers who helped propel China's growth two decades ago and those who are taking strike action today, you'll see that an important generational difference exists. Professor Yu Jianrong, an expert in social issues at the Chinese Academy of Social Sciences (affiliated with the State Council of the People's Republic of China), finds that young rural migrants flocking to the cities in hopes of earning money to aid their poverty-stricken family members in the countryside are different than their parents who came to the city to make extra money for a few years and returned home. Today's young migrant workers are seeking to make a life in the "big city" urban centres, making them less willing to accept the poor working conditions of past generations and fuelling their demands for a better working life.

Low wages are just one hurdle. Combined with skyrocketing housing costs, and the discriminatory *hukou* (residency permit) registration system, which denies rural-born Chinese access to many social services in the big cities in which they now live such conditions make it virtually impossible for migrant workers to climb the social ladder. Even those born in the big cities are subject to a rural *hukou* if that's what their parents had. "They've never been to the countryside; they don't even know what the countryside looks like. They can neither go back to the countryside, nor can they fully enter life in the city. This is a big problem," Professor Yu said of the new generation of migrant workers.

Whether the scattered strikes around the country will grow into a full-fledged labour movement is an open question. The ACFTU remains the only legal trade union in China, and although strikers at the Honda plant in Foshan broke new ground by demanding the right to form their own union, few expect the ruling Communist Party will allow the formation of independent labour organizations.

"So far, we're not seeing co-ordinated action, just opportunistic strikes and a knock-on effect where one strike leads to another, which leads to another," said Geoffrey Crothall, spokesman for the Hong Kong–based China Labour Bulletin. "In the past, strike action tended to be chaotic and haphazard. No one really knew what was going on. Now we're seeing workers demanding to elect their own representatives. That's significant."

A sense of accomplishment lingers among the former staff of the Gloria Plaza over what they their protests achieved. Workers say they simply got tired of being treated poorly and without respect. Although labour unrest has broken out sporadically in China in the past, this new round of strikes represents a new trend as workers organize more effectively, demanding not only pay raises, but also structural reforms for the purpose of engaging in collective bargaining. Realizing that they cannot protect their rights as individuals, workers are banding together in an awareness of the need for collective action.

SOURCES: Jonathan Watts, "Chinese Workers Strike at Honda Lock Parts Supplier," guardian.co.uk (June 11, 2010); Keith Richburg, "Strike at Honda Plant the Latest Sign of Labor Unrest in China," *The Washington Post* (June 12, 2010); Mark MacKinnon "China's Changing Labour Landscape," *CTV News* (June 30, 2010).

heavy use of the procedure may indicate problems. Second, how well does the grievance procedure adapt to changing circumstances? For example, if the company's business turns downward and the company needs to cut costs, how clear are the provisions relating to subcontracting of work, layoffs, and so forth? Third, in multi-unit contracts, how well does the grievance procedure permit local contract issues (such as work rules) to be included and resolved?[55]

From the employees' perspective, the grievance procedure is the key to fair treatment in the workplace, and its effectiveness rests both on the degree to which employees feel they can use it without fear of recrimination and whether they believe their case will be carried forward strongly enough by their union representative. Too many grievances may indicate a problem, but so may too few. A very low grievance rate may suggest a fear of filing a grievance, a belief that the system is not effective, or a belief that union representation is not adequate; on the other hand, just as bad, it may indicate that a weak management has ceded control over the workplace to the union.

As Table 11.8 on page 452 suggests, most grievance procedures have several steps prior to arbitration. Moreover, the majority of grievances are settled during the earlier steps of the process, which is usually desirable both to reduce time delays and to avoid the costs of arbitration, so long as settlements are based on principles and not expediency. If the grievance goes to arbitration, the arbitrator makes a final and binding ruling in the matter.

Where there is a dispute about whether the grievance is arbitrable, unless the collective agreement specifically provides otherwise, an arbitrator's jurisdiction generally will be limited to the interpretation and application of the collective agreement. Accordingly, arbitrators will dismiss a grievance as nonarbitrable if the collective agreement is silent on the issue or the issue to be determined does not fall within the terms of the collective agreement.

What types of issues most commonly reach arbitration? Discharge and disciplinary issues are very common (both in terms of just cause and also appropriateness of disciplinary penalty) as well as issues related to the applicability of seniority in promotion, layoffs, transfers, work assignments, and scheduling. Issues related to compensation, particularly overtime and premium pay, as well as benefits, are also quite common.

What criteria do arbitrators use to reach a decision? In the most common case—discharge or discipline—the arbitrator will consider (1) has the employee given just and reasonable cause for some

Table 11.8 Steps in a Typical Grievance Procedure

EMPLOYEE-INITIATED GRIEVANCE
STEP 1
a. Employee discusses grievance or problem orally with supervisor.
b. Union steward and employee may discuss problem orally with supervisor.
c. Union steward and employee decide (1) whether problem has been resolved or (2) if not resolved, whether a contract violation has occurred.
STEP 2
a. Grievance is put in writing and submitted to production superintendent or other designated line manager.
b. Steward and management representative meet and discuss grievance. Management's response is put in writing. A member of the labour relations staff may be consulted at this stage.
STEP 3
a. Grievance is appealed to top line management and labour relations staff representatives. Additional local or international union officers may become involved in discussions. Decision is put in writing.
STEP 4
a. Union decides whether to appeal unresolved grievance to arbitration according to procedures specified in its constitution and/or bylaws.
b. Grievance is referred to arbitration for binding decision.
DISCHARGE GRIEVANCE (SOMETIMES LESS SERIOUS DISCIPLINE AS WELL)
a. Procedure may begin at step 2 or step 3.
b. Time limits between steps may be shorter to expedite the process.
UNION OR GROUP GRIEVANCE (AND, RARELY, EMPLOYER GRIEVANCES)
a. Union representative initiates grievance at step 1 or step 2 on behalf of affected class of workers or union representatives.

SOURCE: Adapted and revised from Harry Katz, Thomas Kochan, and Alexander Colvin, *An Introduction to Collective Bargaining and Industrial Relations,* 2008. Copyright © 2008 The McGraw-Hill Companies.

sort of discipline by the employer? (2) if so, was the employer's decision to discharge or discipline the employee an excessive response in all of the circumstances of the case? and (3) if excessive, what alternative measure (lesser penalty) should be substituted as just and equitable?[56]

Learn more about due process questions used by arbitrators when making determinations. online with Connect.

LO 5

Describe alternative, less adversarial approaches to labour–management relations.

Alternative Labour–Management Strategies

Although there always have been exceptions to the adversarial approach, a more general transformation to alternative, less adversarial workplace relations has been gaining some ground since the 1980s. This transformation has two basic objectives: (1) to increase the involvement of individuals and work groups in overcoming adversarial relations and increasing employee commitment, motivation, and problem solving, and (2) to reorganize work so that work rules are minimized and flexibility in managing people is maximized. These objectives are especially important for companies that need to be able to shift production quickly in response to changes in markets and customer demands. The specific programs aimed at achieving these objectives include employee involvement in decision making, self-managing employee teams, labour–management problem-solving teams, broadly defined jobs, and sharing of financial gains and business information with employees.

Algoma Steel Inc. is a noteworthy example.[57] In 1992, the company negotiated with the USWA to implement a Joint Workplace Restructuring and Employee Participation Process to address major labour and financial problems. The innovative approach reduced the number of supervisors relative to hourly employees and redefined their role to emphasize coaching and co-ordination, and flattened the organizational structure. Unnecessary layers of management and administration were eliminated coupled with a reduction in overhead costs. Another example is Steffco, a Stelco subsidiary, where a joint labour–management committee was formed in 1990 to examine all plans to subcontract work and to consider possible alternatives. Smaller organizations can also benefit from these initiatives. In Newfoundland and Labrador, for example, two small hydro plants created joint committees to address issues such as health and safety, work and maintenance practices, technological change, and temporary appointments.

Union resistance to such programs has often been substantial, precisely because the programs seek to change workplace relations and the role that unions play. Without the union's support, these programs are less likely to survive and less likely to be effective if they do survive.[58] Union leaders have often feared that such programs will weaken unions' role as an independent representative of employee interests.[59] Despite such understandable union fears, some evidence suggests that these alternative approaches to labour relations—incorporating greater employee participation in decisions, using employee teams, multiskilling, rotating jobs, and sharing financial gains—can contribute significantly to an organization's effectiveness,[60] as well as to workers' wages and job satisfaction.[61]

LABOUR RELATIONS OUTCOMES

The effectiveness of labour relations can be evaluated from management, labour, and societal perspectives. Management seeks to control costs and enhance productivity and quality. Labour unions seek to raise wages and benefits and exercise control over how employees spend their time at work (such as through work rules). Each of the three parties typically seeks to avoid forms of conflict (particularly strikes) that impose significant costs on everyone. In this section we examine several outcomes.

Strikes

Strikes impose significant costs on union members, employers, and society. Fortunately, they are the exception rather than the rule. Very little working time is lost to strikes in Canada (approximately one hour per year per employed worker in 2009[62]). Essentially, a **strike** involves a concerted work stoppage or a refusal to work or to continue to work by employees, or a slowdown of work or other concerted activity on the part of employees in relation to their work that is designed to restrict or limit output. In some jurisdictions, to be valid, a strike must be aimed at compelling the employer to agree to certain terms and conditions of employment,[63] but exceptions may be made for legal work refusals under workplace health and safety legislation[64] and a refusal to cross a lawful picket line.[65] A strike vote in which a majority of workers vote to strike is required before a strike can commence. When workers strike, they receive no pay or benefits from the employer. A union strike fund may provide workers with nominal, if any, compensation.

Employers have the economic weapon of a **lockout** at their disposal. A lockout includes closing a place of employment, a suspension of work, or a refusal by an employer to continue to employ

Strike
A concerted work stoppage or a refusal to work or to continue to work by employees. A strike can also include a slowdown of work or other concerted activity on the part of employees in relation to their work. In all cases, the activity is designed to restrict or limit output.

Lockout
A lockout includes closing a place of employment, a suspension of work, or a refusal by an employer to continue to employ a number of its employees for the purpose of compelling the employees, or employees of another employer, to accept terms and conditions of employment.

a number of its employees for the purpose of compelling such employees, or employees of another employer, to accept terms and conditions of employment.[66] Like strikes, lockouts also have significant economic impacts. A recent lockout of Montreal port workers reportedly cost the employer $800,000 a week.[67] In all but very rare circumstances, both strikes and lockouts are prohibited during the life of a collective agreement.

Picketing

Picketing involves the presence of striking or locked-out workers outside the employer's business premises for the purpose of protesting the labour dispute. Strikers often carry signs and hand out information, and may impede the flow of traffic in and out of the employer's operations.

Picketing is a powerful economic weapon in industrial disputes that can occur in the course of a strike or lockout, but also at other times. Despite its implications for labour relations, few labour relations statutes address or regulate picketing.[68] Although picketing can be lawful or unlawful depending on how it unfolds, no bright line test (clearly defined rule or standard) exists to make this determination. The general rule is that peaceful informational picketing absent any civil or criminal wrong or undue disruption is legal and cannot be prevented.[69]

Wages and Benefits

According to Statistics Canada, public-sector wage gains in 2009 outpaced their private-sector counterparts for the fourth year in a row—2.5 percent versus 1.8 percent, respectively.[70] In addition, union employees in 2009 earned about 18.3 percent more than their nonunion counterparts. Total compensation is generally higher for unionized employees because of the effect of unions on benefits. However, these are raw differences. To assess the net effect of unions on wages more accurately, adjustments must be made for employee and workplace characteristics. We now briefly highlight a few of these.

The union wage effect is likely to be overestimated to the extent that unions can more easily organize workers who are already highly paid or who are more productive. For example, unionization is higher for older workers, those with more education, those with long tenure, and those in larger workplaces.[71] The gap is likely to be underestimated to the extent that nonunion employers raise wages and benefits in response to the perceived "union threat" in the hope that their employees will then have less interest in union representation. When these and other factors are taken into account, it is suggested that the net union advantage in wages, though still substantial, is reduced to 7.7 percent.[72] The union benefits advantage is also reduced, but it remains larger than the union wage effect, and the union effect on total compensation is therefore larger than the wage effect alone.[73]

Beyond differences in pay and benefits, unions typically influence the way pay and promotions are determined. Whereas management often seeks to deal with employees as individuals, emphasizing performance differences in pay and promotion decisions, unions seek to build group solidarity and avoid the possibly arbitrary treatment of employees. To do so, unions focus on equal pay for equal work. Any differences among employees in pay or promotions, they say, should be based on seniority (an objective measure) rather than on performance (a subjective measure susceptible to favouritism). It is very common in union settings for there to be a single rate of pay for all employees in a particular job classification.

Productivity

There has been much debate regarding the effects of unions on productivity.[74] Unions are believed to decrease productivity in at least three ways: (1) the union pay advantage causes employers to use less labour and more capital per worker than they would otherwise, which reduces efficiency across society; (2) union contract provisions may limit permissible workloads, restrict the tasks that particular workers are allowed to perform, and require employers to use more employees for certain jobs than they otherwise would; and (3) strikes, slowdowns, and working-to-rule (slowing down production by following every workplace rule to an extreme) result in lost production.

Competing Through Sustainability

The *Toronto Star*, Union Strike Deal to Save Jobs

The *Toronto Star*, facing declining revenues, reached a deal with its union to save some of the 78 editing jobs that were set to be cut in contemplation of a cost-saving outsourcing arrangement. The newspaper announced a plan in November 2009 that would have seen 70 full-time and eight part-time editorial jobs cut and another 39 full-time and four part-time pre-publishing jobs eliminated in an effort to save more than $4 million a year. *Toronto Star* editor Michael Cooke provided the union 30 days to propose a way to avoid or change the plan to contract out the jobs. The union responded by creating two committees to devise alternatives, resulting in management's ultimate decision to retain some of the workers slated for layoff.

In a memo to staff, Cooke said the company would not proceed with a plan to contract out page production. The company would instead set up a new page production desk that would employ up to 35 full-time staff. The deal, ratified by union members, would result in some job losses; however, the agreement would save the jobs of current page editors who would have been laid off and provide for additional page editor positions to be filled. "The union worked with us on this alternative in full knowledge of the daunting economics we face," Cooke wrote in the memo. "Today's agreement saves some of the 78 editing positions that had been designated for layoff, but over the course of this year our newsroom staff will get smaller by several dozen."

Maureen Dawson, chairwoman of the *Toronto Star* unit of the Southern Ontario Newspaper Guild, said it was not an ideal result, although several jobs were saved. She added, "I'm pleased we were able to stop the outsourcing in editorial and save some of the jobs, but it means that there are still members in both editorial and pre-press who will be leaving involuntarily."

In November 2009, the paper announced what its publisher said would likely be the biggest restructuring in the newspaper's history by offering voluntary buyouts to employees in all divisions of the company. As of January 2010, 166 employees had accepted such voluntary buyouts at the newspaper and the offer had been extended for some other areas of the company.

The deal reached between the union and the *Toronto Star* marks an alternative and increasingly necessary approach to traditional adversarial labour–management relations, in which unions and management take a cooperative and creative approach to tackling challenging economic times and workplace issues facing organizations and their workers.

SOURCES: "*Toronto Star* Publisher Offers Severance Packages, Plans to Contract out Jobs," *The Canadian Press* (November 3, 2009); CBC News, "*Toronto Star*, Union Strike Deal," thestar.com (January 18, 2010); "*Star*, Union Reach Deal to Reduce Job Losses," thestar.com (January 19, 2010).

On the other hand, unions can have positive effects on productivity.[75] Employees, whether members of a union or not, communicate to management regarding how good a job it is doing by either the "exit" or "voice" mechanisms. "Exit" refers to simply leaving the company to work for a better employer. "Voice" refers to communicating one's concerns to management without necessarily leaving the employer. Unions are believed to increase the operation and effectiveness of the voice mechanism.[76] This, in turn, is likely to reduce employee turnover and its associated costs. More broadly, voice can be seen as including the union's contribution to the success of labour–management cooperation programs that make use of employee suggestions and increased involvement in decisions. A second way that unions can increase productivity is (perhaps ironically) through their emphasis on the use of seniority in pay, promotion, and layoff decisions. Although management typically prefers to rely more heavily on performance in such decisions, using seniority has a potentially important advantage—namely, it reduces competition among workers. As a result, workers may be less reluctant to share their knowledge with less senior workers because they do not have to worry about less senior workers taking their jobs. Finally, the introduction of a union may have a "shock effect" on management, pressuring it into tightening standards and accountability and paying greater heed to employee input in the design and management of production.[77]

Although there is evidence that unions have both positive and negative effects on productivity, most studies have found that union workers are more productive than nonunion workers. Nevertheless, it is generally recognized that most of the findings on this issue are open to a number of alternative explanations, making any clear conclusions difficult. For example, unionized establishments are more likely to survive where there is some inherent productivity advantage unrelated to unionism that actually offsets any negative impacts of unionism. If so, these establishments would be overrepresented, whereas establishments that did not survive the negative impact of unions would be underrepresented. Consequently, any negative impact of unions on productivity would be underestimated. Likely, outside of the negative consequences of a strike, there is no reason the presence of a union should materially impact productivity.

Profits and Stock Performance

Even if unions do raise productivity, which is far from clear, a company's profits and stock performance may still suffer if unions raise costs (such as wages) or decrease investment by a greater amount. Evidence shows that unions have a large negative effect on profits and that union coverage tends to decline more quickly in firms experiencing lower shareholder returns, suggesting that some firms become more competitive partly by reducing union strength.[78] Not surprisingly, one study finds that each dollar of unexpected increase in collectively bargained labour costs results in a dollar reduction in shareholder wealth. Other research suggests that investment in research and development is lower in unionized firms.[79] Strikes, although infrequent, lower shareholder returns in both the struck companies and firms (such as suppliers) linked to those companies.[80] These research findings describe the usual effects of unions. The consequences of more innovative union–management relationships for profits and stock performance are less clear.

<table>
<tr><td>LO 6</td></tr>
</table>

Explain how labour relations in the public sector differ from labour relations in the private sector.

THE PUBLIC SECTOR

Swelling government bureaucracies, in conjunction with salaries and working conditions lagging behind those in the private sector, spurred unrest among public civil servants in the early 1960s. Attempts to organize unions were thwarted by governments that refused to grant public-sector workers the right to organize. In 1965, the Canadian Union of Postal Workers staged a nationwide wildcat strike for more than two weeks, demanding that public-sector workers be granted the right to bargain collectively, the right to strike, and improvements in wages and methods of management. The government of Prime Minister Lester Pearson responded by granting public-sector workers the right to bargain collectively in 1967 through the enactment of the Public Service Staff Act (with some exceptions, such as the RCMP). The act gave workers the right to bargain collectively and the right to choose between arbitration or the right to strike to settle a contract.

As in the private sector, changes in the legal framework contributed significantly to union growth in the public sector. By the 1980s, public-sector unions had become among the largest in the country. This remains even truer today, with the public sector boasting a union-density rate more than four times that of the private sector. Public-sector workers including nurses and teachers populate some of the most highly unionized occupations in the country, with the highest rates in public administration, education, utilities, health care and social assistance, and transportation and warehousing.[81] An interesting aspect of public-sector union growth is that much of it has occurred in the service industry and among white-collar employees—groups that have traditionally been viewed as difficult to organize in the private sector.

In contrast to the private sector, public-sector workers face restrictions in their ability to strike. Some public-sector occupations are prohibited from striking altogether, such as police and firefighters. These workers are subject instead to a system of mandatory and binding interest arbitration. In other industries, while the right to strike is not necessarily forbidden, certain employees are designated as "**essential workers**" for the good of public order, health, safety, and welfare, reducing the economic and operational impact of a strike on the employer. Nonetheless, given their size and centralized organization, public-sector strikes remain some of the most volatile and disruptive, and thus effective, strikes today.

Essential Workers
Public-sector workers who are prohibited by statute from striking for the good of public order, health, safety, and welfare.

The Public Service Labour Relations Act governs disputes in the federal public sector. Various other provincial and federal statutes have been enacted implementing distinct procedures, and in some cases designated tribunals, to govern public-sector labour relations in each jurisdiction.

A Look Back

The membership rate, and thus influence, of labour unions in North America and in many other industrial democracies has been on the decline, at least in the private sector. In the meantime, however, as we saw in the opening to this chapter, there continue to be companies where labour unions represent a large share of employees and thus play a major role in the operation and success of those companies. In such companies, whatever the national trend, effective labour relations are crucial for both companies and workers.

Questions

1. Many people picture labour union members as being workers in blue-collar jobs in manufacturing plants. Is that accurate? Are there certain types of jobs where an employer can be fairly certain that employees will not join a union? If so, give examples.

2. Why do people join labour unions? Would you be interested in joining a labour union if given the opportunity? Why or why not? What are the benefits of managing or working within a unionized workplace? What are the drawbacks? As a manager, would you prefer to work with a union or would you prefer that employees be unrepresented by a union? Explain.

3. What led to a change in labour relations at Magna? What was the nature of the change? Do you think it is a sustainable change given that key players from the CAW who facilitated member acceptance of the Framework of Fairness Agreement (FFA) have since retired?

4. Do you think the FFA will ever be fully implemented at Magna? Explain your answer.

Summary

Labour relations statutes create the unionized workplace and establish the rules for its ongoing operation by setting out the rules of conduct that must be followed by employers, unions, and employees during union organizing campaigns and collective bargaining. Legislation also provides for the basic elements of the collective agreement, the grievance and arbitration procedure, strikes, lockouts, unfair labour practices, and procedures for terminating bargaining rights. In a unionized workplace, the union collectively bargains with the employer regarding the terms and conditions of employment on behalf of all the employees in the bargaining unit, resulting in the collective agreement setting out the terms and conditions of employment. With the objective of protecting the respective rights of workers, unions, and management in all aspects of the collective bargaining relationship, labour relations statutes in Canada also aim to facilitate collective bargaining that is carried out promptly and in good faith. Once a collective agreement is in place, the legislative concern for ongoing labour peace is expressed by provisions that promote the expeditious resolution of workplace disputes.

Labour unions seek to represent the interests of their members in the workplace by striving to achieve a more equal playing field among workers and management. Although this may further the cause of industrial democracy, management often finds that unions increase labour costs while setting limits on the company's flexibility and discretion in decision making. As a result, the company may witness a diminished ability to compete effectively in a global economy. Not surprisingly, management in nonunion companies often feels compelled to actively resist the unionization of its employees. This, together with a host of economic, legal, and other factors, has contributed to union losses in membership and bargaining power in the private sector. There are some indications, however, that managements and unions are seeking new, more effective ways of working together to enhance competitiveness while giving employees a voice in how workplace decisions are made.

Key Terms

Agency shop or Rand formula, 431	Duty of fair representation, 435	Maintenance of membership, 432
Arbitration, 448	Duty to bargain in good faith, 436	Mediation, 447
Attitudinal structuring, 443		Picketing, 454
Certification, 438	Essential workers, 457	Ratification, 445
Check-off provision, 431	Integrative bargaining, 443	Strike, 453
Closed shop, 431	Intra-organizational bargaining, 443	Union shop, 431
Conciliation, 447		Voluntary check-off, 432
Distributive bargaining, 443	Lockout, 453	Voluntary recognition, 439

Discussion Questions

1. Why do employees join unions?

2. Why have unions been more successful organizing in Canada than in the United States?

3. What are the benefits and the drawbacks for management and owners of having a union represent employees?

4. What are the general provisions of labour relations legislation in Canada and how do they affect labour–management interactions?

5. What are the features of traditional and nontraditional labour relations? What are the potential advantages of the alternative nontraditional approaches to labour relations?

Self-Assessment Exercise

Would you join a union? Each of the following phrases expresses an opinion about the effects of a union on employees' jobs. For each phrase, circle a number on the scale to indicate whether you agree that a union would affect your job as described by the phrase.

Having a union would result in . . .	Strongly Disagree				Strongly Agree
1. Increased wages	1	2	3	4	5
2. Improved benefits	1	2	3	4	5
3. Protection from being fired	1	2	3	4	5
4. More promotions	1	2	3	4	5
5. Better work hours	1	2	3	4	5
6. Improved productivity	1	2	3	4	5
7. Better working conditions	1	2	3	4	5
8. Fewer accidents at work	1	2	3	4	5
9. More interesting work	1	2	3	4	5
10. Easier handling of employee problems	1	2	3	4	5
11. Increased work disruptions	5	4	3	2	1
12. More disagreements between employees and management	5	4	3	2	1
13. Work stoppages	5	4	3	2	1

Add up your total score. The highest score possible is 65, the lowest 13. The higher your score, the more you see value in unions, and the more likely you would be to join a union.

SOURCE: Based on S. A. Youngblood, A. S. DeNisi, J. L. Molleston, and W. H. Mobley, "The Impact of Work Environment, Instrumentality Beliefs, Perceived Union Image, and Subjective Norms on Union Voting Intentions," *Academy of Management Journal* 27 (1984), pp. 576–590.

Exercising Strategy: Union Workers May Enhance Productivity

Jim Stanford, an economist with the CAW, delivered this stinging rebuke in reporting on a session at the 2009 Canadian Economics Association Conference: "For years, corporate leaders have blamed red tape, taxes, unions, and anything else they could point fingers at for Canada's mediocre productivity record. The more we learn about Canada's productivity failure, however, the more it's clear that the enemy lurks within. It is the failure of Canadian companies to proactively embrace innovation as a business strategy, being content instead with raking in profits from commodities and other less creative activities, that is at the heart of our productivity problems. So while we grapple with the impacts of the current downturn, we must also prepare for the next upturn. And there's no better way to start than by rousing Canada's businesses from their productivity slumber."

In many other articles, including a January 2009 *Toronto Star* report, "Auto Productivity Gives Canada Edge," Stanford has made cogent and articulate arguments that it is false and misleading to blame unionized workers for recent economic woes in the manufacturing sector. Taking into account that Stanford is unapologetic about his soapbox, he says, "Overall, it costs less to assemble a vehicle in terms of labour expenses in a CAW plant than it does at a nonunionized plant in the U.S."

Of course, not everyone is convinced by Stanford and other proponents of the superior skill and dedication of union workers. As the venerable *Economist* magazine put it in February 2007, before the world economy collapsed, "It is not that union workers are lazy, a favourite canard of the right; at least in my experience, union workers are higher quality than you would expect for the job they are doing. However, unions often offer resistance to new work processes that might increase efficiency, and not just ones that would decrease labour demand. A friend whose brother is an engineer for an auto parts supplier often keeps us entertained for hours with stories of the epic (and so far fruitless) battles to do things like install digital gauges, or measure things using the metric system. Unions also spend a lot of time trying to work in featherbedding provisions to their contracts—forcing companies to use more people than are needed for a given job. This makes perfect sense from the standpoint of the union; more people doing a job means more workers paying dues. But it should put a drag on average productivity."

As anyone who has ever been involved for or against a union organizing drive will know, employers will put up stiff resistance to the efforts of a union to acquire bargaining rights. This may be because employers do not believe people like Jim Stanford who trumpet the skill and dedication of union workers. More likely, it is because employers do not want to be constrained by the restrictive provisions of a collective agreement. As good as union workers may be, they may still be collective drags on the productivity of a company simply because of the strict terms and conditions that govern their employment, as negotiated by the trade union that represents them.

For the last word on this question of productivity of unionized workplaces, we will go back in time to a 1998 article in *Scientific American*:

> After nearly a century of union–management warfare in the U.S., a series of nationwide surveys showing that union shops dominate the ranks of the country's most productive workplaces may come as a surprise. In fact, according to Lisa M. Lynch of Tufts University and Sandra E. Black of the Federal Reserve Bank of New York, economic Darwinism—the survival of the fittest championed by generations of hard-nosed tycoons—may be doing what legions of organizers could not: putting an end to autocratic bosses and regimented workplaces.
>
> Lynch and Black correlated the survey data with other statistics that detailed the productivity of each business in the sample. They took as their "typical" establishment a nonunion company with limited profit sharing and without TQM or other formal quality-enhancing methods. (Unionized firms constituted about 20 percent of the sample, consistent with the waning reach of organized labour in the United States.)

The average unionized establishment recorded productivity levels 16 percent higher than the baseline firm, whereas average nonunion ones scored 11 percent lower. One reason: most of the union shops had adopted so-called formal quality programs, in which up to half the workers meet regularly to discuss workplace issues. Moreover, production workers at these establishments shared in the firms' profits, and more than a quarter did their jobs in self-managed teams. Productivity in such union shops was 20 percent above baseline. That small minority of unionized workplaces still following the adversarial line recorded productivity 15 percent lower than the baseline, even worse than the nonunion average.

According to the analysis reported in *Scientific American*, the organization and self-discipline brought to the workplace by a trade union can actually increase productivity so long as employers, working in a cooperative manner with trade unions and their members, move away from an old-fashioned adversarial model toward new business models that rely on workers for innovative ideas and reward them accordingly.

SOURCES: Jim Stanford, "Corporate Canada's Enemy Lurks Within," *The Globe and Mail* (June 5, 2009) at www.theglobeandmail.com/news/opinions/corporate-canadas-enemy-lurks-within/article1171664/ (retrieved July 28, 2011); Tony Van Alphen, "Auto Productivity Gives Canada Edge," *Toronto Star* (January 26, 2009); "Look for the Union Label," *Scientific American*, August 1998 (News and Analysis—Economics) at www3.sympatico.ca/n.rieck/docs/unions.html (retrieved July 28, 2011).

Questions

1. Can unionized plants compete with nonunion plants?

2. What can unionized plants do to enhance productivity because of and not despite the collective agreement?

3. How can nonunion plants learn lessons from the structure of unionized workplaces both to enhance productivity and to make it more difficult for unions to organize their workforces?

4. To what extent do you think unions and their members are responsible to make concessions to aid employers in gaining a competitive and sustainable advantage? What about where the employer is facing bankruptcy?

Managing People: Walmart

No one anticipated that when the Walmart store in Jonquière, Quebec opened in 2001, it would be closed a mere four years later. But that is what happened to the store, which provided 190 jobs for in this small, remote Quebec city. While Walmart executives maintain the closure was due to the store's alleged financial performance, with the closure announced on the heels of employees winning unionization and on the verge of mandatory collective bargaining negotiations, it's hard not to give credence to skeptics who maintain that the closure was based not on money woes, but on anti-union tactics.

By April 2005, six weeks after the closure was announced, 80 percent of the store shelves were vacant, whole sections were closed, and the remaining merchandise was consolidated in the centre of the store. Security guards stood in place of store greeters, ensuring pictures of the skeleton crew of employees and the bleak and unwelcoming image the store now portrayed would not be broadcast to the public—visions that would be certain to render Walmart's omni-present bright yellow smiley-face mascot inconsolable. "This is not what a Walmart is supposed to look like," admits Marc St. Pierre, the store manager.

A little rough around the edges, Jonquière is a city of 60,000 that sits at the edge of inhabited Quebec. To the north is nothing but forest, mountain, and bay all the way to the Arctic Circle. Quebec City is a three-hour drive south, through a wilderness preserve where moose outnumber humans, making highway driving an adventure. Despite its remote setting, far from media capitals, Walmart's abandonment of this north Quebec outpost in the spring of 2005 made news from Tokyo to São Paulo as a lesson in the lengths to which America's largest company will go to crush the threat of unionization. Walmart closed its store in Jonquière only six months after it was certified by the Quebec Commission des relations du travail, Quebec's labour board, as the only unionized Walmart in North America.

With 260 stores in Canada, Walmart is the country's second-largest retail chain. Walmart entered Canada by buying 122 discount department stores from the Canadian subsidiary of Woolco in 1994. (Walmart passed on 22 other Woolco stores, including all 10 of its unionized outlets.) One was in Chicoutimi, which is a sort of white-collar cousin to the blue-collar mill town of Jonquière. In 2001, these two adjacent cities and four smaller towns merged to form Saguenay, which is the largest city in the Saguenay-Lac-St.-Jean region of Quebec. It was about this time that Walmart entered Jonquière, much to the delight of its residents. The 190 jobs that the store brought were equally welcome in an area chronically afflicted by high unemployment.

Even so, a company as anti-union as Walmart was pushing its luck entering Jonquière, a union town whose isolation had historically bred a defiant independence of spirit. The Quebec labour movement was more or less born in the Saguenay region. The area is heavily industrialized; the aluminum smelters and pulp and paper factories that dot the region have been unionized for decades. Labour laws in Canada are more favourable to unionization and are more likely to be vigorously and expeditiously enforced, particularly in Quebec, where the unionization rate is a thriving 40 percent.

Driving Walmart's Jonquière workers into the arms of the United Food & Commercial Workers (UFCW) was an intense atmosphere of submission to Walmart's corporate credo. Says Sylvie Lavoie, a 40-year-old single mother who led the worker rebellion in Jonquière: "Walmart will only choose somebody for promotion who thinks Walmart, sleeps Walmart, and eats Walmart, and who puts Walmart before absolutely everything—before their family even." As a part-timer, Lavoie did not qualify for health insurance and frequently worked weekends while her parents took care of her young daughter, who was not happy about her mother's absences. Lavoie repeatedly applied for the full-time cashier jobs that regularly became available and grew increasingly disenchanted as they were filled by coworkers or by new hires. Things came to a head when a group of cashiers began to talk and realized the inequities among their wage rates.

While three of the store's workers had made efforts to organize with the UFCW in 2002, it wasn't until Lavoie and her coworker joined the effort that the union campaign gained traction, says Herman Dallaire, an organizer for UFCW Local 503 in Quebec City. "The difference was that they were cashiers, which is a big department in the store, and much more popular with their coworkers," Dallaire says. "They also had very strong personalities and were not afraid of the store managers."

In Quebec, a store can be unionized without an employee election. If a majority of the hourly workers sign union cards and if those signatures then are certified by the Quebec Commission des relations du travail, the law requires management to sit down with union representatives and negotiate a collective agreement. If no agreement is reached, a government-appointed arbitrator can impose a contract. In Quebec, if the necessary number of signatures can be collected covertly, a store can be unionized before management even knows an organizing drive is underway.

With Lavoie and her coworker on board, the store soon was driven into bitterly opposed camps. Management began holding mandatory anti-union meetings complete with warnings about what unionization would mean for the future of the store. Complaints of intimidation and harassment came from both sides, as pro-management employees told of organizers pestering them at home at all hours. Some workers "signed the cards just to get some peace," says Noëlla Langlois, a clerk in apparel. "They thought they would vote against [unionizing] in a secret vote."

When the UFCW fell one signature short of the required number for automatic certification, it decided to take its chances by petitioning for a secret vote in April 2004. The move backfired, as the union was voted down 53 percent to 47 percent. The tactless celebration of store managers who taunted union supporters in front of television cameras as they left the store led many who had voted against the union to decide to switch sides.

After a mandated three-month cooling-off period, Lavoie and her allies started over. The second campaign succeeded before management even realized that it had started. The Jonquière store was automatically certified with representation by the UFCW in August 2004.

Two months later, just as the UFCW and Walmart representatives were preparing to begin mandatory contract negotiations, Walmart Canada issued a press release from its headquarters near Toronto. "The Jonquière store is not meeting its business plan," it declared, "and the company is concerned about the economic viability of the store." Nine bargaining sessions produced no results. Succumbing to union demands would have meant adding 30 workers to the payroll, stated Walmart's Pelletier. "We felt the union wanted to fundamentally change the store's business model." Six months after the union was certified, on the same day that the minister of labour referred the parties to arbitration to assist them in reaching a first collective agreement, Walmart announced the closure. Walmart said that it was unable to reach a tentative agreement with the union that would "permit it to operate the store in an efficient and profitable manner." But UFCW Canada spokesman Michael Forman says there was never any indication from Walmart in communications with employees in Jonquière that their store was unprofitable. Forman insists that the announcement by Walmart was an effort "to instill fundamental fear in every Walmart employee that if they try to mix with the union, this is what is going to happen."

Walmart's draconian response to the Jonquière unionists scandalized Quebec. Three of the company's other 46 stores in the province were temporarily closed by bomb threats. A TV broadcaster likened Walmart to Nazi Germany and then apologized. Jean Tremblay, the feisty, populist mayor of Saguenay, gave media interviews by the dozen, denouncing the company. "Because you are big and rich and strong, you can close a store to make your workers in other stores afraid? No!" Tremblay said. "If you want to do business in Quebec—or in Russia or in China—you have to follow the law. And you have to respect the culture."

From his office in Ontario, company spokesman Pelletier insisted that the reasons Walmart gave up on Jonquière had nothing to do with stifling unionism. The store "has struggled from the beginning," he said. "The situation has continued to deteriorate since the union." In Bentonville, Arkansas, H. Lee Scott Jr., Walmart's CEO, seconded Pelletier in a *Washington Post* interview. "You can't take a store that is struggling anyway and add a bunch of people and a bunch of work rules," Scott declared.

A national survey by Pollara Inc., Canada's largest polling organization, found that only 9 percent of Canadians believed that Walmart closed the store in Jonquière because it was struggling financially; it was all about the union. Thirty-one percent of those queried said that they would either do less shopping at its stores or stop going to them altogether—a figure that rose to 44 percent among Quebecers. In another survey taken six months after the Jonquière pullout, Quebecers ranked Walmart 11th out of 12 retail chains for meeting their needs and expectations.

Under Quebec law, a company is legally entitled to shut down a store or a factory for any reason—even to thwart unionization—as long as the closure is permanent. In November 2009, the Supreme Court of Canada quashed a long-fought appeal by Jonquière's former Walmart employees. In a 6–3 ruling, the court ruled that an employer had no legal obligation to stay in business and that it was up to employees to prove that Walmart was engaged in unfair labour practices under Quebec's labour statute and to seek an appropriate remedy, noting that workers could not apply for reinstatement where the workplace no longer existed. The court also upheld an earlier finding by the Quebec Commission des relations du travail that the store closure was "genuine and permanent and that, in itself, according to a long line of cases is 'good and sufficient' reason ... to justify the dismissal," of the employees.

While the decision is striking, its influence outside Quebec, where labour laws differ and do not provide for the same sort of freedoms and leniency in closing down a unionized workplace, is limited. This sentiment is reflected in the dissenting opinion of Justice Rosalie Abella who noted that labour boards elsewhere have "consistently refused to immunize employers who are inspired to close a business—and dismiss employees—by anti-union motives."

Since 2005, other Walmart employees in Canadian locations have secured union certification, but only one other workplace, the workers at Tire & Lube Express at a Walmart in Gatineau, Quebec, reached a collective agreement—imposed by an arbitrator. Walmart washed its hands of the union at the Gatineau garage by closing its doors in October 2008, stating that the new collective agreement with unionized workers had driven up costs by one-third after a Quebec arbitrator imposed a collective agreement that gave the workers a 33 percent wage hike.

In October 2010, the Court of Appeal for Saskatchewan overturned a lower court ruling and upheld the labour board's certification in December 2008, of employees working at a Walmart store in Weyburn, Saskatchewan.

Questions

1. Should employers be entitled to shut down operations to avoid a union? Why or why not?
2. What employer actions might make them more susceptible to union organizing?
3. What might unions do in the future to maintain (or increase) their influence?
4. Should nonunion workers care about what happens to the workers at Walmart and other unionized workers? Why or why not?

SOURCES: Bird Richard, "Canada: Supreme Court Issues Decision in Wal-Mart Closure Case," *Mondaq* (March 12, 2010); Tonda MacCharles, "Top Court Backs Wal-Mart over Union Store Closing," thestar.com (November 27, 2009); "Union Attacks Wal-Mart for Closing Garage," *The Montreal Gazette* (October 17, 2008); Paul Weinberg, "Canada: Closure of First Unionized Wal-Mart Sends Signal," *Inter Press Service* (May 1, 2005); Anthony Bianco, "No Union Please, We're Wal-Mart," *BusinessWeek* (February 13, 2006); "Wal-Mart to Close Unionized Quebec Store," *CBC News* (February 14, 2005); "Wal-Mart Closing Unionized Store," CNNMoney.com (February 9, 2005).

connect **Practise and learn online with Connect.**

CHAPTER

12 Safe, Secure, and Productive Workplaces

Enter the World of Business

Loblaw's Path to Zero

In 2007, struggling to improve profitability and reclaim market share in tough economic times, grocery retail giant Loblaw Companies Limited did something no other major Canadian retailer had been known to do at that time: it created an executive position for health and safety. What would drive such a bold and visible investment in health and safety in a difficult economic and competitive environment, when operations are stretched and resources are in short supply? Jattinder Dhillon, vice president, health, safety and wellness, says Loblaw took this step as part of its "Making Loblaw the Best Again" strategy, and in support of its guiding principle to be "a great place to work." And a great place to work, in Dhillon's view—a view shared by the president and everyone who reports to him—is a *safe* place to work. Dhillon infused his health and safety plan with accountabilities, numbers, reports, and training—measures that in 2008, its first year, resulted in a 34 percent reduction in the frequency of injuries, dramatically surpassing the goal of 10 percent.

With over 1,000 corporate and franchised stores and 139,000 employees, known as "colleagues," Loblaw needed a solid plan. Dhillon and his team responded by developing a five-year plan, *A Path Towards Zero Accidents*, aimed at prevention. "We changed our philosophy," says Dhillon. "We outsourced claims management and freed up resources to focus 100 percent on prevention and on zero tolerance for unsafe behaviours." The *Path Towards Zero* plan is based on four back-to-basic ideas: leadership and commitment, management systems, training, and a focus on behaviours.

It seems intuitive that if the person in the corner office doesn't believe in health and safety and make it a priority, neither will anyone else. So, Dhillon invited senior leaders from all business units to sit on a corporate health and safety steering committee to monitor performance, risks, and initiatives. Without that multidisciplinary focus, Dhillon believed that health and safety would devolve into an isolated, technical, and ultimately ineffective entity that doesn't contribute to the bottom line. Dhillon explains, "By working with operations and engineering to eliminate bending for cashiers, for example, we also increase the number of items these individuals can handle per minute. So now we're using ergonomics to solve a problem and improve efficiency in the business. 'Cost-effective' needs to be part of a health and safety professional's mindset." Talking the language of business also opens the door to the boardroom. Loblaw's governance structure includes a health and safety environment committee on its board of directors. "I present to the board quarterly," says Dhillon. "That's the highest visibility health and safety can have."

Dhillon is clear that in order to have the right discussions with the right people, you need to measure the right things and report the right numbers. Loblaw's management system aligns health and safety processes with operations in all regions, and of course includes hazard assessments, control measures, inspections, training, and more. What distinguishes its system is the reporting: rich in detail with clear pointers to trouble spots. "I get a daily report of incidents across Canada," says Dhillon. "I can give you a breakdown of employee cuts, for example, by store and by department. We immediately go back to the business units, whether it's the deli or the bakery, to talk about work practices: where are knives being used, do we need a cut-resistant glove, are there other ways of doing the work? You can only have those discussions if you have the numbers. And if you're getting the data quarterly, monthly, or even weekly, it's too late." In addition, the reporting system allows Dhillon and his team to use trends, say on slips, trips, and falls from last winter, in planning for next winter.

Like other companies, Loblaw is leveraging e-training and "learning store" initiatives to push learning down through the organization. Learning stores, for example, provide job-specific and health and safety training to a cluster of other stores. But by far the most powerful step Dhillon and his team is taking is "integration." "We're moving away from health and safety training as a separate entity," says Dhillon. "The intent is to integrate it with other operational training." Blending health and safety with everyday ways of doing things is a strategy that works, and saves money.

At the heart of Dhillon's plan is behaviour—specifically, promoting safe ones. "What are the three or four job-specific behaviours that every colleague needs to remember and do excellently each and every time?" he asks. "From a regulatory compliance perspective, sure—you need manuals. But at a grassroots level, let's start with the basics. We used pictograms in our job-specific Key Safe Behaviours guide book to make it as visual as possible." Dhillon says eventually the principles within the guidebook will be integrated into operational training.

Dhillon's vision is about people caring for people. "We need to watch out for one another and not be afraid to coach others," he says. "We need more one-on-one chats than discipline. We need to build contagion so people want to do better. We need to celebrate successes. So yes, we have to do more. We're on a path and we're halfway there."

SOURCE: Adapted from Heidi Croot, "The Loblaw Way: Combating Economic Pressures with Investments in Health & Safety," *The Safety Mosaic,* Summer 2009, Vol. 12, No. 2. Reprinted with permission from *The Safety Mosaic* and Loblaw Companies Limited.

INTRODUCTION

Every year Canadian businesses spend billions of dollars as a result of worker accidents and injuries in terms of lost productivity, turnover, absenteeism, and disability costs. Beyond the fundamental moral and ethical reasons to protect workers' health and safety, employers have a legal duty to provide workers with a safe and healthy place to work. The rewards of a healthy and safe workplace to an organization and its employees are remarkable both in variety and value. Healthy workers are happier and more productive, less likely to be absent or contribute to turnover, and less prone to causing or suffering accidents or injuries at work. As a result of these and other benefits, investments in workplace health and safety produce considerable returns for an employer's bottom line. As will be seen throughout this chapter, more and more companies are implementing health and safety initiatives like Loblaw, recognizing that workplace health and safety is an essential component of strategic HRM.

While the terms *worker* and *employee* are used interchangeably throughout this chapter, it must be pointed out that these terms have different meanings within the context of occupational health and safety legislation. The term *worker* has a much broader definition than *employee* and can include anyone who performs work or supplies services at a workplace or worksite (i.e., employee, contractor, or third-party employee).

EMPLOYEE SAFETY

LO 1

Outline Canadian legislation regulating occupational health and safety.

It is April 6, 1992. The Westray coal mine in Pictou County, Nova Scotia, wins the John T. Ryan safety award. Ironic, given cave-ins at the mine and unheeded and unenforced calls by the Department of Labour for anti-explosion precautionary measures in preceding months—not to mention the litany of health and safety violations recounted by the mine's workers that had been trivialized and disregarded by Westray management. Just over one month later at 5:18 a.m. on May 9, 1992, a methane gas and coal dust explosion rips through a tunnel in the mine, killing all 26 men working underground. In his report of the Westray Mine Public Inquiry, Mr. Justice Peter Richard called the Westray story "a complex mosaic of actions, omissions, mistakes, incompetence, apathy, cynicism, stupidity and neglect."[1] The Westray disaster is one of the worst industrial accidents in Canada's modern history. Like so many others, it is a tragedy that could have been prevented.

Like other aspects of the employment relationship, employee safety is regulated by both the federal and provincial/territorial governments, depending on the jurisdiction. To fully maximize the safety and health of workers, employers need to go well beyond the letter of the law and embrace its spirit. With this in mind, we first spell out the specific protections guaranteed by legislation and then discuss various kinds of health and safety programs that attempt to reinforce these standards.

Occupational Health and Safety Legislation

Although concern for worker safety would seem to be a universal societal goal, comprehensive occupational health and safety legislation did not emerge in this country until the 1970s, propelled largely by the 1976 Ham Royal Commission's *Report of the Royal Commission on the Health and Safety of Workers in Mines*.[2] At that time, a work accident occurred in Canada every seven seconds and roughly 932 workers were killed on the job every year.[3] The report promoted the notion of a system of shared internal responsibility for workplace health and safety by all workplace stakeholders—a principle that stands at the core of modern occupational health and safety legislation.

Today, more than 1,000 workers die in work-related accidents every year in Canada—an average of four workers a day who do not return home to their families.[4] This figure misrepresents the true number of workplace fatalities given that it does not include all deaths genuinely attributable to the workplace, such as in cases of diseases that are likely related to workplace exposures but are not recognized as an occupational disease given the lack of cogent scientific proof.

Occupational health and safety legislation authorizes governments to establish and enforce occupational health and safety standards, administrative requirements, and enforcement mechanisms in respect of the workplace, including workplace inspections and, if appropriate, prosecutions.[5] Much of the research to determine the criteria for specific operations or occupations and for training

Occupational Health and Safety Legislation
The law that authorizes government to establish and enforce occupational health and safety standards, administrative requirements, and enforcement mechanisms in respect of the workplace.

employers to comply with the legislation is carried out by bodies designated by provincial governments, health and safety organizations, and, to some degree, workers' compensation boards, although several other nongovernmental organizations exist that perform research, promote policy, and advocate on behalf of health and safety improvements and initiatives.

LO 2

Discuss current attitudes and approaches relating to health and safety in the workplace.

Internal Responsibility System (IRS)
A system within an organization where every person has direct responsibility for health and safety as an essential part of his or her job.

The Internal Responsibility System   The foundation of occupational health and safety legislation in Canada is the **Internal Responsibility System** (IRS). Stemming from the Ham Royal Commission report, the IRS assigns direct responsibility for health and safety to each person in an organization. Cooperation among workplace parties, joint problem solving, as well as self-monitoring and self-improvement through ongoing communication, regular joint health and safety meetings, and the effective and timely response of management to health and safety issues, is necessary and expected. While it is a shared responsibility in which worker input is a key feature, prudent employers will take the lead in establishing and maintaining an effective IRS and a safe and healthy workplace. This only makes sense, as employers are ultimately responsible should a worker become sick, be injured, or worse, be killed on the job.

Critical to the objective of a safe and healthy workplace is the implementation and periodic review and revision of a comprehensive health and safety policy, procedures for safe operation of equipment, training and promotion of safe practices, rules prohibiting unsafe practices and disciplinary consequences for breaches of rules or other unsafe practices, as well as procedures for responding to accidents or unsafe incidents. In addition to the direct role of employees and employers in the IRS, many others are responsible for contributing to the health and safety culture of the workplace, including the organization's health and safety staff such as doctors, nurses, and various health practitioners. External to the organization, the ministries of labour, and countless health and safety organizations and associations promoting safe practices and health and safety in the workplace all contribute to the effectiveness of the IRS.

Keys to an effective IRS include[6]

1. *Safety First and Safety Always*—A job that cannot be done safely should not be done. This should not be taken to extremes; any work, especially work involving machines, carries inherent risk. Accordingly, the standard must be that every job should be performed without accident each and every time when exercising reasonable care. The goal then is to ensure that reasonable care is always exercised.

   To meet its obligations, the management team must meet a standard of due diligence. The touchstone of due diligence is to take all reasonable precautions for the safety of the workers, and to strive to ensure that all workers exercise reasonable care.

2. *Safety Is Everyone's Responsibility*—The HR group functions in support of the production group. Each manager, supervisor, and worker has direct responsibility for ensuring safe practices throughout the workplace, every hour of every working day.

   This is not simply a statement of good intent; it is a legal responsibility. If members of the management team fail, there are legal consequences. The consequences are personal; managers will not be able to hide behind the company in trying to escape personal responsibility for safety problems.

3. *Safe Work Is Efficient Work*—Experience dictates that there are no shortcuts. While it is tempting to think that dangerous work practices may produce faster results in the short term, this perception is not accurate. Dangerous work practices increase the potential for accidents. Accidents, even relatively minor ones, are time consuming and expensive. Accidents should be considered an unacceptable cost of production. This view is legally and morally sound. It is also good business practice.

Other stakeholders have been assigned duties and responsibilities in achieving the objectives of occupational legislation in some jurisdictions (e.g., constructors, contractors, owners of facilities, professional engineers, licencees, suppliers, and architects). However, within the IRS, the key stakeholders are employers and employees and that will be our focus here. Let's take a closer look at their duties and responsibilities under occupational health and safety legislation.

Employer Duties and Responsibilities   Employers are required by occupational health and safety legislation to take every reasonable precaution to protect the health and safety of their workers. In order to meet this objective, the statute of each jurisdiction prescribes detailed general and specific duties obligating employers to, for example, take steps to implement measures to create and maintain a safe and healthy workplace; provide health and safety devices, equipment, and apparel; conduct inspections; maintain equipment; appoint competent supervisors; train and educate supervisors and workers in health and safety procedures, practices, hazards, and prevention; and create effective and functional health and safety policies and committees. An employer charged with an occupational health and safety offence will need to prove that it exercised "due diligence" in meeting its legal obligations by demonstrating that it recognized the potential for harm, developed a system to prevent the harm from occurring, and took reasonable steps to ensure that the system was working.

LO 3

Describe the roles and responsibilities of various stakeholders in ensuring a safe and healthy workplace.

Although government stakeholders and their partners such as ministries of labour and health and safety associations publish numerous standards, regulators clearly cannot anticipate all possible hazards that could occur in the workplace. Thus, there remains a general duty on employers to be constantly alert for potential sources of harm in the workplace and to correct them.

Supervisors are key players in promoting occupational health and safety given their close proximity, influence upon, and ability to monitor workers' health and safety practices. Like other workplace parties, supervisors are not defined by their titles, but by their day-to-day functions in the workplace. Accordingly, a supervisor within the meaning of occupational health and safety legislation may not necessarily carry that title. A supervisor is generally a person with some direction, control, or authority over workers. Foremen, lead hands, and group leaders, for example, may all fall into this category. Some statutes impose separate general and specific duties on supervisors,[7] while in others a supervisor is simply one of the players involved in meeting an employer's health and safety responsibilities.

Specific director and officer liability is found in some statutes.[8] Regardless, in most jurisdictions, directors and officers of an organization may be personally charged and made liable for violations of occupational health and safety legislation simply in respect of their supervisory or managerial duties.

In addition to the extensive liabilities that arise under the applicable provincial jurisdiction, Bill C-45[9] is federal legislation that is often referred to as the "Westray Bill" in reference to its evolution as a direct consequence of the Westray mine disaster. The Westray Bill amended the Criminal Code of Canada on March 31, 2004, making occupational health and safety negligence a criminal offence. Section 217.1 of the Criminal Code now provides that every person "who undertakes, or has the authority, to direct how another person does work or performs a task is under a legal duty to take reasonable steps to prevent bodily harm to that person, or any other person, arising from that work or task." The real impact of the Westray Bill is to create criminal liability for a corporate entity. For an organization to be convicted, the Crown must prove beyond a reasonable doubt that a representative of the organization breached section 217.1 in a manner showing "wanton or reckless disregard for safety," and that a "senior officer" departed markedly from the standard of care that could be reasonably expected.[10] The offence carries with it a maximum term of life imprisonment for an individual and a fine with no limit for organizations.

In March 2008, a Quebec company, Transpavé, was fined $110,000 for its negligence in the death of 23-year-old Steve L'Écuyer, who was killed when trying to clear a jam in a machine. Transpavé was found to be negligent in allowing L'Écuyer to operate the machine while its safety mechanism was disabled, and for failing to provide L'Ecuyer with proper training on how to safely operate the machine.[11]

Employee Rights, Duties, and Responsibilities   Occupational health and safety legislation recognizes the critical role that employees play in establishing and maintaining a safe and healthy workplace. Like other stakeholders, workers have positive legal duties and responsibilities in furtherance of protecting their own and others' health and safety at work. Employees generally have a duty to follow safety practices and procedures, comply with health and safety instructions, and take all necessary and reasonable precautions to ensure their own and others' health and safety at work. Employees must also cooperate in fulfilling everyone's duties and responsibilities under the legislation and report health and safety hazards, contraventions, and accidents to the employer.

In 2004, an Ontario worker was prosecuted and convicted after the tree he was cutting down fell in the wrong direction onto a live power line, which in turn came in contact with Louis Wheelan, a 19-year old university student who was performing under-brushing and clean-up tasks underneath the line.[12] Wheelan sustained high-voltage electrical burns to 60 percent of his body. Both of Wheelan's legs, his right arm and shoulder, and one finger on his left hand had to be amputated. Wheelan later died from complications arising from his injuries. While the prosecuted worker was not the only one responsible for the accident, the court noted that he was "the last line of defence to protect those workers, and he failed in his obligation to do so. If employers are not going to protect workers, then the workers must protect themselves and each other."[13]

Workers also have the right to refuse unsafe work, giving them a sense of empowerment in respect of their own health and safety. While some jurisdictions place limits on work refusals such that work cannot be refused if it is a normal part of the worker's duties or if the refusal could endanger another person, some jurisdictions merely require that the worker have a reasonably held subjective belief that the work will endanger his or her health or safety or that of another person. To be effective, a worker's right to refuse unsafe work must be respected by other stakeholders, particularly supervisors and employers. Moreover, the right must not be abused by workers—a problem that can manifest itself in workplaces with a high degree of worker unrest or antagonistic labour relations relationships.

Joint Health and Safety Committees   A key aspect of an effective IRS is a joint health and safety committee (JHSC), and in some jurisdictions, health and safety representatives for smaller workplaces. JHSCs are mandated in all jurisdictions, although workplaces with very few workers (fewer than 10 or 20 workers) may be exempted from a formal committee requirement. While committees are merely advisory in nature and have no legal authority to direct specific changes to the workplace, they are nonetheless a critical component of the IRS. Consisting of employee and/ or labour and management representatives, committees provide a forum for cooperative, proactive debate and dialogue of workplace health and safety issues leading to an identification of health and safety problems (ideally before they culminate in accidents), establishing creative solutions, and planning and implementing an effective plan of action. Committees may also participate in activities such as processing worker complaints and suggestions, as well as work refusals, and maintaining or monitoring workplace injury and hazard reports, although they are not legally mandated to do so. Committees are a highly effective vehicle for creating awareness of occupational health and safety in the workplace and promoting the organization's overall health and safety culture. The regular inspections and meetings that committees are expected to carry out in the workplace may be a driving force of this process, but the crucial and instructive value of open and ongoing communication with front-line employees cannot be underestimated.

In the federal sector, employers with more than 300 employees must also establish a policy committee, which acts as a central joint health and safety committee with overarching responsibility for workplace health and safety.[14] The policy committee oversees and coordinates the activities of occupational health and safety committees in the workplace and participates in the development of health and safety policies and programs.

Enforcement Enforcement of occupational health and safety laws is within the domain of the ministries of labour using a system of inspections, investigations, prosecutions, and penalties, including fines and imprisonment. Government health and safety inspectors (or officers) have broad powers flowing from the occupational health and safety statutes in each jurisdiction. With a mandate to enforce occupational health and safety laws, inspectors attend workplaces to investigate a health and safety matter by viewing the scene of the alleged infraction or accident, holding interviews and gathering statements from witnesses; they also have significant powers to search for and seize physical and documentary evidence. Inspectors have the authority to issue orders and directions, request legal opinions, or confer with government lawyers regarding laying charges under the statute, and may testify in a legal proceeding on behalf of the government in respect of charges laid under the legislation. Inspectors also undertake the vital role of monitoring health and safety compliance with a view to preventing health and safety mishaps. Inspections therefore also occur periodically as a proactive measure.

Inspectors are not only enforcement and policing agents. Their expertise in health and safety law makes them a valuable source for guidance and information in respect of interpreting and understanding occupational health and safety laws and in achieving health and safety compliance.

If an inspector finds a violation of health and safety laws, he or she can issue orders or directions designed to remedy the infraction and may require that they be posted in a visible place in the workplace. The inspector's remedial authority in this respect is far-reaching. Stop-work orders, prohibitions on the use of certain equipment or machinery, removal of employees from the workplace until the hazard has been rectified or removed, and banning the use of certain hazardous chemicals or substances are not uncommon.

The inspector's investigation and any orders or directions are the foundation for any charges laid under the statute should the government choose to prosecute the offenders. Charges under health and safety legislation are quasi-criminal in nature and those convicted face jail time varying by jurisdiction from six months to three years, or fines often in the range of tens of thousands of dollars. Fines issued against corporations are much higher; in many cases no maximum penalty exists. In practice, it is not uncommon for fines against corporations to soar well above the $100,000 mark, particularly where a worker has been seriously or fatally injured. In April 2009, Bell Canada was issued a $280,000 fine in respect of the deaths of two workers in June 2007.[15] The workers, employed by Wesbell Communications Technologies, were overcome by the toxic atmosphere inside a manhole where they were working to install new fibre-optic cables for Bell. The fine was the largest ever imposed against a federally regulated employer for a health and safety violation under the Canada Labour Code. For its part in the tragedy, Wesbell was fined $200,000.[16] In May 2010, Ford Motor Company of Canada was fined $850,000 for the deaths of two workers in separate incidents.[17] In one incident on January 31, 2008, a worker was fatally injured at Ford's Oakville assembly plant after being crushed between two forklifts. In the second incident, on January 14, 2009, a worker driving a lift truck carrying an unsecured pallet was killed at Ford's Bramalea parts distribution centre when the pallet struck a storage rack and the worker was crushed between the pallet and the vehicle.

Chemical Hazards Although chemicals (i.e., hazardous substances, materials, toxins, gases, and toxic substances including biological and physical agents) serve many useful purposes both at work and in our homes, they pose serious risks to people and the environment if misused or mishandled, and if proper safety precautions are not taken. Given these risks and the potential for harm, the use, storage, handling, and disposal of chemicals at work is regulated by occupational health and safety legislation and regulations. The standards prohibit the use of some chemicals and place limits and controls on others to eliminate or reduce workers' exposure to these potentially harmful substances. Increasingly, as illustrated in the "Competing Through Sustainability" box, employers are finding that implementing and enforcing safe handling procedures to resolve chemical hazards in the workplace can go a long way toward protecting our environment at the same time.

Chemicals can trigger numerous adverse reactions in a person, ranging from mild skin reactions or eye sensitivity to breathing problems, blindness, burns, cancer and other diseases, and death. Chemical hazards are linked to many occupational diseases, and believed, although not proven, to be the cause of a host of other debilitating and fatal illnesses.

There are hundreds of thousands of chemicals used in industrial settings in North America, with several thousand new chemicals developed each year. For a great number of these chemicals, toxicity data is not available. However, in Canada the **Workplace Hazardous Materials Information System (WHMIS)**, also known as the "right to know" legislation, has been incorporated into occupational health and safety legislation in all jurisdictions. WHMIS works in tandem with the federal Hazardous Products Act,[18] which obligates suppliers who sell or import hazardous materials for use in Canadian workplaces to properly label their products and provide material safety data sheets (MSDSs) to customers and users. MSDSs provide extensive information regarding the chemical's composition, risks, and what to do in the event of potentially harmful exposure. With the purpose of reducing risks in the area of workplace hazardous materials (referred to as "controlled substances" under WHMIS), WHMIS is a national program that requires that workplace hazardous materials be identified and properly labelled, and MSDS sheets must be provided with all chemicals. In addition, workers, supervisors, managers, and anyone else in the workplace who may be exposed to the substances receive proper and adequate training in respect of the identification, control, use, storage, handling, and disposal of the substances. Employers are responsible for ensuring that their workplaces are in compliance with WHMIS and to provide the necessary training and education.

The Effect of Occupational Health and Safety Laws Occupational health and safety legislation has been unquestionably successful in raising the level of awareness of occupational safety. The Association of Workers' Compensation Boards of Canada reported that there were 307,802 compensable workplace injuries resulting in lost time at work in 2008—a significant decline from the peak 620,979 reported almost 20 years earlier in 1989.[19] However, workplace fatalities have actually increased over time, rising from 758 in 1993 to 1,036 in 2008.[20] These figures suggest that, while the legislation may have had a positive impact, it alone cannot solve all the problems of workplace safety.[21] Many industrial accidents are a product of unsafe behaviours, not unsafe working conditions. Because the legislation does not directly regulate employee behaviour, further improvement in the statistical picture may stall unless employees are convinced of the importance of safety at work and put those beliefs into practice—a sentiment recognized by many, including the judge in the above-noted case of Louis Wheelan, who was injured as a result of the tree falling on a power line.

Because conforming to the statute alone does not necessarily guarantee safety, many employers go beyond the letter of the law. In the next section we examine various kinds of employer-initiated safety awareness programs that comply with occupational health and safety law requirements and, in some cases, exceed them.

Understanding and Preventing Workplace Accidents

Perhaps the best line of defence against workplace accidents is understanding why they happen, and in turn, how they can be prevented. Some of the most common types of accidents include trips, slips, or falls; electrical incidents; manual handling/lifting; falling from heights; cuts from

---

Workplace Hazardous Materials Information System (WHMIS)
A Canada-wide system designed to give employers and workers information about hazardous materials in the workplace.

Competing Through Sustainability

Safety Management Goes Green

In the first decade of the new millennium, an increasing number of organizations have incorporated environmental initiatives into their traditional workplace health and safety departments and practices. This is a trend we can expect to continue going forward.

While the alignment of environmental initiatives with health and safety practices has benefitted companies from a cost-efficiency standpoint, it has also helped health and safety managers understand how these two initiatives overlap and flow together. To that end, many environment, and health and safety professionals have worked to ensure common interests converge into mutually beneficial policies and procedures.

Jeremy Shorthouse is one such professional. As the national environmental, health and safety manager for winemaker Vincor Canada, as well as *Canadian Occupational Safety* magazine's Safety Leader of the Year for 2010, Shorthouse knows that safety comes first. He's also aware, though, that sometimes you can protect both your workers and the environment at the same time. He pointed to water specifically as one workplace issue that impacts both workplace safety and the environment.

"One critical crossover is definitely water," said Shorthouse. "Water is a part of our business just because of the fact that we're making wine. There are water additions and constant cleaning and so on, and that water obviously produces slippery floors. The more we can reuse our water the better, because it both saves water and keeps it off the floor. Reducing water usage means reducing slip hazards at our sites and in our cellars."

But the overlap doesn't end there. Chemicals are another big concern. Any chemical agent that can cause harm to the environment tends to have a similar effect on a human being, and vice versa. It's something that Shorthouse and Vincor take very seriously, both with regard to their workers and to the environment. As a company whose products are being consumed by the public, they have to.

"There are definitely chemicals used in our processes," said Shorthouse. "We use sulphur additions to do the wine. Realistically, there's not enough being used that we have to worry about the environment too much, but it does affect the environment of the employee. We have full-face respirators on our workers for that sort of thing."

"On the other side of that, a lot of times we're using very caustic chemicals for our cleaning purposes, which we have to make sure aren't leaked into the sewer system, where they might have an adverse effect. We ensure that our caustic materials are neutralized and have a positive pH level by adding additions. That way they can be taken by the city without causing any problems."

The adoption of interconnected environmental and health and safety departments continues to take place across the country as companies recognize the benefits of uniting these overlapping interests. It's a marriage of mutual interests that Bob Whiting, a senior project manager with the Canadian Centre for Occupational Health & Safety (CCOHS), thinks is a good fit.

"I'd say it's the case that companies do a better job with safety and with environment when the two work together or are grouped together," said Whiting. "There are certainly lots of examples of that. You get better solutions to these sorts of problems when the environmental aspects and health and safety aspects are considered at the same time. With health and safety, I think it's mainly a question of thinking about how a company's work affects the environment, and figuring out how it can cause less of an impact."

Shorthouse feels that the workers themselves are also buying in and becoming more environmentally conscious, which means they are also beginning to understand the impact that environmental issues can have on worker safety.

"Our employees are becoming more focused on reducing and reusing energy and water, and helping out with these sorts of projects in whatever way they can. They're doing this for three reasons: (1) they know they're ultimately helping the bottom line; (2) they know it can help to reduce health and safety risks; and (3) they know we are doing better for the environment."

"I always tell the people in our organization: 'We are a part of the environment. That's where our product comes from: the Earth.'"

SOURCE: Adapted from Taylor Fredericks, "Safety Management Goes Green," *Canadian Occupational Safety*, January 6, 2011. Reprinted with the permission of Annex Printing and Publishing Inc. This article originally appeared in *Canadian Occupational Safety*/www.cos-mag.com.

sharp objects; motor vehicle accidents (including being hit or crushed by a vehicle); burns; fires or explosions; being struck by a falling object; and exposure to harmful chemicals or environments. Common resulting injuries include sprains and strains; hand injuries; back, head, and neck injuries; repetitive strain injuries; and occupational diseases (e.g., cancer, asthma).

Most accidents are preventable. Accidents generally occur because of unsafe acts or unsafe conditions. Of course, accidents can also occur by chance despite the best of safety precautions and procedures, but our focus here is on understanding and taking steps to prevent those accidents over which we can exercise control.

Why should employers care about creating a safe and healthy workplace? Aside from the legal implications and the primary objective of protecting workers, unhealthy, unsafe, and stressful workplaces cost Canadian employers billions of dollars every year in workers' compensation costs, absenteeism, presenteeism (i.e., workers who come to work when ill or injured), short- and long-term disability claims, turnover, and lost productivity.[22] Consider this: 2002 figures from the Ontario Workplace Safety and Insurance Board suggest than an average lost-time workers' compensation claim costs about $12,000—which translates into a $59,000 cost to the company due to further indirect costs (these are figures that are sure to have risen in the decade since). If your company's profit margin is 10 percent, it requires $590,000 in sales to produce a $59,000 profit. Alternatively, if your profit margin is 6 percent, it requires almost $1 million ($983,333) in sales to produce a $59,000 profit. If your company can eliminate just one lost-time injury (average cost $59,000) you have, in effect, created an equivalent profit by increasing your sales by $590,000 at a 10 percent profit margin or $983,333 at a 6 percent profit margin. These figures demonstrate that safety would be a wise top priority even for those employers for whom the primary objective is maximizing the bottom line.

Unsafe Act
A worker's violation of, or disregard for, a safety rule or procedure.

Unsafe Acts An **unsafe act** is directly attributable to human error. Such acts generally involve individual workers violating or disregarding a safety rule or procedure, or turning a blind eye to a safety hazard. Some examples of unsafe acts include knowingly not following established rules or procedures, knowingly disregarding a hazard, willful misconduct, abusing equipment, knowingly using equipment incorrectly, choosing to not use personal protective equipment, failing to properly lock out equipment, removing or making safety devices inoperative, multitasking, and pushing yourself or the equipment beyond its capacity and ability. Unsafe acts also include conduct in the workplace that distracts you or others from focusing on their work. This might include horseplay, bullying or abuse, arguments or yelling, jokes or pranks, or ill-timed conversations. The "it-can't-happen-to-me" syndrome is also particularly dangerous. Workers who are overconfident and believe

Competing Through Technology

Putting Your Guard Up

Changing the operating parameters for a light curtain cost a machine press operator two fingers. [A light curtain is an infrared light installed in front of moving equipment to perform an automatic shutdown when motion is detected, and to prevent an accident.] The worker had set up the light curtain to "mute out" at 60 cm so that he could "hold parts close to the die."

To prevent similar incidents, the employer replaced the light curtain with another that offered floating beams, and implemented a procedure allowing only supervisors to set nonstandard die gap distances. But choosing the most appropriate photoelectric guard in the first place could have prevented the incident.

Photoelectric (optical) presence-sensing devices use a system of light sources and controls that can interrupt a machine's operating cycle. If the light field is broken, the machine stops and will not cycle. These devices are intended only for machines that can be stopped before the worker can reach the danger area.

Their goals, writes author Israel Alguindigue in an article for *Stamping Journal*, are to prevent access to a hazard, eliminate the hazard before access is attained, and prevent the unintended operation of a machine.

Safety devices protect operators and others from residual hazards such as crushing, shearing, cutting, snatching, clamping, trapping, perforating, puncturing, and shock.

Optoelectronic sensors help reduce access time and eliminate the waiting associated with opening doors or hard guards [physical barriers that must be removed in order to obtain access]. In general, they are simple to operate, and help minimize or eliminate repetitive motions. Safety light curtains and scanners can help protect all individuals in and near the hazardous area, not just the operator.

Several criteria need to be considered in selecting optoelectronic safeguarding equipment. National consensus standards help companies that manufacture, integrate, or use machines define the tasks and hazards associated with their machines. The standards also help users estimate risk, determine a corresponding risk reduction strategy, and understand the safeguarding and safety circuit performance requirements for their application.

The fundamental question in implementing safety with optoelectronic sensors is which device to use for which machine. Where suitable, engineering controls such as safety light curtains can be used to safeguard personnel.

SOURCE: Article written by Scott Williams, "Choosing the Right Photoelectric Machine Guard," *Accident Prevention e-News* (April 2009), Industrial Accident Prevention Association. Adapted from Israel E. Alguindigue, "Machine guarding with optoelectronic sensors," at www.thefabricator.com.

---

they are invincible when it comes to health and safety hazards are hazards to themselves and others around them.

Unsafe Conditions   **Unsafe conditions** are also caused by people and can be created at the hands of an individual worker or may be symptomatic of a lax safety atmosphere and workplace culture allowed to fester by supervisors, and ineffective oversight from senior management. Some examples of unsafe conditions include poor housekeeping and clutter, congested areas, deficient and defective equipment, poor ventilation, equipment with no or ineffective safeguards, lack of personal

Unsafe Condition
A physical hazard or inadequate safety programs, policy, or training that poses a risk to the health and safety of workers.

protective equipment, poor visibility including inadequate lighting, poor weather conditions, extreme hot or cold, impractical production standards and targets, inadequate safety programs and policies, and communication thereof, and perhaps most crucial, inadequate training. Identifying and correcting these hazards is an effective way to begin to improve workplace health and safety. The "Competing Through Technology" box on page 477 describes several examples of how technology can be used to make such improvements and eliminate unsafe conditions. Developing and maintaining an effective IRS is key to this process, particularly in larger workplaces where management may have little contact with many of the workers and be less likely to regularly view the workplace. JHSCs and health and safety representatives can play a critical role in assisting in this regard in a manner that is proactive, rather than merely reactive once an accident or incident has occurred. Input and commitment from supervisors and front-line workers is also critical to making this process work given that they are the people working under the conditions day in and day out.

Personal and Occupational Characteristics   Personal and occupational characteristics have been shown to affect the likelihood of accidents occurring.[23] Injury rates are higher among men than women, as well as workers who are less healthy to begin with (i.e., those with chronic health conditions, who are smokers, sedentary, or obese). Moreover, those performing work involving heavy lifting and other physically demanding tasks are much more likely to be injured on the job—the injury rate for this kind of physical work is twice as likely among men and three times as likely among women. Employees working longer hours and rotating shifts are also at a higher risk. In addition, blue-collar workers are at a higher risk than white-collar workers, likely due to the greater prevalence of hazards on the job.

As the Evidence-Based HR feature demonstrates, youths aged 15–24 are also at a higher risk of injury. Young workers' inexperience as well as their lack of concentration in precarious jobs especially when performing part-time, seasonal, contract, and casual work is compounded by the reality that they may not receive the same level of health and safety training as full-time permanent workers. Young workers' high accident rates have led to targeted health and safety campaigns in the last two decades aimed at reducing injuries and raising awareness of young workers' right to be safe and healthy at work, and in hopes of saving young workers' lives. Moreover, a 2009 study by the Institute for Work and Health found that young workers with dyslexia are almost twice as likely to be injured on the job.[24] The study underscores not only the importance of the need for adequate workplace health and safety training, but also the need for the manner of such training to be adjusted according to the individual characteristics of the recipient.

With an ever-growing immigrant population, English is a second language for an increasing number of workers. The language barrier and poor literacy skills of these workers are critical considerations in their health and safety training.[25] Simply handing out safety pamphlets and typical health and safety training procedures will not prevent accidents when the workers do not fully understand what they are reading or being told. If employees can't read or speak English well, managers must instruct them by using some other method or by arranging for communication in their native tongue.

Service industry jobs also tend to have lower accident rates than goods-producing industries.[26] Service industry jobs can include transportation; communication; trade; finance and insurance; real estate; business services; government services; education; health and social services; and accommodation, food and beverages. Goods-producing jobs are in the agriculture, fishing, forestry, mining and oil, manufacturing, and construction sectors. The lower risk in service industry jobs is not all that surprising given the inherently dangerous nature of many of the goods-producing industries.

Excessive worker stress has also been shown to affect workplace health and safety.[27] Although some stressors are external to the organization, many arise from the job or the work environment itself. Regardless of the source of worker stress, employers should implement measures to alleviate

Evidence-Based HR

Every day, an estimated 40 young workers across the country get sick or hurt as a result of their jobs, or even die on the job—that's about one person every 35 minutes. All told, every year over 60,000 young Canadians are disabled or disfigured at work, and about 60 are killed on the job annually. The reasons behind these statistics are many. Research indicates that new workers are more prone to injuries than more seasoned ones, and because young workers tend to change jobs more frequently than their older counterparts, they are "new" on the job longer and more often. For example, according to the Institute for Work and Health, at any given time, 5.3 percent of workers age 15–24 said they were in their first month on the job, compared to 1.1 percent of those over age 25. Working conditions are also part of the problem. Younger workers often undertake physically demanding jobs, and a recent Ontario survey indicated that young workers were also more exposed to unsafe work conditions than older ones. Limited training and supervision contributes to the high rate of young worker injury. A Canadian study of young workers in their first year on the job indicated that less than a quarter had received safety, orientation, or equipment training, and almost half reported receiving no training at all. A U.S. study revealed the alarming statistic that 80 percent of all workplace injuries sustained by younger workers occurred when a supervisor was not around. Finally, intimidation about asking questions or demanding increased safety standards is also a factor. Fearful of being seen as complainers or of losing their jobs, younger workers are unlikely to question just about anything having to do with their working conditions. Throw in some eagerness to please and a little youthful bravado and the statistics become much less surprising.

Governments and employers are working to find ways to reduce these statistics and keep younger workers safe on the job. For example, in British Columbia, the first education and prevention initiatives in support of young worker safety were launched in 1990. In the decade since those programs became widespread, BC reduced its young worker injury rates by over 30 percent. In Ontario, where similar programs are also in place, the decline in young worker injury rates was over 45 percent between 1990 and 2001. While these statistics may seem encouraging, the decrease in worker injury rates was actually less for this age group than for any other age group, and the rate of injury remained stubbornly high—in fact, the highest across all age groups.

So, just how successful are these ongoing prevention and awareness campaigns? There is certainly no shortage of programs and initiatives across the country. The Association of Workers' Compensation Boards of Canada (AWCBC) produces an annual "National Government/ WCB Young Worker Health & Safety Initiatives/Programs Inventory." In 2010, this inventory contained 38 pages of programs and these are just the ones owned or managed by Canadian governments or workers' compensation boards. It's a comprehensive list of resources, which includes research, social marketing, and other products aimed at reaching a broad base of audiences with a vested interest in keeping young people safe on the job—parents, hiring managers and supervisors, educators, community youth workers, and young workers themselves. And, as we saw in the opening story, companies such as Loblaw are taking the initiative and working toward "zero" injuries for all workers. Yet, according to a recent study commissioned by the Canadian Council on Learning Health and the Learning Knowledge Centre Young Adults Work Group, while Canada has made great strides in keeping young workers safe through prevention, education, and regulation, there is a paucity of information on the impact that these efforts are really having on young worker safety. There also seems to be a lot of duplication of effort and the study concluded that greater coordination between government agencies, employers, and researchers would help ensure that the development and delivery of workplace health and safety initiatives for young people was more efficient and effective. If organizations, government, and communities want to keep young workers safe, we are going to have to get better at working together and at finding out what really works.

SOURCES: Association of Workers' Compensation Boards of Canada (AWCBC) *2010 National Government/WCB Young Worker Health & Safety Initiatives/Programs Inventory* at www.awcbc.org/common/assets/english%20pdf/national_inventory_2010.pdf (retrieved May 30, 2011); F. C. Breslin, P. Smith, M. Koehoorn, and H. Lee (2006) "Is the Workplace Becoming Safer?" *Perspectives* July 2006, Statistics Canada Catalogue no. 75-001-XIE, pp. 18–23 at www.statcan.gc.ca/pub/75-001-x/10706/9271-eng.pdf (retrieved May 30, 2011); Institute for Work and Health (2010) *Young Worker Health and Safety: Fast Facts from the Institute for Work & Health* at www.livesafeworksmart.net/english/fast_facts/index.htm (retrieved May 2011); L. Schuyler (2002) "Is Your Teen Safe at Work?" *Reader's Digest* (June 2002) at www.readersdigest.ca/mag/2002/06/teen.html (retrieved May 30, 2011); The Canadian Council on Learning Health and the Learning Knowledge Centre Young Adults Work Group (2009) *Exemplary Practices in Addressing Workplace Health and Safety of Young Adults* at www.accc.ca/ftp/pubs/studies/200908HLKCStudentHealth.pdf (retrieved May 30, 2011); and WorkSafe BC (2011) *Initiatives & Research—Young Worker Strategy* at www2.worksafebc.com/Topics/YoungWorker/WCBInitiatives-YoungWorkerStrategy.asp (retrieved May 30, 2011).

and cope with the situation, given the detrimental impact it has not only on an organization's health and safety, but also productivity and the company's bottom line. Stress-related absences are estimated to cost Canadian employers $3.5 billion a year.[28] Workers afflicted by stress can feel a great deal of pressure, and can become agitated, unfocused, anxious and apathetic. They are also less able to concentrate and make good decisions. Reducing or eliminating stressful working conditions, work redesign, stress management training, a sensitive and supportive management response to worker stress, and early detection and prevention, are effective measures that can help diminish the negative impact of stress on an organization. We discuss the causes of workplace stress and stress management in greater detail later in this chapter.

Jobs that are monotonous and that workers find boring can lead to a greater frequency of workplace accidents. To reduce the impact of the effect of a job that is inherently repetitive, employers should consider changes in the worker's routine, ideally throughout his or her shift, as well as permitting more frequent breaks.

Fatigue is also believed to contribute to a higher number of accidents at work.[29] Fatigue affects a person's focus, reaction time, judgment, and overall ability to perform competently on the job. Workplace conditions that can contribute to fatigue include dim lighting, limited visual acuity (e.g., due to weather), high temperatures, high noise, high comfort, tasks which must be sustained for long periods of time, and work tasks which are long, repetitive, paced, difficult, boring, and monotonous.

Employers can help combat fatigue by providing work environments with good lighting, comfortable temperatures, and reasonable noise levels (or protective hearing equipment to lessen the impact of the noise on workers). In addition, work tasks should provide a variety of interest and tasks should rotate throughout the worker's shift.

Information is a useful tool in designing health and safety strategies that are tailored to meet individual employees' and the organization's needs. However, once employers understand what contributes to unsafe and unhealthy workplaces, and accidents on the job, what can they do to prevent them? In addition to the many approaches already discussed, various initiatives are set out below, including creating a top-down safety commitment and culture, health and safety training and education, selection testing, and safety awareness programs.

Top-Down Safety Commitment and Culture

Safety doesn't necessarily have to start at the top. On the contrary, some of the most effective health and safety programs begin with front-line workers. Regardless of who starts it or how, a commitment from the top is essential to the success of any health and safety program.

There is no better way to lead than by example. When management is genuinely committed to a safe and healthy workplace, an awareness of the importance of safety permeates the workplace and creates a safety culture. This management commitment is emulated by individual workers who exercise diligence in their own commitment to exercising safety at work. Demonstrating a safety commitment requires an active and unwavering dedication to fulfilling occupational health and safety legal obligations, as well as taking the steps necessary to develop, implement, review, and revise health and safety initiatives tailored to the individual organization. Making workplace health and safety a priority also means making health and safety visible through, for example, safety awareness programs, posters, pamphlets, and safety policies and procedures that are properly communicated and easily accessible and within view of workers in their day-to-day jobs. Other measures include training and education; reviewing and discussing safety regularly (e.g., whether at safety-focused meetings, or at routine weekly or biweekly team or department meetings); conducting workplace safety inspections, audits, and analyses to identify and address workplace hazards; and keeping an open-door policy for employees to bring forth any health and safety concerns, issues, or suggestions. JHSCs, safety representatives, or dedicated safety officers can be effective conduits for promoting the safety message throughout the organization and for assisting the employer in carrying out the initiatives and meeting the objectives outlined above.

Health and Safety Training and Education

An effective and comprehensive management health and safety commitment also involves proper health and safety training and education. Training and education is not necessary only to meet the employer's legal obligations, but also to ensure that the employer's health and safety policies and procedures can be effectively put into practice. A well developed policy or procedure is wasted if workers are not aware of it or do not comprehend how to implement it. Training and education must be developed with the needs of the particular organization and individual workers in mind, taking into account not only the content of the training material, but also the method of delivery, the equipment to be used, appropriate training aids, and the most effective type of instructors to deliver the message. Training and education should be periodic to keep health and safety fresh in workers' minds. Moreover, an evaluation of training programs is necessary to ensure that the information is being received and understood as intended.

Selection Testing

Selection testing is a common screening tool used in organizations where highly skilled individuals are sought. However, these tests can also assist employers in assessing an employee's suitability for a job from a health and safety perspective. Tests can assess specific job-related skills and knowledge, aptitude, physical ability, general intelligence, personality characteristics, mental abilities, psychological characteristics, and interests. Testing techniques may involve a demonstration of skills, a simulation, or a written exercise. Of course it is essential to ensure that all selection testing is effective and legally valid.

■ connect™   Learn more about implementing effective and valid selection testing online with Connect.

Safety Awareness Programs

Safety Awareness Programs
Employer programs that attempt to instill symbolic and substantive changes in the organization's emphasis on safety.

Safety awareness programs go beyond compliance with occupational health and safety laws and attempt to instill symbolic and substantive changes in the organization's emphasis on safety. These programs typically focus either on specific jobs and job elements or on specific types of injuries or disabilities. A safety awareness program has three primary components: identifying and communicating hazards, reinforcing safe practices and promoting safety internationally.

Identifying Job Hazards, Analysis, and Communication of Risk   Employees, supervisors, and other knowledgeable sources need to sit down and discuss potential problems related to safety. The **job hazard analysis technique** is one means of accomplishing this (also referred to as a job safety analysis).[30] With this technique, each job is broken down into basic elements, and each is rated for its potential for harm or injury. If there is consensus that a job element has high hazard potential, this element is isolated and potential technological or behavioural changes are considered, developed, and implemented to overcome the hazards. Input from workers who perform the work makes this technique much more effective.

Job Hazard Analysis Technique
A breakdown of each job into basic elements, each of which is rated for its potential for harm or injury.

Another means of isolating unsafe job elements is to study past accidents.[31] This methodology helps managers determine which specific factors and element(s) of a job led to a past accident. The first step in the analysis is to establish the facts surrounding the incident. To accomplish this, all members of the work group involved in or who witnessed the accident give their initial impressions of what happened. Second, the underlying causes of the personal or job factors that could have contributed to the accident are identified. Next, recommendations for establishing proper systems controls, the development of appropriate standards, or the need to ensure compliance with existing adequate standards are discussed. Compiling and analyzing this information allows for conclusions to be drawn in respect of accident trends—where, when, why, and how are accidents occurring and who are they occurring to? From this information, a remedial plan of action can be developed and implemented and risks must be communicated.

Childcare workers at Day Nursery Centre in Winnipeg experienced welcome changes resulting from a job hazards analysis conducted at their workplace.[32] Worker participation combined with management commitment and responsiveness were keys to its success. Workers were suffering from chronic aches and pains, and some had filed workers' compensation claims. Workers who were stooping over a short bench more than 20 times a day to change toddlers' diapers received a new waist-height change table complete with stairs so the toddlers could climb up on their own rather than having to be lifted. Workers were also provided with personal alarms when working alone, adult-sized chairs, and extenders to help clean child-sized tables without bending over.

■ connect™   Learn more about the Hazard Analysis at Canada Border Services Agency (CBSA) online with Connect.

Communication of an employee's risk should take advantage of several media. Direct verbal supervisory contact is important for its saliency and immediacy. Written memos are important because they help establish a paper trail that can later document a history of concern regarding the job hazard. Posters, especially those placed near the hazard, serve as a constant reminder, reinforcing other messages.

In communicating risk, it is important to recognize two distinct audiences. As discussed above, relatively young or inexperienced workers need special attention. Statistics indicate that workers age 15–24 are four times more likely to be injured in their first four weeks of employment.[33] WorkSafeBC reports that young male workers are 70 percent more likely to be injured than any other group.[34] The employer's primary concern with respect to this group is to inform them. However, the employer must not overlook experienced workers. Here, the key concern is to remind them. Research indicates that long-term exposure to and familiarity with a specific threat can lead to complacency.[35] Experienced employees need retraining to jar them from becoming blind to the real dangers associated with their work. This is especially the case if the hazard in question poses a greater threat to older employees. For example, falling off a ladder is a greater threat to older workers than to younger ones. More than 20 percent of such falls lead to a fatality for workers in the 55–65 age group, compared with just 10 percent for all other workers.[36]

Reinforcing Safe Practices One common technique for reinforcing safe practices is implementing a safety incentive program to reward workers for their support and commitment to safety goals. Initially, programs are set up to focus on improving short-term monthly or quarterly goals or to encourage safety suggestions. These short-term goals are later expanded to include more wide-ranging, long-term goals. Prizes are typically distributed in highly public forums (such as annual meetings or events). These prizes usually consist of merchandise rather than cash because merchandise represents a lasting symbol of achievement. A good deal of evidence suggests that such programs are effective in reducing injuries and their cost.[37]

Safety awareness programs can also focus on specific injuries or disabilities where a workplace has a particularly high rate of a particular type of injury.

Promoting Safety Internationally Given the increasing focus on international management, organizations also need to consider how to best ensure the safety of people regardless of the nation in which they operate. Cultural differences may make this more difficult than it seems. For example, a recent study examined the impact of one standardized corporation-wide safety policy on employees in three different countries: the United States, France, and Argentina. The results of this study indicated that the same policy was interpreted differently because of cultural differences. The individualistic, control-oriented culture of the United States stressed the role of top management in ensuring safety in a top-down fashion. However, this policy failed to work in Argentina, where the collectivist culture made employees feel that safety was everyone's joint concern; therefore, programs needed to be defined from the bottom up.[38] The study highlights the need to tailor health and safety management programs to the audience. We discuss the safety issue of bullying in the "Competing Through Globalization" box on page 493.

WORKERS' COMPENSATION

While occupational health and safety laws help to promote health and safety at work and prevent workplace accidents, workers' compensation legislation addresses compensating workers for the workplace injuries they have incurred.[39] In cases where a worker has been fatally injured, workers' compensation provides for survivor benefits to the worker's spouse.

The workers' compensation scheme is a mandatory collective liability system that exists in each jurisdiction in Canada. It is a no-fault system where workers whose employers are registered with the workers' compensation board give up the right to sue their employers for injuries or fatalities sustained in a an accident suffered in the course of employment in return for benefits received from the workers' compensation insurance fund. Employers make regular payments to the workers' compensation board in the form of premiums in return for immunity from lawsuits. The legislation also establishes rights and obligations for employers and employees to promptly report any injuries sustained in the course of employment and to work cooperatively with each other and the board.

In addition to compensating workers for work-related injuries, workers' compensation statutes impose a duty on employers to cooperate in and facilitate the early and safe return to work and recovery of workers who have been injured at work. Throughout this process, workers' compensation boards may provide benefits in the form of compensation for medical and rehabilitative treatments, and assistive devices. Boards also provide skills and occupational training where workers are unable to return to their pre-injury jobs. Boards will assist employers and their employees in determining whether work that the employer has available for a worker to perform is suitable and within the employee's functional abilities based on information from medical practitioners. This may include the board conducting its own ergonomic assessment of the workplace or employee's workstation.

The costs of a claim depend on the extent of an employee's injuries and whether and when that employee can return to work. Employers with high claim costs or frequent accident occurrences will see a rise in their premiums. A workplace injury also has costs beyond those that may become payable to the workers' compensation board; an employee's absence may give rise to hiring and training a temporary replacement. It is estimated that for every dollar that a claim costs the workers' compensation board, the employer incurs another one to four dollars in indirect costs.

While it may seem obvious, it needs to be made clear that the most effective way to reduce the cost of a workplace injury is to prevent the injury from occurring in the first place. The steps and initiatives discussed throughout this chapter are effective ways to meet that objective. However, in the event that an accident occurs, costs can be reduced by returning the employee to work as soon as he or she is medically able to do so, whether on a full-time or reduced-hours basis, and sometimes beginning with modified duties. Designating one or more individuals to deal with workers' compensation claims, and providing them with adequate training and education, is an effective way of ensuring that claims are processed and administered in an organized, timely, and knowledgeable fashion. While this may be performed by a member of the human resources department, some organizations employ occupational health nurses or safety officers who carry out this task. Disability management firms are also available to assist employers in managing workers' compensation claims and in gathering the information necessary from an employee's physician(s) to return the employee to work that is within his or her medical restrictions, in a timely way.

LO 4

Explain the strategic importance of employee wellness programs.

EMPLOYEE WELLNESS PROGRAMS

When employers realized in the 1970s that an unhealthy worker was a liability to productivity, they started to implement programs to encourage workers to adopt healthier lifestyles.[40] Stop-smoking campaigns are a prime early example of wellness campaigns. In the 1980s, the programs expanded to target a wider range of healthy lifestyle practices, marking the beginning of employee wellness programs (recall our definition in Chapter 10). Let's look at some numbers to better understand how employees' unhealthy lifestyles can take a toll on the employer's bottom line.

The Conference Board of Canada calculates that every smoker costs his or her employer approximately $2,500 per year in increased absenteeism, lost productivity, increased group benefit insurance costs, and increased facility maintenance. Research shows that employers can pay an extra $597 per year for each employee who excessively consumes alcohol and $488 per year for every sedentary employee. Employees with four lifestyle risk factors (i.e., sedentary, overweight, smoker, high alcohol intake) are absent over 50 percent more often than those without the risk factors, and cost two to three times more in health costs. Moreover, there is a direct relationship between obesity and the number of workers' compensation claims, lost workdays, medical claims costs, and indemnity claims costs, with the total cost of obesity to Canadian employers estimated at $1.3 billion per year. Obese employees spend about 35 percent more on health services and 77 percent more on medications than people of healthy weight.[41]

What can employers do to improve employee wellness? The variety of employee wellness programs is virtually endless, providing options for employers with modest to abundant resources on hand. Some program ideas include

- On-site gymnasiums, pools, skating rinks, or fitness centres to encourage physical activity;
- Providing healthy foods in on-site cafeterias and vending machines to encourage healthy eating;
- Subsidies to help employees quit smoking, participate in fitness activities, or eat healthier foods;
- On-site health screening, such as cholesterol or blood glucose tests, influenza vaccination clinics, or personal health risk assessments;
- "Lunch and learn" education sessions;
- Stress management training, relaxation and meditation workshops, and self-esteem and assertiveness workshops;
- Informational brochures;
- Health fairs.

Given that a wellness program involves some level of employer financial commitment, and employers are under no legal obligation to promote employee wellness, what exactly is the incentive for employers? Healthier workers are happier and more productive workers. They are absent less frequently, experience less stress, are less likely to become ill or injured (and thus incur prescription drug costs and short- and long-term disability costs for the organization), have better working relationships, are better able to competently perform their jobs, and are less likely to leave the organization—to name just some of the benefits.

And what about that bottom line? Experience tells us that employers who implement wellness programs will receive a return on their investment in the range of $1.15 to $6.15 for every dollar spent. For example, for every $1 BC Hydro spent on the organization's wellness program, the company saved an estimated $3 (after running 10 years). Canada Life Insurance saved $3.43 for every $1 spent on its fitness program. Coors Brewing Company saved $6.15 for every $1 spent on a fitness program, and Telus-BC saved $3 for every dollar spent on corporate health initiatives, within 5 years of launching the program.[42]

Irving Paper, a unionized 375-employee manufacturer in Saint John, New Brunswick, supplements its health and safety program with several health promotion programs and subsidies to encourage healthy lifestyles. Between 1995 and 2000, the company's short-term disability costs dropped by 50 percent, a savings of $800,000, and the number of union grievances fell from 50 to 11 per year. Delta Hotels' implementation of a healthy workplace environment based on "response-ability"—giving the staff more responsibility, accountability, and authority—having more say and control of their work environment, resulted in a turnover rate of 19–22 percent, well below the 40–60 percent rate in the hospitality and tourism sector.[43]

Although implementing a wellness program may be a lengthy undertaking, its benefits to the organization and employees make it a worthwhile endeavour for HRM.

Learn more about seven steps to creating a healthy workplace online with Connect.

ERGONOMICS AND WORKPLACE DESIGN

As discussed in Chapter 4, ergonomics is the science of creating a proper fit between people and their work, taking into account safety, comfort, ease of use, productivity and performance, and aesthetics.[44] Some of the most common ergonomic workplace injuries today are musculoskeletal injuries

LO 5

Discuss various health, safety, and security issues and implications for human resource management.

(MSIs), often referred to as repetitive strain injuries (RSIs). MSIs are injuries that affect tendons, tendon sheaths, muscles, nerves, and joints, and cause persistent or recurring pains most commonly in the neck, shoulders, forearms, hands, wrists, elbows, and lower limbs. Carpal tunnel syndrome, tendonitis, and bursitis are just some examples of common MSIs afflicting today's workers.

Poor work posture or movements, unsuitable workspaces, and unsuitable job processes and design are prime ergonomically based factors contributing to MSIs. The prevalence with which workers spend hours typing on keyboards and clicking a mouse in front of their computers has contributed significantly to the rise of MSIs in today's workplaces. Workers who perform repetitive work, particularly that which is also fast paced, are especially prone to MSIs, although MSIs also frequently arise in workers who perform lifting or loading work that is fairly static without support of the lower limbs, workers exposed to strong vibrations, and workers who work in awkward or uncomfortable positions.

These injuries are the most frequent type of lost-time injuries and the largest source of lost-time workers' compensation claims in Canada. In 2007, in Ontario alone, MSIs accounted for 1.2 million lost working days and $133 million in direct costs.[45] These injuries and their enormous associated costs can be prevented.

Ergonomics can assist in making modifications in workplace design in order to reduce or eliminate ergonomic hazards. Table 12.1 lists suggestions from Ergonomics Canada of signs to watch for in the workplace that often signal the need for ergonomic modifications. This might include new or reconfigured equipment; changes to worker positioning; modifying work techniques or processes; or altering the pace of work or frequency of breaks. There is a wealth of information available from occupational health and safety-focused organizations to assist employers in the use of ergonomics to improve workplace design; the Canadian Centre for Occupational Health and Safety is just one such source. There are also many ergonomic consultants available to assist employers in modifying their workplaces to align with employees' ergonomic needs.

Table 12.1 Is Your Workplace Calling Out for Ergonomic Design?

Ergonomics Canada suggests that the following signs might indicate that your workplace is in need of ergonomic redesign:
• Employees in your workplace, or in certain specific work areas, are experiencing soft-tissue injuries such as tendonitis, back injuries, sore muscles, etc. These are all indicators that the job demands are excessive due to one or a combination of risk factors (e.g., force levels, work postures, repetitive actions, long durations, and/or psychosocial stressors). Accidents and injuries to these workers may be the result of ergonomics issues, for example, inadequate clearances, design of controls and tools, poor design of stairways, lack of appropriate lighting, or poor visibility.
• High rates of general absenteeism and/or worker turnover can be indicators of high levels of physical or mental demand, poor workplace design, and/or poor organizational design.
• A high number of mistakes or requirement for rework on products due to poor quality are often the result of problems such as difficult work processes, high workloads, and fatigue, inadequate communication/information, and poor visibility.
• Poor, or declining, productivity over the course of a shift or over a series of shifts can also mean that the work is not well designed for workers.

SOURCE: Adapted from "How Do I Know When I Need Help in Ergonomics?" Ergonomics Canada (www.ergonomics canada.com/faqs.html). Reprinted by permission of Ergonomics Canada! www.ergonomicscanada.com.

STRESS MANAGEMENT

Your company is downsizing and you fear you're next. Your job is overly demanding with unachievable targets and deadlines. Perhaps you just started a new job and have been assigned a pile of work with little training on how to complete it. Maybe your supervisor approaches his job like a dictator.

Stress is a normal part of life. Undue stress, however, can have a detrimental impact on employees and an organization, particularly where it becomes debilitating. Workers who are under too much stress are more prone to feel rushed and helpless; get angry or upset easily; feel tired, depressed, and anxious; and find it hard to concentrate. Stressed-out workers make more mistakes including being more prone to workplace accidents and injuries; find it hard to make decisions; waste more time; are less creative; and find it hard to get along with coworkers and their bosses. These workers are also less courteous with customers (resulting in customer dissatisfaction and complaints), and miss work more often.[46] Workers under a great deal of stress are also more likely to develop serious illnesses such as heart disease, disorders of the digestive system, MSIs and increases in blood pressure and headaches.[47] One staggering statistic from the Industrial Accident Prevention Association suggests that these workers are five times more likely to develop cancer.[48] Workers under too much stress are also more apt to quit, contributing to the organization's turnover costs.

We have already discussed the staggering statistic that stress-related absences cost Canadian employers about $3.5 billion each year.[49] Research also shows that stress in a business contributes to 19 percent of absenteeism costs and 30 percent of short-term and long-term disability costs. Looking at the problem of stress from a health and safety perspective, research shows that stress in a business contributes to at least 60 percent of workplace accidents, and that frequent conflicts with supervisors or colleagues and high psychological and emotional job demands more than double the risk of being injured in an occupational accident. Stress can also lead to mental illnesses such as depression and anxiety.

The cost of lost productivity to Canadian businesses due to mental illnesses has been estimated at $11.1 billion per year.[50] If nonclinical diagnoses such as burnout are included, that figure swells to $33 billion. Mental illness is also the leading cause of short- and long-term disability claims. Employees who work in unhealthy or unsafe work environments are two to three times more likely to develop mental illnesses. The cost of the consequences of worker stress to health and safety, productivity, and thus profit, means that stress management is an essential part of an organization's health and safety program.

Psychosocial hazards are workplace stressors or work organizational factors that can threaten the mental and physical health of employees. Poor work design, poor management, and unsatisfactory working conditions create a haven for workplace stress. (Table 12.2 provides further examples.) Jobs that place unreasonable demands and pressures on employees and jobs where workers feel they have little control or influence over their work are far more likely to produce stressed out and burned-out employees.

A risk management approach that identifies and assesses stress hazards in the workplace allows an organization to form a plan of action and put it into practice. Table 12.3 on page 488 identifies ways in which an organization can solve and prevent workplace stress.

ALCOHOL AND DRUG ADDICTION

Workers exposed to unhealthy and unsafe work environments are twice as likely to suffer from drug or alcohol addiction.[51] The human-rights aspects of drug and alcohol abuse were covered in Chapter 3 of this text and will not be repeated here, other than to note that drug and alcohol addiction is viewed as a disability warranting the protection of human-rights laws in all Canadian jurisdictions.

Table 12.2   Psychosocial Hazards Contributing to Workplace Stress

- Work overload and time pressure
- Lack of influence or control over how day-to-day work is done
- Lack of social support from supervisors or coworkers
- Lack of training or preparation to do the job
- Too little or too much responsibility
- Ambiguity in job responsibility
- Lack of status rewards (appreciation)
- Discrimination or harassment
- Poor communication
- Lack of support for work/family balance
- Lack of respect for employees and the work they do

SOURCE: Joan Burton "Creating Healthy Workplaces," Industrial Accident Prevention Association (2006) at www.iapa.ca/main/documents/pdf/2004_HWP_Healthy_Workplace_FINAL.pdf.

Table 12.3   Practices for Solving and Preventing Workplace Stress

- Clear organizational structures and processes
- Selection, training, and staff development appropriate to employees' skills, knowledge, and abilities
- Adequate, considerate, supportive, and responsive management
- Clear and appropriate job descriptions
- Changing the demands of work
- Improve employees' control over their work
- Flexible work arrangements
- Encourage support and communication among employees
- Maintaining a workplace free of health and safety hazards
- Improve ergonomic design and physical workplace conditions
- Open, clear, and ongoing communication
- Worker education and training (both skills-based and in respect of stress management)
- Positive social work environment
- Implementation of early detection programs and/or education of managers and supervisors in how to identify stress-related problems at work
- Employee assistance programs

SOURCE: Work Organisation and Stress, URL: http://www.who.int/occupational_health/publications/en/oehstress.pdf on pages 16 and 17. Reprinted by permission of WHO.

The human-rights aspect of substance abuse must be balanced with an employer's obligations under health and safety laws to maintain a healthy and safe workplace for all employees. Substance abuse in the workplace raises critical health and safety issues for other workplace participants as well as the abuser, particularly in safety-sensitive or inherently dangerous jobs. Substance abuse can affect an individual's ability to mentally and physically perform his or her job, causing impaired judgment, slowed reflexes, impaired motor function, drowsiness, and inattention—all of which pose risks to the worker, coworkers, and the public.

The Canadian Centre on Substance Abuse reports that substance abuse costs the Canadian economy more than $22.8 billion.[52] The primary impact of substance abuse on Canadian businesses involves premature death or fatal accidents, injury and accident rates, absenteeism and extra sick leave, and loss of production.

An employer who suspects an employee is under the influence of drugs at work should follow predetermined steps to discreetly remove the employee from his or her workstation, ensuring that each step is properly documented and witnessed by a second member of management, and where applicable, a union representative. All of the steps used to deal with such a situation, including information about the organization's expectations of, and consequences resulting from employees' use of drugs or alcohol in the workplace should be set out in a substance abuse policy. Employers can also offer employees experiencing problems with drugs and alcohol access to an employee assistance program.

Learn more about signs of impairment and a procedure for handling employees suspected of impairment at work online with Connect.

Drug and Alcohol Testing   Employers, especially in safety-sensitive industries, often want to test employees to ensure that they are not impaired by drugs or alcohol at work. Although the goal may be reasonable, decision makers do not always agree. Drug and alcohol testing in employment has limits in Canada. Testing may be permissible only where the employer can meet three stringent conditions set out by the Supreme Court of Canada:

1. The testing policy is rationally connected to the performance of the job;
2. The employer adopted the policy in an honest and good-faith belief that it was necessary to the fulfillment of that legitimate, work-related purpose; and
3. The policy or standard is reasonably necessary to accomplish that legitimate, work-related purpose.

It is on this last step of the test that employers have typically stumbled.

Drug and alcohol testing policies may pertain to pre-employment or pre-access testing, random testing, for-cause testing, or postincident testing. Many employers have failed in defending drug and alcohol testing policies, although the results vary by jurisdiction.

Pre-employment testing is generally impermissible on the basis that it cannot assess actual or future impairment on the job. However, pre-employment testing may be found valid where it meets the Supreme Court's three-step test and there is a sufficient connection to matters of safety.[53] The chances that a pre-employment or pre-access test will be found valid improves where there is evidence of prevalent drug use in the workplace; the organization employs workers in safety-sensitive positions where impairment on the job could lead to significant loss or harm to the impaired worker, coworkers, the public or the environment; *and* the nature of the job is such that the employer cannot adequately monitor the employee at work on a regular basis.

Random drug testing for existing employees is similarly prohibited given that no method exists to accurately measure current impairment.[54] However, random alcohol testing may be appropriate in respect of safety-sensitive positions in some circumstances.

Employers may be able to test employees for drug or alcohol impairment as part of a drug and alcohol policy when there is reasonable cause to test a particular employee. For instance, after an accident or safety infraction, an employer may be able to ask the employee involved to provide a sample for drug or alcohol testing. An employee's behaviour or demeanour and/or the odour of drugs or alcohol also may provide reasonable cause for testing. In addition, an employer may be able to require an employee to undergo drug or alcohol testing as part of a last-chance agreement to accommodate an employee who otherwise might have been dismissed for drug or alcohol impairment. Positive results will require the application of human-rights law and principles of accommodation.

FRAGRANCES IN THE WORKPLACE

For many people, the scent of freshly washed hair, scented creams, or a touch of perfume bring pleasure. However, these smells do not evoke the same reaction in people with scent sensitivities for whom these products can cause irritations and allergic reactions, making scented products in the workplace a health and safety concern.[55] The not-so-pleasurable reactions can include nausea, dizziness, headache, itchy skin, hives, and itchy eyes and nose. A runny nose, wheezing, coughing, difficulty breathing, sore throat, asthma, or asthma-like symptoms, and strange tastes in the mouth are also common reactions.

In recent years, a scent-free movement has gained momentum, finding its way into several Canadian workplaces in the form of scent-free or scent-reduced policies.

connect

Learn more about steps for eliminating problem scents in the workplace online with Connect.

INFLUENZA PANDEMIC

Medical experts have warned us that it is a question of when, not if, a flu pandemic will hit. With the experience of Severe Acute Respiratory Syndrome (SARS) in 2003 and the H1N1 flu in 2009, Canadians are aware of the need to develop adequate procedures to deal with these outbreaks. The impact of a flu pandemic on employers will come in the form of high levels of absenteeism, illness, and disability. Workers may not only become ill themselves, but also may need to stay home to care for sick family members. Moreover, a pandemic could result in entire workplaces being quarantined.

Employers can limit the impact of a flu pandemic on their workplace by developing a contingency plan, educating workers about infectious disease and its symptoms, encouraging healthy hand-washing habits, and providing antiseptic cleanser in the workplace. Educating employees on the benefits of flu vaccinations, holding flu vaccination clinics on-site, keeping the workplace as clean and free of germs as possible, ensuring ventilation systems are operating properly, and asking employees who have any flu symptoms to stay home until they are no longer contagious are other suggested measures.[56]

At a minimum, contingency plans should address alternative arrangements if the workplace has to be quarantined; leave policies; short-term disability issues; the need to modify any human resource policies; organizing remaining staff and replacement workers; working from home: communications, health, and safety issues; and counselling services for employees.

connect

Learn more about seven steps for establishing a contingency plan online with Connect.

LO 6

Discuss the scope and implications of workplace violence and bullying.

WORKPLACE VIOLENCE

At 8:13 a.m. on November 12, 2005, Lori Dupont arrived at work as a recovery room nurse at Hotel-Dieu Grace Hospital in Windsor.[57] Forty-five minutes later, just before 9:00 a.m., her former common-law partner, anesthesiologist Dr. Marc Daniel, emerged from behind a pillar in a room she was preparing for a patient and fatally stabbed her seven times in the back and chest with a 15 cm military-style dagger. Not all cases of workplace violence are as horrific as Lori Dupont's experience. But all violent incidents demand an immediate and diligent response from management. Left unaddressed, seemingly less serious incidents of workplace violence can escalate into an ending as tragic and senseless as that experienced by Dupont.

A 2007 report by Statistics Canada stated that there were more than 356,000 incidents of violence in the workplace in Canada in 2004.[58] Moreover, research indicates that 70 percent of victims of domestic violence are victimized at work.[59]

Workplace violence is any act in which a worker is abused, threatened, intimidated, or assaulted in the course of his or her employment. Beyond physical acts of violence, workplace violence can include threats of violence, verbal and emotional abuse, harassment, intimidating and aggressive behaviour (e.g., throwing objects or slamming fists), abusive language toward another person, bullying, stalking, or obsessively focusing on a grudge, grievance, or romantic interest.[60] See the extensive discussion of bullying in the "Competing Through Globalization" box on page 493. Workplace violence does not always occur between two employees. In fact, it more commonly occurs at the hands of customers, clients, patients (in health-care settings), strangers (e.g., in a robbery), or an acquaintance or family member. Violent behaviour can be attributed to many causes, most of which are external to the workplace. However, a stressful or unhappy work environment can aggravate violent tendencies. Moreover, workplace violence is more likely to occur in organizations without an actively promoted and enforced zero-tolerance workplace violence policy, and in which hiring and retention policies do not adequately screen for potentially violent workers.

The physical and psychological effects of workplace violence are substantial, extending beyond the worker directly involved to coworkers and family members. Victims of workplace violence and those affected by it, such as coworkers, may experience a variety of emotional, psychological, and physical responses, which negatively affect the performance of their work, relationships with coworkers, or their ability to return to the workplace to perform work at all. Anxiety, depression, fear, apathy, headaches, and memory impairment are frequent reactions. Loss of concentration, posttraumatic stress disorder and difficulty making decisions are also common responses.[61] As a consequence, workplace violence has grave effects on an organization. Increased sick leave costs, absenteeism, decreased productivity, and increased staff turnover if employees leave the organization as a result of the violence or its effects are all costly to the organization.

Moreover, workplace violence can create liability for the employer in many legal arenas, including in criminal law under the amendments to the *Criminal Code* enacted by Bill C-45, civil law in the form of actions citing negligence, human-rights law in respect of the employer's responsibility to maintain a workplace free of harassment, and in regard to the employer's obligations to take all reasonable precautions to protect its employees pursuant to occupational health and safety legislation.

The increasing level of violence in the workplace has led many jurisdictions to include provisions in their occupational health and safety statutes dealing explicitly with the protection of workers from workplace violence.[62] In Ontario, such provisions come from a recent amendment to the *Occupational Health and Safety Act*, which came into force on June 15, 2010. The Bill 168 amendments were prompted in part by the recommendations of the jury of the coroner's inquest into the 2005 killing of Lori Dupont. Bill 168 defines "workplace violence" as

(a) the exercise of physical force by a person against a worker, in a workplace, that causes or could cause physical injury to the worker,

(b) an attempt to exercise physical force against a worker, in a workplace, that could cause physical injury to the worker,

(c) a statement or behaviour that it is reasonable for a worker to interpret as a threat to exercise physical force against the worker, in a workplace, that could cause physical injury to the worker.[63]

The amendments implemented by Bill 168 impose six general requirements on employers in Ontario:

1. Develop written policies with respect to violence and harassment in the workplace, post those policies in organizations with more than five employees, and review the policies on at least an annual basis.
2. Develop a program to implement and maintain the workplace violence and harassment policies. The program must include measures to control risk, provide for assistance to be summoned immediately when violence occurs, and deal with incidents of violence, threats, and complaints. The contents of the program must be communicated to workers.
3. Assess the risk of workplace violence and communicate the results of the assessment to the JHSC, health and safety representatives, or the workers themselves where no JHSC or safety representative exists.
4. Take reasonable precautions where the employer is aware, or ought to be aware, that violence is likely to expose a worker to the risk of physical injury in the workplace.
5. Provide information to workers about an individual with a history of violence where workers are likely to encounter that person in the course of their work and where there is a risk of physical injury.
6. Allow workers to refuse unsafe work where workplace violence is likely to endanger their safety.

Lori Dupont's story started long before the morning her life was taken by Marc Daniel. Daniel's erratic and harassing behaviour started more than six months before the murder when their relationship of more than two years ended when he attempted suicide at her home in an effort to exert control over her. Like many other cases of violence, Dupont's murder may have been preventable had better steps been taken to protect her at work. What can employers do to prevent workplace violence from occurring in their organizations?

- Secure top management commitment and worker participation.
- Develop a workplace violence prevention policy and program that communicates and enforces a zero-tolerance approach to workplace violence.
- Identify all factors that contribute to workplace violence.
- Assess the potential for violence in the workplace and in respect of particular jobs and shifts.
- Develop and implement systematic controls to eliminate or minimize workplace violence and the risk of workplace violence.
- Monitor, review, and revise the workplace violence prevention measures in the workplace as necessary.
- Develop and implement written emergency notification procedures in response to situations of workplace violence and measures to assist employees who have experienced workplace violence (e.g., victim assistance programs).
- Attempt to resolve all cases of workplace violence and, failing this, appoint a competent person to investigate the matter.
- Provide thorough information, instruction, and training on workplace violence to each employee.[64]

Other jurisdictions in Canada either have their own workplace violence laws or deal with workplace violence through existing health and safety and human-rights laws. Regardless of the actual legal provisions in place, employers in all Canadian jurisdictions would be well served in following the above requirements and recommendations so as to provide a safe and healthy workplace environment that is proactive in trying to prevent workplace violence and promptly deal with it at an early stage.

Competing Through Globalization

The Office Bully

When we hear the term *bully*, for most of us it conjures up images of young boys being scuffed up on the playground, stuffed into lockers, and mugged of their lunch money. But bullying for many persists far beyond the school-age years. Schoolyard bullies often grow up to get jobs, bringing bullying into the workplace. In fact, the International Labour Organization identified workplace bullying as one of the biggest problems in workplaces today.

In recent years, workplace bullying has become a globally recognized workplace health and safety issue, prompting regulatory responses by several countries worldwide. Aside from Canada, France, Germany, Italy, Sweden, Spain, the Netherlands, Norway, Ireland, the United States, and Australia are just some of the countries that are taking a stand against office bullies.

According to the U.S. Workplace Bullying Institute, 53 million Americans or 35 percent of the American workforce has experienced workplace bullying. Another 15 percent say that they have witnessed workplace bullying or known a family member who was bullied at work. The Institute has become an advocate for legislation that has been introduced in 11 states to outlaw what it calls the "silent epidemic." A few years ago, the Indiana Supreme Court upheld a $325,000 jury verdict for an operating-room employee who claimed a cardiovascular surgeon bullied him by advancing "aggressively and rapidly" with "clenched fists, piercing eyes, beet-red face, popping veins, and screaming and swearing." The employee, who was backed into a corner, reported he put his hands up to protect himself, but the surgeon abruptly walked away. The picture of workplace bullying isn't quite what many would expect—starting with the workplace bully herself. That's right—according to the 2010 U.S. Workforce Bullying Institute Survey, bullying, which is four times more prevalent than unlawful harassment, is perpetrated by females against other females 80 percent of the time.

Regardless of a bully's personal characteristics, bullies are characterized by a pervasive pattern of grandiosity and self-importance, the need of admiration, and a lack of empathy.

Distinct from aggression, workplace bullying is often defined by a persistent pattern of mistreatment of an employee by his or her peers or superiors that jeopardizes the employee's health or career. Consisting typically of demeaning, degrading, cruel, vindictive, or malicious offensive behaviour, bullying is designed to humiliate or undermine a person's self-esteem, dignity, and confidence, and may be carried out in such a subtle and surreptitious manner that it is difficult to say who or what is behind it. Bullying frequently involves an abuse of power, leaving victims feeling hurt, angry, frightened, and powerless. A significant loss in productivity and morale is often the result, as well as high rates of absenteeism, sickness, and staff turnover. And in several more tragic cases—suicide.

While bullying may feel like harassment, workplace harassment has a legal definition supported by legislation designed to protect workers from discriminatory mistreatment as a member of a protected group. A small number of bullying cases involve illegal discriminatory harassment. That's because bullying transcends boundaries of status-group membership. It has been said that bullying is status-blind harassment. In the United States, there is currently no federal law protecting workers from bullying; however, 18 states have instituted various forms of the Healthy Workplace Bill, including leading states such as New York, New Jersey, Illinois, and California.

The Healthy Workforce Bill defines its basic cause of action in this statement: "It shall be an unlawful employment practice to subject an employee to an abusive work environment which exists when the defendant, acting with malice, subjects the complainant to abusive conduct so severe that it causes tangible harm to the complainant."

What does bullying look like? It is often invisible, occurring behind closed doors without witnesses. Office bullies may play mind games or use reverse psychology. They are shallow and superficial, lying and deceiving while slyly charming those around them. Insecurity and lack of empathy fuels a cold satisfaction from launching unwarranted and aggressive attacks. In an article for the *Workplace Violence News*, Randi Barenholtz says that bullying is that which a reasonable person would find hostile, offensive, and unrelated to an employer's legitimate business interests. It may include, but is not limited to, repeated infliction of verbal abuse; physical conduct that a reasonable person would find threatening, intimidating, or humiliating; or the gratuitous sabotage or undermining of a person's work performance.

Malice is the desire to see another person suffer psychological, physical, or economical harm, without legitimate cause of justification (such as being provoked). Bullying can also include one or a series of negative employment decisions such as a termination, demotion, unfavourable reassignment, refusal to promote, or disciplinary action.

Barenholtz describes some of the more common forms of bullying at work:

- Spreading malicious rumours;
- Undermining a person's work;
- Threatening physical abuse;
- Constantly changing work guidelines;
- Withholding necessary information or purposefully giving wrong information;
- Pestering, spying, or intruding on one's privacy;
- Assigning unreasonable duties or workload that are unfavourable to one person;
- Underutilizing; creating a feeling of uselessness;
- Yelling or using profanity;
- Criticizing a person persistently;
- Belittling a person's opinions;
- Unwarranted punishment;
- Blocking applications for training, leave, or promotion;
- Tampering with a person's personal belongings or work equipment.

Employers have a vital role in putting an end to bullying in the workplace. Leading by example and implementing and consistently enforcing a zero-tolerance policy for workplace bullying are important first steps. Educating staff on how to recognize, combat, and cope with office bullying is also critical, as is ensuring that human resource professionals are schooled in how to deal with complaints promptly and diligently.

Individuals who believe they are victims of workplace bullying need to realize that they are not alone. They can take control by breaking the silence and speaking up. They should use the help that is available through the human resource department or union, as well as seeking professional help, or the assistance of support groups.

SOURCES: Randi Barenholtz, "The Workplace Bully Affects 35 Percent of the U.S. Workforce," *Workplace Violence News* (January 4, 2011); L.M. Sixel, "Resisting on-the-Job Bullying," *Houston Chronicle* (May 20, 2011); Emily Kimber, "Dealing with Workplace Bullies," *Canadian Living*, at www.canadianliving.com/life/work/dealing_with_workplace_bullies_2.php (retrieved August 3, 2011).

A Look Back

At the opening and throughout this chapter, we have seen illustrations of the importance of workplace health and safety initiatives for HRM. Employers are gaining an appreciation for the benefits of a healthy and safe workplace by investing in health and safety in both traditional and innovative ways. At the opening of the chapter we learned of Loblaw's health and safety plan to improve health and safety and reduce workplace accidents and injuries. In its 2009 Corporate Social Responsibility Report,[65] Loblaw reported that it has already achieved a 36 percent reduction in total accidents. In 2009 alone, total accidents were reduced by 17 percent, meaning that 1,259 fewer employees were injured at work. Lost-time accidents, which cause an employee to miss his or her next shift, also decreased by 17 percent, resulting in 497 fewer lost-time claims.

Questions

1. What are some other health and safety initiatives that a company such as Loblaw could implement as it pursues its road to zero accidents?

2. Assume that you have taken over the HR function at Loblaw and want to make sure that the health and safety plan is comprehensive. You order a safety audit of the organization, which reveals a high level of worker stress and job dissatisfaction. What do you do?

Summary

Protecting the health and safety of employees is an important aspect of HRM strategy. Employees are the most critical asset in an organization. Unsafe and unhealthy workplaces take a tremendous toll not only on individual workers, but also on the organization. The effects of failing to provide a safe and healthy workplace have wide-ranging implications. As we have seen in this chapter, an employer who makes a serious and steadfast commitment to workplace health and safety will reap the rewards not only in respect of maintaining compliance with legal obligations, but also in worker productivity and measurable improvements to the bottom line.

Key Terms

Internal Responsibility System (IRS), 470
Job hazards analysis technique, 482

Occupational health and safety legislation, 469
Safety awareness programs, 482
Unsafe act, 476

Unsafe conditions, 477
Workplace Hazardous Materials Information System (WHMIS), 474

Discussion Questions

1. Occupational health and safety legislation and the core IRS impose legal duties on several workplace stakeholders. However, no duties are placed on the union. Do you think unions should have legal obligations in respect of occupational health and safety laws and a role in the IRS? If so, to what extent?

2. Given the benefits that organizations reap from an effective health and safety management plan, why do you think so many organizations do not implement these initiatives?

3. Having learned of the significant benefits of making health and safety a priority in the organization, you propose implementing some of the initiatives we have discussed in this chapter in your organization. Top executives are not buying into the idea. How do you go about convincing them that your ideas are worth acting on?

4. You have gained commitment from top management to develop and implement a health and safety management plan including a wellness program. How do you get employees to buy into the organization's commitment to health and safety?

5. Many have suggested that occupational health and safety penalties are too weak and misdirected (aimed at employers rather than employees) to have any significant impact on employee safety. Do you think that occupational health and safety–related sanctions need to be strengthened, or are existing penalties sufficient? Explain your answer.

6. Workers' compensation legislation takes away a worker's right to sue in the event of an injury or accident sustained in the course of employment in exchange for his or her employer's participation in the plan and the benefits the worker receives from the board. Do you think this is a good trade-off for workers? For employers? Why? What would be a workable alternative scheme?

7. Do you think occupational health and safety laws dealing with workplace violence such as Bill 168 in Ontario can help to prevent violence in the workplace? Do you think employers should be held accountable in all cases of acts of violence against their workers?

Self-Assessment Exercise

Research tells us that a person's state of wellness directly affects his or her personal health and the health of the organization. To determine where you are on the wellness scale, take the quiz below.

Scale: 5 = almost always   4 = sometimes   3 = undecided   2 = seldom   1 = almost never

I am able to deal with day-to-day pressures.	1 2 3 4 5
I can resolve issues with family members.	1 2 3 4 5
I can establish friendships easily.	1 2 3 4 5
I am comfortable expressing my feelings with others.	1 2 3 4 5
I am considerate of other people's feelings.	1 2 3 4 5
I take responsibility for my own behaviours.	1 2 3 4 5
I am happy with myself.	1 2 3 4 5
I believe my study habits are adequate.	1 2 3 4 5
I am able to handle my personal finances satisfactorily.	1 2 3 4 5
I am able to effectively schedule my time.	1 2 3 4 5
I feel capable of making important decisions.	1 2 3 4 5
I know how to set and reach goals and objectives.	1 2 3 4 5
I understand the value of computer knowledge.	1 2 3 4 5
I have read a nonfiction book (not for class) in the past six months.	1 2 3 4 5
I am able to successfully confront others.	1 2 3 4 5
I like some private time on occasion.	1 2 3 4 5
I feel skillful in human relations.	1 2 3 4 5
I feel secure going places where I may not know anyone.	1 2 3 4 5

I am able to assert myself when necessary.	1	2	3	4	5
I am able to communicate with others effectively.	1	2	3	4	5
I am within 5–10 pounds of my ideal body weight.	1	2	3	4	5
I understand the seriousness of eating disorders.	1	2	3	4	5
I exercise regularly (20–30 minutes three times per week).	1	2	3	4	5
I know and use ways to handle stress.	1	2	3	4	5
I am knowledgeable about birth control.	1	2	3	4	5
I do not smoke.	1	2	3	4	5
I sleep at least six hours per night on most nights.	1	2	3	4	5
I do not abuse alcohol or binge drink.	1	2	3	4	5
I am comfortable with others who have a different sexual orientation than mine.	1	2	3	4	5
I take time for spiritual growth and development.	1	2	3	4	5
I have been challenged in my beliefs before.	1	2	3	4	5
I make attempts to expand my awareness of different ethnic, racial, and religious groups.	1	2	3	4	5
I am tolerant of others' views about life issues.	1	2	3	4	5
I am able to set personal limits in an intimate relationship.	1	2	3	4	5
I have decided on my academic areas of study.	1	2	3	4	5
I have identified career interests, skills, and abilities.	1	2	3	4	5
I understand job search skills (resume writing, interviewing, etc.).	1	2	3	4	5
I know about available campus resources in my area of study.	1	2	3	4	5
I have a good idea about how marriage, family, and career fit together.	1	2	3	4	5
I am aware of the limits of the earth's natural resources.	1	2	3	4	5
I conserve energy.	1	2	3	4	5
I recycle trash as much as possible (paper, cans, bottles, etc.).	1	2	3	4	5
I enjoy, appreciate, and spend time outside in natural settings.	1	2	3	4	5
I understand the concept of ecological balance.	1	2	3	4	5
I do not pollute the air, water, or earth if I can avoid doing so.	1	2	3	4	5

Add each column (i.e., five ones = 5, six twos = 12, etc.)

Now add the columns together. This will be your total score on the Wellness Quiz.

Scoring

Between 176 and 225: You are a very healthy person in all the dimensions and have a well lifestyle.

Between 125 and 175: You are well in some areas but could use improvement in some of the other areas. You could make some changes to take better care of yourself.

Under 125: You tend to have unhealthy habits and an unhealthy lifestyle. Learn some options to make some lifestyle changes.

SOURCE: Personal Wellness Tools and Resources, "Personal Wellness Quiz" at www.definitionofwellness.com/wellness-resources.html.

Exercising Strategy: Shift Work Raises Risk of Work Injury: UBC Study

Canadians who work night shifts and rotating shifts are almost twice as likely to be injured on the job than those working regular day shifts. Women working the night shift are also more prone to injuries than men, particularly if they work rotating shifts. These are the findings of a study by researchers at the University of British Columbia, published in the *Scandinavian Journal of Work, Environment and Health*, written by Imelda Wong, a PhD Candidate at UBC's School of Environmental Health.

After the International Agency for Research on Cancer reported in 2007 that those who work graveyard shifts appear to have an increased risk for all types of cancer, Wong and her team took a closer look to see what other health effects might be caused by night work. Examining data on more than 30,000 Canadians involved in different types of shift work from 1996 to 2006 from Statistics Canada's Survey of Labour and Income Dynamics, Wong's team found that, unlike the overall rate of workplace injuries in Canada during the study period, the injury rate for night shift workers did not drop.

Wong points to sleepiness as the likely culprit. "I think we can all relate to what it feels like to have a sleepless night. We feel a bit groggy the next day," she told CTV's *Canada AM*. "Well, people who work shift work are constantly sleep deprived and may be more fatigued at work and that does increase the risk of injury."

The risks are higher for women, explained Wong, especially if they worked rotating shifts. "We found with women the risk of injury was more pronounced with both rotating and regular night-shift workers, and for men, the risk was highest among those who worked regular night shifts," she said. Women's greater share of the responsibility for child care and household work means that they have more difficulty maintaining regular sleep schedules, suggest the researchers. "On average, women spend nine hours more per week on household duties than men. And women's primary household duties include child care, which involves daily activities that require more alertness," Wong noted.

The study's findings are particularly significant in today's society where production schedules run around the clock, resulting in more and more Canadians working irregular hours. The number of women in rotating and night shift work increased dramatically by 95 percent during the study period, most notably in the health-care sector. For men, the increase was 50 percent, mostly in manufacturing and trades.

More injuries means real and staggering costs to society, the study found. In 2006 alone, there were 307,000 work-related injury claims linked to shift work, tallying more than $50.5 million in costs to Canada's workers' compensation system. Looking at these figures, no one can quarrel with the researchers' conclusion that both employers and governments need to "consider policies and programs to help reduce the risk of injuries among shift workers."

SOURCES: "Shift Work Raises Risk of Work Injury: UBC Study," *CTV News* (November 3, 2010); "Shift Work Linked to Higher Risk of Work Injury, Canadian Study Finds," *ScienceDaily* (November 3, 2010). at www.sciencedaily.com/releases/2010/11/101102131001.htm (retrieved August 4, 2011).

Questions

1. What kind of health and safety initiatives can organizations implement to reduce the negative effects of the night shift?

2. Do you think that employers should be prohibited from allowing a sleep-deprived worker from working his or her shift? Explain your answer. What kinds of processes could employers put in place to implement this practice?

Managing People: Sustaining Health and Safety Excellence

Few would argue that workplace health and safety is a worthwhile priority. Although turning health and safety objectives into a reality can be an arduous and lengthy task, a dedicated and systematic approach can do wonders for an organization's health and safety record and earn it top marks from health and safety advocates such as the Industrial Accident Prevention Association (IAPA), Canada's leading workplace health and safety organization.

Not too long ago, John Deere Welland Works, which produces front loaders for agricultural and compact utility tractors, rotary cutters, and utility vehicles, was an average safety performer among John Deere's North American facilities. Seeking to turn that record around, the facility implemented a newfound commitment to health safety that was so successful it was chosen to host a Health and Safety Best Practice visit in 2007 as an example for the company's other facilities.

Just how did the facility turn its health and safety vision into a reality? First it hired health and safety director Shawn Finlay. "My job was to make sure safety was here to support the business," explained Finlay. Although the safety department had management's full commitment, it had not been well integrated within the facility's operations.

Finlay and his team implemented several initiatives to help raise safety awareness, drive accountability, and reduce unsafe behaviour: for example, Dupont STOP (safety training observation program), which identifies workers who are performing safely and draws attention to what they're doing in a positive manner; a behaviour-based safety training program called ALERT; continuous improvement teams; and other measures that made health and safety a priority that was both seen and heard.

Finlay also hired co-op students from the University of Waterloo's kinesiology program for four-month placements. The students identified ergonomic risks across the operation and developed a proactive musculoskeletal disorder prevention program. They also redesigned fixtures to reduce or eliminate difficult or awkward manual tasks, including inventing sticks fitted with magnetic ends to reduce bending to pick up metal parts, and introduced ergonomic awareness training where participants learned how to recognize and control awkward work positions.

Instead of merely tracking injuries, Finlay began to identify root causes and take corrective action. Employees were informed about the company's improvements in lost-time injury rates and its enhanced safety program. A positive safety culture began to permeate the workplace, putting safety at the forefront of everyone's mind.

A rigorous housekeeping process has done its part to virtually eliminate injuries from physical hazards and establish a consistent, orderly environment, "because everything has a place now," he says. "Every tool has its place. Everything is properly labelled. We looked at sight lines, space in the work stations, removed unnecessary items that don't add value to our product ... "The result is pride in the workplace, as well as the discipline to maintain it and to continuously improve."

Finlay's efforts have paid off. Of the 46 John Deere plants globally, Welland's safety record improved to rank among the top 10.

According to Finlay, Welland's strides toward safety wouldn't have happened without the commitment from senior management. Safety issues are reviewed with the general manager every morning, and discussed every day with business managers and weekly with staff management. All levels of management participate in the STOP observation program, and the general manager routinely participates in accident investigations. "You're not where you want to be if the safety person is running around doing everything. Everyone is now engaged, including workers, supervisors, and senior management."

"Safety is a never-ending journey," says general manager Donald De Bastiani. "There will always be aspects of our program that can be improved."

Honeywell Specialty Chemicals, a producer of some of the industry's most hazardous materials, also has earned recognition as a leader in workplace health and safety excellence.

Plant manager Dean Palmer explains how Honeywell puts safety first: "Within Honeywell's specialty materials division, which includes Amherstburg, every manager at every level understands that health and safety has to be a fundamental part of how we operate. It is how we operate. If you can't do that successfully, then you don't have a license to operate."

It's not just about health and safety, says Palmer, it's about business. "As the world's leading producer of hydrofluoric acid, Honeywell has recognized that if you don't take the measures to protect the health, safety, and well-being of your workers at a very high level, you're just not sure that you can operate effectively ... There's no grey area. If you're not working safely, you're not working successfully," says Palmer.

Giovanni Grande, environmental safety manager of Honeywell's Amherstburg, Ontario, facility, explains how Honeywell's dedication to health and safety is achieved on a day-to-day basis: "The Amherstburg facility has created a healthy workplace culture where everyone is a step ahead of potential hazards. Workers talk about safety at the start of every shift. During the shift, if someone noticed a coworker's shoe was untied or saw a protruding piece of piping, he or she would alert workers affected, saying 'Heads up, there's a hazard here.'

"From a technical perspective, we had always had tight policies and procedures. But to get to zero and really drill down the things that need to be embedded in people's psyche, you need to address the cultural aspects of health and safety."

Central to Honeywell's health and safety culture is the Structured Safety Process, designed to involve all levels of the organization in safety performance and covering every conceivable aspect of health and safety from meetings and committees to contractor safety and emergency response.

Anticipating safety challenges and issues is an important component of the program. "We'll look at a situation and say, what could go wrong with this? Or what if we lost power in the building? How would we get out of the building safely?"

Honeywell also takes a proactive approach to meeting its personal protective equipment needs—a commitment the Industrial Accident Prevention Association (IAPA) found particularly impressive. In 2000, Honeywell teamed up with two of its suppliers, Draeger Canada and Respirex Inc., to incorporate an acid splash hood into a supplied air breathing system. In 2006 they improved upon the original design so that it works with an air-purifying respirator system that is not tethered, fully protects the eyes, and is sealed around the face. Honeywell also worked with Respirex Inc. to develop rubber pants and a rubber jacket to protect workers from acids.

The IAPA found the plant's wellness initiatives notable as well. In addition to employing a full-time occupational health nurse, an occupational health physician is on site once a week. "We take care of workers as their family doctor would," says Grande. For example, "the average employee's age is 48, so we check the prostates, do blood work, and run cholesterol tests." Three individuals have been diagnosed with elevated prostate-specific antigens and two with elevated cholesterol in the past two years.

"There is an ethical and economic basis supporting our efforts in this area," says Grande. "Our associates' performance, alertness, and safety at work is affected by many factors outside of work, and the better we understand and assist in caring for them, the less likely that one of these conditions will become a factor in their working environment, thereby decreasing the risk of injury or illness."

To companies that strive to create a healthy workplace, Grande offers this advice: "You can't do everything at once. You need a well-defined and realistic plan, and you can't deviate from that plan. If you do, then have a recovery position."

Questions

1. What were the keys to achieving health and safety success for these companies?

2. What are the principles of the approaches applied by John Deere Welland Works and Honeywell that can be applied to other organizations?

3. Both companies have gone beyond what their legal occupational health and safety obligations require. Do you think employers should be legally required to implement the types of initiatives outlined in this article? Why or why not?

SOURCES: "Honeywell Receives Top Level IAPA Health and Safety Award," *The Amherstburg Echo* at www.amherstburgecho.com/ArticleDisplay.aspx?archive=true&e=1921154 (retrieved August 4, 2011); Robert Lee, "Achieving Award-winning Performance," *Accident Prevention e-News* (August 2008).

 **Practise and learn online with Connect.**

Managing Human Resources Globally

Enter the World of Business

From Nunavut to Kosovo: Powering Change and Renewal

The story of FreeBalance Inc. may one day be immortalized in the mythology that we usually reserve for our favourite superheroes. Indeed it is rare for a company to become renowned for battling the wages of war, corruption, and injustice, and restoring order in the world, but that's what this financial management software firm has done in the past and continues to do today—all over the world.

Things started quietly, and the beginnings of FreeBalance were modest and ordinary. Founded in Ottawa in 1984 as Linktek Corporation, the company cut its teeth as a privately held consulting firm specializing in financial software services. After developing a financial management system based on government accounting principles, it acquired the Natural Sciences and Engineering Research Council (NSERC) as its first customer. The word soon spread and the company's financial management system's robust qualities made it the system of choice among Canadian government departments. FreeBalance soon realized it was in the right place at the right time with its ability to lend muscle to public service renewal and decentralization of public finance, a phenomenon then commencing in Canada and many other industrialized countries. FreeBalance kept its focus on government and there were no hints that its real destiny, like that of superheroes, would be played out around the globe. That is, until the Government of Nunavut selected FreeBalance to set up its system of financial accounts and controls, getting Canada's newest territory off to a sound fiscal beginning. It was this event that revealed to FreeBalance the real power of its unique technology, and an understanding of the types of clients that needed it most. With the Nunavut experience now powering the company, FreeBalance began to share its story more widely and to shift its vision to a more altruistic purpose. Soon it would be helping devastated countries work through complex transitions associated with massive change, reconstruction, and fiscal restoration.

The first such opportunity for FreeBalance to see how truly powerful its systems could be arrived in June 1999. That was when the UN Administration Mission in Kosovo (UNMIK) chose FreeBalance to provide the financial management system needed to stabilize the country financially. In such delicate situations, speed is of the essence and the FreeBalance system was operational in 26 days, leading experts at the World Bank to endorse it as the "defacto standard for post-conflict countries where fast deployment is crucial to achieve stability." Since Kosovo, the list of countries and citizens helped by FreeBalance has mushroomed. That led to changes in the way the company had to staff its operations. Most of the work the company now does is far beyond Canadian borders, in remote and tumultuous locations around the world. Small wonder the Jobs page of the FreeBalance website invites applicants to "Make a difference in the world," working with teams in Mongolia, Uganda, Guyana, Afghanistan, Liberia, Sierra Leone, and East Timor (to name a few).

In the past dozen years, this unique Canadian company has ascended into the realm of "flexible global citizenship" as its software repowers one after another of the most disadvantaged countries in the world, delivering development outcomes such as improving the quality of life, health care, and service to citizens, as well as reducing poverty. Small wonder this company, which seeks "strategic thinkers and overachievers who absorb customer problems and articulate thoughtful creative solutions" has an 18–20 percent annual growth rate, and now manages annual budgets worth a quarter trillion ($US) worldwide. It was also named a 2009 Winner of the Canada Export Achievement Awards, but it's clearly more than profit that drives this firm, and there's a reason the company warns job applicants to be ready for the adventure of their professional life. As Manuel Pietra, CEO of FreeBalance, says, "When you have the ability to sell a product that you know is going to improve conditions in a country, you really participate in shaping a nation." It would seem a mere glance at the headlines indicates no end of opportunities for this raised-in-Bytown, global, high-tech company, whose middle name could easily be Sustainability. As Pietra says, "We've seen the transformation of countries that use our software." Not many companies in the world can say that. But then, not many are superheroes either.

SOURCES: Based on "Software Saviours," 2009 Winner Canada Export Achievement Awards Awards at www.exportawards.ca/exportawards/ontario.html (retrieved August 1, 2011); and FreeBalance company website, Company Overview, History and Jobs at www.freebalance.com (retrieved December 12, 2010).

INTRODUCTION

As our opening vignette indicates, the environment in which business competes is rapidly globalizing. More and more Canadian companies, like FreeBalance, are entering international markets by exporting their products overseas, building plants in other countries, and entering into alliances with foreign companies. In 2009, Canadian exports of goods and services totalled $401.8 billion, suffering a 23.6 percent decline brought on by recessionary pressures and with record lows of trade flows in 2009. However, growth of overall exports at 12 percent was indicated for 2010 followed by additional but more moderate gains beyond that.[1]

Indeed, most organizations now function in the global economy. Thus, North American businesses are entering international markets at the same time foreign companies are entering the North American market. Companies are attempting to gain a competitive advantage, which can be provided by international expansion in a number of ways. First, countries with emerging economies are new markets with large numbers of potential customers. For companies that are producing below their capacity, they provide a means of increasing sales and profits. Second, many companies are building production facilities in other countries as a means of capitalizing on those countries' lower labour costs for relatively unskilled jobs. For example, many of the *maquiladora* plants (foreign-owned plants located in Mexico that employ Mexican labourers) provide low-skilled labour at considerably lower cost than in the Canada. In 2008, the average manufacturing hourly wage in Mexico was $2.75, versus more than $25.74 in Canada.[2] Third, the rapid increase in telecommunications and information technology enables work to be done more rapidly, efficiently, and effectively around the globe. With the best university graduates available for $2.00 an hour in India versus $12–$18 an hour in Canada, companies can hire the best talent at a lower cost. And because their day is our night, work done in Canada can be handed off to those in India for a 24/7 work process.[3]

According to a survey of almost 3,000 line executives and HR executives from 12 countries, international competition is the number-one factor affecting HRM. The globalization of business structures and globalization of the economy ranked fourth and fifth, respectively.[4] Deciding whether to enter foreign markets and whether to develop plants or other facilities in other countries, however, is no simple matter, and many human resource issues surface. These include the need to ensure production quality remains high when plants are relocated (to avoid massive recalls), and consideration of ethical issues when operating in environments where human rights are not protected by law and unsafe working conditions prevail.

This chapter discusses the human resource issues that must be addressed to gain competitive advantage in a world of global competition. This is not a chapter on international human resource management (the specific HRM policies and programs companies use to manage human resources across international boundaries).[5] The chapter focuses instead on the key factors that must be addressed to strategically manage human resources in an international context. We discuss some of the important events that have increased the global nature of business over the past few years. We then identify some of the factors that are most important to HRM in global environments. Finally, we examine major issues related to managing expatriate managers. These issues present unique opportunities for firms to gain competitive advantage.

CURRENT GLOBAL CHANGES

Several recent social and political changes have accelerated the movement toward international competition. The effects of these changes have been profound and far reaching. Many are still evolving. In this section we discuss the major developments that have accentuated the need for organizations to gain a competitive advantage through effectively managing human resources in a global economy.

LO 1

Identify the recent changes that have caused companies to expand into international markets.

European Economic Union

European countries have managed their economies individually for years. Because of the countries' close geographic proximity, their economies have become intertwined. This created a number of problems for international businesses; for example, the regulations of one country, such as France, might be completely different from those of another country, such as Germany. In response, six European countries agreed through the Treaty of Rome in 1957 to participate in the European Economic Community (EEC) or "common market" to foster economic and political cooperation. The concept was later expanded, and more countries joined the European Union (EU) established under the Treaty of Maastricht in 1993, which also laid groundwork for development of a single currency among member countries. The EU is a confederation of most of the European nations agreeing to engage in free trade with one another, with commerce regulated by an overseeing body called the European Commission (EC). Within the European Union, legal regulation in the participating countries has become more, although not completely, uniform, and the EU has continued to attract more members. In addition to the previous 15 EU states, as of January 1, 2007, 12 EU accession states—Bulgaria, Cyprus, the Czech Republic, Estonia, Hungary, Latvia, Lithuania, Malta, Poland, Romania, Slovakia, and Slovenia—were added to the EU, expanding the economic zone covered by the European Union to 27 countries. In addition, since 1999, 12 members of the

European Union, and a number of territories such as Andorra and Monaco, have shared a common currency, the euro. This ties the members' economic fates even more closely with one another and although Sweden, Denmark, and the U.K. do not use the euro, Europe has become one of the largest free markets in the world. In addition, the political activities of the European Union have expanded over time, and now include development aid, environmental advocacy, and promotion of human rights and democracy.[6]

North American Free Trade Agreement

The North American Free Trade Agreement (NAFTA) is an agreement among Canada, the United States, and Mexico that has created a free market even larger than the European Economic Community. The United States and Canada already had a free trade agreement since 1989, but NAFTA brought Mexico into the consortium. The agreement was prompted by Mexico's increasing willingness to open its markets and facilities in an effort to promote economic growth.[7] As previously discussed, the *maquiladora* plants exemplify this trend. In addition, some efforts have been made to expand the membership of NAFTA to other Latin American countries, such as Chile.

NAFTA has increased North American investment in Mexico because of Mexico's substantially lower labour costs for low-skilled employees. This has had two effects on employment in North America. First, many low-skilled jobs went south, decreasing employment opportunities for Canadians and Americans who lack higher-level skills. Second, it has increased employment opportunities for Canadians and Americans with higher-level skills beyond those already being observed.[8]

The Growth of Asia

Another important global market lies in Asia. Whereas Japan has been a dominant economic force for over 20 years, recently countries such as Singapore, Hong Kong, and Malaysia have become significant economic forces. In addition, China, with its population of more than 1 billion and trend toward opening its markets to foreign investors, presents a tremendous potential market for goods. In fact, a consortium of Singaporean companies and governmental agencies has jointly developed with China a huge industrial township in eastern China's Suzhou City that will consist of ready-made factories for sale to foreign companies.[9] While Asia has been affected by the recent recession, the main impact has been to only slow its rate of growth. Brazil has also become a major growth market, and indeed it has been speculated that Brazil, Russia, India and China (the BRIC countries) which are now among the largest 10 economies in the world, may overtake most current major economic powers by 2050. Indeed, China may well become the largest economic power in the world much sooner.

General Agreement on Tariffs and Trade

The General Agreement on Tariffs and Trade (GATT) is an international framework of rules and principles for reducing trade barriers around the world. It currently consists of more than 100 member nations. The most recent round of GATT negotiations resulted in an agreement to cut tariffs (taxes on imports) by 40 percent, reduce government subsidies to businesses, expand protection of intellectual property such as copyrights and patents, and establish rules for investing and trading in services. GATT also established the World Trade Organization (WTO) to resolve disputes among GATT members.

These changes—the European Union, NAFTA, the growth of Asia, and GATT—all exemplify events that are pushing companies to compete in a global economy. These developments are opening new markets and new sources of technology and labour in a way that has never been seen in history. However, this era of increasing international competition accentuates the need to manage human resources effectively to gain competitive advantage in a global marketplace. This requires understanding some of the factors that can determine the effectiveness of various HRM practices and approaches.

FACTORS AFFECTING HRM IN GLOBAL MARKETS

Companies that enter global markets must recognize that these markets are not simply mirror images of their home country. Countries differ along a number of dimensions that influence the attractiveness of direct foreign investment in each country. These differences determine the economic viability of building an operation in a foreign location, and they have a particularly strong impact on HRM in the new foreign operation. Researchers in international management have identified a number of factors that can affect HRM in global markets, and we focus on four factors, as depicted in Figure 13.1: culture, education—human capital, the political–legal system, and the economic system.[10]

LO 2
Discuss the four factors that most strongly influence HRM in international markets.

Culture

By far the most important factor influencing international HRM is the culture of the country in which a facility is located. Culture is defined as "the set of important assumptions (often unstated) that members of a community share."[11] These assumptions consist of beliefs about the world and how it works and the ideals that are worth striving for.[12]

Culture is important to HRM for two reasons. First, it often determines the other three factors affecting HRM in global markets. Culture can greatly affect a country's laws, in that laws are often the codification of right and wrong as defined by the culture. Culture also affects human

FIGURE 13.1   Factors Affecting Human Resource Management in International Markets

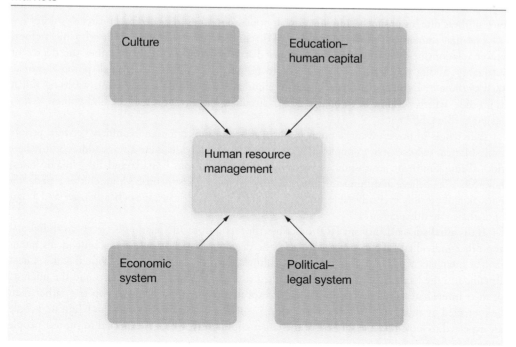

capital, because if education is greatly valued by the culture, then members of the community try to increase their human capital. Finally, as we discuss later, cultures and economic systems are closely intertwined.[13]

However, the most important reason that culture is important to HRM is that it often determines the effectiveness of various HRM practices. Practices found to be effective in Canada and the rest of North America may not be effective in a culture that has different beliefs and values.[14] For example, Canadian companies rely heavily on individual performance appraisal, and rewards are tied to individual performance. In Japan, however, individuals are expected to subordinate their wishes and desires to those of the larger group. Thus, individual-based evaluation and incentives are not nearly as effective there and, in fact, are seldom observed among Japanese organizations.[15]

In this section we examine a model that attempts to characterize different cultures. This model illustrates why culture can have a profound influence on HRM.

Hofstede's Cultural Dimensions In a classic study of culture, Geert Hofstede identified four dimensions on which various cultures could be classified.[16] In a later study conducted with Canadian Michael Bond, he added a fifth dimension that aids in characterizing cultures.[17] The relative cross-cultural value comparisons of Japan, Mexico, Canada, West Africa and the United States on all five dimensions are shown in Table 13.1. It is important to understand that although the scores for the 10 countries included in Table 13.1 appear to measure only whether each country scores high, medium, or low on (power distance (PD), individualism (ID), masculinity (MA), uncertainty avoidance (UA), and long-term orientation (LT), the range of scores creates a continuum that implies conceptual opposites. When examined at the country (societal) level of analysis, the distribution of scores creates two opposite poles for each of Hofstede's dimensions. Thus, the opposite of individualism is collectivism. If a country scores low on the individualism (ID) dimension, its score will then appear near the opposite end of the continuum, meaning it is collectivist in nature. Likewise if a country scores low on masculinity (MA), the culture is considered to be feminine. Finally, when examining cultural attitudes toward time, countries that score low on long-term orientation (LT) are considered to have a short-term orientation toward time. Next, we will describe each of these dimensions including the terms for polar opposites indicated by Hofstede's studies.

The first dimension, **power distance (PD),** concerns how a culture deals with hierarchical power relationships—particularly the unequal distribution of power. It describes the degree of inequality among people that is considered to be normal. Cultures with small power distance, such as those of Denmark and Israel, seek to eliminate inequalities in power and wealth as much as possible, whereas countries with large power distances, such as India and the Philippines, seek to maintain those differences.

Differences in power distance often result in miscommunication and conflicts between people from different cultures. For example, in Mexico and Japan individuals are always addressed by their titles (Señor Smith or Smith-san, respectively). Individuals from Canada and the United States, however, often believe in minimizing power distances by using first names. Although this is perfectly normal, and possibly even advisable among Canadians and Americans, it can be offensive and a sign of disrespect in other cultures.

Individualism–collectivism (ID) describes the strength of the relation between an individual and other individuals in the society—that is, the degree to which people act as individuals rather than as members of a group. In individualist cultures, such as Canada and the United States, Great Britain, and the Netherlands, people are expected to look after their own interests and the interests of their immediate families. The individual is expected to stand on her own two feet rather than be protected by the group. In collectivist cultures, such as Colombia, Pakistan, and Taiwan, people are expected to look after the interest of the larger community, which is expected to protect people when they are in trouble.

Power Distance
One of Hofstede's cultural dimensions; describes how a culture deals with hierarchical power relationships.

Individualism–Collectivism
One of Hofstede's cultural dimensions; describes the strength of the relation between an individual and other individuals in a society.

Table 13.1 Cross-Cultural Value Comparisons

	PD[a]	ID	MA	UA	LT
Canada	39 L[b]	80 H	52 M	48 L	23 L
United States	40 L	91 H	62 H	46 L	29 L
Germany	35 L	67 H	66 H	65 M	31 M
Japan	54 M	45 M	95 H	92 H	80 H
France	68 H	71 H	43 M	86 H	30[c] L
Netherlands	38 L	80 H	14 L	53 M	44 M
Hong Kong	68 H	25 L	57 H	29 L	96 H
Indonesia	78 H	14 L	46 M	48 L	25[c] L
West Africa	77 H	20 L	46 M	54 M	16 L
Russia	95[c] H	50[c] M	40[c] L	90[c] H	10[c] L
China	80[c] H	20[c] L	50[c] M	60[c] M	118 H

[a]PD = power distance; ID = individualism; MA = masculinity; UA = uncertainty avoidance; LT = long-term orientation.

[b]H = top third; M = medium third; L = bottom third (among 53 countries and regions for the first four dimensions; among 23 countries for the fifth). Remember that a country such as China, which scores low in individualism (20L), is considered to be collectivist in nature. This is because collectivism is the opposite of individualism, which is the only cultural dimension being measured.).

[c]Estimated.

SOURCES: Geert Hofstede, "Cultural Constraints in Management Theories," *Academy of Management Executive,* February 1993, Vol. 7, No. 1, p. 91; Geert Hofstede (2005), *Cultures and Organizations: Software of the Mind.* Copyright 2005 Geert Hofstede, pp. 43, 79, 121, 169, 211. Copyright © 1993 by the Academy of Management (NY). Reproduced with permission of the Academy of Management (NY), via the Copyright Clearance Center.

The **masculinity–femininity dimension (MA)** describes the division of roles between the sexes within a society. In "masculine" cultures, such as those of Germany and Japan, what are considered traditionally masculine values—showing off, achieving something visible, and making money—permeate the society. These societies stress assertiveness, performance, success, and competition. "Feminine" cultures, such as those of Sweden and Norway, promote values that have been traditionally regarded as feminine, such as putting relationships before money, helping others, and preserving the environment. These cultures stress service, care for the weak, and solidarity.

The fourth dimension, **uncertainty avoidance (UA),** describes how cultures seek to deal with the fact that the future is not perfectly predictable. It is defined as the degree to which people in a culture prefer structured over unstructured situations. Some cultures, such as those of Singapore and Jamaica, have weak uncertainty avoidance. They socialize individuals to accept this uncertainty and take each day as it comes. People from these cultures tend to be rather easygoing and flexible regarding different views. Other cultures, such as those of Greece and Portugal, socialize their people to seek security through technology, law, and religion. Thus these cultures provide clear rules as to how one should behave.

Finally, the fifth dimension comes from the philosophy of the Far East and is referred to as the **long-term/short-term orientation (LT).** Cultures high on the long-term orientation focus on the future and hold values in the present, such as thrift (saving) and persistence, that will not necessarily provide an immediate benefit. Hofstede found that many Far Eastern countries such as Japan and

Masculinity–Femininity Dimension
One of Hofstede's cultural dimensions; describes the division of roles between the sexes within a society.

Uncertainty Avoidance
One of Hofstede's cultural dimensions; describes how cultures seek to deal with an unpredictable future.

Long-Term/Short-Term Orientation
One of Hofstede's cultural dimensions; describes how a culture balances immediate benefits with future rewards.

China have a long-term orientation. These cultures are oriented toward the past and present, and promote respect for tradition and for fulfilling social obligations. Short-term orientations, on the other hand, are found in North America, Russia, and West Africa.

The current Japanese criticism of management practices in North America illustrates the differences in long-term/short-term orientation. Japanese managers, traditionally exhibiting a long-term orientation, engage in 5- to 10-year planning. This leads them to criticize North American managers, who are traditionally much more short term in orientation because their planning often consists of quarterly to yearly time horizons.

These five dimensions help us understand the potential problems of managing employees from different cultures. Later in this chapter we will explore how these cultural dimensions affect the acceptability and utility of various HRM practices. However, it is important to note that these differences can have a profound influence on whether a company chooses to enter a given country. One interesting finding of Hofstede's research was the impact of culture on a country's economic health. He found that countries with individualist cultures were wealthier; collectivist cultures with high power distance were all poor.[18] Cultures seem to affect a country's economy through their promotion of individual work ethics and incentives for individuals to increase their human capital.

connect

Learn more about Hofstede's dimensions by comparing the Individualism Index (IDV) and national wealth online with Connect.

Implications of Culture for HRM   Cultures have an important impact on approaches to managing people. As we discuss later, the culture can strongly affect the education–human capital of a country, the political–legal system, and the economic system. As Hofstede found, culture also has a profound impact on a country's economic health by promoting certain values that either aid or inhibit economic growth.

More important to this discussion, however, is that cultural characteristics influence the ways managers behave in relation to subordinates, as well as the perceptions of the appropriateness of various HRM practices. First, cultures differ strongly on things such as how subordinates expect leaders to lead, how decisions are handled within the hierarchy, and (most important) what motivates individuals. For example, in Germany, managers achieve their status by demonstrating technical skills, so employees look to them to assign their tasks and resolve technical problems. In the Netherlands, on the other hand, managers focus on seeking consensus among all parties and must engage in an open-ended exchange of views and balancing of interests.[19] Clearly, these methods have different implications for selecting and training managers in the different countries.

Second, cultures may influence the appropriateness of HRM practices. For example, the extent to which a culture promotes an individualistic versus a collectivist orientation will impact the effectiveness of individually oriented human resource management systems. In North America, companies often focus selection systems on assessing an individual's technical skill and, to a lesser extent, social skills. In collectivist cultures, on the other hand, companies focus more on assessing how well an individual will perform as a member of the work group.

Similarly, cultures can influence compensation systems. Individualistic cultures such as those found in North America often exhibit great differences between the highest and lowest-paid individuals in an organization, with the highest-paid individual often receiving 200 times the salary of the lowest. Collectivist cultures, on the other hand, tend to have much flatter salary structures, with the top-paid individual receiving only about 20 times the overall pay of the lowest-paid one.

Cultural differences can affect the communication and coordination processes in organizations. Collectivist cultures, as well as those with less of an authoritarian orientation, value group decision making and participative management practices more highly than do individualistic cultures. When

Evidence-Based HR

While national culture is important, recent research also suggests that its importance may be overstated. Researchers re-examining Hofstede's original work found that while differences existed across nations, significant cultural differences also existed within nations. They further found that the differences in cultures across organizations within countries was larger than the differences across countries. For example, even though both are universities operating within Canada, the culture of Simon Fraser differs substantially from that of McGill (or even the University of Alberta in a neighbouring province.) These results do not imply that one should ignore national culture, but rather that it is important to obtain accurate and current information, engage in critical thinking, and understand important cultural differences at a more micro level than how individuals behave nationally. It's also important to understand changes occurring in the workforce of any country an organization is operating in, particularly because of the growth of globalization and increasing presence and influence of multinational companies now operating where they did not do so in such great numbers before.

It means that certain Canadian HR practices such as pay for performance should not be eliminated from consideration when entering a country such as China, which is very low in individualism and very high in long-term orientation, quite opposite to Canada and the United States, where such practices are used regularly and with great effect. Nor should performance appraisals or merit bonuses (which operate best with a short-term orientation of a year or less) be eliminated from consideration in China. Indeed you will recall the recent implementation of high salaries and performance-based pay among state-owned bank executives in China, discussed in Chapter 9 in this text. In addition, recall that Home Depot made a well-considered decision to implement performance appraisals as part of its HR strategy for managing employees in its new stores in China. Indeed, despite cultural tradition and state funding, Chinese computer manufacturer Lenovo has implemented a merit bonus program, a benefits program, and significant pay differentials among its employees to increase company performance and competitiveness. None of these compensation approaches fit with the stereotype of China as a collective society, but they do indicate that nothing should be assumed in an era of globalization.

In addition, people of varying cultural backgrounds within a nation will be drawn to organizations whose cultures better match their individual, as opposed to national, value systems. For example, a young Japanese worker may grow tired of waiting years for recognition and higher pay in a culture where pay is linked to seniority and decide to "jump ship" to a foreign firm that places less emphasis on age and more emphasis on performance and career development.

All of this means that while managers and HR professionals should be well aware of Hofstede's research and use it as a general guide, they should also do additional research to ensure they are using the most effective human resources practices possible in a changing world where the past, present, and future continue to collide and reshape our notions of "culture."

SOURCES: B. Gerhart and M. Fang, "National Culture and Human Resource Management: Assumptions and Evidence," *International Journal of Human Resource Management* (June 2005), pp. 971–86; G. Milkovich, J. Newman and N. Cole, *Compensation,* (3rd Canadian Edition), McGraw Hill Ryerson, 2010, pp. 318–319.

a person raised in an individualistic culture must work closely with those from a collectivist culture, communication problems and conflicts often appear. As discussed in Chapter 6, much of the emphasis on "cultural diversity" programs in organizations focuses on understanding the cultures of others in order to better communicate with them.

Education–Human Capital

A company's potential to find and maintain a qualified workforce is an important consideration in any decision to expand into a foreign market. Thus, a country's human capital resources can be an important HRM issue. *Human capital* refers to the productive capabilities of individuals—that is, the knowledge, skills, and experience that have economic value.[20]

A country's human capital is determined by a number of variables and therefore countries differ in their levels of human capital. For example, as discussed in Chapter 1, Canada will soon suffer from a human capital shortage in certain areas where jobs being created require skills beyond those of most new entrants into the workforce. A major variable is the educational opportunities available to the labour force. In the Netherlands, for instance, government funding of school systems allows students to go all the way through graduate school without paying.[21] Similarly, the free education provided to citizens in the former Soviet bloc resulted in high levels of human capital, in spite of the poor infrastructure and economy that resulted from the socialist economic systems. In contrast, some developing countries, such as Nicaragua and Haiti, have relatively low levels of human capital because of a lack of investment in education.

A country's human capital may profoundly affect a foreign company's desire to locate there or enter that country's market. Countries with low human capital attract facilities that require low skills and low wage levels. This explains why some North American companies have moved their unionized low-skill/high-wage manufacturing and assembly jobs to Mexico, where they could obtain low-skilled workers for substantially lower wages. Similarly, Japan ships its messy, low-skill work to neighbouring countries while maintaining its high-skill work at home.[22] Countries such as Mexico, with relatively low levels of human capital, might not be as attractive for operations that consist of more high-skill jobs.

Countries with high human capital are attractive sites for direct foreign investment that creates high-skill jobs. In Ireland, for example, more than 25 percent of 18-year-olds attend college, a rate much higher than other European countries. In addition, Ireland's economy supports only 1.1 million jobs for a population of 3.5 million. The combination of high education levels, a strong work ethic, and high unemployment made the country attractive for foreign firms (prior to the country's recent economic crisis) because of the resulting high productivity and low turnover. Similarly, the skills of newly graduated technology workers in India are as high or higher than those found among their counterparts in North America. In addition, because jobs are not as plentiful in India, the worker attitudes are better in many of these locations.[23]

The Political–Legal System

The regulations imposed by a country's legal system can strongly affect HRM. The political–legal system often dictates the requirements for certain HRM practices, such as training, compensation, hiring, firing, and layoffs. In large part, the legal system is an outgrowth of the culture in which it exists. Thus, the laws of a particular country often reflect societal norms about what constitutes legitimate behaviour.[24]

For example, Canada has been a world leader in eliminating discrimination in the workplace. Because of the importance this has in our culture, we also have human rights legislation such as employment equity laws (discussed in Chapter 3) that strongly affect the hiring and firing practices of firms. As a society, we also have strong beliefs regarding the equity of pay systems; thus, pay equity laws are emphasized and the provincial employment standards acts (discussed in Chapter 11), among other laws and regulations, set the minimum wage for a variety of jobs. We also have regulations that dictate much of the process for negotiation between unions and management. These regulations profoundly affect the ways human resources are managed in Canada.

Similarly, the legal regulations regarding HRM in other countries reflect their societal norms. For example, in Germany employees have a legal right to "codetermination" at the company, plant, and individual levels. At the company level, a firm's employees have direct influence on the important decisions that affect them, such as large investments or new strategies. This is brought about through having employee representatives on the supervisory council *(Aufsichtsrat)*. At the plant level, codetermination exists through works councils. These councils have no rights in the economic management of the company, but they can influence HRM policies on issues such as working hours, payment methods, hiring, and transfers. Finally, at the individual level, employees have contractual rights, such as the right to read their personnel files and the right to be informed about how their pay is calculated.[25]

The origins of the European Union provide another example of the effects of the political–legal system on HRM. Still known at the time as the European Economic Community (EEC), the EEC's Charter of December 9, 1989, provides for the fundamental social rights of workers. These rights include freedom of movement, freedom to choose one's occupation and be fairly compensated, guarantee of social protection via social security benefits, freedom of association and collective bargaining, equal treatment for men and women, and a safe and healthful work environment, among others.

Economic System

A country's economic system influences HRM in a number of ways. As previously discussed, a country's culture is integrally tied to its economic system, and these systems provide many of the incentives for developing human capital. In socialist economic systems there are ample opportunities for developing human capital because the education system is free. However, under these systems, there is little economic incentive to develop human capital because there are no monetary rewards for increasing human capital. In addition, in former Soviet bloc countries, an individual's investment in human capital did not always result in a promotion. Rather, it was investment in the Communist Party that led to career advancements.

In capitalist systems the opposite situation exists. There is less opportunity to develop human capital without higher costs. (You have probably observed tuition increases at Canadian universities.) However, those who do invest in their individual human capital, particularly through education, are more able to reap monetary rewards, thus providing more incentive for such investment. In North America, individuals' salaries usually reflect differences in human capital (high-skill workers receive higher compensation than low-skill workers). In fact, research estimates that an individual's wages increase by between 10 and 16 percent for each additional year of schooling.[26]

In addition to the effects of an economic system on HRM, the health of the system can have an important impact. For example, we referred earlier to lower labour costs in India. In developed countries with a high level of wealth, labour costs tend to be quite high relative to those in developing countries. Figure 13.2 on page 514 provides a good example of the different hourly labour costs for manufacturing jobs in various countries.

An economic system also affects HRM directly through its taxes on compensation packages. Thus, the differential labour costs shown in Figure 13.2 do not always reflect the actual take-home pay of employees. Socialist systems are characterized by tax systems that redistribute wealth by taking a higher percentage of a person's income as he or she moves up the economic ladder. Capitalist systems attempt to reward individuals for their efforts by allowing them to keep more of their earnings. Companies that do business in other countries have to present compensation packages to expatriate managers that are competitive in take-home, rather than gross, pay. HRM responses to these issues affecting expatriate managers will be discussed in more detail later in this chapter.

FIGURE 13.2 Average Gross Hourly Compensation (U.S. Dollars) for Production Workers in Several Countries (2009)

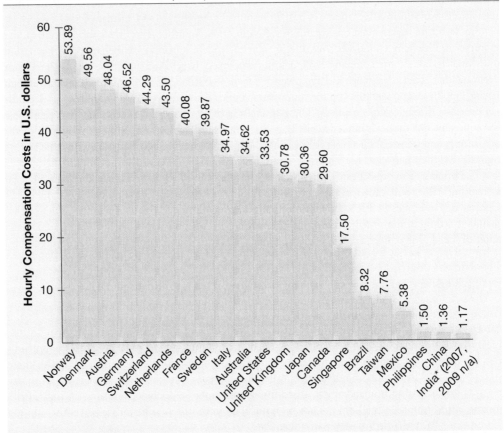

SOURCE: U.S. Bureau of Labour Statistics, http://www.bls.gov/news.release/pdf/ichcc.pdf"www.bls.gov/news.release/pdf/ichcc.pdf. International Hourly Compensation Costs for Production Workers, by Sub-Manufacturing Industry, 1992–2007 (US$) at www.bls.gov/fls/flshcpwindnaics.htm (retrieved September 26, 2011). Hourly compensation costs data were updated on November 20, 2009, to reflect the latest available information.

These differences in economies can have a profound impact on pay systems, particularly among global companies seeking to develop an international compensation and reward system that maintains cost controls while enabling local operations to compete in the war for talent. One recent study examining how compensation managers design these systems indicates that they look at a number of factors including the global firm strategy, the local regulatory/political context, institutions and stakeholders, local markets, and national culture. While they try to learn from the best practices that exist globally, they balance these approaches with the constraints imposed by the local environment.[27] However, not only the hourly labour costs, but also the total cost of employees, affect decisions about where to locate workers. The "Competing through Globalization" box describes how and why cost-cutting strategies in India differ from those in the West.

In conclusion, every country varies in terms of its culture, human capital, legal system, and economic systems. These variations directly influence the types of HRM systems that must be developed to accommodate the particular situation. The extent to which these differences affect

Competing Through Globalization

Managing the Economic Downturn: The Indian Way

As the global recession expands, one often sees different strategies for dealing with it across different countries. For instance, in North America, companies quickly resort to laying off workers as a way of reducing labour costs and keeping headcount in line with production and demand. However, in India, companies rarely default to layoffs.

According to Vasanthi Srinivasan, a professor of organizational behaviour and human resource management at the Indian Institute of Management, Bangalore (IIMB), "There is this paternalistic culture in our organizations, and therefore a sense of a moral obligation on the part of most managers to care for their employees. Organizations in India prefer to hold on to their people as much as possible. The feeling is that the employees have been with us in good times and contributed to the growth of the organization, so how can we let them go in tough times?"

Contrast this with Canada, where 400,000 jobs were lost during the recession; although these jobs were fully recovered within the first year of the downturn, there is no question that terminations occurred when times got tough. In the United States, millions lost their jobs or were downsized. Pothen Jacob, head of the human capital group, Watson Wyatt India, notes the different approach taken in India, saying: "Watson Wyatt's Strategic Rewards Survey reveals that the most common approach in India is a combination of restructuring (67 percent), slower rates of salary increase (51 percent), and a hiring freeze (62 percent). Only a small percentage of companies have considered options such as a reduced workweek (10 percent), broad-based base pay reduction (3 percent), and early retirement (15 percent)." Pay cuts and job cuts do not make as much sense in India because of the lack of a social safety net. Jacob suggests, "In the absence of a structured social net, the implications of a workforce reduction are both economic and emotional."

The implications are emotional because of the social stigma attached to losing a job. Srinivasan says, "Because people work long hours at the workplace and are paid very well, their families tend to believe that they play a crucial role within the organization. If they were to suddenly lose their jobs, it is perceived as a reflection on their competence. The social environment does not understand that one can be asked to leave a job because there is an economic downturn."

SOURCE: "Job Cuts vs. Pay Cuts: In a Slowing Economy What's Better for India?" at http://knowledge.wharton.upenn.edu/india/article.cfm?articleid_4333 (retrieved April 21, 2009).

a company depends on how involved the company is in global markets. In the next sections we discuss important concepts of global business and various levels of global participation, particularly noting how these factors come into play.

MANAGING EMPLOYEES IN A GLOBAL CONTEXT

Types of International Employees

Before discussing the levels of global participation, we need to distinguish between parent countries, host countries, and third countries. A **parent country** is the country in which the company's corporate headquarters are located. For example, Canada is the parent country of Research in Motion (RIM), the company featured in the opening vignette of Chapter 1. A **host country** is the country

Parent Country
The country in which a company's corporate headquarters is located.

Host Country
The country in which the parent country organization seeks to locate or has already located a facility.

LO 3
List the different categories of international employees.

Third Country
A country other than a host or parent country.

Expatriate
An employee sent by his or her company in one country to manage operations in a different country.

Parent-Country Nationals (PCNs)
Employees who were born and live in a parent country.

Host-Country Nationals (HCNs)
Employees who were born and raised in the host, not the parent, country.

Third-Country Nationals (TCNs)
Employees born in a country other than the parent or host country.

LO 4

Identify the four levels of global participation and the HRM issues faced within each level.

in which the parent country organization seeks to locate (or has already located) a facility. Thus the United Kingdom is a host country for Research in Motion because RIM has operations there. A **third country** is a country other than the host country or parent country, and a company may or may not have a facility there.

There are also different categories of employees. **Expatriate** is the term generally used for employees sent by a company in one country to manage operations in a different country. With the increasing globalization of business, it is now important to distinguish among different types of expatriates. **Parent-country nationals (PCNs)** are employees who were born and live in the parent country. **Host-country nationals (HCNs)** are those employees who were born and raised in the host, as opposed to the parent, country. Finally, **third-country nationals (TCNs)** are employees born in a country other than the parent country and host country but who work in the host country. Thus, a manager born and raised in Brazil employed by an organization located in Canada and assigned to manage an operation in Thailand would be considered a TCN.

Research shows that countries differ in their use of various types of international employees. One study revealed that Japanese multinational firms have more ethnocentric HRM policies and practices (they tend to use Japanese expatriate managers more than local host-country nationals) than either European or North American firms. This study also found that the use of ethnocentric HRM practices is associated with more HRM problems.[28]

Levels of Global Participation

We often hear companies referred to as "multinational" or "international." However, it is important to understand the different levels of participation in international markets. This is especially important because as a company becomes more involved in international trade, different types of HRM problems arise. In this section we examine Nancy Adler's categorization of the various levels of international participation from which a company may choose.[29] Figure 13.3 depicts these levels of involvement.

Domestic Most companies begin by operating within a domestic marketplace. For example, an entrepreneur may have an idea for a product that meets a need in the North American marketplace. The individual then obtains capital to build a facility that produces the product or service in a

FIGURE 13.3 Levels of Global Participation

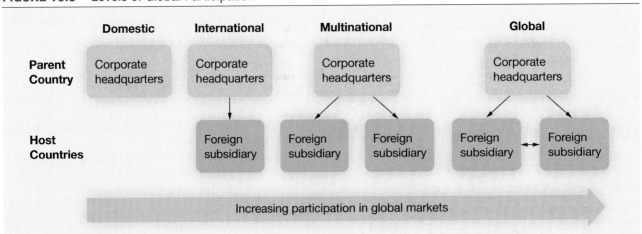

quantity that meets the needs of a small market niche. This requires recruiting, hiring, training, and compensating a number of individuals who will be involved in the production process, and these individuals are usually drawn from the local labour market. The focus of the selection and training programs is often on the employees' technical competence to perform job-related duties and to some extent on interpersonal skills. In addition, because the company is usually involved in only one labour market, determining the market rate of pay for various jobs is relatively easy.

As the product grows in popularity, the owner might choose to build additional facilities in different parts of Canada or North America to reduce the costs of transporting the product over large distances. In deciding where to locate these facilities, the owner must consider the attractiveness of the local labour markets. Various parts of the country may have different cultures that make those areas more or less attractive according to the work ethics of the potential employees. Similarly, the human capital in the different areas may vary greatly because of differences in educational systems. Finally, local pay rates may differ.

Incidentally, even domestic companies face problems with cultural diversity. In North America, for example, the representation of women and visible minorities is increasing within the workforce. These groups come to the workplace with worldviews that differ from those of the traditional white male. Thus, we are seeing more and more emphasis on developing systems for managing cultural diversity within single-country organizations, even though the diversity might be on a somewhat smaller scale than the diversity of cultures across national boundaries.[30]

It is important to note that companies functioning at the domestic level face an environment with very similar cultural, human capital, political–legal, and economic situations, although some variation might be observed across geographic areas.

International As more competitors enter the domestic market, companies face the possibility of losing market share; thus, they often seek other markets for their products. This usually requires entering international markets, initially by exporting products but ultimately by building production facilities in other countries. The decision to participate in international competition raises a host of human resource issues. All the problems regarding locating facilities are magnified. One must consider whether a particular location provides an environment where human resources can be successfully acquired and managed.

Now the company faces an entirely different situation with regard to culture, human capital, the political–legal system, and the economic system. For example, the availability of human capital is of utmost importance, and there is a substantially greater variability in human capital between Canada and other countries than there is among the various provinces in Canada.

A country's legal system may also present HRM problems. For example, France has a relatively high minimum wage, which drives up labour costs. In addition, regulations make it extremely difficult to fire or lay off an employee. In Germany companies are legally required to offer employees influence in the management of the firm. Companies that develop facilities in other countries have to adapt their HRM practices to conform to the host-country's laws. This requires the company to gain expertise in the country's HRM legal requirements and knowledge about how to deal with the country's legal system, and it often requires the company to hire one or more HCNs. In fact, some countries legally require companies to hire a certain percentage of HCNs for any foreign-owned subsidiary.

Finally, cultures have to be considered. To the extent that the country's culture is vastly different from that of the parent organization, conflicts, communication problems, and morale problems may occur. Expatriate managers must be trained to identify these cultural differences, and they must be flexible enough to adapt their styles to those of their host country. This requires an extensive selection effort to identify individuals who are capable of adapting to new environments and an extensive training program to ensure that the culture shock is not devastating.

Multinational   Whereas international companies build one or a few facilities in another country, they become multinational when they build facilities in a number of different countries, attempting to capitalize on lower production and distribution costs in different locations. The lower production costs are gained by shifting production from higher-cost locations to lower-cost locations. For example, some of the major North American automakers have plants all over the world. They continue to shift their production from the United States and Canada where labour unions have gained high wages for their members, to *maquiladora* facilities in Mexico, where the wages are substantially lower. Similarly, these companies minimize distribution and labour costs by locating facilities in central and eastern European countries such as Poland, Hungary, and the Slovak Republic for manufacturing and assembling automobiles to sell in the European market.

The HRM problems multinational companies face are similar to those international companies face, only magnified. Instead of having to consider only one or two countries' cultural, human capital, political–legal, and economic systems, the multinational company must address these differences for a large number of countries. This accentuates the need to select managers capable of functioning in a variety of settings, give them necessary training, and provide flexible compensation systems that take into account the different market pay rates, tax systems, and costs of living.

Multinational companies now employ many "inpatriates"—internal managers from different countries where the company has facilities who are brought in to become part of the corporate headquarters staff. This creates a need to integrate managers from different cultures into the culture of the parent company. In addition, multinational companies now take more expatriates from countries other than the parent country and place them in facilities of other countries. For example, a manager from Scotland, working for a Canadian company, might be assigned to run an operation in South Africa. This practice accentuates the need for cross-cultural training to provide managerial skills for interaction with individuals from different cultures.

Global   Many researchers now propose a fourth level of integration: global organizations. Global organizations compete on state-of-the-art, top-quality products and services and do so with the lowest costs possible. Whereas multinational companies attempt to develop identical products distributed worldwide, global companies increasingly emphasize flexibility and mass customization of products to meet the needs of particular clients. Multinational companies are usually driven to locate facilities in a country as a means of reaching that country's market or lowering production costs, and the company must deal with the differences across the countries. Global firms, on the other hand, choose to locate a facility based on the ability to effectively, efficiently, and flexibly produce a product or service and attempt to create synergy through the cultural differences.

This creates the need for HRM systems that encourage flexible production (thus presenting a host of HRM issues). These companies proactively consider the cultures, human capital, political–legal systems, and economic systems to determine where production facilities can be located to provide a competitive advantage. Global companies have multiple headquarters spread across the globe, resulting in less hierarchically structured organizations that emphasize decentralized decision making. This results in the need for human resource systems that recruit, develop, retain, and use managers and executives who are competent transnationally.

Transnational Scope
A company's ability to make HRM decisions from an international perspective.

Transnational Representation
The multinational composition of a company's managers.

A global (transnational) HRM system is characterized by three attributes.[31] **Transnational scope** refers to the fact that HRM decisions must be made from a global rather than a national or regional perspective. This creates the need to make decisions that balance the need for uniformity (to ensure fair treatment of all employees) with the need for flexibility (to meet the needs of employees in different countries). **Transnational representation** reflects the multinational composition of a company's managers. Global participation does not necessarily ensure that each country is providing managers to the company's ranks. However, this is a prerequisite if the company is to achieve the next attribute. **Transnational process** refers to the extent to which the company's planning and decision-making processes include representatives and ideas from a variety of cultures. This attribute allows for diverse viewpoints and knowledge associated with different cultures, increasing the quality of decision making.

These three characteristics are necessary for global companies to achieve cultural synergy. Rather than simply integrating foreigners into the domestic organization, a successful transnational company needs managers who will treat managers from other cultures as equals. This synergy can be accomplished only by combining selection, training, appraisal, and compensation systems in such a way that managers have a transnational rather than a parochial orientation. However, a survey of 50 companies in Canada and the United States found that global companies' HRM systems are far less transnational in scope, representation, and process than the companies' strategic planning systems and organizational structures.[32]

In conclusion, entry into international markets creates a host of HRM issues that must be addressed if a company is to gain competitive advantage. Once the choice has been made to compete in a global arena, companies must seek to manage employees who are sent to foreign countries (expatriates and third-country nationals). This causes the need to shift from focusing only on the culture, human capital, political–legal, and economic influences of the host country to examining ways to manage the expatriate managers who must be located there. Selection systems must be developed that allow the company to identify managers capable of functioning in a new culture. These managers must be trained to identify the important aspects of the new culture in which they will live as well as the relevant legal–political and economic systems. Finally, these managers must be compensated to offset the costs of uprooting themselves and their families to move to a new situation vastly different from their previous lives. In the next section we address issues regarding management of expatriates.

> **Transnational Process**
> The extent to which a company's planning and decision-making processes include representatives and ideas from a variety of cultures.

Managing Expatriates in Global Markets

We have outlined the major macro-level factors that influence HRM in global markets. These factors can affect a company's decision whether to build facilities in a given country. In addition, if a company does develop such facilities, these factors strongly affect the HRM practices used. However, one important issue that has been recognized over the past few years is the set of problems inherent in selecting, training, compensating, and reintegrating expatriate managers.

In its 2009 Employee Relocation Policy Survey, the Canadian Employee Relocation Council (CERC) reported the average cost of an international relocation of a manager or executive manager to be $92,172 for a permanent relocation; $64,354 for a short-term assignment (three to twelve months) and $105,272 for a long-term assignment.[33] The importance to the company's profitability of managing such moves well (making the right expatriate assignments, managing costs of the entire assignment effectively, and ensuring retention of the expatriate upon return) should not be underestimated. The 2010 Global Relocation Trends Survey conducted by Brookfield Global Relocation Services reveals that total assignment costs can be over $1 million per employee.[34] In the late 1990s the failure rate for expatriate assignments was estimated at between 15 and 40 percent.[35] and the recent Brookfield survey confirms the high end of that estimate, indicating 38 percent of expatriates leave the company within one year of returning to their home country.[36]

In its recently published Talent Mobility 2020 report, PricewaterhouseCoopers (PWC) drew upon its database of survey information from 900 companies on assignment trends spanning the past 18 years, annual global CEO surveys, interviews with its own mobility talent specialists, and extensive surveys among 4,000 Millennials (those born between 1978 and 1999).[37] Combining all sources, the report attempted to discern both current and future trends in foreign assignments and how things might change by 2020. Results indicate that companies are finding other ways to control

> **LO 5**
> Discuss the ways companies attempt to select, train, compensate, and reintegrate expatriate managers.

the cost and risks associated with the types of expatriate assignments described earlier by utilizing additional types of assignments such as frequent travellers, commuters, intraregional assignments, and virtual secondments to customers or suppliers. The number of such assignments has increased 25 percent in the past 10 years and they are predicted to grow a further 50 percent by 2020.[38] In addition, PWC's research indicates that how "our global workforce is sourced, organised and managed will change radically" by 2020.[39] The life stage of employees may be the strongest indicator of who is willing to accept a foreign assignment and the type of assignment that will work the best. Those closer to career peaks may opt for long-term assignments as they have been traditionally managed, or they may prefer a commuter arrangement to maintain work/life balance. Notably, 81 percent of Canadian Millennials surveyed revealed that they want to work abroad, slightly higher than the average of those from all countries (80 percent).[40] Such indications support the report's prediction that by 2020 Millennials will make up the largest portion of international assignees. Further, they will view the world and their careers in a much more boundaryless fashion than did their predecessors, the Boomers. Rather they are likely to follow well-paying opportunities "across functional areas, roles, multiple cultures and economies, without the need to return to their home country until perhaps later in their career."[41]

In the final section of the chapter, we discuss the major issues relevant to the management of expatriate managers. These issues cover the selection, training, compensation, and reacculturation of expatriates.

Selection of Expatriate Managers   One of the major problems in managing expatriate managers is determining which individuals in the organization are most capable of handling an assignment in a different culture. Expatriate managers must have technical competence in the area of operations; otherwise, they will be unable to earn the respect of subordinates. However, technical competence has been almost the sole variable used in deciding whom to send on overseas assignments, despite the fact that multiple skills are necessary for successful performance in these assignments.[42]

A successful expatriate manager must be sensitive to the country's cultural norms, flexible enough to adapt to those norms, and strong enough to make it through the inevitable culture shock. In addition, the manager's family must be similarly capable of adapting to the new culture. These adaptive skills have been categorized into three dimensions:[43] (1) the self dimension (the skills that enable a manager to maintain a positive self-image and psychological well-being), (2) the relationship dimension (the skills required to foster relationships with the host-country nationals), and (3) the perception dimension (those skills that enable a manager to accurately perceive and evaluate the host environment). One study of international assignees found that they considered the following five factors to be important in descending order of importance: family situation, flexibility and adaptability, job knowledge and motivation, relational skills, and extra-cultural openness.[44]

Little evidence suggests that North American companies have invested much effort in attempting to make correct expatriate selections. One researcher found that only 5 percent of the firms surveyed administered any tests to determine the degree to which expatriate candidates possessed cross-cultural skills.[45] More recent research reveals that only 35 percent of firms choose expatriates from multiple candidates and that those firms emphasize only technical job-related experience and skills in making these decisions.[46] These findings glaringly demonstrate that such organizations need to improve their success rate in overseas assignments. As discussed in Chapter 5, the technology for assessing individuals' knowledge, skills, and abilities has advanced. The potential for selection testing to decrease the failure rate and productivity problems of expatriate managers seems promising. For instance, recent research has examined the "Big Five" personality dimensions as predictors of expatriate success (remember these from Chapter 5). For instance, one study distinguished between expatriate success as measured by not terminating the assignment and success as measured by supervisory evaluations of the expatriate. The researcher found that agreeableness, emotional stability, and extraversion were negatively related to the desire to terminate the assignment (i.e., expatriates wanted to stay on the assignment longer), and conscientiousness was positively related to supervisory evaluations of the expatriate.[47]

A final issue with regard to expatriate selection is the use of women in expatriate assignments., Recent evidence indicates that women are overcoming longstanding barriers in North American firms and becoming successful managers in countries where women have not traditionally been promoted to management positions in the past (such as Japan and other Asian counties). For example, Robin Abrams, an expatriate manager for Apple Computer's Hong Kong office, states that nobody cares whether "you are wearing trousers or a skirt if you have demonstrated core competencies." In fact, some women believe that the novelty of their presence among a group of men increases their credibility with locals. Indeed, research suggests that male and female expatriates can perform equally well in international assignments, regardless of the country's cultural predispositions toward women in management. However, female expatriates self-rate their adjustment lower in countries that have few women in the workforce.[48] Research has shown that female expatriates were perceived as being effective regardless of the cultural toughness of the host country[49] and female expatriates feel more strongly than their supervisors that prejudice does not limit women's ability to be successful.[50]

More and more Canadian women are accepting expatriate managerial assignments, overcoming cultural attitudes toward women in other countries and demonstrating that only competency matters in the world of international business.

Learn more about managing expatriates in global markets online with Connect.

■ connect

Training and Development of Expatriates   Once an expatriate manager has been selected, it is necessary to prepare that manager for the upcoming assignment. **Cross-cultural preparation** is the process of educating employees (and their families) who are given an assignment in a foreign country. While there are a number of ways that employees (and their families) can be prepared for an out-of-country assignment, we will focus on cross-cultural training, which may also include some level of language training.

Cross-Cultural Training   To prepare employees for cross-cultural assignments, companies need to provide cross-cultural training. A review of the cross-cultural training literature found support for the belief that cross-cultural training has an impact on effectiveness.[51] In spite of this, cross-cultural training is hardly universal. Most North American companies send employees overseas without any preparation. As a result, the number of employees who return home before completing their assignments is higher for North American companies than for European and Japanese companies.[52] North American companies lose more than $2 billion a year as a result of failed overseas assignments.

To succeed overseas, expatriates (employees on foreign assignments) need to be

1. Competent in their areas of expertise;
2. Able to communicate verbally and nonverbally in the host country;
3. Flexible, tolerant of ambiguity, and sensitive to cultural differences;

LO 6

Discuss the key elements of a cross-cultural preparation program.

Cross-Cultural Preparation
The process of educating employees (and their families) who are given an assignment in a foreign country.

4. Motivated to succeed, able to enjoy the challenge of working in other countries, and willing to learn about the host country's culture, language, and customs;

5. Supported by their families.[53]

One reason for North American expatriates' high failure rate is that companies place more emphasis on developing employees' technical skills than on preparing them to work in other cultures. Research suggests that the comfort of an expatriate's spouse and family is the most important determinant of whether the employee will complete the assignment.[54] Studies have also found that personality characteristics are related to expatriates' desire to terminate the assignment and performance in the assignment.[55] Expatriates who were extroverted (outgoing), agreeable (cooperative and tolerant), and conscientious (dependable, achievement oriented) were more likely to want to stay on the assignment and perform well. This suggests that cross-cultural training may be effective only when expatriates' personalities predispose them to be successful in assignments in other cultures.

Most cross-cultural training programs attempt to create an appreciation of the host country's culture so that expatriates can behave appropriately.[56] This entails emphasizing a few aspects of cultural sensitivity. First, expatriates must be clear about their own cultural background, particularly as it is perceived by the host nationals. With an accurate cultural self-awareness, managers can modify their behaviour to accentuate the effective characteristics while minimizing those that are dysfunctional.[57]

Second, expatriates must understand the particular aspects of culture in the new work environment. Although culture is an elusive, almost invisible phenomenon, astute expatriate managers must perceive the culture and adapt their behaviour to it. This entails identifying the types of behaviours and interpersonal styles that are considered acceptable in both business meetings and social gatherings. For example, Germans value promptness for meetings to a much greater extent than do Latin Americans.

Effective cross-cultural training helps ease an expatriate's transition to the new work environment. It can also help avoid costly or embarrassing mistakes. For example, an expatriate in Japan may wish to bow according to Japanese custom, but it is a subtle business. One should not bow too low to someone lower in status, or not low enough for someone higher in status. How high or low is "just right"? Those in the know say a handshake and a slight bow does the trick.[58]

Methods for cross-cultural training include presentational techniques, such as lectures that expatriates and their families attend on the customs and culture of the host country, immersion experiences, or actual experiences in the home country in culturally diverse communities.[59] Experiential exercises, such as mini-culture experiences, allow expatriates to spend time with a family in Canada from the ethnic group of the host country. For example, an Indian trainer took 20 managers from Advanced Micro Devices on a two-week immersion trip during which the group travelled to New Delhi, Bangalore, and Mumbai, meeting with business persons and government officials.[60] The program required six months of planning, including providing the executives with information on foods to eat, potential security issues, and how to interact in business meetings. For example, Indians prefer a relatively indirect way of entering into business discussions, so the managers were advised to discuss current events and other subjects before talking business.

Research suggests that the degree of difference between North America and the host country (cultural novelty), the amount of interaction with host-country citizens and host nationals (interaction), and the familiarity with new job tasks and work environment (job novelty) all influence the "rigour" of the cross-cultural training method used.[61] Hands-on and group-building methods are most effective (and most needed) in assignments with a high level of cultural and job novelty that require a good deal of interpersonal interaction with host nationals.

∎ connect™   Learn more about cross-cultural training online with Connect.

Language Training   Expatriates must learn to communicate accurately in the new culture. Some firms attempt to use expatriates who speak the language of the host country, and a few provide language training. However, most companies simply assume that the host-country nationals all speak the parent-country's language. Although this assumption might be true, seldom do these nationals speak the parent-country language fluently. Thus expatriate managers must be trained to communicate with others when language barriers exist. See the "Competing through Sustainability" box, which explains how the Four Seasons Regent Hotels and Resorts regards language training of employees as an important part of successful expansion. Table 13.2 on page 525 offers some tips for communicating across language barriers.

Competing Through Sustainability

Ensuring ROI: Getting them Ready and Bringing Them Back

When it comes to sending top talent to other parts of the world, it makes good business sense to think carefully about preparation at both the front and back ends of any foreign assignment. That means preparing employees ahead of time so they can maximize their impact on business. But, it also means ensuring such valuable employees don't leave the company once the assignment is over. The following examples illustrate how to mitigate various opportunities and risks involved in staffing and ending global assignments.

Wherever employees are going in the world, speaking and understanding the local language can help them avoid misunderstandings and gain greater respect from business partners, subordinates, and customers. In the hotel industry, clear communication is essential. If guests have a positive and memorable experience they are much more likely to return, or to book with the same hotel chain in other parts of the world. For example, the Four Seasons Regent Hotel and Resorts is a luxury hotel operations and management group with 22,000 employees worldwide, including approximately 13,000 in international locations. When the Four Seasons faced the challenge of opening a new hotel and resort at Jambaran Bay, Bali, training seemed to be in order. To address such needs, the human resources staff created a self-directed learning centre. The Self Access Learning Center emphasizes communication skills as well as English language skills. Its purpose is to teach skills and improve employees' confidence in their communications. The centre includes video recorders, training modules, books, and magazines. Besides English, the centre also teaches Japanese (the language of 20 percent of hotel visitors) and provides training for foreign managers in Bahasa Indonesian, the native language of Indonesia. The training process begins by administering an English test to potential employees to gauge the level of English training they need. As employees complete each level of the training, they receive a monetary incentive.

The approach has paid off. Travel experts rated the Four Seasons Bali as one of the top hotels in the world. Business has increased steadily since the hotel opened, with guests from North America, Europe, Asia, Australia, and South America. As a result of the training, the Four Seasons is prepared for expansion. As the hotel industry expands in Asia, the Four Seasons now has a trained and talented staff that can be used to meet human resource needs as new resorts are developed. Four Seasons learned that the company must combine the training needs of the local culture with the standards of the company's culture to create a successful international business.

And when it is time to bring employees home from foreign assignments, companies need to prepare both the employee and others well ahead of time, so they don't lose the returning employee during the transition. According to Tom O'Connor, Raytheon's Senior Manager of International Human Resources, various types of communication are key to retention of good people. For example, while on assignment, Raytheon expatriates are required to check in with their North American counterparts regularly so they remain in the loop; "It gives their colleagues an idea of what they've been up to and the value they'll bring back to the business." O'Connor's staff communicates at least twice a year with the expat to ensure they know what's happening with the employee and his or her family—anything that may be meaningful when it comes time to bring the family back home. O'Connor notes that timing is also very important. He feels the expatriate should be contacted about three months before the assignment end date to find out how the employee feels about staying on or coming back to Canada. He says, "If the employee is returning, we contact HR at their home business unit and discuss the person's return date, skill level, interests, and available opportunities." Much will have changed in both the home office and for the employee who has been away, so the idea is to ensure successful reintegration at an appropriate level of the business, along with making sure the new job is geographically where the employee wants to be once back on home turf. These and other similar tactics make sense since the idea is to protect a valuable investment. Lance Richards, senior director and global practices leader with Kelly Services, likens such careful approaches as managing the amortization of an investment, saying, "If you take a $100,000 person and drop them in Beijing for two years, they can easily cost $300,000 per year. If that person then leaves the organization the investment goes out the door too." To prevent such loss, Richards recommends three interventions: (1) don't let disillusionment become part of the return home—ensure the employee returns to a role that is meaningful to him or her; (2) involve the employee as a source of knowledge to others; and (3) coach the expatriate's manager how to manage and retain the expatriate since this is not just an employee, but a valuable investment.

SOURCES: C. M. Solomon, "When Training Doesn't Translate," *Workforce* 76, no. 3 (1997), pp. 40–44; D. McCutcheon, "Repatriation: Bringing Home the Troops," *HR Professional* (April/May 2009).

Steps in Cross-cultural Preparation   The key to a successful foreign assignment is a combination of training and career management for the employee and family. However, as you may understand by now, effective cross-cultural preparation is not a one-shot effort. Foreign assignments involve three phases: predeparture, on-site, and repatriation (preparing to return home). Training is necessary in all three phases. We look now at what types of training are appropriate in each phase of the assignment.

Pre-Departure Phase   Before departure, employees need to receive language training and an orientation to the new country's culture and customs. It is also critical that the family be included in orientation programs.[62] Expatriates and their families need information about housing, schools, recreation, shopping, and health-care facilities in the areas where they will live. Expatriates also must discuss with their managers how the foreign assignment fits into their career plans and what types of positions they can expect upon return.

On-Site Phase   On-site training involves continued orientation to the host country and its customs and cultures through formal programs or through a mentoring relationship. Expatriates and their families may be paired with an employee from the host country who helps them understand

Table 13.2 Communicating across Language Barriers

VERBAL BEHAVIOUR
• *Clear, slow speech.* Enunciate each word. Do not use colloquial expressions.
• *Repetition.* Repeat each important idea using different words to explain the same concept.
• *Simple sentences.* Avoid compound, long sentences.
• *Active verbs.* Avoid passive verbs.

NONVERBAL BEHAVIOUR
• *Visual restatements.* Use as many visual restatements as possible, such as pictures, graphs, tables, and slides.
• *Gestures.* Use more facial and hand gestures to emphasize the meaning of words.
• *Demonstration.* Act out as many themes as possible.
• *Pauses.* Pause more frequently.
• *Summaries.* Hand out written summaries of your verbal presentation.

ATTRIBUTION
• *Silence.* When there is a silence, wait. Do not jump in to fill the silence. The other person is probably just thinking more slowly in the non-native language or translating.
• *Intelligence.* Do not equate poor grammar and mispronunciation with lack of intelligence; it is usually a sign of second-language use.
• *Differences.* If unsure, assume difference, not similarity.

COMPREHENSION
• *Understanding.* Do not just assume that they understand; assume that they do not understand.
• *Checking comprehension.* Have colleagues repeat their understanding of the material back to you. Do not simply ask whether they understand or not. Let them explain what they understand to you.

DESIGN
• *Breaks.* Take more frequent breaks. Second-language comprehension is exhausting.
• *Small modules.* Divide the material into smaller modules.
• *Longer time frame.* Allocate more time for each module than usual in a monolingual program.

MOTIVATION
• *Encouragement.* Verbally and nonverbally encourage and reinforce speaking by nonnative language participants.
• *Drawing out.* Explicitly draw out marginal and passive participants.
• *Reinforcement.* Do not embarrass novice speakers.

SOURCE: From Nancy Adler, *International Dimensions of Organizational Behavior,* 2nd ed., pp. 84–85. Copyright © 1991. South-Western, a part of Cengage Learning, Inc. Reproduced by permission. www.cengage.com/permissions.

the new, unfamiliar work environment and community.[63] Companies also use the Web to help employees on expatriate assignments get answers to questions such as, How do I conduct a meeting here? or What religious philosophy might have influenced today's negotiation behaviour?[64] Knowledge management software allows employees to contribute, organize, and access knowledge specific to their expatriate assignment.

A major reason that employees refuse expatriate assignments is that they can't afford to lose their spouse's income or are concerned that their spouse's career could be derailed by being out of the workforce for a few years.[65] Some "trailing" spouses decide to use the time to pursue educational or other activities that could contribute to their long-term life and career goals. Although it can be difficult to find these opportunities in an unfamiliar place, that's what Nicole Gionet's husband did when she accepted a move to Brussels in 2003. Gionet was destined to play a major role in the merger of Alcatel, a French company with 50,000 employees, and Lucent, a U.S. firm with 30,000 employees. As vice-president of management development for Alcatel Networks Corporation's Fixed Communications Group, Gionet was expected to facilitate the international culture merger for the new entity. It was a great opportunity for Gionet, a Canadian Francophone from Moncton, New Brunswick, so the entire family moved from Ottawa to Brussels in 2003. This meant her husband, an RCMP officer who has been the prime minister's bodyguard, had to take a leave of absence, putting his job on hold until Gionet's work was done in France. He became a "house husband" and full-time parent, something he hadn't had much time for when in Canada. This provided the stable homebase Gionet needed for her new 24/7 responsibilities. Then in 2007, with Gionet's project complete, the family returned to Canada. Although Gionet would have liked to stay on in Europe, her son wanted to attend a Canadian university and her husband was anxious to get back to the job he loved. Gionet then continued her work by commuting between home, Europe, and New Jersey, the location of Lucent's head office.[66]

Repatriation

The preparation of expatriates for return to the parent company and country from a foreign assignment.

Repatriation Phase **Repatriation** prepares expatriates for return to the parent company and country from the foreign assignment. Expatriates and their families are likely to experience re-entry shock (high levels of stress and anxiety when they return because of the changes that have occurred since their departure.) Employees should be encouraged to self-manage the repatriation process.[67] Before they go on the assignment they need to consider what skills they want to develop and the types of jobs that might be available in the company for an employee with those skills.

Aside from re-entry shock, many expatriates decide to leave the company because the assignments they are given upon returning to Canada have less responsibility, challenge, and status than their foreign assignments.[68] To avoid this, employers need to ensure that career-planning discussions are held before the employees leave Canada to clarify the positions they will be eligible for upon repatriation. But career planning sessions are only one method available to employers that have invested heavily in the employee and to realize the full value of the overseas assignment now coming to an end. Astute employers are realizing they must also facilitate re-acculturation of expatriates through a variety of methods, or risk losing the employee during the last stage of the assignment. Because this is such an important aspect of managing expatriates, we discuss re-acculturation of expatriates in greater depth as the conclusion of the chapter.

Virtual Expatriates As you can see, cross-cultural preparation is complex and when such activities are undertaken they require significant (though worthwhile) effort. Perhaps to reduce the amount of cross-cultural preparation required for expatriates, and because of family issues, poor economic times, and security issues, many companies are using virtual expatriates, relying more on short-time assignments, frequent business travel, and international commutes in which an employee lives in one country and works in another.[69] *Virtual expatriates* have an assignment to manage an operation abroad without being located permanently in that country. The employees periodically travel to the overseas location, return, and later use video conferencing and communications technology to manage the operation.[70] Virtual expatriates eliminate exposing the family to the culture shock of an overseas move. This setup also allows the employee to manage globally while remaining in constant touch with the home office. Virtual expatriates are less expensive than traditional expatriates, who can cost companies over three times as much as a host national employee. One major disadvantage of virtual expatriates is that visiting a foreign operation on a sporadic basis may lengthen the time needed to build a local management team, so it will take longer to solve problems because of the lack of a strong personal relationship with local employees. One of the potential difficulties of short-term international assignments is that employees may be perceived as foreigners rather than colleagues because they haven't had the time to build relationships and develop trust among coworkers in their short-term location. Another is that travelling can take a physical and emotional toll on employees as they try to juggle business responsibilities with maintaining contact with family and friends.

Whether the assignment is traditional or virtual in nature, both the expatriate and the employer will need to rely heavily on a wide variety of technological programs and mobile devices to stay in touch and share information required for vital decisions. However, there are problems as well as benefits associated with the use of technology, as the "Competing Through Technology" box illustrates.

Competing Through Technology

Perils of Technology and Globalization

One of the main reasons most companies can even consider doing business internationally is because they know they can transmit digitized information and documents virtually anywhere in the world. Companies also depend on mobile devices (smartphones, laptops, netbooks, cellphones, and tablets) to facilitate dependable around-the-clock communication, to keep projects moving, and to share time-sensitive information. Hence, companies large and small frequently provide mobile devices to employees to support the work they do anywhere in the world. Whether for domestic or international purposes, such virtual leashes clearly enhance productivity.

However, such devices may also create both minor and serious breaches of security, depending on what kinds of limitations and policies are put in place. Such policies are usually drafted by the human resources department in collaboration with the IT department, along with senior management input, and deal with issues such as whether the devices is intended for business use only, or if employees can use them for personal reasons as well. However, with increased use of such devices and more employees working in other parts of the world, and travelling more often to expand into new markets, the question may be asked: Are companies thinking through the security issues connected to mobile devices sufficiently before dispensing such equipment? Recent surveys, discussed below, suggest there is room for improvement and that companies need to be sure they know what they are doing in their efforts to drive profits up and the bottom line down.

In a jointly sponsored survey of 92 European organizations done in 2010, Ovum (a firm specializing in IT and telecommunications) and the European Association for e-Identify and Security found that 70 percent of employees surveyed "say they are allowed to use their corporate devices for personal activities and 48 per cent can use their personally owned mobile devices to connect to corporate systems." In addition, mobile employees are increasingly ignoring laptops in favour of smartphones and tablets, which means that critical information may be stored on smaller, more portable devices that can easily be lost, misplaced, or stolen. And then there is the issue of doing company work, or receiving company e-mails on personal mobile devices, which muddies the picture considerably. Do companies really know who has access to sensitive information? What kind of corporate or personal liability is being incurred when breaches occur? In a survey conducted in October 2010 by Juniper Networks among 6,000 users of mobile devices in 16 countries, 44 percent used them for both personal and business purposes and less than

4 percent used them for business only. Around 70 percent of users in Canada, Japan, and France indicated they use them for personal use only, but a large majority of Chinese, Russian, and Brazilian users employ them for both personal and business reasons. Even more interesting is the fact that 81 percent of all respondents use their devices to log in to their company's network without anyone's permission, most doing so every day.

With post-WikiLeaks awareness, HR specialists and departments around the world may soon need to address the issue of security more aggressively, or suffer embarrassing and costly consequences. Certainly the results of a global study done by iPass among 1,100 mobile enterprise employees (ranging in age from under 21 to over 65) in late 2010 may give pause for thought on the issue. The iPass survey indicated that among those who use their smartphones for work "18 percent of mobile employees have already experienced a relevant security issue with their smartphones," and over a quarter of those users said their smartphones had been lost, stolen, infected with a virus, or hacked. Further, 22 percent of respondents admitted they "breached corporate policy using an unprovisioned smartphone for work when their companies had a stricter smartphone policy in place." Finally, the Ovum study mentioned earlier revealed that "eight out ten respondents believe smartphones expose their business to attack." Such findings would seem to provide a clear mandate for HR to begin driving stricter policies governing use of mobile devices, which somehow avoid restricting the hard work being done by employees living and working in a global world. Who said HR was easy?

SOURCES: The iPass Mobile Workforce Report (November 2010), at www.iPass.com; and S. Dobson, "Smartphones Dial up Challenges for HR, *HR Reporter* (December 13, 2010).

Compensation of Expatriates   One of the more troublesome aspects of managing expatriates is determining the compensation package. While the amount of such packages will vary with the type of job (and level in the organization of the job) for which the expatriate is selected, it is also necessary to examine the exact breakdown of these packages. Most use a balance sheet approach to determine the total package level. This approach entails developing a total compensation package that equalizes the purchasing power of the expatriate manager with that of employees in similar positions in the home country and provides incentives to offset the inconveniences incurred in the location. Purchasing power includes all of the expenses associated with the expatriate assignment. Expenses include goods and services (food, personal care, clothing, recreation, and transportation), housing (for a principal residence), income taxes (paid to federal and local governments), reserve (savings, payments for benefits, pension contributions), and shipment and storage (costs associated with moving and/or storing personal belongings). A typical balance sheet is shown in Figure 13.4.

As you can see from this figure, the employee starts with a set of costs for taxes, housing, goods and services, and reserve. However, in the host country, these costs are significantly higher. Thus the company must make up the difference between costs in the home and those in the host country, and then provide a premium and/or incentive for the employee to go through the trouble of living in a different environment. Table 13.3 provides an idea of just how much these add-ons can cost for an expatriate. As we see, these combined benefits amount to a 114 percent increase in compensation cost above the base pay.

Total pay packages have four components, which must be examined closely by the employer. Each or all of these components may be subject to adjustment depending on anticipated expenses as calculated after taking into account the variances noted in the balance sheet approach. Failure to adjust the package accurately and fairly could undermine fairness of the employee's compensation,

FIGURE 13.4 The Balance Sheet for Determining Expatriate Compensation

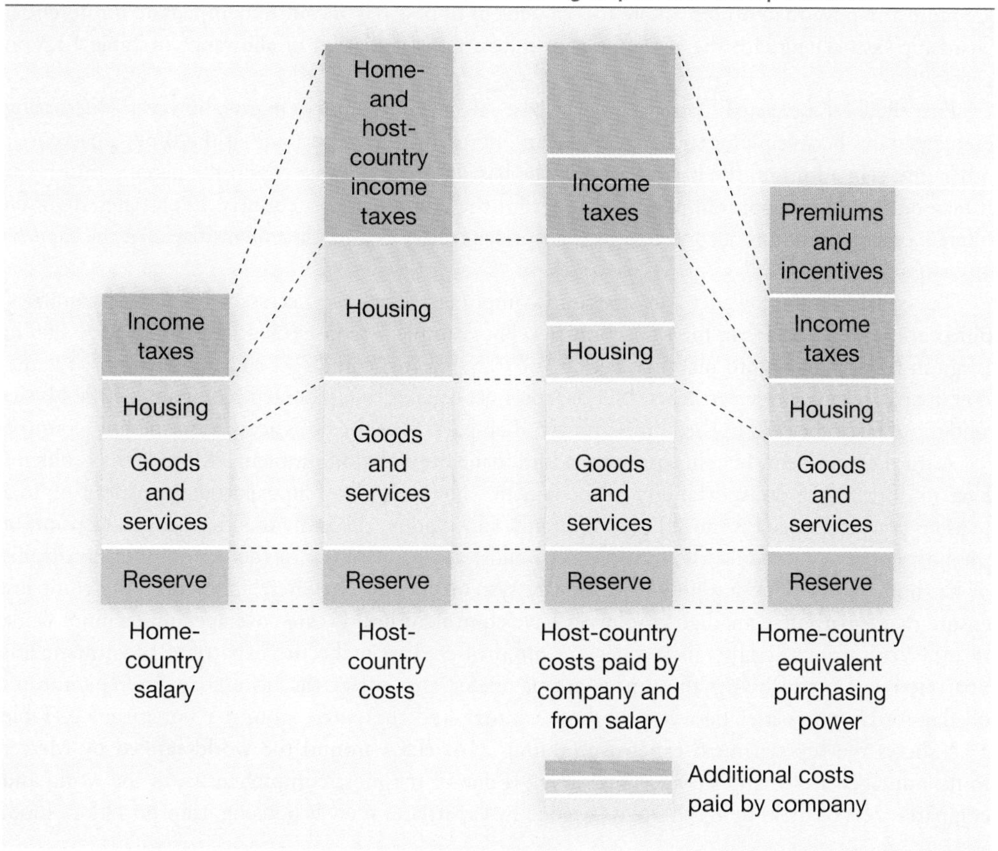

SOURCE: From C. Reynolds, "Compensation of Overseas Personnel," in Joseph Famularo, ed., *Handbook of Human Resource Administration,* 2nd ed., 1986. Copyright © 1986 The McGraw-Hill Companies.

Table 13.3 Average Amount of Allowance as a Percentage of Base Pay

Housing (purchase)	38%
Goods and services (cost of living)	24
Education	22
Position	17
Hardship	13

SOURCE: From B. Fitzgerald-Turner, *HR Magazine,* 1997. Copyright © 1997 by the Society for Human Resource Management. Reprinted with permission of *HR Magazine,* published by the Society for Human Resource Management, Alexandria, VA, via the Copyright Clearance Center.

and the employee's motivation to accept the assignment must also be factored in. Some assignments are more attractive than others. (Note the 13 percent of base pay meant to compensate for potential "hardship" associated with the assignment in the sample calculation of allowance in Table 13.3 on page 529.)

First there is base salary. Determining the base salary is not a simple matter, however. Fluctuating exchange rates between countries may make an offered salary a raise some of the time, a pay cut at other times. In addition, the base salary may be based on comparable pay in the parent country, or it may be based on the prevailing market rates for the job in the host country. Expatriates are often offered a salary premium beyond that of their present salary as an inducement to accept the expatriate assignment.

Tax equalization allowances are a second component. They are necessary because of countries' different taxation systems in high-tax countries. For example, a senior executive earning $100,000 in Belgium (with a maximum marginal tax rate of 70.8 percent) could cost a company almost $1 million in taxes over five to seven years.[71] Under most tax equalization plans, the company withholds the amount of tax to be paid in the home country, then pays all of the taxes accrued in the host country.

A third component, benefits, presents additional compensation problems. Most of the problems have to do with the transportability of the benefits. For example, if an expatriate contributing to a pension plan in Canada is moved to a different country, does the individual have a new pension in the host country, or should the individual be allowed to contribute to the existing pension in his or her home country? What about health care systems located elsewhere? How does the company ensure that expatriate Canadian employees have equivalent health-care coverage and facilities while in other countries? Finally, allowances are often offered to make the expatriate assignment less unattractive. Cost-of-living allowances are payments that offset the differences in expenditures on day-to-day necessities between the host country and the parent country. For instance, Table 13.4 shows the top ten most expensive (among 214) cities around the world ranked by Mercer in its annual cost of living survey. This survey is one of the most comprehensive in the world and compares costs of more than 200 items needed by expatriates such as housing, transportation, food,

Table 13.4 Global Cost of Living Survey: Top 10 Most Expensive Cities in the World for Expatriates, 2010

CITY RANKING—2010
1 Luanda, Angola
2 Tokyo, Japan; London, UK (jointly ranked)
3 Ndjamena, Chad
4 Moscow
5 Geneva
6 Osaka
7 Libreville, Gabon
8 Hong Kong and Zurich (jointly ranked)
9 Copenhagen
10 Singapore

SOURCE: Mercer Human Resource Consulting, "Worldwide Cost of Living—City Rankings, 2010," *Worldwide Global Cost of Living Information Services 2010.*

clothing, household goods, and entertainment. This year the survey included three cities in Africa (Luanda, Ndjamena, and Libreville) which reflects the fact that it has become an important emerging market in the past few years.[72]

Canada's most popular destination for assignees has been shifting in the past decade. In 2000 it was to the (1) U.S., (2) Western Europe, (3) Asia Pacific, and (4) Latin America. However, by 2008, while cross-border assignments to the U.S. still took the number-one spot, the second most likely destination had become the Middle East, followed by Western Europe and Asia Pacific.[73]

Housing allowances ensure that the expatriate can maintain the same home-country living standard. Education allowances reimburse expatriates for the expense of placing their children in private English-speaking schools. Relocation allowances cover all the expenses of making the actual move to a new country, including transportation to and from the new location, temporary living expenses, and shipping and/or storage of personal possessions.

The cost of a North American expatriate working in another country is approximately three to four times that of a comparable North American employee.[74] In addition, "about 38 percent of multinational companies surveyed by KPMG LLP for its 2006 Global Assignment Policies and Practices say overseas assignment programs are 'more generous than they need to be.'"[75] These two facts combined have put pressure on global organizations to rethink their tax equalization strategy and expatriate packages.

Re-Acculturation of Expatriates A final issue of importance to managing expatriates is dealing with the re-acculturation process when the managers re-enter their home country, which we mentioned earlier in our discussion of the repatriation phase. Re-entry is no simple feat. Culture shock takes place in reverse. The individual has changed, the company has changed, and the culture has changed while the expatriate was overseas. According to one source, 60 to 70 percent of expatriates did not know what their position would be upon their return, and 46 percent ended up with jobs that gave them reduced autonomy and authority.[76] Twenty percent of workers want to leave the company when they return from an overseas assignment, and this presents potentially serious morale and productivity problems.[77] Recall as well the findings of the Brookfield survey mentioned earlier, which indicated 38 percent of expatriates leave the company within one year of returning home.[78] If these repatriates leave, the company has virtually no way to recoup its substantial investment in human capital.[79]

Companies are increasingly making efforts to help expatriates through re-acculturation. Two characteristics help in this transition process: communication and validation.[80] *Communication* refers to the extent to which the expatriate receives information and recognizes changes while abroad. The closer the contact with the home organization while abroad, the more proactive, effective, and satisfied the expatriate will be upon re-entry. *Validation* refers to the amount of recognition received by the expatriate upon return home. Expatriates who receive recognition from their peers and their bosses for their foreign work and their future potential contribution to the company have fewer troubles with re-entry compared with those who are treated as if they were "out of the loop." Given the tremendous investment that firms make in expatriate employees, usually aimed at providing global experience that will help the company, firms certainly do not want to lose expatriates after their assignments have concluded. The "Competing through Sustainability" box on page 523 provides suggestions based on Raytheon's experience on how managers can protect their investment in human capital once employees near the end of their foreign assignments.

Finally, one research study noted the role of an expatriate manager's expectations about the expatriate assignment in determining repatriation adjustment and job performance. This study found that managers whose job expectations (constraints and demands in terms of volume and performance standards) and nonwork expectations (living and housing conditions) were met exhibited a greater degree of repatriation adjustment and higher levels of job performance.[81]

Table 13.5 Human Resource Practices That Support Effective Expatriation

STAFFING AND SELECTION
• Communicate the value of international assignments for the company's global mission.
• Ensure that those with the highest potential move internationally.
• Provide short-term assignments to increase the pool of employees with international experience.
• Recruit employees who have lived or who were educated abroad.
TRAINING AND CAREER DEVELOPMENT
• Make international assignment planning a part of the career development process.
• Encourage early international experience.
• Create learning opportunities during the assignment.
• Use international assignments as a leadership development tool.
PERFORMANCE APPRAISAL AND COMPENSATION
• Differentiate performance management based on expatriate roles.
• Align incentives with expatriation objectives.
• Tailor benefits to the expatriate's needs.
• Focus on equality of opportunities, not cash.
• Emphasize rewarding careers rather than short-term outcomes.
EXPATRIATION AND REPATRIATION ACTIVITIES
• Involve the family in the orientation program at the beginning and the end of the assignment.
• Establish mentor relationships between expatriates and executives from the home location.
• Provide support for dual careers.
• Secure opportunities for the returning manager to use knowledge and skills learned while on the international assignment.

SOURCE: From Paul Evans, and Vladimir Pucik, *The Global Challenge: Framework for International Human Resource Management,* 2002. Copyright © 2002 The McGraw-Hill Companies.

In sum, a variety of HR practices can support effective expatriation. In general, the selection system must rigorously assess potential expatriates' skills and personalities and even focus on the candidate's spouse. Training should be conducted prior to and during the expatriate assignment, and the assignment itself should be viewed as a career development experience. Effective reward systems must go beyond salary and benefits, and while keeping the employee "whole" and even offering a monetary premium, should also provide access to career development and learning opportunities. Finally, serious efforts should be made to manage the repatriation process.[82] A summary of the key points is provided in Table 13.5.

A Look Back

FreeBalance is an all Canadian company that reminds us just how successful a small company can get when it looks outside Canadian borders. It is now one of top 100 software companies in Canada and serves over 100 central, regional, and local government organizations around the world, as well as being a top supplier of public expenditure control systems to the Canadian government.

The path to such greatness isn't easy, but FreeBalance seems to have seized every opportunity in its path, and its products make the world a better place every day. Quietly and efficiently, FreeBalance services and financial management software help countries in trouble put the pieces back together again so its citizens can live their lives with greater certainty.

With an increasing number of countries adopting its products as they attempt to overcome the devastating effects of war, environmental disasters, and other critical incidents, FreeBalance may face some challenges. Finding enough of the right people with the right talent to help agencies and governments put their financial house back in order is a unique kind of human resources problem. And the need to find those people quickly adds even more pressure when the outcomes are so important.

Questions

1. Visit the FreeBalance jobs website at www.freebalance.com/company/jobs and examine the company's recruitment approach. Do you think FreeBalance will be able to continue to attract and retain the right kinds of people needed to deliver its unique services and software products around the world? What types of problems might the company encounter when recruiting? How can FreeBalance overcome such problems?

2. How might FreeBalance use expatriate employees as part of its international expansion? What will be the challenges in selecting the right kinds of expatriates?

3. What role is there for local country nationals in offering FreeBalance services around the world?

Summary

Today's organizations are more involved in international commerce than ever before, and the trend will continue. The development of NAFTA, GATT, and the European Union, as well as the economic growth of Asia, have accelerated the movement toward a global market. Companies competing in the global marketplace require top-quality people to compete successfully. This requires that managers be aware of the many factors that significantly affect HRM in a global environment, such as culture, human capital, and the political–legal and economic systems, and that they understand how these factors come into play in the various levels of global participation. Finally, globalization requires that they be adept at developing HRM systems that maximize the effectiveness of all human resources, particularly with regard to expatriate managers. Managers cannot overestimate the importance of effectively managing human resources to gain competitive advantage in today's global marketplace.

Key Terms

Cross-cultural
 preparation, 521
Expatriate, 516
Host country, 515
Host-country nationals
 (HCNs), 516
Individualism–collectivism,
 508

Long-term/short-term
 orientation, 509
Masculinity–femininity
 dimension, 509
Parent country, 515
Parent-country nationals
 (PCNs), 516
Power distance, 508
Repatriation, 526

Third country, 516
Third-country nationals
 (TCNs), 516
Transnational process, 519
Transnational
 representation, 518
Transnational scope, 518
Uncertainty avoidance, 509

Discussion Questions

1. What current trends and/or events (besides those mentioned at the outset of the chapter) are responsible for the increased internationalization of the marketplace?

2. According to Hofstede (in Table 13.1 on page 509), Canada is low on power distance, high on individuality, moderate on masculinity, moderate on uncertainty avoidance, and low on long-term orientation. Russia, on the other hand, is high on power distance, moderate on individuality, low on masculinity, high on uncertainty avoidance, and low on long-term orientation. Many Canadian managers may be tempted to transplant their own HRM practices into Russia when companies seek to develop operations there. How acceptable and effective do you think the following practices will be and why? (a) Extensive assessments of individual abilities for selection? (b) Individually based appraisal systems? (c) Suggestion systems? (d) Self-managing work teams?

3. Think of the different levels of global participation. What companies are you familiar with that exhibit the different levels of participation?

4. Recent research indicates that although Hofstede's research on cultural dimensions is still valid and highly regarded, HR managers should use it as a general guideline, rather than a rigid set of rules when establishing human resource practices in other countries. Other than the example of Lenovo in China, what evidence can you find that companies doing business globally have successfully implemented HR practices where it shouldn't be a good fit culturally in terms of Hofstede's findings? What examples can you find of companies that ignored cultural dimensions in establishing human resource practices, only to regret it later?

5. Think of a time when you had to function in another culture (on a vacation or job). What were the major obstacles you faced, and how did you deal with them? Was this a stressful experience? Why? How can companies help expatriate employees deal with stress?

6. What types of skills do you need to be able to manage in today's global marketplace? Where do you expect to get those skills? What classes and/or experiences will you need?

Self-Assessment Exercise

The following list includes a number of qualities that have been identified as being associated with success in an expatriate assignment. Rate the degree to which you possess each quality, using the following scale and check your score using the scale below. You may also wish to consider asking a classmate or friend who knows you well to complete the assessment (about you) to see how others view you in terms of success in an expatriate assignment:

1 = very low
2 = low
3 = moderate
4 = high
5 = very high

____ Resourcefulness/resilience

____ Adaptability/flexibility

____ Emotional stability

____ Ability to deal with ambiguity/uncertainty/differences

____ Desire to work with people who are different

____ Cultural empathy/sensitivity

____ Tolerance of others' views, especially when they differ from your own

____ Sensitivity to feelings and attitudes of others

____ Good health and wellness

Add up your total score for the items. The higher your score, the greater your likelihood of success. Qualities that you rated low would be considered weaknesses for an expatriate assignment. Keep in mind that you will also need to be technically competent for the assignment, and your spouse and family (if applicable) must be adaptable and willing to live abroad.

SOURCE: Based on P. R. Harris and R. T. Moran, "Rating Scale on Successful Expatriate Qualities," *Managing Cultural Differences,* (3rd ed.) (Houston: Gulf, 1991), p. 569.

Exercising Strategy: Driving Profit by Saving Natural and Human Resources

For many small companies, balancing growth issues such as building sales while still controlling costs is critical to survival. It means that owners must make critical decisions about how much staff to bring on board to keep things going in the right direction, even when cash flow isn't coming in or sales don't meet forecast. Taking one's business global just makes those problems that much more difficult to solve since time zones and distance complicate communication and the ability to be on site to actually see what is happening.

Bioteq Environmental Technologies Inc., is a Vancouver-based developer of technologies in the mining industry, as well as soccer-field-sized waste-water treatment plants. Founded in 1998, the firm had domestic sales of just over $1 million by 2003, but things took a huge leap forward when Bioteq was able to tell customers that sales of metal recovered from contaminated water could be high enough to cover the costs of building and maintaining Bioteq's treatment plants. Suddenly, CEO Brad Marchant found opportunities with global customers to make foreign sales with less risk averse customers in other parts of the world, such as Mexico, China, and Australia, for example, that take a more aggressive approach to technology.

Suddenly in a new league, Marchant had some challenges to work through to ensure such opportunities were captured. For example, he came to realize that "… you shouldn't do business in China; you should do business in a very small part of China." Since Jiangxi province was just beginning to focus on regulations around water treatment, Bioteq focused its efforts on landing a sale with the largest mining firm in the region—Jiangxi Copper Co. But Marchant had no connections there, so he hired a Chinese graduate of environmental engineering at UBC to go to Jiangxi and begin building relations with the company's first potential customer in China. Soon International Trade Canada and the National Research Council stepped in to help build credibility for this all Canadian firm, and Bioteq soon found itself making presentations to willing ears about its high-tech (and high-return) solutions to acid mine drainage and mineral processing woes. By 2007, the deal was in the bag, resulting in an immediate sale to the Chinese of $4.20 million in fees to build a plant, with an additional $2.5 million in annual revenue for years to come. Nice work!

But Marchant knew he needed staff on the ground in China and quickly hired Chinese locals to run things effectively, and to build the company's brand there. This was important because locals knew the business culture and could both run the business and build business without risk of a social faux pas. For example, in China if your host invites you to an exotic wild animal feast don't even consider turning it down or you risk losing the deal. Try everything you are offered—including raccoon and raw snake blood if that's the fare. Would Western tech-mining geeks know this? Probably not. Moreover, the decision to staff locally had another plus. It also freed up Marchant and others who were now anxious to talk to companies in other countries where waste-water treatment and mining regulations are similar to those in Canada. Time is of the essence in the early stages of growth and for Bioteq, the future seems to hold seemingly endless opportunities for global growth. After all, Bioteq is the only company with the unique solution to solve a problem that exists all over the world.

Questions

1. What options for staffing did Bioteq have for consideration when it landed its first deal in China? Do you agree with what Marchant decided to do? Explain why or why not.

2. Why was it wise to hire the Chinese environmental engineering grad to begin exploring the market in Jiangxi province? Was there any risk in doing this? What other options did Marchant have?

3. As Marchant and his team begin exploring other markets around the world, should they follow the same strategy used to open up the Chinese market? What factors might influence their choices over time? How can they prepare even more for future opportunities?

SOURCES: B. Eligh, "Cross-cultural Etiquette 101," Business Travel, *The Globe and Mail*, (October 4, 2003); and "Mining the Middle Kingdom," Canada Export Achievement Awards, 2009 Pacific Award Winner at http://exportawards.ca/exportawards/pacific.html.

Managing People: Mining for Gold

How would you go about "onboarding" senior management and professional employees if your employee-owned ground engineering and environmental services consultancy company operated around the world, with offices in 160 offices in over 30 countries—from Brazil to Russia, and seemingly everything in between? That's the challenge for Golder Associates, a company founded in Canada in 1950, that originally focussed on soil mechanics and ground engineering. Trouble is, services have expanded over the past 60 years and now include natural resources management, environmental and social assessment, environmental management and compliance, decommissioning and decontamination, and planning and design.

Small wonder Golder wanted to get a better grasp on how best to integrate new senior professionals as quickly as possible, whether they joined the company as a new hire, or as part of an acquisition by Golder. To understand the issues, Golder commissioned a study involving 75 senior professionals who had been with the company for under five years to find out what integration barriers they had encountered after joining the company. In other words, what, if anything, got in the way of personal productivity once they were on the job? Interviewers asked 15 questions about "cultural alignment, speed of transition, achieving maximum efficiency in the new position and expectations." Results indicated seven areas of challenge "newbies" encountered when trying to get up to speed, including (1) access to senior mentors, (2) training on company systems and processes; (3) opportunities for networking; (4) improved communication with management (especially comprehending management structure and decision-making processes); (5) clarity of expectations; (6) regular feedback on performance and (7) a structured integration process.

Study participants reported feeling fully integrated with respect to daily project management in less than a year. However, a number said they still didn't "get" Golder's company culture after more than a year. Finally, a few felt they were still at sea with respect to the professional freedom and lack of "informal processes associated with Golder's flat management structure and consensus decision making." In a company that employs over 7,000 people and serves over 6,000 clients, this seems understandable, but for Golder it wasn't acceptable. In a company that states its purpose as "Engineering Earth's Development, Preserving Earth's Integrity" getting newly hired senior professionals up to warp speed as soon as possible is essential.

To solve the problem, Golder developed a four-stage integration program specifically for new senior professionals in their first year of employment. Stage One (Hiring) occurs during the hiring process, where activities include meeting other same-level colleagues, receiving a clear explanation of Golder's unique culture, and frank discussions of mutual expectations. Stage Two (Introduction) occurs in the first week, when the new hire is assigned a senior mentor. Together they work out employee goals and objectives, including opportunities for project involvement. They also create a plan for network building and communication to others about the new hire's arrival. Stage Three (Integration) takes place within the first three months. During this time, mentoring intensifies, training on company systems occurs, and both the mentor and mentee seek networking opportunities that will build contacts quickly. Around this time the employee will also attend a two-day induction course facilitated by long-service Golder professionals. They'll get a chance to share what's happened to them so far, ask questions, and dig deep to close any gaps. Often operating company presidents and other senior management make contributions as well. At the end of three months, the employee receives a performance review and is ready for Stage Four (Management), which continues through the remaining nine months, or the end of the employee's first year. Of course, during that time, mentoring continues and there are two more performance reviews at the six-month and one-year anniversary.

Questions

1. Given the responsibilities new managers and senior professionals are likely to assume at Golder to fulfil the company's purpose of "Engineering Earth's Development, Preserving Earth's Integrity," does the company's new four-stage onboarding program seem adequate for the needs of such professionals? Why or why not?

2. Recognizing that Golder Associates professionals will work all around the world, are there any other activities that Golder could undertake to prepare its new senior-level professionals to reach their highest potential in a new global assignment?

SOURCES: B. Leach, "Maximizing Talent Quickly, Integrating Senior Professionals," *HR Professional,* (July/August 2010); "Golder Fact Sheet," at www.golder.ca/en/modules.php?name=Pages&sp_id=338 (retrieved December 14, 2010).

connect **Practise and learn online with Connect.**

GLOSSARY

360-Degree Feedback Systems A performance appraisal system for managers that includes evaluations from a wide range of persons who interact with the manager. The process includes self-evaluations as well as evaluations from the manager's boss, subordinates, peers, and customers.

Action Learning Teams work on an actual business problem, commit to an action plan, and are accountable for carrying out the plan.

Adventure Learning Learning focused on the development of teamwork and leadership skills by using structured outdoor activities.

Adverse-Effect Discrimination A rule, practice, preference, or restriction that is neutral on its face, but which inadvertently or indirectly operates in a manner that discriminates against an employee or group of employees on a prohibited ground of discrimination.

Agency Shop or Rand Formula A union security provision that requires an employee to pay union membership dues but not to join the union.

Agency Theory A theory focusing on the divergent interests and goals of the organization's stakeholders and the ways that employee compensation can be used to align these interests and goals.

Agent In agency theory, a person (e.g., a manager) who is expected to act on behalf of a principal (e.g., an owner).

Alternative Dispute Resolution (ADR) A method of resolving disputes that does not rely on the legal system. Often proceeds through the four stages of open-door policy, peer review, mediation, and arbitration.

Alternative Work Arrangements Independent contractors, on-call workers, temporary workers, and contract company workers who are not employed full-time by the company.

Analytic Approach Type of assessment of HRM effectiveness that involves determining the impact of, or the financial cost and benefits of, a program or practice.

Appraisal Politics A situation in which evaluators purposefully distort ratings to achieve personal or company goals.

Apprenticeship A work-study training method with both on-the-job and classroom training.

Arbitration A procedure for resolving collective bargaining impasses by which an arbitrator chooses a binding solution to the dispute.

Assessment Centre A process in which multiple raters evaluate employees' performance on a number of exercises.

Assessment Collecting information and providing feedback to employees about their behaviour, communication style, or skills.

Attitude Awareness and Change Program Program focusing on increasing employees' awareness of differences in cultural and ethnic backgrounds, physical characteristics, and personal characteristics that influence behaviour toward others.

Attitudinal Structuring The aspect of the labour–management negotiation process that refers to the relationship and level of trust between the negotiators.

Audit Approach Type of assessment of HRM effectiveness that involves review of customer satisfaction or key indicators (such as turnover rate or average days to fill a position) related to an HRM functional area (such as recruiting or training).

Balanced Scorecard A means of performance measurement that gives managers a chance to look at their company from the perspectives of internal and external customers, employees, and shareholders.

Behavioural Description Interviews (BDI) Structured interviews posing open-ended, experience-based questions that focus on what the applicant has done in the past.

Behaviour-Based Program A program focusing on changing the organizational policies and individual behaviours that inhibit employees' personal growth and productivity.

Benchmark Jobs Key jobs used in pay surveys, that have relatively stable content and are common to many organizations.

Benchmarking Comparing an organization's practices against those of the competition.

Benchmarks© An instrument designed to measure the factors that are important to managerial success.

Bona Fide Occupational Qualification A qualification that is necessary to the performance of a particular job.

Canada/Quebec Pension Plan (CPP/QPP) A mandatory government-sponsored pension plan funded by employers and employees that provides a basic level of income security for working Canadians when they retire or become disabled; administered separately in Quebec.

Career Management System A system to retain and motivate employees by identifying and meeting their development needs (also called development planning systems).

Career Support Coaching, protection, sponsorship, challenging assignments, exposure, and visibility.

Centralization Degree to which decision-making authority resides at the top of the organizational chart.

Certification The process by which the labour board designates the union as the exclusive bargaining agent of employees in the bargaining unit.

Check-Off Provision   A union contract provision that requires an employer to deduct union dues from employees' paycheques.

Climate for Transfer   Trainees' perceptions of characteristics of the work environment (social support and situational constraints) that can either facilitate or inhibit use of trained skills or behaviour.

Closed Shop   A union security provision requiring a person to be a union member before being hired.

Coach   A peer or manager who works with an employee to motivate, help develop skills, and provide reinforcement and feedback.

Cognitive Ability Tests   Tests that include three dimensions: verbal comprehension, quantitative ability, and reasoning ability.

Comparable Worth   A public policy that advocates remedies for any undervaluation of women's jobs (also called pay equity).

Compa-Ratio   An index of the correspondence between actual and intended pay.

Compensable Factors   The characteristics of jobs that an organization values and chooses to pay for.

Competitiveness   A company's ability to maintain and gain market share in its industry.

Compressed Workweeks   Work schedule arrangements whereby employees work the same number of hours normally expected in a traditional five-day workweek, except that the workload is compressed into fewer days of the week, with longer hours worked each day.

Concentration Strategy   A strategy focusing on increasing market share, reducing costs, or creating and maintaining a market niche for products and services.

Conciliation   A procedure for resolving collective bargaining impasses by which a conciliator with no binding authority acts as a facilitator and go-between in the negotiations; sometimes a necessary step before a legal strike or lockout can occur.

Concurrent Validation   A criterion-related validity study in which a test is administered to all the people currently in a job and then incumbents' scores are correlated with existing measures of their performance on the job.

Constructive Dismissal   A unilateral and fundamental change to a material term or condition of employment.

Content Validation   A test-validation strategy performed by demonstrating that the items, questions, or problems posed by a test are a representative sample of the kinds of situations or problems that occur on the job.

Continuous Learning   A learning system that requires employees to understand the entire work process and expects them to acquire new skills, apply them on the job, and share what they have learned with other employees.

Criterion-Related Validity   A method of establishing the validity of a personnel selection method by showing a substantial correlation between test scores and job performance scores.

Cross-Cultural Preparation   The process of educating employees (and their families) who are given an assignment in a foreign country.

Cultural Immersion   A behaviour-based diversity program that sends employees into communities where they interact with persons from different cultures, races, and nationalities.

Defined-Benefit Pension Plan   An employer-sponsored and registered pension plan that guarantees (defines) a specified retirement benefit level to employees typically based on a combination of years of service and age as well as the employee's earnings level (usually the five highest earnings years).

Defined-Contribution Pension Plan   An employer-sponsored and registered pension plan in which an individual account is set up for each employee, to which the employer provides a guaranteed size of contribution; it may also include employee contributions.

Delayering   Reducing the number of job levels within an organization.

Departmentalization   Degree to which work units are grouped based on functional similarity or similarity of work flow.

Development   The acquisition of knowledge, skills, and behaviours that improve an employee's ability to meet changes in job requirements and in client and customer demands.

Direct Applicants   People who apply for a job vacancy without prompting from the organization.

Direct Discrimination   A rule, practice, preference, or restriction that on its face treats a person differently or unequally based on a prohibited ground of discrimination.

Discrimination   A restriction, preference, or distinction based on a prohibited ground, which results in unequal treatment and denies an individual his or her right to the equal protection and benefit of guaranteed human rights and freedoms.

Distributive Bargaining   The part of the labour–management negotiation process that focuses on dividing a fixed economic "pie."

Diversity Management   A strategic initiative designed to capitalize on an organization's diverse talent pool.

Diversity Training   Training designed to improve employee attitudes about diversity and/or develop skills needed to work with a diverse workforce.

Downsizing   The planned elimination of large numbers of personnel, designed to enhance organizational effectiveness.

Downward Move   A job change involving a reduction in an employee's level of responsibility and authority.

Duty of Fair Representation   A common law and statutory duty that the union fairly represent all employees in the bargaining unit, whether or not union members. Unions are prohibited from acting in an arbitrary, discriminatory, or unfair manner.

Duty to Bargain in Good Faith   A duty on employers and unions to make every reasonable effort to collectively bargain with the objective of reaching a collective agreement.

Efficiency Wage Theory   A theory stating that wages influence worker productivity.

E-Learning   Instruction and delivery of training by computers through the Internet or company intranet.

Electronic Human Resource Management (e-HRM)   The processing and transmission of digitized information used in HRM.

Electronic Performance Support Systems (EPSS)   Computer applications that can provide skills training, information access, and expert advice.

Employee Assistance Programs (EAPs)   Employer programs that attempt to ameliorate problems encountered by workers who are drug dependent, alcoholic, or psychologically troubled.

Employee Benefits   Part of an organization's total compensation package and includes both mandatory government-sponsored benefits and voluntary benefits such as life and disability insurance, extended health coverage, additional vacation pay, and a range of other options.

Employee Engagement   The degree to which employees are fully involved in their work and the strength of their commitment to their job and the company.

Employee Share Ownership Plan (ESOP)   An employee ownership plan that gives employers certain tax and financial advantages when shares are granted to employees.

Employee Wellness Programs (EWPs)   Programs designed and sponsored by employers that focus on changing behaviours both during and outside work that could eventually lead to future health problems.

Employment Equity   Initiatives that proactively target women, Aboriginal people, people with disabilities, and visible minorities

to require or encourage preferential treatment in employment practices in an effort to achieve equality in employment.

Employment Insurance (EI)   A mandatory, government-sponsored plan funded by employee and employer contributions that offsets lost income to eligible employees for reasons of job loss, illness, or compassionate leave, and that provides maternity and parental benefits and a variety of other employment initiatives.

Employment Systems Review   An in-depth assessment of all of the employer's systems, policies, and practices, both formal and informal, written and unwritten, as well as collective agreements, and of the manner in which these are implemented, in order to identify barriers to the full participation of designated group members in employment with the employer.

Ergonomics   The science of creating a proper fit between people and their work, taking into account safety, comfort, ease of use, productivity and performance, and aesthetics.

Essential Workers   Public-sector workers who are prohibited by statute from striking for the good of public order, health, safety, and welfare.

Evidence-Based HR   Demonstrating that human resource practices have a positive influence on the company's bottom line or key stakeholders (employees, customers, community, and shareholders).

Exempt Employees   Employees who are not covered by the Employment Standards Act. Exempt employees are not eligible for overtime pay.

Expatriate   An employee sent by his or her company in one country to manage operations in a different country.

Expectancy Theory   The theory that says motivation is a function of valence, instrumentality, and expectancy.

External Analysis   Examining the organization's operating environment to identify strategic opportunities and threats.

External Growth Strategy   An emphasis on acquiring vendors and suppliers or buying businesses that allow a company to expand into new markets.

Flexible Benefits Plan   A benefits plan design that provides employees the chance to choose (within limits) among benefits offered by the employer, to help ensure the plan will more effectively meet the needs of all employees, and to help the employer contain costs.

Flexible Spending Account   An account set up by an employer for each employee that permits pretax contributions to the account to be drawn on to pay for uncovered health care expenses (such as deductibles and copayments).

Flexible Work Schedules A work arrangement whereby an employer permits an employee to select alternative start and end times to the firm's normally scheduled workday, with the proviso that the required total hours will be worked each day and the employee will be present during core business hours (usually 10 a.m. to 3 p.m.) established by the employer.

Forecasting The attempts to determine the supply of and demand for various types of human resources to predict areas within the organization where there will be future labour shortages or surpluses.

Formal Education Programs Employee development programs, including short courses offered by consultants or universities, executive MBA programs, and university programs.

Gainsharing A form of compensation based on group or plant performance (rather than organization-wide profits) that does not become part of the employee's base salary.

Generalizability The degree to which the validity of a selection method established in one context extends to other contexts.

Glass Ceiling A barrier to advancement to higher-level jobs in the company that adversely affects women and minorities. The barrier may be due to lack of access to training programs, development experiences, or relationships (e.g., mentoring).

Goals What an organization hopes to achieve in the medium- to long-term future.

Group Mentoring Program A program pairing a successful senior employee with a group of four to six less experienced protégés.

Group- or Team-Building Methods Training techniques that help trainees share ideas and experiences, build group identity, understand the dynamics of interpersonal relationships, and get to know their own strengths and weaknesses and those of their coworkers.

Hands-On Methods Training methods that actively involve the trainee in learning.

High-Leverage Training Training practice that links training to strategic business goals, has top management support, relies on an instructional design model, and is benchmarked to programs in other organizations.

High-Performance Work Systems Work systems that maximize the fit between the company's social system (employees) and technical system.

Host Country The country in which the parent country organization seeks to locate or has already located a facility.

Host-Country Nationals (HCNs) Employees who were born and raised in the host, not the parent, country.

Human Resource Information System (HRIS) A system used to acquire, store, manipulate, analyze, retrieve, and distribute information related to a company's human resources.

Human Resource Management (HRM) Policies, practices, and systems that influence employees' behaviour, attitudes, and performance.

Human Resource Recruitment Any practice or activity carried on by the organization with the primary purpose of identifying and attracting potential employees.

Human Rights Personal and private rights protected by government through legislation aimed to ensure that individuals are treated equally and can participate freely in society in a manner free from discrimination and harassment based on prescribed grounds such as race; colour; religion or creed; sex; sexual orientation; age; disability; marital status; family status; nationality, ethnicity, or place of origin; or criminal record.

Individualism–Collectivism One of Hofstede's cultural dimensions; describes the strength of the relation between an individual and other individuals in a society.

Intangible Assets A type of company asset including human capital, customer capital, social capital, and intellectual capital.

Integrative Bargaining The part of the labour–management negotiation process that seeks solutions beneficial to both sides.

Interactional Justice A concept of justice referring to the interpersonal nature of how the outcomes were implemented.

Internal Analysis The process of examining an organization's strengths and weaknesses.

Internal Growth Strategy A focus on new market and product development, innovation, and joint ventures.

Internal Responsibility System (IRS) A system within an organization where every person has direct responsibility for health and safety as an essential part of his or her job.

Intra-Organizational Bargaining The part of the labour–management negotiation process that focuses on the conflicting objectives of factions within labour and management.

Involuntary Turnover Turnover initiated by the organization (often among people who would prefer to stay).

Job Analysis The process of getting detailed information about jobs.

Job Description A list of the tasks, duties, and responsibilities that a job entails.

Job Design The process of defining the way work will be performed and the tasks that will be required in a given job.

Job Enlargement Adding challenges or new responsibilities to an employee's current job.

Job Enrichment The process of enriching jobs that are boring, repetitive, or low in scope through interventions such as ensuring workers have opportunities for input into important organizational decisions involving their work.

Job Evaluation An administrative procedure used to measure internal job worth.

Job Experiences The relationships, problems, demands, tasks, and other features that employees face in their jobs.

Job Hazard Analysis Technique A breakdown of each job into basic elements, each of which is rated for its potential for harm or injury.

Job Redesign The process of changing the tasks or the way work is performed in an existing job.

Job Rotation The process of systematically moving a single individual from one job to another over the course of time. The job assignments may be in various functional areas of the company or movement may be between jobs in a single functional area or department.

Job Satisfaction A pleasurable feeling that results from the perception that one's job fulfills or allows for the fulfillment of one's important job values.

Job Specification A list of the knowledge, skills, abilities, and other characteristics (KSAOs) that an individual must have to perform a job.

Job Structure The relative pay of jobs within an organization.

Leading Indicator An objective measure that accurately predicts future labour demand.

Learning Management System (LMS) Technology platform that automates the administration, development, and delivery of a company's training program.

Lockout A lockout includes closing a place of employment, a suspension of work, or a refusal by an employer to continue to employ a number of its employees for the purpose of compelling the employees, or employees of another employer, to accept terms and conditions of employment.

Long-Term Disability Plan A form of income for longer periods of absence from work due to nonwork-related chronic illness or disability.

Long-Term/Short-Term Orientation One of Hofstede's cultural dimensions; describes how a culture balances immediate benefits with future rewards.

Maintenance of Membership Union rules requiring members to remain members for a certain period of time (such as the length of the union contract).

Managing Diversity The process of creating an inclusive environment that allows all employees to contribute to organizational goals and experience personal growth.

Marginal Employee An employee performing at a barely acceptable level because of lack of ability and/or motivation to perform well, not poor work conditions.

Marginal Tax Rate The percentage of an additional dollar of earnings that goes to taxes.

Masculinity–Femininity Dimension One of Hofstede's cultural dimensions; describes the division of roles between the sexes within a society.

Mediation A procedure for resolving collective bargaining impasses by which a mediator with no formal authority acts as a facilitator and go-between in the negotiations.

Mentor An experienced, productive senior employee who helps develop a less experienced employee.

Merit Increase Grid A grid that combines an employee's performance rating with the employee's position in a pay range to determine the size and frequency of his or her pay increases.

Merit Pay Annual increases to base pay that are usually linked to performance appraisal ratings.

Minimum Wage The lowest hourly wage an employer is legally allowed to pay an employee in the relevant province or territory of Canada for which such wages are determined.

Motivation to Learn The desire of the trainee to learn the content of a training program.

Myers-Briggs Type Indicator® Personality Inventory (MBTI)® A personality assessment tool used for team building and leadership development that identifies employees' preferences for energy, information gathering, decision making, and lifestyle.

Needs Assessment The process used to determine if training is necessary.

New Technologies Current applications of knowledge, procedures, and equipment that have not been previously used. Usually involves replacing human labour with equipment, information processing, or some combination of the two.

Nonbenchmark Jobs Jobs that are unique to organizations and that cannot be directly valued or compared through the use of market surveys.

Occupational Health and Safety Legislation The law that authorizes government to establish and enforce occupational health and safety standards, administrative requirements, and enforcement mechanisms in respect of the workplace.

Offshoring   Exporting jobs from developed countries to countries where labour and other costs are lower.

On-the-Job Training (OJT)   New or inexperienced employees learning through observing peers or managers performing the job and trying to imitate their behaviour.

Opportunity to Perform   Trainees are provided with or actively seek experience using newly learned knowledge, skills, or behaviour.

Organizational Analysis   A process for determining the business appropriateness of training.

Organizational Socialization   A process by which new employees are transformed into effective members of the company.

Outcome Fairness   The judgment that people make with respect to the outcomes received relative to the outcomes received by other people with whom they identify.

Outplacement Counselling   Counselling to help displaced employees manage the transition from one job to another.

Outsourcing   The practice of having another company provide services.

Parent Country   The country in which a company's corporate headquarters is located.

Parent-Country Nationals (PCNs)   Employees who were born and live in a parent country.

Pay Equity   Equal pay for work of equal value.

Pay for Performance   Variable forms of pay designed to recognize and reward employees' performance that are based on measures of individual or group contributions to the organization's success; sometimes called incentive pay, variable pay, or performance-based pay.

Pay Grades   Jobs of similar worth or content grouped together for pay administration purposes.

Pay Level   The average pay, including wages, salaries, and bonuses, of jobs in an organization.

Pay Policy Line   A mathematical expression that describes the relationship between a job's pay and its job evaluation points.

Pay Structure   The relative pay of different jobs (job structure) and how much they are paid (pay level).

Performance Appraisal   The process through which an organization gets information on how well an employee is doing his or her job.

Performance Feedback   The process of providing employees information regarding their performance effectiveness.

Performance Management   The means through which managers ensure that employees' activities and outputs are congruent with the organization's goals.

Performance Planning and Evaluation (PPE) System   Any system that seeks to tie the formal performance appraisal process to the company's strategies by specifying at the beginning of the evaluation period the types and level of performance that must be accomplished in order to achieve the strategy.

Person Analysis   A process for determining whether employees need training, who needs training, and whether employees are ready for training.

Picketing   Picketing involves the presence of striking or locked-out workers outside the employer's business premises for the purpose of protesting the labour dispute. Strikers often carry signs and hand out information, and may impede the flow of traffic in and out of the employer's operations.

Power Distance   One of Hofstede's cultural dimensions; describes how a culture deals with hierarchical power relationships.

Predictive Validation   A criterion-related validity study that seeks to establish an empirical relationship between applicants' test scores and their eventual performance on the job.

Presentation Methods   Training methods in which trainees are passive recipients of information.

Principal   In agency theory, a person (e.g., an owner) who seeks to direct another person's behaviour.

Procedural Justice   A concept of justice focusing on the methods used to determine the outcomes received.

Profit Sharing   A compensation plan in which payments are based on a measure of organization performance (profits) and do not become part of the employees' base salary.

Progression of Withdrawal   Theory that dissatisfied individuals enact a set of behaviours in succession to avoid their work situation.

Promotions   Advancement into positions with greater challenge, more responsibility, and more authority than the employee's previous job.

Prosocial Motivation   The degree to which people are energized to do their jobs because it helps other people.

Protean Career   A career that is based on self-direction with the goal of psychological success in one's work.

Psychological Contract   Expectations of employee contributions and what the company will provide in return.

Psychological Harassment   Vexatious behaviour in the form of repeated and hostile or unwanted conduct, comments, actions, or gestures, that affects an employee's dignity or psychological or physical integrity and that adversely affects an employee's work environment.

Psychosocial Support Serving as a friend and role model, providing positive regard and acceptance, and creating an outlet for a protégé to talk about anxieties and fears.

Quantitative Ability Concerns the speed and accuracy with which one can solve arithmetic problems of all kinds.

Range Spread The distance between the minimum and maximum amounts in a pay grade.

Rate Ranges Different employees in the same job may have different pay rates.

Ratification A vote of bargaining unit members to accept a tentative collective agreement settlement reached between the union and management bargaining teams (or otherwise proposed for settlement).

Reasonable Accommodation Adjustments that employers are legally obligated to make to their policies, practices, and expectations to ensure that an employee is not subject to discriminatory treatment based on a prohibited ground of discrimination. Commonly referred to as the duty to accommodate.

Reasoning Ability A person's capacity to invent solutions to many diverse problems.

Reengineering Review and redesign of work processes to make them more efficient and improve the quality of the end product or service.

Referrals People who are prompted to apply for a job by someone within the organization.

Registered Pension Plans Retirement plans sponsored by employers that are registered according to the Income Tax Act and subject to federal and provincial pension standards legislation.

Reliability The consistency of a performance measure; the degree to which a performance measure is free from random error.

Repatriation The preparation of expatriates for return to the parent company and country from a foreign assignment.

Role Behaviours Behaviours that are required of an individual in his or her role as a jobholder in a social work environment.

Sabbatical A leave of absence from the company to renew or develop skills.

Safety Awareness Programs Employer programs that attempt to instill symbolic and substantive changes in the organization's emphasis on safety.

Selection The process by which an organization attempts to identify applicants with the necessary knowledge, skills, abilities, and other characteristics that will help it achieve its goals.

Self-Directed Learning A program in which employees take responsibility for all aspects of learning.

Self-Efficacy The employees' belief that they can successfully learn the content of a training program.

Self-Service Giving employees online access to HR information, online enrollment in programs and services, and completing online attitude surveys.

Sexual Harassment Any unwanted verbal comment or physical contact of a sexual nature, or that is based on a person's sex or gender that the harasser knew was unwelcome or reasonably ought to have known was unwelcome.

Share Options An employee ownership plan that gives employees the opportunity to buy the company's shares at a previously fixed price.

Short-Term Disability Plan Benefits plans that provide income security to employees for short periods of absence from work due to nonwork-related illness or injury.

Sick Leave Programs Employer-sponsored benefit plans that often provide full salary replacement to employees for a limited period of time and which may be based on length of service.

Simulation A training method that represents a real-life situation, allowing trainees to see the outcomes of their decisions in an artificial environment.

Situational Interview An interview procedure where applicants are confronted with specific future-based issues, questions, or problems that are likely to arise on the job.

Six Sigma Training An action training program that provides employees with defect-reducing tools to cut costs and certifies employees as green belts, champions, or black belts.

Skill-Based Pay Pay based on the skills employees acquire and are capable of using.

Strategic Choice The organization's strategy; the ways an organization will attempt to fulfill its mission and achieve its long-term goals.

Strategic Human Resource Management (SHRM) A pattern of planned human resource deployments and activities intended to enable an organization to achieve its goals.

Strategy Formulation The process of deciding on a strategic direction by defining a company's mission and goals, its external opportunities and threats, and its internal strengths and weaknesses.

Strategy Implementation The process of devising structures and allocating resources to enact the chosen strategy.

Strike A concerted work stoppage or a refusal to work or to continue to work by employees. A strike can also include a slowdown of work or other concerted activity on the part of employees in relation to their work. In all cases, the activity is designed to restrict or limit output.

Succession Planning The identification and tracking of high-potential employees capable of filling higher-level managerial positions.

Sustainability The ability of a company to survive and exceed in a dynamic competitive environment, based on an approach to organizational decision making that considers the company's ability to make a profit without sacrificing the resources of its employees, the community, or the environment.

Systemic Discrimination Unintentional discrimination that arises from a pattern of behaviour that is rooted in established stereotypes, attitudes, and value systems that perpetuates the relative disadvantage of a protected group.

Talent Management A systematic planned strategic effort by a company to attract, retain, develop, and motivate highly skilled employees and managers.

Task Analysis The process of identifying the tasks, knowledge, skills, and behaviours that need to be emphasized in training.

Telecommuting The practice of using technology to complete work traditionally done in the workplace in another location, such as the employee's home.

Third Country A country other than a host or parent country.

Third-Country Nationals (TCNs) Employees born in a country other than the parent or host country.

Total Quality Management (TQM) A cooperative company-wide effort to continuously improve the ways people, machines, and systems accomplish work.

Training A planned effort to facilitate the learning of job-related knowledge, skills, and behaviour by employees.

Training Design Process A systematic approach for developing training programs.

Training Outcomes A way to evaluate the effectiveness of a training program based on cognitive, skill-based, affective, and results outcomes.

Transfer of Training The use of knowledge, skills, and behaviours learned in training on the job.

Transfer The movement of an employee to a different job assignment in a different area of the company.

Transitional Matrix Matrix showing the proportion (or number) of employees in different job categories at different times.

Transnational Process The extent to which a company's planning and decision-making processes include representatives and ideas from a variety of cultures.

Transnational Representation The multinational composition of a company's managers.

Transnational Scope A company's ability to make HRM decisions from an international perspective.

Uncertainty Avoidance One of Hofstede's cultural dimensions; describes how cultures seek to deal with an unpredictable future.

Undue Hardship The limit upon an employer's duty to accommodate an employee under human rights legislation.

Union Shop A union security provision that requires all existing and future employees to join and maintain membership in the union.

Unsafe Act A worker's violation of, or disregard for, a safety rule or procedure.

Unsafe Condition A physical hazard or inadequate safety programs, policies, or training that poses a risk to the health and safety of workers.

Upward Feedback Managerial performance appraisal that involves subordinates' evaluations of the manager's behaviour or skills.

Utility The degree to which the information provided by selection methods enhances the effectiveness of selecting personnel in real organizations.

Validity The extent to which a performance measure assesses all the relevant—and only the relevant—aspects of job performance.

Verbal Comprehension A person's capacity to understand and use written and spoken language.

Vesting Rights Rights to a pension to be paid upon retirement earned by members of a pension plan once a specified minimum period of time has been worked with the employer sponsoring the plan (up to two years in Canada).

Virtual Reality Computer-based technology that provides trainees with a three-dimensional learning experience. Trainees operate in a simulated environment that responds to their behaviours and reactions.

Virtual Teams Teams that are separated by time, geographic distance, culture, and/or organizational boundaries and rely almost exclusively on technology for interaction between team members.

Voluntary Check-Off A union security provision wherein members of the union have union dues deducted by the employer only at their request, and there is no requirement to join the union.

Voluntary Recognition Voluntary recognition occurs where the employer agrees in writing to recognize the union as the exclusive bargaining agent of employees in the bargaining unit.

Voluntary Turnover Turnover initiated by employees (often whom the company would prefer to keep).

Workers' Compensation A mandatory government-sponsored insurance plan funded by employers that provides wage-loss benefits, health care, survivor benefits, and rehabilitative services to eligible employees with work-related injuries or diseases.

Workforce Utilization Review A comparison of the proportion of workers in protected subgroups with the proportion that each subgroup represents in the relevant labour market.

Workplace Hazardous Materials Information System (WHMIS) A Canada-wide system designed to give employers and workers information about hazardous materials in the workplace.

Wrongful Dismissal An allegation against a former employer by a terminated employee that wrongful termination of the employment contract has occurred due to failure (on the part of the employer) to provide just cause for termination of employment.

Chapter 1

Page 3: CP Photo/AP Photo/Richard Drew; page 21: © Image Source/PunchStock; page 27: Comstock/PunchStock.

Chapter 2

Page 39: THE CANADIAN PRESS/Darren Calabrese.

Chapter 3

Page 77: Comstock/PunchStock; page 96: Juan Silva/The Image Bank/Getty Images.

Chapter 4

Page 125: THE CANADIAN PRESS Images/Mario Beauregard; page 139: © AP Photo/ The Joblin Globe/T. Rob Brown; page 157: © Ryan McVay/Getty Images/DAL.

Chapter 5

Page 165: Photo courtesy of MNP; page 186: Adamgregor/Dreamstime.com.

Chapter 6

Page 209: AFP/Getty Images; page 218: © The McGraw-Hill Companies/Lars A. Niki, photographer/DAL.

Chapter 7

Page 253: PRNewsFoto/I Love Rewards; page 266: © Ryan McVay/Getty Images/DAL.

Chapter 8

Page 301: CP Photo/AP Photo/Elizabeth Dalziel; page 320: Aj-brugge/Dreamstime.com; page 331: Mathieu Belanger/Reuters/Landov.

Chapter 9

Page 345: THE CANADIAN PRESS/Trevor Hagan; page 365: LWA Photographer's Choice/ Getty Images; page 367: © Bob Daemmrich/PhotoEdit.

Chapter 10

Page 381: Photo: Robert Puskajler; page 389: Helen Ashford/Workbook Stock/Getty Images; page 404: © CORBIS/All Rights Reserved.

Chapter 11

Page 421: *Toronto Star*/GetStock.com; page 446: THE CANADIAN PRESS/Graham Hughes.

Chapter 12

Page 467: CP Photo/Ryan Remiorz.

Chapter 13

Page 503: CP Photo/AP Photo/Anjum Naveed; page 521: LWA/The Image Bank/Getty Images.

ENDNOTES

Chapter 1

1. A. S. Tsui and L. R. Gomez-Mejia, "Evaluating Human Resource Effectiveness," in *Human Resource Management: Evolving Rules and Responsibilities*, ed. L. Dyer (Washington, DC: BNA Books, 1988), pp. 1187–1227; M. A. Hitt, B. W. Keats, and S. M. DeMarie, "Navigating in the New Competitive Landscape: Building Strategic Flexibility and Competitive Advantage in the 21st Century," *Academy of Management Executive* 12, no. 4 (1998), pp. 22–42; J. T. Delaney and M. A. Huselid, "The Impact of Human Resource Management Practices on Perceptions of Organizational Performance," *Academy of Management Journal* 39 (1996), pp. 949–969.

2. F. Hansen, "2006 Data Bank Annual," *Workforce Management* (December 11, 2006), p. 48.

3. SHRM-BNA Survey No. 66, "Policy and Practice Forum: Human Resources Activities, Budgets, and Staffs: 2000–2001," *Bulletin to Management*, Bureau of National Affairs Policy and Practice Series (June 28, 2001) (Washington, DC: Bureau of National Affairs).

4. CHRP, CCHRA Human Resources Professionals in Canada: Revised Body of Knowledge and Required Professional Capabilities (October 2007), p. 4 at www.chrp.ca/rpc/body-of-knowledge (retrieved June 7, 2011).

5. Grossman, "New Competencies for HR," *HR Magazine* (June 2007), p. 58.

6. "The Thinkers 50," at www.thinkers50.com/profile/31/2009 (retrieved June 13, 2011); "Colloquia Prize" at http://daveulrich.com (retrieved June 13, 2011).

7. S. Dobson, "Employers Brace for G20. *Canadian HR Reporter*," (June 2010), pp. 1, 31.

8. A. Halcrow, "Survey Shows HRM in Transition," *Workforce* (June 1998), pp. 73–80: J. Laabs, "Why HR Can't Win Today," *Workforce* (May 1998), pp. 62–74; C. Cole, "Kodak Snapshots," *Workforce* (June 2000), pp. 65–72; W. Ruona and S. Gibson, "The Making of Twenty-First Century HR: An Analysis of the Convergence of HRM, HRD, and OD," *Human Resource Management* 43 (2004), pp. 49–66.

9. Towers Perrin, *Priorities for Competitive Advantage: An IBM Study Conducted by Towers Perrin*, 1992.

10. CHRP, *Hire a CHRP, The Strategic Advantage, Survey Results—Business Leaders Value the CHRP* at www.chrpa.ca (retrieved September 2010).

11. L. Claus and J. Collison, *The Maturing Profession of Human Resources: Worldwide and Regional View* (Alexandria, VA: Society for Human Resource Management, 2005).

12. Mysalary.com (Canada), "HR Generalist III, Base Salary, National Average, August 2010," at www.salary.com/salary/index.asp (retrieved August 11, 2010).

13. L. Claus and J. Collison, *The Maturing Profession of Human Resources: Worldwide and Regional View* (Alexandria, VA: Society for Human Resource Management, 2005).

14. J. Wiscombe, "Your Wonderful, Terrible HR Life," *Workforce* (June 2001), pp. 32–38.

15. Hansen, "Top of the Class."

16. R. Grossman, "Putting HR in Rotation," *HR Magazine* (March 2003), pp. 50–57.

17. CCHRA, "About Us," at www.cchra.ca/about-us (retrieved August 24, 2010).

18. S. Klie, "It Pays to Have HR Designation," *Canadian HR Reporter* (April 2010), pp. 1, 12.

19. A. Jones, "Evolutionary Science, Work/Life Integration, and Corporate Responsibility," *Organizational Dynamics* 32 (2002), pp. 17–31.

20. A. Fox, "Get in the Business of Being Green," *HR Magazine* (June 2008), p. 45.

21. P. Owusu, "Conference Board of Canada—July 9, 2010—Month at a Glance: Canada's Job Machine Is Still Rolling" (Ottawa: Conference Board of Canada, 2010).

22. A. Cowan and R. Wright. *Valuing Your Talent: Human Resources Trends and Metrics* (Ottawa: Conference Board of Canada (June 2010), pp. 9–11.

23. Ibid., p. ii.

24. Ibid., p. 8.

25. Human Resources and Skills Development Canada, *Looking Ahead: A 10-Year Outlook for the Canadian Labour Market* (2006–2015) (Ottawa: HRSDC, 2006).

26. M. Hilton, "Skills for Work in the 21st Century: What Does the Research Tell Us?" *Academy of Management Executive* (November 2008), pp. 63–78; "Manufacturing: Engine of US Innovation," *National Association of Manufacturing* (October 4, 2006) at www.nam.org (retrieved January 21, 2009); Human Resources and Skills Development Canada, *Looking Ahead: A 10-Year Outlook for the Canadian Labour Market* (2006–2015) (Ottawa: HRSDC, 2006).

27. Human Resources and Skills Development Canada, *Looking Ahead: A 10-Year Outlook for the Canadian Labour Market* (2006–2015) (Ottawa: HRSDC, 2006).

28. Ibid.

29. Ibid.

30. Canadian Manufacturers and Exporters. *20/20 Building Our Vision for the Future: The Future of Manufacturing in Canada, Perspectives and Recommendations on Workforce Capabilities* (Ottawa: CME 2005) pp. 9–10.

31. Ibid.

32. Ibid., p. 31.

33. Ibid., p. 3.

34. J. Barney, *Gaining and Sustaining a Competitive Advantage* (Upper Saddle River, NJ: Prentice Hall, 2002).

35. L. Weatherly, *Human Capital: The Elusive Asset* (Alexandria, VA: 2003 SHRM Research Quarterly).

36. WestJet. WestJetCulture, Fact Sheet, Corporate Profile and Backgrounder at www.westjet.com/guest/en/aboutUs/corporateProgfile/westJetCulture, www.westjet.com/pdf/

investorMedia/westjetBackgrounder.pdf, and www.westjet.com/pdf/investorMedia/investorFactSheet.pdf (retrieved August 10, 2010).

37. Westjet. "WestJet Named as One of the Best Employers in Canada," News Release (December 31, 2009) at westjet2.mediaroom.com/index.php?s=43&item=406 (retrieved June 7, 2011).

38. Ibid.

39. L. Bassi, J. Ludwig, D. McMurrer, and M. Van Buren, *Profiting from Learning: Do Firms' Investments in Education and Training Pay Off?* (Alexandria, VA: American Society for Training and Development, 2000).

40. P. Drucker, *Management Challenges for the 21st Century* (New York: HarperBusiness, 1999); Howard N. Fullerton Jr., "Labor Force Projections to 2008: Steady Growth and Changing Composition," *Monthly Labor Review* (November 1999), pp. 19–32.

41. CBC News, "GM Closes Windsor Plant, Ending an Era" (July 28, 2010) at www.cbc.ca/canada/windsor/story/2010/07/28/wdr-gm-plant-closing.html (retrieved June 7, 2011).

42. Edmunds Inside Line. "General Motors Building Opel Astra in Russia" (July 29, 2010) at www.Insideline.com/opel/asta/general-motors-building-open-astra-in-russia.html (retrieved August 1, 2010).

43. J. O'Toole and E. Lawler III, *The New American Workplace* (New York: Palgrave McMillan, 2006).

44. D. M. Rousseau, "Psychological and Implied Contracts in Organizations," *Employee Rights and Responsibilities Journal* 2 (1989), pp. 121–129.

45. D. Rousseau, "Changing the Deal While Keeping the People," *Academy of Management Executive* 11 (1996), pp. 50–61; M. A. Cavanaugh and R. Noe, "Antecedents and Consequences of the New Psychological Contract," *Journal of Organizational Behavior* 20 (1999), pp. 323–340.

46. Towers Watson. *The Shape of the Emerging 'Deal': Insights from Towers Watson's 2010 Global Workforce Study, 2010* (Toronto: Towers Watson, 2010).

47. Towers Watson, "Engaging and Retaining Top Performers," *Workforce Snapshots* at www.towerswatson.com (retrieved August 2, 2010).

48. R. Vance, *Employee Engagement and Commitment* (Alexandria, VA: Society for Human Resource Management, 2006).

49. J. Gibbons, "Employee Engagement: A Review of Current Research and Its Implications," in A. Cowan and R. Wright eds. *Valuing your Talent Human Resources Trends and Metrics* (Toronto: The Conference Board of Canada, 2010), p. 5.

50. For examples, see M. Huselid, "The Impact of Human Resource Management Practices on Turnover, Productivity, and Corporate Financial Performance," *Academy of Management Journal* 38 (1995), pp. 635–672; S. Payne and S. Webber, "Effects of Service Provider Attitudes and Employment Status on Citizenship Behaviors and Customers' Attitudes and Loyalty Behavior," *Journal of Applied Psychology*

91 (2006), pp. 365–368; J. Hartner, F. Schmidt, and T. Hayes, "Business-Unit Level Relationship between Employee Satisfaction, Employee Engagement, and Business Outcomes: A Meta-analysis," *Journal of Applied Psychology* 87 (2002), pp. 268–279; I. Fulmer, B. Gerhart, and K. Scott, "Are the 100 Best Better? An Empirical Investigation of the Relationship between Being a 'Great Place to Work' and Firm Performance," *Personnel Psychology* 56 (2003), pp. 965–993; "Working Today: Understanding What Drives Employee Engagement," *Towers Perrin Talent Report* (2003).

51. S. Klie, "Lower Employee Engagement Tied to Declining Manager Effectiveness," *Canadian HR Reporter* (December 14, 2009), pp. 14–16.

52. *Talent Management: The State of the Art* (Stamford, CT: Towers-Perrin, 2005).

53. Society for Human Resource Management, *Workplace Visions* 5 (2000), pp. 3–4.

54. Canadian Manufacturers and Exporters. *20/20 Building Our Vision for the Future: The Future of Manufacturing in Canada, Perspectives and Recommendations on Workforce Capabilities* (Ottawa: CME 2005), p. 47.

55. Statistics Canada. *The Canadian Labour Market at a Glance 2007* Labour Statistics Division, pp. 68, 70.

56. Ibid., pp. 59, 111.

57. R. S. Kaplan and D. P. Norton, "The Balanced Scorecard—Measures That Drive Performance," *Harvard Business Review* (January–February 1992), pp. 71–79; R. S. Kaplan and D. P. Norton, "Putting the Balanced Scorecard to Work," *Harvard Business Review* (September–October 1993), pp. 134–147.

58. The Royal Bank of Canada, "Donations" at www.rbc.com/donations/index.html (retrieved August 2010).

59. RBC, "Corporate Responsibilities" at www.rbc.com/responsibility/approach/recognition.html (retrieved June 13, 2011).

60. J. R. Jablonski, *Implementing Total Quality Management: An Overview* (San Diego: Pfeiffer, 1991).

61. National Quality Institute, Canada Awards of Excellence (CAE) *Overview* at www.nqi.ca/Awards/Overview.aspx (retrieved August 4, 2010).

62. Statistics Canada. *The Canadian Labour Market at a Glance 2007*, Labour Statistics Division, Catalogue no. 71-22-2X. p. 89.

63. Statistics Canada. *Canada's Changing Labour Force 2006*, Catalogue no. 97-559, p. 6.

64. Human Resources and Skills Development Canada, *Looking Ahead: A 10-Year Outlook for the Canadian Labour Market (2006–2015)* (Ottawa: HRSDC, 2006).

65. Statistics Canada. *Canada's Changing Labour Force 2006*, Catalogue no. 97-559, p. 29.

66. Ibid., p. 26.

67. Human Resources and Social Development Canada, *Advancing the Inclusion of People with Disabilities* (2006), SDDP-042-12-06E, Catalogue no HS4-27/2006E, pp. 48–49.

68. Ibid., p. 29.

69. Statistics Canada. *Projections of the Diversity of the Canadian Population, 2006 to 2031*, Statistics Canada, 91-551X. p. 16.

70. T. H. Cox and S. Blake, "Managing Cultural Diversity: Implications for Organizational Competitiveness," *The Executive* 5 (1991), pp. 45–56.

71. J. Ledvinka and V. G. Scarpello, *Federal Regulation of Personnel and Human Resource Management*, 2nd ed. (Boston: PWS-Kent, 1991).

72. N. Lockwood, *The Glass Ceiling: Domestic and International Perspectives* (Alexandria, VA: Society for Human Resource Management, 2004).

73. Catalyst Inc. *Canadian Women in Business Pyramid* (Toronto: Catalyst Inc, 2010) at www.catalyst.ca (retrieved August 6, 2010).

74. M. Pastin, *The Hard Problems of Management: Gaining the Ethics Edge* (San Francisco: Jossey-Bass, 1986); T. Thomas, J. Schermerhorn, Jr., and J. Dienhart, "Strategic Leadership of Ethical Behavior in Business," *Academy of Management Executive* 18 (2004), pp. 56–66.

75. N. Crawford. "Leading by Example," *HR Professional Magazine* (June/July 2008), p. 32.

76. Hewitt. Best Employers Studies Canada, *Benefits of High Engagement* at http://was2.hewitt.com/bestemployers/canada/pages/emp_benefits.htm (retrieved June 7, 2011).

77. G. F. Cavanaugh, D. Moberg, and M. Velasquez, "The Ethics of Organizational Politics," *Academy of Management Review* 6 (1981), pp. 363–374.

78. "Manufacturing: Engine of US Innovation," *National Association of Manufacturing* (October 4, 2006) at www.nam.org (retrieved January 21, 2009).

79. C. Hill, *International Business* (Burr Ridge, IL: Irwin/McGraw-Hill, 1997).

80. The Conference Board of Canada. "Executive Summary 2009," *How Canada Performs: A Report Card on Canada* (Toronto: The Conference Board of Canada, 2010), p. 1.

81. RIM, "Company" at www.rim.com/company (retrieved August 2010).

82. C. Hymowitz, "IBM Combines Volunteer Service, Teamwork to Cultivate Emerging Markets," *The Wall Street Journal* (August 4, 2008), p. B6.

83. J. Schramm, "Offshoring," *Workplace Visions* 2 (Alexandria, VA: Society for Human Resource Management, 2004); P. Babcock, "America's Newest Export: White Collar Jobs," *HR Magazine* 49 (4) 2004, pp. 50–57.

84. The Conference Board of Canada. "Executive Summary 2009," *How Canada Performs: A Report Card on Canada* (Ottawa: The Conference Board of Canada, 2010). Details & Analysis: Education and Skills.

85. F. Hansen, "U.S. Firms Going Wherever the Knowledge Workers Are," *Workforce Management* (October 2005), pp. 43–44.

86. Jim Hopkins, "To Start Up Here, Companies Hire Over There," *USA Today* (February 10, 2005) at www.usatoday.com.

87. J.R. Baldwin & W. Gu, *Offshoring and Outsourcing in Canada*, Statistics Canada (May 2008), Catalogue no. 11F0027M—no. 055, p. 15, Table 5: "The Share of Services Imports by Training Partners."

88. Ibid., p. 20.

89. Ibid., p. 15.

90. E-mail communication from Lyn Basket, vice president Sales and Marketing, Pure & Co. (August 25, 2010).

91. I. Brat, "A Joy (stick) to Behold," *The Wall Street Journal* (June 23, 2008), p. R5; and www.standens.com/leaf-springs.html.

92. A. Weintraub, "High Tech's Future Is in the Toy Chest," *BusinessWeek* (August 26, 2002), pp. 124–126.

93. *2002 Benefits Survey* (Alexandria, VA: Society of Human Resource Management Foundation, 2002).

94. P. Choate and P. Linger, *The High-Flex Society* (New York: Knopf, 1986); P. B. Doeringer, *Turbulence in the American Workplace* (New York: Oxford University Press, 1991).

95. J. A. Neal and C. L. Tromley, "From Incremental Change to Retrofit: Creating High-Performance Work Systems," *Academy of Management Executive* 9 (1995), pp. 42–54.

96. K. A. Miller, *Retraining the American Workforce* (Reading, MA: Addison-Wesley, 1989).

97. S. Moffett, "Separation Anxiety," *The Wall Street Journal* (September 27, 2004), p. R11.

98. "Virtual Working Conditions," e-mail communication from Lyn Baskett, vice president, Sales and Marketing, Pure & Co. (August 25, 2010).

99. Ibid.

100. A. Gupta, "Expanding the 24-Hour Workplace," *The Wall Street Journal* (September 15–16, 2007), pp. R9, R11.

101. T. Peters, "Restoring American Competitiveness: Looking for New Models of Organizations," *The Executive* 2 (1988), pp. 103–110.

102. "Outstanding Training Initiatives: Capital One: Audio Learning in Stereo," *Training* (March 2006), p. 64.

103. M. J. Kavanaugh, H. G. Guetal, and S. I. Tannenbaum, *Human Resource Information Systems: Development and Application* (Boston: PWS-Kent, 1990).

104. M. A. Huselid, "The Impact of Human Resource Management Practices on Turnover, Productivity, and Corporate Financial Performance," *Academy of Management Journal* 38 (1995), pp. 635–672; U.S. Dept. of Labor, *High-Performance Work Practices and Firm Performance* (Washington, DC: U.S. Government Printing Office, 1993); J. Combs, Y. Liu, A. Hall, and D. Ketchen, "How Much Do High-Performance Work Practices Matter? A Meta-analysis of Their Effects on Organizational Performance," *Personnel Psychology* 59 (2006), pp. 501–528.

105. B. Becker and M. A. Huselid, "High-Performance Work Systems and Firm Performance: A Synthesis of Research and

Managerial Implications," in *Research in Personnel and Human Resource Management* 16, ed. G. R. Ferris (Stamford, CT: JAI Press, 1998), pp. 53–101; A. Zacharatos, J. Barling, and R. Iverson, "High Performance Work Systems and Occupational Safety," *Journal of Applied Psychology* 90 (2005), pp. 77–93.

106. B. Becker and B. Gerhart, "The Impact of Human Resource Management on Organizational Performance: Progress and Prospects," *Academy of Management Journal* 39 (1996), pp. 779–801.

107. P. Wright, *Human Resource Strategy: Adapting to the Age of Globalization* (Alexandria, VA: Society for Human Resource Management Foundation, 2008).

108. S. Csoka and B. Hackett, *Transforming the HR Function for Global Business Success* (New York: Conference Board, 1998), Report 1209-19RR.

109. Towers Perrin, *Priorities for Competitive Advantage*.

110. L. Cassiani, "Wanted: Strategic VP HR," *Canadian HR Reporter*, 14 (4) (February 26, 2001), p. 9.

Chapter 2

1. J. Barney, "Firm Resources and Sustained Competitive Advantage," *Journal of Management* 17 (1991), pp. 99–120.

2. L. Dyer, "Strategic Human Resource Management and Planning," in *Research in Personnel and Human Resources Management,* ed. K. Rowland and G. Ferris (Greenwich, CT: JAI Press, 1985), pp. 1–30.

3. *Webster's New American Dictionary.*

4. J. Quinn, *Strategies for Change: Logical Incrementalism* (Homewood, IL: Richard D. Irwin, 1980).

5. M. Porter, *Competitive Strategy: Techniques for Analyzing Industries and Competitors* (New York: Free Press, 1980).

6. R. Miles and C. Snow, *Organizational Strategy, Structure, and Process* (New York: McGraw-Hill, 1978).

7. P. Wright and G. McMahan, "Theoretical Perspectives for Strategic Human Resource Management," *Journal of Management* 18 (1992), pp. 295–320.

8. D. Guest, "Human Resource Management, Corporate Performance and Employee Well-Being: Building the Worker into HRM," *Journal of Industrial Relations* 44 (2002), pp. 335–358; B. Becker, M. Huselid, P. Pinckus, and M. Spratt, "HR as a Source of Shareholder Value: Research and Recommendations," *Human Resource Management* 36 (1997), pp. 39–47.

9. P. Boxall and J. Purcell, *Strategy and Human Resource Management* (Basingstoke, Hants, U.K.: Palgrave MacMillan, 2003).

10. F. Biddle and J. Helyar, "Behind Boeing's Woes: Chunky Assembly Line, Price War with Airbus," *The Wall Street Journal* (April 24, 1998), pp. A1, A16.

11. Wikipedia, http://en.wikipedia.org/wiki/Air_Canada (retrieved September 27, 2010).

12. K. Martell and S. Carroll, "How Strategic Is HRM?" *Human Resource Management* 34 (1995), pp. 253–267.

13. K. Golden and V. Ramanujam, "Between a Dream and a Nightmare: On the Integration of the Human Resource Function and the Strategic Business Planning Process," *Human Resource Management* 24 (1985), pp. 429–451.

14. P. Wright, B. Dunford, and S. Snell, "Contributions of the Resource-Based View of the Firm to the Field of Strategic HRM: Convergence of Two Fields," *Journal of Management* 27 (2001), pp. 701–721.

15. J. Purcell, N. Kinnie, S. Hutchinson, B. Rayton, and J. Swart, *Understanding the People and Performance Link: Unlocking the Black Box* (London: CIPD, 2003).

16. P. M. Wright, T. Gardner, and L. Moynihan, "The Impact of Human Resource Practices on Business Unit Operating and Financial Performance," *Human Resource Management Journal* 13 no. 3 (2003), pp. 21–36.

17. C. Hill and G. Jones, *Strategic Management Theory: An Integrated Approach* (Boston: Houghton Mifflin, 1989).

18. W. Johnston and A. Packer, *Workforce 2000: Work and Workers for the Twenty-First Century* (Indianapolis, IN: Hudson Institute, 1987).

19. "Labor Letter," *The Wall Street Journal* (December 15, 1992), p. A1.

20. P. Wright, G. McMahan, and A. McWilliams, "Human Resources and Sustained Competitive Advantage: A Resource-Based Perspective," *International Journal of Human Resource Management* 5 (1994), pp. 301–326.

21. P. Buller, "Successful Partnerships: HR and Strategic Planning at Eight Top Firms," *Organizational Dynamics* 17 (1988), pp. 27–42.

22. M. Hitt, R. Hoskisson, and J. Harrison, "Strategic Competitiveness in the 1990s: Challenges and Opportunities for U.S. Executives," *The Executive* 5 (May 1991), pp. 7–22.

23. P. Wright, G. McMahan, B. McCormick, and S. Sherman, "Strategy, Core Competence, and HR Involvement as Determinants of HR Effectiveness and Refinery Performance." Paper presented at the 1996 International Federation of Scholarly Associations in Management, Paris, France.

24. N. Bennett, D. Ketchen, and E. Schultz, "Antecedents and Consequences of Human Resource Integration with Strategic Decision Making." Paper presented at the 1995 Academy of Management Meeting, Vancouver, BC, Canada.

25. Golden and Ramanujam, "Between a Dream and a Nightmare."

26. J. Galbraith and R. Kazanjian, *Strategy Implementation: Structure, Systems, and Process* (St. Paul, MN: West, 1986).

27. B. Schneider and A. Konz, "Strategic Job Analysis," *Human Resource Management* 27 (1989), pp. 51–64.

28. P. Wright and S. Snell, "Toward an Integrative View of Strategic Human Resource Management," *Human Resource Management Review* 1 (1991), pp. 203–225.

29. S. Snell, "Control Theory in Strategic Human Resource Management: The Mediating Effect of Administrative Information," *Academy of Management Journal* 35 (1992), pp. 292–327.

30. R. Schuler, "Personnel and Human Resource Management Choices and Organizational Strategy," in *Readings in Personnel and Human Resource Management,* 3rd ed., ed. R. Schuler, S. Youngblood, and V. Huber (St. Paul, MN: West, 1988).

31. B. Gerhart and G. Milkovich, "Employee Compensation: Research and Practice," in *Handbook of Industrial and Organizational Psychology,* 2nd ed., ed. M. Dunnette and L. Hough (Palo Alto, CA: Consulting Psychologists Press, 1992), pp. 481–569.

32. D. Balkin and L. Gomez-Mejia, "Toward a Contingency Theory of Compensation Strategy," *Strategic Management Journal* 8 (1987), pp. 169–182.

33. S. Cronshaw and R. Alexander, "One Answer to the Demand for Accountability: Selection Utility as an Investment Decision," *Organizational Behavior and Human Decision Processes* 35 (1986), pp. 102–118.

34. P. MacDuffie, "Human Resource Bundles and Manufacturing Performance: Organizational Logic and Flexible Production Systems in the World Auto Industry," *Industrial and Labor Relations Review* 48 (1995), pp. 197–221; P. McGraw, "A Hard Drive to the Top," *U.S. News & World Report* 118 (1995), pp. 43–44.

35. M. Huselid, "The Impact of Human Resource Management Practices on Turnover, Productivity, and Corporate Financial Performance," *Academy of Management Journal* 38 (1995), pp. 635–672.

36. B. Fulmer, B. Gerhart, and K. Scott, "Are the 100 Best Better? An Empirical Investigation of the Relationship between Being a 'Great Place to Work' and Firm Performance," *Personnel Psychology* 56 (2003), pp. 965–993.

37. J. E. Delery and D. H. Doty, "Modes of Theorizing in Strategic Human Resource Management: Tests of Universalistic, Contingency and Configurational Performance Predictions," *Academy of Management Journal* 39 (1996), pp. 802–883; D. Guest, J. Michie, N. Conway, and M. Sheehan, "Human Resource Management and Corporate Performance in the UK," *British Journal of Industrial Relations* 41 (2003), pp. 291–314; J. Guthrie, "High Involvement Work Practices, Turnover, and Productivity: Evidence from New Zealand," *Academy of Management Journal* 44 (2001), pp. 180–192; J. Harter, F. Schmidt, and T. Hayes, "Business-Unit-Level Relationship between Employee Satisfaction, Employee Engagement, and Business Outcomes: A Meta-Analysis," *Journal of Applied Psychology* 87 (2002), pp. 268–279; Watson Wyatt, Worldwide, "Human Capital Index®: Human Capital as a Lead Indicator of Shareholder Value" (2002).

38. M. Bhattacharya, D. Gibson, and H. Doty, "The Effects of Flexibility in Employee Skills, Employee Behaviors, and Human Resource Practices on Firm Performance," *Journal of Management* 31 (2005), pp. 622–640.

39. D. Guest, J. Michie, N. Conway, and M. Sheehan, "Human Resource Management and Corporate Performance in the UK," *British Journal of Industrial Relations* 41 (2003), pp. 291–314; P. Wright, T. Gardner, L. Moynihan, and M. Allen, "The HR Performance Relationship: Examining Causal Direction," *Personnel Psychology* 58 (2005), pp. 409–476.

40. P. Wright, *No Strategy: Adaptive to the Age of Globalization* (Arlington, VA: SHRM Foundation, 2008).

41. M. Porter, *Competitive Advantage* (New York: Free Press, 1985).

42. C. Lawton, "How HP Reclaimed Its PC Lead over Dell" (June 2007); "Can Dell's Turnaround Strategy Keep HP at Bay?" (September 2007), *Knowledge@Wharton,* http://knowledge. wharton.upenn.edu/article.cfm?articleid1799.

43. R. Schuler and S. Jackson, "Linking Competitive Strategies with Human Resource Management Practices," *Academy of Management Executive* 1 (1987), pp. 207–219.

44. R. Miles and C. Snow, "Designing Strategic Human Resource Management Systems," *Organizational Dynamics* 13, no. 1 (1984), pp. 36–52.

45. A. Thompson and A. Strickland, *Strategy Formulation and Implementation: Tasks of the General Manager,* 3rd ed. (Plano, TX: BPI, 1986).

46. "Towers Perrin and Watson Wyatt to Combine to Form Towers Watson" (June 28, 2009); TowersWatsonpress, www.towersperrin.com/tp/showdctmdoc.jsp?country=global &url=Master_Brand_2/global/Press_Releases/2009/2009 0628/2009_06_28.htm (retrieved October 1, 2010).

47. J. Schmidt, *Making Mergers Work: The Strategic Importance of People* (Arlington, VA: SHRM Foundation, 2003).

48. Uyen Vu, "HR's Role in Mergers, Acquisitions," *Canadian HR Reporter* (December 4, 2006), p. 17.

49. Anonymous, Energy: Company Expects to Shed Another $100M. "Suncor Cutting Corporate Fat, CEO Says," QMI Agency, *The London Free Press* (February 3, 2010).

50. S. Pearlstein, "Corporate Cutback Yet to Pay Off," *Washington Post* (January 4, 1994), p. B6.

51. K. Cameron, "Guest Editor's Note: Investigating Organizational Downsizing—Fundamental Issues," *Human Resource Management* 33 (1994), pp. 183–188.

52. Quinn, *Strategies for Change.*

53. H. Schultz and D. Yang, *Pour Your Heart Into It* (New York: Hyperion, 1987).

54. R. Pascale, "Perspectives on Strategy: The Real Story behind Honda's Success," *California Management Review* 26 (1984), pp. 47–72.

55. Templin, "A Decisive Response to Crisis."

56. P. Wright and S. Snell, "Toward a Unifying Framework for Exploring Fit and Flexibility in Strategic Human Resource Management," *Academy of Management Review* 23, no. 4 (1998), pp. 756–772.

57. H. Behar, *It's Not about the Coffee: Lessons for Putting People First from a Life at Starbucks* (New York, NY: Penguin Group, 2007).

58. T. Stewart, "Brace for Japan's Hot New Strategy," *Fortune* (September 21, 1992), pp. 62–76.

59. B. Dunford, P. Wright, and S. Snell, "Contributions of the Resource-Based View of the Firm to the Field of Strategic HRM: Convergence of Two Fields," *Journal of Management* 27 (2001), pp. 701–721.

60. C. Snow and S. Snell, "Staffing as Strategy," vol. 4 of *Personnel Selection* (San Francisco: Jossey-Bass, 1992).

61. T. Batten, "Education Key to Prosperity—Report," *Houston Chronicle* (September 7, 1992), p. 1B.

62. Schultz and Yang, Pour Your Heart Into It.

63. G. McMahan, University of Texas at Arlington, personal communications.

64. P. Wright, S. Snell, and P. Jacobsen, "Current Approaches to HR Strategies: Inside-Out vs. Outside-In," *Human Resource Planning* (in press).

65. A. S. Tsui and L. R. Gomez-Mejia, "Evaluating HR Effectiveness," in *Human Resource Management: Evolving Roles and Responsibilities,* ed. L. Dyer (Washington, DC: Bureau of National Affairs, 1988), pp. 1-187–1-227.

66. D. Ulrich, "Measuring Human Resources: An Overview of Practice and a Prescription for Results," *Human Resource Management* 36, no. 3 (1997), pp. 303–320.

67. P. Wright, G. McMahan, S. Snell, and B. Gerhart, *Strategic HRM: Building Human Capital and Organizational Capability,* Technical report (Ithaca, NY: Cornell University, 1998).

68. S. Caudron, "HR Is Dead, Long Live HR," *Workforce* (January 2003), pp. 26–29; Society for Human Resource Management, *HR's Evolving Role in Organizations and Its Impact on Business Strategy* (Alexandria, VA: Society for Human Resource Management, 2008); "The Buying Services Game" *HR Magazine* (November 2008), pp. 77–82.

69. P. Babcock, "A Crowded Space," *HR Magazine* (March 2006), pp. 68–74.

70. M. Rafter, "Promise Fulfilled," *Workforce Management* (September 2005), pp. 51–54.

71. T. Starner, "Managing the Handoff," *Human Resource Executive* (March 2, 2005), pp. 1, 18–25; S. Westcott, "Should It Stay or Go?" *Human Resource Executive* (May 16, 2005), pp. 30–33.

72. S. Greengard, "Building a Self-Service Culture That Works," *Workforce* (July 1998), pp. 60–64.

73. R. Broderick and J. W. Boudreau, "Human Resource Management, Information Technology, and the Competitive Edge," *Academy of Management Executive* 6 (1992), pp. 7–17.

74. P. Wright, "Strategies and Challenges of the Chief Human Resource Officer: Results of the First Annual Cornell/CAHRS Survey of CHROs," Technical report, 2009.

75. Ibid.

76. J. Paauwe, *Human Resource Management and Performance: Unique Approaches for Achieving Long-Term Viability* (Oxford: Oxford University Press, 2004).

Chapter 3

1. Constitution Act, 1867.
2. Constitution Act, 1867, s.91.
3. Constitution Act, 1867, s.92.
4. Dickason v. University of Alberta (1992) 95 D.L.R. (4th) 439 at para. 23.
5. Vriend v. Alberta, [1998] 1 S.C.R. 493 at para. 61.
6. Canadian Charter of Rights and Freedoms, s.1.
7. Canadian Charter of Rights and Freedoms, s.33.
8. (Federal) Canadian Human Rights Act; (AB) Human Rights, Citizenship and Multiculturalism Act; (BC) Human Rights Code; (MB) Human Rights Code; (NB) Human Rights Act; (Nfld. & Lab.) The Human Rights Code; (NS) Human Rights Act; (ON) Human Rights Code; (PEI) Human Rights Act; (QB) Charter of Human Rights and Freedoms; (SK) Saskatchewan Human Rights Code; (NWT) Human Rights Act; (NU) Human Rights Act; (YT) Human Rights Act.
9. New Brunswick's Human Rights Act explicitly prohibits only sexual harassment.
10. *Jubran v. North Vancouver School District No. 44* (2002), 42 C.H.R.R. D/273 (B.C.H.R.T.), quashed on judicial review 45 C.H.R.R. D/249 (B.C.S.C.), rev'd 253 D.L.R. (4th) 294, 2005 B.C.C.A. 2001.
11. The Supreme Court of Canada eliminated any distinction between the legal test to be applied to different types of discrimination in *British Columbia Public Service Employee Relations Commission v. B.C.G.E.U.* (1999), 176 D.L.R. (4th) 1 (S.C.C.) ("Meiorin").
12. *Central Alberta Dairy Pool v. Alberta (Human Rights Commission),* [1990] 2 S.C.R. 489.
13. *British Columbia (Public Service Employee Relations Commission) v. BCGSEU,* [1999] 3 S.C.R. 3 ("Meiorin").
14. *Syndicat des Employées de Techniques Professionnelles et de Bureau d'Hydro-Québec, section local 2000 v. Hydro-Québec* (2008), 294 D.L.R. (4th) 407 (S.C.C.).
15. *British Columbia Public Service Employee Relations Commission v. B.C.G.E.U.* (1999), 176 D.L.R. (4th) 1 (S.C.C.) ("Meiorin").
16. *Wiens v. Inco Metals Inc.* (1988), 9 C.H.R.R. D/4795 (Ont. Bd. Inq.).
17. *Pillai v. Lafarge Canada Inc.,* 2003 BCHRT 26.
18. *Jones v. C.H.E.Pharmacy Inc.,* 2001 B.C.H.R.T. 1.
19. *Adga Group Consultants Inc. v. Lane,* 2008 CanLII 39605 (Ont. Div. Ct.).
20. *Large v. Stratford (City),* [1995] 3 S.C.R. 733.
21. *Etobicoke (Borough) v. Ontario (Human Rights Commission),* [1982] 1 S.C.R. 202.

22. *McKinney v. University of Guelph*, [1990] 3 S.C.R. 229; *Vilven v. Air Canada* 2009 FC 367.

23. *Commission des droits de la personne et des droits de la jeunesse c. Bombardier inc. (Bombardier Aerospace Training Center)*, 2010 QCTDP 16 (CanLII); Quebec Human Rights Tribunal Release, "Bombardier Inc. sentenced to pay damages Canadian Pilot of Pakistani Origin Wins Major Discrimination Suit," December 8, 2010, www2.cdpdj.qc.ca/Documents/Bombardier_december%202010_AN.pdf.

24. *Sheridan v. Sanctuary Investments Ltd.* (1999), 33 C.H.R.R. D/4664 (B.C. H.R.T.).

25. *Waterman v. National Life Assurance Co. of Canada* (1993), 18 C.H.R.R. D/176 (Ont. Bd. Inq.).

26. *Vriend v. Alberta*, [1998] 1 S.C.R. 493 (S.C.C.).

27. *Hislop v. Canada (Attorney General)*, [2007] S.C.J. No. 10; *M. v. H.*, [1999] 2 S.C.R. 3.

28. *Wamsley v. Ed Green Blueprinting*, 2010 HRTO 1491 (CanLII).

29. *Cameron v. Giorgio & Lim Restaurant* (1993), 21 C.H.R.R. D/79 (N.S. Bd. Inq.).

30. *Barnes v. Thomas Stratton Warehousing Co. Inc.* (1993), 22 C.H.R.R. D/427 (Nfld. Bd. Inq.).

31. *Cameron v. Giorgio & Lim Restaurant* (1993), 21 C.H.R.R. D/79 (N.S. Bd. Inq.).

32. *Irving v. Medland* (1985), 6 C.H.R.R. D/2842 (Man. Bd. Adj.).

33. *Janzen v. Platy Enterprises Ltd.*, [1989] 1 S.C.R. 1252.

34. *Van Berkel v. MPI Security Ltd.* (1996), 28 C.H.R.R. D/504 (B.C.H.R.C.).

35. *Smith v. Menzies Chrysler*, 2009 HRTO 1936 (CanLII).

36. *Canada (Human Rights Commission) v. Canada (Armed Forces)*, [1999] 3 F.C. 653.

37. *McNulty v. G.N.F. Holdings Ltd.* (1992), 16 C.H.R.R. D/418 (B.C.H.R.C.); *McLellan v. Mentor Investments Ltd.* (1991), 15 C.H.R.R. D/134 (N.S. Bd. Inq.).

38. Canadian Human Rights Commission, "Anti-Harassment Policies for the Workplace: An Employer's Guide, Part 4: Checklist for an Anti-Harassment Policy: Medium and Large Organizations," www.chrc-ccdp.ca/publications/anti_harassment_part3-eng.aspx#part4.

39. *An Act Respecting Labour Standards*, R.S.Q., c. N-1.1.

40. *Occupational Health and Safety Act*, 1993, S.S. 1993, c. O-1.1, sections 2 (1) (l), 3 (c).

41. *An Act Respecting Labour Standards*, section 81.18.

42. Manitoba, Northwest Territories, Quebec, and Yukon Territories.

43. *Dupuis v. British Columbia Ministry of Forests* (1993), 20 C.H.R.R. D/87 (B.C.H.R.C.); *Nova Scotia Construction Safety Assn. v. Nova Scotia* (Human Rights Commission) (2006), 24 N.S.R. (2d) 321 (C.A.).

44. *Ontario Labour Relations Act*, 1995, s.54.

45. An Act Respecting Equal Access to Employment in Public Bodies and Amending the Charter of Human Rights and Freedoms. R.S.Q., chapter A-2.01 (April 1, 2009).

46. Statistics Canada, "Women in Canada: Paid Work 1976–2009," at www.statcan.gc.ca/daily-quotidien/101209/dq101209a-eng.htm (retrieved December 9, 2010).

47. Human Resources and Skills Development Canada, "Employment Equity Act: Annual Report 2009," (2010) at www.hrsdc.gc.ca/eng/labour/publications/equality/annual_reports/2009/cover.shtml).

48. Statistics Canada, "Average Earnings by Sex and Work Pattern (Full-time Workers)," (2008).

49. Statistics Canada, "Average Earnings by Sex and Work Pattern (Full-time Workers)," (2008).

50. Human Resources and Skills Development Canada, "Employment Equity Act: Annual Report 2009," (2010) at www.hrsdc.gc.ca/eng/labour/publications/equality/annual_reports/2009/cover.shtml.

51. Statistics Canada, 2006 Census: Data Table, Catalogue number: 97-564-XCB2006002.

52. Human Resources and Skills Development Canada, "Employment Equity Act: Annual Report 2009," (2010) at www.hrsdc.gc.ca/eng/labour/publications/equality/annual_reports/2009/cover.shtml.

53. CBC News, "Canada's Aboriginal Population Tops Million Mark: StatsCan," at www.cbc.ca/canada/story/2008/01/15/aboriginal-stats.html (retrieved January 15, 2008).

54. Statistics Canada, "Canadians in Context—People with Disabilities, Indicators of Well-being in Canada," at www4.hrsdc.gc.ca/.3ndic.1t.4r@-eng.jsp?iid=40#M_1).

55. Statistics Canada, Perspectives on Labour and Income, "Disability in the Workplace," (February 2006 vol. 7, no. 2) at www.statcan.gc.ca/pub/75-001-x/10206/9096-eng.htm.

56. Statistics Canada, 2006 Census: Data Products, Topic-based Tabulations, "Labour Force Activity (8), Visible Minority Groups (15), Immigrant Status and Period of Immigration (9), Highest Certificate, Diploma or Degree (7), Age Groups (9) and Sex (3) for the Population 15 Years and Over of Canada, Provinces, Territories, Census Metropolitan Areas and Census Agglomerations, 2006 Census—20% Sample Data," 2006 Census.

57. Statistics Canada, "The Daily," (April 2, 2008) at www.statcan.gc.ca/daily-quotidien/080402/dq080402a-eng.htm.

58. Statistics Canada, "Study: Projections of the Diversity of the Canadian Population: 2006–2031," at www.statcan.gc.ca/daily-quotidien/100309/dq100309a-eng.htm (retrieved March 9, 2010).

59. Reports of private-sector employers are submitted to Human Resources and Social Development Canada and reports of public sector employers are submitted to the Public Service Human Resources Management Agency of Canada.

60. Employment Equity Act, s.5.

61. Employment Equity Act, s.6.

62. Human Resources and Skills Development Canada, "Guidelines for the Employment Equity Act and Regulations, Document 1: Overview of Employment Equity," at www.hrsdc.gc.ca/eng/lp/lo/lswe/we/legislation/guidelines/doc1.shtml#steps.

63. Employment Equity Act, s.15.

64. Statistics Canada, "Women in Canada: Economic Well-being," at www.statcan.gc.ca/daily-quotidien/101216/dq101216c-eng.htm (retrieved December 16, 2010).

65. (AB) Human Rights, Citizenship and Multiculturalism Act, s.6; (BC), Human Rights Code, s.12; (MB) Employment Standards Code, s.82 (1); (NB) Employment Standards Act, s.37.1; (Nfld. & Lab.) Human Rights Code, s.11; (NS) Labour Standards Code, s.57; (ON) Employment Standards Act, 2000, s.42; (PEI) Human Rights Act, s.7; (SK) The Labour Standards Act, s.17; (NWT) Human Rights Act, s.9 (YT) Employment Standards Act, s.44. Section 19 of Quebec's Charter of Human Rights and Freedoms requires equal pay for equal work.

66. (CAN) Canadian Human Rights Act, s.11 (YT) Human Rights Act, s.15; (MB) The Pay Equity Act; (NB) Pay Equity Act, 2009; (NS) Pay Equity Act; (ON) Pay Equity Act; and (PEI) Pay Equity Act; (QB) Pay Equity Act.

67. BCE, "Bell Canada and CEP Reach Agreement on Pay Equity—Current and former employees to vote on settlement," at www.bce.ca/en/news/releases/corp/2006/05/15/73604.html (retrieved May 15, 2006).

68. *Public Service Alliance of Canada v. Canada Post Corporation*, 2010 FCA 56 (CanLII).

69. Adapted from Emily Mathieu, "Company Shows PRIDE against Discrimination," at www.thestar.com/Business/article/589483 (retrieved February 19, 2009).

70. "Canada's Best Diversity Employers," at www.canadianimmigrant.ca/careers/workplaceissues/article/3252.

71. www.canadastop100.com/diversity.

72. "Canada's Best Diversity Employers," at www.canadianimmigrant.ca/careers/workplaceissues/article/3252.

73. Ibid.

74. Martha L. Maznevski, and J. J. DiStefano, "The Mortar in the Mosaic: A New Look at Composition, Process, and Performance in Decision-Making Groups." Paper presented at the Academy of Management 1996 Annual Meetings.

75. "Canada's Best Diversity Employers," at www.canadianimmigrant.ca/careers/workplaceissues/article/3252.

76. Canadian Human Rights Commission, "*Framework for Documenting Equality Rights*," (2010) at www.chrc-ccdp.ca/pdf/framework_equality.pdf.

77. Ibid.

78. Ibid.

Chapter 4

1. L. Hawkins and N. Shirouzo, "A Tale of Two Auto Plants," *The Wall Street Journal* (May 24, 2006), pp. B1–B2.

2. D. Ilgen and J. Hollenbeck, "The Structure of Work: Job Design and Roles," in *Handbook of Industrial & Organizational Psychology*, 2nd ed., ed. M. Dunnette and L. Hough (Palo Alto, CA: Consulting Psychologists Press, 1991), pp. 165–208.

3. R. Griffin, Task Design: *An Integrative Approach* (Glenview, IL: Scott Foresman, 1982).

4. B. Brocka and M. S. Brocka, *Quality Management: Implementing the Best Ideas of the Masters* (Homewood, IL: Business One Irwin, 1992).

5. G. L. Stewart and M. R. Barrick, "Team Structure and Performance: Assessing the Mediating Role of Intrateam Process and the Moderating Role of Task Type," *Academy of Management Journal* 43 (2000), pp. 135–148.

6. G. S. Van der Vegt, B. J. M. Emans, and E. Van de Vliert, "Patterns of Interdependence in Work Teams: A Two-Level Investigation of the Relations with Job and Team Satisfaction," *Personnel Psychology* 54 (2001), pp. 51–70.

7. F. P. Morgeson, M. D. Johnson, M. A. Campion, G. J. Medsker, and T. V. Mumford, "Understanding Reactions to Job Redesign: A Quasi-Experimental Investigation of the Moderating Effects of Organizational Context on Perceptions of Performance and Behavior," *Personnel Psychology* 59 (2006), pp. 333–363.

8. C. M. Barnes, J. R. Hollenbeck, D. T. Wagner, D. S. DeRue, J. D. Nahrgang, and K. M. Schwind, "Harmful Help: The Costs of Backing-up Behaviors in Teams," *Journal of Applied Psychology* 93 (2008), pp. 529–539.

9. S. Hamm, "Big Blue Shift," *BusinessWeek,* June 5, 2006, pp. 108–110.

10. www-03.ibm.com/industries/ca/en/education/k12/contact.html; and www-03.ibm.com/industries/ca/en/education/k12/solutions/index.html.

11. A. L. Kristof-Brown, B. D. Zimmerman, and E. C. Johnson, "Consequences of Individuals' Fit at Work: A Meta-analysis of Person–Job, Person–Organization, Person–Group, and Person–Supervisor Fit," *Personnel Psychology* 58 (2005), pp. 281–342.

12. M. Schminke, M. L. Ambrose, and R. S. Cropanzano, "The Effect of Organizational Structure on Perceptions of Procedural Fairness," *Journal of Applied Psychology* 85 (2000), pp. 294–304.

13. T. Neff and J. Citrin, "You're in Charge: Now What?" *Fortune,* January 24, 2005, pp. 109–120.

14. H. Moon, J. R. Hollenbeck, S. E. Humphrey, D. R. Ilgen, B. West, A. Ellis, and C.O.L.H. Porter, "Asymmetrical Adaptability: Dynamic Structures as One-Way Streets," *Academy of Management Journal* 47 (2006), pp. 681–696.

15. M. D. Johnson, J. R. Hollenbeck, D. R. Ilgen, S.E. Humphrey, C. J. Meyer, and D. K. Jundt, "Cutthroat

Cooperation: Asymmetrical Adaptation of Team Reward Structures," *Academy of Management Journal* 49 (2006), pp. 103–120.

16. J. R. Hollenbeck, H. Moon, A. Ellis, B. West, D. R. Ilgen, L. Sheppard, C. O. Porter, and J. A. Wagner, "Structural Contingency Theory and Individual Differences: Examination of External and Internal Person–Team Fit," *Journal of Applied Psychology* 87 (2002), pp. 599–606.

17. B. Schlender, "Ballmer Unbound: How Do You Impose Order on a Giant Runaway Mensa Meeting?" *Fortune,* January 26, 2004, p. 123.

18. E. Primoff and S. Fine, "A History of Job Analysis," in *The Job Analysis Handbook for Business, Industry, and Government,* ed. S. Gael (New York: Wiley, 1988), pp. 14–29.

19. W. Cascio, *Applied Psychology in Personnel Management,* 4th ed. (Englewood Cliffs, NJ: Prentice Hall, 1991).

20. J. Walker, *Human Resource Strategy* (New York: McGraw-Hill, 1992).

21. D. A. Hofmann, F. P. Morgeson, and S. J. Gerras, "Climate as a Moderator of the Relationship between Leader–Member Exchange and Content-Specific Citizenship: Safety Climate as an Exemplar," *Journal of Applied Psychology* 88 (2003), pp. 170–178.

22. A. K. Weyman, "Investigating the Influence of Organizational Role on Perceptions of Risk in Deep Coal Mines," *Journal of Applied Psychology* 88 (2003), pp. 404–412.

23. L. E. Baranowski and L. E. Anderson, "Examining Rater Source Variation in Work Behavior to KSA Linkages," *Personnel Psychology* 58 (2005), pp. 1041–1054.

24. G. T. Milkovich, J. Newman, and N. Cole, *Compensation,* 3rd Canadian ed. (Toronto: McGraw-Hill Ryerson, 2010).

25. National Occupational Classification, *Job Descriptions, An Employers' Handbook*, through Human Resources and Social Development Canada, Catalogue no. HS4-33/2007 at www5. hrsdc.gc.ca/NOC/English/NOC/2006/pdf/JobDescriptions. pdf (retrieved October 23, 2010).

26. Government of Canada, *Working in Canada, Labour Market Projections* at www.workingincanada.gc.ca/content_pieces-eng. do?cid=1403 (retrieved October 23, 2010).

27. E. McCormick and R. Jeannerette, "The Position Analysis Questionnaire," in *The Job Analysis Handbook for Business, Industry, and Government,* pp. 880–901.

28. E. C. Dierdorff and M. A. Wilson, "A Meta-analysis of Job Analysis Reliability," *Journal of Applied Psychology* 88 (2003), pp. 635–646.

29. M. K. Lindell, C. S. Clause, C. J. Brandt, and R. S. Landis, "Relationship between Organizational Context and Job Analysis Ratings," *Journal of Applied Psychology* 83 (1998), pp. 769–776.

30. F. P. Morgeson and M. A. Campion, "Social and Cognitive Sources of Potential Inaccuracy in Job Analysis," *Journal of Applied Psychology* 82 (1997), pp. 627–655.

31. D. S. DeRue, J. R. Hollenbeck, M. D. Johnson, D. R. Ilgen, and D. K. Jundt, "How Different Team Downsizing Approaches Influence Team-level Adaptation and Performance," *Academy of Management Journal* 51 (2008), pp. 182–196.

32. F. Hanson, "A Leg Up in Down Times," *Workforce Management* (January 19, 2009), p. 14.

33. C. O. Trevor and A. J. Nyberg, "Keeping Your Headcount When All About You Are Losing Theirs: Downsizing, Voluntary Turnover Rates, and the Moderating Role of HR Practices," *Academy of Management Journal* 51 (2008), pp. 259–276.

34. M. Campion and P. Thayer, "Development and Field Evaluation of an Interdisciplinary Measure of Job Design," *Journal of Applied Psychology* 70 (1985), pp. 29–34.

35. J. R. Edwards, J. A. Scully, and M. D. Brtek, "The Measurement of Work: Hierarchical Representation of the Multimethod Job Design Questionnaire," *Personnel Psychology* 52 (1999), pp. 305–324.

36. F. P. Morgeson and S. E. Humphrey, "The Work Design Questionnaire (WDQ): Developing and Validating a Comprehensive Measure for Assessing Job Design and the Nature of Work," *Journal of Applied Psychology* 91 (2006), pp. 1312–1339.

37. F. Taylor, *The Principles of Scientific Management* (New York: W. W. Norton, 1967) (originally published in 1911 by Harper & Brothers).

38. R. Griffin and G. McMahan, "Motivation through Job Design," in *OB: The State of the Science,* ed. J. Greenberg (Hillsdale, NJ: Lawrence Erlbaum Associates, 1993).

39. R. Hackman and G. Oldham, *Work Redesign* (Boston: Addison-Wesley, 1980).

40. A. M. Grant, "The Significance of Task Significance," *Journal of Applied Psychology* 93 (2007), pp. 108–124.

41. A. M. Grant, E. M. Campbell, G. Chen, K. Cottone, D. Lapedia, and K. Lee, "Impact and Art of Motivation Maintenance: The Effects of Contact with Beneficiaries on Persistence Behavior," *Organizational Behavior and Human Decision Processes* 103 (2007), pp. 53–67.

42. M. Schrage, "More Power to Whom?" *Fortune* (July 23, 2001), p. 270.

43. A. A. Grandey, G. M. Fisk, and D. D. Steiner, "Must 'Service with a Smile' Be Stressful?" *Journal of Applied Psychology* 90 (2005), pp. 893–904.

44. J. B. Carson, P. E. Tesluk, and J. A. Marrone, "Shared Leadership in Teams: An Investigation of Antecedent Conditions and Performance." *Academy of Management Journal* 50 (2007), pp. 1217–1234.

45. F. W. Bond, P. E. Flaxman, and D. Bunce, "The Influence of Psychological Flexibility on Work Redesign: Mediated Moderation of a Work Reorganization Intervention," *Journal of Applied Psychology* 93 (2008), pp. 645–654.

46. W. E. Byrnes, "Making the Job Meaningful All the Way Down the Line," *BusinessWeek* (May 1, 2006), p. 60.

47. J. A. Colquitt and R. F. Piccalo, "Transformational Leadership and Job Behaviors: The Mediating Role of Core Job Characteristics," *Academy of Management Journal* 49 (2006), pp. 327–340.

48. "How Do I Know When I Need Help in Ergonomics?" Ergonomics Canada at www.ergonomicscanada.com/faqs.html.

49. S. Sonnentag and F. R. H. Zijistra, "Job Characteristics and Off-the-Job Activities as Predictors of Need for Recovery, Well-Being, and Fatigue," *Journal of Applied Psychology* 91 (2006), pp. 330–350.

50. S. Mewman, M. A. Griffen, and C. Mason, "Safety in Work Vehicles: A Multilevel Study Linking Safety Values and Individual Predictors to Work-related Driving Crashes," *Journal of Applied Psychology* 93 (2008), pp. 632–644.

51. D. K. Berman, "Technology Has Us So Plugged into Data, We Have Turned Off," *The Wall Street Journal,* November 10, 2003, pp. A1–A2.

52. J. Baker, "From Open Doors to Gated Communities," *BusinessWeek* (September 8, 2003), p. 36.

53. A. Aston, "Who Will Run the Plants?" *BusinessWeek* (January 22, 2007), p. 78.

54. D. W. Jarrell, *Human Resource Planning: A Business Planning Approach* (Englewood Cliffs, NJ: Prentice Hall, 1993).

55. P. Coy, "Global Overcapacity," *BusinessWeek* (February 16, 2009), p. 26.

56. L. Chappel, "Toyota Plants Idling, But Workers Aren't," *Workforce Management* (September 8, 2008), pp. 22–24.

57. M. Conlin, "Savaged by the Slowdown," *BusinessWeek* (September 17, 2001), pp. 74–77.

58. S. Mohammad, "Pardon Me, Friend, But You're in My Job," *Canadian Business* (October 26, 2009), p. 125.

59. J. P. Guthrie, "Dumb and Dumber: The Impact of Downsizing on Firm Performance as Moderated by Industry Conditions," *Organization Science* 19 (2008), pp. 108–123.

60. J. McGregor, A. McConnon, and D. Kiley, "Customer Service in a Shrinking Economy," *BusinessWeek* (February 19, 2009), pp. 34–35.

61. C. D. Zatzick and R. D. Iverson, "High-Involvement Management and Workforce Reduction: Competitive Advantage or Disadvantage?" *Academy of Management Journal* 49 (2006), pp. 999–1015.

62. P. P. Shaw, "Network Destruction: The Structural Implications of Downsizing," *Academy of Management Journal* 43 (2000), pp. 101–112.

63. J. Schu, "Internet Helps Keep Goodwill of Downsized Employees," *Workforce* (July 2001), p. 15.

64. C. O. Trevor, and A. J. Nyberg, "Keeping Your Headcount When All About You Are Losing Theirs: Downsizing, Voluntary Turnover Rates, and the Moderating Role of HR Practices," *Academy of Management Journal* 51 (2008), pp. 259–276.

65. E. Frauenheim, "Technology Forcing Firms to Shed More Light on Layoffs," *Workforce Management* (January 19, 2009), pp. 7–8.

66. J. Holton, "You've Been Deleted," *Workforce Management* (September 11, 2006), p. 42.

67. J. Marquez, "The Would-be Retirees," *Workforce Management* (November 3, 2008), pp. 24–28.

68. J. S. Lublin and S. Thurm, "How Companies Calculate Odds in Buyout Offers," *The Wall Street Journal* (March 27, 2006), pp. B1–B2.

69. S. A. Johnson and B. E. Ashforth, "Externalization of Employment in a Service Environment: The Role of Organizational and Customer Identification," *Journal of Organizational Behavior* 29 (2008), pp. 287–309.

70. J. Marquez, "Inside Job," *Workforce Management* (February 12, 2006), pp. 19–21.

71. M. Kripalani, "Call Center? That's So 2004," *BusinessWeek* (August 7, 2006), pp. 40–41.

72. S. Hamm, "Outsourcing Heads to the Outskirts," *BusinessWeek* (January 22, 2007), p. 56.

73. W. Zellner, "Lessons from a Faded Levi-Strauss," *BusinessWeek* (December 15, 2003), p. 44.

74. A. Meisler, "Think Globally, Act Rationally," *Workforce* (January 2004), pp. 40–45.

75. A. Tiwana, "Does Firm Modularity Complement Ignorance? A Field Study of Software Outsourcing Alliances," *Strategic Management Journal* 29 (2008), pp. 1241–1252.

76. S. E. Ante, "Shifting Work Offshore? Outsourcer Beware," *BusinessWeek* (January 12, 2004), pp. 36–37.

77. P. Engardio, "The Future of Outsourcing," *BusinessWeek* (January 30, 2006), pp. 50–58.

78. Donna Lero, Julia Richardson, and Karen Korabik, "Cost Benefits Review of Work Life Balance Practices—2009," submitted to the Canadian Association of Administrators of Labour Legislation (CAALL), p. 41 at www.caall-acalo.org/docs/Cost-Benefit%20Review.pdf (retrieved May 4, 2011).

79. Ibid. p. 41.

80. *CN v. Canada* (Canadian Human Rights Commission), [1987] 1 S.C.R. 1114.

81. E. Brynjolfsson and L. Hitt, "The Productivity Paradox of Information Technology," *Communications of the ACM* (December 1993), pp. 66–77.

82. "Seven Critical Success Factors for Using Information Technology," *Total Quality Newsletter* (February 1994), p. 6.

83. J. E. Rigdon, "Technological Gains Are Cutting Costs in Jobs and Services," *The Wall Street Journal* (February 24, 1995), pp. A1, A5, A6.

84. R. Broderick and J. W. Boudreau, "Human Resource Management, Information Technology, and the Competitive Edge," *Academy of Management Executive* 6 (1992), pp. 7–17.

85. S. E. O'Connell, "New Technologies Bring New Tools, New Rules," *HRMagazine* (December 1995), pp. 43–48; S. F. O'Connell, "The Virtual Workplace Moves at Warp Speed," *HRMagazine* (March 1996), pp. 51–57.

Chapter 5

1. C. K. Stevens, "Antecedents of Interview Interactions, Interviewers' Ratings, and Applicants' Reactions," *Personnel Psychology* 51 (1998), pp. 55–85.

2. A. E. Barber, J. R. Hollenbeck, S. L. Tower, and J. M. Phillips, "The Effects of Interview Focus on Recruitment Effectiveness: A Field Experiment," *Journal of Applied Psychology* 79 (1994), pp. 886–896.

3. D. S. Chapman and D. I. Zweig, "Developing a Nomological Network for Interview Structure: Antecedents and Consequences of the Structured Selection Interview," *Personnel Psychology* 58 (2005), pp. 673–702.

4. R. Kanfer, C. R. Wanberg, and T. M. Kantrowitz, "Job Search and Employment: A Personality–Motivational Analysis and Meta-Analytic Review," *Journal of Applied Psychology* 86 (2001), pp. 837–855.

5. Department of National Defence Advertisements, *London Free Press*, March 13, 2002, and *Western News*, March 27, 2003.

6. S. L. Rynes and A. E. Barber, "Applicant Attraction Strategies: An Organizational Perspective," *Academy of Management Review* 15 (1990), pp. 286–310.

7. S. Klie, "Employee Branding: Getting Employees to Come to You," *Canadian HR Reporter* (November 19, 2007), p. 10.

8. Ibid.

9. D. Foust, "How to Pick a Business Brain," *BusinessWeek* (February 20, 2006), p. 104.

10. G. Gloeckler, "Sidestepping the GMAT," *BusinessWeek* (August 8, 2005), pp. 71–72.

11. S. Klie, "Employee Branding: Getting Employees to Come to You," *Canadian HR Reporter* (November 19, 2007), p. 9.

12. Canada's Top 100 Employers www.canadastop100.com/history.html and www.canadastop100.com/competitions.html (retrieved October 29, 2010).

13. Meyer Norris Penny at http://was2.hewitt.com/bestemployers/canada/pdfs/BES_CaseStudies_2010_MNP.pdf.

14. S. Klie, "Employee Branding: Getting Employees to Come to You," *Canadian HR Reporter* (November 19, 2007), p. 9.

15. F. Lievens and S. Highhouse, "The Relation of Instrumental and Symbolic Attributes to a Company's Attractiveness as an Employer," *Personnel Psychology* 56 (2003), pp. 75–102.

16. J. E. Slaughter, M. J. Zickar, S. Highhouse, and D. C. Mohr, "Personality Trait Inferences about Organizations: Development of a Measure and Assessment of Construct Validity," *Journal of Applied Psychology* 89 (2004), pp. 85–103.

17. D. R. Avery, "Reactions to Diversity in Recruitment Advertising—Are Differences Black and White?" *Journal of Applied Psychology* 88 (2003), pp. 672–679.

18. M. E. Brooks, S. Highhouse, S. S. Russell, and D. C. Mohr, "Familiarity, Ambivalence, and Firm Reputation: Is Corporate Fame a Double-Edged Sword?" *Journal of Applied Psychology* 88 (2003), pp. 904–914.

19. D. N. Cable and K. Y. Yu, "Managing Job Seekers' Organizational Image Beliefs: The Role of Media Richness and Media Credibility," *Journal of Applied Psychology* 91 (2006), pp. 828–840.

20. R. S. Schuler and S. E. Jackson, "Linking Competitive Strategies with Human Resource Management Practices," *Academy of Management Executive* 1 (1987), pp. 207–219.

23. G. Colvin, "How to Manage Your Business in a Recession," *Fortune* (January 19, 2009), pp. 88–93.

22. M. Orey, "Hang the Recession, Let's Bulk Up," *BusinessWeek,* February 2, 2009, pp. 80–81.

23. J. Collins, "How Great Companies Turn Crisis Into Opportunity," *Fortune* (February 2, 2009), p. 49.

24. C. R. Wanberg, R. Kanfer, and J.T. Banas, "Predictors and Outcomes of Networking Intensity among Job Seekers," *Journal of Applied Psychology* 85 (2000), pp. 491–503.

25. G. Van Hoye and F. Lievens, "Tapping the Grapevine: A Closer Look at Word-of-Mouth as a Recruitment Source," *Journal of Applied Psychology* 94 (2009), pp. 341–352.

26. Y. Saint-Cyr, "Most Successful Recruitment Source," *HR infodesk, Canadian Payroll and Employment Law at Work* (August 2008) at www.hrinfodesk.com/preview.asp?article=26068 (retrieved June 23, 2011).

27. A. Halcrow, "Employers Are Your Best Recruiters," *Personnel Journal* 67 (1988), pp. 42–49.

28. J. McGregor, "I Can't Believe They Took the Whole Team," *BusinessWeek* (December 18, 2006), pp. 120–122.

29. S. Begley, "Behind 'Shortage' of Engineers: Employers Grow More Choosy," *The Wall Street Journal* (November 16, 2005), pp. A1, A12.

30. J. Smith, "Is Online Recruiting Getting Easier?" *Workforce* (September 2, 2001), p. 25.

31. B. R. Dineen, S. R. Ash, and R. A. Noe, "A Web of Applicant Attraction: Person–Organization Fit in the Context of Web-Based Recruitment," *Journal of Applied Psychology* 87 (2002), pp. 723–734.

32. B. Dineen and R. A. Noe, "Effects of Customization on Applicant Decisions and Applicant Pool Characteristics in a Web-based Recruiting Context," *Journal of Applied Psychology* 94 (2009), pp. 224–234.

33. CMA British Columbia at www.cmabc.com.

34. K. Maher, "Blogs Catch on as Recruiting Tool," *The Wall Street Journal* (September 28, 2004), p. B10.

35. A. Singh, "Podcasts Extend Recruiters Reach," *The Wall Street Journal* (April 24, 2006), p. B3.

36. S. Moretti, "Facebook Using Canada as Testing Ground," QMI Agency, *London Free Press* (November 4, 2010).

37. E. White, "Ernst & Young Reaches Out to Recruits on Facebook," *The Wall Street Journal* (January 8, 2007), p. B5.

38. D. Mattioli, "Who's Reading On-Line Resumes? Identity Crooks," *The Wall Street Journal* (October 17, 2006), p B9.

39. Job Bank "About Us," at www.jobbank.gc.ca/abs-eng.aspx (retrieved November 14, 2010).

40. A. McConnon, "A Headhunter Searches for a Second Life," *BusinessWeek* (January 26, 2009), pp. 80–81.

41. P. Smith, "Sources Used by Employers When Hiring College Grads," *Personnel Journal* (February 1995), p. 25.

42. J. W. Boudreau and S. L. Rynes, "Role of Recruitment in Staffing Utility Analysis," *Journal of Applied Psychology* 70 (1985), pp. 354–366.

43. R. Hawk, *The Recruitment Function* (New York: American Management Association, 1967).

44. K. D. Carlson, M. L. Connerly, and R. L. Mecham, "Recruitment Evaluation: The Case for Assessing the Quality of Applicants Attracted," *Personnel Psychology* 55 (2002), pp. 461–494.

45. C. K. Stevens, "Effects of Preinterview Beliefs on Applicants' Reactions to Campus Interviews," *Academy of Management Journal* 40 (1997), pp. 947–966.

46. M. S. Taylor and T. J. Bergman, "Organizational Recruitment Activities and Applicants' Reactions at Different Stages of the Recruitment Process," *Personnel Psychology* 40 (1984), pp. 261–285.

47. L. M. Graves and G. N. Powell, "The Effect of Sex Similarity on Recruiters' Evaluations of Actual Applicants: A Test of the Similarity–Attraction Paradigm," *Personnel Psychology* 48 (1995), pp. 85–98.

48. A. Meisler, "Little White Lies," *Workforce* (November 2003), pp. 88–89.

49. J. P. Wanous, *Organizational Entry: Recruitment, Selection and Socialization of Newcomers* (Reading, MA: Addison-Wesley, 1980).

50. P. Hom, R. W. Griffeth, L. E. Palich, and J. S. Bracker, "An Exploratory Investigation into Theoretical Mechanisms Underlying Realistic Job Previews," *Personnel Psychology* 51 (1998), pp. 421–451.

51. J. M. Phillips, "The Effects of Realistic Job Previews on Multiple Organizational Outcomes: A Meta-analysis," *Academy of Management Journal* 41 (1998), pp. 673–690.

52. P. G. Irving and J. P. Meyer, "Reexamination of the Met-Expectations Hypothesis: A Longitudinal Analysis," *Journal of Applied Psychology* 79 (1995), pp. 937–949.

53. Y. Ganzach, A. Pazy, Y. Hohayun, "Social Exchange and Organizational Commitment: Decision-Making Training for Job Choice as an Alternative to the Realistic Job Preview," *Personnel Psychology* 55 (2002), pp. 613–637.

54. C. Collins, "The Interactive Effects of Recruitment Practices and Product Awareness on Job Seekers' Employer Knowledge and Application Behaviors," *Journal of Applied Psychology* 92 (2007), pp. 180–190.

55. J. Welch and S. Welch, "So Many CEO's Get This Wrong," *BusinessWeek* (July 17, 2006), p. 92.

56. C. H. Van Iddekinge and R. E. Ployhart, "Developments in the Criterion-Related Validation of Selection Procedures: A Critical Review and Recommendations for Practice," *Personnel Psychology* 61 (2008), pp. 871–925.

57. D. D. Robinson, "Content-Oriented Personnel Selection in a Small Business Setting," *Personnel Psychology* 34 (1981), pp. 77–87.

58. M. V. Rafter, "Assessment Providers Scoring Well," *Workforce Management* (January 19, 2009), pp. 24–25.

59. E. Zimmerman, "What Are Employees Worth?" *Workforce,* (February 2001), p. 36.

60. R. A. Posthuma, F. R. Morgeson, and M. A. Campion, "Beyond Employment Interview Validity: A Comprehensive Narrative Review of Recent Research and Trends over Time," *Personnel Psychology* 55 (2002), pp. 1–81.

61. R. Pingitore, B. L. Dugoni, R. S. Tindale, and B. Spring, "Bias against Overweight Job Applicants in a Simulated Interview," *Journal of Applied Psychology* 79 (1994), pp. 909–917.

62. F. Hanson, "Keeping Interviews on Point to Stay Out of Legal Hot Water," *Workforce Management* (August 14, 2006), pp. 44–45.

63. M. A. McDaniel, D. L. Whetzel, F. L. Schmidt, and S. D.Maurer, "The Validity of Employment Interviews: A Comprehensive Review and Meta-Analysis," *Journal of Applied Psychology* 79 (1994), pp. 599–616; A. I. Huffcutt and W. A. Arthur, "Hunter and Hunter (1984) Revisited: Interview Validity for Entry-Level Jobs," *Journal of Applied Psychology* 79 (1994), pp. 184–190.

64. C. H. Middendorf and T. H. Macan, "Note-Taking in the Interview: Effects on Recall and Judgments," *Journal of Applied Psychology* 87 (2002), pp. 293–303.

65. Information gathered from Tom Janz, Lowell Hellervik, and David C. Gilmore, *Behavior Description Interviewing: New, Accurate, Cost Effective* (Boston and Toronto: Allyn and Bacon, 1986) and *The Employment Interview: Theory, Research, and Practice,* edited by Robert W. Eder and Gerald R. Ferris (Newbury Park, California: Sage, 1989).

66. Paul C. Green, *Building Robust Competencies, Linking Human Resource Systems to Organizational Strategies* (Jossey-Bass Publishers, San Francisco,1999), pp. 76–78.

67. M. A. McDaniel, F. P. Morgeson, E. B. Finnegan, M. A. Campion, and E. P. Braverman, "Use of Situational Judgment Tests to Predict Job Performance: A Clarification of the Literature," *Journal of Applied Psychology* 86 (2001), pp. 730–740.

68. A. P. J. Ellis, B. J. West, A. M. Ryan, and R. P. DeShon, "The Use of Impression Management Tactics in Structured

Interviews: A Function of Question Type?" *Journal of Applied Psychology* 87 (2002), pp. 1200–1208.

69. S. Maurer, "A Practitioner-Based Analysis of Interviewer Job Expertise and Scale Format as Contextual Factors in Situational Interviews," *Personnel Psychology* 55 (2002), pp. 307–327.

70. W. C. Byham, "Can You Interview for Integrity?" *Across the Board* (March 2004), pp. 34–38.

71. T. Libby, "Surviving the Group Interview," *Forbes,* March 24, 1986, p. 190; Dipboye, *Selection Interviews: Process Perspectives* (Cincinnati, OH: South-Western, 1991) p. 210.

72. Y. Ganzach, A. N. Kluger, and N. Klayman, "Making Decisions from an Interview: Expert Measurement and Mechanical Combination," *Personnel Psychology* 53 (2000), pp. 1–21.

73. C. Tuna, "How to Spot Resume Fraud," *The Wall Street Journal* (November 13, 2008), p. C1.

74. S. F. Dingfelder, "To Tell the Truth," *Monitor on Psychology* (March 2004), pp. 22–23.

75. A. Davis, J. Pereira, and W. M. Bulkeley, "Security Concerns Bring Focus on Translating Body Language," *The Wall Street Journal* (August 15, 2002), pp. A1–A3.

76. J. S. Lublin, "Bulletproofing Your References in the Hunt for a New Job," *The Wall Street Journal* (April 7, 2009), p. C1.

77. M. R. Barrick and R. D. Zimmerman, "Reducing Voluntary Turnover through Selection," *Journal of Applied Psychology* 90 (2005), pp. 159–166.

78. S. Pustizzi, "Résumé Fraud Gets Slicker and Easier," CNN.com (March 11, 2004), p. 1.

79. N. Schmitt, F. L. Oswald, B. H. Kim, M. A. Gillespie, L. J. Ramsey, and T. Y. Yoo, "The Impact of Elaboration on Socially Desirable Responding and the Validity of Biodata Measures," *Journal of Applied Psychology* 88 (2003), pp. 979–988.

80. N. Schmitt and C. Kunce, "The Effects of Required Elaboration of Answers to Biodata Questions," *Personnel Psychology* 55 (2002), pp. 569–587.

81. M. Barnekow-Bergkvist, U. Aasa, K. A. Angquist, and H. Johansson, "Prediction of Development of Fatigue during a Simulated Ambulance Work Task from Physical Performance Tests," *Ergonomics* 47 (2004), pp. 1238–1250.

82. J. Hogan, "Structure of Physical Performance in Occupational Tasks," *Journal of Applied Psychology* 76 (1991), pp. 495–507.

83. N. D. Henderson, M. W. Berry, and T. Matic, "Field Measures of Strength and Fitness Predict Firefighter Performance on Physically Demanding Tasks," *Personnel Psychology* 60 (2007), pp. 431–473.

84. J. Hogan, "Physical Abilities," in *Handbook of Industrial & Organizational Psychology,* 2nd ed., ed. M. D. Dunnette and L. M. Hough (Palo Alto, CA: Consulting Psychologists Press, 1991).

85. The Guide to Screening and Selection in Employment, Canadian Human Rights Commission (March 2007), p. 5 (©

Minister of Public Works and Government Services, 2007, Catalogue no. HR21-21/2007E-PDF 978-662-45271-3).

86. M. Schoeff, "Skill Levels of U.S. Grads Leave Employers Cold," *Workforce Management* (April 7, 2007), p. 14.

87. J. Smerd, "New Workers Sorely Lacking Literacy Skills," *Workforce Management* (December 10, 2007), p. 6.

88. M. J. Ree, J. A. Earles, and M. S. Teachout, "Predicting Job Performance: Not Much More Than g," *Journal of Applied Psychology* 79 (1994), pp. 518–524.

89. J. F. Salagado, N. Anderson, S. Moscoso, C. Bertua, and F. De Fruyt, "International Validity Generalization of GMA and Cognitive Abilities: A European Community Meta-Analysis," *Personnel Psychology* 56 (2003), pp. 573–605.

90. J. A. LePine, J. A. Colquitt, and A. Erez, "Adaptability to Changing Task Contexts: Effects of General Cognitive Ability, Conscientiousness, and Openness to Experience," *Personnel Psychology* 53 (2000), pp. 563–593.

91. D. Foust, "How to Pick a Business Brain," *BusinessWeek* (February 20, 2006), p. 104.

92. G. Gloeckler, "Sidestepping the GMAT," *BusinessWeek* (August 8, 2005), pp. 71–72.

93. L. Lavelle, "Is the MBA Overrated?" *BusinessWeek* (March 20, 2006), pp. 78–79.

94. F. P. Morgeson, M. A. Campion, R. L. Dipboye, J. R. Hollenbeck, K. R. Murphy, and N. Schmitt, "Reconsidering the Use of Personality Tests in Personnel Selection Contexts," *Personnel Psychology* 60 (2007), pp. 683–729.

95. E. Freudenheim, "Personality Testing Controversial, but Poised to Take Off," *Workforce Management* (August 14, 2006), p. 38.

96. V. Knight, "Personality Tests as Hiring Tools," *The Wall Street Journal* (March 15, 2006), p. B1.

97. D. Goleman, "Sometimes, EQ Is More Important than IQ," CNN.com (January 14, 2005), p. 1.

98. M. A. Shaffer, D. A. Harrison, H. Gregersen, J. S. Black, L. A. Ferzandi, "You Can Take It With You: Individual Differences and Expatriate Effectiveness," *Journal of Applied Psychology* 91 (2006), pp. 109–125.

99. J. M. Hunthausen, D. M. Truxillo, T. N. Bauer, and L. B. Hammer, "A Field Study of Frame of Reference Effects on Personality Test Validity," *Journal of Applied Psychology* 88 (2003), pp. 545–551.

100 N. Schmitt and F. L. Oswald, "The Impact of Corrections for Faking on the Validity of Non-cognitive Measures in Selection Contexts," *Journal of Applied Psychology* (2006), pp. 613–621.

101. S. A. Birkland, T. M. Manson, J. L. Kisamore, M. T. Brannick, and M. A. Smith, "Faking on Personality Measures," *International Journal of Selection and Assessment* 14 (December 2006), pp. 317–335.

102. N. L Vasilopoulos, J. M. Cucina, and J. M. McElreath, "Do Warnings of Response Verification Moderate the Relationship between Personality and Cognitive Ability?" *Journal of Applied Psychology* 90 (2005), pp. 306–322.

103. C. H. Van Iddekinge, P. H. Raymark, and P. L. Roth, "Assessing Personality with a Structured Employment Interview: Construct-Related Validity and Susceptibility to Response Inflation," *Journal of Applied Psychology* 90 (2005), pp. 536–552.

104. R. Mueller-Hanson, E. D., Heggestad, and G. C. Thornton, "Faking and Selection: Considering the Use of Personality from Select-In and Select-Out Perspectives," *Journal of Applied Psychology* 88 (2003), pp. 348–355.

105. C. Palmeri, "Putting Managers to the Test," *BusinessWeek* (November 20, 2006), p. 82.

106. C. Winkler, "Job Tryouts Go Virtual: Online Job Simulations Provide Sophisticated Candidate Assessments," *HR Magazine* (September 2006), pp. 10–15.

107. E. White, "Walk a Mile in My Shoes," *The Wall Street Journal* (January 16, 2006), B3.

108. A. Hedger, "Six Ways to Strengthen Staffing," *Workforce Management* (January 15, 2007).

109. K. Maher, "Win in a Competition, Land on Square that Offers Job," *The Wall Street Journal* (June 1, 2004), p. B10.

110. J. Puliyenthuruthel, "How Google Searches—For Talent," *BusinessWeek* (April 11, 2005), pp. 32–34.

111. W. Arthur, E. A. Day, T. L. McNelly, and P. S. Edens, "Meta-Analysis of the Criterion-Related Validity of Assessment Center Dimensions," *Personnel Psychology* 56 (2003), pp. 125–154.

112. C. E. Lance, T. A. Lambert, A. G. Gewin, F. Lievens, and J. M. Conway, "Revised Estimates of Dimension and Exercise Variance Components in Assessment Center Postexercise Dimension Ratings," *Journal of Applied Psychology* 89 (2004), pp. 377–385.

113. F. L. Schmidt and J. E. Hunter, "The Validity and Utility of Selection Methods in Personnel Psychology: Practical and Theoretical Implications of 85 Years of Research Findings," *Psychological Bulletin* 124 (1998), pp. 262–274.

114. Employment Standards Act, Revised Statutes of Ontario, 1990, Chapter E14, Part XII, Section 46-49, p. 24.

115. J. E. Wanek, P. R. Sackett, and D. S. Ones, "Toward an Understanding of Integrity Test Similarities and Differences: An Item-Level Analysis of Seven Tests," *Personnel Psychology* 56 (2003), pp. 873–894.

116. D. S. Ones and C. Viswesvaran, "Gender, Age, and Race Differences on Overt Integrity Tests: Results across Four Large-Scale Job Applicant Data Sets," *Journal of Applied Psychology* 83 (1998), pp. 35–42.

117. M. R. Cunningham, D. T. Wong, and A. P. Barbee, "Self-Presentation Dynamics on Overt Integrity Tests: Experimental Studies of the Reid Report," *Journal of Applied Psychology* 79 (1994), pp. 643–658.

118. V. M. Catano, W. Wiesner, R. Hackett and L. Methot, *Recruitment and Selection in Canada*, 4th ed., Nelson Series in Human Resources Management (Toronto: Nelson, 2010), pp. 396–401.

119. F. S. Schmidt and J. E. Hunter. 1998. "The Validity and Utility of Selection Methods in Personnel Psychology: Practical and Theoretical Implications of 85 years of Research Findings." *Psychology Bulletin* 124: (1998), pp. 262–274.

120. D. Lindsay, "True Lies [Job Applicant Writes an 'Integrity' Test]," *This* (January/February) 1998 p. 4 and "Honesty Tests," CBC, *The National*, n.d.

121. Employment Standards Act, Revised Statutes of Ontario, 1990, Chapter E14, Part XII, Section 46-49, p. 24.

122. M. E. Paronto, D. M. Truxillo, T. N. Bauer, and M. C. Leo, "Drug Testing, Drug Treatment, and Marijuana Use: A Fairness Perspective," *Journal of Applied Psychology* 87 (2002), pp. 1159–1166.

123. K. R. Murphy, G. C. Thornton, and D. H. Reynolds, "College Students' Attitudes toward Drug Testing Programs, *Personnel Psychology* 43 (1990), pp. 615–631.

124. N. Chserbinin, "Ontario Raises the Bar for Accommodation," *Canadian Employment Law Today*, Issues no. 549, January 27, 2010, p. 1.

125. Ibid., p. 6.

126. R. Skinulis, "Murphy's Law," *HR Professional* (October–November 2008), p. 34.

Chapter 6

1. T. T. Baldwin, C. Danielson, and W. Wiggenhorn, "The Evolution of Learning Strategies in Organizations: From Employee Development to Business Redefinition," *Academy of Management Executive* 11 (1997), pp. 47–58; J. J. Martocchio and T. T. Baldwin, "The Evolution of Strategic Organizational Training," in *Research in Personnel and Human Resource Management* 15, ed. G. R. Ferris (Greenwich, CT: JAI Press, 1997), pp. 1–46.

2. D. Day, *Developing Leadership Talent* (Alexandria, VA: SHRM Foundation, 2007); M. London, *Managing the Training Enterprise* (San Francisco: Jossey-Bass, 1989); C. McCauley and S. Heslett, "Individual Development in the Workplace," in *Handbook of Industrial, Work, and Organizational Psychology*, vol. 1, ed. N. Anderson, D. Ones, H. Sinangil, and C. Viswesveran (London: Sage Publications, 2001), pp. 313–335.

3. R. W. Pace, P. C. Smith, and G. E. Mills, *Human Resource Development* (Englewood Cliffs, NJ: Prentice Hall, 1991); W. Fitzgerald, "Training versus Development," *Training and Development Journal* (May 1992), pp. 81–84; R. A. Noe, S. L. Wilk, E. J. Mullen, and J. E. Wanek, "Employee Development: Issues in Construct Definition and Investigation of Antecedents," in *Improving Training Effectiveness in Work Organizations,* ed. J. K. Ford (Mahwah, NJ: Lawrence Erlbaum, 1997), pp. 153–189.

4. Towers Perrin HR Services, *Talent Management: The State of the Art* (Chicago, IL: Towers Perrin, 2005) at www.towers perrin.com.

5. A. P. Carnevale, "America and the New Economy," *Training and Development Journal* (November 1990), pp. 31–52.

6. J. M. Rosow and R. Zager, *Training: The Competitive Edge* (San Francisco: Jossey-Bass, 1988).

7. D. Miller, "A Preliminary Typology of Organizational Learning: Synthesizing the Literature," *Strategic Management Journal* 22 (1996), pp. 484–505; ed. S. Jackson, M. Hitt, and A. DeNisi, *Managing Knowledge for Sustained Competitive Advantage* (San Francisco: Jossey-Bass, 2003).

8. R. Noe, *Employee Training and Development*, 4th ed. (New York: Irwin/McGraw-Hill, 2008).

9. Ibid.

10. R. A. Noe, "Trainees' Attributes and Attitudes: Neglected Influences on Training Effectiveness," *Academy of Management Review* 11 (1986), pp. 736–749.

11. T. T. Baldwin, R. T. Magjuka, and B. T. Loher, "The Perils of Participation: Effects of Choice on Trainee Motivation and Learning," *Personnel Psychology* 44 (1991), pp. 51–66; S. I. Tannenbaum, J. E. Mathieu, E. Salas, and J. A. Cannon-Bowers, "Meeting Trainees' Expectations: The Influence of Training Fulfillment on the Development of Commitment, Self-Efficacy, and Motivation," *Journal of Applied Psychology* 76 (1991), pp. 759–769.

12. M. E. Gist, C. Schwoerer, and B. Rosen, "Effects of Alternative Training Methods on Self-Efficacy and Performance in Computer Software Training," *Journal of Applied Psychology* 74 (1989), pp. 884–891; J. Martocchio and J. Dulebohn, "Performance Feedback Effects in Training: The Role of Perceived Controllability," *Personnel Psychology* 47 (1994), pp. 357–373; J. Martocchio, "Ability Conceptions and Learning," *Journal of Applied Psychology* 79 (1994), pp. 819–825.

13. L. H. Peters, E. J. O'Connor, and J. R. Eulberg, "Situational Constraints: Sources, Consequences, and Future Considerations," in *Research in Personnel and Human Resource Management,* ed. K. M. Rowland and G. R. Ferris (Greenwich, CT: JAI Press, 1985), vol. 3, pp. 79–114; E. J. O'Connor, L. H. Peters, A. Pooyan, J. Weekley, B. Frank, and B. Erenkranz, "Situational Constraints Effects on Performance, Affective Reactions, and Turnover: A Field Replication and Extension," *Journal of Applied Psychology* 69 (1984), pp. 663–672; D. J. Cohen, "What Motivates Trainees?" *Training and Development Journal* (November 1990), pp. 91–93; Russell, Terborg, and Powers, "Organizational Performance."

14. C. E. Schneier, "Training and Development Programs: What Learning Theory and Research Have to Offer," *Personnel Journal* (April 1974), pp. 288–293; M. Knowles, "Adult Learning," in *Training and Development Handbook,* 3rd ed., ed. R. L. Craig (New York: McGraw-Hill, 1987), pp. 168–179; R. Zemke and S. Zemke, "30 Things We Know for Sure about Adult Learning," *Training* (June 1981), pp. 45–52; B. J. Smith and B. L. Delahaye, *How to Be an Effective Trainer,* 2nd ed. (New York: John Wiley and Sons, 1987).

15. E. Holton III and T. Baldwin, eds, *Improving Learning Transfer in Organizations* (San Francisco: Jossey-Bass, 2003); J. B. Tracey, S. I. Tannenbaum, and M. J. Kavanaugh, "Applying Trained Skills on the Job: The Importance of the Work Environment," *Journal of Applied Psychology* 80 (1995), pp. 239–252; P. E. Tesluk, J. L. Farr, J. E. Mathieu, and R. J. Vance, "Generalization of Employee Involvement Training to the Job Setting: Individual and Situational Effects," *Personnel Psychology* 48 (1995), pp. 607–632; J. K. Ford, M. A. Quinones, D. J. Sego, and J. S. Sorra, "Factors Affecting the Opportunity to Perform Trained Tasks on the Job," *Personnel Psychology* 45 (1992), pp. 511–527.

16. Ford, Quinones, Sego, and Sorra, "Factors Affecting the Opportunity to Perform Trained Tasks on the Job."

17. Ibid.; M. A. Quinones, J. K. Ford, D. J. Sego, and E. M. Smith, "The Effects of Individual and Transfer Environment Characteristics on the Opportunity to Perform Trained Tasks," *Training Research Journal* 1 (1995/96), pp. 29–48.

18. G. Stevens and E. Stevens, "The Truth about EPSS," *Training and Development* 50 (1996), pp. 59–61.

19. R. D. Marx, "Relapse Prevention for Managerial Training: A Model for Maintenance of Behavior Change," *Academy of Management Review* 7 (1982), pp. 433–441; G. P. Latham and C. A. Frayne, "Self-Management Training for Increasing Job Attendance: A Follow-up and Replication," *Journal of Applied Psychology* 74 (1989), pp. 411–416.

20. "Putting the Distance into Distance Learning," *Training* (October 1995), pp. 111–118.

21. A. F. Maydas, "On-line Networks Build the Savings into Employee Education," *HR Magazine* (October 1997), pp. 31–35.

22. D. Picard, "The Future Is Distance Training," *Training* (November 1996), pp. s3–s10.

23. E. Wagner and P. Wilson, "Disconnected," *TD* (December 2005), pp. 40–43; J. Bronstein and A. Newman, "IM Learning," *TD* (February 2006), pp. 47–50.

24 E. Wagner and P. Wilson, "Disconnected," *TD* (December 2005), pp. 40–43.

25. S. Boyer and B. Lambert, "Take the Handcuffs off Sales Team Development with Self-Directed Learning," (November 2008), pp. 62–66.

26. What Is Apprenticeship? Human Resources and Skills Development Canada at www.hrsdc.gc.ca/eng/workplaceskills/trades_apprenticeship/what_is.shtml (retrieved December 3, 2010).

27. A. H. Howard III, "Apprenticeships," in *The ASTD Training and Development Handbook,* pp. 803–813.

28. M. Weinstein, "Virtually Integrated," *Training* (April 2007), p. 10; A. Hira, "The Making of a UPS Driver," *Fortune* (November 12, 2007), pp. 118–129; P. Ketter, "What Can Training Do for Brown," *T + D* (May 2008), pp. 30–36.

29. N. Adams, "Lessons from the Virtual World," *Training* (June 1995), pp. 45–48.

30. Ibid.

31. H. Dolezalek, "Virtual Vision," *Training* (October 2007), pp. 40–46.

32. P. Galagan, "Second That," *T+D* (February 2008), pp. 34–37.

33. M. Hequet, "Games That Teach," *Training* (July 1995), pp. 53–58.

34. G. P. Latham and L. M. Saari, "Application of Social Learning Theory to Training Supervisors through Behavior Modeling," *Journal of Applied Psychology* 64 (1979), pp. 239–246.

35. M. Rosenberg, *E-Learning: Strategies for Delivering Knowledge in the Digital Age* (New York: McGraw-Hill, 2001).

36. "Learning Management Systems: An Executive Summary," *Training* (March 2002), p. 4.

37. D. Sussman, "The LMS Value," *TD* (July 2005), pp. 43–45.

38. D. Brown and D. Harvey, *An Experiential Approach to Organizational Development* (Englewood Cliffs, NJ: Prentice Hall, 2000); J. Schettler, "Learning by Doing," *Training* (April 2002), pp. 38–43.

39. R. J. Wagner, T. T. Baldwin, and C. C. Rowland, "Outdoor Training: Revolution or Fad?" *Training and Development Journal* (March 1991), pp. 51–57; C. J. Cantoni, "Learning the Ropes of Teamwork," *The Wall Street Journal* (October 2, 1995), p. A14.

40. P. Froiland, "Action Learning," *Training* (January 1994), pp. 27–34.

41. H. Lancaster, "This Kind of Black Belt Can Help You Score Some Points at Work," *The Wall Street Journal* (September 14, 1999), p. B1; S. Gale, "Building Frameworks for Six Sigma Success," *Workforce* (May 2003), pp. 64–66.

42. J. DeFeo, "An ROI Story," *Training and Development* (July 2000), pp. 25–27.

43. S. Gale, "Six Sigma Is a Way of Life," *Workforce* (May 2003), pp. 67–68.; and McKesson Canada at www.mckesson.ca/en/products/programs/six_sigma.aspx.

44. McKesson Canada website, About Us, Six Sigma www.mckesson.ca/en/about-us/six-sigma (retrieved July 4, 2011).

45. K. Kraiger, J. K. Ford, and E. Salas, "Application of Cognitive, Skill-Based, and Affective Theories of Learning Outcomes to New Methods of Training Evaluation," *Journal of Applied Psychology* 78 (1993), pp. 311–328; J. J. Phillips, "ROI: The Search for Best Practices," *Training and Development* (February 1996), pp. 42–47; D. L. Kirkpatrick, "Evaluation of Training," in *Training and Development Handbook,* 2nd ed., ed. R. L. Craig (New York: McGraw-Hill, 1976), pp. 18-1–18-27.

46. J. Gordon, "Eye on ROI," *Training* (May 2007), p. 43–45.

47. H. Dolezalek, "The Path to Inclusion," *Training* (May 2008), pp. 52–54.

48. S. E. Jackson and Associates, *Diversity in the Workplace: Human Resource Initiatives* (New York: Guilford Press, 1992).

49. B. Gerber, "Managing Diversity," *Training* (July 1990), pp. 23–30; T. Diamante, C. L. Reid, and L. Ciylo, "Making the Right Training Moves," *HR Magazine* (March 1995), pp. 60–65.

50. S. M. Paskoff, "Ending the Workplace Diversity Wars," *Training* (August 1996), pp. 43–47.

51. D. C. Feldman, *Managing Careers in Organizations* (Glenview, IL: Scott Foresman, 1988); D. Reed-Mendenhall and C. W. Millard, "Orientation: A Training and Development Tool," *Personnel Administrator* 25, no. 8 (1980), pp. 42–44; M. R. Louis, B. Z. Posner, and G. H. Powell, "The Availability and Helpfulness of Socialization Practices," *Personnel Psychology* 36 (1983), pp. 857–866; C. Ostroff and S. W. J. Kozlowski Jr., "Organizational Socialization as a Learning Process: The Role of Information Acquisition," *Personnel Psychology* 45 (1992), pp. 849–874; D. R. France and R. L. Jarvis, "Quick Starts for New Employees," *Training and Development* (October 1996), pp. 47–50.

52. J. H. Greenhaus and G. A. Callanan, *Career Management,* 2nd ed. (Fort Worth, TX: Dryden Press, 1994); D. C. Feldman, *Managing Careers in Organizations* (Glenview, IL: Scott Foresman, 1988); D. Hall, Careers In and Out of Organizations (Thousand Oaks, CA: Sage, 2002).

53. D. T. Hall, "Protean Careers of the 21st Century," *Academy of Management Executive* 11 (1996), pp. 8–16; Hall, *Careers In and Out of Organizations.*

54. D. M. Rousseau, "Changing the Deal while Keeping the People," *Academy of Management Executive* 11 (1996), pp. 50–61; D. M. Rousseau and J. M. Parks, "The Contracts of Individuals and Organizations," in *Research in Organizational Behavior* 15, ed. L. L. Cummings and B. M. Staw (Greenwich, CT: JAI Press, 1992), pp. 1–47.

55. C. Ansberry, "A New Blue-Collar World," *The Wall Street Journal* (June 30, 2003), p. B1.

56. M. B. Arthur, P. H. Claman, and R. J. DeFillippi, "Intelligent Enterprise, Intelligent Careers," *Academy of Management Executive* 9 (1995), pp. 7–20.

57. K. R. Brousseau, M. J. Driver, K. Eneroth, and R. Larsson, "Career Pandemonium: Realigning Organizations and Individuals," *Academy of Management Executive* 11 (1996), pp. 52–66.

58. M. B. Arthur, "The Boundaryless Career: A New Perspective of Organizational Inquiry," *Journal of Organization Behavior* 15 (1994), pp. 295–309; P. H. Mirvis and D. T. Hall, "Psychological Success and the Boundaryless Career," *Journal of Organization Behavior* 15 (1994), pp. 365–380; M. Lazarova and S. Taylor, "Boundaryless Careers, Social Capital, and Knowledge Management: Implications for Organizational Performance," *Journal of Organizational Behavior* 30 (2009), pp. 119–139; D. Feldman and T. Ng, "Careers: Mobility, Embeddedness, and Success," *Journal of Management* 33 (2007), pp. 350–377.

59. Harris Interactive, Emerging workforce study (Ft. Lauderdale, FL: Spherion, 2005) at www.spherion.com/pressroom/L. Chao, "What GenXers Need to Be Happy at Work," *The Wall Street Journal* (November 29, 2005), p. B6; E. Kaplan-Leiserson, "The Changing Workforce," *TD* (February 2005), pp. 10–11.

60. R. Noe, *Employee Training and Development*, 4th ed. (New York: McGraw-Hill, Irwin, 2008).

61. C. Waxer, "Course Review," *Human Resource Executive* (December 2005), pp. 46–48.

62. C. Waxer, "Bank of Montreal Opens Its Checkbook in the Name of Employee Development," *Workforce Management* (October 24, 2005), pp. 46–48.

63. J. Bolt, *Executive Development* (New York: Harper Business, 1989); M. A. Hitt, B. B. Tyler, C. Hardee, and D. Park, "Understanding Strategic Intent in the Global Marketplace," *Academy of Management Executive* 9 (1995), pp. 12–19.

64. A. Howard and D. W. Bray, Managerial Lives in Transition: *Advancing Age and Changing Times* (New York: Guilford, 1988); Bolt, *Executive Development*; J. R. Hinrichs and G. P. Hollenbeck, "Leadership Development," in *Developing Human Resources,* ed. K. N. Wexley (Washington, DC: BNA Books, 1991), pp. 5-221–5-237; Day, *Developing Leadership Talent.*

65. M. Weinstein, "Personalities & Performance," *Training* (July/August 2008), pp. 36–40.

66. S. K. Hirsch, *MBTI Team Member's Guide* (Palo Alto, CA: Consulting Psychologists Press, 1992); A. L. Hammer, *Introduction to Type and Careers* (Palo Alto, CA: Consulting Psychologists Press, 1993).

67. G. C. Thornton III and W. C. Byham, *Assessment Centers and Managerial Performance* (New York: Academic Press, 1982); L. F. Schoenfeldt and J. A. Steger, "Identification and Development of Management Talent," in *Research in Personnel and Human Resource Management*, ed. K. N. Rowland and G. Ferris (Greenwich, CT: JAI Press, 1989), vol. 7, pp. 151–181.

68. B. B. Gaugler, D. B. Rosenthal, G. C. Thornton III, and C. Bentson, "Meta-Analysis of Assessment Center Validity," *Journal of Applied Psychology* 72 (1987), pp. 493–511; D. W. Bray, R. J. Campbell, and D. L. Grant, *Formative Years in Business: A Long-Term AT&T Study of Managerial Lives* (New York: Wiley, 1974).

69. R. G. Jones and M. D. Whitmore, "Evaluating Developmental Assessment Centers as Interventions," *Personnel Psychology* 48 (1995), pp. 377–388.

70. www.steelcase.com/en/pages/homepage.aspx.

71. C. D. McCauley and M. M. Lombardo, "Benchmarks: An Instrument for Diagnosing Managerial Strengths and Weaknesses," in *Measures of Leadership*, pp. 535–545; "Benchmarks©—Overview," at www.ccl.org (retrieved March 28, 2006).

72. C. D. McCauley, M. M. Lombardo, and C. J. Usher, "Diagnosing Management Development Needs: An Instrument Based on How Managers Develop," *Journal of Management* 15 (1989), pp. 389–403.

73. S. B. Silverman, "Individual Development through Performance Appraisal," in *Developing Human Resources,* pp. 5-120–5-151.

74. M. W. McCall Jr., M. M. Lombardo, and A. M. Morrison, *Lessons of Experience* (Lexington, MA: Lexington Books, 1988).

75. R. S. Snell, "Congenial Ways of Learning: So Near yet So Far," *Journal of Management Development* 9 (1990), pp. 17–23.

76. R. Morrison, T. Erickson, and K. Dychtwald, "Managing Middlescence," *Harvard Business Review* (March 2006), pp. 78–86.

77. McCall, Lombardo, and Morrison, *Lessons of Experience;* M. W. McCall, "Developing Executives through Work Experiences," *Human Resource Planning* 11 (1988), pp. 1–11; M. N. Ruderman, P. J. Ohlott, and C. D. McCauley, "Assessing Opportunities for Leadership Development," in *Measures of Leadership,* pp. 547–562; C. D. McCauley, L. J. Estman, and P. J. Ohlott, "Linking Management Selection and Development through Stretch Assignments," *Human Resource Management* 34 (1995), pp. 93–115.

78. S. Thurm, "Power-Sharing Prepares Managers," *The Wall Street Journal* (December 5, 2005), p. B4.

79. M. London, *Developing Managers* (San Francisco: Jossey-Bass, 1985); M. A. Campion, L. Cheraskin, and M. J. Stevens, "Career-Related Antecedents and Outcomes of Job Rotation," *Academy of Management Journal* 37 (1994), pp. 1518–1542; M. London, *Managing the Training Enterprise* (San Francisco: Jossey-Bass, 1989).

80. Ibid.

81. D. C. Feldman, *Managing Careers in Organizations* (Glenview, IL: Scott Foresman, 1988).

82. J. M. Brett, L. K. Stroh, and A. H. Reilly, "Job Transfer," in *International Review of Industrial and Organizational Psychology: 1992,* ed. C. L. Cooper and I. T. Robinson (Chichester, England: John Wiley and Sons, 1992); D. C. Feldman and J. M. Brett, "Coping with New Jobs: A Comparative Study of New Hires and Job Changers," *Academy of Management Journal* 26 (1983), pp. 258–272.

83. D. T. Hall and L. A. Isabella, "Downward Moves and Career Development," *Organizational Dynamics* 14 (1985), pp. 5–23.

84. H. D. Dewirst, "Career Patterns: Mobility, Specialization, and Related Career Issues," in *Contemporary Career Development Issues,* ed. R. F. Morrison and J. Adams (Hillsdale, NJ: Lawrence Erlbaum, 1991), pp. 73–108.

85. D. Flacks, "Building on Old-School Ethics and Integrity," *Toronto Star* (November 20, 2010), p. M7.

86. Ibid.

87. C. J. Bachler, "Workers Take Leave of Job Stress," *Personnel Journal* (January 1995), pp. 38–48.

88. K. Lunau, "When the Going Gets Tough," *Macleans* (October 14, 2009) at www2.macleans.ca/2009/10/14/when-the-going-gets-tough/2/.

89. D. B. Turban and T. W. Dougherty, "Role of Protégé Personality in Receipt of Mentoring and Career Success," *Academy of Management Journal* 37 (1994), pp. 688–702; E. A. Fagenson, "Mentoring: Who Needs It? A Comparison of Protégés' and Nonprotégés' Needs for Power, Achievement, Affiliation, and Autonomy," *Journal of Vocational Behavior* 41 (1992), pp. 48–60.

90. K. E. Kram, *Mentoring at Work: Developmental Relationships in Organizational Life* (Glenview, IL: Scott Foresman, 1985); K. Kram, "Phases of the Mentoring Relationship," *Academy of Management Journal* 26 (1983), pp. 608–625; G. T. Chao, P. M. Walz, and P. D. Gardner, "Formal and Informal Mentorships: A Comparison of Mentoring Functions and Contrasts with Nonmentored Counterparts," *Personnel Psychology* 45 (1992), pp. 619–636; C. Wanberg, E. Welsh, and S. Hezlett, "Mentoring Research: A Review and Dynamic Process Model," in *Research in Personnel and Human Resources Management,* ed. J. Martocchio and G. Ferris (New York: Elsevier Science, 2003), pp. 39–124.

91. E. White, "Making Mentorships Work," *The Wall Street Journal* (October 23, 2007), p. B11; E. Holmes, "Career Mentors Today Seem Short on Advice but Give a Mean Tour," *The Wall Street Journal* (August 28, 2007), p. B1; J. Sandberg, "With Bad Mentors It's Better to Break Up than to Make Up," *The Wall Street Journal* (March 18, 2008), p. B1.

92. L. Eby, M. Butts, A. Lockwood, and A. Simon, "Protégés' Negative Mentoring Experiences: Construct Development and Nomological Validation," *Personnel Psychology* 57 (2004), pp. 411–447; M. Boyle, "Most Mentoring Programs Stink—but Yours Doesn't Have To," *Training* (August 2005), pp. 12–15.

93. G. F. Dreher and R. A. Ash, "A Comparative Study of Mentoring among Men and Women in Managerial, Professional, and Technical Positions," *Journal of Applied Psychology* 75 (1990), pp. 539–546; T. D. Allen, L. T. Eby, M. L. Poteet, E. Lentz, and L. Lima, "Career Benefits Associated with Mentoring for Protégés: A Meta-Analysis," *Journal of Applied Psychology* 89 (2004), pp. 127–136; R. A. Noe, D. B. Greenberger, and S. Wang, "Mentoring: What We Know and Where We Might Go," in *Research in Personnel and Human Resources Management,* ed. G. Ferris and J. Martucchio (New York: Elsevier Science, 2002), pp. 129–174; R. A. Noe, "An Investigation of the Determinants of Successful Assigned Mentoring Relationships," *Personnel Psychology* 41 (1988), pp. 457–79; B. J. Tepper, "Upward Maintenance Tactics in Supervisory Mentoring and Nonmentoring Relationships," *Academy of Management Journal* 38 (1995), pp. 1191–1205; B. R. Ragins and T. A. Scandura, "Gender Differences in Expected Outcomes of Mentoring Relationships," *Academy of Management Journal* 37 (1994), pp. 957–971.

94. B. Kaye and B. Jackson, "Mentoring: A Group Guide," *Training and Development* (April 1995), pp. 23–27.

95. D. B. Peterson and M. D. Hicks, *Leader as Coach* (Minneapolis, MN: Personnel Decisions, 1996).

96. D. Coutu and C. Kauffman, "What Coaches Can Do for You," *Harvard Business Review* (January 2009), pp. 91–97.

97. J. Toto, "Untapped World of Peer Coaching," *TD* (April 2006), pp. 69–71.

98. D. T. Jaffe and C. D. Scott, "Career Development for Empowerment in a Changing Work World," in *New Directions in Career Planning and the Workplace,* ed. J. M. Kummerow (Palo Alto, CA: Consulting Psychologists Press, 1991), pp. 33–60;

99. L. Summers, "A Logical Approach to Development Planning," *Training and Development* 48 (1994), pp. 22–31; D. B. Peterson and M. D. Hicks, *Development First* (Minneapolis, MN: Personnel Decisions, 1995).

100. D. Brown, "TD Gives Employees Tool to Chart Career Paths, "*Canadian HR Reporter* (June 20, 2005); BBM Human Resource Consultants at www.Bbmcareerdev.com/career solutions_careeradvisor.php (retrieved December 5, 2010).

101. Catalyst website:, "Canadian Women in Business," (Pyramid published March 2011) at www.catalyst.org/publication/198/canadian-women-in-business (retrieved July 6, 2011).

102. U.S. Department of Labor, *A Report on the Glass Ceiling Initiative* (Washington, DC: U.S. Department of Labor, 1991).

103. P. J. Ohlott, M. N. Ruderman, and C. D. McCauley, "Gender Differences in Managers' Developmental Job Experiences," *Academy of Management Journal* 37 (1994), pp. 46–67; D. Mattioli, "Programs to Promote Female Managers Win Citations," *The Wall Street Journal* (January 30, 2007), p. B7.

104. L. A. Mainiero, "Getting Anointed for Advancement: The Case of Executive Women," *Academy of Management Executive* 8 (1994), pp. 53–67; J. S. Lublin, "Women at Top Still Are Distant from CEO Jobs," *The Wall Street Journal* (February 28, 1995), pp. B1, B5; P. Tharenov, S. Latimer, and D. Conroy, "How Do You Make It to the Top? An Examination of Influences on Women's and Men's Managerial Advancement," *Academy of Management Journal* 37 (1994), pp. 899–931.

105. P. Tharenou, "Going Up? Do Traits and Informal Social Processes Predict Advancement in Management?" *Academy of Management Journal* 44 (2001), pp. 1005–1017.

106. U.S. Department of Labor, *A Report on the Glass Ceiling Initiative;* R. A. Noe, "Women and Mentoring: A Review and Research Agenda," *Academy of Management Review* 13 (1988), pp. 65–78; B. R. Ragins and J. L. Cotton, "Easier Said Than Done: Gender Differences in Perceived Barriers to Gaining a Mentor," *Academy of Management Journal* 34 (1991), pp. 939–951.

107. W. J. Rothwell, *Effective Succession Planning,* 2nd ed. (New York: AMACOM, 2001).

108. M. W. McCall Jr., and M. M. Lombardo, "Off the Track: Why and How Successful Executives Get Derailed," *Technical Report* no. 21 (Greensboro, NC: Center for Creative Leadership, 1983); E. V. Veslor and J. B. Leslie, "Why Executives Derail: Perspectives across Time and Cultures," *Academy of Management Executive* 9 (1995), pp. 62–72.

Chapter 7

1. J. D. Shaw, M. K. Duffy, J. L. Johnson, and D. E. Lockhart, "Turnover, Social Capital Losses, and Performance," *Academy of Management Journal* 48 (2005), pp. 594–606.

2. R. Batt, "Managing Customer Services: Human Resource Practices, Quit Rates, and Sales Growth," *Academy of Management Journal* 45 (2002), pp. 587–597.

3. I. S. Fulmer, B. Gerhart, and K. S. Scott, "Are the 100 Best Better? An Empirical Investigation of the Relationship between Being a 'Great Place to Work' and Firm Performance," *Personnel Psychology* 56 (2003), pp. 965–993.

4. M. Boyle, "Happy People, Happy Returns," *Fortune* (January 22, 2007), p. 100.

5. J. P. Guthrie, "High-Involvement Work Practices, Turnover, and Productivity: Evidence from New Zealand," *Academy of Management Journal* 44 (2001), pp. 180–190.

6. S. S. Masterson, "A Trickle-Down Model of Organizational Justice: Relating Employees' and Customers' Perceptions of and Reactions to Fairness," *Journal of Applied Psychology* 86 (2001), pp. 594–604.

7. K. M. Kacmer, M. C. Andrews, D. L. Van Rooy, R. C. Steilberg, and S. Cerrone, "Sure Everyone Can Be Replaced ... But at What Cost? Turnover as a Predictor of Unit-Level Performance," *Academy of Management Journal* 49 (2006), pp. 133–144.

8. M. Riketta, "The Causal Relation between Job Attitudes and Performance: A Meta-analysis of Panel Studies," *Journal of Applied Psychology* 93 (2008), pp. 472–481.

9. A. Cowan and R. Wright, "Valuing Your Talent: Human Resources Trends and Metrics," Conference Board of Canada (June 2010), p. 42.

10. J. D. Shaw, N. Gupta, and J. E. Delery, "Alternative Conceptualizations of the Relationship between Voluntary Turnover and Organizational Performance," *Academy of Management Journal* 48 (2005), pp. 50–68.

11. J. Sullivan, "Not All Turnover Is Equal," *Workforce Management* (May 21, 2007), p. 42.

12. J. Lublin, "Keeping Clients by Keeping Workers," *The Wall Street Journal* (November 20, 2006), p. B1.

13. J. Banks, "Turnover Costs," *Workforce Management* (June 23, 2008), p. 22.

14. S. C. Payne and S. S. Weber, "Effects of Service Provider Attitudes and Employment Status on Citizenship Behaviors and Customers' Attitudes and Loyalty Behavior," *Journal of Applied Psychology* 91 (2006), pp. 365–378.

15. G. A. Gelade and M. Ivery, "The Impact of Human Resource Management and Work Climate on Organizational Performance," *Personnel Psychology* 56 (2003), pp. 383–404.

16. B. Schneider, P. J. Hanges, D. B. Smith, and A. N. Salvaggio, "Which Come First, Employee Attitudes or Organizational Financial and Market Performance?" *Journal of Applied Psychology* 88 (2003), pp. 838–851.

17. D. W. Baruch, "Why They Terminate," *Journal of Consulting Psychology* 8 (1944), pp. 35–46; J. G. Rosse, "Relations among Lateness, Absence and Turnover: Is There a Progression of Withdrawal?" *Human Relations* 41 (1988), pp. 517–531.

18. C. E. Labig and I. B. Helburn, "Union and Management Policy Influences on Grievance Initiation," *Journal of Labor Research* 7 (1986), pp. 269–284.

19. E. R. Burris, J. R. Detert, and D. S. Chiaburu, "Quitting before Leaving: The Mediating Effects of Psychological Attachment and Detachment on Voice," *Journal of Applied Psychology* 93 (2008), pp. 912–922.

20. M. L. Ambrose and M. Schminke, "The Role of Overall Justice Judgments in Organizational Research: A Test of Mediation," *Journal of Applied Psychology* 94 (2009), pp. 491–500.

21. D. A. Harrison, D. A. Newman, and P. L. Roth, "How Important Are Job Attitudes? Meta-analytic Comparisons of Integrative Behavioral Outcomes and Time Sequences," *Academy of Management Journal* 49 (2006), pp. 305–325.

22. E. A. Locke, "The Nature and Causes of Job Dissatisfaction," in *The Handbook of Industrial & Organizational Psychology,* ed. M. D. Dunnette (Chicago: Rand McNally, 1976), pp. 901–969.

23. A. Cowan and R. Wright, "Valuing Your Talent: Human Resources Trends and Metrics," Conference Board of Canada (June 2010), p. 41.

24. C. O. Trevor and D. L. Wazeter, "Contingent View of Reactions to Objective Pay Conditions: Interdependence among Pay Structure Characteristics and Pay Relative to Internal and External Referents," *Journal of Applied Psychology* 91 (2006), pp. 1260–1275.

25. S. C. Currall, A. J. Towler, T. A. Judge, and L. Kohn, "Pay Satisfaction and Organizational Outcomes," *Personnel Psychology* 58 (2005), pp. 613–640.

26. B. M. Meglino, E. C. Ravlin, and C. L. Adkins, "A Work Values Approach to Corporate Culture: A Field Test of the Value Congruence Process and Its Relationship to Individual Outcomes," *Journal of Applied Psychology* 74 (1989), pp. 424–433.

27. R. Eisenberger, F. Stinghamber, C. Vandenberghe, I. L. Sucharski, and L. Rhoades, "Perceived Supervisor Support: Contributions to Perceived Organizational Support and Employee Retention," *Journal of Applied Psychology* 87 (2002), pp. 565–573.

28. P. Lattman, "Does Thank You Help Keep Associates?" *The Wall Street Journal* (January 24, 2007).

29. S. C. Payne and A. H. Huffman, "A Longitudinal Examination of the Influence of Mentoring on Organizational Commitment and Turnover," *Academy of Management Journal* 48 (2005), pp. 158–168.

30. G. C. Ganster, M. R. Fusiler, and B. T. Mayes, "Role of Social Support in the Experience of Stress at Work," *Journal of Applied Psychology* 71 (1986), pp. 102–111.

31. B. A. Gerhart, "How Important Are Dispositional Factors as Determinants of Job Satisfaction? Implications for Job Design and Other Personnel Programs," *Journal of Applied Psychology* 72 (1987), pp. 493–502.

32. E. F. Stone and H. G. Gueutal, "An Empirical Derivation of the Dimensions along Which Characteristics of Jobs Are Perceived," *Academy of Management Journal* 28 (1985), pp. 376–396.

33. L. W. Porter and R. M. Steers, "Organizational, Work and Personal Factors in Employee Absenteeism and Turnover," *Psychological Bulletin* 80 (1973), pp. 151–176.

34. D. Isen, "Reduce Employee Turnover, Build Customer Loyalty," *Workforce Management* (May 19, 2008), p. 34.

35. J. R. Hackman and G. R. Oldham, "Motivation through the Design of Work," *Organizational Behavior and Human Performance* 16 (1976), pp. 250–279.

36. E. C. Dierdorff and J. K. Ellington, "It's the Nature of the Work: Examining Behavior-based Sources of Work-Family Conflict," *Journal of Applied Psychology* 93 (2008), pp. 883–892.

37. A. M. Grant, "Relational Job Design and the Motivation to Make a Prosocial Difference," *Academy of Management Review* 32 (2007), pp. 393–417.

38. A. M. Grant, "Does Intrinsic Motivation Fuel the Prosocial Fire? Motivational Synergy in Predicting Persistence, Performance, and Productivity," *Journal of Applied Psychology* 93 (2007), pp. 48–58.

39. A. M. Grant, "The Significance of Task Significance," *Journal of Applied Psychology* 93 (2007), pp. 108–124.

40. A. M. Grant, E. M. Campbell, G. Chen, K. Cottone, D. Lapedia, and K. Lee, "Impact and Art of Motivation Maintenance: The Effects of Contact with Beneficiaries on Persistence Behavior," *Organizational Behavior and Human Decision Processes* 103 (2007), pp. 53–67.

41. A. Cowan and R. Wright, "Valuing Your Talent: Human Resources Trends and Metrics," Conference Board of Canada (June 2010), p. 41.

42. J. Applegaste, "Plan an Exit Interview," CNNMoney.com (November 13, 2000), pp. 1–2.

43. J. Lynn, "Many Happy Returns," CNNMoney.com (March 2, 2001), pp. 1–2.

44. M. Laff, "Performance Management Gives a Shaky Performance," *T + D* (September 2007), p. 18; A. Fox, "Curing What Ails Performance Reviews," *HR Magazine* (January 2009), pp. 52–56.

45. E. Pulakos, *Performance Management* (San Francisco: Wiley-Blackwell, 2009); K. Murphy and J. Cleveland, *Performance Appraisal: An Organizational Perspective* (Boston: Allyn & Bacon, 1991).

46. J. Cleveland, K. Murphy, and R. Williams, "Multiple Uses of Performance Appraisal: Prevalence and Correlates," *Journal of Applied Psychology* 74 (1989), pp. 130–135.

47. M. Beer, "Note on Performance Appraisal," in *Readings in Human Resource Management,* ed. M. Beer and B. Spector (New York: Free Press, 1985).

48. R. Schuler and S. Jackson, "Linking Competitive Strategies with Human Resource Practices," *Academy of Management Executive* 1 (1987), pp. 207–219.

49. L. King, J. Hunter, and F. Schmidt, "Halo in a Multidimensional Forced-Choice Performance Evaluation Scale," *Journal of Applied Psychology* 65 (1980), pp. 507–516.

50. B. R. Nathan, A. M. Mohrman, and J. Millman, "Interpersonal Relations as a Context for the Effects of Appraisal Interviews on Performance and Satisfaction: A Longitudinal Study," *Academy of Management Journal* 34 (1991), pp. 352–369; M. S. Taylor, K. B. Tracy, M. K. Renard, J. K. Harrison, and S. J. Carroll, "Due Process in Performance Appraisal: A Quasi-experiment in Procedural Justice," *Administrative Science Quarterly* 40 (1995), pp. 495–523; J. M. Werner and M. C. Bolino, "Explaining U.S. Courts of Appeals Decisions Involving Performance Appraisal: Accuracy, Fairness, and Validation," *Personnel Psychology* 50 (1997), pp. 1–24.

51. S. Bates, "Forced Ranking," *HR Magazine* (June 2003), pp. 63–68; A. Meisler, "Deadman's Curve," *Workforce Management* (July 2003), pp. 44–49; M. Lowery, "Forcing the Issue," *Human Resource Executive* (October 16, 2003), pp. 26–29.

52. Ibid.

53. F. Blanz and E. Ghiselli, "The Mixed Standard Scale: A New Rating System," *Personnel Psychology* 25 (1973), pp. 185–99; K. Murphy and J. Constans, "Behavioral Anchors as a Source of Bias in Rating," *Journal of Applied Psychology* 72 (1987), pp. 573–577.

54. P. Smith and L. Kendall, "Retranslation of Expectations: An Approach to the Construction of Unambiguous Anchors for Rating Scales," *Journal of Applied Psychology* 47 (1963), pp. 149–155.

55. Murphy and Constans, "Behavioral Anchors"; M. Piotrowski, J. Barnes-Farrel, and F. Esrig, "Behaviorally Anchored Bias: A Replication and Extension of Murphy and Constans," *Journal of Applied Psychology* 74 (1989), pp. 823–826.

56. U. Wiersma and G. Latham, "The Practicality of Behavioral Observation Scales, Behavioral Expectation Scales, and Trait Scales," *Personnel Psychology* 39 (1986), pp. 619–628.

57. Latham and Wexley, Increasing Productivity through Performance Appraisal.

58. T. Patten Jr., *A Manager's Guide to Performance Appraisal* (New York: Free Press, 1982).

59. M. O'Donnell and R. O'Donnell, "MBO—Is It Passe?" *Hospital and Health Services Administration* 28, no. 5 (1983), pp. 46–58; T. Poister and G. Streib, "Management Tools in Government: Trends over the Past Decade," *Public Administration Review* 49 (1989), pp. 240–248.

60. D. McGregor, "An Uneasy Look at Performance Appraisal," *Harvard Business Review* 35, no. 3 (1957), pp. 89–94.

61. E. Locke and G. Latham, *A Theory of Goal Setting and Task Performance* (Englewood Cliffs, NJ: Prentice Hall, 1990).

62. S. Carroll and H. Tosi, *Management by Objectives* (New York: Macmillan, 1973).

63. G. Odiorne, *MBO II: A System of Managerial Leadership for the 80s* (Belmont, CA: Pitman, 1986).

64. R. Rodgers and J. Hunter, "Impact of Management by Objectives on Organizational Productivity," *Journal of Applied Psychology* 76 (1991), pp. 322–326.

65. R. Heneman, K. Wexley, and M. Moore, "Performance Rating Accuracy: A Critical Review," *Journal of Business Research* 15 (1987), pp. 431–448.

66. T. Becker and R. Klimoski, "A Field Study of the Relationship between the Organizational Feedback Environment and Performance," *Personnel Psychology* 42 (1989), pp. 343–358; H. M. Findley, W. F. Giles, and K. W. Mossholder, "Performance Appraisal and Systems Facets: Relationships with Contextual Performance," *Journal of Applied Psychology* 85 (2000), pp. 634–640.

67. L. Axline, "Performance Biased Evaluations," *Supervisory Management* (November 1991), p. 3.

68. K. Wexley and R. Klimoski, "Performance Appraisal: An Update," in *Research in Personnel and Human Resource Management* (vol. 2), ed. K. Rowland and G. Ferris (Greenwich, CT: JAI Press, 1984).

69. F. Landy and J. Farr, *The Measurement of Work Performance: Methods, Theory, and Applications* (New York: Academic Press, 1983).

70. G. McEvoy and P. Buller, "User Acceptance of Peer Appraisals in an Industrial Setting," *Personnel Psychology* 40 (1987), pp. 785–797.

71. D. Antonioni, "The Effects of Feedback Accountability on Upward Appraisal Ratings," *Personnel Psychology* 47 (1994), pp. 349–356.

72. Murphy and Cleveland, *Performance Appraisal: An Organizational Perspective.*

73. J. Bernardin and L. Klatt, "Managerial Appraisal Systems: Has Practice Caught Up with the State of the Art?" *Public Personnel Administrator* (November 1985), pp. 79–86.

74. Fox, "Curing What Ails Performance Reviews."

75. H. Heidemeier and K. Moser, "Self-Other Agreement in Job Performance Rating: A Meta-Analytic Test of a Process Model," *Journal of Applied Psychology* 94 (2008), pp. 353–370.

76. M. W. Horrigan, "Employment Projections to 2012: Concepts and Context," *Monthly Labor Review* 127 (2004), pp. 3–11.

77. J. Bernardin, B. Hagan, J. Kane, and P. Villanova, "Effective Performance Management: A Focus on Precision, Customers, and Situational Constraints," in *Performance Appraisal: State of the Art in Practice,* ed. J. W. Smither (San Francisco: Jossey-Bass, 1998), pp. 3–48.

78. R. Hoffman, "Ten Reasons You Should Be Using 360-Degree Feedback," *HR Magazine* (April 1995), pp. 82–84.

79. S. Sherman, "How Tomorrow's Best Leaders Are Learning Their Stuff," *Fortune* (November 27, 1995), pp. 90–104; W. W. Tornow, M. London, and Associates, *Maximizing the Value of 360-Degree Feedback* (San Francisco: Jossey-Bass, 1998); D. A. Waldman, L. E. Atwater, and D. Antonioni, "Has 360-Degree Feedback Gone Amok?" *Academy of Management Executive* 12 (1988), pp. 86–94.

80. L. Atwater, P. Roush, and A. Fischthal, "The Influence of Upward Feedback on Self- and Follower Ratings of Leadership," *Personnel Psychology* 48 (1995), pp. 35–59; J. F. Hazucha, S. A. Hezlett, and R. J. Schneider, "The Impact of 360-Degree Feedback on Management Skill Development," *Human Resource Management* 32 (1993), pp. 325–351; J. W. Smither, M. London, N. Vasilopoulos, R. R. Reilly, R. E. Millsap, and N. Salvemini, "An Examination of the Effects of an Upward Feedback Program over Time," *Personnel Psychology* 48 (1995), pp. 1–34; J. Smither and A. Walker, "Are the Characteristics of Narrative Comments Related to Improvements in Multirater Feedback Ratings over Time?" *Journal of Applied Psychology* 89 (2004), pp. 575–581; J. Smither, M. London, and R. Reilly, "Does Performance Improve Following Multisource Feedback? A Theoretical Model, Meta-analysis, and Review of Empirical Findings," *Personnel Psychology* 58 (2005), pp. 33–66.

81. D. Bracken, "Straight Talk about Multirater Feedback," *Training and Development* (September 1994), pp. 44–51; K. Nowack, J. Hartley, and W. Bradley, "How to Evaluate Your 360-Feedback Efforts," *Training and Development* (April 1999), pp. 48–52.

82. A. Tversky and D. Kahneman, "Availability: A Heuristic for Judging Frequency and Probability," *Cognitive Psychology* 5 (1973), pp. 207–232.

83. K. Wexley and W. Nemeroff, "Effects of Racial Prejudice, Race of Applicant, and Biographical Similarity on Interviewer Evaluations of Job Applicants," *Journal of Social and Behavioral Sciences* 20 (1974), pp. 66–78.

84. D. Smith, "Training Programs for Performance Appraisal: A Review," *Academy of Management Review* 11 (1986), pp. 22–40.

85. G. Latham, K. Wexley, and E. Pursell, "Training Managers to Minimize Rating Errors in the Observation of Behavior," *Journal of Applied Psychology* 60 (1975), pp. 550–555.

86. J. Bernardin and E. Pence, "Effects of Rater Training: Creating New Response Sets and Decreasing Accuracy," *Journal of Applied Psychology* 65 (1980), pp. 60–66.

87. E. Pulakos, "A Comparison of Rater Training Programs: Error Training and Accuracy Training," *Journal of Applied Psychology* 69 (1984), pp. 581–588.

88. H. J. Bernardin, M. R. Buckley, C. L. Tyler, and D. S. Wiese, "A Reconsideration of Strategies in Rater Training," in *Research in Personnel and Human Resource Management,* vol. 18, ed. G. R. Ferris (Greenwich, CT: JAI Press, 2000), pp. 221–274.

89. K. Wexley, V. Singh, and G. Yukl, "Subordinate Participation in Three Types of Appraisal Interviews," *Journal of Applied Psychology* 58 (1973), pp. 54–57; K. Wexley, "Appraisal Interview," in *Performance Assessment,* ed. R. A. Berk (Baltimore: Johns Hopkins University Press, 1986), pp. 167–185; D. Cederblom, "The Performance Appraisal Interview: A Review, Implications, and Suggestions," *Academy of Management Review* 7 (1982), pp. 219–227; B. D. Cawley, L. M. Keeping, and P. E. Levy, "Participation in the Performance Appraisal Process and Employee Reactions: A Meta-analytic Review of Field Investigations," *Journal of Applied Psychology* 83, no. 3 (1998), pp. 615–663; H. Aguinis, *Performance Management* (Upper Saddle River, NJ: Pearson Prentice Hall, 2007); C. Lee, "Feedback, Not Appraisal," *HR Magazine* (November 2006), pp. 111–114.

90. W. Giles and K. Mossholder, "Employee Reactions to Contextual and Session Components of Performance Appraisal," *Journal of Applied Psychology* 75 (1990), pp. 371–377.

91. E. Locke and G. Latham, *A Theory of Goal Setting and Task Performance* (Englewood Cliffs, NJ: Prentice Hall, 1990).

92. H. Klein, S. Snell, and K. Wexley, "A Systems Model of the Performance Appraisal Interview Process," *Industrial Relations* 26 (1987), pp. 267–280.

93. M. London and E. M. Mone, "Managing Marginal Performance in Organizations Striving for Excellence," in *Human Resource Dilemmas in Work Organizations: Strategies for Resolution,* ed. A. K. Korman (New York: Guilford, 1993), pp. 95–124.

94. C. Balthazard, "Legal Fever Catching," Pulse Survey, *Canadian HR Reporter* (November 1, 2010), p. 11.

95. S. Dobson, "Human Rights Costs Growing Concern," *Canadian HR Reporter* (July 12, 2010), p. 1.

96. Website for B.C. Human Rights Tribunal at www.bchrt.bc.ca/index.htm (retrieved July 11, 2011).

97. S. Dobson, "Human Rights Costs Growing Concern," *Canadian HR Reporter* (July 12, 2010), p. 1.

98. K. Maher, "Big Employer Is Watching," *The Wall Street Journal* (November 4, 2003), pp. B1, B6.

99. "A. Miedema and A. Pushalik, "How, and When, Employers Should Monitor Employees," *Canadian HR Reporter* (November 2, 2009), p. 17.

100. Ibid, pp. 17, 18.

101. A. Miedema and A. Pushalik, "How, and When, Employers Should Monitor Employees," Tips for Employers, *Canadian HR Reporter* (November 2, 2009), p. 17.

102. J. Payne, "Termination for Cause Update, A Briefing for Human Resources Professionals," Presentation notes (March 22, 2001), p. 1 at www.nelligan.ca/e/PDF/termination forcause.pdf (retrieved January 30, 2011).

103. Ibid.

104. J. Payne, "Termination for Cause Update, A Briefing for Human Resources Professionals," Presentation notes (March 22, 2001) p. 2, at www.nelligan.ca/e/PDF/termination forcause.pdf (retrieved January 30, 2011).

105. L. Goodfellow, "Constructive Dismissal: A Primer," *Canadian Employment Law Today* (June 30, 2010); 560, p. 4.

106. Ibid.

107. Ibid., p. 5.

108. A. G. Tekleab, R. Takeuchi, and M. S. Taylor, "Extending the Chain of Relationships among Organizational Justice, Social Exchange, and Employee Reactions: The Role of Contract Violations," *Academy of Management Journal* 48 (2005), pp. 146–157.

109. D. P. Skarlicki and R. Folger, "Retaliation in the Workplace: The Roles of Distributive, Procedural, and Interactional Justice," *Journal of Applied Psychology* 82 (1997), pp. 434–443.

110. C. M. Holmvall, and D. R. Bobocel, "What Fair Procedures Say About Me: Self-Construals and Reactions to Procedural Fairness," *Organizational Behavior and Human Decision Processes* 105 (2008), pp. 147–168.

111. H. Y. Li, J. B. Bingham, and E. E. Umphress, "Fairness from the Top: Perceived Procedural Justice and Collaborative Problem Solving in New Product Development," *Organization Science* 18 (2007), pp. 200–216.

112. P. Dvorak, "Firing Workers Who Are a Bad Fit," *The Wall Street Journal* (May 1, 2006), p. B5.

113. T. A. Judge, B. A. Scott, and R. Ilies, "Hostility, Job Attitudes and Workplace Deviance: A Test of a Multilevel Model," *Journal of Applied Psychology* 91 (2006), pp. 126–138.

114. B. J. Tepper, "Relationship among Supervisors' and Subordinates' Procedural Justice Perceptions and Organizational Citizenship Behaviors," *Academy of Management Journal* 46 (2003), pp. 97–105.

115. T. Simons and Q. Roberson, "Why Managers Should Care About Fairness: The Affects of Aggregate Justice Perceptions on Organizational Outcomes," *Journal of Applied Psychology* 88 (2003), pp. 432–443.

116. K. K. Spors, "If You Fire People, Don't Be a Jerk About It," *The Wall Street Journal* (December 22, 2008), pp. C1–C2.

117. C. S. Spel and T. C. Blum, "Adoption of Workplace Substance Abuse Prevention Programs: Strategic Choice and Institutional Perspectives," *Academy of Management Journal* 48 (2005), pp. 1125–1142.

118. S. E. Needleman, "More Employers Help the Laid Off Find Jobs," *The Wall Street Journal* (April 1, 2009), p. C1.

Chapter 8

1. J. S. Adams, "Inequity in Social Exchange," in *Advances in Experimental Social Psychology,* ed. L. Berkowitz (New York: Academic Press, 1965); P. S. Goodman, "An Examination of Referents Used in the Evaluation of Pay," *Organizational Behaviour and Human Performance* 12 (1974), pp. 170–195; C. O. Trevor and D. L. Wazeter, "A Contingent View of

Reactions to Objective Pay Conditions: Interdependence among Pay Structure Characteristics and Pay Relative to Internal and External Referents," *Journal of Applied Psychology* 91 (2006), pp. 1260–1275; M. M. Harris, F. Anseel, and F. Lievens, "Keeping Up with the Joneses: A Field Study of the Relationships among Upward, Lateral, and Downward Comparisons and Pay Level Satisfaction," *Journal of Applied Psychology* 93, no. 3 (May 2008), pp. 665–673; Gordon D. A. Brown, Jonathan Gardner, Andrew J. Oswald, Jing Qian, "Does Wage Rank Affect Employees' Well-being?" *Industrial Relations* 47, no. 3 (July 2008), p. 355.

2. J. B. Miner, *Theories of Organizational Behaviour* (Hinsdale, IL: Dryden Press, 1980); B. Gerhart and S. L. Rynes, *Compensation: Theory, Evidence, and Strategic Implications* (Thousand Oaks, CA: Sage, 2003).

3. The Harbour Report™ North America 2008, www.oliver wyman.com.

4. T. Van Alphen, "Ford Canada under Pressure to Cut Labour Costs," *Toronto Star* (October 14, 2009) at theStar.com (retrieved February 5, 2011).

5. "CAW Members at Ford Approve New Agreement," (November 1, 2009) at www.caw.ca/en/8019.htm (retrieved February 5, 2011).

6. B. Gerhart and G. T. Milkovich, "Organizational Differences in Managerial Compensation and Financial Performance," *Academy of Management Journal* 33 (1990), pp. 663–691; E. L. Groshen, "Why Do Wages Vary among Employers?" *Economic Review* 24 (1988), pp. 19–38; Gerhart and Rynes, *Compensation.*

7. M. L. Williams, M. A. McDaniel, N. T. Nguyen, "A Meta-Analysis of the Antecedents and Consequences of Pay Level Satisfaction," *Journal of Applied Psychology* 91 (2006), pp. 392–413; M. C. Sturman, C. O. Trevor, J. W. Boudreau, and B. Gerhart, "Is It Worth It to Win the Talent War? Evaluating the Utility of Performance-Based Pay," *Personnel Psychology* 56 (2003), pp. 997–1035; B. Klaas and J. A. McClendon, "To Lead, Lag or Match: Estimating the Financial Impact of Pay Level Policies," *Personnel Psychology* 49 (1996), pp. 121–141. S. C. Currall, A. J. Towler T. A. Judge, and L. Kohn, "Pay Satisfaction and Organizational Outcomes," *Personnel Psychology* 58 (2005), pp. 613–640; M. P. Brown, M. C. Sturman, and M. J. Simmering, "Compensation Policy and Organizational Performance: The Efficiency, Operational, and Financial Implications of Pay Levels and Pay Structures," *Academy of Management Journal* 46 (2003), pp. 752–762; Eric A. Verhoogen, Stephen V. Burks, and Jeffrey P. Carpenter, "Fairness and Freight-Handlers: Local Labour Market Conditions and Wage-Fairness Perceptions in a Trucking Firm," *Industrial & Labour Relations Review* 60, no. 4 (July 2007), p. 477.

8. G. A. Akerlof, "Gift Exchange and Efficiency-Wage Theory: Four Views," *American Economic Review* 74 (1984), pp. 79–83;

J. L. Yellen, "Efficiency Wage Models of Unemployment," *American Economic Review* 74 (1984), pp. 200–205.

9. S. L. Rynes and G. T. Milkovich, "Wage Surveys: Dispelling Some Myths about the "Market Wage," *Personnel Psychology* 39 (1986), pp. 71–90.

10. B. Gerhart and G. T. Milkovich, "Employee Compensation: Research and Practice," in *Handbook of Industrial and Organizational Psychology,* 2nd ed., ed. M. D. Dunnette and L. M. Hough (Palo Alto, CA: Consulting Psychologists Press, 1992).

11. G. T. Milkovich, J. M. Newman, and B. Gerhart, *Compensation,* 10th ed. (New York: McGraw-Hill/Irwin, 2010).

12. D. Tyson, *Canadian Compensation Handbook* (Aurora, ON: Aurora Professional Press, 2002), pp. 40–41.

13. Ibid.

14. D. Tyson, *Canadian Compensation* (Aurora, ON: Aurora Professional Press, 2002) pp. 48–49, 52; and G. T. Milkovich, J. Newman, and N. Cole, *Compensation*, 3rd Canadian ed. (Whitby, ON: McGraw-Hill Ryerson, 2010), pp. 83–85.

15. D. Tyson, *Canadian Compensation Handbook*, (Aurora, ON: Aurora Professional Press, 2002), pp. 45–48.

16. G. T. Milkovich, J. Newman, and N. Cole, *Compensation*, 3rd Canadian ed. (Whitby, ON: McGraw-Hill Ryerson, 2010) pp. 86–95.

17. B. Gerhart, G. T. Milkovich, and B. Murray, "Pay, Performance, and Participation," in *Research Frontiers in Industrial Relations and Human Resources,* ed. D. Lewin, O. S. Mitchell, and P. D. Sherer (Madison, WI: IRRA, 1992).

18. C. H. Fay, "External Pay Relationships," in *Compensation and Benefits,* ed. L. R. Gomez-Mejia (Washington, DC: Bureau of National Affairs, 1989).

19. J. P. Pfeffer and A. Davis-Blake, "Understanding Organizational Wage Structures: A Resource Dependence Approach," *Academy of Management Journal* 30 (1987), pp. 437–455; M. A. Carpenter and J. B. Wade, "Micro-Level Opportunity Structures as Determinants of Non-CEO Executive Pay," *Academy of Management Journal* 45 (2002), pp. 1085–1103.

20. C. M. Solomon, "Global Compensation: Learn the ABCs," *Personnel Journal,* July 1995, p. 70; R. A. Swaak, "Expatriate Management: The Search for Best Practices," *Compensation and Benefits Review* (March–April 1995), pp. 21.

21. *1997–1998 Survey of Geographic Pay Differential Policies and Practices* (Rochester, WI: Runzeimer International).

22. "International Cost of Living Ranking," www.Xpatulator.com (retrieved February 23, 2011).

23. E. E. Lawler III, *Pay and Organizational Development* (Reading, MA: Addison-Wesley, 1981).

24. R. Folger and M. A. Konovsky, "Effects of Procedural and Distributive Justice on Reactions to Pay Raise Decisions,"

Academy of Management Journal 32 (1989), pp. 115–130; H. G. Heneman III and T. A. Judge, "Compensation Attitudes," in S. L. Rynes and B. Gerhart, eds., *Compensation in Organizations* (San Francisco: Jossey-Bass, 2002), pp. 61–103; J. Greenberg, "Determinants of Perceived Fairness of Performance Evaluations," *Journal of Applied Psychology* 71 (1986), pp. 340–342; H. G. Heneman III, "Pay Satisfaction," *Research in Personnel and Human Resource Management* 3 (1985), pp. 115–139.

25. J. Greenberg, "Employee Theft as a Reaction to Underpayment of Inequity: The Hidden Cost of Pay Cuts," *Journal of Applied Psychology* 75 (1990), pp. 561–568.

26. Adams, "Inequity in Social Exchange"; C. J. Berger, C. A. Olson, and J. W. Boudreau, "The Effect of Unionism on Job Satisfaction: The Role of Work-Related Values and Perceived Rewards," *Organizational Behaviour and Human Performance* 32 (1983), pp. 284–324; P. Cappelli and P. D. Sherer, "Assessing Worker Attitudes under a Two-Tier Wage Plan," *Industrial and Labour Relations Review* 43 (1990), pp. 225–244; R. W. Rice, S. M. Phillips, and D. B. McFarlin, "Multiple Discrepancies and Pay Satisfaction," *Journal of Applied Psychology* 75 (1990), pp. 386–393.

27. Cappelli and Sherer, "Assessing Worker Attitudes."

28. R. M. Kanter, *When Giants Learn to Dance* (New York: Simon & Schuster, 1989); E. E. Lawler III, *Strategic Pay* (San Francisco: Jossey-Bass, 1990); "Farewell, Fast Track," *BusinessWeek* (December 10, 1990), pp. 192–200; R. L. Heneman, G. E. Ledford, Jr., and M. T. Gresham, "The Changing Nature of Work and Its Effects on Compensation Design and Delivery," in S. L. Rynes and B. Gerhart, eds., *Compensation in Organizations.*

29. Lawler, *Strategic Pay;* G. Ledford, "3 Cases on Skill-Based Pay: An Overview," *Compensation and Benefits Review,* March–April 1991, pp. 11–23; G. E. Ledford, "Paying for the Skills, Knowledge, Competencies of Knowledge Workers," *Compensation and Benefits Review,* July–August 1995, p. 55; Heneman et al., "The Changing Nature of Work." G. Ledford, "Factors Affecting the Long-term Success of Skill-based Pay," *WorldatWork Journal,* First Quarter (2008), pp. 6–18. J. Canavan, "Overcoming the Challenge of Aligning Skill-based Pay Levels to the External Market," *WorldatWork Journal,* First Quarter (2008), pp. 18–24. E. C. Dierdorff and E. A. Surface, "If You Pay for Skills, Will They Learn? Skill Change and Maintenance Under a Skill-Based Pay System," *Journal of Management* 34 (2008), pp. 721–743.

30. Ledford, "3 Cases."

31. Heneman et al., "The Changing Nature of Work."

32. T. D. Wall, J. M. Corbett, R. Martin, C. W. Clegg, and P. R. Jackson, "Advanced Manufacturing Technology, Work Design, and Performance: A Change Study," *Journal of Applied Psychology* 75 (1990), pp. 691–697.

33. J.P. Womack, Daniel T. Jones, and Daniel Roos, *The Machine That Changed the World, The Story of Lean Production,* (New York: Harper Perennial, 1990), p. 56.

34. Lawler, Strategic Pay.

35. Ibid.; Gerhart and Milkovich, "Employee Compensation."

36. B. C. Murray and B. Gerhart, "An Empirical Analysis of a Skill-Based Pay Program and Plant Performance Outcomes," *Academy of Management Journal* 41, no. 1 (1998), pp. 68–78.

37. Ibid.; N. Gupta, D. Jenkins, and W. Curington, "Paying for Knowledge: Myths and Realities," *National Productivity Review* (Spring 1986), pp. 107–123; J. D. Shaw, N. Gupta, A. Mitra, and G. E. Ledford, "Success and Survival of Skill-Based Pay Plans," *Journal of Management* 31 (2005), pp. 28–49.

38. Data from U.S. Bureau of Labour Statistics web site, www.bls.gov.

39. "Production Plants and Joint Ventures in America," www.Brose.com at www.brose.com/ww/en/pub/company/international_locations/locations_of_production/america/london.htm (retrieved Feb. 23, 2011).

40. Education at a Glance 2010: OECD Indicators © OECD 2010 at www.oecd.org/edu/eag2010 (retrieved February 4, 2011).

41. C. Sparks and M. Greiner, "U.S. and Foreign Productivity and Labour Costs," *Monthly Labour Review* (February 1997), pp. 26–35.

42. E. Faltermayer, "U.S. Companies Come Back Home," *Fortune* (December 30, 1991), pp. 106ff; M. Hayes, "Precious Connection: Companies Thinking about Using Offshore Outsourcing Need to Consider More than Just Cost Savings," *Information Week Online* at www.informationweek.com (retrieved October 20, 2003).

43. G. Robertson, "TD Chief's Compensation Rises 8 Per Cent After Bank Books Record Profit in 2010," *The Globe and Mail Report on Business* (February 24, 2011); and Doug Alexander and Sean B. Pasternak, "Royal Bank and Toronto Dominion Profits Top Estimates" (March 3, 2011) at www.bloomberg.com/news/2011-03-03/royal-bank-toronto-dominion-profits-top-estimates-on-higher-lending-fees.html.

44. A. Farnham, "The Trust Gap," *Fortune* (December 4, 1989), pp. 56ff; Scott McCartney, "AMR Unions Express Fury," *The Wall Street Journal* (April 17, 2003).

45. D. M. Cowherd and D. I. Levine, "Product Quality and Pay Equity between Lower-Level Employees and Top Management: An Investigation of Distributive Justice Theory," *Administrative Science Quarterly* 37 (1992), pp. 302–320.

46. "Employment Standards" and "Your Guide to the Employment Standards Act 2000," Ontario Ministry of Labour at www.labour.gov.on.ca/english/es/pubs/guide/index.php and Employment Standards, Human Resources and Skills Development Canada at www.hrsdc.gc.ca/eng/labour/employment_standards/index.shtml.

47. "Pay Equity" Fact Sheet, The National Association of Women and the Law at www.nawl.ca/en/allissues/les-femmes-le-travail-et-legalite/payequity.

48. Pay Equity Commission, "What Is Pay Equity?" at www.payequity.gov.on.ca/peo/english/faqs.html#equity (retrieved February 5, 2010).

49. Pay Equity Commission, "Who Does the Pay Equity Act Apply To?" at www.payequity.gov.on.ca/peo/english/faqs.html#equity (retrieved February 5, 2010).

50. B. Gerhart and N. El Cheikh, "Earnings and Percentage Female: A Longitudinal Study," *Industrial Relations* 30 (1991), pp. 62–78; R. S. Smith, "Comparable Worth: Limited Coverage and the Exacerbation of Inequality," *Industrial and Labour Relations Review* 61 (1988), pp. 227–239.

51. W. T. Bielby and J. N. Baron, "Men and Women at Work: Sex Segregation and Statistical Discrimination," *American Journal of Sociology* 91 (1986), pp. 759–799.

52. Gerhart, "Gender Differences in Current and Starting Salaries"; B. Gerhart and G. T. Milkovich, "Salaries, Salary Growth, and Promotions of Men and Women in a Large, Private Firm," in *Pay Equity: Empirical Inquiries,* ed. R. Michael, H. Hartmann, and B. O'Farrell (Washington, DC: National Academy Press, 1989); K. W. Chauvin and R. A. Ash, "Gender Earnings Differentials in Total Pay, Base Pay, and Contingent Pay," *Industrial and Labour Relations Review* 47 (1994), pp. 634–49; M. M. Elvira and M. E. Graham, "Not Just a Formality: Pay System Formalization and Sex-Related Earnings Effects," *Organization Science* 13 (2002), pp. 601–617.

53. Gerhart, "Gender Differences in Current and Starting Salaries"; B. Gerhart and S. Rynes, "Determinants and Consequences of Salary Negotiations by Graduating Male and Female MBAs," *Journal of Applied Psychology* 76 (1991), pp. 256–262.

54. G. F. Dreher and R. A. Ash, "A Comparative Study of Mentoring among Men and Women in Managerial, Professional, and Technical Positions," *Journal of Applied Psychology* 75 (1990), pp. 539–546.

55. "Canada Pension Plan and Old Age Security," Human Resources and Skills Development at www.hrsdc.gc.ca/eng/oas-cpp/index.shtml (retrieved February 5, 2011).

56. "Employment Insurance," Service Canada at www.servicecanada.gc.ca/eng/sc/ei/index.shtml (retrieved February 5, 2011).

57. Workers Compensation, Human Resources and Skills Development Canada at www.hrsdc.gc.ca/eng/labour/workers_compensation/index.shtml (retrieved February 5, 2011).

Chapter 9

1. We draw freely in this chapter on several literature reviews: B. Gerhart and G. T. Milkovich, "Employee Compensation: Research and Practice," in *Handbook of Industrial and Organizational Psychology,* vol. 3, 2nd ed., ed. M. D. Dunnette and L. M. Hough (Palo Alto, CA: Consulting Psychologists Press, 1992); B. Gerhart and S. L. Rynes, *Compensation: Theory, Evidence, and Strategic Implications* (Thousand Oaks, CA: Sage, 2003); B. Gerhart, "Compensation Strategy and Organization Performance," in S. L. Rynes and B. Gerhart, eds., *Compensation in Organizations: Current Research and Practice* (San Francisco: Jossey-Bass, 2000), pp. 151–194; B. Gerhart, S. L. Rynes, and I. S. Fulmer, "Compensation," *Academy of Management Annals* 3 (2009).

2. B. Gerhart and G. T. Milkovich, "Organizational Differences in Managerial Compensation and Financial Performance," *Academy of Management Journal* 33 (1990), pp. 663–691.

3. E. Deci and R. Ryan, *Intrinsic Motivation and Self-Determination in Human Behaviour* (New York: Plenum, 1985); A. Kohn, "Why Incentive Plans Cannot Work," *Harvard Business Review* (September–October 1993).

4. R. Eisenberger and J. Cameron, "Detrimental Effects of Reward: Reality or Myth?" *American Psychologist* 51, no. 11 (1996), pp. 1153–1166; S. L. Rynes, B. Gerhart, and L. Parks, "Personnel Psychology: Performance Evaluation and Compensation," *Annual Review of Psychology* (2005).

5. D. R. Dalton, M. A. Hitt, S. T. Certo, and C. M. Dalton, "The Fundamental Agency Problem and Its Mitigation: Independence, Equity, and the Market for Corporate Control," *Academy of Management Annals* (2007), pp. 1–64; R. A. Lambert and D. F. Larcker, "Executive Compensation, Corporate Decision Making, and Shareholder Wealth," in *Executive Compensation,* ed. F. Foulkes (Boston: Harvard Business School Press, 1989), pp. 287–309.

6. L. R. Gomez-Mejia, H. Tosi, and T. Hinkin, "Managerial Control, Performance, and Executive Compensation," *Academy of Management Journal* 30 (1987), pp. 51–70; H. L. Tosi Jr. and L. R. Gomez-Mejia, "The Decoupling of CEO Pay and Performance: An Agency Theory Perspective," *Administrative Science Quarterly* 34 (1989), pp. 169–189.

7. K. M. Eisenhardt, "Agency Theory: An Assessment and Review," *Academy of Management Review* 14 (1989), pp. 57–74.

8. R. E. Hoskisson, M. A. Hitt, and C. W. L. Hill, "Managerial Incentives and Investment in R&D in Large Multiproduct Firms," *Organizational Science* 4 (1993), pp. 325–341; M. Bloom and G. T. Milkovich, "Relationships among Risk, Incentive Pay, and Organizational Performance," *Academy of Management Journal* 41 (1998), pp. 283–297.

9. Eisenhardt, "Agency Theory."

10. Ibid.; E. J. Conlon and J. M. Parks, "Effects of Monitoring and Tradition on Compensation Arrangements: An Experiment with Principal–Agent Dyads," *Academy of Management Journal* 33 (1990), pp. 603–622; K. M. Eisenhardt, "Agency- and Institutional-Theory Explanations: The Case of Retail

Sales Compensation," *Academy of Management Journal* 31 (1988), pp. 488–511; Gerhart and Milkovich, "Employee Compensation."

11. G. T. Milkovich, J. Hannon, and B. Gerhart, "The Effects of Research and Development Intensity on Managerial Compensation in Large Organizations," *Journal of High Technology Management Research* 2 (1991), pp. 133–150.

12. G. T. Milkovich and A. K. Wigdor, *Pay for Performance* (Washington, DC: National Academy Press, 1991); Gerhart and Milkovich, "Employee Compensation"; Gerhart and Rynes, *Compensation: Theory, Evidence, and Strategic Implications.*

13. C. Trevor, B. Gerhart, and J. W. Boudreau, "Voluntary Turnover and Job Performance: Curvilinearity and the Moderating Influences of Salary Growth and Promotions," *Journal of Applied Psychology* 82 (1997), pp. 44–61; C. B. Cadsby, F. Song, and F. Tapon, "Sorting and Incentive Effects of Pay-for-Performance: An Experimental Investigation," *Academy of Management Journal* 50 (2007), pp. 387–405; A. Salamin and P. W. Hom, "In Search of the Elusive U-Shaped Performance-Turnover Relationship: Are High Performing Swiss Bankers More Liable to Quit?" *Journal of Applied Psychology* 90 (2005), pp. 1204–1216; J. D. Shaw, and N. Gupta, "Pay System Characteristics and Quit Patterns of Good, Average, and Poor Performers," *Personnel Psychology* 60 (2007), pp. 903–928.

14. R. D. Bretz, R. A. Ash, and G. F. Dreher, "Do People Make the Place? An Examination of the Attraction–Selection–Attrition Hypothesis," *Personnel Psychology* 42 (1989), pp. 561–581; T. A. Judge and R. D. Bretz, "Effect of Values on Job Choice Decisions," *Journal of Applied Psychology* 77 (1992), pp. 261–271; D. M. Cable and T. A. Judge, "Pay Performances and Job Search Decisions: A Person–Organization Fit Perspective," *Personnel Psychology* 47 (1994), pp. 317–348.

15. E. E. Lawler III, *Strategic Pay* (San Francisco: Jossey-Bass, 1990); Gerhart and Milkovich, "Employee Compensation"; Gerhart and Rynes, *Compensation: Theory, Evidence, and Strategic Implications;* B. Gerhart, C. Trevor, and M. Graham, "New Directions in Employee Compensation Research" in G. R. Ferris (ed.), *Research in Personnel and Human Resources Management* (London: JAI Press, 1996), pp. 143–203; M. Beer and M. D. Cannon, "Promise and Peril in Implementing Pay-for-Performance," *Human Resource Management* 43 (2004), pp. 3–20.

16. R. D. Bretz, G. T. Milkovich, and W. Read, "The Current State of Performance Appraisal Research and Practice," *Journal of Management* 18 (1992), pp. 321–352; R. L. Heneman, "Merit Pay Research," *Research in Personnel and Human Resource Management* 8 (1990), pp. 203–263; Milkovich and Wigdor, *Pay for Performance;* Rynes, Gerhart, and Parks, "Personnel Psychology: Performance Evaluation and Compensation."

17. Compensation Planning Outlook 2011, Conference Board of Canada, p. 7.

18. Bretz et al., "Current State of Performance Appraisal."

19. Ibid.

20. Ibid.

21. W. E. Deming, *Out of the Crisis* (Cambridge, MA: Center for Advanced Engineering Study, Massachusetts Institute of Technology, 1986), p. 110.

22. Ibid.

23. Ibid.

24. Trevor et al., "Voluntary Turnover."

25. Rynes and Gerhart, *Compensation: Theory, Evidence, and Strategic Implications.*

26. Rynes, Gerhart, and Parks, "Personnel Psychology: Performance Evaluation and Compensation."

27. R. Folger and M. A. Konovsky, "Effects of Procedural and Distributive Justice on Reactions to Pay Raise Decisions," *Academy of Management Journal* 32 (1989), pp. 115–130; J. Greenberg, "Determinants of Perceived Fairness of Performance Evaluations," *Journal of Applied Psychology* 71 (1986), pp. 340–342.

28. Rynes, Gerhart, and Parks, "Personnel Psychology: Performance Evaluation and Compensation."

29. B. Gerhart and S. Rynes, "Determinants and Consequences of Salary Negotiations by Graduating Male and Female MBAs," *Journal of Applied Psychology* (1991), pp. 256–262; Gerhart and Rynes, *Compensation: Theory, Evidence, and Strategic Implications.*

30. E. A. Locke, D. B. Feren, V. M. McCaleb, K. N. Shaw, and A. T. Denny, "The Relative Effectiveness of Four Methods of Motivating Employee Performance," in *Changes in Working Life,* ed. K. D. Duncan, M. M. Gruenberg, and D. Wallis (New York: Wiley, 1980), pp. 363–388; for a summary of additional evidence, see also Gerhart and Rynes, *Compensation: Theory, Evidence, and Strategic Implications.*

31. Gerhart and Milkovich, "Employee Compensation."

32. Top 100 Employers in Canada website, Company profiles (retrieved March 9, 2011).

33. This idea has been referred to as the "share economy." See M. L. Weitzman, "The Simple Macroeconomics of Profit Sharing," *American Economic Review* 75 (1985), pp. 937–953. For supportive empirical evidence, see the following studies: J. Chelius and R. S. Smith, "Profit Sharing and Employment Stability," *Industrial and Labour Relations Review* 43 (1990), pp. 256S–273S; B. Gerhart and L. O. Trevor, "Employment Stability under Different Managerial Compensation Systems," Working Paper 1995 (Cornell University: Center for Advanced Human Resource Studies); D. L. Kruse, "Profit Sharing and Employment Variability: Microeconomic Evidence on the Weitzman Theory," *Industrial and Labour Relations Review* 44 (1991), pp. 437–453.

34. Gerhart and Milkovich, "Employee Compensation"; M. L. Weitzman and D. L. Kruse, "Profit Sharing and Productivity," in *Paying for Productivity*, ed. A. S. Blinder (Washington, DC: Brookings Institution, 1990); D. L. Kruse, *Profit Sharing: Does It Make a Difference?* (Kalamazoo, MI: Upjohn Institute, 1993); M. Magnan and S. St-Onge, "The Impact of Profit Sharing on the Performance of Financial Services Firms," *Journal of Management Studies* 42 (2005), pp. 761–791.

35. T. Van Alphen, "GM Employees in Canada Should Get Bonuses Too: CAW," *The Toronto Star*, www.thestar.com (February 14, 2011) at www.thestar.com/business/article/938870--gm-employees-in-canada-should-get-bonuses-too-caw (retrieved July 15, 2011).

36. Compensation Planning Outlook 2011, Conference Board of Canada, p. 7.

37. Gerhart and Rynes, *Compensation: Theory, Evidence, and Strategic Implications.*

38. "New Data Show Widespread Employee Ownership in U.S.," National Center for Employee Ownership at www.nceo.org/library/widespread.html.

39. "Executive Compensation: Taking Stock," *Personnel* 67 (December 1990), pp. 7–8; "Another Day, Another Dollar Needs Another Look," *Personnel* 68 (January 1991), pp. 9–13; J. Blasi, D. Kruse, and A. Bernstein, *In the Company of Owners* (New York: Basic Books, 2003).

40. I. Huss and M. Maclure, "Broad-based Stock Options Plans Take Hold, *Canadian HR Reporter* (July 17, 2000) pp. 13, 18.

41. Gerhart and Milkovich, "Organizational Differences in Managerial Compensation."

42. Compensation Planning Outlook 2011, Conference Board of Canada, p. 11.

43. *CICA Handbook*, Part II, Section 3870 and IFRS 2.4, 2.10, and 2.11.

44. Corey Rosen, *EBRI Databook on Employee Benefits* (Washington, DC: Employee Benefit Research Institute, 1995) at www.nceo.org, updated February 14, 2008.

45. D. Jones and T. Kato, "The Productivity Effects of Employee Stock Ownership Plans and Bonuses: Evidence from Japanese Panel Data," *American Economic Review* (June 1995), pp. 391–414.

46. Thomas P. Edmonds, Cindy D. Edmonds, Frances M. McNair, and Philip R. Olds, *Fundamental Accounting Concepts*, 5th ed. McGraw-Hill Higher Education 2006, Online Learning Centre, Student ed., Glossary at http://highered.mcgraw-hill.com/sites/0072989432/student_view0/glossary.html.

47. *CICA Handbook*, Part II, Section 3870 and IFRS 2.4, 2.10, and 2.11.

48. C. Jensen, Research and Legislation on ESOPs Could Have Positive Effects for Canada," at www.axiomnews.ca/NewsArchives/2009/January/January19.html.

49. Ibid.

50. C. Beatty and H. Schachter, *Employee Ownership—The New Source of Competitive Advantage*, John Wiley and Sons, 2002, p. 244.

51. Canada's Top 100 Employers 2011 website at www.canadastop100.com/national/ (retrieved March 6, 2011).

52. Ibid.; T. H. Hammer, "New Developments in Profit Sharing, Gainsharing, and Employee Ownership," in *Productivity in Organizations,* ed. J. P. Campbell, R. J. Campbell and Associates (San Francisco: Jossey-Bass, 1988); K. J. Klein, "Employee Stock Ownership and Employee Attitudes: A Test of Three Models," *Journal of Applied Psychology* 72 (1987), pp. 319–332.

53. J. L. Pierce, S. Rubenfeld, and S. Morgan, "Employee Ownership: A Conceptual Model of Process and Effects," *Academy of Management Review* 16 (1991), pp. 121–144.

54. J. G. Belcher, "Gainsharing and Variable Pay: The State of the Art," *Compensation and Benefits Review* (May/June 1994), pp. 50–60, in G. Milkovich, J. Newman and N. Cole, *Compensation*, 3rd Canadian ed., (Whitby, ON: McGraw Hill Ryerson, 2010), p. 251.

55. Compensation Planning Outlook 2011, Conference Board of Canada, p. 7

56. R. T. Kaufman, "The Effects of Improshare on Productivity," *Industrial and Labour Relations Review* 45 (1992), pp. 311–322; M. H. Schuster, "The Scanlon Plan: A Longitudinal Analysis," *Journal of Applied Behavioural Science* 20 (1984), pp. 23–28; M. M. Petty, B. Singleton, and D. W. Connell, "An Experimental Evaluation of an Organizational Incentive Plan in the Electric Utility Industry," *Journal of Applied Psychology* 77 (1992), pp. 427–436; W. N. Cooke, "Employee Participation Programs, Group-Based Incentives, and Company Performance: A Union–Nonunion Comparison," *Industrial and Labour Relations Review* 47 (1994), pp. 594–609; J. B. Arthur and L. Aiman-Smith, "Gainsharing and Organizational Learning: An Analysis of Employee Suggestions over Time," *Academy of Management Journal* 44 (2001), pp. 737–754; J. B. Arthur and G. S. Jelf, "The Effects of Gainsharing on Grievance Rates and Absenteeism over Time," *Journal of Labour Research* 20 (1999), pp. 133–145.

57. D. E. Tyson, *Canadian Compensation Handbook* (Aurora, ON: Aurora Professional Press, 2002), pp. 203–206.

58. T. L. Ross and R. A. Ross, "Gainsharing: Sharing Improved Performance," *The Compensation Handbook*, 3rd ed., ed. M. L. Rock and L. A. Berger (New York: McGraw-Hill, 1991).

59. T. M. Welbourne and L. R. Gomez-Mejia, "Team Incentives in the Workplace," *The Compensation Handbook,* 3rd ed; E. Siemsen, S. Balasubramanian, and A. V. Roth, "Incentives That Induce Task-Related Effort, Helping, and Knowledge Sharing in Workgroups," *Management Science* 10 (2007), pp. 1533–1150.

60. R. S. Kaplan and D. P. Norton "Using the Balanced Scorecard as a Strategic Management System," *Harvard Business Review* (January–February 1996), pp. 75–85.

61. M. C. Jensen and K. J. Murphy, "Performance Pay and Top-Management Incentives," *Journal of Political Economy* 98 (1990), pp. 225–264; A stronger relationship between CEO pay and performance was found by R. K. Aggarwal and A. A. Samwick, "The Other Side of the Trade-off: The Impact of Risk on Executive Compensation," *Journal of Political Economy* 107 (1999), pp. 65–105; A. J. Nyberg, I. S. Fulmer, B. Gerhart, and M. A. Carpenter, "The Future of Agency Theory in Executive Compensation Research: Separating Fact from Fiction." Unpublished working paper. Also, these observed relationships actually translate into significant changes in CEO pay in response to modest changes in financial performance of a company, as made clear by Gerhart and Rynes, *Compensation: Theory, Evidence, and Strategic Implications.*

62. M. C. Jensen and K. J. Murphy, "CEO Incentives—It's Not How Much You Pay, But How," *Harvard Business Review* 68 (May–June 1990), pp. 138–153. The definitive resource on executive pay is B. R. Ellig, *The Complete Guide to Executive Compensation,* 2nd ed. (New York: McGraw-Hill) 2007.

63. C. E. Devers, A. A. Cannella, G. P. Reilly, and M. E. Yoder, "Executive Compensation: A Multidisciplinary Review of Recent Developments," *Journal of Management* 33 (2007), pp. 1016–1072; W. G. Sanders and D. C. Hambrick, "Swinging for the Fences: The Effects of CEO Stock Options on Company Risk Taking and Performance, *Academy of Management Journal* 50 (2007), pp. 1055–1078.

64. Gerhart and Milkovich, "Organizational Differences in Managerial Compensation."

65. CIBC Management Proxy Circular, CIBC Notice of Annual Meeting of Shareholders (February 25, 2010), p. 32 at www.cibc.com/ca/pdf/about/proxy-circular-10.pdf.

66. CIBC Management Proxy Circular, CIBC Notice of Annual Meeting of Shareholders (February 25, 2010), p. 38, at www.cibc.com/ca/pdf/about/proxy-circular-10.pdf.

67. CIBC Management Proxy Circular, CIBC Notice of Annual Meeting of Shareholders (February 25, 2010), p. 34, at www.cibc.com/ca/pdf/about/proxy-circular-10.pdf.

68. L. Young, "Executive Compensation Reform," *HR Professional* (September 2010) pp. 22–25.

69. 2010 Building High Performance Boards, Canadian Coalition for Good Governance (March 2010) at www.ccgg.ca/site/ccgg/assets/pdf/CCGG_Building_High_Performance_Boards_Final_March_2010.pdf (retrieved March 2, 2011).

70. Executive Compensation Principles at www.ccgg.ca/site/ccgg/assets/pdf/2009_Executive_Compensation_Principles.pdf (retrieved March 5, 2011).

71. J. Cutcher-Gershenfeld, "The Impact on Economic Performance of a Transformation in Workplace Relations," *Industrial and Labour Relations Review* 44 (1991), pp.

241–260; Irene Goll, "Environment, Corporate Ideology, and Involvement Programs," *Industrial Relations* 30 (1991), pp. 138–149.

72. L. R. Gomez-Mejia and D. B. Balkin, *Compensation, Organizational Strategy, and Firm Performance* (Cincinnati: South-Western, 1992); G. D. Jenkins and E. E. Lawler III, "Impact of Employee Participation in Pay Plan Development," *Organizational Behaviour and Human Performance* 28 (1981), pp. 111–128.

73. D. I. Levine and L. D. Tyson, "Participation, Productivity, and the Firm's Environment," in *Paying for Productivity.*

74. T. Welbourne, D. Balkin, and L. Gomez-Mejia, "Gainsharing and Mutual Monitoring: A Combined Agency–Organizational Justice Interpretation," *Academy of Management Journal* 38 (1995), pp. 881–899.

75. Ibid.

76. A. Colella, R. L. Paetzold, A. Zardkoohi, and M. J. Wesson, "Exposing Pay Secrecy," *Academy of Management Review* 32 (2007), pp. 55–71; J. Schaubroeck et al., "An Under-Met and Over-Met Expectations Model of Employee Reactions to Merit Raises," *Journal of Applied Psychology* (March 2008), pp. 424–434.

77. Blinder, *Paying for Productivity.*

78. Hammer, "New Developments in Profit Sharing"; Milkovich and Wigdor, *Pay for Performance;* D. J. B. Mitchell, D. Lewin, and E. E. Lawler III, "Alternative Pay Systems, Firm Performance and Productivity," in *Paying for Productivity.*

79. Kaufman, "The Effects of Improshare on Productivity"; M. H. Schuster, "The Scanlon Plan: A Longitudinal Analysis," *Journal of Applied Behavioural Science* 20 (1984), pp. 23–28; J. A. Wagner III, P. Rubin, and T. J. Callahan, "Incentive Payment and Nonmanagerial Productivity: An Interrupted Time Series Analysis of Magnitude and Trend," *Organizational Behaviour and Human Decision Processes* 42 (1988), pp. 47–74.

80. C. R. Gowen III and S. A. Jennings, "The Effects of Changes in Participation and Group Size on Gainsharing Success: A Case Study," *Journal of Organizational Behaviour Management* 11 (1991), pp. 147–169.

81. L. Hatcher, T. L. Ross, and D. Collins, "Attributions for Participation and Nonparticipation in Gainsharing-Plan Involvement Systems," *Group and Organization Studies* 16 (1991), pp. 25–43; Mitchell et al., "Alternative Pay Systems."

82. B. R. Ellig, "Compensation Elements: Market Phase Determines the Mix," *Compensation and Benefits Review* 13 (3) (1981), pp. 30–38; L. R. Gomez-Mejia and D. B. Balkin, *Compensation, Organizational Strategy, and Firm Performance* (Cincinnati, Ohio: South-Western Publishing, 1992); M. K. Kroumova and J. C. Sesis, "Intellectual Capital, Monitoring, and Risk: What Predicts the Adoption of Employee Stock Options?" *Industrial Relations* 45 (2006), pp. 734–752; Y. Yanadori and J. H. Marler, "Compensation Strategy: Does Business Strategy Influence Compensation in High-Technology Firms?" *Strategic*

Management Journal 27 (2006), pp. 559–570; B. Gerhart, "Compensation Strategy and Organizational Performance" in S. L. Rynes and B. Gerhart (eds.), *Compensation in Organizations* (San Francisco: Jossey-Bass, 2000).

83. A. J. Baker, "Stock Options—A Perk That Built Silicon Valley," *The Wall Street Journal* (June 23, 1993), p. A20.

Chapter 10

1. U.S. Bureau of Labor Statistics, Economic News Release (June 8, 2011), Employer Costs for Employee Compensation—March 2011, Table 1. Civilian workers, by major occupational and industry group at www.bls.gov/news.release/ecec.t01.htm (retrieved July 25, 2011).

2. James H. Dulebohn, Janice C. Molloy, Shaun M. Pichler, Brian Murray, "Employee Benefits: Literature Review and Emerging Issues," *Human Resource Management Review* 19 (2009), pp. 86–103. Joseph J. Martocchio, *Employee Benefits,* 2nd ed. (New York: McGraw-Hill, 2006).

3. H. W. Hennessey, "Using Employee Benefits to Gain a Competitive Advantage," *Benefits Quarterly* 5, no. 1 (1989), pp. 51–57; B. Gerhart and G.T. Milkovich, "Employee Compensation: Research and Practice," in *Handbook of Industrial and Organizational Psychology,* vol. 3, 2nd ed., ed. M. D. Dunnette and L. M. Hough (Palo Alto, CA: Consulting Psychologists Press, 1992); J. Swist, "Benefits Communications: Measuring Impact and Value," *Employee Benefit Plan Review,* September 2002, pp. 24–26.

4. R. Ehrenberg and R. S. Smith, *Modern Labor Economics: Theory and Public Policy,* 7th ed. (Upper Saddle River, NJ: Addison Wesley Longman, 2000).

5. B. T. Beam Jr. and J. J. McFadden, *Employee Benefits,* 6th ed. (Chicago: Dearborn Financial Publishing, 2000)

6. The organization and description in this section draws heavily on Beam and McFadden, *Employee Benefits.*

7. Service Canada, "The Canada Pension Plan Retirement Pension," (March 2010) at www.servicecanada.ca.

8. S. Cooper, *The New Retirement* (Toronto: Viking Canada, 2008), p. 85.

9. "Employment Insurance Extension of Self-Employed Canadians Comes Into Effect: Represents One of the Most Significant Enhancements to the EI Program in a Decade," Government of Canada Press Release (February 1, 2010) at www.canada.gc.ca.

10. Service Canada website at www.servicecanada.ca.

11. K. Marshall, "Employer Top-ups," *Perspectives* (February 2010), p. 10.

12. J. V. Nackley, *Primer on Workers' Compensation* (Washington, DC: Bureau of National Affairs, 1989).

13. Beam and McFadden, *Employee Benefits,* p. 81.

14. A.H. Wheeler, "Pathophysiology of Chronic Back Pain" (2002) at www.emedicine.com.

15. J. R. Hollenbeck, D. R. Ilgen, and S. M. Crampton, "Lower Back Disability in Occupational Settings: A Review of the Literature from a Human Resource Management View," *Personnel Psychology* 45 (1992), pp. 247–278; J. J. Martocchio, D. A. Harrison, and H. Berkson, "Connections between Lower Back Pain, Interventions, and Absence from Work: A Time-Based Meta-Analysis," *Personnel Psychology* (2000), p. 595.

16. Employee Benefit Research Institute, Value of Benefits Constant in a Changing World: Findings from the 2001 EBRI/MGA Value of Benefits Survey (March 28, 2001) at www.ebri.org (retrieved July 26, 2011).

17. Table 1. Employer-sponsored Non-wage Benefits, Survey of Labour and Income Dynamics 2000 in K. Marshall, "Benefits of the Job," Perspectives on Labour and Income, The Online Edition (May 2003).

18. Beam and McFadden, *Employee Benefits,* 6th ed.

19. Beyond Benefits II: Disability Plans an Absence Management in Canadian Workplaces," Conference Board of Canada (June 2010), p. 15 and 20.

20. Ibid., p. 15.

21. Ibid., p. 15 and 16.

22. Ibid., p. 11.

23. P. Gougeon, "Shifting Pensions," *Perspectives* (May 2009), p. 16 and 17, Statistics Canada Catalogue no. 75-001-X M.

24. S. LaRochelle-Cote, Garnett Picto, and John Myles, "Income Replacement during the Retirement Years," *Perspectives* (August 2010), Statistics Canada Catalogue no. 75-001-X.

25. "Pension Guide for Members of Federally Regulated Pension Plans," Office of the Superintendent of Financial Institutions (OSFI) (June 2009) at www.osfi-bsif.gc.ca/app/DocRepository/1/eng/pension/guides/mem_guide_e.pdf (retrieved July 26, 2011).

26. S. LaRochelle-Cote, Garnett Picto, and John Myles, "Income Replacement during the Retirement Years," *Perspectives* (August 2010), Statistics Canada Catalogue no. 75-001-X.

27. N. Stewart and A. Cowan, "Compensation Planning Outlook 2011, Playing It Safe in the Face of an Unsteady Economic Recovery," Conference Board of Canada 2010, p. 12 and 13.

28. S. Dobson, "Pensioners Fight Back in Bankruptcy," *Canadian HR Reporter* (November 2, 2009), p. 3.

29. "Pension Promise," CBC documentary (nd).

30. "Rethinking Retirement: The Impact of Proposed Changes to Bankruptcy Priorities—a Risky Proposition, Issue 1, Towers Watson (December 2010) at www.towerswatson.com.

31. Ibid.

32. J. Fierman, "How Secure Is Your Nest Egg?" *Fortune* (August 12, 1991), pp. 50–54.

33. T. Pikorski, "Minimizing Employee Benefits Litigation through Effective Claims Administration Procedures," *Employee Relations Law Journal* 20, no. 3 (Winter 1994–1995) pp. 421–431.

34. B. J. Coleman, *Primer on Employee Retirement Income Security Act,* 3rd ed. (Washington, DC: Bureau of National Affairs, 1989).

35. *Continental Can Company v. Gavalik,* summary in *Daily Labor Report* (December 8, 1987): "Supreme Court Lets Stand Third Circuit Ruling That Pension Avoidance Scheme Is ERISA Violation," no. 234, p. A-14.

36. T. Williams, "Penson Plan Guidelines," *HR Professional* (February/March 2005), p. 16

37. A. L. Gustman, O. S. Mitchell, and T. L. Steinmeier, "The Role of Pensions in the Labor Market: A Survey of the Literature," *Industrial and Labor Relations* 47 (1994), pp. 417–438.

38. E. P. Lazear, "Why Is There Early Retirement?" *Journal of Political Economy* 87 (1979), pp. 1261–84; Gustman et al., "The Role of Pensions."

39. P. Cappelli, *The New Deal at Work: Managing the Market-Driven Workforce* (Boston: Harvard Business School Press, 1999).

40. S. Dorsey, "Pension Portability and Labor Market Efficiency," *Industrial and Labor Relations* 48, no. 5 (1995), pp. 276–292.

41. DeCenzo and Holoviak, *Employee Benefits,* 6th ed.

42. S. L. Grover and K. J. Crooker, "Who Appreciates Family Responsive Human Resource Policies: The Impact of Family-Friendly Policies on the Organizational Attachment of Parents and Non-parents," *Personnel Psychology* 48 (1995), pp. 271–288; T. J. Rothausen, J. A. Gonzalez, N. E. Clarke, and L. L. O'Dell, "Family-Friendly Backlash: Fact or Fiction? The Case of Organizations' On-Site Child Care Centers," *Personnel Psychology* 51 (1998), p. 685; M. A. Arthur, "Share Price Reactions to Work-Family Initiatives: An Institutional Perspective," *Academy of Management Journal* 46 (2003), p. 497; J. E. Perry-Smith and T. Blum, "Work-Family Human Resource Bundles and Perceived Organizational Performance," *Academy of Management Journal* 43 (2000), pp. 1107–1117.

43. Employment Insurance: Guide for Supplemental Unemployment Benefit Program (SUB), Government of Canada, Service Canada, at www.servicecanada.gc.ca/eng/cs/sub/documents/sub.pdf (retrieved July 26, 2011).

44. K. Marshall, "Employer top-ups," *Perspectives* (February 2010), Statistics Canada Catalogue no. 75-001X, pp. 5–8, 11.

45. Ibid., p. 10.

46. S. Miles, "Career Interrupted," *Canadian HR Reporter* (December 13, 2010), p. 22.

47. "The Families and Work Institute's 1998 Business Work–Life Study," at www.familiesandwork.org. Results based on a nationally representative survey of employers having 100 or more employees.

48. Canada's Top 100 Employers, TD Bank Financial Group, Top Employer Profile, Health and Family Friendly Benefits at www.eluta.ca/top-employer-td-bank (retrieved July 26, 2011).

49. E. E. Kossek, "Diversity in Child Care Assistance Needs: Employee Problems, Preferences, and Work-Related Outcomes," *Personnel Psychology* 43 (1990), pp. 769–791.

50. R. Broderick and B. Gerhart, "Nonwage Compensation," in *The Human Resource Management Handbook,* ed. D. Lewin, D. J. B. Mitchell, and M. A. Zadi (San Francisco: JAI Press, 1996).

51. Dulabohn et al., "Employee Benefits."

52. Hennessey, "Using Employee Benefits to Gain a Competitive Advantage."

53. A. C. Monheit and P. F. Cooper, "Health Insurance and Job Mobility: The Effects of Public Policy on Job-Lock," *Industrial and Labor Relations Review* 48 (1994), pp. 86–102.

54. Beam and McFadden, *Employee Benefits.*

55. R. Lieber, "New Way to Curb Medical Costs: Make Employees Feel the Sting," *The Wall Street Journal* (June 23, 2004), p. A1.

56. M. Barringer and O. S. Mitchell, "Workers' Preferences among Company-Provided Health Insurance Plans," *Industrial and Labor Relations Review* 48 (1994), pp. 141–152.

57. Anonymous, "Exploring the Future of Health Benefits," *Benefits Canada* (March 2009), p. S1.

58. N. Mrkvicka, "The Cost Also Rises," *Benefits Canada* (November 2010), p. 71.

59. Wellness Councils of America, "101 Ways to Wellness," www.welcoa.org, 2001; Wellness Councils of America, "A Guide to Developing Your Worksite Wellness Program," www.welcoa.org, 1997.

60. Company profiles, Top 100 Employers in Canada at www.canadadstop100.com/national.

61. D. A. Harrison and L. Z. Liska, "Promoting Regular Exercise in Organizational Fitness Programs: Health-Related Differences in Motivational Building Blocks," *Personnel Psychology* 47 (1994), pp. 47–71.

62. J. C. Erfurt, A. Foote, and M. A. Heirich, "The Cost-Effectiveness of Worksite Wellness Programs for Hypertension Control, Weight Loss, Smoking Cessation and Exercise," *Personnel Psychology* 45 (1992), pp. 5–27.

63. N. Mrkvicka, "The Cost Also Rises," *Benefits Canada* (November 2010), p. 71.

64. J. C. Erfurt, A. Foote, and M. A. Heirich, "The Cost-Effectiveness of Worksite Wellness Programs for Hypertension Control, Weight Loss, Smoking Cessation and Exercise."

65. 2009/2010 North American Staying@Work Report: The Health and Productivity Advantage, National Business Group on Health, Towers Watson (originally published by Watson Wyatt Worldwide), pp. 3, 7.

66. Figure 1, Global Average Medical Trends 2006–2011, *2011 Global Medical Trends Survey Report*, p. 3 Towers Watson at www.towerswatson.com.

67. H. Gardner, unpublished manuscript (Cheyenne, WY: Options & Choices, 1995).

68. Hewitt Associates. www.hewitt.com.

69. Beam and McFadden, *Employee Benefits.*

70. M. Wilson, G. B. Northcraft, and M. A. Neale, "The Perceived Value of Fringe Benefits," *Personnel Psychology* 38 (1985), pp. 309–320. Similar results were found in other studies reviewed by H. W. Hennessey, P. L. Perrewe, and W. A. Hochwarter, "Impact of Benefit Awareness on Employee and Organizational Outcomes: A Longitudinal Field Experiment," *Benefits Quarterly* 8, no. 2 (1992), pp. 90–96; MetLife, Employee Benefits Benchmarking Report at www.metlife.com (retrieved June 24, 2007).

71. M. C. Giallourakis and G. S. Taylor, "An Evaluation of Benefit Communication Strategy," *Employee Benefits Journal* 15, no. 4 (1991), pp. 14–18; Employee Benefits Research Institute, "How Readable Are Summary Plan Descriptions for Health Care Plans," *EBRI Notes* (October 2006) at ebri.org.

72. J. Abraham, R. Feldman, and C. Carlin, "Understanding Employee Awareness of Health Care Quality Information: How Can Employers Benefit?" *Health Services Research* 39 (2004), pp. 1799–1816.

73. Beam and McFadden, *Employee Benefits;* M. W. Barringer and G. T. Milkovich, "A Theoretical Explanation of the Adoption and Design of Flexible Benefit Plans: A Case of Human Resource Innovation," *Academy of Management Review* 23 (1998), pp. 305–324.

74. For supportive evidence, see A. E. Barber, R. B. Dunham, and R. A. Formisano, "The Impact of Flexible Benefits on Employee Satisfaction: A Field Study," *Personnel Psychology* 45 (1992), pp. 55–75; E. E. Lawler, *Pay and Organizational Development* (Reading, MA: Addison-Wesley, 1981).

75. Towers Watson, *Update on Benefits Trends, Postretirement Benefit Plan Design* (September 2010), p. 2, at www.towers watson.ca.

Chapter 11

1. J. T. Dunlop, *Industrial Relations Systems* (New York: Holt, 1958).

2. C. Kerr, "Industrial Conflict and Its Mediation," *American Journal of Sociology* 60 (1954), pp. 230–245.

3. Walton, R. and R. McKersie, *A Behavioral Theory of Labor Negotiations: An Analysis of a Social Interaction System* (New York: McGraw-Hill, 1965); Walton and McKersie, *Behavioral Theory of Labor Negotiations*, 2nd ed. (Ithaca, NY: ILR Press, 1991); R. Walton, J. Cutcher-Gershenfeld, and R. McKersie, *Strategic Negotiations: Theory of Change in Labor–Management Relations* (Cambridge, MA: Harvard Business School Press, 1994).

4. H. C. Katz and T. A. Kochan, *An Introduction to Collective Bargaining and Industrial Relations,* 3rd ed. (New York: McGraw-Hill, 2004).

5. S. Webb and B. Webb, *Industrial Democracy* (London: Longmans, Green, 1897); J. R. Commons, *Institutional Economics* (New York: Macmillan, 1934).

6. C. Kerr, J. T. Dunlop, F. Harbison, and C. Myers, "Industrialism and World Society," *Harvard Business Review,* February 1961, pp. 113–126.

7. Katz and Kochan, *An Introduction to Collective Bargaining.*

8. Anthony Bianco, "No Union Please, We're Wal-Mart," *BusinessWeek* (February 13, 2006) at www.businessweek.com/ magazine/content/06_07/b3971115.htm; (retrieved August 10, 2011). Carolyn King, "Union Claims Legal Victory vs Wal-Mart Canada in 2 Provinces," *The Wall Street Journal* (October 15, 2010).

9. Human Resources and Skills Development Canada, "Union Membership in Canada—2009 (Revised January 15, 2010)."

10. It is mandated by statute in Manitoba and Quebec; (MB) Labour Relations Act, s.76; (QB) Labour Code, s.47. It is mandatory at the request of the union in other jurisdictions: (CAN) Canada Labour Code, s.70; (ON) Labour Relations Act, 1995, s.47 (excluding the construction industry). See also (BC) Labour Relations Code, s.6 (3) (f), which provides that it is an unfair labour practice for an employer to refuse to include a union dues clause in the parties' first collective agreement. It may require the written consent of the employee: (AB) Labour Relations Code, s.27; (NB) Industrial Relations Act, s.9; (Nfld. & Lab.) Labour Relations Act, s.35; (NS) Trade Union Act, s.60; (PEI) Labour Act, s.45 (2)–(5); (SK) Trade Union Act, s.32. See also (BC) Labour Relations Code, s.16. It can also be negotiated by the parties into their collective agreement: (PEI) Labour Act, s.45 (1). Some statutes provide for exemptions from union security clauses and union dues check off where they come into conflict with a person's religious beliefs. Where a religious exemption is found, the amount equivalent to the union dues is submitted to a registered charity. The exemption may preclude the employee from entitlement to some or all of the protections and benefits in the collective agreement.

11. Statistics Canada, "Unionization 2010," *Perspectives*, Catalogue no. 75-001-X, October 2010.

12. United States Bureau of Labor Statistics, www.bls.gov.

13. Statistics Canada, "Unionization 2010," *Perspectives*, Catalogue no. 75-001-X, October 2010.

14. The Fraser Institute, "Fraser Alert: Explaining Canada's High Unionization Rates," (August 2005) (www.tvo.org/theagenda/ resources/pdf/Highunionrate4.pdf).

15. "The Social Determinants of Health in Manitoba," Manitoba Federation of Labour (July 27, 2010).

16. (CAN) Canada Labour Code, s.3 (1); (AB) Labour Relations Code, s.1 (l) (i); (BC) Labour Relations Code, s.1 (1); (MB) Labour Relations Act, s.1; (NB) Industrial Relations Act, s.1 (1); (Nfld. & Lab.) Labour Relations Act, s.2 (1) (m); (NS) Trade Union Act, s.2 (2) (a); (ON) Labour Relations Act,

1995, s.1 (3); (PEI) Labour Act, s.7 (2) (b); (QB) Labour Code, s.1 (l); (SK) Trade Union Act, s.2 (f) (i).

17. In respect of Ontario, see the Agricultural Employees Protection Act, S.O. 2002, c.16; *Dunmore v. Ontario* (Attorney General), 2002 CLLC 220-004 and *Fraser v. Attorney General of Ontario*, 301 D.L.R. (4th) 335 (Ont. C.A.), leave to appeal to Supreme Court of Canada granted 2009 CanLII 15013 (SCC).

18. Police are explicitly included in two provinces: (NS) Trade Union Act, s.2 (1) (k) (i); (PEI) Labour Act, s.7 (1) (h).

19. (CAN) Canada Labour Code, s.6; (AB) Labour Relations Code, s.4; (MB) Labour Relations Act, ss.3, 4 (3); (NB) Industrial Relations Act, s.1 (1) (8); (Nfld. & Lab.) Labour Relations Act, s.3; (ON) Labour Relations Act, 1995, ss.3, 4; (QB) Labour Code, ss.1 (l) (3)–(3.3) (4) (5) (6), 4; (PEI) Labour Act, ss.7 (1) (i) (2).

20. (CAN) Canada Labour Code, s. 3 (1). Professional employees are defined by the application of specialized knowledge typically gained through university or institutional studies and their membership or eligibility for membership in a professional organization that regulates the profession.

21. (AB) Labour Relations Code, s1 (l) (ii); (NS) Trade Union Act, s.2 (2) (b); (ON) Labour Relations Act, 1995, s. 1 (3) (a); (PEI) Labour Act, s.7 (2) (a).

22. (CAN) Canada Labour Code, s.94 (3); (AB) Labour Relations Code, s.149; (BC) Labour Relations Code, ss.5, 6 (3); (MB) Labour Relations Code, ss.7, 9, 17; (NB) Industrial Relations Act, ss.3 (2) (3) (4); (Nfld. & Lab.) Labour Relations Act, ss.23–26; (NS) Trade Union Act, ss.53 (3), 58; (ON) Labour Relations Act, 1995, ss.72, 76; (PEI) Labour Act, s.10 (1); (QB) Labour Code, ss.13, 14; (SK) Trade Union Act, s.11 (1).

23. (CAN) Canada Labour Code, s.94 (1); (AB) Labour Relations Code, ss.148; (BC) Labour Relations Code, ss.6 (1); (MB) Labour Relations Act, ss.6 (1); (NB) Industrial Relations Act, s.3 (1); (Nfld. & Lab.) Labour Relations Act, s.23 (1); (NS) Trade Union Act, s.53 (1); (ON) Labour Relations Act, 1995, s.70; (PEI) Labour Act, s.10 (1) (a); (QB) Labour Code, s.12; (SK) Trade Union Act, s.11 (1) (b).

24. (CAN) Canada Labour Code, s.94 (3) (a); (AB) Labour Relations Code, s.149 (a); (BC) Labour Relations Code, s.6 (3) (a); (MB) Labour Relations Act, s.7; (NB) Industrial Relations Act, s.3 (4); (Nfld. & Lab.) Labour Relations Act, ss.24 (1), 25 (2); (NS) Trade Union Act, s.53 (3) (a) (i); (ON) Labour Relations Act, 1995, s.72; (PEI) Labour Act, s.10 (1); (SK) Trade Union Act, s.11 (1).

25. (CAN) Canada Labour Code, s.94 (3) (b); (AB) Labour Relations Code, s.149 (b); (BC) Labour Relations Code, s.6 (3) (c); (NB) Industrial Relations Act, s.3 (2) (b); (Nfld. & Lab.) Labour Relations Act, ss.24 (1) (b); (NS) Trade Union Act, s.53 (3) (b); (ON) Labour Relations Act, 1995, s.72; (PEI) Labour Act, s.10 (1) (c). See also Hollinger Canadian Newspapers, LP and CEP (2001), 81 CLRBR (2d) 77 (SK).

26. (ON) Labour Relations Act, 1995, s.82 (PEI) Labour Act, s.10 (1) (f); (SK) Trade Union Act, s.11 (1).

27. With the exception of Quebec.

28. (CAN) Canada Labour Code, ss. 95 (h) (i), 96; (AB) Labour Relations Code, s.151 (f) (h); (BC) Labour Relations Code, s.9; (MB) Labour Relations Act, ss.8 (e), 19 (d); (NB) Industrial Relations Act, ss.5 (2) (3), 6 (2) (3) (4); (Nfld. & Lab.) Labour Relations Act, s.28 (1); (NS) Trade Union Act, ss.54, 58; (ON) Labour Relations Act, 1995, ss.76, 87 (2); (PEI) Labour Act, s.10 (2) (e); (QB) Labour Code, s.13; (SK) Trade Union Act, s.11 (2) (a).

29. (CAN) Canada Labour Code, s.95 (c); (AB) Labour Relations Code, s.151 (c); (BC) Labour Relations Code, s.4 (2); (MB) Labour Relations Act, as.5 (2) (3); (NB) Industrial Relations Act, ss.5 (1), 6 (1); (NS) Trade Union Act, s.54 (c); (ON) Labour Relations Act, 1995, s.71; (PEI) Labour Act, s.10 (2) (a); (QB) Labour Code, s.12.

30. See for example (CAN) Canada Labour Code, s.95; (AB) Labour Relations Code, ss.22, 151, 152; (MB) Labour Relations Act, ss.8, 19, 23, 24; (NS) Trade Union Act, ss.54, 58 (1); (Nfld. & Lab.) Labour Relations Act, ss.30, 33 (ON) Labour Relations Act, ss.51, 71, 73 (2), 74, 75.

31. (CAN) Canada Labour Code, s.37; (AB) Labour Relations Code, s.153; (BC) Labour Relations Code, s.12 (1) (a); (MB) Labour Relations Code, s.20; (Nfld. & Lab.) Labour Relations Act, s.130; (ON) Labour Relations Act, 1995, s. 74; (QB) Labour Code, s.47.2; (SK) Trade Union Act, s.25.1. The statutory duty in Nova Scotia is limited to certain employees: (NS) Trade Union Act, s.54A (3).

32. (CAN) Canada Labour Code, s.50; (AB) Labour Relations Code, s.60; (BC) Labour Relations Code, ss.11, 47; (MB) Labour Relations Act, ss.26, 62, 63 (1); (NB) Industrial Relations Act, s.34; (Nfld. & Lab.) Labour Relations Act, s.71; (NS) Trade Union Act, s.35 (a); (ON) Labour Relations Act, 1995, s.17; (PEI) Labour Act, s.22 (a); (QB) Labour Code, s.53; (SK) Trade Union Act, ss.11 (1) (c), 33 (4).

33. Neither the Alberta nor Nova Scotia statutes provide for partisan nominees: (AB) Labour Relations Code, s.8; (NS) Trade Union Act, s.16.

34. H. N. Wheeler, J. A. McClendon and R.D. Weikle, "The Individual Decision to Unionize," *Labor Studies Journal* (September 1998), 34–54.

35. (CAN) Canada Labour Code, s.29 (2); (AB) Labour Relations Code, s.33; (BC) Labour Relations Code, ss.18 (1), 19 (1), 24 (1) (Majority support is required where there is another bargaining agent); (MB) Labour Relations Act, s.40 (1); (NB) Industrial Relations Act, s.14 (2); (Nfld. & Lab.) Labour Relations Act, s.47 (1); (NS) Trade Union Act, s.23 (1); (ON) Labour Relations Act, 1995, s.8 (2); (PEI) Labour Act, s.12 (1); (QB) Labour Code, ss.28, 32; (SK) Trade Union Act, 6 (1.1).

36. For example, see (CAN) Canada Labour Code, s.28; (MB) Labour Relations Act, s.40 (1); (NB) Industrial Relations Act, s.14 (2)–(5).

37. See, for example (AB) Labour Relations Code, s.42; (ON) Labour Relations Act, 1995, s.18 (3); (PEI) Labour Act, s.19. There are no specific provisions for voluntary recognition in the Canada Labour Code, but it is contemplated in s.24.1. In some circumstances, a voluntarily recognized union is deemed to have been certified in Nova Scotia and Prince Edward Island once a collective agreement is entered and filed with the board or minister of labour: (NS) Trade Union Act, s.30 (1) (2); (PEI) Labour Act, s.19 (3).

38. (CAN) Canada Labour Code, s.99.1; (BC) Labour Relations Code, ss.14 (4) (f), 14 (5); (MB) Labour Relations Act, s.41; (NB) Industrial Relations Act, s.106 (8) (e); (Nfld. & Lab.) Labour Relations Act, s.47 (8); (NS) Trade Union Act, s.25 (9); (ON) Labour Relations Act, 1995, ss.11 (1) (2), 111 (5). See also (QB) Labour Code, ss.29, 31. But see (SK) Trade Union Act, s.9. See also Teamsters, Local Union No. 31 and Transx Ltd., 2000 CLLC 220-031 (C.I.R.B.); Cardinal Transportation B.C. Inc. and CUPE, Local 561 (1996), 34 CLRBR (2d) 1 (BC); L & L Painting and Decorating, [2007] OLRB Rep. Sept./Oct. 887 (ON); K.D. Clair Construction Ltd., [2008] O.L.R.D. No. 756 (ON).

39. (CAN) Canada Labour Code, s.25 (1); (AB) Labour Relations Code, s.38 (1); (BC) Labour Relations Code, s.31; (MB) Labour Relations Act, s.43; (Nfld. & Lab.) Labour Relations Act, s.44; (NS) Trade Union Act, s.25 (15); (ON) Labour Relations Act, 1995, s.15; (PEI) Labour Act, s.15; (SK) Trade Union Act, s.9.

40. J. A. Fossum, *Labour Relations,* 8th ed. (New York: McGraw-Hill, 2002), p. 149.

41. (CAN) Canada Labour Code, s.80; (BC) Labour Relations Code, s.55; (MB) Labour Relations Act, s.87; (Nfld. & Lab.) Labour Relations Act, ss.81–83; (ON) Labour Relations Act, 1995, s.43; (QB) Labour Code, ss.93.1–93.9; (SK) Trade Union Act, s.26.5. The Alberta, New Brunswick, Nova Scotia and Prince Edward Island statutes do not have first agreement arbitration provisions. But see CUPE and Lab. Rel. Bd. (N.S.) (1983), 1 D.L.R. (4th) 1 (SCC).

42. R. E. Walton and R. B. McKersie, *A Behavioral Theory of Negotiations* (New York: McGraw-Hill, 1965).

43. Fossum, *Labour Relations.* See also C. S. Loughran, *Negotiating a Labour Contract: A Management Handbook,* 2nd ed. (Washington, DC: Bureau of National Affairs, 1990).

44. T. A. Kochan, *Collective Bargaining and Industrial Relations* (Homewood, IL: Richard D. Irwin, 1980).

45. R. Fisher and W. Ury, *Getting to Yes* (New York: Penguin Books, 1991).

46. Kochan, *Collective Bargaining and Industrial Relations.*

47. (CAN) Canada Labour Code, ss. 71, 72; (AB) Labour Relations Code, s.65 (1) (2); (BC) Labour Relations Code, s.74; (MB) Labour Relations Act, s.67 (1); (NB) Industrial Relations Act, s.36; (Nfld. & Lab.) Labour Relations Act, s.79 (1); (NS) Trade Union Act, s.37; (ON) Labour Relations Act, 1995, ss.16 (4), 18 (1) (2); (PEI) Labour Act, s.25; (QB) Labour Code, s.55. Although in some jurisdictions the appointment is discretionary, it is mandatory in Ontario and Manitoba upon the application of one of the parties. In Saskatchewan and Quebec, conciliation boards can be appointed only at the discretion of the minister: (SK) Trade Union Act, s.22; (QB) Labour Code, s.55.

48. (CAN) Canada Labour Code, s.105; (AB) Labour Relations Code, s.65 (1) (2); (BC) Labour Relations Code, ss.76, 77; (MB) Labour Relations Act, s.95; (NB) Industrial Relations Act, s.70; (Nfld. & Lab.) Labour Relations Act, s.80; (NS) Trade Union Act, s.40; (ON) Labour Relations Act, 1995, s.19; (QB) Labour Code, s.94.

49. (AB) Labour Relations Code, s.64; (NB) Industrial Relations Act, s.70 (1); (Nfld. & Lab.) Labour Relations Act, s.80 (1).; (ON) Labour Relations Act, 1995, s.19. However, a mediator can be appointed solely on the initiative of the minister in Manitoba: (MB) Labour Relations Act, s.95 (2).

50. (CAN) Canada Labour Code, ss.87.4, 87.5, 87.7; (AB) Labour Relations Code, ss.112, 113; (BC) Labour Relations Code, ss.72, 73; (NB) Public Service Labour Relations Act, R.S.N.B. 1973 c. P-25, s.43.1; (Nfld. & Lab.) Public Service Collective Bargaining Act, R.S.N.L. 1990, P-42, s.10; (ON) Crown Employees Collective Bargaining Act, 1993, S.O. 1993, c.38, ss.30–35, 37–42; (QB) Labour Code, ss.111.0.10–111.0.26, 111.10–111.20.

51. H. C. Katz and T. A. Kochan, *An Introduction to Collective Bargaining and Industrial Relations,* 3rd ed. (New York: McGraw-Hill, 2004).

52. (CAN) Canada Labour Code, ss.51–55; (MB) Labour Relations Act, ss.83–86; (SK) Trade Union Act, s. 43.

53. (Nfld. & Lab.) Labour Relations Act, s.99 (2); (NS) Act, s.48; (PEI) Labour Act, s.36 (3); (QB) Labour Code, s.107; (SK) Trade Union Act, s.34. A reopener clause allows parties to address issues that have such a substantial impact on the bargaining unit that the parties have agreed the issue cannot wait to be negotiated until the expiry of the collective agreement. The reopener clause allows them to reopen the collective agreement midterm to negotiate the issue.

54. Kochan, *Collective Bargaining and Industrial Relations,* p. 386.

55. Alternative criteria would be efficiency, equity, and worker voice. John W. Budd and Alexander J. S. Colvin, "Improved Metrics for Workplace Dispute Resolution Procedures: Efficiency, Equity, and Voice," *Industrial Relations* 47, no. 3 (July 2008), p. 460.

56. *Wm. Scott & Co. Ltd.,* [1977] 1 C.L.R.B.R. 1 (P.C. Weiler), p.5.

57. Human Resources and Skills Development Canada, "Evaluation of the Labour–Management Partnerships Program

(LMPP)— Final Report" (March 1998) at www.hrsdc.gc.ca/ eng/cs/sp/hrsdc/edd/reports/1998-000389/sp-ah062e.pdf.

58. Ibid.

59. Ibid.

60. M. Alexander, "A Comprehensive Model for Introducing and Implementing Workplace Change and Improving Labour–Management Relations: Merging the Techniques, Processes and Skills of Organization Development with the Realities of Labour–Management Development," (1998) at www.modern timesworkplace.com/good_reading/GRLabor/FeatureArticle. pdf; Kochan and Osterman, *Mutual Gains;* J. P. MacDuffie, "Human Resource Bundles and Manufacturing Performance: Organizational Logic and Flexible Production Systems in the World Auto Industry," *Industrial and Labor Relations Review* 48, no. 2 (1995), pp. 197–221; W. N. Cooke, "Employee Participation Programs, Group-Based Incentives, and Company Performance: A Union–Nonunion Comparison," *Industrial and Labor Relations Review* 47, no. 4 (1994), pp. 594–609; C. Doucouliagos, "Worker Participation and Productivity in Labor-Managed and Participatory Capitalist Firms: A Meta-Analysis," *Industrial and Labor Relations Review* 49, no. 1 (1995), pp. 58–77; L. W. Hunter, J. P. MacDuffie, and L. Doucet, "What Makes Teams Take? Employee Reactions to Work Reforms," *Industrial and Labor Relations Review* 55 (2002), pp. 448–472; S. J. Deery and R. D. Iverson, "Labor–Management Cooperation: Antecedents and Impact on Organizational Performance," *Industrial and Labor Relations Review* 58 (2005), pp. 588–609; James Combs, Yongmei Liu, Angela Hall, and David Ketchen, "How Much Do High-Performance Work Practices Matter? A Meta-Analysis of Their Effects on Organizational Performance," *Personnel Psychology* 59, no. 3 (2006), pp. 501–528.

61. Robert D. Mohr and Cindy Zoghi, "High-Involvement Work Design and Job Satisfaction," *Industrial & Labor Relations Review* 61, no. 3 (April 2008), pp. 275–296; Paul Osterman, "The Wage Effects of High Performance Work Organization in Manufacturing," *Industrial and Labor Relations Review* 59 (2006), pp. 187–204.

62. Human Resources and Skills Development Canada, *Indicators of Well-Being in Canada, Work—Strikes and Lockouts* at www4. hrsdc.gc.ca/.3ndic.1t.4r@-eng.jsp?iid=14 (retrieved July 28, 2011).

63. (AB) Labour Relations Code, s.1 (v); (MB) Labour Relations Act, s.1; (NS) Trade Union Act, s.2 (1) (v).

64. (BC) Labour Relations Code, s.1 (1); (NB) Industrial Relations Act, s.1 (1).

65. (BC) Labour Relations Code, s.1 (1).

66. (CAN) Canada Labour Code, s.3 (1); (AB) Labour Relations Code, s.1 (p); (BC) Labour Relations Code, s.1 (1); (MB) Labour Relations Act, s.1; (NB) Industrial Relations Act, s.1 (1); (Nfld. & Lab.) Labour Relations Act, s.2 (1) (p); (NS) Trade Union Act, s.2 (1) (o); (ON) Labour Relations Act,

1995, s.1 (1); (PEI) Labour Act, s.7 (1) (k); (QB) Labour Code, s.1 (h); (SK) Trade Union Act, s.2 (j.2).

67. "Montreal Port Deal Reached," CBC News, July 22, 2010.

68. However, see (AB) Labour Relations Code, s.84; (BC) Labour Relations Code, ss.65–67; (NB) Industrial Relations Act, s.104; (Nfld. & Lab.) Labour Relations Act, s.128.

69. *Pepsi-Cola Canada Beverages (West) Ltd. v. RWDSU, Local 558,* [2002] 1 S.C.R. 156 (SCC); *Art Gallery of Ontario and OPSEU, Local 535,* [1989] OLRB Rep. June 537 (ON).

70. Sharanjit Uppal, Statistics Canada, "Unionization 2010," at www.statcan.gc.ca/pub/75-001-x/2010110/pdf/11358-eng.pdf.

71. Ibid.; Statistics Canada, "*Perspectives on Labour and Income,*" September 2002, 3 no. 9, Catalogue no. 75-001-XIE at www. statcan.gc.ca/pub/75-001-x/75-001-x2002009-eng.pdf.

72. Ibid.

73. Jarrell and Stanley, "*A Meta-Analysis*"; R. B. Freeman and J. Medoff, *What Do Unions Do?* (New York: Basic Books, 1984); L. Mishel and M. Walters, "*How Unions Help All Workers,*" Economic Policy Institute Briefing Paper (August 2003), www.epinet.org.

74. J. T. Addison and B. T. Hirsch, "Union Effects on Productivity, Profits, and Growth: Has the Long Run Arrived?" *Journal of Labour Economics* 7 (1989), pp. 72–105; B.T. Hirsch, "Unionization and Economic Performance: Evidence on Productivity, Profits, Investment, and Growth," *Public Policy Sources No. 3* at http://oldfraser.lexi.net/publications/ pps/3/#Introduction.

74. R. B. Freeman and J. L. Medoff, "The Two Faces of Unionism," *Public Interest* 57 (Fall 1979), pp. 69–93; L. Mishel and P. Voos, *Unions and Economic Competitiveness* (Armonk, NY: M. E. Sharpe, 1991); M. Ash and J. A. Seago, "The Effect of Registered Nurses' Unions on Heart-Attack Mortality," *Industrial and Labour Relations Review* 57 (2004), p. 422; C. Doucouliagos and P. Laroche, "What Do Unions Do to Productivity? A Meta-Analysis," *Industrial Relations* 42 (2003), pp. 650–691.

76. Freeman and Medoff, "Two Faces."

77. S. Slichter, J. Healy, and E. R. Livernash, *The Impact of Collective Bargaining on Management* (Washington, DC: Brookings Institution, 1960); Freeman and Medoff, "Two Faces"; Statistics Canada, "*Perspectives on Labour and Income,*" September 2002, vol.3 no.9, Catalogue no. 75-001-XIE at www.statcan.gc.ca/pub/75-001-x/75-001-x2002009-eng.pdf.

78. B. E. Becker and C. A. Olson, "Unions and Firm Profits," *Industrial Relations* 31, no. 3 (1992), pp. 395–415; B. T. Hirsch and B. A. Morgan, "Shareholder Risks and Returns in Union and Nonunion Firms," *Industrial and Labour Relations Review* 47, no. 2 (1994), pp. 302–318. Hristos Doucouliagos and Partice Laroche, "Unions and Profits: A Meta-Regression Analysis," *Industrial Relations.* 48, no. 1 (January 2008), p. 146.

79. Addison and Hirsch, "Union Effects on Productivity." See also B. T. Hirsch, *Labour Unions and the Economic Performance of Firms* (Kalamazoo, MI: W. E. Upjohn Institute, 1991); J. M. Abowd, "The Effect of Wage Bargains on the Stock Market Value of the Firm," *American Economic Review* 79 (1989), pp. 774–800; Hirsch, *Labour Unions*.

80. B. E. Becker, and C. A. Olson, "The Impact of Strikes on Shareholder Equity," *Industrial and Labour Relations Review* 39, no. 3 (1986), pp. 425–438; O. Persons, "The Effects of Automobile Strikes on the Stock Value of Steel Suppliers," *Industrial and Labour Relations Review* 49, no. 1 (1995), pp. 78–87.

81. Sharanjit Uppal, Statistics Canada, "Unionization 2010," at www.statcan.gc.ca/pub/75-001-x/2010110/pdf/11358-eng.pdf.

Chapter 12

1. Justice K. Peter Richard, Commissioner, "The Westray Story: A Predictable Path to Disaster, Report of the Westray Mine Public Inquiry" (November 1997) at www.gov.ns.ca/lwd/pubs/westray (retrieved August 1, 2011).

2. Ham Royal Commission (Toronto: Ontario Ministry of the Attorney General, 1976).

3. Dr. Paul Rohan, "The Trend of Work Injuries in Canada," *Canadian Family Physician* (June 1978) pp. 576–582.

4. Association of Workers' Compensation Boards of Canada, "Number of Fatalities by Jurisdiction, 1993–2008," at www.awcbc.org/common/assets/nwisptables/fat_summary_jurisdiction.pdf.

5. (CAN) Canada Labour Code, R.S.C. 1985, c. L-2; (AB) Occupational Health and Safety Act, R.S.A. 2000, c. 0-2; (BC) Workers Compensation Act, R.S.B.C. 1996, c. 492; (MB) Workplace Safety and Health Act, C.C.S.M c.W210; (NB) Occupational Health and Safety Act, S.N.B. 1983, c. O-0.2; (Nfld. & Lab.) Occupational Health and Safety Act, R.S.N.L. 1990, c. 0-3; (NS) Occupational Health and Safety Act, R.S.N.A. 1996, c. 7; (ON) Occupational Health and Safety Act, R.S.O. 1990, c. O.1; (PEI) Occupational Health and Safety Act, S.P.E.I. 2004, c.42; (QB) An Act Respecting Occupational Health and Safety, R.S.Q. c. S-2.1; (SK) Occupational Health and Safety Act, 1993 S.S. 1993, c.O-1.1; (YT) Occupational Health and Safety Act, R.S.Y.T. 2002, c. 159; (NWT & NU) Safety Act, R.S.N.W.T. 1988, c. S-1.

6. Jamie Knight, C. Kontra, and C. Nassar, *HR Manager's Guide to Health and Safety* (3rd ed.), Thomson Carswell: Toronto, 2010.

7. British Columbia, Newfoundland and Labrador, Ontario and Yukon Territories.

8. (CAN) Canada Labour Code, s.149 (2); (AB) Occupational Health and Safety Act, s.1; (BC) Workers Compensation Act, s.121; (NWT) Mine Health and Safety Act, s.3

9. An Act to Amend the Criminal Code, S.C. 2003, c.21.

10. Criminal Code, s.22.1.

11. "Transpavé Faces Penalty in Landmark Workplace Death," *CBC News* (February 27, 2008).

12. *R. v. Campbell*, [2004] O.J. No. 129 (Ont. C.J.) (QL).

13. *R. v. Campbell*, para. 86.

14. (CAN) Canada Labour Code, s.134.1 (1).

15. "Bell Fined $280,000 for Deaths of Cable Workers," *The Toronto Star* (May 27, 2009) at www.thestar.com/article/609589 (retrieved August 4, 2011).

16. "Telecommunications Company Fined $200,000 After Two Workers Killed," Ontario Ministry of Labour Newsroom (July 22, 2009).

17. "Auto Manufacturer Fined $850,000 After Workers Killed," Ontario Ministry of Labour (May 25, 2010).

18. R.S.C. 1985, c. H-3.

19. "Number of Accepted Time-loss Injuries, by Jurisdiction, 1982–2008," Association of Workers' Compensation Boards of Canada at www.awcbc.org/common/assets/nwisptables/lti_summary_jurisdiction.pdf.

20. "Number of Fatalities, by Jurisdiction, 1993–2008," Association of Workers' Compensation Boards of Canada atwww.awcbc.org/common/assets/nwisptables/fat_summary_jurisdiction.pdf.

21. R. L. Simison, "Safety Last," *The Wall Street Journal* (March 18, 1986), p. 1.

22. "Healthy Workplaces, What? Why? How?" Industrial Accident Prevention Association, 2007 at www.iapa.ca/main/documents/pdf/2006_hwp_short.pdf.

23. Kathryn Wilkins and Susan G. Mackenzie, "Work Injuries," Statistics Canada, *Health Reports* (August 2007), p. 5.

24. "Young People with Dyslexia May Be at Higher Risk of Work Injuries," Institute for Work & Health (August 17, 2009) at www.iwh.on.ca/at-work/58/dyslexia-linked-to-higher-risk-of-work-injury-among-youth (retrieved August 4, 2011).

25. Robert Scherer, James D. Brodzinski, and Elaine A. Crable, "The Human Factor—Human Failings as Main Cause of Workplace Accidents," *HR Magazine* (April 1993) at http://findarticles.com/p/articles/mi_m3495/is_n4_v38/ai_14345057/ (retrieved August 4, 2011).

26. F. Curtis Breslin, Peter Smith, Mieke Koehoorn, and Hyunmi Lee, "Is the Workplace Becoming Safer?" Statistics Canada, *Perspectives on Labour and Income* (July 2006), pp. 18–23.

27. "Work Organisation and Stress," World Health Organization, 2003 at www.iapa.ca/main/documents/pdf/StressTextmater.pdf.

28. Joan Burton, "Creating Healthy Workplaces," Industrial Accident Prevention Association, 2006 at www.iapa.ca/main/documents/pdf/2004_HWP_Healthy_Workplace_FINAL.pdf.

29. "Fatigue," Canadian Centre for Occupational Health and Safety (July 5, 2007) at www.ccohs.ca/oshanswers/psycho social/fatigue.html; Stanley Coren, "Sleep Deficit, Fatal Accidents, and the Spring Shift to Daylight Savings Time," 1998, Presented at INABIS '98—5th Internet World Congress on Biomedical Sciences at McMaster University, Canada (December 7–16) at www.mcmaster.ca/inabis98/occupational/ coren0164/index.html.

30. N.A. Keith and E. Ranking, *A Practical Guide to Occupational Health and Safety Compliance in Ontario* (3rd ed.) (Aurora, ON: Canada Law Book, 2006, p.175; "Job Safety Analysis," Canadian Centre for Occupational Health and Safety (May 29, 2008) at www.ccohs.ca/oshanswers/hsprograms/job-haz. html (retrieved August 4, 2011).

31. N.A. Keith and E. Ranking, *A Practical Guide to Occupational Health and Safety Compliance in Ontario* (3rd ed.) (Aurora, ON: Canada Law Book, 2006), pp.185–188.

32. "Big Changes for Workers After Job Hazard Analysis," Manitoba Federation of Labour Occupational Health Centre, *Focus on Occupational Health and Safety* (February 2007), pp. 1, 3.

33. "MOL Enforcement Blitz: Young and New Worker Safety," Industrial Accident Prevention Association (May 2010).

34. "Young Workers Have the Worst Injury Record in B.C.: Be a Survivor," WorkSafeBC at www.llbc.leg.bc.ca/public/pubdocs/ bcdocs/369585/campaign_survivor.pdf.

35. T. Markus, "How to Set Up a Safety Awareness Program," *Supervision* 51 (1990), pp. 14–16.

36. J. Agnew and A. J. Saruda, "Age and Fatal Work-Related Falls," *Human Factors* 35 (1994), pp. 731–736.

37. B. Sosin, "The Trick to Creating the Most Effective Safety-Incentive Program; Done Right, Safety-Incentive Programs Recognize Employees for Improved Performance as Well as Motivate Workers to Maintain Stellar Safety Records—The Power of Incentives," *HR Magazine* (September 2003) at http://findarticles.com/p/articles/mi_m3495/is_9_48/ ai_108315183/ (retrieved August 4, 2011); R. King, "Active Safety Programs, Education Can Help Prevent Back Injuries," *Occupational Health and Safety* 60 (1991), pp. 49–52.

38. M. Janssens, J. M. Brett, and F. J. Smith, "Confirmatory Cross-Cultural Research: Testing the Viability of a Corporation-wide Safety Policy," *Academy of Management Journal* 38 (1995), pp. 364–382.

39. (CAN) Government Employees Compensation Act, R.S.C., 1985, c. G-5; (AB) Workers' Compensation Act, R.S.A. 2000, c. W-15; (BC) Workers Compensation Act, R.S.B.C. 1996, c. 492; (MB) Workers Compensation Act, C.C.S.M. c. W200; (NB) Workers' Compensation Act, R.S.N.B. 1973, c. W-13 and Workplace Health, Safety and Compensation Commission Act, S.N.B. 1994, c. W-14; (Nfld. & Lab.) Workplace Health, Safety and Compensation Act, R.S.N.L. 1990, c. W-11; (NS) Workers' Compensation Act, S.N.S. 1994–95, c. 10;

(NWT) Workers' Compensation Act, S.N.W.T., 2007, c. 21; (NU) Workers' Compensation Act, Consolidation of, S.Nu. 2007, c.15; (ON) Workplace Safety and Insurance Act, 1997, S.O. 1997, c. 16, Sch. A; (PEI) Workers Compensation Act, R.S.P.E.I. 1988, c. W-7.1; (QB) An Act respecting industrial accident and occupational diseases (R.S.Q., c. A-3.001), Workers' Compensation Act, R.S.Q. c. A-3 and An Act Respecting Indemnities for Victims of Asbestosis and Silicosis in Mines and Quarries, R.S.Q., c. I-7; (SK) Workers' Compensation Act, 1979, S.S. 1979, c. W-17.1; (YT) Workers' Compensation Act, S.Y. 2008, c. 12.

40. Joan Burton, "Creating Healthy Workplaces," Industrial Accident Prevention Association, 2006 at www.iapa.ca/ main/documents/pdf/2004_HWP_Healthy_Workplace_ FINAL.pdf; Joan Burton, "The Business Case for a Healthy Workplace," Industrial Accident Prevention Association, 2008 at www.iapa.ca/main/documents/pdf/fd_business_case_ healthy_workplace.pdf.

41. Ibid.

42. Joan Burton, "Creating Healthy Workplaces," Industrial Accident Prevention Association (2006) at www.iapa.ca/ main/documents/pdf/2004_HWP_Healthy_Workplace_ FINAL.pdf; "The Business Case for a Healthy Workplace," Industrial Accident Prevention Association, 2008 at www. iapa.ca/main/documents/pdf/fd_business_case_healthy_ workplace.pdf.

43. Ibid.

44. "How Do I Know When I Need Help in Ergonomics?" Ergonomics Canada at www.ergonomicscanada.com/faqs.html.

45. "April Inspection Blitz: Musculoskeletal Disorders," *Accident Prevention e-News* (April 2009), Industrial Accident Prevention Association.

46. "Understanding Stress at Work," Industrial Accident Prevention Association (June 2006).

47. "Work Organisation and Stress," World Health Organization (2003), p. 8 at www.iapa.ca/main/documents/pdf/ StressTextmater.pdf.

48. Joan Burton, "The Business Case for a Healthy Workplace," Industrial Accident Prevention Association, 2008, pp. 4–5, at www.iapa.ca/main/documents/pdf/fd_business_case_healthy_ workplace.pdf.

49. Ibid.

50. Ibid.

51. Ibid.

52. "The Costs of Substance Abuse in Canada 2002: Highlights," March 2006, Canadian Centre on Substance Abuse.

53. *Chiasson v. Kellogg Brown & Root (Canada) Co.*, 2007 ABCA 426 (CanLII); *Vancouver Shipyards Co. v. U.A., Local 170*, 2006 CarswellBC 3405 (B.C. Arb. Bd.); *Milazzo v Autocar Connaisseur* (2003) 47 C.H.R.R. D/468. More recently, the Tribunal followed this finding in *Dennis v. Eskasoni Band Council*, 2008 CHRT 38.

54. *Entrop v. Imperial Oil*, [2000] 50 O.R. (3d) 18 C.A.; *Imperial Oil Limited v. Communications, Energy & Paperworkers Union of Canada, Local 900*, [2009] O.J. No. 2037 (QL).

55. "When Fragrances Offend," *Health & Safety Report* (January 2007), Canadian Centre for Occupational Health and Safety at www.ccohs.ca/newsletters/hsreport/issues/2007/01/ezine.html#inthenews (retrieved August 4, 2011).

56. Jamie Knight and Laura Karabulut, *Public Health in the Workplace* (3rd ed.) (Aurora, ON: Thomson Reuters Canada, 2010), pp. 25–26, 33–34.

57. Jason Contant, "Shock & Tell," *Occupational Health and Safety Canada* (April/May 2008) at www.ohscanada.com/25years/best_editorial/5.VIOLENCE.aspx (retrieved August 4, 2011).

58. Statistics Canada, "Study: Criminal Victimization in the Workplace," *The Daily* (February 16, 2007) at www.statcan.gc.ca/daily-quotidien/070216/dq070216a-eng.htm (retrieved August 4, 2011).

59. Joan Riggs, "Workplace Violence Prevention Think Tank: October 29–30, 2008," Centre for Research & Education on Violence Against Women and Children.

60. Eric M. Roher, *Violence in the Workplace* (3rd ed.) (Toronto: Thomson Reuters Canada, (2010), pp.11–12; Norman A. Keith and Goldie Bassi, *Human Resources Guide to Preventing Workplace Violence* (2nd ed.) (Aurora, ON: The Cartwright Group, 2010), p. 20.

61. Eric M. Roher, *Violence in the Workplace*, p. 8; Norman A. Keith and Goldie Bassi, *Human Resources Guide to Preventing Workplace Violence*, pp.11–12.

62. (CAN) Canada Occupational Health and Safety Regulations, SOR/86-304, Part XX; (AB) Occupational Health and Safety Code 2009, Part 27; (BC) Occupational Health and Safety Regulation 296/97, ss.4.27–4.31; (MB) Workplace Safety and Health Regulation 217/2006, Part 11; (Nfld. & Lab.) Occupational Health and Safety Regulations, 2009, Part III; (NS) Violence in the Workplace Regulations 209/2007; (ON) Occupational Health and Safety Act, ss.1, Part III.0.1; (PEI) P.E.I. Reg. EC180/87, Part 52; (SK) Occupational Health and Safety Act, 1993, ss.2, 3, 14 and Occupational Health and Safety Regulations, 1996, R.R.S. C.0-1.1, Reg. 1, s.37; (QB) Labour Standards Act, s.81.18.

63. *Bill 168 Implementation Guide*, Thomson Reuters Canada, 2010; Laura K. Karabulut, "Bill 168: Workplace Violence and Harassment," Filion Wakely Thorup Angeletti LLP 2010 Annual Firm Seminar, June 2010 at www.filion.on.ca/seminar-2010.

64. Norman A. Keith and Goldie Bassi, *Human Resources Guide to Preventing Workplace Violence*, pp. 93–94; "Violence Prevention in the Workplace," Human Resources and Skills Development Canada, 2009.

65. "2009 Corporate Social Responsibility Report," Loblaw Companies at www.loblaw.ca/en/csr_2009/work/w_health.htm.

Chapter 13

1. "The Moment of Truth—Global Export Forecast Summary Export," Global Export Forecast Summary Fall 2010, Table 21: Canadian Exports by Sector at www.edc.ca/publications/gef/english/index.htm (retrieved December 12, 2010).

2. "Global Manufacturing Wage Gap Impacted by Falling Dollar," *Manufacturing & Technology News* (February 28, 2008) at www.allbusiness.com/labor-employment/worker-categories/11419898-1.html (retrieved December 20, 2010).

3. D. Kirkpatrick, "The Net Makes It All Easier—Including Exporting U.S. Jobs," *Fortune* at www.fortune.com/fortune/print/0,15935,450755,00.html (May 2003).

4. Towers Perrin, *Priorities for Competitive Advantage: A Worldwide Human Resource Study* (Valhalla, NY: Towers Perrin, 1991).

5. R. Schuler, "An Integrative Framework of Strategic International Human Resource Management," *Journal of Management* (1993), pp. 419–460.

6. Europa website, Summaries of EU Legislation, Institutional Affairs, Building Europe Through the Treaties: Treaty Establishing the European Economic Community, EEC Treaty—Original Text (non-consolidated version) at http://europa.eu/legislation_summaries/institutional_affairs/treaties/treaties_eec_en (retrieved August 10, 2011).

7. L. Rubio, "The Rationale for NAFTA: Mexico's New 'Outward Looking' Strategy," *Business Economics* (1991), pp. 12–16.

8. H. Cooper, "Economic Impact of NAFTA: It's a Wash, Experts Say," *The Wall Street Journal*, Interactive Edition (June 17, 1997).

9. J. Mark, "Suzhou Factories Are Nearly Ready," *Asian Wall Street Journal* (August 14, 1995), p. 8.

10. R. Peiper, *Human Resource Management: An International Comparison* (Berlin: Walter de Gruyter, 1990).

11. V. Sathe, *Culture and Related Corporate Realities* (Homewood, IL: Richard D. Irwin, 1985).

12. M. Rokeach, *Beliefs, Attitudes, and Values* (San Francisco: Jossey-Bass, 1968).

13. L. Harrison, *Who Prospers? How Cultural Values Shape Economic and Political Success* (New York: Free Press, 1992).

14. N. Adler, *International Dimensions of Organizational Behavior*, 2nd ed. (Boston: PWS-Kent, 1991).

15. R. Yates, "Japanese Managers Say They're Adopting Some U.S. Ways," *Chicago Tribune* (February 29, 1992), p. B1.

16. G. Hofstede, "Dimensions of National Cultures in Fifty Countries and Three Regions," *Expectations in Cross-Cultural Psychology*, eds. J. Deregowski, S. Dziurawiec, and R. C. Annis (Lisse, Netherlands: Swets and Zeitlinger, 1983).

17. G. Hofstede, "Cultural Constraints in Management Theories," *Academy of Management Executive* 7 (1993), pp. 81–90.

18. G. Hofstede, "The Cultural Relativity of Organizational Theories," *Journal of International Business Studies* 14 (1983), pp. 75–90.

19. G. Hofstede, "Cultural Constraints in Management Theories."

20. S. Snell and J. Dean, "Integrated Manufacturing and Human Resource Management: A Human Capital Perspective," *Academy of Management Journal* 35 (1992), pp. 467–504.

21. N. Adler and S. Bartholomew, "Managing Globally Competent People," *The Executive* 6 (1992), pp. 52–65.

22. B. O'Reilly, "Your New Global Workforce," *Fortune* (December 14, 1992), pp. 52–66.

23. A. Hoffman, "Are Technology Jobs Headed Offshore?" Monster.com, http://technology.monster.com/articles/offshore.

24. J. Ledvinka and V. Scardello, *Federal Employment Regulation in Human Resource Management* (Boston: PWS-Kent, 1991).

25. Conrad and Peiper, "Human Resource Management in the Federal Republic of Germany."

26. R. Solow, "Growth with Equity through Investment in Human Capital," The George Seltzer Distinguished Lecture, University of Minnesota.

27. M. Bloom, G. Milkovich, and A. Mitra, "Toward a Model of International Compensation and Rewards: Learning from How Managers Respond to Variations in Local Host Contexts," working paper 00-14 (Center for Advance Human Resource Studies, Cornell University: 2000).

28. R. Kopp, "International Human Resource Policies and Practices in Japanese, European, and United States Multinationals," *Human Resource Management* 33 (1994), pp. 581–599.

29. Adler, *International Dimensions of Organizational Behavior.*

30. S. Jackson and Associates, *Diversity in the Workplace: Human Resource Initiatives* (New York: Guilford Press, 1991).

31. Adler and Bartholomew, "Managing Globally Competent People."

32. Ibid.

33. 2009 Canadian Relocation Policy Survey, Canadian Employee Relocation Council, p. 9, at www.cerc.ca (retrieved January 3, 2011).

34. Y. Hemeda, "Containing Cost of Relocation a Balancing Act," *Canadian HR Reporter*, 23, 16 (September 20, 2010), p. 25.

35. N. Forster, "The Persistent Myth of High Expatriate Failure Rates: A Reappraisal," *International Journal of Human Resource Management* 8, no. 4 (1997), pp. 414–434.

36. Y. Hemeda, "Containing Cost of Relocation a Balancing Act," *Canadian HR Reporter*, 23, 16 (September 20, 2010), p. 25.

37. Talent Mobility 2020: The next generation of international assignments, Pricewaterhousecoopers (2010) at www.pwc.com/us/en/hr-management/publications/index.jhtml/?IsIssue=ISSUE&PubId=352&IssueID=6056.

38. Ibid., p. 6.

39. Ibid., p. 3.

40. Ibid., p. 15.

41. Ibid., p. 13.

42. M. Mendenhall, E. Dunbar, and G. R. Oddou, "Expatriate Selection, Training, and Career-Pathing: A Review and Critique," *Human Resource Management* 26 (1987), pp. 331–345.

43. M. Mendenhall and G. Oddou, "The Dimensions of Expatriate Acculturation," *Academy of Management Review* 10 (1985), pp. 39–47.

44. W. Arthur and W. Bennett, "The International Assignee: The Relative Importance of Factors Perceived to Contribute to Success," *Personnel Psychology* 48 (1995), pp. 99–114.

45. R. Tung, "Selecting and Training of Personnel for Overseas Assignments," *Columbia Journal of World Business* 16, no. 2 (1981), pp. 68–78.

46. Moran, Stahl, and Boyer, Inc., *International Human Resource Management* (Boulder, CO: Moran, Stahl, & Boyer, 1987).

47. P. Caligiuri, "The Big Five Personality Characteristics as Predictors of Expatriates' Desire to Terminate the Assignment and Supervisor Rated Performance," *Personnel Psychology* 53 (2000), pp. 67–88.

48. P. Caligiuri and R. Tung, "Comparing the Success of Male and Female Expatriates from a U.S.-based Multinational Company," *International Journal of Human Resource Management* 10, no. 5 (1999), pp. 763–782.

49. L. Stroh, A. Varma, and S. Valy-Durbin, "Why Are Women Left at Home? Are They Unwilling to Go on International Assignments?" *Journal of World Business 3* 5, no. 3 (2000), pp. 241–255.

50. A. Harzing, *Managing the Multinationals: An International Study of Control Mechanisms* (Cheltenham: Edward Elgar, 1999).

51. J. S. Black and M. Mendenhall, "Cross-Cultural Training Effectiveness: A Review and Theoretical Framework for Future Research," *Academy of Management Review* 15 (1990), pp. 113–136.

52. R. L. Tung, "Selection and Training of Personnel for Overseas Assignments," *Columbia Journal of World Business* 16 (1981), pp. 18–78.

53. W. A. Arthur Jr. and W. Bennett Jr., "The International Assignee: The Relative Importance of Factors Perceived to Contribute to Success," *Personnel Psychology* 48 (1995), pp. 99–114; G. M. Spreitzer, M. W. McCall Jr., and Joan D. Mahoney, "Early Identification of International Executive Potential," *Journal of Applied Psychology* 82 (1997), pp. 6–29.

54. J. S. Black and J. K. Stephens, "The Influence of the Spouse on American Expatriate Adjustment and Intent to Stay in Pacific Rim Overseas Assignments," *Journal of Management* 15 (1989), pp. 529–544; M. Shaffer and D. A. Harrison, "Forgotten Partners of International Assignments: Development and Test of a Model of Spouse Adjustment," *Journal of Applied Psychology* 86 (2001), pp. 238–254.

55. M. Shaffer, D. A. Harrison, H. Gregersen, J. S. Black, and L. A. Ferzandi, "You Can Take It with You: Individual Differences and Expatriate Effectiveness," *Journal of Applied Psychology* 91 (2006), pp. 109–125; P. Caligiuri, "The Big Five Personality Characteristics as Predictors of Expatriate's Desire to Terminate the Assignment and Supervisor-Rated Performance," *Personnel Psychology* 53 (2000), pp. 67–88.

56. P. Dowling and R. Schuler, *International Dimensions of Human Resource Management* (Boston: PWS-Kent, 1990).

57. Adler, *International Dimensions of Organizational Behavior.*

58. B. Eligh, "Cross-cultural Etiquette 101, *The Globe and Mail* (October 4, 2003), p. T10.

59. J. S. Black and M. Mendenhall, "A Practical but Theory-Based Framework for Selecting Cross-Cultural Training Methods," in *Readings and Cases in International Human Resource Management,* ed. M. Mendenhall and G. Oddou (Boston: PWS-Kent, 1991), pp. 177–204.

60. P. Tam, "Culture Course," *The Wall Street Journal* (May 25, 2004), pp. B1, B12.

61. S. Ronen, "Training the International Assignee," in *Training and Development in Organizations,* ed. I. L. Goldstein (San Francisco: Jossey-Bass, 1989), pp. 417–453.

62. E. Dunbar and A. Katcher, "Preparing Managers for Foreign Assignments," *Training and Development Journal* (September 1990), pp. 45–47.

63. P. R. Harris and R. T. Moran, *Managing Cultural Differences* (Houston: Gulf, 1991).

64. J. Carter, "Globe Trotters," *Training* (August 2005), pp. 22–28.

65. C. Solomon, "Unhappy Trails," *Workforce* (August 2000), pp. 36–41.

66. V. Held, "International Relations, Canadian HR Professionals Find Success Working Abroad," *HR Professional* (February/ March 2007), vol. 24, no. 1, pp. 57, 59.

67. H. Lancaster, "Before Going Overseas, Smart Managers Plan Their Homecoming," *The Wall Street Journal* (September 28, 1999), p. B1; A. Halcrow, "Expats: The Squandered Resource," *Workforce* (April 1999), pp. 42–48.

68. Harris and Moran, *Managing Cultural Differences.*

69. J. Cook, "Rethinking Relocation," *Human Resources Executive* (June 2, 2003), pp. 23–26.

70. J. Flynn, "E-Mail, Cellphones, and Frequent-Flier Miles Let 'Virtual' Expats Work Abroad but Live at Home," *The Wall Street Journal* (October 25, 1999), p. A26; J. Flynn, "Multinationals Help Career Couples Deal with Strains Affecting Expatriates," *The Wall Street Journal* (August 8, 2000), p. A19; C. Solomon, "The World Stops Shrinking," *Workforce* (January 2000), pp. 48–51.

71. R. Schuler and P. Dowling, *Survey of ASPA/I Members* (New York: Stern School of Business, New York University, 1988).

72. Mercer Human Resource Consulting, "Worldwide Cost of Living Survey 2010—City Rankings" Worldwide Global Cost of Living Information Services 2010, June 29, 2010 at www.mercer.com.au/press-releases/1383810 (retrieved January 7, 2011).

73. Extracted from S. Cummins, "A LookAhead: Trends in Assignment Types, Destinations and Pay," HR Adviser (Spring 2010) at www.mercer.com, ORC's Expert View Archive.

74. C. Joinson, "No Returns: Localizing Expats Saves Companies Big Money and Can Be a Smooth Transition with a Little Due Diligence by HR," *HRMagazine* 11, no. 47 (2002), p. 70.

75. J. J. Smith, "Firms Say Expats Getting Too Costly, but Few Willing to Act" (2006), *SHRM Online* at www. shrm.org/global/library_published/subject/nonIC/CMS_018300. asp (retrieved March 9, 2007).

76. C. Solomon, "Repatriation: Up, Down, or Out?" *Personnel Journal* (1995), pp. 28–37.

77. "Workers Sent Overseas Have Adjustment Problems, a New Study Shows," *The Wall Street Journal* (June 19, 1984), p. 1.

78. Y. Hemeda, "Containing Cost of Relocation a Balancing Act," *Canadian HR Reporter*, 23, 16 (September 20, 1010), p. 25.

79. J. S. Black, "Coming Home: The Relationship of Expatriate Expectations with Repatriation Adjustment and Job Performance," *Human Relations* 45 (1992), pp. 177–192.

80. Adler, *International Dimensions of Organizational Behavior.*

81. Black, "Coming Home."

82. P. Evans, V. Pucik, and J. Barsoux, *The Global Challenge: International Human Resource Management* (New York: McGraw-Hill, 2002), p. 137.

LEARNING OBJECTIVES

Chapter 1: Human Resource Management: Gaining a Competitive Advantage

LO1: Discuss the roles and activities of a company's human resource management function and the competencies HR professionals need today. (page 6)
LO2: Discuss the implications of changes in the economy, the makeup of the labour force, environmental issues, and ethics for company sustainability. (page 11)
LO3: Discuss how human resource management helps meet the needs of various stakeholders. (page 19)
LO4: Discuss some of the challenges companies must overcome and the strategies required to compete in the global marketplace. (page 23)
LO5: Identify the challenges of technology and discuss high-performance work systems. (page 26)
LO6: Discuss the transformation of the HRM function. (page 29)

Chapter 2: Strategic Human Resource Management

LO1: Describe the differences between strategy formulation and strategy implementation. (page 43)
LO2: List the components of the strategic management process. (page 44)
LO3: Discuss the role of the HRM function in strategy formulation and its linkages to the process. (page 47)
LO4: Discuss the more popular typologies of generic strategies and the various HRM practices associated with each. (page 50)
LO5: Describe the different HRM issues and practices associated with various directional strategies. (page 55)
LO6: Describe steps HRM can take to maximize its value and become a true strategic partner in the organization. (page 62)
LO7: Examine the role of the chief human resources officer. (page 67)

Chapter 3: The Legal Environment: Equality and Human Rights

LO1: Describe how various levels of government shape the legal environment for HRM in Canada. (page 79)
LO2: Explain the importance of the Canadian Charter of Rights and Freedoms and human rights legislation, and their implications for HRM. (page 82)
LO3: Discuss what constitutes discrimination and requirements for reasonable accommodation. (page 84)
LO4: Explain various concepts of discrimination and HRM's role in prevention and elimination of such behaviours. (page 85)
LO5: Explain employment equity legislation and describe the four designated groups. (page 106)
LO6: Describe what is required to implement and promote employment equity programs. (page 110)
LO7: Explain pay equity and its implications for HRM. (page 112)
LO8: Develop approaches for managing and promoting diversity effectively. (page 113)

Chapter 4: Analysis and Design of Work and Human Resource Planning

LO1: Analyze and organization's structure and work-flow process, identifying the output, activities, and inputs in the production of a product or services. (page 127)
LO2: Understand the importance of job analysis in strategic human resource management. (page 136)

LO3: Choose the right job analysis technique for a variety of human resource activities. (page 138)
LO4: Identify the tasks performed and the skills required in a given job. (page 140)
LO5: Understand the different approaches to job design and various trade-offs that may be required. (page 140)
LO6: Discuss how to align a company's strategic direction with its human resource planning and determine the labour demand and supply for workers in various job categories. (page 146)
LO7: Discuss various ways of eliminating a labour surplus and avoiding a labour shortage. (page 149)
LO8: Discuss the types of new technologies that can be considered in redesigning jobs organization-wide, and planning of the HRM function. (page 157)

Chapter 5: Recruitment and Selection

LO1: Describe the various recruitment policies that organizations adopt to make job vacancies more attractive. (page 168)
LO2: List the various sources from which job applicants can be drawn, their relative advantages and disadvantages, and the methods for evaluating them. (page 171)
LO3: Explain the recruiter's role in the recruitment process, challenges the recruiter faces, and the opportunities available. (page 177)
LO4: Establish the basic standards of selection methods, including reliability, validity, and generalizability. (page 180)
LO5: Discuss how the particular characteristics of a job, organization, or applicant affect the utility of any test. (page 183)
LO6: List the common methods used in selecting human resources and the degree to which each method meets selection method standards. (page 184)
LO7: Describe the various legal requirements in recruitment processes and selection decisions. (page 197)

Chapter 6: Training and Strategic Development of People

LO1: Discuss the relationship between training and development and how the two can contribute to companies' business strategy. (page 211)
LO2: Explain the steps involved in a systematic approach to training in organizations, including needs assessment, various presentation methods available, and evaluation. (page 213)
LO3: Explain the importance of organizational socialization, the onboarding process, and other special training solutions. (page 225)
LO4: Explain how employees development contributes to strategies related to employee retention, developing intellectual capital, and business growth. (page 228)
LO5: Discuss current trends using formal education for development. (page 229)
LO6: Relate how assessment of personality type, work behaviours, and job performance can be used for employee development. (page 231)
LO7: Explain how job experiences can be used for skill development. (page 233)
LO8: Develop successful mentoring and coaching programs. (page 237)
LO9: Discuss the steps and responsibilities in the development planning process. (page 240)